The Handgun

The Handgun

GEOFFREY BOOTHROYD

THE SPORTSMAN'S PRESS · LONDON

This edition published in 1988 by
The Sportsman's Press

© Geoffrey Boothroyd 1988

First published 1970

All rights reserved. No part of this publication may be reproduced, stored in a retrieval system, or transmitted in any form or by any means, electronic, mechanical, photocopying, recording or otherwise, without the prior permission of the copyright owner.

British Library Cataloguing in Publication Data
Boothroyd, Geoffrey, *1925–*
The handgun.—2nd ed.
1. Pistols – to 1987
I. Title
683.4′32′09

ISBN 0–948253–27–4

Printed in Great Britain at The Bath Press, Avon

For my Family
who have been patient

Contents

Introduction

For almost a quarter of a century I have been fascinated by the handgun, by its history, by its use, and by the long and continued process of development that has led from the hand cannon of the fourteenth century to the automatic pistol of today.

The first 'handgun' I ever owned (and I still have it) was a Webley and Scott air pistol, and it was with the aid of this that I was first taught the basic principles of safety, and was also made aware of the sense of responsibility that must accompany the ownership of any firearm. Following the air pistol came a succession of revolvers and automatic pistols, and then, one day, I was given a flintlock pistol. This immediately aroused an interest in the ancestors of my cartridge weapons, and the subsequent acquisition of a Colt Pocket Pistol, the model of 1849, served only to stimulate it.

With the growth of this new interest, I found that friends accumulated even more rapidly than my collection. The more knowledgeable, through their kindness and tolerance, not only increased the pleasure I gained from our mutual interests, but also broadened the scope of my activities. Many of them had developed a specific interest in one highly specialised aspect of the subject. Some concentrated on flintlock pistols, percussion pistols or metallic ammunition, some on handloading or on repairs and home gunsmithing; others concentrated on target shooting or on the combat use of the handgun. The range, from the practical to the esoteric, was almost limitless. In discussion, or through correspondence, I would often find that some particular aspect, one that I might formerly have tended to treat with disdain, was really of considerable interest. Anything that even marginally affects or influences one's own speciality should not be lightly scorned.

But the very natural desire to find out more about a subject can all too often be frustrated by lack of opportunity or, more often, by lack of information. In this book, I have therefore endeavoured to collect together as much information as possible on the handgun and, as the theme to link the many aspects of the subject, I have taken that of the technological development not only of the handgun itself but also of the methods of manufacture. Originally manufacture meant 'to make by hand'; today the usual meaning is 'to make by machine', and in no field has this change been of more significance than in the field of handgun production.

In addition, a rightful emphasis has been placed on the importance of the individual, on those men whose efforts revolutionised both design and manufacture until, gradually, the handgun of today evolved. It is my hope that this book may bring about a more complete realisation of the immense effort and years of endeavour that finally culminated in so deceptively simple a weapon as the .22 automatic pistol. Such an understanding of the past adds to appreciation of the present, and the value of a prized antique is only enhanced if it is set in its correct historical perspective.

During the several years I have spent in writing this book, a number of people have contributed most generously of their time, patience and knowledge, and I cannot let this opportunity pass without paying tribute to their great kindness and unfailing courtesy when faced with my continued demands for information, advice or assistance.

As always, Peter A. Bedford and R. H. Walton deserve special mention both for their encouragement and advice, and for providing hard won facts and data, the result of their long study of the subject. I am especially grateful to Colonel Franklin S. Allen, Jr., of the United States Air Force who provided valuable information and generously made available a number of the photographs that came out of a joint project with Don Chandler. I should also like to include Carl H. Moisel of Quebec, whose help with the complexities of German military pistols was of great value, and R. Caranta of Aix-en-Provence for his help with regard to the later French pistols. For valuable assistance on the earlier French military pistols, I have to thank G. Demaison, and to Iwan Hedman of Sweden I must express my appreciation for material that he supplied and for his help in obtaining relevant literature. My thanks also go to Dr Heinz Zatschek of Vienna and F. Hediger of Switzerland for advice and information on arms made in their respective countries.

It is a pleasure to acknowledge my appreciation of the help received from the officials of the following museums: The Armouries of H.M. Tower of London; the Royal Scottish Museum, Edinburgh; the Heeresgeschichltiches Museum, Vienna; the Tøjhusmuseet, Copenhagen; the Kungl. Armemuseum, Stockholm; the Nederlands Leger-enWapenmuseum, Leiden; M. Jean Puraye, Conservateur du Musée d'Armes de Liege. In particular I wish to express my thanks to J. G. Scott and R. Roddon of the Glasgow Museums and Art Galleries and to the staff of the Museum for their considerable assistance during the several photographic sessions they kindly arranged for me. I must equally include J. F. T. Thomson, M.A., F.L.A., Director of the Dick Institute, Kilmarnock, who gave me valuable help on the research side and on the further photographic work I undertook there.

For access to and information on patent material I acknowledge the help of Mr Hamilton of the Commercial Library and Mrs Hillhouse of the Mitchell Libraries, Libraries Department, Corporation of Glasgow.

The decision to use the original patent drawings solved certain problems but created others, not the least of which was the problem of reproduction since many of the drawings were in the form of extremely fine engravings and some were of considerable age. I am particularly grateful to Mr Nicholas Flower of Cassell and Co., who undertook the difficult task of photographing these drawings on my behalf, and to Mr T. Rees and the library staff of the Science Museum, South Kensington, London, without whose help this exercise would not have been possible. To retain authenticity, the key letters have not been deleted and have, in certain instances, been used in the text. To have added a key for each drawing would have added needless complexity and would have been of dubious value.

From the many manufacturers and dealers, I met with unfailing co-operation. Although no doubt greatly harassed by their own day-to-day problems, they nevertheless always found time to answer queries and to provide literature, catalogues, material and illustrations. In Britain these included Webley and Scott Ltd., Birmingham; L. LePersonne and Co. Ltd., London; Salter and Varge Ltd., London; and Arthur E. S. Matthews Ltd., London. Help in abundance was provided by Imperial Metal Industries (Kynoch) Ltd., Birmingham, in particular by Roy Goodman, and also by Imperial Chemical Industries Ltd., Nobel Division, Ayrshire.

Considerable assistance was also received from the firms of Albrecht Kind, Hunstig and Waffen-Franconia, Wuerzburg, both of Western Germany, and I also wish to express my appreciation of the help provided by the Commercial Office of the Spanish Embassy in London.

The true American liberality of Smith and Wesson, Colt, Hi-Standard and Ruger was equalled only by that of Carl Walther and Mauser-Werke AG. Advice and material on a similar scale were made available by Hammerli Ltd., by SIG of Neuhausen and by V. Bernadelli of Gardone. To Armi Beretta I wish to pay especial tribute not only for their help but also for the courtesy I received during my visit to their factory in 1964. I gained equal personal pleasure from my visit to the factory of Aldo Uberti in Gardone and from my interesting conversation with Signora Uberti. I have especial pleasure in acknowledging the help and assistance received from M. René Laloux, President of Fabrique Nationale, M. J. Demey, Chef de Service and M. Ernest Vervier, Chief Designer, all of whom made my visit to the FN factory at Herstal a fascinating and rewarding experience. My requests for information from Astra, Unceta y Cia and Gabilondo y Cia were answered with true Basque courtesy, and prompt and considerate assistance was received from the French firms of Manufrance, Manufacture d'Armes des Pyrenées and Manufacture d'Armes Automatiques, Bayonne. Officials of the Birmingham Proof House, the Banc d'Epreuves of Liege and the Banco di Prova of Gardone contributed help and advice, in particular Signor Giuseppe Zambonardi, Chief of the Proof Department at Gardone, who devoted so much time to me during my visit, and M. Edmonds-Alt, General Manager of the Banc d'Epreuves of Liege, whose unfailing courtesy and kindness contributed greatly to the success of my visit to this important centre of gunmaking.

I acknowledge with gratitude the assistance given by the City of Glasgow Police and by the Chief Constable who gave permission for me to examine and photograph weapons in the Glasgow Police Collection. Claude Blair and B. T. Batsford Ltd., very kindly gave me permission to reproduce four drawings from Mr Blair's book *Pistols of the World*.

All photographs acknowledged to the Tower of London are Crown Copyright Reserved.

W. A. C. Paton, R. Dalgleish, Ian Frame, R. D. Nicoll, J. W. Dickinson, D. B. Fraser, John A. Smith and Lindsay Allan not only gave me permission to photograph weapons in their possession but also allowed me to pull them apart. For their co-operation I am naturally extremely grateful, but I am even more so for their touching faith in my ability to put their weapons back together again.

The difficult and unenviable task of translating literature, catalogues, letters, documents, etc. was carried out with commendable accuracy by J. Henry Weber, Dr H. S. Sloane and E. Gianinni, to whom I am also indebted for the use they allowed me to make of their wide knowledge of European affairs. To J. Henry Weber and W. A. C. Paton go my especial thanks for their help in the tremendous task of proof reading.

In writing this book I laboured under the comforting delusion that when the typescript had been finished most of my problems would vanish. This, of course, was not the case, for there were many difficulties and problems to be surmounted before the typescript could become a recognisable book. My task during this period was made considerably easier by the help received from my publishers, and it is also a great pleasure to place on record the debt I owe to Brian Rawson for his constant help and encouragement during the time the text was being edited. The value of a book of this type would be greatly diminished without an effective index, and for her work in this connection I have to thank Miss Hebe Jerrold.

Unless otherwise indicated, I must accept personal

responsibility for the photographs. For the technically inclined, these were taken on Ilford F.P.3 negative material and were printed on Agfa paper. The cameras used were the 6 × 9 cm Linhof Super Technica and a $2\frac{1}{4}''$ square Rollei.

Finally, I have to thank Val Gauld who retyped my typescript and whose helpful suggestions were much appreciated, and also Margaret I. Cowden who helped me greatly during the final stages of revision.

Geoffrey Boothroyd

Glasgow, Scotland.
January 1970

Author's Note to the second English Edition

It is now eighteen years since the first edition of this book was published and although two American editions followed the original British edition the book rapidly went out of print in the country of origin and, to my delight (though sadly not to my profit) the price on the second hand market rose and then continued to rise!

When I was approached regarding a new British edition I have to admit that I was delighted. I felt that the critical acclaim that *The Handgun* had received over the years, and indeed even recently, in the *Handgun Digest*, merited a new edition. After careful consideration I decided that the book could be brought up-to-date within the original framework if the last chapter was deleted and replaced by new material.

Over fourteen thousand words have been written and new illustrations provided to record recent handgun history. It is my hope that this text substitution will be well received and the loss of the original text accepted.

I have to thank my Publisher for his support and encouragement, to Sue Coley who edited this edition and also my wife, Nancy, who proof read the final chapter and whose help did much to lighten the workload.

Geoffrey Boothroyd
Glasgow, 1988

Note on Abbreviations used in the Text

The student of firearms must learn to live with a perverse, aggravating and, at times, totally inconsistent nomenclature. There is no short cut through the tangle, and the inadequacy of descriptive terms allied to a capricious and often illogical attempt at classification, tends to confuse and mystify the beginner. With experience, the terms are related to the context and to the period, so that, always with a wary eye open for synonyms, the serious student retires behind a protective barrier of jargonese, insulated from lesser mortals in much the same way as a lawyer, doctor or scientist. The study of firearms has suffered from the lack of a Linnaean system. We have inherited a terminology which, like Topsy, 'has just growed', and, to add to the problem, it is multi-lingual 'contrangelment' where even the British and the Americans are separated by a common language.

A belief that at least some of the difficulties could be resolved in the present work was short-lived, but as evidence of good faith, if nothing else, a short list of common and currently used abbreviations is given which may provide some slight solace and remove one possible cause of confusion.

ACP	Automatic Colt Pistol
AEP	Anciens Etablissements Pieper
CF	Centre-fire
DA	Double Action
DWM	Deutsche Waffen-und Munitionsfabriken AG
FN	Fabrique Nationale d'Armes de Guerre SA
ISU	International Shooting Union (also UIT)
IWK	Industrie-Werke Karlsruhe AG
MAB	Manufacture d'Armes Automatiques, Bayonne
MAC	Manufacture d'Armes de Chatellerault
MAP	Manufacture d'Armes des Pyrenées
MAS	Manufacture d'Armes de St. Etienne
MAT	Manufacture d'Armes de Tulle
NP	New Police
NRA	National Rifle Association
NSRA	National Small-bore Rifle Association
OWG	Oesterreichishe Werke-gws-Anstalt
PF	Pin-fire
RF	Rim-fire
RFM	Rim-fire Magnum
RIC	Royal Irish Constabulary
RWS	Rheinisch-Westfälische Sprengstoff-Adien Gesellschaft
SA	Single Action
SAA	Single Action Army
SACM	Societé Alsacienne de Constructions Mécaniques
SAGEM	Societé d'Applications Générales Electriques et Mécaniques
SFM	Societé Française des Munitions de Chasse, de Tir et de Guerre
SIG	Schweizerische Industrie Gesellschaft
S&W	Smith and Wesson
UIT	Union Internationale de Tir (also ISU)
WCF	Winchester Centre-fire
WMR	Winchester Magnum Rim-fire
WR	Westley Richards
WRF	Winchester Rim-fire
W&S	Webley and Scott

Chapter One

From Matchlock to Flintlock

For six centuries man has laboured to perfect the gun. Much of this work is undocumented, confused and obscure. We do not know with any certainty who discovered gunpowder, but the use of a chemical agency to propel a missile instead of human muscle and sinew caused a revolution in the established methods of warfare. The invincibility of the proud armoured knight, the skill and strength of the archer and the impregnability of the fortress were all challenged by this new and destructive force.

The ancestors of the firearm family were in use by the year 1300, and these patriarchs would be described today as artillery or cannon. The early products were crude, but they evolved to become things of size and power, and when in 1453, the Sultan Mohamet II of Turkey laid siege to Constantinople, he boasted a cast bronze cannon seventeen feet long. This monster, known as the Dardanelles gun, was reputed to hurl a half ton ball for almost a mile and it can be seen to this day in the Tower of London.

Such guns were of immense prestige value and their arrival outside the walls of a mediaeval fortress often resulted in the surrender of the inhabitants without a shot being fired. Capable of battering down the defensive walls and buildings, these cumbersome weapons were, however, of little value against an army in the field. What was needed was a hand cannon, a light weapon capable of being carried, loaded and fired by one man. Given sufficient men so armed, firepower could be properly deployed and effectively utilised.

An early 'hand cannon', one of the few surviving specimens, has a bore or calibre of 0.7″ and a barrel length of just over 12″. This gun (missing the shaft) was excavated in 1849 on the site of a robber baron's stronghold near Tannenberg in Germany. The castle was utterly destroyed in 1399 so there is little doubt that the Tannenberger Buchse dates from the fourteenth century. Many similar guns are recorded in the manuscripts of the fourteenth and early fifteenth centuries and, as changes and developments took place, the general contours of a recognisable gun slowly began to appear. Such guns were difficult to use and lacked accuracy.

Many problems confronted the user of the hand cannon. First of all, the powder charge had to be poured in at the muzzle, followed by the ball. The touch-hole was then primed. The wooden stock or shaft could either be supported under the right arm or placed on the ground; the left hand supported the barrel, and care had to be taken to ensure that the touch-hole was uppermost. The touche, a hot coal or hot rod, would then have to be checked and, if necessary, reheated from a convenient brazier or fyrpanne. In addition to observing the target, the cannoneer had simultaneously to use his right hand to make sure that the touche was directed on to the touch-hole. Three handed soldiers would have been useful, but in their absence a third hand was provided by the invention of the serpentine. This was an 'S' shaped piece of metal provided with a pivot attached to the side of the gunstock. The upper arm of the serpentine terminated in a clamp or a small tube, the lower arm being longer and therefore heavier so that the serpentine would naturally assume a near vertical position. Instead of using glowing coal, hot wire or glowing splint, a wick or match was used, fashioned from a loosely twisted rope of hemp soaked in saltpetre and spirits of wine to make it burn slowly and steadily. The use of the match reduced the dependence of the soldier on the fyrpanne and, of greater importance, allowed him to take a rudimentary aim. After he had loaded the gun, he fastened the glowing end of the match in the clamp of the serpentine, and then, when he pulled the lower arm of the serpentine, the match described an arc to come into contact with priming powder previously placed in a small depression surrounding the touch-hole, so causing it to ignite and the gun to discharge.

Great advances took place during the fifteenth century. Improvements were made in the form and general appearance of the gun stock; the quality of the match was bettered to increase reliability, and the touch-hole was moved from the top to the right hand side of the barrel. The saucer shaped depression developed into a pan projecting at right angles and provided with a hinged sliding cover. This prevented the loss of priming powder either from spillage or the effects of wind and helped to keep it dry in the event of light rain. The crude serpentine was ultimately replaced by the first gunlock—the matchlock.

In the earliest matchlock models, a 'C' shaped serpentine was attached to an axle which passed through the lock plate. The axle or tumbler was provided with a slotted arm through which the end of a pivoted lever or sear protruded, and to the other end of the sear was attached the 'tricker' or trigger. When the trigger was pulled, the sear caused the tumbler and attached serpentine to rotate, bringing the glowing end of the match down on to the priming. After firing, a flat spring returned the mechanism when the trigger bar was released. This lock had five pieces of mechanism, and the names of four are still in use today: tumbler, sear, sear spring and trigger. A later type of matchlock, the button lock, speeded up ignition by a rearrangement of the lockwork so that the serpentine was actuated by spring pressure. In this type of lock, the serpentine was pulled back or cocked by hand and a match inserted into the jaws. A light touch on a button trigger released the sear spring, and the resultant pressure revolved the tumbler and brought the lighted end of the match down on to the priming. The most sophisticated form of matchlock was the snap or tinder lock which used a small piece of tinder or match held in a tube. This was ignited immediately before use, so eliminating the long dangling length of match which festooned the commoner varieties of matchlock.

Today, such weapons as these might appear sadly lacking in refinement, but it is remarkable that most of the important principles successfully adopted in the course of the following centuries were at least tried by the matchlock gunmaker. For example, trigger guards were an early innovation; rifling appeared about the year 1500; and attempts were made to design breechloaders and weapons capable of repeating fire.

In Europe the matchlock in one or another of its many and varied forms remained the standard military weapon until the beginning of the eighteenth century. In Asia, except in the Near East with its close contacts with Europe, ignition by means of a lighted match was employed until modern times.

Due to both political and physical isolation, firearms in Japan followed a distinct and entirely separate pattern. According to tradition, they were first introduced in 1542 from mainly Portuguese sources. Japanese craftsmen copied these weapons and developed the snapping matchlock, a type which enjoyed only a limited popularity in Europe.

Matchlocks were used in Japan until the mid-nineteenth century and although some were converted to percussion, the main transition was from matchlock to breechloading cartridge weapons. No intermediate Japanese forms such as the wheellock and flintlock appear to have been made.

To cunning craftsmen seeking improvements, the main disadvantage of the matchlock was the lighted match. Even when lit, it required constant adjustment and attention, apart from being a considerable hazard near gunpowder. The light from the match—'as though from glow-worms in the night'—frequently prevented a successful ambush or foiled a surprise attack. On the other hand, the matchlock was cheap, easy to manufacture, and a man could be taught its use far more quickly than he could be trained as a skilled archer.

The widespread use of the matchlock is reflected in the numerous and often puzzling names which describe the variations evolved to meet some specific need. Perhaps the term 'musket' is the one which is least confusing since this has always meant a heavy military arm. First used by the Spanish to describe a new type of firearm introduced by the Duke of Alva into the Spanish service about 1550, the terms 'musket' and 'musketeer' are still in common use.

Both the spirit of the age and the lengthy and complex business of handling and loading a matchlock musket are best shown in a series of engravings from *The Management of Arms, Arquebuses, Muskets and Pikes* by Jacob de Gheyn, published in 1608. The musketeer swaggers through the pages of this book in a delightful variety of costumes displaying his dexterity with powder and shot flask, patron (the forerunner of the cartridge), loading stick, forked rest and burning match. Two other arms were the shorter, lighter caliver which could be used without a rest, and the petronel used by the cavalry. The term 'arquebus' and its variants, 'hak-buchse', 'hacquebut' or 'hagbutt' has given rise to considerable speculation but there is now some measure of agreement that, originally, this group of terms meant a gun having a small projection underneath the barrel, designed to hook over a wall and so take up some of the recoil. In German, 'hak' means hook and 'buchse' means gun, but in time the usage altered so that arquebus came to mean a light gun fired without a rest—subsequently a wheellock as opposed to a matchlock.

The Arquebus. From Jacob de Gheyn's *Management of Arms.* (British Museum)

In this brief coverage of early arms history, no mention has been made of the pistol. If we accept the general definition of this term—'a small hand gun, held in one hand when fired'—it is apparent that the firing mechanism of neither the hand cannon nor the matchlock was suitable for adaptation to a light and handy weapon. A lighted match was difficult enough to manage on foot let alone on horseback! Some weapons which today could be called pistols were made in Europe, but often they were combination arms. A number of breechloading pistols—consisting of a round shield with a pistol barrel projecting through the boss—were made for Henry VIII between 1544 and 1547 and still survive in the Tower of London. Matchlock pistols were also made in Japan and occasionally in India, but as far as Europe was concerned, the 'one hand gun' had to wait for the next important invention, the wheellock.

The Musket. From Jacob de Gheyn's

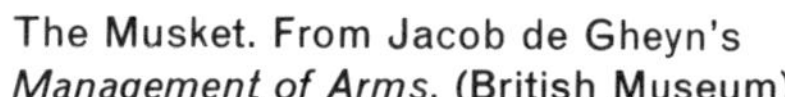

Management of Arms. (British Museum)

The originator of the wheellock is really unknown although there is evidence that one of the greatest geniuses of history, Leonardo da Vinci, designed a feasible though hardly practical wheellock somewhere about 1508. It is likely that the first practical locks resulted from the work of several men. What is of importance, is that this new lock made the pistol a practical weapon: for the first time a firearm could be carried

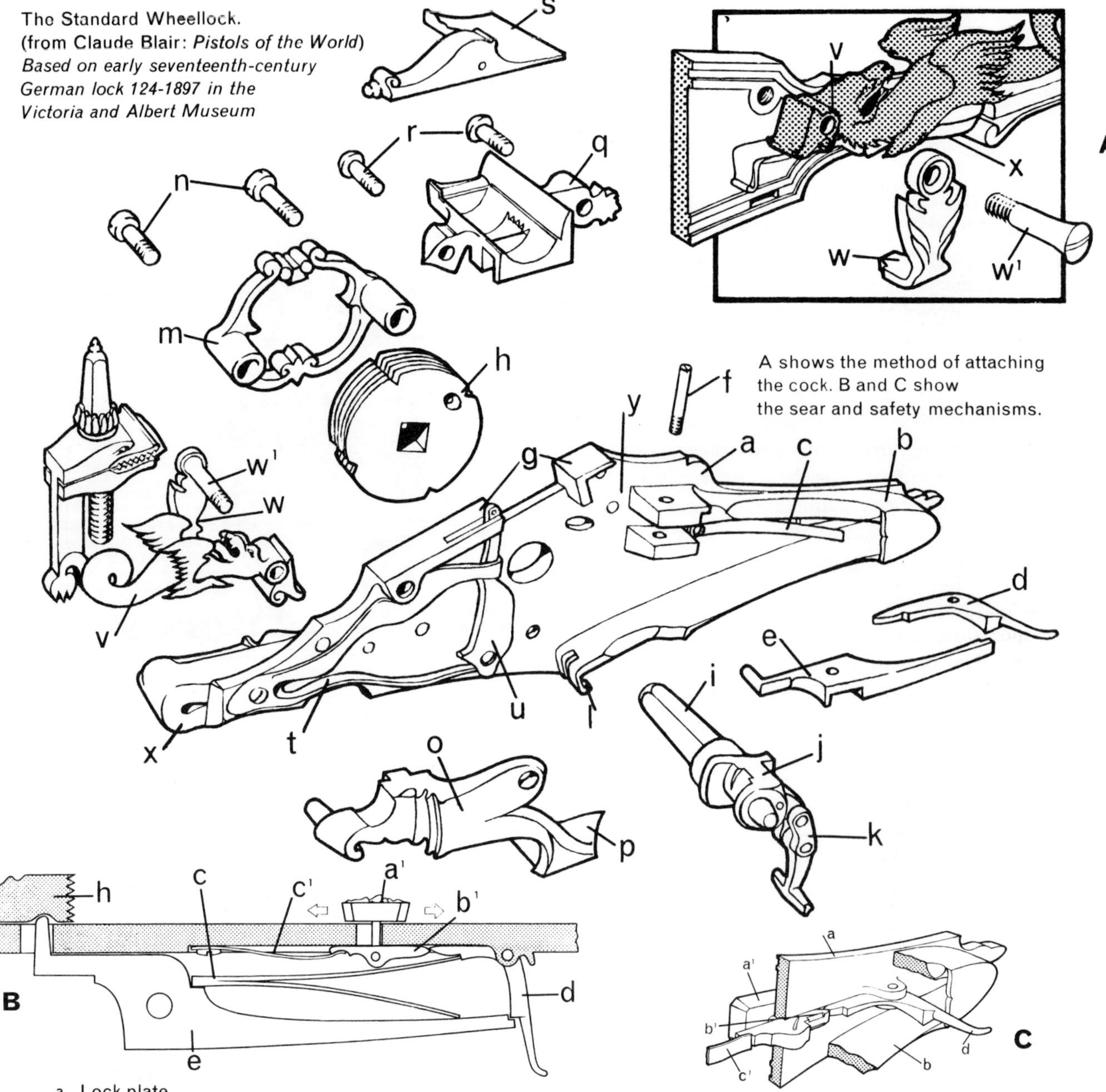

The Standard Wheellock.
(from Claude Blair: *Pistols of the World*)
Based on early seventeenth-century German lock 124-1897 in the Victoria and Albert Museum

A shows the method of attaching the cock. B and C show the sear and safety mechanisms.

a Lock plate
b Mainspring
c Sear spring
d Trigger lever
e Sear lever
f Sear pivot pin securing sear lever to *y*
g Shoulders on which the pan *q* is supported
h Wheel with square hole for the spindle *i* and a circular recess in which the nose of the sear *e* engages
i Wheel spindle
j Portion of *i* round which the transmission chain *k* winds. To the left is the cam that opens the pan cover automatically as the wheel unwinds by striking the lever *u*
k Transmission chain terminating in a toggle that engages with the mainspring at *l*
l End of mainspring shaped to receive the toggle on *k*
m Ring-shaped wheel cover
n Screws for attaching *m* to the lock plate
o Bridle supporting the inner end of the wheel spindle *i* with mainspring stop at *p*
p Mainspring stop on *o*
q Pan, slotted for the wheel and the edge of the lock plate to which it is attached at *g*
r Retaining screws for *q*
s Sliding pan cover pivoted to the top of *u*
t Pan cover spring
u Pan cover arm, pivoted at the bottom
v Cock, the neck chiselled in the form of a wyvern. The lower jaw of the dog-head is movable
w Cock bridle
w' Cock pivot screw
x Cock spring
y Lugs between which the sear lever is pivoted. The upper one also serves to secure the end of the mainspring
a' External knob of sliding safety catch
b' Safety catch lever which engages over the toe of the trigger lever *d*
c' Safety catch spring

Detached German wheellock with the wheel recessed into the lockplate.

concealed, or be laid aside in some convenient place, and yet be ready to fire at a moment's notice.

The operation of the wheellock was similar to the modern flint petrol lighter in that a hardened steel disc with grooves cut on its periphery was mounted on an axle. Attached to the axle was a small chain connected to a very strong mainspring. Rotation of the wheel, by means of a spanner on the squared end of the axle, caused the mainspring to be tensioned and, when the lock was fully spanned, or wound up, a sear engaged a depression in the side of the wheel. The whole of the mechanism was mounted on a lock plate, part of the top of which was fashioned into a priming pan through which the edge of the wheel projected. Also attached to the lock plate was the doghead, a spring loaded swinging arm provided with jaws which held the pyrophoric material, pyrites. The flash pan was provided with a cover having an internal linkage which automatically slid it aside when the lock was operated.

To charge a wheellock pistol, powder and ball were introduced, the lock was spanned, the flashpan was filled with powder and the cover was slid across the top to prevent loss of the priming. With the pyrites firmly secured in the jaws of the doghead, this arm was swung over until the pyrites pressed against the flashpan cover. At this stage the pistol was ready to fire and could be laid aside.

On firing, the trigger released the sear which permitted the wheel to rotate for three-quarters of a turn with great rapidity. The instant the wheel began to spin, a cam on the axle operated a linkage which opened the pan cover, the pyrites came into contact with the now rapidly spinning wheel, and the result was a copious production of sparks. By this means the priming was ignited, fire flashed through the touch-hole into the barrel and the gun was discharged. Four basic types of wheellock appeared and are broadly classified as follows:

1. Those in which the wheel was mounted externally on the lock plate.
2. Those where the external wheel was partially or wholly covered or shielded.
3. The Tschinke, in which not only the wheel but much of the mechanism was uncovered and mounted on the outside of the lock plate.
4. Later wheellocks which employed internal mounting, the wheel being recessed in the back of the lock plate.

The origin of the first wheellock pistols is as difficult to determine as the name of the inventor of the lock mechanism itself. Early combination wheellock pistols were made in Italy and these formidable weapons were pistols combined with crossbows, war hammers and even maces. They appear to have been made in Venice about 1520, but authenticated early sixteenth century Italian wheellocks are rare and it is to Germany that we must turn to discover more; it is there that one of the earliest 'I didn't know the gun was loaded' stories is to be found in the *Chronica newer Geschicten* under the intriguing title, 'How Laux Pfister Shot a Whore in Constance'.

It appears that the lady in the story had been invited to the room of a young blood of Augsburg in Constance. Doubtless wishing to impress the lady, he started to toy with a loaded gun, pressed the trigger and shot 'the whore through the chin so that the bullet passed through the back of her neck'. Our gun-happy friend had to pay the lady forty florins and a further twenty florins per annum for life plus other incidental expenses. Aside from the unexpected outcome of the young man's amorous proclivities, the moral is as apt today as it was over four centuries ago: that it is foolhardy to play with guns, particularly those in which the mechanism is unfamiliar. The author of the above piece, William Rem, records that the gun lock 'functioned in such a way that when the trigger was pressed, it ignited itself and so discharged the piece'.

The occurrence of such accidents and the use of concealable weapons for nefarious purposes had the inevitable result. The Emperor Maximilian I banned manufacture of the dangerous wheellocks in 1517, and other authorities followed suit with particular emphasis placed on wheellocks short enough to be carried beneath the clothing. Although those charged with the protection and welfare of the citizen viewed the wheellock pistol with disfavour, the performance and undoubted value of the pistol for military purposes began to be recognised—in particular, its suitability for cavalry.

Turbulent Europe at the time of the Emperor Charles V (1519–1555) was an excellent proving ground for the wheellock pistol and the new tactics that accompanied its use. The mounted German 'reiters' of Charles V formed up into ranks fifteen or sixteen deep and charged the enemy. When in range, the first rank fired their pistols (each man carried at least two) and then wheeled to right or left, while the manoeuvre was repeated by succeeding ranks. In theory, the retiring ranks would reload and wheel again to the attack, so producing a form of continuous fire.

It was as an aid to loading that cartridges made their first effective appearance although, as early as 1500, mention had been made by Leonardo da Vinci of paper tubes containing individual powder charges. The early cartridge was really only a container for a charge of powder though sometimes the bullet was included. Loading, particularly in the heat of battle, was greatly simplified if the paper tube was torn open by the teeth and the charge poured into the barrel of the gun followed by the ball. The paper container was then used as wadding. The cartridge box was developed as protection and, worn on the person, was known as a patron—today the German word for cartridge. The derivation of the word 'cartridge' is from the French 'cartouche' and

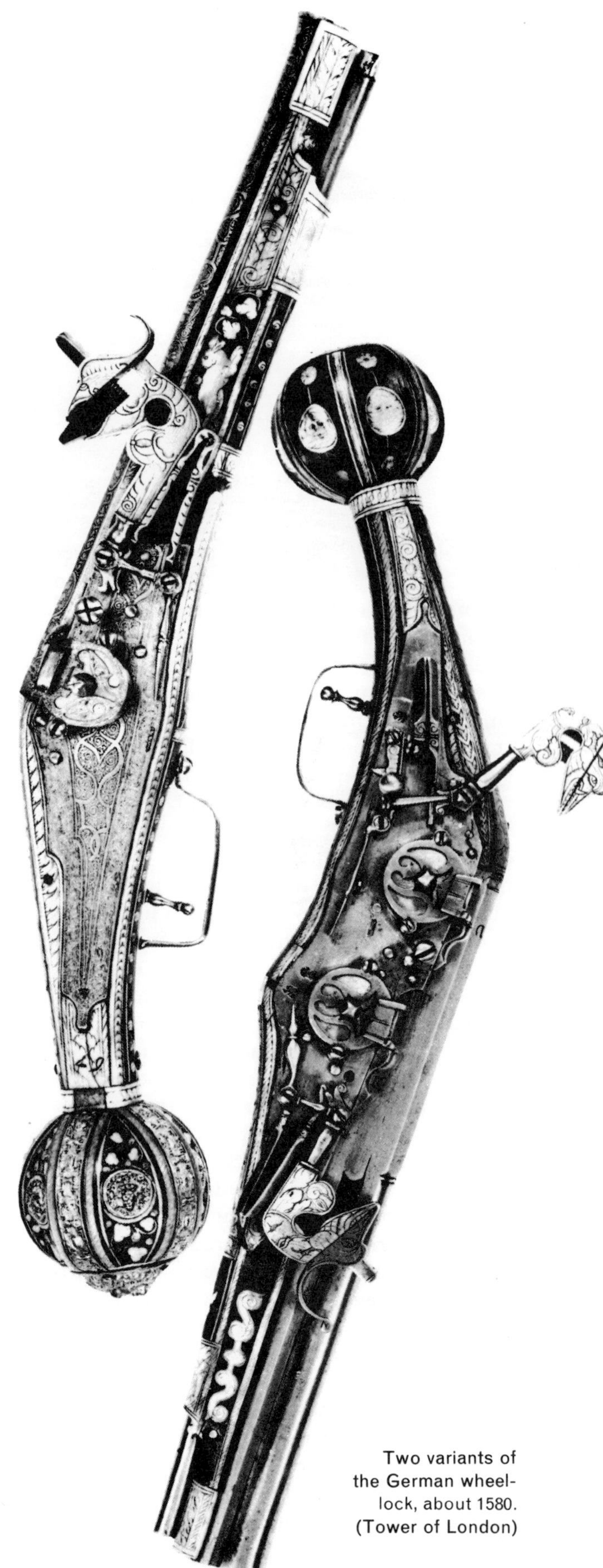

Two variants of the German wheellock, about 1580. (Tower of London)

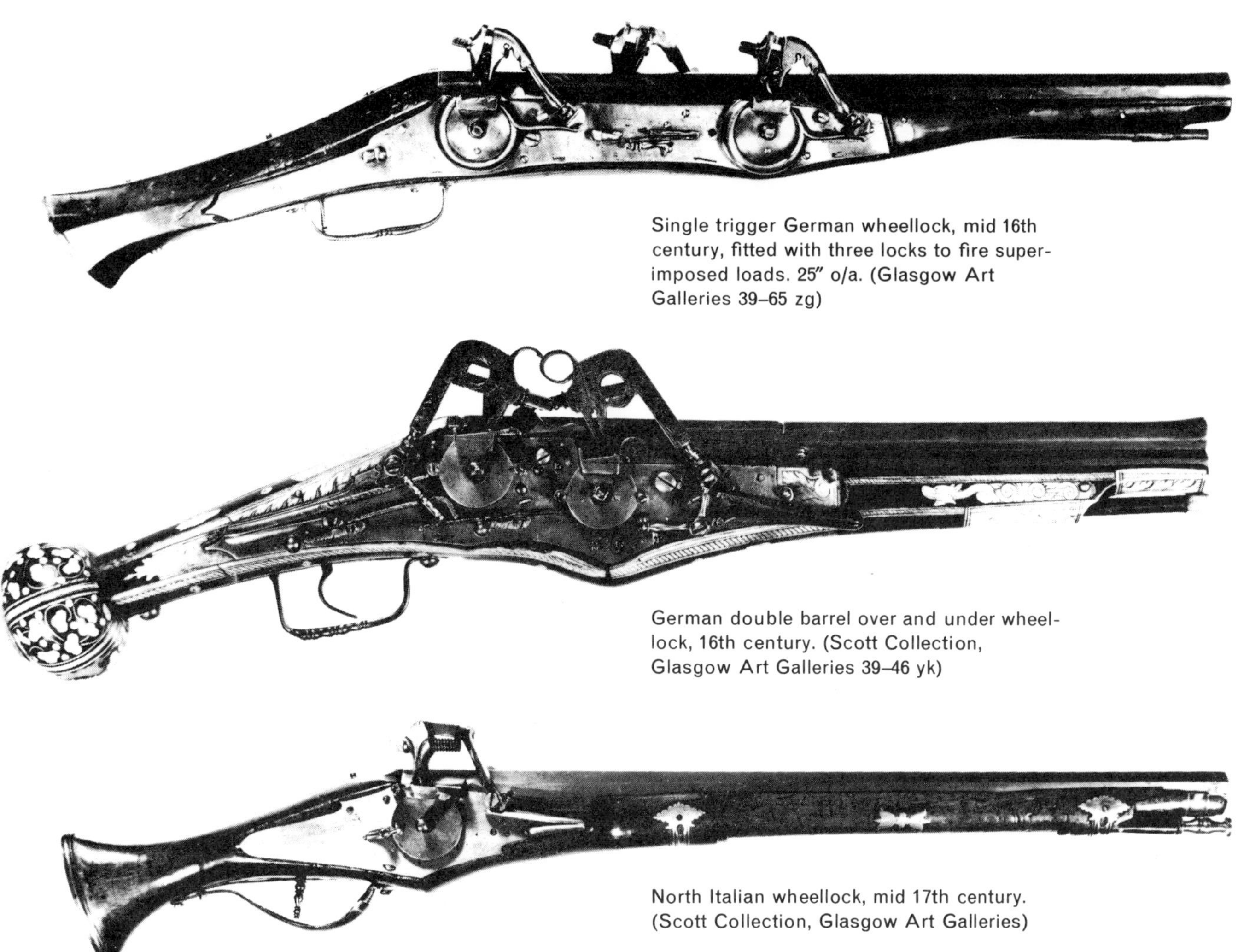

Single trigger German wheellock, mid 16th century, fitted with three locks to fire superimposed loads. 25″ o/a. (Glasgow Art Galleries 39–65 zg)

German double barrel over and under wheellock, 16th century. (Scott Collection, Glasgow Art Galleries 39–46 yk)

North Italian wheellock, mid 17th century. (Scott Collection, Glasgow Art Galleries)

originally meant a large wooden box containing up to three hundred musket balls.

The etymology of the word 'pistol' is not so straightforward. Italy, as we have seen, has some claim to the honour of being the birthplace of the wheellock pistol, and the name is said to come from the city of Pistoia. A counter claim comes from Czechoslovakia, where it is maintained that 'pistol' is derived from a short Bohemian handgun known as a pist'ala or pipe. Several other derivations have been proposed but none have been completely accepted. Heavy powerful pistols were also known as 'dagges' or 'dags' in England and to a lesser extent in Germany, but the origin of this term is unknown and it was little used after the sixteenth century.

To the modern eye, the wheellock pistols of the sixteenth century are most ungainly in appearance and, to say the least, somewhat cumbersome. One type which evolved had a butt set at a very slight angle to the axis of the barrel. Another, known as a 'Puffer' had the butt set at an acute angle, terminating in a round ball which tended to become overemphasised towards the end of the century. At first sight this large ball would appear to make an excellent club if the owner was unable to reload in the pressure of battle, an impression strengthened by looking at some of the early pictorial illustrations of knightly combat. Unfortunately, however, the ball butt of the Puffer would not have withstood such rough treatment since it was only secured to the stock by a peg, and its purpose appears to have been to facilitate the withdrawal of the pistol from an all-enveloping protective holster.

By far the greatest number of wheellock pistols were made in the great German gunmaking centres of Nurnberg, Augsburg and Munich, but

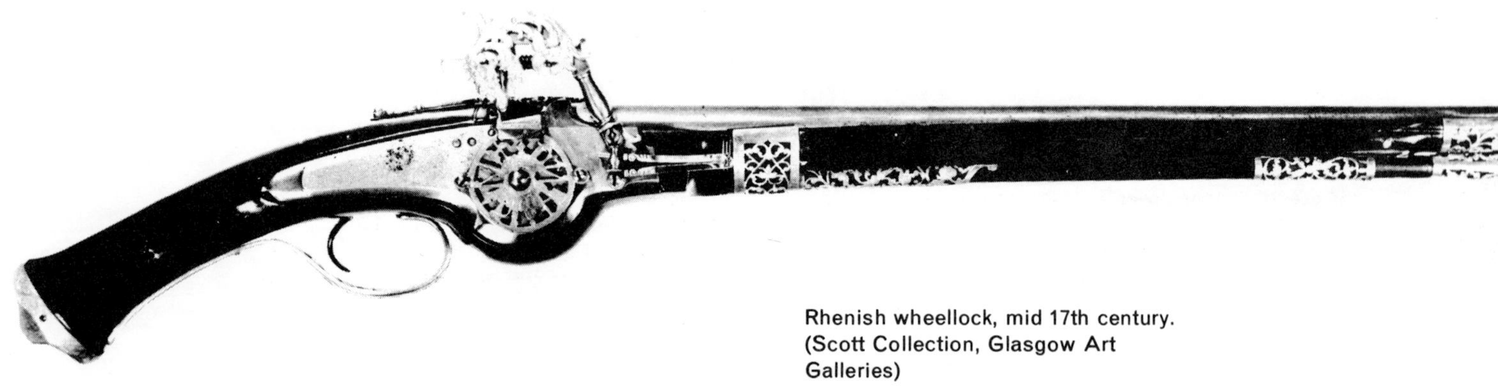

Rhenish wheellock, mid 17th century. (Scott Collection, Glasgow Art Galleries)

due to the influence of trade and the migration of gunmakers, difficulty often arises in establishing the origin of particular weapons. Such confusion occurs between Italian and German wheellock pistols during the second half of the sixteenth century, but there is no doubt that by this time Brescia in the North of Italy had established a tradition in the manufacture of firearms, a tradition that continues to the present day.

Although initially influenced by German design and decoration, the French evolved a wheellock mechanism of their own and, by the end of the sixteenth century, French pistols had entirely lost the angularity still evident in German weapons and possessed a charm and grace that can be appreciated even by the practical modern pistol-user.

Most of our knowledge of these early pistols has been gained from a close study of the weapons to be seen in the great museums or collections of Europe and America. Wheellock pistols were never cheap, but the German master gunsmith fortunate enough to possess a princely patron devised 'improvements' either to increase the safety, the rate of fire or the certainty of operation. Pistols were made having one barrel above another, each served by a separate lock, as were pistols capable of firing three shots. The charges were superimposed and fired successively. The potential purchasers of such marvels of mechanical ingenuity behaved much as the wealthy gun enthusiast of today and the extra expense of decoration was felt to be more than justified. The wooden furniture of the pistol was carved and inlaid with precious metals, ivory, horn, bone or mother of pearl, and the metal parts of the lock-work, the barrel, the trigger guard and mounts were engraved, blued, gilt or enamelled. The Italian gunsmiths of Brescia were renowned for their metal chiselling in high relief and, with their equally unerring instinct for line, they produced some of the finest pistols, ones which today still delight us with their craftsmanship.

Because of their artistry, weapons such as these have survived—often in princely collections—when a plain undecorated arm might well have been scrapped because of technical obsolescence. The appetite of the Emperor Charles V for firearms was, for example, insatiable, and evidence of the quality of workmanship demanded by him can be seen in a collection of wheellock arms in the Real Armeria, Madrid. Although wheellocks were not the sole prerogative of princes, the relative expense of even a pistol of military quality meant that their distribution was restricted to those who were best fitted to use them. Repairs also presented a problem, for although the local blacksmith could repair a matchlock, special training was necessary to master the intricacies of the more complicated wheellock.

While the wealthy toyed with their expensive and highly decorated wheellocks and those less well endowed struggled with the vagaries of the matchlock, a new type of lock appeared which from rude and obscure beginnings rose to a pinnacle of mechanical and artistic perfection by the end of the eighteenth century. Instead of the smouldering match with its simple lock or the complex mechanism of the wheellocks, this new device copied the age-old action of striking sparks with flint and steel to produce fire. It is known today as the Dutch snaphaunce.

The basic principle of all the 'flint and steel' locks was to secure a piece of specially shaped flint in the jaws of a pivoting arm, known as the cock, so that, when the trigger was pulled, a strong mainspring impelled the flint to sweep in an arc so that it struck against the steel which was

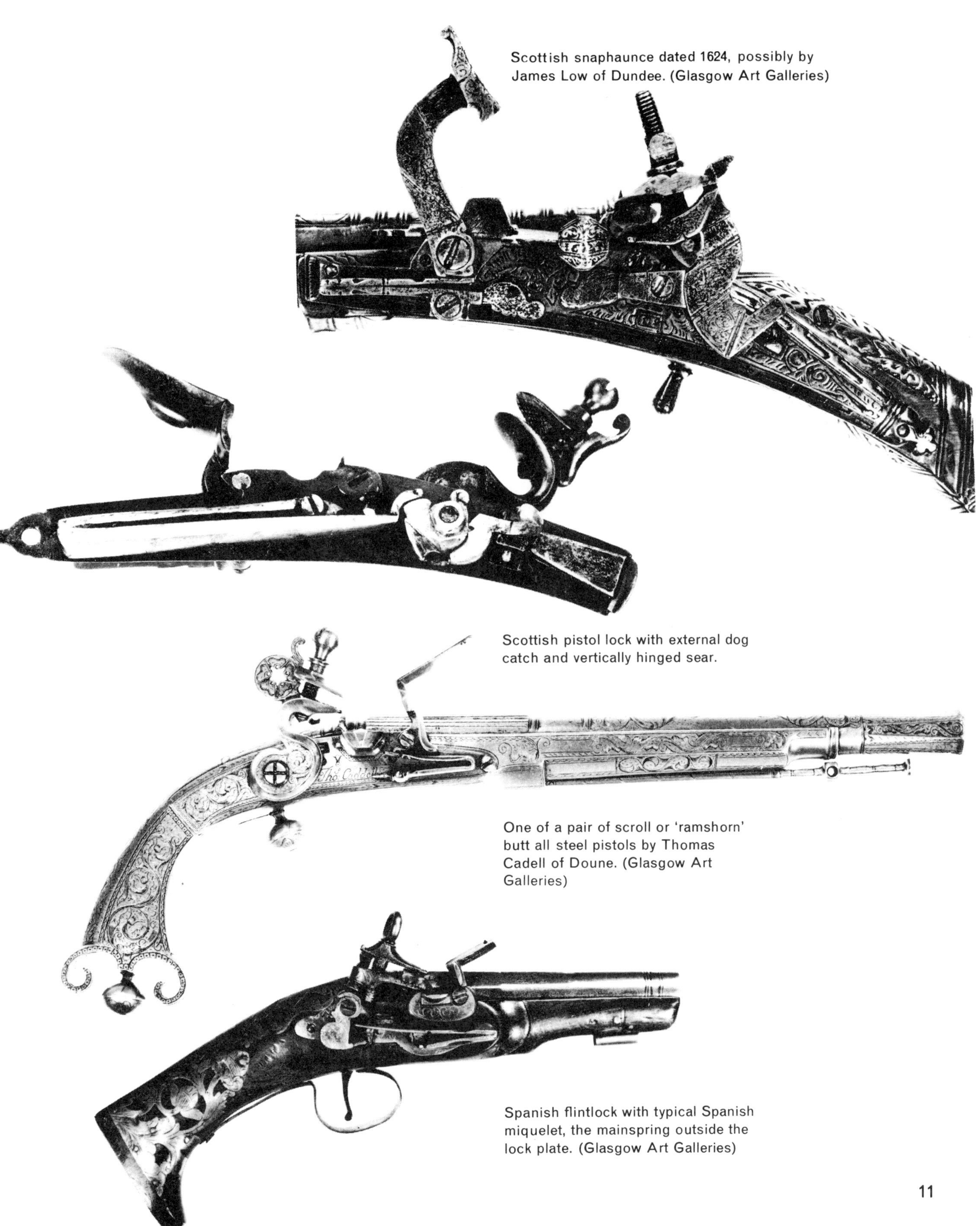

Scottish snaphaunce dated 1624, possibly by James Low of Dundee. (Glasgow Art Galleries)

Scottish pistol lock with external dog catch and vertically hinged sear.

One of a pair of scroll or 'ramshorn' butt all steel pistols by Thomas Cadell of Doune. (Glasgow Art Galleries)

Spanish flintlock with typical Spanish miquelet, the mainspring outside the lock plate. (Glasgow Art Galleries)

cock, tumbler and sear mechanism were similar to the French system, but the Italian lock remained true to its snaphaunce ancestry with pan cover and steel separate, and the cover opened automatically with the rotation of the tumbler. It is the excellent line and superb decoration of these pistols that today catch the eye of the visitor to a museum or collection. However, the artistry and grace of line suffered from over-elaboration towards the end of the seventeenth century, and pistols became vehicles for applied art rather than weapons. Certainly, their look of 'rightness' which can be discerned by the modern pistolman gradually becomes more difficult to detect as the years go by and the flamboyance of the decoration increases.

A basic variant of the flint and steel or snapping lock was the mechanism known today as the miquelet or Mediterranean lock, of which there were two differing versions, the Spanish and the Italian. Although the Spanish version was the more efficient, some doubt exists as to whether credit for the actual invention can rightfully be given to Spain. Two theories are put forward: the first that the Spanish miquelet was an adaptation of the Italian; the second, perhaps less tenable, that it evolved separately and at a later date.

The Spanish miquelet caused the mainspring to push upwards against the heel or rear of the cock, but the Italian lock made it act downwards on the toe or front of the cock. In both types the mainspring was fitted on the outside of the lock plate. The most important feature of all miquelet locks was that the steel and the pan cover were combined into one 'L' shaped component which became known as the hammer, battery or, in America, the frizzen.

We have seen that with the snaphaunce the pistol could be loaded and primed, the pan cover closed and the cock drawn back in readiness to fire. All that then had to be done to ensure that the loaded weapon could be carried safely was to see that the steel was 'out of battery'. Such an operation was not possible in locks which employed the combined steel and pan cover, since with the cock in the forward or uncocked position, the pan cover, by virtue of its design, had to be open. Should the pistol be loaded and primed the cover had to be shut and, of necessity, the steel would be in battery and the weapon liable accidentally to discharge. This was overcome by the provision of a safety or half cock device.

In the miquelet lock, the safe position was achieved by using a sear with two arms, and in both the Spanish and Italian versions the sear operated horizontally through the lock plate. Both arms of the sear in the Spanish lock passed through the lock plate ahead of the cock, the half cock sear being formed as a stud and the full cock sear as a flat blade. In the Italian version of the miquelet, one arm of the sear engaged the toe of the cock to provide the half cock position, while the full cock position was obtained by the second sear to the rear of the cock engaging the heel.

In Spain, credit for the invention of the miquelet lock is given by the Madrid gunmaker Isidro Soler to Simon Marquarte II. Soler wrote one of the few early technical books on gunmaking in 1795, the *Compendio Historico*. A writer contemporary with Marquarte, Alonzo Martines de Espinar, merely mentions that Marquarte made more miquelet locks than those of other types and testifies to the excellence of his workmanship. Simon Marquarte II was the son of the Simon Marquarte brought to Spain from Germany by the gun loving Charles V. He himself was gunmaker to both Philip III and Philip IV and although he may not have invented the Spanish miquelet, there is little doubt that he contributed to its perfection. During the first quarter of the seventeenth century this type of lock became increasingly popular in Spain and gradually replaced the matchlock and the wheel-lock.

To modern eyes, the Spanish miquelet lock (with its huge jawed cock and uncompromisingly right-angled steel and pan cover) appears crude and angular, lacking both grace and symmetry. Nevertheless, the virtues of the mechanism were many. It was simpler than the snaphaunce and consequently cheaper. It was less likely to go wrong. That it was highly effective there can be little doubt, for it remained in use in Spain until the day of the flint and steel locks was past. The Spanish lock never became popular in Western Europe, but guns using some variant of this basic design did achieve widespread distribution and, in their regionally developed forms, found successful and long-lived application throughout what we know today as the Balkans and the Middle East. Only in Morocco was the supremacy of the miquelet challenged, and here the Dutch snaphaunce was well established, surviving in a fossilised form until comparatively recent times. Like the Northern Italians already mentioned, the Spanish gunmakers were famous for the excellence of their gun barrels. The secret behind their excellence, according to Isidro Soler, was the use of Biscayan horseshoes.

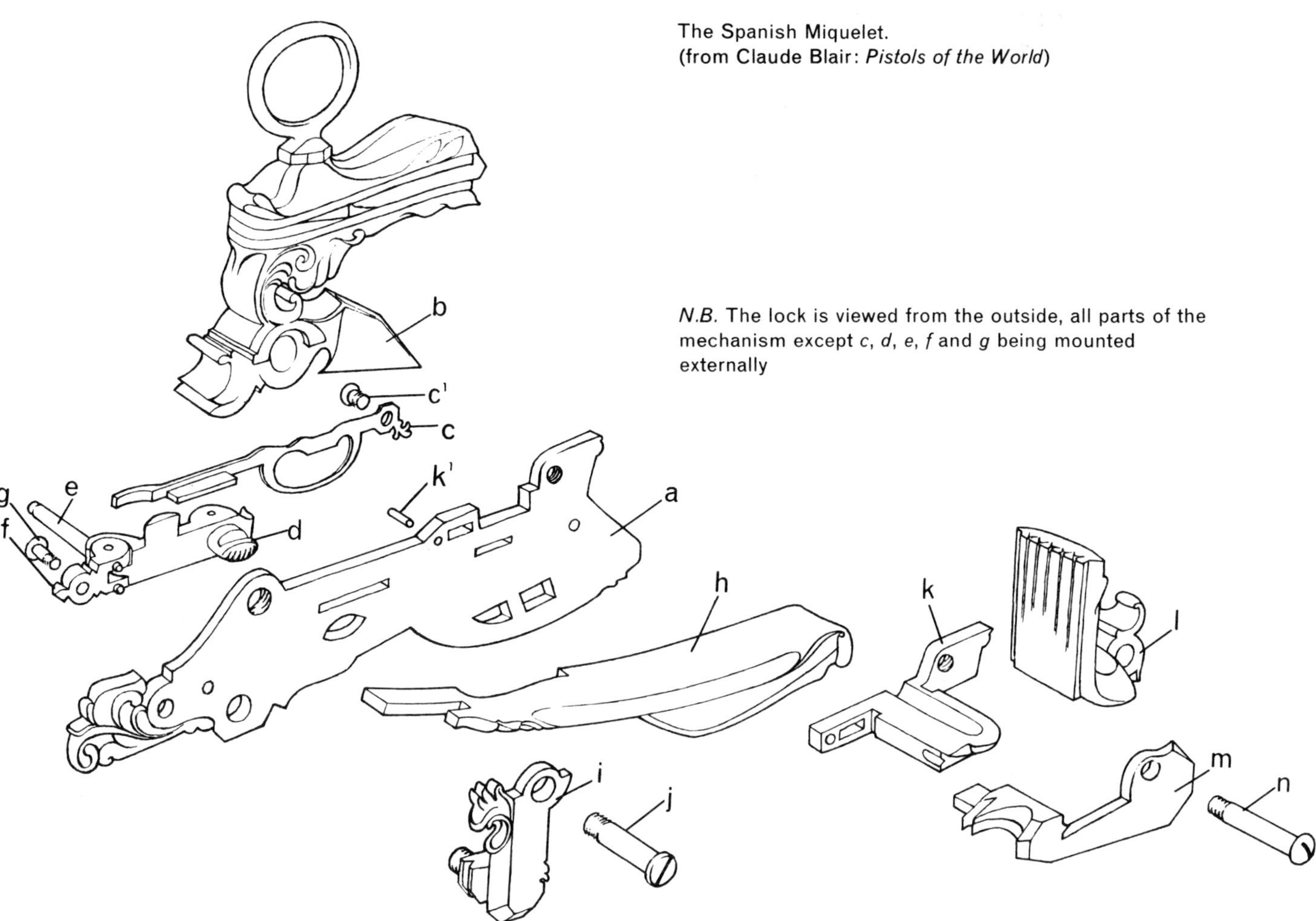

The Spanish Miquelet.
(from Claude Blair: *Pistols of the World*)

N.B. The lock is viewed from the outside, all parts of the mechanism except *c*, *d*, *e*, *f* and *g* being mounted externally

- *a* Lock plate
- *b* Cock with toe to engage sears *c* and *d* and heel to act against mainspring *h*
- *c* Full cock sear lever with retaining screw *c*
- *d* Half cock held by vertical pivot to the sear lever. Pressure on the trigger lever *e* causes this last to move out, so withdrawing the sear. At the same time the lug on the upper edge of the sear lever presses the end of the full cock sear lever *c* back, so withdrawing its sear
- *e* Trigger lever
- *f* Bracket, screwed to the lock plate, to which the half cock sear lever is pivoted
- *g* Retaining screw for *f*
- *h* Mainspring
- *i* Cock bridle
- *j* Cock pivot screw
- *k* Pan, secured by pin k^1 and screw *n*
- *l* Combined steel and pan cover
- *m* Bridle for *l*
- *n* Pivot screw for *l*, also serving to retain the forward end of *m*

Based on a lock of 1790 in the Victoria and Albert Museum (No. M.714-1927)

Throughout the later history of gunmaking, continued reference is made to the use of horseshoes and horseshoe nails for barrel forging. The reason behind this apparently peculiar choice of raw material is simply that it was a constant and reliable source of iron of known quality. According to Soler, this secret was discovered by a German gunsmith, Nicholas Bis, who had been brought to Spain in 1691 by Charles II. Rightly disturbed by the quality of Spanish barrels, many of which burst under test, Bis realised that the poor performance of the barrels was due to defective material and not to faulty workmanship. Deciding that Biscayan iron possessed the most desirable qualities for his purpose, Bis developed a complicated forging technique which proved to be highly successful in practice. Since other Spanish makers followed his example, the reputation of Spanish barrels became such that all Europe clamoured for them.

From an appearance point of view, three main

types of flint and steel pistol were produced in Spain. The first differed little in general style from those made elsewhere in Europe except that the majority were fitted with the miquelet lock—of which the Madrid gunmaker, as befitted a man who worked in the capital, created a variant with the mainspring inside the lock plate, though it conformed in outward appearance to better quality European locks. The second has no generally accepted name but, despite its rather odd appearance, had an unusually effective grip, as only practical experience can confirm. The third type, invariably fitted with a miquelet lock and having a distinctive, almost bizarre appearance, was the ball butted pistol which was made in Ripoll in the province of Catalonia and was unlike any other made elsewhere in Spain. Ripoll pistols were characterised by very short stocks terminating in a ball butt, the stock being covered with a metal inlay. Another feature was the use of a spur trigger guard, a device which we shall come across again. The gunmakers of Ripoll disappear from history with regrettable suddenness. Somewhat like the makers of Scottish pistols at Doune in Perthshire, the Ripoll gunsmiths produced quite distinctive weapons but, whereas it was sheer economic adversity that caused the demise of the Scottish craftsmen at Doune, harsh and bloody warfare wiped out the Ripoll makers when the town was entirely destroyed during the Spanish Civil War of 1839.

The Spanish miquelet had emerged as a distinctive and practical mechanism by the end of the sixteenth century, and it continued to be used in Spain although, elsewhere, the French lock achieved supremacy in all but the more backward areas where firearms were made. The differences between the Spanish and Southern Italian locks have already been mentioned, the miquelet being confined in Italy to the South dominated by the gunmakers of Naples. We have also seen how the Northern Italian makers had produced in Brescia perhaps the finest snaphaunce pistols ever made, but even the exuberance of the Brescian at his most flamboyant was overshadowed by the Neapolitan artist. Similar but slightly less elaborate pistols were made in Sicily and Sardinia. Since these makers did not sign their work, understandable doubt exists concerning the exact origin of those pistols, which tend

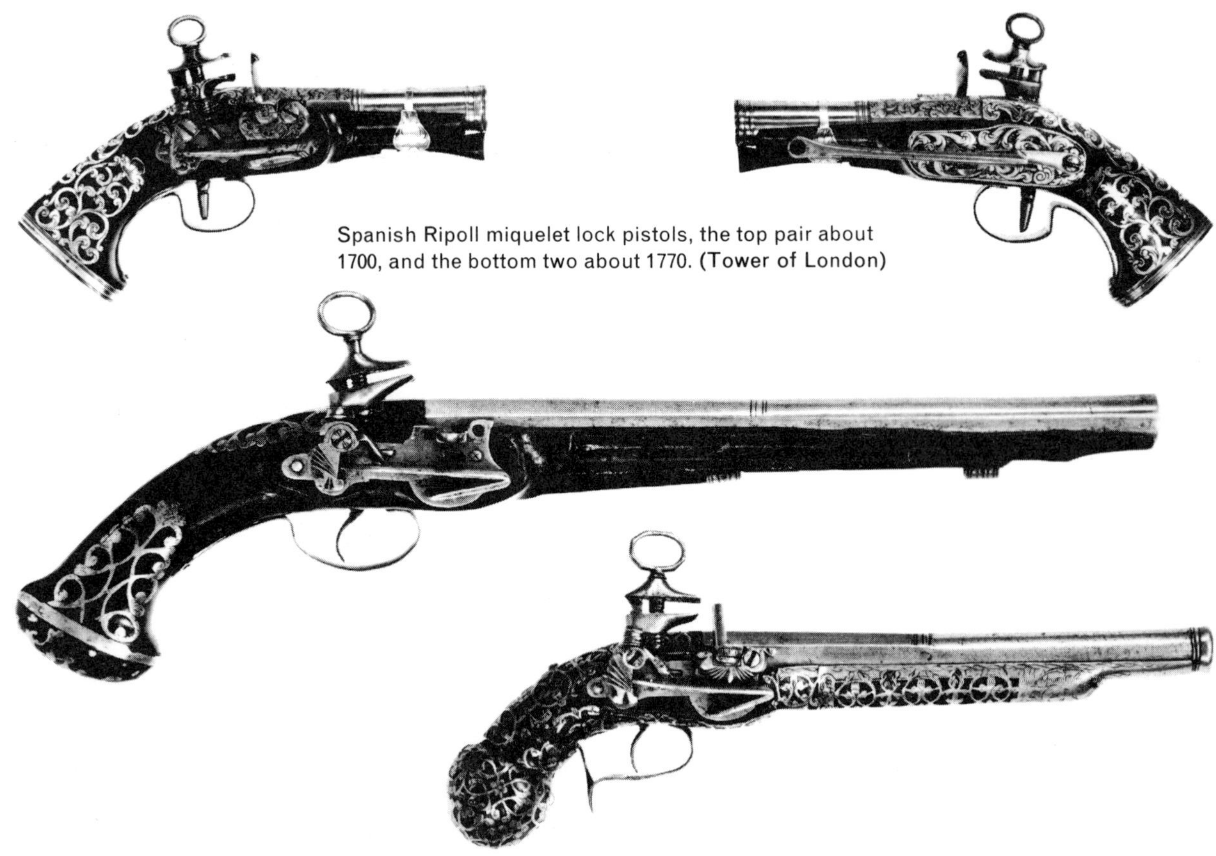

Spanish Ripoll miquelet lock pistols, the top pair about 1700, and the bottom two about 1770. (Tower of London)

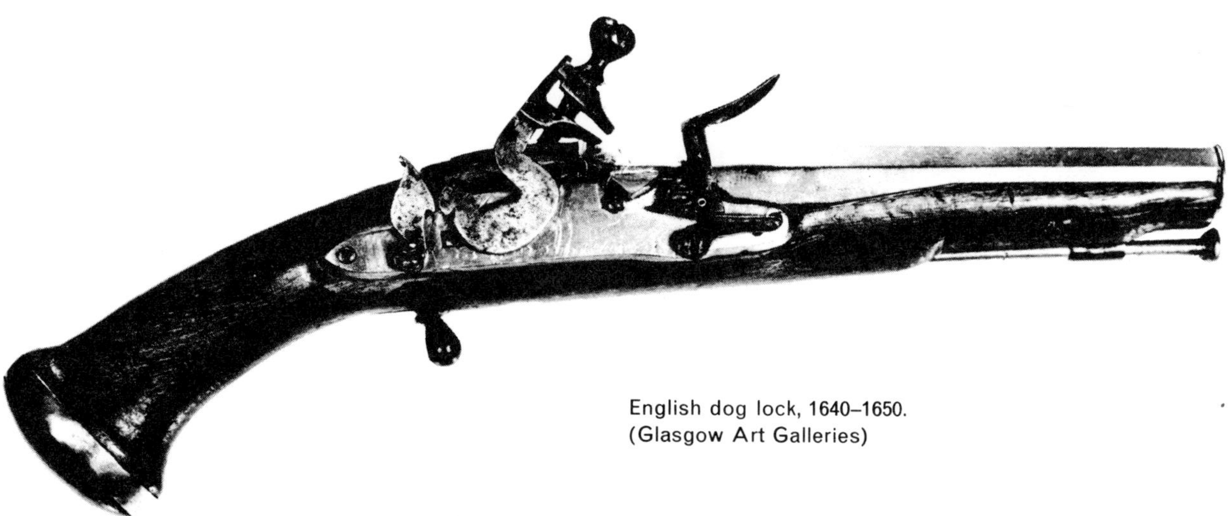

English dog lock, 1640–1650.
(Glasgow Art Galleries)

to mystify the specialist collector, but delight the eye of even those who have no interest in firearms.

If only for reasons of national pride, mention must be made of the so-called English lock which combined the features of the snaphaunce and the miquelet. Relatively few sixteenth century English pistols have survived and most of the information we have is gained from a study of their representation in early paintings. Brief mention has been made of the Dutch snaphaunce, which is supposed to have appeared during the latter part of the sixteenth century, but it is difficult to differentiate between early snaphaunce locks and to decide whether or not they were of English or Dutch origin. The task of the researcher is additionally complicated by the problem of the terminology of the period.

There is no doubt that by the early part of the seventeenth century gunmaking in England had progressed to such an extent that a peculiarly English type of lock had been developed which was used on pistols of English manufacture. Known to present day collectors as the English dog lock, this mechanism employed a sear which acted horizontally through a hole in the lock plate and was pivoted on a vertical pin resembling the sear mechanism of the wheellock. The cock and tumbler or axle were forged in one piece, unlike the later flintlocks. The steel and pan cover were also made in one piece but, unlike the miquelet, the steel was curved instead of being straight. A feature common to many of these English locks was the provision of an additional safety feature—a hook-shaped catch or dog fitted to the outside of the lock plate. This catch engaged in a recess cut in the tail of the cock as the latter was drawn back to just beyond the half cock position. Another feature of the early English lock was the provision of a buffer mounted externally on the lock plate which arrested the forward movement of the cock and prevented the jaws of the cock from smashing into the pan. Although known as a dog lock, some of these English locks will be found without the dog catch and, towards the end of its short life, further modifications were made in that the sear, while still acting horizontally, no longer protruded through the lock plate but engaged in two notches or bents cut in the tumbler.

Without doubt, the most important of the gun locks to appear was the French lock, the true flintlock. Unlike the discoveries and inventions already discussed, the invention of this particular lock can be attributed with reasonable certainty to one man, Marin le Bourgeois, who was born into a family of armourers, locksmiths and clockmakers at Lisieux in Normandy, in the middle of the sixteenth century. By any standards, Marin le Bourgeois was remarkably talented, for his work included painting, sculpture, the making of musical instruments and other 'ingenious mechanical contrivances'. That he was thoroughly familiar with a wide range of firearms can be taken for granted, and it is known that he made a crossbow and an air rifle in addition to the more conventional weapons. A man of such wide attainments could not long escape the attention of the Court, and in 1598 Henri IV appointed him valet-de-chambre, a conventional title designed to free him from the authority of the Paris craft guilds. After Henri's death in 1610, Marin continued to work for his successor, Louis XIII, until his death in 1634. The earliest surviving French flintlock, now in the Hermitage Museum, Leningrad, bears the inventory No. 152 of the personal Cabinet d'Armes of Louis XIII and must have been made between the years 1605 and 1615.

In what way did the French lock of le Bourgeois differ from the snaphaunce and the miquelet? The new lock can best be described as a hybrid, for the combined steel and pan cover of the miquelet was joined to the inside mechanism of the snaphaunce but the sear was arranged quite differently. Instead of moving horizontally through the lock plate, it moved vertically and engaged in bents cut in the tumbler to provide the half and full cock positions. As the mechanism was improved and refined, the stop which arrested the forward fall of the snaphaunce cock was eliminated. Instead, the cock of the true flintlock was provided with a shoulder on the inside face which came into contact with the top edge of the lock plate when the cock was in the forward position. By the middle of the seventeenth century a further improvement appeared which simplified the fixing of the cock to the tumbler.

Throughout the sixteenth century the German gunmakers had been pre-eminent, but the seventeenth century saw the emergence of the French as leaders in both design and technical development. The French makers equalled the Germans in ingenuity but, in addition, were able to combine with that ingenuity an elegance of form that is totally lacking in, for example, the ball-butted Puffer, the German wheellock pistol. This is not to say that with the invention of the true flintlock,

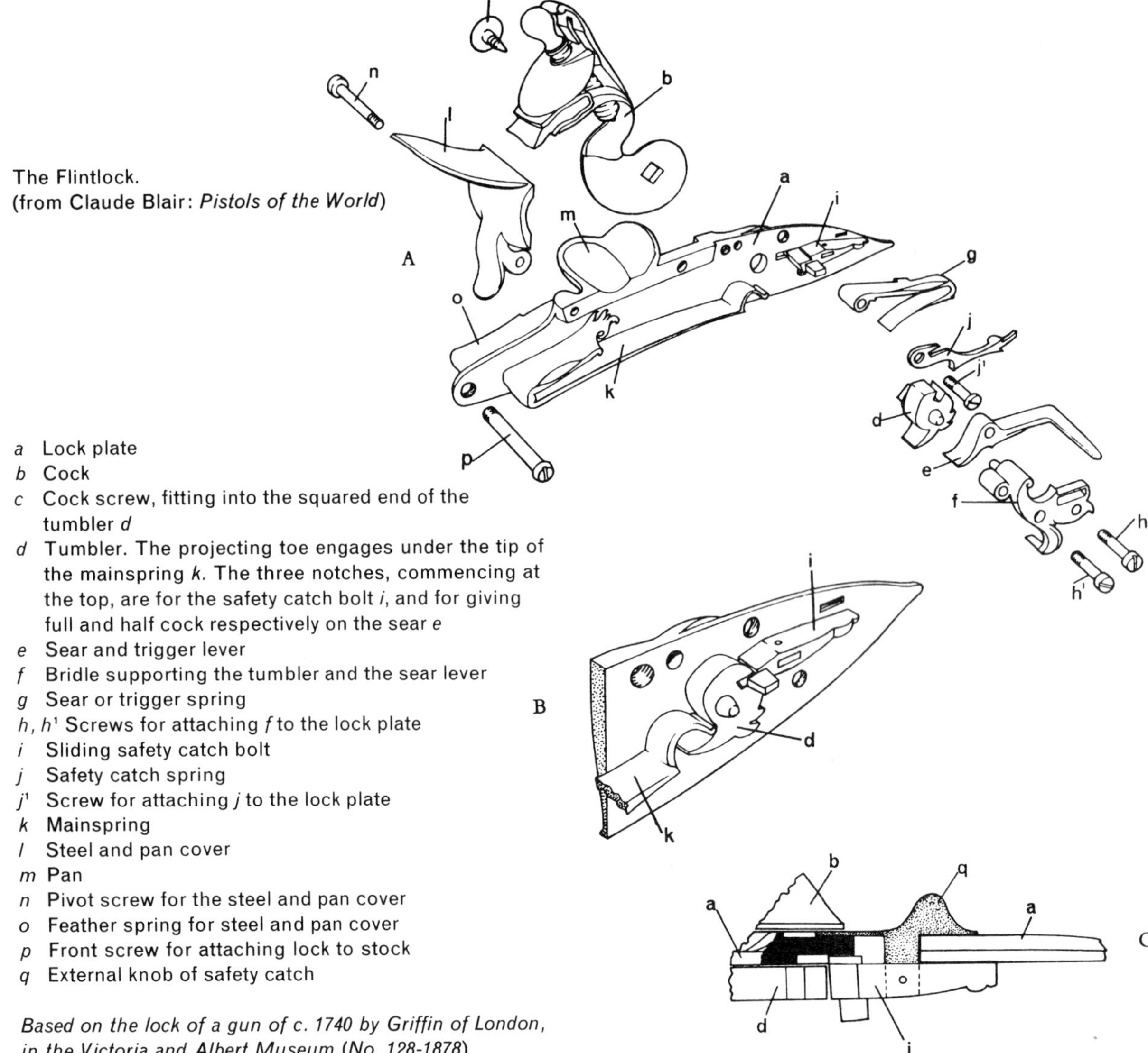

The Flintlock.
(from Claude Blair: *Pistols of the World*)

a Lock plate
b Cock
c Cock screw, fitting into the squared end of the tumbler *d*
d Tumbler. The projecting toe engages under the tip of the mainspring *k*. The three notches, commencing at the top, are for the safety catch bolt *i*, and for giving full and half cock respectively on the sear *e*
e Sear and trigger lever
f Bridle supporting the tumbler and the sear lever
g Sear or trigger spring
h, *h*' Screws for attaching *f* to the lock plate
i Sliding safety catch bolt
j Safety catch spring
j' Screw for attaching *j* to the lock plate
k Mainspring
l Steel and pan cover
m Pan
n Pivot screw for the steel and pan cover
o Feather spring for steel and pan cover
p Front screw for attaching lock to stock
q External knob of safety catch

Based on the lock of a gun of c. 1740 by Griffin of London, in the Victoria and Albert Museum (No. 128-1878)

all owners of wheellocks threw them away to buy the new style of weapon. Wheellocks continued to be made, one outstanding maker being Pierre Bergier of Grenoble. A number of his pistols were in the Cabinet d'Armes of Louis XIII and were distinguished by their ability 'pour tirer dans l'eau'. It is unlikely that the maker intended them for submarine warfare; the idea was to produce a lock mechanism that would function in the rain. This was achieved by making the lock totally enclosed and by taking the utmost care in manufacture to combine the necessary close tolerances with ease and certainty of operation.

Although both maker and patron in early seventeenth century France retained their individual preferences for the type of mechanism most suitable for pistols and other weapons, the flintlock became steadily more popular than its rivals and, as increasing care and ingenuity were lavished on its improvement, the new mechanism became more and more widely adopted. But, although it was destined to reign supreme in Western Europe, it met with considerable opposition in Italy and also in Germany—the traditional home of the wheellock.

Gunmakers were not, however, entirely preoccupied with lock mechanisms. During the seventeenth and eighteenth centuries various types of breechloaders were made, some with hinged barrels into which were introduced separate chambers provided with a pan and cover, while an alternative system, the turn-off or screw barrel, made possible extremely effective pistols. The turn-off breechloading pistol, although made throughout Western Europe, had particular success in England and, by the early 1700's, had evolved into perhaps the most attractive type of pistol ever made in this country, the so-called Queen Anne pistol.

The turn-off system possessed undoubted advantages. The simple construction involved the barrel being made in two parts, the front portion internally threaded at the rear so that it could be screwed on to an externally threaded portion of the breech chamber. The breech was chambered to take a ball of very slightly larger calibre than the barrel proper, and behind it was a chamber for the powder charge with a vent communicating to the flash pan.

To load a turn-off or screw barrelled pistol, the barrel was first of all unscrewed, and a few pistols were provided with special swivels or linkages between the barrel and stock in order to prevent

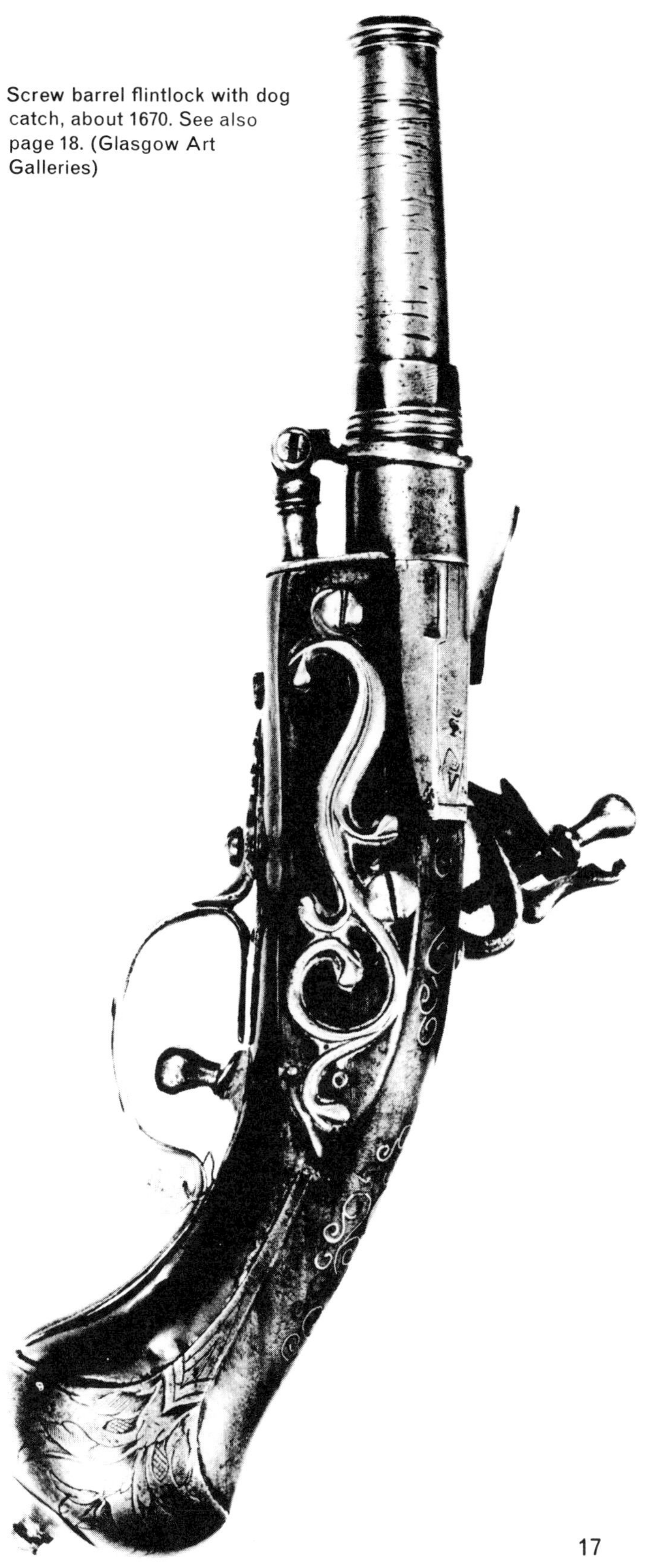

Screw barrel flintlock with dog catch, about 1670. See also page 18. (Glasgow Art Galleries)

the barrel being dropped—of particular importance for a horseman's pistol. In earlier weapons, the barrel could be unscrewed by hand, but later a key was provided which either engaged a lug at the rear of the barrel or, in the shape of a plug, entered internal grooves at the muzzle. With the barrel unscrewed, the powder charge was introduced and a ball placed in a cup-shaped recess at the end of the breech chamber. The barrel was then screwed back into place, the pistol primed and cocked, and it was then ready to fire.

This operation was far slower than the traditional loading from the muzzle with the aid of a ramrod, but the breechloading system had the great advantage of making the pistol shoot both harder and with greater accuracy. Another factor which made the system of value was that it permitted effective shooting with short pocket pistols, so much so that the screw barrel system remained in use until the development of cartridge loading.

Screw barrel flintlock with dog catch, about 1670, with barrel unscrewed. (Glasgow Art Galleries)

Harman Barne, gunmaker to Prince Rupert, and from 1660 to 1661 to Charles II, was perhaps one of the earliest English gunmakers to make his mark in history. An immigrant from the Low Countries, Barne was established in business during the reign of Charles I, and took the side of the Royalists during the Civil War. The famous story of Prince Rupert's shots at the weathercock gives some idea of the skill of both the marksmen and gunmakers of the period.

When the Royalist Army halted its march in the town of Stafford on 13 September 1642, Prince Rupert, keen to demonstrate the accuracy of his pistols, fired a shot at the weathercock on the steeple of St Mary's Church, hitting the tail of the weathercock. The prince's uncle, Charles I, remarked that the shot was a lucky fluke, whereupon the prince fired his second pistol with equally accurate results. The pistols used are described as 'screwed horseman's pistols' and here we run into some difficulty with terminology. During the seventeenth century, the term 'screwed' meant a rifled barrel (screw barrel later coming into use to describe 'turn-off' barrels), and since Barne was the prince's gunmaker and made both turn-off and rifled pistols, there is some doubt as to what type of pistol was actually used. However, since the range at which the shots were fired was sixty paces, the assumption must be that they were rifled turn-off pistols. To add to the confusion, the turn-off or screw barrel pistol is today more generally known as a cannon-barrel pistol, for it became the practice to decorate the muzzle with a baluster lip in imitation of a cannon.

Several chamber loading pistols with drop down barrels (similar to a modern shotgun) are recorded. One example can be seen in the Birmingham Museum, but it would appear that they enjoyed a limited popularity compared with the turn-off type of breech loader.

Repeating systems of varying degrees of complexity appeared during the seventeenth century, but all suffered from a basic inadequacy in construction materials. Moreover, the very high degree of craftsmanship required restricted the output, since none but the most highly skilled were able to translate the ingenious schemes of the inventor into effective practice. Foremost amongst the inventors of magazine repeating weapons were the Kalthoffs, who came from the famous German metal working town of Solingen. One member of the family, Caspar, was making repeating weapons in London during the mid-seventeenth century, and arrived in this country from Copenhagen. Both Kalthoff and Harman Barne made repeating magazine guns based on a cylindrical breech block mounted on a vertical axis, but yet another London gunmaker, John Dafte, produced an effective revolver capable of firing six shots which employed automatic rotating of the cylinder, unlike the earlier matchlock and wheellock 'revolvers' in which the cylinders had to be rotated by hand.

Interest in repeating mechanisms certainly existed but, although Samuel Pepys, the famous diarist, recorded on 3 July 1662, 'a gun to discharge seven times, the best of all devices I ever saw, and very serviceable, and not a bauble, for it is much approved of and many thereof made', such weapons must have been fabulously expensive and restricted to a fortunate few. Two years later, Pepys recorded on 4 March, 'by coach to my Lord Sandwich, with whom I spoke, walking a good while with him in his garden ... There were several people by trying a new fashion gun brought my Lord this morning, to shoot off often, one after another, without trouble or danger, very pretty.'

Of far more practical value, although perhaps less interesting, were the 'turn-over' pistols which became popular in France during the mid-seventeenth century, and were capable of firing two shots one after the other. These pistols were highly effective weapons, having one barrel over the other, each barrel being provided with its own separate flash pan and pan cover. With the pistol

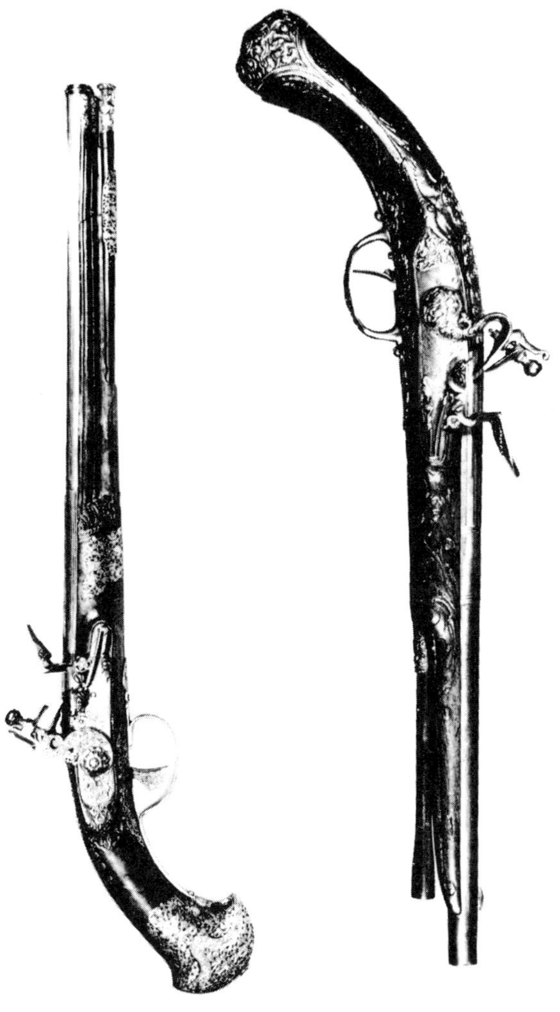

One of a pair of Brescian flintlocks. (Royal Scottish Museum)

Brescian flintlock. (Royal Scottish Museum)

Pair of flintlocks, about 1721, by J. Hawkins of London.

loaded and primed, the top barrel could be fired, the cock re-set and the barrel rotated on a central axis so that their position were reversed and the second barrel fired by the same lock. Usually, a catch was provided to lock the barrels in the firing position. Pistols of this type were also made in Germany (Wender pistols) and were exceptionally popular in Holland.

The end of the seventeenth century saw the flintlock in one or another of its regional forms firmly in the ascendant and the pistol equally well established as a valuable and distinct type of firearm. Groups of craftsmen had emerged competent to produce highly decorative works of art or ingenious mechanical contrivances, and in addition to the renowned centres of gunmaking such as Brescia, Suhl in Thuringia, Ferlach in Austria, Paris, Madrid and London, the seventeenth century saw the establishment of Birmingham and Liege as centres for the manufacture of firearms.

The inclusion of London as one of the world's great gunmaking centres towards the close of the seventeenth century is of course arguable, but by the end of Queen Anne's reign (1702–1714) the English gunmaker had well and truly laid the foundations of a reputation which eventually became the envy of Europe.

Many factors contributed towards this immense increase in stature and prestige. The age of Queen Anne is rightly regarded as a major turning point in English history. Apart from the military successes of Marlborough, which humbled the might of Louis XIV, art, craft and science flourished. Arising from the demands for arms occasioned by the unrest on the Continent, the gunmaker also prospered.

This period also saw the final abolition of the matchlock from the line regiments of the British Army and an endeavour to establish a rational system of manufacture for military arms. Previously, details of manufacture had been left to the separate contractors but, with the establishment of standard patterns for muskets, fusils, carbines and pistols, the Ordnance Office in the Tower of London gained increasing control, regulating both the quality of workmanship and the price, and even influencing design. The demand for pistols was far below that for muskets and less attention was paid to the need for standardisation. Despite the increase in capacity of both the Birmingham and London makers, relatively large purchases of pistols were made from the Continent and, since the pistol is perhaps the most

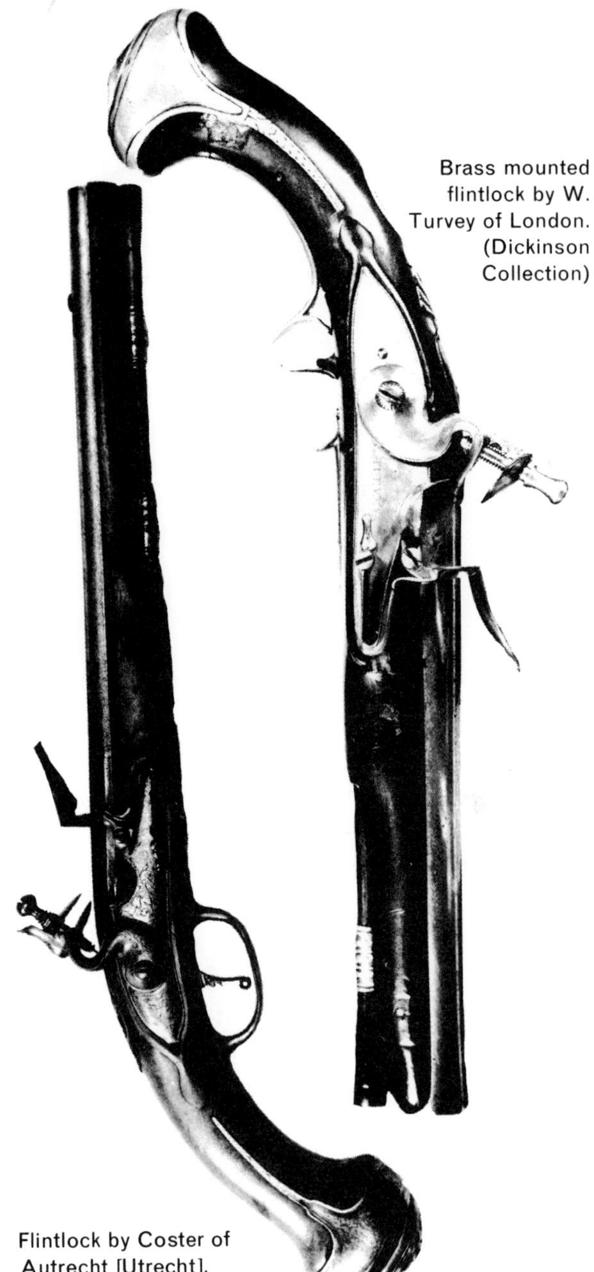

Brass mounted flintlock by W. Turvey of London. (Dickinson Collection)

Flintlock by Coster of Autrecht [Utrecht].

personal of arms, individuals often preferred to acquire them privately, thus ensuring a higher quality arm, though it had to be one that used issue ammunition. Further confusion exists due to the practice of regiments buying their own arms, and the problem of classification of Service weapons presents some difficulty.

Two dimensions which aid identification are the barrel length and the bore or calibre. Until the late nineteenth century, the internal diameter of the barrel was known by the 'bore' size which was determined by the number of solid lead balls of bore diameter obtainable from a pound of lead. Thus, a 20 bore pistol would accept a round ball of nominal .615″ in diameter, twenty of which would weigh one pound. One early attempt at standardisation took place in 1630, for the military wheellock pistol was re-

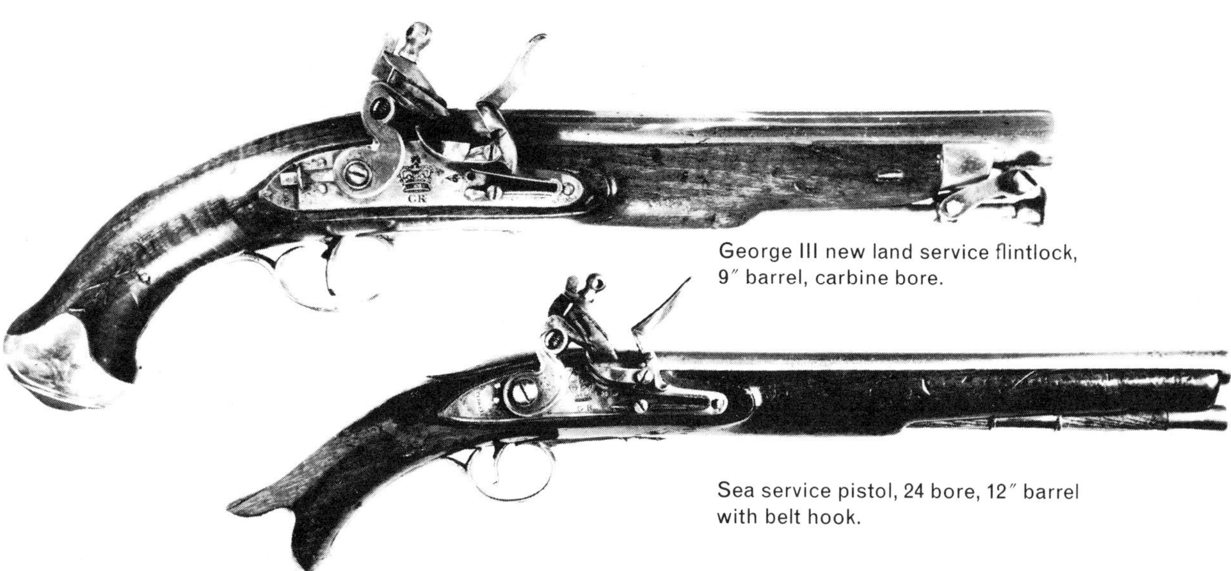

George III new land service flintlock, 9″ barrel, carbine bore.

Sea service pistol, 24 bore, 12″ barrel with belt hook.

'Duck's Foot' flintlock by Jacques of London.

The same from above. (Glasgow Art Galleries)

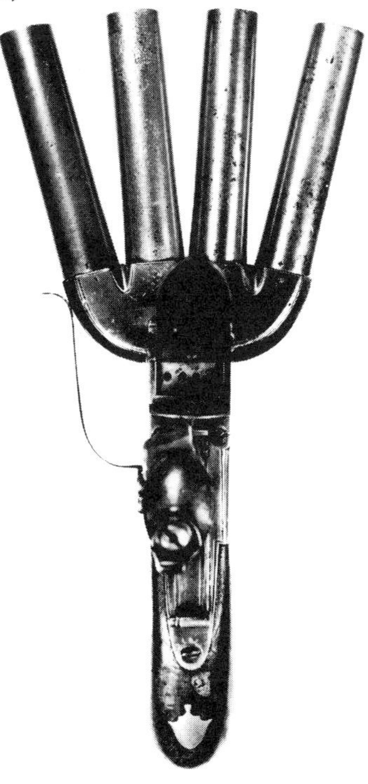

quired to have a barrel length of 18″, taking bullets 24 to the pound 'rowleing in'. Later, when it was demonstrated that the shorter barrel was equally effective, an attempt was made to reduce the barrel length to 16″, and by the time of Queen Anne it had come down to 14″. Such pistols were full stocked to the muzzle and furnished with brass trigger guards, side plates and butt caps. The butt caps were rounded and provided with decorative ears which often extended along the grip, the length of which appears to have been determined by the whim of the maker or, perhaps, the vagaries of fashion.

In the course of the reigns of the first three Georges, the barrel of the Service pistol became even shorter and there was a tendency for the bore to increase from pistol bore (24) to carbine bore (16) while the butt-caps lost their long decorative side pieces or ears. In addition, the rounded contour of cock and lock plate changed to a flat section and the swan-necked cock was replaced by the so-called reinforced cock. The raised decorative apron around the barrel tang was lost, but, in compensation, general efficiency was higher. By the end of the century, the barrel length had been reduced to 9″ and, instead of the ramrod being housed in brass pipes and liable to accidental loss, an effective form of captive ramrod was fitted which greatly simplified loading. As might be expected, flintlock weapons were affected by adverse weather and a simple type of waterproof pan was adopted.

Pistols used by the Navy were generally similar to the Service horse pistol and often fitted with a steel belt hook attached to the left hand side of the stock. One type of pistol which gained in popularity throughout the eighteenth century was the blunderbuss pistol. Such pistols were often carried by naval officers and were intended for close range hand-to-hand combat, a feature of the boarding tactics so successfully employed at this time. Similar weapons also formed part of the armoury of stage coach guards on mail coaches who were issued by the Post Office with a blunderbuss and two horse pistols, the necessary ammunition, a post-horn and a timepiece. The following were instructions issued to mail guards by Thomas Hasker in July, 1816:

> 'As many accidents have happened by the improper loading of firearms although the Guards have positive orders not to fire them wantonly it is deemed proper to state them, that the top of the powder horn is a sufficient charge for the blunderbus with 10 or 12 shot the size of a pea. That for the pistols two thirds of such a charge is proper. That they must be particular to ram the charge well that air may not be confined between or beyond the charge, and that they keep their arms clean and never loaded above a week.'[1]

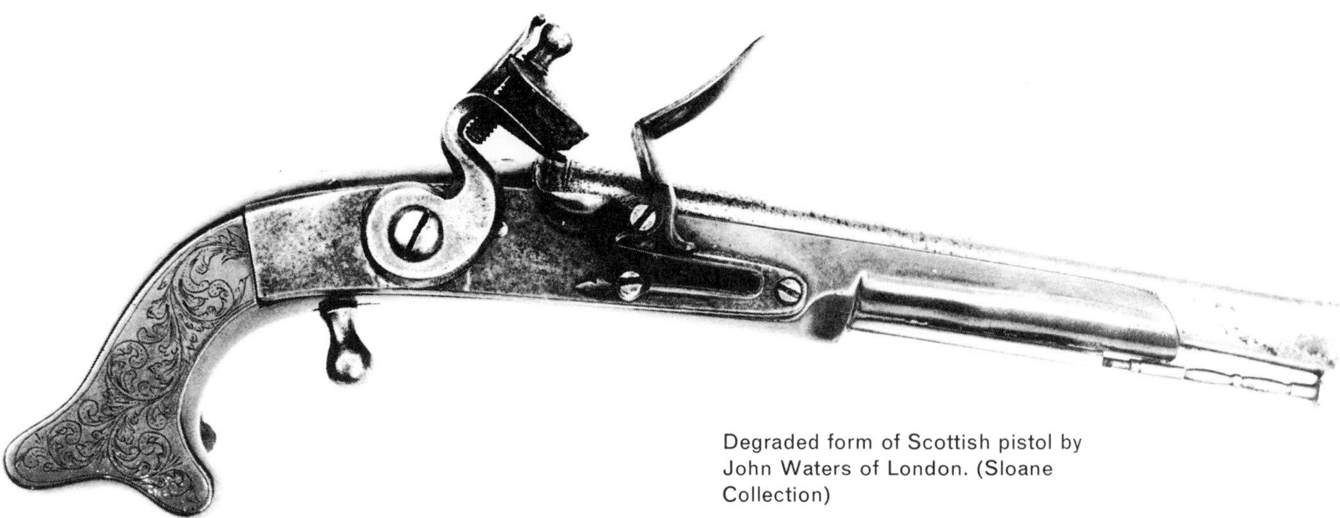

Degraded form of Scottish pistol by John Waters of London. (Sloane Collection)

Towards the end of the century, another type of pistol makes a brief appearance, the 'Mob' or 'Duck's Foot' pistol. These pistols were arranged to fire four shots simultaneously, the separate barrels diverging horizontally so as to spread the shots over a wide front. Such pistols, as the name implies, were specifically intended for dealing with unruly mobs and were suitable for use by tough sea captains, prison officers and the like. If fired into a tightly packed mob. someone was bound to get hit.

In addition to the many variations of the standard Service pistol for issue to the Army and Navy, many similar sound, sturdy pistols were bought by the Government for issue to Coast Guards, Revenue Officers, Prison Guards and the Guards of Mail Coaches. Many of these pistols because of the conditions of service, were fitted with brass barrels and, in addition to the maker's name on the lock plate, carried the Crown and 'G.R.' cypher found on all other Service arms.

The most unusual of the issue Service weapons was undoubtedly the Scottish all metal pistol mentioned earlier. During the turbulent times of the early eighteenth century, it was customary for a Highland soldier allotted the task of keeping the peace to carry a musket, basket hilted broadsword, dirk, targe and pistol. The pistol was worn under the left armpit, butt forward and attached to the cross belt by means of a 5″ long belt hook. Even if one assumes that the early Highland soldier provided his own pistol, the task of outfitting the later regiments must have been beyond the productive capacity of the indigenous Scottish firearm maker and, in addition, the cost of a hand-made pistol would have been excessive.

However, impelled either by Highland parsimony or by the business acumen of the Birmingham and London makers, certain of the Highland Regiments were eventually provided with Scottish pistols, some of which were made by Isaac Bissel (1745-1780) of Birmingham, and some of which are attributed to John Waters (1724–1776) of London. The pistols were of two different

[1] E. Vale: *The Mail Coach Men of the Late 18th Century*.

types. Those bearing London Proof Marks had brass or gunmetal stocks terminating in a kidney shaped butt which appears to be a degraded form of the true so-called Heart-butt pistol. The pistol marked Bissel were all steel, the butt being of the scroll or ramshorn type, although the term best employed for these Birmingham imitations is 'claw butted'. As far as can be ascertained, the unusual practice of issuing non-commissioned officers and men with 'side pistols' continued until 1789, although the officers, of course, carried them until much later.

The true Highland pistol received its death blow from the far cheaper English imitations, and the epitaph of the village of gunmakers at Doune in Perthshire is recorded in the Statistical Account of Scotland of 1789: 'There is now', it states, 'very little demand for Doune pistols owing to the low price of pistols made in England'.

To what degree these pistols saw actual military use is a matter for some conjecture, and an illuminating but unromantic light is cast on the Highlander's preference for broadsword and dirk by the Order of the Day given by Lord George Murray at Culloden in 1746: 'The Highlanders to be in their kilts and nobody to throw away their guns'.

The picturesque practice of wearing Scottish pistols as part of military dress uniforms finally died out when the officers of the 92nd Regiment, the Gordon Highlanders, ceased to wear their pistols in 1865. The type of pistol worn represents the last stage in the final degradation of an antique form of pistol. The Highland dress pistol of the nineteenth century, sometimes bearing the name of a well-known gunmaker, often the name of a haberdasher or accoutrement maker, retained the all metal construction and vestiges of the form, outline and decoration of its illustrious forbear, but the grace and splendour of the original had been lost.

The first skirmish of the American War of Independence took place at Lexington on the morning of 19 April 1775, and possibly more has been written by both sides about this war than about any other conflict of the eighteenth century, at least as far as the use of firearms is concerned.

The patriots had been accumulating arms and ammunition at Concord, a small village some twenty miles from Boston, and, on 18 April, a mixed British force under the command of Major John Pitcairn, which included eight hundred Royal Marines, set off in darkness along the Concord road, with the object of seizing these warlike stores. The movement of British troops aroused the patriots and the alarm was spread. By the time the British had reached Lexington the local militia, some seventy strong, were formed up on the village green—having been warned by Paul Revere, whose exploits on that night have been immortalised in Longfellow's poem, 'Paul Revere's Ride'. The rebels were ordered to disperse and, in the following confusion, someone fired. The volley was returned and the militia dispersed, but by the time the British had reached Concord most of the stores had been moved to safety. Two months later at the Battle of Bunker's Hill on 17 June, Major Pitcairn was killed and the pistols he carried are now the property of the Lexington Historical Society. Made by John Murdoch of Doune in Perthshire, they are typical all steel Scottish pistols slightly over twelve inches in length with the usual belt hook and are of the 'ramshorn' butt type. There is a legend that the first shot of the War of Independence was fired from a Scottish pistol, but although one could imagine Pitcairn firing a shot from his pistol to gain attention, it is more likely that the first shot came from the musket of one of the understandably nervous militia men.

Yet another pair of Scottish pistols is associated with the War of Independence but this time they were characteristic examples of the type known by modern collectors as 'lobe butted'. These pistols are preserved at Chateau Lafayette, Chavaniac-Lafayette, Haute-Loire, France, and were bequeathed by General George Washington to the Marquis de Lafayette in accordance with the terms of his will which stated: 'To General de la Fayette I give a pair of finely wrought steel pistols, taken from the enemy in the Revolutionary War'. No hint is given as to the original owner but we know that the pistols were made by Thomas Murdoch, who was working in Leith, near Edinburgh, in 1774. That these Scottish pistols have survived is not surprising since, by any standards, they are unusual and fascinating weapons. Other pistols of the Revolutionary period have also survived and their history is known. The majority were, however, personal arms, privately purchased, and even if they lacked the unique character of the Scottish all steel pistol, their owner would obviously have been proud of them and they would have borne his name or family crest and often, in addition, his

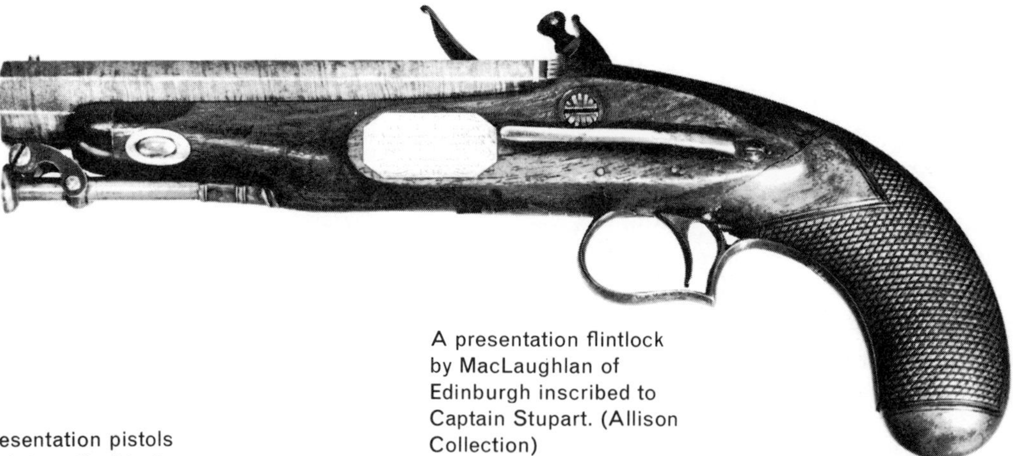

A presentation flintlock by MacLaughlan of Edinburgh inscribed to Captain Stupart. (Allison Collection)

One of a pair of presentation pistols by Thomas Murdoch inscribed to the Marquis de Bouillé.

regiment. One such pistol, made by Ketland and Co., Birmingham, between 1767 and 1776, was owned by Captain James Boucher of the 31st Regiment of Foot (later redesignated the 1st East Surrey Regiment). The 31st arrived in Canada from England in 1776, and we find that the only officer serving with the regiment with a surname commencing with 'B' was Captain Boucher. Since the Ketland pistol is marked on the side plate '31st Regt.' and has the monogram 'J.B.' in script on the escutcheon, the identity of the owner is established with some measure of certainty. Despite diligent research on the part of the present owner of this pistol, no information concerning the fate of Captain James Boucher has come to light and it is possible that he did not survive the loss of his pistol.

Pistols were often presented to individuals as a token of esteem from their colleagues, and a typical example is the 16 bore given to Captain Stupart who fought at the battle of Waterloo. The pistol bears the crest of the Stupart family and a silver plate inscribed 'Presented to Capt. Stupart by the non-commissioned officers and men of his troop of the Royal Scots Greys as a small token of their esteem and regard. 1816'.

By the end of the eighteenth century, the gun-rooms of most of the noble houses of Europe could boast several splendid, magnificently decorated firearms, products of master gunmakers from France, Germany, Italy and Spain. Such weapons, however, lie outside the scope of this work which is primarily concerned with technology rather than decoration.

It has already been said that, as far as military

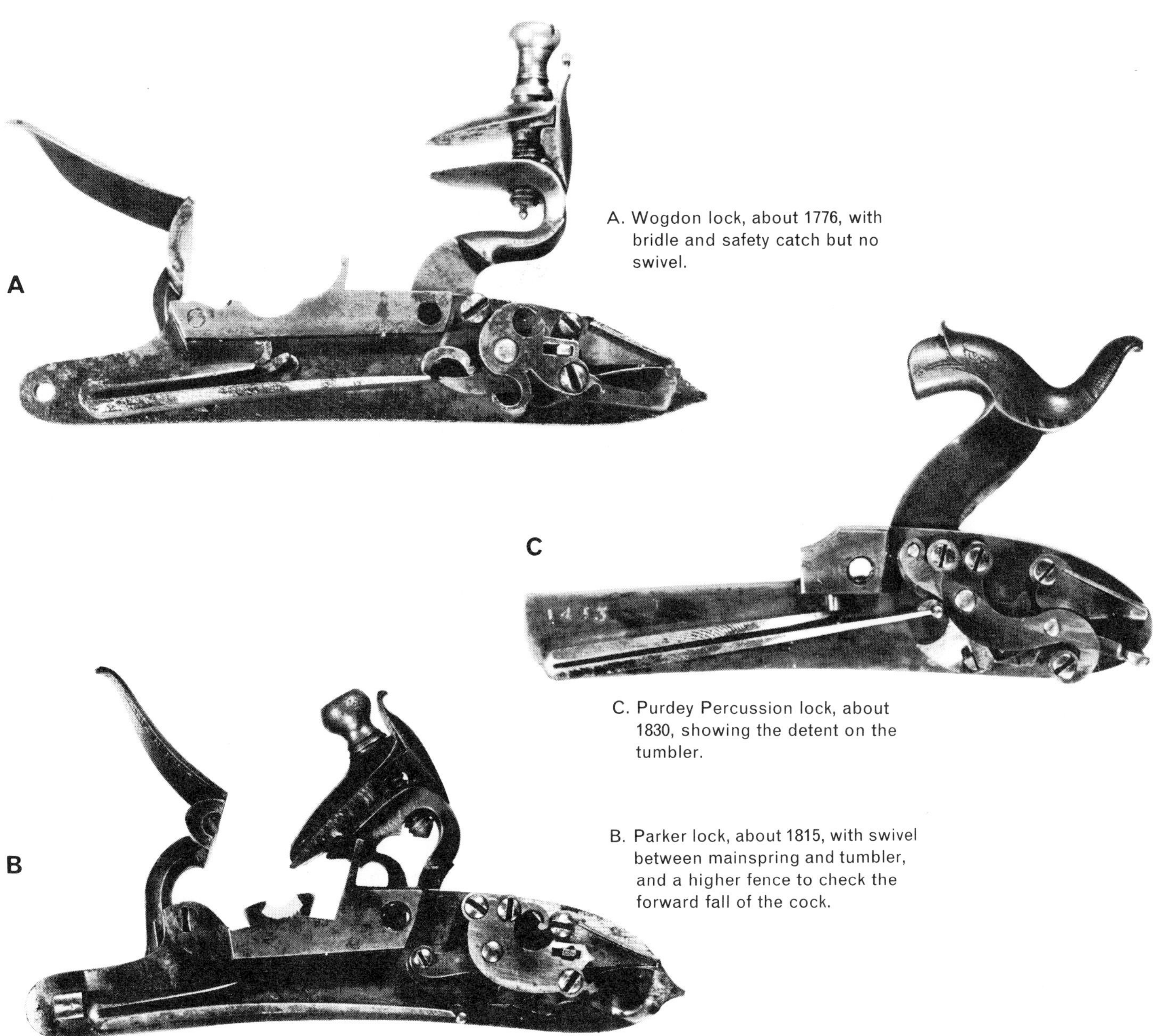

A. Wogdon lock, about 1776, with bridle and safety catch but no swivel.

C. Purdey Percussion lock, about 1830, showing the detent on the tumbler.

B. Parker lock, about 1815, with swivel between mainspring and tumbler, and a higher fence to check the forward fall of the cock.

weapons were concerned, the whole of the flintlock period was characterised by a lack of technical innovation. Pistols tended to become shorter and of heavier calibre and, as greater care was taken in the finishing of the lockwork, their operation became more certain and positive. Such improvements in the actual construction of the pistol can be attributed to the greater degree of specialisation within the gunmaking trade as a whole, and this is reflected in small items such as the screws used to assemble locks. Screws which were accurately made and carefully threaded undoubtedly contributed to the smoother working of gun locks, and the availability of soundly constructed locks of standard pattern greatly eased the problem of the gun assembler. But this was also a factor that tended to restrict experimentation and contributed in no small measure to the conservatism which was a feature of the period. Such changes as did take place were easily accommodated within the existing concept of the mechanism. On English locks, a bridle appeared to provide additional support for the pan cover hinge screw. In the seventeenth century a similar improvement had been made inside the lock by using a bridle to act as an additional bearing for the tumbler and this, coupled with the later introduction of a steel link or swivel between the mainspring and the tumbler, resulted in a considerable reduction in friction, greatly increasing the speed of the lock. Previously, the mainspring had terminated in a hook which acted directly on the tumbler and at least one maker, Ketland of Birmingham, had placed a small roller at the toe of the spring. This system, however, was not as popular as the swivel, although we do

Innes pistol lock showing the small bearing wheel between the feather spring and the tail of the pan cover.

find it being used later on Colt revolving pistols, the roller being on the hammer rather than on the spring itself.

A similar little roller also made its appearance as a friction-reducing bearing between the feather spring and the pan cover. This invention appears to have been introduced between 1780 and 1790, and on most locks the roller is attached to the spring, the end being bifurcated. On some locks, the roller will be found on the pan cover itself when, in addition, there is a small cam fitted to the spring to modify the opening action of the pan cover.

Reference has been made earlier to the Queen Anne cannon-barrelled or 'turn-off' pistol. In pistols of this type the lock plate was not separate but formed an extension of the barrel, the pan being attached directly to the breech beneath the vent. By 1750, a logical development of this method of construction, the box lock, was introduced which was even more compact and particularly suited to the manufacture of pocket pistols. The box lock represented the first real advance in design since the flintlock became established. From the beginnings of the first recognisable firearm, gunmakers had been content to attach the all-important lock mechanism to the side of the stock and here, with relatively few unimportant exceptions, it remained. The Queen Anne cannon-barrelled pistol represented the first departure from the accepted design con-

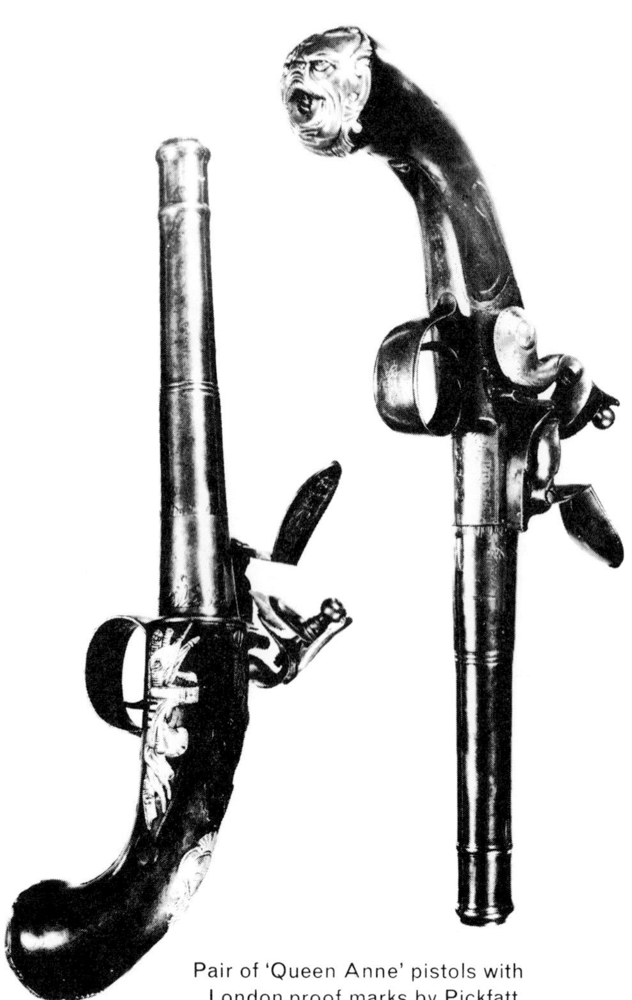

Pair of 'Queen Anne' pistols with London proof marks by Pickfatt.

cept in that the lock plate, trigger plate and butt strap were forged as part of the breech, and the whole formed what was to be called in later years the action body of the pistol. Looked at another way, the action body represented three sides of a box. If the cock was then moved from the outside to the inside of one of the walls, and the priming pan from the side to the top of the breech, and if two more sides were provided (one opposite to the side which carried the cock originally, and one as top), the result created was, in effect, the box lock. The box had five metal sides, the sixth being provided by the end of the wooden stock. One further alteration remained to be made—the combining of cock and tumbler—and this was quite simply accomplished by cutting the notches or bents into the cock itself.

This rigid and quite roomy box, with the centrally disposed cock, allowed space for the accommodation of additional refinements. One could, for example, make the box wider and mount two barrels side by side at the front. Two separate locks mounted inside the box produced a compact double barrelled pistol.

To reduce cost and complexity, a variant of this type appeared having a single cock, the flash pan being divided into two parts, one of which was provided with a sliding cover which could be opened or closed by means of a thumb catch mounted on the side of the action. A broad hinged pan cover of the usual type covered both sides of the pan. Such a pistol would be loaded in the normal manner and, in the case of multiple

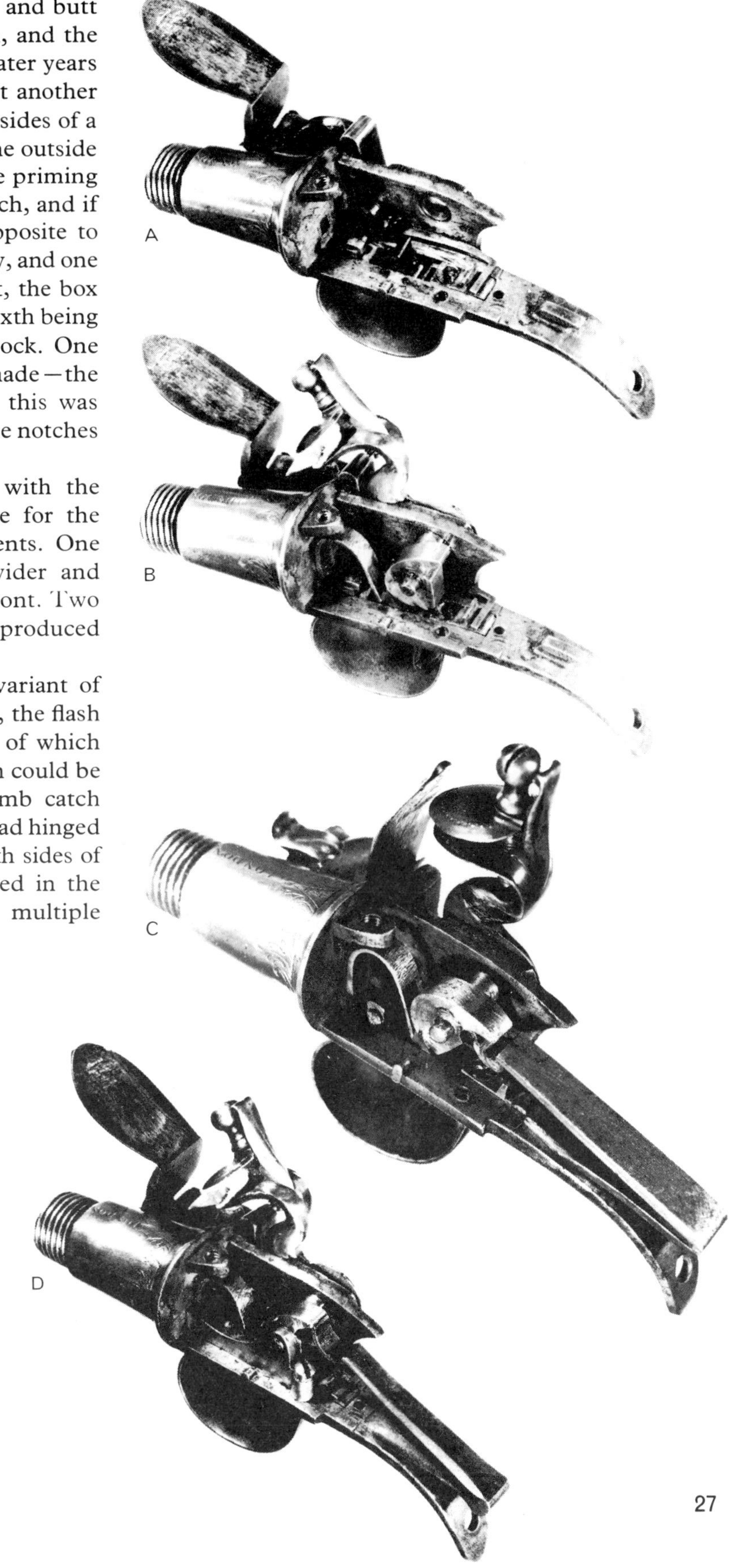

A. Basic action body with trigger attached.

B. Tumbler, cock and trigger spring fitted.

C. Mainspring fitted.

D. Bridle fitted to support tumbler.

barrelled pistols, an internal key was used to engage in grooves cut internally at the muzzle – which might at first glance be taken for rifling. With the barrels removed (they were usually numbered to correspond with the breech chambers), the breech was disclosed with a central chamber for the charge of black powder, the face cupped to form a seat for the ball. With powder and ball in place, the barrels were screwed on and the pistol primed. The left hand portion of the pan was then isolated by operating the cut-off. Brought to full cock with the pan cover down, the right hand barrel could be fired. Brought back to full cock again, the pan cover was closed and the cut-off opened, and the left hand barrel could then be discharged.

An alternative system was to arrange the barrels vertically, one above the other, in which case the cut-off system was unsatisfactory. For over and under pistols the tap action was employed. The pan was mounted centrally as before but its shape was rectangular with sloping sides, front and rear. At the base of the pan was a cylindrical steel drum mounted transversely across the action body. The drum was spring loaded and provided with an external tap or lever. The tap could only be moved to either the three o'clock or six o'clock positions. With the tap in the three o'clock position the solid face of the drum showed, and in the six o'clock position the surface of the drum displayed a deep groove with a central vent hole. The body of the pistol was provided with two vents, one from the front face of the pan to the upper barrel, the second from the bottom of the drum housing to the lower barrel.

The method of operation was as follows. The barrels would be loaded in the manner described above, the cock brought back to the half cock position and secured by the safety catch. If this was mounted on top of the action, the hammer and, by means of an extension, the pan cover could be locked, the latter in the closed position. Alternatively, the cock only could be locked by moving the trigger guard forward. The pan was

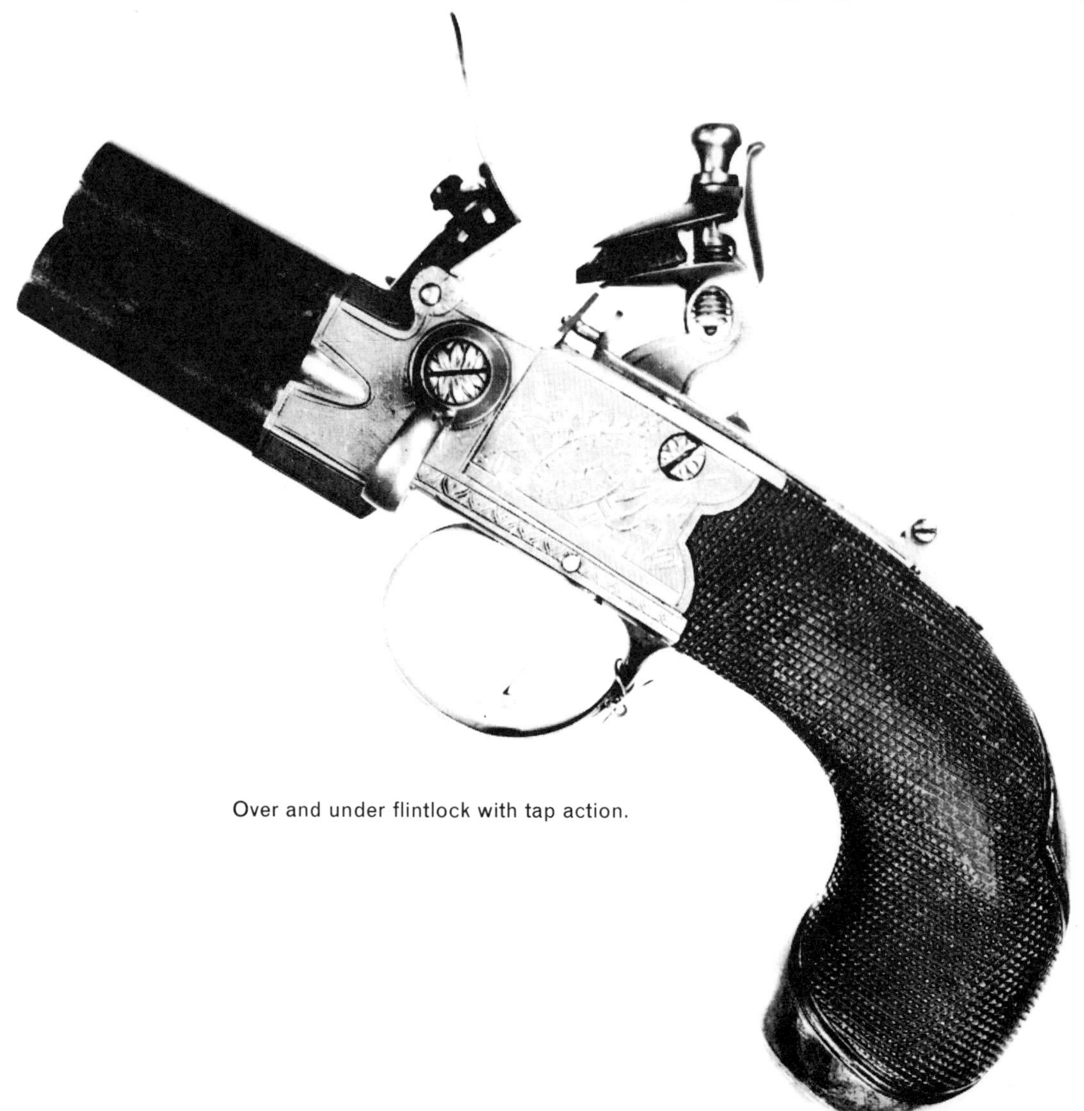

Over and under flintlock with tap action.

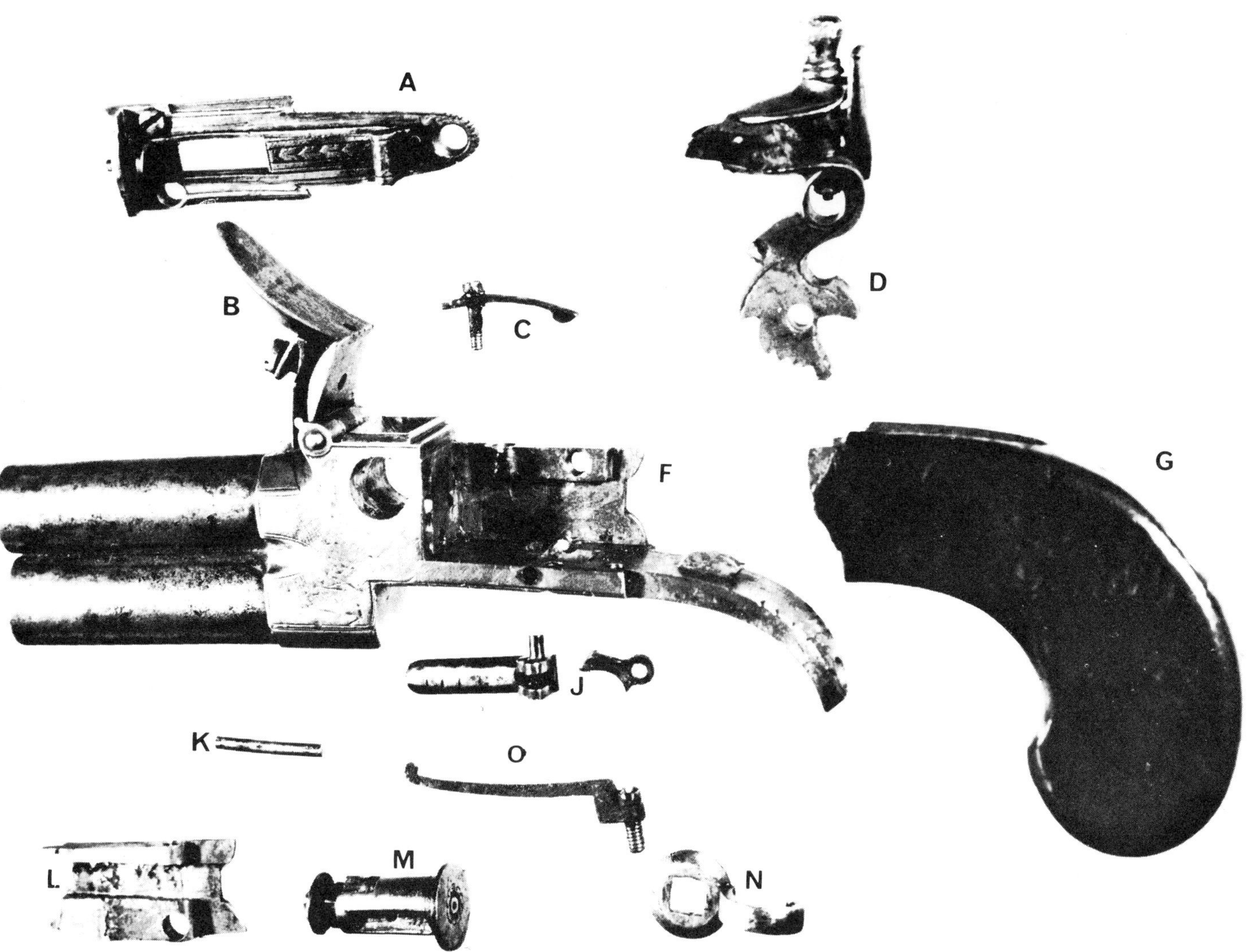

Dismantled double barrel flintlock with tap action, mainspring not shown.

A. Top plate with sliding safety.
B. Steel and pan cover.
C. Trigger spring.
D. Cock.
E. Upper barrel.
F. Frame.
G. Butt.
H. Lower barrel.
J. Trigger pin with sear.
K. Trigger pin.
L. Side plate.
M. Tap plug.
N. Tap lever.
O. Tap indexing spring.

then primed with the tap in the six o'clock position so that the groove in the drum was also primed. The tap was then turned to the three o'clock position. If the safety catch was released, the pan closed and the action cocked and fired, the priming in the pan would discharge the top barrel via the vent in the pan wall. Then the pistol was again cocked, the pan closed and the tap turned to the six o'clock position. When the pistol was fired again, the priming contained in the groove of the drum flashed and ignited the charge in the lower barrel via the vent in the body of the drum and the vent between the drum housing and the lower barrel. If a fully loaded and primed pistol was fired with the tap in the six o'clock position, both barrels would, of course, be fired simultaneously. Box lock pistols with either sliding or revolving (tap action) cut-offs, or a combination of both, were made with one, two, three or four barrels. Four barrelled pistols were also made which fired each barrel successively, two barrels at one time or all four barrels at once. Single barrel tap action pistols were made capable of firing two successive shots, the loads being superimposed and the barrel in two sections. The rear section had an internal vent which communicated with the front barrel, the tap providing two priming charges.

Variations of the screw barrel box lock appear to have been endless. In the smaller pocket pistols the provision of a secure safety device coupled with a folding trigger made it possible to have a very compact pistol that could be carried with safety in the pocket fully loaded and brought into action with the minimum of delay. The folding trigger fitted into a recess underneath the action

Four barrelled tap action flintlock showing the two cocks and pans. (Glasgow Art Galleries)

body and, as the cock was drawn back, the trigger hinged downward and was brought into use by a projection on the bottom of the cock, the sear being pivoted and kept in constant engagement by means of an additional spring. The trigger itself was spring loaded so that, when not required, it could be pushed forward and would snap back into its housing. The inside of the box-like action provided ample room for the accommodation of this additional mechanism, and the spring arm for the drum of the tap action pistol was housed in the action body as well.

Relatively few screw barrelled box lock pistols were rifled. The centrally disposed cock and flash pan precluded the fitting of sights and, in any case, pistols of this type were intended for close range defence; they were made to be pointed at an opponent rather than aimed. With the emphasis on close quarter use, it is not surprising that box lock pistols were fitted with small folding bayonets. A patent was taken out by John Waters of Birmingham in 1781 (No. 1284) which described 'pistols with a bayonet', the bayonet being connected by a 'spring, slide, hinge or otherwise'. A hinge at the muzzle was the most common form, and the bayonet, when released, was swung from its underneath position either alongside or on top of the barrel where it was subsequently locked into position by means of a spring.

Effective bayonets of this type were also fitted to the 'bell mouthed' blunderbuss boarding pistols sometimes carried by naval officers. When fitted to the smaller pocket box lock pistol, the bayonet had to be reduced from an effective 6″ to 8″ in length to not much more than a pocket knife in size, so its value was correspondingly reduced. On pocket weapons its value was possibly more intimidating than effective but, when confronted by a determined man with an empty pistol, the sinister 'whoosh' as the bayonet flicked over into the locked position may well have deterred all but the most determined aggressor. The release for the bayonet could be either a separate catch or a separate trigger, but on some pistols the tip of the blade was retained by a special notch in the trigger guard. Bayonets could not be fitted to screw barrelled pistols and, with these particular weapons, there was, of course, the ever present risk of losing the key for unscrewing the barrels. To avoid this annoyance, pocket pistols were sometimes provided with a hinged lever attached to the barrel which could not be lost, and pairs of single barrel pistols were sometimes made with a suitable aperture in the butt which served as a key—providing both pistols were available.

The box lock was also used in conjunction with the turn-over barrel system, the smaller pocket pistol being provided with two or four barrels, each barrel having the steel and flash pan attached to it. Typical of this class of pistol were the all steel multi-barrelled weapons made in Liege, many of which bore the name, Segalas, (London). Although there was an actual London maker by the name of Israel Segalas who worked between 1715 and 1740, the pistols attributed to him were wooden-stocked sidelocks, as were those made by his son, Israel Segalas the Younger, who later became Warden of the London Gunmakers Company and subsequently Proof Master. It is generally accepted that none of the pistols bearing the name Segalas in any one of the fourteen known variant spellings, were made by Israel Segalas and, in spite of the London, Londres or Londini engraved on the action, Liege would have been more appropriate. Such pistols were, however, made in considerable numbers and can be regarded as the forerunners of the immense flood of cheap percussion box lock pistols which were to pour into the market throughout the first half of the nineteenth century.

Four barrelled flintlock with combined tap and slide action, by Dobson and Baker of London.

The last quarter of the eighteenth century was a period of immense importance. Following the accession of George III in 1760, changes took place in Britain which had a decisive effect on the manufacture of arms, particularly of pistols. Eventually, these changes were to sweep away the skills of the individual craftsman and result in the production of a machine made pistol on which craftsmanship was confined to embellishment.

The greatest obstacle hindering the provision and repair of military firearms was the lack of standardisation of component parts. The French were the first fully to appreciate this situation and, in 1717, all Government armouries were instructed to follow the measurements of a standard pattern and to adhere as closely as possible to a uniform method of manufacture. The problem of putting such an instruction into practice with the engineering techniques then available was formidable but, by 1763, the French had issued the first standard military flintlock pistol and, by 1777, the armouries of St Etienne and Charleville were producing a new cavalry pistol which differed very considerably from its predecessor and

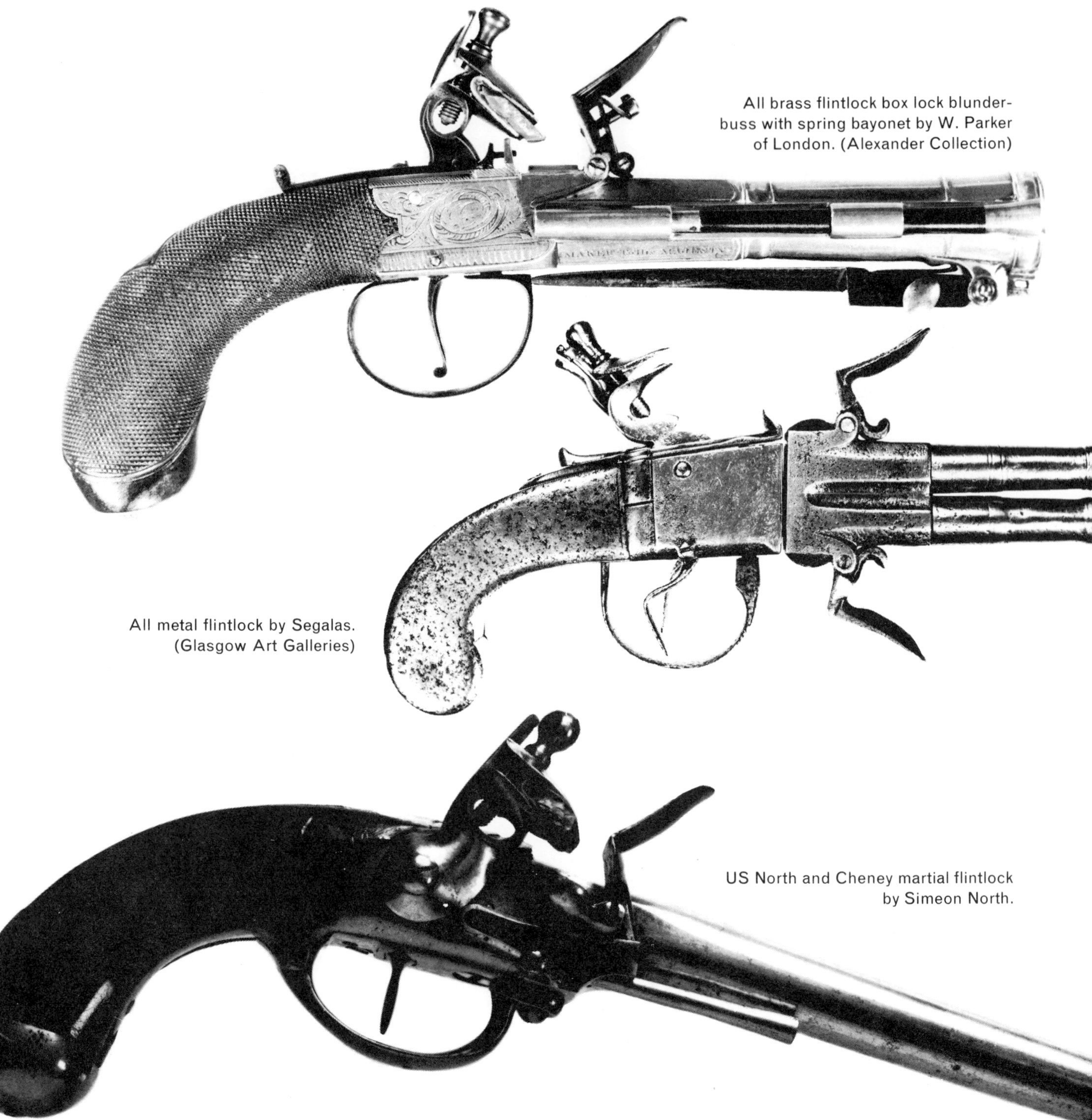

All brass flintlock box lock blunderbuss with spring bayonet by W. Parker of London. (Alexander Collection)

All metal flintlock by Segalas. (Glasgow Art Galleries)

US North and Cheney martial flintlock by Simeon North.

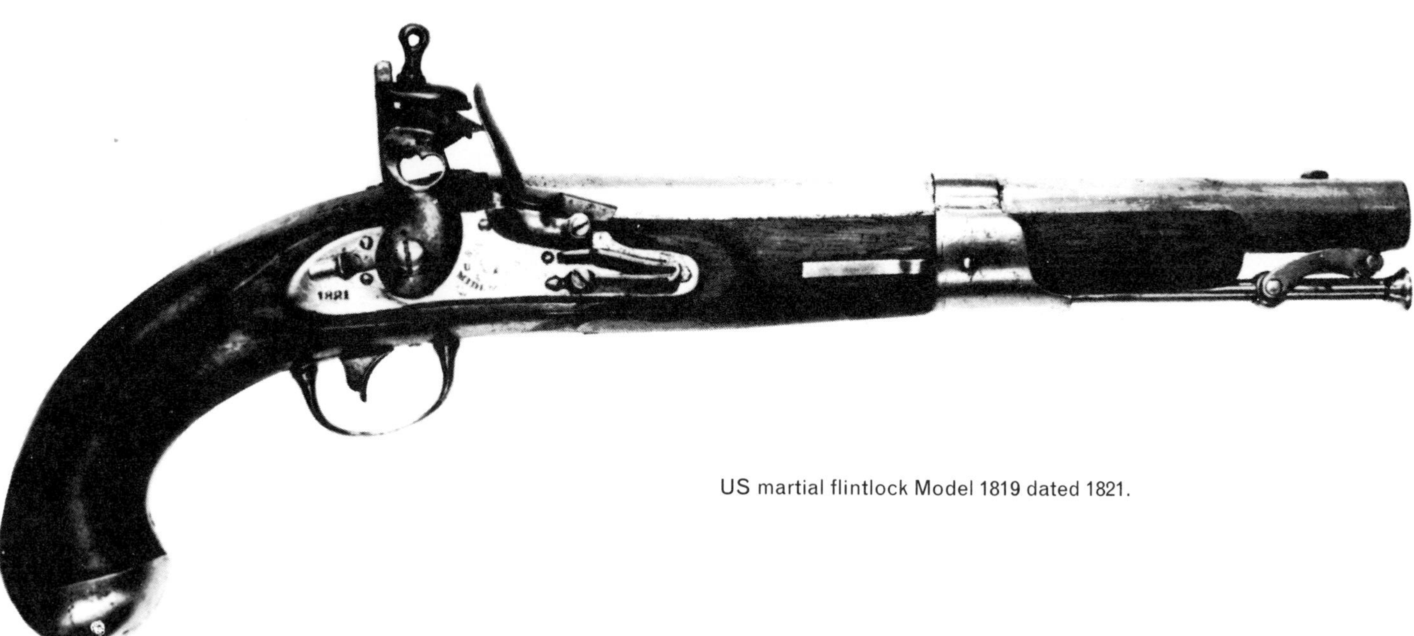

US martial flintlock Model 1819 dated 1821.

resembled no other contemporary military pistol.

The Model 1777 could be regarded as a simplified version of the English Queen Anne pistol, but it was muzzle loading and not a screw barrel pistol. Of approximately 14 bore (.69″), the round barrel was $7\frac{1}{2}''$ long, tapering towards the muzzle. This was attached to a breech frame of brass which housed the lockwork, and the pan, made of the same material, was cast integrally with the frame. The iron cock was mounted externally.

Apart from its unusual design, at least to military eyes, this pistol is of importance since it was the first military pistol to be manufactured for the newly emergent government of the United States. In 1799 a contract for 500 of these pistols at a price of $6.50 each was obtained by Simeon North of Berlin, Conn., in association with his brother-in-law, Elisha Cheney. The only important difference between the French and American pistols is that the US model, known as the 'North and Cheney', had a barrel one inch longer than the French original. Although some of the French pistols were fitted with a belt hook, none of the 2,000 North and Cheney pistols eventually manufactured possessed this attachment. Such is the importance accorded to this, the first US martial pistol, that, today, a North and Cheney pistol in mint condition would probably fetch about $4,000 from a collector. There can be little doubt that the success of Simeon North owed much to the pioneering work of Eli Whitney, inventor of the cotton gin and the father of the 'American' system, the production in volume, by means of gauges, of standardised and interchangeable parts.

These developments foreshadowed events which by the mid-nineteenth century had almost completely revolutionised the manufacture of handguns. Before examining the results of factory mass-production, let us take a last and nostalgic look at the traditional pistol towards the end of the flintlock period.

The high quality of workmanship and design attained by the individual maker is nowhere better exemplified than in the flintlock duelling pistol. In Britain, pistols specially designed for duelling first made their appearance between 1780 and 1790 and evolved from the better quality holster pistol. The need for such specialised weapons was in part due to the decline in the fashion of wearing a sword with everyday dress, and in part to the realisation that the pistol was a great equaliser, for the successful combatant no longer depended on greater physical strength or dexterity. Once the pistol had been accepted as a tool for settling arguments between gentlemen, efforts were directed towards perfecting a weapon designed to meet the formalised ritual of the occasion.

Of equal importance was the loading of these specialised weapons. The slapdash methods advocated for reloading military pistols allowed for the fact that rate of fire took precedence over accuracy. With duelling the opposite was true.

The first requisite was that the bullet mould, usually supplied with the pistol, should cast a perfectly spherical ball of such a size that, when wrapped in one thickness of greased linen, it could be forced into the barrel by the pressure of the thumb. Linen was employed because its uniform quality and strength made it less liable to tear. In the case of the rifled pistols that were later employed for both duelling and target use, the patched ball was of such a size that it exactly fitted the barrel, and the bullet was started into the rifling with a tap from a leather faced mallet (often included in the pistol case), thereafter being driven home with a steady pressure of the ramrod. The mould used in casting bullets was of the normal 'pincer' type which often incorporated a sprue cutter, the cutter being used to remove the sprue, the metal that had solidified in the passage (sprue hole) through which the lead ran into the mould. A rough and ready clipping of the sprue was satisfactory for normal use but, as greater care was needed for bullets to be used in the precision duelling pistol, special cutters were employed whose blades were shaped to suit the curvature of the ball. The fastidious would remove any irregularities on the surface of the bullet with a fine file. After this careful trimming, the bullets were weighed to eliminate those that might contain a hidden flaw or cavity, so that the whole process tended to produce bullets of equal weight and identical shape.

Before the pistol was loaded, it was thoroughly cleaned and the vent cleared with a pricker to remove any obstruction that might cause a misfire or 'flash in the pan'. The pan was primed with fine powder but care was taken not to overfill, for this could result in caking. The pan cover was closed and, even though the cock might be in the safe or half cock position, the prudent would apply the safety catch, if one was fitted. The pistol was primed before it was loaded to avoid any possibility of the main charge finding its way out through the vent due to the pressure created in the barrel when the ball was rammed home, since such a loss would inevitably cause inaccuracy. The next operation was to charge with powder.

Merely pouring a measured volume of powder down the barrel did not suffice for the precise duellist. Amongst the various tools to be found in the pistol case was a special charger designed to be attached to the ramrod or, alternatively, to the cleaning rod. When the measure had been screwed in position and every care taken to avoid volume variation, the pistol barrel was placed muzzle downwards over the charger and rod until the measure reached the chamber. Both pistol and charger were then inverted, the powder was deposited exactly where required, and none adhered to the side of the barrel. The normal powder charge for a duelling pistol was rather lighter than that for the common pistol of equivalent bore, the average being less than one drachm (modern contraction, dram, equal to 27.3 grains avoirdupois, 1.638G metric).

The bullet was introduced as previously described and seated on the powder, care being taken to avoid an air space. Conversely, enthusiastic ramming could over-compress the powder, which might result in caking and, as a result, in erratic ignition. In the case of flintlock pistols, the flint had naturally to be carefully selected, properly packed in the jaws of the cock and properly secured by the capstan screw. It only remained for the safety catch to be released, the pistol to be cocked, and the weapon was ready to fire. These painstaking attentions to detail would have been superfluous if the pistol itself had not been made to the highest possible standards, and the qualities which distinguish the highly specialised duelling pistol were not developed overnight. Throughout the period there was a process of constant transition, so that the slim, almost feminine deadliness of the dueller of the 1790's became, by the mid-nineteenth century, that highest expression of the pistol maker's art and craft, the heavier, very masculine target pistol. Finally, even this was submerged by the flood of machine made pistols.

Allied to the problem of deciding whether or not a particular example is a true duelling pistol purely on evolutionary grounds, there is an additional difficulty presented by the fact that pistols were often made for some other specific purpose, but could be used for duelling should the occasion arise. Typical of this class were the 'Officer's Pistols', usually of plain military type but of higher quality finish and workmanship, and sometimes provided with a detachable shoulder stock. In order to take advantage of Government issue ammunition, this class of pistol was of 16 bore, the same calibre as both the 'carbine bore' issue pistol and the carbine itself. It must be remembered that three sizes of issue pistol were in use and, for a time, concurrently. The musket bore pistol of nominal 12 bore, taking a ball of 14½ to the pound, the carbine bore pistol of nominal 16 bore, taking a ball of 20 to the pound, and the pistol bore weapon of from 20-24 bore, using a ball 34 to the pound. Better quality pistols for officer's use were made to suit ammunition supplied in all these calibres, but the rather distinctive hybrid, suitable for service use but capable of both duelling and target work, was made as large as 16 bore to suit the carbine bore ammunition. Such pistols tend slightly to

Flintlock duelling pistol by Wogdon and Barton, about 1795. (Alexander Collection)

confuse the picture and only experience, coupled with the 'feel', can indicate whether or not they were used for duelling.

The true duelling pistol first appeared as a transitional type about 1770–75. Full stocked to the muzzle, the butt was more curved than the contemporary holster pistol and had flattened sides. A barrel length of 12″ was later reduced to 10″. The shape was octagonal at the breech, changing to round halfway towards the muzzle, and at this point a baluster turn was introduced.

During the next twenty years, subtle changes took place. There was less drop to the stock and, to compensate, the butt became more deeply curved until, on pistols by H. W. Mortimer, it was so incurved that it nearly resembled the crook of a walking stick. This fashion was almost a trademark of Mortimer pistols and was not followed by other makers to the same extent.

The flattened sides of the butt tended to disappear about 1790 and, ten years prior to this, checkering had made its first appearance in a rudimentary form. Before long, the style of checkering became individualistic, and Mortimer favoured a broad, deeply cut design with an additional fine pattern of stars inside the basic diamond. Two other makers whose style of checkering was distinctive were John Twigg and Durs Egg. Twigg, along with Joseph Griffin and John Tow, was perhaps the first of the great London gunmakers responsible for the emergence of the duelling pistol as a distinct type of weapon, a pistol which was both eminently suitable for its purpose and possessed definite visual attraction by virtue of line and form rather than applied decoration. The dates during which Twigg was active are open to some dispute. Carey suggests 1760 to 1780, but this is too early by about ten years; other authorities credit John Twigg with the introduction of the full octagonal barrel about 1770. The reason behind this change of fashion is difficult to discover, but it may have been weight distribution—the reason why weights are hung on the end of the barrels of today's target pistols. For the type of shooting expected of duelling pistols, there is no doubt that the very difficult question of balance would have been an important factor. The change was certainly not dictated by reasons of cost, since a full octagon barrel would be more expensive to make than the earlier style, due to the problem of filing the flats not only absolutely smooth, but true.

John Twigg was one of the greatest English gunmakers and John Manton, who rose to be his foreman, was but one of the many gunmakers who learned their trade and their appreciation of fine craftsmanship from Twigg before setting up on their own.

The period from 1780 onward was one of intense rivalry in fashionable gunmaking and one man who emerged to gain his share of the lucrative business to be had from rich and noble patronage, was Durs Egg. A fondness for the products of one special maker is perhaps irrational, but my own liking for Durs Egg is due to an acquaintance with a duelling pistol of his at a stage when the mysteries of the flintlock were first being explained to me. I have never equalled the shooting done with this particular pistol using

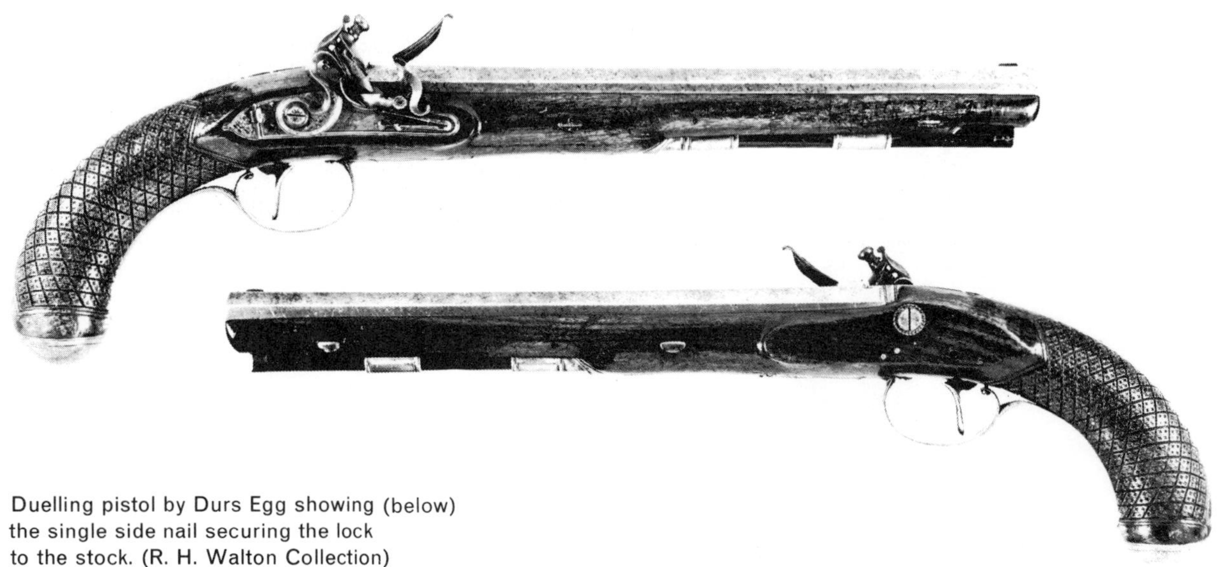

Duelling pistol by Durs Egg showing (below) the single side nail securing the lock to the stock. (R. H. Walton Collection)

any other flintlock, and for this reason I shall always hold the Durs Egg dueller in the highest esteem. Equally, I favour the products of the 1780-1790 period—the light 10″ octagon barrel full stocked to the muzzle, the grace of the swan-neck cock where every line is right, and that indefinable something which tells one at once that the pistol fits the hand, like the handshake of a friend.

Egg was an immigrant, having learned his trade in Switzerland and Paris before setting up his business in London in 1772. Like Henry Nock, he was a contractor to the Board of Ordnance. Many of the splendid firearms made by Durs Egg are preserved at Windsor Castle, his royal patron having been the Prince of Wales, later George IV. Royal patronage confirmed his success and the large number of pistols and sporting guns which bear his signature are an indication of the demand for his work. In addition to producing quality weapons, Durs Egg continued to work for the Board of Ordnance. Some of the more unusual weapons made by him were the prototype breechloading military rifles made for Patrick Ferguson and, for a contract received in 1784, a breechloading carbine with a 'tip-up' action. This design was a copy of that attributed to Guiseppe Crespi of Milan, and one of these carbines is at present in the Scott Collection, Glasgow.

Egg's considerable fortune, amassed as a result of the demand for arms during the Napoleonic Wars, suffered severely from his association with the Swiss gun designer, S. J. Pauly, with whom he

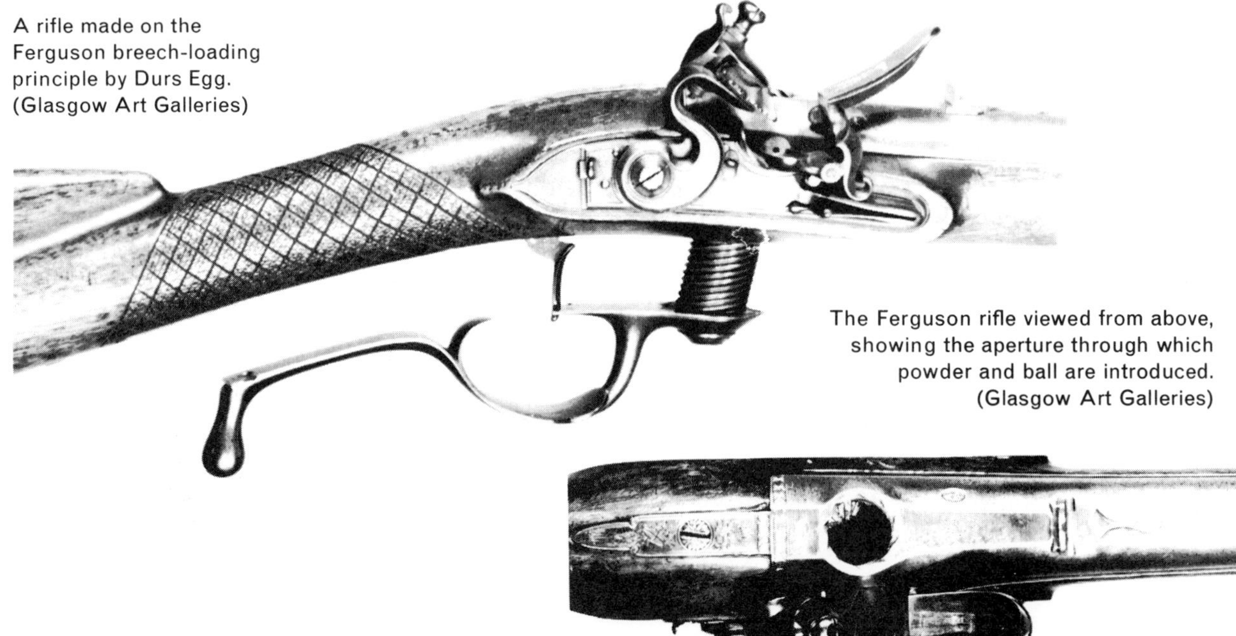

A rifle made on the Ferguson breech-loading principle by Durs Egg. (Glasgow Art Galleries)

The Ferguson rifle viewed from above, showing the aperture through which powder and ball are introduced. (Glasgow Art Galleries)

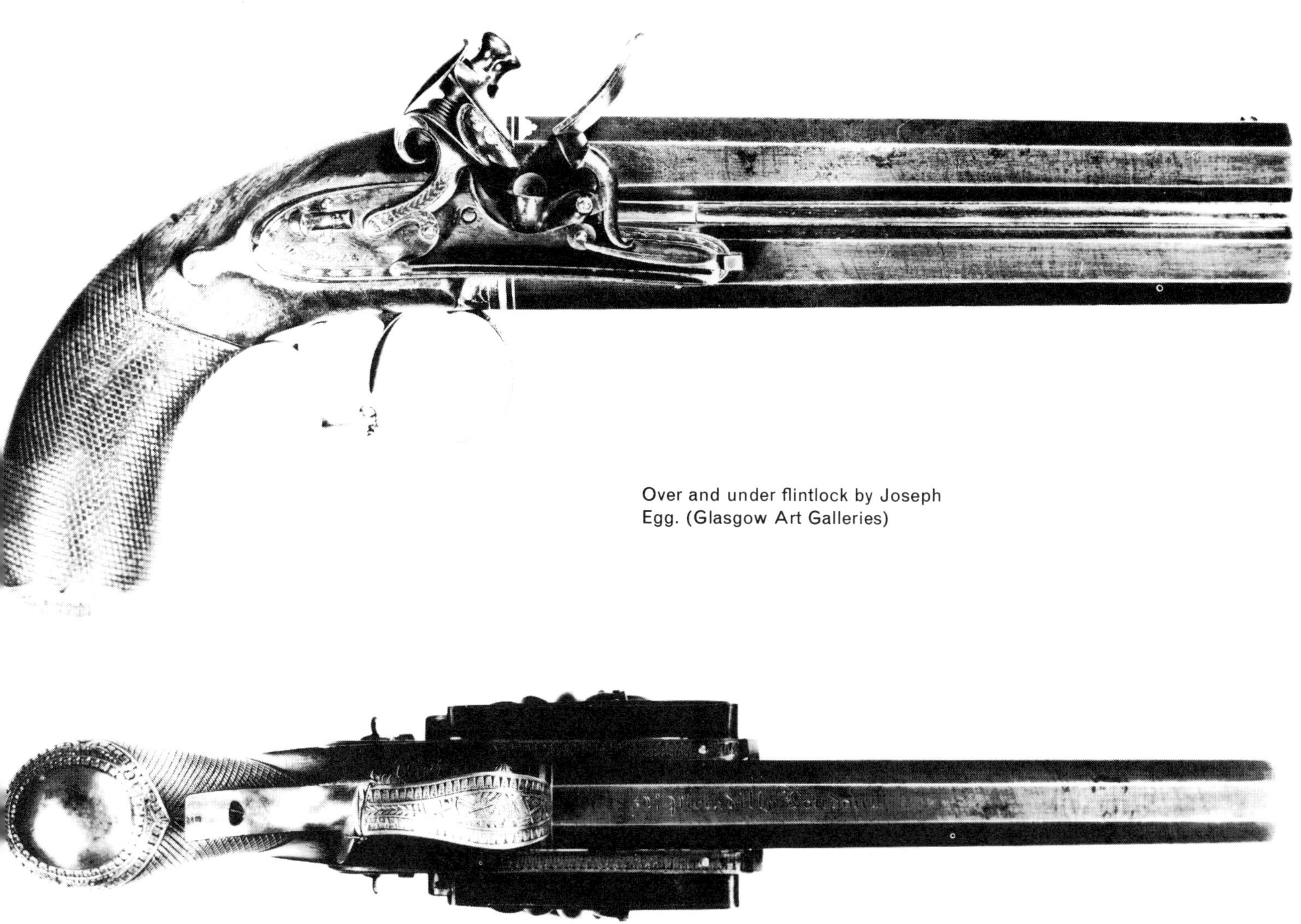

Over and under flintlock by Joseph Egg. (Glasgow Art Galleries)

Detail of engraving on the over and under flintlock by Joseph Egg. (Glasgow Art Galleries)

made a disastrous attempt to produce an airship. Egg died in London at the age of 86, on the verge of bankruptcy.

At No. 1 Piccadilly, London, there was another Egg, Joseph, a nephew of Durs Egg. He first appeared in London prior to 1800 and, in 1807, entered into partnership with the London gunmaker, Henry Tatham. In 1815, Joseph Egg set up in business on his own in Piccadilly, where he remained until his death in 1837. Both Henry Tatham and Joseph Egg made fine duelling pistols, but Egg was responsible for a distinctive type of lock with an external mainspring which, though he never patented it, he may have invented. In the Scott Collection in Glasgow there is a very fine over and under double flintlock pistol by Joseph Egg which employs an external mainspring which, linked to the cock, also serves as a 'hammer spring', the original but somewhat confusing term for the spring which actuated the steel and pan cover. External mainsprings were of value in the construction of double barrelled pistols since they considerably reduced the overall width, particularly in the case of the over and under pistols. Similar locks were employed by Egg on single barrelled pistols and also by a famous provincial maker, Jeremiah Patrick of Liverpool.

Unlike his namesake, Joseph Egg left a flourishing business which lasted until 1880 under the guidance of his sons and grandsons. Two patents were granted to Joseph Egg for automatic priming magazines: No. 4727 in 1822 and No. 6829 in 1835. Egg was also a claimant to the honour of being the inventor of the copper percussion cap, and his later trade cards are so inscribed. If his claim could be proved, Joseph Egg would rightly take his place as one of the

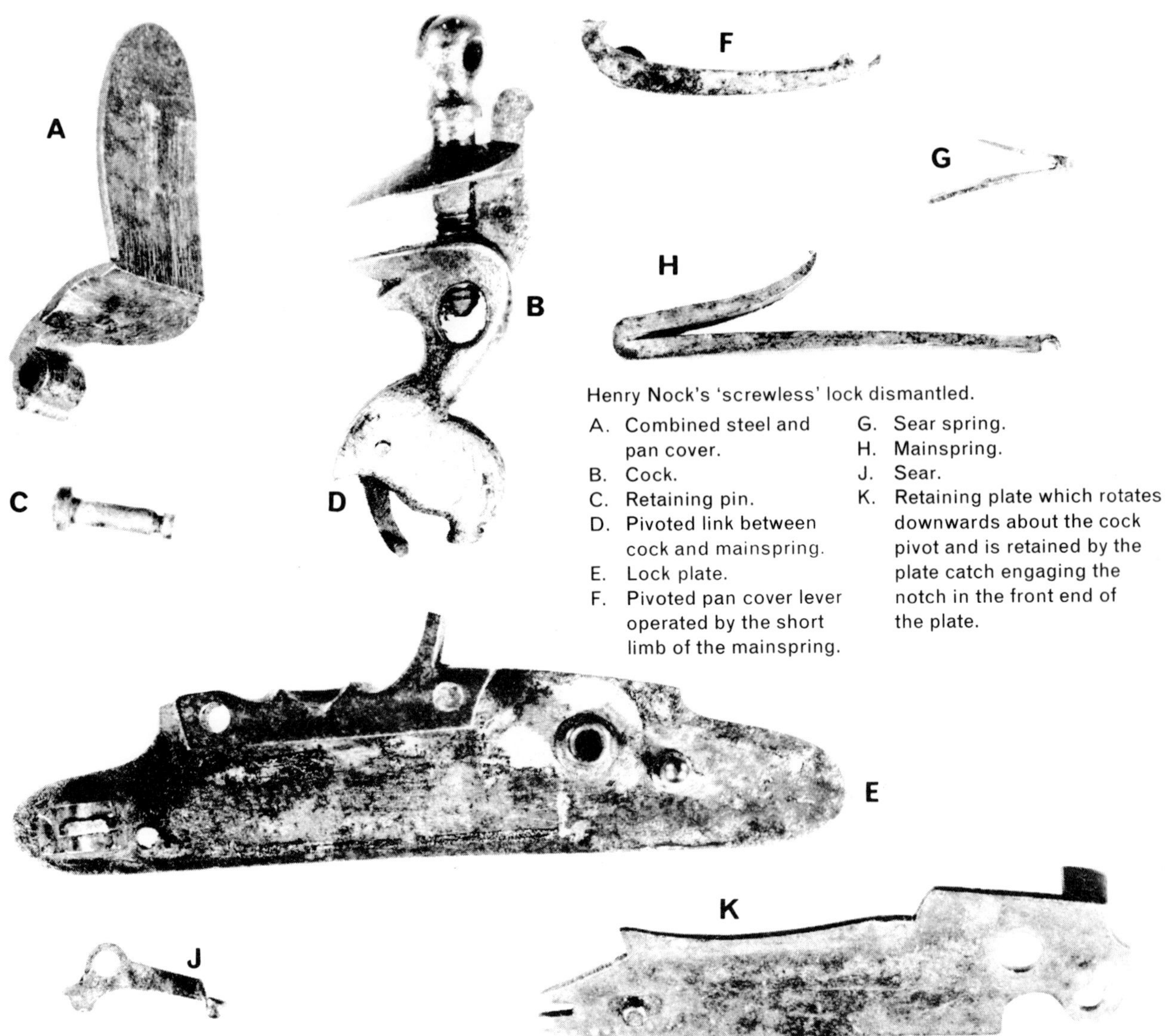

Henry Nock's 'screwless' lock dismantled.

A. Combined steel and pan cover.
B. Cock.
C. Retaining pin.
D. Pivoted link between cock and mainspring.
E. Lock plate.
F. Pivoted pan cover lever operated by the short limb of the mainspring.
G. Sear spring.
H. Mainspring.
J. Sear.
K. Retaining plate which rotates downwards about the cock pivot and is retained by the plate catch engaging the notch in the front end of the plate.

most important figures in the whole history of firearms.

The list of London makers of high quality firearms is a lengthy one. Like his contemporaries, Henry Nock also made duelling pistols, although originally he was a lock maker and was later to become an important contractor to the Board of Ordnance. First recorded in business in 1771 in the Parish of St Andrews, Nock, as a gunmaker of quality, subsequently moved to No. 10 Ludgate Street, near St Paul's Cathedral (now Ludgate Hill). He was responsible for several inventions relating to firearms, not all of which received the attention their undoubted merit deserved.

Elegant in its simplicity, the enclosed screwless lock, which Nock appears to have made first of all in 1785, would seem to have been a highly desirable innovation and one eminently suitable for military purposes. If we take the $4\frac{3}{4}''$ pistol lock shown in the illustration as an example, it will be found to have the Crown and 'GR' cypher in the centre of the lock plate and, at the rear, 'H. Nock'.

Secured to the stock by one screw which entered the internally threaded axle on which the cock was swung, all the components were mounted between the main plate and the inside locking plate. With the cock removed from the stock, a small catch on the inside front of the lock could be pushed forward and the locking plate moved downwards. This released the tension on the sear spring and the lock plate could be lifted off. The sear spring and sear were then free to be removed. The mainspring had to be compressed and unhooked from the link connecting it to the cock, after which both the mainspring and cock could be taken from the lock plate. The pan cover and steel could be removed by pushing out a retaining pin. The shorter arm of the mainspring bore against a lever, pivoted at one end, and at the other end of this lever was mounted a roller bearing which acted against a cam on the pan cover and steel.

The lock was extremely easy to dismantle and, by virtue of the link, mainspring and roller bearing on the pan cover, the action was smooth and quick. The only screw threads were those on the cock capstan screw and the internal thread to receive the side nail or screw securing the lock to the stock. A measure of interchangeability was apparently achieved and it is strange that this lock did not meet with the success it undoubtedly deserved. Possibly it appeared at the wrong time and was an easy prey to those twin enemies of invention, conservatism and established convention. The enclosed screwless lock was never patented but, in 1787, Henry Nock was granted Patent No. 1598 for 'breeching applicable to all kinds of guns and other fire arms'.

Nock's breech was an improvement on the chamber breech plug which made its appearance about 1770 as an alternative to the common breech plug. The latter was a simple screwed plug which closed the breech end of the barrel, the face of the plug being sometimes provided with a recess across it for the purpose of holding a greater depth of powder opposite the touch-hole. Externally, the chamber plug appeared much the same; the alterations were internal. Instead of the 'V' shaped notch, there was a narrow central chamber communicating with the touch-hole.

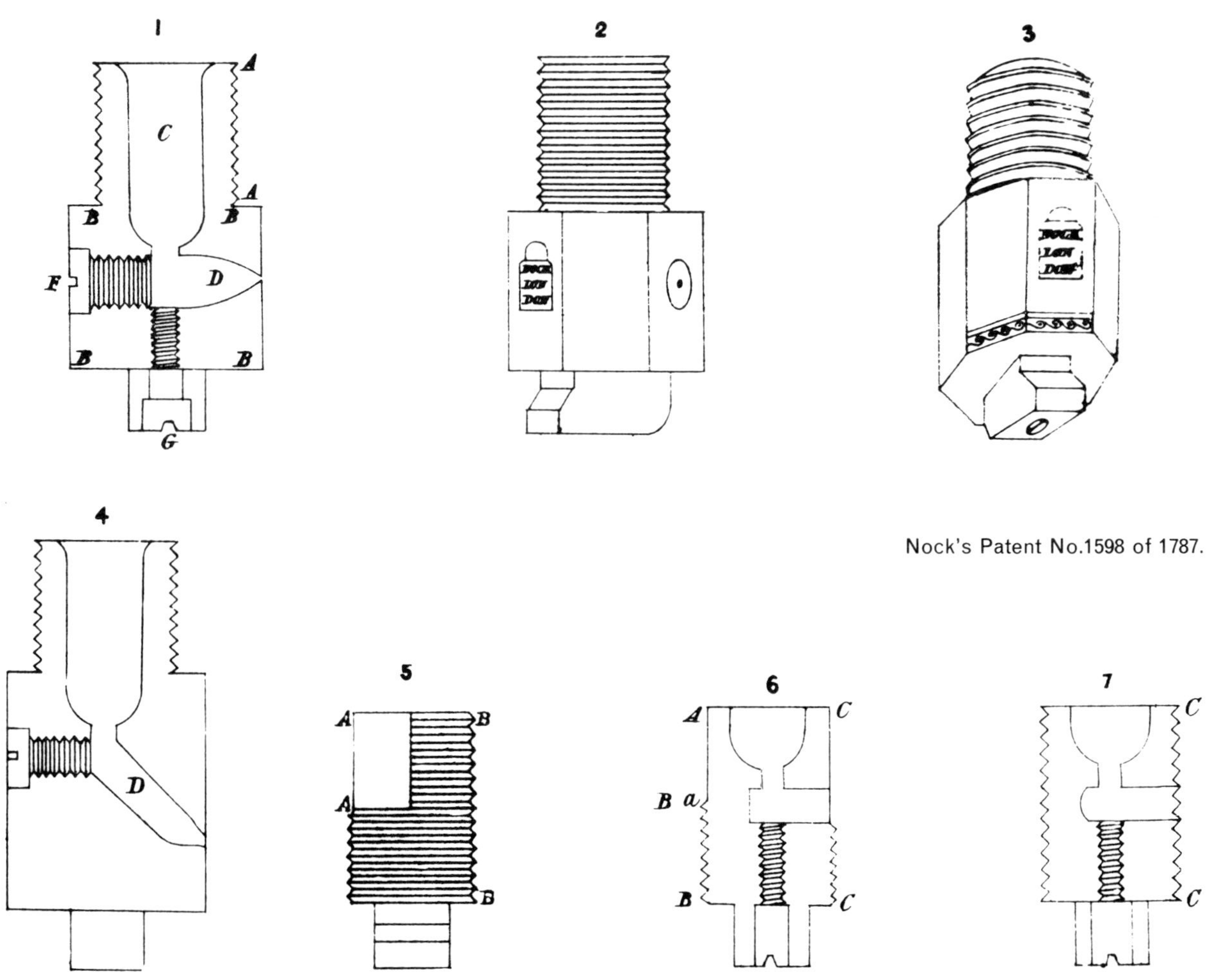

Nock's Patent No.1598 of 1787.

In Nock's improvement the rear portion of the plug was also enlarged to conform with the contours of the barrel, the touch-hole being in the head of the plug rather than passing through the wall of the barrel as in the case of the common breech plug. A screw was fitted opposite the touch-hole in order to facilitate manufacture and to aid in cleaning the anterior chamber.

Improvements of Nock's original design were made by others, the most notable being Joseph Manton's 'recessed' breech, patented in 1792 (No. 1865). This employed Nock's principle but reduced the ignition time by placing the lock nearer to the centre of the barrel. The use of chamber breech plugs did much to improve the ignition of the powder and a further refinement was for the touch-hole or vent to be lined with gold or platinum. The intention was to eliminate the corrosion that might lead to enlargement of the vent and a reduction in performance. Platinum was considered to be superior, since, being harder, it was less liable to blow out. Gold or platinum was also used for the cartouche or oblong plug of precious metal inlaid on the top of the breeching to carry the maker's name or mark. The value of these metals has increased so much, that many fine pistols of this period will be found minus both vent plug and cartouche—a practice in my opinion, comparable to robbing the dead of their gold fillings.

On duelling pistols and better quality weapons, the hook breech was employed, the hook engaging in a slot cut in a separate tang which remained attached to the stock. Flat slides or cross bolts, instead of the soft iron pins employed for cheaper weapons, secured the barrel to the stock, and two slides were used on full stocked weapons. When the slides were withdrawn, the barrel was simply unhooked and detached, and there was no need to unscrew the tang screw, as there was on weapons without the hook breech. The centre of the slide was usually slotted and pinned to the stock so that it could not be inadvertently fully withdrawn and lost. About 1790, oval silver plates were let into the stock to protect the wood and to act as bearings for the barrel slides.

During the last ten years of the eighteenth century, the lock plate became smaller. The priming pan had much attention lavished on it and, on better quality pistols, it became narrower and more spoon shaped. It was also by now separate from the fence and the bridle, a development which allowed moisture to flow freely past the pan instead of being directed into it. Locks of this quality were, of course, fitted with the link swivel between mainspring and tumbler and with the roller bearing between feather spring and pan cover. An examination of the internals of such locks will reveal that the extremely high standard of finish, the result of painstaking polishing, was not merely confined to the outside. Internally, best quality locks were a visual delight, the bridle often being pierced with scroll work. Equally, the short arm of the mainspring frequently terminated in a formalised decoration.

Amongst the leaders of fashion at the end of the century were Wogdon, Mortimer and the Mantons. Robert Wogdon appears to have been a maker of duelling pistols to the exclusion of anything else: so popular were his pistols among the duelling set, that once an argument had gone beyond the law it was referred to as 'Wogdon's Case'. In a poem published in London in 1782 entitled 'Stanzas on Duelling' by an Irish Volunteer, the first of forty verses is as follows:

> Hail Wogdon Patron of that leaden death
> Which waits alike the bully and the brave,
> As well might art recall departed breath,
> As any artifice your victims save.

Such indeed is fame.

Above all, Wogdon was a maker of accurate pistols. Great care was taken to ensure that the pistol fitted the client and emphasis was placed on the practical aspect, that the pistol would shoot where it was supposed to. Little appears to be known about Wogdon: his place of business was in the Haymarket, London, and possibly he started there some time prior to 1770. His pistols have a distinctive style of their own and yet the only word to describe their appearance would be conservative. Most were full stocked to the muzzle, the early ones having barrels made in the French style, round in section with a flat rib in the sighting plane. Careful examination will also show that these barrels were 'swamped', in other words they tapered from the breech towards the muzzle and then flared out. An alternative term would be 'necked', and this form of barrel was encountered occasionally until the end of the duelling period.

A pair of Wogdon pistols in the collection of W. A. C. Paton are silver mounted and, although restored, there is ample evidence of the skill and craft of the maker. The silver hallmark is dated 1776, and the silver mounts were the work of John King, a member of the King family who

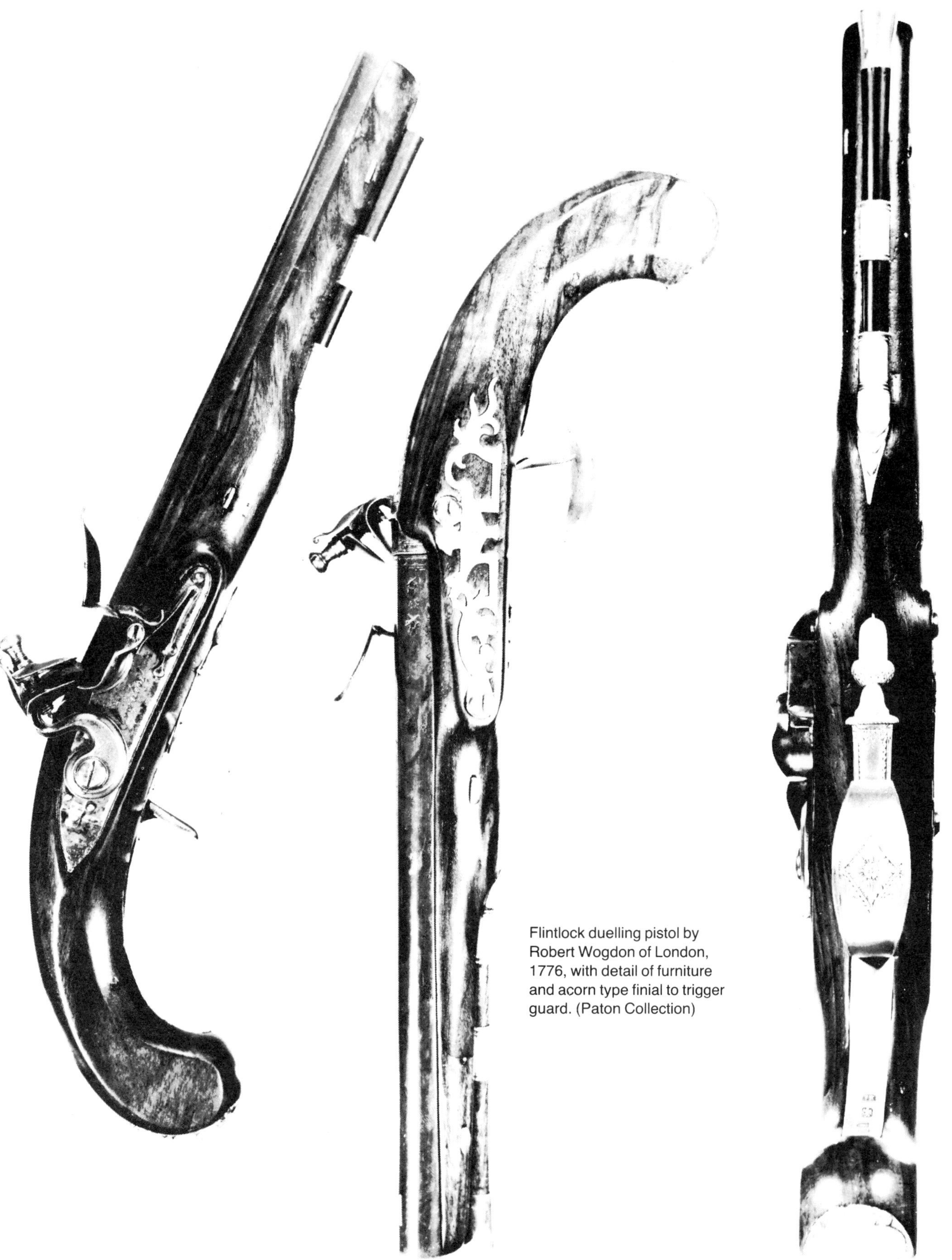

Flintlock duelling pistol by Robert Wogdon of London, 1776, with detail of furniture and acorn type finial to trigger guard. (Paton Collection)

produced the majority of the mounts used by the London gunmakers during the eighteenth century. The trigger guard finial is of the acorn type and the guard itself is a simple bow secured to the stock by two pins. Also pinned to the stock are the ramrod pipe and tail pipe. A silver side plate, cast and pierced with rococo scrolls, and a cast silver butt plate depicting a buxom Britannia complete the silver furniture. The effect of the silver against the dark walnut of the stock is most pleasing and considerably enhances the appearance. As one would expect, the stock is continued to the muzzle, and the butt is gracefully curved and flattened. Thus, the form is both elegant and entirely practical since the pistol points naturally on the line of sight.

The lock is of simple construction and lacks both the roller on the pan and a swivel on the tumbler. The safety bolt engages a slot in the tumbler and bolts at the half cock. The name Wogdon in flowing script is engraved on the outside of the plate, and there are no internal marks.

Of 38 bore, the barrel is swamped and in the French style. It is secured to the stock by two flat slides, and has a hook which engages the false breech. A broad 'U' rear sight with central narrow 'V' of reasonable proportions is forged as part of the false breech and a silver blade foresight is dovetailed into the barrel. The sights are sensible, but absence of any lateral adjustment would make aiming off necessary. There is a common breech plug with a 'V' slot and the vent is gold lined. On the flat of the barrel 'Wogdon' is engraved in script followed by 'London' in upper case roman. The ramrod is protected by a brass tip and equipped with a sheathed worm for extracting the charge. The trigger is of the simple single 'set' type, the mechanism of which remained unaltered for many years.

The set trigger first appeared as a separate mechanism in the middle of the sixteenth century and was particularly valuable on firearms which employed a powerful mainspring, for example the wheellock. The set trigger is still employed today both for rifles and pistols, and the effect is to make it possible to fire with a very light pressure—so light that it will have the minimum disturbing effect on the aim. With a single set trigger this is accomplished by pushing forward the trigger to engage a catch, and this action compresses a strong spring. The catch is operated by a light spring which, on single set triggers, also acts as the trigger return spring, since, with the single set trigger, the lock can be released either in the normal manner or by employing the set device. With the trigger set or cocked and the mainspring compressed, a light touch on the trigger releases the catch and the trigger bar, impelled by the spring, strikes the sear tail a sharp blow, so releasing the lock.

The use of the set trigger required an alteration to the mechanism of the lock, and this was the addition of a 'detent'. With the normal trigger, a steady pressure is maintained upon the sear making it impossible, in a well-constructed lock, for the nose of the sear to engage the half cock bent and so arrest the fall of the cock. With the set trigger, a sharp percussive blow is given to the tail of the sear and, to prevent the nose engaging the half cock bent, a small pivoted side plate (the detent) is employed which shrouds the half cock bent and effectively prevents accidental engagement.

The set trigger mechanism employed on pistols is relatively simple but it is subject to malfunctioning due to oxidation and gumming of the lubricant. The presence of a malfunction may not always be obvious since, even if the set mechanism will not operate, this does not impair the normal function of the trigger. Some set triggers will be encountered with provision for adjusting the spring tension of the trigger spring, and others where the let off can be modified to suit the requirements of the individual. Such adjustments are made by a small capstan screw in the trigger plate and the presence of such a screw is a visual indication that a set trigger is fitted.

As was perhaps appropriate, Wogdon pistols were used in some of the most famous duels. One in particular was the meeting between the Duke of York and Colonel Lennox of the Coldstream Guards, which took place on Wimbledon Common on 27 May 1789, and in which neither of the combatants was injured. An equally famous encounter was the duel between Vice President Aaron Burr of America and General Alexander Hamilton, Secretary of the Treasury, which took place in 1804. Hamilton was killed but, despite much popular resentment, Aaron Burr was able to resume his position in the Senate barely four months after the incident. One of the pistols used by the principals in the Duke of York *vs* Colonel Lennox duel is illustrated in W. W. Greener's book, *The Gun and Its Development*. It bears a commemorative silver plate and Greener describes the weapon as 'a notable duelling pistol'. The illustration shows a half stocked pistol with octagonal barrel and a spur trigger guard. It is unusual in that the barrel lacks both the rib and pipe normally fitted to carry the ramrod.

Spur trigger guards were fitted to the pistols made by H. W. Mortimer, perhaps the best known of the gunmakers bearing the name Mortimer. Tradition has it that the first Mortimer served in the army of Charles I, but on the relationship of the various gunmaking Mortimers who were in business in the late eighteenth century, history is regrettably reticent.

Hervey Walklate or Henry William Mortimer (his given names are in some doubt) was in business at 89 Fleet Street, London, by 1780. His early pistols are easily identified by the hooked, incurving butt mentioned earlier, and he later adopted the spur trigger guard which became fashionable about 1795. On many of the duelling pistols I have handled, the spur trigger guard has felt more of a hindrance than an asset, but Mortimer seems to have placed the spur in a more agreeable position as far as I am concerned, and it does help to control the pistol. On many spur trigger guards the position of the spur appears to have been dictated more by the need for style than by practical reasons but, on Mortimer pistols, especially those with set triggers, it is a valuable aid to shooting.

Duelling pistols were sold in pairs, cased in oak or Honduras mahogany. Indeed, not only duelling pistols but the better quality officers' pistols, carriage and pocket pistols, were also furnished with cases. For inferior quality weapons, brightly coloured flannel bags seemed to suffice. A case was lined with baize and provided with compartments. The centre rectangular compartment separated the two pistols and housed the powder flask. The manufacture of these containers was a trade on its own, requiring the work of specialists. For identification, it can be noted that the earlier fashion was to employ a brass inlaid drop handle in the centre of the lid.

Although there was variation in the number and quality of the tools provided—which might include powder flask, cleaning rod, mainspring cramp, etc.—the disposition of the various compartments underwent little change. A delightful and interesting practice was the use of trade labels which today are often a source of valuable information.

These labels vary from a mere statement of the vendor's name and address to a skilful and often picturesque example of the best engraver's art. H. W. Mortimer appears to have preferred the more lavish type of presentation and may well have set the trend. An early label gives the following information: 'H. W. Mortimer, Gun Maker to His Majesty, 89, Fleet Street, London, Wholesale, Retail, and for Exportation'. The centre pedestal bearing this information is surmounted by the Royal Arms and on either side are two gentlemen in the sporting dress of the period with the appropriate dead game and an unusually sagacious gun dog. This label was drawn by Thomas Stothard, a noted artist (1755–1834), and the engraver was Thomas Holloway. A later label provides additional information and, although the form and style remain the same, the unicorn has now a somewhat proud and haughty look instead of the slightly startled appearance apparent on the earlier plate. Mr Mortimer has been joined by his son and instead of the rather bald statement, 'for

Thomas Elsworth Mortimer's trade label.

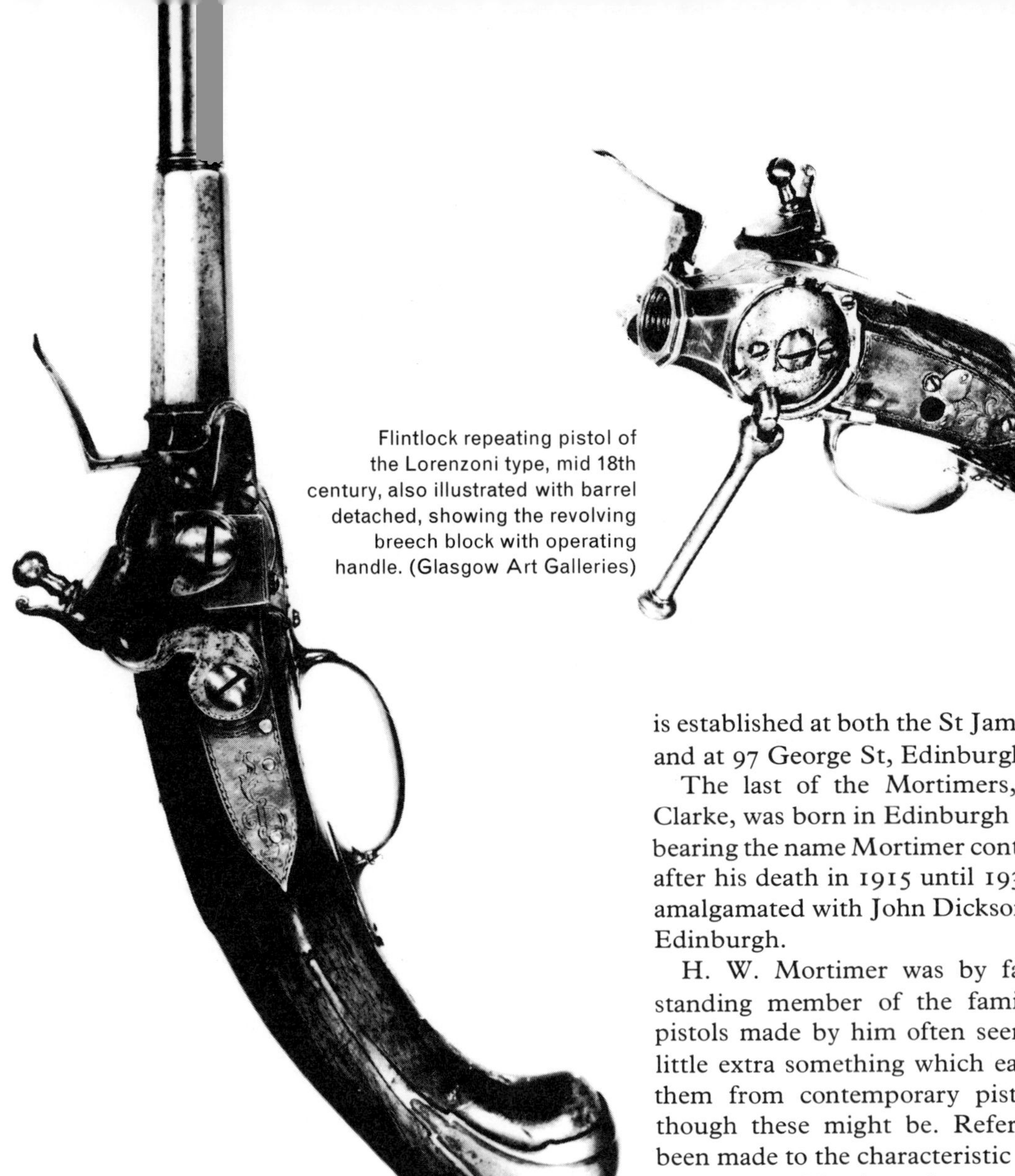

Flintlock repeating pistol of the Lorenzoni type, mid 18th century, also illustrated with barrel detached, showing the revolving breech block with operating handle. (Glasgow Art Galleries)

exportation', we find that the Mortimers are Gun Makers to the United States of America and the Hon. East India Company, and can supply Fine Gunpowder flints and Patent Shot. An even later plate provides the information that H. W. Mortimer and Son have now been joined by T. Mortimer.

At this point the history of the Mortimer family becomes somewhat complicated and the exact relationship between Thomas J. Mortimer, in business at 44 Ludgate Hill, and Thomas Elsworth Mortimer, in business at 34 St James' Street, is difficult to unravel. About 1820, Thomas Elsworth opened a branch in Edinburgh to which the whole business was later transferred, and it is from a later trade plate that confirmation is obtained. On this we read that Thomas Elsworth Mortimer, Rifle, Gun and Pistol Maker, is established at both the St James' Street address and at 97 George St, Edinburgh.

The last of the Mortimers, Thomas Alfred Clarke, was born in Edinburgh in 1840, but guns bearing the name Mortimer continued to be made after his death in 1915 until 1939, when the firm amalgamated with John Dickson and Son, also of Edinburgh.

H. W. Mortimer was by far the most outstanding member of the family, and duelling pistols made by him often seem to possess that little extra something which easily distinguishes them from contemporary pistols, pre-eminent though these might be. Reference has already been made to the characteristic shape of the butt. In addition, Mortimer decorated the termination of the butt with spiral grooves which meet in a quite delightful, yet unobtrusive shell design.

Not content with the production of conventional weapons, Mortimer revived the Lorenzoni magazine system, named after the mid-seventeenth century Florentine gunmaker Michele Lorenzoni. An improvement on the Kalthoff system, the Lorenzoni magazine repeater carried the separate charges of powder and ball in two tubular magazines in the butt. The revolving breech block was provided with two chambers corresponding to the openings of the two magazines. To load the weapon it was held muzzle downward and the breech block was rotated to charge the chambers. When rotated in an anticlockwise direction, the ball was placed into the breech of the barrel and further rotation resulted in the powder chamber being brought into line with the barrel so forming a temporary breech. Automatic priming of the pan was yet another feature of the system, the priming powder being contained in a separate magazine, two cams on the revolving breech cocking the cock and closing the pan cover.

Two men who had a decisive effect on the appearance of the duelling pistol and, indeed, upon the gunmaking world, were the brothers Manton. To avoid any accusation of favouritism —for each had, and still has, his staunch adherents—their considerable contributions to gunmaking are considered in order of age.

John Manton, the elder half-brother, the son of a Lincolnshire farmer, was born about 1760. He may have served his apprenticeship with Twigg and he was certainly foreman at Twigg's before setting up in business on his own at 6 Dover Street, in what is now the heart of Mayfair. John Manton's guns were always marked quite simply, but with evident pride, 'Manton, London'. He appears to have received a Royal Warrant as 'gunmaker to H.R.H. the Prince of Wales' about 1800. Sometime after 1820, the firm changed its style to 'John Manton and Son', and in 1834, John Manton died, although the firm remained active until 1848.

The younger brother, Joseph, was born in 1766 and in 1795 he opened a shop at 27 Davies Street, Berkeley Square. His guns bore the name Joseph Manton in full. Joseph is credited with a number of 'inventions' or improvements to the flintlock system. For example, his improved trigger, patented in 1792, employed a light spring arranged so that the trigger blade remained in contact with the sear tail, consequently eliminating loose movement of the trigger. Also patented in 1792 was the breech already referred to, and eleven years later a 'hammer' with a grooved pan cover to permit the escape of air. One of Joseph's more important inventions related to shotguns, and this was the patent elevated rib, a considerable aid to sighting double barrel guns. This patent was one of the many matters about which the two brothers disagreed, and John Manton, who contested the validity of the patent, demonstrated a gun in court which he stated he had made during his service with Twigg over twenty years before.

A safety catch, the 'Gravitating Stop', which was intended to prevent accidental discharge of the gun during loading or whilst being carried in the near vertical, was yet another attempt by Joseph to attract custom. The celebrated Colonel Peter William Lanoe Hawker, author of the famous *Instructions to Young Sportsmen*, to whose patronage Joseph Manton undoubtedly owed much of his fame, acknowledged the value of the gravitating stop, but cautioned that it must be kept very clean, otherwise malfunctioning was likely to occur. Hawker hastened to add that this 'was a caution to a slovenly shooter and not as an imperfection in the plan'. Hawker has nothing to say about the value of the Manton musical lock, a curved spring attached to the trigger plate which was struck by a pin attached to the trigger so that, when the lock was cocked, 'a pleasant and musical sound' was produced. Further patents by Manton refered to percussion locks, but these will be covered later.

Brother John also protected his ideas, but the number of patents to his name is rather less. They were mainly concerned with improvements to gun locks with the purpose of achieving faster and more positive ignition. In company with most of the gunmakers towards the end of the flintlock period, both Mantons pursued the chimera of the waterproof lock. Although by careful attention to design and by meticulous fitting of cover to pan, the ingress of water might be prevented, none of the 'improved' locks were proof against damp and this deficiency was not finally resolved until the appearance of the percussion lock.

Viewed dispassionately, the greatest impact of the Mantons was on style and fashion, and many of their improvements were designed more to catch the attention of their rich and fashionable clientele than to effect a decisive or radical alteration in basic design. But it cannot be denied that both men turned out pistols of superlative quality and the considerable changes which occurred in the appearance of the duelling pistol during the early years of the nineteenth century owe much to the efforts of the brothers Manton.

It must not be imagined that all changes were universally adopted. Just as there were those who accepted the new styles, there were also those who rejected them and, indeed, cheaper pistols continued to be made without incorporating many of the improvements found on the more costly weapons.

The most distinctive change was to the stock. Instead of continuing to the muzzle, the stock was reduced so that it ended approximately half way along the barrel, terminating in a horn or metal cap. Seen very occasionally on full stocked pistols, the saw-handled butt came into favour about 1805, and is encountered in a variety of forms. Pistols with this form of stock were peculiarly British and the fashion persisted into the percussion period. The butt extended back over the top of the hand, and individuality was displayed in both the shape and length of this extension; in some it was truncated, in others it was quite lengthy and terminated in a sharp point. With both saw handle and spur trigger guard, one would expect to find this combination providing a very firm grip. This has not been my own experience and, although I do not find the pointed extension distracting to the sight picture (some extensions had a 'sight' groove), none of the saw-handled duelling pistols I have fired or handled have fitted my hand with the same sense of belonging as do the butts of the conventional type of fully developed duelling pistol.

Several of the pistols made during this period of experimentation with the new style were not aesthetically satisfying. Half stocks, saw handles and spur guards need to be blended together before a satisfactory whole can be obtained. In particular, the rounded shape of the older style of guard does not suit the heavier appearance of the new style pistol of the early 1800's, but it was not long before a most graceful guard was developed and harmony restored.

In addition to changes in the stock, the octagonal barrel which had been very popular with full stocked pistols became more massive, measuring up to one inch across the flats at the breech. With the loss of half the wooden fore-end, an alternative means of securing the ramrod became necessary, so a rib was attached to the bottom flat of the barrel. A simple cylindrical ramrod pipe was then fitted to this rib. Even if the thickness of the barrel had not been increased, the addition of this rib would have created the impression of weight and solidarity which characterises the later duelling pistol. With the shorter fore-end, there was room for only one cross bolt to secure the barrel instead of the two used formerly. Silver plates to protect the wooden furniture continued to be used, but these could now be rectangular instead of oval.

About 1805, platinum tended to replace gold for the lining of the vent and there is some evidence to show that John Manton was the first to use this harder and more durable metal for such a purpose.

Although the ethics of the duelling code frowned upon the use of rifled pistols, there were those who perhaps gained some extra confidence by using them, and there were gunmakers ready to meet the demand. Joseph Manton went so far as to introduce his secret rifling which could not be detected by a cursory glance at the muzzle. But rifled flintlock duelling pistols were comparatively rare, and would have been of advantage only to the skilled duellist who practised target shooting and knew exactly where his pistols shot.

Duelling pistols of the highest quality were made during this, the golden age of British pistol making, and it is instructive to take a look at a pistol of the late flintlock period—a typical saw-handled pistol of 1815 by William Parker, 233 High Holborn, London—and to compare it with the earlier Wogdon. Established about 1790, Parker made flintlock pocket pistols, holster pistols and blunderbusses, and it was his pistols that were used to arm the police in London following their re-organisation by Sir Robert Peel in 1829. The usual trade label inside the lid of the case informs all and sundry that W. Parker is gun-

William Parker's trade label.

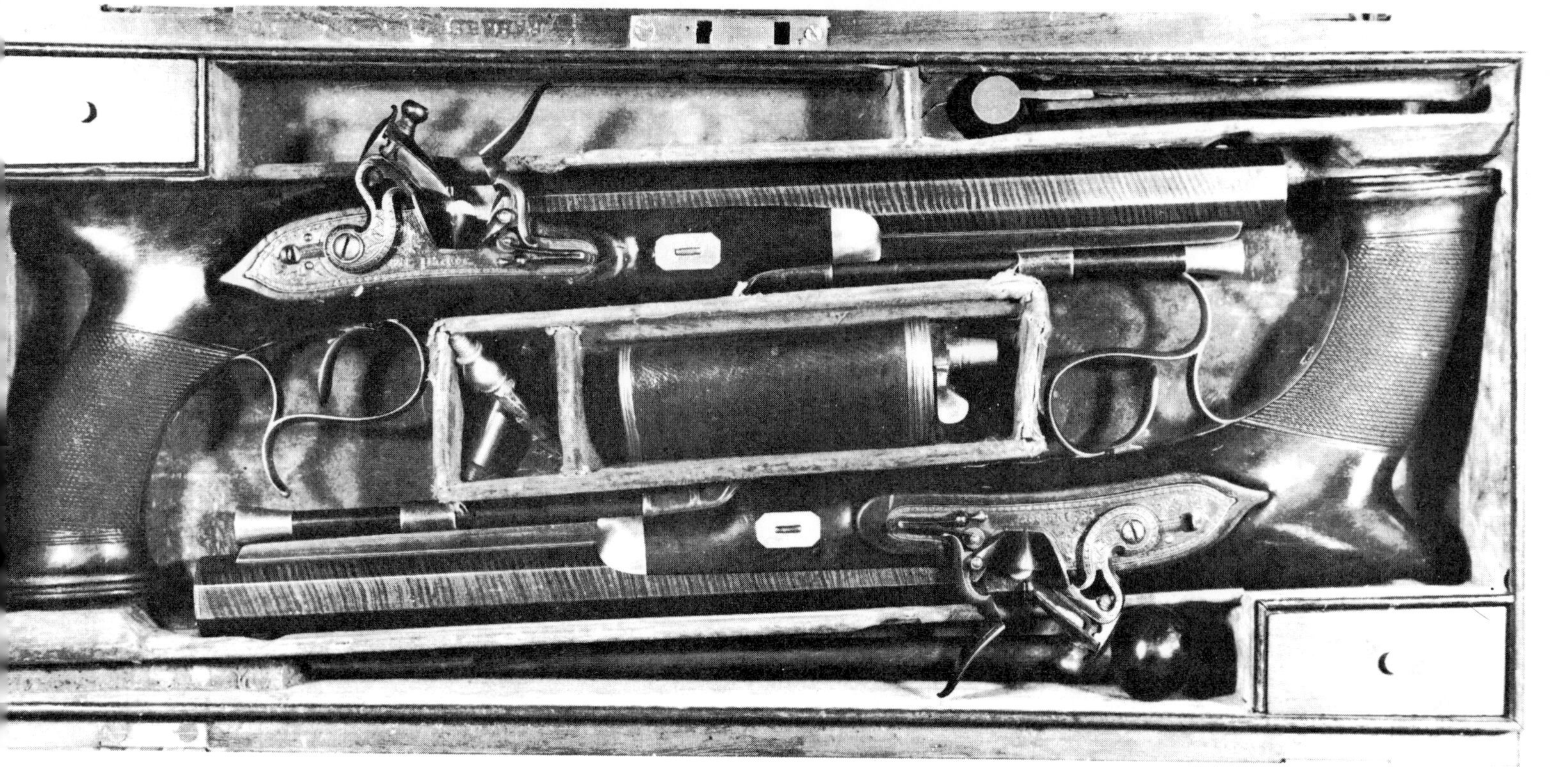

Cased pair of Parker saw-handled duelling pistols, about 1815.

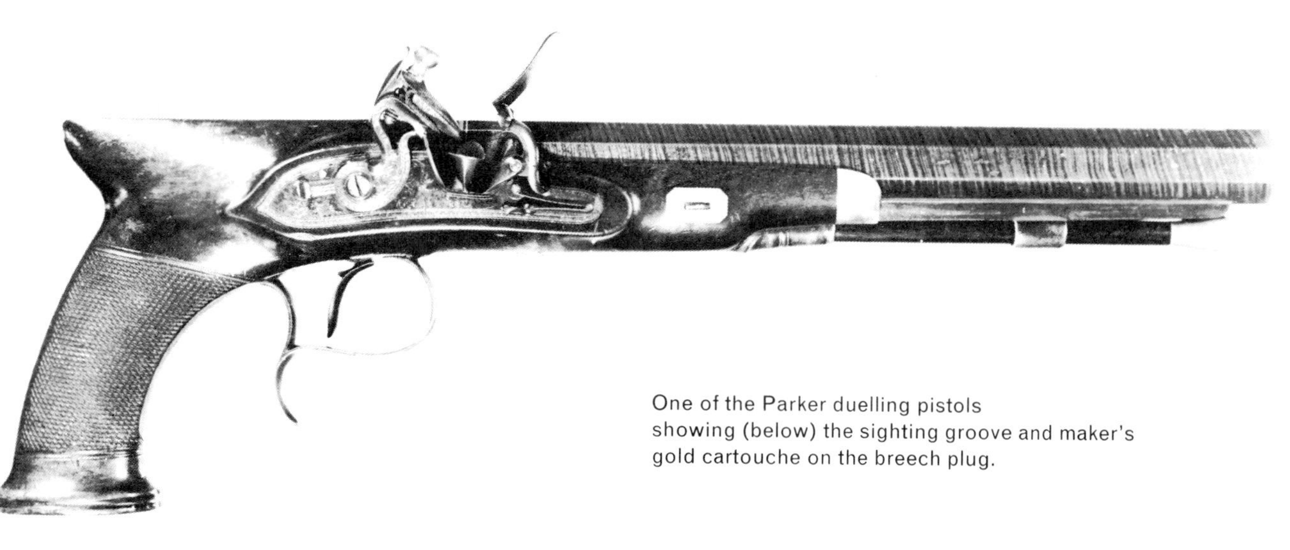

One of the Parker duelling pistols
showing (below) the sighting groove and maker's
gold cartouche on the breech plug.

maker to His Majesty and the Hon. Board of Ordnance. Lesser mortals might think that such an important man would not deign to serve them, but he is reassured by the statement, 'Merchants, dealers and others supplied with all kinds of firearms of the best quality on the lowest terms and shortest notice'.

Regarding terms and delivery, we have to accept Mr Parker's reassurance, but the pair of pistols speak for themselves, for they are excellent. As could be expected, they are cased and provided with the normal tools—bullet mould, mainspring cramp, powder flask etc.—all of the same good quality. When the pistols are taken out, the first impression is of weight and size. The visual appearance is also striking: dark walnut stocks, browned barrel and furniture, gold lining at the breech and gold lined pan. Quite massive magnificence.

Barrel length is 9″, smooth bore, octagon. Internal diameter .625″ or 19 bore. At the breech it is $\frac{31}{32}$″ across the flats, tapering to $\frac{15}{16}$″ at the muzzle. Chamber breeching is employed in company with a platinum vent, but the cartouche bearing the maker's name, 'W. Parker, Holborn, London', is in gold, as are the two decorative lines on the breech plug. The barrel proper bears the legend 'Gun Maker to His Majesty' on the top flat, and underneath the appropriate London proof marks is the number of the pistol, 3043. The barrel, which is secured to the stock by one loop and the usual hook breech, is provided with a bottom rib to carry the ramrod pipe. As can be seen from the illustration, the saw handled butt extension is quite sharply pointed and there is a sighting groove along the top. This groove is continued along the tang of the false breech, into which is dovetailed the rear sight. The rear sight has a deep 'V', and the foresight is a silver bead relieved at the front and dovetailed into the barrel.

The stock carries a silver rectangular escutcheon plate on the left side, and rectangular silver plates protecting the stock in the vicinity of the barrel cross bolt. The fore-end of the half stock terminates in a plain silver cap, but the lower ramrod pipe, which is of steel, is attached to the stock by a screw instead of being pinned. A spur trigger guard of elegant and appropriate shape is fitted to the stock by means of a screw immediately behind the pineapple type finial, and the screw passes through the stock into the lower part of the false breech. At the rear of the guard, the tang is secured by a wood screw. The use of screws instead of pins makes the task of dismantling somewhat easier, and the use of a bolt to tie the trigger guard and false breech together increases the strength considerably.

A single set trigger of similar design to that fitted to the Wogdon pistols is used, but the workmanship is of a slightly higher standard. No adjustment is provided for 'let off' and the trigger plate carrying the mechanism is simply let into the stock and retained in position by the trigger guard. The butt terminates in an oval cut-off flat pommel into which is inset a flat engraved steel cap secured by a screw.

The lock is of very high quality, and the cock is of the open-necked instead of the more fragile 'swan-necked' type. This variant of the swan-necked cock made its appearance about 1800, and may have been copied from the style adopted by Nicolas Noel Boutet of Versailles. But even this more robust type of cock was liable to fracture and the prudent flintlock owner was advised to carry both a spare cock and a spare hammer or steel. The later English open-necked cock differed in one important respect from its predecessors, namely the means employed to arrest its fall. The Dutch snaphaunce and the English dog lock had employed a buffer mounted externally on the lock plate against which the breast of the cock abutted. The later flintlock employed a shoulder on the inside of the cock and, when this struck the top edge of the lock plate, its fall was arrested. With the open-necked cock the bottom jaw was suitably modified so that, on falling, it struck the rear fence which was designed to accept it. The internal shoulder could then be abolished. The open-necked cock appears to have been used on box lock pistols before it gained popularity on sidelock weapons. Yet another style of cock appeared about 1810, and this is known as the reversed 'C' type. Here again, the fall was arrested by the modified fence rather than by the internal shoulder.

As to the other parts, a rain proof pan, inlaid with gold, enhances the appearance of the lock plate and the inside of the pan cover has a trumpet shaped recess, doubtless designed to aid ignition. There is, of course, a roller on the feather spring, and both the screw for the feather spring and the screw for the pan cover bridle enter from inside the lock plate, no doubt a minor point, but one which gives the lock a neater appearance. The pan and pan cover are very much smaller than previously, the pan being similar to a deep but narrow spoon. The cover and steel are mounted on a curved arm and this permits the cover and pan to be so positioned that full advantage is taken of the flattened breech plug.

The safety catch mounted behind the cock locks or bolts the tumbler, and the triangular safety catch spring fits between the two limbs of the sear spring. Since the pistol is fitted with a set trigger, there is a detent on the tumbler, but it is a rather unusual one in that it is fitted in the centre of the tumbler rather than on the face, as was the common practice. Both the bent and the sear nose are reinforced, the reinforcement or broadening possibly serving to strengthen the mechanism at these critical points, but also to reduce friction since the moving parts which are relieved do not have sliding contact against the lock plate. The mainspring is linked to the tumbler by a swivel and, as a whole, the lock is very smooth and sweet in operation.

There is only one side nail, and all that remains of the side plate, formerly so popular, is a small engraved cup which serves to protect the stock, and through which the side nail passes. The front or bar of the lock is held in place by a small hook projection which engages the head of a screw buried in the inletting of the stock.

These pistols by Parker may be taken as typical examples of the style and design features of 'best' quality weapons at the end of the flintlock period. Weapons such as these were turned out by the elite of the London makers, and they are weapons which cannot be faulted even by the most critical examination. There were, of course, many provincial makers whose work was the equal of the best London gunmaker, but most of the ones who established a reputation either moved to the capital or set up premises there in order to benefit from a London address.

One of the first to compete with the London makers was William Ketland of Birmingham. Many pistols by Ketland will be found to bear a London address and carry London proof marks. As there was no Proof House in Birmingham until 1813, several makers established Proof Houses of their own and, under the direction of Nathaniel Nye, a distinguished mathematician, they carried out proof for themselves. A recognised Proof House was erected in Weaman Street by Thomas Galton and another private Proof House was operated by Ketland.

The Ketland mark, crossed sceptres surmounted by a crown, acquired an excellent reputation as a guarantee of sound workmanship. This mark was similar to that adopted in a slightly modified form (by the addition of a letter 'V' for the view mark and 'BPC' for the proof mark) as the official mark for the Birmingham Proof House from the time of its establishment until 15 April 1904. The private Proof Houses were able to operate because the Ordinances of 1670 had only given the Gunmaker's Company of London the right to enforce proof in London and the suburbs or within ten miles thereof. The Act of 1813, however, made it an offence to sell any gun barrel in England and Wales without having such a barrel proved and duly marked at the London or Birmingham Proof House.

In the early part of the nineteenth century, Birmingham could truly be regarded as the arsenal of the world, and firms such as Ketland were large scale contractors for military arms throughout the Napoleonic Wars. From figures obtained regarding firearms made in England and received in Ordnance Stores, the combined efforts of the London trade and Government factories totalled 845,477, whereas the figure for Birmingham was 1,827,889. These are total figures for muskets and pistols during the years 1804 to 1815. If it is realised that barrels and locks for arms produced by the London trade were to a large extent furnished by Birmingham barrel and lock makers, the total production of piece parts and finished arms becomes quite remarkable.

An even greater impact on the London gunmakers of quality was made by William Westley Richards, who, severing connections with his family concern, built a factory at 82 High Street, Birmingham, in 1812 and, as early as 1815, had established a retail outlet in the heart of fashionable London, at 170 Bond Street. William Bishop was agent for Westley Richards in London and he was a man well known to the sporting fraternity for, to quote the famous Colonel Hawker again, the impoverished shooter 'has only to pay a visit to Mr Bishop, where he will get, at reduced prices, the guns of almost every mechanic in London, and some of them entirely new, with every article, as it came packed from the gunmaker, to the gentleman, who raised the wind on it'. William Westley Richards was considered by many to be 'Joe Manton the Second' and the high quality of the guns he made, coupled with the sales technique and great personal charm of 'the Bishop of Bond Street', established the company on a very firm basis. The eldest son succeeded his father in 1855, and further enhanced the reputation.

Not everyone sought the glamour of a London

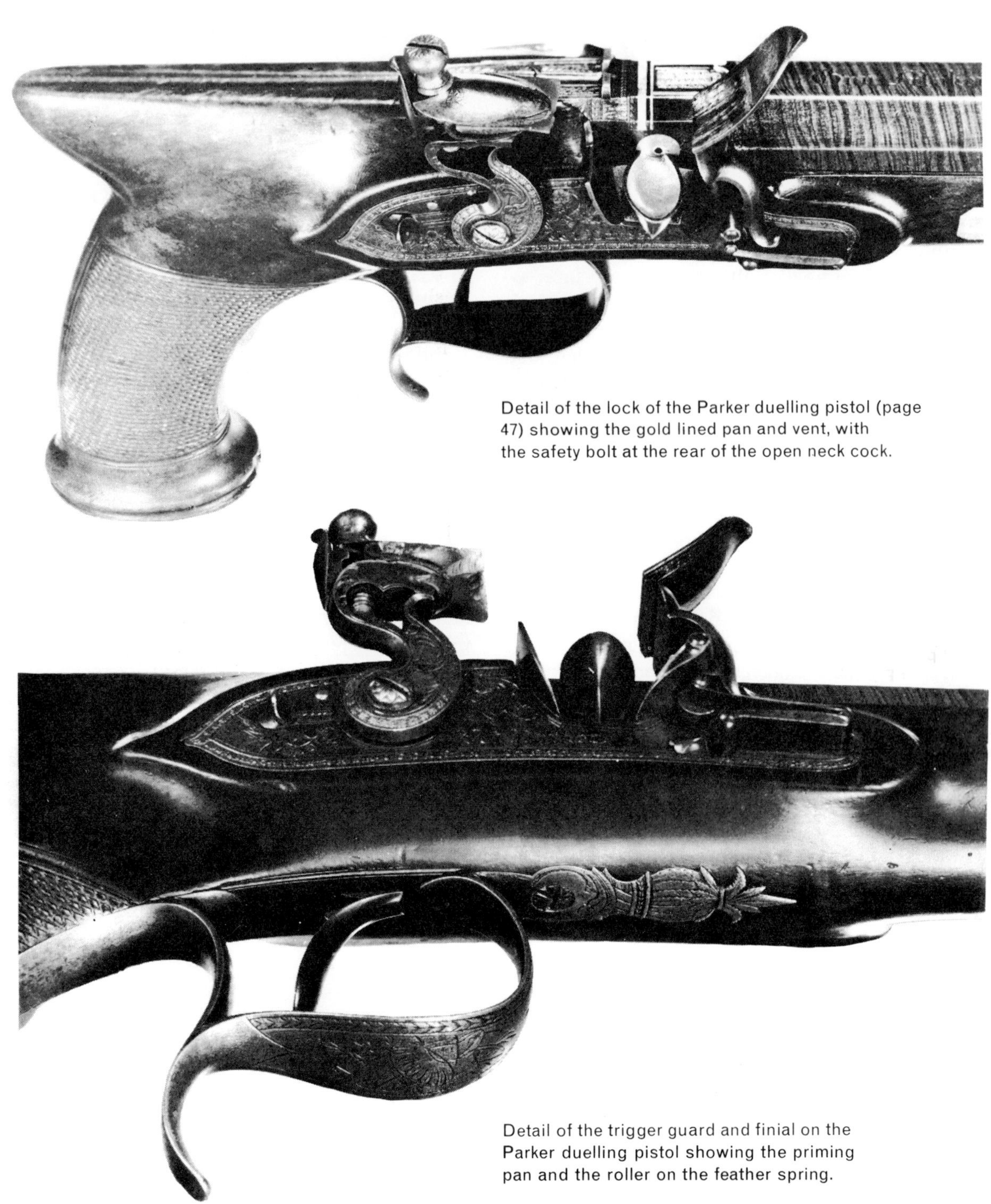

Detail of the lock of the Parker duelling pistol (page 47) showing the gold lined pan and vent, with the safety bolt at the rear of the open neck cock.

Detail of the trigger guard and finial on the Parker duelling pistol showing the priming pan and the roller on the feather spring.

address. To take one example in the north of England, Patrick of Liverpool made superb duelling pistols of a distinctive style and impressive appearance. In Edinburgh, the capital city of Scotland, the traditions of the past had not been entirely forgotten and, although the famous all steel pistol had degenerated into a mere ornament for Highland Dress, new reputations were being established. Innes, MacLauchlan, Thompson, Wallace—all these men made Edinburgh the gunmaking capital of the North, and the products of their skill during the nineteenth century were the equal of any in Britain.

In Dublin, as one might expect, the makers of duelling pistols flourished. Without doubt the greatest were the Rigby family. The first John

Rigby started up his workshop in Dublin in 1735, and a London branch was opened in 1866. During the latter half of the nineteenth century the family specialised in rifles, and in this field gained a well-merited world-wide reputation. The firm of Rigby was one of the very few to survive the transition from the handmade flintlock, through the percussion era, into the age of the modern breechloading cartridge.

To accomplish this required constant adaptation, and none of the great gunmakers in England adopted the widespread use of machine tools that was to characterise the production of the revolver and, later, of the automatic pistol. Double rifles, rifles and shotguns, the finishing of which is still largely a matter for hand craftsmen, have managed to survive even into this automated age, but the flintlock duelling pistol and the percussion duelling and target pistol were the last products of an industry which was extinguished by 1850.

At this point we come almost to the end of a remarkable period in the history of gunmaking. Quality, craftsmanship, individuality, the perfection of even the smallest detail, these are some of the factors that immediately strike one in any critical examination of pistols made in the course of it. For the craftsman it was truly a golden age when the direction was towards the perfection of his art. It has often been said of Joseph Manton that he would take components put aside as finished by his workman and would then work away on them until they were finished to his satisfaction. This tale may be apocryphal, but it nevertheless serves to illustrate the philosophy of gunmaking at the time: absolute perfection the prime consideration.

The years between 1790 and 1850 saw Britain the undisputed leader in the manufacture of pistols as weapons, as opposed to pistols as vehicles for applied art. The close of this era saw the decline of craftsmanship in pistol making;

Cased pair of smooth bore flintlock pistols by Fatou of Paris. (Glasgow Art Galleries)

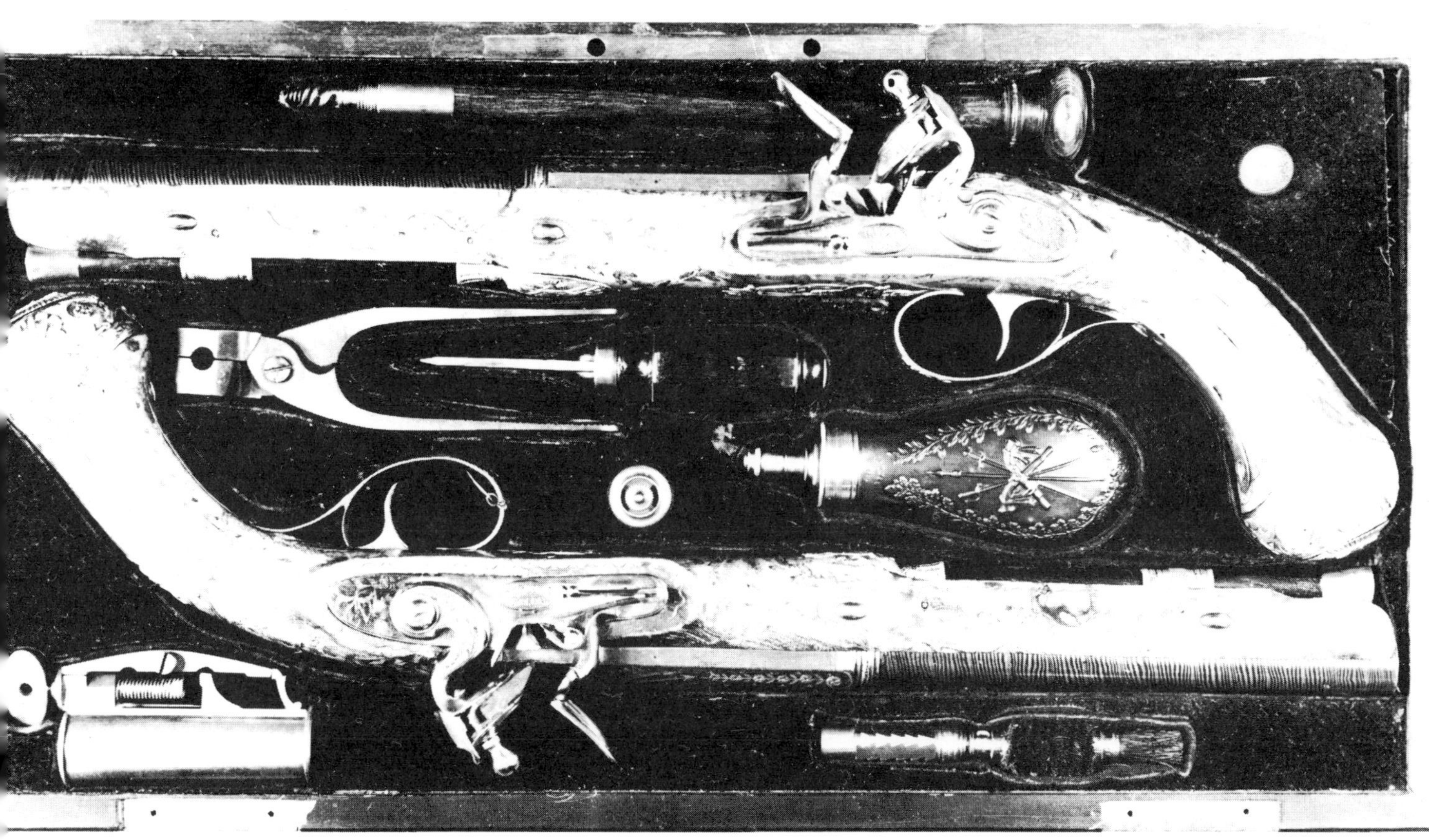

the skilled hand of the master craftsman was replaced by the automatic machine tool, and lack of capital, coupled with a chronic inability to foresee future trends resulted in the extinction of British pistol manufacture as a virile and expanding industry almost before it was born.

The only other country to produce duelling pistols with definable national characteristics was France. During the latter half of the reign of Louis XV, French gunmaking was dominated by the master craftsman of Paris, the most outstanding of whom was Jean Baptiste Laroche. Laroche was appointed Arquebusier du Roi during the reign of Louis XV and specialised in making the many presentation pieces which were given away by the French Monarch for services rendered to the Crown. Weapons of this type were rarely, if ever, used, and do not come within the scope of this work, but they do serve to indicate a basic style, provided that the riot of ornamentation can be ignored. The pair of flintlock holster pistols made about 1760 by Laroche and his son, signed 'Les La Roche', now in the Victoria and Albert Museum, are possibly the most richly decorated pistols ever made.

During the interminable squabbles that distracted Europe towards the end of the eighteenth century, French military requirements were met by the arsenals of St Etienne, which had been reorganised as a Royal manufactory in 1764. Tulle, in the Department of the Correze, south of Limoge, reached a similar status some thirteen years later. Two other establishments, Charleville and Maubeuge, are both situated on the borders of what is now Belgium, and Charleville, the first of the Royal Manufactories, was established as such in 1688. Maubeuge did not exist until 1704, and the manufactory was transferred to Chatellerault in 1830.

Not all the weapons made by the State factories were of plain military design and, in fact, in 1792, after the French Revolution, the demand for *armes de luxe* was considerable. During the period of the Directory, the Consulate and the Empire (1792—1814), presentation arms were made and given to distinguished French and foreign officers and to people of importance throughout Europe. By far the greatest number and most important of these weapons were made at the Versailles factory, established in 1792.

In terms of total production, however, Versailles was the least important of the State factories. The output of pistols between 1802 and 1814 was 2,346 as compared with St Etienne where, during a similar period, 163,072 pistols were manufactured. It was in the artistic field that Versailles made its greatest contribution, and no important arms collection can be regarded as complete unless it is graced by a pair of pistols signed 'Boutet'.

Nicholas Noel Boutet was related to some of the finest gunsmiths in France. His father, Noel Boutet, had been Arquebusier des Cheveau-légers du Roi, and his father-in-law, Desaintes, was Arquebusier ordinaire du Roi. The French Revolution and the execution of Louis XVI terminated his appointment as Royal Gunmaker, but such was his ability that, despite the radically altered political situation, he was appointed Directeur Artiste of the State Factory at Versailles. In 1794 a special workshop was set up for the production of *armes de luxe* under Boutet, and his craftsmen were recruited from France and Liege. In 1800 Napoleon Bonaparte, then first Consul, granted an eighteen year concession to Boutet and the terms of the contract included the delivery of 12,000 firearms per annum to the army and the training of pupils, so that the traditions of French gunmaking might be preserved.

Without doubt, the best work of the Manufacture Nationale de Versailles was between 1800 and 1815, but during the last year of this period the workshop was virtually sacked and plundered by the victorious Allies after the Battle of Waterloo.

Boutet presentation pistols were generally rifled, and the majority were full stocked to the muzzle. The half stocked pistols do not possess the same finished appearance, giving the impression that the pistol was originally a full stocked weapon, and there is not the same appearance of style as with the half stocked British pistol. But, in form, the presentation pistols follow the same general line. Characteristic of Boutet's design is the right-angled butt terminating in a flat pommel. The general styling is reminiscent of H. W. Mortimer's walking stick butts, although the immediate impression is not as pleasing. With the less costly weapons, the stock has a curiously hump-backed appearance which, allied to a rather extravagant treatment of the pommel, results in a decided lack of balance. Boutet's pistol locks are most impressive; the fantastically high finish obtained and the graceful sweeping curve of the cock are a delight. Characteristic of Boutet's later work is the acute angle of the jaw

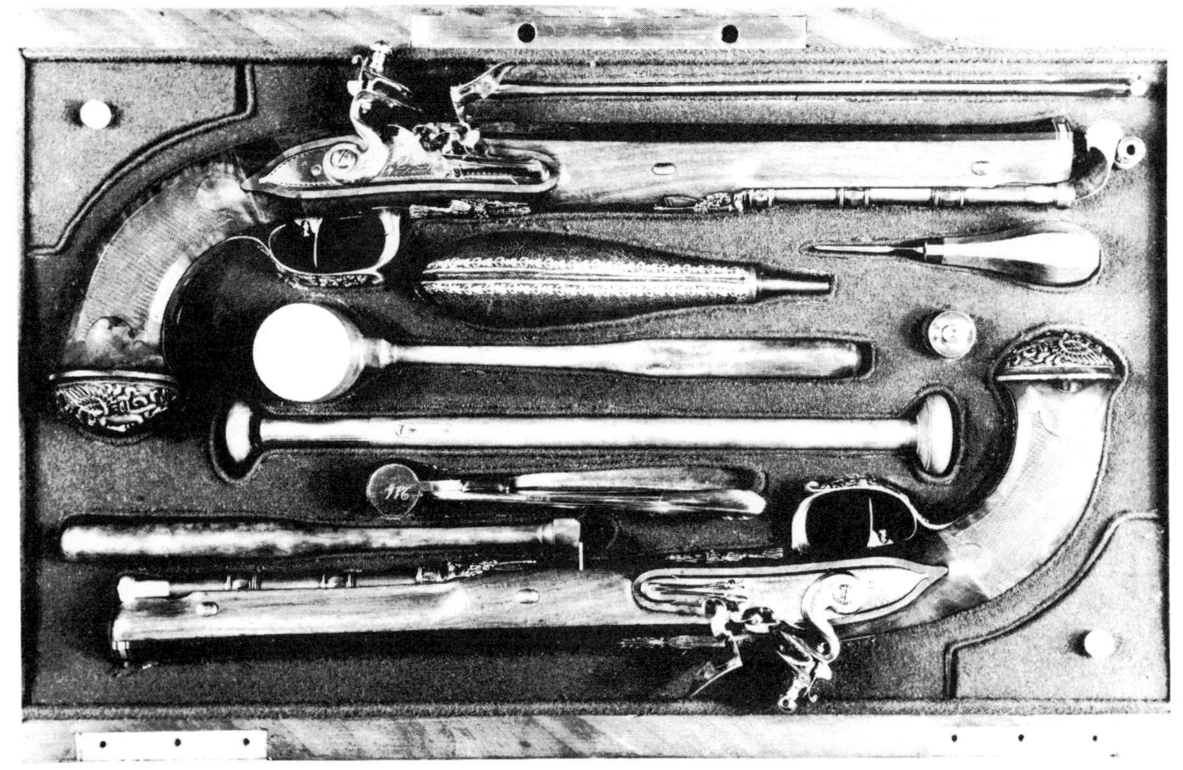

Pair of presentation flintlock pistols by Boutet of Versailles. (Glasgow Art Galleries)

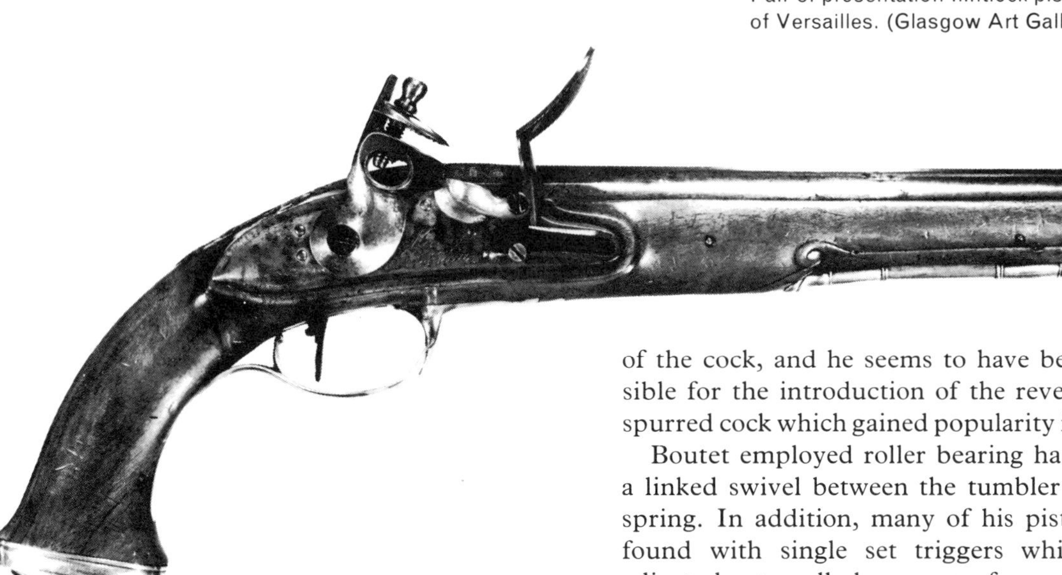

Flintlock pistol by Boutet of Versailles. (Glasgow Art Galleries)

of the cock, and he seems to have been responsible for the introduction of the reversed 'C' or spurred cock which gained popularity in Britain.

Boutet employed roller bearing hammers and a linked swivel between the tumbler and mainspring. In addition, many of his pistols will be found with single set triggers which can be adjusted externally by means of a capstan screw. It was standard practice to fit octagonal barrels to these pistols, the barrel being slightly necked in the upper half. Rifling was of the poly-groove type, and some barrels had in excess of a hundred fine-tooth grooves.

A superb example of Boutet's work can be seen in the Glasgow Museum, a cased single pistol complete with all accessories. An immediate impression is made by the superb finish, the en-

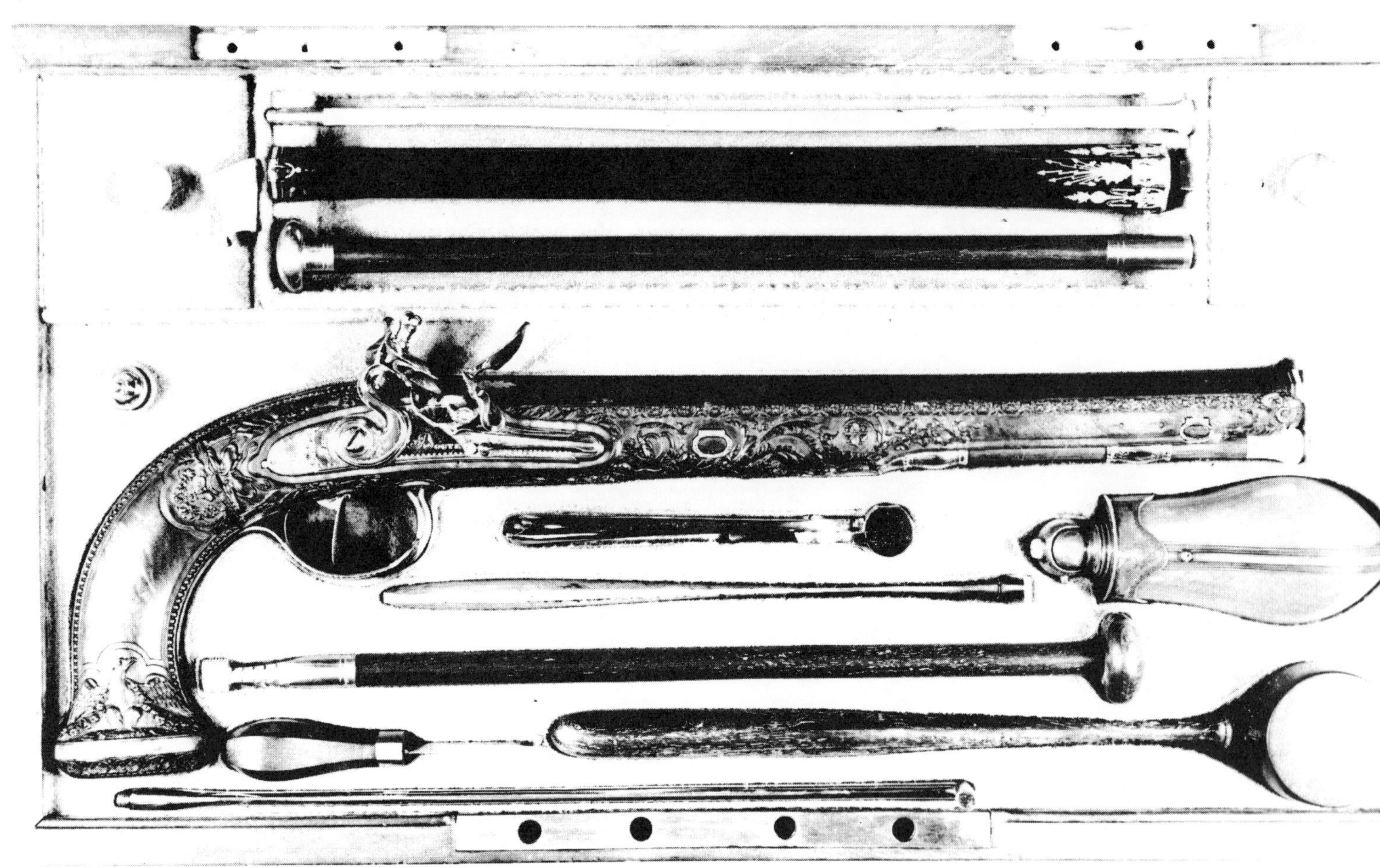

Cased single pistol by Boutet of Versailles. (Glasgow Art Galleries)

graved steel furniture, the jewel-like polish on the steel lock, and by the stock, incredibly carved with eagles, sphinxes, hounds and elaborate foliage. A delightful and unusual feature is the use of minute oval drop handles recessed into the fore-end and hinged to the barrel cross bolts. The barrels (the case contains a spare) are finished in a beautiful deep lustrous blue, decorated at the muzzle and breech. The cleaning rod, loading stick, powder flask and bullet mould are of equally high quality, and these accessories, together with the gun, fit into a recessed case. In Britain compartmented cases were the fashion.

Pistols such as these were fantastically expensive and, as is often the case when quality is the sole consideration, their manufacture was not financially rewarding and Boutet was often beset by money troubles. The products of Boutet's workshop at Versailles were signed 'Directeur Artiste' during the Napoleonic period; after the restoration in 1814, he signed 'Manufacture royale à Versailles'. Boutet finally moved to Paris where he set up in business at 87 Rue Richlieu under the title 'arquebusier ordinaire du Roi et des Princes'. He died in Paris in 1833.

In Germany and Austria, preoccupation with the wheellock had inhibited the development of the flintlock, and only one family of German gunmakers, the Kuchenreuters of Regensburg, were of sufficient stature to be known and sought after outside their own country. Even in a country where it was traditional for gunmaking to be carried on from generation to generation, the Kuchenreuters were remarkable. Nineteen members of the family are recorded by Støckel to have been gunmakers, from the mid-seventeenth to the twentieth century. Most members of the family specialised in the manufacture of pistols and, during the late eighteenth and early nineteenth centuries, their pistols, although plain and unostentatious, became renowned for accuracy.

The gunmakers in America will feature largely in later chapters. Pistols of the quality described in this chapter were either imported from Europe or made up from imported components. Locks in particular were imported from specialist manufacturers in Wolverhampton and Birmingham. Very few high quality flintlock pistols of purely domestic manufacture are available for study today, and such pistols as have survived are likely to have been the work of immigrant gunmakers who were able to find and retain a market for their old world skills.

The period covered by the so-called Kentucky pistol was from the post Revolutionary War to about 1840. The majority of the pistols that have survived are flintlock—those that are percussion are invariably conversions. Full stocked to the muzzle in walnut or cherry—later examples are in curly maple—many stocks will be found with a deep reddish stain characteristic of the old Pennsylvania German 'violin' finish. The pistols will also often be found either silver or brass mounted and, as the silver was obtained from the coinage of the period, it is rare to encounter silver 'touch' or hall marks. The calibres of these pistols vary from .36 to .50 and only the later examples are rifled. The majority of the barrels are of iron, though some early examples are of brass.

Only rarely are pistols encountered with indigenous locks; early pistols had locks of German origin and later locks were obtained from Birmingham. Kentucky pistols lacked the originality and grace of the Kentucky rifle but, in the early nineteenth century, gunsmiths working mainly on the eastern seaboard turned out duelling pistols of high quality. It is difficult to assess the domestic work content of these pistols since it is likely that not only locks but also furniture were imported, and the problem is further complicated by the fact that many of the gunsmiths had been trained in England.

Such a state of affairs was not destined to last long, for the extraordinarily rapid rise of American technology, due in no small measure to the relatively few skilled craftsmen available, resulted in the utilisation of machine tools and their rapid integration into the craft industries.

As we shall see in the next chapter, the largely hand-made single shot pistol of superb quality continued to be made in Britain, France, Belgium and Germany during at least part of the first half of the nineteenth century. Such weapons even survived the transition from flint to percussion but, unlike the high quality shotgun and double rifle, the pistol as a hand-made individual creation was utterly vanquished by the mass-produced products of the new gun factories. The pistol maker vanishes from history; in his stead appears the gun designer.

Notes to Chapter One

The brief historical survey undertaken in this chapter is intended as an outline. For those who wish to study the development of firearms to 1800 in greater detail there is fortunately an extensive and wide range of literature available. As a general introduction *The Treasury of the Gun* by Harold L. Peterson (New York, 1962) and, equally well illustrated, *The Age of Firearms* by Robert Held (London, 1959) can both be recommended.

For the more serious student *European and American Arms* by Claude Blair (London, 1962) and *The Art of the Gunmaker: Vol. 1, 1500-1660; Vol. 2, 1660-1830* by J. F. Hayward (London, 1962) provide a comprehensive survey of firearms development and ornamentation. One of the most important works on the flintlock is *The Flintlock, its Origin and Development* by Torsten Lenk, edited by Hayward (London, 1964).

Specialist interests are catered for by *Le Armi da Fuoco Portatili Italiane* by General Agostino Gaibi (Milan, 1962) and a companion work *Armi e Armature Italiane* by Aldo Mario Aroldi (Milan, 1961).

Further suggestions for additional reading are *British Military Firearms 1650-1850* by H. L. Blackmore (London, 1961) and the classic *English Pistols and Revolvers* by J. N. George, first published in 1938. The quality of the illustrations in the second reprint is much improved. *European Hand Firearms of the 16th, 17th and 18th Centuries* by Jackson and Whitelaw is also now available although the plates in this reproduction are rather darker than those in the original.

The serious student will greatly benefit by membership of the Arms and Armour Society, and details can be obtained from the Hon. Secretary, 40 Great James St, London, W.C.1. The Society publishes a Journal and details of new publications of interest to members.

The importance of actually seeing weapons cannot be overemphasized. A list of Museums which will amply repay a visit is given in the notes at the end of the last chapter.

Chapter Two

Forsyth and the Detonating Principle

The most remarkable feature regarding the invention of the detonating principle was that this discovery was made, not by a Manton, a Mortimer or indeed by any of the ingenious gunmakers of the first years of the nineteenth century, but by an obscure Scottish clergyman.

Some of the curious chemical family of initiatory explosives or exciting detonants had already been discovered when, on 13 March 1800, Edward Charles Howard reported to the Royal Society upon 'a new fulminating mercury' he had discovered. A reference to fulminate of gold will be found in the unabridged edition of Pepys' diary for 11 November 1663, and fulminate of silver had been made in France by Count Claude Louis Berthollet in 1788. Referring to the terrible properties of fulminate of silver, Nicholson wrote in 1795: 'When it has been once obtained it can no longer be touched.' Mercury fulminate was safer to handle but even the intrepid Charles Howard was seriously injured during his researches into the mysteries of this irascible compound.

Another equally excitable family of compounds, the chlorates, received considerable attention during the eighteenth century. Potassium chlorate had been discovered by Berthollet in 1786, and he showed how it could be substituted for the saltpetre in gunpowder. A more powerful and violent explosive was obtained, but the manufacture presented problems and, as a propellant, its action was too violent and not amenable to control.

Whilst the chemists were investigating these choleric compounds and the gunmakers were continuing in their efforts to perfect and improve the flintlock, the Reverend Alexander John Forsyth was ministering to his flock and, in his leisure hours, amusing himself with scientific study and shooting wildfowl on the loch near the Manse of Belhelvie.

It was at the Manse, some eight miles north of Aberdeen, that Forsyth had been born on 28 December 1768. Educated at King's College, Aberdeen, he graduated Master of Arts in 1786 and, having decided to enter the Church, he was licensed for the Ministry in 1790. Shortly afterwards his father died and the parish petitioned that the son should be presented with the living that the father had held for fifty-two years.

With his interest in chemistry and mechanics, and no doubt fully acquainted with the work that had been done in both France and England on detonating compounds, it is not surprising that Forsyth should have experimented with chemical means of speeding up the ignition of the powder charge in his fowling piece. The story goes that, when out fowling, Forsyth had missed many a bird because they were scared by the flash from the priming of his flintlock. A hood was fitted over the pan to hide the flash but, unsatisfied with this expedient, Forsyth went on to experiment with fulminate of mercury and potassium chlorate, first of all as propellants. Like others before him, he found that any slight advantages were more than outweighed by the hazards, so he then experimented with using detonating mixtures as priming. These mixtures could be ignited all right by the sparks from a flint, but often the priming failed to ignite the charge and all that resulted was 'a flash in the pan'.

Further work showed that slightly better

results were obtained when the detonating mixture was ignited by a blow, but success was not achieved until the detonating mixture was confined and the flame of ignition was directed into the powder charge. These trials were carried out using an iron tube about 9″ long provided with a touch-hole, adjacent to which was a cup containing the detonating powder. If the charge was wadded, even with a thin piece of paper, ignition occurred each time without fail.

By 1805 a successful gun lock had been made which Forsyth fitted to his fowling piece and used that season. In the spring of 1806 he took the gun with him to London where it was shown to Lord Moira, then Master General of Ordnance. At Lord Moira's invitation, Forsyth set up a workshop in the Tower of London and, having obtained leave from the Aberdeen Presbytery, he set to work to produce a robust lock suitable for use with either musket or cannon. Before he had fully completed his work, Moira was replaced by John Pitt, the second Earl of Chatham and brother to William Pitt the Younger. Chatham lacked many of his brother's qualities and he precipitately ordered Forsyth 'to take himself and all his rubbish from the Tower'. Forsyth returned home in disgust and, on 11 April 1807, took out Patent No. 3032 for his invention. Since his invention had been rejected by the military, he then decided to try his luck elsewhere and accordingly, in 1808, set up in business at No. 10 Piccadilly, London. His assistant was James Purdey, who had been one of Manton's pupils and was later to become very famous on his own account. Forsyth remained actively connected with the business until 1819, when he returned to his parochial duties. At the same time the business was transferred to 8 Leicester St, Leicester Sq., and the firm continued to be listed as gunmakers until 1845.

The first commercially successful Forsyth lock was the well-known scent bottle type, introduced in 1808. The scent bottle lock or, as it was then known, the magazine lock, offered a number of important advantages. In an advertisement of the period it was claimed that 'there was rapid and complete inflammation of the whole of the charge of gunpowder, prevention of loss of force through the touch-hole and perfect security against rain or damp in the priming. No flash from the pan and less risk of accidental discharge'. The latter claim was due to the fact that not only had the user the security of the half cock and the safety bolt but, in addition, the magazine could be put in such a position that even if the lock were cocked and the trigger pulled, the gun would not go off.

That Forsyth licensed others to make his patent lock is clear from the *Edinburgh Evening Courant* for Saturday, 6 May 1809, when the following interesting advertisement appeared.

'Forsyth's Patent Gunlock. Innes, Gunmaker to his Majesty, being appointed sole manufacturer for Scotland begs leave to inform the nobility and gentlemen who have done him the honour of making enquiry after this important discovery that he has now completed an assortment of double and single guns on this construction which he can now recommend with confidence, several sportsmen both in England and this country having used them last season and found them infinitely superior to guns with the flint lock. The priming is impervious to damp, the inflammation instantaneous making the aim much more certain and from the complete ignition of the charge the effect produced in the firing of the gun is increased one third both in strength and closeness.

'The application of this lock to rifle guns has been found of singular advantage.

'Good workmen will meet with liberal encouragement.'

Innes was a gunmaker of considerable repute and in addition to sporting guns and rifles he also made a wide range of pistols. It is very likely that as well as making pistols on the Forsyth principle, Innes would have been asked to convert flintlock pistols. I have never seen a specimen by Innes so converted, but I did have an opportunity some time ago to examine an extremely interesting pair of Manton duelling pistols. Apart from providing an opportunity to examine the Forsyth conversion, they also demonstrated the prevailing uncertainty of the times, at least as regards ignition systems.

The Manton pistols were made between 1805 and 1810 and are typical of Joseph Manton's work. The barrels are .486″ in diameter, say 40 bore, and weigh 2 lbs. Ten inches in length, they are $\frac{15}{16}$″ across the flats at the muzzle and very nearly an inch wide at the breech. The barrels bear no name, but the breech plug carries a rectangular cartouche in platinum with 'Joseph Manton, London' and a crown inset. The plug, which is of the Manton recessed type, is fitted with a platinum vent and has a thin platinum decorative inlaid line. The barrels are rifled with Manton's secret rifling, the grooves being very shallow and half the width of the lands. This

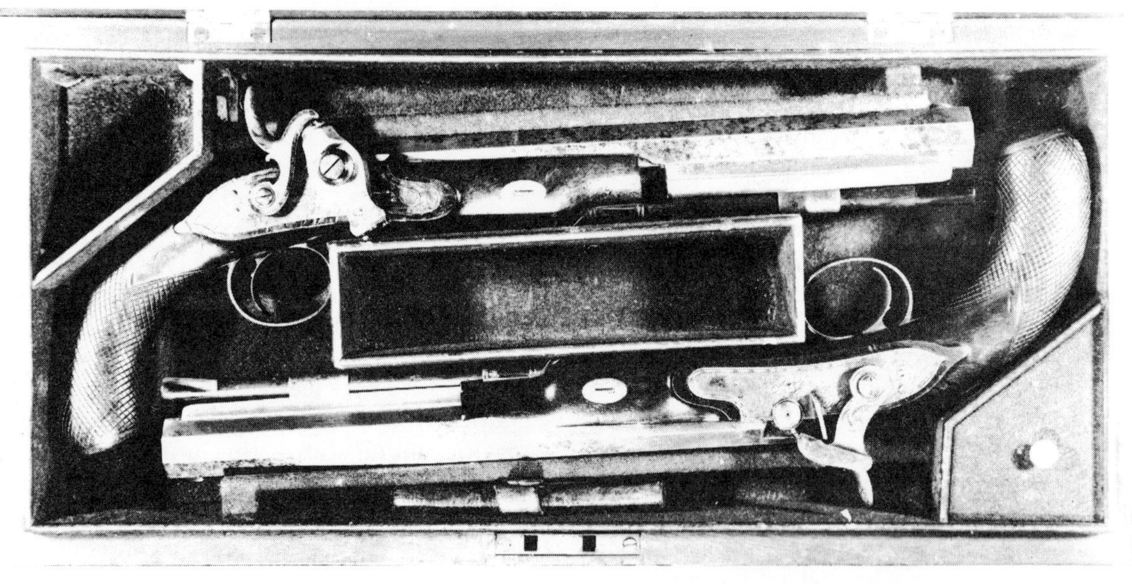

Cased pair of Manton pistols, the one above with the Forsyth 'scent bottle' percussion lock (interchangeable type) and with a cap lock.

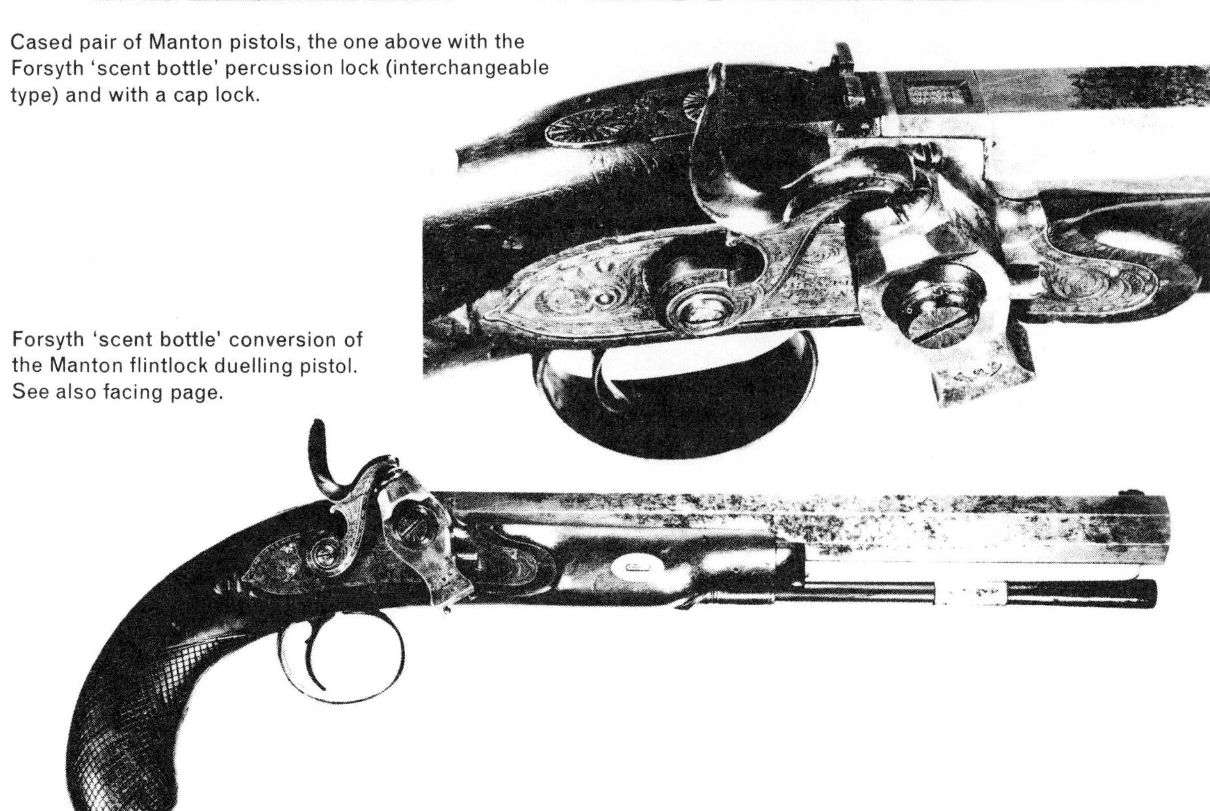

Forsyth 'scent bottle' conversion of the Manton flintlock duelling pistol. See also facing page.

secret rifling is very difficult to detect and would escape cursory examination. The false breech carries a broad 'U' type rear sight dovetailed into the breech immediately behind the breech plug, and this sight has facilities for lateral adjustment by means of a cramp. The main screw securing the false breech tang passes through the stock into the trigger plate, and a screw through the trigger plate engages the base of the false breech, providing ample security. Instead of set triggers, these pistols are fitted with Manton's improved trigger, the subject of his Patent No. 1893, dated 5 July 1792. In the words of the patent abridgement, 'the trigger has a spring screwed to the frame (trigger plate) and the end of the spring is turned to act through a notch in the trigger whereby the trigger is kept close to the rear of the lock by the spring and is prevented from shaking'. This was a most useful invention and was very widely adopted.

Of plain design but excellent workmanship, the pistols are half stocked and the ramrod is carried by one pipe attached to a rib underneath the barrel. The butt is lightly checkered and terminates in a rounded steel butt cap with a vestigial tang. Oval silver plates protect the stock where the

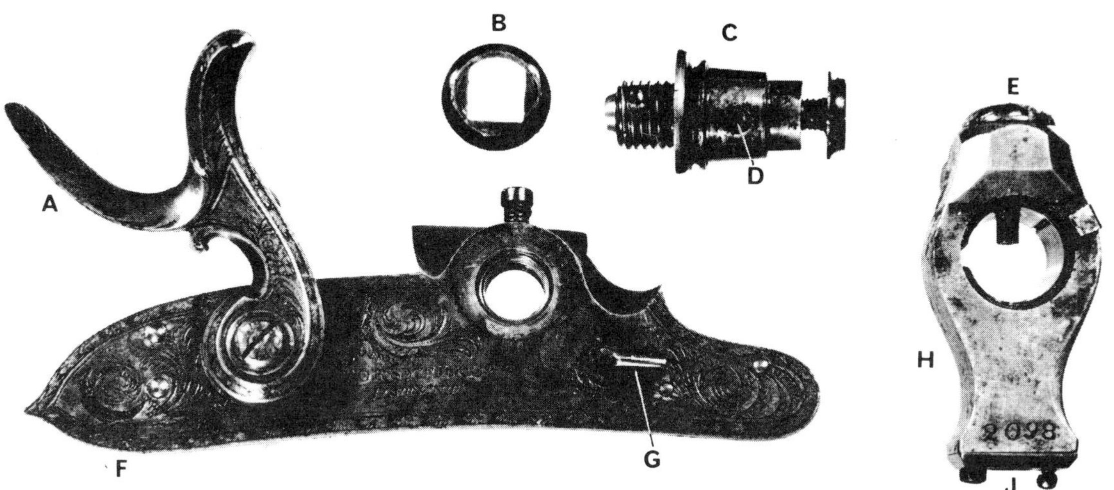

Forsyth 'scent bottle' percussion lock dismantled.

A. Cock or hammer.
B. Retaining washer.
C. Screwed taper plug.
D. Priming pan.
E. Spring loaded striker.
F. Lock plate.
G. Magazine stop.
H. Priming magazine.
J. Cover plate.
K. Platinum lined vent.
L. Barrel.

barrel pin passes through the wood. A horn tip finishes the fore-end, and a simple lower pipe is pinned to the stock.

Most of the weight of these pistols is in the barrel; to me they lack balance and, for this reason, pointability. It is in the locks that the greatest interest is aroused since one of the pair is fitted with a Forsyth roller magazine or scent bottle lock.

The lock plate is four inches in length and bears the legend, 'Forsyth and Co. Patent'. There is a formalised edge decoration to the plate and cock, and light scroll engraving. The mechanism of the lock is simple; it lacks a safety bolt but a detent guards the half cock bent of the tumbler. The centre top edge of the plate is raised to conform with the contour of the Manton recessed breech plug and it is thickened at this point. A tapped hole $\frac{5}{16}''$ in diameter passes through the lock plate and into this is screwed the plug of the Forsyth magazine. The plug itself is quite complex and most carefully made. The threaded portion is $\frac{5}{16}''$ in length and has a shoulder which butts against the lock plate when the plug is screwed home. The screwed portion has a blind hole which mates with a tapped hole in the lock plate. A screw through the tapped hole locates the plug and ensures that it is correctly orientated. A narrow hole passes completely through the plug at the screwed end and terminates in a platinum bushed vent, the bush being slightly conical on the outside and designed to mate with the vent in the barrel. The other end of this passage is tapped to take the large-headed screw that secures the magazine to the barrel. The barrel is tapered, and in the middle of the tapered section there is a small recess with a central passage (referred to by Forsyth as the 'touch-hole') which communicates with the passage drilled axially through the barrel. The end of the barrel terminates in a 'D' shaped section which accommodates the washer securing the magazine to the tapered portion.

The magazine is 1.9″ high, 0.85″ wide and 0.4″ thick. A tapered hole passes through the broadest portion, above which is housed the spring loaded detonating pin or 'exploding rod'. In the bottom section of the magazine is a parallel hole 0·2″ in diameter forming the magazine proper.

The hole is 0·8″ long and is closed at the lower end by a pivoted rectangular cover plate, in the centre of which is a hole with a horn plug to act as an explosion disc in the event of the fulminate in the magazine exploding accidentally. On the type of lock under examination, the barrel or pivot screws into the lock plate, since this lock is of the detachable type and can be removed and replaced by the original flintlock if desired. On locks intended to be permanent fixtures, the 'barrel' screws directly into the breeching and takes the place of the vent.

Fulminating composition is introduced into the magazine by sliding the cover plate aside. The cock is then drawn back to the half cock position and the spring loaded catch protruding through the lock plate in front of the magazine is depressed. The whole magazine assembly is then rotated anticlockwise through 180 degrees. This rotation is restricted by a stop on the rear of the magazine which limits the extent of travel since it abuts against the shoulder of the barrel, part of which is recessed. With the magazine in the inverted or priming position, approximately one eighth of a grain of priming is deposited in the recess in the barrel. The magazine is returned to the firing position and is locked into battery by the spring catch. When the cock is drawn back and released by the trigger, the nose strikes the detonating pin, the lower face of which ignites the tiny charge of fulminate. The flash passes through the vent into the central flash hole and then through the original vent of the pistol, igniting the main charge. To re-prime, the cock is drawn back to the half cock position and the operation repeated until the priming is exhausted. Enough priming is contained in the magazine for about twenty-five shots. The whole operation takes less than eight seconds, considerably less than required to prime a flintlock, and there is, of course, no need to adjust or change flints.

There were several minor variations of the magazine lock, none of which overcame its somewhat ungainly bulk. Although it was used on pistols converted from flint to percussion, a far neater and better adapted system here was that of Forsyth's sliding magazine. An additional refinement was the use of a link between the cock and the magazine containing the loose priming powder which permitted the automatic operation of the priming magazine. When the cock was drawn back, the link caused the magazine to slide to the rear so charging the 'touch-hole'; when the trigger was pulled the link slid the magazine forward out of the way as the cock fell. The nose of the cock was fitted with a detachable firing pin which could be replaced when the tip became eroded.

After reading the advertisements extolling the virtues of the Forsyth system, one wonders why the flintlock remained so long in use. The percussion Brunswick rifle was not adopted until 1836, and it was 1839 before orders were given to convert existing stocks of flintlock arms to the percussion system. Much of this conversion work was carried out by the Darlaston lock makers in the Midlands, who reaped considerable benefit from making 'cushion' locks—a somewhat odd term for the new percussion lock and one which illustrates how changes in name can produce difficulties for the researcher.

The comments of contemporary writers illustrate the mood of the period and give some insight into the apparently senseless delay on the part of the Military Authorities and the reluctance of sportsmen to become readily converted to the new system.

The first consideration was one of cost. A Forsyth lock alone cost as much as a good quality flintlock gun. It was possible and often desirable to convert an existing flintlock weapon to percussion; this gave the benefits of the new system without the expense of a completely new weapon, and a favourite pistol or fowling piece did not have to be prematurely retired due to the march of progress. The Manton pistol discussed earlier is an example of such a conversion.

It was of great importance to clean the lock carefully after use due to the extremely corrosive nature of the fulminating powder. At 10/6d. per ounce, this was expensive and not universally obtainable. Also, in spite of the claims made, the priming was not impervious to damp. Forsyth himself appears to have abandoned the use of mercury fulminate, and one formula for the detonating powder was potassium chlorate, sulphur and lycopodium or club moss. The club moss was supplied as a fine yellow powder remarkable for its combustibility but liable to a deterioration of its inflammable properties because of damp. Forsyth supplied a formula for making up the detonating powder and Colonel Hawker's version runs:

'One ounce of oxymuriate of potash,
One eighth of an ounce of superfine charcoal,
One sixteenth of an ounce of sulphur,

Mixed with gum arabic water, and then dried. It should be mixed up in wood for fear of accident.'

Yet another formula was:

'Five of oxymuriate,
Two of sulpur and
One of charcoal.'

Hawker then goes on to say: 'I merely give the recipe, in case a sportsman should be in a place where he cannot buy the composition, as I presume that no one in his senses would run the risk of being blown up, in order to make, perhaps indifferently, what he could so cheaply purchase in perfection'.

Despite the disadvantages of the loose powder, and the risk of premature explosion in the priming magazine (which Forsyth provided against with his 'explosion disc'), both the scent bottle and sliding magazine types of lock were widely copied, particularly on the continent.

With the exception of the lock patented by the Parisian gunmaker Prelat in 1810, which was an unashamed copy of the Forsyth scent bottle lock, most of the other patented locks employing loose detonating powder incorporated automatic priming on similar lines to the Forsyth sliding magazine lock. Typical of such systems was the lock patented by Joseph Contriner of Vienna, where the magazine was attached to the cock or hammer by a link and was capable of sliding in an arc. Contriner made detonating locks on several of the variant Forsyth principles. All the ones I have seen have been excellent examples of the gunmaker's art, as befitted a gunmaker in the capital city of the Habsburgs.

As an alternative to the use of loose powder in small grains, the detonating mixture could be made up into small pellets or pills. One of the earliest locks to cater for this was patented in February 1816 (No. 3985) by Joseph Manton. A special hollow plug just under a $\frac{1}{4}''$ in diameter and slightly less than one inch long, was fitted to a specially adapted hammer and retained by a spring. The plug, provided with a floating firing pin, also contained the detonating pellet. When the lock was fired the flash passed through the central hole in the plug and through a vent in the anvil and so to the powder charge. A box containing 24 plugs was provided and these could be kept ready charged, since it was quicker to change the entire plug than to re-prime.

The pellet lock was not one of Manton's successes, since Forsyth brought a successful action for patent infringement; nor was the system well received by the discriminating clientele of the 'King of Gunmakers'.

For those who wished, apparatus was available or could be made, to produce the little detonating pellets. Cohesion of the grains was obtained by the use of gum arabic, varnish or wax. The opportunity to examine one make of pellet was provided a few years ago and analysis showed that the pellets, which weighed about 20 mg and were approximately 2mm in diameter, consisted essentially of mercury fulminate coated with rouge (iron oxide). Pellets such as these were sold in glass bottles and special dispensers were manufactured to simplify the task of placing an individual pellet on to the pivot or nipple. The nipples were similar to those later employed for the copper percussion cap, but were shorter and wider. An annular depression or hollow to receive the pellet was provided and systems such as that invented by William Westley Richards in 1821 (British Patent No. 4611) used to prevent inadvertent loss of the pellet. Richards' system used a pivoted arm with a cap fitting over the end of the nipple. When the hammer fell, the cover was automatically flicked out of the way. The patent covered the use of priming powder either loose or in pelletted form and featured a priming magazine.

Priming magazines for use with loose powder and pellets also appeared which were incorporated into the hammer or made in the form of tubes along the barrel. In one form or another, pellet locks continued to be manufactured until finally vanquished by the copper percussion cap system.

Yet another detonating system was the tube lock. Although never as popular as the copper cap, the tube lock undoubtedly had its devotees. Undaunted by the failure of his 1816 pellet lock, Joseph Manton tried again and, in 1818, patented a tube lock (British Patent 4285); in this venture he was rewarded with considerably more success. The primer consisted of a tube of thin metal, open at both ends and filled with detonating powder. The tube was placed on a grooved anvil attached to the lock plate and at right angles to the touch-hole. To retain it in position a weak spring or forked lever could be employed or, alternatively, a snap cover. Although judged to be an infringement of the Forsyth Patent, this patent did not have long to run, and before long tube locks were widely sold both in Britain and on the continent. The Manton tube was about $\frac{5}{8}''$ long and $\frac{1}{16}''$ in diameter. Since it was inserted

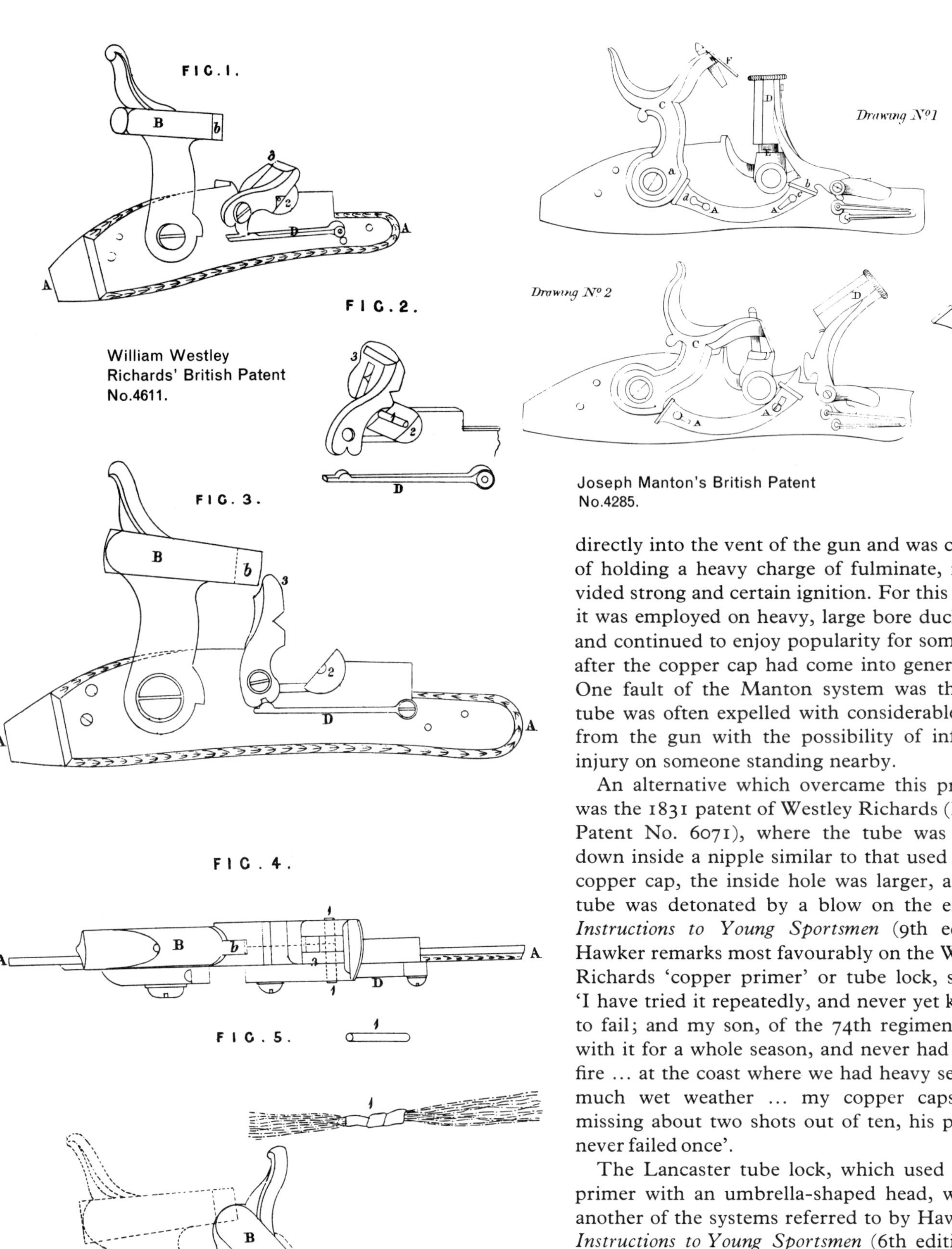

William Westley Richards' British Patent No.4611.

Joseph Manton's British Patent No.4285.

directly into the vent of the gun and was capable of holding a heavy charge of fulminate, it provided strong and certain ignition. For this reason it was employed on heavy, large bore duck guns and continued to enjoy popularity for some time after the copper cap had come into general use. One fault of the Manton system was that the tube was often expelled with considerable force from the gun with the possibility of inflicting injury on someone standing nearby.

An alternative which overcame this problem was the 1831 patent of Westley Richards (British Patent No. 6071), where the tube was thrust down inside a nipple similar to that used on the copper cap, the inside hole was larger, and the tube was detonated by a blow on the end. In *Instructions to Young Sportsmen* (9th edition) Hawker remarks most favourably on the Westley Richards 'copper primer' or tube lock, saying: 'I have tried it repeatedly, and never yet knew it to fail; and my son, of the 74th regiment, shot with it for a whole season, and never had a miss fire ... at the coast where we had heavy seas and much wet weather ... my copper caps were missing about two shots out of ten, his primers never failed once'.

The Lancaster tube lock, which used a tube primer with an umbrella-shaped head, was yet another of the systems referred to by Hawker in *Instructions to Young Sportsmen* (6th edition) as 'the safest of all detonators'. With claim and conflicting counterclaim not only between the different systems, but also amongst the variations within a system, the prospective purchaser of a new gun cannot have had an easy time selecting the one best suited to his purpose. Equal indecision characterised the attitude of the military.

In Austria the tube lock gained favour due to the work of a Milanese craftsman, Giuseppe Console. In 1812 Console invented a loose powder magazine protected against moisture and, in 1825, a system of ignition based on fulminate of mercury. His tube or capsule lock, invented in 1830, was submitted to the Austrian Government and adopted as a means of converting existing flintlocks. The Console lock was modified and improved by Vincent Augustin, an Austro-Hungarian army officer who became Master of Ordnance and Master Gunner in 1849 and was in charge of the Arsenal in Vienna during its formative years.

One of the drawbacks in the use of tube primers was the greater difficulty of repriming, coupled with the problem of devising a suitable and effective magazine system to contain and feed them. A rival system was the patch lock which possibly appeared slightly earlier than the pellet lock and which contained the priming between two paper patches in a similar manner to the caps still employed for toy cap guns. Usually the patch was placed in a special recess in the detachable nose of the hammer. The nipple or pivot (sometimes called the peg) had a central hole and was undoubtedly the forerunner of the later true percussion cap nipple.

The most outstanding development of the patch lock was Christian Sharps' disc primer patented in 1852 (US Patent No. 9308), which comes very much into the category of those 'I don't believe it' stories. An examination of the patent increases this feeling of unreality for here is a system that depends upon throwing a flat disc of fulminate into the air in the direction of the nipple. The disc is trapped in mid-air by the falling hammer just before being crushed on the nipple. This system was applied to both rifles and pistols and in practice it functioned extremely well. However, J. H. Walsh (Stonehenge), the author of *The Shotgun and Sporting Rifle*, sounded a note of caution: 'This plan acts very well when free from the action of the wind, but if it is at all submitted to the agent, the disc is blown away and the consequence is a miss-fire!' Yet another of these ingenious American devices was the Butterfield disc primer.

The logical solution to this problem of automatic priming was to connect the separate caps or primers together in the form of a tape. The best known and most successful tape priming system was that invented by an American dentist, Dr Edward Maynard, who took out his patent in 1845, claiming the manufacture of primers 'in a continuous series', the primers fed by the movement of the lock.

Relatively few types of firearms were made to use the Maynard tape primer, but a very great number were manufactured of each type and consequently, with the exception of the copper cap percussion weapon, the Maynard tape primer became the most common magazine primer system.

Dr Maynard's description of his primer was as follows: 'The detonating material of the Maynard Primer is in the form of Little Lozenges each about one-sixth of an inch wide and one thirtieth of an inch thick. These lozenges are enclosed between two narrow strips of strong paper cemented together and rendered waterproof and incombustible. The single strip thus formed is a little less than one fourth of an inch wide, is very stiff and firm and contains four of these lozenges (each of which is a charge) in every inch of its length, the charges forming projections, of their own shape, on one side, having considerable and equal spaces between them; the other side of the strip being one flat and even surface.

'One of these strips, containing fifty or more or less charges, is coiled up and placed in a magazine in the lock, and is fed out by the action of the lock, one charge each time the hammer is raised. When the hammer descends it cuts off and fires the charge fed out upon the vent (or nipple, if one is used) of the gun, thus igniting the powder of the cartridge within the barrel.'

To feed this tape two distinct types of mechanism were employed. The first used a 'finger' to feed the tape from the coil into a position above the nipple. The second system employed a 'feeding wheel' similar to a pinion with very coarse teeth.

Maynard firearms were made by the Maynard Arms Co., Washington: the Maynard Gun Co., Chicopee Falls, Massachusetts; and by the Massachusetts Arms Co., also in Chicopee Falls. The United States Army standardised the Maynard tape lock in 1855 and continued its use until about 1860. Both the Springfield rifle-musket of 1855 and the Springfield pistol carbine Model of 1855 employed the Maynard tape primer system with the 'finger' feeding system.

The 'cog wheel' form of tape magazine was used on the Massachusetts Arms Co. revolver which was unusual in that it could be fired with either tape or copper cap primers.

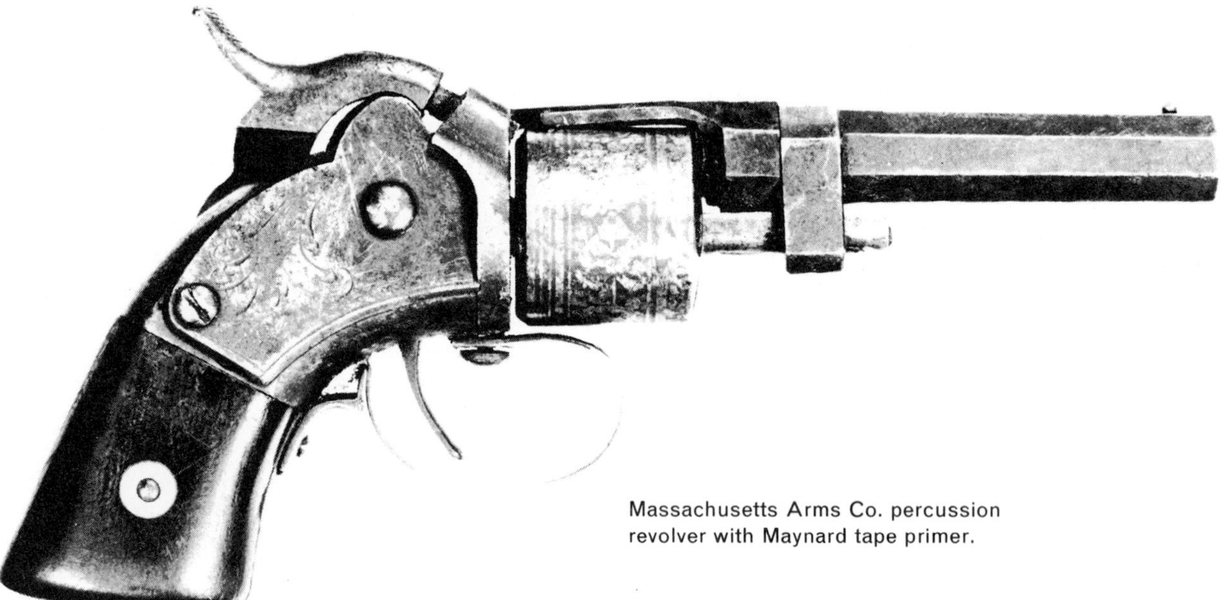

Massachusetts Arms Co. percussion revolver with Maynard tape primer.

An interesting variant of the basic Maynard system was the Ward 'Magazine Hammer'. Instead of the magazine for the tape being part of the lock plate, the roll of Maynard caps was carried in a special recess in the thickened head of the hammer. A movable lid provided access to the magazine, and the act of cocking the hammer fed a single primer over the vent of the nipple.

Although not a tape primer, Baron Charles-Louis-Stanilaus Heurteloup's continuous tube primer deserves mention, since it too falls into that class of invention which, even on close examination, should not work, but which in practice actually does.

The Heurteloup, Maynard and Ward systems all made use of a hammer with a cutting edge which cut the priming immediately before the flat hammer nose caused detonation. With the Maynard tape this posed no problem since, as mentioned by Dr Maynard, 'there was considerable and equal spaces between the charges'. Not so with the earlier 'continuous' Heurteloup priming. The Baron was granted three British patents. The first, No. 6611 taken out in 1834, referred to the use of a long tube made of soft metal 'or other suitable material'; the detonating powder was contained inside this tube, 'a portion of the tube being cut off by a cutting edge or knife attached to the cock'. The tube could be contained in a chamber or groove in the stock 'and is advanced by a suitable mechanism'. The first reaction to this idea is that the extremely sensitive detonating powder would be ignited by the cutting action of the knife.

In his second patent, No. 7980 taken out in 1839, Heurteloup explains the 'suitable mechanism' referred to in his original patent. The continuous priming was fed by the action of a small cog or serrated wheel which was rotated by a connecting arm attached to the tumbler of the lock and operated each time the lock was cocked.

Difficulty must have been encountered with the priming tube since an alteration to the formula of the original mixture, which consisted of 'five parts chlorate of potash, one part sulphur and one and a half parts of charcoal', was made in the third patent taken out in 1841, No. 9084. Heurteloup states that the original priming composition was liable to ignite 'beyond the part struck' and it was also possible for it to continue to burn 'like a slow match'. A modified priming consisting of 'chlorate of potash itself or a mixture of 48 parts of chlorate of potash, 1 part of sulphur and 1 part of charcoal, all finely powdered', was advocated. This mixture was put into tubes of pewter about one tenth of an inch in diameter. Machinery for the manufacture and filling of the tubes was also described as well as the forming of the tubes into a flat tape. Trials were carried out by the British Government in 1837 but the results were not conclusive although, in a report issued in 1838, the wish was expressed that improvements to the Baron's invention would 'lead eventually to the discovery of what they (the Committee) consider the grand desideration for Military Service namely, a simple, safe and durable self priming musket'.

It was four years after Heurteloup patented his invention in the United States in 1841, that

Maynard patented his, and the appearance and efficiency of the tape priming system was so improved by placing the magazine on the lock plate that tape priming was adopted for military service, the very result that Heurteloup had been so keen to obtain for his own system.

The most successful and most widely adopted percussion system was that which employed the copper cap, though considerable efforts were made by inventors during the first half of the nineteenth century to find some alternative which would provide self-priming.

The inventor of the small metal thimble with internal priming is not known. It is almost certain that the pellet and patch locks which employed a peg, pivot or nipple screwed into the breech appeared first of all. Shortly afterwards someone had the bright idea of placing the detonating compound inside a metal thimble or cap which would fit securely on to the stem of the nipple. Many people have laid claim to the invention, many researchers have advanced the claims of others, but, apart from the fact that Prelat first patented the copper cap in July 1820, all else is conjecture. In Britain the invention was claimed by Joseph Egg, who told Captain Lacy, author of *The Modern Shooter,* that the first copper cap had 'been made out of an old pennypiece'. James Purdey claimed that he had made the first cap from the tag of an old umbrella. Colonel Hawker himself, in *Instructions to Young Sportsmen* (6th edition), tells how he had hit upon the plan of a perforated nipple, with the detonating powder contained in the crown of a small cap, and how Joe Manton had converted a gun to Hawker's design. In the same edition Hawker modestly refers to his claim: 'I do not mean to say that I was the inventor of it—very probably not'.

Yet another claimant was Joshua Shaw, an English artist resident in America. Shaw's patent for a copper cap was granted in 1822 in America; in Britain, David patented a 'compound lock' in 1822, which could either function as a flintlock or a percussion lock. The nipple was made to turn on a hollow axis so that either the nipple or a priming pan could be used, and the lower jaw of a special cock was blunt-ended so that it would serve as a hammer. A similar type of lock was made by the noted London gunmaker, Ezekial Baker.

Once the principle of the copper cap had been discovered attempts were then made to improve the system and to eradicate some of the problems which attended its use. The danger with early caps was due to the fragmentation of the metal cap itself. Hawker refers to the number of sportsmen who were severely cut about the face by fragments, himself included. This was overcome by careful selection of the copper to eliminate brittleness and also by the use of a fluted skirt to the cap. It was essential that the cap fitted the nipple correctly. If too loose it could be lost inadvertently, and if too tight a misfire would result due to the cushioning of the hammer blow.

Caps were made in a wide range of sizes and the prices of best quality waterproof caps by the English makers Eley and Joyce were 1/6d. for a box containing 250, or 5/6d. per 1,000. When ordering caps, it was advised that a nipple should be sent at the same time to ensure the correct fit, both as to length and diameter.

A variant type of cap, and one which is still manufactured, is the 'top hat' cap made with a

The second of the Manton duelling pistols converted to percussion by the drum and nipple method (see page 58).

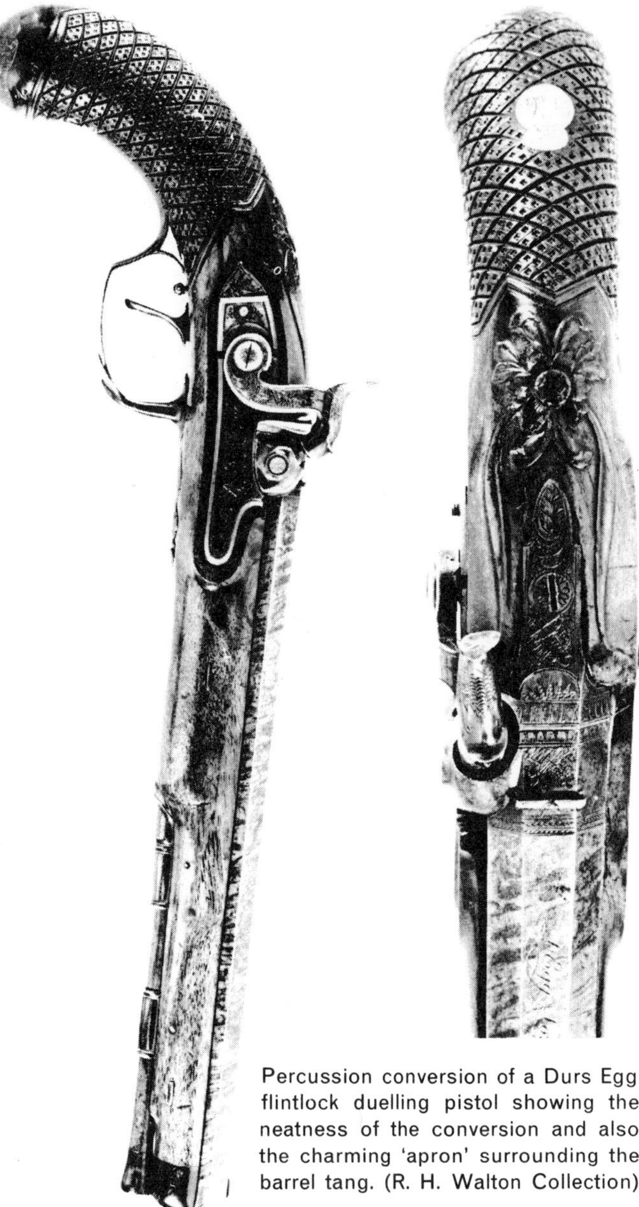
Percussion conversion of a Durs Egg flintlock duelling pistol showing the neatness of the conversion and also the charming 'apron' surrounding the barrel tang. (R. H. Walton Collection)

'brim'. This type of cap was originally designed for use with nipples provided with a hinged guard which held the cap securely on the nipple. Another type was that patented in 1830 by Samuel Smith, the London gunmaker. The Smith Patent Imperial Cap was designed for use with a special nipple larger in diameter than the common nipple, and with a raised centre portion round the vent. The cap, 'so that it can be easily handled', was made large to correspond with the nipple and was formed with a central cup to contain the priming. One of the advantages of the copper cap system was the ease with which flint guns could be converted. The easiest method was to fit a steel striker into the jaws of the cock in place of the flint and to replace the pan cover and steel with a converter. This was a pan cover with a nipple screwed in so that a cap placed on the nipple would be struck by the steel striker. If the user found difficulty in obtaining caps, the weapon could easily be changed back to flint and steel ignition.

The more usual form of conversion, however, was to fit a screw plug carrying the nipple into the vent, the original flint cock being replaced by a percussion hammer. An example of such a conversion, the second of the Manton pair of duelling pistols, is illustrated on page 65.

An alternative method of conversion was to fit a new breeching. The original breech plug was removed and a new plug fitted complete with boss to receive the nipple. If the original lock was of good quality it could be adapted by the removal of the flash pan, pan cover and feather spring, the original screw holes being filled in. A new hammer was of course necessary and the outline of the lock plate was altered to conform with the new breeching. Such conversions were common, and it was not unusual for a weapon to be converted from flint to Forsyth 'scent bottle' and then to a pill lock, finally ending up with the copper cap system.

It is not easy to establish any chronological classification of the wide variety of percussion lock systems, and at some time it must have been possible to buy at least one example of each. Indeed, the gun room of a keen sportsman might well have contained Forsyth scent bottle locks, pellet or patch locks, tube locks and a firearm fitted with a tape lock.

Because of the ease of conversion from one system to another, few examples of percussion locks other than the copper cap and the Maynard tape system survive today; those that do are prized by collector and historian alike because of the important part they have played in the development of firearms.

Notes to Chapter Two

References not mentioned elsewhere concerning Forsyth will be found in *The Reverend Alexander John Forsyth, M.A., LL.D., and his Invention of the Percussion Lock* by Major General Sir A. J. Forsyth, Aberdeen, 1909. A reprint of the original was published in 1955.

Information on Forsyth's sliding magazine system appears in 'Forsyth's Sliding Magazine Detonating Pistols' an article by P. A. Bedford published in *Black Powder*, Vol. 5, No. 6.

Chapter Three
The Percussion Pistol Perfected

We have already seen that the owner of an costly and often highly prized flintlock duelling pistol might go to the expense of converting it to one or another of the percussion systems. Fortunately, many did not, since the practice of duelling was going out of favour.

As might be expected, the army was the last stronghold of the duel, and it was an encounter between Lieut-Colonel Fawcett of the 55th Regiment and his brother-in-law, Lieut. Munro of the Royal Horse Guards—in which Fawcett, a distinguished officer, was killed—that led to the formation of the Association for the Suppression of Duelling. Pressure by the Association finally led to the amendment of the Articles of War in 1844, and the penalties imposed were such as to deter all but the most foolish and hot-headed. The last encounter which took place on English soil was between two French refugees in 1852.

The true duelling pistol probably ceased to be made in England after about 1840–45, and most of the pistols made in the third and fourth decades of the nineteenth century are better described as 'target pistols in the duelling style'. In spite of the volume of literature on duelling, it should also be remembered that the majority of people in 'society' never fought a duel, and few even witnessed one.

Acknowledged to be one of the best pistol shots in Britain, Captain Horatio Ross, born in 1801, was completely averse to the practice of duelling and, although he spent some time in the army, in the 14th Light Dragoons, he neither received nor sent a challenge. Ross acted as second on sixteen occasions but, believing no doubt that the second's first responsibility was to bring about a reconciliation, he never actually saw a duel fought.

In later years Captain Ross spoke reminiscently of a curious match that he had with Lord Vernon. 'Vernon had agreed to shoot a match with Lord Kennedy for £200 a side at 200 yards distance with rifles. Lord Vernon, or rather, as he then was, the Hon. George Vernon, came to the Red House for breakfast, and went to the ground to fire some practice shots. He made very bad practice indeed, and was evidently nervous, so I offered to shoot five shots with my pistol at 100 yards against his rifle for £5 and actually beat him.'

Ross goes on to say that 'Lord Kennedy arrived, looking ghastly, and said to me, "it's no use, I must be beaten. I have never been to bed. I have been up all night at Crockford's and have lost £3,000!" '[1] He did, in fact, shoot so badly that he lost the match.

Ross himself was never beaten in any match—and in those days pistol shooting was inevitably accompanied by a sizeable wager. He was also equally well known for his rifle shooting and his son, Edward C. R. Ross, was the first winner of the Queen's Prize at the National Rifle Association's inaugural meeting at Wimbledon in 1860. Marksmanship appeared to run in the family.

Several types of target/duelling pistol were made during the percussion period. The first was almost identical in form to its flint counterpart. This was the half-stocked saw-handled pistol usually fitted with the spur guard. The pistol is by J. D. Dougall of Glasgow, a maker later famous

[1] *The Sporting Mirror, Vol. III.* p. 153 (London, 1882).

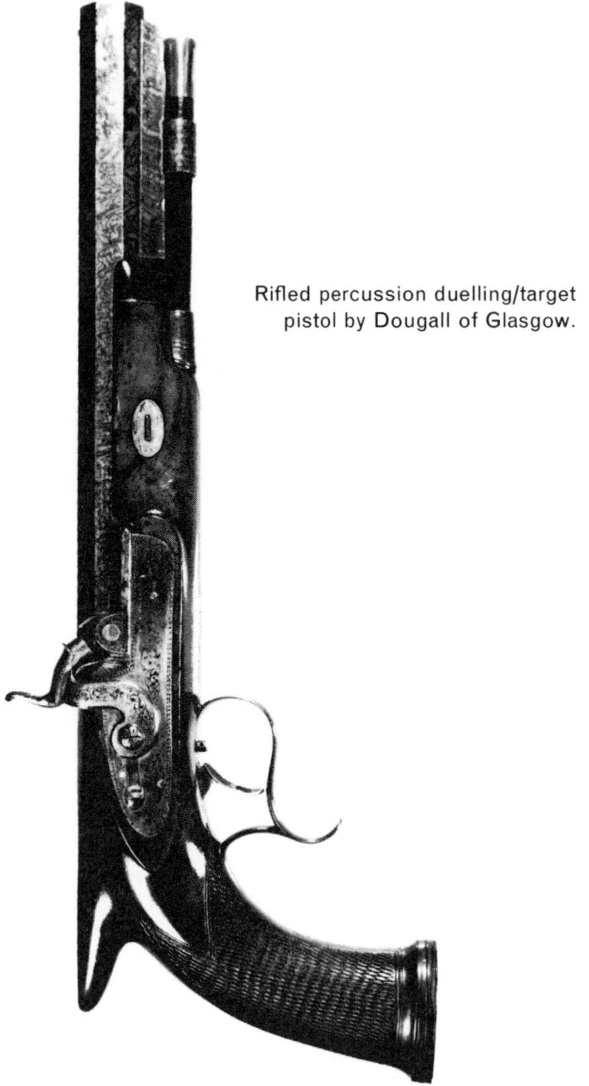

Rifled percussion duelling/target pistol by Dougall of Glasgow.

for his staunch advocacy of the pin-fire cartridge. The Dougall pistol is fairly typical of its type, its massive appearance being borne out by its weight of two and a quarter pounds. The barrel is rifled with nine hemispherical grooves, the bore being just over the half inch at 34 bore. Octagonal for its entire length, the barrel tapers slightly towards the muzzle and is 9″ in length, including the breeching. It bears Birmingham marks and the maker's name, and is pleasantly browned.

The breeching carries a screw-in nipple on the right hand side, the base of the nipple being squared to permit removal with a suitable key. A solid platinum plug closes the hole drilled across the breeching. Some breechings were provided with a removable screw to permit the cleaning of the various passages which conveyed the flash from the priming to the charge. It was also common practice to use a platinum plug with a small vent, one reason being to avoid a build up of pressure under the charge, of particular importance in the case of long barrelled sporting guns.

The barrel of a percussion target/dueller differed from its flint predecessor in one other respect. A metal projection on the right hand side of the barrel in front of the nipple housing will usually be found on bar-lock duellers. This was not normally used when the front of the lock plate was fully inletted and, apart from presenting a finished appearance to the pistol, it may have been of some value in preventing the flash from the cap from getting inside the lock plate and causing corrosion.

The lock of this pistol is of good quality and, as a set trigger is provided, it has a detent. The half cock safety bolt is behind the hammer on the outside of the lock plate, but it bolts the tumbler rather than the hammer. The set trigger is pushed forward to cock the mechanism and the set pressure can be adjusted by a capstan screw located immediately in front of the trigger. Rudimentary sights are fitted and the engraving is minimal though well executed.

Although very muzzle-heavy, the pistol is not unpleasant to shoot but the tip of the saw-handle tends to distract the eye when the pistol is being aimed.

The distinctive feature of the illustrated Manton pistols is the use of back action locks. This type of lock is easily identified since the greater proportion of the lock plate is behind the hammer. Internally, the mainspring will be found behind the tumbler, rather than in front as is the case with the front action or bar-lock.

Back action locks were rarely employed on flint guns since the normal bar-lock was ideally arranged, the bar providing a mount for the pan and bridle and space to accommodate the feather spring. Where the pan and bridle were mounted on the barrel or fore-end—on, for example, double barrelled turn-over weapons—it was obviously advantageous to have the bulk of the lock behind the breech so as not to interfere with the 'turn-over' action.

Back action locks became popular during the 1820's for both percussion pistols and long guns. The locks were mortised into the wrist of the stock and this tended to lighten the fore-end. Since the lock could be contoured to the form of the stock by curving not only the lock plate but also the limbs of the lock, a cleaner outline could also be produced. A disadvantage was that the stock itself might be weakened due to the amount of wood removed during the inletting of the lock mechanism.

Apart from the use of back action locks and the stock form, the construction of these pistols was typical of the period. The barrel group was unchanged but, as can be seen, the false breech tang was now secured by two screws, the first through the tang proper into the trigger plate, the second through the trigger plate into the base of the false breech. A further screw secured the rear of the trigger plate, the screw passing into the stock. This method of construction differed from earlier flintlock practice (as exemplified by the Parker flint pistol) in that on these pistols the trigger plate was located by the inletting and retained in place by the trigger guard. The later construction was far more robust and allowed for greater precision in assembly.

After he left Forsyth in order to set up on his own, James Purdey established the world famous business that today still bears his name at No. 314½ Oxford St, London. The pair of pistols illustrated, engraved with his name, have fortunately survived undamaged, including case and accessories, and they serve as a nostalgic reminder of past glories.

It is well worth while having a close look at them, for they represent that last freedom of expression in British pistol making, a freedom that was to be greatly diminished with the development of the machine tool, and then further restricted due to the use of mass production techniques. The first impression is one of deceptive simplicity: the pistols owe little to applied decoration; their charm and

Percussion duelling pistol by Joseph Manton, about 1830. (Paton Collection)

A. Barrel.
B. Hook.
C. Barrel loop.
D. Ramrod pipe.
E. False breech.
F. Stock.
G. Trigger plate.
H. Trigger guard.
J. Back action lock.
K. Cap.
L. Worm.
M. Ramrod.

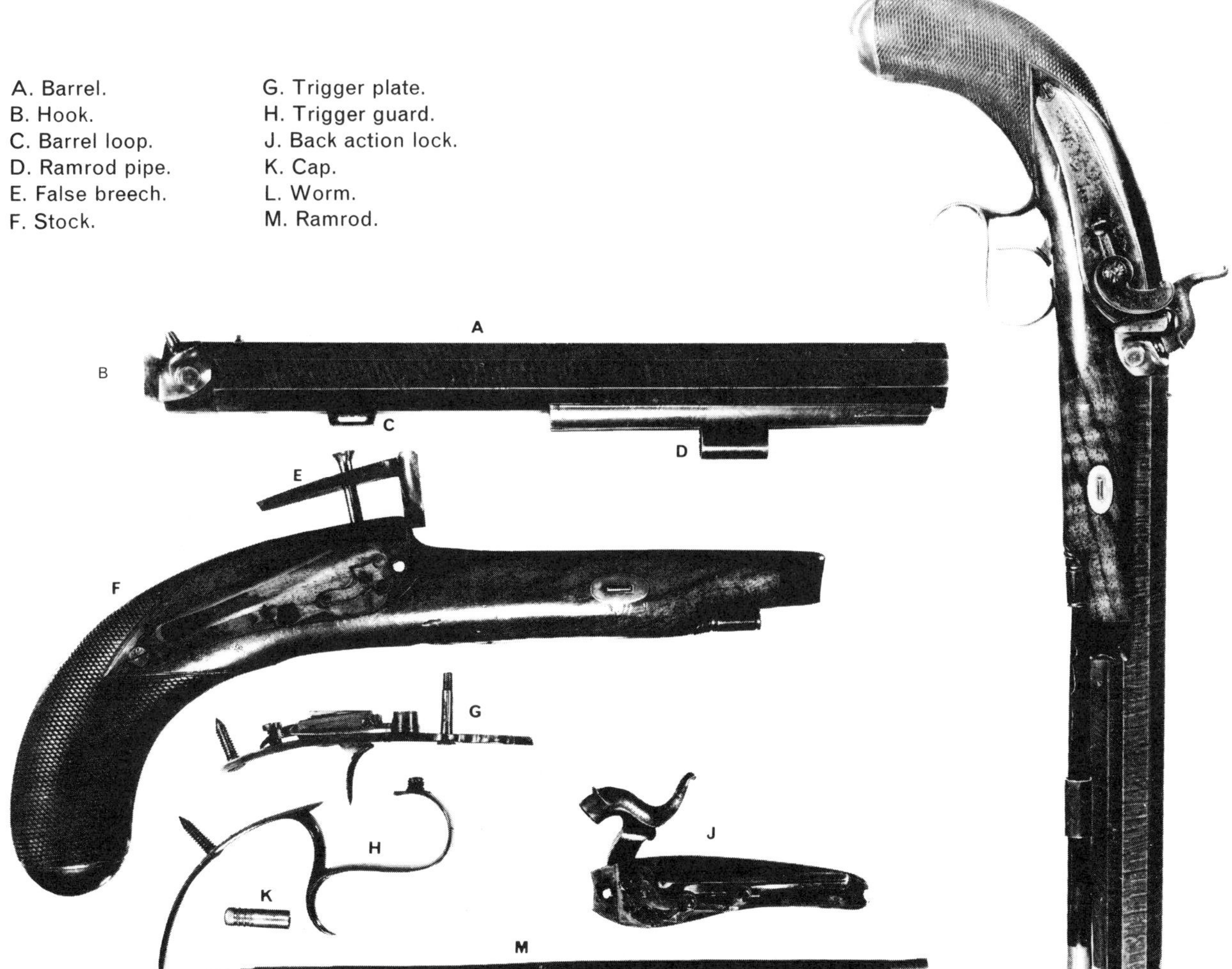

James Purdey's trade label.

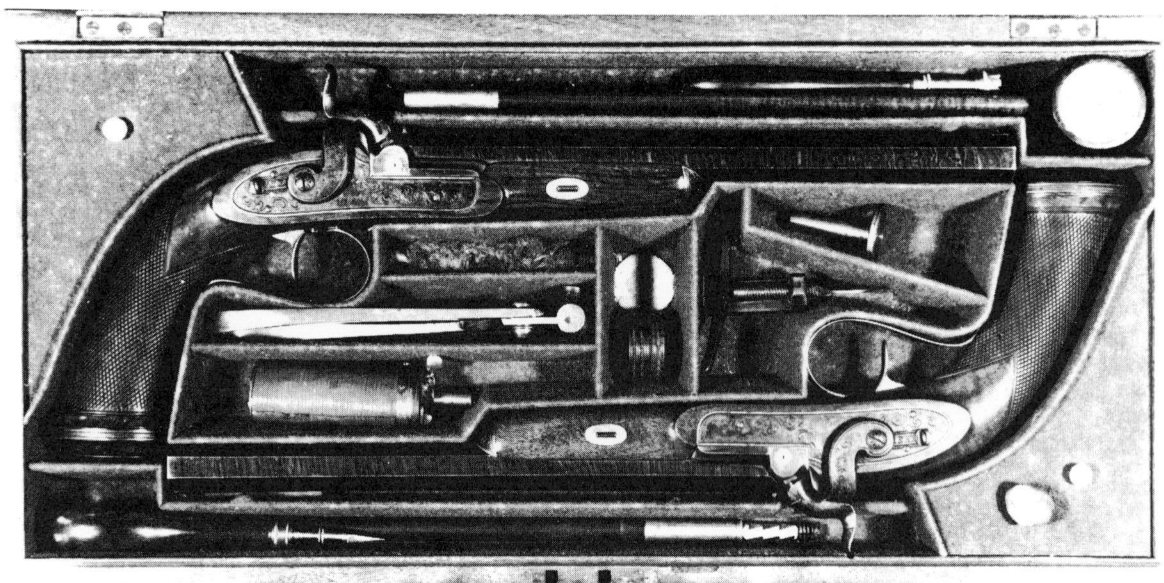

Cased pair of Purdey percussion duelling/target pistols. (Paton Collection)

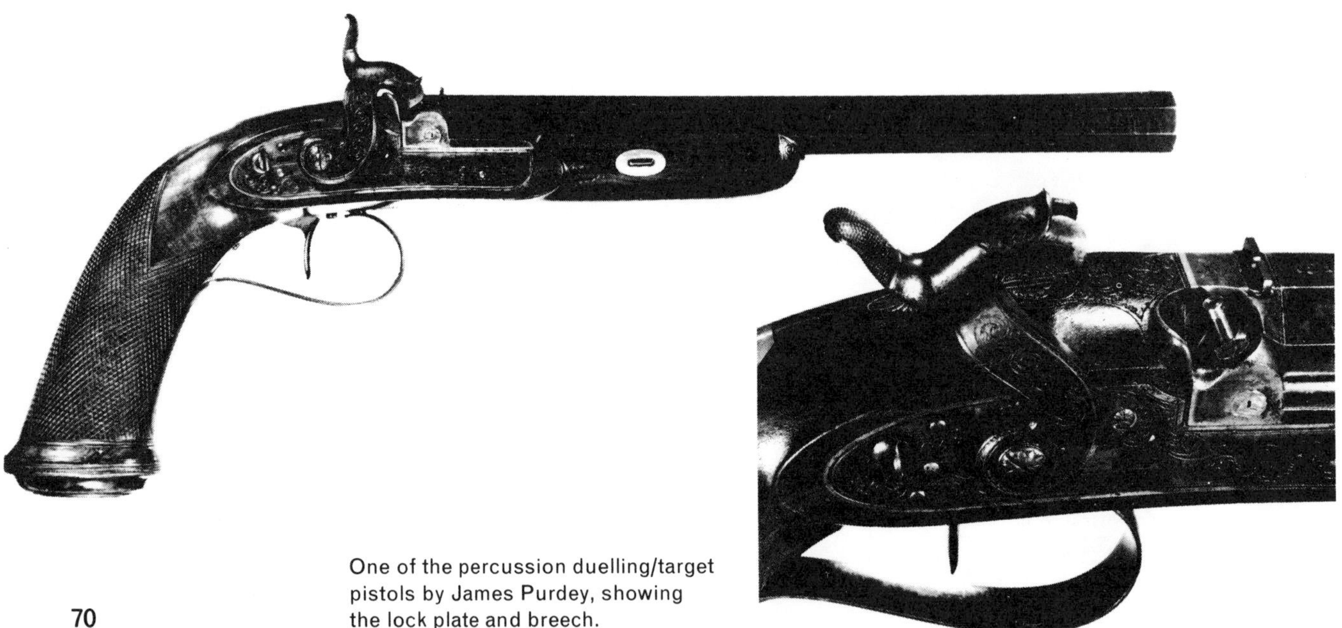

One of the percussion duelling/target pistols by James Purdey, showing the lock plate and breech.

appeal rely almost entirely on elegance of line.

During the percussion period there was considerable experimentation with the shape of the stock, the flat pommel featured on the saw-handled pistol being increasingly employed on the conventional style of stock. Graceful flowing curves gave way to increased angularity and a new style of trigger guard appeared. This permitted the pistol to be supported in the same way as the spur guard did but, in my own opinion, with increased comfort. Metal butt caps were also employed, the cap provided with a spring loaded lid inside which was a cavity that could be used to carry a small supply of caps, or perhaps a spare nipple, as the owner's fancy dictated.

These somewhat subtle changes in stock shape can be recognised from the illustrations, but a full appreciation of their practical effect on the handling qualities of the pistol can only be gained by actual use.

An immediate reaction to the Purdey pistols is 'what has happened to the ramrod?'. The practice of making pistols without a fitted ramrod appears to have gained ground about 1830. The increasing use of rifled pistols for target work and the need to employ well fitting patched bullets meant that the simple ramrod was no longer a practical means of loading. Since it would have been impossible to carry the mallet on the pistol, the sensible alternative was to keep all the impedimenta for loading in the pistol case, and the illustration shows the loading mallet fitted into the case. A simple bullet mould with a sprue cutter can also be seen, the mould being the work of W. Davis of Birmingham. As it cast a ball slightly over the bore size of 58 gauge, even this on its own would have been a tight fit; when the one inch diameter patch was used a loading mallet was essential to start the ball in the rifling. Ten inches in length, the octagon barrel is slightly necked, being 0.9″ at both muzzle and breech and 0.8″ in the centre. The rifling is hemispherical with twelve grooves.

Sights are carried on the barrel proper; the foresight is a silver bead, the rear sight a deep 'U'. Both are dovetailed, with lateral movement allowed to correct the sighting.

Assembly of the pistol differs slightly from that employed on the Manton pistols since the false breech is attached by one screw into the woodwork, a second screw passing upwards through the trigger plate into the front of the false breech. The tail of the trigger plate is attached to the stock by one screw; the guard is provided with one screw on the tang, and the front of the guard screws into the trigger plate. A single set trigger of conventional design is fitted and the workmanship is of a high standard.

The lock plate is also of conventional design. The lock employs a detent, and the safety bolts into the tumbler rather than into the rear face of the hammer. One centre side nail secures the lock plate, the precise inletting making additional screws unnecessary.

Of simple construction, entirely free from superfluous ornamentation or gadgetry, these pistols are beautifully made and of the highest quality. Although they could have been used for duelling, they were undoubtedly target pistols, built to provide a precise instrument for the man who wished to exercise his skill at a target which would not shoot back.

In France and Belgium duelling pistols continued to be made, but design stagnated and, as the years went by, the muzzle loading duelling pistol became somewhat of an anachronism, although the Parisian gunmakers Gastinne-Renette included muzzle loading and breech-loading 'pistolets de tir' until comparatively recently. The breechloading pistols were made on two systems—a 'bascule' with drop-down barrel and the 'pistolets à glissiere' where the barrel slid forward for loading.

Both the French and Belgian makers produced percussion pistols on the style of the master Boutet with half stock and over emphasised pommels, but, by 1835, the duelling/target pistol had acquired the form that predominated throughout the remainder of its existence.

The fore-end was short and the curved butt deeply fluted. Spur trigger guards were the rule rather than the exception and emphasis was placed on barrel decoration. Either deep etching was employed to bring out the figure, or else flutes were cut to modify the barrel contour.

Cases were recessed rather than compartmented and a lavish array of tools furnished. Ramrods were rarely fitted to the pistol and the case contained a loading stick and mallet which, in the case of 'armes de luxe', were as lavishly ornamented as the pistols.

In Germany the *arme blanche* was considered to be more appropriate, and the output of duelling pistols in Germany and Austro-Hungary was small. In France not only were these pistols used for target practice and duelling proper, but also for a 'duelling game', invaluable for practice should one's honour be called in question.

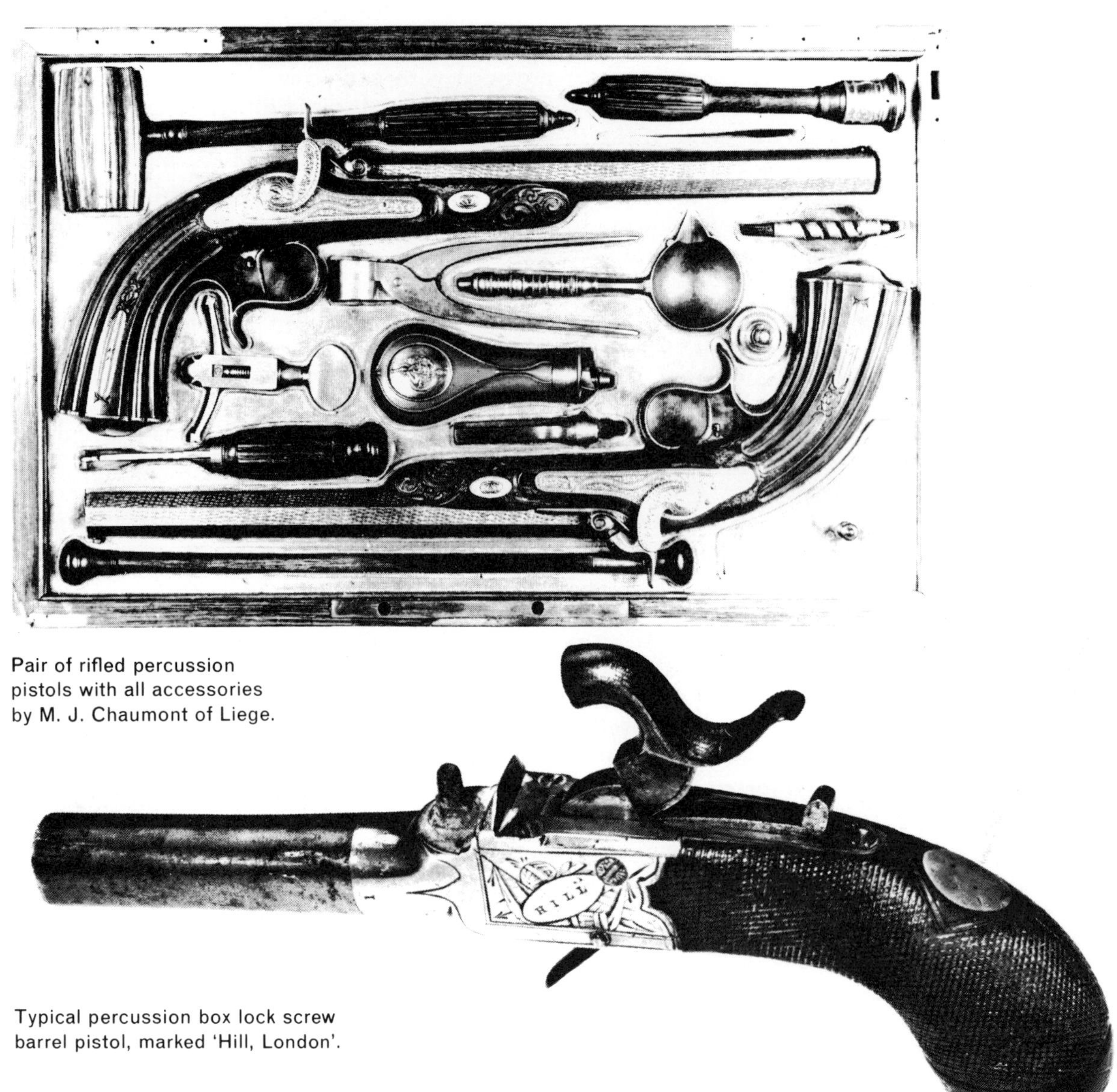

Pair of rifled percussion pistols with all accessories by M. J. Chaumont of Liege.

Typical percussion box lock screw barrel pistol, marked 'Hill, London'.

A special frangible bullet was perfected for practice duelling, where the bullet was propelled by the cap only. It was advised that practice should not take place at distances of less than twenty metres, and the participants wore face masks and gloves. Later, instead of wearing gloves, special hand shields were fitted to the pistols, and it was then important not to lower the pistol until one's opponent had fired.

Should practice take place in winter, it was important to ensure that the bullets were not allowed to freeze, as this could well destroy their frangible properties and result in injury. It was equally important to ensure that the pistols did not get too hot, for in this case the bullets would not take the rifling.[1] The careful 'duellist' almost needed a special compartment in his pistol case for a thermometer!

Continental duelling/target pistols lacked the almost macabre quality of the more sombre British pistol, a severely functional instrument. The rather florid style of the French and Belgian duellers detracted from the essentially businesslike aspect, best seen in duelling pistols made in Britain at the turn of the century.

A class of pistol made in immense numbers throughout the percussion period and which, in fact, survived in an abased form until about 1930, was the box lock screw barrelled pocket pistol. Differing little mechanically from their flintlock predecessors, they were usually fitted with a folding trigger and were made in all qualities from the 'best' to the appalling. Differing equally in size from a tiny toy to a formidable

[1] Winant: *Automatic Pistol Shooting* p. 96 (London 1916).

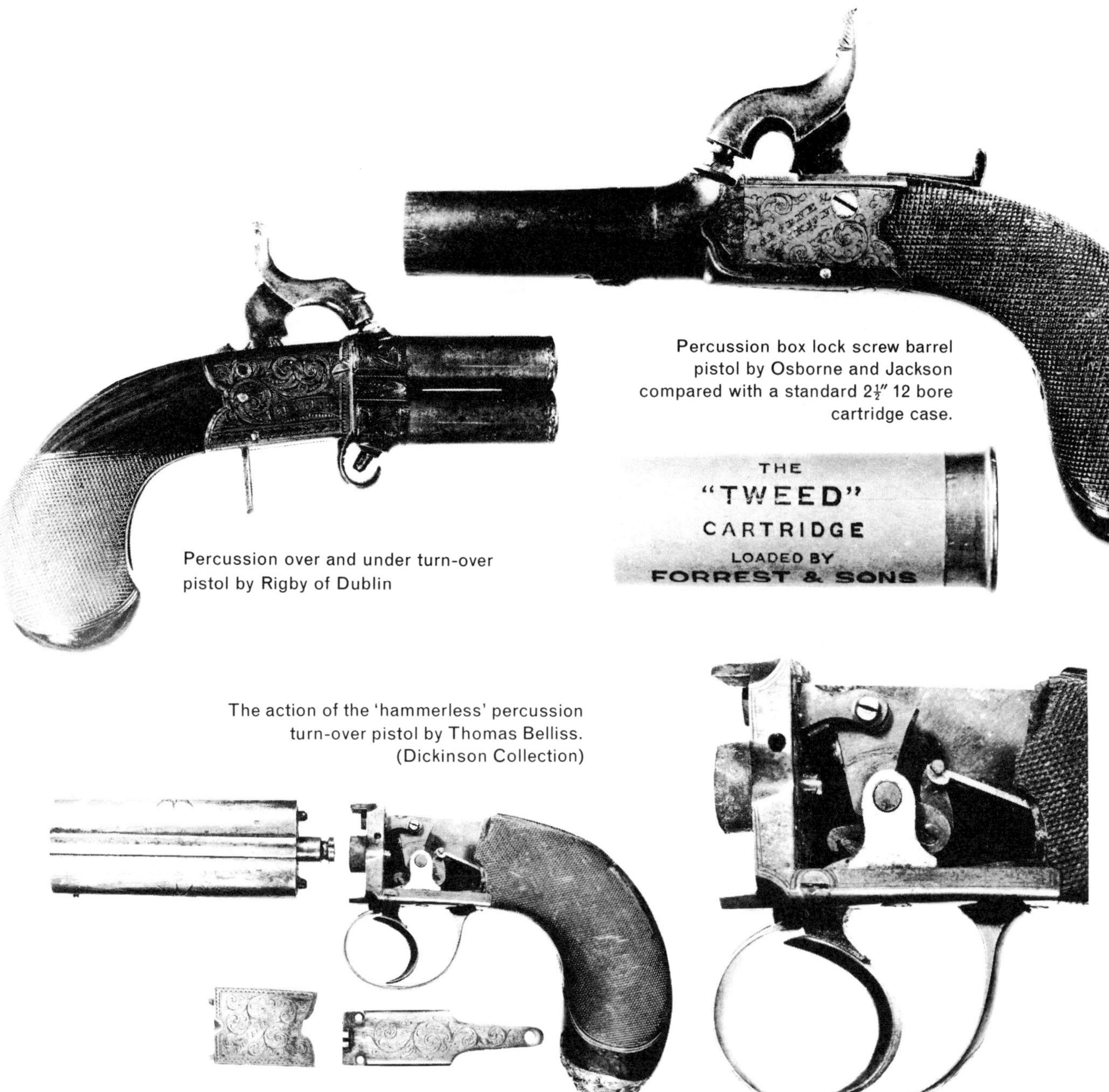

Percussion box lock screw barrel pistol by Osborne and Jackson compared with a standard 2½″ 12 bore cartridge case.

Percussion over and under turn-over pistol by Rigby of Dublin

The action of the 'hammerless' percussion turn-over pistol by Thomas Belliss. (Dickinson Collection)

single shot self-defence weapon, the box lock is of importance since, free from the restrictions imposed by the steel and pan cover, the full potentiality of the box lock could be exploited, and this action formed the basis for a range of multi-shot weapons characterised by their simplicity and effectiveness.

The simple box lock proved to be amazingly adaptable. For example, two barrels could be attached to the front of the box and, by simple rearrangement, two locks with external side-hammers could be provided to produce a small but effective double barrelled pistol. A variation which simplified the lock work was the double barrelled turn-over screw pistol. A side or centrally mounted hammer could be employed and, after the first shot had been fired, it was only the work of a moment to re-cock the hammer, rotate the barrels through 180 degrees and fire a second shot.

An interesting variation on the common theme is the pistol by Thomas Belliss which illustrates an early 'hammerless' or self-cocking action. With the barrels loaded and the nipples capped it is only necessary to pull the trigger for the first shot, rotate the barrels (which are locked into battery by a spring inside the 'box') and pull the trigger again. In this action the tumbler is fitted with a striker which protrudes through the lock plate. At the bottom of the tumbler is a link swivel on to which is hooked the mainspring. In front is a hooked spring loaded link so arranged that it engages the trigger sear. When the trigger is pulled back the link rotates the tumbler, drawing back the striker. A camming surface on the sear disengages the nose of the sear from the hook,

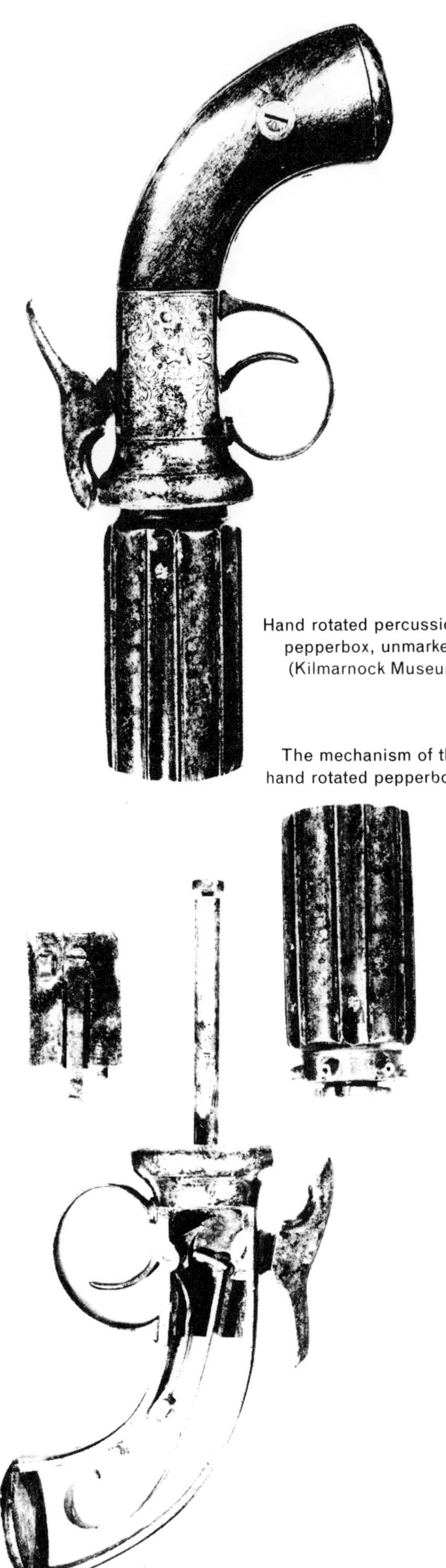

Hand rotated percussion pepperbox, unmarked. (Kilmarnock Museum)

The mechanism of the hand rotated pepperbox.

and this, when released, permits the tumbler to rotate under the influence of the mainspring, so impelling the striker forward to fire the capped nipple of the uppermost barrel. This well made pistol would have been an extremely effective close quarter self-defence weapon.

Since the box lock was ideally suited to accommodate the turn-over barrel system, it was an easy matter to increase the number of barrels. Simple revolving barrel pistols were made with four, five and six barrels, the one illustrated having six barrels of .360 bore. The nipples are at right angles to the line of the bore and the barrel cluster is machined out of the solid. The frame is a single forging; the lock work, as can be seen, is very simple and somewhat crudely made. The hammer has the usual half and full cock bents, and the mainspring is linked by means of a rectangular link which was the subject of a patent taken out by Westley Richards in 1852, although the pistol itself is probably rather earlier. The barrel group is mounted on a pin which screws into the standing breech, and is secured by one pan headed screw. Cylinder rotation is anticlockwise, and the crudely cut 'star' at the rear of the barrel group is indexed and held in battery by the spring fitted to the removeable side plate. Although very crudely made, there is a minimum to go wrong and hand-rotation of the barrel group is positive.

This type first appeared about 1820 and, since it employed a rotating or revolving barrel, it was, by definition, a revolver. But, in modern usage, the term revolver is applied only to an arm with a single barrel and a rotating cylinder, and multi-barrelled firearms of the same general type are known as pepperboxes. When the term pepperbox first came into use is uncertain. From an examination of the dismantled weapon, it can be seen how this mechanism could be altered to include automatic rotation of the barrel group and if, in addition, we add the self-cocking mechanism, it will be appreciated that the transition from hand-rotated pepperbox to a self-cocking self-rotating pistol was by no means difficult to achieve within the framework of the simple box lock.

It will be shown later how the pepperbox evolved and how the true revolver made its appearance as a practical weapon.

The sidelock continued to be employed on both single and multi-barrelled pistols until this type of weapon was finally vanquished by the mass-produced revolver. The lock, either bar or back action, was inletted into the stock, the latter, in the case of multi-barrelled weapons which did not employ a fore-end, being attached to the breech by a bottom and top strap. With half or full stocked conventional single barrel pistols the layout was on the lines already described for duelling pistols.

With two barrels and two locks, one at each side of the butt, it becomes evident that the amount of woodwork that had to be removed to accommodate all the mechanism was excessive and serious weakening of the stock could result. For this reason, there appeared a mutation or half-breed. In pistols where two or more barrels were to be used and box lock construction avoided, a semi-box lock appeared using side plates but with the top and bottom straps considerably extended both as to length and width. This system was of particular use on double barrelled pistols with a left and right hand lock and external hammers. Using this system four barrelled turn-over pistols were practicable, which I suppose could be termed box locks with external side hammers.

During the percussion period both the turn-over system with or without screw barrels and the 'over and under' pistol enjoyed considerable popularity and were made in both the pocket and the larger belt sizes.

A simple but very ingenious solution to the problem of providing repetitive fire was that used by William and John Rigby of Dublin. Rigby made three and four barrelled pistols with all metal stocks, each barrel being provided with its own percussion nipple. The barrels were detachable for loading and numbered consecutively to ensure that the correct barrel was re-fitted to the

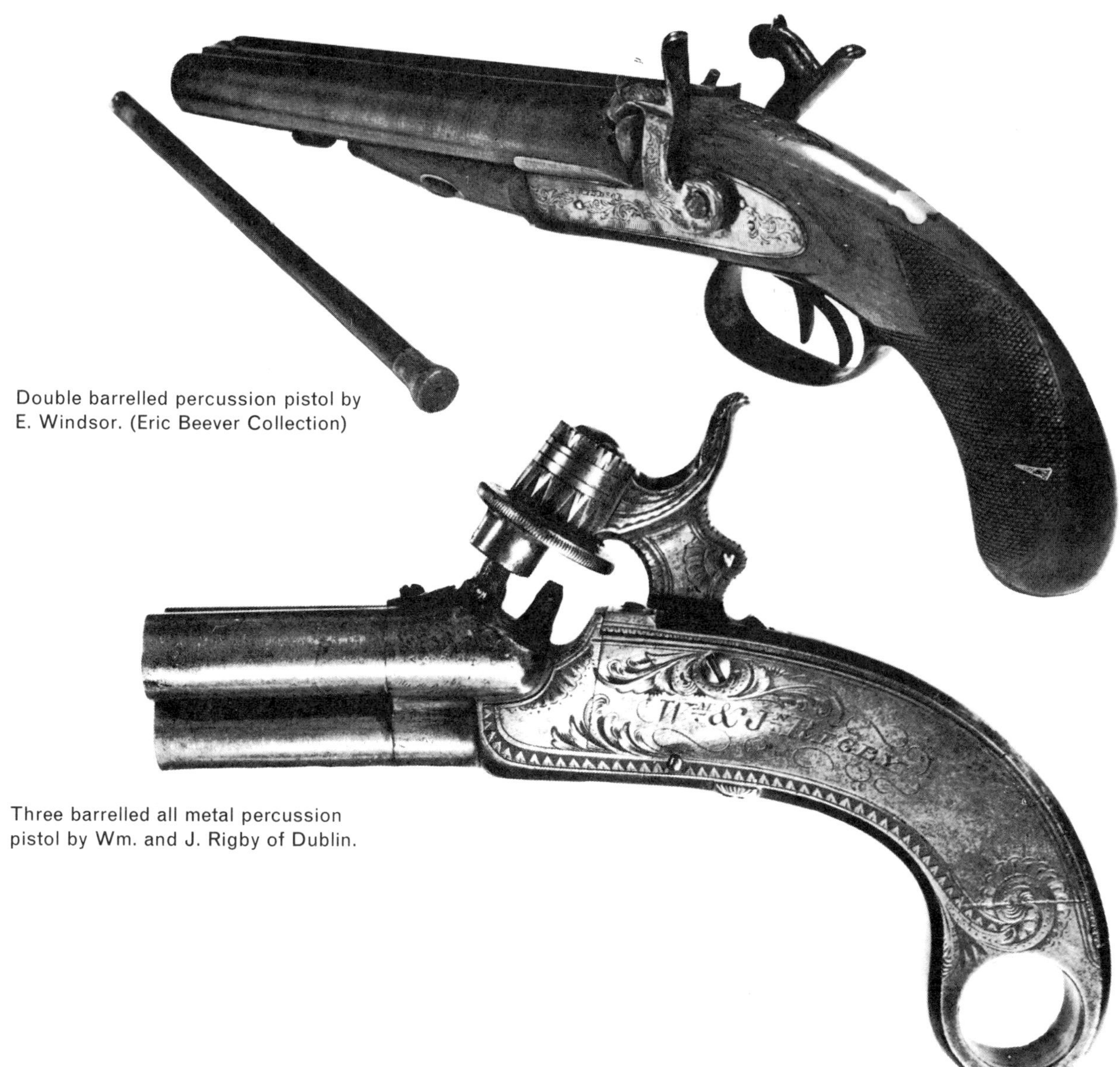

Double barrelled percussion pistol by E. Windsor. (Eric Beever Collection)

Three barrelled all metal percussion pistol by Wm. and J. Rigby of Dublin.

appropriate breech. The reason for this was that, as these pistols were made long before the days of unified screw threads, not all the threads would mate. The most unusual feature of the pistol is that the striker was offset and attached to a circular plate which could be manually rotated so that the striker would hit each of the capped nipples and fire the loaded barrels in turn. Being made by Rigby, the lock had Rigby's 'Extra-notch' which permitted the hammer to be withdrawn to a safe position clear of the nipple, but sufficiently close to prevent the loss of a loosely fitting cap. The idea of a rotating striker will be encountered again; on Sharp's four barrel cartridge derringer, for example, it was rotated automatically. The Rigby, as befits the product of a very notable gunmaker, is extremely well made and, being all metal and provided with a suitable hole in the stock, could be also be used as a knuckleduster should the multiplicity of shots fail or the number of assailants be greater than the number of shots available.

A rather more complicated solution was that devised by H. Colleye. His pistol employed a ring trigger and a four shot vertical block magazine. This type became common on some variant cartridge forms, but the use of a vertical magazine with four superimposed chambers, each with a countersunk nipple, was unusual. The Colleye pistols were made in Belgium and were of good quality, those I have seen having good engraving and an attractive finish.

Until the perfection of the percussion revolver and its acceptance as a military weapon, single or double barrelled belt pistols varying from 16 to 24 bore were popular, and were carried by officers for military use. The increasing disfavour with which duelling was viewed reduced the need for a military side arm which could be employed for duelling, and the shorter belt pistol which, if of the over and under pattern, had the decided advantage of a second shot, was more easily carried and equally effective at close range.

The classification of percussion pistols is to some extent arbitrary, at least as regards the non-military types. The terms 'duelling', 'target', 'holster', 'carriage' and 'pocket' are to some extent self-explanatory, and it will have already been realised that, with only a few exceptions, it is not always possible, since many pistols were made to serve more than one specific purpose, to draw a sharp and distinctive line between each type. One class of self-defence percussion pocket pistol, the Deringer, merits attention if only

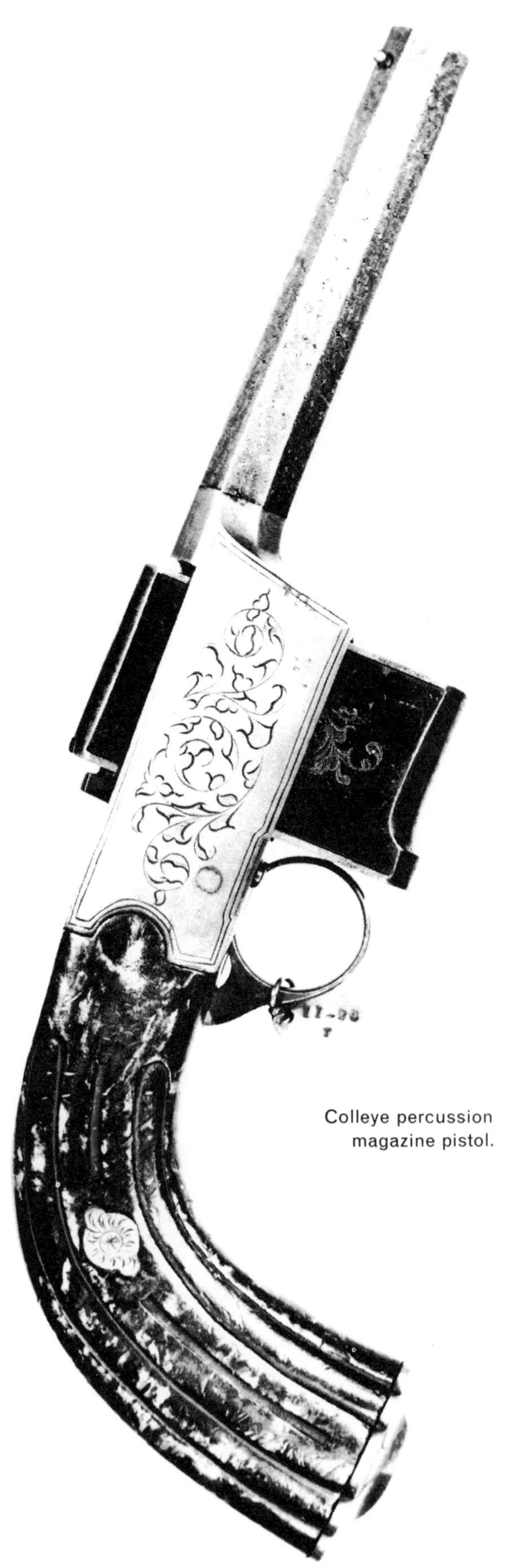

Colleye percussion magazine pistol.

Colleye percussion magazine pistol with magazine detached.

because the name of the maker has passed into the English language—'derringer'—a short pistol.

Henry Deringer was the eldest son of an American gunsmith of German extraction born in Easton, Pennsylvania, in 1786. After serving his apprenticeship, Deringer moved to Philadelphia where he started to make firearms in 1806, beginning with flintlock rifles and pistols, and later moving on to percussion weapons. He also became a contractor to the US Army.

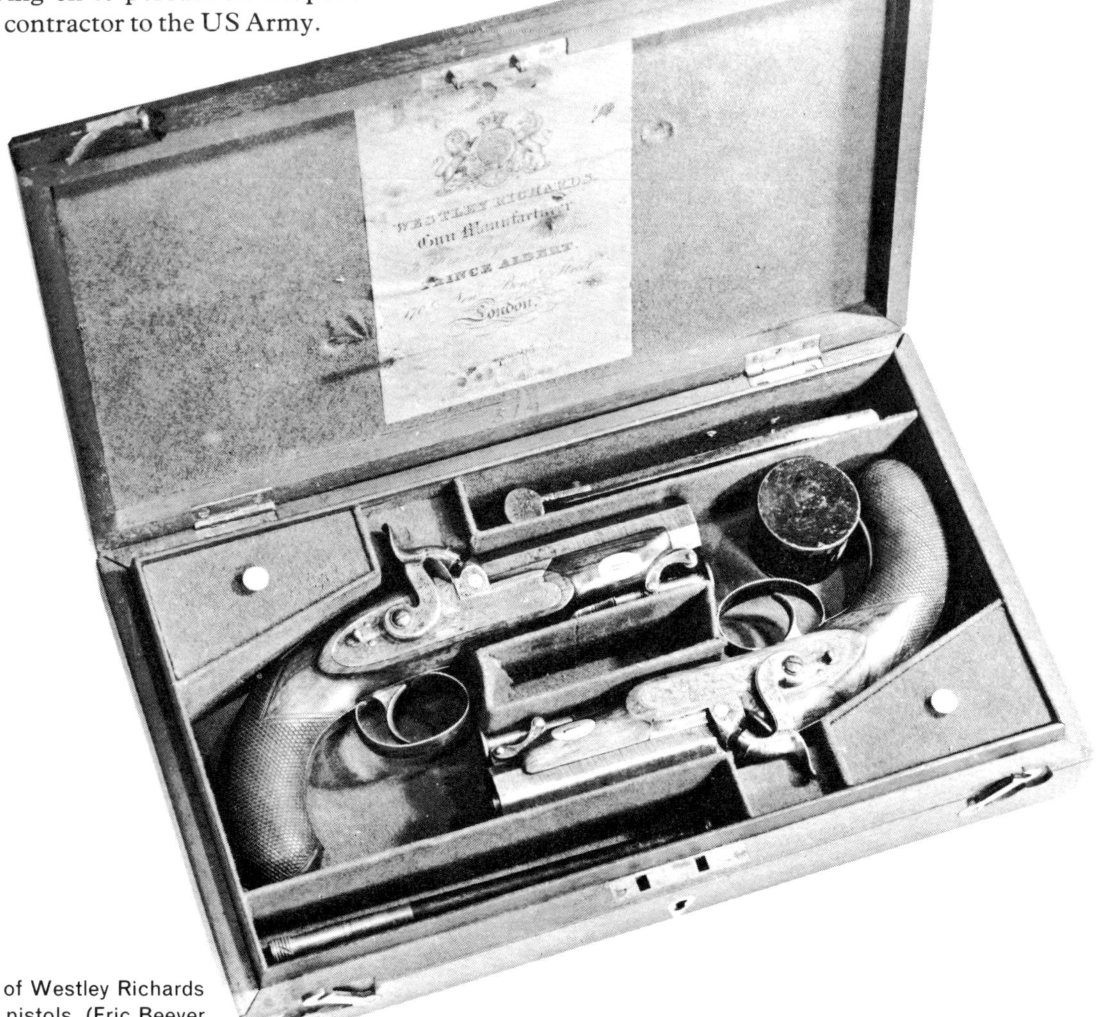

Cased pair of Westley Richards percussion pistols. (Eric Beever Collection)

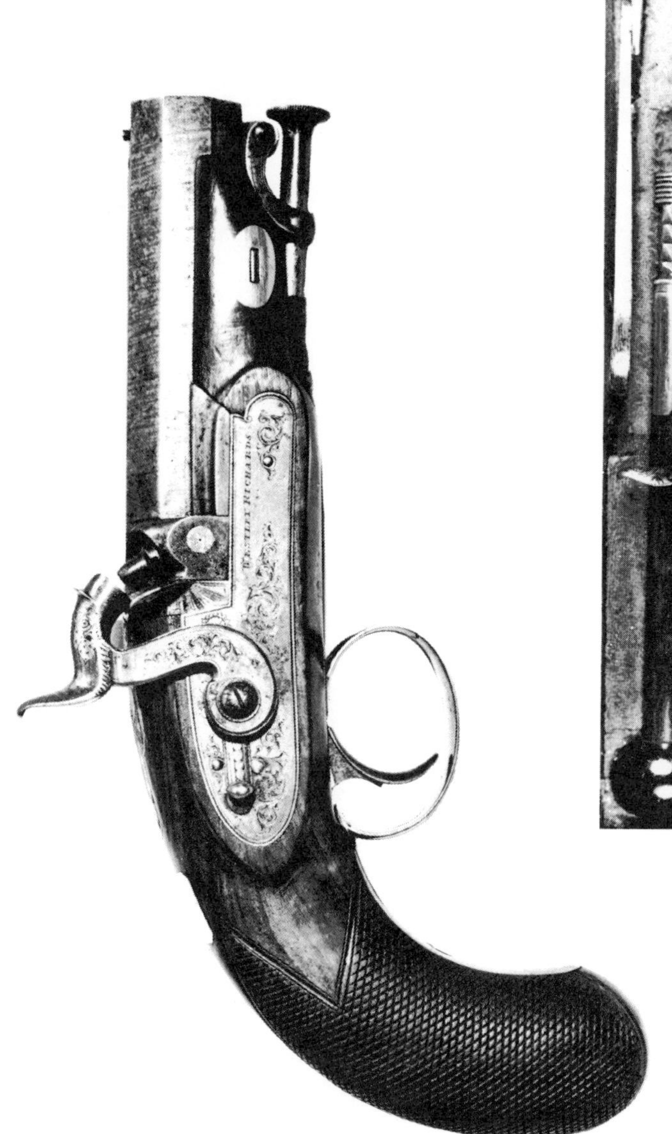

One of the cased pair of Westley Richards percussion pistols. shown on page 77. (Eric Beever Collection)

Cased pair of percussion pocket pistols by Clough of Bath. (Kilmarnock Museum)

The pocket Deringer pistol was well made and of conventional construction. The barrel was attached by the usual screw passing through the barrel tang into the trigger plate, and by a flat bolt through the fore-end and barrel loop. A back action sidelock was fitted and on most pistols the mounts were of german silver. Barrel lengths varied from just under an inch up to four inches and calibre from .33 to .51. Stocks were usually of American walnut, but pistols with metal stocks and even ivory stocks are also known. The barrels were apparently manufactured from rifle barrels cut down and the marking 'Deringer Philada' always appeared on the lock plate and breech.

The fame, or rather the notoriety, of the Deringer was due to the number of homicides in which these pistols featured, culminating in the assassination of President Lincoln by John Wilkes Booth. As the murder weapon was identified by name, the ensuing international publicity resulted in the generic use of the word derringer to describe any small pistol which could be carried without inconvenience and which was suitable for emergency use at close quarters. Henry Deringer never produced any pocket

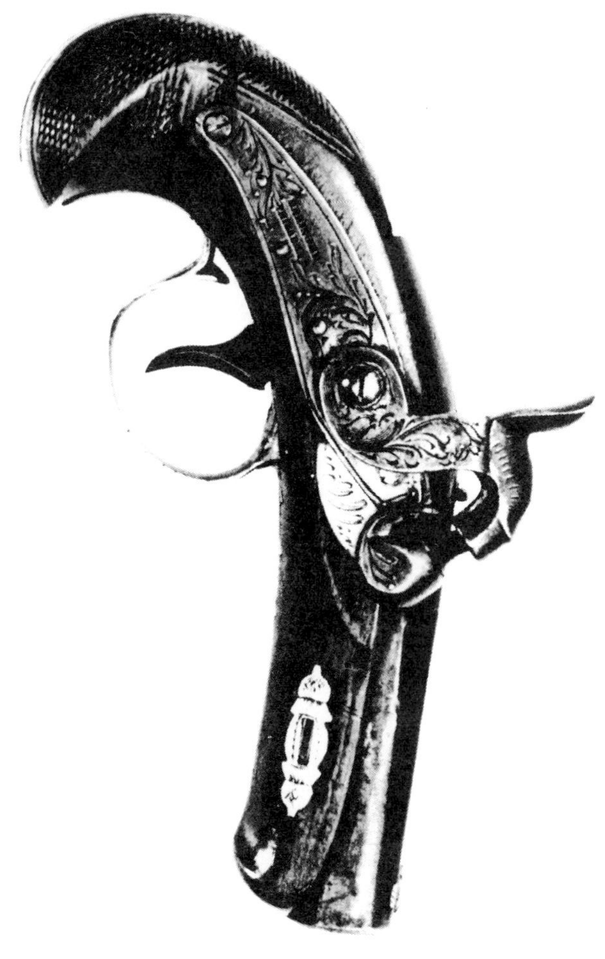

Deringer percussion pistol.
(Wallis and Wallis)

pistols other than with percussion cap ignition, but the name derringer was applied not only to the many imitations of his basic, but unpatented design, but also to the numerous cartridge pocket pistols which followed. An attempt was made to differentiate between pistols made by Deringer himself and those made by others by spelling Deringer with one 'r' and the generic term with two, derringer. This distinction is recent and by no means universally accepted.

Percussion pistols of military issue were simple in design and not markedly dissimilar to their flintlock forbears. Distinct national characteristics were evident and, on economic grounds, the earliest percussion pistols issued were, of course, conversions. The simplest method was employed and, to reduce cost, the original lock was adapted by removing the flash pan and cover and fitting a percussion hammer in place of the cock.

Any study of British Military pistols is made somewhat difficult due to the official attitude towards them. By 1838, following a number of trials with different systems, the authorities had made up their minds to adopt the percussion cap —the delay no doubt due to the erratic performance of the early caps. If too soft, the hammer would force part of the cap metal into the orifice of the nipple and so effectively 'spike' the weapon; if too hard and brittle, injury to the man firing the gun or to his companion could result—the type of accident referred to by Colonel Hawker.

It is to Frederick Joyce, a London chemist, that much of the credit for improving the performance of the percussion cap must go, not only as regards blocked nipples and fragmenting caps, but also as regards the equally important reduction of the corrosive effect on the firearm of the residues from the cap. The firm of F. Joyce and Co. was founded about 1828 and, together with the firm of Eley Bros., founded by William Eley a few years previously, they were the sole suppliers of percussion caps to the Government.

For civilian use, caps made by the French firm of Gevelot, in which the skirt of the cap was grooved according to the design of the Belgian gunmaker Mangeot, were for a time highly regarded and became widely adopted. For Government use, however, the 'top hat' type of cap was employed.

Cap composition underwent considerable modification. Mercury fulminate alone, when used in sufficient volume to ignite the powder with certainty, produced excessive pressure which deformed the cap, and modifiers such as potassium chlorate and antimony sulphide were therefore incorporated. Caps containing potassium chlorate and antimony sulphide only were used for a time, but the addition of fulminate and ground glass to increase sensitivity soon became the usual practice.

Caps manufactured by Eley had an internal metal foil cover over the priming composition, whereas caps manufactured by Joyce were waterproofed by the use of an inflammable varnish 'which in no way detracted from their certainty and sharpness of fire'.

The man responsible for the design of the first percussion military pistols used by the British was George Lovell, who began his career in Government Service as a clerk in the Royal Carriage Department at Woolwich in 1805. In 1816 he was appointed Store-keeper of the

Enfield factory and, in 1840, became Inspector of Small Arms and in charge of production.

In 1837 yet another attempt was made to standardise military weapons. Lovell suggested that the musket size ball of 14½ to the pound should become the standard ball, and in this he had the backing of no less a person than the Duke of Wellington. The Duke proposed three weapons, a smooth bore musket, a rifle and a carbine; the pistol, 'an ineffectual weapon', was to be discarded.

Fortunately for the narrative, the pistol does not disappear from history. As far as can be gathered, it was abolished as a cavalry arm in 1838, although the Lancers were allowed to retain one each—the alternative, the much favoured carbine, would have interfered with the management of the lance. In other cavalry regiments only Squadron Majors and Trumpeters were allowed pistols.

The low regard in which the pistol was held was largely due to the emphasis placed on the use of the sword. The cavalry tactics employed by Marlborough had achieved such success that the use of the *arme blanche* had become hallowed by tradition, and it is really not surprising that the cavalry pistol as such had lost favour and that its necessary improvement had been neglected. In practice its main use had been to shoot wounded horses and recalcitrant soldiers—and to light fires.

Even the carbine was little used for, according to Sir H. Havelock (*A History of Cavalry*), the men were too tightly uniformed for dismounted work and 'They even found difficulty in remounting so tight were their overalls'.

Seen in the light of contemporary thought, it is no wonder that Lovell's first percussion pistol was somewhat uninspired. Of decidedly massive appearance and, like all of Lovell's arms, well made, it would have served as a most useful club. Of musket bore (.753″), the Pattern 1842 Smooth Bore pistol fired a ball weighing 14½ to the pound and tipped the scales at slightly over 3 lbs. In appearance it closely resembled the Enfield series of percussion long arms. The 9″ barrel was fitted with a captive swivel rammer at the muzzle, and the pistol was full stocked and brass mounted.

A similar pistol of this period was the East India Company pistol which differed slightly in the shape of the stock, and had a smaller trigger guard and heavier brass mounts. It was again smooth bored, and the calibre was slightly less at .653 nominal carbine, or 16 bore.

A similar series of smaller pistols with 6″ barrels were issued to the Navy as Sea Service pistols. The calibre was .56″ and, as many of these pistols were made from converted flintlock stores, there was a considerable lack of uniformity. Sea Service pistols issued to both the Navy and the Coast Guard were of course fitted with belt hooks and many of these short and comparatively handy weapons saw service in the Colonies.

The last of Lovell's smooth bore pistols was the Police pocket model of 1848, made for the Irish Constabulary. The overall length of this pistol was 9″ and it was of semi-box lock construction with a centrally disposed hammer and a captive ramrod, the upper pipe for which was mounted on a rib under the barrel, and the tail pipe was immediately in front of the trigger guard.

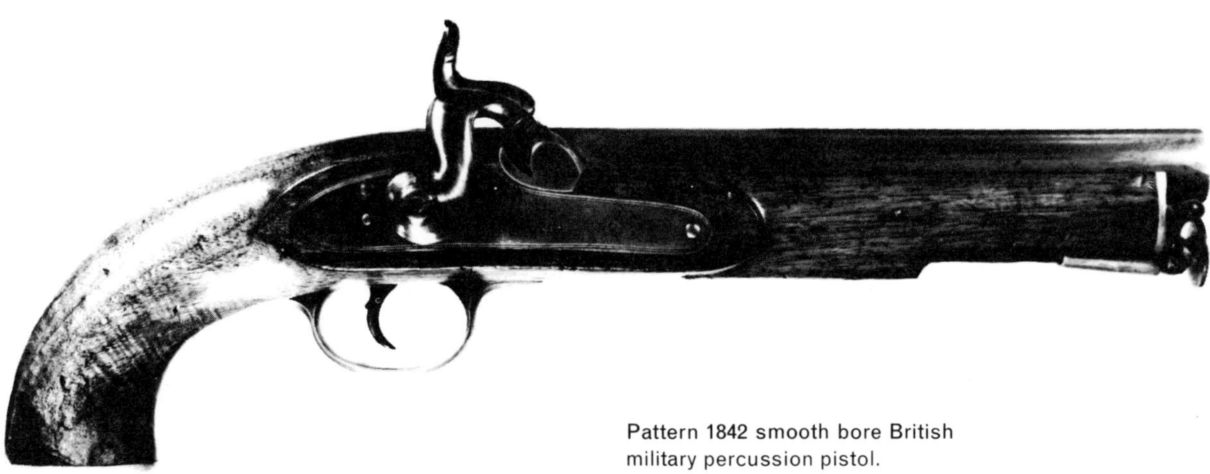

Pattern 1842 smooth bore British military percussion pistol.

Enjoying, as J. N. George succinctly puts it in *English Pistols and Revolvers,* 'the somewhat unusual distinction of having been obsolete at the actual time when it was first issued', the 10″ rifled Cavalry Pistol of 1856 was of the same calibre as the .577 Enfield Rifle Musket Pattern of 1853 and, as one might imagine, it bears the imprint of George Lovell's hand in its general design.

This pistol, as it originally appeared, had a 'pillar' or 'tige' breech, the invention of Colonel Thouvenin and a modification of the earlier Delvigne chamber breech of 1826. Both these systems were designed to ease the problem of loading a rifled barrel from the muzzle. The problem was a difficult one: if the bullet was made small enough in diameter to pass down a fouled barrel it was too small to grip the rifling on its way out, and the benefit of having a rifled barrel was lost. The French solution was, in the case of the chamber breech, to leave an annular ring at the breech upon which a loosely fitting ball could be expanded by blows from a heavy rammer. The 'tige' system employed a stout central pillar around which lay the powder charge and upon which the ball was expanded. Neither of these systems was entirely satisfactory as the desirable properties of the bullet—concentricity and absence of deformity—tended to be lost by the pounding it received, and, in the case of the rifle, the labour involved induced a measure of fatigue and unsteadiness which affected the rifleman's aim.

Traditional English 'pincer' type single cavity bullet mould with sprue cutter.

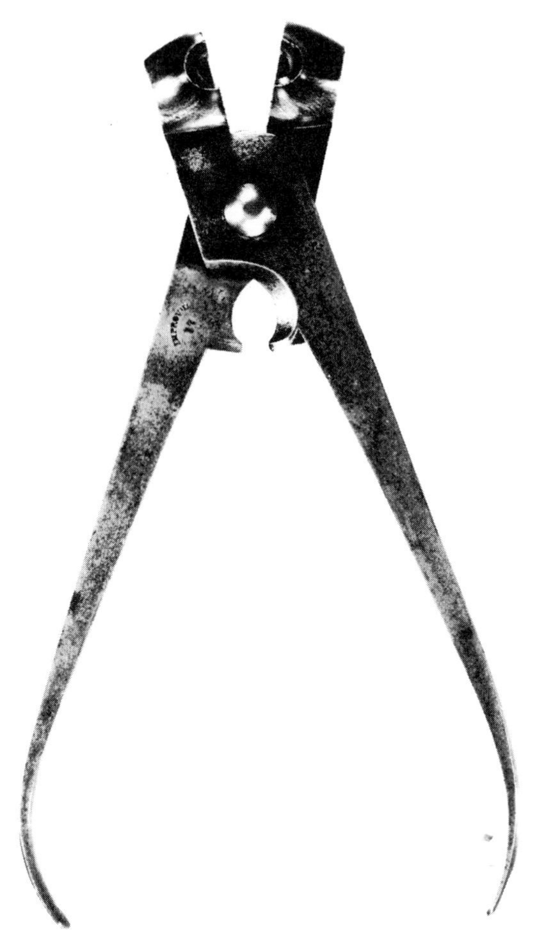

The second pattern of Cavalry Pistol dispensed with the tige, this being made possible by improvements in the ammunition.

The accuracy potential of the duelling or target pistol was to a great extent dependent upon the care taken both in preparing the round ball and in loading. With the advent of the rifled pistol we have already seen the necessity of using a mallet in order to introduce the patched ball into the rifling, and with pistols of precision it was no hardship to clean out the barrel and remove black powder fouling between each shot if necessary.

With the military pistol such painstaking care was neither possible nor desirable. To obtain increased accuracy, the design of the pistol or the projectile would have to be modified to allow for rapid loading. Fortunately for the pistol user, these problems were even more pressing in the case of the rifle. Mechanical solutions to the problem had been tried; the two groove rifling of Captain Berners and the four grooved rifling of General John Jacob had special bullets provided, with one or two bands to correspond with the rifling. The famous Whitworth had hexagonal rifling and a hexagonal mechanically fitting bullet. With the Whitworth, supreme accuracy was attainable, as the writer can testify from personal experience, but the problem of fouling was a major one.

The next solution was to deform the bullet after loading, as with the chamber and pillar rifles, but this system was discarded for the reasons mentioned above. Emphasis was then placed on bullet design and, in 1841, Captain Minie, an instructor at the School of Vincennes, modified a hollow bullet patented by Delvigne in 1841 by scooping out the base and inserting an iron cup. The idea was that the pressure of the powder gases drove the cup into the base of the bullet and caused the sides to expand into the rifling. This type of bullet and the Minie rifle were adopted by the French to replace the 'tige' rifle and, in 1851, the Minie Rifled Musket was approved by the British and the first was issued in 1852.

The 'Minnie', as it became known in Britain, was not a success. The famous Birmingham gunmaker Greener, who claimed prior right to the invention of the expanding principle, was understandably indignant at being pipped at the post. Subsequently his claims, effectively prosecuted by the Member of Parliament for Birmingham, Mr Scholefield, were acknowledged by an award of £1,000 in 1857 for 'the first public suggestion of the principle of expansion, commonly called the Minie principle'.

One of the troubles with the Minie was that the iron cup was sometimes driven right through the bullet, and Greener somewhat spitefully remarked on one occasion that he had seen 'as many as sixteen rings extracted from one barrel which had been returned as "foul" '.

Tremendous interest was aroused in the progress of the development of small arms and ammunition during the second half of the nineteenth century. Much of this was no doubt due to the atmosphere of the times, but a contributory factor was the establishment of the Volunteers and also the National Rifle Association, which, following the inaugural meeting at Wimbledon in 1860, did much to foster and encourage interest in rifle shooting. Pistol shooting, however, was sadly neglected until the efforts of Major Charles Ford resulted in the first Revolver Competition being held in 1885.

Until the adoption of the Snider breech loader following the trials of 1864, much speculation, trial and experiment had attended the important matter of deciding which was the most suitable bullet design. It was agreed that the elongated bullet was preferable to the spherical and much effort was expended in finding the optimum proportions of the conical and cylindrical parts of the cylindro-conoidal bullet.

A fearsome array of bullet designs appeared and in Britain a new bullet of modified Minie shape, designed by the gunmaker Pritchett, was finally adopted. Pritchett received an award of £1,000 in 1854 for the use of his bullet, which, although hollow based, lacked the Minie cup. Later a new bullet with a box wood plug was introduced with a diameter of .55″ and a length of 1.09″.

This lengthy digression serves as an introduction to the ammunition used with the Cavalry Rifle Pistol, similar to that finally used with the Enfield Rifle Musket Pattern of 1853. The bullet diameter was .568″; the weight, as one might expect, was less, 390 grains as against 530 grains, and the powder charge was reduced from 2½ drams of RFG (Rifle Fine Grained) to a more manageable one dram. The second pattern of pistol discarded the pillar breech and employed five groove rifling. In 1858 the 8″ rifled pistol India Cavalry Pattern No. 1 was approved and in 1861, a similar pistol was approved for the British Service. Some of these pistols were fitted with detachable shoulder stocks where the stock was provided with a metal 'tongue' which could be passed through a slot in the butt of the pistol and secured in position. Known as the Yeomanry Rifled Pistol Carbine, this weapon, as its name implies, could be used as either a pistol or a carbine, a compromise of dubious value, but one which has been proposed, accepted and rejected for almost as long as there have been pistols to which shoulder stocks could be fitted.

The pattern of development in America was not dissimilar to that in Britain, although the official flintlock pistols issued to the United States forces showed less diversity of pattern, due perhaps to the influence of the machine tool. Both French and British patterns influenced design and a bore size of 0.54″ had been standardised by 1816. The US Pattern 1836 flintlock smooth bore pistol was the last of the flint and steel pistols and many were converted to percussion by the traditional drum and nipple method, with new percussion hammers.

The first percussion pistol made under contract for the United States was the Model 1842 Navy of .54 calibre. Made by Nathan Peabody Ames, it owed much to George Lovell, particularly with regard to the lock which employed an enclosed hammer. Lovell had produced a back action lock in 1831, which he admitted had been inspired by earlier work done by Nock, but it had met with little encouragement in Britain and had been criticised on the grounds that its construction was likely to induce internal rusting and swelling of the stock in wet weather.

This attitude might be thought due to innate British conservatism, and the Americans must have considered the theoretical advantages of greater strength and reduced liability to damage of more importance. Locks of this pattern were also more amenable to machine production.

In appearance this 6″ barrelled pistol differed

from its British contemporaries since, although it was brass mounted and fitted with an iron swivel captive ramrod, it had a broad barrel band which gave it a French or German look. In this respect it followed established American practice which favoured the barrel band as opposed to the cross bolt method of securing the barrel adopted by the British.

The US Army Model 1842 was again of .54 calibre but had a longer barrel and was fitted with a conventional lock with an external hammer. It was brass mounted, a linked swivel ramrod was fitted, and a similar barrel band was again employed to secure the barrel to the stock. The illustration shows a contract arm manufactured by H. Aston and Co., Middletown, Conn., and is so marked.

Henry Aston was born in London on 2 December 1803 and arrived in America in either 1819 or 1820. He worked for Simeon North, the first official manufacturer of pistols for the United States Government, and was later employed by Nathan Starr and Sons, also of Middletown, Conn. In 1845 he started business on his own account in Middletown, where he continued to live until his death in 1864. As was common practice, the date of manufacture was marked on the lock of US martial pistols, and those made by Aston on his first contract for 30,000 were dated from 1846 until 1850.

In addition to the smooth bore pistols made by Ames, both smooth bore and rifled pistols of the same pattern were made by Henry Deringer of Philadelphia. Total production of these pistols was probably not in excess of 4,000. Those made for the Navy are marked USN. Pistols marked

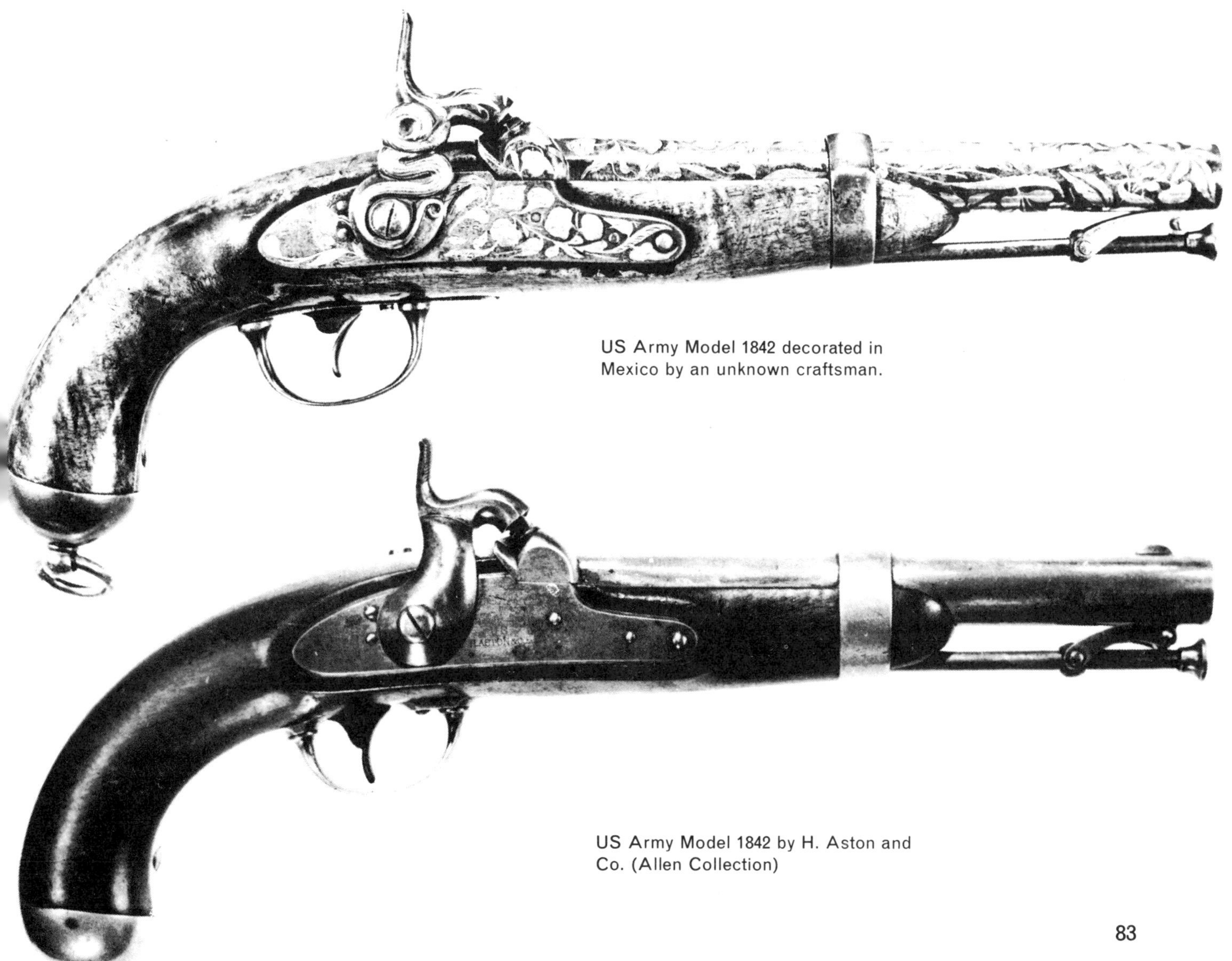

US Army Model 1842 decorated in Mexico by an unknown craftsman.

US Army Model 1842 by H. Aston and Co. (Allen Collection)

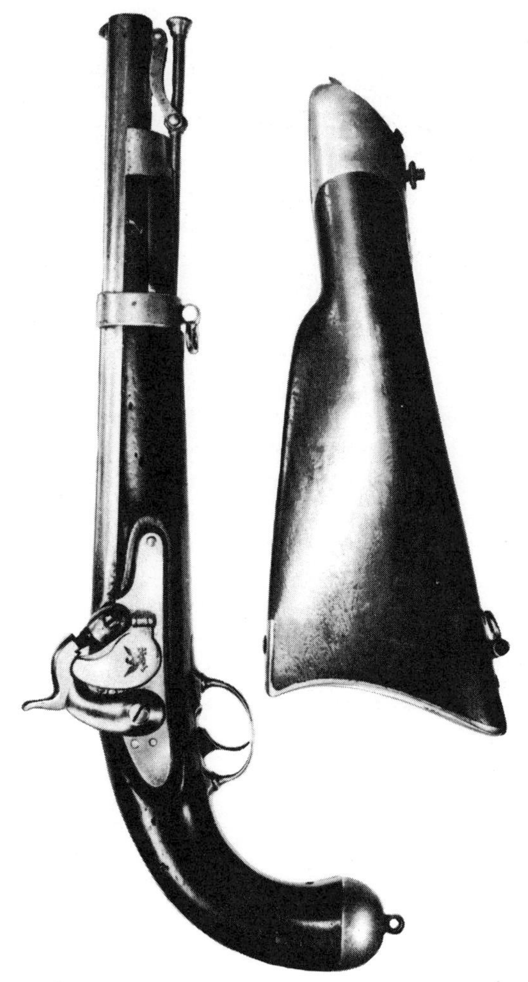

Springfield 1855 pistol carbine with Maynard tape primer. (Allen Collection)

UNR may have been made for the US Mounted Rifles or the US Revenue Service. For Naval Service a small number of the barrels were tinned to prevent corrosion.

The last of the main sequence military single shot muzzle loading pistols made for the US Government was the Model 1855 pistol carbine. The model shown was manufactured by the Springfield Armoury and is fitted with the Maynard tape primer. Of .58 calibre it is a particularly handsome arm especially when the detachable shoulder stock is fitted. A very rare variant was the Model 1855 as made by the Harper's Ferry Armoury and marked 'Harper's Ferry' on the lock plate. It differs from the Springfield product in that Maynard's primer is not fitted and the barrel band is ¼″ further back from the muzzle.

As with the Enfield rifled pistol, the Springfield pistol carbine was not a success. When the cavalry stooped to using pistols they preferred a revolver, while the heavy cavalry or Dragoons wanted a carbine. It has been said that a shoulder stock converts a good pistol into a bad rifle and this was undoubtedly the case with these obsolete single shot muzzle loaders. The point of aim changed when the stock was fitted and they were slow and difficult to load on horseback, especially when fouled. However, the idea had been in use since the seventeenth century and we shall continue to encounter pistols with detachable shoulder stocks as we progress through the years up to the present day.

French military single shot muzzle loading percussion pistols present a slightly more complicated picture. This is due first of all to the wider employment of percussion conversions, and secondly to the greater variety of military flintlocks that were available for such conversion.

The spirit of adventure which had resulted in the manufacture of the famous French cavalry pistol Model of 1777, known as 'à la Mandrin' from the name of a famous French smuggler, seems to have been lacking during that even greater adventure, the French Revolution. The new designs produced during the period of the Consulate and the First Empire and manufactured by the French Government Arsenals reverted to the conventional sidelock. The first of these, the Modèle an 9 (Model of Year 9 of the Revolution, the Calendrier républicain having come into effect on 22 September 1793) was made in tremendous numbers and was widely used by the French during the Napoleonic Wars. The pistol was characterised by a rather cumbersome barrel band which was absent in the second of the Revolutionary pistols, the Modèle an 13, where it was replaced by a simpler barrel band.

This barrel band became a fore-end cap in the next model, the Modèle 1816. For each model one finds the usual Naval and Police variants differing in barrel length and calibre; in the case of the Navy, a belt hook was fitted if not previously provided. An abbreviated list of the conversions which took place is given below:

Pistol Model an 9 and an 13 converted to percussion 1841, rifling added 1854.

Pistol Model 1816 and 1822 converted to percussion 1841, rifling added 1854.

Police Model 1822 converted to percussion 1841.

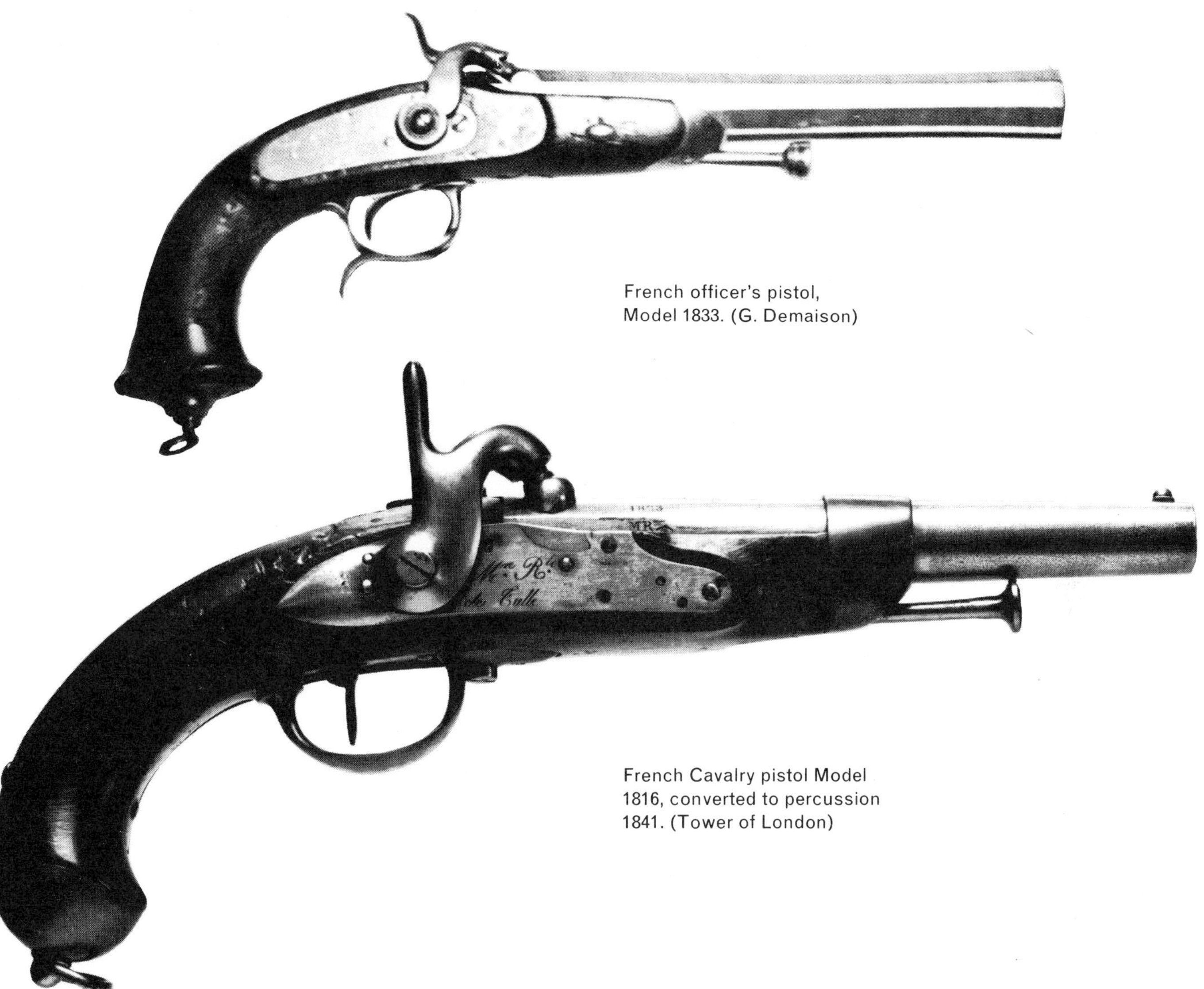

French officer's pistol, Model 1833. (G. Demaison)

French Cavalry pistol Model 1816, converted to percussion 1841. (Tower of London)

No regulation pistols for officers were issued before an 12. During the Revolution pistols were seized from the 'aristos' or from the enemy and were redistributed to Republican officers, and in many cases such pistols, especially 'Pistolets de Luxe', were presented as prizes to honour a brilliant feat of arms. Also popular were the smaller box lock pocket pistols known in France as 'Pistolets à l'Ecossaise', a semantic shift liable to cause confusion in direct translation since in English the term 'Scottish Pistol' refers to an entirely different type of weapon.

With the return of the Bourbon family and the restoration of the Monarchy in 1815, new models were designed for the use of officers, the Models 1814 and 1816, and in 1833 the only really interesting military pistol of the period was produced, the Officer's Model of 1833. It was half stocked and fitted with a back action lock known as 'à la Pontcharra', and was of importance since it was one of the first military firearms to employ the Delvigne chamber breech. The diameter of the chamber was slightly smaller than that of the multi-grooved rifled barrel, and the 17mm (about .69″) round ball employed could be loaded with relative ease. It was rammed down two or three times to ensure expansion. Present day experimentation with these pistols shows that accuracy is quite good, and consistent hits in the centre of a figure target at 25 yards are not difficult to achieve.

The use of heavy calibre over and under percussion rifled pistols by British officers is paralleled in France; in 1855 such a pistol with back action locks and a fluted butt was designed for staff-officers. As in Britain, the military pistol was never considered to be an important piece of equipment, and it was not until the collapse of Sedan during the Franco-Prussian War of 1870 that serious consideration was given by the French Military Authorities to the use of the handgun—and by this time the term handgun had become synonymous with revolver. The French Navy had been quicker off the mark and had adopted the Lefaucheux pin-fire revolver in 1858.

To catalogue the percussion military single shot pistols employed by the European armies until the adoption of the revolver would present somewhat of a problem and, since the majority bear a marked resemblance to the French pistols already mentioned, they are of little interest to anyone except the military pistol specialist. There are of course certain pistols which for one reason or another deserve mention.

Giuseppe Console has been referred to earlier, and the Console lock, improved by Vincent Augustin, was adopted by the Imperial and Royal Austro-Hungarian Cavalry in 1844. With the interesting exception of the use of the tube lock on a military pistol, the Austrian Cavalry pistol shows strong French influence, but is slightly unusual in being full stocked to the muzzle. The majority made were smooth bore with a calibre of 16.9mm, though a rifled version did also appear. The last percussion single shot pistol used by the Austrians was the rifled Cavalry pistol of 1859 (System Lorenz) which employed four grooves and was of 13.9mm calibre. The revolver was adopted in 1870.

Russian Cavalry pistols are to be found with a ring hammer, a type of hammer used in place of the normal spurred hammer and designed to avoid entanglement with the reins and other accoutrements of the cavalry man. Ring hammers were also used on German, Belgian and Scandinavian pistols, pistol carbines and carbines.

The various Germanic states exercised a measure of individuality in their choice of military pistols and, even when the type is identical, the furniture in one case might be iron and, in another case, brass. This state of affairs continued until Prussian influence resulted in a greater measure of uniformity being adopted throughout what was to become, in 1871, the German Empire.

Amongst the various German states, the most widely used Cavalry pistol appears to have been the Prussian half stocked cannon-barrelled pistol with spur trigger guard. The earlier pistols were percussion conversion, and the original flintlock feather spring was retained to actuate the nipple protector that replaced the pan cover and steel. Ramrods were not fitted either to these pistols or to the later Model 1850, and a separate rod was attached to the ammunition pouch. The Prussian pistols bore the Royal Crown on the lock plate as well as the name of the manufacturing arsenal, Danzig, Potsdam, Spandau or Suhl.

Full stocked pistol carbines with detachable shoulder stocks and carbine type swivels were also used. The diversity of types can be explained by the fact that each of the separate German states had its own Arsenal. The famous Mauser Factory at Oberndorf, for example, was originally the Government Arsenal of Wuerttemburg, which did not become part of the German Empire until 1871.

The Dreyse needle-fire pistol Model of 1856 had a limited issue to Cavalry, but the pistol cannot have enjoyed the tremendous success of the Model 1841 Dreyse Zundnadelgewehr, the first breechloading military rifle ever to chamber a cartridge complete with primer, propellant and projectile, and a weapon which decisively affected the course of history. This rifle was 'the magic wand with which the various Germanic States were united to form Germany under the Hohenzollern dynasty'. Pistols had a far less decisive effect on the course of history, and it was not until 1879 that the 10.6mm revolver was issued, and pistols and pistol-carbines were relegated to obscurity.

If the pistol-carbine was greatly favoured in both Austro-Hungary and Germany, it was even more so in Scandinavian countries. The histories of Norway, Sweden and Denmark are closely linked together: Norway was, for example, under Danish rule until 1814 when she accepted the suzerainty of the Swedish crown, becoming finally independent in 1905. It is not surprising therefore that their military weapons exhibit strong family resemblances.

The last of the Danish Cavalry flintlocks was the Model of 1807, a smooth bore full stocked pistol of 16 bore (17.5mm) and fitted with an 'internal' lock of similar design to that invented by Henry Nock and later used on the US Navy percussion pistol of 1842. These pistols were manufactured at the Kronborg Arms Factory near Helsingör and, in 1815, some were fitted with detachable shoulder stocks; later in 1827, the use of these stocks was abolished.

Whether or not any of these pistols were converted to percussion is open to debate. An experi-

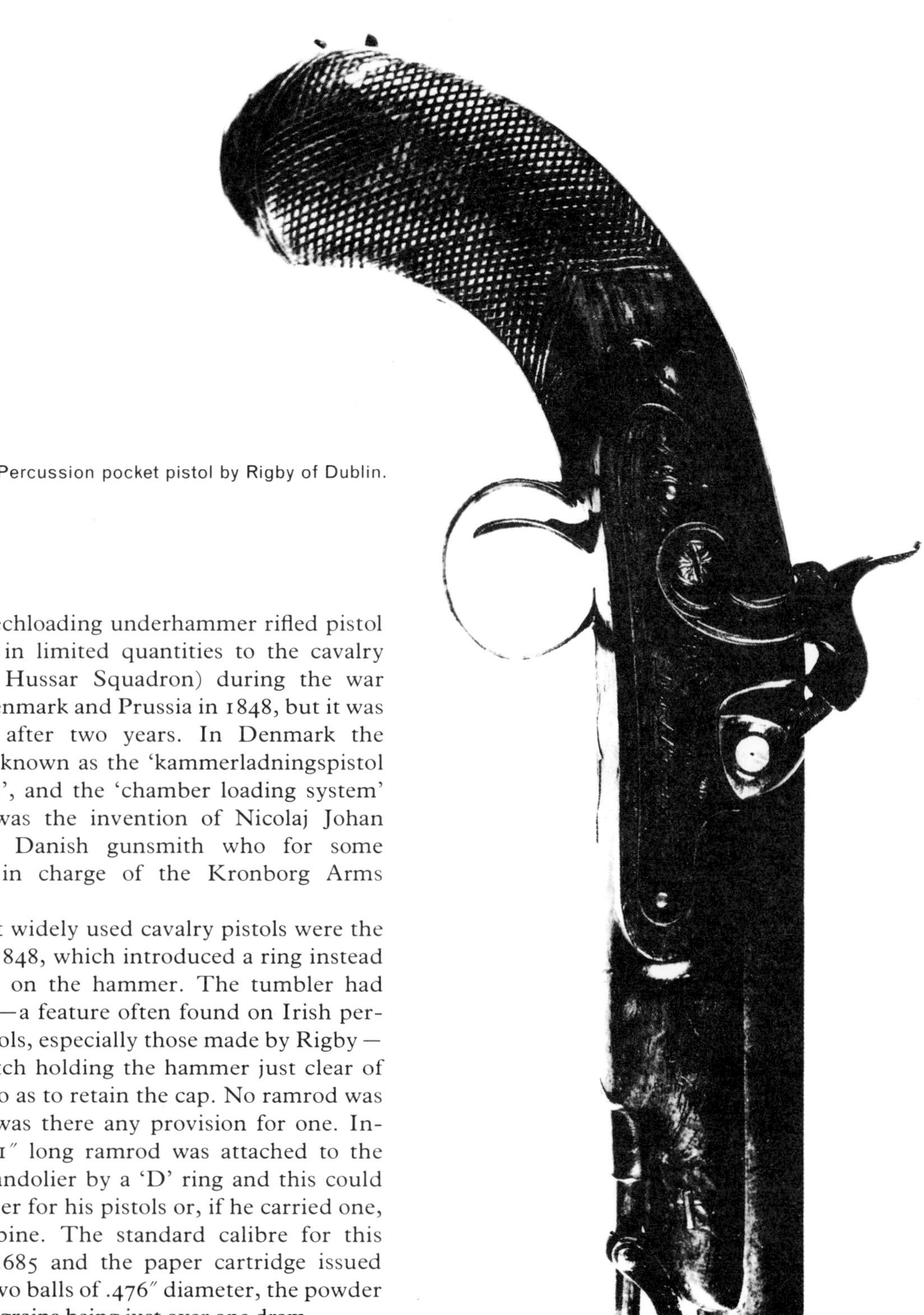
Percussion pocket pistol by Rigby of Dublin.

mental breechloading underhammer rifled pistol was issued in limited quantities to the cavalry (Volunteer Hussar Squadron) during the war between Denmark and Prussia in 1848, but it was withdrawn after two years. In Denmark the design was known as the 'kammerladningspistol model 1841', and the 'chamber loading system' employed was the invention of Nicolaj Johan Löbnitz, a Danish gunsmith who for some years was in charge of the Kronborg Arms Factory.

The most widely used cavalry pistols were the Models of 1848, which introduced a ring instead of the spur on the hammer. The tumbler had three bents—a feature often found on Irish percussion pistols, especially those made by Rigby—the first notch holding the hammer just clear of the nipple so as to retain the cap. No ramrod was fitted, nor was there any provision for one. Instead, an 11″ long ramrod was attached to the trooper's bandolier by a 'D' ring and this could be used either for his pistols or, if he carried one, for his carbine. The standard calibre for this pistol was .685 and the paper cartridge issued contained two balls of .476″ diameter, the powder charge at 27 grains being just over one dram.

The Model of 1848 was made under contract in Liege by two concerns, those of Remille and Renkin, and also by the Kronborg factory in Denmark. Pistols such as these were also used during the later invasion of Denmark by the Prussians in 1864 and were not replaced by the revolver until 1865.

Other military pistols employed by Denmark were the Royal Horse Guards pistol, a percussion conversion from the French an 9—the conversion being carried out in France—and the 1848 Navy pistol, also a conversion, which employed the Jessen 'internal hammer' lock. The last of the official issue pistols was that used by the Schleswig Gendarmerie. These pistols, supplied by Auguste Francotte of Liege, employed a ring hammer and were half stocked and supplied with a detachable shoulder stock.

In Norway and Sweden the cavalry were issued with two pistols, one a smooth bore (flankør) pistol and the other a rifle bore (studser) pistol. One detachable shoulder stock was issued with each pair of pistols. The Norwegian pistols appear to have been made as flintlocks and later to have been converted to percussion at the Kongsberg Arms Factory, Drammen, in southern Norway. Swedish pistols were manufactured by the firm of Husqvarna which had been originally established as the Royal Small Arms Factory in 1689 in the central province of Småland. The factory and township served the Swedish crown until 1757 and then passed into private hands, finally becoming a joint stock company in 1867.

The majority of these pistols, for which Liege was again an important source, were full stocked to the muzzle with a heavy brass barrel band at the muzzle. A rather odd 'L' shaped side plate, again of brass, was used and both the trigger guard and butt cap were made of the same material. The first of the Norwegian percussion pistols was a conversion of the Model 1831 flintlock, and both smooth bore and rifled conversions were issued as the Model 1831/46 in 1846. The last of these conversions was carried out in 1855, the single shot muzzle loaders being replaced by 11mm single action Lefaucheux revolvers which were issued to the Cavalry and Artillery in 1864.

The Swedish pistols were first converted from flintlock in 1849 and the rifled versions were, on conversion, fitted with a 'tige' or pillar breech. The Model of 1850, the smooth bore 'flankørpistol', was a massive weapon weighing nearly three pounds if the shoulder stock is included. The overall length was 40cm., just over 18″, the barrel slightly over $11\frac{1}{2}$″ and the bore 20mm. The rifled version was similar except that the calibre was reduced to 14.85mm. The method of dismounting the barrel is particularly interesting: the breech tang screw was removed and, with the hammer at half cock, the barrel was pushed

Swedish Model 1850 percussion pistol carbine, the smooth bore 'flankørpistol'.

forward for a quarter of an inch, thus releasing a hook underneath the barrel from a cross pin fitted to the fore-end nose cap. The whole operation was very quick and easy.

The first revolvers were issued to the Swedish Artillery in 1863, but it was not until the mid 1870's that their use became general.

The percussion single shot muzzle loading pistol had a relatively short life. As a military weapon it appears to have been just tolerated and no more. This is hardly surprising if one thinks of the cavalry man supposed to use it. First of all he had to manage his horse, possibly pretty jumpy after a charge. Then he had to reform ranks, a carbine in one hand, a pistol in the other, and very possibly the reins between his teeth. On top of all that, if he had fired his weapons, he was faced with having to reload. His ramrod might have been separate, attached to the bandolier holding his supply of made-up paper cartridges, but, if it was a captive one, he would have had to withdraw it from either pistol or carbine. The nipples (except in the case of pistols with the Maynard tape primer) had to be re-capped and he would certainly have dropped some of the caps before getting one securely on to the nipple. At the same time, he had to ensure that he did not drop his most important weapon, the sword!

In view of the problems and difficulties with which the cavalrymen had to contend it is hardly surprising that the *arme blanche* retained its position of importance even after the appearance of reliable cartridge loading revolvers and semi-automatic weapons.

It is generally accepted that the percussion revolver did much to raise firearms in the estimation of the cavalryman, and the first successful use of these new weapons was in America. The British were not slow to follow the American example, not only in the use but also in the manufacture of this new and effective arm. Only a brief interval of time separated the heavy cumbersome single shot muzzle loading cavalry pistol from the percussion and later breechloading revolver, but the chief and most remarkable change was in the means by which these two weapons were made.

This revolution in the method of manufacture swept away the age old traditions of gunmaking, at least as far as the pistol is concerned, and the hand of the craftsman, whether he was good, bad or indifferent, was replaced by the tireless energy and greater overall precision of the machine tool.

Notes to Chapter Three

The most relevant works of reference for this chapter are *British Military Firearms, 1650-1850* by Howard L. Blackmore (London, 1961), *Eldhandvapen, Vol. II* by J. Alm (Stockholm, 1933), *Duelling Pistols* by John A. Atkinson (London, 1964), *Early Percussion Firearms* by Lewis Winant (New York, 1956), *Henry Deringer's Pocket Pistol* by John E. Parsons (New York, 1952) and *Handfeuerwaffen, Vol. I* by Jaroslav Lugs (Berlin, 1962).

For information on French military pistols of this period I am indebted to George Dumaison of Paris and to information that has appeared in the *Journal* of Les Arquebusiers de France. Details of membership of this society can be obtained by writing to 137 Avenue de la République, Montrouge (Seine), France.

Chapter Four

The Machine Tool, its Influence and Effect on Firearms Manufacture

Before we take a closer look at the effect of the percussion system on the design of handguns, consideration must be given to the tremendous changes which took place over a relatively short period of time due to the adoption of the system of interchangeable manufacture.

Mention has previously been made of the early attempts in France to manufacture firearms on the interchangeable principle, and Joseph Wickham Roe's definition of the term, as stated in *English and American Tool Builders*, may help to avoid confusion.

According to Roe, the interchangeable principle is 'the art of producing complete mechanisms, the corresponding parts of which are so nearly alike that any part may be fitted into any of the given mechanisms'. This does not include the manufacture of separate parts similar to one another, but which do not fit permanently into a mechanism. The interchangeable system, developed by and for gunmakers, had a decisive effect on firearm design generally and on the handgun in particular. Once perfected, the system made possible the manufacture in mass not only of firearms, but also of clocks, sewing machines and typewriters, and it is today the basis of modern industry.

The first step towards 'mass production' was the appearance of 'specialisation'. Instead of one man making an entire firearm himself, separate craftsmen specialised in specific operations and, in the centres of arms manufacture such as Birmingham, Liege, St. Etienne, Suhl and the Valtrompia in Brescia, specialist individuals and groups of individuals appeared who were solely concerned with the manufacture of one component or a related group of components. In barrel making for example, the barrel welders produced the rough tube, the barrel borers made true the hole down the middle and the barrel grinders finished the outside surface. On muzzle loading guns, the breech forgers and stampers made and fitted the breech plugs together with the breechers and filers. The making of ribs either for the ramrod or to secure two barrels together lay in the province of the rib makers.

Similarly, with the rest of the gun, there were those who specialised in stockmaking, in making furniture such as trigger guards, in butt plates etc., and—the élite of the trade—the lockmakers. If we add barrel browners, hardeners, spring makers and engravers it is not surprising that by the mid-nineteenth century it was possible to list over thirty separate crafts or trades, all of which contributed in some way to the making of a complete gun.

This method of manufacture carried on with simple hand tools was highly successful, but this very success engendered complacency, extreme specialisation, secrecy and introspection, and herein lay the seeds of ultimate and inevitable destruction. The skill of the individual craftsman gave way in due course to the skill built into a specialised machine tool.

Supplies of fuel, raw material and power were the factors which influenced the growth of firearms manufacture in any particular locality. In the early days timber and then coal were required; there was also the need for easily worked iron ore and for water as a source of power to aid in the extraction and working of the iron. The Val Trompia in the Province of Brescia in Northern

The Beretta workshop in Gardone in the sixteenth century. (Beretta)

Italy is a classic example of the suitable geographical location. The history of metal working here, in particular the manufacture of weapons, goes far back into history; according to tradition the ancient Roman colony of Brixia made weapons for the wars between the Romans and the Etruscans. The availability of timber and iron ore, and of power from the River Mella, coupled with the metal working skills of the inhabitants of the valley, more than explain the early establishment of what was to become a flourishing arms industry. The centre of the industry was Gardone and, by 1567, 'arquebuses of every sort' were being made there. By the seventeenth century specialisation had already come in, with barrels made at Gardone, while the nearby village of Marcheno specialised in gun locks, and gun furniture was made at Lumezzane.

A similar pattern developed in and around Birmingham, where gunmaking as a distinct industry dates from the last quarter of the seventeenth century. By 1692 a group of Birmingham gunmakers had contracted to supply the Government with two hundred snaphaunce muskets per month. Half of the muskets, according to the trial order agreed on 5 January 1693, 'shall have flatt locks engraven, the other half Round Locks and that all of them shall have brass pipes cast and brass heel plates and all the stocks varnished, and to have six Good thrids in the Breech screws, and that all the said Gun Stocks shall be well made and Substantiall and none of them Glewed'.

William Bourne, Thomas Moore, John West, Richard West and Jacob Austin on behalf of themselves and the rest of the Birmingham gunmakers were to be paid seventeen shillings each for these arms, which had to be dispatched in quantities of one hundred, carriage being paid at the rate of three shillings per hundredweight.

The first order for 'trade muskets' was obtained in 1698 and for over two centuries Birmingham supplied the major part of the demand for this class of weapon. The gun industry in Birmingham was concentrated in the small district around St Mary's Church, the 'gun quarter', for not only was much of the 'material'—the components—manufactured in this area, but the firms there exercised a virtual monopoly in the work of 'setting up' or assembling guns, particularly those of higher quality. The tendency towards specialisation could be clearly seen and, since this method of manufacture entailed the frequent transport of part-finished and completed components from one workshop to another, the advantages of having the workshops near to each other is evident.

The Birmingham gunmakers enjoyed the further advantage of being able to draw on the productive capacity of a wider area, for certain trades became well established in the Black Country and both Wednesbury and Darlaston produced gun barrels and gun locks, though the manufacture of gun barrels declined after the Napoleonic Wars. In Wednesbury this decline was turned to good effect for large stocks of welded barrels were made into gas pipes.

The master gunmaker or entrepreneur seldom possessed a large workshop. His function was to purchase at the best possible price the forgings and part-finished components, and to redistribute them to specialised craftsmen who were responsible for finishing and assembly. The degree to which the master gunmaker exercised control over the finished gun was to a large extent dependent on the type of trade in which he was engaged and also, of course, the scale of his activities.

He would purchase material from the barrel-makers, lock makers, trigger and trigger guard makers, gun furniture makers and, if engaged on the manufacture of military weapons, from yet another specialist branch of the trade, the bayonet forgers.

Engaged in each of these separate trades were completely independent manufacturers, some of whom were large enough to employ many workers in their own workshop and also to provide work for outworkers who either rented a bench in a large shop or carried out their trade at home. At the other end of the scale were the 'little masters' who employed only one or two assistants. In the mid-nineteenth century in Darlaston, then an important centre of the gun lock trade, there were five or six workshops employing twenty journeymen each and some twenty or thirty little masters.

Many of these small specialist firms gained international reputations and, although their names were often hidden away inside lock plates or merely indicated by cryptic initials, their fame and the high quality of their workmanship was a byword in the trade.

In *The Industrial Development of Birmingham and the Black Country,* G. C. Allen describes a typical section of the gun quarter in Birmingham and I used, until recently, to visit the area he describes and found there what can only be described as a perfect example of fossilised industry.

The premises of the master gunmaker stood on the main street, with an archway in the centre above which was a faded, peeling and scarcely legible sign carrying the legend, 'H. Morris, Gun and General Engraver'. The passageway through the arch communicated with two courtyards surrounded by workshops in two and three storeyed blocks. Every workshop consisted of one or two rooms in which the various operations of setting up guns were carried out, each by a 'little master'. In the great days of gunmaking in Birmingham all these shops would have been fully occupied and, by visiting each in turn, one could have seen the entire sequence of operations from the receipt of a rough forging of a trigger guard or of tubes from the barrel welders, right the way through to the finished gun. I was only able to see the last remaining vestiges of what must have been a hive of industry, served by an army of small boys scurrying to and fro with barrels, actions, lockwork and gun furniture, some with agreed instructions, others seeking a little master who would perform the required operations on perhaps a pair of barrels for a definite price.

I became quite friendly with Mr Morris, the engraver, and his shop, typical of the small Birmingham workshop, had remained unchanged for over half a century. It was approached through the courtyard and up two flights of outside wooden stairs which were a danger to life and limb, particularly after dark. Lit by gas and heated by a cast iron coke stove, the workshop walls were lined with benches on which lay a profusion of tools and of cardboard and tin boxes, all in a state of indescribable confusion. The proprietor had his own bench against a window with a north light and, after dark, work would be carried on by the light of an incandescent gas mantle, the glare softened by a mask of tissue paper. Electric light was not favoured by Mr Morris, and the hissing of the gas jets, the cosy warmth of the stove and the sound of tools in use created a strong sense of atmosphere which I can recall with ease and with considerable pleasure to this day. My visits were, of course, made in what can only be called the twilight of the British gun trade and during the occasional evenings spent in this workshop it was interesting to see how the old customs were still carried on. Many of the specialist workers in the trade had left; the lure of more congenial working conditions, higher wages, pension schemes and the like, had drawn them into the modern light industry of the Midlands. In the evenings, however, they could still earn extra money at their old craft and, from five o'clock onwards, men would pass into the workshop from the twentieth century world outside and each would go to his bench, one making trigger plates from the rough forgings, another shaping guards and yet another working on an action recently received from the hardeners. At nine o'clock the files and gravers would be laid on the bench, and coats and hats would be put on in time for a glass of beer at the local before closing time. All the work had been done entirely by hand and the skill with which file, chisel and hammer were wielded was delightful to watch.

Dickson's in Edinburgh, the last remaining gunmaker in Scotland, the workshop where the setting up of the famous Round Action shotgun is carried out, presents a similar picture, and in the workshops of the Artigiani in Gardone, the Italian equivalent to the little master, the traditional side by side double shotgun is still being made under a similar organisation and by time-honoured methods.

But the survival of craft gunmaking is nowadays restricted to the sporting double barrelled shotgun and it is problematical how long this will last.

In view of the very high degree of specialisation that, even from an early date, characterised the manufacture of firearms, it is rather surprising that no attempts were made to gather workers together in small factories, since it was fully realised that the constant movement of part-finished components from one small workshop to another was expensive and, for the larger manufacturer, the co-ordination of the effort of a large number of small workshops and outworkers can have by no means been an easy task.

The reasons of course were many. Until the introduction of machinery compelled the gunmaker to establish a factory, he had little inducement to do so: a factory was suited only to large scale production, and the market was almost entirely restricted to military weapons. Here, the difficulty lay in the wide fluctuation in demand which meant that the factory owner had to establish a unit capable of meeting maximum demand and yet bear the cost of keeping it idle during times of depression. Under the prevailing system the burden could be thrown on to the workers themselves, many of whom might find employment in allied working trades, and for this reason the gun trade exhibited quite remarkable powers of expansion and contraction.

A possible additional contributory factor was the appearance of the 'truck system', a system of paying wages, not in cash, but in goods of one description or another. After the Napoleonic Wars conditions were particularly bad in Darlaston, then the centre of the lock trade, and many of the workmen had to manage on as little as four shillings a week. The truck system only served to aggravate conditions, for the outworker who asked to be paid for his week's labours would be told: 'Money—what's money for? We've got good bread, rice and good bacon.' The Truck Act of 1831 did nothing to alleviate the conditions, for outworkers were not covered and the system continued—which may have accounted for the rather odd, at least to the modern eye, combination of trades which are to be found listed in the old Directories.

Bowlker, Richard, 23, Peck Lane, Birmingham, 1774-1777. Gun-maker, Victualler and Pawnbroker.

Burt, Richard, Whittal St., Birmingham. 1785. Gunsmith and Victualler.

Dunn, Joseph. 8, Upper Priory, Birmingham. 1767-1770. Gun-maker and Publican.

Freeth, John. Market Place, Walsall. 1770–1781. Gunsmith and Grocer.

Jevon, John. 'Three Swans' Dudley St, Wednesbury. 1817. Best gun-lock maker, Victualler.

Round, Joseph. 'Turks Head Inn', Wednesbury. 1817. Victualler, maltster, gas-pipe and gun barrel maker.

Spittle, Joseph. 'Blue Ball', Hall End,

Wednesbury. 1817. Victualler and gun lock filer.

The evils of the system are evident from a letter written in 1864 under the pseudonym 'Fair Play' which stated: 'I think that the masters are not aware of the unjust way in which the foremen deal with the employed. For instance, they always give the most work to those who will allow them the most money for so doing. It may be as well to state that the foremen are paid very good wages, and I think it rather hard at such times as these, that the men should have to pay from 10–15% out of their wages to the foremen, for I can assure you sir, that such is being done at one of our largest gunlock and furniture manufactories in Birmingham at the present time; and there are men who keep public houses, who, by paying the foreman so much per cent get most of the work for their own houses, and the poor man has to go to these houses for his work, and allow the publican about 20% besides spending part of his hard-earned wages in the house.'

This letter shows that the abuses continued even after the establishment of factories, but much of the old independent spirit of the gun trade managed to survive. In many of the larger gun factories the men were entirely independent of the owner of the factory in which they worked. They would rent their own 'stands'—which comprised a bench, a vice and a gas jet—and, if the employer could not give them enough, they would take in outside work. The usual rent was 1/– per bench and 6d. per week for gas, with an additional 1/– or 1/6d. for every man employed by the worker and 6d. for every boy. Even as late as 1870 it was impossible to induce the men to give up their old time prejudices. The foremen at the Birmingham Small Arms Company, where a number of Darlaston lock and spring filers had been engaged, found it impossible to eradicate practices hallowed by time. 'These men still followed the practice of a hundred years previously—they still resorted to 'fiddle drilling' (i.e. bow and breast drilling) when, by going a few yards, they could use power machinery. They still used tallow dip candles (purchased by themselves) when tempering springs, although the Company had offered to supply them with Russian Tallow free. They would not do tempering after 10 o'clock in the morning, owing to their superstitious belief that springs tempered after that hour would break.'

Such habits and traditions managed to survive the impact of the factory system as they had survived the application of power to tasks formerly carried out by sheer muscle. From the sixteenth century until well into the nineteenth the most important source of this power both in Europe and in North America was the water wheel, and it is no exaggeration to say that, in many instances, local industry survived due entirely to the availability of water when both fuel and raw material had long vanished. Water power was used to work ore-crushing plants, and to provide both the blast for furnaces and the power for hammer and rolling mills. The water wheel even retained its immense industrial importance long after the invention of the steam engine—one of the commonest early uses of which was to provide a constant head of water.

A forge at the moment when the hammer hits the die blocks and red hot bar material is forged into a recognisable shape, in this case the frame of an automatic pistol.

In a series of articles which appeared in *The Engineer* in 1859 reference was made 'to a peace-full looking factory, some twelve miles from London ... busy with the labour of hundreds of men engaged in the construction of an almost ceaseless stream of the most deadly small arms which has ever been contrived by man'. This rather florid introduction leads into a guided tour of the Royal Small-Arm Manufactory at Enfield commencing with 'the large yard, which contains in its centre the storage reservoir for the water supply to drive the two water wheels'.

Similarly, a visitor to the Springfield Armoury, Springfield, Massachusetts (which as one might expect was sited on the Connecticut River) would no doubt be taken to view the watershops. The blast for the rows of forges in the forge shop was provided by bellows worked by water power and, in another building where iron bars were rolled out and cut into lengths suitable for forging the barrels, water power also drove the machinery for shaping wooden stocks, as well as the grinding wheels—which were some five or six feet in diameter and were used for barrel grinding—and the machines employed for the final polishing operation.

Horse shoe nail stubs before and after being welded into a bar.

At Enfield, barrels were made from best quality wrought iron supplied in the form of 'skelp', a bar 16″ in length, 4″ in width and weighing about 10 lbs. The skelp was heated red-hot and then passed through a pair of bending rollers so constructed that the flat skelp was turned into a tube, the two long edges being brought together. The tube was then reheated and passed through welding rollers which had one series of cylindrical grooves and another series of conical grooves gradually lessening in diameter and depth. The edges of the tube were united when it was passed through the cylindrical grooves; then, with a mandril of iron rod inside, the passage through the conical grooves consolidated the weld. The lump for the nipple seat was then welded on to the rough barrel at the breech end, and the barrel itself was subsequently rough and smooth bored. The final operation was the grinding and straightening.

Common barrels were made in much the same way except that the welding was carried out by hand. Both hand and power hammer forging were used in the manufacture of twist barrels which, instead of being welded longitudinally, were welded spirally, the skelp being wound spirally round a mandril. The strength of these barrels was not only dependent on the skill of the barrel welder but was also related to the quality of the iron. For many years the firm of Marshall and Mills of the Monway Works, Wednesbury, was renowned for the quality of its iron: not only was it supplied to Birmingham makers, but also to both the British and United States governments.

An important source of raw material was the scrap from metal working operations, and a highly profitable branch of iron forging formerly carried out in the Midlands was that known as 'Swaff Iron Forging' (probably a corruption of 'swarf'). This was a process based on workshop scrap—iron and steel filings, cuttings from barrel boring, chips from lock plates etc. These cuttings were collected by the boys in each shop and sold to the Swaff Forger. They were then first of all immersed in dilute sulphuric acid, the action of

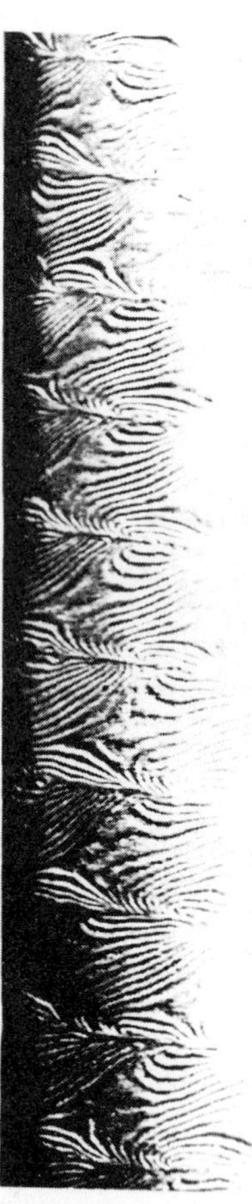

A range of Belgian damascus barrels. From left to right: non-twisted brown damascus; 'Prince Albert' brown damascus; Turkish etched damascus; Boston single band etched damascus.

the acid causing the pieces of scrap to adhere together. After draining, the resultant mass was then heated to welding heat in an air furnace and subsequently beaten into a bar with light hammers. These Swaff Iron bars were sold to gun forgers for forging patent breeches, lock plates and gun furniture.

The gun barrel welders often employed metal which had not been purchased from the iron maker—old horseshoe nails, waste iron from the nailing shops and scrap steel from the spring and bayonet factories. This sort of material was widely employed in the manufacture of 'figured iron' barrels, those made from a mixture of iron and steel. Such barrels, after finishing and polishing, were traditionally 'browned' by chemical oxidation processes, the mild etch received during this process emphasising the 'figured' structure of the barrel. They were used for better quality pistols and often the beautiful patterns obtained depended on the process employed in the actual manufacture of the figured iron, on the proportion of steel and iron used, and on the method of working and the extent of the etch. The browning process could merely emphasise the structure by a difference in colour, or it could actually remove metal so that the finished barrel presented an appearance akin to engraving.

A considerable amount of ingenuity was exercised by the barrel makers both in their choice of raw material and in the processes employed, particularly in the manufacture of one type of figured barrel, the damascus barrel. This type of barrel was widely used for sporting guns and, to a lesser extent, for pistols. Rods of iron and steel were piled into 'faggots' and the bundle of rods

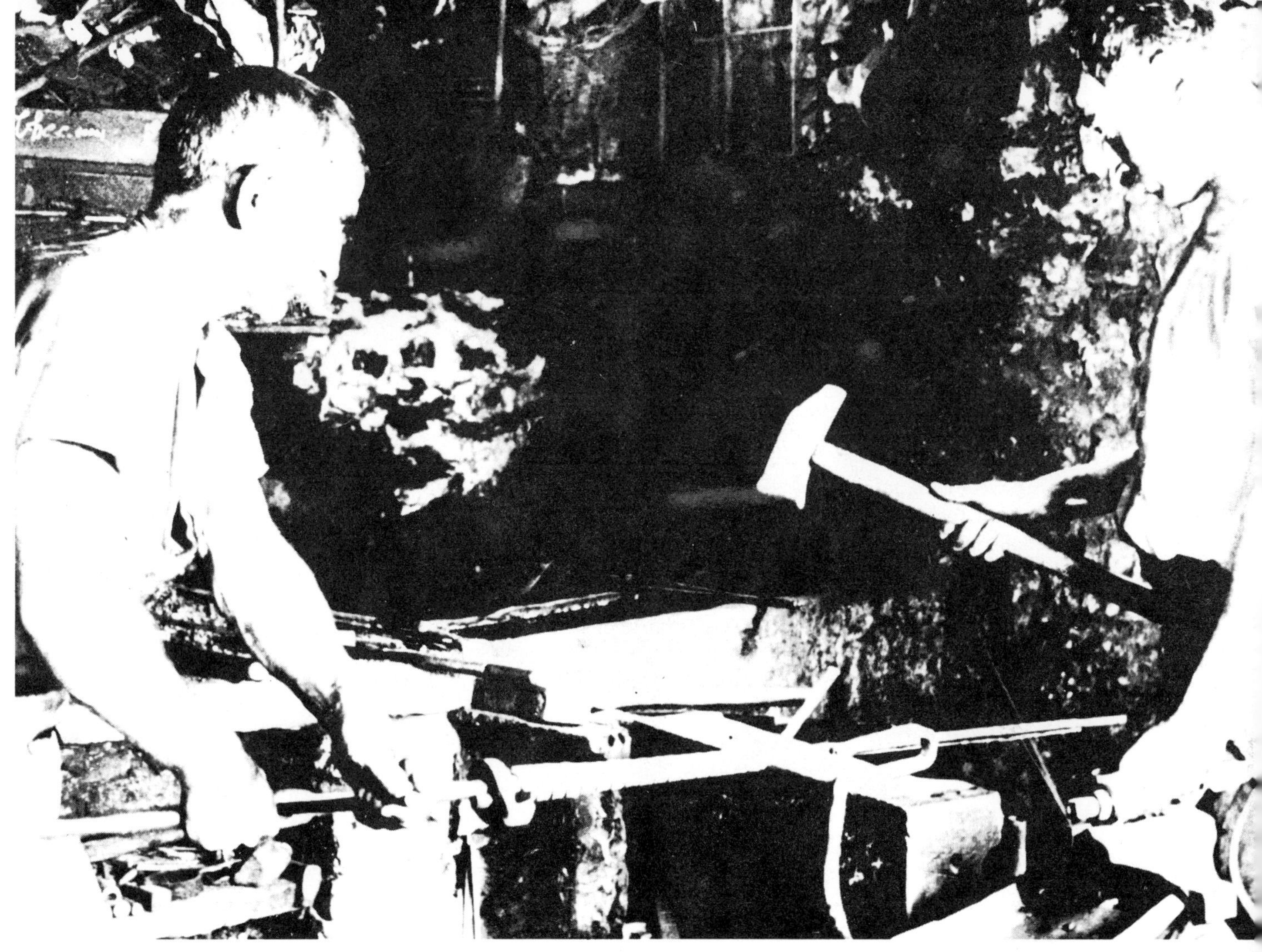

Making a damascus barrel; the band or ribbon being wound round the mandrel. The breech end is to the left.

was held securely together during the subsequent forging process by placing one end into a rectangular hoop of iron provided with a handle. The rods were packed by introducing a wedge, and the bundle was forged by hand, either with the use of a tilt hammer or, in later years, of a steam hammer. After forging, the faggot would, of course, be reduced in cross section and considerably elongated. The faggots so produced were then reheated and twisted. One end was placed in a block and the other in a rotating head which, when turned, twisted the faggot. A man armed with a pair of tongs stood by to ensure that no part of it was twisted more than any other. On completion, the twisted faggots were welded into coils either singly or in multiples. Each barrel required a minimum of two coils, one for the muzzle and the other for the more robust breech end. The variations in manufacture, the proportions of iron and steel used, and the method of laying the faggots, all produced barrels having a distinctive appearance when finished. The names used to describe the various grades of barrel were many: sham dam, twopenny iron, charcoal iron, stub twist, stub damascus, single iron damascus, two iron damascus, laminated steel and so on. Best quality barrels were relatively expensive and it was possible to gain some idea of the barrel quality by appearance. The fact that damascus barrels were appreciably more expensive than plain barrels led to the practice of plating a thin layer of damascus figured iron over the top of a plain barrel in order to simulate the genuine article. The more unscrupulous would even go so far as to 'paint on' the pattern and so delude the prospective purchaser into believing that he had a damascus barrel when in fact it was very likely to be a barrel of poor quality.

A forging for the frame of the Browning High Power automatic pistol. (Fabrique Nationale)

The same forging after machining. (Fabrique Nationale)

The availability of Whitworth and Siemens steel barrels during the latter part of the nineteenth century resulted in a fall in the demand for fine damascus barrels. The highly skilled and laborious techniques formerly employed gradually became extinct until, in 1930, the last fine damascus barrels were made by the firm of J. Delcour-Dupont of Nessonvaux in the Vesdres Valley not far from Liege in Belgium.

Barrels were now made by drilling through solid bar, by rolling or drawing pierced blanks, or they were rolled hollow by the Mannesmann process, all techniques which were part of the new industrial technology and no longer a craft occupation.

A similar revolution took place in the manufacture of the lockwork and, of less importance in the consideration of handguns, the stock. Before this revolution, the various parts of the lock—the lock plate, tumbler, sear, bridle and hammer—were hand forged with hammer and anvil, as were the mainspring and sear spring. The rough forgings were finished by hand filing, and, after hardening, the lock was then assembled. No elaborate machinery was needed and manufacture was largely on the old domestic basis with husbands, wives and children taking part, each making a contribution to the finished product. The first change that took place was the introduction of hot stamping. Patent No. 7712, taken out in 1838 by George Round, Lock Filer, and Samuel Whitford, Die Sinker, described the new process. In the preamble, the aims and intent were clearly set forth: 'The manufacture of gun and pistol locks, plates, hammers, sears, tumblers, bridles etc., by stamps, dies and presses instead of hammers, anvils and a few other tools'. Among the advantages claimed were that parts could be produced to exactly the same shape and could therefore be interchangeable. In the case of lock plates for flint guns, a stamp with an 150 lb. hammer was to be employed and there were two dies to produce the correct shape. A further series of operations was needed to form the pan and fence. Tools were also made for the removal of the fraize or flash of excess metal and, after deflashing, the parts were shaken in a 'rattling box' or rumbled to remove the scale formed during the heating operation. Sets of finishing dies were then used, the parts being heated 'warm red' and struck twice, 'which makes it exceedingly smooth'. The necessary holes were pierced by a small press.

This was a beginning. But, although increased accuracy was obtainable and much of the skill formerly needed in hand forging was eliminated by the use of dies, hand filing was still necessary for the final finishing. The real revolution came when the skill needed to perform this final operation was built into the machine.

The lathe is undoubtedly the most important of the family of machine tools, but until the middle of the eighteenth century it remained remarkably primitive, the common type being the 'pole lathe' in which the workpiece was driven by a cord passed round it and attached at one end to the top of a springy pole mounted near the ceiling as a horizontal cantilever, and at the other to a foot treadle. A lathe of this type gave the work an oscillatory motion only half of which could be utilised, but from it developed boring machines and screw cutting machines.

All present day copying or profile turning lathes can trace their ancestry back to Blanchard's gun stock lathe and here we must go back to the Springfield Armoury on the banks of the Connecticut River where Thomas Blanchard was employed for several years as a designer and where he improved and invented numerous machines for firearm manufacture. Blanchard's first machine (which is still preserved in the Armoury Museum) was used for turning shoe lasts, his next for turning gun stocks. The Blanchard lathe for turning irregular shapes operated on the pantograph system using a master gun stock and, although it looks more like a primitive hand loom than a machine tool, it was the earliest of the specialist machine tools developed for interchangeable arms manufacture. When installed, its degree of accuracy was such that improvements had to be made to the metal working tools. Blanchard also designed an inletting machine for fitting locks to the stocks which used the actual lock plates as formers. Blanchard lathes were manufactured by the Ames Manufacturing Company who exported over 400 stocking machines of the Blanchard type to European Governments and arms manufacturers.

The workshops and the factories of the Massachusetts and Connecticut gunmakers were the cradle of the 'American' system, the interchangeable system brought to perfection. Accurate and specialised machine tools and the adoption of the use of limit gauges (this latter factor had thwarted previous French attempts) ensured success and, whereas the British machine tool makers had supplied tools for the building of the world's railways, it was the Americans who supplied the tools and the know-how for the armouries of Europe. Practically all the machine tools installed when the Enfield Small Arms Factory was re-established in 1855 were of American origin. Not content with supplying the tools, the Americans also exported the 'know-how'. James H. Burton, who had been at the Harper's Ferry armoury and who had also worked with the Ames Manufacturing Company, came over to England to supervise the installation of the machinery at Enfield and also to take charge of production.

The background to the decision made by the British Government to establish a small factory of their own as an alternative to advertising for a contract under the old Ordnance system is given by the celebrated engineer James Nasmyth, the inventor of the steam hammer, in his autobiography. Nasmyth had worked as personal assistant to Henry Maudslay, the pioneer of precision engineering, before setting up in business on his own account, and he was well qualified to advise the Government on matters connected with machine tools.

'In 1853 I was appointed a member of the Small Arms Committee for the purpose of re-modelling and in fact, re-establishing, the Small Arms Factory at Enfield. The wonderful success of the needle gun in the war between Prussia and Denmark in 1848, occasioned some alarm amongst our military authorities as to the state of affairs at home. The Duke of Wellington to the last proclaimed the sufficiency of "Brown Bess" as a weapon of offence and defence, but matters could no longer be deferred. The United States Government, though possessing only a very small standing army, had established at Springfield a small arms factory, where, by the use of machine tools specially designed to execute with the most unerring precision all the details of muskets and rifles, they were enabled to dispense with mere manual dexterity, and to produce arms to any amount. It was finally determined to improve the musketry and rifle systems of the English Army. The Government resolved to introduce the American system by which arms might be produced much more perfectly, and at a great diminution of cost. It was under such circumstances that the Small Arms Committee was appointed.

'Colonel Colt had brought to England some striking examples of the admirable tools used at Springfield (Hartford) and he established a manufactory at Pimlico for the production of his well-known revolvers. The committee resolved to make a personal visit to the United States Factory at Springfield. My own business engagements at home prevented my accompanying the Members who were selected; but as my friend John Anderson (now Sir John) acted as their guide, the committee had in him the most able and effective helper. He directed their attention to the most important and available details of that admirable establishment; the United States Government acted most liberally in allowing the committee to obtain every information on the subject; and the heads of the various departments, who were intelligent and zealous, rendered them every attention and civility.

'The members returned home enthusiastically

delighted with the results of the enquiry. The committee immediately proceeded with the entire remodelling of the Small Arms Factory at Enfield. The workshops were equipped with a complete series of special machine tools, chiefly obtained from the Springfield Factory. [The machinery was in fact supplied by Robbins and Lawrence and the Ames Mfg. Co.] The United States Government also permitted several of their best and most experienced workmen and superintendents to take service under the English Government.'

During the visit of this commission, Major Ripley, Superintendent of the Springfield Armoury from 16 April 1841 to 16 August 1854, ordered ten muskets which had been manufactured in ten successive years from 1843 to 1853 to be stripped and the parts reassembled at random. As a result of this visit, 157 special machine tools were ordered, made up of 74 milling machines, 23 drilling machines, five tapping machines and seven edging machines. The remainder were special machines for threading, boring, rifling, turning and so on.

Eli Whitney.

The earliest attempt to build skill into machine tools and to establish interchangeable manufacture can be accredited to a French gunsmith LeBlanc and, in 1785, Thomas Jefferson, then the US Minister to France, reported that he had visited LeBlanc's workshops and had been handed a box of parts sufficient to make 50 musket locks. 'I put several of them together myself taking pieces at random, as they came to hand, and they fitted in a most perfect manner. The advantages of this, when arms need repair, are evident.' He then added: 'The principle of establishing the margins of error plus or minus which are tolerable for critical dimensions and then enforcing them in the workshop by means of suitable gauges is essential to the success of the system'.

One of the American engineers who grasped these principles and applied them was Eli Whitney, to whose work some reference has already been made. Born in 1765, Whitney is probably best known for his invention of the cotton gin, and it was in order to exploit this invention that, in 1793, he went into partnership with Phineas Miller. His rewards, however, were meagre and, in 1798, he turned his attention to the manufacture of firearms. After obtaining his first contract from the American Government in 1798, Whitney set about building a factory at Whitneyville, outside the city of New Haven in Connecticut, but, since all the machinery had to be designed and built from scratch, it took two years to get it into operation.

In 1812, when he applied for another contract for 15,000 muskets, Whitney stated that his objective was 'to make the same parts of different guns, as the locks for example, as much alike each other as the successive impressions of a copper plate engraving'. The United States Government officials were sceptical, so Whitney went to Washington taking with him ten pieces of each part of a musket. Before a distinguished assembly, he selected components at random from the piles of parts in front of him and successfully assembled ten muskets.

After Whitney's death in 1825, the business was carried on by Eli Whitney Blake and Philos Blake, his nephews. In 1842 his son, Eli Whitney

Junior, came of age and took over the management of the armoury, contributing improvements in barrel drilling and advocating the use of steel for barrels. The company continued in existence until 1888 when the plant was sold to the Winchester Repeating Arms Co.

Alongside the figure of Eli Whitney stands that of Simeon North. Also born in 1765, North began his career in 1795 by making scythes in an old mill adjoining his farm. It is not known when he first began to manufacture pistols but, when he obtained his initial government contract in 1799, he carried out the work with the aid of his brother-in-law, Elisha Cheney, a clockmaker who supplied the pins and screws. Some years later, in 1811, North was elected Lieut.-Colonel of the Sixth Connecticut Regiment, an appointment which gave him considerable pleasure and which accounts for references made to Colonel North.

By 1813 North was employing forty or fifty men and, since his original factory at Berlin, Connecticut, was no longer large enough, additional premises were being built at Middletown. It was also in this year that he contracted to furnish the United States Government with 20,000 pistols, and the agreement contained the following significant clause: 'The component parts of the pistols are to correspond so exactly that any limb or part of one pistol may be fitted to any other pistol of the twenty thousand'. North died in Middletown in 1852, having manufactured some 50,000 martial pistols and about the same number of long arms for the United States Government.

The work of both Whitney and North has tended to overshadow the contribution to the ultimate success of the interchangeable parts system made by John Hancock Hall. On 21 May 1811 Hall patented his own design for a rising receiver action but when, in 1813, he obtained an order for one hundred rifles, he was unable to execute it. His problem was the impracticability of low volume production; only a large order could warrant the expense of erecting a factory and of providing water power and all the necessary machinery. The result was that Hall went to work at the national armoury at Harpers Ferry, where he eventually received a contract to supervise the manufacture of one thousand rifles of his own pattern. Five years were spent in tooling up, the contract was completed in 1824, and these firearms were the first to be made in quantity in a national armoury with uniform and interchangeable parts. Equally, although they were never popular—criticism was often directed at the leakage of gas at the joint between the receiver and the barrel—the carbines made on the Hall breechloading system were also the first percussion firearms to be issued as a standard weapon to US troops. Possibly one reason why Hall does not receive due credit is because the Hall 1833 percussion carbine was manufactured entirely by Simeon North, a later batch of flintlock carbines were made at Harpers Ferry in 1837 and, in 1838, North contracted for a further order for percussion weapons which incorporated some of his own modifications. Hall himself died in 1841.

Over the years, as manufacturing techniques improved and the tolerances were decreased, the term 'interchangeable' altered its meaning. The degree of interchangeability found satisfactory in 1812 would not have been satisfactory in 1850; even by 1828 Simeon North was contracting to supply firearms 'the parts of which should be interchangeable, not only in the lot contracted for, but that they may be exchanged in a similar manner with the rifles made or making at the national armouries'.

Between them, Eli Whitney and Simeon North started a chain reaction, the results of which still affect us today. It was in building on the foundations that they had laid down that one man, Samuel Colt, came to exercise an influence on manufacturing methods greater than that of any other man of his generation.

Colt was born in Hartford, Connecticut, on 19 July 1814. When he was seven his mother died and shortly afterwards his father's business failed. At the age of ten he was apprenticed to a bleacher and dyer and he also worked as a farm labourer. A rather sporadic schooling ceased when he was sixteen and he signed on as a seaman for a voyage to India. The first model of his design for a revolving pistol is supposed to have been whittled out of wood on the return journey. In 1831 his first pistols were made by a gunsmith and several more were produced in Baltimore between 1833 and 1835. Patent protection in both Britain and France was obtained in 1835, followed by his first United States patent in 1836. The Patent Arms Manufacturing Company was formed in March 1836 and a four storey factory was built at Paterson, New Jersey, on the banks of the Passaic River. Due to shortage of capital, the revolving pistols and rifles made at Paterson were fabricated part by machinery and part by hand. Perhaps for this reason costs were relatively high and, in spite of diligent efforts by Colt to interest the Government, the necessary substantial orders did not materialise. In 1837 an US Army board reported 'that from its complicated character, its liability to accident and other reasons, this arm was entirely unsuited to the general purposes of the service'. Despite this disappointment, Colt persevered and was rewarded by a small order from the newly independent Republic of Texas.

A further Government trial in 1840 was more favourable, but by no means enthusiastic. The lack of orders, coupled with internal dissension within the company, resulted in lawsuits and, in 1842, the Paterson factory ceased business.

The Colt Armoury at Hartford.
(English and American Tool Builders)

Samuel Colt.

With no factory but with his patent right intact, Colt was offered a contract for one thousand pistols. Although no doubt inured to the vagaries of the arms business, it must have seemed ironical to Colt that the order he had been seeking in vain for several years had come when he was no longer able to manufacture in his own factory. Undaunted, Colt sought out Eli Whitney Junior, who had both the necessary capital and the factory at Whitneyville. Colt had to assign his government contract to Whitney, the agreement being that Colt would receive any profit over cost of manufacture after providing certain bonus payments to Whitney.

A further order for one thousand pistols encouraged Colt to re-establish himself in business and, in 1847, premises were obtained in his native Hartford. By 1853 continued expansion had resulted in growing pains, and these premises had become inadequate. A tract of land on the river front, known as the South Meadows, was therefore purchased and, since the land was subject to flooding, a protective dike 30 feet high and $1\frac{3}{4}$ miles long was built. On the reclaimed land a 500 ft. long building in the shape of an 'H' was erected, some 1,400 machines, the majority built on the premises, were installed and special tools and fixtures were made, the cost of which almost equalled that of the machines. Such an investment in tooling was unparalleled. The original building made of Portland stone was destroyed by fire two years after Colt's death in 1869, and the loss of machinery—including a beam engine of 300 h.p. and a double horizontal engine of 400 h.p.—was estimated at $800,000. The factory was rebuilt under the supervision of Elisha King Root who had joined Colt in 1849 and who, on Colt's death, became president of the company.

Root was yet another of the New England mechanical geniuses and inventors. He invented an improved drop hammer and worked out a whole system of jigs, tools and fixtures. Of Root it has been said: 'the credit for the revolver belongs to Colt; for the way they were made, mainly to Root'.

The Colt armoury during Root's time was the largest private armoury in the world. It was also the training ground and finishing school for a number of men who were to play no small part in raising the United States to the position of

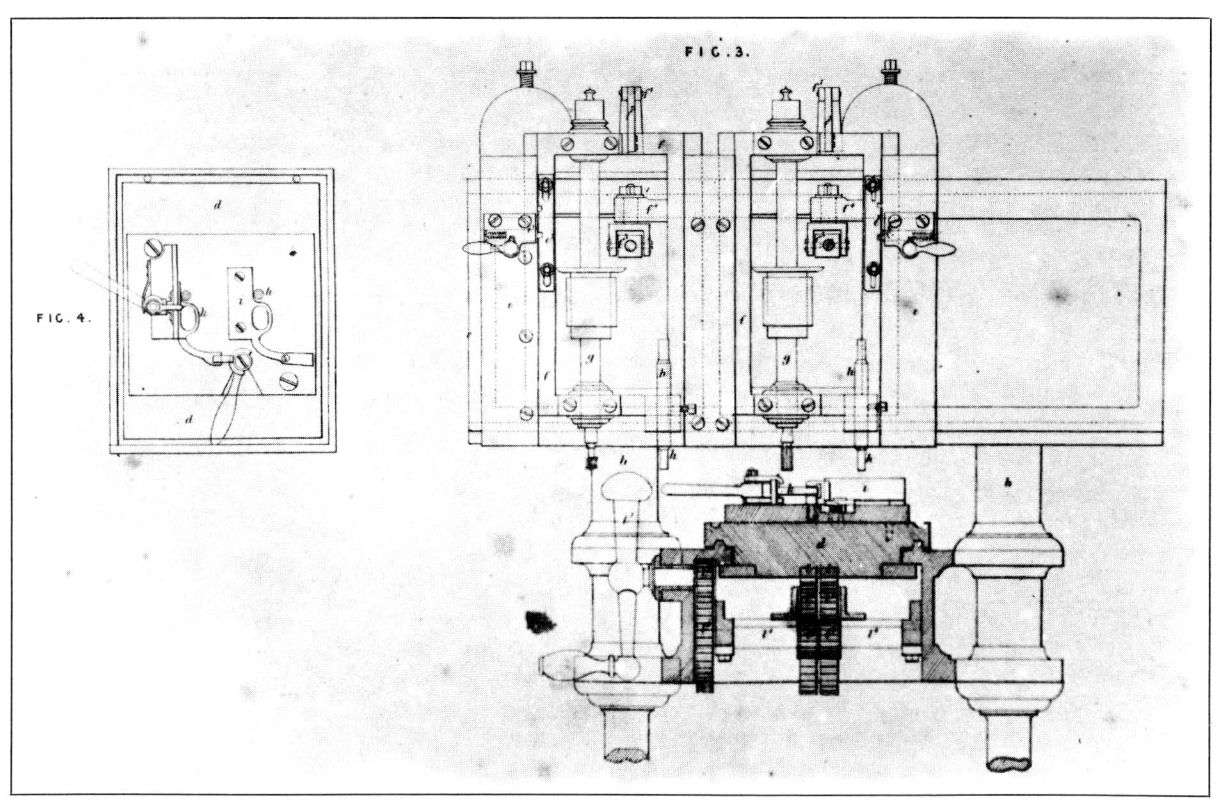

Colt's Patent No.861 of 1854, Sheet 5, showing a machine for the milling of the trigger guard and strap together with the fixture for holding the components.

Colt's Patent No.861 of 1854 showing a vertical multiple spindle drill and the fixture for drilling the hammer.

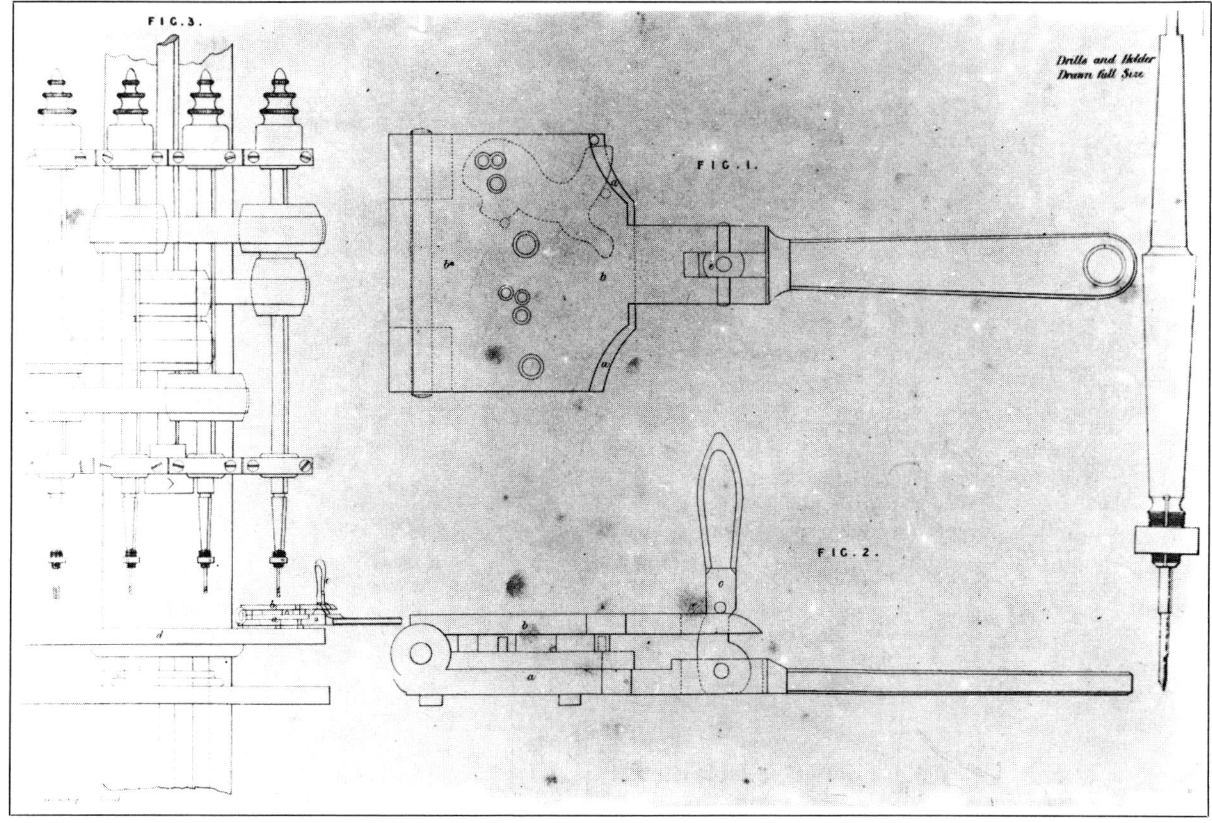

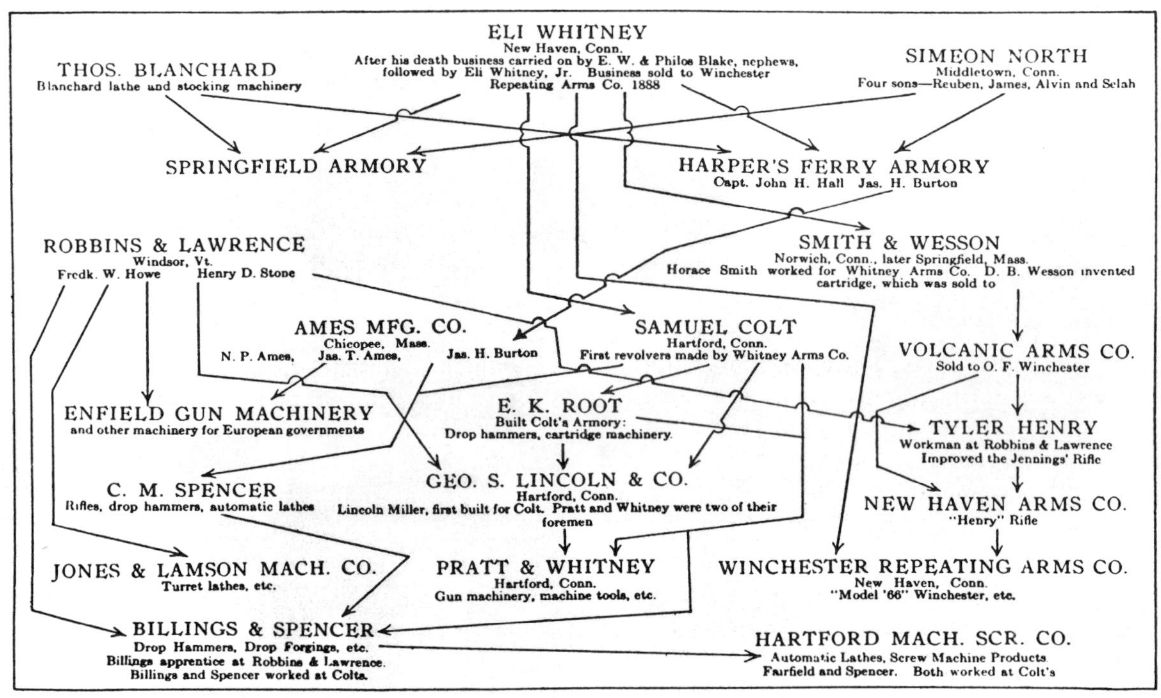

The genealogy of the American gunmakers. (English and American Tool Builders)

industrial supremacy that it enjoys today. Some of these men, such as F. Alexander Thuer, Charles B. Richards and Alexander Mason, will be discussed further when consideration is given to the individual Colt models. Others like Francis A. Pratt and Amos Whitney (of the same family as Eli Whitney), Charles E. Billings and Christopher M. Spencer, formed partnerships, the companies they founded exercising an important influence on the later age of automation.

Francis Pratt worked for two years in the Colt Armoury, Whitney for four years. In 1860 Pratt and Whitney started out on their own, no doubt having gained valuable experience as a result of the time spent at Colt's. The Pratt and Whitney Company was formed in 1869, its main business being the manufacture of machine tools for making firearms and sewing machines. Following the receipt of orders from the German Government, the firm equipped the armouries of Spandau, Erfurt and Danzig, and in later years their successful endeavours in establishing standards for the engineering industry contributed in no small way to the rise of the company to its position as one of the leaders of the machine tool industry.

Billings went to Colt's when he was twenty one and became their expert on drop forging. Later he joined forces with Spencer and together they formed the Billings and Spencer Company of Amherst, Massachusetts. It was here that Spencer developed the automatic lathe, its basis a standard Pratt and Whitney lathe to which was added Spencer's 'brain wheel', a large diameter cam wheel. As this revolved, the steel cams bolted to its periphery engaged followers which actuated the chuck, turret and slides. Accurate profile cutters appeared between 1848 and 1852 and multiple spindle machines by 1859. The need for drilling large numbers of holes with precision led to the replacement of the old spearpoint drill by the modern twist drill, but the demand for these drills could only be met by the machine tool and, since no machine was available which could form the spiral flutes, one was designed and built by the firm of Brown and Sharpe. The result was the first truly universal milling machine.

Less than fifty years spans the gap between the percussion single shot muzzle loading pistol and the cartridge loading revolver. Both belong to the nineteenth century: one traces its ancestry back to the beginnings of the pistol as a recognisable weapon; the other, unchanged in its essentials, is still manufactured today. The influence of the machine tool on the handgun was decisive, and the demands made by the arms manufacturer on the infant machine tool industry were equally far reaching in their effect.

The machine tool of today. Two slides for the Walther P-38 being machined on a RUMAG miller, and right, a multiple spindle drilling machine operating on the Walther P-38 frame which is held in a fixture not dissimilar to that used by Colt a hundred years earlier. (Walther)

Notes to Chapter Four

In recent years, the more liberal interpretation of the meaning of history has focused attention on the social economic and technological factors which have moulded modern society. Until comparatively recently the technological factor has been largely ignored. As we have seen, its importance in the narrow field of firearms development cannot be overemphasised, but unfortunately the literature is scant and difficult of access.

Before a detailed study of the technology of the manufacture of firearms is undertaken however, the broader aspects of the subject can be considered by reference to *A History of Technology* by Singer, Hall and Williams (Clarendon Press, Oxford) or to the sequel to this large and important work, *A Short History of Technology* by Derry and Williams (Clarendon Press, Oxford).

The more specialised literature is rather unevenly divided amongst the various branches, and the history of the machine tool is poorly represented. The most important work is *English and American Tool Builders* by J. W. Roe (New Haven, 1916) and a later work *Tools for the Job* by L. T. C. Rolt (London, 1965).

Information on the organisation of the gun trade in Birmingham is given in *The Industrial Development of Birmingham and the Black Country* by G. C. Allen (London, 1929).

For information on the Birmingham gun trade I am especially indebted to Miss Dorothy Young who allowed me to extract details from the thesis which she compiled for her Master of Commerce degree and which deals exhaustively with the 'History of the Birmingham Gun Trade'. Other works consulted included *The Cause of Decay in a British Industry* by 'Artifex & Opifex', *The Industrial History of Birmingham* edited by S. Timmins, *Wednesbury Workshops* by F. W. Hackwood and *A History of Warwickshire* by S. Timmins. A detailed account of the Royal Small Arm Manufactory, Enfield, will be found in the issue of *The Engineer* for 25 March 1859, and reference should also be made to Samuel Colt's address to the Institute of Civil Engineers on 25 November 1851.

Information on the history of the machine tool is contained in '100 Years of Progress in Development of American Metalworking Equipment' by Guy Hubbard in *Automotive Industries* for 1 September 1955, and in 'Metal-Cutting Machine Tools' by W. Steeds in *The Chartered Mechanical Engineer*, Vol. II No. 6, 1964.

Chapter Five

The Development of the Percussion Revolver

The lengthy but very necessary digression into the complexities of mass production has rather broken the thread of the narrative. In Chapter Three the cavalry of Europe were left galloping to and fro engaged in their interminable struggle for supremacy. When they eventually discarded their clumsy and ineffectual single shot pistols, they rearmed with cartridge loading revolvers and, in so doing, missed a phase in handgun development—the short but exciting era of the percussion revolver.

With very few exceptions the percussion revolver was the weapon of only two countries, America and Great Britain. Both possessed the manufacturing potential to produce them and both were engaged in conflict, the first to unite a continent, the second to unite an Empire.

Throughout the history of firearms, efforts have been continuously directed towards the pressing need to increase fire power. With the muzzle loading long gun, ease and speed of reloading dominated the military mind, and ingenious men made unceasing efforts to perfect some effective system of repetitive fire. Such systems as were actually realised in practice—multiple superimposed charges, multiple barrels, magazine systems like the Lorenzoni and the Kalthoff, and the numerous revolving systems—were inevitably restricted in use because of expense and the not inconsiderable problems of manufacture. Even had these considerations been disregarded, their very complexity made their use under aggressive conditions extremely difficult, while repairs could really only be carried out by a skilled craftsman.

These problems were swept aside by two important developments. The first was the perfection of a simple and reliable means of ignition, the percussion cap; the second was the appearance of suitable machine tools, coupled with their employment in sequence. The mechanical complexity of the flintlock repeating firearm with its concomitant problems was banished by the first; the second permitted manufacture in quantity to the necessary degree of accuracy and at a price which ensured a wide and expanding market.

The weapon which eventually appeared was the percussion revolver. As has been said before, a revolver is theoretically any firearm employing either a number of barrels or a cylinder with a number of chambers arranged around a central axis, where the barrel group or cylinder rotates to bring each barrel or chamber into battery in front of the firing mechanism. Today, however, the term revolver is restricted to those weapons which employ a rotating cylinder and a single barrel, and by common usage is confined to a handgun, the revolver pistol. Those weapons which use rotating barrels are today known as pepperboxes, and those which employ chambers arranged like the spokes of a wheel are known as radial or turret guns. It can, in fact, be assumed that the pepperbox was the first system to be invented, and that the weight of such an arm was very probably the reason for the appearance of the true revolver.

Matchlock and wheellock revolving arms required that the barrel group or cylinder be rotated by hand. A locking system was employed to ensure alignment of the barrel group with the firing mechanism and, in the case of the revolver,

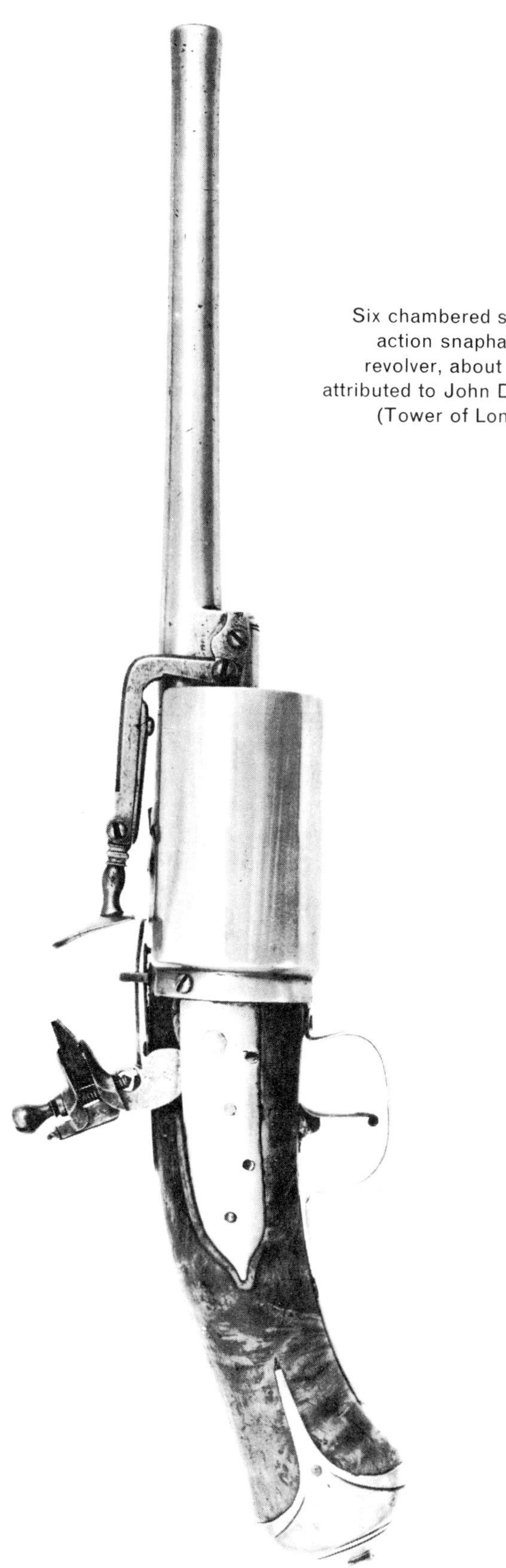

Six chambered single action snaphaunce revolver, about 1680, attributed to John Dafte. (Tower of London)

to ensure that the chambers would align with the single barrel. In addition, it was necessary to re-prime between each shot and the weapons that appeared were regarded by their affluent owners more as interesting and ingenious curiosities than as practical firearms.

Flint and steel ignition systems made it possible for each barrel or chamber to be provided with a pan and steel. In the case of the snaphaunce type a link was used to slide back the pan cover, but this was not required on any weapon employing the combined steel and pan cover, the true flintlock. The next stage was to eliminate the need to rotate the cylinder or barrel group by hand and then to devise a method of automatic priming to reduce the multiplicity of priming pans. The latter consideration was not of great importance on weapons with three or four chambers, but it was essential for eliminating the 'Christmas Tree' effect where more than three consecutive shots were required.

What is perhaps the earliest surviving specimen of automatic cylinder rotation is now in the Tower of London Armouries. Although unsigned, it is attributed to the London maker John Dafte and can be dated about the third quarter of the seventeenth century. The method employed to achieve the rotation of the cylinder is of the greatest interest since it was almost identical to that adopted by Colt—a method still used in that remarkable survival of a past age, the famous Colt Single Action Army Revolver. A signed example of Dafte's work, a carbine, is to be found in the Colt Museum at Hartford.

A very complete description of Dafte's revolver is to be found in J. N. George's *English Pistols and Revolvers*, and the following condensed account is based on it.

A back action sidelock was employed and a pawl linked to the breast of the cock engaged a six toothed ratchet cut on the base of the cylinder, engagement being ensured by a small 'V' spring between the pawl and the cock. As the cock was drawn back, the pawl rotated the cylinder through one sixth of a complete revolution, so bringing the next chamber into line with the barrel. It was of the greatest importance to make certain that the chamber was lined up with the barrel and securely retained in battery at the time of discharge, and, since cylinder locking or bolting was vital, the Dafte revolver was provided with a spring catch which engaged a notch appropriately provided on the cylinder.

With the pistol as it at present survives, it is

necessary to draw back the cock and bring the steel into battery. Separate priming pans are provided for each chamber, each with its own cover. A link on the cock opens each pan cover in turn the moment the flint held in the jaws of the cock strikes the steel. From his examination of the weapon, George concluded that the maker had intended to provide automatic means whereby the separate steel was returned to battery after each shot. Had this mechanism survived, it would have been possible to fire six shots from the pistol merely by drawing back the cock for each shot.

The difficulty of ensuring chamber and barrel alignment was bypassed in an ingenious though rather brutal fashion by the immigrant Huguenot gunmaker Jacques Gorgo who worked in London during the late seventeenth century. Rather than devise locking systems, Gorgo used a barrel with a cone shaped breech end. The bullet leaving the cylinder was deflected into the bore by the cone and, although simple in concept, accuracy must have been adversely affected. Gorgo's system was also employed by another gunmaker, Andrew Dolep who worked in England at about the same time as Gorgo, and modifications of the system continued to be used and are often undetected. Reference will be made later to convergently bored chambers where the bullet has to change direction as it enters the barrel.

By the middle of the eighteenth century the pepperbox type of construction had gained favour and a number of flintlock pepperboxes with different signatures, but all bearing a remarkable resemblance to each other, have survived.

Work which has been done, notably by R. Bedford, shows that this type of pistol was invariably seven barrelled. Each barrel was screwed into a cylindrical breeching, with the seventh barrel in the centre of the cluster. The breeching had a central arbor at the rear of which were six teeth. The teeth, together with a spring loaded roller mounted in the action body, ensured the correct alignment of the hand rotated barrel group. To load the pistol, the barrels were removed from the breeching, each chamber was charged with powder and ball, and the barrels were then replaced in the same way as with the turn-off or screw barrel pistol. The breeching was provided with six touch-holes and, since the breeching entered a closely fitting annular shield, the priming could not be lost. To prime, the pan cover mounted on the top of the shield was opened and, as the barrel group was rotated,

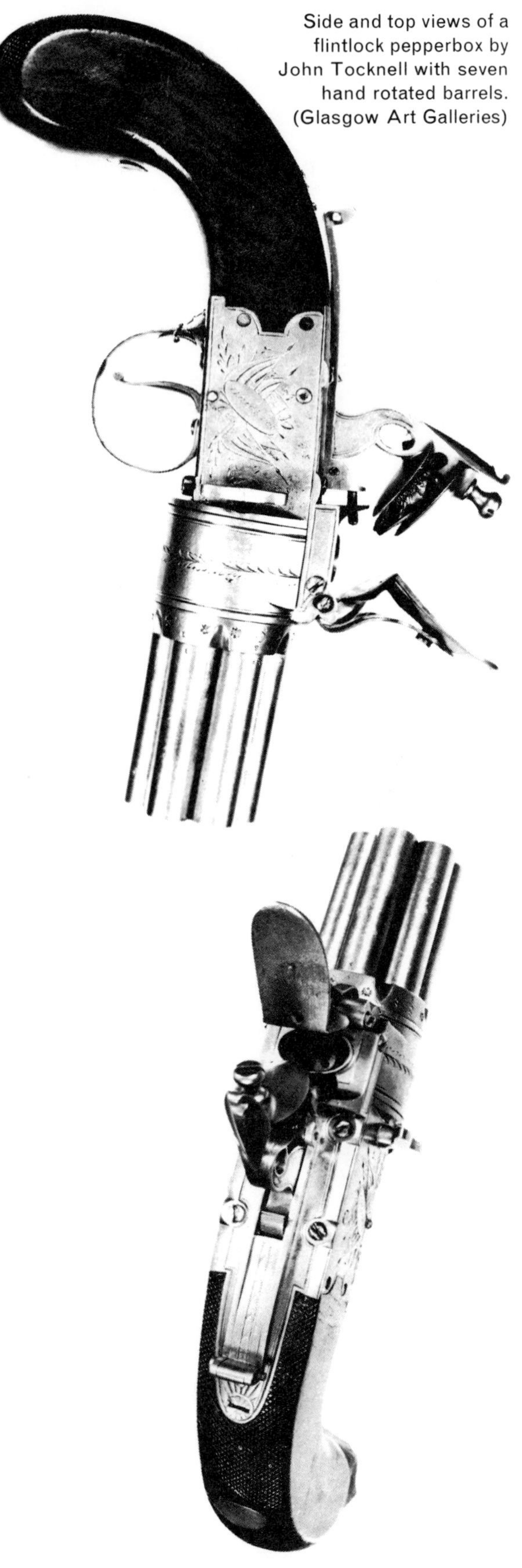

Side and top views of a flintlock pepperbox by John Tocknell with seven hand rotated barrels. (Glasgow Art Galleries)

priming powder could be introduced into each of the pans. To fire the pistol, the pan cover was closed and the cock drawn back. Following each shot these two operations were repeated.

Mention has only been made of six priming pans, although the pistol has seven barrels. The answer is that the central barrel was fired in conjunction with one of the barrels on the periphery of the group so that for each complete loading there was one discharge where two shots were fired simultaneously. The bore of the pistol illustrated is 8mm or .313 (150 bore) and it is signed by John Tocknell of Brighton. Tocknell, however, was a general gunsmith, incapable of making a pistol to the very high standards necessary to ensure safe and positive functioning, and, in Bedford's opinion, the maker was very probably Henry Nock. The remainder of the pistol is conventional: once again the versatile box lock was employed and a safety catch of conventional type fitted.

A mechanically operated flintlock pepperbox which can be dated rather earlier than the hand rotated type mentioned above is to be found in the Glasgow Art Galleries and Museum. As can be seen, it is a very handsome pistol indeed, with an overall length of 11″. Unfortunately it carries no maker's signature, the only marks being those of the London Proof House and the number identification for each barrel. A similar pair of pistols by Kolbe, who worked in London between 1730 and 1737, is preserved in the armouries at Windsor Castle (No. 798).

To load the pistol shown, the cannon barrels had to be unscrewed from the breeching using the internal key provided, and each barrel had

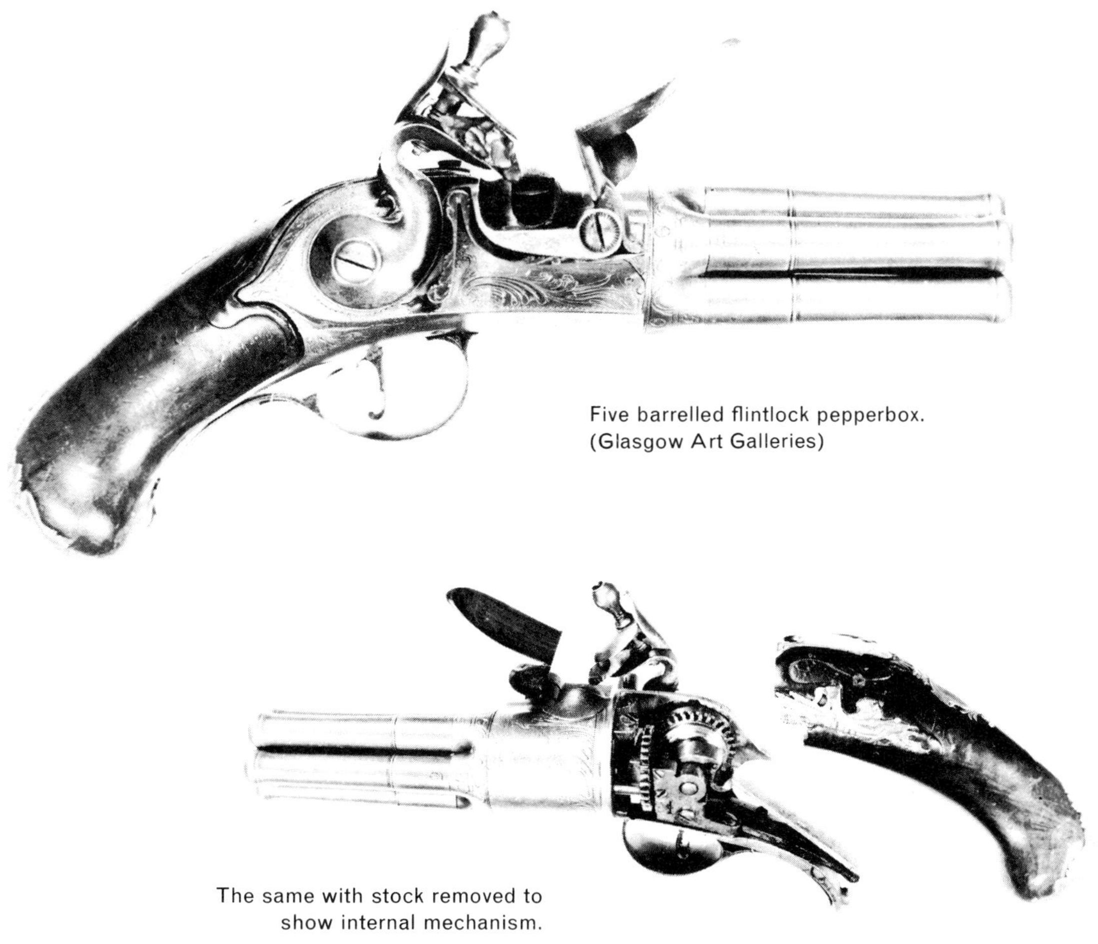

Five barrelled flintlock pepperbox. (Glasgow Art Galleries)

The same with stock removed to show internal mechanism.

then to be primed separately. Additional security to prevent multiple discharge was provided by a spring loaded flap which opened at the appropriate moment. The barrels were mechanically rotated by means of a pinion attached to the tumbler. This pinion can be seen in the illustration showing the stock removed, as can the manner in which it meshes with a further pinion mounted at right angles to it. To fire, all that was necessary was to draw back the cock: this rotated the barrel group and at the same time closed the pan cover by means of an internal linkage—the linkage that is missing on the Dafte revolver described earlier.

In the opening years of the nineteenth century emphasis again swung back to the last of the flintlock revolvers, the Collier. Some doubt still surrounds the precise origin of this particular design and current research tends to credit it to Captain Artemus Wheeler of Concord, Massachusetts. Wheeler patented his system in America on 10 June 1818. A British patent (No. 4315) was taken out by Elisha Haydon Collier on 24 November 1818, and a fellow Bostonian, Cornelius Coolidge, patented the system in France.

As patented, when the cock was drawn back, the Collier cylinder revolved automatically by means of a coil spring which periodically had to be tensioned. The idea does not appear to have been used on pistols and manufacturing problems possibly restricted it to experimental arms. The distinguishing features of the system were the provision of a positive seal between the chamber mouth and the barrel, and the equally positive alignment.

Inadequate sealing led not only to the escape of

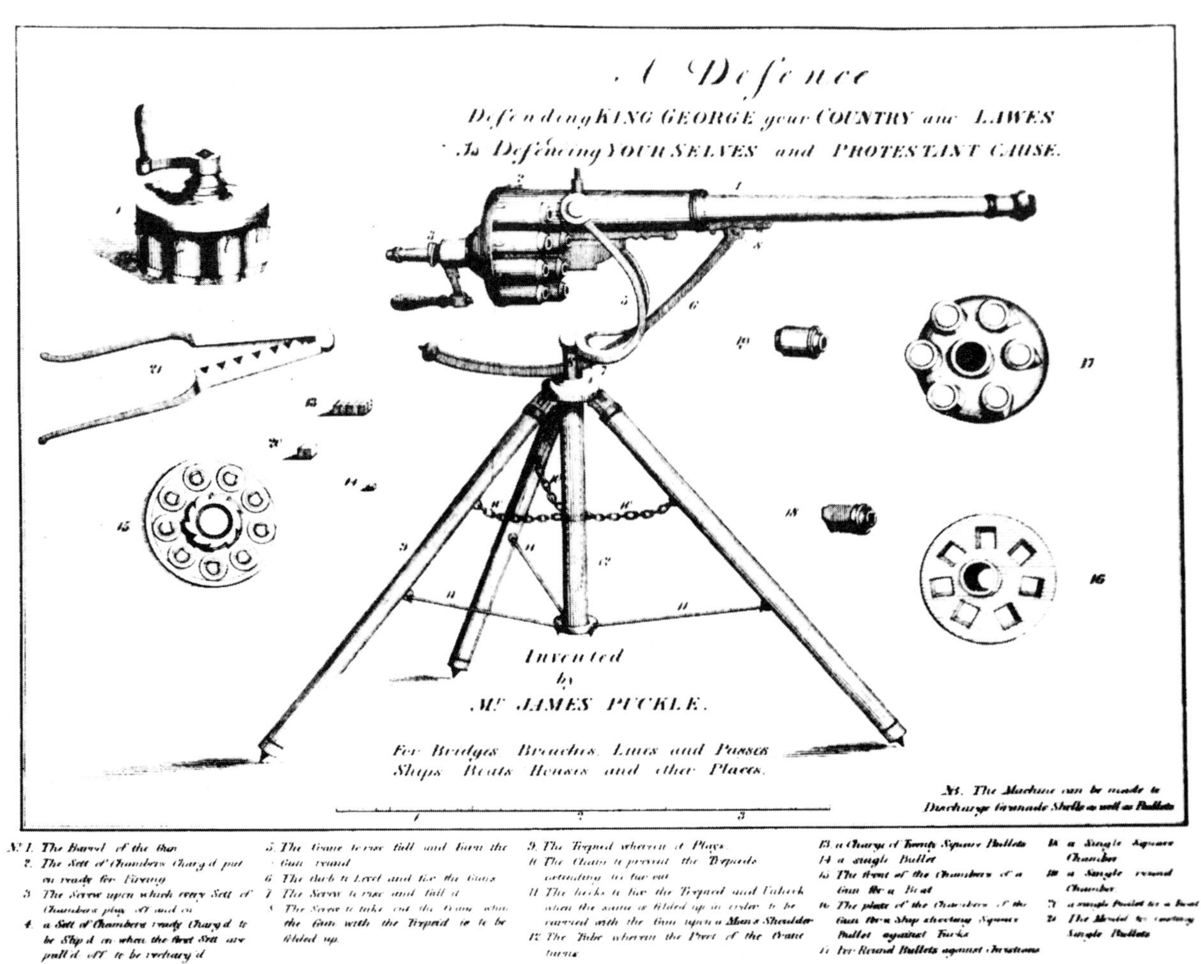

James Puckle's famous patent of 1717.

gas at the junction of cylinder and barrel—resulting in loss of pressure and consequent reduction in muzzle velocity—but also to the possibility of a multiple discharge, all the chambers being fired at once due to the flash spreading from one to the next. In the Collier the mouth of the cylinder was recessed, the cone formed fitting over the breech end of the barrel. Locking was achieved by means of a wedge which thrust forward the cylinder when the cock fell.

The need to provide a positive seal had been appreciated by James Puckle nearly a hundred years earlier in connection with his 'portable gun or machine, called a Defence'. In the Puckle gun the system was reversed, the barrel being countersunk and security obtained by the use of a screw crank which had to be unscrewed after each shot so that the cylinder could be rotated manually. Puckle's invention is perhaps best remembered because of the curious reference in his patent of 1717 to the fact that the shape of chambers and of the bullets may be varied, some 'for shooting square bullets against Turks' others for shooting 'round bullets against Christians'. A reciprocating cylinder to eliminate gas leakage between cylinder and barrel was again employed during the percussion revolver period and we shall also encounter it during the era of the cartridge revolver.

The other interesting feature of the Collier was its automatic priming device. Two variations appeared, the first operated by means of a toothed ratchet and the second by means of a linkage. The magazine was mounted above the pan cover, and the container was closed by a rotating steel plug containing three recesses. Each time the mechanism was operated the plug revolved and deposited the powder contained in one of the recesses into the pan. Collier, who described himself on his trade labels as a 'Cylinder Gun Manufacturer', sold revolver pistols, shotguns and rifles from his London premises, and tried without success to interest the British Government in the military potential of his weapon. Meanwhile, in America, Wheeler had been trying to interest the US Navy in his version of the revolving gun with the same lack of success.

Apparently, an appreciable quantity of Collier arms were sold, but, although a few were made on the percussion system, there was no further development, and they do not appear to have influenced the evolution of the revolver in any decisive manner.

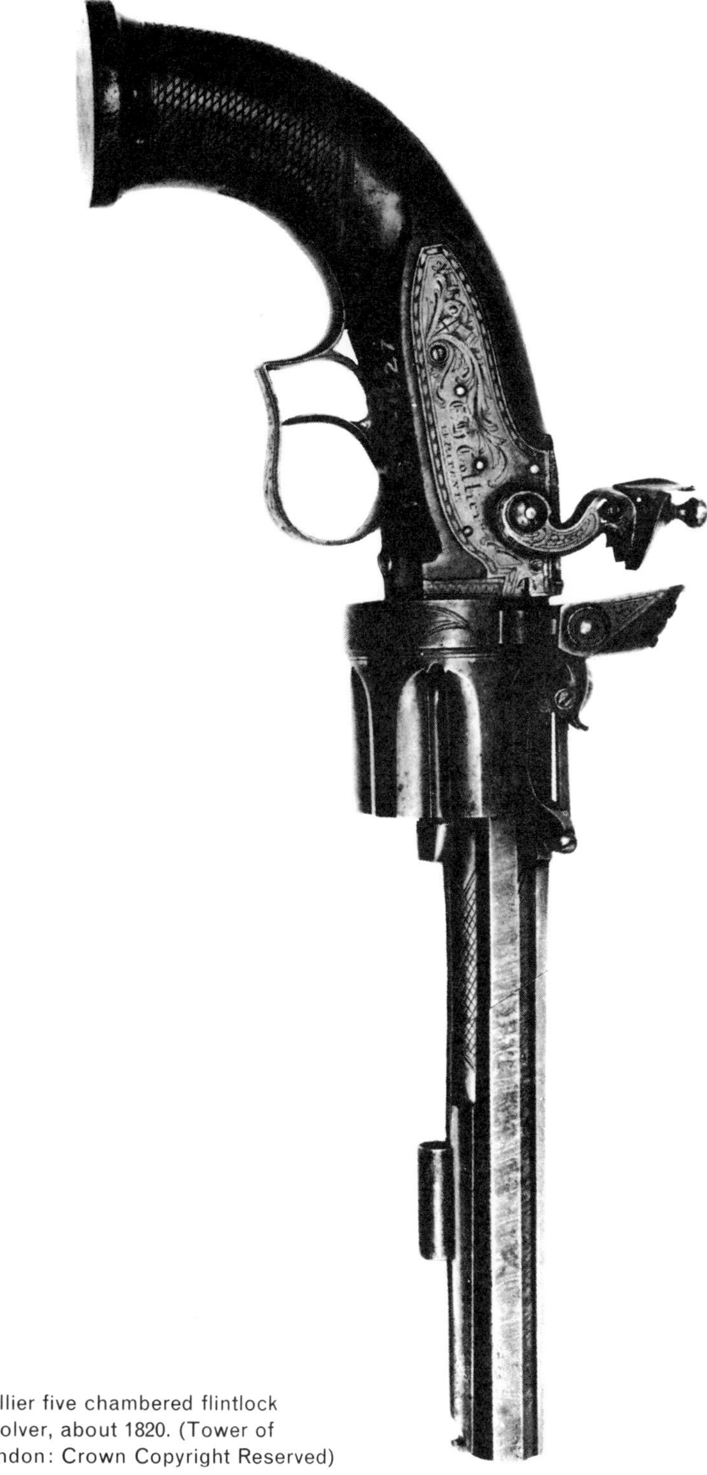

Collier five chambered flintlock revolver, about 1820. (Tower of London: Crown Copyright Reserved)

The hand rotated pepperbox (page 74) seems to have been the first revolving arm to employ the percussion cap system in England and, doubtless because of the low cost and ease of manufacture, this class of pistol continued to be made even after the development of more sophisticated weapons incorporating barrel rotation and a self-cocking system. In the absence of engraved presentation pieces, the actual date of manufacture of most percussion pepperboxes of English provenance is difficult to establish. The patent records of the period contribute little since many of the features employed were already in common use. In a patent (No. 8704) taken out by Joseph Rock Cooper in 1840, the claims made were qualified by the statement: 'I would remark that although I have necessarily shown many parts which are old and well known I do not claim the same and further in carrying out my several improvements variations may be made in some of the parts without departing from my invention so long as the modes of action claimed as my invention be substantially retained'. Since a similar disclaimer could equally well be incorporated into other patents referring to pepperbox type weapons, precise dating of many of the specific 'improvements' which appear during the period 1825–1855 is virtually impossible.

As, therefore, no understanding of the evolution of the revolving pistol can be obtained from the written record, the only alternative is to adopt a system of classification of known examples and to draw conclusions which may not be chronologically accurate but which will at least bring some order to what may appear to be haphazard trial and error on the part of the gunmaker.

The mechanisms employed can be divided into two distinct types. The first is the 'thumb cocking' or 'single action', the second 'self-cocking' or 'trigger action'. Although the term 'double action' is often applied to trigger action weapons, I have restricted its use to pistols which appeared somewhat later, and in which both trigger action and single action are combined. Otherwise an additional term such as combined single and double action would be needed to describe the vast majority of modern cartridge loading revolvers.

In the case of the single action pepperbox the mechanism was ready made and based once again on the box lock. The advantage of being able to rotate the barrels by the simple expedient of cocking the hammer had been appreciated for some time, and the use of a pawl linked to the hammer acting upon a ratchet at the breech end of the barrel group presented no difficulties. Since the idea was not a new one, the trouble and expense of securing patent protection—with the decided probability of expensive litigation—would not seem justifiable, but, in America, the brothers Barton and Benjamin M. Darling were in fact granted a patent for the first American pepperbox in 1836, and claimed the rotation of the cylinder by cocking the lock. As far as is known, patent protection for this idea was not sought elsewhere. The Darling central hammer self-rotating pepperboxes were crude and ungainly by contemporary British standards and achieved no success outside the country of their origin.

Single external hammer pepperboxes also appeared employing a lock mechanism which can be traced back to the Queen Anne pistol, and with mechanical rotation of the barrels once again a feature. This was accomplished by the pawl and ratchet method.

Four barrelled pistols were also made and, at this point, the distinction between the 'turn-over' system and the pepperbox becomes rather fine. These pistols were usually made with two hammers, the first and second shots being fired by pressing the front and then the rear trigger. The hammers would then be cocked and the barrels rotated through 180 degrees to permit the second pair of barrels to be discharged. If only one hammer was fitted, the barrels had to be turned through 90 degrees after each shot and the benefit of having two consecutive shots was forfeited.

Once mechanical rotation and the locking of the barrels had been perfected, the way was open for the next step, the self-cocking action. In America, the first of these mechanisms was patented by Ethan Allen in 1837. The lock was shown applied to a single shot pistol, but in practice it was applied chiefly to pepperbox pistols. A second patent granted in 1845 referred to improvements in the mechanism for rotating the cylinder and also to a feature which permitted the self-cocking mechanism to be operated manually if so desired—the true double action. Some later production models, lacking a spur on the hammer, continued to incorporate this type of mechanism but, in the absence of the spur, the value of the single action feature was dubious.

Allen conducted his business on strong family lines. He first went into partnership with his brother-in-law, Charles Thurber, and subsequently with another brother-in-law, Thomas P. Wheelock. Later, Sullivan Forehand and Henry C. Wadsworth joined the firm; both were sons-in-law and, when Allen died in 1871, they continued the business under their own names until Wadsworth retired in 1890. The firm, then trading under the name Forehand Arms Co., ceased operations in 1900.

Allen's firm is best known for the pepperboxes it manufactured until 1871. These were extremely popular, and the most common type was a self-cocking bar hammer six shot pistol, the distinctive feature of which was the sharply

Percussion bar hammer pepperbox by J. and B. Smith of London.

Percussion pepperbox marked 'Improved Revolver'.

angled butt. Calibres ranged from .28 to .40, and four and five shot variants were also made. A contemporary advertisement extolling the virtues of the pistol stated 'that it can be discharged six times with almost the rapidity of thought ... they can be fired the moment they are taken from the pocket with one hand only, and are no larger than the ordinary pocket pistol. Can be carried in the pocket without the least inconvenience. For travellers, housekeepers, Captains and planters they are an indispensable article as persons both male and female, can with this Pistol protect their lives and property if attacked by several persons.'

Other American pepperbox makers included Blunt and Syms and Robbins and Lawrence. Robbins and Lawrence manufactured an unusual pepperbox patented by George Leonard (US Patent No. 7493 of 1850) in which the striker revolved and the barrel group was fixed. In 1855 W. W. Marston of New York patented an extraordinary pepperbox mechanism (US Patent No. 13,581) employing thirty-three letters and numbers to identify components on his patent drawing. It is doubtful if any of these complex pistols were manufactured, but pepperboxes of a more conventional design will be found bearing the name of Marston in one style or another. A rarer type of American pepperbox, superficially similar to the Allen ones, was the Manhattan—manufactured with 3, 5 and 6 shot barrel groups and in various barrel lengths.

As the American philosophy of manufacture became increasingly associated with mass production techniques, the scope for individual variations lessened. Europe, however, lacked the machinery, the capital and the incentive to adopt similar techniques, and minor variations on the basic system continued to occur.

British bar hammer pepperboxes bear a decided resemblance to the American Allen type and, although many exhibit fine external workmanship and decoration, a plain and often rough finish is immediately evident once the mechanism is examined. British self-cocking pepperboxes made towards the end of the period when this type of weapon was popular show remarkable similarity to each other, and one is forced to the conclusion that, even if the individual gunmakers whose names appear in such profusion hand finished their wares, the major components must have come from a restricted source. As with the sporting rifle and shotgun, the inability of the small gunmaker to compete against an organised

Six barrelled pepperbox by J. Blanch and Sons, .400 calibre, self-cocking and with bar hammer. (Kilmarnock Museum)

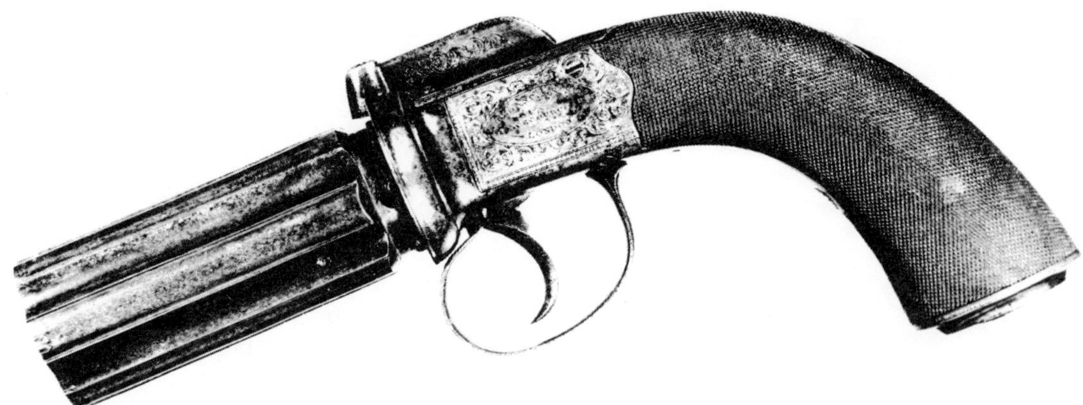

and specialist industry resulted, first of all, in dependence on the Birmingham trade for piece parts and later in complete dependence for the entire weapon. It was only in deference to past tradition, that the weapon would be engraved by the true manufacturer with the vendor's name and address. On the other hand, if a particular weapon became sufficiently popular—as the bar hammer pistols of the round butt type did in the 1840's—greater variety became possible. The demand was then sufficient to make individual manufacture economic, and the larger and more fashionable gunmakers could demand and obtain from the manufacturer detail design changes which would ensure for 'their' pistol some distinguishing feature which would no doubt appeal to a discriminating clientele.

Square butt pepperboxes of the bar hammer type appeared about 1850, and the decline in demand for the pepperbox over the next ten years is reflected in the falling standard of workmanship.

By reason of their construction, all bar hammer pepperboxes were fitted with nipples at right angles to the bore. Most employed a shield with a cut out for the hammer and provision to cap the nipples. With the combination of vertical nipples, sensitive caps (due to the relatively light hammer blow—a feature of the self-cocking action) and the enclosing shield, the possibility of an inadvertent multiple discharge was considerable. Some makers attempted to overcome this problem by recessing the nipples and dispensing with the shield.

A few British pepperboxes, by reason of their design or workmanship, are obviously the product of an individual maker, and such pistols, with their delightful blend of beauty and utility, immediately stand out from their contemporaries. Their rarity further enhances their value.

One such pistol was the enclosed hammer self-cocking pepperbox manufactured by Charles J. Smith of London under patents obtained in 1845 (British Patent No. 10,667). The lock mechanism was similar to the Belliss turn-over pistol (see page 73) and employed a horizontal striker linked to the tumbler and conventional barrel rotating and locking mechanism. The nipples were in line with the axis of the barrels and partitions were employed to separate them. A distinctive feature of the Smith pistol was the self-priming feature which depended on fulminate pellets instead of percussion caps, although the latter, by 1845, were well established.

The pepperbox was first and foremost a close quarter self defence weapon but, due to the limitations of design, its inherent defects severely restricted its usefulness. Except at point blank range the pepperbox was wildly inaccurate, partly because of the short barrels (the length was restricted by considerations of weight) and also because of the long and excessively heavy trigger pull required to operate the self-cocking mechanism. In addition, the centrally disposed hammer lay directly in the line of sight—a problem which was overcome in the case of pistols made on the Mariette system patented in Belgium in 1837. Little is known of Mariette, and such information as is available is scant and contradictory. It is even doubtful if Mariette manufactured any of the pepperboxes which bore his name and the most likely theory is that he was

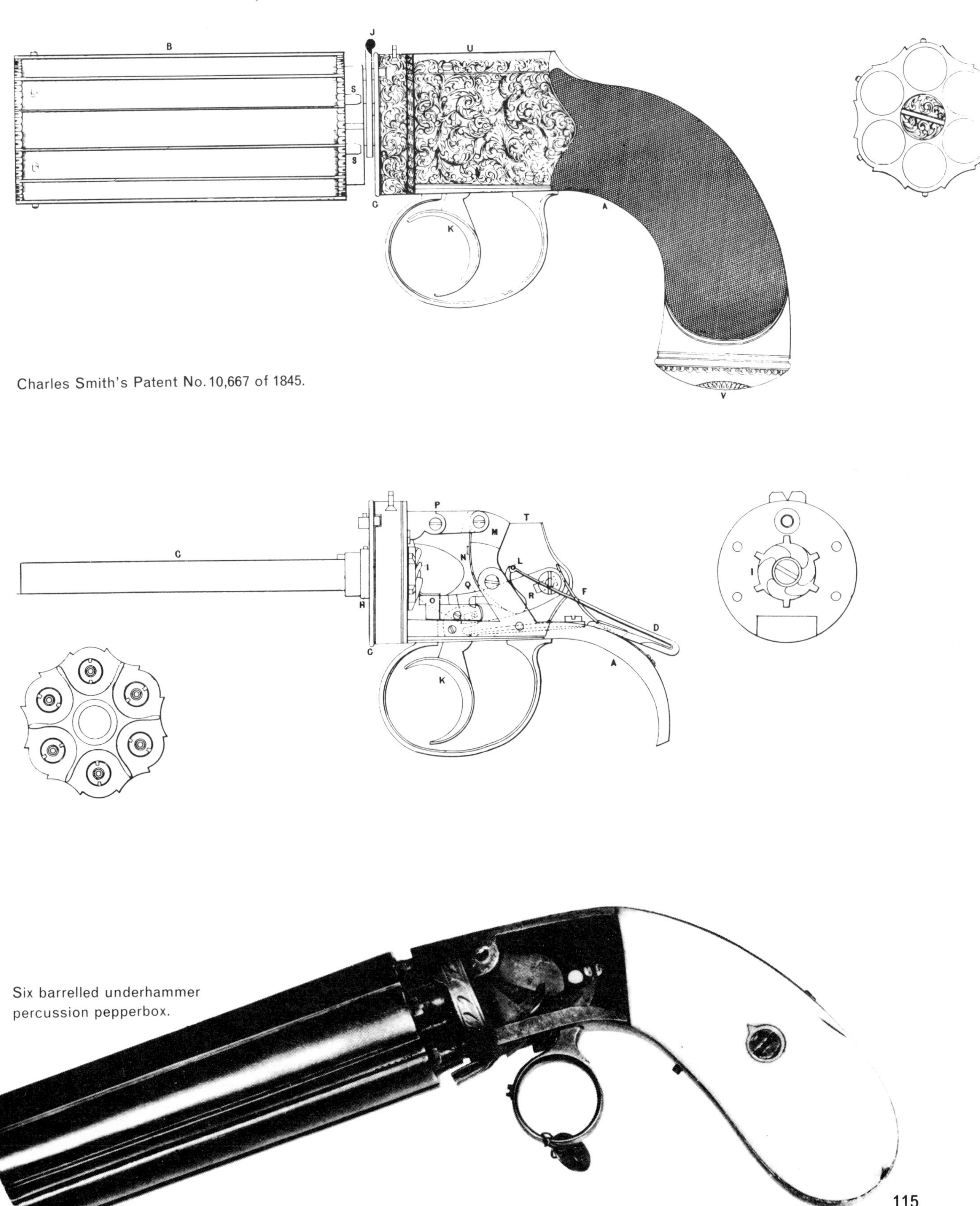

Charles Smith's Patent No. 10,667 of 1845.

Six barrelled underhammer percussion pepperbox.

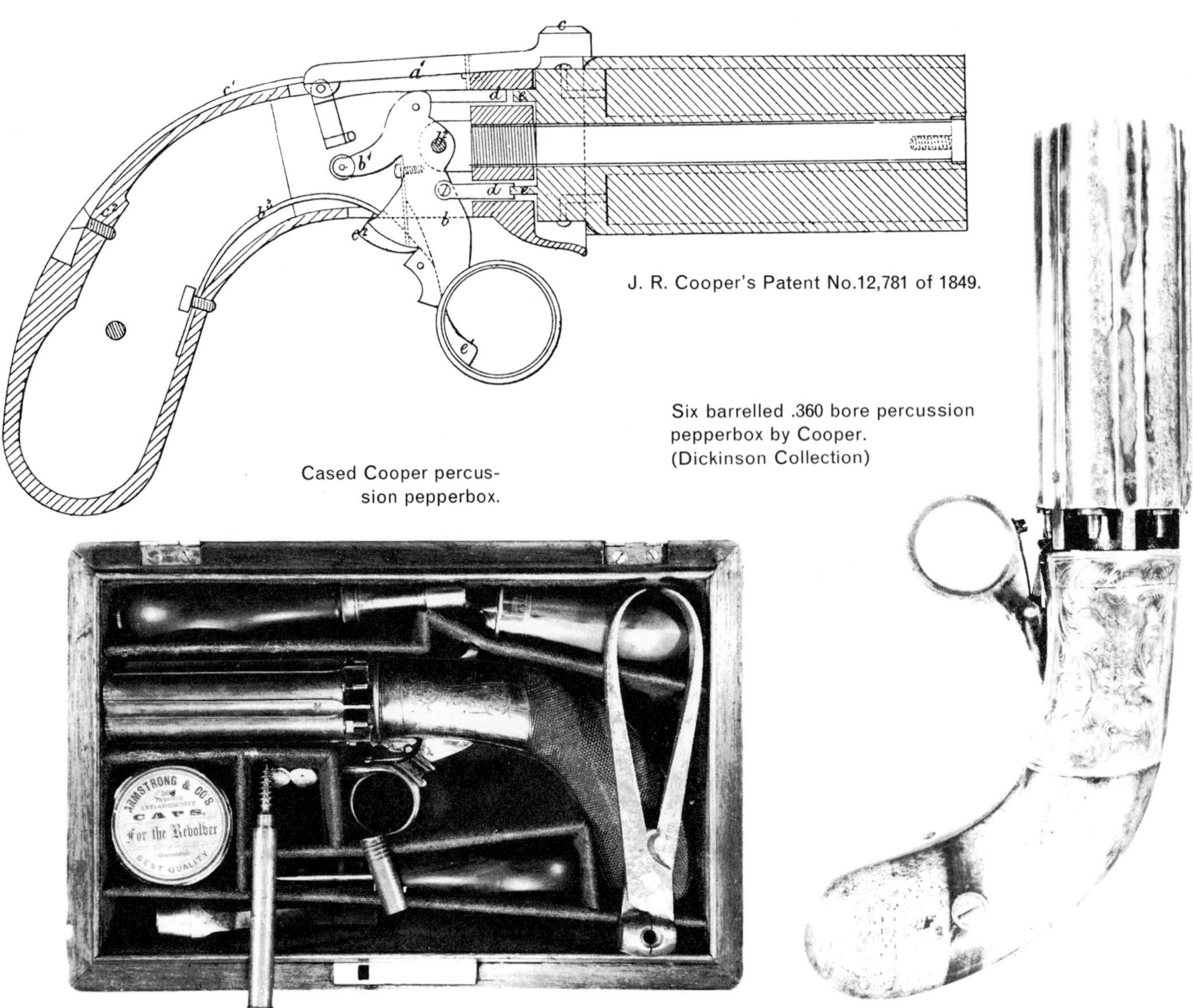

J. R. Cooper's Patent No.12,781 of 1849.

Six barrelled .360 bore percussion pepperbox by Cooper. (Dickinson Collection)

Cased Cooper percussion pepperbox.

the patentee only of many and varied pistols based on his system.

The Mariette was distinguished by the use of nipples in line with the axis of the bore and by an underhammer operated by a ring trigger. Due to the number of separate manufacturers, there were many variants, the most bizarre being the French and Belgian 24 and 18 shot pepperboxes which, because of their extreme bulk, might more accurately be described as flowerpots.

The Mariette system was not patented in Britain, but similar pepperboxes were manufactured by Joseph Rock Cooper and others, under Cooper patents. The majority of the pepperboxes bearing the legend 'J. R. Cooper Patent' or 'J. R. Cooper Patentee' employed the underhammer system attributed to Mariette. The one illustrated, a .360 bore with $3\frac{1}{2}''$ barrels and Birmingham Proof Marks, is not a particularly well made example. It also lacks the safety catch, and the nipples fitted are of a different pattern. In the twenty-one patents he took out over a period of thirty years, Cooper never in fact obtained protection for the most important of his pistols, and very considerable research would be needed to discover which of his patents actually protected original ideas and which relied more on intimidation.

The cased Cooper which bears no identification other than the legend 'J. R. Cooper's Patent' is typical of the series. Of .360 bore it is six barrelled and the barrel cluster is $3''$ in length. A sliding safety catch which bolts the barrel cluster is fitted on the top strap, and the only unusual feature is the rather ornate ring trigger. Acanthus leaf engraving is minimal but the pistol is well finished and the rounded butt is fully and carefully checkered. Furnished with the case is a standard W. Davies 'pincer' bullet mould, marked 105, casting a ball .355″ in diameter. There is a patch cutter marked 100 and a small, but incomplete, ramrod incorporating a screw worm for withdrawing the charge. A turnscrew and small bronzed powder flask complete the equipment. Caps manufactured by Armstrong and Co. 'for the Revolver' together with felt wads remain in the case due to the thoughtfulness, or perhaps the forgetfulness, of a previous owner.

Rarely encountered are the Cooper bar hammer pepperboxes usually marked 'J. R. Cooper Reg'd. 7 Dec. 1843'. This series of pistols will be found with both ring triggers and folding triggers. The mechanism used was conventional, and similar to that described in Patent No. 8347, Fig. 23, dated 1840, but again the protection sought did not cover the self-cocking mechanism.

From the marking 'Reg'd' (Registered) it is apparent that Cooper sought protection under the Non-ornamental or Useful Designs Act of 1843 which was possibly brought in to ease the difficulty of obtaining protection for minor ideas. The Patent Law Amendment Act of 1852 and the centralisation of Patent Offices lessened the need for the 1843 Act, and also simplified and cheapened patent protection, with the result that the number of patents granted in 1853 was nearly twice that granted in the previous year.

With the appearance of cheap, robust and accurate revolvers in the 1850's, interest in the pepperbox began to wane. Multi-barrelled pistols with non-rotating barrels continued to be made and, as replicas of the originals, are still manufactured today. Such pistols were and are cartridge loading and, although some people class them as pepperboxes, I personally prefer, on purely arbitrary grounds, to restrict the term to weapons with multiple barrels having parallel axes and capable of rotation.

Both pin-fire and centre-fire cartridge pepperboxes were also manufactured, but these will be

J. R. Cooper's Patent No.8347 of 1840.

FIG. 20.

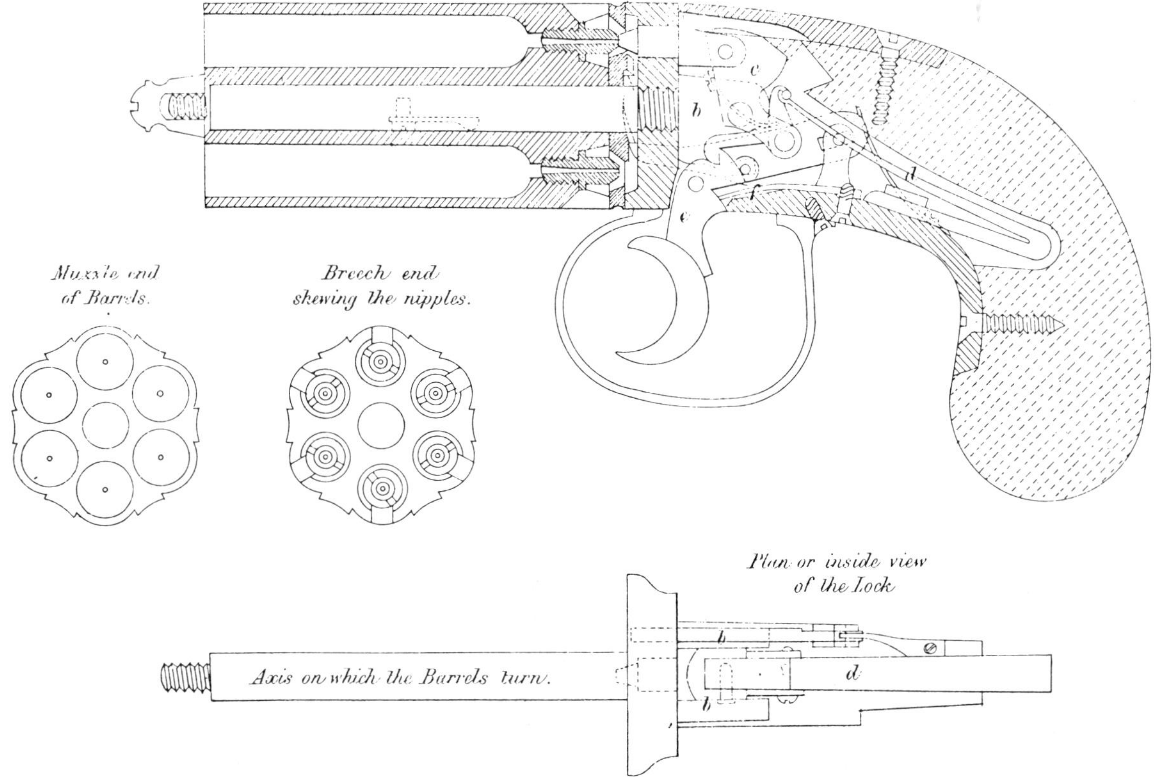

considered later. Entirely for reasons of cost, they were never as popular as the percussion pepperbox.

Before we examine the further development of the revolver, however, some mention must be made of the unique and short-lived 'transition' revolver, the link between the percussion pepperbox and the 'true' revolver with rotating cylinder and single barrel. Alternatively, it may be regarded as an expedient, a design based on a type of mechanism in common use and, in the absence of patent protection, available to anyone who wished to construct weapons along those lines. The transitional revolver perpetuated the basic defects of the pepperbox—heavy trigger pull and the use of unpartitioned nipples—but it had the important advantage of low cost and was simple to manufacture. Of more importance, the design was such as to permit the British maker to produce weapons in competition with the machine-made Colt by largely traditional methods which did not require substantial capital investment. One such competitor, Robert Adams, manufactured a revolver on the 'American System' of interchangeable components. The makers of the transitional revolver sought to exploit a market largely created by Colt, and they achieved a limited success by offering a wide range of revolving pistols to cater for all pockets. The finest examples were of high quality finish and were supplied in the traditional mahogany cases with all the accessories the wealthy had come to expect.

The desirable qualities of the revolver were increased accuracy and range, repetitive fire and a

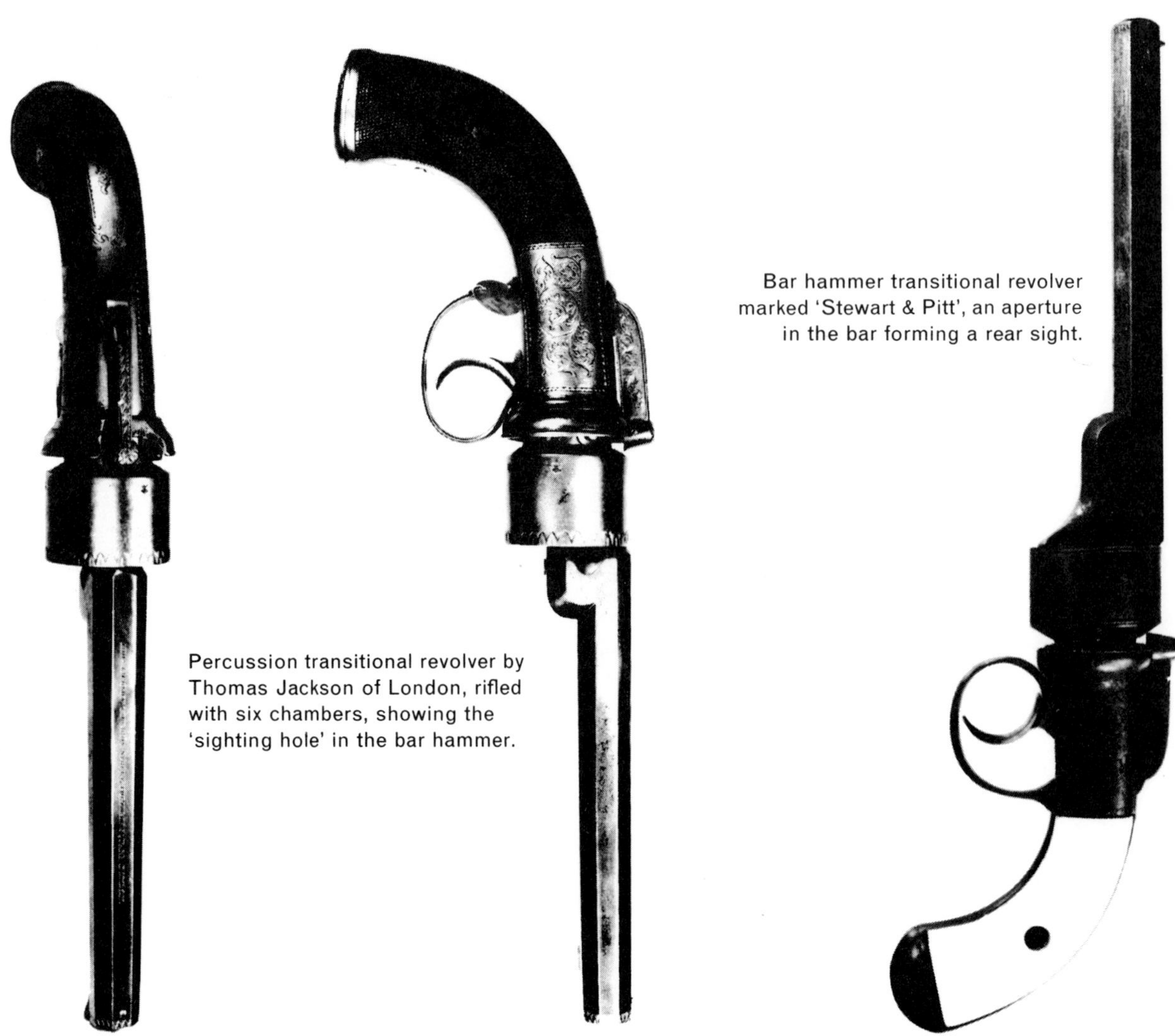

Percussion transitional revolver by Thomas Jackson of London, rifled with six chambers, showing the 'sighting hole' in the bar hammer.

Bar hammer transitional revolver marked 'Stewart & Pitt', an aperture in the bar forming a rear sight.

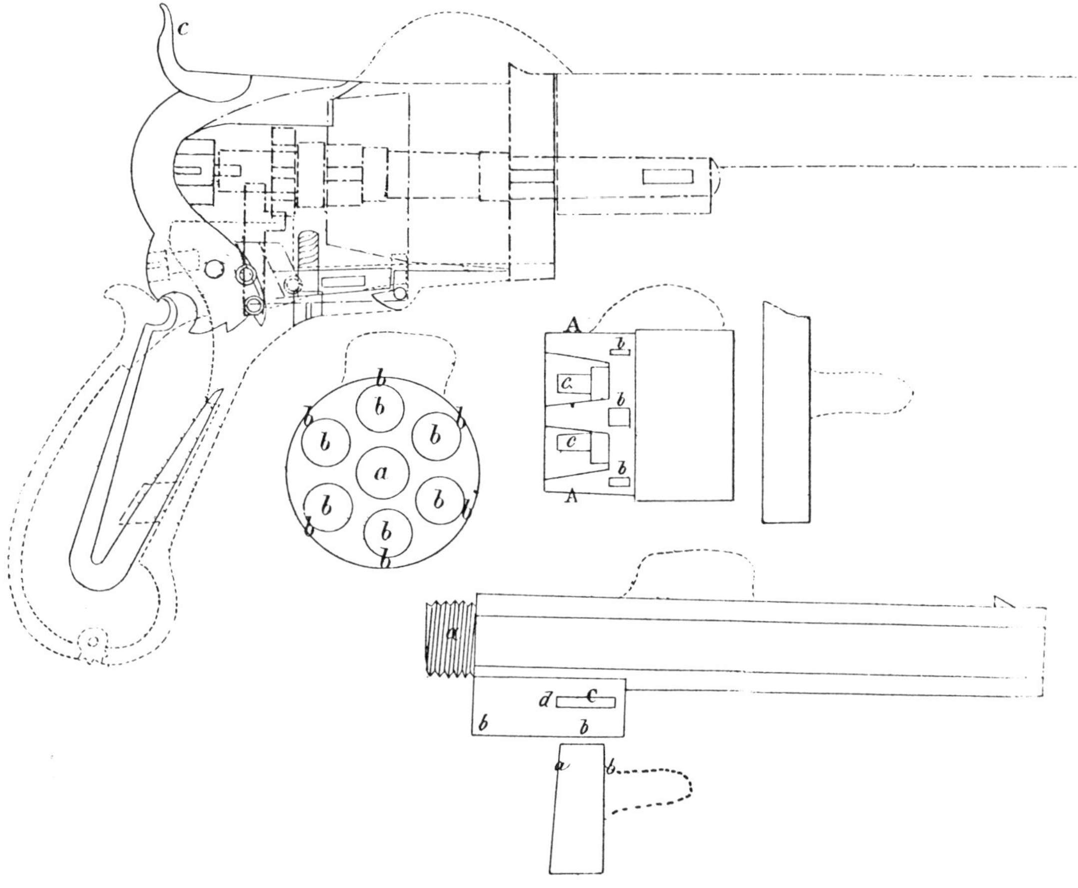

Colt's Patent No.6909 of 1835.

reduction in weight and bulk. These aims had already been achieved by Samuel Colt in America and his patent taken out in Britain in October 1835 (British Patent No. 6909) and his later American Patent No. 138 issued on 25 February 1836 had a decisive effect on handgun design.

The revolving rifle and pistol shown in the specifications were in fact never manufactured although the principles outlined in the specification were employed and strenuously defended by Colt until the expiry of the patents in 1857. He had first sought patent protection in Britain due to a peculiarity of British Patent Law which meant that, had he obtained protection in America prior to application in Britain, his patents in the latter would have been invalidated.

Colt's success was due to a number of factors: the care with which the specifications were drawn, the assiduity with which any infringement was contested, the simplicity of the mechanism itself, and the continued research and experiment to eliminate faults and to improve not only the basic design but also the methods of manufacture.

The features of the basic design were the rotation of the cylinder by cocking the hammer, the locking of the cylinder at the moment of discharge, the use of centrally placed nipples the axes of which were in line with the bore, and the use of partitions to separate the nipples and prevent simultaneous discharge. Later patents covered the loading and priming of the pistol without disconnecting the breech, and also the use of a lever rammer.

The employment of machinery both dictated the form of the pistol and permitted its manufacture in considerable numbers. It can therefore be said that the Colt was the prototype of all modern revolvers and also the first to be used on a large scale as a military weapon.

Since probably as much effort was expended in attempting to evade the Colt patents as was devoted to basic design improvements, it could be said that they had an inhibiting effect, but when they expired, the tremendous success of the Colt in America greatly influenced Colt's competitors and established the 'single action' as the American revolver.

The common British transition revolver was self-cocking, the frame and action entirely derived from the pepperbox, and in its simplest form it was cheaply and crudely made. The defects of the pepperbox were perpetuated, and since, as can be seen from the illustrations, the barrel was merely screwed on to the cylinder spindle, accuracy was not improved. The specimen shown is six chambered, the $4\frac{3}{4}''$ barrel rifled with 3 grooves, and the lands and grooves of equal width. Access to the lockwork is gained

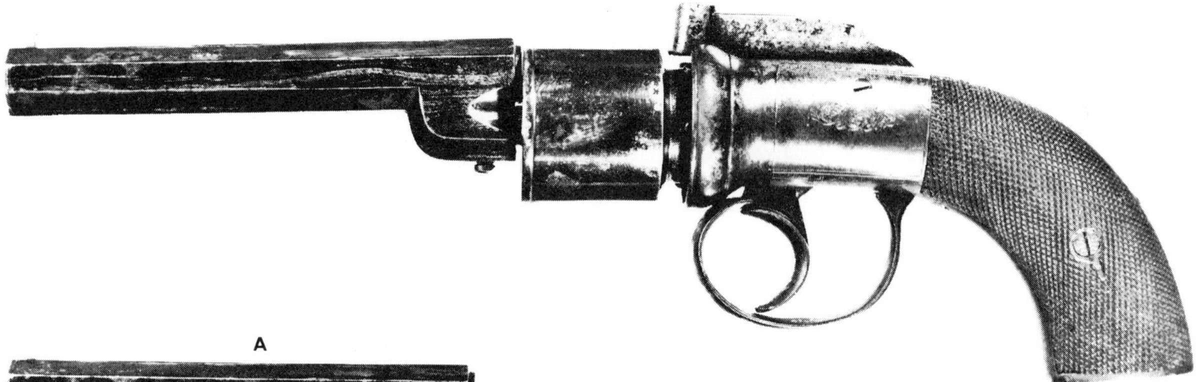

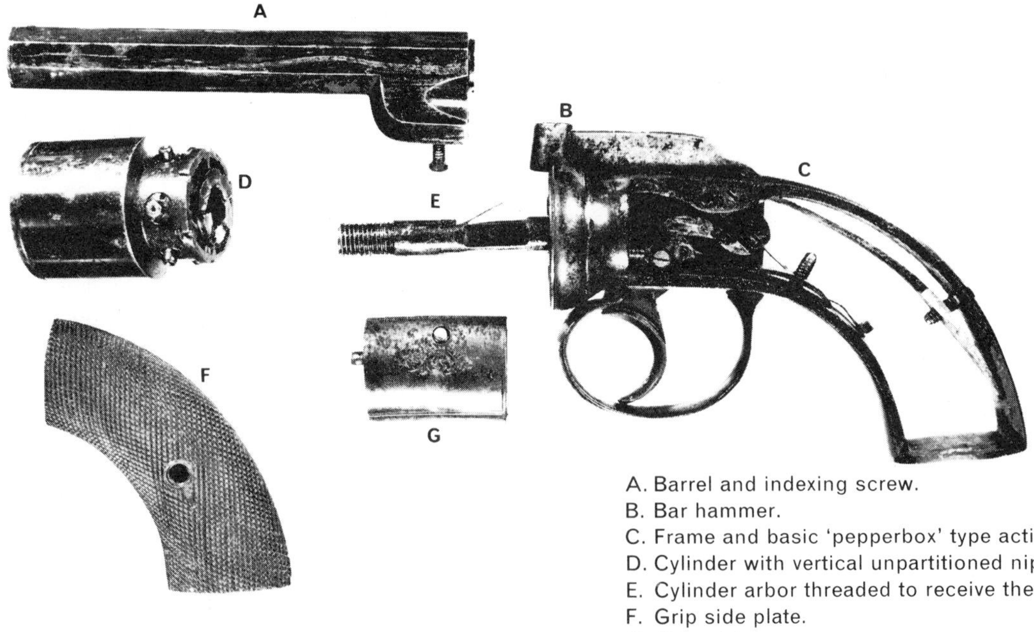

English transitional percussion revolver. (R. Dalgleish Collection)

The cylinder.

A. Barrel and indexing screw.
B. Bar hammer.
C. Frame and basic 'pepperbox' type action.
D. Cylinder with vertical unpartitioned nipples.
E. Cylinder arbor threaded to receive the barrel.
F. Grip side plate.
G. Side plate.

through a side plate attached to the frame by a single screw, additional security being given by the pin at the front of the plate which enters a recess in the frame. Cylinder rotation is achieved by the pepperbox 'lifter' bolted to the side of the frame engaging the ratchet at the rear of the cylinder. The cylinder is bolted by a pin linked to the trigger which protrudes through the standing breech and enters the elongated holes again formed at the rear of the cylinder. The slots cut in the periphery of the cylinder behind the vertical nipples are to provide a 'safe' position for the hammer either during loading or whilst a loaded pistol is being carried. A pin on the hammer engages these slots and so prevents cylinder rotation. The basic defect lies in the method of mounting the barrel. Additional rigidity was obtained by adding a bottom strap between the frame and the barrel, as can be seen from the illustration.

One man who set out to improve the transitional revolver was T. K. Baker, a gunmaker of Fleet St, London. In April 1852 he took out Registered Design No. 3230 which covered an alteration to the standard pepperbox bar hammer to permit thumb cocking by providing a long spur at the rear. The internal mechanism of the pepperbox was altered to eliminate the self-cocking action. Baker's 'improvement', however, stands slightly apart from the main line of development, where the next stage was represented by the single action transitional type which still owed something to the pepperbox, but was, in effect, an attempt to build a revolver on the traditional principles of British gunmaking.

The beautifully made example by J. Wilson, London (page 122) must have been an entirely satisfactory revolver since it is extremely easy to cock and points well. In addition, very adequate sights are provided and, as is common with many of the revolvers of this type, the hammer is both offset and angled to the right to permit an unobstructed view of the sights. Barrel length is $5\frac{3}{4}''$, the barrels are rifled with 16 fine grooves, and the bore is .440. The cloverleaf cylinder has six chambers of .460 bore, the mouth of each recessed to permit the breech of the barrel to enter and so ensure minimum gas escape. The cylinder reciprocates, and the forward motion is provided by a square sectioned bolt which passes through the standing breech and is impelled forward by the breast of the hammer. The return motion of the cylinder, which disengages the mouth of the chamber from the rear of the barrel, is effected by a horseshoe shaped spring attached to the barrel group, and it comes into operation when the hammer is cocked. There is no provision for a rammer; the usual practice was for a small wooden one to be supplied in the pistol case.

English transitional percussion revolver with bottom strap.

A similar pistol retailed by Alexander Martin of Glasgow (page 123) is, however, fitted with a rammer. Although mechanically similar to the Wilson pistol, one important difference lies in the fact that the nipples are deeply recessed and are, in effect, separated by partitions. This pistol again uses the reciprocating cylinder principle, and the figure 8 shaped spring can be seen attached to the barrel group. The square bolt which pushes the cylinder forward can also be seen protruding through the lock plate to the left of the cylinder lock.

Patents covering the gas seal principle had been taken out by Moore and Harris in 1852, and also by Philip Webley in 1858. The Webley patent described the use of a bolt pushed forward by the breast of the hammer similar to that employed on the Wilson and Martin pistols. The principal retailers of 'gas seal' revolvers were Baker, Lang, Witton and Daw and Parker Field and Sons, all of London. The Parker Field revolver illustrated (page 124) was sold complete with accessories in a splendid case inside the lid of which was the trade label. Such evidence as is available indicates that Joseph Lang was the first in the field with this design, but revolvers of this general type, both with and without the gas seal feature, will be found to bear the names of quite a numbers of retailers.

Percussion revolvers of the transitional type were also manufactured in Belgium and four examples are illustrated (page 125). The Colleye, in common with the remainder of this group, has horizontal partitioned nipples and a ring trigger, and the barrel, which lacks a rammer, is attached to the cylinder arbor by a cross pin or wedge. This method appears to have been a popular one since it was also employed by both Pirlot et Fresart and by J. J. Rissack, the two examples of whose work have attached rammers very similar to those employed by Colt. All four pistols are well made,

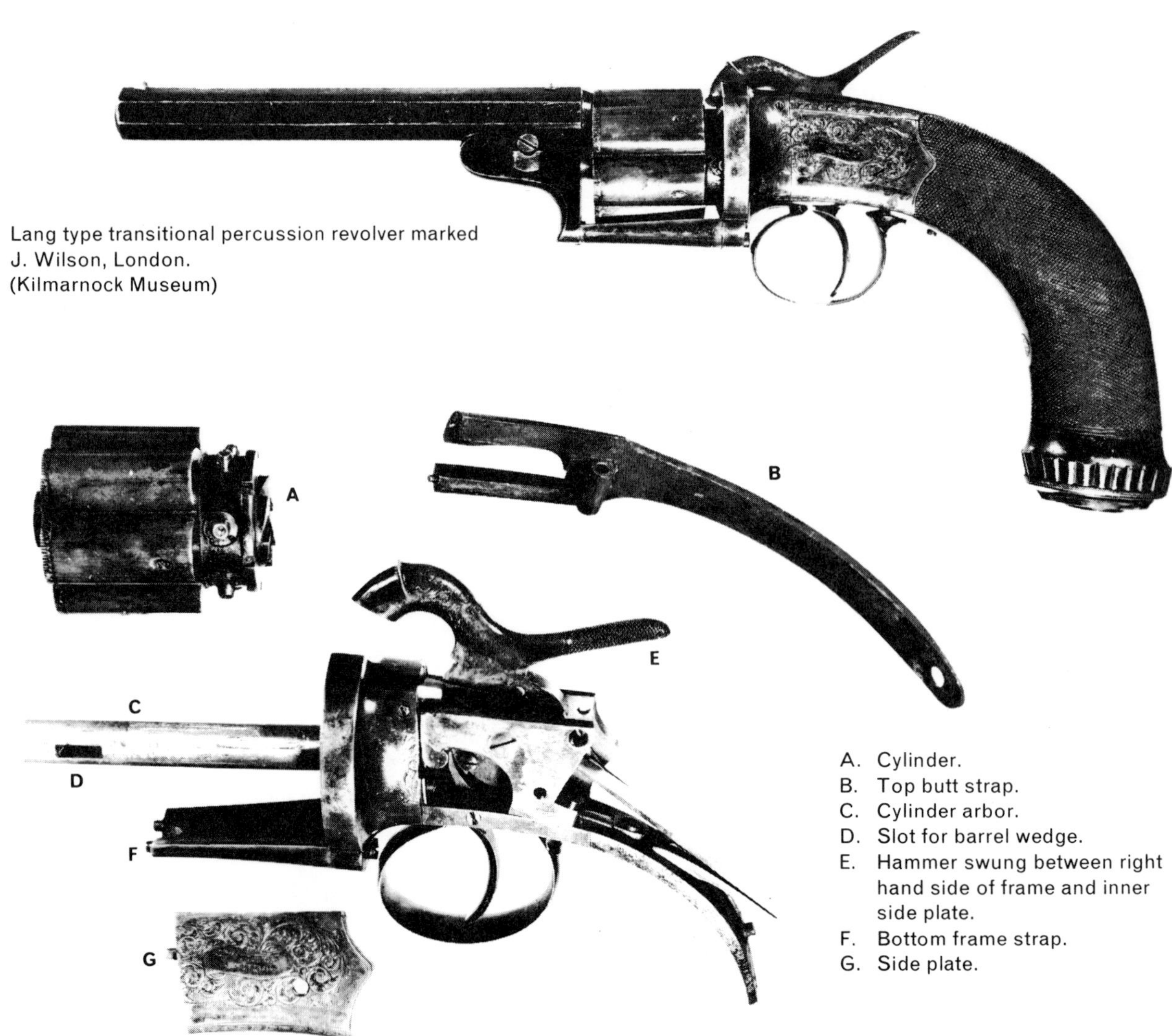

Lang type transitional percussion revolver marked J. Wilson, London. (Kilmarnock Museum)

A. Cylinder.
B. Top butt strap.
C. Cylinder arbor.
D. Slot for barrel wedge.
E. Hammer swung between right hand side of frame and inner side plate.
F. Bottom frame strap.
G. Side plate.

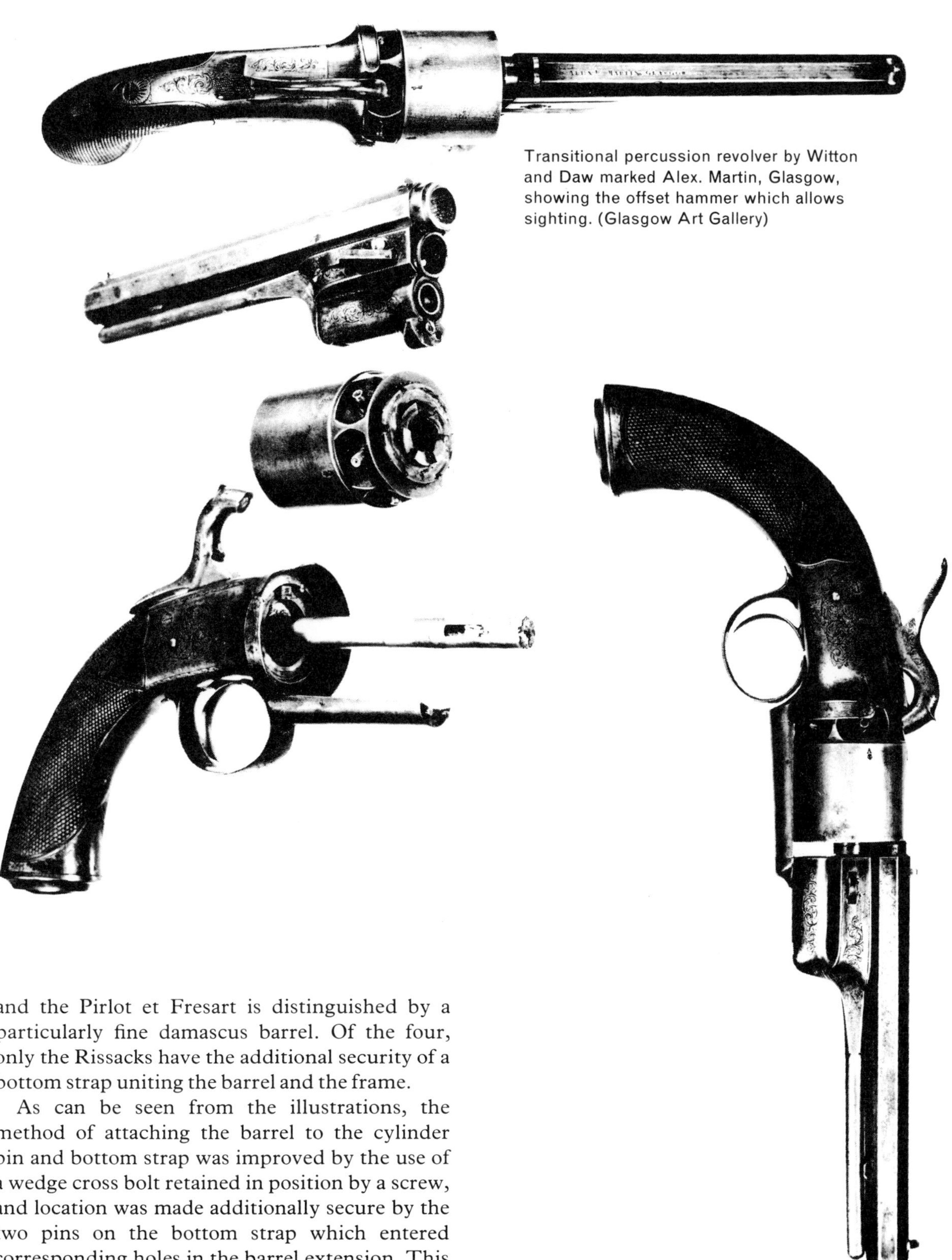

Transitional percussion revolver by Witton and Daw marked Alex. Martin, Glasgow, showing the offset hammer which allows sighting. (Glasgow Art Gallery)

and the Pirlot et Fresart is distinguished by a particularly fine damascus barrel. Of the four, only the Rissacks have the additional security of a bottom strap uniting the barrel and the frame.

As can be seen from the illustrations, the method of attaching the barrel to the cylinder pin and bottom strap was improved by the use of a wedge cross bolt retained in position by a screw, and location was made additionally secure by the two pins on the bottom strap which entered corresponding holes in the barrel extension. This system was similar to that employed by Colt on his 'open top' percussion revolvers.

Considerable ingenuity was devoted to the design of attached rammers. With the Witton and

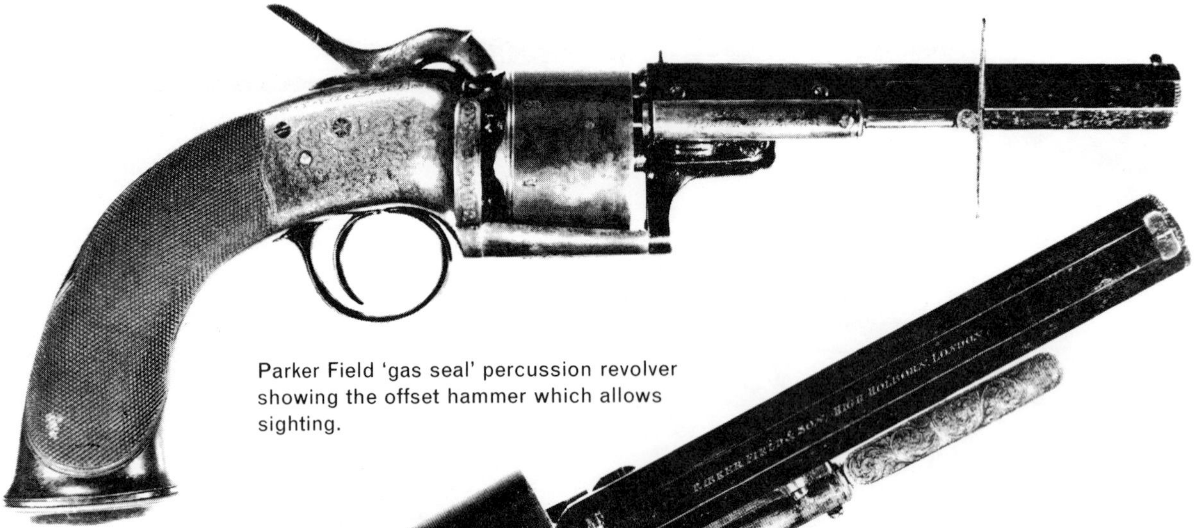

Parker Field 'gas seal' percussion revolver showing the offset hammer which allows sighting.

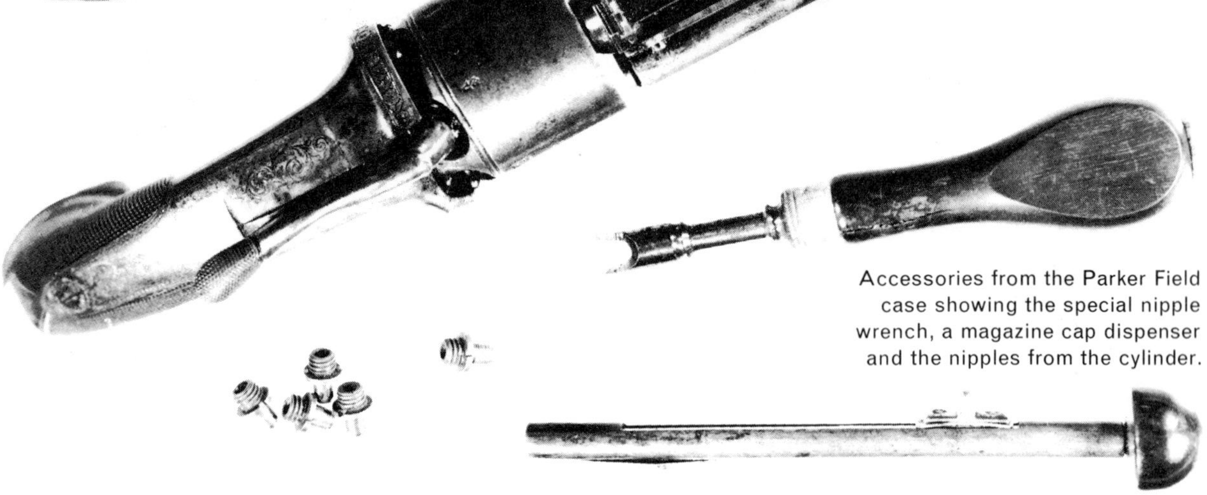

Accessories from the Parker Field case showing the special nipple wrench, a magazine cap dispenser and the nipples from the cylinder.

Parker Field trade label.

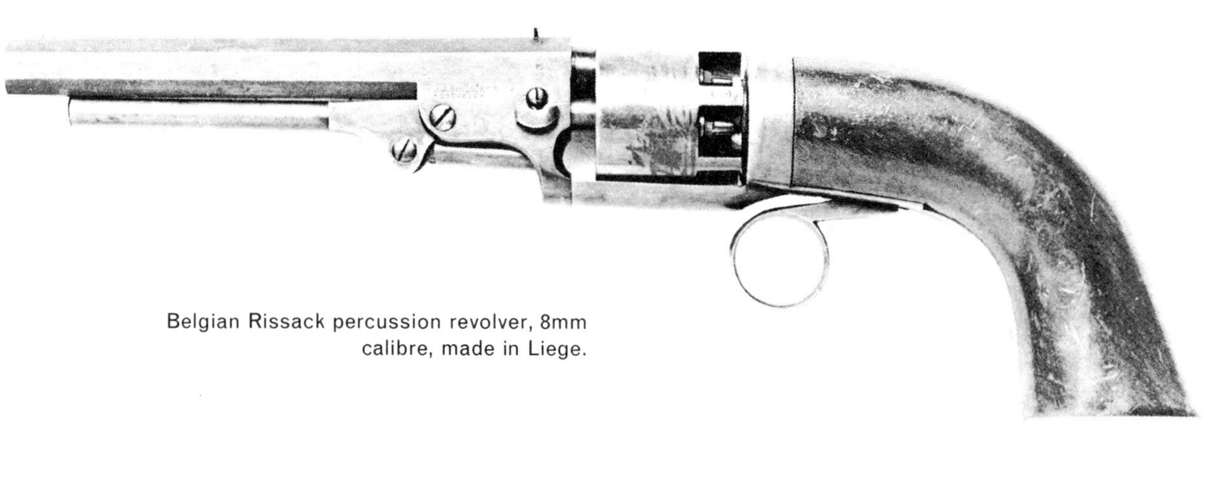

Belgian Rissack percussion revolver, 8mm calibre, made in Liege.

Belgian Pirlot et Fresart percussion revolver with attached rammer.

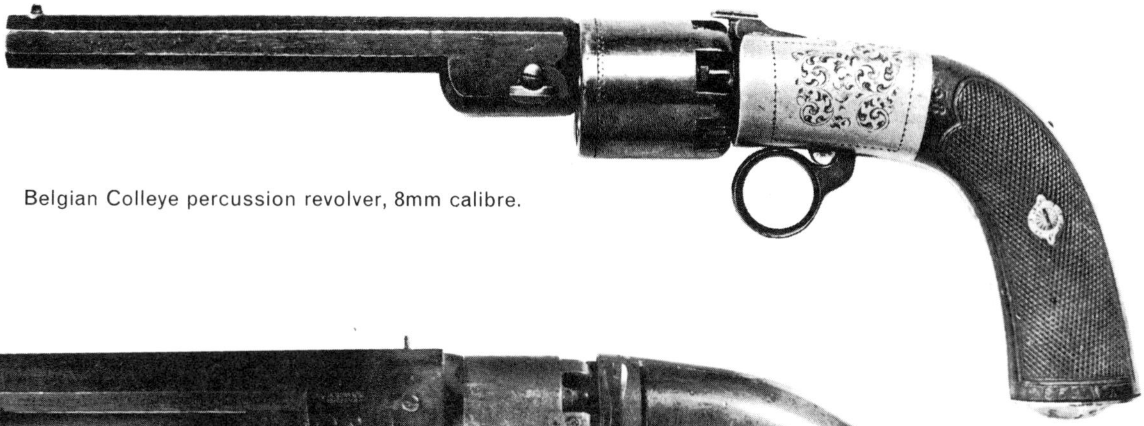

Belgian Colleye percussion revolver, 8mm calibre.

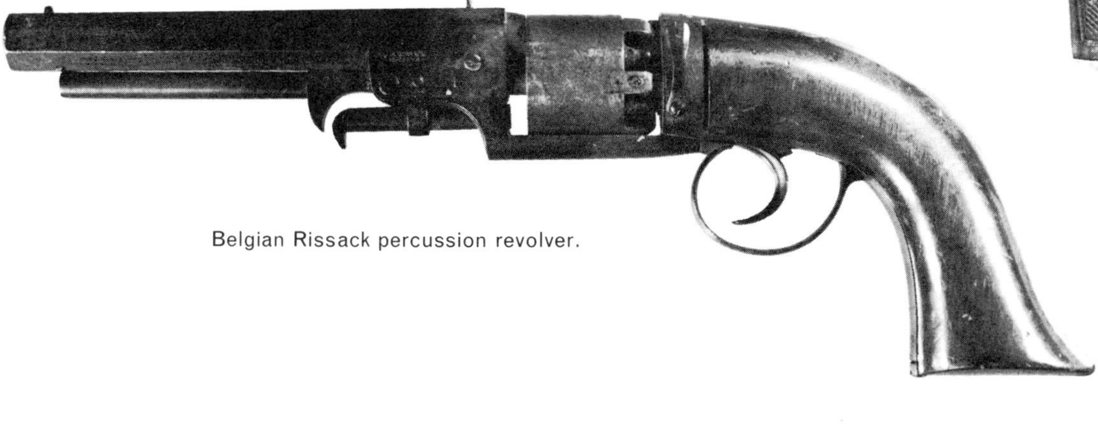

Belgian Rissack percussion revolver.

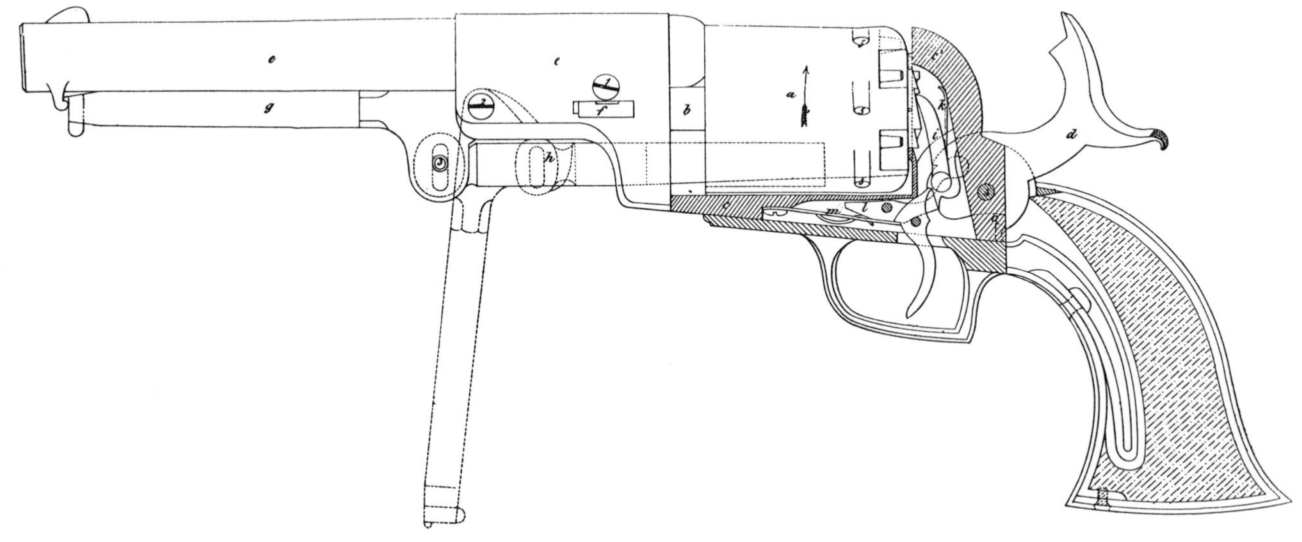

Colt's Patent No.12,668 of 1849.

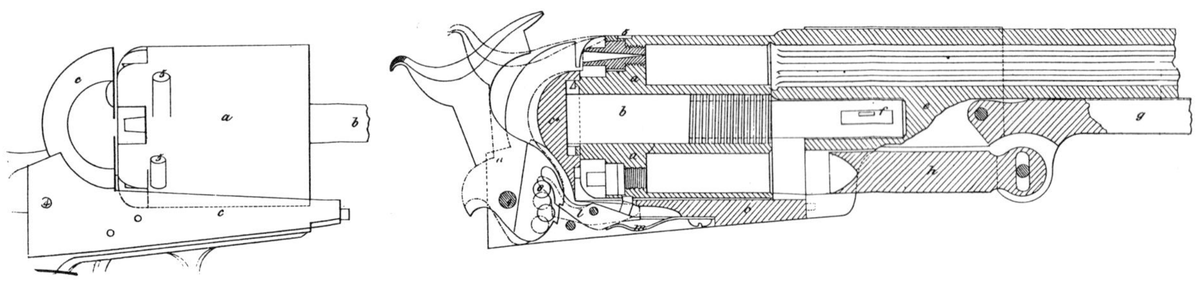

Daw, it was hinged under the barrel and, being a compound rammer, was capable of seating the bullet quite firmly. Simple plunger rammers were also employed and, on revolvers retailed by Parker Field and Sons, 233 High Holborn, London, they incorporated a 'T' shaped head which was hinged to fold along the barrel when not in use.

With many of the early revolvers it was necessary to remove the barrel before the pistol could be reloaded. In the case of the Colt Paterson models, a special powder flask with five nozzles was then placed in position over the cylinder, each nozzle corresponding with a chamber. With the powder introduced, the ball was placed on the mouth of the chamber and rammed home using a special combination tool, one end of which was inserted into the slot in the cylinder pin. The handle of this tool was provided with a removable head which, when unscrewed, discharged the nipple wrench, and which also contained the pricker provided to clear the nipple.

On later Paterson pistols a loading lever was attached and, as with British pistols with attached rammers, a special powder flask with an offset nozzle was provided to charge the cylinder 'in situ'.

The transition revolver as such was not a feature of the American pattern of revolver development. Some revolvers, such as the Butterfield, which employed a disc primer magazine patented by Jesse S. Butterfield on 14 June 1859, are definitely unusual to modern eyes. Butterfield revolvers were made by John H. Krider of Philadelphia and, like many other undistinguished revolvers, saw limited use during the American

Civil War more through force of circumstance than because of any real merit.

Based on volume of production, revolvers by Colt, Remington and Starr were the most important of those manufactured in America, and these pistols will be dealt with in the next chapter.

Notes to Chapter Five

A detailed survey of pepperbox firearms is given in *American, British and Continental Pepperbox Firearms* by Jack Dunlap (California, 1964). Reference should also be made to 'Seven for Six' by R. Bedford in *Guns Review,* (Vol. 7, No. 2).

Detailed information on British Transitional Revolvers will be found in *Black Powder* (the Journal of the Muzzle Loader's Association of Great Britain), Vol. 8, No. 3. This remains, with the exception of *The Revolver 1818-1865* by Taylerson, Andrews and Frith (London, 1968), the only definitive published up-to-date material on the subject and was the result of work by John Bell, John Philpott and P. A. Bedford.

The whole of this period is covered by J. N. George in his *English Pistols and Revolvers,* but George's treatment should be considered in the light of the additional material mentioned above.

Chapter Six
Colonel Colt and his Competitors

Samuel Colt did more to shape the course of the development of the handgun than possibly any other individual. He was an inventor and an engineer. He was able to choose the right man for the right job and he was capable of exploiting these personal factors to the full. Inventiveness and manufacturing capability laid the foundations of his success, and the combination of having the right product at the right price and of backing it up by vigorous salesmanship and effective publicity, produced what was, in effect, a new philosophy of business. Colt had one other advantage: he happened to be born at the right time.

The early history of the Colt enterprise has already been covered. The first revolvers manufactured by Colt were the folding trigger Paterson models, the .36 large holster pistol or Texas Model, the .31 and .34 belt models, and the .28, .31 and .34 pocket pistols. Later variant models were fitted with attached loading levers and could have different barrel lengths. Since the series was partly 'made by hand', minor differences can be found by the specialist, but these are of little significance except to the dedicated Colt collector. The year 1848 was an important one: during the course of it the new Hartford factory was established and a new series of revolvers was put on the market, the massive .44 calibre Dragoons. Mechanically, the Dragoon differed little from its predecessors except that it was a 'six shooter', whereas all previous Paterson models had had five chambers. Patient investigation by specialists has resulted in the classification of the Dragoon series and the following is that adopted by Serven.

1. *Whitneyville-Walker Dragoon Pistols.*

As mentioned earlier, the Paterson venture failed in 1842, and the Whitneyville-Walker pistols were the first to be manufactured following a lapse of five years. Credit must be given to Captain Samuel H. Walker, an ex-Texas Ranger and US Army officer, for inducing Colt to continue in the gun business. To what extent Walker influenced the design of the first Colt Dragoon is hard to say, but changes were apparently made before approval of the final design was given and manufacture of the pistol started at the Whitneyville factory of Eli Whitney Jnr.

Historically the most important of the Dragoon series, the Whitneyville-Walker had a 9″ barrel and the cylinder, marked 'Model U.S.M.R.' and 'Colt's Patent', was engraved with a soldier and an Indian fight scene. The barrel marking was 'Address Saml. Colt New York City'. As can be seen from the illustration, the frame was curved at the rear and there was a square backed brass trigger guard. The cylinder had oval locking slots and the trigger and cylinder bolt screws did not pass completely through the frame. The major variation was in the design of the latch for the loading lever. Initially the spring catch was located near the hinge as shown, but this was later altered in favour of an end latch. Finish on these pistols was case hardening for the frame, hammer and loading lever; the trigger guard was polished brass and the remainder blued.

2. *Whitneyville-Hartford Dragoon Pistols.*

Few of these pistols were manufactured and, since they were made during the period when production facilities were being transferred from

Whitneyville to the Pearl St. factory at Hartford, they can, in a production sense, be regarded as transition models. Finish on these pistols was similar to the earlier version except that the grip strap and trigger guard were sometimes plated. The barrel length was reduced to $7\frac{1}{2}''$ and the cylinder was also shortened from $2\frac{7}{16}''$ to $2\frac{3}{16}''$, resulting in a reduction in weight from 4 lbs. 9 oz. to 4 lbs. 2 oz. An end latch was used on the loading lever and the barrel wedge entered from the left instead of the right.

3. *Hartford Dragoon, First Model.*

Since it is likely that any necessary production or design alterations were made during the actual transition period, and that production was stabilised, the changes were only changes of detail. The major feature was that the join between the frame and butt was straight instead of curved, and that the trigger and bolt screws passed through the frame. The legend 'U.S. Dragoons' appeared on the cylinder.

4. *Hartford Dragoon, Second Model.*

The significant alteration on this model was the substitution of rectangular locking slots on the cylinder for the oval slots used previously. During the production run of this model, the original 'V' mainspring was changed to a flat spring and a bearing wheel for the spring was added to the hammer.

5. *Hartford Dragoon, Third Model.*

This was the first Dragoon to be offered in both $7\frac{1}{2}''$ and $8''$ barrel lengths. The traditional square backed trigger guard was changed to a rounded back, and two sizes of guard were made, one

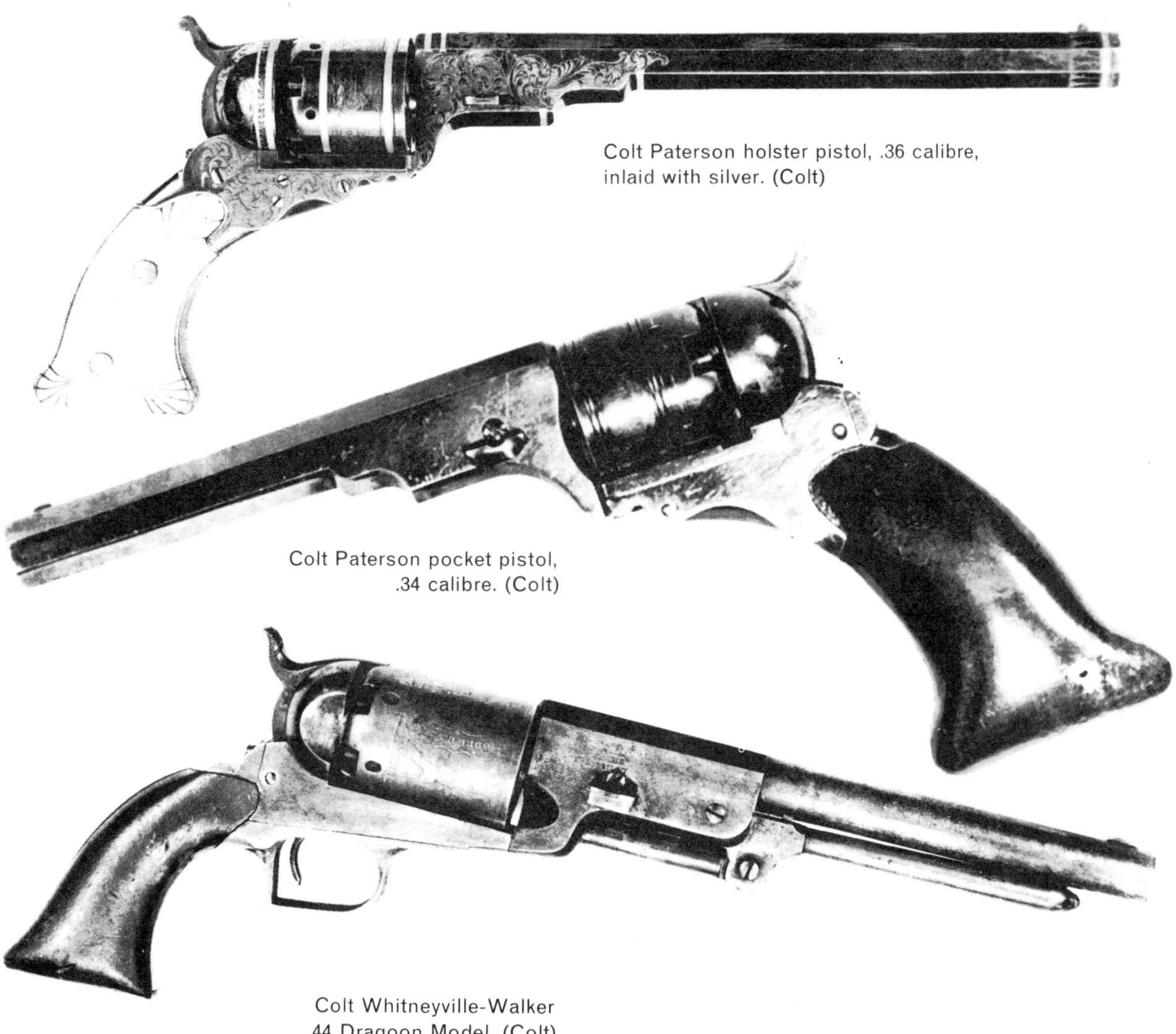

Colt Paterson holster pistol, .36 calibre, inlaid with silver. (Colt)

Colt Paterson pocket pistol, .34 calibre. (Colt)

Colt Whitneyville-Walker .44 Dragoon Model. (Colt)

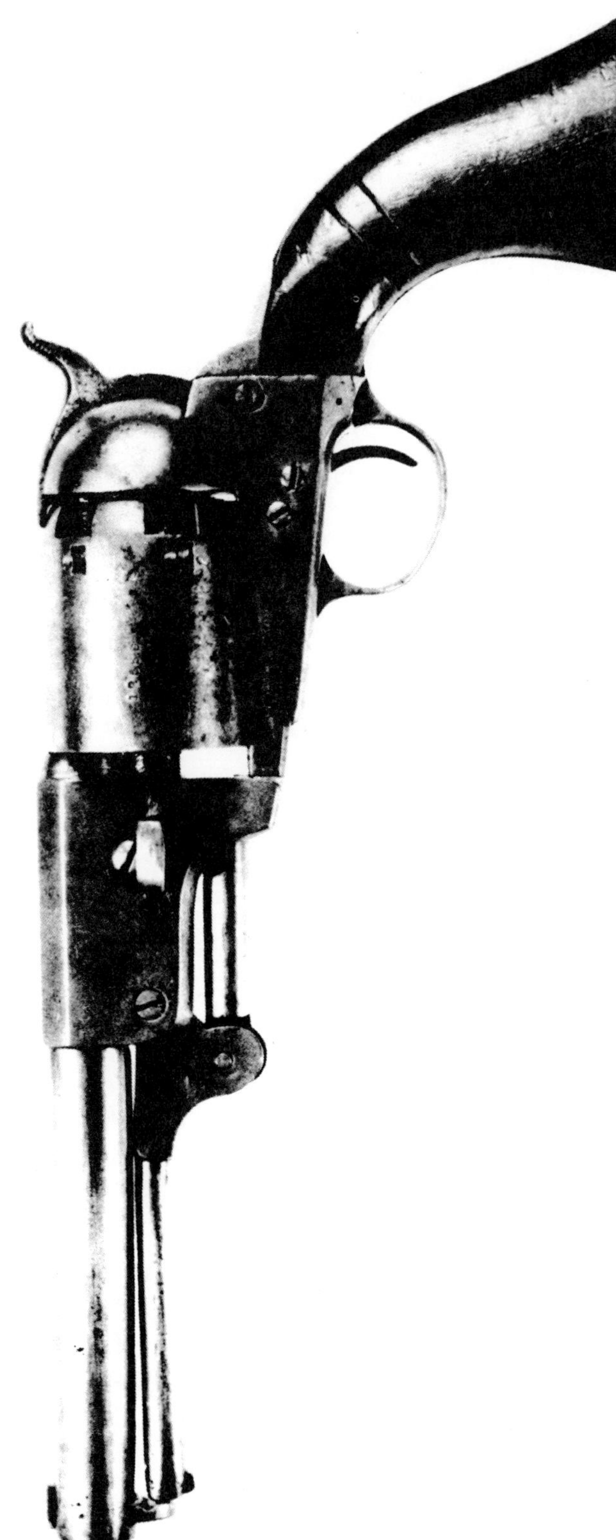

Colt Third Model, Hartford Dragoon. (Col. F. S. Allen)

larger than the other to permit use with gloves.

6. *Hartford-English Dragoons.*

These were Third Model Dragoons manufactured at Hartford especially for the British market. They were shipped to the London Sales Office and sold with English-made cases and English Dixon powder flasks.

7. *Belgian Dragoons.*

Colt licensed the manufacture of his pistols in Belgium, and the Liege-made Dragoons followed the Hartford pattern with variations to the type of barrel. Some will be found with full octagonal barrels and others with fluted barrels in the contemporary Belgian manner. In addition to those made under licence, many copies were manufactured; the licensing system proved difficult to operate, and the exercise was finally abandoned. It is interesting that, at one stage, Colt proposed to supply Belgian manufacturers with Hartford components for finishing and assembly—a practice subsequently adopted by American manufacturers to this day with rather greater success. It must, however, be remembered that Colt originated the idea.

8. *American Imitations.*

Most of the domestic copies of the Dragoon were made during the Civil War by manufacturers in Texas. Since they were largely hand-made, there were many variants, and these are of particular interest to the collector of Americana of the Civil War period and to the collector of Dragoon pistols in that they have been passed off as the genuine product. Provision for a shoulder stock was made on a few Second Model Dragoons and, on the Third Model, the recoil shield was altered on those intended for use with the detachable shoulder stock. One shoulder stock was issued with each pair of pistols, the stocks being marked with the serial numbers of both pistols.

The Dragoon was manufactured between 1847 and 1860, but continued to be listed by Colt until 1863.

Production of pocket pistols at Hartford began with the 'Little Dragoon', a five chambered .31 calibre pistol supplied in 3″, 4″, 5″ and 6″ barrel lengths. Early models had no loading lever and the end of the cylinder arbor was recessed so that the arbor could be used to seat the ball in the cylinder, the barrel, of course, having been removed. The first series, characterised by square backed trigger guards, was replaced

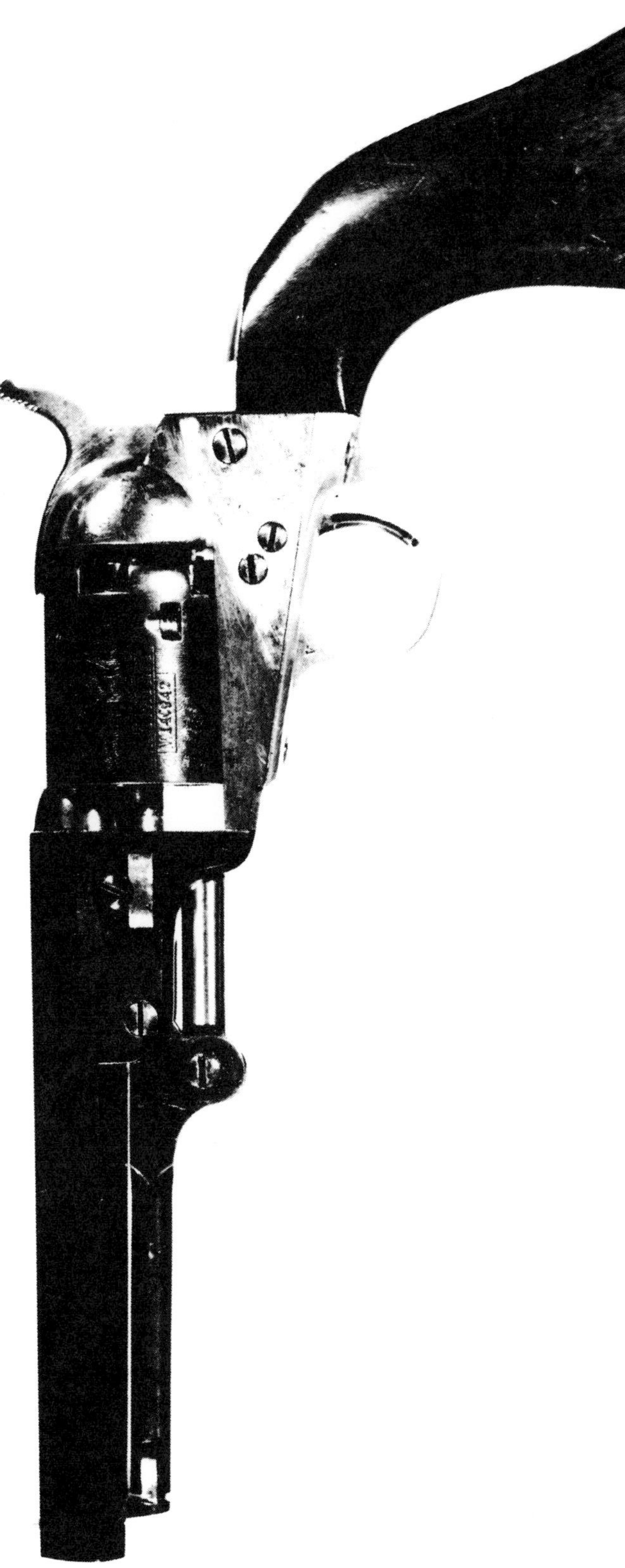

Colt Model 1849 .31 pocket pistol.

by the so-called Model 1849 Pocket pistol which, in general, followed the design of the previous model, although there were differences in detail. The illustration shows the common version of this pistol, with octagonal barrel and five chambered cylinder (some six chambered pistols were made in 1860) engraved with the stage-coach hold-up scene and marked with the number of the pistol and 'Colt's Patent'. Six variations in the marking on the barrel have been recorded, two of which are for London Colts.

The next pistol in the series was the Navy Belt Model or Model of 1851, and this can be regarded as the big brother to the pocket model. Of .36 calibre, it was six chambered and was usually fitted with a $7\frac{1}{2}''$ barrel. Early models had the square backed trigger guard and an open notch instead of a slot for the barrel wedge, the wedge being above the wedge screw instead of below. Cylinders were engraved with the scene of the Naval engagement between ships of the Texas Navy and the Mexican Navy, together with the date of the battle, 16 May 1843.

Navy pistols made in Colt's London factory carried British Proof Marks and those supplied to the British Government carried additional acceptance markings such as 'W.D.' and the broad arrow. Some Navy pistols were made for use with detachable shoulder stocks, and the recoil shield was notched and the frame fitted with stud screws.

Possibly the least attractive of the Colt percussion pistols was the Model of 1855, the Root side hammer pocket pistol. The basic patent for this pistol was granted to Elisha K. Root on 25 December 1855 (US Patent No. 13,999). Root, as we saw in Chapter Four, designed much of the machinery in the Colt factory, but his pocket pistol, from the standpoint of both design and serviceability, was not as good as the other percussion pistols made at Hartford. The Model 1855 pistols were, however, the first Colt revolvers to have a top strap over the cylinder and a screw-in barrel, and they were also the first to use the 'creeping' rammer. Made in both .28 and .31 calibre and with barrel lengths of $3\frac{1}{2}''$ and $4\frac{1}{2}''$, the sheath trigger and external hammer were distinctive features.

Not all of Colt's ideas were successful. There is, in the Colt collection, an experimental pistol where the cylinder is rotated by 'curved diverging grooves', a method that will be encountered later. Colt, however, did not develop the idea, though he went to the trouble of protecting it by

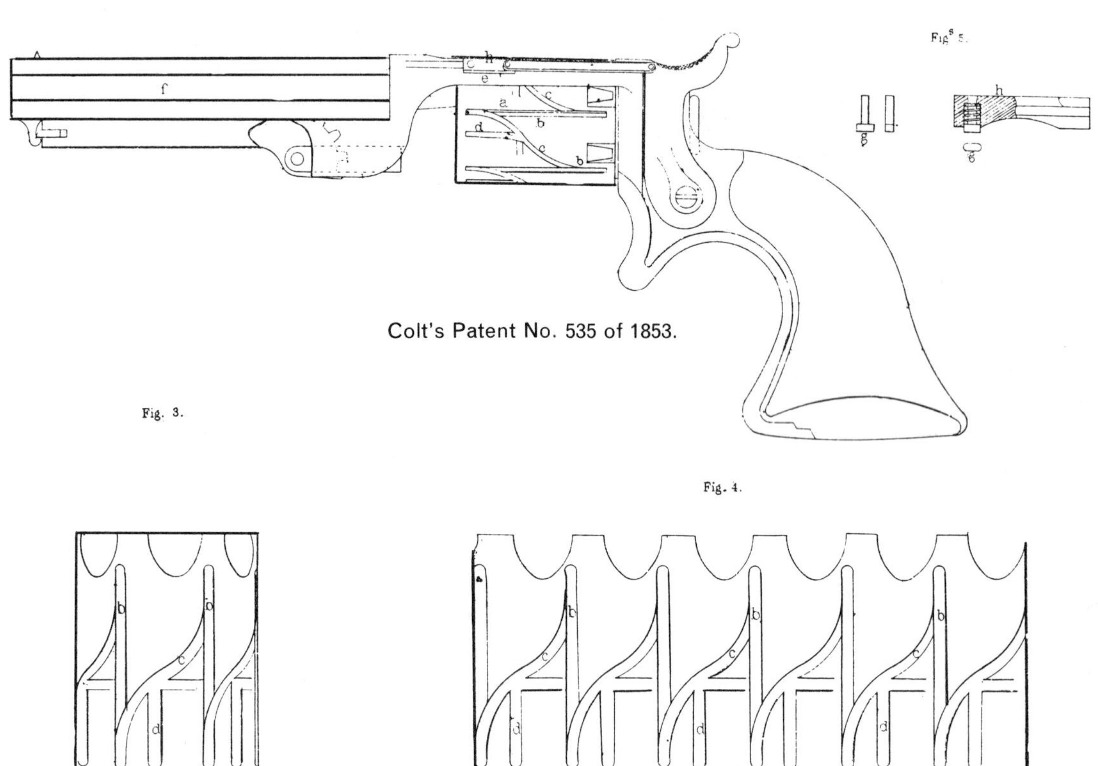

Colt's Patent No. 535 of 1853.

patent (British Patent No. 535 of 1853).

Without doubt the most widely used of all the Colt percussion pistols, the Army Holster Pistol Model of 1860 (34% of the pistols purchased by the US Ordnance Dept. during the Civil War were of the 1860 Model) featured the 'streamlined' look. Of .44 calibre and designed to replace the famous Dragoon, the Army was similar in internal construction, the only design alteration of significance being the adoption of the 'creeping' loading lever used on the Roots side hammer pistol, instead of the hinged type used previously. In order to accommodate the larger calibre, the cylinder was of greater diameter at the front with a rebated section at the rear. A variation was the use of a fluted instead of a plain cylinder, though this meant losing the ship scene that the latter, like the Navy pistols, usually carried.

Originally 7½″, the barrel length was later standardised at 8″ and, at 2 lbs. 11 oz., the weight showed a significant reduction from the 4 lbs. 2 oz. of the Dragoon. The 1860 Army Holster pistols provided for a detachable shoulder stock and there were two sizes of grip—one the Army size, the other the smaller Navy size. Manufacture of these pistols began in 1860 and was discontinued in 1872 after approximately 200,000 had been made, including cartridge conversions.

The round barrelled Navy Belt pistol or Model of 1861 was very similar to the 1860 Army. Of .36 calibre instead of .44, the cylinder lacked the rebated rear, and the bar of the frame was not cut away. The barrel length was standardised at 7½″ and the round cylinder bore the legend 'Colt's Patent' and the serial number of the pistol. The ship scene was again used and the marking at the top of the barrel read 'Address Col. Saml. Colt New-York U.S. America'.

In my opinion, this is one of the most pleasant of the Colt percussion pistols to handle. Although the one I have bears no trace of its original finish, it is very tight and shoots extremely well, bearing in mind the absence of proper sights. As with all of the series, the rear sight is formed by a notch in the hammer and any variation in the hammer position causes an alteration in elevation.

The size and shape of the grip has, in my view, never been bettered for a single action revolver and, carried forward without alteration, it was used on the famous Colt Single Action Army cartridge revolver.

Two other pistols must be included in the percussion Colt series, the first being the five chambered .36 calibre Pocket Pistol with the

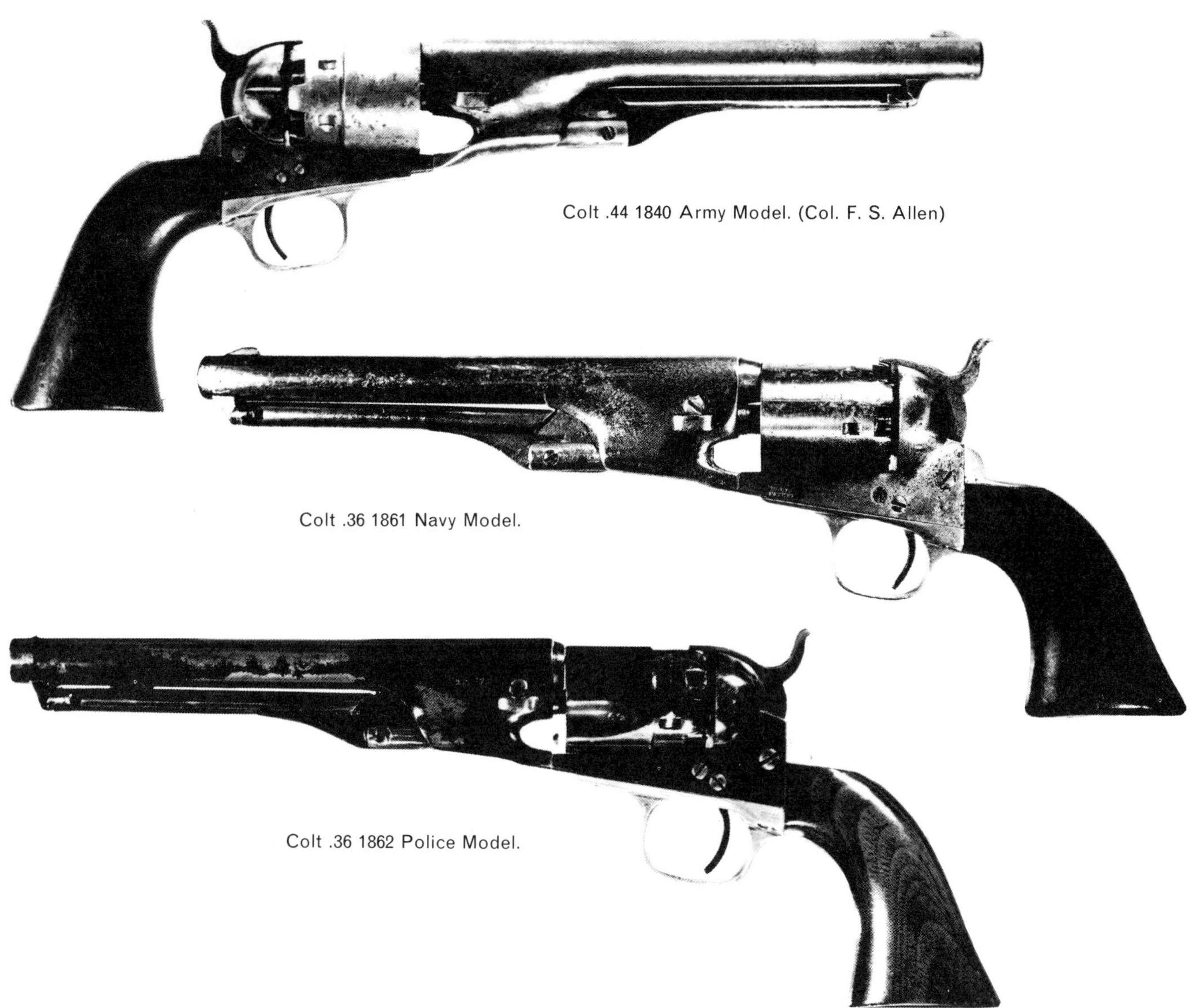

Colt .44 1840 Army Model. (Col. F. S. Allen)

Colt .36 1861 Navy Model.

Colt .36 1862 Police Model.

rebated round cylinder. Furnished with 4½″, 5½″ and 6½″ barrels, this was based on the 1849 .31 pocket pistol, the original frame being 'stepped down' in a similar manner to the 1860 Army to accommodate the rebated cylinder.

The second—and the last of the percussion Colts—was the Police Pistol Model of 1862. This pistol again shows how, with standardised production, changes could be wrought and new models introduced with a minimum of re-tooling or disturbance to manufacture. The frame of the Police Model was identical to the .36 calibre Pocket Pistol, the differences being in the use of a round barrel and a fluted, rebated cylinder. The example illustrated has a 6½″ barrel, this being the longest standard length, though it was also available with 4½″ and 5½″ barrels. Despite the fact that the five chambered Police Model lacked the extra shot of the Navy, it was lighter and handier and apparently highly regarded by officers during the Civil War. The specimen shown is finished entirely in blue with the exception of the sides of the hammer and the polished brass of the back strap and trigger guard. Markings are the usual address on the top of the barrel, 'Pat. Sept. 10th. 1850' on the cylinder and, on the left hand side of the frame, 'Colt's Patent'. The calibre marking is on the left hand side of the trigger guard, '.36 Cal', and the pistol also carries London Proof Marks both on the barrel and between each chamber of the cylinder.

The basic US patents of Sam Colt expired in 1857, and the competition which had hitherto been kept at bay quickly appeared keen to take advantage of, and gain a share in, a most lucrative market. Domestic competition was provided by

Remington, Starr, Savage, Whitney and many others. Some of the models which appeared were almost direct copies of the Colt—notably those made by the Manhattan Fire Arms Mfg. Co. and by the Metropolitan Arms Co., both of New York. During the Civil War, copies of the 1851 .36 Navy were made by manufacturers in the Confederacy—for example Griswold and Gunnison and Rigdon and Ansley, both of Georgia.

Colt also established a factory in Britain to manufacture his pistols, and the history of this enterprise will be dealt with in the next chapter.

The story of Colt in Europe is somewhat complex. The majority of Colt pattern pistols were made in Belgium at Liege, some under Colt patents. Others were copies and, as might be expected, there was a wide variation in quality. Colt's European patents were obtained in 1849 and were valid for fourteen years. His first agent in Belgium, Devos-Sera, was appointed by William E. Newton, a London Patent Agent and the man who protected Colt's European interests. The Belgian gunmakers objected to the high prices they had to pay for Colt components—whether from Hartford or London—and they complained that their profits were not high enough. Added to the licensing problems, Colt had to fight patent infringements and, in an attempt to make his position more secure, a new Belgian agent was appointed, J. Sainthill of Brussels. In spite of his efforts, however, Colt's interests in Europe were more productive of trouble than profit and, with the closure of his London factory in 1856, Colt decided to cut his losses and concentrate manufacture at the Hartford factory. Of the Belgian 'Colts' made, those by N. Gillon were probably the best and an example of his work can be seen in the Tower of London Collection.

Six chambered percussion revolver by Ancion et Cie. of Liege. Not a true Colt copy, but a competitive pistol. (W. A. C. Paton Collection)

Of all the European legitimate Colt revolvers, pirates, fakes and imitations, those made by the Kaiserlich-Königlich Machine Works at Innsbruck in Austria are perhaps the best documented.

In 1849 the KK Machine Works had received a sample Colt revolver from America, together with the manufacturing rights for a period of five years. A few months later, in August, an Austrian patent was granted to Joseph Ganahl, Chairman of the Board of Directors, which gave him the right to manufacture Colt revolvers and rifles, the revolver submitted being the 1848 Dragoon.

Apparently the factory manufactured the Dragoon, but modifications kept the weight down to just over 2 lbs. and the proportions were reduced to more manageable size. Two production variants have been identified, the differences being in the trigger guard and butt length.

Following approval by the Austrian Board of Ordnance, Innsbruck-manufactured revolvers were issued to the Austrian Imperial Navy, or Kriegs-Marine, and the pistols and accessories were marked 'KM' under a crown and appear to have been used by the Austrian Navy during the 1860's. The pistols were supplied to 'other ranks' with an open top holster of distinctly modern design, provided with pockets to accommodate the capper and either a spare loaded cylinder or ammunition in the form of packets of cartridges. Markings on the Austrian Colt in addition to the Government 'KM' included the legend 'KKP Maschin-Fabrik Innsbruck' (Imperial and Royal Privileged Machine Factory) on the right hand side of the frame under the cylinder.

In America, Colt's chief competitor was probably the old-established firm of E. Remington and Sons, Ilion, New York. Eliphalet Remington I was a prosperous blacksmith, and tradition has it that his son made his first gun at his father's forge. It was so successful at the local turkey shoots that, by about 1816, he was getting orders for other guns. By 1828 he was making complete weapons in a new factory at Ilion, and, by 1845, government contracts for service arms had been obtained and mass production techniques were being employed. In addition to long guns, Remington also made pistols and, in 1857, he began the manufacture of a percussion revolver designed and patented by Fordyce Beals. The first revolver designed by Beals, the famous 'walking beam' model, was patented in 1854, manufactured by Eli Whitney Jnr., and illustrates the extremes to which it was necessary to go to evade patents—in this case Colt's. Whitney, who had patented a solid frame ring trigger revolver in 1854, had overlooked the potential of the solid frame feature and had neglected to include it in his claim. The Whitney Beals also employed a solid frame, but its main interest lay in the method employed to rotate the cylinder. The actual mechanism was concealed behind the two curved side plates attached to each side of the frame which enclosed the lower half of the cylinder. The ring trigger was connected to a double ratchet which engaged offset cylinder stops or notches at each end of the cylinder. As the trigger was moved forward to the position shown in the illustration, the cylinder was rotated, rotation being completed as the trigger was brought back to the rear position. At this point it bore against the sear (sometimes spelled scear or sceare) under the frame and released the hammer which had previously been manually cocked.

The Remington Beals First Model, based on Beals' US patents dated 24 June 1856 and 26 May 1857, differed from the original Beals design in that conventional means were used to rotate the cylinder, the odd feature being that the pawl was mounted externally on the left hand side of the frame. This pistol, a rather crude looking .31 calibre five shot revolver, was manufactured from 1857 to 1858, and approximately 2,500 were made. Differing only slightly in the arrangement of the mechanism, the Second Model Beals manufactured from 1858 to 1860, was again of .31 calibre and again single action, but in this model a sheath trigger was used.

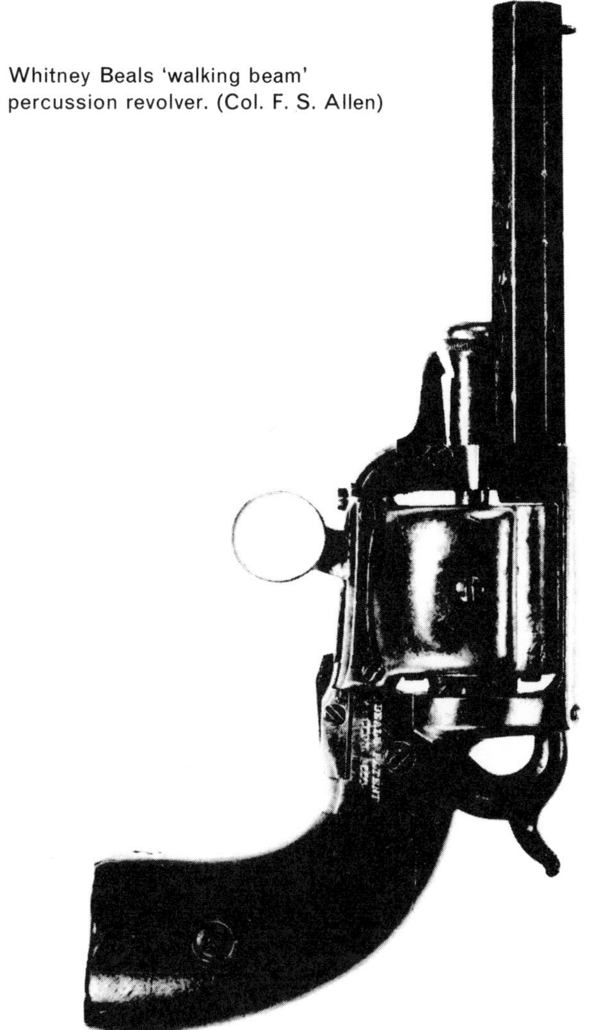

Whitney Beals 'walking beam' percussion revolver. (Col. F. S. Allen)

In the Third Pocket Model a lever rammer was fitted, and this rammer, patented by Beals in 1858, was the basis of the rammer design employed in the remainder of the Remington pistols. Since it acted as the cylinder pin retainer, the rammer had to be lowered before the cylinder pin could be withdrawn to remove the cylinder. Also of .31 calibre, this model employed the external pawl, but its appearance foreshadowed the 'Remington look' faithfully adhered to in the later series.

The first of what can be referred to as the 'service pistols' was the Beals Army Revolver. This model, made from 1860 to 1862, was a six chambered .44 calibre weapon with an 8″ barrel. In sharp contrast to the Colt series, it had a solid frame and the butt straps were part of the frame forging. Finish was blued except for the case hardened hammer and the polished brass trigger guard, the removal of which provided access to the mechanism. Considerably more robust than the Colt, and possessing almost the same feel, the Beals Army Model set the pattern for the whole range of Remington revolvers, even including the Remington Army Model cartridge revolver of 1875.

Similar to the Army Model, the Beals Navy was of .36 calibre and can be distinguished by the smaller web on the lever rammer. The 1861 Army and 1861 Navy Models which followed were attempts to improve on the Beals models. The lever rammer was provided with a cut out portion which permitted the cylinder pin to be withdrawn without lowering the rammer. The cylinder pin, when fully seated, was retained by a friction spring. Because of the 'improvement', there was a distinct space between the lever rammer and the barrel, and this feature, since this idea was later abandoned, is an aid to identification, as is the lack of cut out on the frame for the cylinder pin wings and the fact that these were the first models in which the barrel threads were visible—the frame being chamfered at this point.

The .44 calibre New Model Army illustrated was the last of the Remington single action percussion revolvers and, in my opinion, the best percussion revolver of American manufacture. Since the Elliot patent rammer used on the 1861 Models was discarded, there was no gap between the lever and the frame, and the rammer had to be lowered before the cylinder pin could be withdrawn. To take it out completely, the lever rammer assembly itself had to be removed by unscrewing one screw. This feature of the New Model Army and Navy revolvers was designed to prevent the inadvertent loss of the cylinder pin. The modification to the rammer assembly was simple but most effective. For the first time, effective safety notches were cut into the cylinder so that the hammer could be lowered between the nipples, at the same time locking the cylinder.

The dismantled pistol is a modern replica of the .44 New Model manufactured by Aldo

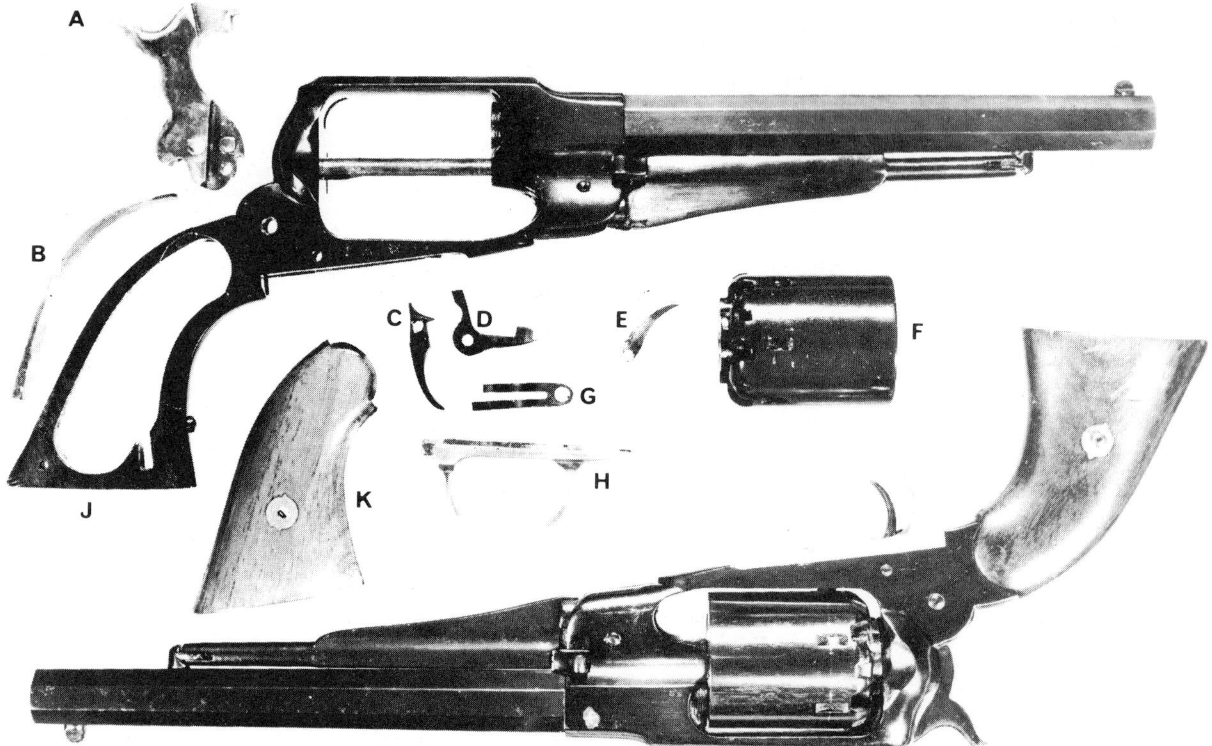

A dismantled replica, made by Aldo Uberti, of the .44 Remington New Model Army, with the assembled original below.

A. Hammer.
B. Mainspring.
C. Trigger.
D. Cylinder bolt.
E. Hand.
F. Cylinder.
G. Trigger and cylinder bolt spring.
H. Trigger guard.
J. Main frame.
K. Grip.

Uberti of Gardone, Italy, and the second illustration shows how the internal mechanism as well as the general appearance has been faithfully copied, although the actual parts are not interchangeable.

Three other single action percussion pistols were made by Remington during this period. The New Model Belt Revolver was a smaller version of the New Model Navy, also .36 calibre but, at 2 lbs. 2 oz., it was 8 oz. lighter. An even smaller version was the New Model Police Revolver, manufactured in $3\frac{1}{2}''$, $4\frac{1}{2}''$, $5\frac{1}{2}''$ and $6\frac{1}{2}''$ barrel lengths. The last of the series was the .31 calibre New Model Pocket Revolver. As with the Police Model, the size reduction was obtained at the expense of one shot, both pistols being five chambered. The New Model Pocket had a sheath trigger and, together with the Belt and Police Models, was offered in a wider range of finishes than the larger Service Models. As an alternative to the full blue, a nickel-plated frame or full nickel-plating was offered and special plating or engraving was available to order.

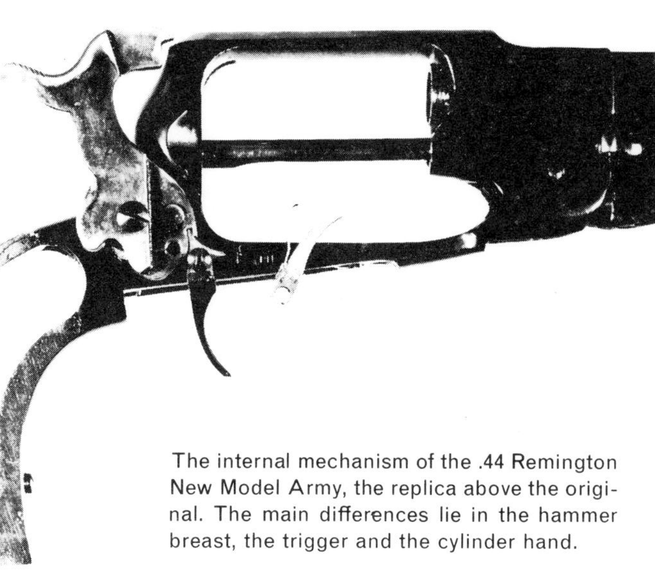

The internal mechanism of the .44 Remington New Model Army, the replica above the original. The main differences lie in the hammer breast, the trigger and the cylinder hand.

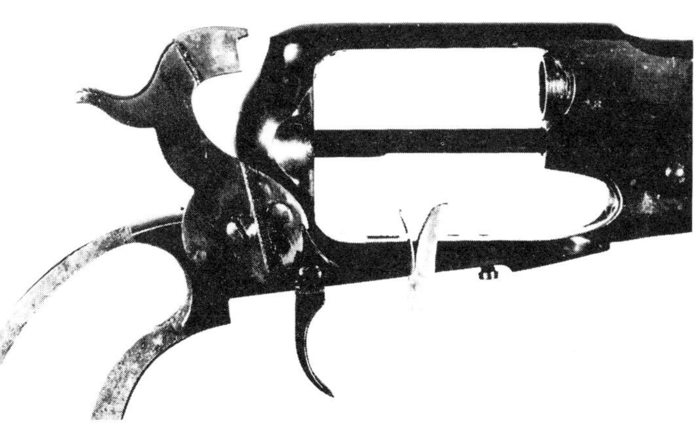

Most of these models continued in production until 1888, as did the two double action Models manufactured by Remington. The first of these was the Remington Rider Pocket .31 Double Action Revolver which appeared in 1860. Based on Rider's Patents of 1858 and 1859, the Rider Pocket is immediately distinguishable by its curious 'mushroom' cylinder. Rider also designed a single-shot smooth bore .170 calibre derringer which, apart from its unusual appearance, was of all brass construction and left in a natural brass finish.

The second was the double action version of the New Model Belt Revolver and, except for the trigger positioned in the middle of the guard, there is nothing to distinguish it from the single action model. Remington's interest in pistols ceased with the discontinuation of their automatic pistol in 1934, but, as we shall see later, a pistol, albeit of extremely unusual design, has once again been put on the market bearing the name Remington.

On the basis of number manufactured, the Starr percussion revolver could claim to be the third most successful American pistol of the period. The system employed was radically different again and the method of construction used can best be seen from the illustration of the dismantled Starr .44 calibre Single Action Model which bears the patent date, 15 January 1856, on the right hand side of the frame. This US patent was actually a percussion pepperbox patent and refers to the self-cocking mechanism employed on the self-cocking revolvers manufactured by Starr. A later US patent, of 4 December 1860, details the fully developed self-cocking revolver as does British Patent No. 880 of 7 April 1860.

The 1860 patent refers first of all to the frame design which, as can be seen, was made in two parts connected by a hinge joint. The upper part of the frame, to which was attached the barrel and loading lever, was hinged to the lower part; the forked top strap was hooked over the recoil shield and retained in position by a large knurled top strap screw which, together with the hinge pin, held the frame together. When the top strap screw was removed (no tools needed) the pistol could be 'broken' and the cylinder removed. The cylinder was mounted in the frame by a short ogival pin at the front, immediately behind which there was a collar to restrict forward movement. The rear bearing for the cylinder was formed by the ratchet wheel which, on assembly, entered the recoil shield and was supported by the bearing machined in the face of the shield. The cylinder on the double action Starr had no divisions between the nipples, but these were themselves recessed. The Patent covering the single action Starr, US Patent No. 42,435 of 19 April 1864, was obtained by Thomas Gibson.

The first of the series was the 1858 .36 calibre self-cocking or double action revolver. With the exception of the lock mechanism, it was similar in appearance to the single action model illustrated, but the lock mechanism, although referred to as double action, is perhaps best described as selective double action.

The .36 calibre pistol weighed 3 lbs. 3 oz., had a 6″ barrel and, like the two other Starr revolvers, was six shot. The nipples were inclined slightly outward and were separated by divisions. The .44 double action, at 2 lbs. 12 oz., was lighter, also had a 6″ barrel, but was $\frac{3}{8}$″ shorter overall than the twelve inch .36.

On the selective double action versions of the Starr there was a small slide at the rear of the trigger. With the slide pushed upwards, the pistol could be operated as a self-cocking revolver, and repetitive fire was obtained merely by pulling and releasing the trigger or 'firing lever' as it was referred to in the Starr literature. For single action or thumb cocking, the slide was moved

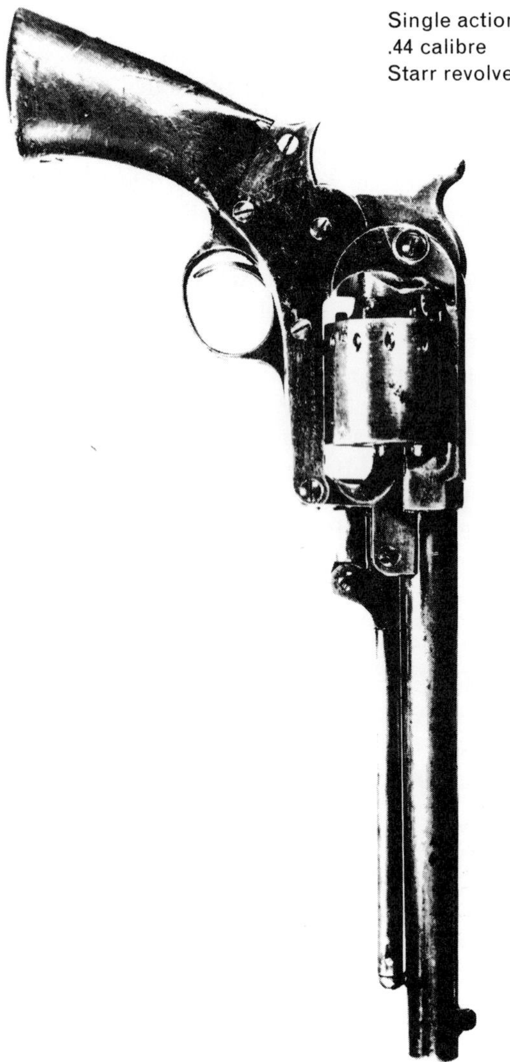

Single action .44 calibre Starr revolver.

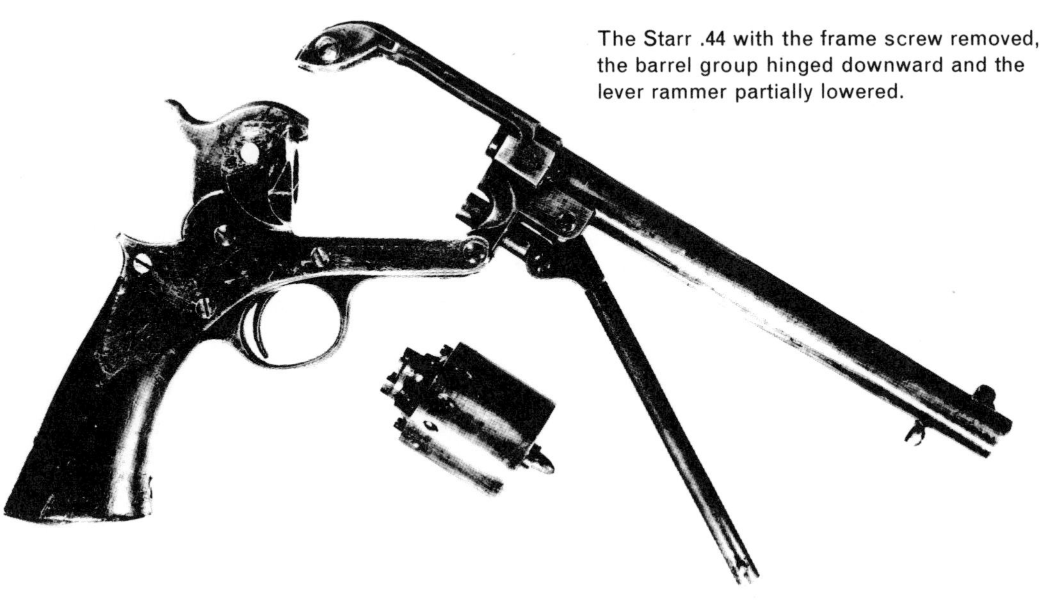

The Starr .44 with the frame screw removed, the barrel group hinged downward and the lever rammer partially lowered.

down and the hammer could then be drawn back by the thumb and released by the 'fine' trigger as with normal single action weapons. The 'fine' trigger at the rear of the trigger guard was, in fact, the trigger proper. The firing lever cocked the hammer and bolted the cylinder, the slide at the rear pressing against the 'fine' trigger—a simple pivoted lever which disengaged the sear of the 'fine' trigger from the notch in the hammer and so released it.

The above sounds somewhat complicated and the operation was by no means as simple as with the Beaumont-Adams true double action pistol which had appeared in England three years earlier. The Starr was, however, the first effective American revolver to employ a self-cocking action.

The reason for introducing a single action version some five years later was undoubtedly due to price considerations. The double action Starr revolvers were more expensive than their competitors and the relative complexity of the mechanism may have tended to inhibit sales. The extremely well made single action appeared only in .44 calibre with an 8″ barrel, and had twelve locking notches in the cylinder so that the cylinder could be locked with the hammer safely down between the nipples—a feature lacking on the double action models. All the Starrs lack the feel and balance of the Colts and Remingtons and, in my opinion, are not as pleasant to shoot.

Issued to the Union Army in 1863 at a price of $20.00 complete with accessories, the Savage .36 calibre Model 1861 was perhaps the most unusual of the Civil War percussion revolvers to be purchased in any quantity—approximately 10,000 being bought by the Union Government. It was patented by Henry S. North and Edward Savage of Middletown, Connecticut, the patents being taken out in 1856, 1859 and 1860—when the patentees formed the Savage Revolving Fire Arms Company.

The Savage, at 3 lbs. 7 oz., was one of the heavier of the percussion pistols of the period and also one of the longest; with its $7\frac{1}{8}$″ barrel it had an overall length of $14\frac{1}{4}$″. The top hammer was on the right of the frame and the nose was canted over to strike the nipple through a hole in the top strap. As can be seen, the nipples were deeply recessed and the reciprocating cylinder provided a gas seal at the moment of discharge. The trigger and finger (cocking) lever were both inside a massive trigger guard, the latter, when drawn back, cocking the hammer and, after withdrawing

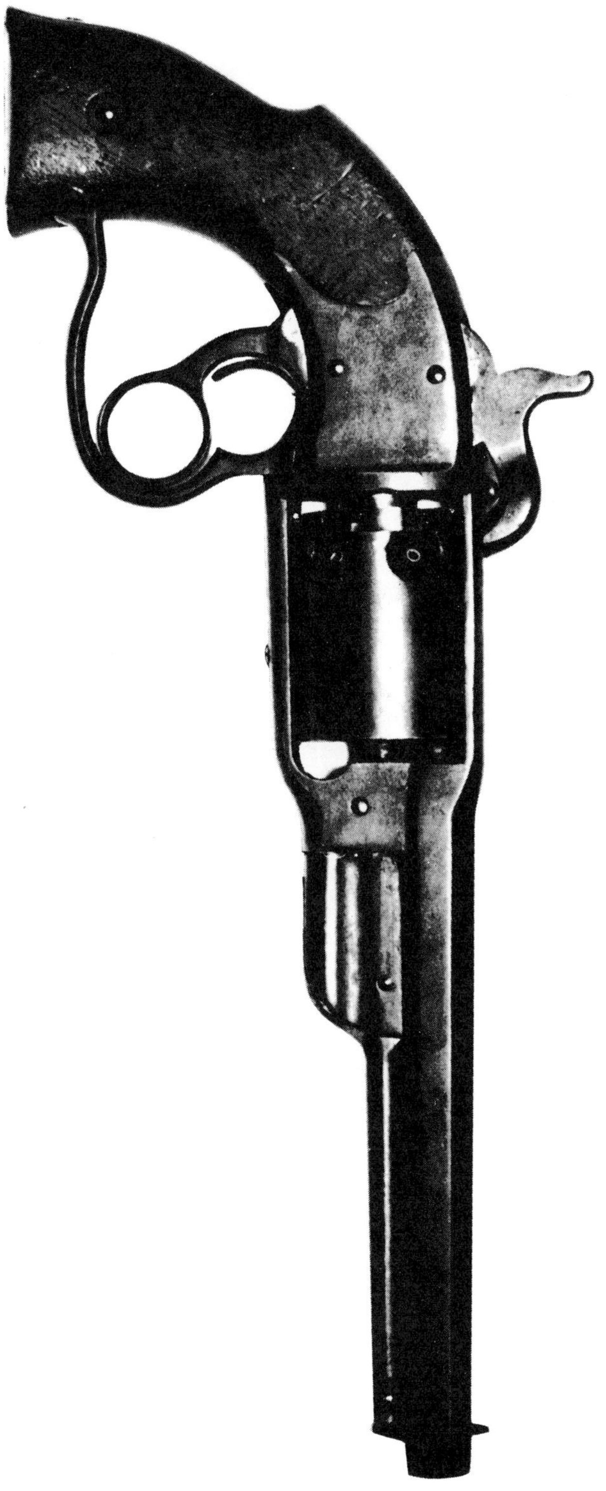

The Savage .36 Model 1861.

Allen and Wheellock percussion revolver. (Kilmarnock Museum)

it from the breech end of the barrel, rotating the cylinder.

Of slightly less conventional appearance, the Allen and Wheellock Belt Pistol is of interest because of its unusual rammer. From the illustration it can be seen that the lever formed part of the trigger guard when in the closed position. When the guard was pushed down and forwards, the teeth formed as part of the guard engaged teeth cut in the rammer, so forcing the rammer to the rear and seating the ball. Limited purchases of the .44 version of this pistol were made by the Union Army and it can be classed as a martial percussion revolver, but it was also made in a variety of styles and with both a central hammer, as shown, and an external one.

With a somewhat checkered production history, the Rogers and Spencer .44 calibre Army Model was based on patents taken out by Austin T. Freeman of Binghampton, New York, in 1862 and, known as the Freeman, had been originally manufactured by C. B. Hoard at Watertown, New York. The firm of Rogers and Spencer, also of New York, had manufactured the Pettingill six shot 'hammerless' self-cocking revolver which, due to the complexity of its mechanism, had proved a failure. Seeing lucrative Government contracts slipping through their fingers, they seized on the Freeman as an alternative and acquired the rights to manufacture it. The example shown has a $7\frac{1}{2}''$ octagonal barrel and weighs just on 3 lbs. It has been used for shooting recently and, fitted with modern target sights, the present owner reports that it shoots quite accurately.

In this brief review of American percussion

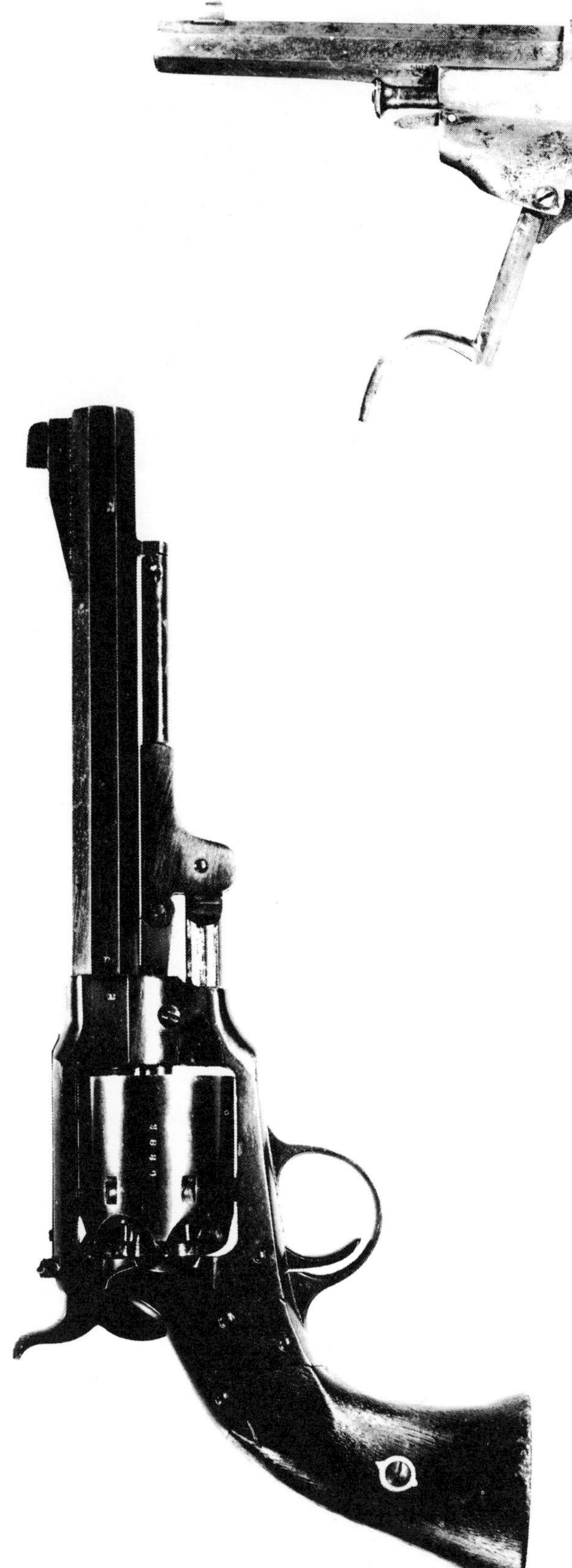

Rogers and Spencer percussion revolver fitted with modern target sights. (Col. F. S. Allen)

revolvers it will be apparent that two dominant factors have emerged. The first is that the successful revolvers were mechanically simple, and the second that their manufacture was based on what we would today refer to as mass production techniques. The capital locked up in extremely expensive tooling restricted any major variation in model design, with the result that the different models were all permutations of an established theme which allowed for minor design improvements and advances, but avoided any costly modifications which would, in addition, have caused a major disruption of production.

It is equally obvious that there was no absence of inventive genius. The large manufacturing concerns such as Colt and Remington relied almost entirely, however, on their proven bread and butter models coupled with sound manufacturing techniques and volume production.

Elsewhere the position was rather different. Both Britain and Western Europe lacked the technological know-how of this new means of manufacture and, for a time, they either depended on American machine tools or else attempted to produce large quantities of weapons by the old and cheaper hand techniques. As a result, quality suffered.

In the next chapter an attempt will be made to follow the development of the revolver in Britain and Europe, and to discuss some of the men who influenced the pattern of progress.

Notes to Chapter Six

More has been written about Samuel Colt than about any other personality connected with firearms. Some of the more important works are *The Whitney Firearms* by Claud Fuller (Huntington, 1946), *Colt Firearms from 1836* by James E. Serven (Santa Ana, 1964), *Colt—The Man, The Arms, The Company* by J. L. Mitchell (Harrisburg, 1959) and *The Story of Colt's Revolver* by William B. Edwards (Harrisburg, 1953).

Articles in the *American Rifleman* on particular Colt models are: Colt Paterson (February 1960 and March 1962), Colt Hartford-Walker (September 1956, November 1961 and May 1963), Colt Pocket Model of 1849 (April 1957 and June 1964), Colt Navy Model 1851 (April 1958, May 1959 and September 1964), Colt Model of 1855 (June 1961), Colt .44 Army Model of 1860 (January 1954, February 1955, December 1956 and May 1959) and Colt Navy Model 1861 (May 1959 and September 1964).

Data on other American percussion revolvers will be found in *Remington Handguns* by C. L. and C. R. Karr (Harrisburg, 1956). Relevant articles in the *American Rifleman* are: Remington New Model Pocket Revolver (May 1955 and February 1963), Remington New Model .44 (May 1959 and April 1961), Remington New Model Belt .36 (May 1955, July 1955 and May 1959), Remington .44 Army Model 1861 (January and July 1954) and Remington Model 1861 .36 (May 1959).

The Confederate Brass-Framed Colt and Whitney by W. A. Albaugh (Falls Church, 1955) and *United States Martial Pistols and Revolvers* by Col. Arcadi Gluckman (Harrisburg, 1939) provide data on some of the less well known American percussion revolvers.

Chapter Seven
The Percussion Revolver in Britain

John Nigel George, to whom all who profess an interest in firearms will be for ever indebted, quite rightly, in his book *English Pistols and Revolvers*, draws attention to the importance of the year 1851. This was the year of the 'Great Exhibition of the Works of Industry of all Nations' and, beneath the arches of Paxton's Crystal Palace in Hyde Park, were housed examples of the art of gunmaking from both Britain and abroad.

As might be expected, Colonel Samuel Colt, super-salesman, took advantage of this marvellous shop-window to display his wares and, at the same time, the opportunity was taken to present suitably engraved specimens of his work to important people likely to influence the course of affairs in his favour.

In addition, on 25 November 1851, Colt delivered a paper 'On the Application of Machinery to the manufacture of Rotating Chambered-Breech Fire-Arms, and the peculiarities of those Arms' to the Institute of Civil Engineers—an Institute of which he was subsequently elected an Associate Member in May 1852. Colt opened his remarks by stating that it was not his intention to enter upon a history of firearms but, despite this disclaimer, he went on to discuss, in some detail, their historical development. Reference was then made to the excellence of Colt arms, and instances were given of their successful use in the field. The actual manufacture of revolvers by machinery was treated in very general terms, the emphasis placed on the product rather than on how it was manufactured. At the conclusion of the paper, the meeting was addressed by the Honourable Abbot Lawrence, the United States Minister, who felt convinced that 'the arm would have a fair trial in England, and that no undue prejudice would be permitted to prevail'.

As time was to show, the Minister's sanguine hopes were to be dashed. Patriotic prejudice, coupled with the thought of commercial losses should the 'Yankee Adventurer' realise his ambition, resulted in ferocious attacks on Colt, his pistols and his method of manufacture, particularly following the establishment of his English factory in London and his attempts to get his pistols adopted by the British Government.

Colt's main adversary was a London gunmaker, Robert Adams, who had patented a five chambered self-cocking revolver on 24 February 1851 (British Patent No. 13,527). Both men took part in a spirited encounter during the discussion period which followed Colt's address to the Institute of Civil Engineers. The meeting was well padded with Colt's friends (all doubtless recipients of suitably engraved Colt presentation models) and Adams did not have the chance to put forward the merits of his own pistol until an opportunity was afforded by a Mr J. Freeman who said that during the course of the Great Exhibition he had been attracted, in the American department, to Colonel Colt's revolvers, and had perceived their merits. He begged, however, 'to direct attention to a similar pistol made by Messrs. Deane, Adams and Deane and would ask one of these gentlemen to explain wherein its merits consisted'.

Adams sprang to his feet, flourished his pistol, and explained to those present the merits and advantages of his design and method of operation.

The pistol that Adams described is what we today would call the Deane, Adams and Deane Model of 1851. It was available in .500 (36 bore), .442 (54 bore) and .32 (120 bore). Variations in calibre, whilst affecting overall dimensions, did not significantly alter the appearance of the different sizes of pistol, and the general 'line' of the Adams was to become that of the British revolver. Just as the ancestry of the Colt Single Action Army can be traced back to the percussion Colts, the basic line of the Adams can still be seen in the last of the British cartridge revolvers.

The Americans, most of whom have the idea that anything worthwhile in nineteenth century revolver development originated from their side of the Atlantic, often express surprise that the first commercially successful solid frame percussion revolver was invented and manufactured in Britain, as was the trigger action and the later 'double action'.

In the Adams, the barrel, lock frame and top strap were all forged out of one piece of iron. The cylinder with its five chambers revolved on a centre-pin. The pin was retained by a spring but could be drawn out either partially, so that the cylinder could be removed, or completely to facilitate cleaning. The ratchet was not formed as part of the cylinder but was separate and, by taking out two screws, could be removed or replaced should wear affect its operation.

The lockwork is of great interest and can best be understood by referring to the illustration where the principal parts are shown, and by looking at the patent drawing for Adams' specification. The trigger and hammer are mounted on transverse pins through the frame. On the

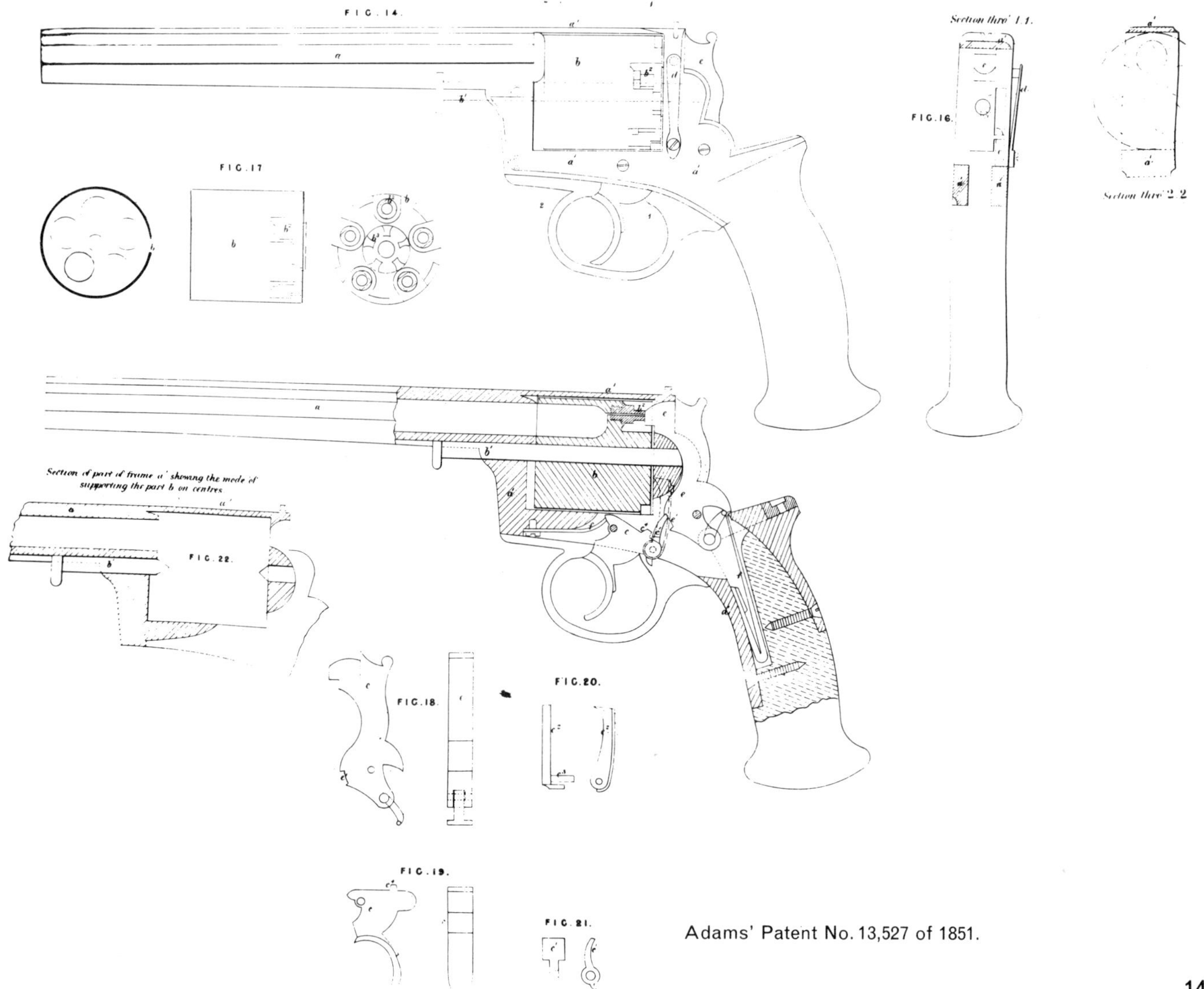

Adams' Patent No. 13,527 of 1851.

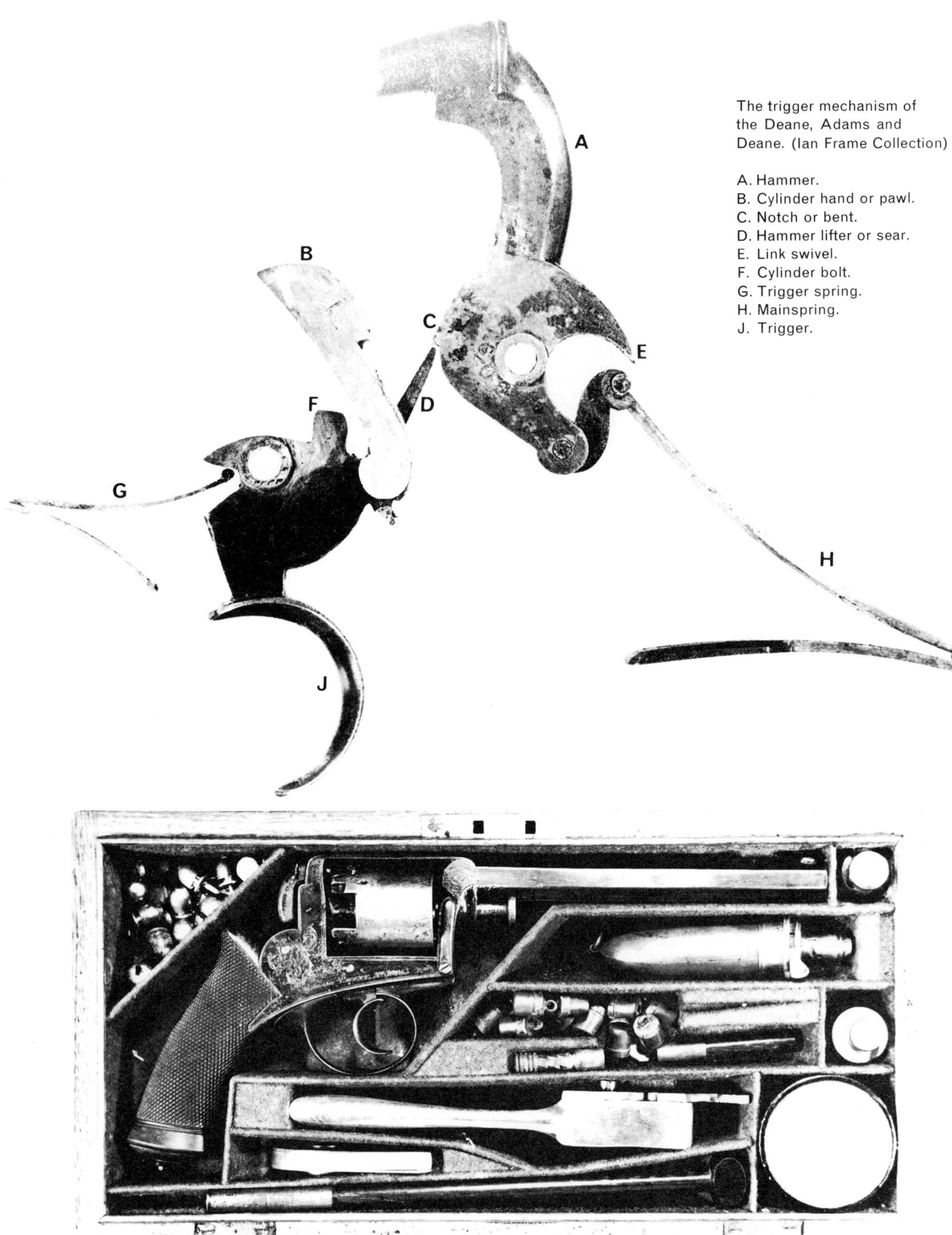

The trigger mechanism of the Deane, Adams and Deane. (Ian Frame Collection)

A. Hammer.
B. Cylinder hand or pawl.
C. Notch or bent.
D. Hammer lifter or sear.
E. Link swivel.
F. Cylinder bolt.
G. Trigger spring.
H. Mainspring.
J. Trigger.

Cased Deane, Adams and Deane 54 bore percussion revolver.

patent drawing the trigger return spring is housed under the front of the trigger guard and is a leaf spring. On the actual example illustrated the return spring is the 'V' spring beloved by the British gunmaker, and is retained by the guard, no screws being used. The 'V' mainspring is attached to the front strap and a rectangular hole fits over a lump forged as part of the strap or, more often, the lump is separate and riveted to the strap, a method of attachment used on box locks for many years. The link swivel which we first met on the improved flintlock is employed to attach the mainspring to the hammer and, so far, we are on familiar ground.

If we refer to the pepperbox action (page 117), it will be remembered that the hammer was lifted by a hooked link attached to it. As the trigger was pulled the link was brought forward, lifting the hammer until the hook was disengaged by the camming action of the trigger.

Now look at the Adams. Here the hammer is pushed upwards by what Adams calls a 'hammer lifter'. This is the small lever at Fig 21 in the patent drawing, and it can be seen from the illustration that, as the lifter moves upwards, it will ultimately be pushed forward out of the notch on the hammer by the camming action of the breast of the hammer. When this happens, the hammer will fall, the nose striking the cap on the nipple and so firing the charge. When the trigger is released, it returns to its original position impelled by the trigger return spring. The ratchet pawl or cylinder hand has a pin at the bottom end (Fig 20 on the drawing) which passes through the rear of the trigger and at the same time locates the hammer lifter. The lifter is kept in contact with the hammer by a small flat spring, the upper end of which is attached to the pawl, the lower end acting on the lifter. The effect of this spring is to press the lifter to the rear and the pawl forward. (If the ends of these two limbs are pressed together they will fly apart.) The forward movement of the pawl is restricted by the fact that its nose acts against the ratchet teeth at the rear of the cylinder and, even when not engaged, its forward movement is still restricted by the passage formed in the standing breech through which it acts. At this stage we have been able to lift and release the hammer and rotate the cylinder. Arrangements have now to be made to lock the cylinder in battery at the moment of firing. This is achieved by the projecting stop formed on the trigger which, when the trigger is pulled back, moves upward through a hole in the bar of the action and contacts a projection machined at the rear of the cylinder.

As far as the mechanism was concerned, one other provision had to be made. So that the chambers may be loaded and capped, they must be free to rotate. Since there is no half cock notch as appears on the single action, this cannot be done unless the trigger is pulled slightly back. Since holding back the trigger the correct amount to achieve free rotation of the cylinder would be difficult, and possibly dangerous, Adams provided a hammer stop on the left hand side of the frame immediately in front of the hammer. To load the Adams, the trigger is pulled slightly to raise the hammer and the spring loaded hammer stop is pushed inwards and the trigger released. The hammer lock or safety permits the pistol to be carried fully loaded and ready for use since, when the trigger is pulled, the spring stop moves outwards of its own accord allowing the hammer to strike the capped nipple.

Looking at the patent drawing and the illustrations of the various types of Adams Model 1851, the absence of a lever rammer is immediately apparent. Bullets for the Adams were cast with a small tang (covered by an 1851 patent) and both round ball and conical bullets could be cast from the mould supplied with the pistols. This mould —the 'rat tails' are clearly visible in the illustration—was furnished with a special sprue cutter and will be found to be marked 'Registered 28 November, 1851', this being the Registered Designs Act already referred to. This mark may also be found on Adams' moulds which do not cast 'spiked' bullets. The spike was designed to fix a felt wad to the base of the bullet and a wad cutter was provided. The mould is 54 bore and the wad cutter slightly larger, 52 bore. With the wad attached, the tail of the ball or bullet could be peened over to eliminate the possibility of the two becoming separated and then, according to Robert Adams, the assembly could be pressed into the cylinder with the finger after the powder charge had been introduced from a suitable flask.

Early Adams rifling employed three broad grooves with narrow lands and, according to Adams, 'every portion to which self acting tools had been found applicable, was planed, bored, turned, slotted and rifled by machinery'.

Unfortunately, I have not been able to trace any information concerning the type of machine tools employed by Adams, and the term 'self acting' which he used to describe them does not imply that they possessed 'inbuilt' skill. They

Cased Deane, Adams and Deane, marked Rigby, Dublin. (R. Dalgleish Collection)

1851 Model Adams 36 bore, No. 176, marked Deane, Adams and Deane.

could well have been similar to the 'first generation' machine tools employed by Maudslay, Nasmyth and Whitworth. Stress was, however, laid on the use of 'special steam machinery', but it is very questionable if full advantage was taken by Robert Adams of the techniques available, although later evidence is available regarding the tools and techniques adopted for the manufacture of the John Adams breechloader.

From an examination of a number of the Deane, Adams and Deane variants, hand working was still employed for finishing. The American technique was to avoid hand work even at this stage if possible. Specialist tools were developed for each single operation, whereas the European idea was to employ general purpose tools which could be used for a variety of jobs. For this reason, an examination of the internal mechanism of a Colt will show little evidence of hand work, whereas, in the case of the Deane-Harding for instance, hand working is very evident. On balance, the external finish of British revolvers was better than their American counterparts, whereas internally they were slightly inferior.

The 1851 Adams presents further problems regarding manufacture. On close examination, there are a number of design and constructional variations, and it becomes apparent that the 1851 series were actually made by different manufacturers. The assessment is further complicated by the fact that many of the revolvers bear the names of retailers only and evidence as to the manufacturer has to be sought by dismantling the pistol to search for identification markings.

If we assume that the pistol shown is an early Adams, we at least have a starting point, and the

36 bore Deane, Adams and Deane percussion revolver, No.7351 R.

54 bore Deane, Adams and Deane percussion revolver, No. 30253 B.

variants encountered can be examined in relation to this particular example. The pistol bears the serial number 176 and is marked on the top strap, 'Deane, Adams and Deane, Makers to H.R.H. Prince Albert'. The address given is 30 King William St, London Bridge, London. The manufacture of revolvers took place on the other side of the Thames in the vicinity of what is now London Bridge Railway Station in Bermondsey —premises in Weston Street being no doubt rented from the then South Eastern Railway Company.

As would be expected, this Adams, which is 36 bore, lacks a rammer, but it is unusual in that the frame is chamfered to match the contour of the trigger guard, a feature not seen on later specimens.

It would be reasonable to assume that this pistol was made by Adams in London and that the forgings were supplied by specialist contractors. This is borne out by the initials 'W.T.' on the frame under the butt, although it is more likely that W. Tranter did much more than just supply the part-machined forgings.

How many of the Adams 1851 type revolvers were actually made by Adams is not known and, indeed, it is difficult to discover the extent of the work done on revolvers which originated at the Bermondsey Works. A similar 'Dragoon' Adams, No. 7351 R of 36 bore, is also illustrated and the differences in the frame are apparent.

A later Adams of 54 bore (.442″) bears the legend 'T. E. Mortimer, Edinburgh' on the top strap and is marked on the left hand side of the frame 'Adams Patent 1851'. The number is 30253B and this, coupled with the name

'I. Brazier' underneath the frame adjacent to the trigger guard, indicates that the pistol was manufactured by Brazier of Wolverhampton, a noted gun and gunlock manufacturer. Detail differences will be seen between this pistol and the next Adams, made by William Tranter of Birmingham. This pistol, again of 54 bore, is distinguished by being fitted with Tranter's patent rammer which is shown attached to the left side of the frame. On the top strap the name of the vendor, 'Wm. & J. Rigby, Dublin', is engraved and the lower frame carries the legend 'Adams Patent', but the date has been defaced by the insertion of the pin to carry the rammer. The rammer is marked 'W. Tranter's Patent No. 50' and the serial number is 20229Y. With the butt removed, the batch number of the pistol is revealed — 8299 — and also the initials 'W.T.'

The fitting of the lever rammer dates the pistol as being post-1853, assuming that the rammer was fitted when the pistol was manufactured and that it is not a later addition. This type of rammer is covered by Tranter's patent No. 2921, dated 16 December, 1853 and was employed on Tranter-made Adams and also on First Model 'Double Trigger' Tranters which will be discussed later.

Detail differences in construction already referred to can be seen from the illustrations and include the shape of the butt and the fact that the Brazier-Adams has a butt trap. Use of the rammer on the Tranter-Adams and the difference in shape of the hammer safety catch should also be noted; the Tranter version is straight and that on the Brazier-Adams is curved. Trigger guards differ slightly (the Tranter is rounded at the front edge), the rear bearing for the cylinder pin on the Tranter is dovetailed into the frame, and there are differences in the machining of the locking surfaces at the rear of the cylinder. The Tranter-Adams has five-grooved rifling and the Brazier-Adams, three grooved rifling. Both pistols bear London proof marks and there is a $\frac{1}{4}''$ difference in the barrel length, the Tranter-Adams being the longer at $6\frac{5}{8}''$.

Both pistols are cased, the earlier Brazier-Adams being provided with a small brass-tipped wooden ramrod to ease the strain on the fingers when pushing home the Adams felt wadded bullet. Cleaning rods, bullet moulds, powder flask etc. are common to both sets; also turnscrews, nipple wrenches, oil bottle and provision in the case for a supply of percussion caps — those in the Tranter-Adams case are modern,

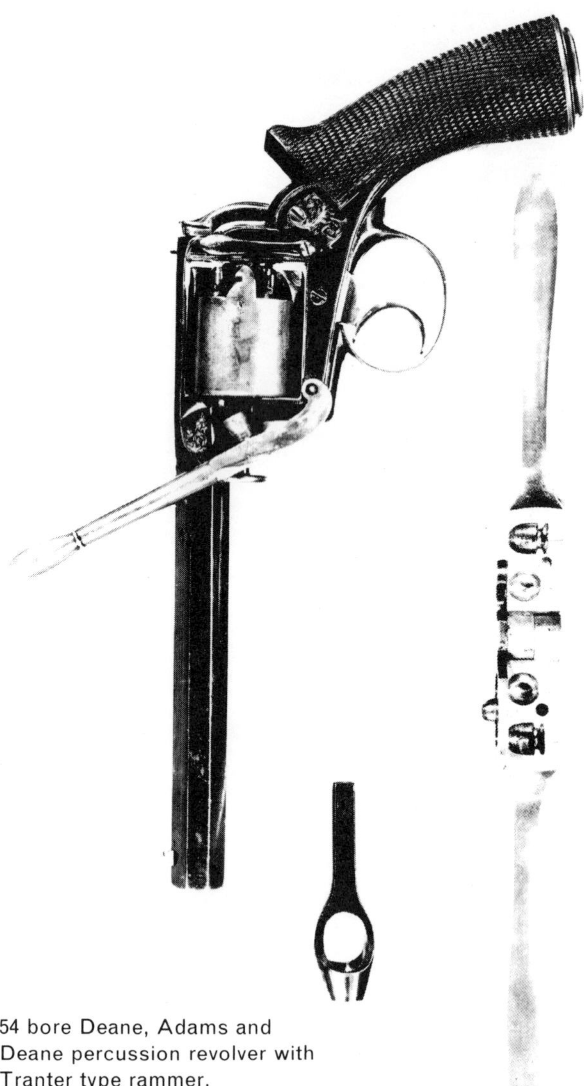

54 bore Deane, Adams and Deane percussion revolver with Tranter type rammer.

those in the Brazier-Adams contemporary and marked 'T. E. Mortimer' on a paste-on label.

In addition to being manufactured by Brazier and Tranter, Adams revolvers were also made by other firms, both in Britain and in Belgium.

About 1855, modifications were made to the angle of the butt, the more streamlined shape which resulted being similar to that of the Beaumont-Adams (page 156). In addition, a permanently attached rammer, known as 'Rigby's rammer', was fitted. This was similar to the Tranter rammer but, instead of being removable, it was attached by a screw and, when not in use, was hinged back to lie along the frame. The wooden butt was inletted to accommodate the handle.

During the time Robert Adams was organising the manufacture of his pistols, his rival was equally active. Samuel Colt had his eye on

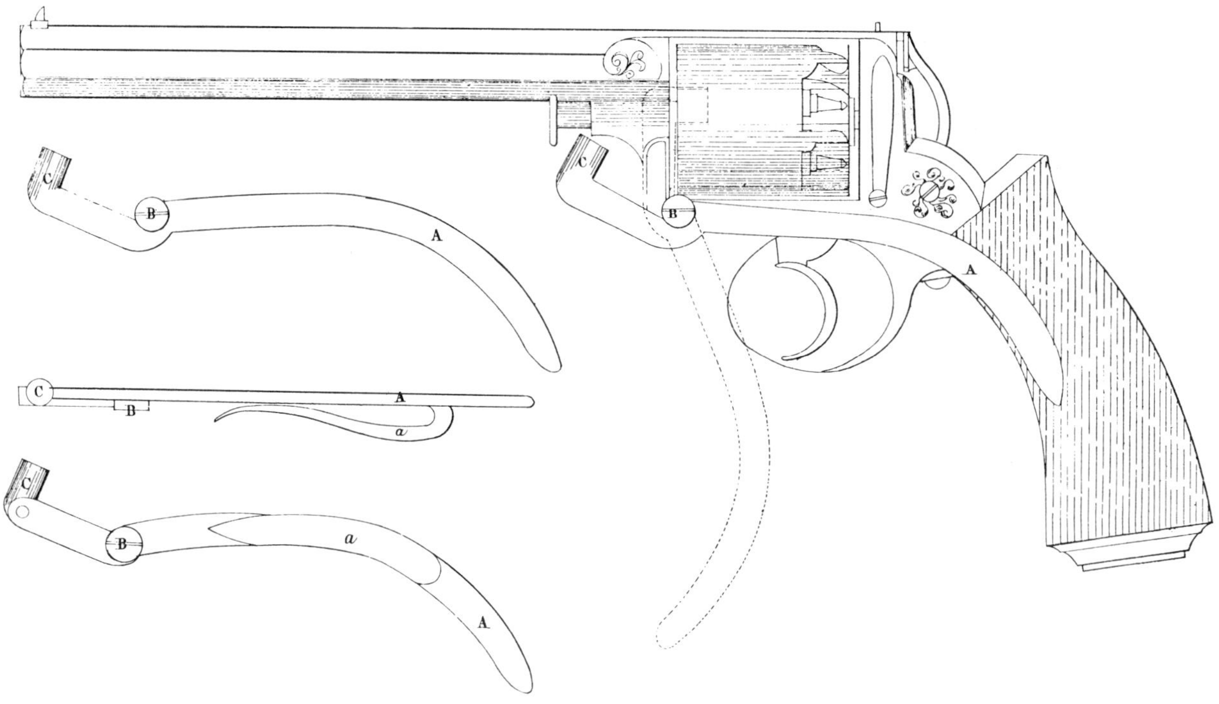

Rigby's Patent No.1976 of 1854.

Government contracts for Service pistols and, in 1853, his factory in Bessborough Place, Millbank, by Vauxhall Bridge in London, was in production. A Sales Office was opened at 1 Spring Gardens, Cockspur St, and later moved to 14 Pall Mall.

Initially, production at the factory was confined to the assembly of Hartford manufactured components, carried out under the eye of key personnel from the American factory. For political reasons the works manager was British, no less a person than the Secretary of the Institute of Civil Engineers, Mr Charles Manby. With the exception of the American staff, the bulk of the people employed were unskilled and had no knowledge of 'the art and mysterie of gunmaking'.

Unlike the factories of Adams, Brazier, Tranter and others, we know something of the London Colt factory. In 1854 it was visited by Charles Dickens, and later, on 27 May 1854, he published an article in his magazine *Household Words*. The first part dealt with the historical aspect of the revolver and it is likely that this was culled from a publicity hand-out, very probably the text of Colt's address to the Institute of Civil Engineers. Dickens described the Colt pistol in highly commendatory terms and subsequently wrote about his tour of the factory.

No apologies are needed for including a full transcript of this section of the article, for it is of great interest, not only because it is a gun factory, but also because it was the first 'mass production' factory to be established outside America. The techniques of production and also the method of establishing the factory have been faithfully followed by every American firm that subsequently established manufacturing facilities in this country, and it also served as a model for English manufacturers.

'We are on the threshold of Colonel Colt's factory, in the sombre and smoky region of Millbank. Under the roof of this low, brickbuilt, barrack-looking building, we are told that we may see what cannot be seen under one roof elsewhere in all England—the complete manufacture of a pistol, from dirty pieces of timber and rough bars of cast steel, till it is fit for the gunsmith's case. To see the same thing in Birmingham and in other places where firearms are made almost entirely by hand labour, we should have to walk about a whole day, visiting many shops carrying on distinct branches of the manufacture; not to speak of the toolmakers, the little screw and pin makers; all of whose work is done here. "We are independent people", says my informant, "and are indebted to no one, save the engine and fixed machine makers." This little pistol which is just put into my hand will pick into more than two hundred parts, every one of which parts is made by a machine. A little skill is required in polishing the wood, in making cases, and in guiding the machines; but mere strength of muscle, which is so valuable in new societies, would find no market here—for the steam engine—indefatigably toiling in the hot, suffocating smell of rank oil, down in the little stone chamber below—performs nine-tenths of all the work that is done here. Neat, delicate-handed, little girls do the work that brawny smiths still do in other gun-shops. Most of them have been sempstresses and dressmakers, unused to factory work, but have been induced to conquer some little prejudice against it, by the attraction of better pay than they could hope to get by needle-work. Even the men have, with scarcely an exception, been hitherto ignorant of gunmaking. No recruiting sergeant ever brought a more miscellaneous group into the barrack-yard, to be drilled more rapidly to the same duty, than these two hundred hands have been. Carpenters, cabinet-makers, ex-policemen, butchers, cab-men, hatters, gas-fitters, porters, or, at least, one representative from each of those trades, are steadily drilling and boring at lathes all day in upper rooms. Political economists tell us that the value of labour will find its level as surely as the sea: and so, perhaps it will: but it is a sort of sea that does not right itself quickly enough to prevent a great deal of misery; that is always recognised and deplored; but for which the best mathematicians of the school have not yet been able to find a remedy. For Science, with her two centuries of pedigree, has become a little aristocratic, and does not bend her genius down to many incidents of individual wretchedness which humbler folks cannot shut their eyes to. Perhaps if men who have learnt but one trade, and have grown old in it, could be as easily absorbed into another, when desirable, as these new gunsmiths are, the working world would go more smoothly than it does. The girls here earn from two to three shillings per day; the boys the same. The men get from three to eight shillings per day of ten hours; while one or two, being quick, clever, and reliable, are paid regularly twelve shillings per day. What is commonly called piece-work is not the system usually adopted here. It has been found to tempt the men to hurry their work at the expense of a neat finish, and the manager prefers to give a workman six months' trial, during which he learns his business of gun-making by machinery, and is also sure by that time to have shown what wages he is worth. Only twelve of these people are Americans; one or two Germans; the rest are English.

'Listening to these facts as my conductor communicates them, we pass into a long room hung with targets as they appeared after firing at them with Colt's revolvers. All the bullet marks are, of course, very near the bull's eye—which, I hope I am not presumptuous or depreciatory of the great Colt invention in attributing in some measure to the marksman. Beyond this is the store room, lined with wooden racks up to the ceiling, which are almost naked now, only five pistols of all the number that are made here—six hundred a week—being at this moment in store. For there is a new government order for the Baltic; and as fast as they are finished the pistols are sent away, packed in deep cases, that look very large indeed, considering that they are only for five-and-twenty single pistols each. But the conical balls and bullet-moulds, powder-flasks and percussion caps take up more room than the pistols themselves.

'Out of the hot atmosphere, and the all-pervading odour of hot oil, we pass a yard ancle deep in iron chips (which make a dry hard road in all weathers, very destructive to leather) into a long out-building, in which the only genuine smiths are at work. Here the very beginning of the pistol is made; if we except the cutting and polishing of the stock, which have been already described in these pages. There is little of the noise of a smithy here except the roaring of the furnaces. A workman rams the end of a long bar of steel into the fire; and, taking it out glowing with heat, strikes a bit off the end as if it were a stick of peppermint; while his companion, giving it a couple of rough taps upon the anvil, drops the redhot morsel into a die. This die is a plug-hole shaped something like a horse-shoe, at the foot of a machine, bearing a painful resemblance to a guillotine. While they have been breaking off the bit of steel, a huge screw has been slowly lifting up the iron hammer-head, which plays the part of the axe in the guillotine: and now the great hammer drops, and with one stroke beats the piece of iron to the form of the die. It has cooled to a black heat now, and is shaped something like the sole of a very narrow shoe; but it must be heated again, and

Benjamin Cogswell's trade label.

the heel end must be beat up at right angles to the long part—taking care that it be bent according to the grain of the metal, without which it will be liable to flaw. Thus the shield, and what may be called the body of the pistol, are made in an instant.

'In Birmingham, the barrels of fire-arms are made of old nails that have been knocked about, and which are melted, rolled into sheets, twisted again, and beaten about, till they are considered to be tougher and less likely to burst; but the American gunsmiths know nothing about this. They merely beat the end of the bars of cast steel again and beat it with steam hammers; for it would not do to draw it through holes, as thick wire is drawn, or to roll it as with ordinary round bars. These hammers are fixed, five in a frame, where they quiver with a chopping noise too rapidly to count the strokes, over a little iron plate, never touching it, though coming very close. Into the first of these the smith thrusts the red end of the bar, and guides it till it is beaten square. The next hammer beats it smaller, but still square: the next hammer beats it smaller and longer still, but rounder. The fourth hammer beats it quite round, and the fifth strikes off the exact length for the barrel. This gradual process is absolutely necessary, for the steel will not bear being beaten round the first time; and, although five barrels may be thus forged in one minute, the rapid strokes of these hammers are said to make it quite as tough as the Birmingham plan; which seems to be borne out by the results at the Proof House. On the same floor, the barrels and cylinders, after polishing, are case-hardened, and tinted blue, by burning in hot embers; processes which are well known.

'Across the yard strewn with chips of iron

again, and through the tool room, where men are turning great screws and other bolts and portions of machinery, we mount to the first floor, and enter a long room filled with machines, and rather more redolent of hot rank oil. Considering that the floor supports a long vista of machinery in full action, the place looks clean and neat, and is not very noisy. Girls quietly attending to the boring and rifling of the barrels — having nothing to do but to watch the lathe narrowly, and drop a little oil upon the borer with a feather now and then — men drilling cylinders, holding locks to steam files, cutting triggers, slotting screws, treating cold iron everywhere as if it was soft wood, to be cut to any shape, without straining a muscle. It would be difficult and tedious to describe these machines minutely, although they are very interesting to a spectator, and cannot, I believe, be seen elsewhere. Every one of them is a simple lathe; but it is in the various cutters, borers, and riflers that the novelty and ingenuity exist. Where the thing to be made is of eccentric shape, the cutter is of eccentric shape also; and although the superintendent of each machine acquires more or less skill by practice, it is in the perfection of these cutters and borers that the guarantee for uniformity consists. The bores of barrels and cylinders must be mathematically straight, and every one of the many parts must be exactly a duplicate of another. No one part belongs, as a matter of course, to any other part of one pistol; but each piece may be taken at random from a heap, and fixed to and with the other pieces until a complete weapon is formed;

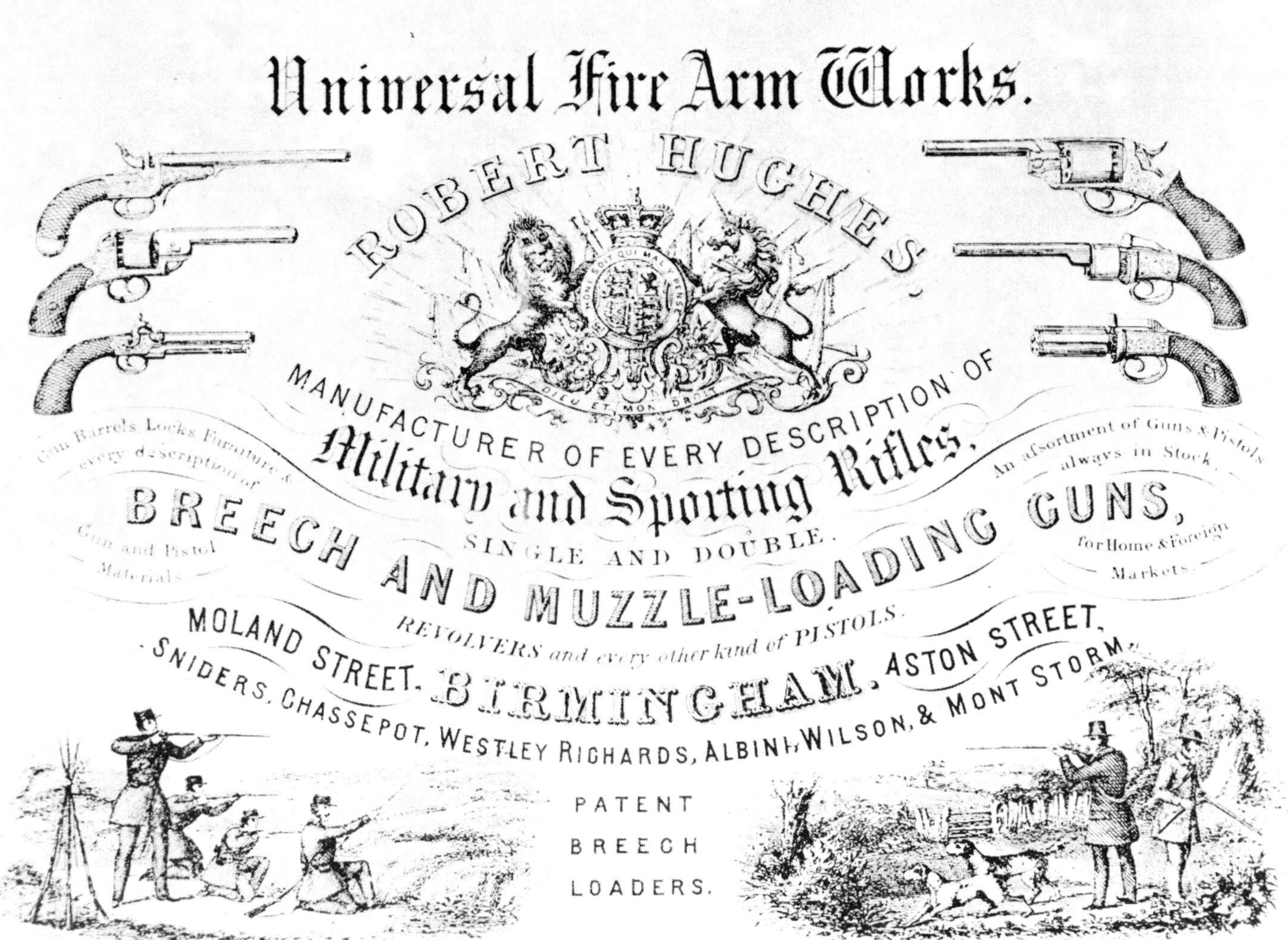

Robert Hughes' trade label for the Universal Fire Arms Works.

that weapon being individualised by a number stamped upon many of its component parts. The advantage of these contrivances is obvious. In every case of revolvers are placed, when sold, a number of such parts of a pistol as are most liable to accident; and, with these, any soldier or sailor may, in a few minutes, repair his own weapon. Seventy-odd out of a hundred of the injured revolvers picked up on the battle-field during the Mexican war were repaired with bits of other pistols on the spot.

'In the top floor, just above this, men and women, with black hands and faces, are polishing at lathes still moved, as everything is moved, by the steam engine in the hot stone chamber below. Everybody gets a slice of his thirty horse-power; and my conductor says, they have still plenty of power to spare, as if steam power were an article like gas or water, to be laid on whenever it is wanted from a distant reservoir. Such, indeed, it is; though when carried far, as I saw it by a belt across the yard, much of the force, of course, is wasted. Here is our friend, the butcher, still wearing a blue smock, and very busy polishing cylinders. His work spins so rapidly that red-hot particles of emery fly off and lodge upon his face, which is specked and spotted all over in rather a comical manner. He gets a hit in the eye sometimes (for he will not wear spectacles), which causes great pain; but not more than is occasioned by the minute chips of steel which trouble the workmen down stairs, and which have to be taken out with a magnet; or, when they stick in, by scraping the eye with the sharpest knife that can be found. The butcher is very quiet and intent upon his work, as the manager enters with me; but the American close to us is singing a song when we come in, and does not think of leaving off —not he. The girls have a natural shame of black hands and faces, though they cannot help themselves, and look more closely down at their work while strangers are near, than the neat and tidy girls below.

'All this time we have been seeing only the making of little bits of a pistol. Pausing a moment, to see the engraving of a ship in full sail, and other ornamental work—including the maker's name stamped by great pressure on the cylinder—we come into a great room, where all the minute portions are brought to be examined. Here, by means of gauges, but chiefly by the practised eye of the superintendent, each separate article is examined, and rejected if in the slightest degree faulty. From this room the various parts are served out to the workmen who put them together and turn out the complete revolver.

'Every revolver being equal to six single pistols, they are rarely spoken of as braces. Most customers take only a single revolver and the name of every purchaser being recorded, and the number, which is marked on many parts of the weapon, being noted at the same time some curious identifications occur. Several anecdotes are related of persons who have been traced by the revolver in their possession. In the skirmishing in Florida, the death of many poor fellows whose names were unknown, and who were found killed, was certified to their friends by publishing the number of the pistol in their belt, or grasped in their stiff hands. There is a revolver, says my conductor, which was brought to me to repair, some months since. I recognised it, by the number, in a moment for one stolen from here long ago, and I think the man who brought it saw I did, for he never came to fetch it away again. In cases of murder perpetrated by a Colt's revolver, the weapon itself, if ever one should be so used, would become a conclusive evidence.

'Here is the proving-room, where the pistols undergo a preparatory trial, before being sent up for the regular government proof. It is by no means, the dark, mysterious iron-plated room, in which I have been taught to believe that guns are proved; but an ordinary workshop, with two square wooden pipes, fixed horizontally, and open at the end, breast high. I am invited to prove a pistol, by firing it into one of these pipes, which, I am told, afford sufficient protection to the firer in case of a barrel bursting—an event, pains were taken to assure me, of very rare occurrence. After a little practice, I find that a mere novice may, with one hand, discharge the six rounds as rapidly as the eye can wink.

'My companion has nothing more to show me except the baths and the reading room, supplied chiefly with newspapers, for the benefit of the workmen; so I bid him good day, and go out of the smell of hot rank oil, to enjoy more keenly the cool breeze that is blowing from the river.'

We must leave Charles Dickens appreciatively sniffing the breezes from the River Thames and visit the Colt Sales Office to inspect two models that were manufactured in London, the Model 1851 .36 calibre Navy and the .31 calibre Pocket Model of 1849. These pistols were marked 'Address. Col. Colt. London' but it must be remembered that Hartford-made pistols destined for the British market were also similarly marked.

On British-made Colts the simple '—' at the beginning and end of the lettering had an additional spearhead and, on the stamp 'Colt's Patent' on the left hand side of the frame, the letter 's' in 'Colt's' was broken.

The walnut grips on London-made Colts were better shaped than on the Hartford models and there were detail variations in the machining of the nipple housing in the cylinder and in the cross hatching on the hammer spur, where British-made pistols had a border.

In all, some 40,000 .36 Navy pistols and about 10,000 .31 Pocket pistols were made by Colt's London Armoury before the factory was closed in 1856, but the London venture was not without its problems and difficulties. The steam engine which supplied power for the machinery did not give satisfaction and the American management grumbled about the climate. Dependence on unskilled labour was reflected in the quality of the product and semi-skilled operators had to be employed at higher rates. The fact that London-made Colts were better finished than their American counterparts was due to the more critical eye of the British customer who demanded the standard of external finish to which he was accustomed. Finally, with the end of the Crimean War in April 1856, demand fell and, although the British Board of Ordnance had purchased a considerable number of Colt Navy revolvers (marked with the Broad Arrow and 'W.D.' and with the 'T.P.' which denoted that they had been proved at the Tower), Colt despaired of obtaining contracts of sufficient size to warrant the continuation of manufacture in Britain. In this he was proved right. The Beaumont-Adams was finally adopted and, with its adoption, the Colt-Adams controversy was finally concluded. Colt's decision to close the London factory was also influenced by the increase in capacity of the Hartford plant which was now capable of meeting the demand at less cost.

The closure of the London factory by no means ended the influence of Colt or Colt arms. A depot was established at 14 Pall Mall, and Charles Frederick Dennett and the Baron Friederich Kunow Waldemar August von Oppen served as agents and looked after the interests of the Colt Company in Britain. The later Colts, as we shall see, were marked 'Colt's Pt. F.A. Mfg. Co. Hartford, Ct. U.S.A. Depot 14, Pall Mall, London', the Sales Office being at 14 Glasshouse St, Piccadilly Circus.

Even before the Colt factory had closed its doors, the opposition was strengthening its position. On 9 February 1856, the London Armoury Company was provisionally registered, and among the shareholders were several people whom we shall meet again as we follow the development of the English percussion revolver, including Robert Adams, Frederick Edward Blackett Beaumont, John Deane (the senior partner in the firm Deane, Adams and Deane), William Harding and James Kerr. The new company obtained premises in Henry St, Bermondsey. The steam engine and machine tools were transferred to the new factory from the Weston Street premises and, by 1857, production appears to have settled down.

In addition to new premises, it is likely that the London Armoury Company also benefitted from the employment of additional machinery and they certainly had an improved product—the Beaumont-Adams double action revolver of 1855 which had already been manufactured by Deane, Adams and Deane and was a considerable advance on its predecessors.

The history of the Beaumont-Adams is of great interest since this pistol was the first true double action revolver to be produced in commercial quantities. To trace the development of the Beaumont-Adams, we must return to 1853 and to Robert Adams' patent specification No. 2712 of 22 November. At first glance, there is little difference between the drawings for the 1851 patent and those which accompanied the 1853 patent, but 'the improvements are intended to obviate an objection which has been very generally made to such class of fire-arms when the same are cocked, by the act of pulling the trigger, which is that the strength of effort necessarily called into force when pulling the trigger to cause the barrels to revolve and to overcome the mainspring prevents that steadiness of aim which is requisite for correct shooting'. These improvements consisted of the addition of a small, spring loaded pawl and an extra notch or bent on the breast of the hammer, together with the provision of a small spring located in the breast of the hammer, the purpose of which will later become obvious.

According to R. Bedford, this type of action was in production for a very short time and was made concurrently with the ordinary Adams 1851 revolvers. This is borne out by the fact that F. B. E. Beaumont patented his double action mechanism in 1855, British Patent No. 374 of 20 February, and thus rendered the Adams 1853

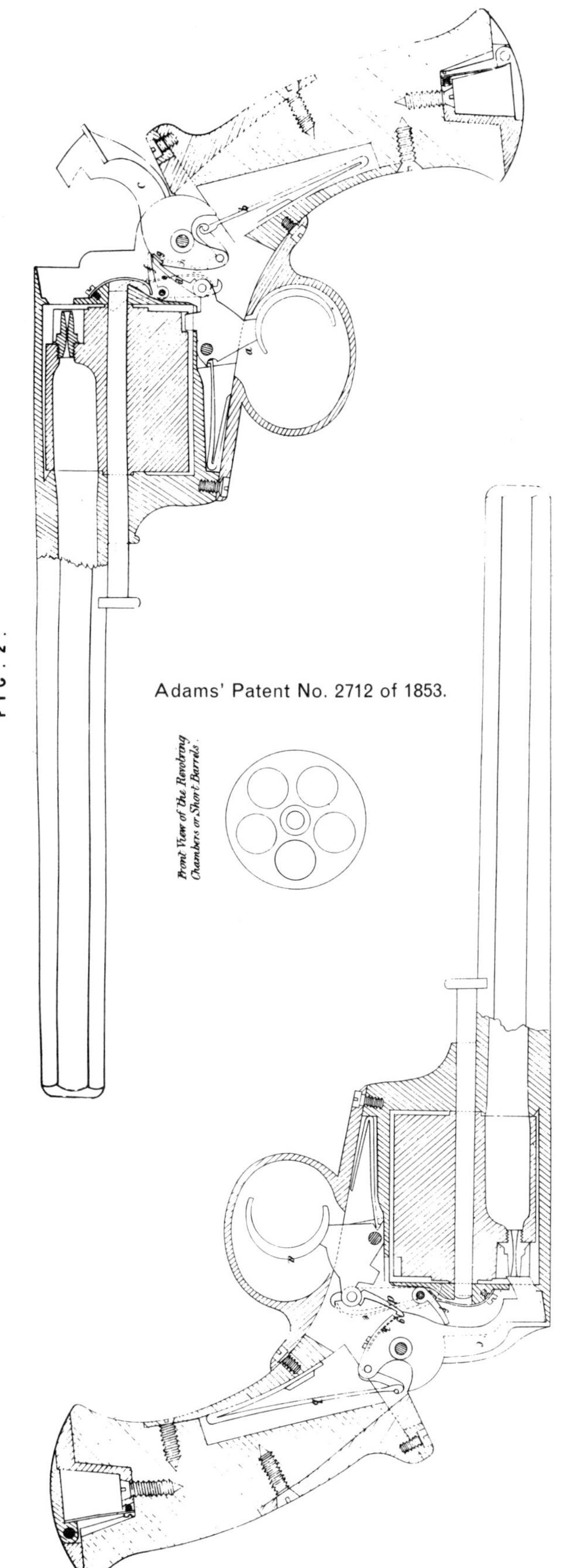

action obsolescent. The very appropriate term 'hesitation action' has been given to the Adams mechanism by R. Bedford, and it aptly describes this important link in the chain of development of the double action mechanism.

In use, the hesitation action operated as follows. The trigger was pulled back, rotating the cylinder and cocking the hammer. At full cock, the spring loaded pawl, (f) on the patent drawing, engaged the upper notch in the hammer breast. This, in effect, propped the hammer back at full cock. If the trigger was released slightly, the lifter, or 'driver' as Adams preferred to call it, was disengaged by a small spring in the breast of the hammer so that, when pressure was again applied to the trigger, the lifter then pushed the pawl out of engagement and so released the hammer.

The pistol shooter of today who has used both the 'long action' Smith and Wesson and the Colt for rapid aimed double action shooting will appreciate the benefits that the 'hesitation action' provided. Although the Smith and Wesson action is not a hesitation action, it is possible to 'hold on' to the trigger prior to firing and to use this pause to correct the aim. The great protagonist of this method of double action shooting was the late Ed. McGivern.

A spur on the hammer of the hesitation action would make it possible to thumb cock the action, but it must be stressed that the cylinder would not rotate. This is what Beaumont did, but he altered the pawl or catch slightly from the original Adams and also provided a means whereby the cylinder would be rotated if the pistol were thumb cocked.

It will be remembered that, on single action or thumb cocking mechanisms, the limb that rotated the cylinder was attached to the hammer. On the Adams, the cylinder hand was attached to the trigger. To achieve true double action and be able to rotate the cylinder both by pulling the trigger and by thumb cocking, there had to be some positive connection between the hammer and the trigger. The illustration shows how this was done. The trigger and cylinder hand is much the same as that used on the Adams self-cocker, but the lifter is different. On the Beaumont-Adams, it is pierced by a rectangular hole into which the hook on the hammer breast can enter. With the mechanism assembled, it can be seen that, when the hammer is drawn back by the thumb, the hook will engage the hole in the lifter and lift the rear of the trigger. This, in turn, will cause the cylinder hand to

Beaumont's Patent No.374 of 1855.

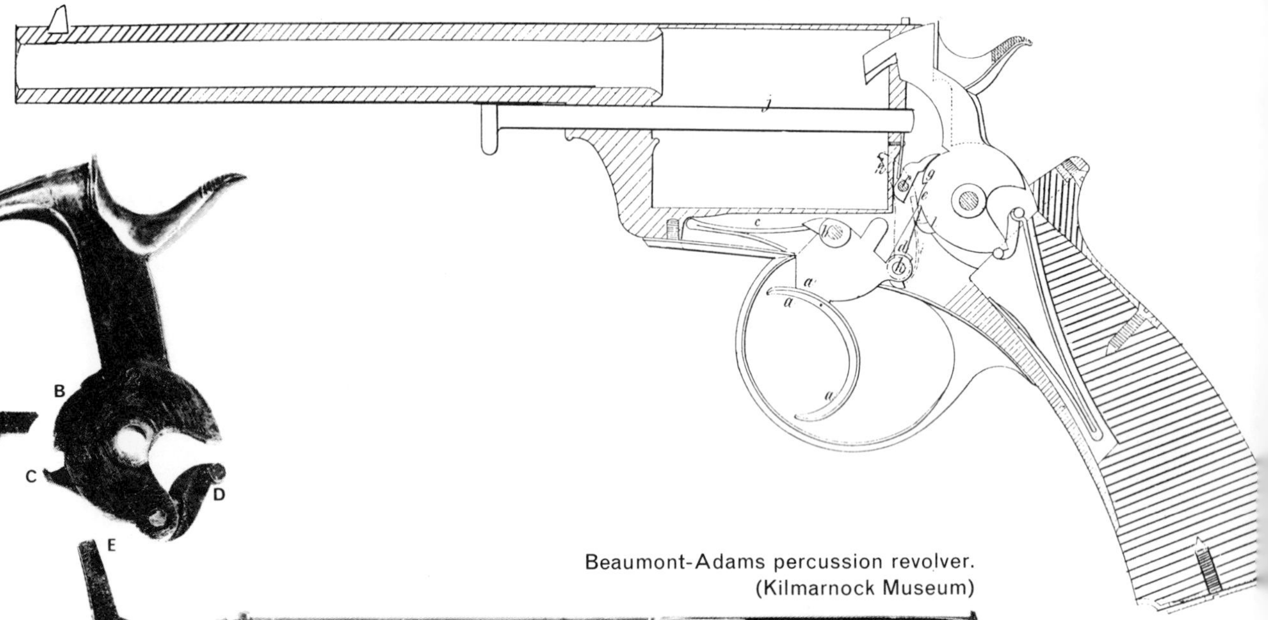

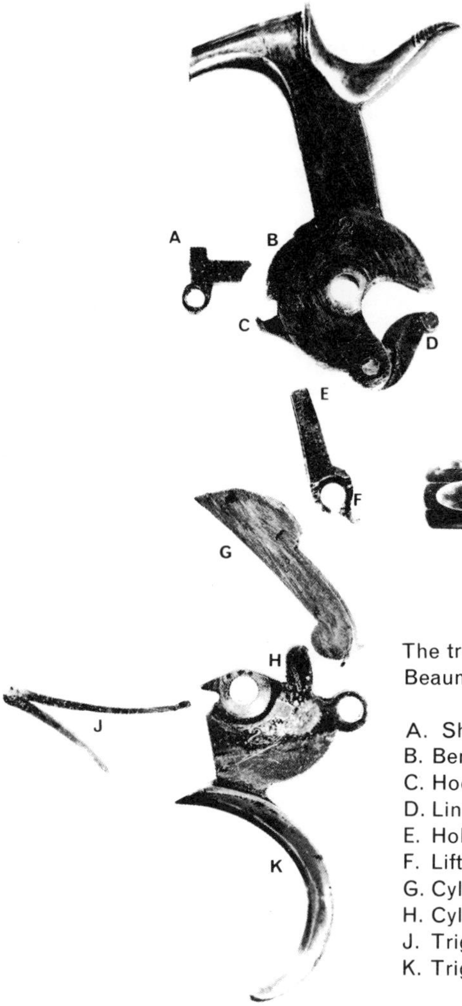

Beaumont-Adams percussion revolver.
(Kilmarnock Museum)

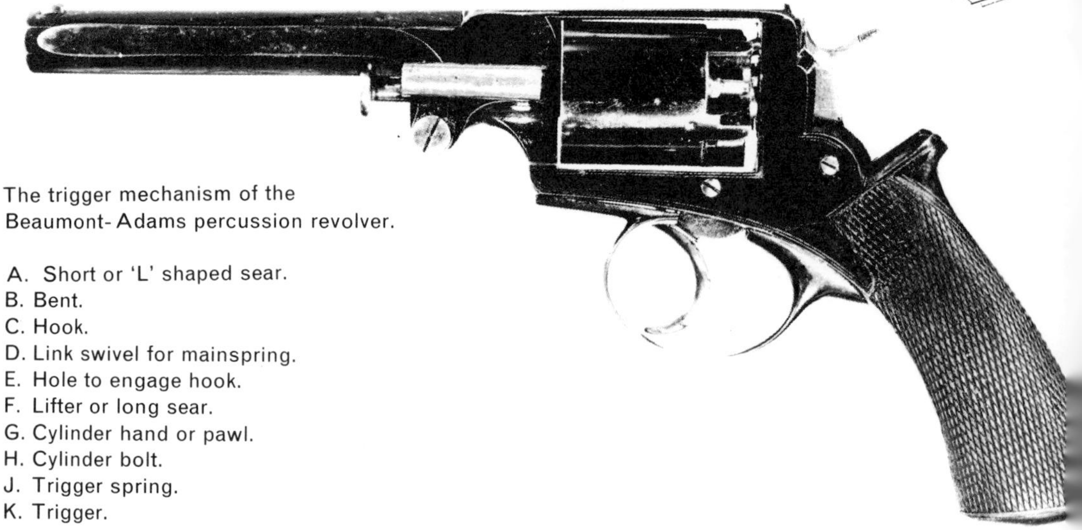

The trigger mechanism of the Beaumont- Adams percussion revolver.

A. Short or 'L' shaped sear.
B. Bent.
C. Hook.
D. Link swivel for mainspring.
E. Hole to engage hook.
F. Lifter or long sear.
G. Cylinder hand or pawl.
H. Cylinder bolt.
J. Trigger spring.
K. Trigger.

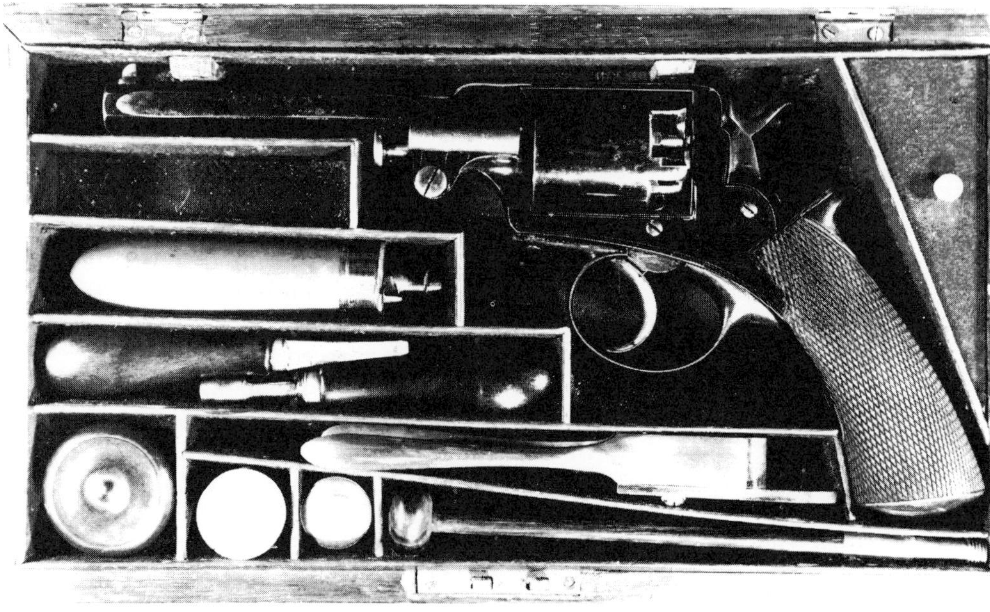

Cased Beaumont-Adams percussion revolver.

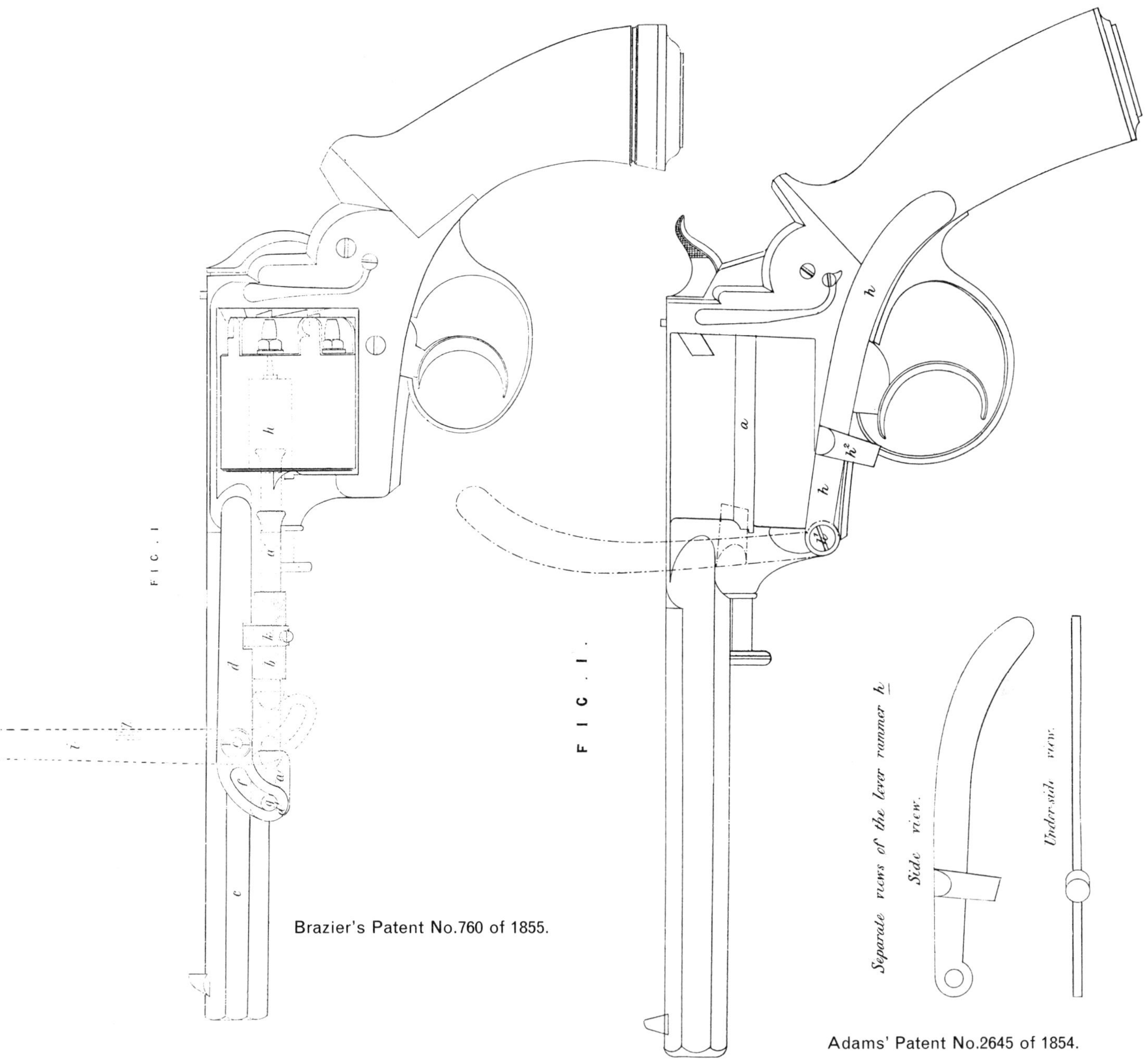

Brazier's Patent No.760 of 1855.

Adams' Patent No.2645 of 1854.

rotate the cylinder. With the hammer at full cock, the 'L' shaped short sear will be pressed into the full cock bent on the hammer by a spring which lies behind it, attached to the frame. To release the hammer, the trigger is pulled and the lifter, due to the camming action of the bottom surface of the hook, will move slightly forward and the top will then push the 'L' shaped short sear out of engagement. The hammer will fall and fire the pistol, the mechanism returning to the original position impelled by the 'V' shaped trigger return spring. The mechanism is simple and quite effective. There is a possibility that the pawl could become inoperative due to clogging with dirt or dried oil, but the pistol could still be fired trigger action.

Externally, the Beaumont-Adams can be recognised by the spur on the hammer, and the earliest type of rammer fitted was the simple lever patented by Robert Adams (British Patent No. 2645 of 1854). Some self-cocking Adams revolvers, however, were fitted with the Brazier rammer (British Patent No. 760 of 5 April 1855) in which the lever lay along the side of the barrel. This was invented by Joseph Brazier, a member of the famous family of Wolverhampton gunlock manufacturers, but was more complicated than the later Kerr rammer patented in July of the same year (British Patent No. 1722) which superceded both the earlier rammers. Where the Brazier lever was pulled upward and forward, the Kerr moved upward and to the rear to seat the bullet in the chamber. There was, however, another rammer invented by Richard Brazier and used with his patent double action revolver. Specimens of this are extremely rare,

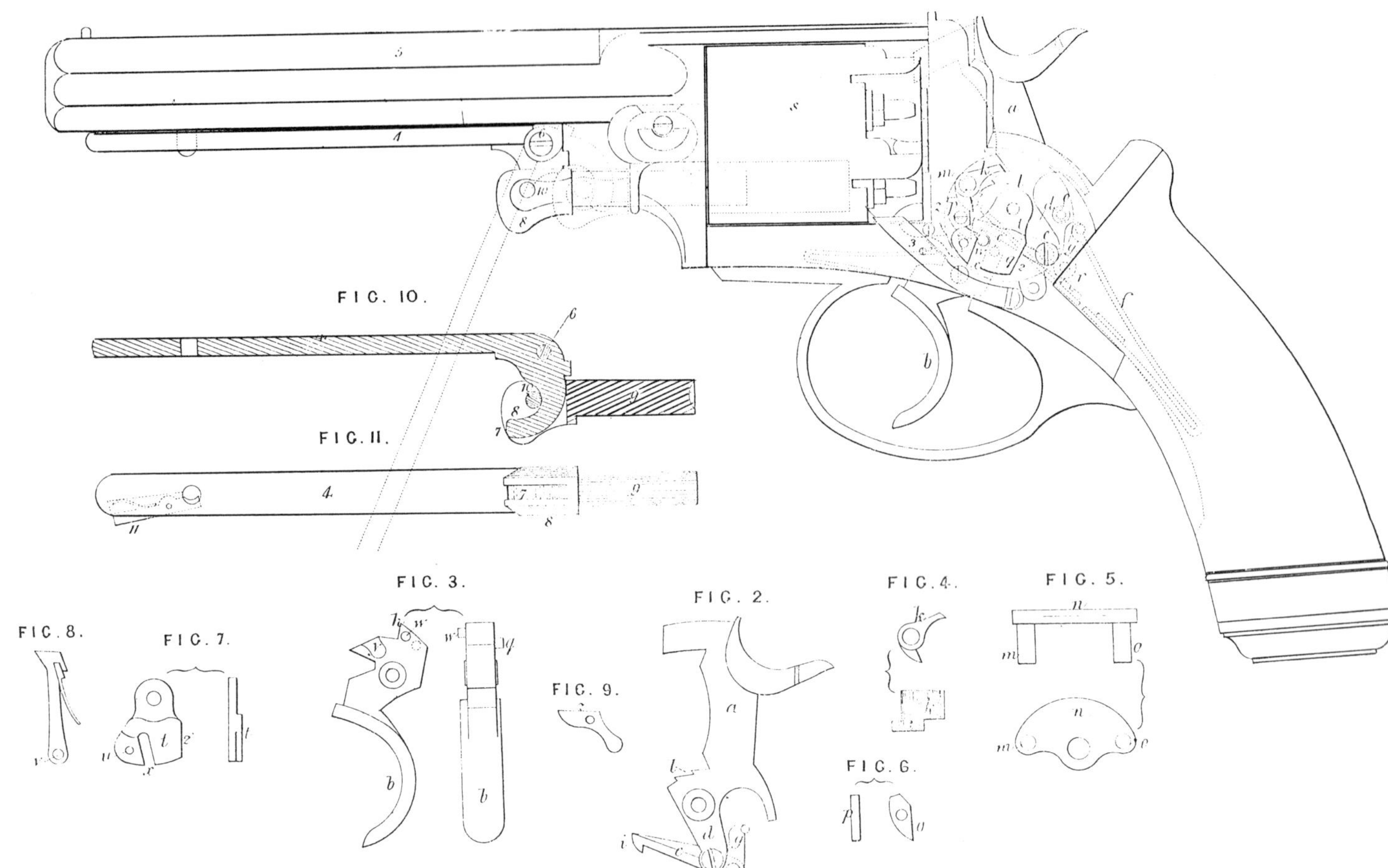

Brazier's Patent No.1593 of 1858.

.500 Beaumont-Adams percussion revolver No.51809 damascened in gold.

no doubt due to the complexity of the lockwork as shown by the drawing for his British Patent No. 1593 of 1858.

There was no spring loaded plunger on the Beaumont-Adams to provide a half cock position. This was obtained by an extra bent on the hammer breast into which the pawl dropped, so that the pistol could be carried safely when fully loaded and also so that the cylinder could rotate freely during the loading operation.

With the .500 Beaumont-Adams, the slide which locks the cylinder can be seen at the rear of the frame, while the spring previously employed on the Adams to retain the cylinder pin has now been replaced by a small screw. This method of retaining the cylinder pin was patented in 1859.

Following the usual trials, the 54 bore (.442″)

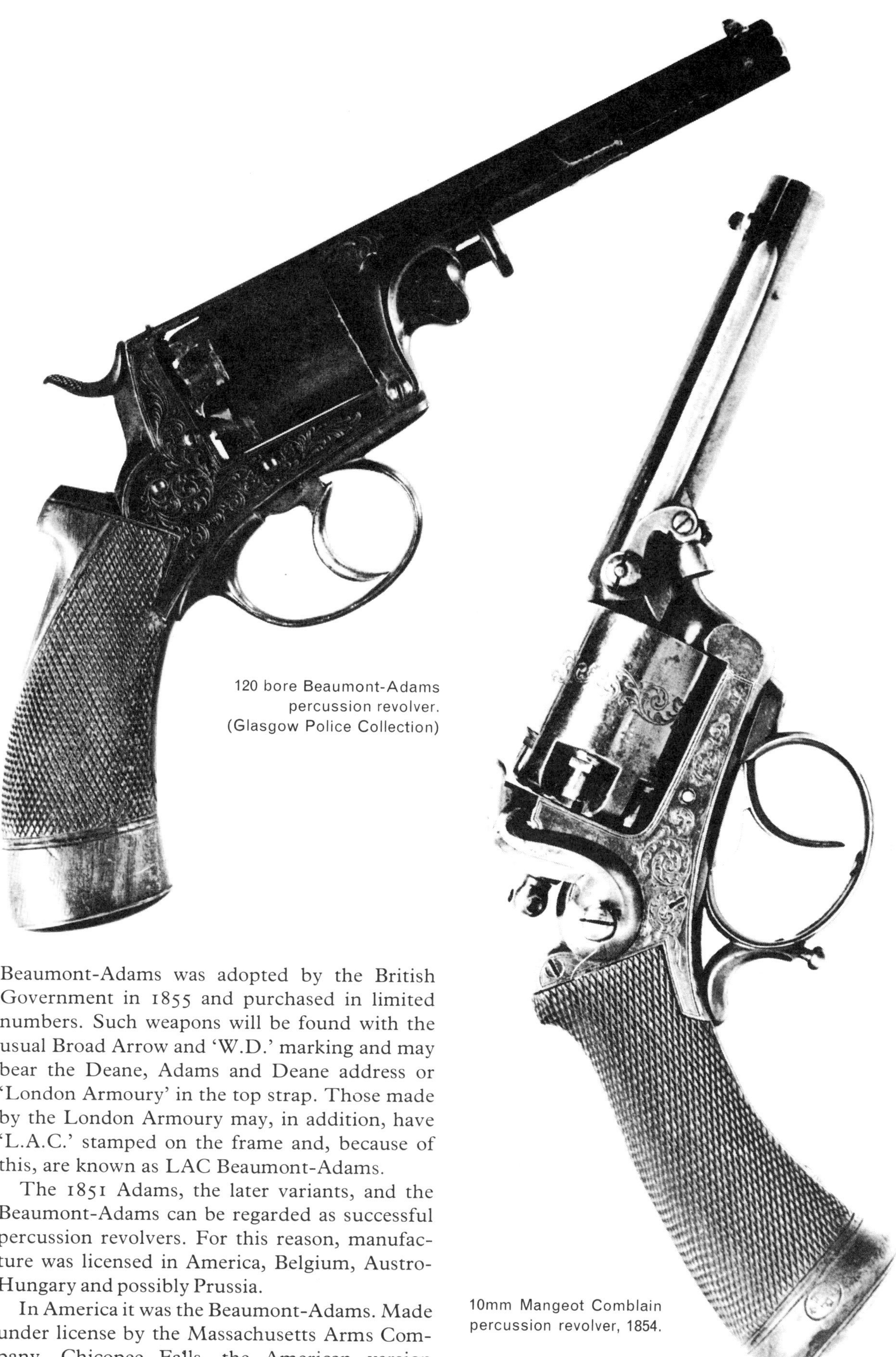

120 bore Beaumont-Adams percussion revolver. (Glasgow Police Collection)

10mm Mangeot Comblain percussion revolver, 1854.

Beaumont-Adams was adopted by the British Government in 1855 and purchased in limited numbers. Such weapons will be found with the usual Broad Arrow and 'W.D.' marking and may bear the Deane, Adams and Deane address or 'London Armoury' in the top strap. Those made by the London Armoury may, in addition, have 'L.A.C.' stamped on the frame and, because of this, are known as LAC Beaumont-Adams.

The 1851 Adams, the later variants, and the Beaumont-Adams can be regarded as successful percussion revolvers. For this reason, manufacture was licensed in America, Belgium, Austro-Hungary and possibly Prussia.

In America it was the Beaumont-Adams. Made under license by the Massachusetts Arms Company, Chicopee Falls, the American version differed only slightly from its British prototype

54 bore percussion revolver by John Adams.

and appears to have been in production from 1857 to 1861. During the Civil War a number of .36 calibre military pistols—five chambered and with a 6″ barrel and three grooved rifling—were bought by the US Government, and, in all, they purchased over a thousand Beaumont-Adams, some of them imported from England.

Modified Adams 1851 self-cocking revolvers were manufactured by Antonin Vincenc Lebeda in Prague. A noted gunmaker of the first half of the nineteenth century, Lebeda was born in Breslau and later worked in Vienna before becoming established in Prague in 1820. Adams revolvers attributed to Lebeda used a slightly modified self-cocking action based on Mangeot's patents in which a trigger stop was formed by a spring in the trigger guard. With the spring compressed, a stop protruded through the guard against which the tip of the trigger abutted immediately prior to releasing the hammer. The aim could be corrected at this point and the stop released, a final pressure on the trigger discharging the pistol. Mangeot was later associated with Comblain in the production of a side hammer percussion revolver which enjoyed little success.

In Belgium several manufacturers produced the Adams under license, the best known being possibly Pirlot Frères of Liege, who appear to have been active from about 1840 to 1870. Both Eugene Pirlot and Gustave Pirlot were members of the adminstrative commission of the Banc d'Epreuves des Armes à Feu. Pirated versions were no doubt made and the presence of British proof marks is no guarantee of domestic manufacture, since Belgian proofs may often be located in addition to the London ones.

Possibly the most interesting of the Adams series is the Beaumont-Adams illustrated in the *Journal of the Society for Army Historical Research, Vol. 35, No. 143*. The article on 'Early British Regulation Revolvers' by R. Scurfield mentions the Prussian Navy 9mm revolver, the specimen illustrated being dated 1870 and marked 'Suhl'. Further research has proved abortive.

The last muzzle loading revolver bearing the name Adams was the 1866 John Adams manufactured by the Adams Patent Small Arms Company formed by Robert Adam's brother John after he left the London Armoury Company.

Few muzzle loading John Adams revolvers were made and consequently this pistol has been rather neglected. Nevertheless it is of importance since it was virtually identical with the John Adams .450 centre-fire revolver adopted by the British Government. John Adams took out several patents relating to firearms, three of which deserve mention: No. 2824 taken out in 1857, No. 1758 of 1861 and No. 1959. The last was obtained in 1866 and refers to the rammer used on the 1866 percussion revolver. This pistol, in sharp contrast to the previous Adams revolvers, was six chambered and, instead of being forged in one piece, the frame was 'built-up'. The first Adams patent mentioned described a somewhat complicated pistol with the barrel and top strap made separately but this pistol does not appear to have been manufactured on a commercial basis. The second patent, that of 1861, referred to a breechloading revolver so arranged that cartridges could be loaded at the breech. Alternatively, by employing a cylinder provided with nipples, the pistol could be used as a muzzle loader.

With its 'built-up' construction, the barrel and frame for the cylinder were formed in one piece which fitted into a slot machined into the lock frame. This part of the pistol, as the name implies, carried the lockwork, hammer etc. The general arrangement of the pistol can be seen from the illustration of the partially dismantled .450 centre-fire Adams (page 213).

The lockwork is essentially the same as the Beaumont-Adams except that the 'L' shaped pawl of the Beaumont action has been moved free from its position in front of the breast of the hammer where it was actuated by the lifter. In the John Adams action it lies beneath the hammer and, in effect, becomes a secondary trigger operated by the back of the trigger proper, the tail protruding through the frame and trigger guard. The spring which causes the secondary trigger or auxiliary sear to engage the half and full cock bents in the hammer, is mounted on the same stud that carries the mainspring.

This arrangement became quite popular and variations were widely adopted on centre-, pin- and rim-fire revolvers. The origin of this type of double action mechanism can be traced to William Tranter's double trigger mechanism, first patented in 1853, No. 212 of 28 January. Next to Adams pistols, those made by William Tranter were possibly the most popular.

The eldest son of a blacksmith, Tranter was apprenticed by his father to a gunmaker and, after completing his apprenticeship, he started his own business with a small legacy left to him by an uncle. His first premises were in St Mary's Square, Birmingham, and, in 1846, he was joined by a younger brother, David, who acted as business manager. In the early 1860's he built a new and spacious factory on what was then the outskirts of Birmingham, at Aston. In its day, the Tranter factory was the most extensive pistol-making establishment in the Midlands and, with the pistol-making side of the business augmented by Government contracts for Snider rifles, the concern prospered. But, in 1885 (David Tranter had died the year before), William Tranter ran into financial difficulties and sold the business to his friend George Kynoch, who had established his ammunition factory at Witton in 1862. The factory continued to make firearms until 1900 and we shall learn more about its activities in a later chapter. In 1926 the old Tranter factory was bought by the Hercules Cycle Company, and was finally demolished in 1961.

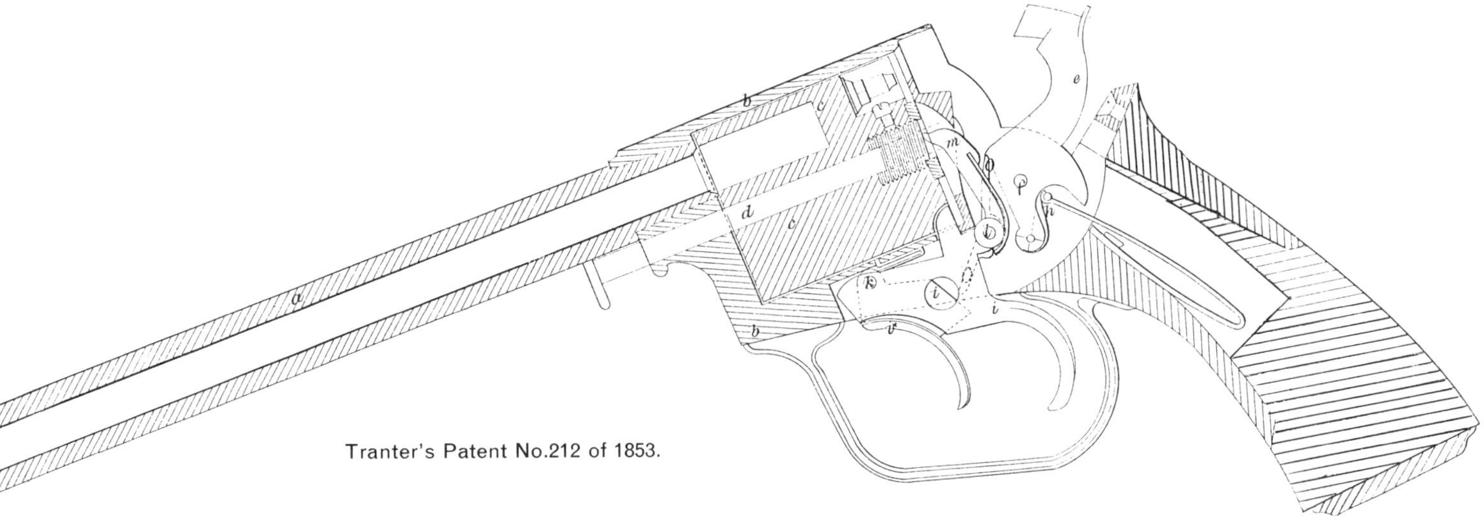

Tranter's Patent No.212 of 1853.

Percussion arms made at the factory showed a striking resemblance to the Robert Adams revolvers, and this is hardly surprising since the Tranter was built under Adams patents and, as we have already seen, Tranter had himself manufactured Adams revolvers for Robert Adams.

Tranter percussion revolvers are divided into two types, the Double Trigger Models and the later Single Trigger Models. Three variants of the Double Trigger Model are recognised. The First Model had a detachable rammer similar to that fitted to the Adams (page 148). The Second Model had a rammer fitted to the left hand side of the frame by a key pivot and barrel hook, and it could be removed from the pistol by turning it to the appropriate position—the key slot can be seen

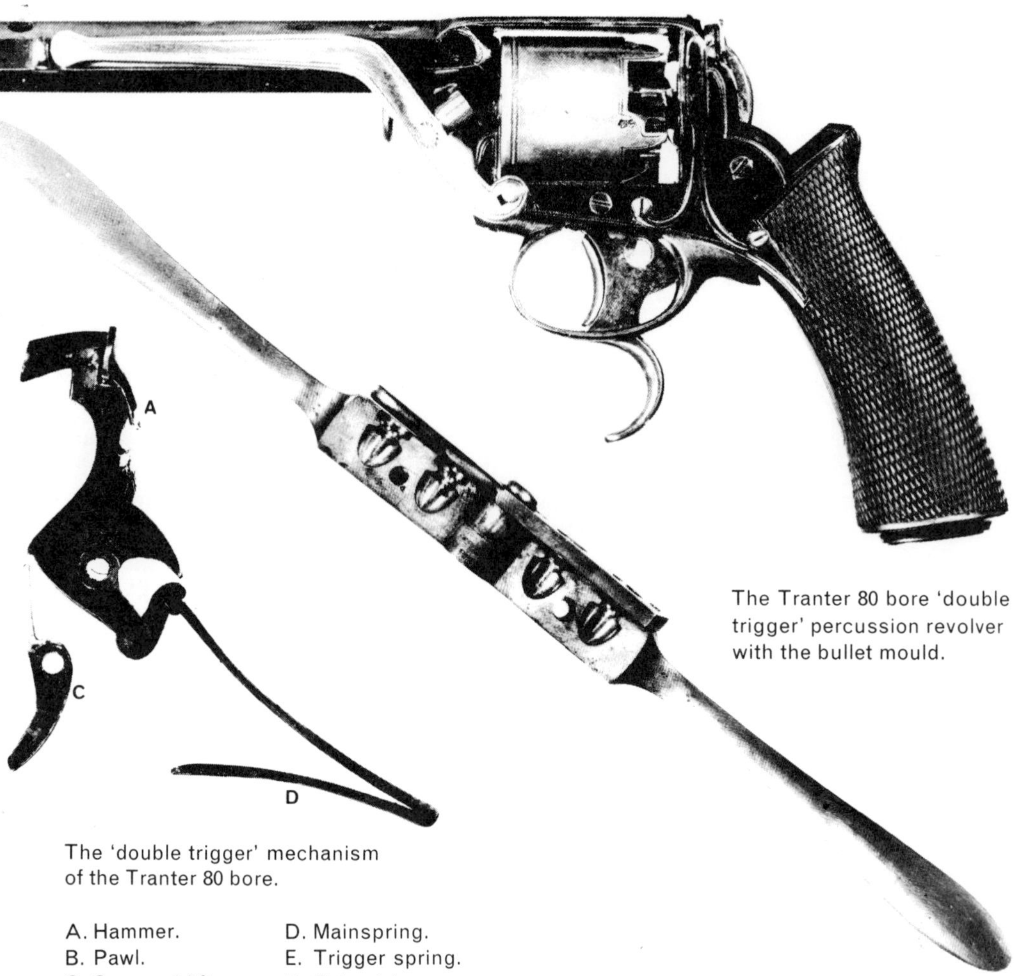

The Tranter 80 bore 'double trigger' percussion revolver with the bullet mould.

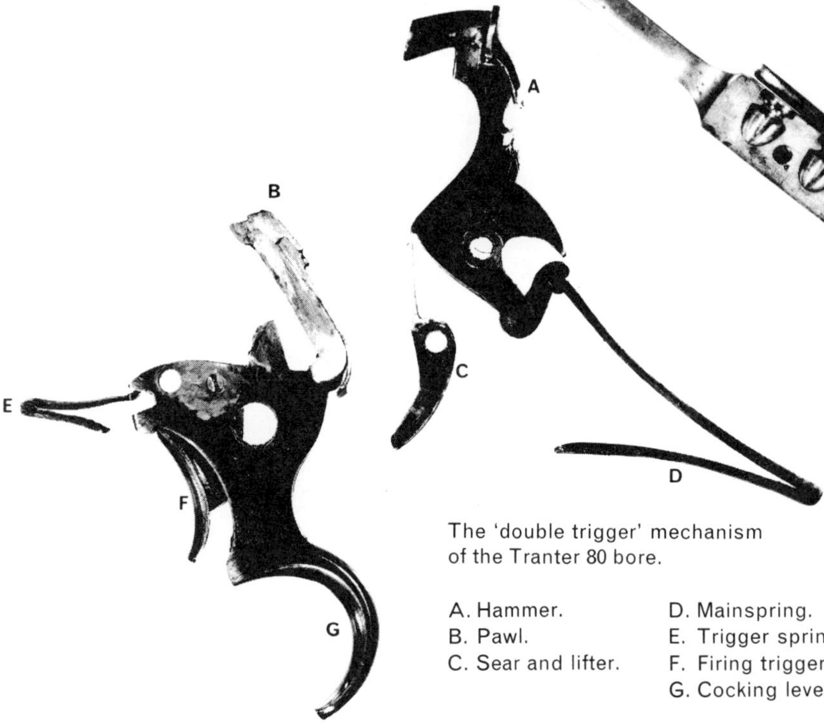

The 'double trigger' mechanism of the Tranter 80 bore.

A. Hammer.
B. Pawl.
C. Sear and lifter.
D. Mainspring.
E. Trigger spring.
F. Firing trigger.
G. Cocking lever.

The Tranter 80 bore cased with accessories.

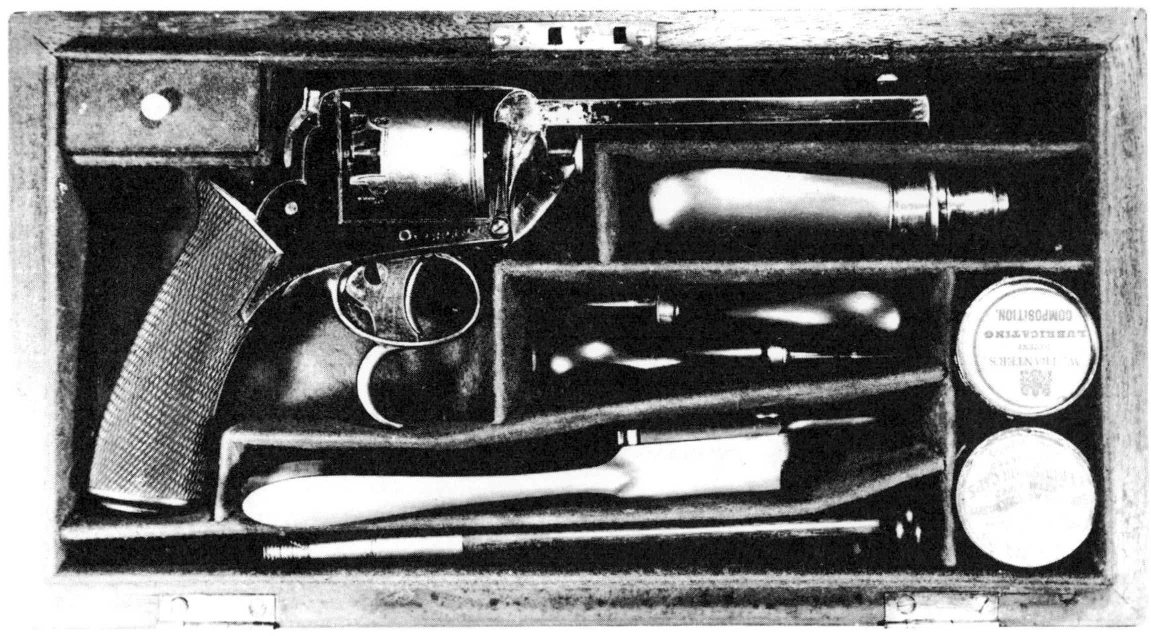

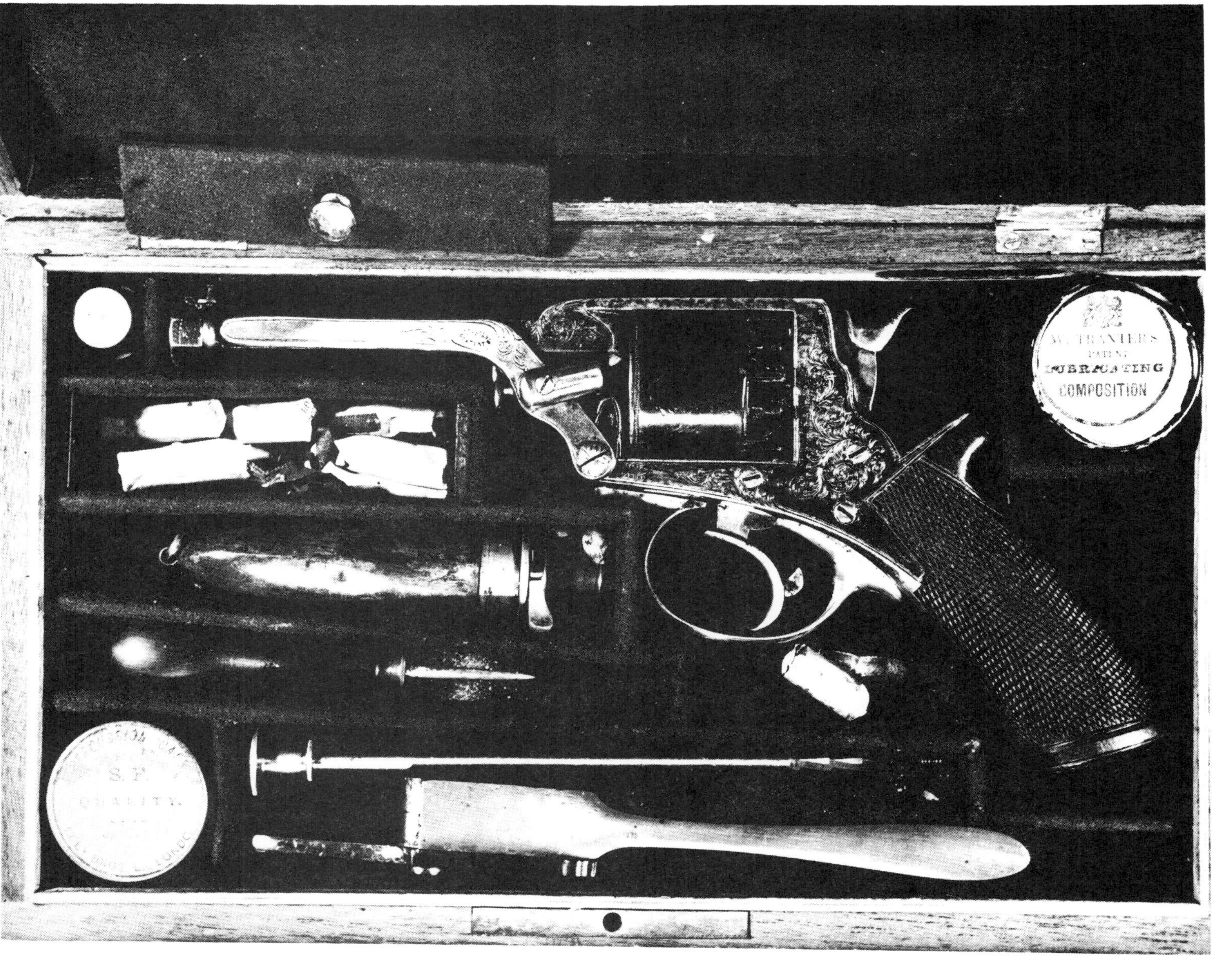

80 bore Fourth Model Tranter (1856) percussion revolver.

in the illustration. The Third Model presented a more streamlined outline and, attached to the pistol by a screw, the rammer differed in that the plunger was pivoted to the lever instead of being formed integrally. The double trigger mechanism was used on all three models and the arrangement of the component parts can be seen in the illustration of the detached lockwork. The trigger proper was hinged inside the cocking lever carrying the cylinder bolt, to which was attached the cylinder hand and the sear and lifter. The cocking lever lay outside the trigger guard and was pulled back by the second finger. When fully drawn back, it acted as a spur to steady the pistol and at the same time cocked the hammer and rotated and locked the cylinder. The trigger could then be pulled, and the blade of the trigger pressing against the tail of the lifter made it act as a sear to release the hammer. Operated in this manner, deliberate aimed fire was possible but, if rapid fire was called for, the trigger and cocking lever were pulled simultaneously, resulting in 'cocking action' rapid fire.

Despite contemporary comment 'that one could not be expected to play "cornet à piston" on one's revolver in the middle of an engagement', Tranter's double trigger action proved to be effective and entirely practical and, since the pistols were particularly well made, they enjoyed an enviable and well-deserved reputation. The safety catch on the double trigger models was an improvement on the Adams. On the Adams, the trigger had to be pulled slightly back to raise the hammer so that the safety could be pressed in towards the frame. The Tranter safety was completely automatic; the pistol could be carried without danger when loaded and capped, and the cylinder rotated freely during loading. Externally, the catch consisted of a spring bifurcated at the tail and mounted on the left hand side of the frame, to which it was attached by two screws. At the top a rectangular block was formed which passed through the frame in front of the hammer. This block was pushed out of the way of the falling hammer by the cylinder hand, the extension to which can be seen immediately behind the ratchet pawl.

The double trigger models were so popular that they continued to be manufactured even after the introduction of the later single trigger double action series. Tranter's attention to detail can also be seen in his bullet design. The mould supplied for use with his pistols cast a bullet with a deep groove above the base. Cased pistols were supplied with a tin of 'W. Tranter's Patent Lubricating Composition', consisting of beeswax and tallow, and, after the bullets had been dipped into the molten lubricant, withdrawn and allowed to cool, the grooves were filled by it. A supply of these bullets could be kept on hand and loading was consequently simple and speedy. Bullet diameter for the 80 bore pistol was .392″, the mouth of the chamber was .400″, but, since it tapered to .388″ at the base, the bullet was held firmly and, after loading, there was no need to apply additional lubricant to eliminate the possibility of a multiple discharge. Since the lubricant was carried into the barrel, fouling was reduced. Both the patent bullet and the mould were described in Tranter's Patent No. 2921 of 16 December 1853.

Cylinder withdrawal was again simple and speedy. The cylinder pin was formed with two slots cut in the shaft and, on the right hand side of the frame in front of the cylinder, a spring-loaded pin passed through the frame and engaged the slots so that the pin was either retained in the fully home position or else withdrawn so that the cylinder could be removed.

Third Model Tranter revolvers were manufactured in 38, 54, 80 and 120 bore sizes, but the First and Second Models were either not made in 120 bore, or were very rare. None of the double trigger models could, of course, be thumb cocked since there was no hook on the lifter to connect the hammer with the trigger. One variant of the double trigger model, the so-called 'Export' Model had a 'treble action'. This mechanism was referred to in Tranter's patent of 1856, and the hammer had a spur which permitted thumb cocking in addition to the use of the cocking lever. Most of these models appear to have been made for export and few will be found bearing the names of English vendors. Tranter's 1856 Patent, No. 1913 of 16 August, covered a number of ideas on trigger mechanisms, one of which was employed on his double action single trigger revolver. The later rim-fire and centre-fire revolvers employed the same basic mechanism with slight variations. With the double action mechanism of the 1863 Tranter rim-fire revolver (page 217), the obvious feature is the small lug visible at the back of the trigger. When the trigger was pulled, this passed through a slot in the guard and struck the auxiliary sear, which could be engaged in the half or full cock bents on the hammer. Tranter employed the same lifter for the self-cocking action. Sometimes the hook was on

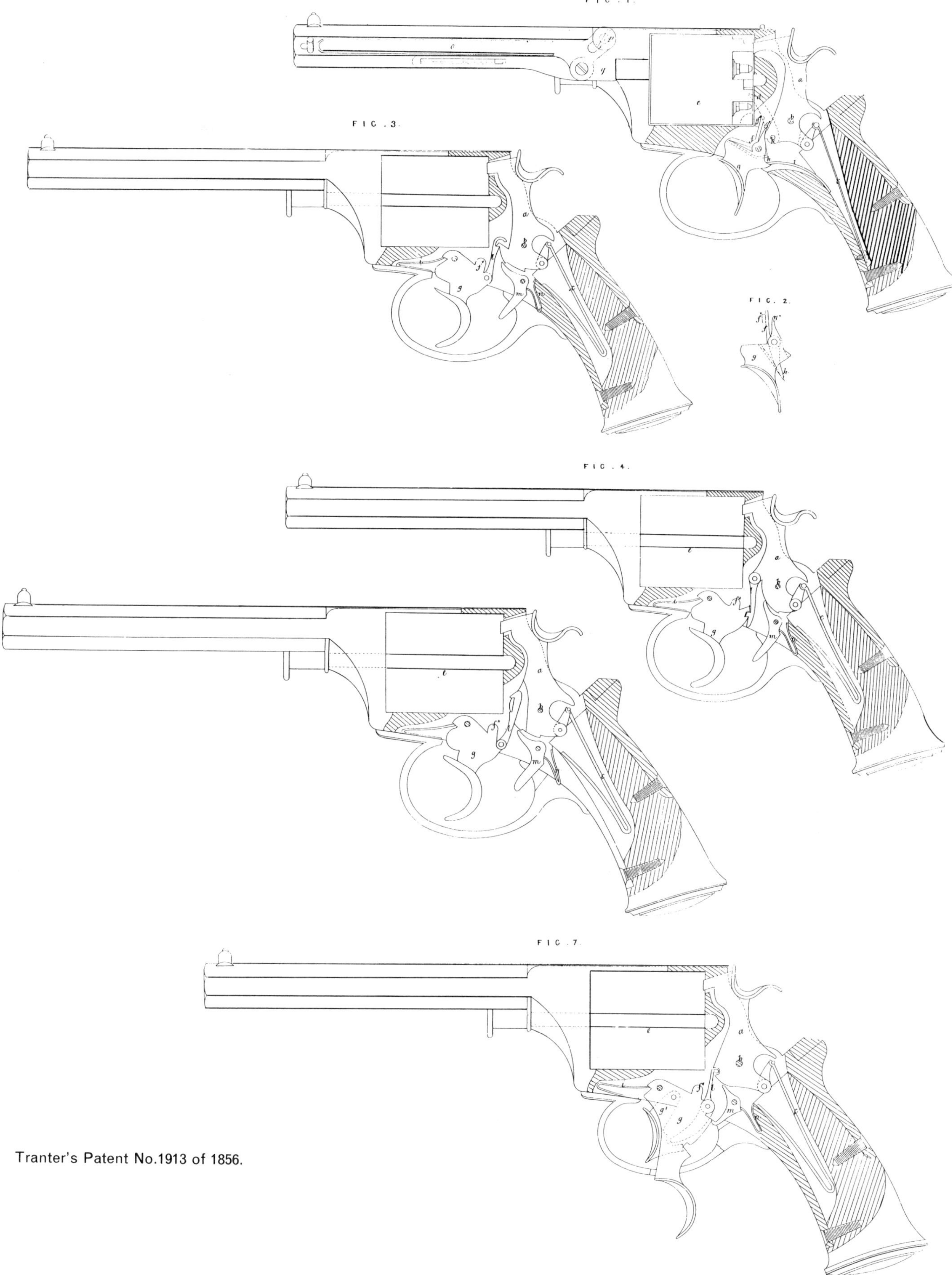

Tranter's Patent No.1913 of 1856.

Tranter single trigger Fourth Model percussion revolver, showing hinged cylinder lock. See also facing page.

the hammer breast; alternatively, it could be formed as part of the lifter. It is debatable which system was the better, and equally so are the relative merits of allowing the tail of the sear to protrude through the lock plate or, as on the Tranter, of providing a lug on the rear of the trigger. In my own opinion, the Tranter system is preferable, since the external tail of the sear on some of the revolvers which have employed this type of operation is sharply pointed and, although it has never happened, I have always had a fear of getting a finger caught between the trigger and the shark's tooth of the sear.

Bearing a close resemblance to the Beaumont-Adams, the Deane-Harding percussion revolver represented a most important evolutionary advance in the design of the double action mechanism, although the revolver itself was not highly regarded by contemporary users. The adverse opinion of Lord Roberts is well known, and is quoted by J. N. George: 'It is an arm, which could always be depended upon to get out of order at a critical moment'. Although never a Service

Cased 80 bore single trigger Tranter percussion revolver.

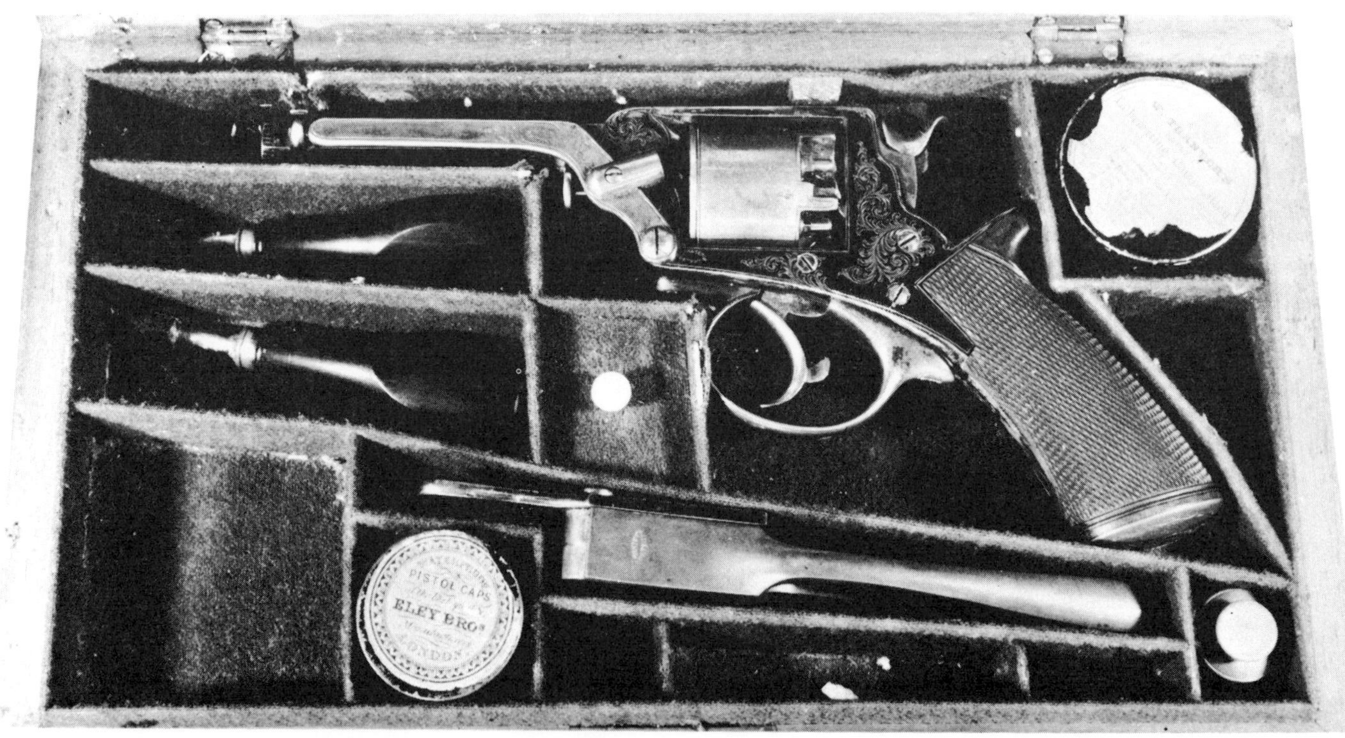

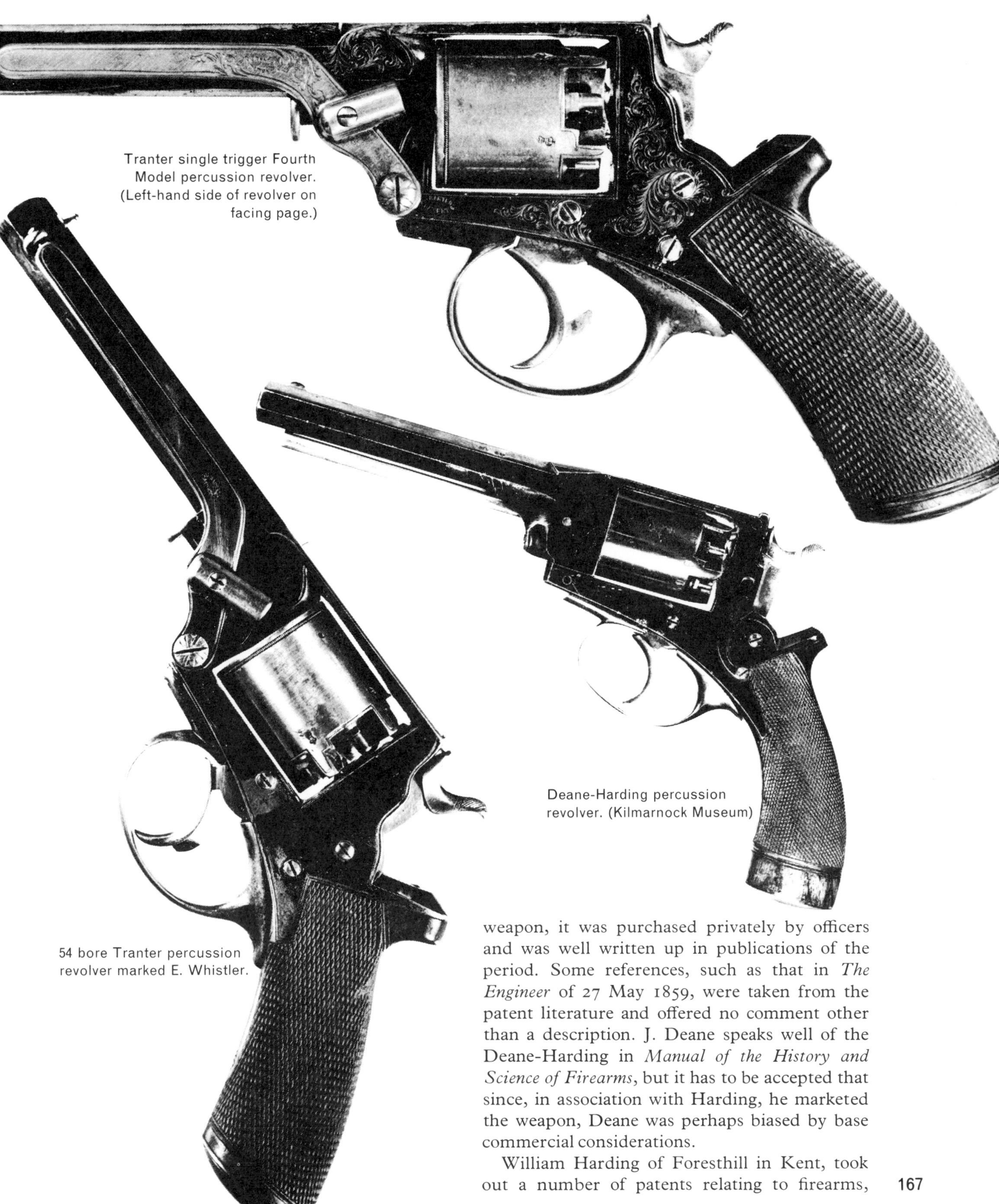
Tranter single trigger Fourth Model percussion revolver. (Left-hand side of revolver on facing page.)

Deane-Harding percussion revolver. (Kilmarnock Museum)

54 bore Tranter percussion revolver marked E. Whistler.

weapon, it was purchased privately by officers and was well written up in publications of the period. Some references, such as that in *The Engineer* of 27 May 1859, were taken from the patent literature and offered no comment other than a description. J. Deane speaks well of the Deane-Harding in *Manual of the History and Science of Firearms*, but it has to be accepted that since, in association with Harding, he marketed the weapon, Deane was perhaps biased by base commercial considerations.

William Harding of Foresthill in Kent, took out a number of patents relating to firearms,

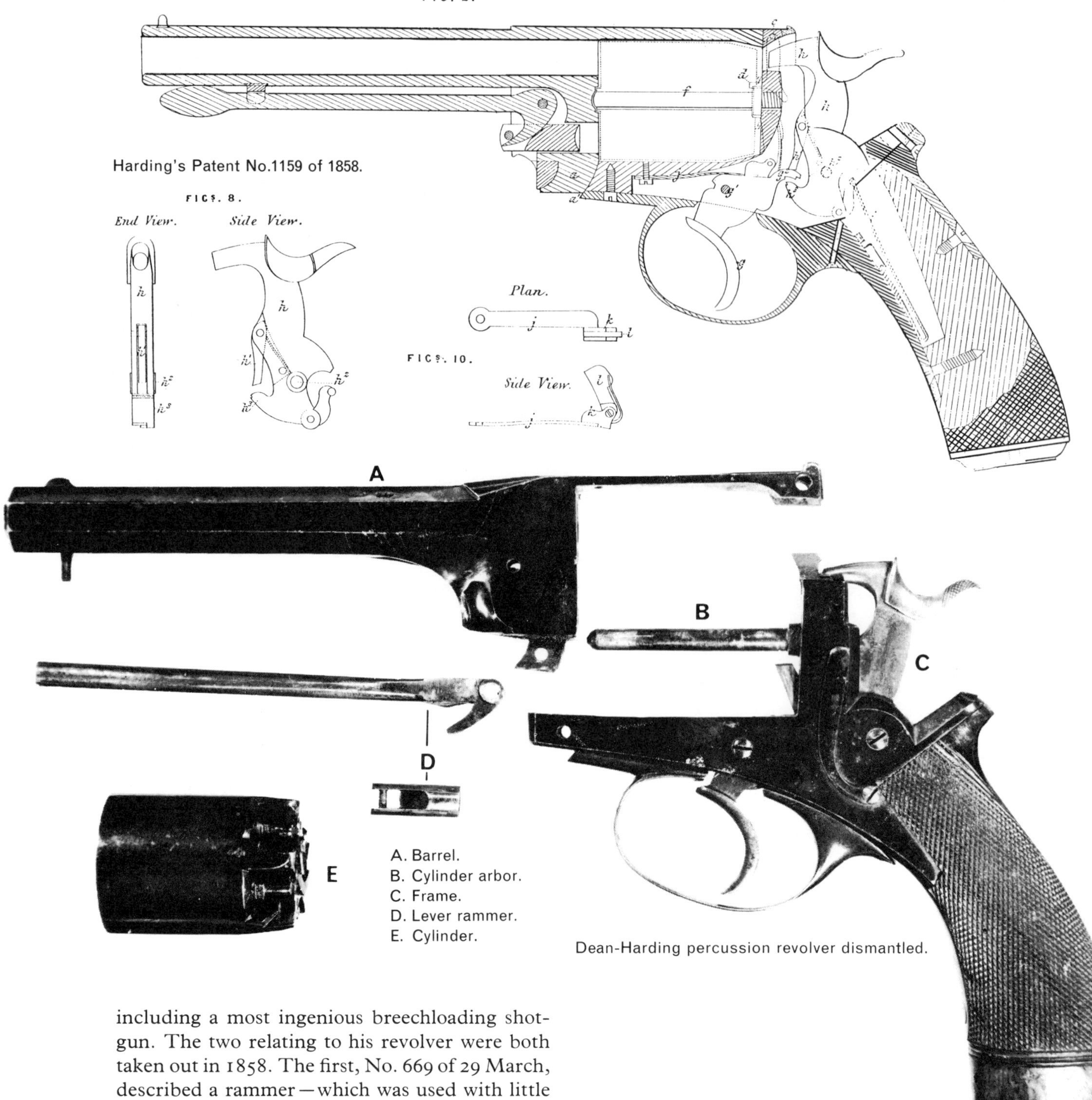

Harding's Patent No.1159 of 1858.

A. Barrel.
B. Cylinder arbor.
C. Frame.
D. Lever rammer.
E. Cylinder.

Dean-Harding percussion revolver dismantled.

including a most ingenious breechloading shotgun. The two relating to his revolver were both taken out in 1858. The first, No. 669 of 29 March, described a rammer—which was used with little variation on all the production variants of the Deane-Harding—and a conventional type of double action mechanism.

An auxiliary sear was used, mounted in the same position as that on the Beaumont-Adams, the major difference being in the 'lifter' which, instead of pushing upwards on the hammer, reverted to the earlier pepperbox type of lifter by which it was no doubt inspired. The double action mechanism of Patent No. 669 does not appear to have ever been used on a production revolver. Two months later Harding's Patent No. 1159 appeared, and is of considerable importance in that an entirely new double action mechanism was described, one which, in basic essentials, is still employed to this day. Both the 'lifter' and secondary sear or trigger previously employed by both Beaumont and Tranter were dispensed with, and a new component or limb was introduced which Harding called a 'rule jointed rod'. The mechanism can best be understood from the illustration. When trigger or self-cocking action was employed, the extension at the rear of the trigger engaged the 'rule jointed rod', the rod acting as a lifter and so rotating the hammer. When the hammer was at full cock, the two components were disengaged and the hammer fell, discharging the weapon. When the trigger was released, it returned to its original position, the extension moving aside the spring loaded rod. When single action or thumb cocking was employed, the trigger extension engaged a bent which, in the normal way, can be seen on the hammer proper. On the patent application, provision was made for both a half and full cock bent, but only the full cock bent is employed on the specimen illustrated, and a spring loaded safety catch is fitted to provide a half cock position. Both the cylinder bolt and hand were mounted on a common pivot, and the cylinder bolt was formed as part of the trigger return spring. The arrangement for locking and rotating the cylinder was perhaps the weakest part of the mechanism and the one most likely to provide cause for complaint in actual use.

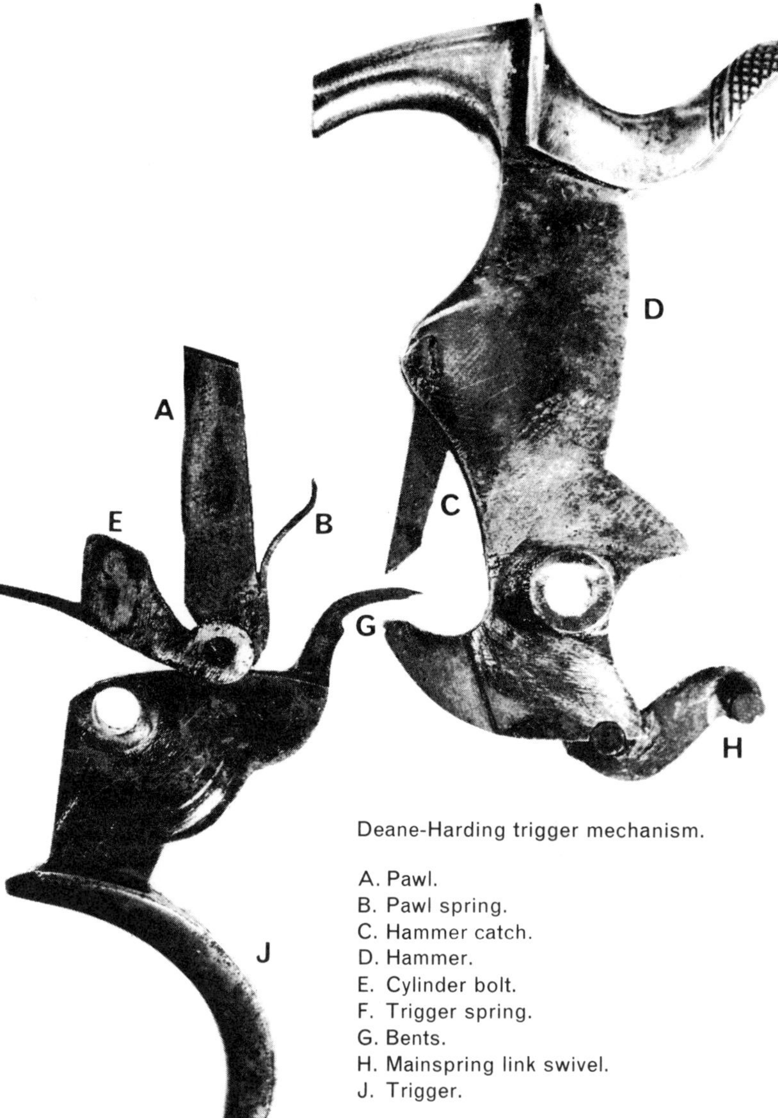

Deane-Harding trigger mechanism.

A. Pawl.
B. Pawl spring.
C. Hammer catch.
D. Hammer.
E. Cylinder bolt.
F. Trigger spring.
G. Bents.
H. Mainspring link swivel.
J. Trigger.

With that delightful but aggravating inconsistency to which gun designers, manufacturers and writers seem heir, the descriptive but unwieldy term 'rule jointed rod' became known as the 'hammer catch' in Britain. Colt in America called it a 'strut', and Smith and Wesson a 'sear'. In this work, the trigger which holds the hammer at half or full cock will be referred to as the 'sear', that part of the hammer which it engages as the 'bent', and, on double action mechanisms, the spring loaded limb attached to the hammer will be known as the 'hammer catch'.

Harding's hammer catch has been and is employed by the majority of revolver manufacturers and, for this reason alone, Harding's otherwise undistinguished revolver merits our attention.

The pistol illustrated is of 54 bore (80 and 120 bore versions were also made) with a 6″ barrel, rifled with four narrow equidistant grooves. The rammer is quite simple and effective and the pistol is finished externally to the customary high standard. The internal mechanism, however, shows evidence of rather crude hand finishing which was no doubt responsible for the unreliability of the functioning. Although this particular specimen has seen very little use, firing from full cock on single action was not always satisfactory and cylinder rotation was not positive. 'Stonehenge', writing in 1859, mentioned the Deane-Harding, stressing that the *principle* on which the pistol was made was without equal, but damning by implication the lack of other desirable qualities. The frame was formed in two pieces and the cylinder pin was screwed into the standing breech. Three variants of the Deane-Harding are recognised by modern collectors, the differences being so slight as to be of interest only to the specialist.

The Kerr revolver was both robust and well made. It enjoyed less popularity in Britain than either the Adams or the Tranter but was highly regarded in those parts of the world where the services of one's own gunmaker were not easily obtainable. The principle features of the Kerr

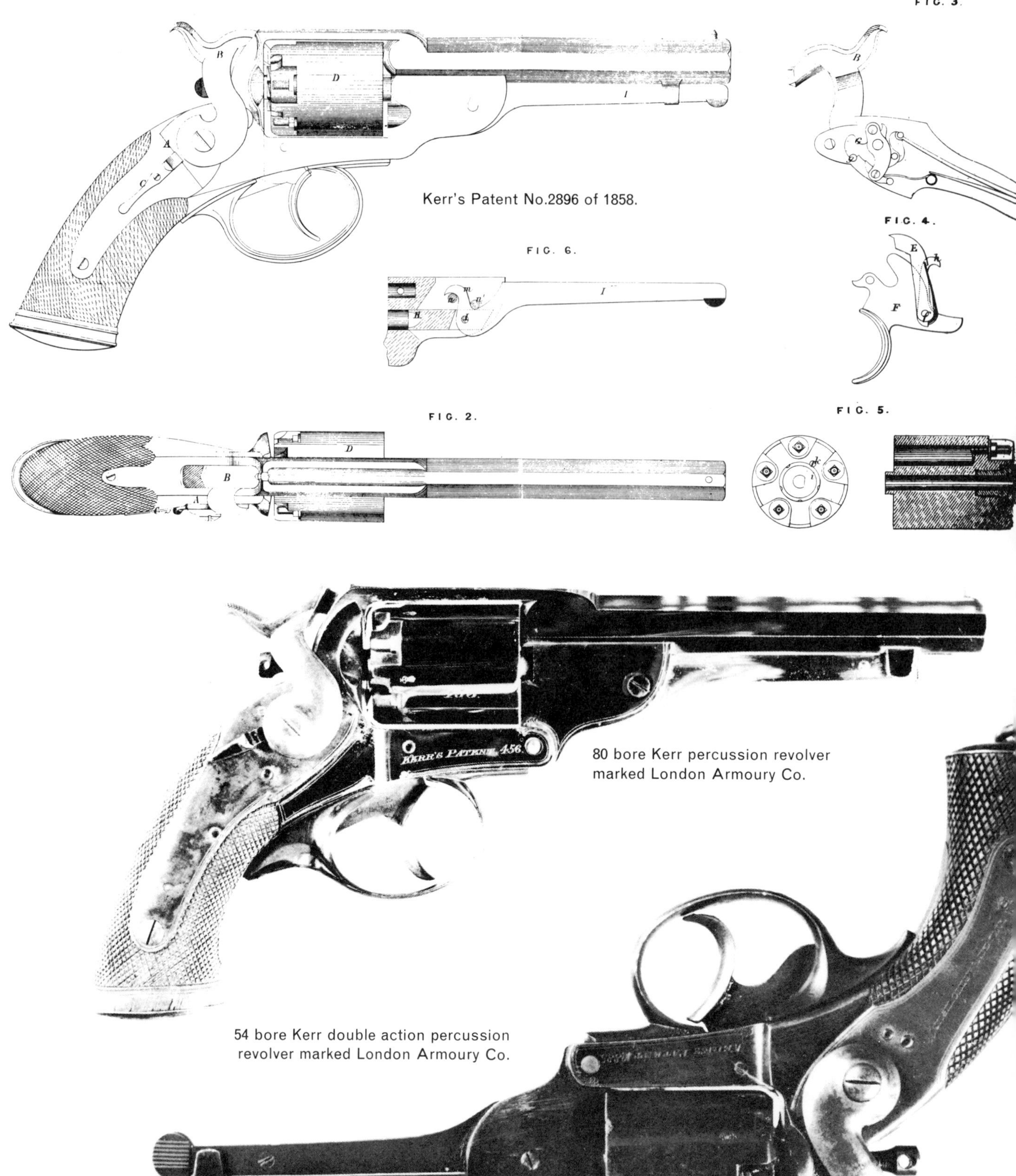

Kerr's Patent No.2896 of 1858.

80 bore Kerr percussion revolver marked London Armoury Co.

54 bore Kerr double action percussion revolver marked London Armoury Co.

revolver were the employment of an 'ordinary gun lock' and a rammer housed under the barrel. The back action side lock meant that an external side hammer had to be employed and, owing to the design of the rammer lever, the cylinder pin was introduced from the rear of the frame and the protruding head (which has a transverse hole through it to ease the task of removal) can be seen in the illustration. A two piece frame was used on all Kerr revolvers, the barrel and top strap being an integral forging attached to the remainder of the frame by two screws. As far as is known, only 54 and 80 bore sizes were manufactured, and all models were five chambered and had five grooved rifling with a right hand twist. Basic design features are covered in Kerr's Patents, No. 2896 of 17 December 1858, and No. 242 of 26 January 1859.

In addition to the variation in calibre, the earlier models were single action, the later versions double action. Both employed conventional side locks which could be easily and quickly removed for repair or cleaning, and repairs beyond the capability of the owner could be carried out by a gunsmith conversant with this type of lock. The only visible external difference between the single and double action variants was in the shape of the trigger blade.

James Kerr was associated with the London Armoury Company from about 1859 until the Company went into liquidation in 1867, after which he continued in business on his own account at 54 King William Street. To add to the confusion, the Kerr family formed the second London Armoury Company in 1894. When retailed by the original London Armoury Company, the Kerr revolver could be marked 'London Armoury' or 'London Armoury Co.', bore the legend 'Kerr's Patent', and was often engraved with a retailer's name. The 80 bore pistol, for example, bears 'William Landell, 106 Trongate, Glasgow', on the top strap. This firm was still in business as general ironmongers until quite recently, and some years ago I visited the premises in search of information concerning their gun vending activities. Although situated on one of the main thoroughfares of the city, the shop still clung to the traditions and style of the past and, as I entered, the scent of history was in the air. Neither of the two old gentlemen who appeared to answer my questions had ever actually sold guns themselves—the firearms side of the business ceased prior to 1900—but one of them remembered that somewhere they still had an old Colt revolver. A search, which lasted nearly half an hour, brought to light an 1849 .31 calibre Colt pocket pistol which changed hands for the price of a bottle of whisky and now forms part of my collection.

The 80 bore double action Kerr—which bears Landell's name as the retailer—is in splendid condition and, although the case does not contain the full complement of tools and accessories, it has the loading, cleaning and operating instructions inside the lid. These outline the reasoning behind the inventor's method of construction, a reasoning that appears to have been accepted by his customers, since not only was the Kerr revolver used by officers of the Confederate Army during the American Civil War, but the 54 bore model was also, according to J. N. George, adopted by the Portuguese Government. Some were certainly manufactured by Orbea Hermanos of Eibar, Spain, but whether the Orbea Brothers had a licensing arrangement with Kerr or marketed a pirated version is not known.

Without doubt, the most confusing series of percussion pistols are those attributed to the brothers Webley. Philip Webley was apprenticed to Benjamin Watson, gun lock filer, with whom he served his seven years indentures. In 1835 he joined his brother James, and they set up as gun lock makers, percussioners etc. in Weaman St, Birmingham. Three years later Philip married Caroline, the eldest daughter of William Davis, and, in 1845, he bought his father-in-law's business as a gun implement maker. A large proportion of the bullet moulds found by the fortunate collector in cased pistol sets will be found to bear the initials 'W.D.' which, in the absence of the Broad Arrow Government mark, stand for 'William Davis' and not 'War Department'. Webley continued this lucrative side of the gun business and, in addition, furnished turnscrews, wadding punches and gun furniture as well as gun and pistol locks.

During 1853 both Philip and James Webley took out patents upon which the Webley single action revolvers were based.

The first patent, No. 305 of 4 February, was under the name of Philip Webley and referred to the method of using a hinge to attach the barrel to the frame, so facilitating the removal of the cylinder. James Webley's Patent No. 743 of 29 March described a cylinder pin, the middle of which was made square 'so as to arrest any fouling deposits'. Philip Webley's second patent, No. 2127 of 14 September, describes the lockwork

Either Double or Single Action.

KERR'S NEW PATENT REVOLVING PISTOL.

1st. By the introduction of the ordinary back-action Gun-lock, which, with the addition of one limb only, revolves the cylinder, this revolver is rendered as simple as any single-barrel pistol.

The lock can be cleaned by any one conversant with fire-arms, and it can be repaired by any Gun-maker or Armourer, thereby obviating the objections which have been hitherto raised to the general use of Revolvers, from the complicated nature of their action.

2nd. The lock being fitted into the stock in the usual method is completely closed up, no wet or dirt can get inside it; the exploded caps cannot be blown off the nipples into the action, rendering the pistol useless for the time, and the limbs of the lock are not exposed to injury by the gas from the discharge (as in other revolvers), which soon rusts and spoils them.

3rd. A raised boss or shield protects the nipples, and prevents the chance of accident by anything striking the caps, in suddenly withdrawing it from the holster, belt, or otherwise.

4th. The body and barrel being separate, enables the former to be case-hardened, which adds greatly to its strength.

5th. A very simple and powerful lever is used for the ramrod; it is placed under the barrel, and has a spring catch, which prevents its being shaken out by the recoil in shooting, and the plunger working in a hole drilled true with the axis of the bore of the cylinder, insures the ball being correctly inserted.

6th. Simplicity and strength have been studied in the general construction of the pistol.

DIRECTIONS FOR LOADING.

Explode a cap on each nipple (when loading for the first time after the pistol has been cleaned), draw up the hammer to half-cock, so that the cylinder may rotate—put the full charge of powder in each chamber (three-eighths or four-eighths of a drachm for the 80 gauge, and four-eighths, or five-eighths for the 54 gauge), then insert the bullet, taking care in ramming it home that none of the powder is shaken out of the chamber.

Fine grain powder is the best—soft lead must always be used, and the bullets properly greased.

DIRECTIONS FOR CLEANING.

Remove the cylinder—which is done by unturning the fly-pin on the left hand side of the pistol till it stops, withdraw the rod and the cylinder will come out. Clean out the cylinder and barrel with either oil or water; if the latter, they must be properly greased afterwards. Before replacing the cylinder, oil the cylinder rod. After the cylinder is replaced, the fly-pin must be turned back again till it stops.

If necessary to take off the lock put it at full cock, and unscrew the side screws, give the cock a tap with the handle of the turn-screw, and it will come out like an ordinary gun-lock.

In replacing the lock the trigger must be held quite back, and the lock dropped into its place at full cock—the stud of the tumbler will fall into the hook or link attached to the trigger. If the lock is in its proper position, on removing the hand from the trigger it will remain back. Care must then be taken that the side screws are turned right home.

To bolt the Pistol.—Rest the nose of the Cock on the Cylinder between the nipples, and push the Bolt into the Cock which will have the effect of locking Cock, Cylinder, and Trigger.

Instructions for loading, cleaning and using the Kerr patent revolver.

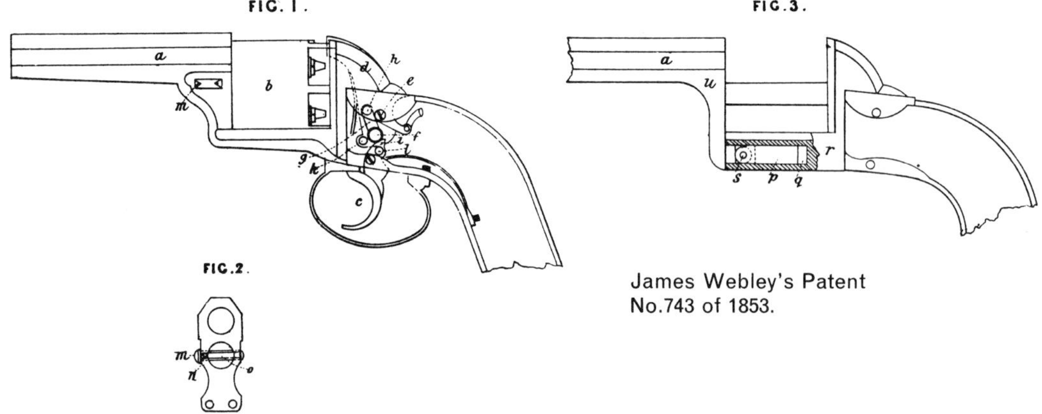

James Webley's Patent No.743 of 1853.

for a revolver based on his earlier patent.

The whole series of single action James Webley revolvers were, like the Colt percussion models, open framed and distinguished by the large spur on the hammer provided as an aid to speedy thumb cocking. Three basic sizes of pistol were produced, the Holster, Belt and Pocket Models. The largest was the 48 bore Holster, then the 64 bore Belt and finally the Pocket Models in both 90 and 120 bore calibres. For convenience, the series has been divided into three models or variants, the classification adopted by A. W. F. Taylerson.

The First Model employed a hinged frame

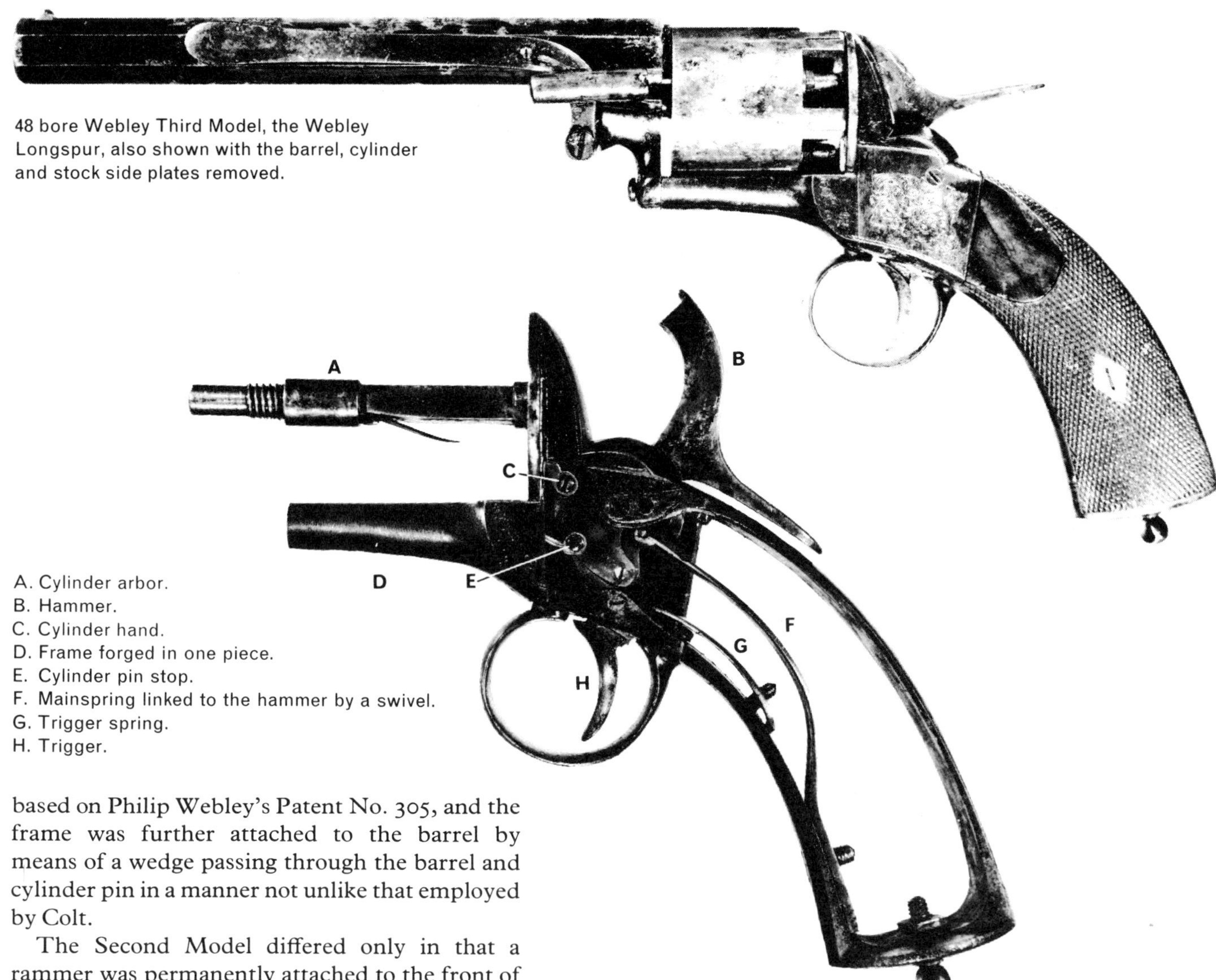

48 bore Webley Third Model, the Webley Longspur, also shown with the barrel, cylinder and stock side plates removed.

A. Cylinder arbor.
B. Hammer.
C. Cylinder hand.
D. Frame forged in one piece.
E. Cylinder pin stop.
F. Mainspring linked to the hammer by a swivel.
G. Trigger spring.
H. Trigger.

based on Philip Webley's Patent No. 305, and the frame was further attached to the barrel by means of a wedge passing through the barrel and cylinder pin in a manner not unlike that employed by Colt.

The Second Model differed only in that a rammer was permanently attached to the front of the right hand side of the frame and folded back along it. The earlier variant was provided with a separate rammer (normally kept in the pistol case) which pivoted on a peg provided at the right hand, breech end of the barrel.

The 48 bore Third Model had a simple lever rammer with loose head permanently attached to the left hand side of the barrel. The hinged frame feature was discarded in favour of a simpler means of attaching the lower barrel extension by a screw passing through the extension into the frame, the barrel being attached to a screw threaded cylinder pin.

The mechanism of the Webley 'Longspur' was simple and rather fragile. The cylinder hand (or pawl) was attached to the breast of the hammer and kept in contact with the cylinder ratchet by means of a long and ineffective spring attached to the frame behind the hammer pivot screw. The cylinder stop was also attached to the hammer somewhat lower down than the hand, and the cylindrical rod of the stop passed through the bar of the action and engaged the web at the rear of the cylinder. On most of the Holster and Belt pistols an additional cylinder lock (not visible on the illustration) was provided which blocked the cylinder at the moment of discharge. This was operated by the trigger sear and locked into grooves formed between the webs of the cylinder. The absence of these locking grooves can be seen in the illustration of the 90 bore Pocket Model. The variation in rammers can also be noted, the Pocket Model having an open slot and large thumbscrew instead of the cheese headed screw employed for barrel retention on the Holster Model.

As might be expected, examples of the James

Webley Third Model 90 bore pocket percussion revolver. (R. H. Walton Collection)

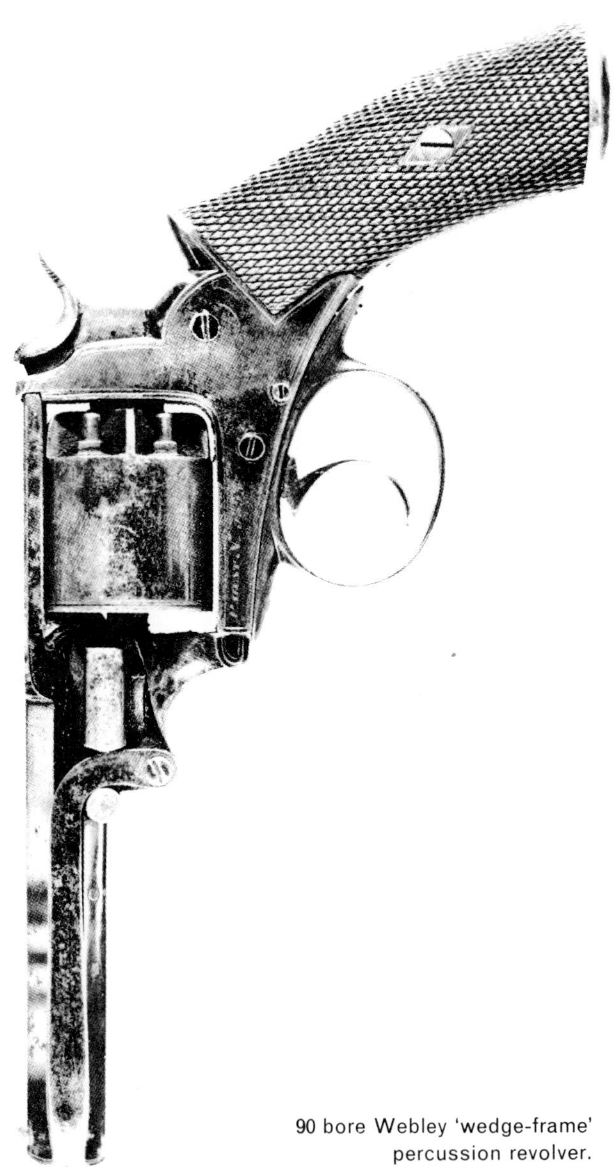

90 bore Webley 'wedge-frame' percussion revolver.

Webley 'Longspur' exhibited many minor differences in both design and construction since they were largely hand made. They were usually marked 'James Webley, Patentee' or 'Webley's Patent' on the frame, the back strap often bearing the flamboyant 'By Her Majesty's Royal Letters Patent'.

By 1868 James Webley had apparently ceased to manufacture revolvers, and the by then obsolete 'Longspur' series faded into an obscurity only recently dispelled by the modern specialist researcher.

Although Philip Webley retailed James Webley revolvers, he also marketed a very similar revolver bearing his own name. It was perhaps slightly more graceful in outline than the James Webley and can be distinguished by the charming 'S' curve of the rammer attached to the left hand side of the frame, a rammer very similar to the one employed by Tranter, with the head formed as part of the lever. The internal mechanism was also different, embodying the 'L' shaped combined cylinder hand and bolt mentioned in Philip Webley's Patent No. 2127.

The need to introduce a more up-to-date pistol with a stronger frame having increased rigidity was met by the appearance of the Webley 'Wedge Frame' series of double action pistols. At first glance, these five chambered revolvers appear to have a solid frame but, on closer examination, it will be found that the barrel and top strap were forged in one piece and the lock frame was separate, the junction being at the front of the bar and the top of the standing breech. The two parts were secured by the typical wedge passing through the barrel extension and a slot in the cylinder pin. Two main types are recognised, the

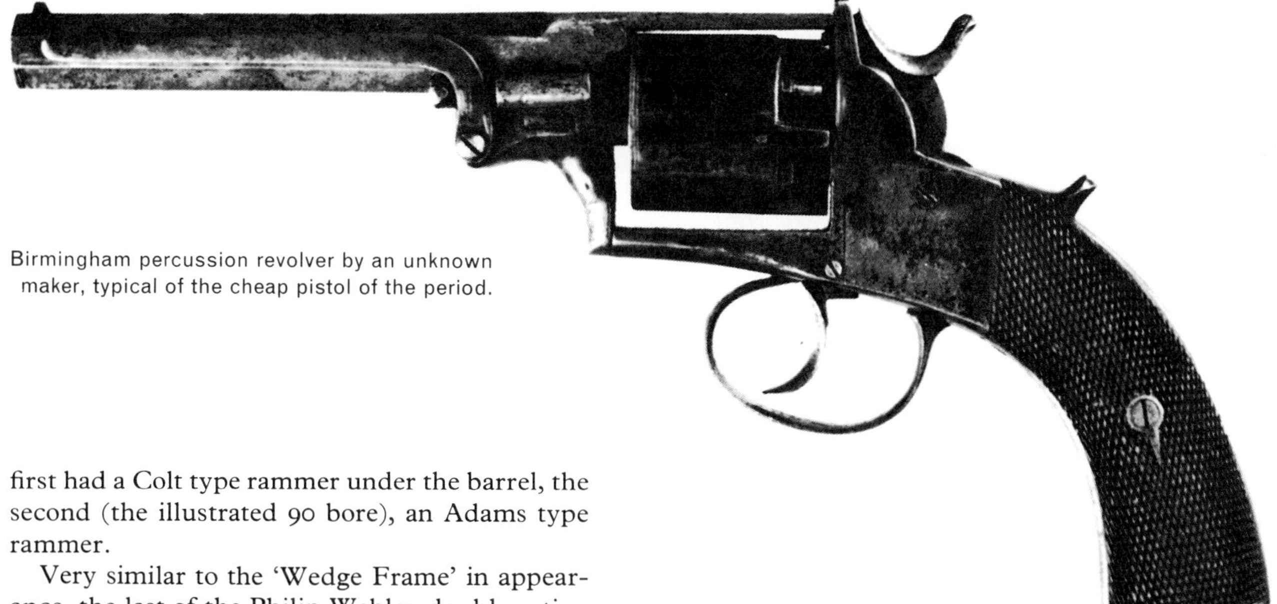
Birmingham percussion revolver by an unknown maker, typical of the cheap pistol of the period.

first had a Colt type rammer under the barrel, the second (the illustrated 90 bore), an Adams type rammer.

Very similar to the 'Wedge Frame' in appearance, the last of the Philip Webley double action percussion pistols was made with a solid frame. The barrel, unlike the Adams and Tranter, was separate and screwed into the frame.

None of the many variants of the double action Webley revolvers were particularly distinguished, and their interest lies mainly in the fact that they were the precursors to what was to become the most important series of British cartridge revolvers, and ultimately the only revolvers manufactured by a commercial concern in this country.

The name of Webley has been associated with a distinct class of percussion revolver characterised by the open frame, self-cocking action and generally cheap construction. The term 'amorphous' used by P. A. Bedford is perhaps the most descriptive. Typical of this type of revolver is the specimen illustrated, which is unmarked except for the Birmingham proof marks on the cylinder and barrel. As a group they were mechanically degraded—the mechanism being of the pepperbox or transitional revolver type—and the features can easily be understood from the illustration. Pistols in this group, which can be found with a spur or prawl on the backstrap but also without this annoying appendage, were fitted with different types of rammer, with barrels screwed on to the cylinder pin and with barrels secured by a cross bolt. Very cheaply made and of poor quality, cost reduction was carried to extreme lengths. A close examination of some of these pistols will show that the barrels were only partly rifled for one or two inches at the muzzle—sufficiently to deceive the casual purchaser—the remainder being 'smooth bored' and not apparent unless the barrel was removed and viewed from the breech end.

Webley catalogues illustrated better quality revolvers of this general type which bore an external similarity to the Bentley series of self-cocking revolvers manufactured by Joseph Bentley of Birmingham and Liverpool. Four basic variants of the Bentley are at present recognised. All were open frame with the Colt type barrel securing wedge. The earlier models employed Bentley's famous safety catch, a spring loaded lever fitted to the nose of the hammer. The catch was operated by a small button which, when the hammer was drawn slightly back to clear the nipple partitions, was pressed by the thumb. Since the hammer nose passed through an aperture formed at the top of the standing breech, the front limb of the safety catch was raised and prevented the hammer going completely forward. When the pistol was to be fired, the hammer was drawn back by the trigger and the spring loaded safety catch automatically disengaged. Two other features of the Bentley series are of interest. The later version employed an unusual rammer, the head formed as a quick pitch screw. A thumb lever was provided which, when rotated, caused the head to move sufficiently to seat the bullet in the chamber. This rammer formed part of Bentley's patent No. 768 of 1854, and the Bentley 'safety hammer bolt or catch' and the basic mechanism of the self-cocking action were covered in his patent No. 960 of 1852. The only interesting feature of the latter is the combined cylinder bolt

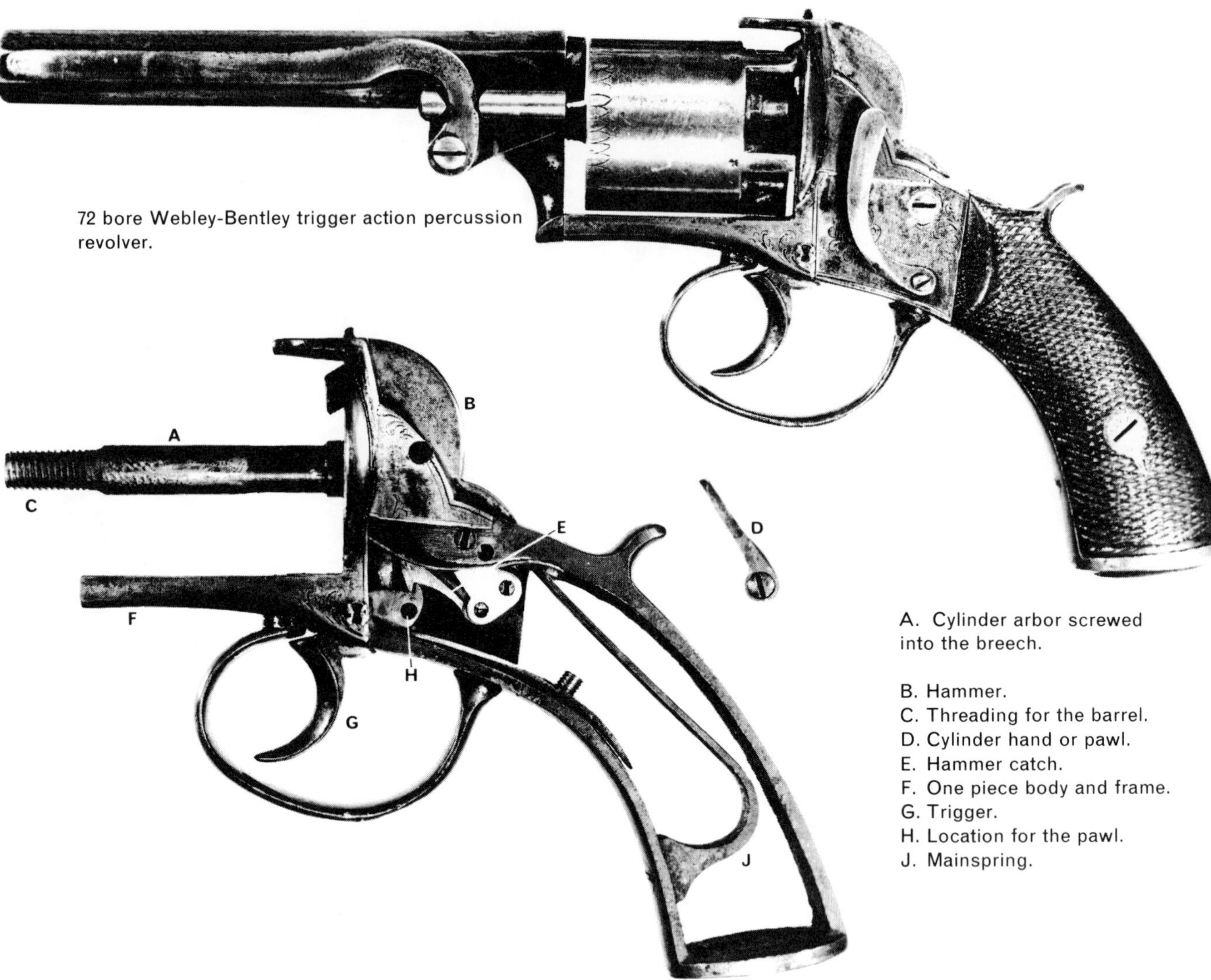

72 bore Webley-Bentley trigger action percussion revolver.

A. Cylinder arbor screwed into the breech.

B. Hammer.
C. Threading for the barrel.
D. Cylinder hand or pawl.
E. Hammer catch.
F. One piece body and frame.
G. Trigger.
H. Location for the pawl.
J. Mainspring.

and trigger return spring which was unusual in that it was fitted to the top of the bar of the action. The rear part of the spring had two lugs, the lower projecting through the bar to act on the trigger, the upper serving as a cylinder bolt. Another patent (No. 780 of 1856) taken out by Bentley, referred to his patent cylinder bolt, and his lock mechanism was protected by No. 2657 of 1857.

Even less well known than the Bentley were the very unusual series of percussion revolvers patented and manufactured by William Westley Richards of Birmingham. Founded in 1812, the firm of Westley Richards is happily still with us at the time of writing. Both father and son contributed greatly to the development of the rifle and sporting shotgun. Westley Richards were the first gunmakers to market the Anson and Deeley action for shotguns and rifles. The venture into the revolver business was not characterised with the signal success which the firm later enjoyed in other fields but, as can be seen from the illustrations of two of the three models manufactured, their revolvers, if not successful in the commercial sense, were at least highly original. Both pistols illustrated are self-cocking and they share with a later rare side hammer single action model (Richards' Patent No. 911) the absence of a bottom strap to the frame. The top strap was made integrally with the barrel and secured to the frame by a thumb catch. A similar device was used to attach the barrel extension to the cylinder pin. Not encountered on any other British percussion pistol, this type of construction was, however, employed in America, notably by the Massachusetts Arms Co. (page 64) revolvers manufactured under Wesson and Leavitt's patents. Even these are rare, since the newly-formed company was successfully sued by Samuel Colt for infringement of his patents before it had got into its stride, and production was consequently curtailed.

The Westley Richards revolvers do have two

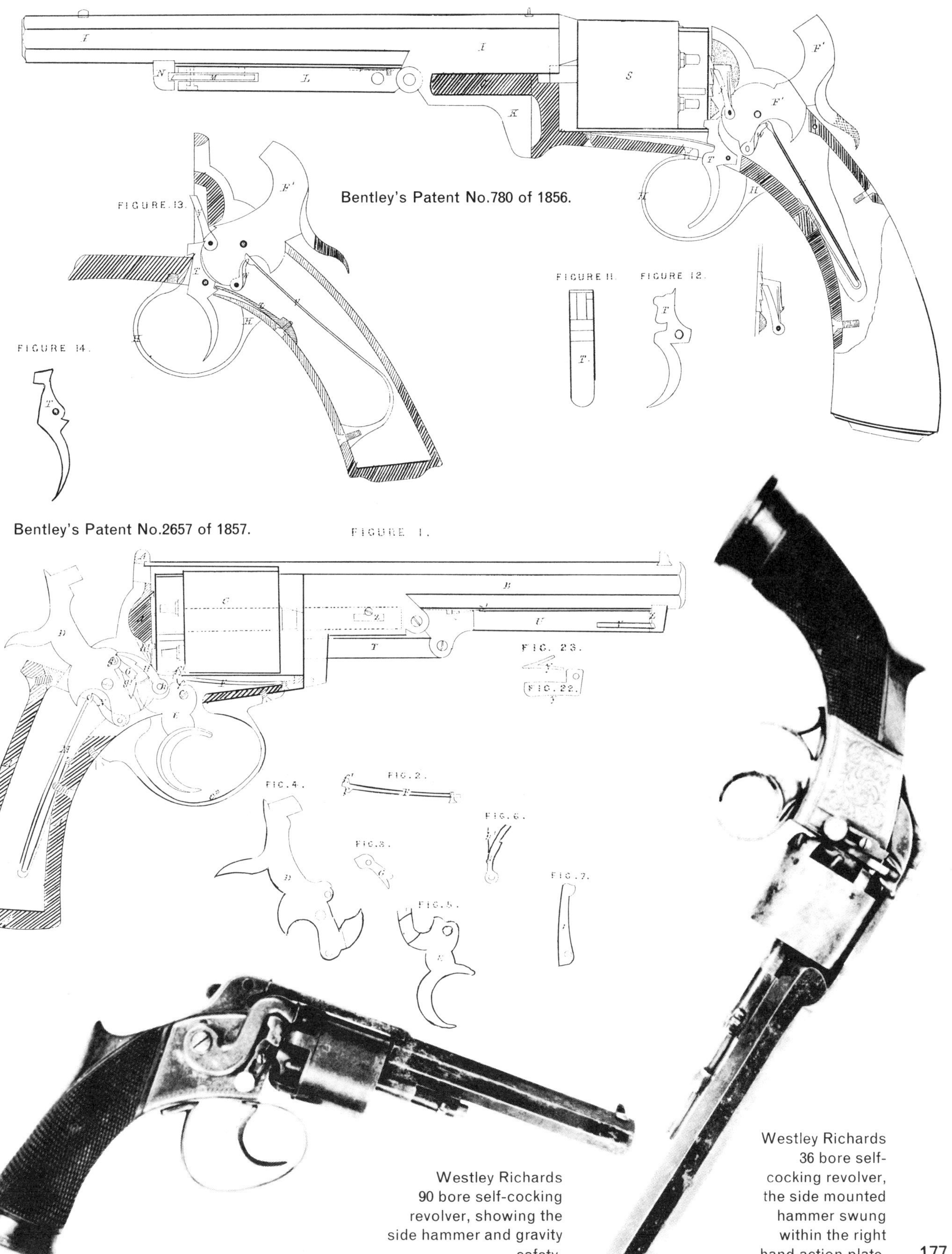

Bentley's Patent No.780 of 1856.

Bentley's Patent No.2657 of 1857.

Westley Richards 90 bore self-cocking revolver, showing the side hammer and gravity safety.

Westley Richards 36 bore self-cocking revolver, the side mounted hammer swung within the right hand action plate.

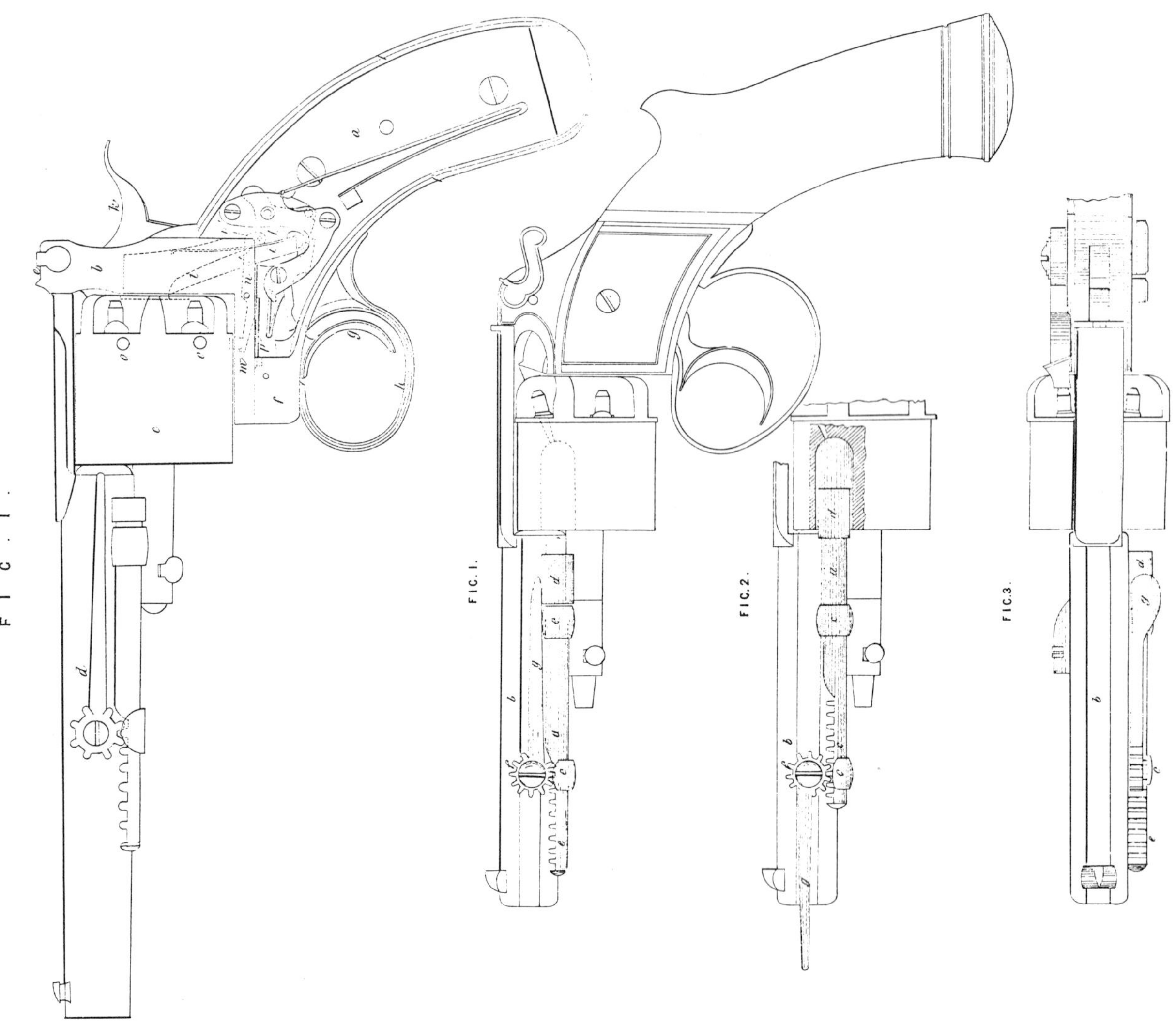

Richards's Patent No.911 of 1855. Richards's Patent No.993 of 1854.

other interesting features. The first is the rather unusual rammer, based on a rack and pinion mechanism (Patent No. 993), and the second is the method of bolting the hammer clear of the nipples during loading. The safety was similar to the Manton 'Patent Gravitating Stops' used by 'Old Joe' on his sporting guns and briefly mentioned earlier. As with the Manton safety, the Westley Richards device had to be kept scrupulously clean otherwise it failed to function, since the safety slide, fitted to the right hand side of the frame, was pushed upward to prevent the hammer falling on the nipple. When the hammer was slightly raised, it was supposed to disengage by virtue of its own weight, a plug of platinum being used to increase the weight of the slide.

Of the remaining identifiable and distinct British percussion revolvers, mention should be made of the Moore and Harris, whose patent, No. 69, was obtained on 1 October 1852. The only specimen I have seen was similar to the patent drawing, the frame hinged at the standing breech, and the barrel extension locking with a spring loaded stud on the bar of the frame. An interesting feature was the reciprocating cylinder designed to effect a gas seal, the system of operation almost identical to that illustrated on page 122, a bolt pushing forward against a spring to seat the chamber mouth against the barrel.

Two 'hammerless' revolvers appeared in 1853, the Harvey and the Pennell, and both were 'hand made'. The Harvey appeared in two basic types, the first with a saw handled butt as in Harvey's Patent No. 1298 of 26 May 1853, and the second

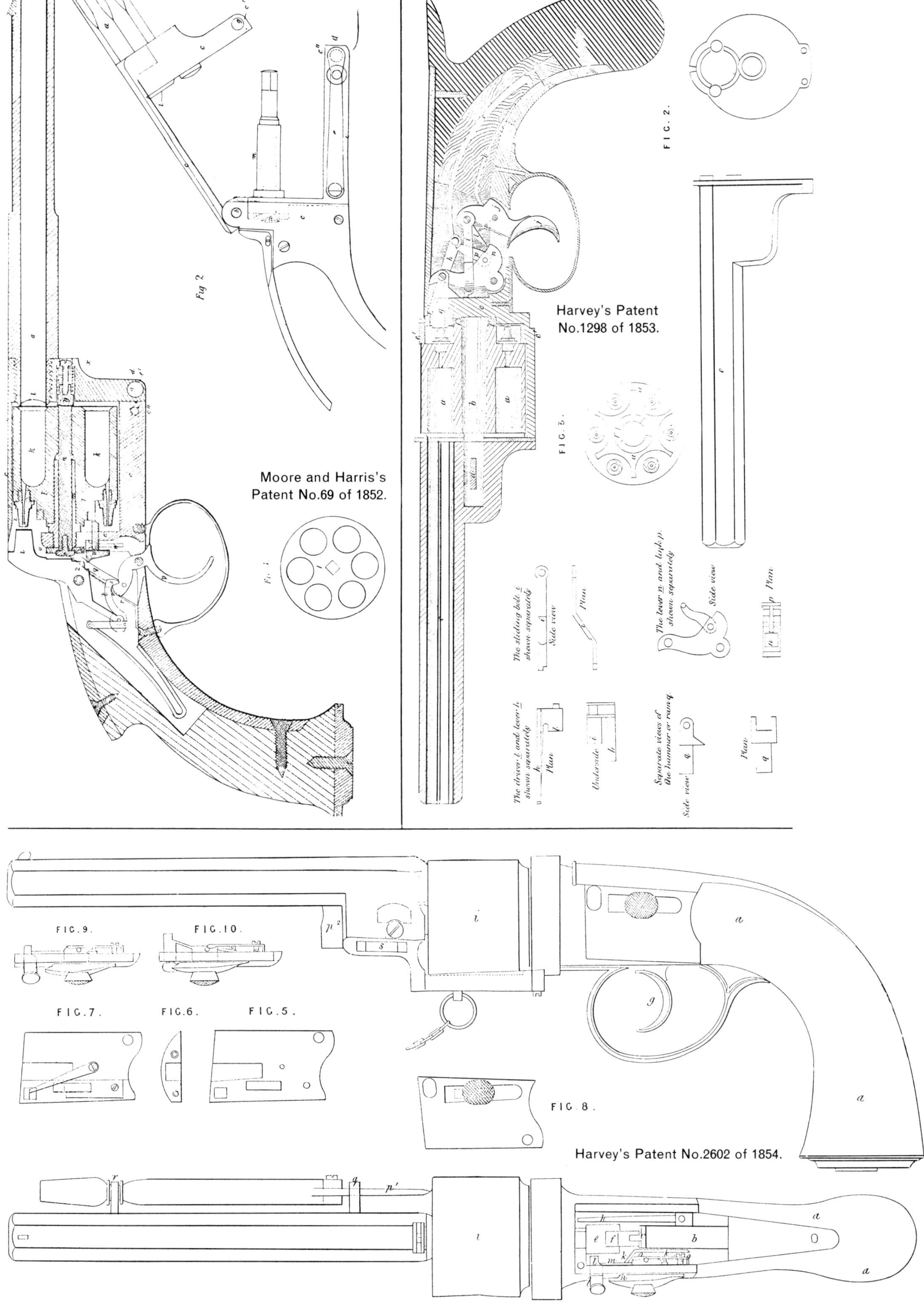

Moore and Harris's Patent No.69 of 1852.
Harvey's Patent No.1298 of 1853.
FIG. 2.
FIG. 3.
The sliding bolt i shown separately
Side view
Plan
The lever n and lug p. shown separately
Side view
Plan
The driver h and lever h shown separately
Plan
Underside
Separate views of the hammer or ram q.
Side view
Plan
FIG.9.
FIG.10.
FIG.7.
FIG.6.
FIG.5.
FIG.8.
Harvey's Patent No.2602 of 1854.

with a normal stock. The general appearance of the later version can be seen from Harvey's Patent No. 2602 of 1854. This drawing also illustrates the rather odd rammer which was attached to the barrel by a spring catch and also served as a nipple key and turnscrew.

On the Pennell specimen examined there was no provision for a rammer but, since the barrel and cylinder could be easily removed, the short loading stick (in the pistol case) would be employed to seat the balls firmly home. Examples with Pennell's rammer, which can be seen in the illustration filed with his patent No. 1038 of 1853, do exist, but the functioning of this detachable rammer may have been suspect in practice.

Both revolvers were six chambered and had octagonal barrels. Those specimens seen were of

Bailey's Patent No.1634 of 1858.

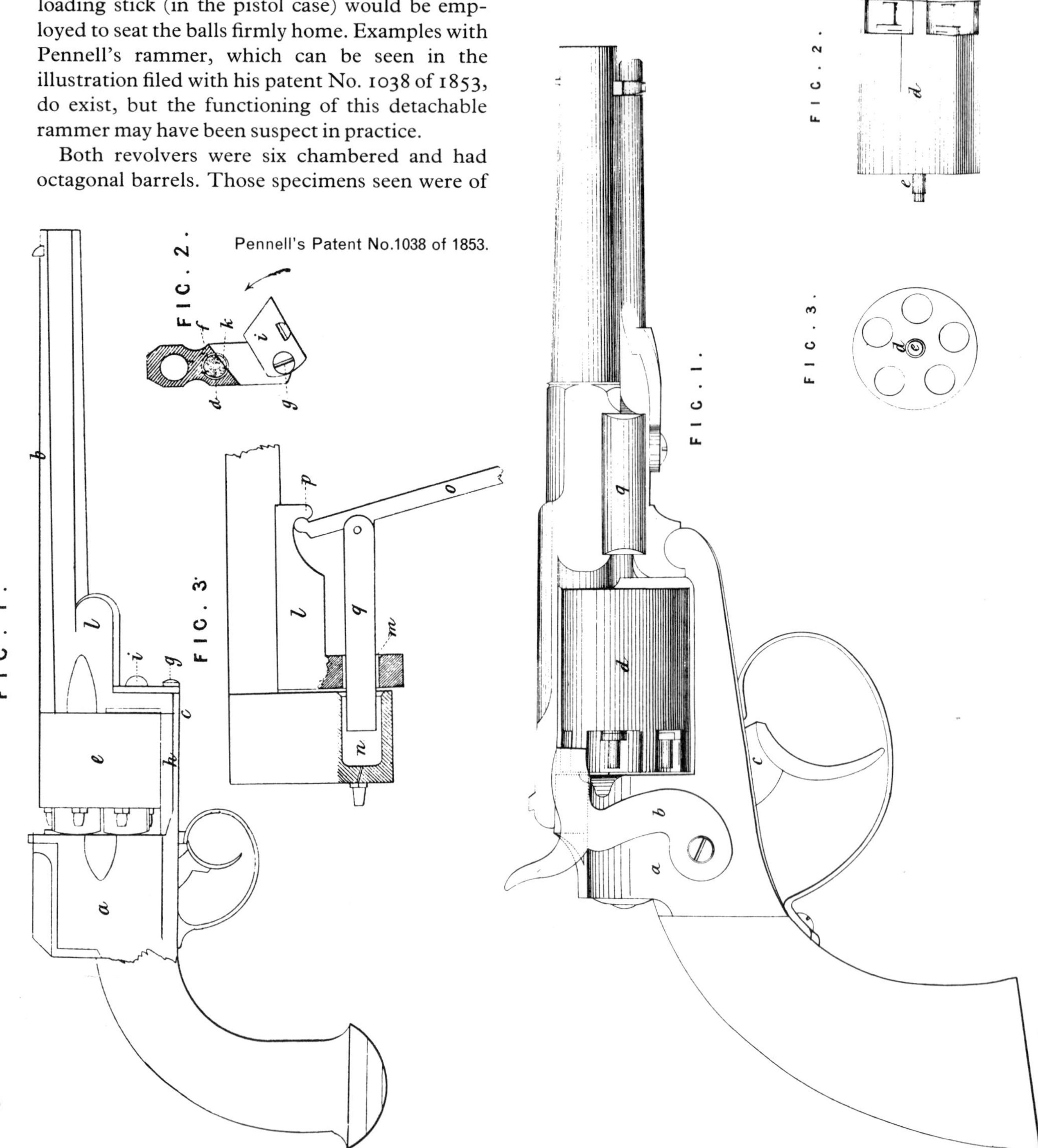

Pennell's Patent No.1038 of 1853.

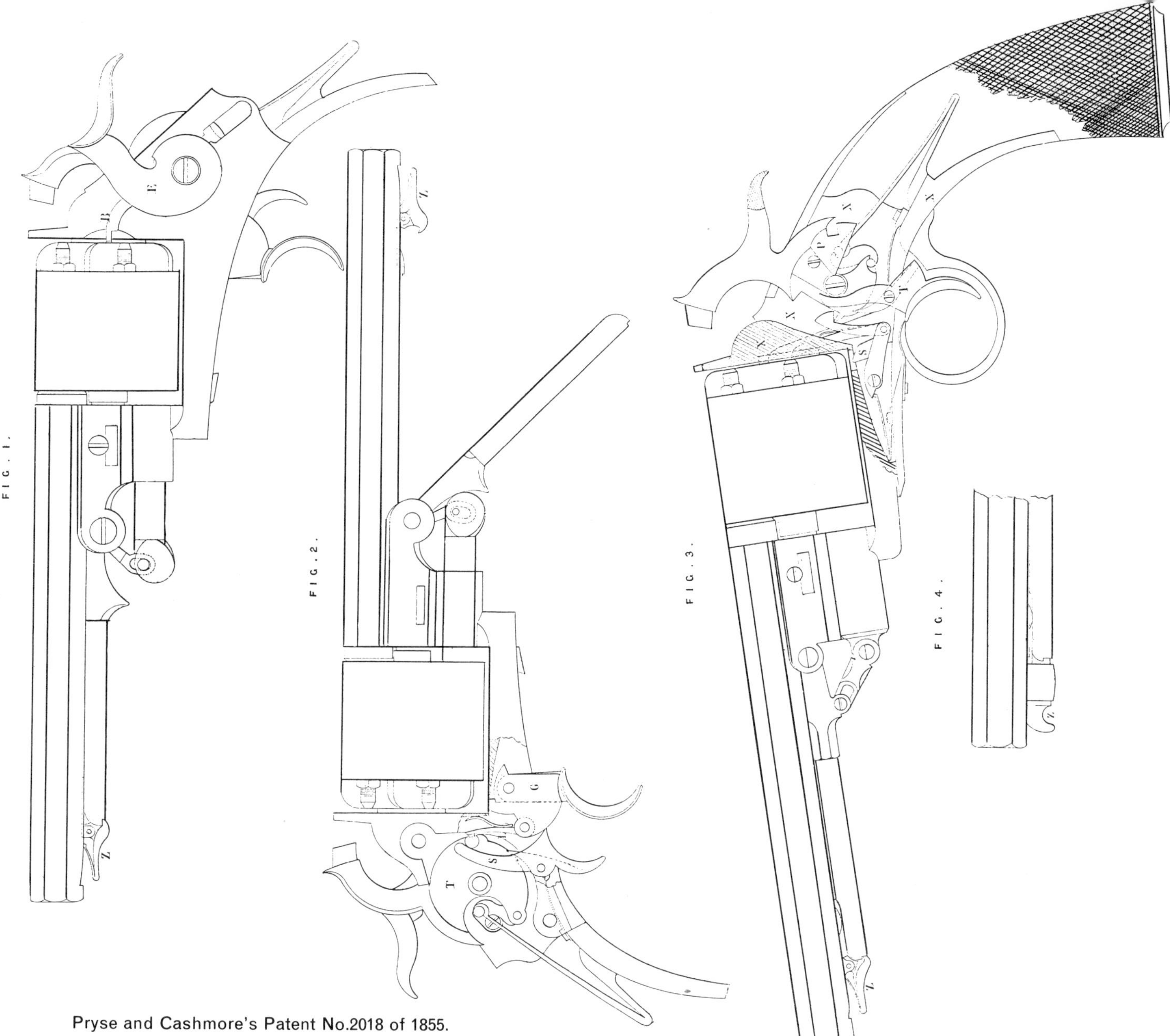

Pryse and Cashmore's Patent No.2018 of 1855.

54 bore and very well finished, but the self-cocking action would hinder accurate shooting at long ranges due to the long and heavy trigger pull.

Yet another even rarer percussion revolver is that patented by T. Bailey (British Patent No. 1634 of 1858) with a side hammer similar to the Kerr and with a separate barrel frame assembly. The general appearance of this revolver can be seen in the patent drawing.

Contemporary literature on percussion revolvers is regrettably scarce and often biased. For some reason, George H. Daw's series of percussion revolvers has had extensive coverage, although only one of the models that he made is ever illustrated, and the same woodcut is always used. There is some doubt as to who made the Daw revolver, but it was covered by British Patent No. 2018 taken out in 1855 by Charles Pryse of Birmingham and Paul Cashmore of West Bromwich. Known to the modern collector as the 'Standard' Model, it was made in 120, 80, 54 and 38 bores, and the .500 or 38 bore version is illustrated. Contemporary references to the Daw made favourable mention of the fact that both front and rear sights were mounted on the barrel and, since the pistol lacked a top strap, the sight base was necessarily shorter than would be the case with a solid or wedge frame pistol with top strap. Mention was also made of the form of the recoil shield which, unlike the Colt, had no cut in the side for putting the caps on the nipples. Daw's arrangement was certainly ingenious since capping was carried out with the hammer at half cock. The hammer nose had 'ears' which closed the gap in the recoil shield when it was down. Pins were employed on the rear face of the cylinder to

38 bore percussion revolver by George Daw.

lock into a notch in the hammer nose, and both prevented the cylinder from revolving and allowed the weapon to be carried safely when fully loaded. No less a person than General Jacob of Scinde Irregular Horse fame stated that 'this is the best and most convenient revolver to which my attention has been directed'. Captain Llewellyn Jewitt of the 1st Derbyshire Rifles also spoke highly of the Daw in his *Rifleman's Manual*, as did Lt. Hans Busk, Victoria Rifles, in his book, *The Rifle And How to Use It*. This contemporary praise must, however, be taken with some reserve since Busk, for example, treats both the Adams and the Deane-Harding with scant respect—'I consider them inferior in every respect to Colt's and to be liable to serious objections which cannot be urged against the original [Colt] arm'. Unfortunately we are left in the dark as to the nature of these serious objections. Busk, incidentally, does not even mention the Tranter, which most certainly enjoyed a favourable reputation.

A complete history of the percussion revolver has yet to be written. There are those intriguing specimens which lack documentation, and where little or nothing is known about the inventor or manufacturer. There are also those where documentary proof is available, but where no specimens have survived—if, indeed, any were made. One example is the self-cocking Needham revolver which bore a resemblance to the Westley Richards and is well illustrated in the drawings with British Patent No. 2184 of 1853. No examples, however, appear to have survived. Another 'unknown' is Williams' patent revolver of 1853, an example of which may be lying forgotten in a drawer, awaiting discovery.

The present day revival of interest in the percussion revolver, coupled with the availability of suitable powder and caps, permits the enthusiast to form his own opinion of its merits. The demand for 'shooting' percussion revolvers is so great that a new industry has been established, the manufacture of 'replica' weapons. At present restricted to revolvers of American origin, commercial pressure may yet result in the making of replicas of the Adams and Tranter. For the present, those wishing to shoot English percussion revolvers have to find original and increasingly expensive specimens in order to enjoy this aspect of handgunning.

By the end of the percussion period, the revolver had been developed to such a stage of mechanical perfection that many percussion pistols

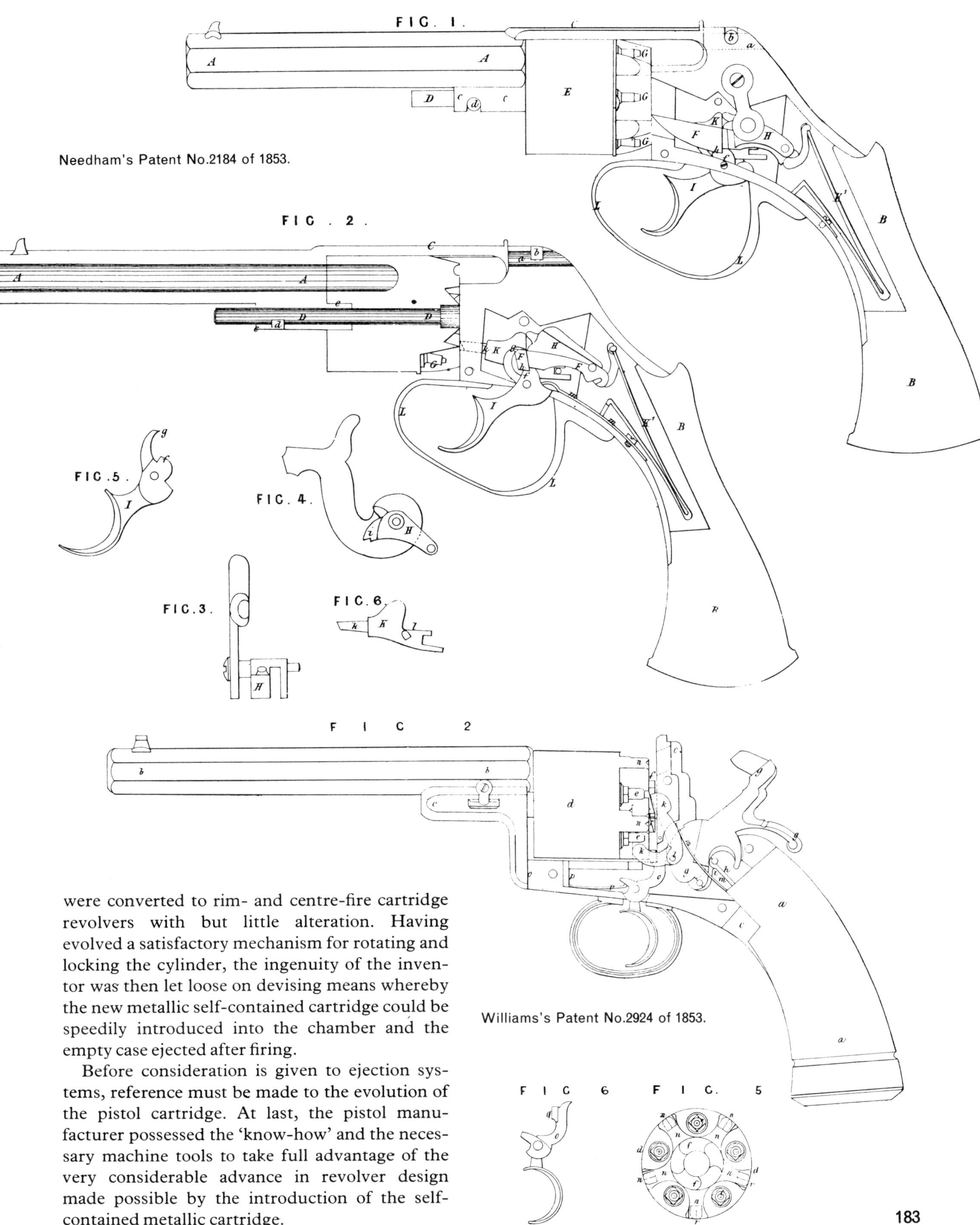

Needham's Patent No.2184 of 1853.

Williams's Patent No.2924 of 1853.

were converted to rim- and centre-fire cartridge revolvers with but little alteration. Having evolved a satisfactory mechanism for rotating and locking the cylinder, the ingenuity of the inventor was then let loose on devising means whereby the new metallic self-contained cartridge could be speedily introduced into the chamber and the empty case ejected after firing.

Before consideration is given to ejection systems, reference must be made to the evolution of the pistol cartridge. At last, the pistol manufacturer possessed the 'know-how' and the necessary machine tools to take full advantage of the very considerable advance in revolver design made possible by the introduction of the self-contained metallic cartridge.

Notes to Chapter Seven

In addition to text references to the manufacture of Colt revolvers in Britain, mention should also be made of 'Colt's London Navy Revolver' by Joseph G. Rosa in *Guns Review* (Vol. 5, No. 2) and of 'Address Col. Colt London' by Howard L. Blackmore in *Gun Digest* (12th edition, 1958).

English percussion revolvers lack the extensive bibliography of their American counterparts. Apart from J. N. George, most of the useful material has been contributed by a small group of enthusiasts whose work has appeared in *The Journal of the Arms and Armour Society*. The most relevant articles are: 'Percussion Revolvers, the Hesitation Action' (Vol. IV), 'Deane and Adams, The London Armoury Company' (Vol. II), 'James Webley Single Action Revolvers' (Vol. II) and 'The Adams Patent of 1853' (Vol. IV).

Much valuable information is also contained in articles published in *Black Powder*. Here again, the most relevant are: 'Deane and Adams' (Vol. 7, No. 7), 'Webley' (Vol. 6, No. 12), 'Beaumont Adams' (Vol. 10, No. 3), 'Kerr' (Vol. 7, No. 12), 'Tranter' (Vol. 6, No. 9), 'Deane Harding' (Vol. 7, No. 12, with additional notes in Vol. 8, No. 2), 'Witten and Daw' (Vol. 8, No. 3 and Vol. 8, No. 6), 'Bentley' (Vol. 7, No. 4), 'Westley Richards' (Vol. 7, No. 8) and 'G. H. Daw' (Vol. 8, No. 6). More recently, the appearance of *The Revolver 1818–1865* by Taylerson, Andrews and Frith (London, 1968) has done much to dispel a great deal of the mystery which surrounded the English percussion revolver.

Attention should also be drawn to a detailed examination of the Adams percussion revolver in 'The Percussion Revolver of Lt. Col. George James Ambrose' by J. Darwent in *Guns Review* (Vol. 5, No. 8).

I am personally indebted to R. G. Goodman for much valuable information on the history of Tranter's factory, and also for his comments on my interpretation of such facts as are available.

Chapter Eight

The Development of the Cartridge

If we accept the term 'cartridge' to mean any disposable container for a single load for a firearm, then the history of the development of the cartridge is almost as long as that of the firearm and certainly just as complicated. The earliest cartridge was simply a means of cheaply and conveniently carrying, ready for use, one charge of powder. The powder was contained in a paper wrapped case which was opened by tearing the paper cover with the fingers or, more often, with the teeth, and the contents were then poured from the container into the barrel, the paper being either discarded or used as wadding to stop the bullet falling out of the barrel. By the early seventeenth century it had become common practice to attach the ball to the paper container by means of a sprue or flange; later it was wrapped inside the paper case together with the powder. Such cartridges were either made by the individual purely as a matter of convenience or were manufactured to a standard pattern for military use.

The successful development of the percussion revolver into a practical weapon of increased fire power emphasised the inadequacy of the paper cartridge and, due to the significant reduction in calibre, increased the problems of making and using the traditional form of cartridge. What was wanted was a cartridge containing both powder and ball which could be loaded into the chamber complete and rammed home ready for use.

Once the need had been established, men ingenious and men astute appeared eager to promote their ideas and inventions. Some were condemned from the outset because of complete impracticability, others because neither the machinery nor the materials were then available to translate a sensible idea into practice. Specially designed firearms were required to handle some of the cartridges proposed and, either because such weapons could not be manufactured by existing techniques or because of the commercial risk inevitable with any new and untried idea, many of the ideas remained on paper, some to reappear a century later when the climate of opinion was more favourable to their adoption.

The percussion revolver required a cartridge containing both powder and ball, and one that had to be sufficiently robust to withstand reasonable handling, impervious to damp and capable of being ruptured after it had been safely loaded into the chamber. It was also desirable that, if the necessity arose, the weapon could be loaded with separate powder and ball. These requirements were met by the combustible cartridge. Originally, the paper case was nitrated so that it would ignite from the flash from the percussion cap, and be consumed by the burning of the powder charge. One alternative employed by Robert Adams was a metal container, the end closed by nitrated paper. Another was to make a completely combustible cartridge by using a mixture of gunpowder and collodion which was compressed in a mould, dried and attached to the base of the bullet by either glue or collodion. This technique resulted in a reasonably waterproof cartridge, but it was fragile and easily liable to accidental damage. Probably the most successful revolver cartridge of the percussion period was the Hayes 'skin' cartridge.

British Patent No. 2059, dated 4 September 1856, was taken out by Captain John Montague

Hayes, RN, and described 'an improvement in the construction of cartridges for firearms'. In manufacture 'a skin of membrane (prepared from the gut of animals, pigs or birds or reptiles) is used instead of paper for cartridges, which are made without a seam. A covering of net-work or thread may be used to strengthen the cartridge.'

The Hayes cartridge in its final form owed something to the work of men like William Thomas Eley who had patented a cheaper version of the Adams patent 'Dustbin' cartridge in 1854. Eley's specification (No. 2487) employed the projecting tang method of fixing the case containing the propellant charge to the base of the bullet but, instead of using a metal case as did Adams, a 'paper or flexible' case was used.

In 1855 the idea was developed further by Eley and Samuel Colt who took out a joint patent (No. 1324) in which the powder container was formed from sheet foil, and the lapped joints sealed with waterproof cement. The most important feature of this patent was the provision of a detachable outer paper case to protect the cartridge. The case had to be removed before the cartridge was inserted into the chamber and a piece of tape was attached to the end to facilitate this.

The Colt-Eley tin-foil cases were not entirely successful due to the residue remaining in the chamber after firing, but the paper protective case was a most useful idea and one which came into common use.

An improvement on the original Hayes cartridge was made by William Montgomery Storm (US Patent No. 33,611 of 1861) in which the membrane was treated with gutta-percha varnish

Various early types of cartridge.

Top row, left to right: Adams 'Dustbin' cartridge; Adams bullet with 'tail'; Tranter's bullet with wide lubricant groove; Eley nitrated paper combustible cartridge; bullet with nitrated paper powder container; paper wrapper for a Colt cartridge.

Bottom row, left to right: Eley combustible cartridge; Eley skin cartridge with thread reinforcement; case for the Eley cartridge; cartridge and case for the .44 Colt.

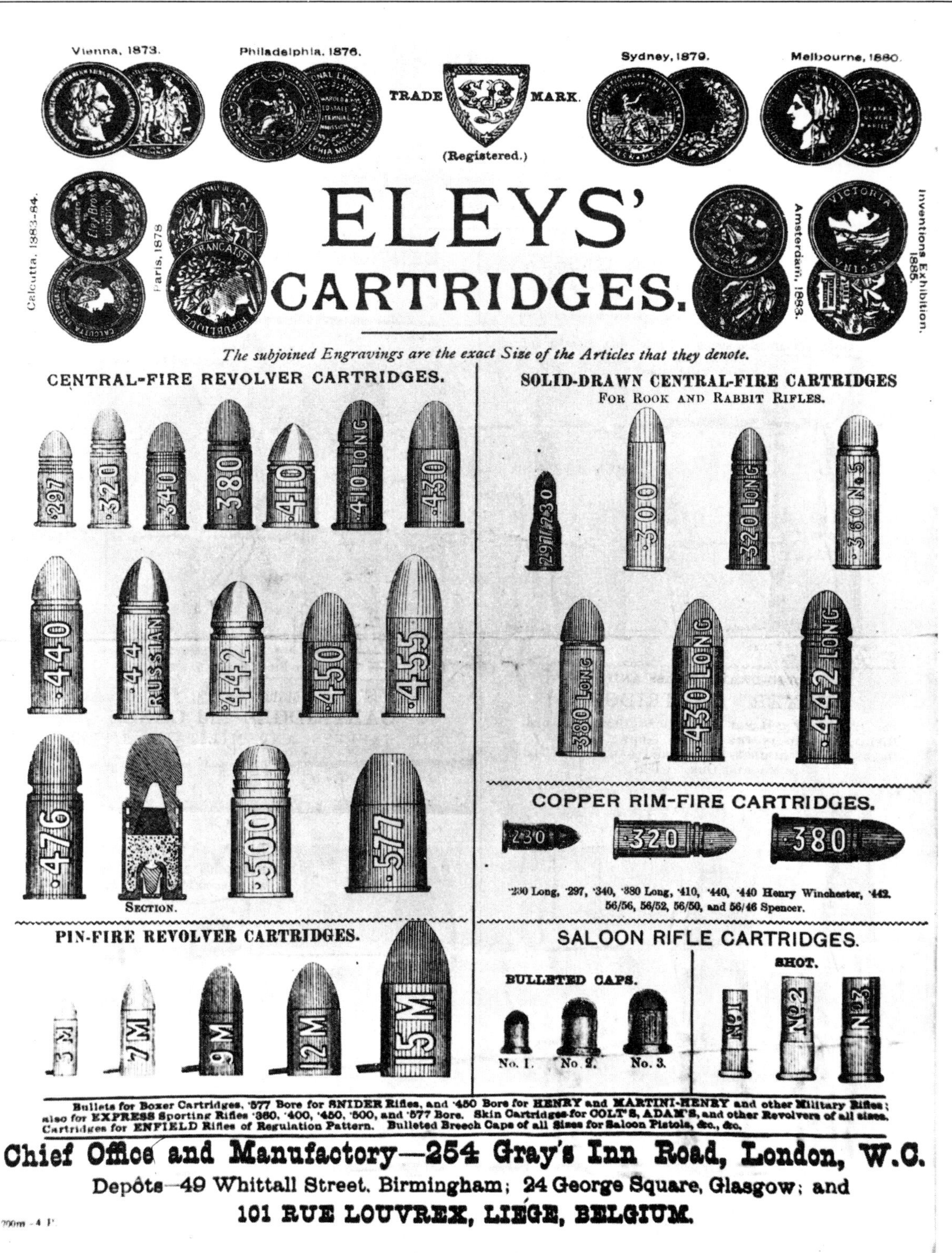

An Eley Brothers' ammunition advertisement.

to render the cartridge waterproof and also brittle so that it would fragment when forced by the rammer into the chamber. The Hayes cartridge was sold in America under both Hayes' and Storm's patents, and was manufactured by Broux and Mall of London.

Skin cartridges of English manufacture with their paper protective jacket appear to have survived the passage of time remarkably well. The use of animal gut seems to have been replaced by thin nitrated tissue paper towards the end of the muzzle loading era, the tissue container being attached to the bullet either by thread or by adhesive. The illustration gives an idea of the general appearance of some of these skin cartridges. This type of cartridge remained in use until about 1890, Eley Bros. deleting them from their catalogues after 1889.

Both the chronology and classification of the early nineteenth century cartridges is difficult. Concurrently with the development of the externally primed combustible cartridge, efforts were being made to develop the breechloading as opposed to muzzle loading cartridge. As we have already seen with the muzzle loading cartridge, both paper and metal were used and, for the rifle, external as well as internal priming.

The idea of loading firearms from the breech instead of from the muzzle was not new and it is remarkable how very few of the apparently revolutionary ideas of the nineteenth century were. Most of the successful ones were a result of relatively minor improvements and the difficulty lies in tracing the true ancestry of a successful idea back to the man who first thought of it and, in order to preserve a reasonable line of connective thought, to disregard many of the undoubtedly interesting and sometimes amusing backwaters of progress.

The first satisfactory self-primed metallic cartridge, and one which made the introduction of the breechloader a practical proposition, was the pin-fire cartridge. Credit for inventing this is given to Casimir Lefaucheux who had developed an effective pin-fire cartridge for shotguns. Improvements were made by Bush of London in 1841, Houiller in 1846, and many others. Lefaucheux exhibited a pin-fire cartridge arm at the Great Exhibition in London in 1851 and, in 1854, his son, Eugene Gabriel Lefaucheux, secured British Patent protection for a single action thumb cocked pistol (J. H. Johnson's Patent No. 955) employing pin-fire cartridges.

Originally the case was built up, much as is the

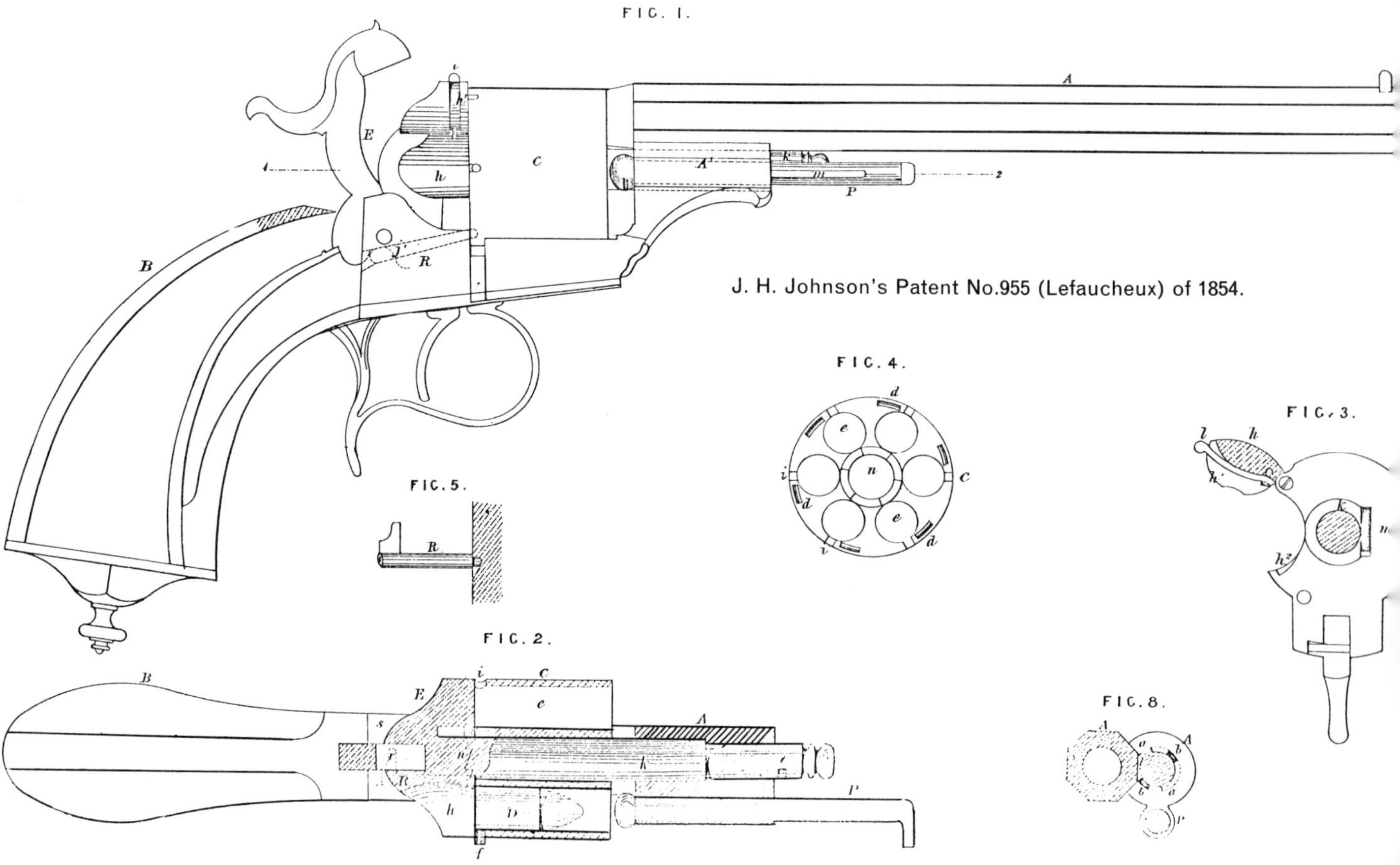

J. H. Johnson's Patent No.955 (Lefaucheux) of 1854.

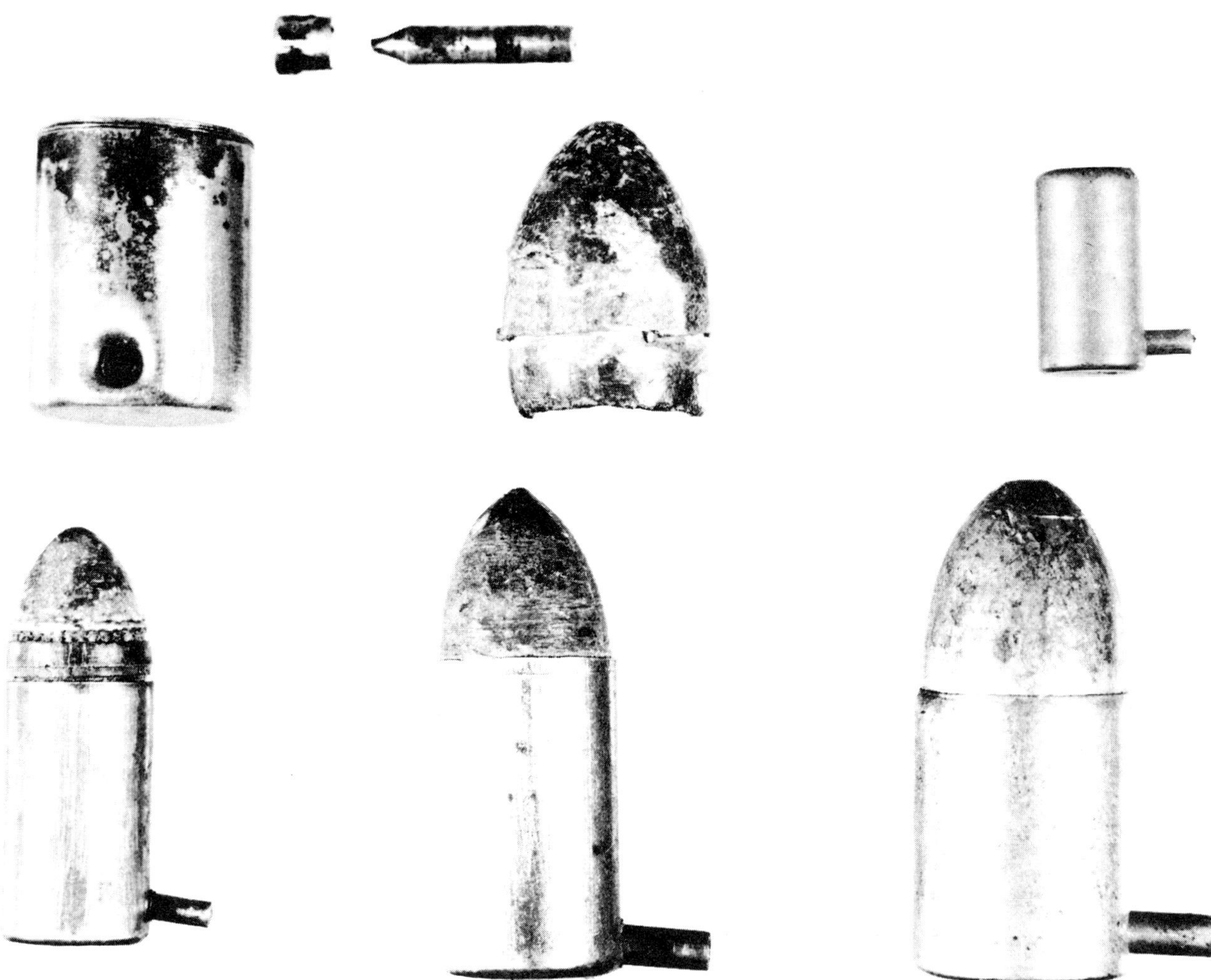

Various pin-fire cartridges.

Top row, left to right: 12mm case with cap and pin; 12mm bullet; 5mm blank.
Bottom row, left to right: 7mm; 9mm; 12mm.

modern shotgun case, with a paper tube attached to a copper head. Later, the whole case was made from copper and drawn in one operation from a circular blank. The cup-shaped pressing so produced was trimmed at the neck, and a hole was pierced in the wall near the base. A cardboard base with a rectangular hole cut in the middle was then pressed into the case and a percussion cap placed in the depression in the centre of the base wad. The cap was retained in place by a pin introduced through the hole in the wall of the case and, when the cartridge was loaded into the chamber of the weapon, the blow from the hammer striking the pin ignited the cap and then the charge.

The method of construction of the later brass pin-fire cartridge can be seen from the illustration. The pin and small cap are in fact removable and the cartridge is reloadable. With the larger pin-fire shotgun cases, special tools for reseating the pin to the correct depth were obtainable, and similar tools for pin-fire revolver cases were often included in cased sets and resembled a pair of thin nosed pliers for introducing the cap, the jaws having a slot to aid withdrawal of the pin.

Manufactured until the mid-1930's by European cartridge companies, the pin-fire revolver cartridge has to a great extent been neglected in both the American and British literature. The importance of the pin-fire system has been clouded by the enormous number of very cheap and poor quality continental pin-fire revolvers which were sold until manufacture ceased shortly before the Second World War. This neglect has tended to obscure the importance of the pin-fire, for not only was it the true metallic breechloading cartridge—the method of construction solved the problem of obturation—but it was also, as we shall later see, the first breechloading metallic cartridge to be adopted for military use.

Obtainable in 5, 7, 9, 12, and 15mm calibres, the thin metal case of the pin-fire cartridge momentarily expanded when the charge was fired and, for a critical moment, became, in effect, part of the gun. It was this obturation that sealed the open breech and made the breechloader a practical proposition. The disadvantage was that the cartridge could be loaded in one position only as the protruding striker pin had to fit into a notch cut into the rear of the chamber wall. The protruding pin was also a possible source of danger for, if accidentally struck, the cartridge might go off. On the credit side, the pin was a useful means of extracting the fired cases, and it was also a visible indication of whether or not the case had been fired. The smallest pin-fire cartridge, 2mm, is still made for watch charm blank pistols and, for its tiny size, makes a surprising noise. Some of the objections to the pin-fire cartridge were overcome with the introduction of the rim-fire, a class of cartridge that is still in widespread use to this day, albeit in one calibre only.

Just as the name Lefaucheux became almost synonymous with 'pin-fire', so the credit for the rim-fire system has been given to Louis Nicolas Auguste Flobert although, in all probability, the actual idea may have originated with Houiller, who described a variant of the idea in his 1847 patent which also referred to improvements in pin-fire cartridges. There is, however, no evidence that Houiller ever manufactured ammunition or arms on his system. On the other hand, Flobert certainly did, and to such effect that certain sizes of rim-fire ammunition are still to be found in ammunition makers' catalogues under his name.

The earliest Flobert rim-fire cartridges do not have the well defined rim we see on the .22 rim-fire of today. The base of the case was swelled slightly to prevent it being driven into the bore by the force of the hammer blow, since the hammer performed the dual function of breech block and firing pin. Also we can assume that, at the time of its inception, Flobert did not have the necessary tooling or techniques needed to manufacture cartridges with a true rim.

The Flobert cartridge and the rifle and pistols designed to be used with it were intended for indoor target practice and, when Flobert exhibited his wares at the London Exhibition of 1851, considerable interest was aroused. The tiny Flobert cartridge consisted of a simply drawn copper case not much larger than a percussion cap and undoubtedly derived from it. The fulminate was contained in the head of the case and acted as both ignitor and propellant, there being no separate charge of black powder. The low velocities which resulted were quite adequate for target shooting and the sport became quite popular. 'Breechloading practice pistols' as they were then known, were made in three sizes, the No. 1 or 6mm size was 'bulleted breech cap' or of the same calibre as the No. 3, but loaded with shot.

Until quite recently the descendants of these early cartridges were still manufactured as Flobert or Saloon cartridges. The other name for the No. 1 or 6mm size was 'bulleted breech cap' or BB cap. Instead of the round ball, a cylindrical bullet with a conical nose was loaded into the No. 1 case and the result was the Gallery Conical or CB ammunition. Both shot and blank cartridges were produced in Britain and, in the No. 3 or 9mm calibre, the shot loads in both the short and long cartridges were very popular, used in the No. 3 bolt action smooth bore Garden Guns, for dealing with small rodents.

On the continent Flobert cartridges were made in 5, 6, 7, and 9mm calibres with both round ball and conical bullets; shot cartridges in the same calibres were also available.

An even smaller rim-fire, the 4mm, although never loaded in Britain, was, and still is, very widely used on the Continent for indoor target shooting.

Another rim-fire, the Bosquette, made in 5, 6, 7 and 9mm sizes, can also be encountered, and the 6mm is still used in France for twelve metre rifle and pistol shooting. Yet another Flobert design, the Bosquette was intended for use with rifled weapons, the Flobert having been originally for smooth bores. The bullet shape was such that it cut nice clean holes in paper targets, and this was the type of ammunition used by the French Societés de Flobertistes before World War One. Because of its accuracy up to twenty yards, it became popular for shooting small birds at close range in garden shrubbery or 'groves'—hence its name.

These rim-fires can almost be regarded as fossilised; advances in manufacturing techniques since they were first produced have had an effect on the method of manufacture, but ballistically there has been little improvement either as regards performance or development. Similarly, with the weapons in which these cartridges were used, the breech mechanisms retained their original simplicity. In order to retain a share of the market, it was necessary to reduce costs to the absolute minimum, with the result that quality suffered.

It was left to the Americans to realise the potentiality of the rim-fire cartridge and to devise the techniques and machinery for producing an improved cartridge, the Smith and Wesson 'No. 1 Pistol Cartridge' or the .22 short. This cartridge, developed by Douglas B. Wesson in 1856–58, was undoubtedly inspired by the Flobert but differed in that a cylindro-conoidal bullet was used, the actual charge consisting of between three and four grains of black powder. The priming was in the rim of the cartridge case instead of across the head and, for the first time, it was possible to form a true rim. The case length was increased to accommodate the powder charge and, by 1871, it has been estimated that the .22 short was being made at the rate of 100,000 per day.

The practical difficulties of turning out thousands of these little cartridges per day, all identical and made to close tolerances, cannot be over-emphasised. Using a combined blanking and cupping punch and die, the first operation was to form a cup from a sheet of copper of the required thickness and quality. After this, the cups had to be annealed before they could be drawn, and the scale formed on the copper had to be removed by rumbling and pickling in dilute sulphuric acid. Any traces of the pickling acid had to be removed by washing—soda and soft soap solutions were used at one time—and the cups then had to be dried.

Annealing restored the ductility, and further drawing could now be carried out. The cup was pushed through a die by a punch, the diameter was reduced and the length of the cup increased. Three separate drawing operations were needed, together with the intermediate annealing, washing and drying processes, before the cups went to the next operation, 'trimming'. This was necessary because the movement of metal during the drawing operations might mean that the mouth of the cup was not perfectly straight and perhaps cracks might have occurred which had to be removed; it was, of course, essential to standardise the length of the cup. With trimming complete, the cup had been transformed into a 'case' except for the formation of the rim or head. Heading was carried out on completely automatic machines where the case was pushed into the die until the head emerged to be struck by the heading 'bunter'; this upset the head close to the die face and so formed the rim. The headed case was then pushed out of the die by the next case, which was carried into the die by the heading punch.

After heading, the cases were washed before being passed to the priming department. Priming was placed inside the case head and the case was then spun so that centrifugal force caused the priming to be distributed equally inside the rim. The priming was then dried and the operation complete.

Two methods were used for manufacturing the bullets. The oldest method was to cast slugs of lead into a cast iron mould and subsequently swage the slugs into the proper shape. In the second method the casting operation was eliminated and the bullets were manufactured in a special machine which also cut and formed them.

With both case and bullet completed, the next operations were loading, the assembly of the seperate components and the provision of a correct charge of powder. The powder charge and insertion of the bullet was carried out by automatic machinery as was the crimping of the bullet into the case. At this point, the bullet itself was cannelured, the indentations formed serving to hold the grease lubricant used to prevent leading of the bore of the rifle or pistol barrel.

Relatively little change has taken place in the actual manufacturing techniques, but there has been an improvement in the materials used for dies and punches and also in the drawing lubricants. Initially, each operation was conducted separately, and components were transferred by hand from one interstage operation to the next. With automation, the separate processes have been combined as far as possible, with the result that one machine performs a number of related operations consecutively and output per machine has been gradually increased. These machines require little attention from the machine operator other than to see that the raw material is fed to them and the product is removed. Besides making cartridges, this type of manipulative tool has also taken over the boring, repetitive tasks of making such things as nails, wood screws and nuts and bolts. Even today their often uncanny skill can excite the admiration of people seeing them in operation for the first time, and one tends to

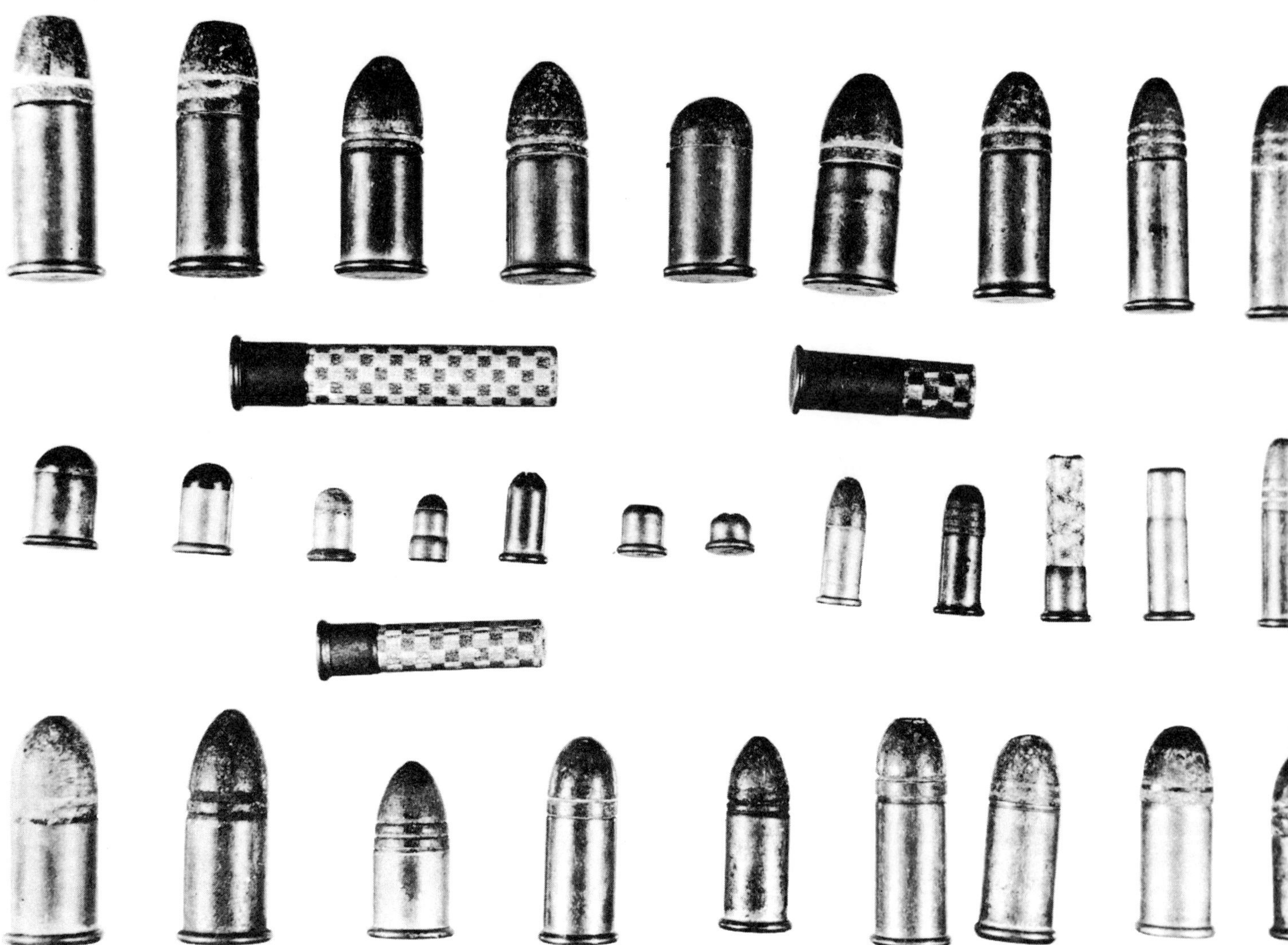

A selection of rim-fire cartridges both past and present, illustrating the variety manufactured.

forget that the men who designed them and made them work are long since dead and buried.

The complexity and cost of the machinery required for manufacturing ammunition on a reasonable scale inevitably influenced the development and organisation of the industry. This fact, coupled with the desire to secure the supplies of raw materials needed to keep the factories in full production—brass, copper, primers and propellants—led to the horizontal and vertical integration of the industry and to the formation of large and powerful ammunition interests who, in turn, were swallowed up by the even larger chemical concerns of the twentieth century. It is interesting to reflect that the humble .22 rim-fire is still very much with us in spite of the advances in metallurgy and propellants, and the .22 short of a hundred years ago is not markedly dissimilar, in external appearances at least, to the .22 short fired from the specialised rapid-fire automatic pistols of today.

For about ten years the rim-fire cartridge reigned supreme in America. Of the .22 short and long, the .25 and the .30 short and long, the short versions were particularly popular in a variety of arms, for example the Sharps four barrelled pistol first made in the 1860's, and the Remington, Colt and Marlin revolvers. The .32 short saw use in cheap, pocket pistols and also the Remington Rider magazine pistol. The .32 long has a much longer history and was only discontinued as late as 1963. First used in the No. 2 Smith and Wesson of 1861, it was gradually replaced over the years by the .32 Smith and Wesson centre-fire, but remained a popular rifle cartridge until the mid-1920's. Displaced by the .38 centre-fire, the .38

Various sectioned metallic cartridges.
Top, left to right: pin-fire, rim-fire.
Centre: centre-fire with folded head construction.
Bottom: .45 ACP with anvil, cap and bullet, the case being solid head with a centre flash hole.

short and long rim-fire cartridges appear to have been useful but, unlike the .41 short, they perhaps lacked glamour. The .41 short was first made for the Moore's 'Patent Metallic Pistol, Derringer's Pattern' of 1863, later to be known as the National and then as the Colt No. 1 Derringer. As well as being chambered in a host of lesser known cartridge derringer pistols, the .41 rim-fire was the cartridge used by the famous Remington Double Derringer, the favourite hide-away gun of the river-boat gambler, dance-hall girl, outlaw and lawman, and in modern centre-fire guise is still a favourite with those who require the maximum punch from the minimum package.

With sixteen grains of black powder instead of the ten loaded into the short version, the .41 long saw use in the famous Colt 'Cloverleaf' revolver of 1871. The most famous of all the large rim-fires, the .44 Henry, was born on 16 October 1860, when B. Tyley Henry was granted US Patent No. 30446 for the Henry Rifle, the old Volcanic, originally manufactured as both a rifle and a pistol and based on patents taken out by Smith and Wesson in 1854. The Volcanic Company was bought out by Oliver Fisher Winchester who formed the New Haven Arms Company, later to become the Winchester Repeating Arms Co. The Volcanic, redesigned by Henry to chamber the .44 rim-fire, late became the .44 Winchester Model 1866, the first of many lever action rifles and the foundation upon which the fame and fortune of Winchester was well and truly laid. Few revolvers employed the .44 Henry—most were conversions from percussion—and although this cartridge appears to have been discontinued about 1920, the 'H' headstamp still found on every Winchester rim-fire cartridge helps preserve the name.

A very rare American rim-fire, the .46 short, appears to have been used only for conversions of the .44 Remington Army percussion, the barrel of which was of larger diameter than its nominal calibre designation would suggest.

The largest rim-fire handgun cartridge manufactured in America, the .50 Remington Pistol, was loaded with 32 grains of black powder and a 290 grain bullet. The Remington Navy Model 1865 Rolling Block single shot pistol was the first cartridge pistol, and the only single shot one, to be adopted by the United States, with the exception of flare pistols and special survival weapons.

The earliest breechloading cartridge pistols sold in Britain were the Flobert Saloon pistols, open frame pin-fire revolvers and unashamed copies of the .22 rim-fire Smith and Wesson. The first British manufacturer to exploit the market for breechloading revolvers was William Tranter who took out his first patents for these in 1863. The Tranter series of rim-fire revolvers appear to have been the first commercially successful domestic revolvers and were made in .422, .380, .320 and .230 calibres. The .442 was the equivalent of the 54 bore percussion Army revolver and the actual case diameter was .450. The Tranter .230 was known as the Tranter No. 1 and the .320 as the Tranter No. 2. The series of British rim-fires was as follows: .442, .440, .380, .380 long, .340, .320, .320 long, .297 and .230.

The cartridge manufacturer had two different

supply problems. On the one hand, there were cartridges designed to fit the newly introduced rim-fire revolvers and, on the other, cartridges for those percussion revolvers which had been converted to breechloading. In carrying out a conversion it was obviously far cheaper to leave the barrel alone and provide suitable cartridges, the cases for which could be accommodated in chambers specially provided in the replacement cylinders supplied. Two of the cartridges in calibres later to be discarded were the .442 and the .340. The first, as we have seen, was designed to be used in the 54 bore percussion revolver and the second was suitable for conversions of the very popular 120 bore size. Both were also made as centre-fire cartridges and were employed in centre-fire conversions of percussion as well as in new breechloading pistols.

Very few of the rim-fire cartridges were marked with a calibre designation, the .442 being a notable exception. It is easy to imagine the problems that the changeover from percussion to rim- and centre-fire produced. The 1860's and 70's might well have been the dream age of the gun fanatic, for the shops of the gunmakers would have been full of percussion revolvers, conversions, and both rim- and centre-fire revolvers, whilst the problem of holding stocks of powder and ball, skin cartridges and the new metallics must have presented quite a headache.

Many of the gunmakers and dealers left with stocks of muzzle loading weapons offered them at 'greatly reduced prices' and, as an added inducement, extolled the virtues of these weapons as 'being well adapted for foreign service, or where breech-loading ammunition is not readily available'.

On the continent, in addition to the 'standard' Flobert series of rim-fire cartridges, the .320 and .380 in both long and short versions were very popular for cheap 'self-defence' rim-fire revolvers, as was the .350/9mm rim-fire—a purely continental cartridge not listed by either American or British manufacturers. The only European power to use rim-fire revolvers on a significant scale were the Swiss, who adopted a modification of the Chamelot-Delvigne in 1873. In common with most rim-fire cartridges, the bullet was externally lubricated and at .430″ in diameter the metric calibre designation was 10.4mm. Later, in 1878, the Swiss service revolvers were converted to 10.4mm centre-fire.

The rim-fire was certainly a great advance on the muzzle loading skin cartridge and it was more successful than the pin-fire, but in the larger calibres it had several defects. It was difficult to distribute the priming evenly around the rim, particularly with the larger cases, and misfires were relatively common. Also, the proportion of priming compound to propellant was excessive and resulted in high pressures and ruptured rims. By virtue of the design, the head of the case tended to become convex on firing and this, particularly in the case of revolvers, caused increased friction between the head and the recoil shield. In addition, the cases were not normally reloadable.

It was for these reasons that the rim-fire was eventually ousted by the centre-fire in all but the .22 calibre, and the story of the development of the centre-fire cartridge is longer and even more complex than that of the pin- or rim-fire.

Today it is generally accepted that the earliest examples of the centre-fire cartridge were those produced by Samuel Johannes Pauly, who was born in Switzerland in 1766. This remarkable and versatile Swiss inventor took out his first important patent in France in 1812. During his stay in Paris, it is recorded that Pauly employed a Prussian lock maker, von Dreyse, and he was also associated with the noted Parisian gunmaker Prelat. Pauly's experiments in Paris were cut short by the fall of the city to the Allies on 5 April 1814 and he came to London, where, on 4 August 1814, he quickly took out British Patent No. 3833 in respect of an 'Apparatus for Discharging Firearms by means of Compressed Air'. This was not as might be imagined a kind of air gun but a method of using hot compressed air to ignite 'explosive powder'.[1]

Pauly unfortunately did not reap the benefits of his pioneer work and even his adventure in ballooning with the famous gunmaker Durs Egg ended in failure. Meanwhile Johann Nikolaus von Dreyse continued to experiment with self-igniting cartridges and, in 1840, the Prussian Army adopted the Dreyse needle gun which proved to be an highly effective arm for its day, and was used both in the short war against Denmark in 1864 and with spectacular success against the Austrians in the war of 1866. The Dreyse was also used against the French in the Franco-Prussian War of 1870–71, but the French had the superior Chassepot. Pistols were made

[1] Full details of Pauly's patents are given in *Pauly, Gun Designer* by W. Reid (JAAS, Vol. II), Vol. 22, 27 October 1866 and Vol. 22, 17 November 1866.

using both the Pauly centre-fire system and Dreyse's needle-fire ignition, but they were not widely used. The Dreyse Model 1856 pistol was apparently issued to the Prussian Cavalry in 15.4mm calibre, but further information on both the pistol and its Service use is lacking.

Nikolaus von Dreyse was born in Sommerda in 1787, the son of a master locksmith. The firm of Waffen und Munitionsfabrik von Dreyse was organised to manufacture his breechloading rifles and his son, Franz von Dreyse, was also connected with the firm. After 1901 the company became known as the Rheinische Metallwaren und Maschinenfabrik and, although a series of automatic pistols were manufactured under the name Dreyse, they were, in fact, designed by Louis Schmeisser.

A series of needle-fire revolvers were manufactured by Dreyse about 1860, most of them being marked 'F. Dreyse, Sommerda', and these appear to have been made under patents obtained by George Leopold Ludwig Kufahl who, in his specification of 1852, gave his address as Christopher Street, Finsbury, London. Kufahl's patents refer to needle-fire rifles and revolvers and, although Kufahl's needle-fire revolver does not appear to have been made in Britain, an experimental rifle bearing his name and generally similar to that described in the patent specification is to be found in the Dick Institute, Kilmarnock. Possibly, however, a similar needle-fire revolver was made in this country but has since been lost.

Kufahl needle-fire revolver by Dreyse of Sommerda. (Tower of London)

Many efforts were made to combine the centre-fire ignition system of the Pauly or Dreyse with an entirely gas-tight construction similar to the Flobert or the Lefaucheux pin-fire case. If we accept that Pauly was the first to use a metallic centre-fire reloadable cartridge, the fulminate contained in a depression in the centre of the cartridge head, then Clement Pottet was the first to make a gun which used a metallic centre-fire cartridge with an ordinary copper cap attached to it. Pottet, like Dreyse, had worked for Pauly in Paris and his cartridge shows Pauly's influence.

In Britain, Joseph Needham patented his needle-fire cartridge in 1852. This differed from the Dreyse in that the priming was contained in a shallow cup attached to a card wad at the base of the case. In the Dreyse needle-fire cartridge the priming was attached to the paper wadding or sabot which held the bullet.

With the Dreyse type cartridge the needle had to pass through the base of the cartridge and through the powder charge before it could reach the priming. With Needham's ball or bullet cartridge the needle passed through a thin copper disc which was already perforated (the small hole covered by an external paper patch), through a thin cardboard disc, again perforated, and into the priming. The base wads, powder, bullet wad and bullet were contained in a thin brass cylinder held together by an outside envelope of several layers of brown paper. Several makers, Rigby was one, produced rifles for these cartridges, and dissection of the cartridges shows several small differences in construction. So far all the cartridges discussed have been of 'built-up' construction, and eventually, by a process of gradual evolution, the built-up cartridge with a brass head and a paper tube became (if we except the all-plastic type) the shotgun cartridge of today. With rifles and pistols, however, such cases had their defects since not only the bullet but also the paper case was likely to leave the muzzle when fired. Cartridges were therefore made where the paper case was ignited so that all that had to be removed after firing was the brass head, and this could be reloaded. With the modern Flobert shot cartridge this still applies; the paper tube separates from the head and travels through the bore intact—disintegrating on leaving the muzzle—and only the cartridge head is extracted.

The desire to increase the case strength led to the development in America of metallic cases fired by external ignition. This was, however, a rather retrograde step since, although they were breechloading, these cartridges reverted to the system employed by the breechloading percussion cap firearms with consumable cartridges. Amongst the many types of externally ignited cartridge made and developed during the stress of war in America, the Maynard, in its improved form, was perhaps the most successful. The early Maynard cartridge employed a parallel brass tube with a small hole in the centre of the base, and was loaded with a lubricated bullet. How the case was to be extracted after being fired is not known but this difficulty was appreciated for, in 1859, Edward Maynard obtained a further patent which referred to the provision of a large diameter steel disc, also perforated, which was soldered to the base of the original cartridge and provided a rim that could be grasped by the fingers to extract the case.

The importance of the rim may not be fully appreciated. Not only did it serve as a means of extracting the fired case, but it also ensured correct positioning of the cartridge in the chamber. Without a rim, 'headspace', to use a modern term, would be variable and a misfire could result.

Yet another small evolutionary step was taken when George Woodward Morse, an American engineer, took out US Patent No. 20,727 in 1858 and also British Patent No. 1164 in the same year. This was a modification of his previous patent No. 20,214 taken out earlier in 1858, and it illustrated a brass tube with a 'V'-shaped wire, the ends of which were soldered to the inside wall of the case. The point of the 'V' was level with the base of the tube and acted as an anvil for a percussion cap. The annular space between the cap and the tube was filled with an annular rubber disc.

The difficulties of producing a satisfactory solid drawn centre-fire cartridge case were not caused by lack of ideas—these, as can be seen from the patent literature, were plentiful—but by the problems of translating these ideas into practice. Also, in America, when all the effort should have been directed towards the goal of manufacturing a satisfactory centre-fire cartridge, much time and energy was being spent in attempting to evade the patent of Rollin White. It was this that led to the production of perhaps the most bizarre series of revolvers and cartridges ever made.

To follow the story, we have to go back to the time when Horace Smith and Daniel B. Wesson patented the mechanism that was later to evolve into the Winchester Model 1866 rifle. Under their patents of 1854, Smith and Wesson made both rifles and pistols for 'loaded ball' ammunition. We have seen something of the problems involved in manufacturing cartridge cases, and allied to this was the difficulty of providing some means of ignition. Smith and Wesson had no such troubles; they dispensed with the cartridge case entirely. The ammunition used by their repeating arms and by similar arms later made by the Volcanic Repeating Arms Co. consisted of a cylindro-ogival lead bullet made with a small cavity in the base. This cavity was filled with black powder and the priming was contained in a small copper disc backed up by a piece of cork set in the base of the 'cartridge'. There was no case in the accepted sense of the word. These cartridges were, of course, centre-fire, but, although the basic toggle link breech mechanism was entirely satisfactory and the rifles and pistols received many glowing tributes, particularly with regard to the rapidity of fire, the commercial success of these weapons was restricted.

The calibres furnished were, by the standards of the times, rather small and the weapons lacked a satisfactory gas seal at the breech, a common failing with most of the early breechloaders. Perhaps the most unsatisfactory feature, however, was the lack of power. A .38 calibre Volcanic bullet had a black powder charge of $6\frac{1}{2}$ grains to propel a bullet weighing 100 grains. As a comparison, the .41 rim-fire derringer cartridge fired a bullet weighing 130 grains propelled by a 13 grain powder charge. It was left to B. Tyler Henry to solve the problems and usher into the world the rifle which was to become the Winchester.

Smith and Wesson themselves concentrated on

revolvers and on the development of their .22 rim-fire cartridge, and it was only when they were almost ready to market their breechloading rim-fire revolver that they were made aware of Rollin White's patent. No revolvers based on the Rollin White patent were, in fact, ever marketed and very possibly no one would have ever heard of his name had it not been for the fact that, in his patent No. 12,648 of 1855, White claimed that his invention included 'extending the chambers through the rear of the cylinder for the purpose of loading them at the breech from behind'.

And this, of course, was precisely what Smith and Wesson had intended to do themselves with their new rim-fire cartridge. They could, of course, have ignored the Rollin White patent and risked an action for infringement. Such an action might have been fought successfully, since the idea of boring completely through the cylinder of a revolver was not entirely new, and pin-fire weapons manufactured by Lefaucheux of France had already appeared on the market in Europe and had no doubt even been sold in America.

The ways of the law, however, are by no means simple and, in spite of evidence of prior usage, there was nothing to indicate with any reasonable degree of certainty that the courts would decide in their favour. A further and more important point was that, even if they were successful, they would gain no exclusive rights, and the way would then be clear for their competitors also to manufacture pistols with bored-through cylinders.

In the event, an agreement was reached between Smith and Wesson and Rollin White which permitted manufacture on a royalty basis, and Smith and Wesson very shrewdly inserted a proviso that White should defend his patent claims against any infringement.

Smith and Wesson very soon had reason to congratulate themselves warmly on their foresight and business acumen for, no sooner had they started to market their rim-fire revolvers, than other makers began to sell revolvers that were clearly infringements of the basic Rollin White patent. As agreed, White took steps to defend his claims and, in November 1863, these were upheld in favour of Smith and Wesson by the Federal Circuit Court in the District of Massachusetts (Case No. 17,535; Smith and Wesson *vs.* Allen, Federal Cases Circuits and Districts Courts, 1789–1880).

As a result of this ruling, thousands of revolvers were turned over to Smith and Wesson and were sold by them with the added legend, 'manufactured for Smith and Wesson'. One such revolver, a conventional single action brass framed seven shot .22 rim-fire, is illustrated and is marked 'Made for Smith and Wesson by Lowell Arms Co.'

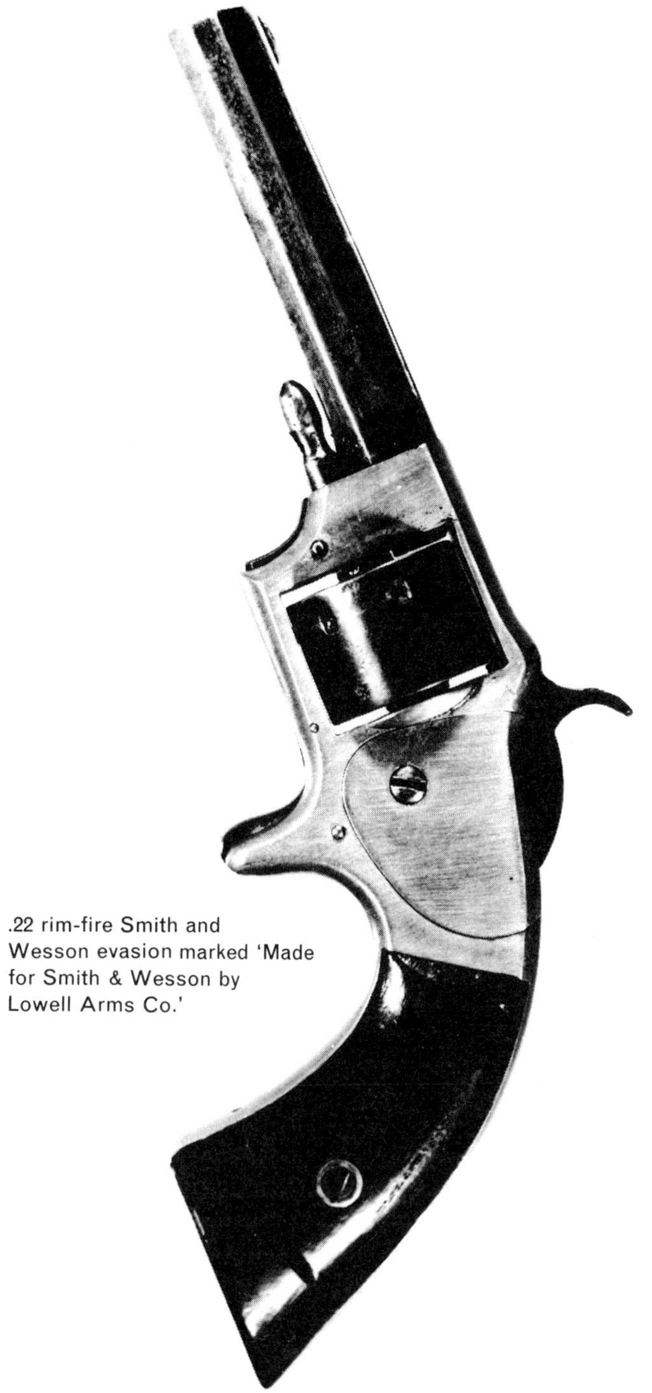

.22 rim-fire Smith and Wesson evasion marked 'Made for Smith & Wesson by Lowell Arms Co.'

There was little that was conventional about the revolvers made expressly for the purpose of evading the Rollin White Patent. The first of

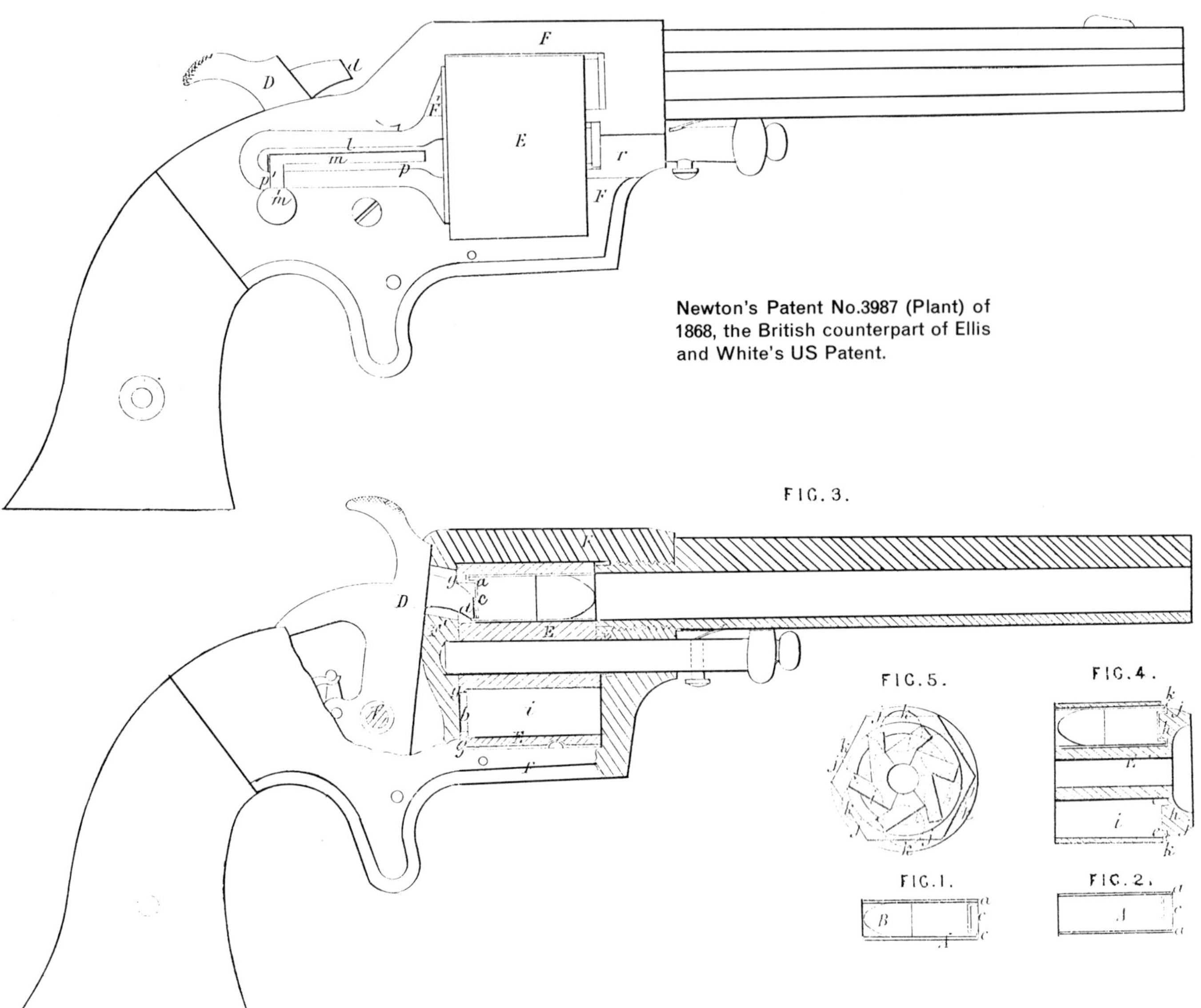

Newton's Patent No.3987 (Plant) of 1868, the British counterpart of Ellis and White's US Patent.

these evasions to reach the market was the Plant, manufactured by the Plant Manufacturing Co., New Haven, under Ellis and White's patents.

In 1859 Willard C. Ellis and John N. White of Springfield were granted Patent No. 24,726 for the first front loading, self-contained metallic cartridge revolver. The feature of this patent was the fact that the revolver cylinder was not bored entirely through, although there was a small opening at the rear to allow the hammer nose to strike the interior of the hemispherical base of the patent cartridge known today as a 'hollow-base' or 'cup-primer' cartridge. This base, dished inwardly, contained the fulminate. The cartridges and improvements to the cylinder were described in Patent No. 39,318 of 1863, and further improvements to the system were patented by Henry Reynolds, who invented an ejection rod attached to the back of the frame (US Patent No. 42,688 of 1864). When pushed forward through the small opening in the rear of each chamber, it ejected the fired cases from the front of the cylinder. Ellis and White revolvers were made by Plant and by Merwin and Bray. The .28 calibre example shown was manufactured by the Eagle Arms Co. of New York and is generally similar to both the solid frame Plant and the Merwin and Bray. In terms of sales, the most successful of the front loading revolvers marketed in an endeavour to avoid infringing the Rollin White patent, were the 'teat-fire' revolvers. Revolvers using this system were made in .32 and .45 calibres, but few of the larger calibre have survived and it is reasonable to suppose that few were manufactured.

The teat-fire system was patented by Daniel Moore who had manufactured a revolver which infringed the all-powerful White patent. Moore's teat-fire patent was granted in 1863 (US Patent No. 38,321), and revolvers were manufactured under it by the Moore Patent Fire Arms Co. until about 1867, manufacture being continued by the National Arms Co. until 1870.

The Moore cartridge (illustrated with the .32 Moore revolver) was .335″ in diameter and $3\frac{1}{8}$″ in length. The .32 calibre bullet was contained entirely within the case in a similar manner to the Plant cup-primer cartridge, and was located by a circumferential groove or cannelure $\frac{15}{32}$″ from the case mouth. The priming was contained in the small teat at the base of the cartridge.

To load the single action Moore type revolver the loading gate, in front of the cylinder, was swung downwards and the cartridges pushed into the front of each chamber. After loading, the gate was then swung back into the position shown in the illustration to prevent the cartridges from falling out. Later models incorporated an extraction extension which served to push the fired cases out of the cylinder, and a small cut-out for this purpose can be seen in the recoil shield.

.28 Smith and Wesson evasion made by the Eagle Arms Co. of New York.

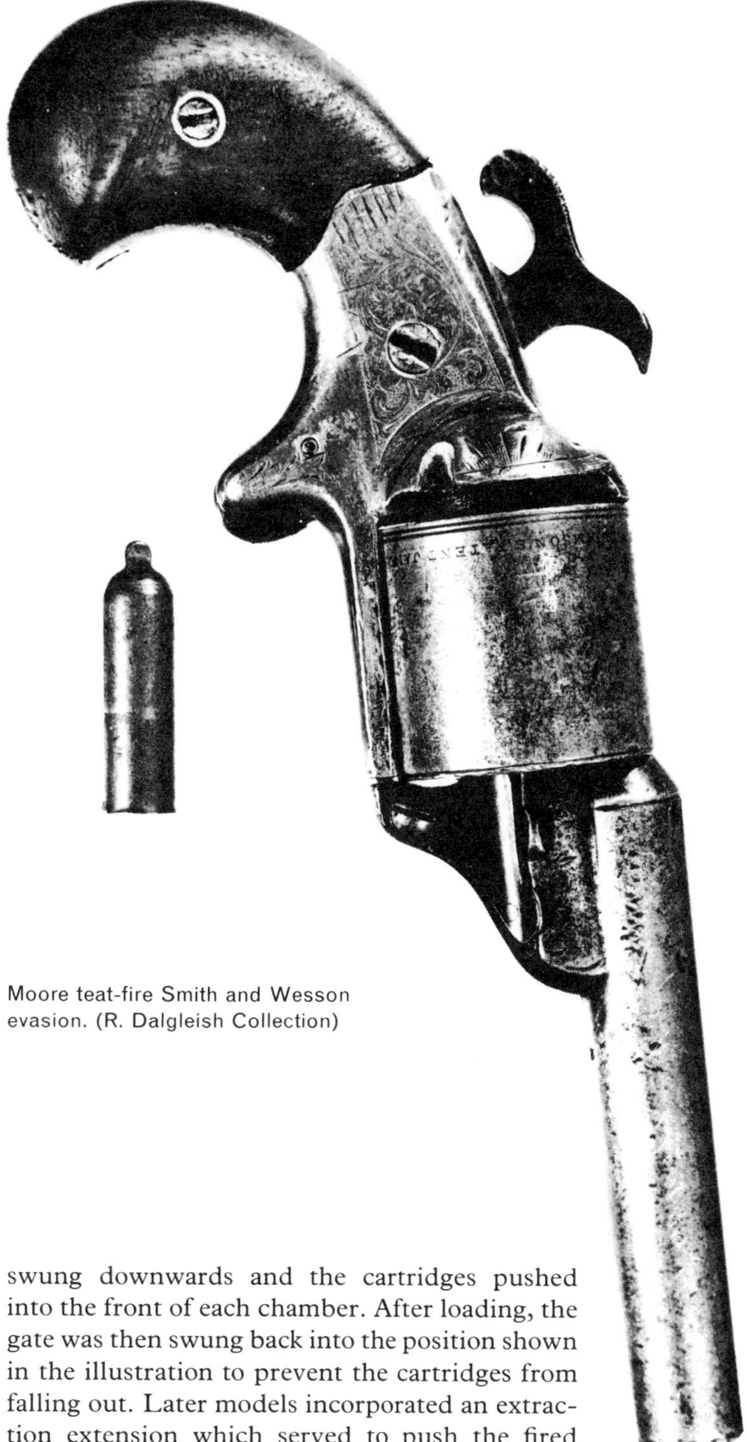

Moore teat-fire Smith and Wesson evasion. (R. Dalgleish Collection)

The strangest of the Rollin White or Smith and Wesson 'evasions' was the Crispin revolver. Invented by Colonel Silas Crispin and patented by him in October 1865 (US Patent No. 50,224), this revolver had a hinged frame and a two part cylinder, both front and rear sections of which rotated. When the action was opened, the barrel hinged downward, the front portion of the cylinder being attached by its own cylinder pin to the front part of the frame, the rear portion remaining attached to the standing breech.

A very special cartridge was required and this was the subject of Crispin's Patent No. 49,237 granted in August 1865. This was a self-contained metallic cartridge, but the fulminate was contained in a raised annular belt formed towards the mouth of the case.

To load the Crispin, the cartridges were inserted into the front section of the cylinder and the action was closed so that the rear of the cartridges were then seated in the rear of the cylinder which was not bored entirely through. The fulminate loaded belts of the cartridges were then at the junction between the two sections of the cylinder and, since the cartridges acted as dowel pins, both sections of the cylinder had to turn as one. The rear section of the cylinder had small cut-outs appropriately placed so that the firing pin could strike the annular belt of the cartridge and so fire the round.

Crispin apparently took out a previous patent on a centre-fire cartridge of built-up construction but, although it can be regarded as a link in the evolution of the centre-fire, the patent does not appear to have been utilised on a practical basis. Lacking the unusual features of his belted primer cartridge—certainly the most peculiar cartridge ever put into production—his earlier cartridge inventions are now forgotten. If one had to think up a selling point for the Crispin revolver, probably the only one that could be successfully put forward is that it required no mechanical means of ejection since, when the cylinder was opened, the fired cartridges could easily be removed by hand.

The revolvers so far discussed have all employed special cartridges. The ingenious Slocum was designed to use standard rim-fire cartridges, but still had to be so constructed as not to infringe the White patent. This was achieved by loading the cylinder from the side. The Slocum, if nothing else, was a testament to the ingenuity of man and an illustration of how far people will go to achieve their objective. Had the Slocum been merely an exercise to see how the problem could be solved it would have been remarkable enough, but the revolver was actually manufactured on a commercial basis and people not only bought them but apparently thought highly of the system.

Frank Slocum's patent, obtained in 1863 (US Patent No. 38,204), described the method of side loading into a cylinder 'which is not open at the rear end' (except for a small slot for the hammer nose). The chambers for the cartridges were sliding tubes which fitted into troughs cut into the cylinder proper, and these tubes were arranged to slide forward over a fixed 'stationary piston' or ejecting rod. With the hammer at half cock, the chamber opposite the ejecting rod was unlatched and pushed forward, and the cartridge was then dropped into the trough and the tube chamber pushed back. This operation had to be carried out for each cartridge but, after firing, the fired case would drop out of the trough of its own accord, and was prevented from sticking in the sliding chamber by the ejecting rod.

Yet another revolver which employed standard rim-fire cartridges was the Pond. Once again the cylinder was not bored entirely through and the rim-fire cartridges were dropped into each chamber at the front and followed by tubes or 'thimbles', the internal diameter corresponding to that of the cartridge case, the outside diameter to that of the rim. The rear of the cylinder was provided with notches through which the hammer nose could enter to strike the rim of the cartridge, and a somewhat complicated extraction system was employed to eject the fired cases and to separate the cases from the thimbles.

The only pin-fire 'evasion' marketed in America was the Polain, and details of this unusual revolver are to be seen in British Patent No. 2210 of 28 August 1865. Prosper Polain of Brussels later patented his invention in America (US Patent No. 53,548 of 27 March 1866).

The Polain is of interest since its construction foreshadowed later developments in simultaneous extraction. The cartridges were introduced through lateral openings in the cylinder in a similar manner to the Slocum, but they were then moved forward into separate open-ended chambers resembling the 'tubes' of the Pond, but differing in that they were carried in a group on a rotating disc. To load the pistol, the barrel assembly was unlocked by moving a lever, and the barrel assembly could then be drawn forward, taking with it the disc and the attached 'open-ended' chambers or tubes. Cartridges were then loaded through the apertures in the side of the cylinder, and the barrel was returned and locked in its former position.

Rollin White's patent lasted for fourteen years and, shortly after it expired in 1869, an attempt was made to obtain a seven year extension. This was vetoed by President Grant who stated that 'justice to the government and to the

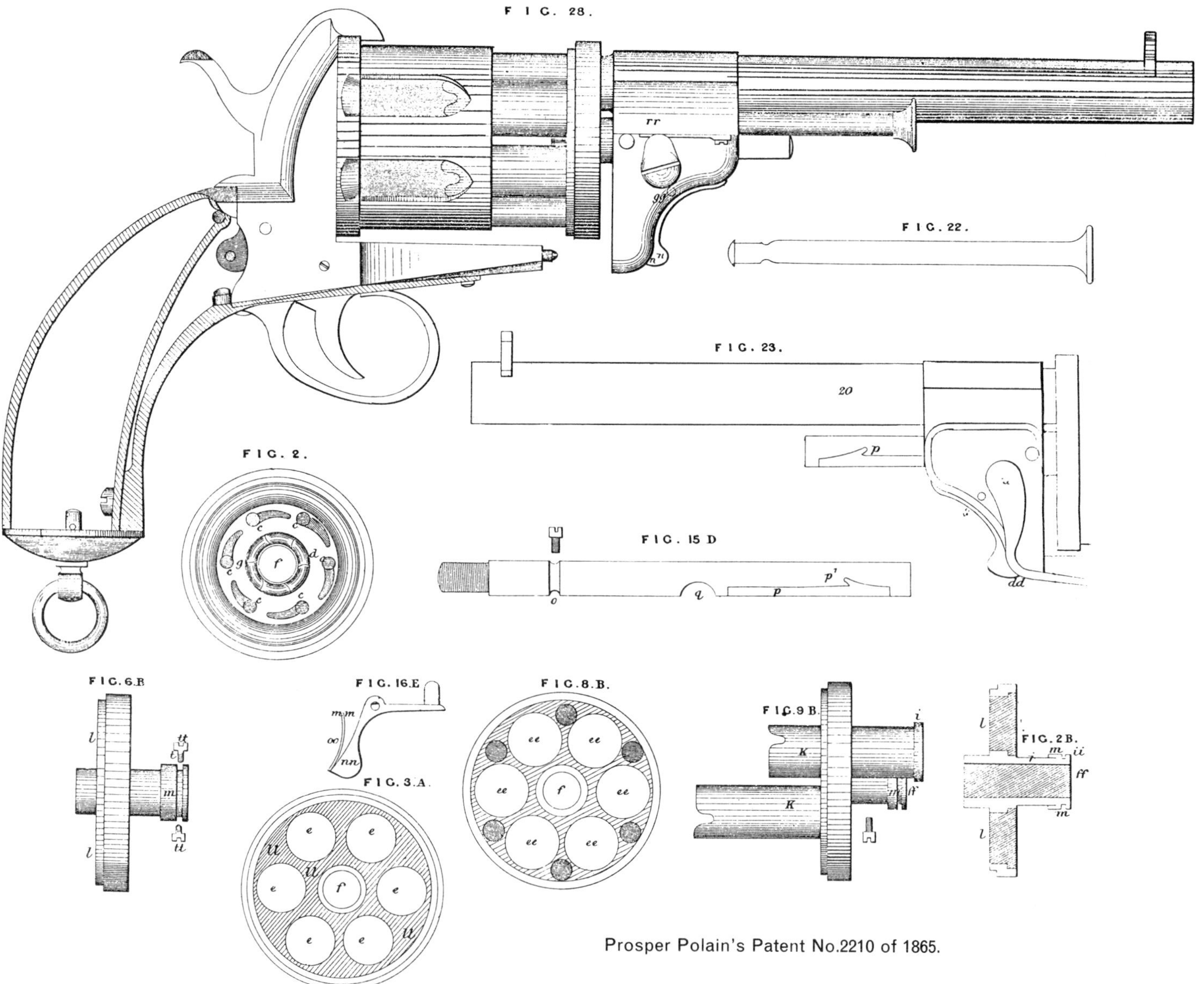

Prosper Polain's Patent No.2210 of 1865.

public forbids this patent from being renewed'.

One can only guess at the frustration which the American revolver manufacturers must have felt during the period of White's all-powerful patent. No doubt the most annoyed was Samuel Colt, particularly if the story that Rollin White offered him his invention and was turned down is true. Colt, it will be remembered, died in 1862 and consequently did not live to see the first 'cartridge' Colt. This was the brain-child of F. Alexander Thuer, a Prussian immigrant who had joined Colt's in 1849. Restricted as Colt's were by the Rollin White patent, and mindful of the very great number of percussion Colt revolvers in the hands of the public, it is not surprising that Thuer's method of dealing with the problem of cartridge loading was to patent, in 1868, a means of converting percussion revolvers.

The conversion was available in .31, .36 and .44 calibres, and the standard conical bullet cast by the Colt mould was employed. Black powder was the propellant, but it was also necessary to have the tapered brass Thuer cartridge case and what Colt's still called 'caps'—what we would today call 'primers'. In addition, lubricating wads were provided to be placed between the bullet and the powder in the assembled cartridge. Colt's supplied a set of five reloading tools which enabled the owner to de-cap the fired case, re-cap and reload.

Modifications to the standard Colt revolver consisted of boring through the percussion cylinder and turning off a part of the rear. A conversion ring (fitted with a rebounding firing pin and an ejecting lever) was then attached to the rear of the cylinder, and was capable of part rotation independent of the front part of the cylinder. The rimless, tapered, centre-fire, metallic, reloadable cartridges were loaded into the front of the cylinder and, with the conversion ring turned to the right, the firing pin, driven by the hammer, fired the cartridge in line with the barrel. When the ring was turned to the left, snapping the hammer caused the ejecting lever to give a sharp blow to the fired case in the chamber second to the right of the hammer, and the ejecting lever was so arranged that it could be used to eject a loaded cartridge without risk.

A slight alteration was necessary to the rammer face, and it was also customary to deepen the groove on the right hand side of the barrel lug to permit loading and ejecting without the barrel being removed. Very few Thuer-converted Colts have survived, and from this it may be assumed that only a limited number of such conversions were carried out.

When the Rollin White patent expired in 1869, the field was open to a number of more effective breechloading conversions, and since no patent evasion was necessary, these were greatly simplified.

In Britain, where there were none of the restrictions that had hampered revolver development in America, further work on centre-fire cartridges had resulted in British Patent No. 137 of 1866, granted to Colonel Edward Mounier Boxer of the Royal Laboratory at Woolwich. This was for a cartridge whose case was made from coiled sheet brass 0.003″ thick with an outside paper wrapper. A later patent, No. 2,653, also taken out in 1866, suggested modifications to the design, and these culminated in the Pattern II Boxer cartridge which was approved for use with the Snider breechloading conversion of the Enfield rifle in December 1866.

A series of modified cartridges, nine in all, were produced, each distinguished by an appropriate 'Mark'. The appearance of the first Boxer cartridge raised a storm of objections, and it was asserted that Colonel Boxer could lay no claim to any part of the cartridge since the prior patents of Daw, Cornish and Rigby entirely covered the principles of construction. The *Saturday Review* summed up a lengthy article by stating that 'in substance Colonel Boxer took a Metford bullet, grooved it, put it into a Rigby case and labelled the result "The Boxer Cartridge" '.

The Boxer case was very similar to the previous cartridge cases developed for shotguns and not markedly dissimilar to the present paper case with brass head, the cap chamber or battery cup acting as a rivet to hold the paper tube base wadding and the brass head together. The Boxer, however, was slightly more complex in that the cap chamber had also to attach the later iron disc which served as the extracting rim. This type of construction was used for the .577 Snider cartridge and for the .577/.450 necked Martini-Henry cartridge. It was not until the Army were involved in a real shooting war that the deficiencies of the Boxer type of construction became apparent. After firing, the case could become jammed in the rifle, and the iron base could be torn off by the extractor; the case was also liable to damage if roughly handled and was susceptible to damp with a consequent risk of misfire. Assembly of the various components of the cartridge was carried out by hand, and the manufacture of the Boxer was largely dependent on manual labour.

Since errors and omissions in assembling the various components could lead to quite disastrous results if the defective cartridge was fired, the Martini-Henry cartridge had a small hole cut in the base to permit inspection after assembly. The complaints continued to increase as the demands of the service increased, and reached a peak in the quite disastrous reverses of the Sudan campaigns where, in spite of every effort to ensure that rifles and cartridges were kept free from sand, it was common to find that over 25% jammed after firing only two or three rounds.

Drawn brass cases of English manufacture were available by 1876, and the Mark II solid drawn Martini-Henry cartridge was introduced in 1885.

The difficulties encountered with the Boxer type cartridge did not loom so large with the revolver cartridge although it was manufactured on much the same principle. The first 'issue' breechloading metallic cartridge revolver, a conversion from the muzzle loading revolvers previously in use, went to the Naval Service. The cartridge, generally known as the 'Adams' was made from a seamless drawn cup with an internal paper wad to reinforce the base. The base and rim consisted of a blackened wrought iron disc .510″ in diameter, the three components being secured by a hollow copper rivet which, when the flash hole had been pierced, served as a battery or chamber for the copper percussion cap and flat brass anvil.

The original charge was 13 grains of 'Shell FG' black powder (later known as 'Pistol' powder) behind a 225 grains pure lead bullet

.765″ long and .455″ in diameter. The bullet was round-nosed, hollow-based and provided with two cannelures to carry the beeswax lubricant. It was retained in the case by three equidistant stab marks visible on the outside of the case. The assembly of the case components resulted in the base of the case being dished inwardly and, when the iron discs were found to buckle, brass discs were substituted in the Mark II pattern and improvements in manufacturing techniques eliminated the dishing.

The Adams cartridge was not declared obsolete until 1894 and, apart from primer set-back which tended to mar the smooth rotation of the cylinder, the Adams cartridge appears to have performed in a generally satisfactory manner. There were, however, two objections: firstly the low power, and secondly the fact that 'built-up' construction was not entirely suitable for self-extracting revolvers.

The adoption of the Enfield revolver in 1880 resulted from the need to provide a more powerful revolver than the .450 Adams. A new cartridge was designed, the first two types of which had a bullet .455″ in diameter, the third .477″.

Practically nothing is known of the Mark I .455″ Enfield, but the Mark II, approved in November 1880, was the first solid-drawn pistol cartridge with integral primer pocket to be issued to the British service.

The case length was increased from .690″ to .870″ which allowed an increase in the powder charge from 13 to 18 grains of powder. Although the case diameter remained the same at .479″, the rim diameter was increased from .510″ to .534″, the increase aiding extraction.

A Boxer type primer, consisting of the separate cap and flat anvil, continued to be employed and was housed in the deep primer pocket formed in the base of the case. Bullet weight went up from 225 grains to 265 grains and, instead of pure lead, an alloy of twelve parts lead to one part tin was used.

The Mark III Enfield cartridge had the same case, but the bullet diameter was increased to .477″ in front of the cannelures, the base diameter remaining the same at .455″. On close examination, this gives the bullet a somewhat 'swollen-headed' appearance. As in the case of the Adams and the earlier Marks of Enfield, the bullet was hollow-based, but the Mark III was provided with a clay base plug.

With the adoption of the Webley revolver

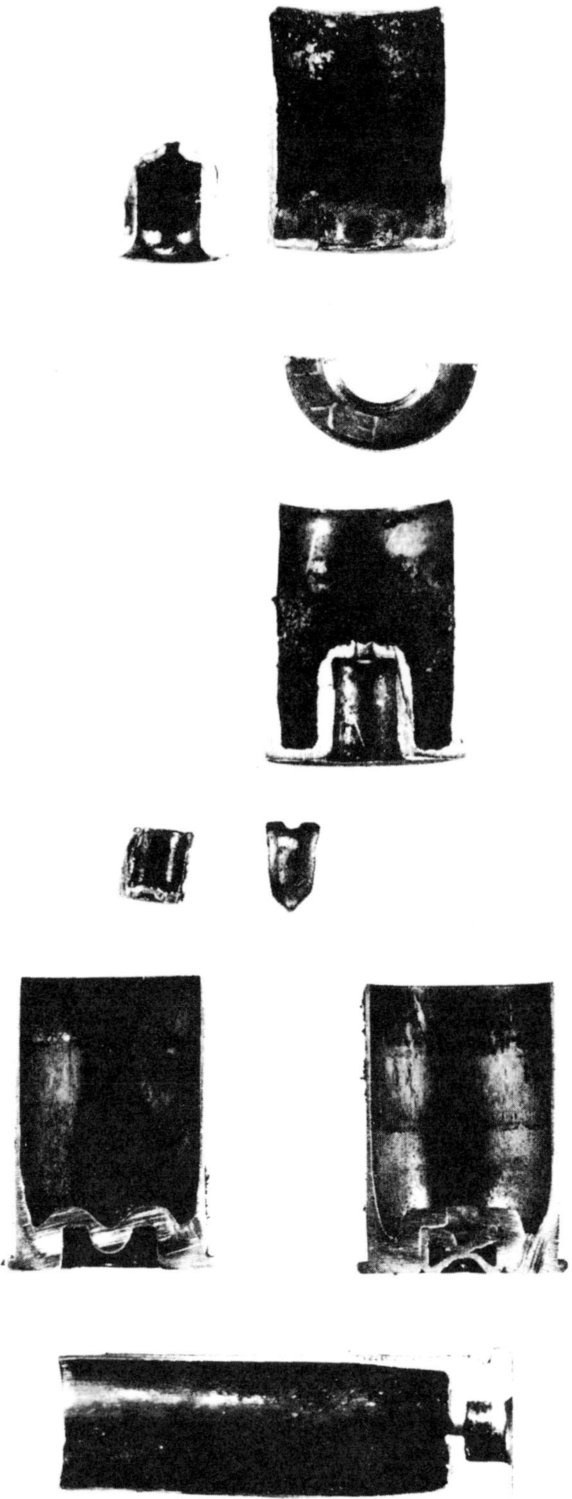

Sectioned centre-fire metallic cartridges.

Top to bottom, left to right: 'Boxer' type with separate rim attached to the case by the cap chamber; solid drawn case with 'arrow' anvil; folded head .455 Berdan type primer; folded head with seperate 'Boxer' type primer; flat base .44 Remington Magnum.

Mark I in 1887, yet another cartridge appeared—'cartridge, small-arm, ball, pistol, Webley (Mark I)', to give the newcomer its full military designation. The case had the same overall dimensions as the Enfield but the primer pocket was different. The old type flat anvil was discarded and a circular dished anvil employed instead. The change in the type of primer also meant that the primer pocket was not as deep, although it was greater in diameter.

In 1894, the introduction of cordite as the propellant in place of black powder resulted in further changes. Initially, the original Mark I Webley case was used, but experience showed that a better performance would result if the air space in the case were reduced. The difference in bulk between 18 grains of black powder and 6.5 grains of cordite was such that it proved possible to reduce the case length from .870″ to .760″ with the Mark II and subsequent variations. Another important change with the Mark II was the substitution of a Berdan type primer for the Boxer type previously used. The anvil of the Berdan type was formed as part of the case, as can be seen from the illustrations of the sectioned cartridge cases. The various Marks of .455″ cartridge differed in the type of bullet loaded and the amount of propellant.

With the introduction of the Webley Self-Loading Pistol, a rimless cartridge appeared which, in its Service form, brings us up-to-date as far as the cartridge case is concerned. The original 'balloon' construction—where the cap chamber intruded into the interior of the case—has, as a result of improvements in the primer, been gradually reduced; in general the primer diameter is greater, the length less. In the final form shown in the illustration (.44 Remington Magnum), the base of the interior of the cartridge is formed flat. This so-called 'solid head' construction provides increased strength and is now employed with both Boxer and Berdan type primers.

Many of the improvements in both the design of the cartridge case and in its manufacture started in America, the lead being taken in the late 1860's by Frankford Arsenal, the US Government establishment. Early experiments were with 'inside primed' cartridges where the fulminate was held in place against the base of the cartridge by means of a cup or anvil. To all outward appearances, the cartridge looked like a rim-fire. Very complete data on the work carried out at Frankford is contained in the *Ordnance Memoranda No. 14, Metallic Cartridges,* first published in 1873 and subsequently reprinted.

Internally primed cartridges were manufactured with either the Martin bar anvil or Colonel S.V. Benet's cup system. Benet's inside primed cartridges were employed in the Remington Model 1865 single shot pistols and look like rim-fire cartridges except for the indentations in the case wall which serve to retain the inside primer system. Benet also experimented with externally primed cases and successfully formed the primer pocket in one piece of metal. He employed a separate anvil similar to the Boxer, and it was after seeing these cartridges that Colonel Hiram Berdan patented his centre-fire cartridge in which the anvil was formed as part of the case, the so-called teat-anvil.

The first Berdan patent was obtained in 1866, US Patent No. 53,388. In this, the anvil was thrown up from the bottom of the primer pocket to one side. In 1868, Berdan obtained an additional cartridge patent, No. 82,587, covering a drawn metal, folded head cartridge with the anvil thrown up from the centre of the primer pocket, and with two vents punched through the pocket at each side of the anvil.

The cap used with the Berdan case was invented by A. C. Hobbs, an employee of the Union Metallic Cartridge Co., and was patented by him in 1869. Essentially it was an adaptation of the common percussion cap, and the patent was concerned with the location and shape of the detonating pellet inside.

To Berdan can be given the credit for forming the anvil as part of the case, and although he did not patent a cap for this type of case, his name is now associated with small arms cartridge caps which lack an internal anvil.

For a cap with an internal anvil, the term 'primer' is often used. The original Boxer-type employed a flat anvil shaped rather like an arrowhead which, after the fired cap had been removed from the case, could be re-used, new caps only being required.

This type of cap and anvil continued to be used for British shotgun cartridges until 1932 when the flat anvil was replaced by the 'tubular' one which considerably reduced gas leakage past the cap. The shape of the modern pistol and rifle cartridge anvil was finalised over half a century ago and, although modifications to the basic design will be encountered, these anvils are now made from hard brass and produced on a single action press from narrow strip stock. A single punch and die can be employed or up to five sets of tools. After the anvil has been blanked and formed it is then washed and assembled in the cap, after the cap has been charged.

Considerable care is required during the entire operation of primer or cap manufacture, not only to safeguard the operatives but also to ensure that all tolerances are held within rigid specification. Otherwise the primer either cannot be inserted into the primer pocket or, in being inserted, is damaged, resulting in a misfire. One other type of primer is manufactured for American and Continental shotgun cartridges. In this, the cap and anvil are assembled inside a battery cup and, when the cartridge has been fired and is de-capped for reloading, the entire primer assembly is removed. The old 'thick rim' Perrin revolver cartridge employed a primer system of this type. Also known as the 'French rim', this cartridge was developed about 1865 for Lefaucheux revolver conversions to centre-fire, and was available in 7mm, 9mm and 12mm sizes. The thick rim sealed the pin-fire grooves at the rear of the cylinder. With British type shotgun cartridges, where the battery cup remains as part of the case, only the cap and anvil are removed.

Today the different varieties of cap and primer have multiplied but, as we shall see in the section on handloading, efforts have been made to standardise on primer sizes and very considerable advances have been made in the priming charge itself. The cartridge case is now either rim-fire or centre-fire, all other types being obsolete, and rim-fire cartridges are restricted to low power ammunition only. Two primer systems are used for centre-fire cartridges: the Boxer with attached anvil and the Berdan where the anvil is formed as part of the cartridge case.

Rimmed or flanged cartridges are generally restricted to single shot pistols and revolvers, while rimless cartridges, with a groove instead of a rim, are used in automatic or self-loading pistols, although there are one or two exceptions where rimless cartridges are used in revolvers with special half-moon clips.

Amongst the earliest examples of 'rimless' cartridges were those invented by Sylvester Hayward Roper for use in his four shot revolving shotguns made by the Roper Sporting Arms Co. of Hartford. These shotguns were made from about 1866 until the early 1880's but the cartridges used are of further interest since they employed a head of smaller diameter than the case. In this, they anticipated a development designed to permit the use of very large cartridges in breech mechanisms originally designed for much smaller cases. Today such cartridges are known as rebated rimless.

Rimless cartridges became widely adopted with the introduction of vertical box magazines for repeating rifles where, as any user of the SMLE (Short Rifle, Magazine Lee-Enfield) will be only too well aware, the use of rimmed rounds presents problems if the cartridges are not loaded correctly.

In addition to these types of case, there is one other, the semi-rim, again used in automatic pistols. The specific uses and merits of each type will be discussed later. The chemistry of cartridges will also be left alone since we are here mainly concerned with the mechanics and with one other component of the cartridge—in many respects the most important—the bullet.

Lead has been traditionally employed for the projectile from the earliest days of firearms. We have seen how the round ball of the muzzle loader was replaced by the cylindrical bullet with either a round or ogival nose. Other alterations to the actual shape of the bullet consisted of providing either a hollow base to ensure expansion or, more rarely, a hollow nose to increase the effect of the bullet on impact. Grease grooves or cannelures also came into use and, in early cartridges, were left outside the case mouth. This is still the case with the modern .22 rim-fire, but improvements in bullet lubricant have reduced the pick-up of dirt, one of the reasons why the bullet was seated inside the case so that the grease grooves were covered by the case mouth.

Early externally lubricated revolver cartridges will be found to have a bullet diameter equal to the case diameter. The bullet, if examined, will have a base slightly reduced in diameter so that it can enter the case mouth. Many cartridges were 'heel seated' in this fashion until, overtaken by the march of progress, they were banished from the ammunition makers' catalogues.

The popularity of some was such that the cartridge was brought up to date by the substitution of an internally lubricated bullet for the original heel seated bullet and, due to the difference in bullet diameter, the bullet was provided with a deep hollow in the base so that, when fired, the skirt would expand and fill the rifling. Others, such as the .320 and the .380 originally introduced in Britain in the late 1860's, are still manufactured today by some cartridge companies in almost their original form, except for the substitution of modern smokeless powders.

Due to the problems that would have been created if black powder had had to be used, the availability of smokeless powder was an important factor in the development of satisfactory self-loading or semi-automatic pistols. The reduction in fouling considerably eased the difficulties of the automatic pistol designer and ensured the practical success of this type of weapon.

The movement of the cartridge from the magazine to the chamber in an automatic pistol is generally quite rapid and somewhat violent. With the exception of the .22 rim-fire, relatively soft lead bullets do not function well through auto-pistols, and the standard type of bullet is therefore round nosed and metal-jacketed.

The technique of producing metal clad bullets was perfected in the mid-1880's by Major Rubin, Director of the Government Laboratories at Thun, Switzerland. It was whilst serving with the Swiss Army that he developed the modern composite bullet consisting of a lead core enveloped in a jacket of a copper-nickel alloy. Subsequently a great deal of work was carried out on jacketing materials, and this was usually aimed at reducing cost or at improving performance by reducing metallic fouling, since clad bullets are not normally lubricated.

Most of the early automatic pistols were relatively low-powered and attempts were made to overcome this deficiency by the use of soft-nose, hollow-point and other bullet variations. The most unusual was the Westley Richards version of the very popular .30 Mauser (7.63mm) cartridge known as the WR All-Range or, in German, as the 'pilz' or mushroom bullet. Most of the hollow-point and soft-nosed bullets made for use with automatic pistols enjoyed only a brief popularity, and their use today is the exception rather than the rule. Of all the unusual bullet designs, that used with the .35 Smith and Wesson auto-pistol cartridge is the only one which merits description.

Smith and Wesson's venture into the pocket automatic pistol market was not a commercial success. The .32 automatic cartridge (7.65mm Browning) had been introduced by Fabrique Nationale in 1900 and Smith and Wesson had left things a little late when their own cartridge was brought out in 1913. Although described as a .35 the bullet diameter at .306″ average was very little different to the .308″ or the 7.65mm.

At this point it may be as well to point out that there is neither sense nor reason in many of the names by which we know and attempt to identify revolver and auto-pistol cartridges. The 7.65mm Browning is also known as the .32 ACP (Automatic Colt Pistol) and as the .30 Browning. The cartridge nomenclature designation may be related to the bullet diameter, the bore diameter, the groove diameter or the case diameter; on the other hand, it may bear no relation to any of these dimensions and be a purely arbitrary figure selected by the manufacturer for political, prestige or sales promotional reasons. Also it will be appreciated that dimensional variations occur between different manufacturers of the same nominal cartridge. Prestige and sales promotion may have had something to do with the naming of the Smith and Wesson auto-pistol cartridge but, because of their traditional dislike of full-jacketed bullets, Smith and Wesson designed a bullet which they termed a 'half-mantle'. The nose was metal clad so that it would not be deformed during chambering, but the bearing surface of the bullet was left unclad and the two parts were anchored together by slots being provided in the cap or mantle through which the lead core would pass on swaging.

The 'half-mantle' bullet might have had a promising future but for the deceptive and inaccurate designation. Prospective purchasers were deterred by the possibility of finding supplies difficult to obtain and, although the .35 cartridge might be expected to be more powerful than the .32 ACP, the performance was, in fact, inferior. Manufacture was discontinued in 1921; a remodelled pistol was re-issued as a standard .32 automatic in 1924, but the entire exercise was finally abandoned in 1937.

Smith and Wesson were also responsible for yet another unusual bullet design. This was the 'self-lubricating' bullet invented by Douglas B. Wesson in which a central hollow core was provided with lubricant. The core was closed at the base by a brass plug, and four minute passages were made from the core to the point of the bullet, emerging at the shoulder. When the cartridge was fired the brass plug was forced up the core, driving the lubricant out of the passages and lubricating the bore.

To sum up, the bullet may be made of lead, either cast or swaged, or of an alloy of lead and a hardening agent, perhaps tin or antimony. With the exception of the .22 rim-fire, lead bullets are not normally commercially available for automatic pistols and composite bullets are used to avoid deformation during feeding from the magazine into the chamber. The cladding or mantle may be cupro-nickel or steel, the steel being clad itself with a thin film of copper or cupro-nickel to eliminate rusting. Gilding metal, an alloy of copper and zinc, is also used, sometimes under a trade name such as 'Lubaloy' or 'Nobeloy'.

The case into which the bullet is loaded may be rimmed (flanged) or rimless. If the cartridge is rimless, the bullet is not crimped into the case since, in the absence of the rim, the case mouth is used to obtain the correct headspace for the cartridge. An alternate design is the semi-rim (for example the Colt Super .38) where sufficient flange is left to prevent the cartridge going too far into the chamber instead of having the mouth of the case strike against a shoulder in the barrel, as with rimless cartridges. The rim or flange serves two purposes; the first is to provide a means whereby the fired case can be extracted, and the second is to ensure proper positioning of the cartridge in the chamber. In the rimless versions the groove is provided for extraction.

As always, there are exceptions to most attempts to systemise a random collection of facts. The exception in this case is the 6.5mm Bergmann automatic pistol cartridge manufactured for the Bergmann automatic pistol, one of the earliest of the plain 'blow-back' automatics, which appeared on the market in 1895. The case was both 'bottle-necked' and tapered and, as it originally appeared, lacked both rim and extractor groove. The extractor groove was not needed since the case was literally blown out of the chamber as the action opened, and a rim was not required since the case was seated on the taper.

We have seen how, with the semi-rimmed Colt Super .38, the case seats, or is positioned by, the rim of the case—as with a rimmed revolver cartridge—and how the mouth of the case may be employed for this purpose—for example, the .45 Colt Auto and the 9mm Parabellum or Luger. The descriptive term 'bottle-necked' is used to describe a cartridge case where the case diameter is greater than that of the bullet so that the neck must be reduced in size or 'necked down' to fit it. This type of case is commonly employed for rifles to provide increased powder accommodation without unduly increasing the length, and the shoulder of the rimless case seats against an equivalent shoulder in the chamber.

Bottle-necked cases are also slightly tapered to facilitate extraction, but the extreme taper encountered on the early Bergmann cases is no longer used. Since, when the cartridge is fired, the case or 'shell' expands due to the pressure created, the hardness and quality of the brass generally used are of extreme importance. The case is usually slightly smaller than the chamber and, if the brass is too soft, the case expands but does not spring back again when the pressure falls, so resulting in extraction difficulties. If, on the other hand, the brass is too hard, the case may very probably split or crack, and gas at high pressure will leak into the action with possibly disastrous results. Optimum hardness differs, and the case mouth is usually softer than the base. Excessive hardness of the brass where the bullet is seated can result in the case mouth cracking during firing, or even during storage, due to stresses set up during manufacture. I have at present 500 rounds of .256 bottle-necked rifle ammunition in original boxes, and each case has cracked at the mouth. The attention now given to neck annealing has fortunately resulted in such sad happenings becoming increasingly rare; the ammunition mentioned was made in 1920.

In the case of revolvers, bullets have to be tightly seated into the case to prevent 'creep', the bullet moving forward out of the case due to inertia effects. This can happen with hand-loaded ammunition if the crimp is not tight, and the bullet can move sufficiently forward to emerge from the cylinder and prevent rotation, so tying-up the gun. On the other hand, the bullet, if inadequately seated, can, when the cartridge is being chambered in an automatic pistol, be driven back into the case. It is also important that the complete cartridge should be sealed against deterioration, which could be caused either by the ingress of oil from the chamber—as could happen if a weapon were left loaded for any length of time—or by the ingress of moisture. Three methods are currently employed to keep the bullet firmly attached to the case. Firstly, if the cartridge seats on the rim or shoulder, the case mouth can be crimped into a groove or cannelure provided in the bullet. A second method is to indent or 'stab' the case into a cannelure or even into the bullet envelope. The third method applies where the cartridge has to seat on the case mouth; as this cannot be deformed, the case is crimped behind the bullet or, alternatively, the interference between the clad bullet and case mouth is so adjusted that the two are a tight fit.

Present day ammunition consists of bullet, case (or shell), cap or primer and the propellant charge or powder. The development of smokeless powders will be dealt with later, but enough has been said regarding the other components of the cartridge to indicate that the evolution of a satisfactory self-contained metallic cartridge was a lengthy and rather complicated business involving many people in many different countries. A large number of individuals contributed something, the efforts of several being commemorated in the use of their names to describe a particular cartridge or component. Since many contributions were made by anonymous individuals employed by ammunition companies whose names have passed into history, much of the work is unrecorded.

Take a closer look at the next cartridge you hold in your hand, be it the humble .22 rim-fire, a 7.65mm Browning or the .44 Magnum. There can be few other manufactured articles of similar size that have had so much time, attention and money lavished on their perfection, and so much ingenuity devoted to their development. Without the deceptively simple metallic cartridge, the modern firearm as we know it would not exist.

Notes to Chapter Eight

In recent years there has grown up a considerable interest in the historical development of the metallic cartridge and also in cartridge collecting. Of particular interest to the collector is 'The Cartridge Collector', a monthly feature by Frank Wheeler in *The Gun Report,* P.O. Box 111, Aledo, Illinois, USA.

Other works of interest include *Cartridges of the World* by Frank C. Barnes (Gun Digest Co., Chicago, 1965), *Cartridges Headstamp Guide* by H. P. White and B. D. Munhall (Bel Air, 1963), *Cartridges* by Hershell C. Logan (Huntingdon, 1948), *Cartridges for Collectors* by F. A. Datig (California, 1958), *Centrefire Metric Pistol and Revolver Cartridges* by H. P. White and B. D. Munhall (Washington, 1948) *DWM Cartridges 1896-1956* by F. A. Datig (California, 1962), *Metallic Cartridges* by T. J. Treadwell (New York, 1950), *DWM Munitions-Katalog No.* 3 (a reprint of the original by the Gun Digest Co., 1958), *Small Arms and Ammunition in the United States Service* by B. K. Lewis (Washington, 1960), *Textbook of Small Arms*, 1929 (HMSO, 1929) and *Cartridge Manufacture* by D. T. Hamilton (New York, 1916).

I am also indebted to R. Caranta, Aix-en-Provence, for information on French metallic pistol cartridges and to F. Hediger, Lenzburg, for his help and advice on Swiss military cartridges. My debt to R. G. Goodman is also acknowledged.

Chapter Nine
The Cartridge Revolver

One undoubted advantage that the percussion revolver had possessed had been that there was no need to make provision for extracting the fired metallic cartridge case. In the development of the self-contained metallic cartridge revolver during the last quarter of the nineteenth century, therefore, much of the work had to be devoted to the design of efficient extraction systems, and we can divide those that evolved into two separate classes: revolvers where there was provision for extracting single fired cases, and those where all the cartridges in the cylinder were simultaneously extracted, whether they had been fired or not.

When considering the mechanism of the cartridge revolver, we must also bear in mind that the earlier divisions into which we placed the percussion revolver—single action, cocked either by the thumb or by the trigger, and double action, with both thumb and trigger action cocking—still obtain.

In order to ensure an accurate description of the type of revolver, a third classification has to be introduced, that of 'solid frame' and 'hinged frame'. The term 'hinged frame' will also be employed to describe certain types of revolver frame which 'opened' even if they did not actually hinge in the accepted sense of the term.

As always, there will be those weapons which cannot properly fit into these groups and, where their importance merits description, separate reference will be made to them.

If we exclude the 'Smith and Wesson Evasions', that peculiar but interesting series of revolvers made in America which we met in the last chapter, one separate group of revolvers merits mention—the transitional cartridge percussion conversion or, to borrow a French term, the 'transformed' revolver. The revolver manufacturer with a stock of percussion revolvers on his hands could either attempt to sell them at reduced rates as already mentioned, or he could convert existing stocks to metallic cartridge. In order to maintain production during the transition, slight design modifications could be made, using existing machine tools, jigs and fixtures, until a more up-to-date design could be introduced. The individual was faced with the same problem as his predecessor during the transition from flint to percussion. 'Had these new-fangled metallic cartridges come to stay? Should I buy a new revolver or have my old percussion revolver converted?' To be on the safe side, if the conversion allowed the use of metallic cartridges as well as the well tried separate powder and ball, all the better. The new cartridges were expensive; they were certainly more convenient but appropriate supplies might not always be readily available. Black powder, caps and lead were always obtainable, and the user of the percussion revolver complete with bullet mould was to some extent self-sufficient.

These were some of the reasons which lay behind the appearance of percussion conversions to either rim- or centre-fire metallic cartridge revolvers. The weapons themselves fall into two categories, those converted from existing stocks by the original manufacturer and those subsequently converted from revolvers already in use as percussion weapons.

A typical example of such a conversion is illustrated. Originally, this was a 120 bore Beaumont-Adams five chambered percussion

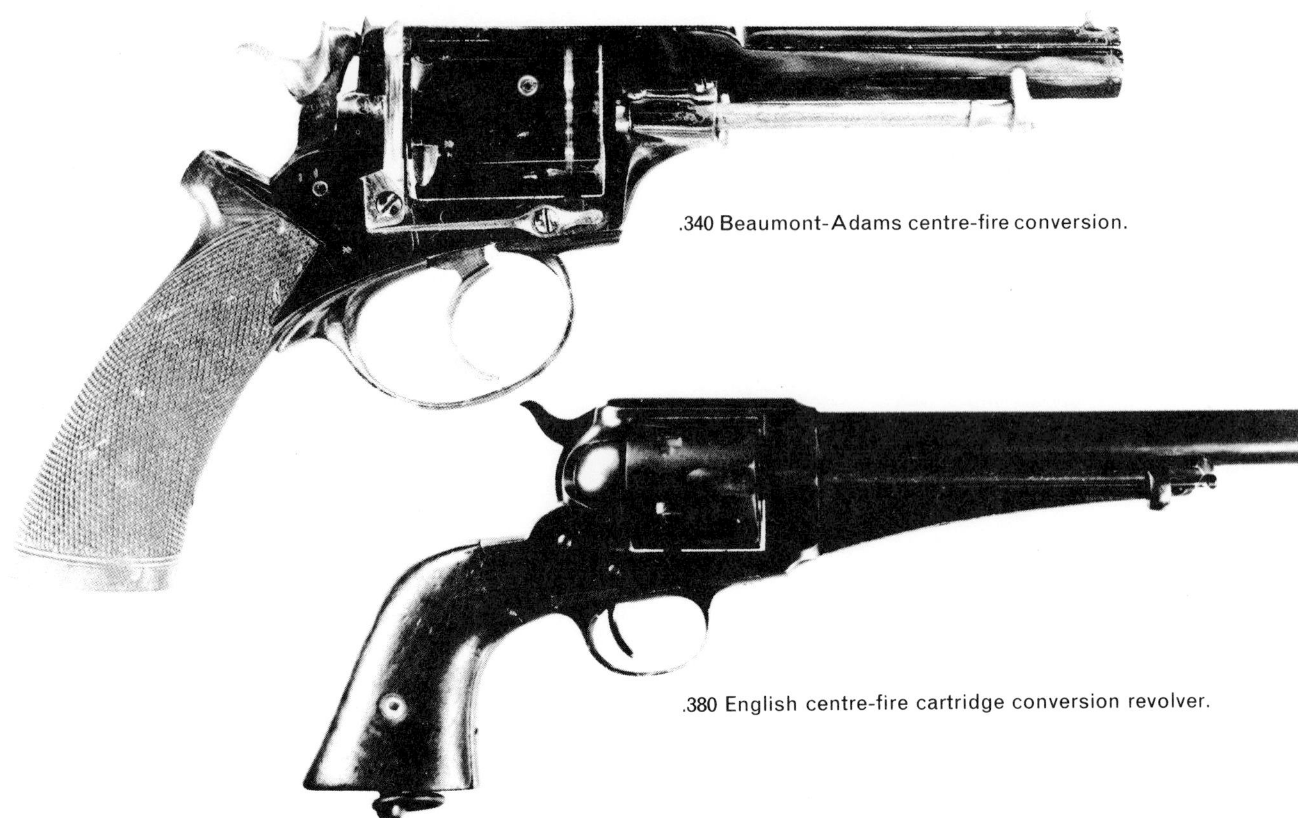

.340 Beaumont-Adams centre-fire conversion.

.380 English centre-fire cartridge conversion revolver.

revolver, but it was later converted to .340 centre-fire metallic. As originally sold by Thos. Conway, 15 Blackfriars St, Manchester, the pistol may have been fitted with a lever rammer of the Kerr type (see page 156), but this was removed during the conversion. In its place a lump was brazed to the right hand side of the frame which carries the ejector rod. This lump was provided with a small spring-loaded pin which entered a dimple in the rod to prevent the rod from moving to the rear and entering a chamber inadvertently. Location of the pin and dimple was ensured by an extension on the head of the rod which prevented it rotating. The pin retaining the cylinder pin was moved from the right hand side of the frame to the left, and a spring loaded gate was provided on the right hand side of the frame to permit the introduction and ejection of cartridges. The gate swung to the rear and was simply attached by a hinge screw, forward movement being prevented by an extension to the insert frame modification which reduced the size of the hole through which the hammer striker operated. The hammer nose was, of course, modified and the original cylinder was replaced by a cartridge cylinder bored straight through for the .340 centre-fire cartridge.

From the manner in which this conversion was carried out (and from the presence of Birmingham Proof Marks on the cylinder) it is reasonable to assume that it was undertaken by a Birmingham gunsmith and that the pistol was subsequently refinished and reblued.

The .380 revolver illustrated is typical of the very cheap early Birmingham-made cartridge revolvers which often possessed a veneer of quality due to the standard of polishing and blueing but lacked any technical merit. The small spring which can be seen attached to the barrel, and which served to prevent the ejector rod from sliding loosely to and fro, was an obvious afterthought; such crude modifications would not have been tolerated on a pistol with any pretence to quality.

An improvement on the simple rod type ejector was that patented by C. B. Richards in America. The Richards conversion, US Patent No. 117,461 of 25 July 1871, was for the Colt Model 1860 Army and consisted of a conversion breech plate which carried a spring-loaded firing pin and a laterally opening gate. An alteration was needed to the recoil shield to permit the installation of the conversion breech plate, and the side of the barrel had to be milled to

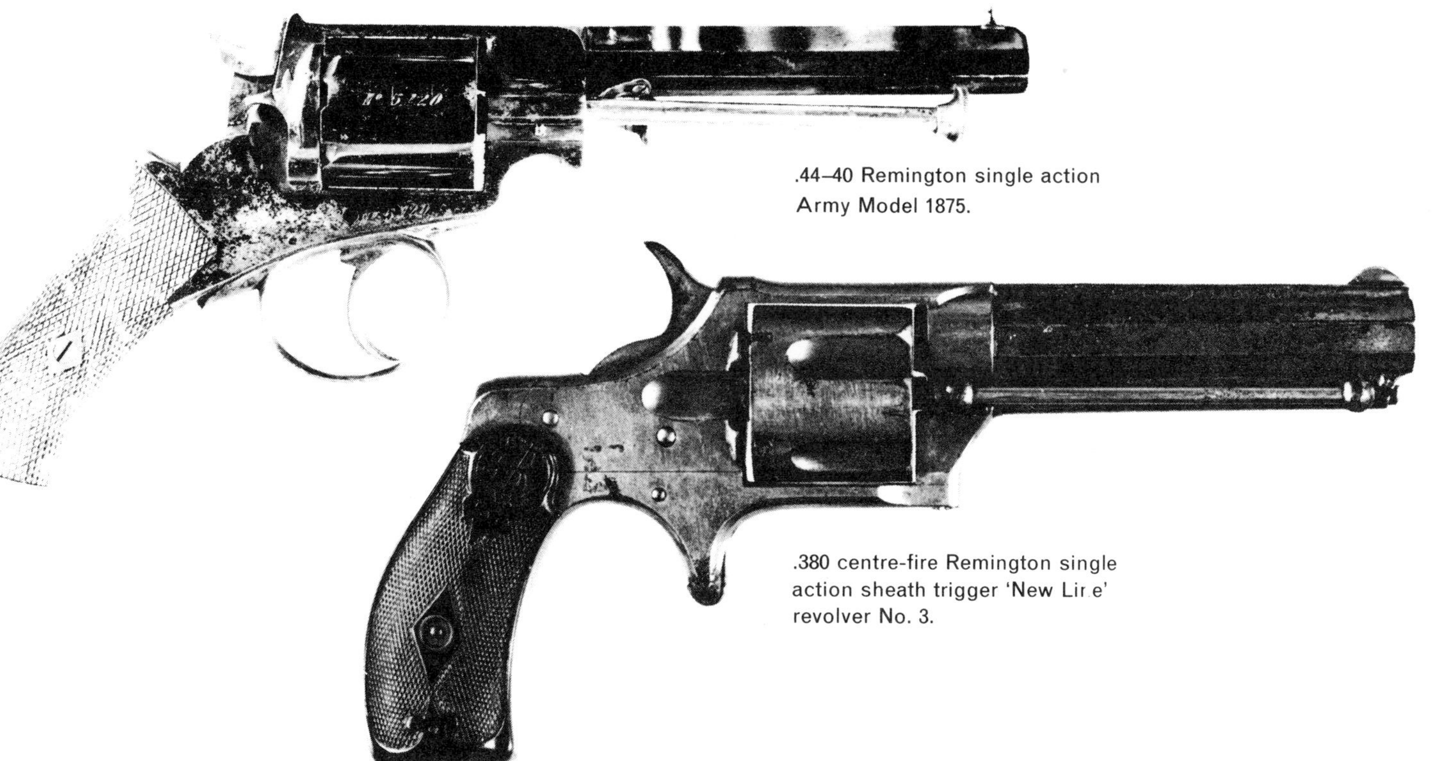

.44–40 Remington single action Army Model 1875.

.380 centre-fire Remington single action sheath trigger 'New Line' revolver No. 3.

accept the ejector case which housed the ejector rod and its return spring. This system was later modified by W. Mason in his patent No. 128,644 of 1872, and the ejector case and rod employed were essentially similar to those used for the famous Colt Single-Action Army Model. Both of these conversions were for a .44 centre-fire cartridge, but there was a further .44 rim-fire variant which dispensed with the conversion breech plate, the recoil shield being cut away and provided with a loading gate. The transition from this model to the solid frame Single Action Army was only a minor step.

The advantages of the Mason spring-loaded rod ejector were such that this system is still employed on the modern Colt Single Action Army Models currently manufactured by Colt, and also on the Ruger series of single action revolvers. As with any system, advantages and disadvantages can be emphasised in order to condone or condemn. The spring return of the ejector rod speeds up the extracting cycle and simplifies the mechanism since no locking devices are needed to prevent the extractor rod from inadvertently entering the chamber mouth. The system lacks power and, if a stubborn case is encountered, the ejector has to be pressed against a solid surface with the risk of bending the rod or breaking off the finger plate.

A similar type of rod ejector was fitted to the Remington Model 1875 Army Revolver and to the later Model 1890 both of which were cartridge developments of the Remington percussion single action revolvers.

An even simpler type of rod ejector was fitted to the Remington New Line Series of revolvers which were brought out in 1873. These revolvers were based on William S. Smoot's US Patent No. 143,855 of 1873. The New Line Revolver No. 1 was .30 rim-fire, the No. 2, .32 rim-fire, and the No. 3, .380 centre-fire. Two styles were produced of the No. 3 Model, the first having the standard 'bird's head' grip, the second (illustrated) having a modified saw handle grip. All were single action, were fitted with sheath triggers, and were five chambered. With the exception of the Model 51 Automatic Pistol, Remington manufactured no pistols between 1895 and comparatively recently.

An alternative to the spring-loaded rod ejector which, even when the spring was separately mounted as on the Remington, had the disadvantage of bulk, was the swivel ejector rod patented by John Adams, British Patent No. 2258 of 1872. The design of this rod can be seen from the patent drawing and also from the illustration of the John Adams .450 centre-fire Model 1872 Mark III Army revolver.

The original version of this revolver was a conversion of the London Armoury Company Beaumont-Adams to .450 centre-fire and was

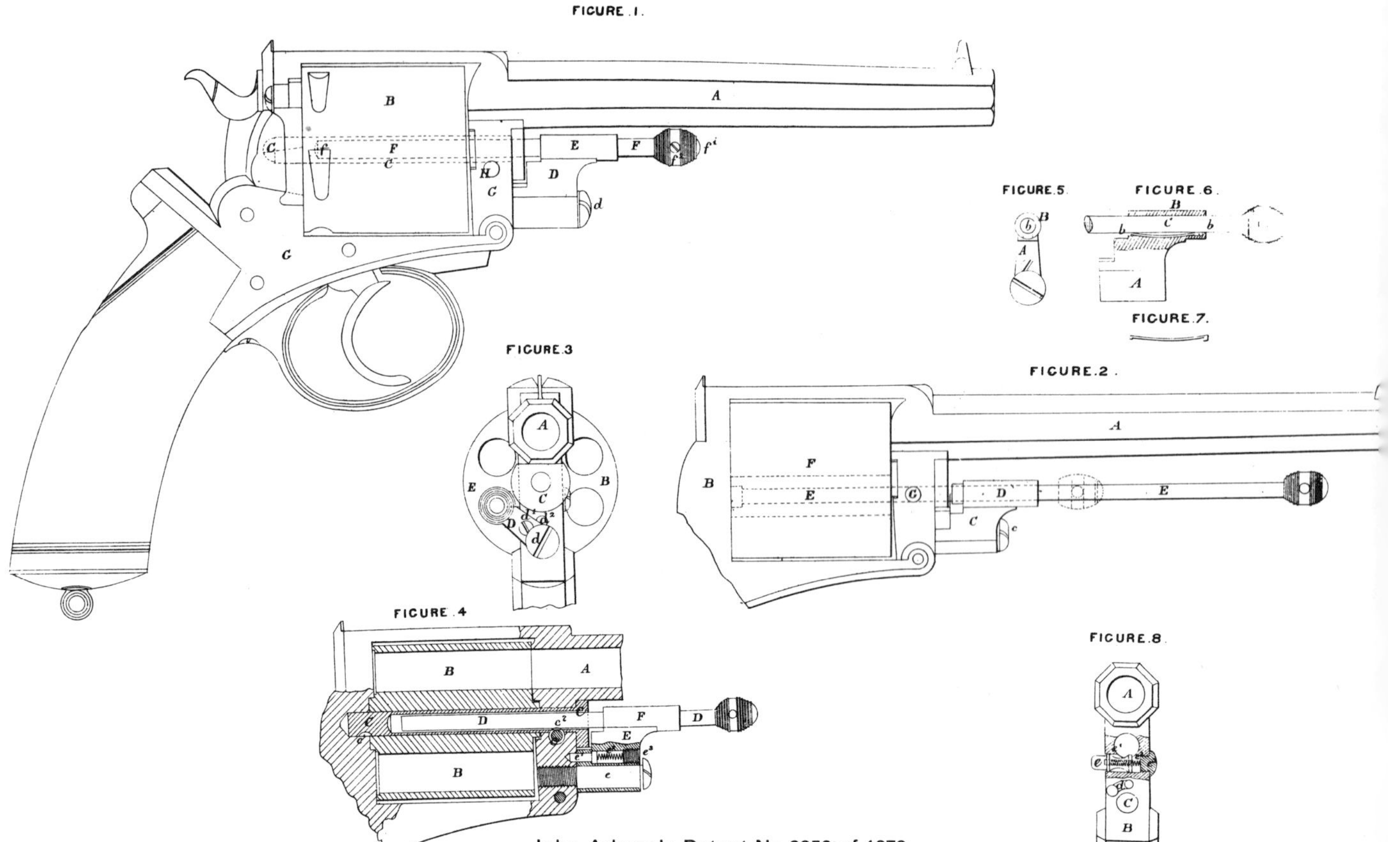

John Adams's Patent No.2258 of 1872.

adopted by the British Army in 1868. The conversion was carried out in accordance with John Adams' British Patent of 1867 which covered the loading gate design and a simple rod ejector. The first true John Adams revolver was the Government Model Mark II and it is likely that manufacture of this model was concurrent with conversions of the Beaumont-Adams to

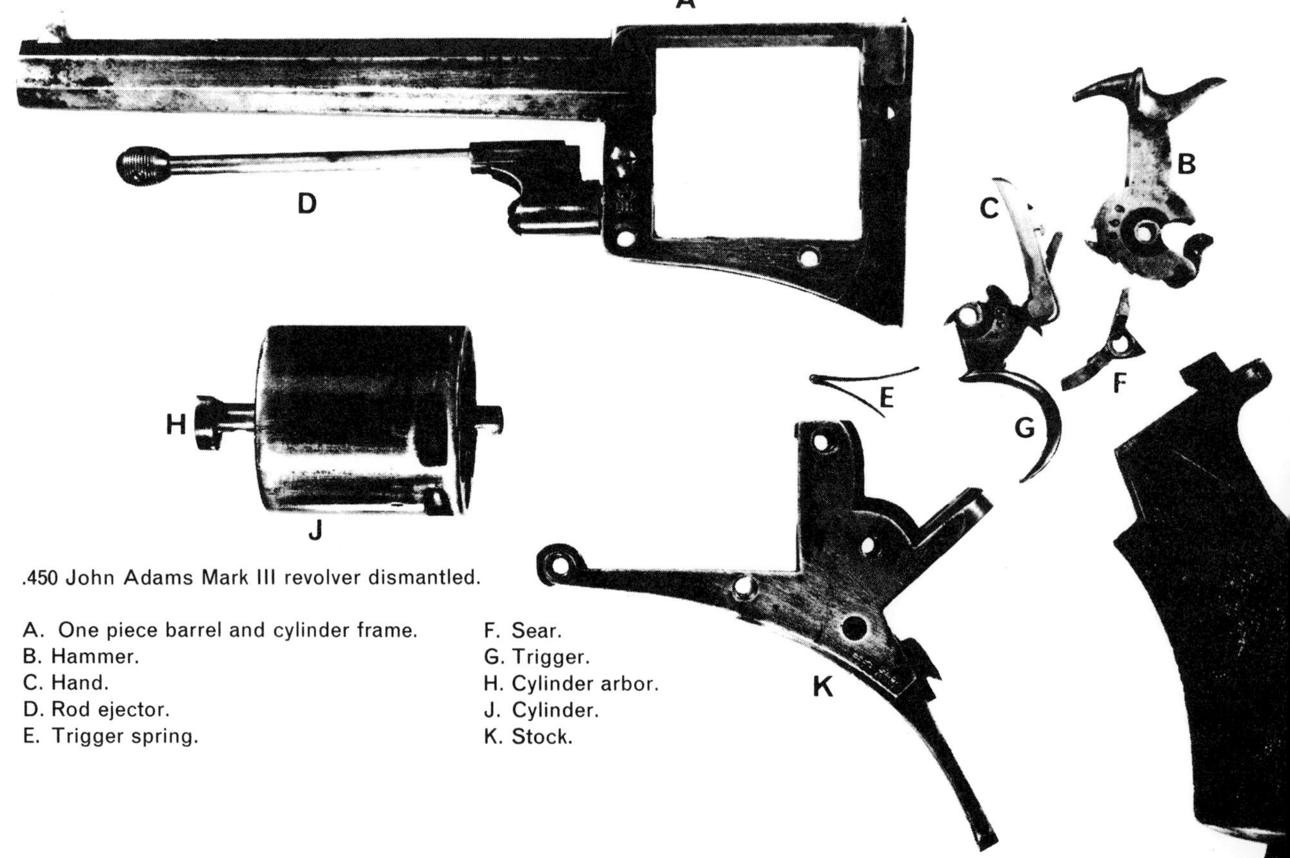

.450 John Adams Mark III revolver dismantled.

A. One piece barrel and cylinder frame.
B. Hammer.
C. Hand.
D. Rod ejector.
E. Trigger spring.
F. Sear.
G. Trigger.
H. Cylinder arbor.
J. Cylinder.
K. Stock.

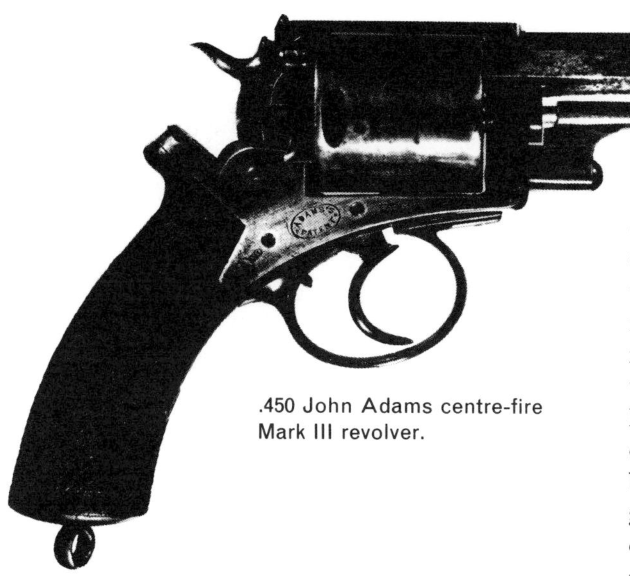

.450 John Adams centre-fire Mark III revolver.

centre-fire. The Adams's Patent Small Arms Company was incorporated on 15 August 1864, and its address was 391 Strand, London. From the contemporary advertisement it will be noticed that 'this company is now converting the Service .54 Gauge Revolvers (Beaumont-Adams) to this system for H.M's. War Department etc.' It will also be noticed that already difficulties were being encountered with the two systems of calibre designation. The advertisement refers to the .54 gauge, note the '.' (point), and the old gauge sizes are already being confused with the decimal inch sizes used for cartridge weapons. The revolver shown in the advertisement is the Mark II, the Mark I being the percussion conversion. The John Adams revolver differed in one important respect from the Beaumont-Adams; instead of being made from one forging, it was made from two separate forgings, the barrel and cylinder frame, and the lock frame. This was done possibly to facilitate machining of the frame, but also to avoid infringement of the Robert Adams master patent. The lock work is similar to the Beaumont-Adams (see page 156) except for the arrangement of the 'secondary trigger'.

According to contemporary accounts the barrel and frame were forged together from best Marshall's iron and the square opening for the cylinder was then drilled out. The barrel was drilled on a vertical boring machine, after which the forging was placed on a rudimentary milling machine (Fig. 1 on p. 214.) consisting of a lathe headstock unit which carried the rotary cutters, the work being mounted on a cross slide in a suitable fixture. In this first operation, both sides of the frame were plain surface milled simultaneously and were gauged to width. The barrel was machined using the same basic machine, but with a different fixture, the eight flats being produced one after another by suitable indexing. The same machine (Fig. 2.) also squared the end of the frame by using the fixture marked 'A'. Internal recesses were machined out by the cutters on the machine in Fig. 4, and the tooling shown in Fig. 5. was for machining the lock frame to receive the lock work and cylinder frame. This series of engravings shows how, by employing a standard basic machine or a series of such machines, together with the appropriate fixtures and circular cutters, the arduous labour previously required to shape gun parts by hand-filing was eliminated.

After the basic machining had been completed, the barrels were then rifled to a pitch of one turn in two feet. Five grooves, each $\frac{1}{4}''$ wide, were cut with lands $\frac{1}{16}''$ wide. The cylinders consisting of sections cut from a round bar were forged solid after which they were set up and drilled through. Lock parts were forged in dies and subsequently hand finished with a file. The bore of the barrel as laid down was .443″ and all parts were gauged. If, for example, the barrel accepted a gauge of .446″ it was rejected.

The rod ejector fitted to the John Adams Mark II or 1867 model revolver was locked in position

John Adams's advertisement from *The Engineer* of 1870.

THE GOVERNMENT BREECH-LOADING REVOLVER.

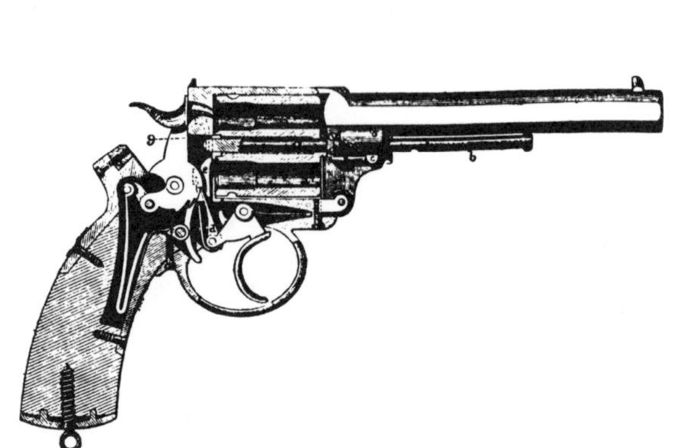

MR. JOHN ADAMS' REVOLVER.

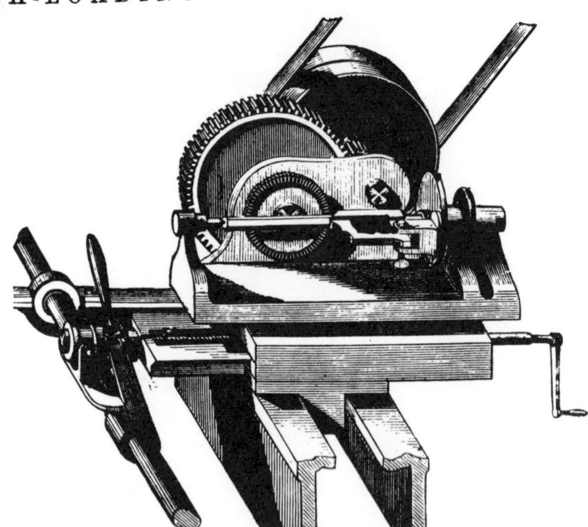

FIG. 3.—MACHINE FOR FACING "BACK-ENDS."

FIG. 1.—MACHINE FOR GAUGING THE FRAMES.

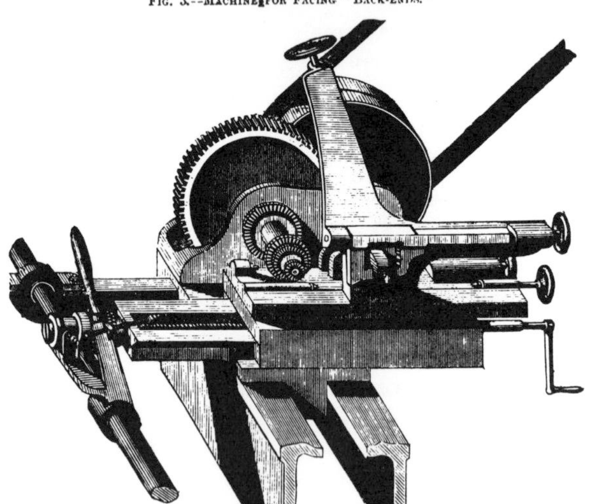

FIG. 4.—MACHINE FOR CUTTING SLOTS IN THE FRAMES.

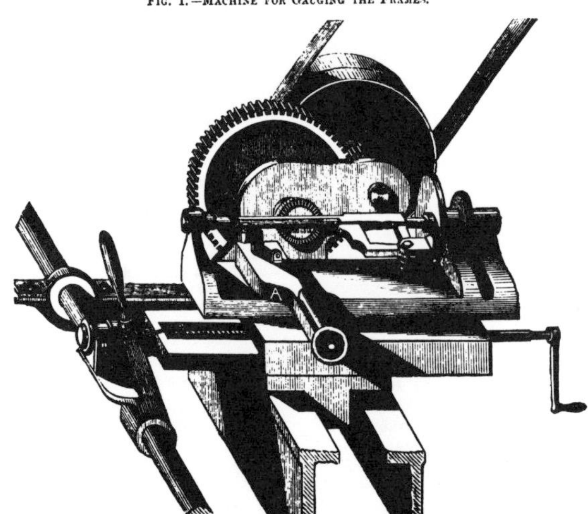

FIG. 2. -MACHINE FOR SHAPING BARRELS.

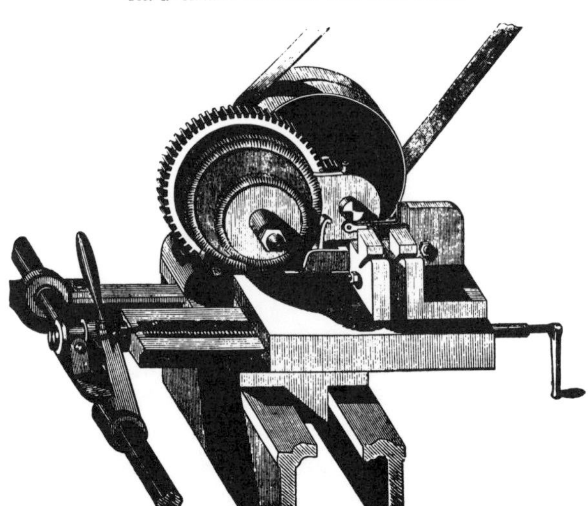

FIG. 5.—MACHINE FOR CUTTING SLOTS IN THE "BACK-ENDS."

THE adaptation of the breech-loading principle to military rifles was very naturally followed by a general expression of opinion that the exigencies of the service required a similar change in the revolvers in the hands of our navy. We have repeatedly pointed out the advantages which would accrue from such a change, and later on our popular contemporary, the *Pall Mall Gazette*, went further, and while expatiating on the advantages offered by the breech over the muzzle-loader, commended the Government upon their choice of Mr. Adams' pistol, and the ammunition specially designed for it by Colonel Boxer. Since that time large numbers of these weapons have been made and many experiments conducted, all of which have proved the correctness of official judgment. We have much pleasure, therefore, in laying before our readers illustrations of the arm itself, and of some of the machinery employed in its manufacture.

We think that a mere inspection of our engraving will sufficiently explain the construction of the pistol, but we have nevertheless indicated some of the leading features by letters,

Some of the basic machinery used in manufacturing the John Adams revolver. From *The Engineer* for 8 May 1868.

John Adams Model 1868 revolver.

by a small lever under the rod housing. The loading gate was pivoted at the top and lifted upwards to open instead of downwards as with the Colt. The gate was hinged to a small plate which was not forged as part of the frame but was inserted into a dovetail cut in the frame and then peened over.

The Mark III version was so marked on the left hand side of the frame in front of the cylinder and was, as has been mentioned, fitted with the swivel rod ejector. The Adams was also available for civilian purchase. Although it was a serviceable weapon, the general finish left much to be desired and, in this respect, it cannot be compared to the Colt. The original Adams Patent Small Arms Company went out of business in 1881, shortly after the Government had approved the Enfield revolver. This, as we shall see, was manufactured not by a private contractor but at the Royal Small Arms Factory at Enfield.

A somewhat mysterious series of revolvers was marketed by the London Armoury Co., the correct style being James Kerr and Co. (successors to the London Armoury Co. Ltd.). The example illustrated, a solid frame rod ejector .450 centre-fire 'Army' revolver, is typical of the 'trade' revolvers of superior quality whose manufacturers are, as yet, unknown. The significant feature of this revolver was the method of removing the cylinder; the axis pin was retained by a spring-loaded catch which, when depressed, made it possible for the pin to be withdrawn and the cylinder removed.

The disadvantage of the simple rod ejector, that of lack of power, was overcome by William Tranter's patent rod, or 'plunger' ejector as

.450 James Kerr (London Armoury Company) centre-fire revolver.

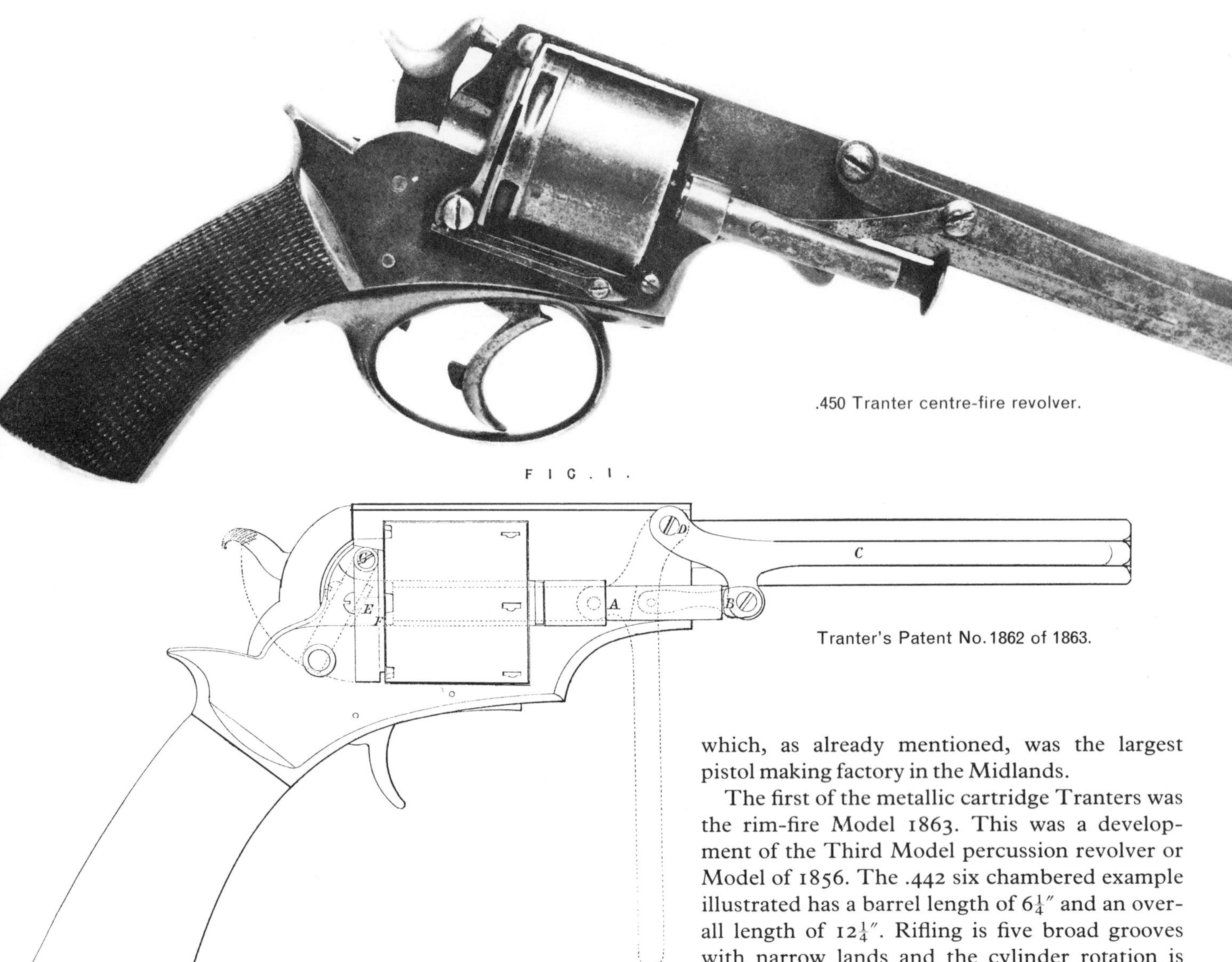

.450 Tranter centre-fire revolver.

Tranter's Patent No. 1862 of 1863.

Tranter called it in British Patent No. 1862 of 1863. As can be seen from the patent drawing, this was a simple variation of the muzzle loading lever rammer, but it was unusual in that it was intended to act on the case mouth rather than on the base of the case.

A variant of this ejector will be found on a number of British revolvers, the modification being designed to simplify manufacture. The example shown is a .450 centre-fire marked 'Tranter's Patent' and, in the absence of evidence to the contrary, may well have been made by him. The origin of these 'trade' revolvers is in considerable doubt, since they often lack both the manufacturer's mark and the retailer's name. Tranter, however, certainly had the capacity to manufacture at his works at Aston, Birmingham, which, as already mentioned, was the largest pistol making factory in the Midlands.

The first of the metallic cartridge Tranters was the rim-fire Model 1863. This was a development of the Third Model percussion revolver or Model of 1856. The .442 six chambered example illustrated has a barrel length of $6\frac{1}{4}''$ and an overall length of $12\frac{1}{4}''$. Rifling is five broad grooves with narrow lands and the cylinder rotation is clockwise. The frame of the pistol is forged in one piece but, in common with most Tranters, the barrel was made separately. The trigger mechanism has already been discussed (see page 163).

Access to the lock work is by means of a removable side plate on the left hand side of the action body, a most useful feature since it permits cleaning with the minimum disturbance. This side plate is secured by one screw which passes through the centre of the hammer screw. Adequate support is provided for the hammer bearing, but the plate can still be removed without disturbing the hammer, and the functioning of the parts verified. This feature was common to many of the Tranter revolvers and can also be seen on the .380 centre-fire. As with the percussion revolver, the action is provided with a half cock notch or bent so that the hammer can be withdrawn to the rear sufficiently to permit the rotation of the cylinder during loading.

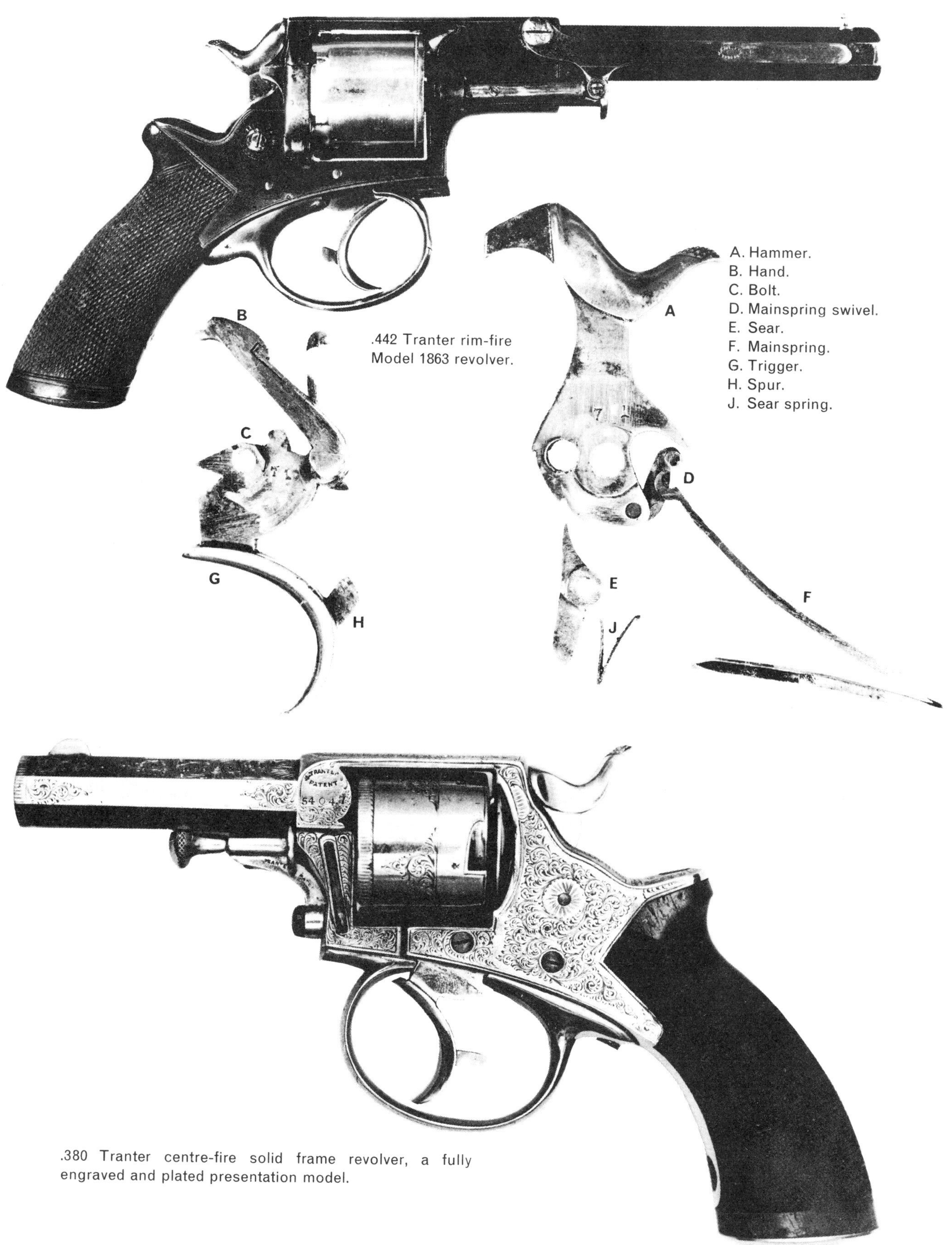

.442 Tranter rim-fire Model 1863 revolver.

.380 Tranter centre-fire solid frame revolver, a fully engraved and plated presentation model.

Cartridges are introduced by unlatching a downward hinging loading gate on the right hand side of the action body, but this is not as convenient or as quick as the spring-loaded gate used on the Colt SAA. The cylinder can quickly be removed by depressing a spring-loaded lever which lies parallel to the barrel axis on the left hand side of the frame in front of the cylinder. The frame has, in fact, been extended to accommodate it. Rim-fire .442 ammunition is not plentiful today, but I have been able to use this pistol sufficiently to gain a good impression of its practical worth. It is very well made and, because of its weight, pleasant to shoot. This particular example was sold by Trulock Brothers, 11 Essex Bridge, Dublin, and is so marked on the barrel. Both the frame and the ejector lever bear the legend 'W. Tranter's Patent' and the former also carries the number of the pistol, 5345. As one would expect, Birmingham Proof Marks are to be found on both barrel and cylinder. The pistol was originally sold in a splendid mahogany case with provision for fifty cartridges and the usual cleaning tools.

It is of interest to compare the rim-fire revolver with the later centre-fire version shown here which employed the identical ejector lever system but incorporated a firing pin in the frame, the nose of the hammer being shrouded. This firing mechanism was covered by Tranter's Patent No. 285 of 1868. It is, however, difficult, if not impossible, to attempt model designation by patent dates, desirable though this might be. Patented features such as the 1868 firing pin can be identified, but this will also be found on revolvers employing the much earlier lever ejector of 1863, and equally on later weapons fitted with the rod ejector of 1868.

In the later .450 Tranter Army revolver the ejector was altered to a swivel type patented in 1871, in which the swivel was provided with a spring to align the rod with the chamber.

In what was possibly the last of the Tranter Army solid frame series, a return was made to the simple rod ejector mounted inside a tube, the tube being attached to the frame by two screws. This revolver also dispensed with the spring catch on the loading gate, the gate being kept either open or closed by a spring under the hinge. The retaining spring for the cylinder pin was removed from the side of the frame to the pin itself, and there were some slight modifications to the action, the separate spring formerly employed for the secondary sear being eliminated by

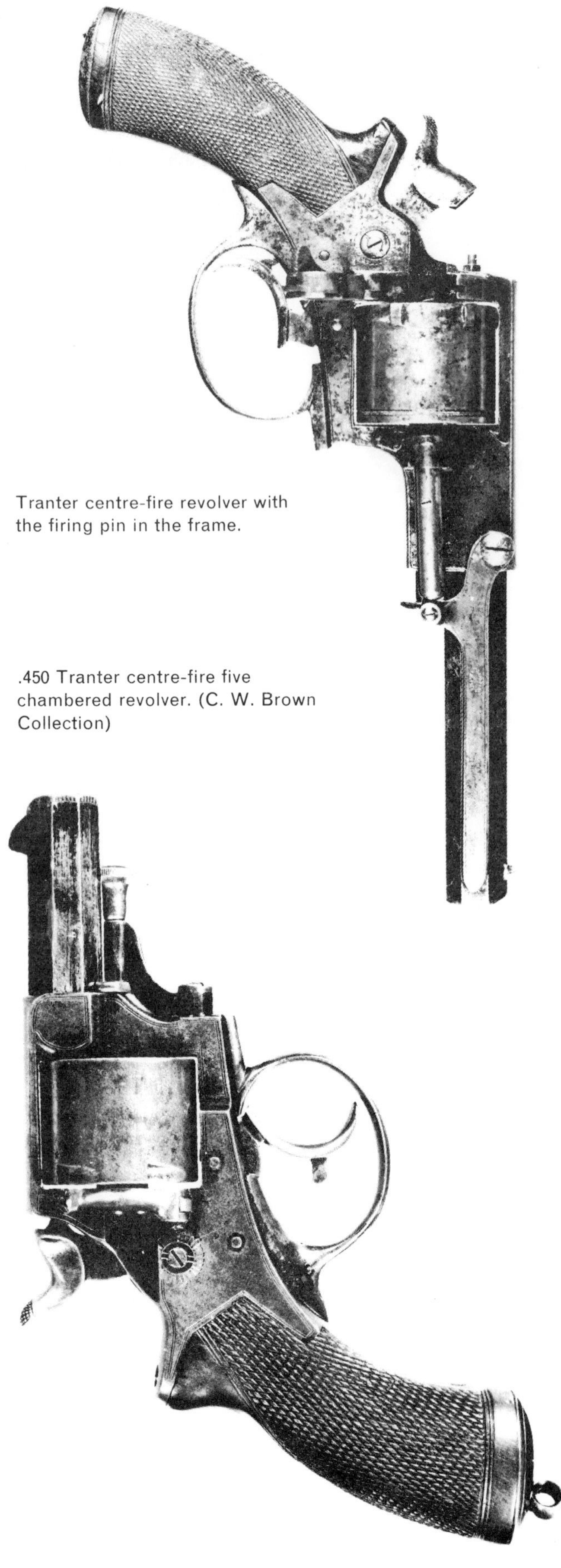

Tranter centre-fire revolver with the firing pin in the frame.

.450 Tranter centre-fire five chambered revolver. (C. W. Brown Collection)

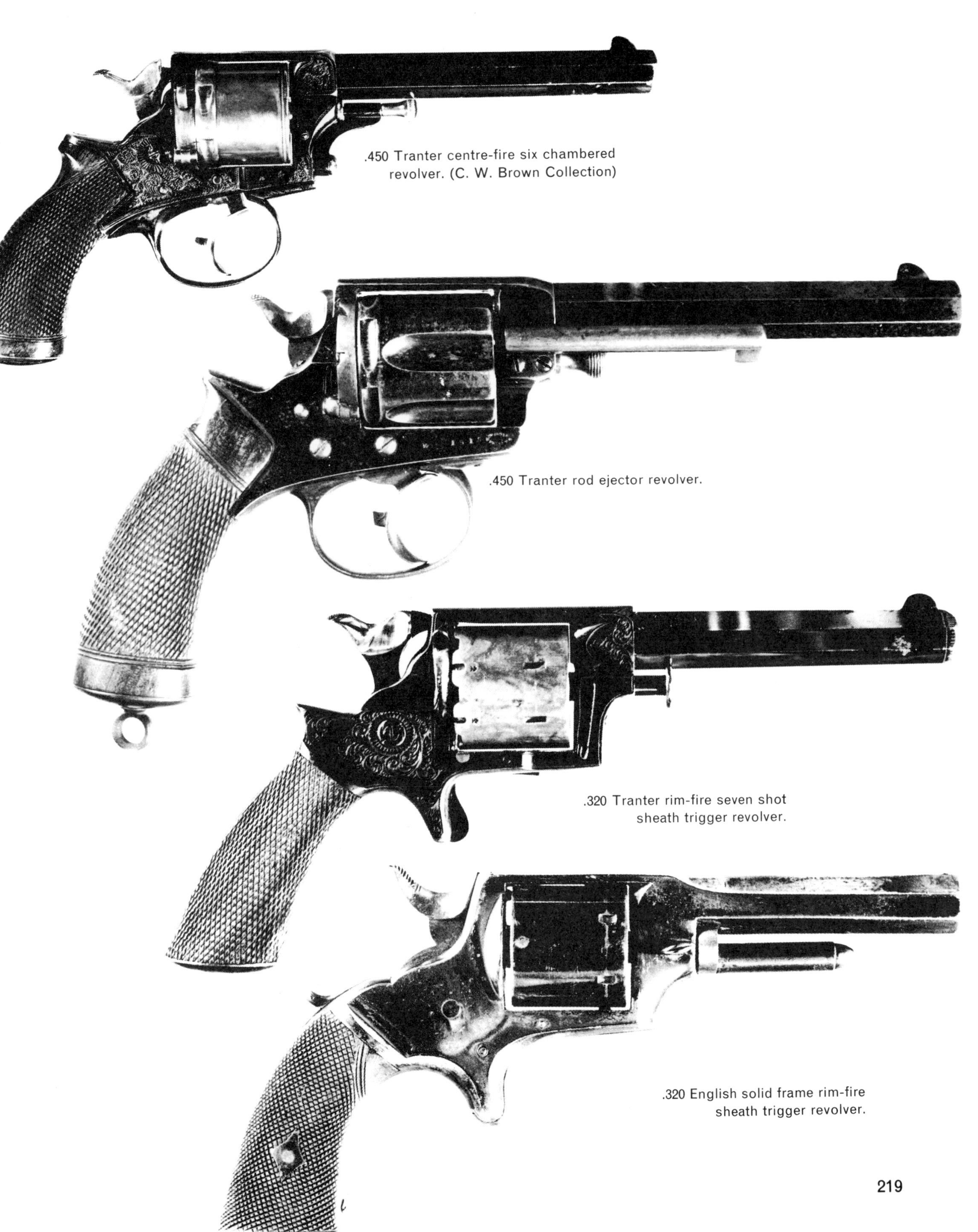

.450 Tranter centre-fire six chambered revolver. (C. W. Brown Collection)

.450 Tranter rod ejector revolver.

.320 Tranter rim-fire seven shot sheath trigger revolver.

.320 English solid frame rim-fire sheath trigger revolver.

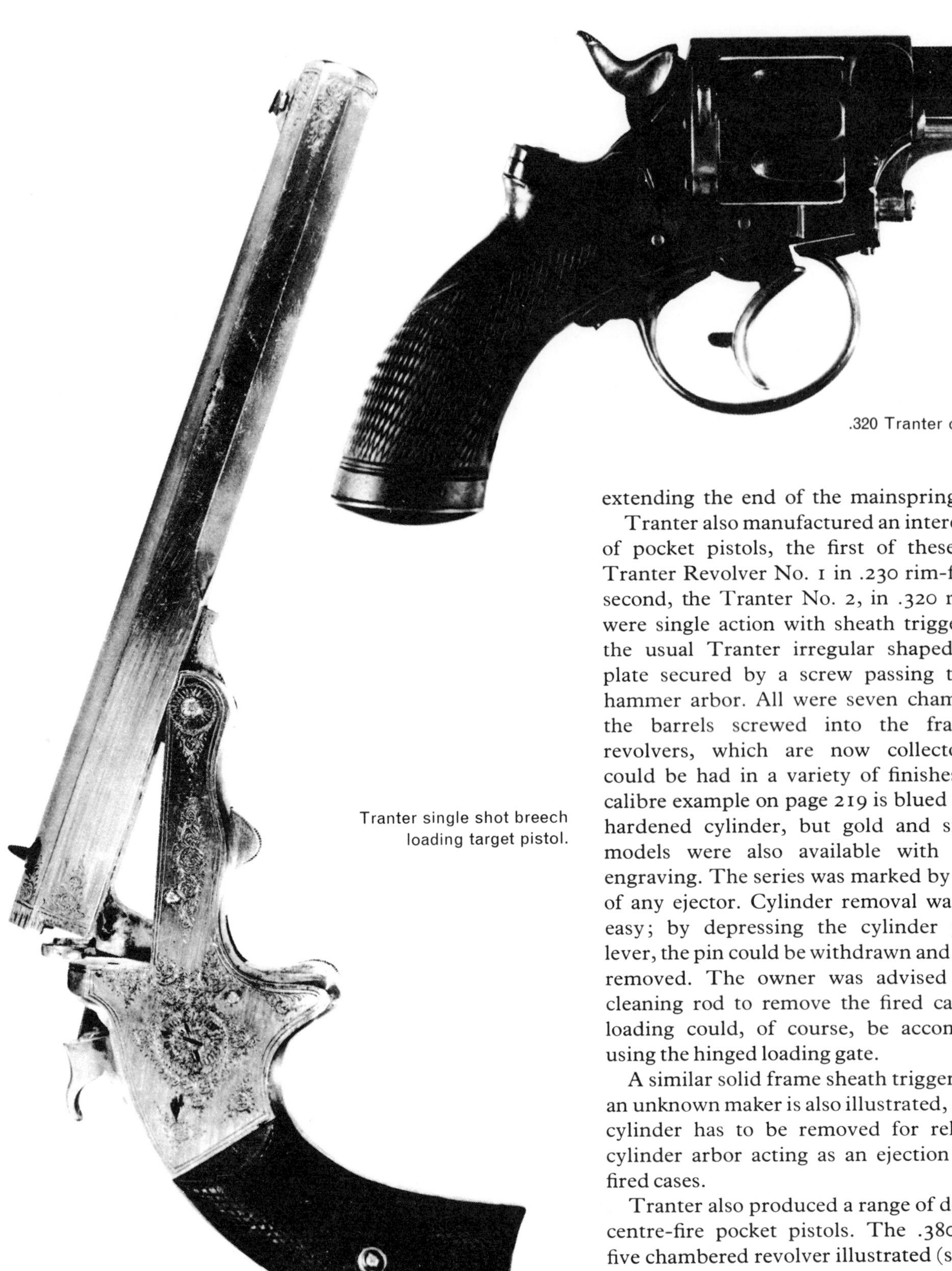

.320 Tranter centre-fire five shot revolver.

Tranter single shot breech loading target pistol.

extending the end of the mainspring.

Tranter also manufactured an interesting range of pocket pistols, the first of these being the Tranter Revolver No. 1 in .230 rim-fire, and the second, the Tranter No. 2, in .320 rim-fire. All were single action with sheath triggers and had the usual Tranter irregular shaped inspection plate secured by a screw passing through the hammer arbor. All were seven chambered with the barrels screwed into the frame. These revolvers, which are now collector's pieces, could be had in a variety of finishes. The .320 calibre example on page 219 is blued with a case-hardened cylinder, but gold and silver plated models were also available with or without engraving. The series was marked by the absence of any ejector. Cylinder removal was quick and easy; by depressing the cylinder pin locking lever, the pin could be withdrawn and the cylinder removed. The owner was advised to use the cleaning rod to remove the fired cases, but re-loading could, of course, be accomplished by using the hinged loading gate.

A similar solid frame sheath trigger revolver by an unknown maker is also illustrated, and here the cylinder has to be removed for reloading, the cylinder arbor acting as an ejection rod for the fired cases.

Tranter also produced a range of double action centre-fire pocket pistols. The .380 centre-fire five chambered revolver illustrated (see page 217) bears no retailer's name but carries the usual 'Tranter's Patent' on the frame and on the swivel ejector. Not only did this type of ejector push out the fired cases, but the swivel arm also retained the cylinder pin and the spring arm. Although

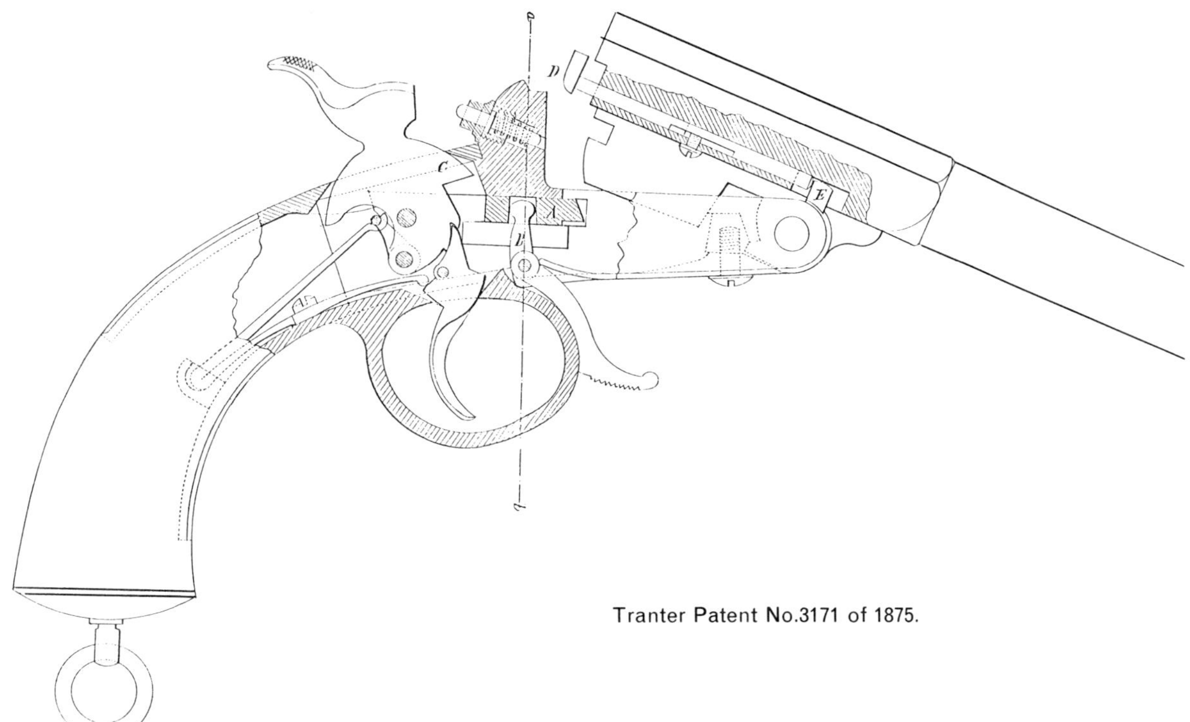

Tranter Patent No.3171 of 1875.

only 7½″ overall and with a barrel just under 3″, the Tranter pocket model is easy to shoot and has a man-sized trigger guard. A later version of this pistol had a fluted cylinder. Tranter was also responsible for the manufacture of a rather fine single shot Saloon or target pistol. The .380 centre-fire version is illustrated, but it was also available in .230 and .320 rim-fire. A variation of this pistol with a separate firing pin will be seen in the patent illustration for Tranter's Patent No. 3171 of 1875.

One other important revolver by Tranter will be encountered, the hinge frame simultaneous ejector, and this will be dealt with in a later chapter. Tranter appears to have gone out of business in 1885, a year after his younger brother David died. The factory was sold to George Kynoch who, much to the annoyance of his fellow directors on the board of Kynoch, ran several private businesses. The Kynoch Gun Factory was one of these, but it was unsuccessful and was sold yet again to Henry Schlund, formerly Kynoch's Works Manager. Tranter will, however, be referred to again later, but the closing of the factory marked the end of competitive revolver manufacture in Britain. In 1887 the Webley Mark I was accepted as the standard sidearm for the British Army and, until recent times, Webleys enjoyed a virtual monopoly of the military revolver market.

The handguns manufactured by P. Webley and Son have been exhaustively covered by William C. Dowell in *The Webley Story* and no new or additional material can be offered. Even so, it is necessary to outline the history of this company here in order to preserve continuity.

The early history was covered in Chapter Seven, but its fortunes can be said to have been laid with the introduction of the Webley double action solid frame RIC Models in 1867. The original version of this revolver is illustrated on page 222, and this particular example is fitted with an ivory grip inscribed 'Presented to R. S. Benson Esq., Sept. 1873, by a few College Friends'. There are many variants of the original RIC, the name derived for the Royal Irish Constabulary, who adopted this revolver in 1868, the year of its foundation.

In the first model it will be seen that the cylinder locking notches were at the front end, locking being achieved by a spring-loaded bolt in the bar of the frame. The trigger mechanism is a variation of the Tranter mechanism (see page 162), except that the spur on the rear of the trigger is done away with, the secondary sear or trigger being lengthened to protrude through the lock plate. The action of the later RIC models more closely resembled the Tranter since the extra limb required for locking the cylinder was discarded, locking being accomplished by an extension on the trigger which engaged projections at the rear of the cylinder. The later Webley can be identified by these projections and by the swell or hump on the top strap necessary to provide clearance for the cylinder projections. This modification reduced the number of limbs in the mechanism, and the small screw about which the earlier cylinder bolt pivoted can be seen in front of the trigger screw. Both models employed an unusual swivel rod ejector mounted on a clip which fitted round the barrel in front of the frame. The ejector rod was housed in the hollow cylinder

.442 Webley RIC First Model revolver.

axis pin and, when required, was pulled forward and the arm swivelled to one side to enter the appropriate chamber. Cartridges were introduced through a spring-loaded gate on the right hand side of the frame. The early RIC revolvers were chambered for the .442 centre-fire cartridge which was later given the official title of 'Cartridge, SA Ball, .442 Mark I'. Later versions of the RIC revolver were chambered for the .450, .476, .455 and .430 cartridges as well as for the .44 Winchester and .45 Colt.

Subsequent variants of the RIC Model introduced the swivel ejector originally patented by John Adams—where the pivot screw entered the left hand side of the frame—and similar to that employed by Tranter. The next modification was to recess the cylinder locking grooves, and this led to the 1880 RIC Model and variants. This was the last of the series with smooth cylinders, the example illustrated bearing the name of Daniel Fraser, Edinburgh, a famous Scottish gunmaker renowned for his sporting rifles. In 1883 an 'improved' version of the RIC Model appeared, the first to have a grooved cylinder. The true RIC Models had six chambers and closely resembled each other. As with any successful and popular article, however, there were those who sought to share some of the profitability by offering similar articles at a reduced price. This happened with the Webley RIC Model and other gunmakers, particularly in Belgium, copied the basic Webley design, while even less reputable makers copied the copies.

This was particularly so with yet another highly successful Webley product, the Bulldog series of five chambered pocket revolvers.

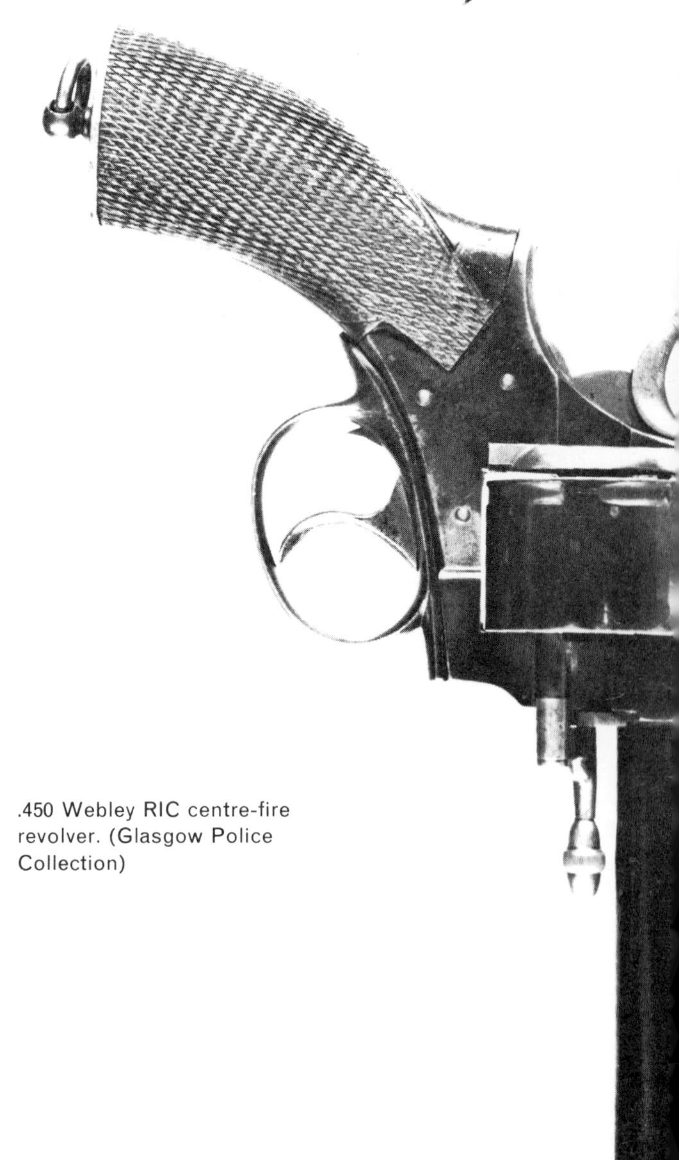

.450 Webley RIC centre-fire revolver. (Glasgow Police Collection)

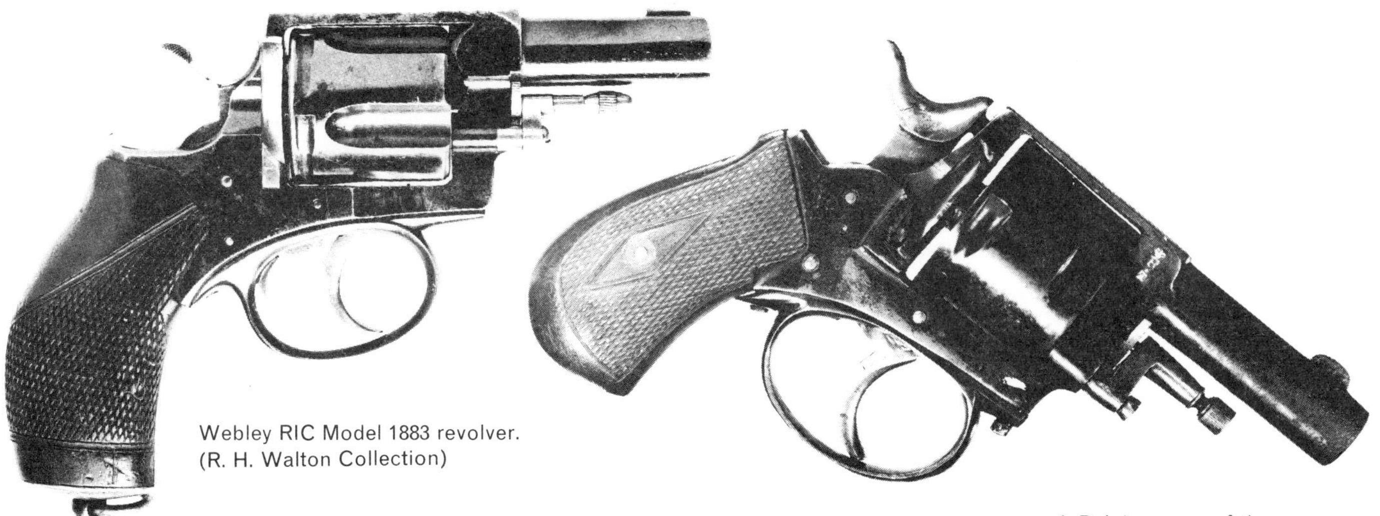

Webley RIC Model 1883 revolver.
(R. H. Walton Collection)

A Belgian copy of the Webley Bulldog.

These were again of solid frame construction and there is a strong resemblance between the short barrel RIC revolvers and the Bulldogs. The early Bulldogs had a smooth cylinder, the version manufactured after 1883 having a grooved one. In contrast to the RIC series, the Bulldog revolvers were five chambered, and the shape of the stock was also different. The Bulldog was fitted with a 'bird's head' or 'parrot beak' stock, the two half plates being secured to the one piece butt strap by a single transverse screw, while the RIC series had a one piece wooden stock, the straps terminating in a butt plate to which a lanyard swivel was often fitted.

The first Bulldog was chambered for the .442 centre-fire cartridge. This was followed by a .44 rim-fire version and later by a .450 centre-fire. The Webley Bulldog was probably the most widely copied British revolver ever made. A Belgian copy of the Bulldog in .38 calibre is illustrated, but the majority appear to have been chambered for the .32 cartridge. Copies were made in Belgium, Germany, Spain and America. Most followed the original lines of the Webley quite closely, and several can be found with a lever safety catch. Apart from the legend 'British Bulldog', few bore any indication of the manufacturer. An exception was the British Bulldog made by Sullivan Forehand and Henry C. Wadsworth, the sons-in-law of the famous Ethan Allen. The firm of Forehand and Wadsworth of Worcester, Massachusetts, was in business from 1871 until 1890 and, in addition to making copies of the Webley Bulldog—which, with the exception of the trigger mechanism, were very similar—they manufactured quite a

.577 Webley revolver chambered for the .577 Boxer cartridge, the original stock replaced by the present oversize one.

range of inexpensive revolvers bearing names such as Bull Dog, Swamp Angel and Terror. Wadsworth retired in 1890, but the firm continued under the name Forehand Arms Co. until 1900.

Webley's also made a range of Civilian Pocket Models generally similar to the RIC series, but the most interesting of the range, before the introduction of the hinged frame group of revolvers, were the solid frame Army Express Models made in both double and single action. The swivel ejector was replaced by a rod ejector very similar to that fitted to the Tranter (see page 219) and a new barrel contour was adopted which foreshadowed the style today associated with the name Webley.

The most formidable Webley revolver was undoubtedly the .577, one of the earliest solid frame pistols manufactured by Webleys for the centre-fire cartridge. Six chambered for the .577 Boxer with 28 grains of black powder and a 295 grain soft lead bullet, it packed more punch than any other revolver made before or since—with the exception of the latest heavy magnum revolvers. Weapons such as this were popular during the second half of the nineteenth century since they were capable of stopping fanatical savages. Similar reasons dictated the development of the multi-barrelled pistols made by Lancaster and others which were again chambered for the .577 cartridge.

Without doubt the most famous rod ejector revolver is the Colt Single Action Army Model sometimes called the Model of 1873. We could, with quite adequate reason, go even further and state that the Colt SAA is the most famous revolver of all time. Just as the name 'Winchester' to many people means 'repeating rifle', so the name Colt is synonymous with revolver and, in particular (at least to the Anglo-American), with that type of revolver associated with the opening of the American West.

The Single Action Army Model was not the first cartridge Colt revolver. Three quite distinct models pre-dated it. The first of these was C. B. Richard's cloverleaf cylinder Model of 1871, called by Colt the House Pistol. This was unusual in revolvers of the time in having only four chambers. It is at once recognisable by the shape of the cylinder, the cluster of four chambers resembling a cloverleaf. Furnished with 3″ and $1\frac{1}{2}$″ barrels, this pistol was single action, had a sheath trigger and a rod ejector underneath the barrel. It is also of importance since it was the first 'solid frame' Colt cartridge revolver to be made. Charles B. Richards, the inventor, was the Assistant Factory Superintendent at Colt's Hartford factory and, as mentioned earlier in this chapter, had been responsible for a method of converting percussion revolvers to use standard metallic cartridges.

The .41 rim-fire House Pistol with the cloverleaf cylinder was later modified, and a similar pistol with a five chambered round cylinder introduced. The last of the Colt 'open frame' revolvers was the little .22 Pocket Model. Like the House Pistol, the frame of the .22 Pocket Pistol was of bronze, and either .22 short or long rim-fire cartridges could be introduced into the seven chambered cylinder through the groove in the right hand recoil shield. Of far wider distribution were the Colt New Line Pocket revolvers.

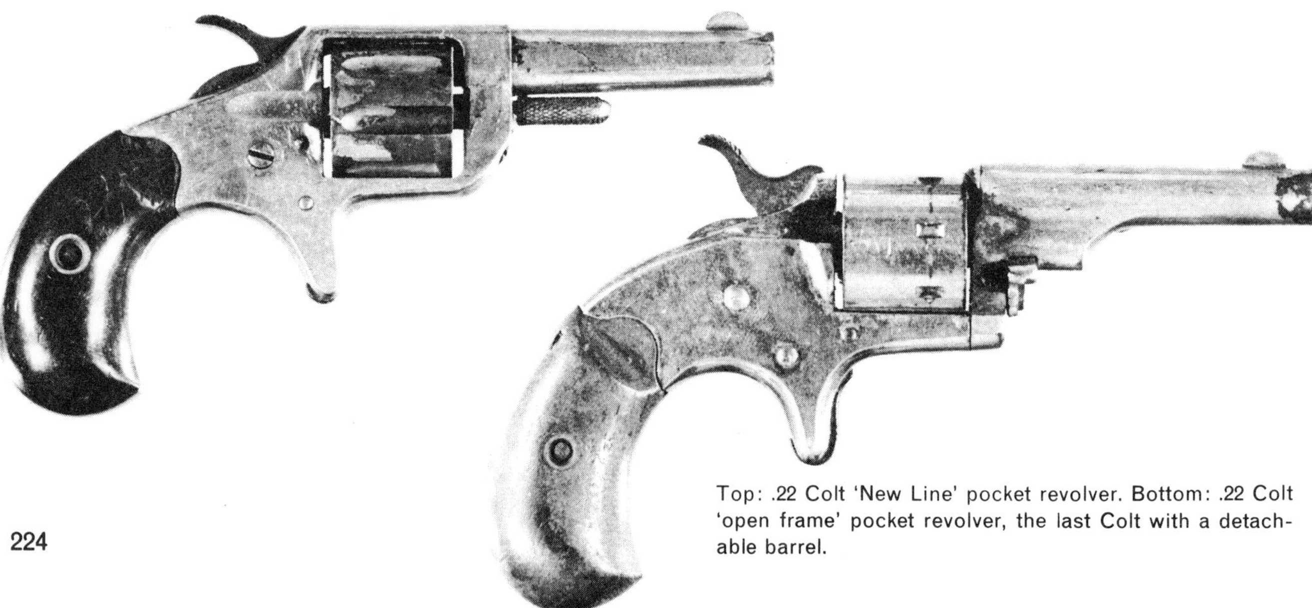

Top: .22 Colt 'New Line' pocket revolver. Bottom: .22 Colt 'open frame' pocket revolver, the last Colt with a detachable barrel.

These solid frame pistols with screw-in barrels were first manufactured in 1873 and could be obtained in the following calibres.

.22 short and long rim-fire.
.30 short and long rim-fire.
.32 short and long rim-fire.
.32 short and long Colt centre-fire.
.38 short and long rim-fire.
.38 short and long Colt centre-fire.
.41 short and long rim-fire.
.41 short centre-fire.

The .32 and .38 Colt centre-fire long and short cartridges were adaptations of the British .320 and .380 revolver cartridges of the 1860's. As originally made, the outside lubricated bullets were heel seated. Later the .32 long Colt was introduced with inside lubrication, the bullet diameter being reduced so that it would enter the case, and a deep base cavity ensured expansion into the rifling.

The .38 long Colt (also known as the Colt Navy) was similarly modernised and in 1894 appeared as the .38 Colt Army with an inside lubricated bullet. Both cartridges were interchangeable and the Army version gradually replaced the original. As was then the practice, the case length was increased to cover the lubricant grooves in the bullet.

The Colt revolvers which handled these cartridges bore a close resemblance to one another. All were five chambered, with the exception of the .22 which was seven chambered. The .22 also differed from the other calibre models in that the barrel had flattened sides and the frame was bronze instead of steel. According to Serven, the earliest of these revolvers had locking slots on the periphery of the cylinder, but most of those seen today have locking slots on the breech face of the cylinder between the chambers (William Mason's US Patent of 1874).

The .32 calibre model illustrated was carried for many years by the wife of an Army officer in India, and legend has it that the gallant lady employed the pistol to good effect on more than one occasion. Loading could not have been very speedy since the cylinder pin had to be withdrawn by pressing a small button on the left hand side of the frame. The cylinder could then be removed and the fired cases poked out with the cylinder pin. A fresh load could either be introduced with the cylinder removed, or else the pistol could be reloaded, one cartridge at a time, through the slot in the recoil shield. The barrel bears the usual Colt legend, 'Colt's PT. F.A. Mfg. Co. Hartford Ct. U.S.A.' in two lines and the particular example illustrated also bears Mason's patent date under the barrel, 'Pat. Sept. 15, 1874'. On other examples, the side of the barrel can frequently be found etched with the calibre, 'Colt New 32', in a cartouche.

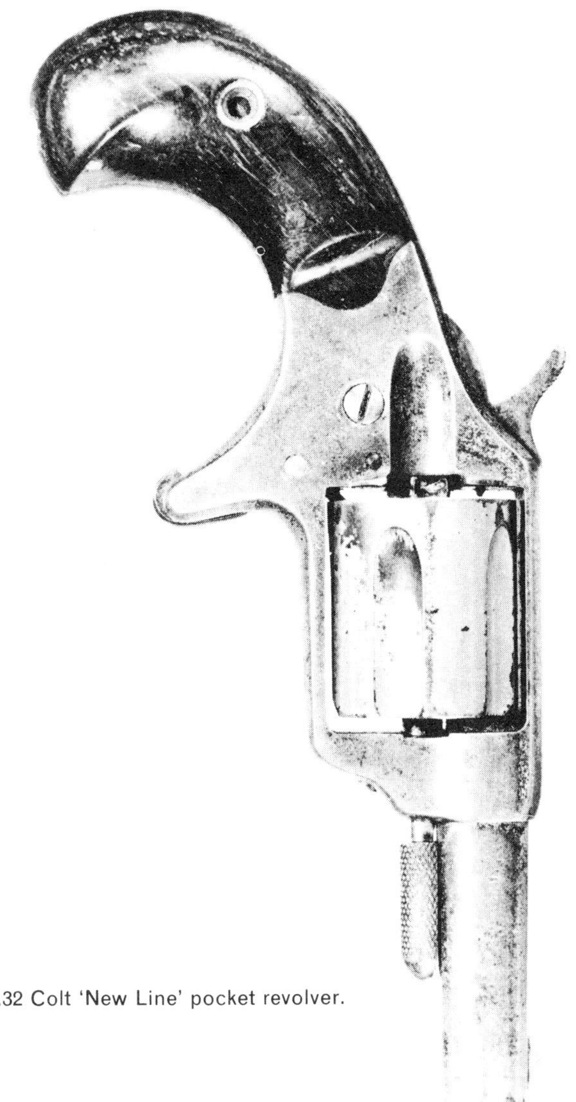

.32 Colt 'New Line' pocket revolver.

A very similar series of revolvers known as the New Line Police and House series then appeared, those fitted with $4\frac{1}{4}''$, 5″ and 6″ barrels having a rod ejector. The short $2\frac{1}{4}''$ barrel versions had no ejector, the cylinder pin serving instead. The difference between the Pocket and the Police and House models lay chiefly in the shape of the butt. The Pocket had the bird's head grip, the Police and House version a flat base butt with hard rubber stock, the Police model illustrating a 'cop and robber' motif in relief.

Colt was by no means the only maker of this type of pistol. Many firms which bore names

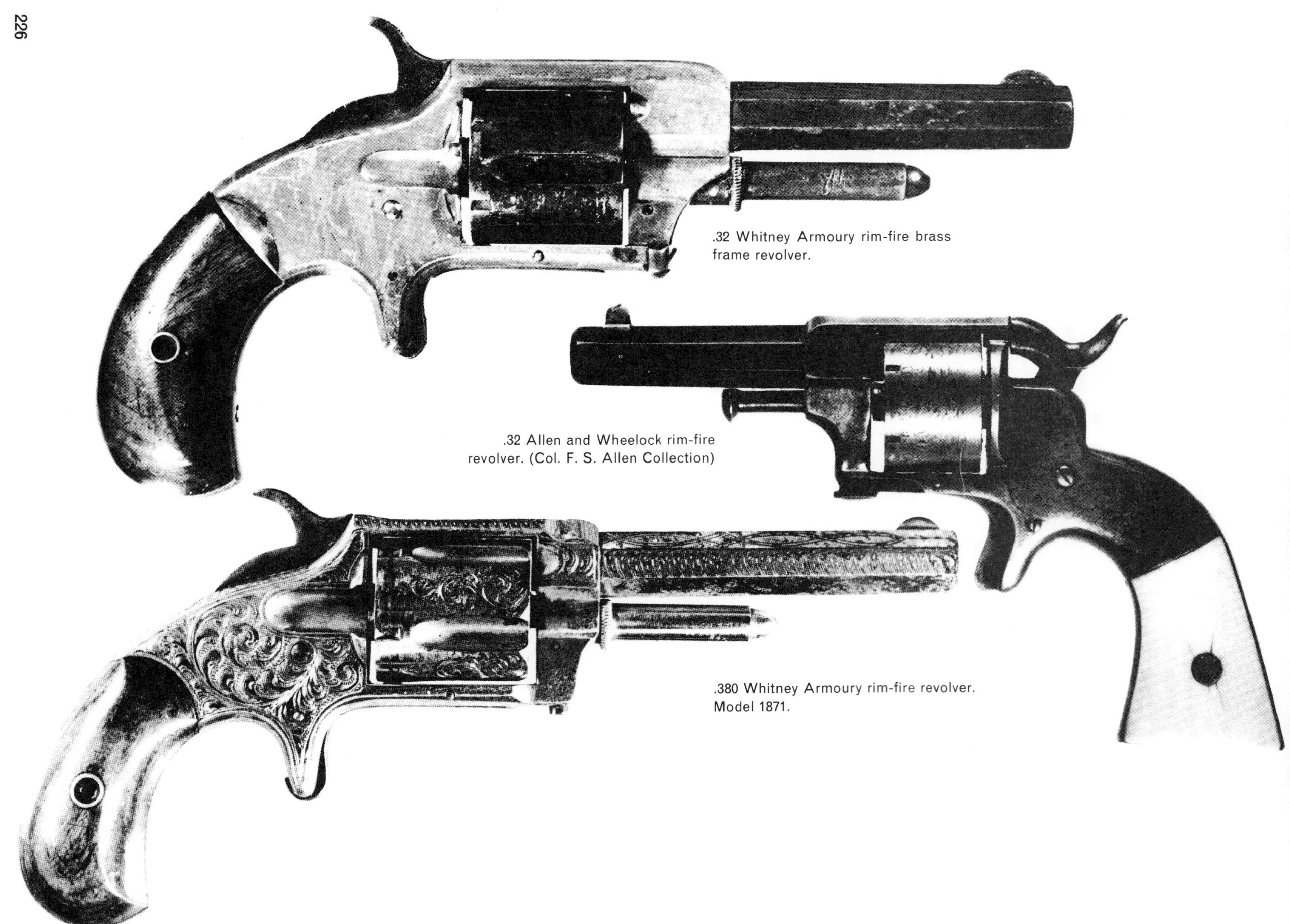

.32 Whitney Armoury rim-fire brass frame revolver.

.32 Allen and Wheelock rim-fire revolver. (Col. F. S. Allen Collection)

.380 Whitney Armoury rim-fire revolver. Model 1871.

made famous during the percussion period survived into the cartridge era. Allen and Wheellock, whose pepperboxes were discussed earlier, also manufactured the little side hammer rim-fire revolver illustrated, the basic patents for which were obtained in 1856. Equally, reference has already been made to the Armoury operated by Eli Whitney and later, in 1842, taken over by his son. The Whitney Armoury manufactured an immense number of weapons during the American Civil War, and later produced a solid frame single action revolver lacking a rod ejector, the cartridges being removed from the cylinder by means of an extension to the cylinder pin, in a similar manner to that employed by the Colt New Line Police and House revolvers. One of the examples illustrated has a brass frame and is chambered for the .32 rim-fire cartridge, while the other is a nicely engraved .38 version. The importance of the Whitney Armoury in the development of the American firearms industry has, as yet, not been accurately defined. Although it ceased operations in 1888, its activities spanned nearly a century and were mainly concerned with contract arms, not the least of these being the Colt Whitneyville Dragoons. Had Eli Jnr. not made the Dragoon percussion revolver for Colt, the remarkable Colt story might have ended somewhat differently.

Although of interest to the Colt collector, these early cartridge models do not have the appeal, the fascination, of the larger Colt Single Action Army. This remarkable revolver merits considerable attention, if only because of the span of years over which it was produced. I cannot think of any other reasonably complicated mass-produced article which has been manufactured, virtually unchanged in outward appearances, for so long a time. It is quite astonishing in this day of planned obsolescence to hold the .450 Boxer Colt No. 38918 in the hand and reflect that it was manufactured in 1876 and will shortly be 100 years old. Of even more staggering import is the fact that you or I could purchase a similar revolver (except for the calibre) today.

The real and mythical portrayal of the part played by the Colt SAA in the opening of the American West in books, films and television tends perhaps to obscure the fact that this was a military weapon and that sales were not confined to the cowboy, outlaw, lawman and fast gunslinger whose proficiency with the 'Colt', both real and imaginary, has done so much to perpetuate the Colt legend.

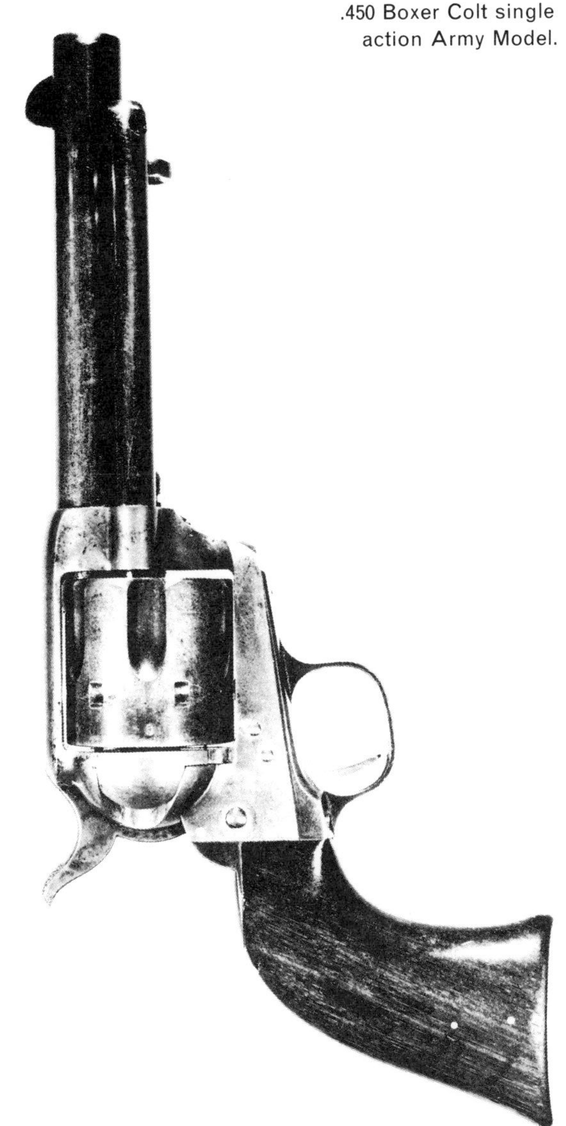

.450 Boxer Colt single action Army Model.

The ancestry of the Model 1873 is easy to trace, and a good starting point is the Model 1860 Army percussion revolver, always remembering that, mechanically, the history goes back even further. After the 1860 Army, we saw how the stop-gap conversions were introduced, those by Mason and those by Richards. Then came the .44 rim-fire, the Model 1872, the direct ancestor of the Colt SAA. The new model was made with a solid frame into which the barrel was screwed. There were also minor improvements to the mechanism, but in essence the old and well tried single action mechanism was employed relatively unchanged, at least in principle. There were the same few parts: hammer, hand, cylinder bolt, trigger and three springs—mainspring, handspring and a bifurcated spring which operated both the cylinder bolt and the trigger. The original military issue was, of course, six chambered and had a $7\frac{1}{2}''$ barrel. The first contract secured by Colt's in 1873 was for the supply of 8,000 .45 calibre revolvers to the US Government, and by 1890 just over 37,000 had been ordered. In addition to being issued to the US Army, these revolvers were used by the State Militia and various departments of the Federal Government. Custer's Seventh Cavalry, some twelve companies of which were engaged at one time or another in the famous battle of the Little Big Horn in June 1876, were also armed with the Colt SAA. Present evidence is that General Custer himself was armed with a pair of Webley RIC revolvers, but since he had been fortunate enough to receive quite a large number of presentation revolvers at one time or another, the truth of the matter is still open to speculation. At this stage in its development, the .45 Army Colt was very similar to the .450 Boxer Colt illustrated. The revolver was finished in blue except for the frame which was case-hardened and left with the case-hardening colours showing. A one-piece walnut grip was fitted and the cylinder pin was retained by a single screw which passed through the frame at an angle. The ejector rod head was round with a small central hole.

Capable of being used with both the .45 Government cartridge and the .45 Colt cartridge, contemporary opinion expressed by the judges at the Centennial Exhibition held in Philadelphia in 1876 was:

'A military weapon extracting the discharged shells singly; combining strength and simplicity of action, not liable to get out of order; readily taken apart and easily cleaned; having entire

.450 Boxer Colt single action Army Model.

A. Hammer.
B. Back strap screws.
C. Back strap.
D. Hand.
E. Barrel and action body assembly.
F. Hammer screw.
G. Mainspring.
H. Back strap screw.
J. Trigger guard screw.
K. Cylinder pin.
L. Sear and bolt spring.
M. One piece stock.
N. Trigger guard.
O. Cylinder pin bushing.
P. Cylinder.
R. Trigger and bolt screws.
S. Trigger.
T. Cylinder bolt.

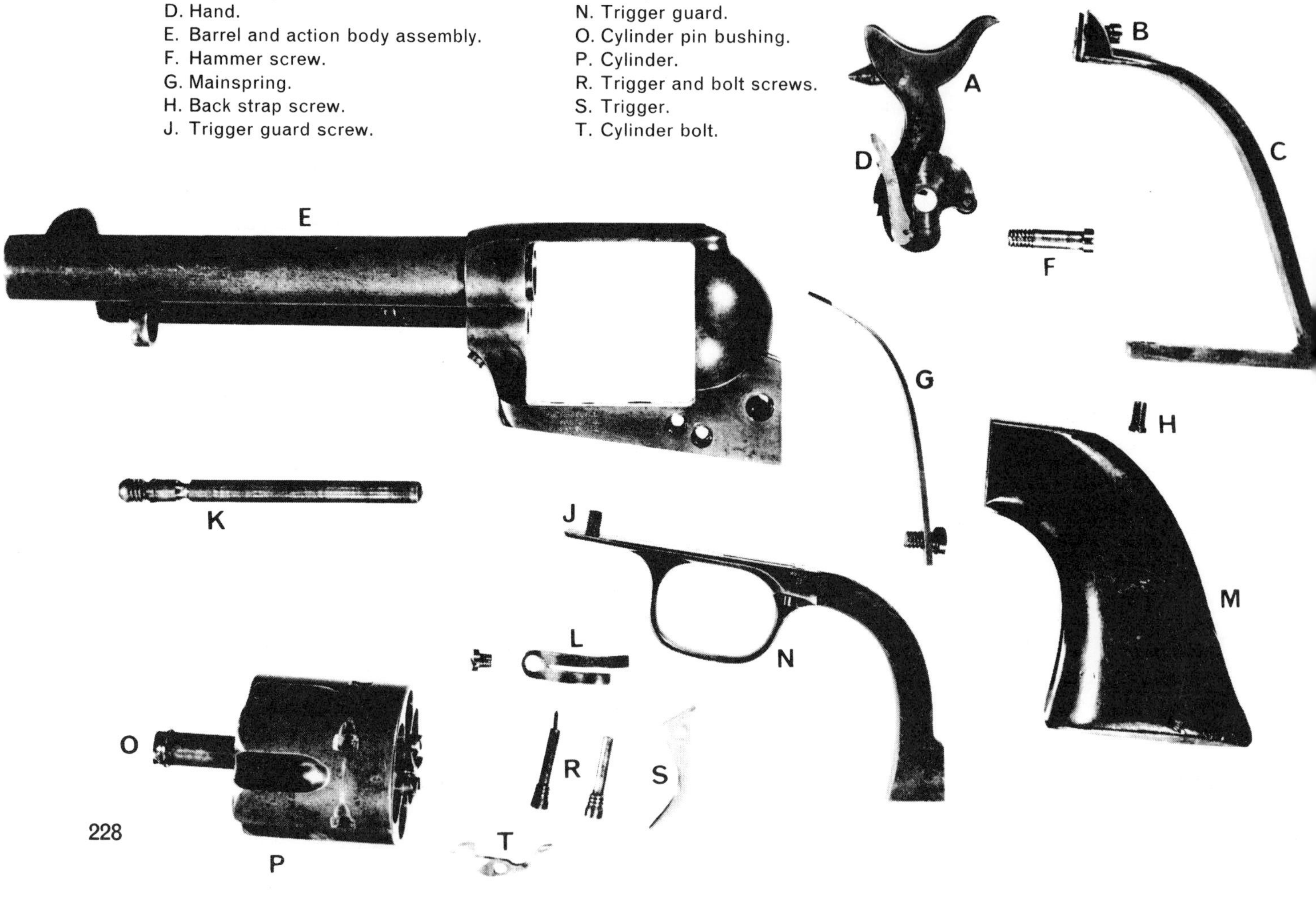

interchangeability of parts; with a high order of finish. Commended for durability and actual service in the hands of a soldier.'

Since several of the parts were liable to break, the ruggedness of the Colt has perhaps been overstressed. The important feature was, however, that it could still be made to fire even if some of the parts were either broken or missing. Equally, repairs could easily be carried out since the Colt could be dismantled down to the last component in a few minutes and, due to the interchangeable method of manufacture, new parts could be fitted by almost anyone.

One of the main rivals of the Colt during the last decades of the nineteenth century was the Smith and Wesson Schofield. This however, was condemned because of the multiplicity of parts, its only attractive feature being the 'automatic' ejection. Even this was denigrated since it was stated 'that Cavalry officers do not pay much attention to the quality of rapid ejection . . . since they do not carry on the person more than twelve rounds of ammunition'.

Another contender was the Remington Model 1875. This revolver, along with the Colt and the Smith and Wesson, was subjected to a number of tests by the US Ordnance Board, one of which was for endurance. This called for 250 rounds to be fired through the revolvers under test, after which they were allowed to remain for forty-eight hours uncleaned. A further fifty rounds were then fired. The Colt emerged from these tests without receiving adverse comment, but both of its competitors were condemned for excessive fouling and difficulty of operation. Yet another revolver tested was the Forehand and Wadsworth, but it, too, was damned with faint praise, objections being made to the greater weight, poor balance, greater number of parts and lack of rigidity. Government adoption of the Colt, and its continued use even after the development of more sophisticated revolver systems, undoubtedly helped to sway public opinion in favour of the Colt, and there is no doubt that this revolver was pre-eminently the weapon for the frontiersman and traveller.

Known at the factory as the Model P, the Single Action Army was chambered for the Winchester .44–40 cartridge in 1878 and, in this calibre, was advertised as the 'Frontier Six Shooter' and was so marked on the left side of the barrel.

The name 'Peacemaker', as applied to the .45 calibre Colt Single Action, appears to have been first used by the sales conscious Colt agents, but the term was one which had been applied to duelling pistols very much earlier, in *Charles O'Malley, The Irish Dragoon*,[1] where we find Count Considine taking 'the small mahogany box which contained his peacemakers under his arm and leading the way to the stables'.

Throughout the long life of the Colt SAA there have been few manufacturing changes. Until serial number 150,000, for instance, the method of securing the cylinder pin followed a basic design where the pin was retained by a small pointed screw which entered the front of the frame and was angled upward to lock it. There were two types of screw head; the earlier was shaped to agree with the contour of the frame, the later had a slightly dished head which simplified manufacture and did not detract in any way from the appearance. Mason's patent of 1874 introduced an improved system which locked the cylinder pin by a transverse spring-loaded bolt which passed through the frame under the pin. The cylinder pin and cylinder could, by this means, be quickly removed without the need for a turnscrew. Although it provided an easier method of removing the cylinder, Mason's transverse bolt (which came into use about 1890), unless kept clean and properly adjusted, could result in the pin moving forward under the inertia effect caused by prolonged firing.

There were several sizes of ejector rod housings and lengths of ejector rod, the standard housing length being four inches. The ejector rod head on the early models was round and had a small hole in the centre; later models were fitted with an ejector rod head which conformed to the barrel contour and was much neater. The original stocks were made in one piece and were almost identical to the percussion Navy stocks. Later, hard rubber stocks were offered, made in two separate panels and retained by a stock screw. These stocks had the rampant Colt in an oval and the earliest design also showed an eagle with outstretched wings and the motto, 'E Pluribus Unum'. De luxe factory stocks of best walnut, ivory or pearl were also available with a small inlaid metal medallion showing a rampant colt and the word 'Colt'.

Three grades of factory engraving were available, A, B, and C, the A grade being the cheapest. In the standard range, barrel lengths were 3″, 3½″, 4″ (the House or Storekeeper's Model with

[1] By Charles James Lever (Dublin 1841).

A comparison of frame design. The centre pistol is the Colt 'Flat Top' Target Model without ejector; the lower pistol is a Colt 'Bisley' Model with the spring loaded transverse cylinder bolt; the top pistol has the original pointed screw method of securing the cylinder bolt.

A comparison showing the 'round' ejector head on the upper Colt SAA as related to the later version which is contoured to the barrel. The lower pistol has the 'Winans' type foresight.

.45 Colt Single Action Army revolver.
(Col. F. S. Allen Collection)

no ejector), $4\frac{3}{4}''$ (ending flush with the end of the ejector rod housing), $5\frac{1}{2}''$ and $7\frac{1}{2}''$. Longer barrels could be had to order, at one time the cost being one dollar for each additional inch of barrel.

Cylinders were all six chambered and, with the exception of a few reworked double action cylinders identified by extra long flutes, there was little external variation throughout the years.

Chamber boring on the .455 and possibly the .476 British calibres was different since it was necessary to accommodate the increased rim diameters of cartridges intended for use with star simultaneous ejectors. Any significant increase in the centre-line diameter of the chambers would have meant an alteration not only in the cylinder diameter but also in the frame size, and, since one of the basic tenets of the 'American system' would have been violated, this could not be carried out. To overcome the problem, the chambers were bored convergently, i.e. if the axes were continued they would eventually meet. The rim diameter of the Boxer .450 cartridge was 0.505″, and of the .455, 0.530″. If the .455 cartridge was loaded into the Boxer .450 cylinder, the rims overlapped and only five cartridges could be loaded. The .45 Colt rim diameter was 0.505″ and, since the cylinder was designed for this calibre, there were no problems with the cartridge.

The degree of divergence was slight and cannot be detected except by careful measurement with the appropriate equipment. For the standard cylinder, the pitch diameter of the chambers was 1.495″ and, on the .455 cylinder, 1.525″. This allowed the standard cylinder cartridges to be used with a maximum rim diameter of 0.507″, and the .455 cylinder cartridges with rim diameters up to 0.572″. Cylinder diameter was also increased slightly from 1.646″ to 1.666″. Work on this problem was carried out by the writer in 1959 and, although Colt's were not able to confirm that this practice was adopted by the factory, the facts speak for themselves and the dimensional variations recorded are well outside acceptable factory tolerances.

The use of divergent cylinder boring has already been mentioned and will come up again when we deal with .22 revolver conversion systems. Normally the degree of divergency can be easily verified. In the case of the .455 Colt, it is impossible to verify visually whether or not the chambers are parallel, but, due to the difference in rim sizes, alteration to the standard cylinder was necessary and divergent boring was the answer. Minor modifications were also necessary on Colt SAA revolvers chambered for the rimfire cartridge. Four such calibres were available, the .22 short, long and long rifle, the .22 WRF, .32 and .44 rim-fire. A chisel shaped firing pin replaced the standard firing pin and the frame aperture was altered.

The centre-fire calibres available were: .32 Colt, .32 S & W, .32–20 and .32–44, .38 short and long Colt, .38 S & W, .38–44, .38 Special, .357 Magnum, .380 Eley, .38–40 WCF, .41 short and long Colt, .44 German and .44 Russian, .44 S & W and .44 S & W Special, .44–40 WCF, .45 Colt, .45 ACP, .450 Boxer, .450, .455 and .476 Eley.

Colts can very occasionally be encountered in other calibres and one examined recently was chambered for the .44 Evans and was so marked. This cartridge was made for the American Evans repeating rifle first introduced about 1875. Very

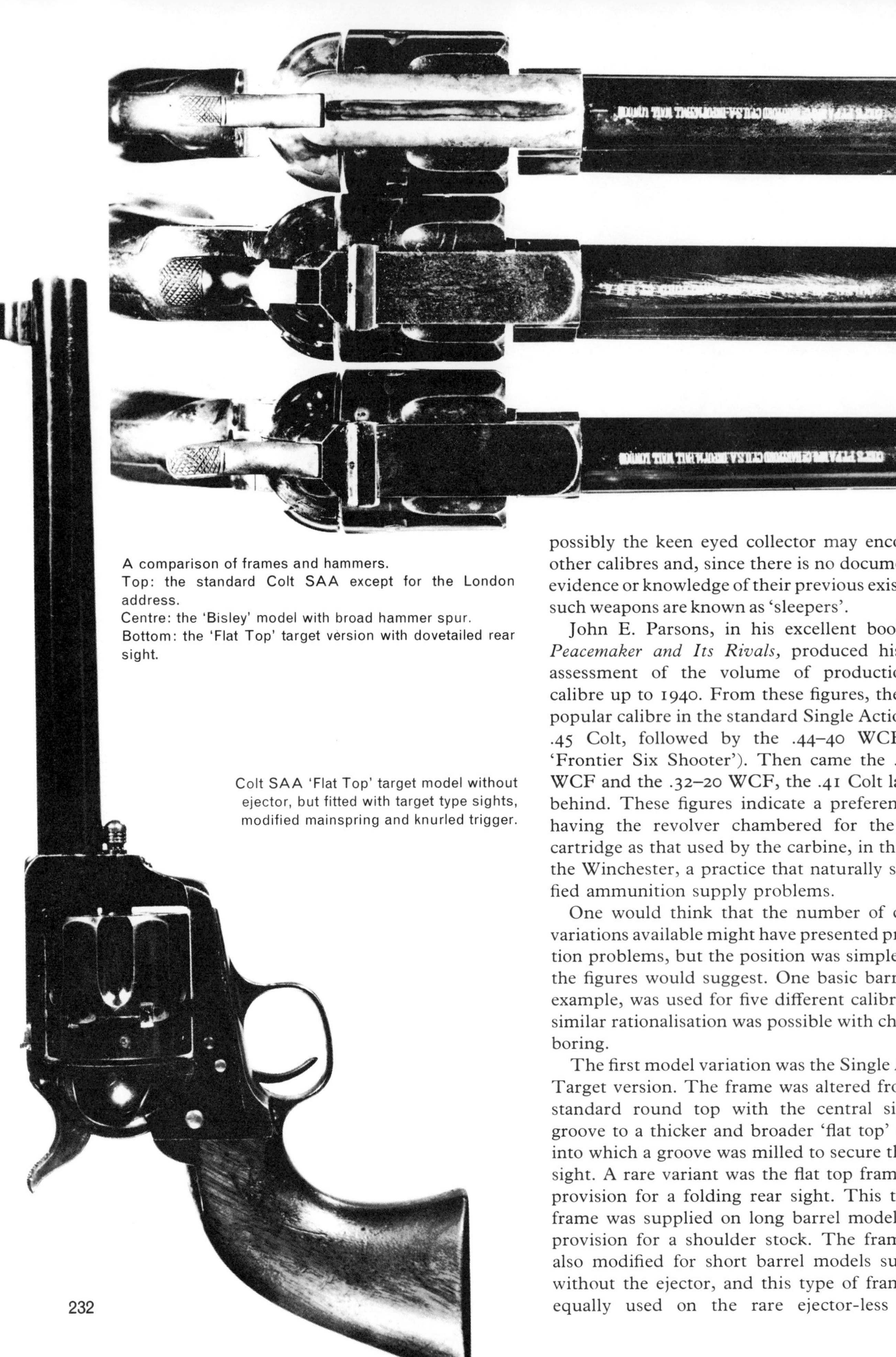

A comparison of frames and hammers.
Top: the standard Colt SAA except for the London address.
Centre: the 'Bisley' model with broad hammer spur.
Bottom: the 'Flat Top' target version with dovetailed rear sight.

Colt SAA 'Flat Top' target model without ejector, but fitted with target type sights, modified mainspring and knurled trigger.

possibly the keen eyed collector may encounter other calibres and, since there is no documentary evidence or knowledge of their previous existence, such weapons are known as 'sleepers'.

John E. Parsons, in his excellent book *The Peacemaker and Its Rivals,* produced his own assessment of the volume of production by calibre up to 1940. From these figures, the most popular calibre in the standard Single Action was .45 Colt, followed by the .44–40 WCF (the 'Frontier Six Shooter'). Then came the .38–40 WCF and the .32–20 WCF, the .41 Colt lagging behind. These figures indicate a preference for having the revolver chambered for the same cartridge as that used by the carbine, in this case the Winchester, a practice that naturally simplified ammunition supply problems.

One would think that the number of calibre variations available might have presented production problems, but the position was simpler than the figures would suggest. One basic barrel, for example, was used for five different calibres and similar rationalisation was possible with chamber boring.

The first model variation was the Single Action Target version. The frame was altered from the standard round top with the central sighting groove to a thicker and broader 'flat top' design into which a groove was milled to secure the rear sight. A rare variant was the flat top frame with provision for a folding rear sight. This type of frame was supplied on long barrel models with provision for a shoulder stock. The frame was also modified for short barrel models supplied without the ejector, and this type of frame was equally used on the rare ejector-less target models. Triggers were standard except for the Single Action Target Models where a checkered trigger was sometimes fitted. The increased interest in target shooting prompted the introduction of a special version of the Single Action in 1894, which was known, for obvious reasons, as the Bisley Model.

The Bisley was similar to the Single Action in mechanical essentials. The rear of the frame was slightly deeper and the hammer spur lower to allow easier and faster cocking without shifting the grip on the butt. Internally, the mainspring was provided with a link swivel connection to the hammer, and the hammer and mainspring (which had a bifurcated end) could not be interchanged with the Single Action components where the mainspring was flat-ended and there was a central groove for the roller bearing on the hammer. The alteration in the grip straps and stock are immediately apparent as is the larger trigger guard. The screws securing the back strap to the frame entered underneath the strap, and two piece stocks had therefore to be employed as, otherwise, these screws could not be removed.

On the Bisley Model the trigger was $\frac{5}{16}$" wide offering a much broader surface to the trigger finger than the standard trigger which was only half the width, and the Bisley trigger was also checkered.

During its brief life—it was discontinued in 1912—the Bisley gained many successes in competitive shooting and was highly thought of in Britain. Sights fitted to both the SAA and the Bisley varied. The SAA employed the sighting groove and a fixed blade foresight. Variations of the blade were available, and the type fitted to the lower of the two Single Action Army pistols illustrated (see page 230) was known as the Winans type after the noted revolver shot who first introduced it. Whether or not it was a factory variant is not known, but it seems likely.

The foresight on the target models of the SAA and the Bisley was interchangeable and was attached by a screw to a slotted square based sight block. The normal type was a simple blade (as on the .455 Bisley illustrated), but an alternative was the Paine bead sight (as on the Colt SAA 'flat top' illustrated), named after Ira Paine. Other sights were also fitted, but this is likely to have been done by the owner of the pistol rather than by the factory.

Various markings were carried on both the SAA and the Bisley. The Colt legend appeared on the top of the barrel and, on revolvers intended

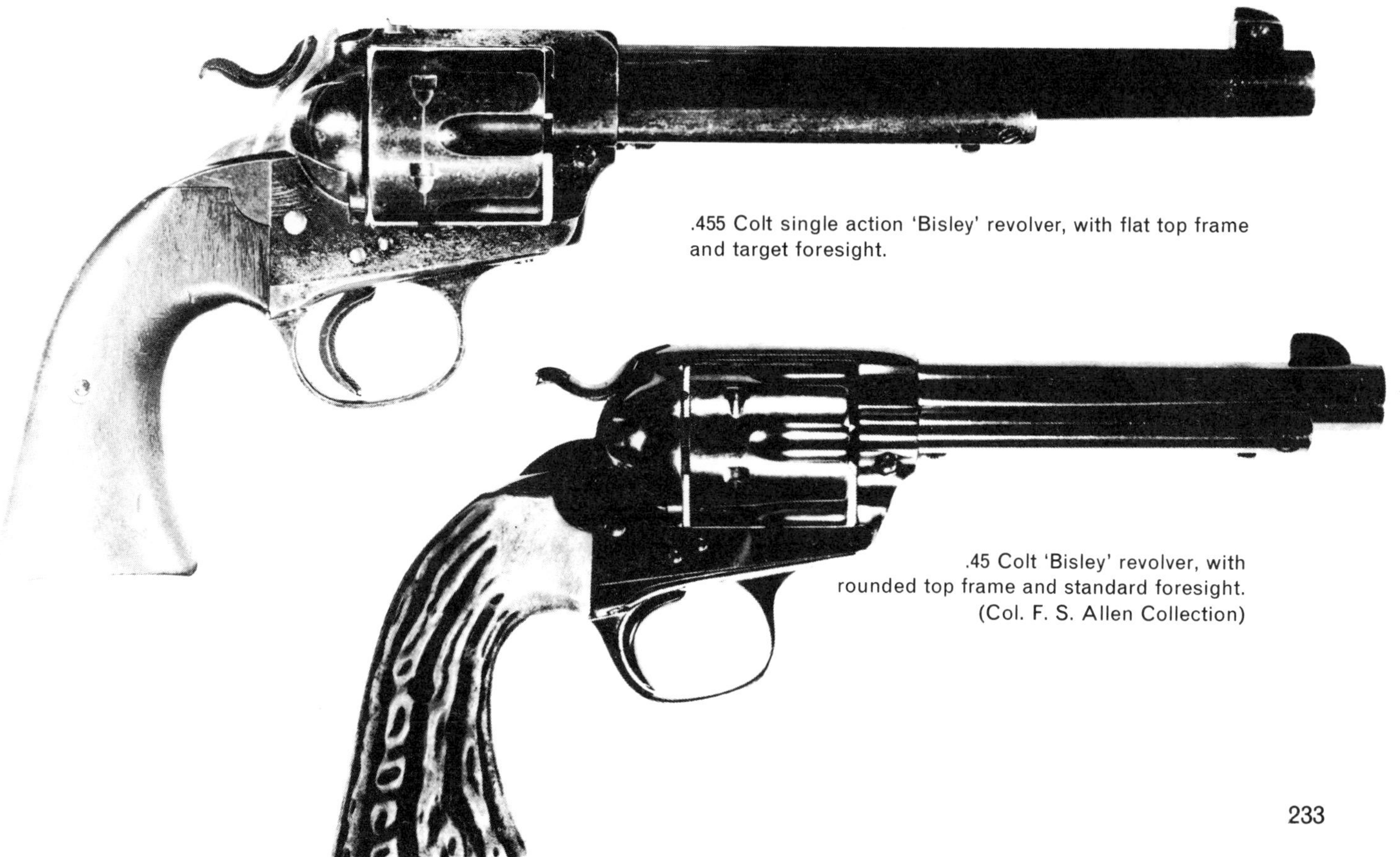

.455 Colt single action 'Bisley' revolver, with flat top frame and target foresight.

.45 Colt 'Bisley' revolver, with rounded top frame and standard foresight. (Col. F. S. Allen Collection)

The .45 Colt SAA of today.

A comparison of the Colt 'Flat Top' and the Colt 'Bisley', the distinctive differences lying in the lower back strap of the 'Bisley' and its larger guard and lower hammer spur.

for the British market, 'Depot 14, Pall Mall London' was added to the usual Hartford address. Calibre markings were stamped on the left hand side of the barrel at the breech end and, on the early models, the calibre designation appeared on the trigger guard: '.450 B' for .450 Boxer. Finish on the standard model was all blue except for the frame, loading gate and hammer. Target models were blued all over. Nickel or silver plating could be had from the factory at extra cost.

Production of the Single Action Army ceased in 1941. At the end of World War Two, the price of a second-hand SAA began to rise, and the demand increased to such an extent that it became profitable to manufacture replicas.

Sturm Ruger introduced their .22 'Single Six' in 1953 and followed it with the .357 Magnum in 1955. Although these were single action revolvers shaped in the classic mould of the Colt SAA, they were not, however, replicas.

In 1955, by popular demand, Colt's recommenced manufacture of the Single Action Army Model and, to indicate post war manufacture, the serial numbers of post-1955 SAA Colts have the letters SA following the serial number.

Since 1955 several variants of the basic model have either been introduced, or, as with the Sheriff's Model, re-introduced. The .45 Colt Sheriff's Model was offered again in 1961. A 3″ barrel without ejector rod was fitted and these guns were made by Colt's under contract with the Centennial Arms Corporation of Chicago.

In 1958 Colt's re-introduced their famous Buntline Special in .45 Colt calibre only. The history of the original Buntline Special started in 1876 when Colt's produced a special Single Action for the Philadelphia Centennial Exhibition called 'Colt's pistol with carbine barrel and attachable stock'. The standard SAA could be had with a barrel up to $7\frac{1}{2}$″ in length; the special long barrel models had 10″ and 16″ barrels but, according to the factory records, only thirty of these were made between 1876 and 1884. The name Buntline, according to tradition, is due to the interest shown in these 'specials' by Edward Z. C. Judson who wrote some of the earliest 'Western' fiction. Judson's pen name was Ned Buntline, and the story goes that he saw these pistols at the Exposition, bought five at the then price of $26 each, and then presented them to five famous Western Frontier Marshalls: Wyatt Earp, Neal Brown, Charley Bassett, Bat Masterson and Bill Tilghman. The presentation is supposed to have taken place in Dodge City, Kansas, and this is the reason why these revolvers bear their 'collectors' name, 'Buntline Specials'. Colt's have since capitalised on this legend and currently market four 'Buntline Specials', but as the addition of a shoulder stock would violate the US Federal Firearm Act, the modern Buntlines have no provision for fitting one. The New Frontier Buntline Special is built on the New Frontier Single Action Army frame, this model having been first introduced in 1963 with a $5\frac{1}{2}''$ barrel and Colt Accro click adjustable rear sight. The rear sight is recessed into the top of a 'flat top' frame and a Baughman quick draw pattern ramp foresight is provided. Calibres of the New Frontier available are .357 Magnum (also .38 S & W Special), .44 Special and .45 Colt. The Buntline version has a $12''$ barrel and is available in .45 Colt only.

The standard Buntline Special is a $12''$ barrel variant of the current Single Action Army and is again available in .45 Colt only. The Single Action Army can be had in $4\frac{3}{4}''$, $5\frac{1}{2}''$ and $7\frac{1}{2}''$ barrel lengths and in .357 Magnum, .44 Special and .45 Colt.

In 1958 Colt introduced a .22 rim-fire version of the SAA known as the Colt Frontier Scout. The new gun is about four-fifths the size of the SAA, has a barrel length of $4\frac{3}{4}''$ and weighs 1 lb. 7 ozs. empty. The frame of the Frontier Scout is of aluminium alloy; the barrel, cylinder and the remainder of the working parts are of steel. A cylinder gate of standard SAA design is fitted but the ejector rod housing is a plain round tube instead of being specially shaped, as in the original design, to fit against the side of the barrel. Made in one piece, the grip frame of the Frontier Scout differs from the original which was made in two pieces joined together by a screw. The mainspring is pressed into a recess in the grip frame instead of being fastened by a screw, and the usual roller on the hammer which serves to reduce friction has been eliminated. Various other small detail changes have been made to ease manufacture, reduce costs and, in certain respects, to improve durability. All the screws employed have nylon washers under the heads to avoid loosening—a frequent source of annoyance with the original models. (This trouble can be overcome on the original by coating the screw threads with varnish or lacquer, which does not hinder removal and does help to prevent the screws slackening off in service.)

.22 Colt 'Frontier Scout'. (Colt)

This model became available as the Buntline Scout in 1959. The original Frontier Scout was finished in blue with a white aluminium frame. Later an all blue version was offered, and this is also the finish of the Buntline Scout. Calibre is again .22 long rifle and the barrel length is $9\frac{1}{2}''$ as against the $4\frac{3}{4}''$ of the Frontier Scout. In 1959 the Buntline Scout was offered in .22 Winchester

Magnum rim-fire, and subsequently the three basic Frontier Scout Models, Q.1 (Blue), K.3 (Nickel) heavy frame and K.1 (Blue) heavy frame could be had in .22 long rifle, .22 Magnum rim-fire, or with an extra interchangeable cylinder so that both calibres could be fired in the same gun.

The collector of the future will be even more confused than the collector of today since, in addition to the present three short barrel versions and the two Buntline long barrel versions, several 'commemorative models' of the Frontier Scout have been made by Colt's. The first of these was the gold plated 'Pony Express Frontier Scout'. Intended for the 'collectors' market, the production of this special model was limited to 1,000 copies numbered consecutively from 1 to 500 in two series. The first series had the suffix E for east, the second the suffix W for west since, at the ceremonies which took place during July 1960, five hundred riders rode in each direction between St. Joseph and Sacramento. These commemorative revolvers were supplied in a special fitted case and the barrels were stamped '1860–1 Russell, Majors and Waddell Pony Express Centennial Model 1960–61'.

In 1962 another souvenir model was marketed by Colt's through a special dealer. This .22 Frontier Scout was known as the Colt New Mexico 50th Anniversary Model and the barrel was marked '1912—New Mexico Golden Anniversary—1962'. Included in the cased outfit is a bronze commemorative medallion. Again in 1964 Colt's produced a limited number of Frontier Scouts for controlled sale by private distributor marked '1864-Nevada "Battle Born"—1964'. This souvenir firearm was based on the heavy frame Frontier Scout, but the cylinder was unfluted and simulated mother of pearl plastic stocks were fitted.

It is very likely that further commemorative models will be manufactured differing slightly from the standard range, and this practice may extend to the large centre-fire Single Action Army.

With nine current variants on the selling range, five rim-fire and four centre-fire, the 'saga of the single action' has yet to run its course and there is every possibility that in the very near future the Single Action Army will appear in a special commemorative model, the Centennial Single Action, to honour the quite remarkable achievement of one hundred years of almost continuous manufacture.

The gold plated Colt SAA model used by the artist Richard Chopping on the dust jacket for the last of Ian Fleming's 'James Bond' novels, *The Man with the Golden Gun.*

Before we leave the story of the Single Action, several aspects of its use and handling should be mentioned. Single Action Colts with serial numbers below 165,000 should be used with black powder loads only. Ten years later, in 1906, when the serial numbers had reached 288,000, Colt's guaranteed all arms as being suitable for either black powder or smokeless.

In loading the Single Action the hammer should be drawn back to the half cock position, the second 'click'. The trigger should not be touched, and the sear will then snap into the half cock safety bent. If the hammer is at full cock, it should be released by carefully lowering it; it can then be drawn back to the half cock position. With the hammer in this position, the cylinder is free to rotate for both loading and unloading, and the chambers line up with the loading gate. The factory instructions state that if the SAA is new or a sound second-hand model, it can safely be carried with all six chambers loaded. In practice, it is safer to load five chambers only since, in lowering the hammer after loading six rounds, the thumb could accidentally slip off the hammer spur. The possibility of an accidental discharge is particularly likely when placing the hammer in the first bent or safety position since the hammer has to be lowered gently almost on to the frame and then drawn slightly back to engage the safety bent. For this reason it is very useful to have an empty chamber under the hammer.

An additional factor is that, if the revolver is fully loaded and the hammer is left in the safety notch, a blow on the hammer could break the trigger sear or chip off the bent—for instance, if the full loaded revolver were allowed to drop on the floor. Under these conditions, the force might be sufficient both to cause the damage and to discharge the gun.

On second-hand SAA revolvers intended for use and not merely collector's pieces, the mechanism should be examined by a competent authority to ensure that damage has not been caused to the safety and half cock bents by the practice of slip-hammer shooting or fanning. Parts for the Single Action Army are still available and it is safer to have the revolver examined and the trigger and hammer replaced if any signs of abuse or damage can be detected, or if there is any irregularity in performance.

To dismantle the SAA, check that the revolver is unloaded. Remove the cylinder by opening the unloading gate and withdrawing the cylinder pin (retained on early models by a screw and on later models by a spring-loaded cross bolt). Draw back the hammer to half cock and push the cylinder out of the frame on the right. On revolvers fitted with one piece stocks the straps have to be removed first. Remove the back strap by unscrewing the two screws at either side of the hammer, and then the single front back strap screw at the toe of the butt. Then remove the mainspring screw and take off the trigger guard by unscrewing the three guard screws. (Remember which screws came from where, so that they can be put back in the original position when reassembling.) The bifurcated bolt and trigger spring under the frame should now be taken out, and the two screws which pass through the frame be unscrewed so that the trigger and bolt can be removed. The hammer screw should then be taken out, and the hammer with attached cylinder hand and hand spring withdrawn downwards. Assembly is accomplished in the reverse order and, as the trigger and bolt screws are of different lengths due to the taper of the frame, they must be replaced in their original positions. The cylinder has an internal bushing which can be withdrawn for cleaning and lubrication. Tighten all screws using the correct size of screwdriver and, if the revolver is to be used extensively, use a lacquer on the screw threads to prevent slackening off and possible loss.

The simple rod ejector, although today typified by the Colt Single Action Army, was first employed by that somewhat despised series of pin-fire revolvers which are identified by the name Lefaucheux, and it is regrettable that the importance of the Lefaucheux has been obscured by the enormous numbers of cheap copies with which we automatically associate the term 'pin-fire revolver'. The original version was developed by Eugene Lefaucheux, son of the famous Parisian gunmaker Casimir Lefaucheux, the man responsible for the first effective pin-fire shotgun cartridge. Eugene Lefaucheux patented the use of the pin-fire cartridge in a conventional revolver in 1854 and, following trials by the French Navy, the Lefaucheux was adopted for use in 1858. The Lefaucheux Model 1858 was a single action, six chambered pin-fire revolver, calibre 10.7 mm (.42″), with a simple rod ejector mounted on the right side of the frame. A recoil shield was used, on the right hand side of which was the loading gate, hinged at the top and provided with a spring catch at the bottom. The frame was 'open top', and the barrel group was attached to the cylinder pin. The so-called Navy Model had a rounded trigger guard and the civilian version differed in that a small spur was fitted to it.

The importance of the Lefaucheux lies in the fact that it was the first metallic cartridge handgun to be officially adopted for service use by any military power. The 1858 Model was later

Pin-fire Lefaucheux revolver manufactured and engraved in Liege.

modified and, in 1867, both variants were again adapted by the provision of a guide for the ejector rod which was brazed to the barrel. In 1873, the Model 1858 pin-fires were converted to centre-fire and modified from single to double action. Such conversions are known as Model 1858 'Transformé'. Very nearly all the Model 1858 revolvers were made by the Manufacture de St-Etienne. The Lefaucheux revolver was also adopted by Norway, Denmark and Sweden. Norway adopted an 11mm single action version for cavalry and artillery in 1864, the officer's model differing in that it had an octagonal instead of a round barrel. Also issued for officer's use were the double action versions with both round and octagonal barrels. In 1898, the Kongsberg Arms Factory modified some of the original Lefaucheux revolvers by adding a top strap which was screwed to the barrel, passed over the top of the cylinder and was attached to the standing breech. A rear sight (previously formed on the hammer nose) was fitted to this top strap. The Kongsberg factory also manufactured Lefaucheux revolvers, but apparently less than 250 were actually delivered. There is considerable doubt as to whether the Paris factory of Eugene Lefaucheux had the manufacturing capacity to produce all the weapons which bore the legend 'E. Lefaucheux Brte. S.G.D.S. à Paris' and it seems likely that much of the work was done at St. Etienne and by various gunmakers in Liege.

In the earlier Lefaucheux models, the barrel was forged as one piece with the lower part of the frame. In later versions, an extension to the barrel was attached to the frame by a screw, and there were variations in the stock shape, the 'saw handle' being particularly popular. Of all the many variants, the most bizarre were undoubtedly the twelve and twenty shot revolvers. The example illustrated on page 240 bears neither maker's name nor any proof marks, but it is very obviously a Lefaucheux and the frame has been modified by the addition of a top strap from the barrel to the standing breech. The twelve chambered cylinder was machined internally to reduce weight, and, with the rod ejector swivelling downwards in an arc, more than one empty case could be ejected without rotating the cylinder. Solid frame, rod ejector Lefaucheux revolvers were also made, and one example with an octagonal barrel and folding trigger is shown.

Another distinct class of 'revolver' associated with the pin-fire cartridge was the pin-fire pepperbox or 'self-cocking fist pistol' (coups de

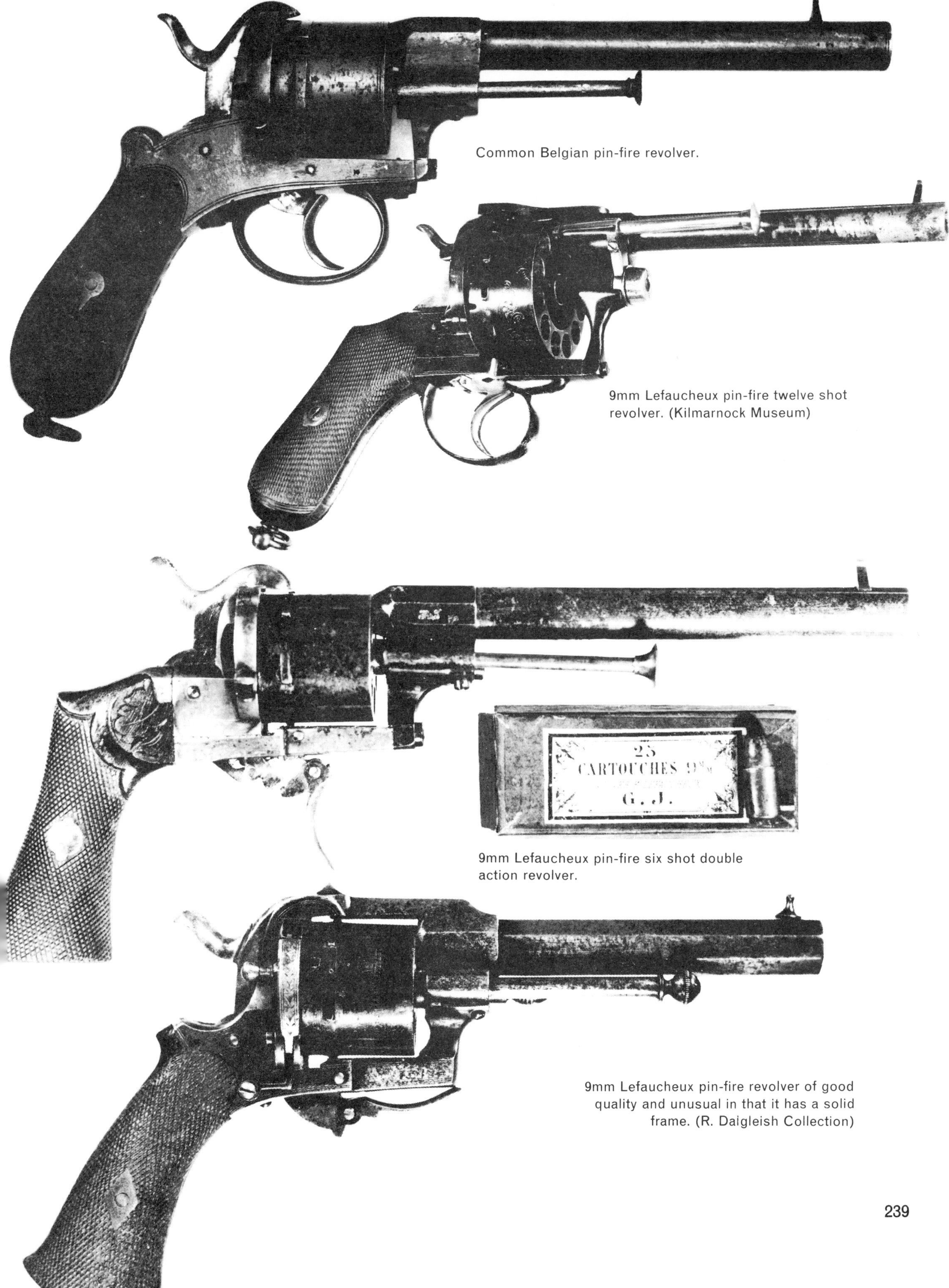

Common Belgian pin-fire revolver.

9mm Lefaucheux pin-fire twelve shot revolver. (Kilmarnock Museum)

9mm Lefaucheux pin-fire six shot double action revolver.

9mm Lefaucheux pin-fire revolver of good quality and unusual in that it has a solid frame. (R. Dalgleish Collection)

A poor quality Belgian pin-fire revolver.

7mm rim-fire cartridge pepperbox marked 'Deprez Bte.'

poing). Many of these were made with easily demountable cylinders, and the lever for unscrewing the cylinder pin can be seen on the folding trigger example marked 'Deprez Bte.'.

Last but by no means least, is the hinge frame pin-fire revolver which lacks any maker's name or mark and employs the standard rod ejector. The hinged barrel is locked by means of an eccentric cross bolt operated by an external lever.

With pistols of this period yet another method of removing the fired case can be encountered, where the ejector rod, mounted in the butt of the pistol, was unscrewed and withdrawn, and the fired cases poked out of the chambers. Although delightfully simple, this method had the disadvantage that the rod could easily be lost. A rod attached to the pistol was preferable, and this was the method used with great success on the early Smith and Wesson revolvers, the first cartridge loading revolvers to achieve widespread use in America.

In fact the Smith and Wesson No. 1 Revolver achieved a 'first' in more than one respect. It was the first American cartridge revolver and the first successful rim-fire cartridge revolver in the world. The means whereby Smith and Wesson acquired a virtual monopoly of the manufacture of metallic cartridge revolvers in America has been dealt with in a previous chapter. The first revolver that the company made was a seven shot single action .22 rim-fire with a sheath trigger and a frame hinged at the top which tipped up so that the cylinder could be removed. When this had been done, each chamber could then be placed over the ejecting rod mounted under the barrel and the fired cases pushed out, one at a time.

All the versions of the Model No. 1 had a cylinder stop in the top strap. This was in the form of a pivoted lever, the rear end raised by a tiny cam on the hammer nose. The rear sight was also formed at the rear of the cylinder stop lever. Three variants of the basic model were made. The rare Model No. 1 First Issue had a hinged hammer nose and there was a small circular inspection plate on the left side of the frame which was itself contoured. In the Model No. 1, Second Issue, an irregularly shaped side plate was fitted and the sides of the frame were flat. The original Model No. 1 was made from 1857 to 1859, and the Model No. 1 Second Issue from 1859 to 1868.

The last variant of the .22 Model No. 1 was the Third Issue which differed in having a 'bird's

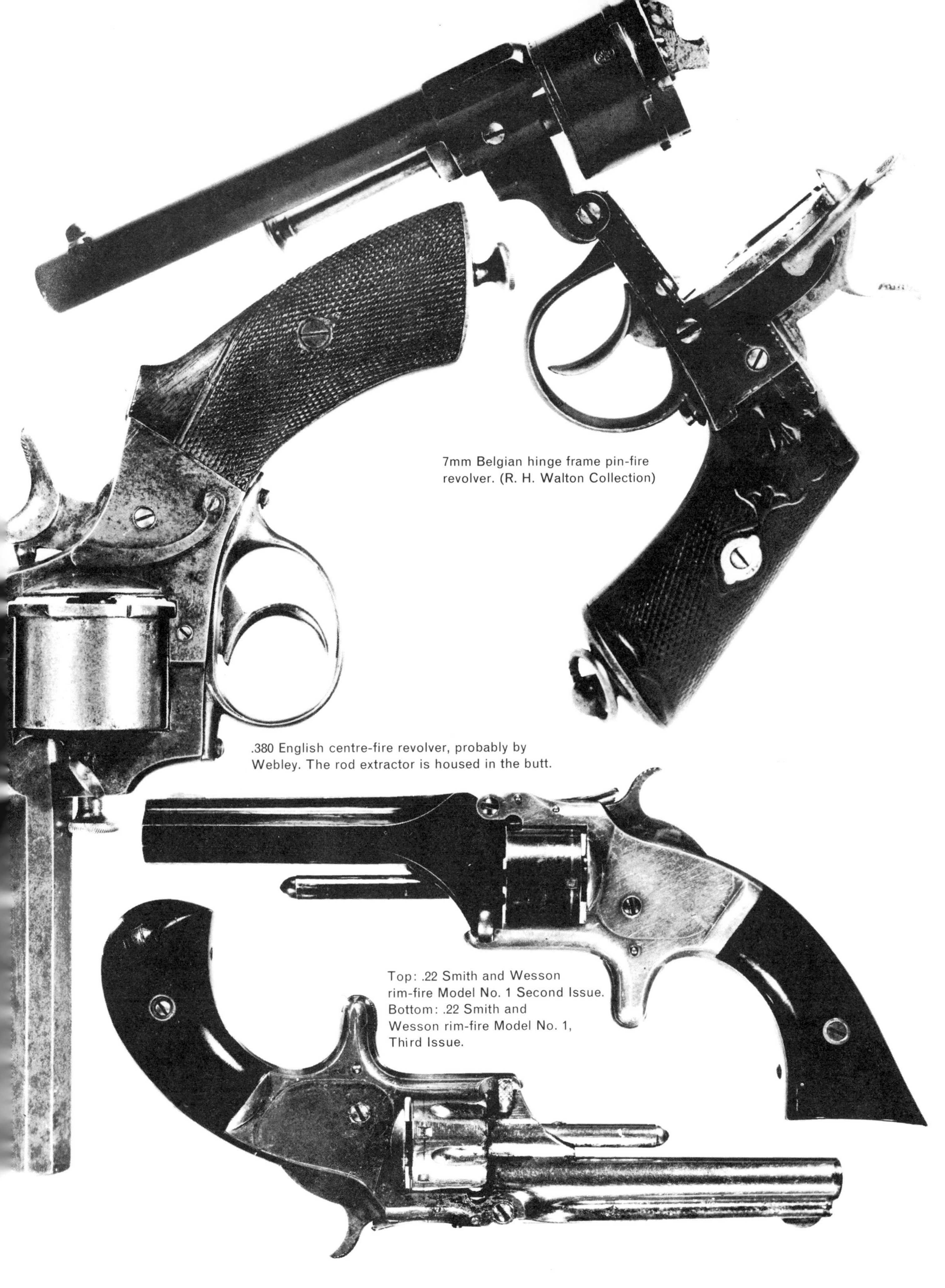

7mm Belgian hinge frame pin-fire revolver. (R. H. Walton Collection)

.380 English centre-fire revolver, probably by Webley. The rod extractor is housed in the butt.

Top: .22 Smith and Wesson rim-fire Model No. 1 Second Issue. Bottom: .22 Smith and Wesson rim-fire Model No. 1, Third Issue.

which was single action and had six chambers, closely resembled the earlier .22 rim-fire. The similar Model 1½, again .32 calibre but only five chambered, first appeared in 1865. The original Model 1½ was the only one to have the cylinder stop located in the bottom strap of the frame rather than in the top strap. Later versions had the cylinder stop in the top strap and a round butt, the final one having a rounded barrel and fluted cylinder.

The .32 calibre Models No. 2 and 1½ were widely copied, and a British-made copy of the Model No. 2 six chambered .32 rim-fire is illustrated, this example engraved with the vendor's name, 'Charles Ingram, Glasgow' on the top strap.

The year 1869 was important for Smith and Wesson since their all-important patents expired and their monopoly came to an end. The little

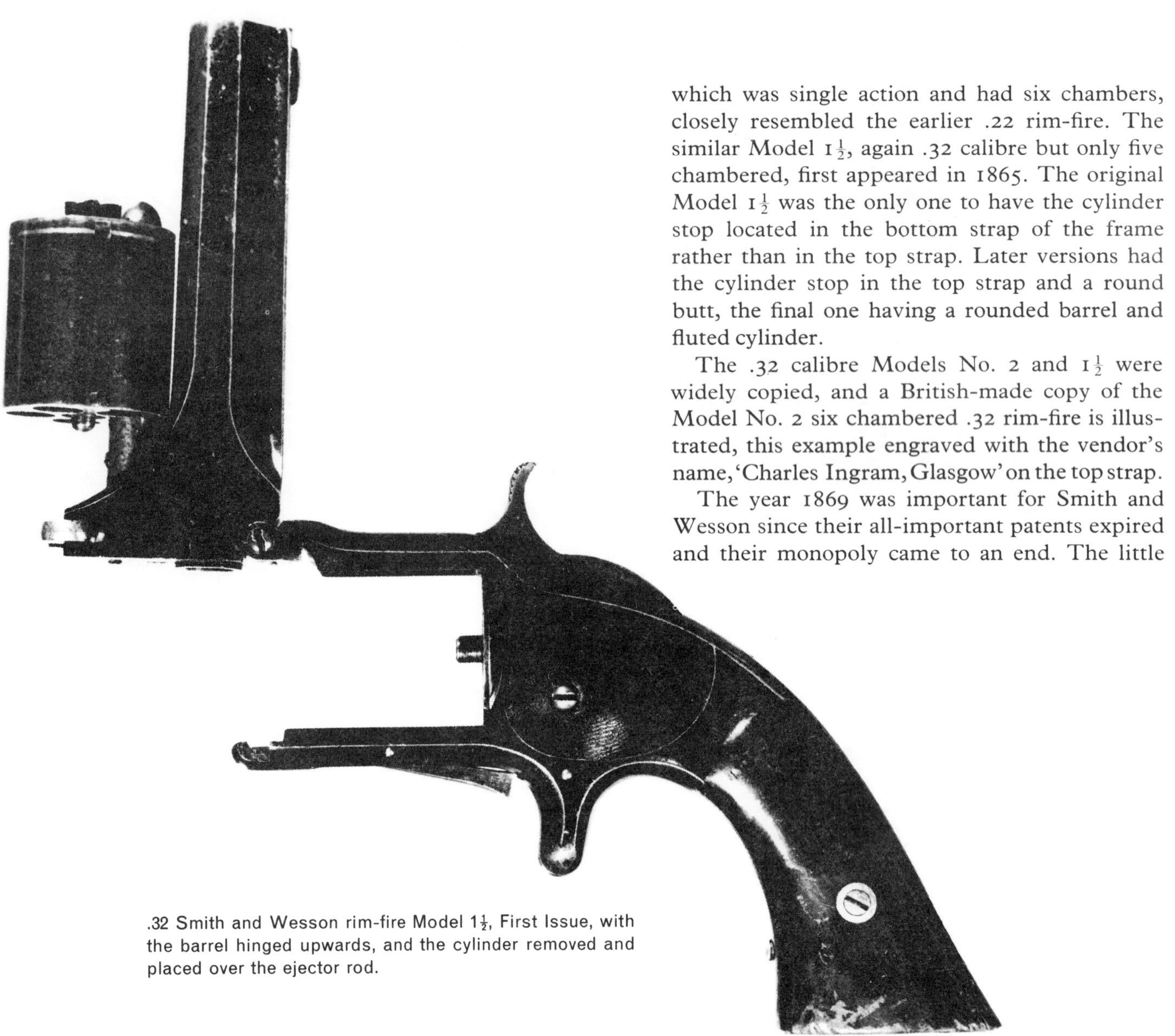

.32 Smith and Wesson rim-fire Model 1½, First Issue, with the barrel hinged upwards, and the cylinder removed and placed over the ejector rod.

head' grip, a round barrel with integral top rib and a fluted instead of a smooth cylinder. This version was made from 1868 until 1879. Apart from those revolvers already discussed which evaded the Smith and Wesson/Rollin White patents, there were others which, following a successful court case, were held to be infringements of the basic patent. Revolvers made by the Manhattan Fire Arms Co., by Moore's Patent Fire Arms Co., and by several other firms, were allowed to be sold provided they were stamped 'Made for Smith and Wesson'. Smith and Wesson also purchased revolvers from such firms to fill outstanding war orders, the manufacturers paying royalties to Smith and Wesson.

In 1861, the first of a range of .32 calibre rim-fire revolvers appeared. In design and general appearance the Smith and Wesson Model No. 2,

.22 short rim-fire revolvers had been an outstanding success in spite of their woefully inadequate stopping power and, although competition had been driven underground in America, copies had been made in Britain and Europe, notably by Webley. Smith and Wesson were alive to the inadequacies of their product and, in addition, were aware that rival manufacturers would be tooling up ready to swamp the market with imitations of their revolver once patent protection lapsed. It was vital therefore to have something new, original and preferably much superior ready to put on the market in order to retain their pre-eminent position. Two things were needed. The first was greater stopping power, which could be achieved by increasing the calibre. The second was a means of speeding up the loading, as something far quicker

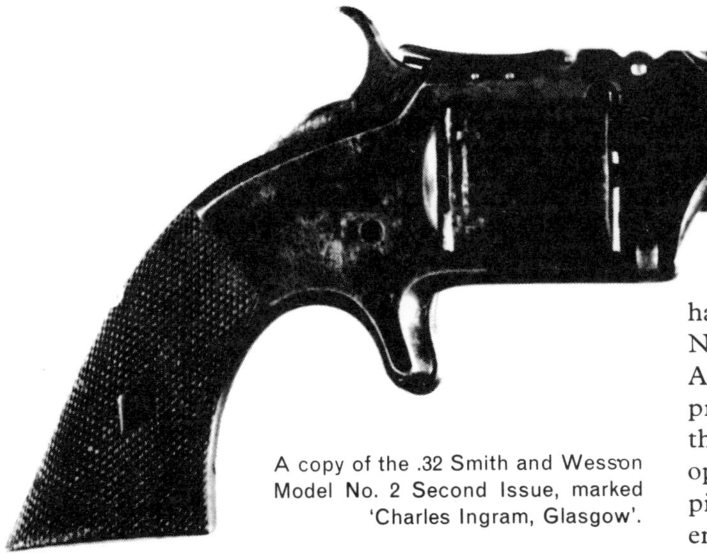

A copy of the .32 Smith and Wesson Model No. 2 Second Issue, marked 'Charles Ingram, Glasgow'.

was needed than the business of unlatching the frame, removing the cylinder and poking out each fired case.

The first requirement was met by the introduction of a new centre-fire cartridge, the .44 Smith and Wesson, later to be known as the .44 Smith and Wesson American to avoid confusion with a later improvement, the .44 Smith and Wesson Russian. The new cartridge was somewhat similar to the British .442 and was the first outside primed, reloadable brass cased revolver cartridge to be manufactured in commercial quantities in America. The first .44 S & W American cartridges were made about 1870 and they remained in production until the 1940's. As the bullet was heel seated, its diameter was the same as that of the outside of the case and it was externally lubricated. The new revolver to handle this cartridge was the Smith and Wesson No. 3, later known as the Smith and Wesson American. It differed completely from its predecessors in that the barrel was hinged at the front of the frame and tipped downwards to open. The extractor, operated by a rack and pinion mechanism, automatically ejected the six empty cases when the revolver was 'broken'. Of .44 nominal calibre the new revolver was single action and had an 8″ barrel, the overall length being 13½″, the weight 42½ ozs.

The hinged opening of the action was based on a patent taken out by W. C. Dodge in America, and protection in Britain was granted by British Patent No. 2050 of 1865. Associated with the design was C. A. King who had patented the system for simultaneous ejection of empty, fired cases. Daniel B. Wesson acquired both patents, and a later British Patent (No. 1510) was granted to Smith and Wesson in 1869. One of the drawings filed with this application shows details of the ejector mechanism. This, as can be seen, was based on a segment of a cog wheel enclosed in the hinge joint of the frame, and this acted on a rack so that, when the action was opened, the extractor rod 'A' moved rearward to expel the cartridges. (As the system was not selective, both fired and unfired cartridges were ejected.) The rack was

.44 Smith and Wesson No. 3, First Model. (R. H. Walton Collection)

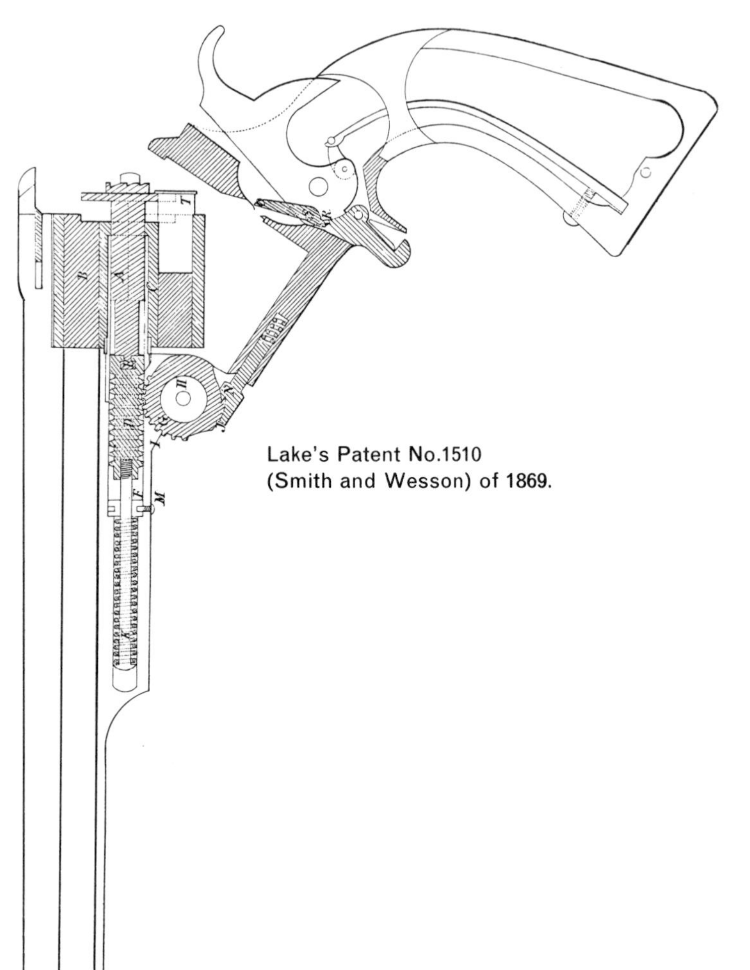

Lake's Patent No.1510 (Smith and Wesson) of 1869.

then retracted under the influence of the return spring 'K' so that the star ejector came flush with the rear face of the cylinder, and the pistol could be reloaded and the action closed. The high standards set in the manufacture have been religiously adhered to by Smith and Wesson to the present day. The American Model of 1869 was a splendid arm usually finished in the famous deep Smith and Wesson blue, but also available as a nickel plated model if desired.

A similar hinged frame revolver was that patented by Piddington on behalf of Captain Tackels (British Patent No. 2662 of 1872). This was tested in the Swiss revolver trials of 1871, but was eliminated and does not appear subsequently to have been commercially exploited.

Another variant was the breechloading double action centre-fire revolver with a tip-down barrel patented by Frederick Tolhausen on behalf of Michel Javelle of St. Etienne (British Patent No. 1362 of 1861). Speedy reloading was accomplished by replacing a discharged cylinder with a loaded one, but this early solution was overtaken by later ejection systems which obviated the need to carry spare cylinders. Javelle revolvers are comparatively rare.

Smith and Wesson had previously made unsuccessful efforts to interest the US Government in large calibre metallic cartridge revolvers, but, in 1870, Ordnance Board approval won them an order for 1,000 No. 3 revolvers. This was the

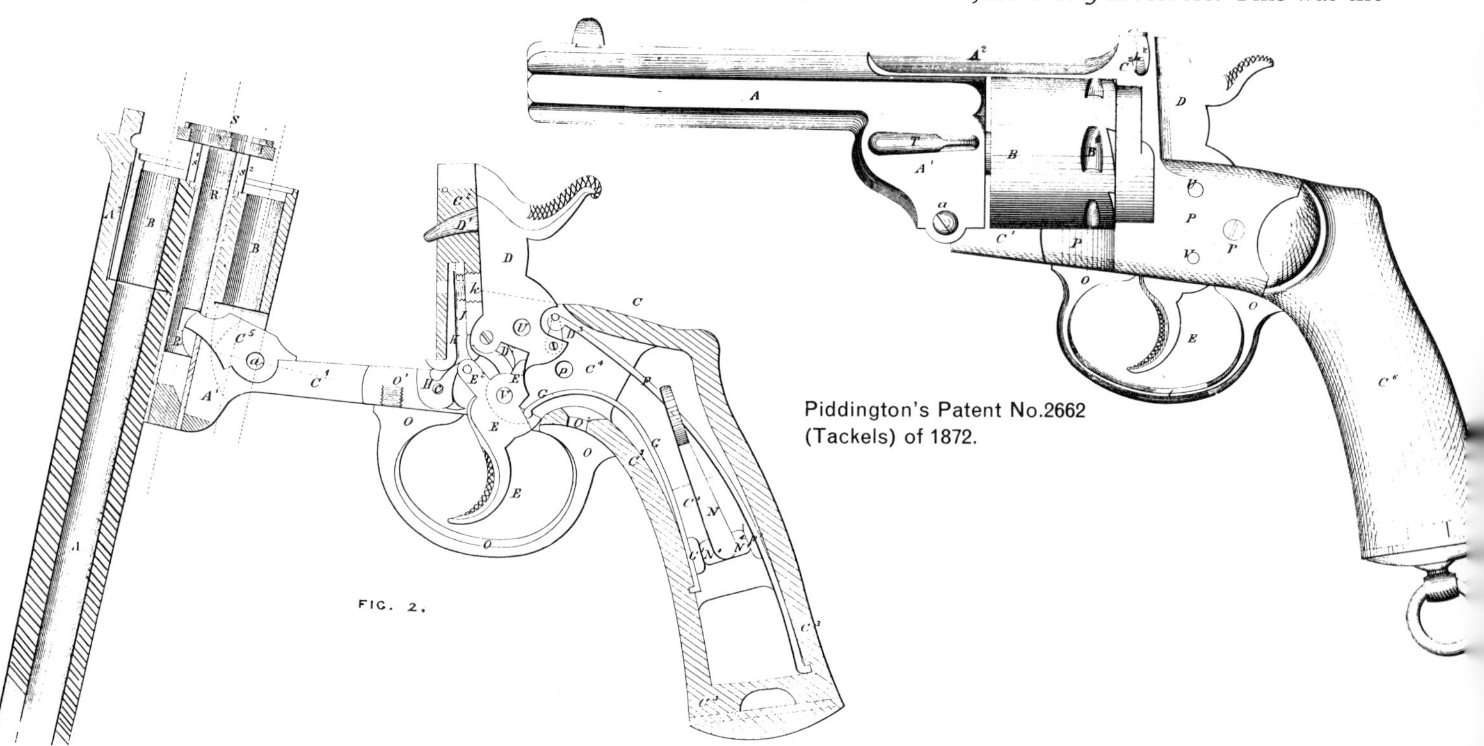

Piddington's Patent No.2662 (Tackels) of 1872.

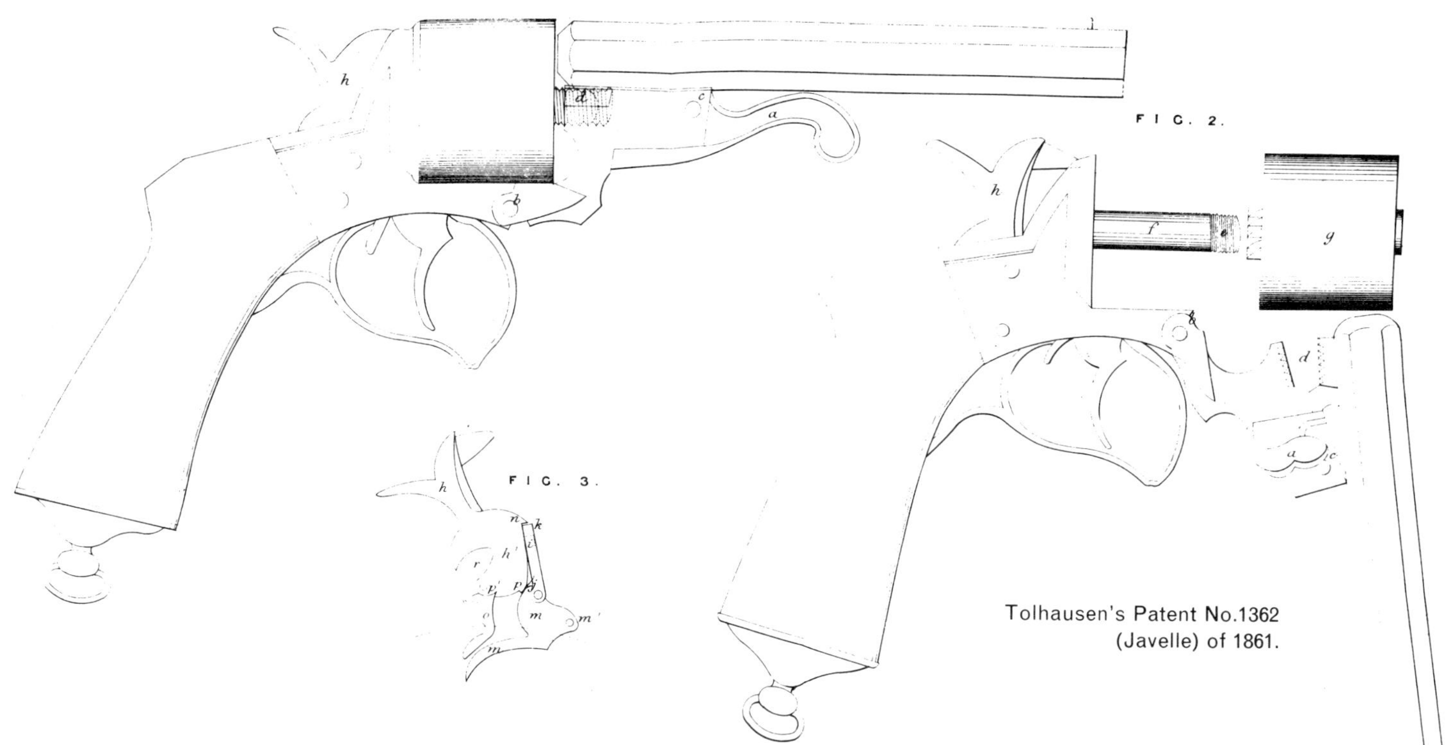

Tolhausen's Patent No.1362 (Javelle) of 1861.

sum total of revolvers ordered by the Army, since reports from the field indicated that the weapon was too frail for the arduous conditions of service use and that frequent repairs were necessary to both the lock and the ejector mechanism. The Army still stuck to the single shot pistol, the Remington Rider rolling block, but in a later series of trials the Colt Single Action was adopted.

Smith and Wesson were undaunted by this rejection for the simple reason that they had another customer interested in their wares.

In 1870 Horace Smith sold his interests in the firm to Daniel B. Wesson but, since Smith and Wesson was already a name to be reckoned with in the arms world, he allowed his name to remain in the firm's title. Shortly afterward, preliminary discussions having been completed with their important customer, Smith and Wesson signed a contract for the supply of 20,000 revolvers with Major General Alexander Gorloff, the Russian Military Attaché to the United States.

Several changes in the original No. 3 Model were requested by the Russians, the most obvious being in the shape of the frame. The original American model had a most suitable streamlined frame which was entirely satisfactory for single action shooting since it allowed the pistol to recoil in the hand and brought the hammer spur nearer to the thumb for faster cocking. The Russians asked that a hump or 'prawl' be provided on the back strap to prevent the hand of the shooter sliding up the grip, the very thing that the accomplished single action pistol shot allows to happen. With the prawl on the back strap, all that happens is that, when the gun recoils, the prawl digs into the tender web between thumb and forefinger and can result in acute discomfort. The other equally useless encumbrance was the provision of a spur on the trigger guard. Due to these additions, the Smith and Wesson Russian Military Model was quite distinctive and, on revolvers supplied on the original order, markings in Russian appeared on the barrel; the civilian version bore the legend 'Russian Model' in English. During the production life of this model, several manufacturing changes were made, but these are of little significance. By far the most important feature of the Russian Model was the cartridge employed. The .44 Smith and Wesson Russian cartridge was undoubtedly the most accurate and popular cartridge of its day. It differed from the American cartridge in that it was slightly longer in the case, averaging 0.955″ against 0.88″, and the bullet diameter was reduced to equate with the inside diameter of the case. On specimens measured by the writer, the bullet for the American cartridge averages .44″, and that for the Russian .43″. Early specimens of the Russian cartridge were outside lubricated, but the lubricant grooves were later seated inside the case.

Yet another variant of the Model No. 3 was the Turkish Model. No dates are available regarding the manufacturing run, but over 5,000 were produced. Whether the Turks bought these revolvers in time to use them against the Russians in the War of 1877 is uncertain, but their order might well have been placed as a result of the effective use of the Smith and Wesson Russian Model in the hands of the Czarist armies. The model supplied to the Ottoman Empire was

.44 Smith and Wesson No. 3, Second Model.

similar to the earlier American Model except that it was chambered for a .44 calibre rim-fire cartridge and the inscription on the barrel was in Turkish.

The basic No. 3 revolver is now recognised to have two variants or types. The 'improved' or 2nd model had a slight bulge in the frame at the trigger pin to accomodate a larger pin (an alteration requested by the Russians) and a notch or groove in the hammer overlapping a projection on the barrel catch. This feature was patented in 1863 by John C. Howe and prevented the cartridge from being fired if the barrel was not securely latched. The 2nd model dates from late 1871, but revolvers manufactured after that date may not all have incorporated these improvements.

A variation of this latch is to be found on the Schofield version of the No. 3, where the incorporated improvements were the work of Col. George W. Schofield. The basic patent was obtained in 1871, and a contract was signed for 3,000 pistols to be delivered to the US Ordnance Department. The .45 calibre Schofield can be regarded as an improved version of the No. 3 or American Model and, in place of the rather complicated rack and pinion extractor mechanism, a simple cam release was substituted. The barrel latch of the American model was strengthened and instead of being hinged to the barrel, was attached to the frame. As manufactured for the Army, the Schofield had a 7″ barrel with the usual rib along the top. Six thousand were ordered by the Army, many were sold to civilians and they were also popular with US Marshalls and the employees of Wells Fargo and the American Express Co.

The .45 Smith and Wesson cartridge was much shorter and less powerful than the .45 Colt. It must be admitted that the original .45 Colt with forty grains of black powder was perhaps too much for the ordinary average pistolman to handle and, on practical grounds, there was justification for the reduction in the load. The shorter Smith and Wesson cartridge could be used in the Colt SAA and was also known as the .45 Colt Government. The .45 Colt, with its case length of 1.27″, could not, however, be used in the Smith and Wesson Schofield, the cartridge case length of which averaged 1.110″. Interchangeability was one way only and the .45 Smith and Wesson cartridge first made in 1875 was discontinued in 1939.

As will have been only too apparent, the terminology of the various Smith and Wesson 'vintage' revolvers is somewhat complicated, and matters get worse instead of better with the proliferation of variants and improvements of the Model No. 3. The most important of these was the single action Model No. 3 New Model which, introduced in 1879, was chambered for the .44 Russian, the .44 Russian gallery or target load and the British .450.

In the hands of such outstanding pistol shots as Ira Anson Paine and the Bennetts, W. W. and his younger brother Fred, the Model No. 3 New Model achieved scores that had only been previously possible with out and out target pistols such as the single shot Stevens 'Lord Model'. In Britain, the American revolver expert Walter Winans swept the board with his Smith and Wesson, and the activities of such gentlemen demonstrated without doubt the accuracy potential of the revolver in the hands of men who had spent the necessary time in training. In both Britain and America competitive shooting was, in the 1880's, a matter for the revolver and not the specialised target pistol, and only in the last few years has the revolver been seen less and less on the target ranges, being displaced first of all by the .22 automatic and the single shot

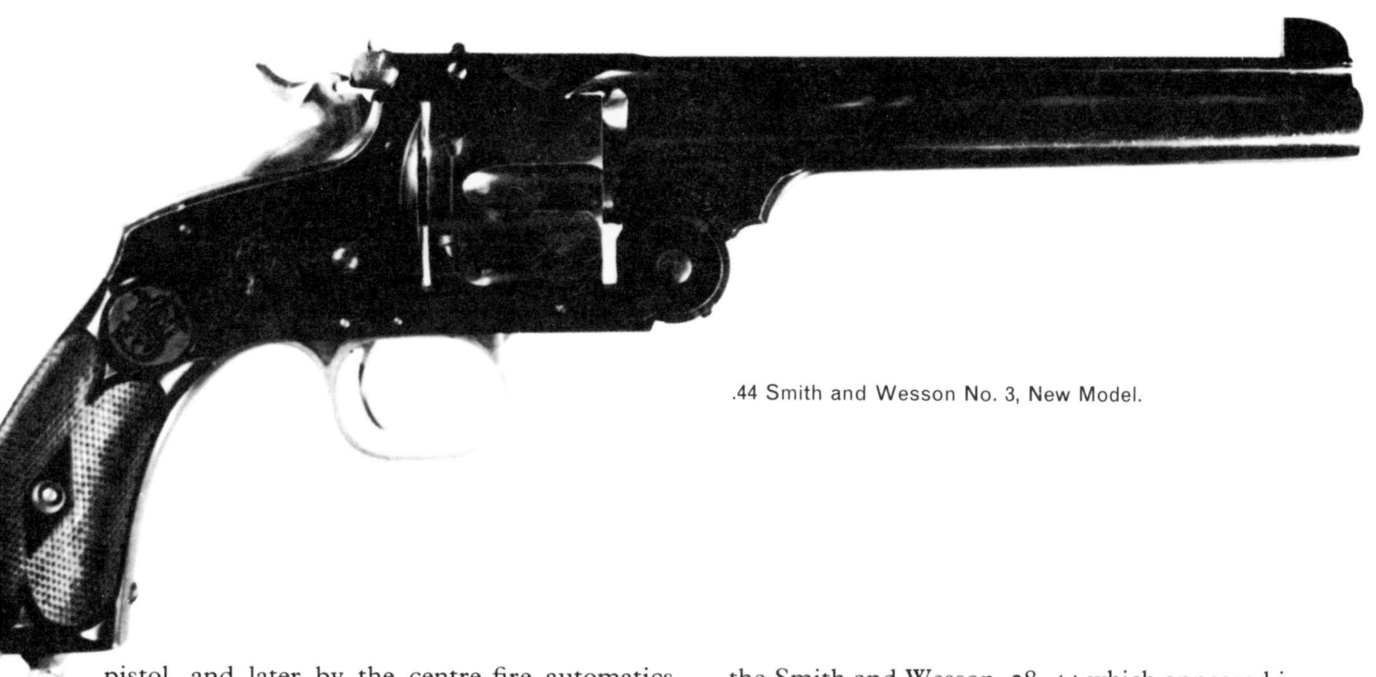

.44 Smith and Wesson No. 3, New Model.

pistol, and later by the centre-fire automatics.

Smith and Wesson were alive to the publicity that these revolver matches aroused and the No. 3, chambered for the .44/40 Winchester cartridge, appeared as the Frontier Model. It was also chambered for the .32–44 and the .38–44 Smith and Wesson. These cartridges must not be confused with the .38–40 Winchester centre-fire introduced in 1870 for the Winchester rifle and also used in both the Colt Single Action and the Smith and Wesson No. 3. The .38–40 WCF is, in fact, about .40 calibre but the –40 in the designation is to indicate the original black powder charge. The .32–44 and .38–44 S & W were special target cartridges developed for the No. 3 single action revolver, and the –44 refers to the frame size of the revolver and not to either calibre or powder charge. The case length was the same as that of the cylinder and the bullets were seated entirely within the case, being supported by the case and cylinder until the front of the bullet entered the rifling. The .38–44 was designed and built by Smith and Wesson and the Union Metallic Cartridge Co. to the order of Ira Paine in 1886. Shortly afterwards F. E. Bennett ordered the first .32–44. Two loadings were available, the lighter load with round ball intended for indoor 'gallery' shooting.

Smith and Wesson's advertisement of the period stated that 'the .32–44 and the .38–44, in the Russian Army Model frame, are the chosen arm of marksmen desiring a lighter charge and an almost imperceptible recoil'. 'The Russian Model .44, .32–44 and .38–44 are fitted with rear elevating sights and wind gauge when desired'.[1] The original .38–44 must not be confused with the Smith and Wesson .38–44 which appeared in 1931, this being a special cartridge loaded by Remington for use in .38 calibre revolvers built on the .44 calibre frame. The designation .38–44 was dropped after a few years probably because of the risk of confusion.

Not content with the successes achieved on the target ranges, Smith and Wesson introduced a new pocket model which was placed on the market in time for the Philadelphia Centennial Exhibition of 1876. This was known as the .38 Model No. 2 but, mainly because of the confusion with earlier models, collectors of today refer to this revolver as the 'Baby Russian'. Both the First and Second Models were five chambered single action revolvers with sheath triggers, and the Second Model embodied changes based on the patents obtained by Daniel B. Wesson and James Henry Bullard in 1877 which eliminated the longer housing under the barrel. Without doubt the most interesting feature of the new pocket model was the cartridge, the .38 Smith and Wesson, which became almost the standard cartridge for pocket pistols in America and was widely used throughout the rest of the world. This cartridge was also adopted by Britain as the .380/200 for military use—the '200' indicating the bullet weight, the loading being equivalent to the .38 S & W Super Police cartridge. A year later a .32 calibre version of this revolver was introduced which employed the new .32 Smith and Wesson cartridge. The New Model 1½ replaced the old rim-fire .32, and the new centre-fire cartridge rapidly ousted

(1) In A. C. Gould's *Modern American Pistols and Revolvers* (Boston, 1894).

A copy of the .32 Smith and Wesson Safety Hammerless by Maltby, Henley and Co., New York.

A Spanish copy of a .38 Smith and Wesson by Fa de Trocaola Aranzabal y Cia, Eibar.

the .320 European pocket pistol cartridge.

In 1880 a double action .38 appeared, and its five versions are very confusing for the collector of today. Externally similar to the single action top break models, the double action version had a bow-shaped trigger guard instead of the sheath trigger of the single action, and the mechanism permitted both thumb cocking and trigger action. The variations in design were restricted to the contour of the side plate and the cylinder locking bolt. A .32 calibre version also appeared in 1880 and, in 1881, a .44 calibre which contemporary literature refers to as the .44 Navy.

This series of double action simultaneous ejection revolvers were amongst the most successful ever marketed. The principle features were copied in America, Belgium, Germany and Spain and, as has already been mentioned, the .32 and .38 Smith and Wesson cartridges became standard for this size of weapon. Many of these copies bore no proof marks and, in order to avoid legal action, the 'maker's name' was altered. In one case the legend on the barrel reads 'Smill and Welson, Sprangeeld, Mus. E.U.A.' The patent dates were similarly garbled. A .38 copy where the manufacturer has signed his name is illustrated, the maker being Fa. de Trocaola Aranzabal y Cia, Eibar (Spain).

When the Smith and Wesson Safety Hammerless revolver was announced in 1887, the press referred to a 'new departure' in revolver design. This phrase apparently appealed to Smith and Wesson for it was subsequently used as a model designation. The Safety Hammerless was not, however, unique, for it was not the first hammerless revolver, nor indeed the first self-cocking or trigger action revolver. Both the top break, hinged frame features and the simultaneous ejection were already well tried, and the only new departure was the incorporation of a butt safety device which prevented cocking and firing until the safety lever had been depressed. The safety grip was in the back strap and, when depressed by the normal grip on the pistol prior to firing, the top of the grip, which was pivoted at the bottom, moved inwards to depress a pivoted latch out of the way of the internal hammer. With the grip safety not engaged, the latch projected from the wall of the frame and prevented the hammer from being cocked. In addition to this feature, Smith and Wesson emphasised the heavy trigger pull and stressed that this made it difficult for children to fire the pistol. Made in both .32 and .38 Smith and Wesson calibres the New Departure, Safety

Hammerless was offered in either blue or nickel finish and a variety of barrel lengths. Five variants or models of the .38 were made and two models of the .32. The Safety Hammerless was in production from 1887 until 1940, and both American and European copies can again be encountered. The example illustrated is a .32 'hammerless' revolver marked 'Maltby, Henley & Co., New York'. The safety hammerless was not, however, copied to the same extent as the standard double action top-break series.

During the period under review, Smith and Wesson also manufactured a .32 calibre revolving 'rifle', which was really nothing more than a modified No. 3 Russian revolver with barrel lengths of 16″, 18″ or 20″. The butt was slotted and provided with a detachable wooden stock, and the frame was modified for the attachment of a hard rubber fore-end. The cartridge was specially developed with 17 grains of powder and a bullet weighing 100 grains. This cartridge could be used in the .32–44 No. 3 revolver already mentioned and was relatively popular until Winchester appeared with their .32–20 WCF cartridge. The Smith and Wesson 'rifle' was not a success. The old story that 'a shoulder stock converts a good pistol into an indifferent carbine' still held good and less than a thousand 'rifles' were manufactured in a five year production run which ended in 1885. An added cause of annoyance with revolving rifles in general is the gas leak between the cylinder and barrel; if the left hand supports the rifle by holding the fore-end, this can be unpleasant, and the fact that the gas leak on a rifle is very much closer to the face than with a one hand gun only makes matters worse.

Smith and Wesson had considerably more success with their next venture. In 1891 they decided to improve the single action .38. The sheath trigger was replaced by a bow guard and a rebounding lock was introduced. This was patented by Wesson and Bullard, US Patent No. 198,228 of 18 December 1877, and was first introduced on the single action .32 model. Half-cocking to free the cylinder was no longer necessary and, with a six inch barrel, the Model 1891, as it was known, was an excellent target revolver using the .38 S & W cartridge. From the basic frame of the Model 1891 was then developed a highly successful single shot target pistol. The first of these single shot pistols were of .38 calibre, but later they were also made in .32. Since the original grips were rather on the small side for target shooting, special oversize interchangeable

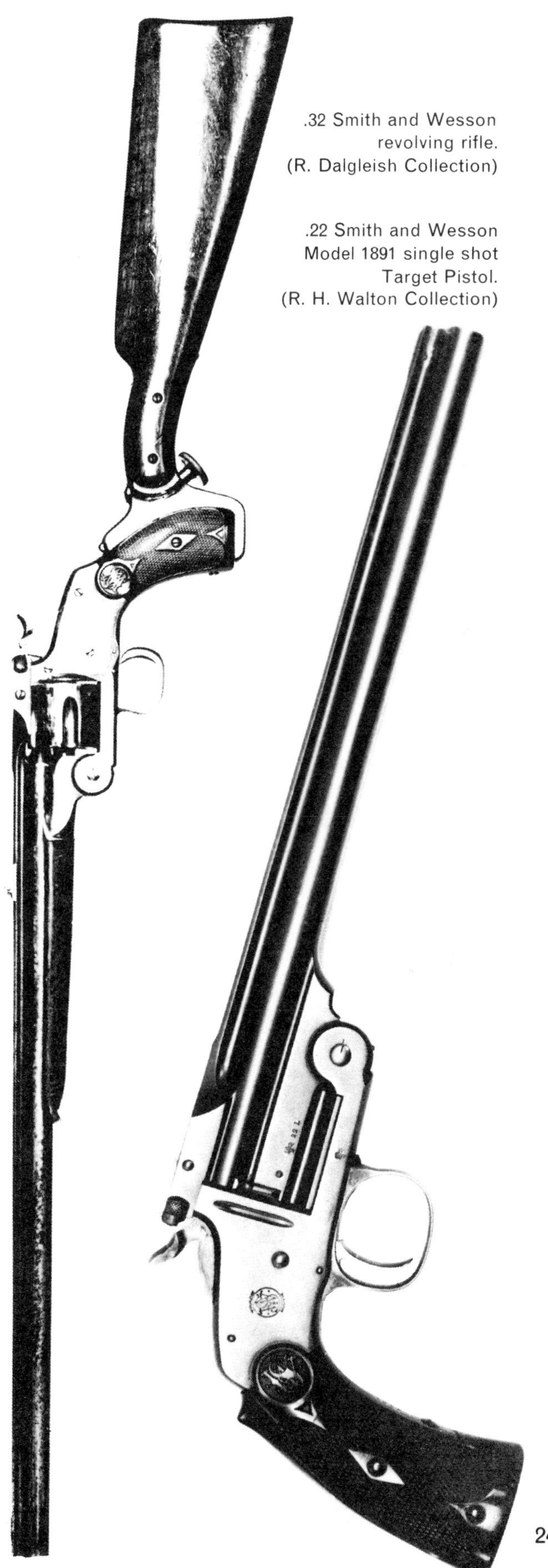

.32 Smith and Wesson revolving rifle. (R. Dalgleish Collection)

.22 Smith and Wesson Model 1891 single shot Target Pistol. (R. H. Walton Collection)

hard rubber grips were introduced. In 1893 the single shot pistol was also available in .22 calibre and, with the right accessories, both a handy pocket revolver and an excellent single shot target pistol could be had for minimum expense.

Variations on the basic theme were produced until 1909 when the 'Perfected' target pistol, adapted from the later double action model revolver, was introduced. These special target single shot pistols became very popular and again illustrate the theme of 'interchangeable manufacture' since, by employing the same basic components, an entire range of models could be manufactured for specialist purposes with a minimum of disturbance to production and a minimum capital outlay on machine tools and tooling.

In March 1895 Smith and Wesson introduced an entirely new revolver which abandoned the hinged frame upon which much of their success had been based. Successive models were introduced on the new system in which the cylinder was mounted on a crane or yoke and swung out to the left for loading and unloading. The hinged frame principle soon ceased to be the Smith and Wesson trademark, and before long only low powered pocket revolvers were made on this system in America, as, for example, the Iver Johnson, the Hopkins and Allen and the Harrington and Richardson.

The Smith and Wesson system was without doubt the basis of one of the more successful types of revolver, and hinged frame simultaneous revolvers directly inspired by the original have been manufactured in countless numbers, particularly in pocket size and in all qualities from the utterly atrocious to the barely acceptable. Many bear spurious markings, others 'for Smith and Wesson ctg' with the 'for' and the abbreviation for cartridge so small that the casual purchaser sees only the name Smith and Wesson.

Military use of the Smith and Wesson No. 3 has been discussed. One other major power, Japan, adopted a 9 mm revolver which employed the basic Smith and Wesson ejection system, but the Japanese Model 26 (1893), issued as a cavalry pistol, was trigger action only, the hammer lacking a spur for thumb cocking. The lock work was European rather than American in design, the quick dismounting with a hinged side plate owing something to Nagant, the lock and frame construction similar to the Austrian Gasser.

The disadvantage of the Smith and Wesson system was the inadequacy of the simple barrel latch, an inadequacy overcome in other hinged frame actions such as the Webley. In addition, alternative methods of simultaneous ejection were developed, and these will be discussed in the next chapter. As far as the European versions are concerned, the subject is complicated by inventions and improvements to the lockwork which, for the sake of continuity, will be treated as they arise.

Notes to Chapter Nine

Of particular value to those interested in weapons of the period covered in this chapter is a recent book, *The Revolver* 1865-1888 by A. W. F. Taylerson (London, 1966). A detailed study of Webley pistols and revolvers is contained in *The Webley Story* by William C. Dowell (Leeds, 1952) and equal coverage of Colt weapons is given in *Colt Firearms* by James E. Serven (5th edition, Santa Ana, 1964). Remington cartridge revolvers are mentioned in *Remington Handguns* by C. L. and C. R. Karr, (3rd edition, Harrisburg, 1956) and reference should also be made to *Smith and Wesson Hand Guns* by R. C. McHenry and W. F. Roper (Harrisburg, 1958) and to *Smith and Wesson Revolvers* by John E. Parsons (New York, 1957).

The Peacemaker and its Rivals by John E. Parsons (New York, 1950) can be recommended for the Colt collector.

Interesting contemporary mention is made of revolvers in *The Modern Sportsman's Gun and Rifle Vol. II* by J. H. Walsh (London, 1884) and also in *The Gun and its Development* by W. W. Greener (London, 1910), where the ninth is generally regarded to be the best edition.

Chapter Ten
Simultaneous Extraction Revolver Systems

By the end of the nineteenth century the design of the revolver had become standardised and several recognisable 'national' types had emerged. In America the market was dominated by the solid frame 'swing out' cylinder designs of Colt and Smith and Wesson, except where earlier designs were still used to satisfy the tremendous demand for cheap, simple pocket revolvers.

Britain, losing her revolver manufacturers one by one, relied entirely on the hinged frame Webley which, with its simultaneous ejection and strong barrel latch, was deservedly successful in both the military and civilian spheres. The gradual demise of the British revolver industry resulted in an increasing dependence on foreign weapons, particularly American, in time of war.

In Europe, several revolver designs emerged, but the main concern lay in improvements to the lock work and in providing facilities for quick and easy dismounting. Simultaneous ejection systems—with one notable exception, the Galand—did not become widely adopted, at least for military weapons. Interest was centred around solid frame rod ejection revolvers of the Chamelot-Delvigne type, improved and modified by Nagant, Schmidt and Gasser. The adoption of the automatic pistol for military use resulted in the stagnation of revolver design, civilian pocket and self-defence revolvers being based on successful British and American designs such as the Webley RIC and Bulldog, and the Smith and Wesson. Conversions and copies of European military revolvers were also made in tremendous numbers both for domestic use and for export to many of the markets formerly served by British and American manufacturers.

5.75mm Velodog folding trigger revolvers from a WUM catalogue of about 1930.

In the period between the First and Second World Wars the large continental merchanting houses offered cheap copies of the Webley Bulldog and Webley RIC revolvers, a wide range of 7.65 mm folding trigger solid frame weapons, and the Velodog revolvers in 5.75 mm calibre. In addition, there were Belgian made Nagant system seven chambered revolvers in 8 mm Lebel, 7.62 mm Nagant and .32–20 WCF. These were available together with copies of the hinged frame Smith and Wesson pocket models mainly in .32 and .38 calibre, Spanish copies of the 'swing out cylinder' Smith and Wesson Military and Police Model, and similar, widely advertised copies, made by the Belgian firm of Pieper and bearing the trade name 'Bayard'. Some of these copies sold for as little as $6.00 whereas the original Smith and Wesson, also available in the same catalogue, would be priced at over $50.00.

To the Anglo-American three names were of importance in the design and manufacture of revolvers: Colt, Smith and Wesson, and Webley. The importance of the contribution made by European designers and inventors has largely been ignored and is in danger of being forgotten. Some of this work will be discussed as we follow the development of the revolver until, at last, the supremacy of this system of repetitive fire is challenged by the self-loading pistol.

Hinged frame revolvers had been developed in Europe and an early example was the Devisme patented by L. F. Devisme of Paris. The construction of this revolver can be seen in the drawing which accompanied Brooman's Specification No. 2990 of 30 December 1858. L. F. Devisme may have been associated with F. P. Devisme, a French gunmaker with premises at 36 Boulevard des Italiens, Paris, but actual specimens of the Devisme revolver, in either 9 mm or 12 mm centre-fire, carry Liege proof marks and manufacture may have been entirely carried on in Belgium. The Devisme was quite advanced for its day. The frame, hinged at the base of the standing breech, was locked by the lever (i) which also rotated the barrel sleeve (c) to which was attached the rod ejector (e). When the pistol was closed and locked, the rod ejector and housing lay under the barrel. Unlocking moved the ejector to a position in front of one of the chambers so that a fired case could be extracted. Loading with this system would be far quicker than through a side gate, but extraction was certainly no faster. On the basis of the distribution of serial numbers, the quantity manu-

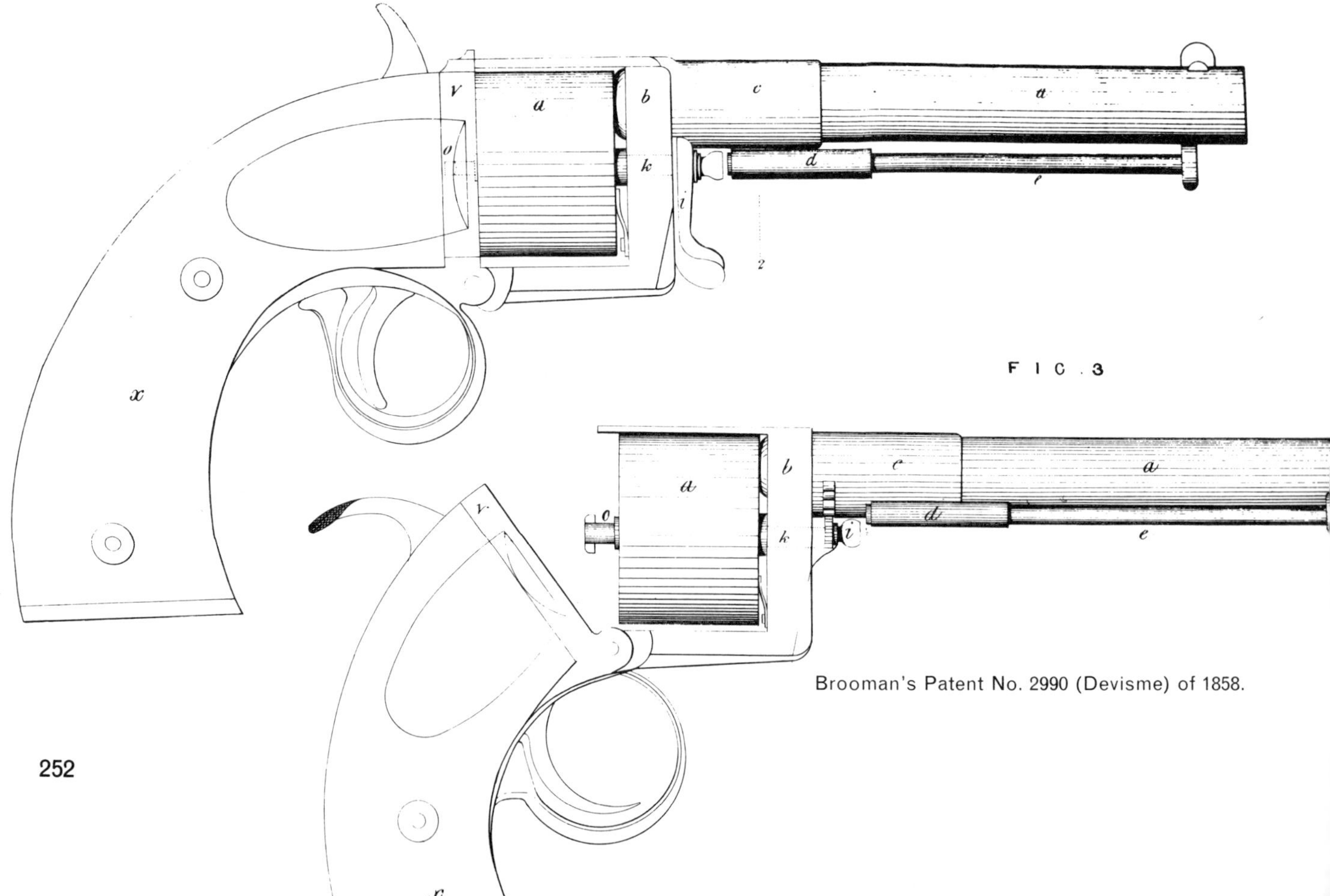

Brooman's Patent No. 2990 (Devisme) of 1858.

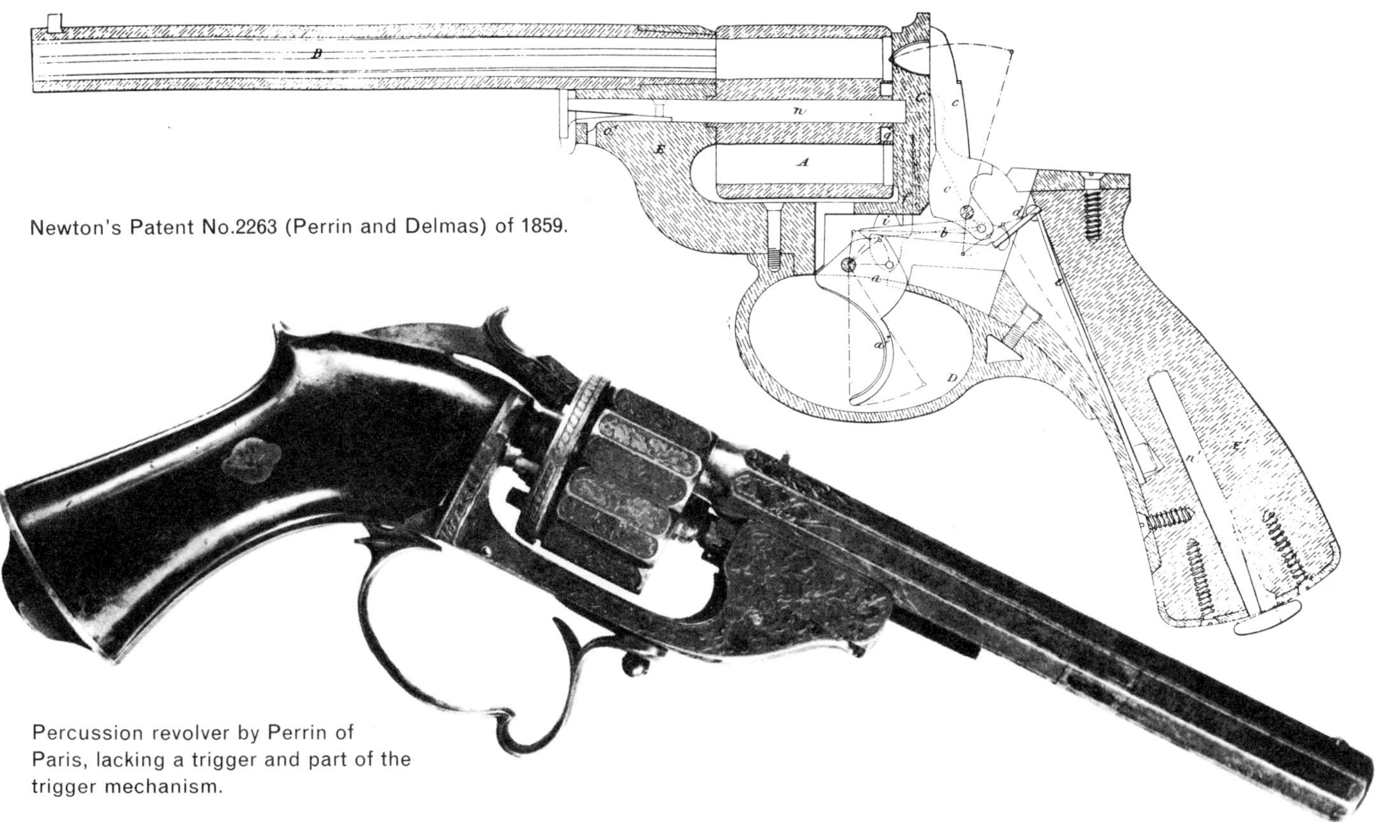

Newton's Patent No.2263 (Perrin and Delmas) of 1859.

Percussion revolver by Perrin of Paris, lacking a trigger and part of the trigger mechanism.

factured is not likely to have exceeded 1,000, and the reason for the commercial failure of the Devisme, despite its advanced ammunition and ingenious construction, is likely to have been the relatively poor locking provided by the small cross-pin (o) which entered locking slots in the standing breech.

The French gunmaker Perrin obtained protection for his ideas of cartridge revolvers and on a centre-fire cartridge with British Patent No. 2263 of 1859 which was taken out by A. V. Newton (an important British Patent Agent) and was subsequently assigned to Perrin and Delmas. The revolver illustrated in the above drawing which accompanied the specification was self-cocking, the mechanism based on that used for the pepperbox. On some models, cartridge extraction was by means of a rod ejector (the 1874 edition of Larousse states that Perrin was the inventor of this system), on others the rod was housed in the butt. The Perrin was a rather ungainly weapon, its appearance not improved by the somewhat Baroque trigger guard which was a feature of many of the models manufactured. The inventor apparently attempted to obtain military approval for his revolver, but his efforts were unsuccessful and Perrin is today better known for his 'thick rim' cartridge than for his revolvers, although some were sold during the American Civil War and apparently saw service on a rather limited scale.

In Belgium, a 'tip-up' variant was also used by A. Spirlet of Liege, and was again patented in Britain—Piddington's Patent No. 2107 of 1870. The Spirlet can be dated slightly before the British patent date and the examples extant bear a close resemblance to the patent drawing. Although it featured simultaneous extraction, the system was not automatic; the extractor was operated by a plunger under the barrel, the knob (g) of which had to be struck against a suitably hard object to operate the mechanism. This type of frame will be encountered later and was quite popular in Europe. The calibre was 11.5 mm and the trade mark 'A. Spirlet et Cie' will usually be found on the barrel.

A variant of the Spirlet, another hinged frame centre-fire revolver with simultaneous extraction, is also illustrated on page 255. This example was made by A. Fagnus and Co. of Liege. A different locking system was employed by the firm of Henrion, Dassy and Heuschen (Manufacture d'Armes HDH), also of Liege, who appears to have specialised in large capacity revolvers; the

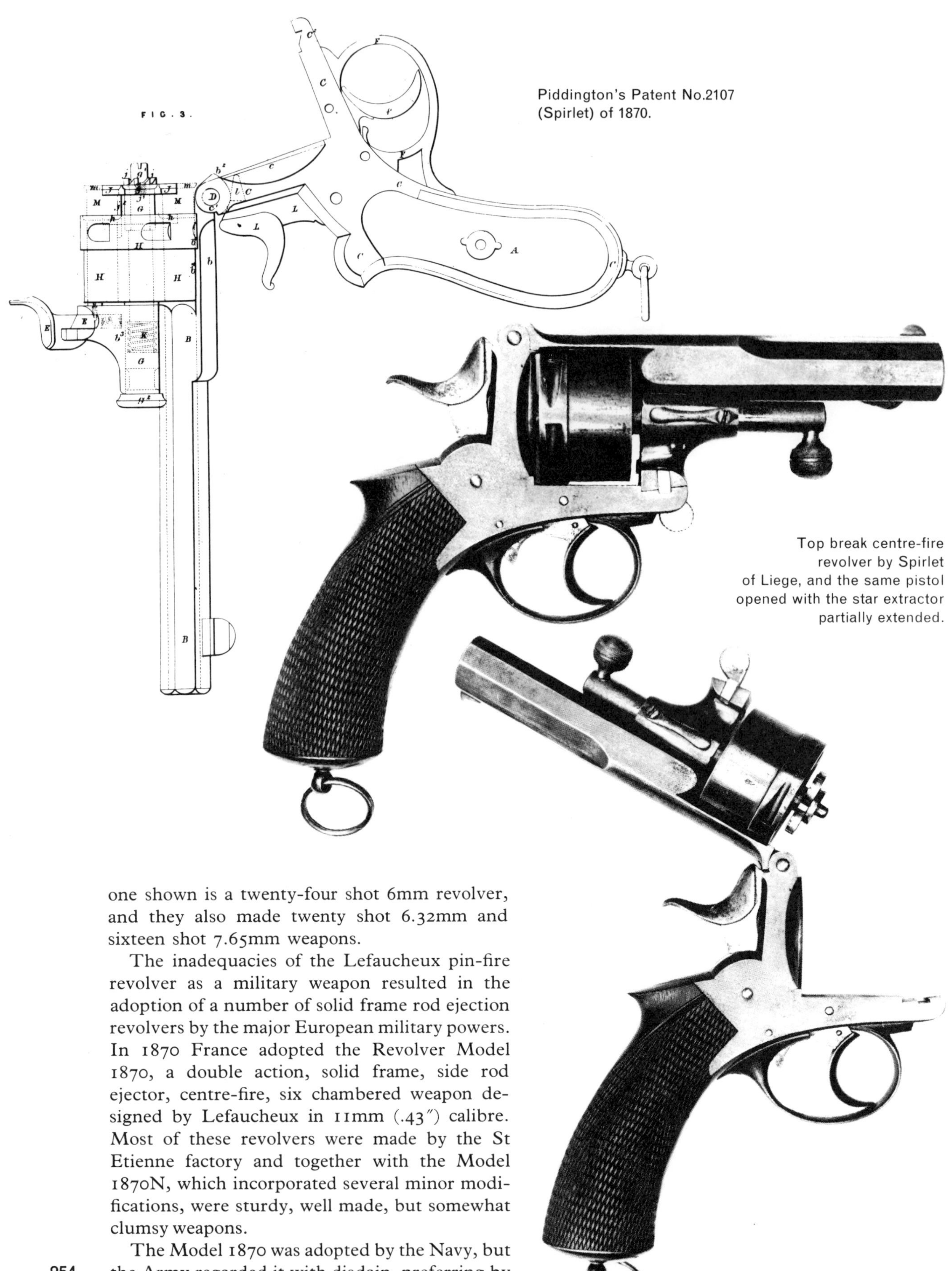

Piddington's Patent No.2107 (Spirlet) of 1870.

Top break centre-fire revolver by Spirlet of Liege, and the same pistol opened with the star extractor partially extended.

one shown is a twenty-four shot 6mm revolver, and they also made twenty shot 6.32mm and sixteen shot 7.65mm weapons.

The inadequacies of the Lefaucheux pin-fire revolver as a military weapon resulted in the adoption of a number of solid frame rod ejection revolvers by the major European military powers. In 1870 France adopted the Revolver Model 1870, a double action, solid frame, side rod ejector, centre-fire, six chambered weapon designed by Lefaucheux in 11mm (.43″) calibre. Most of these revolvers were made by the St Etienne factory and together with the Model 1870N, which incorporated several minor modifications, were sturdy, well made, but somewhat clumsy weapons.

The Model 1870 was adopted by the Navy, but the Army regarded it with disdain, preferring by

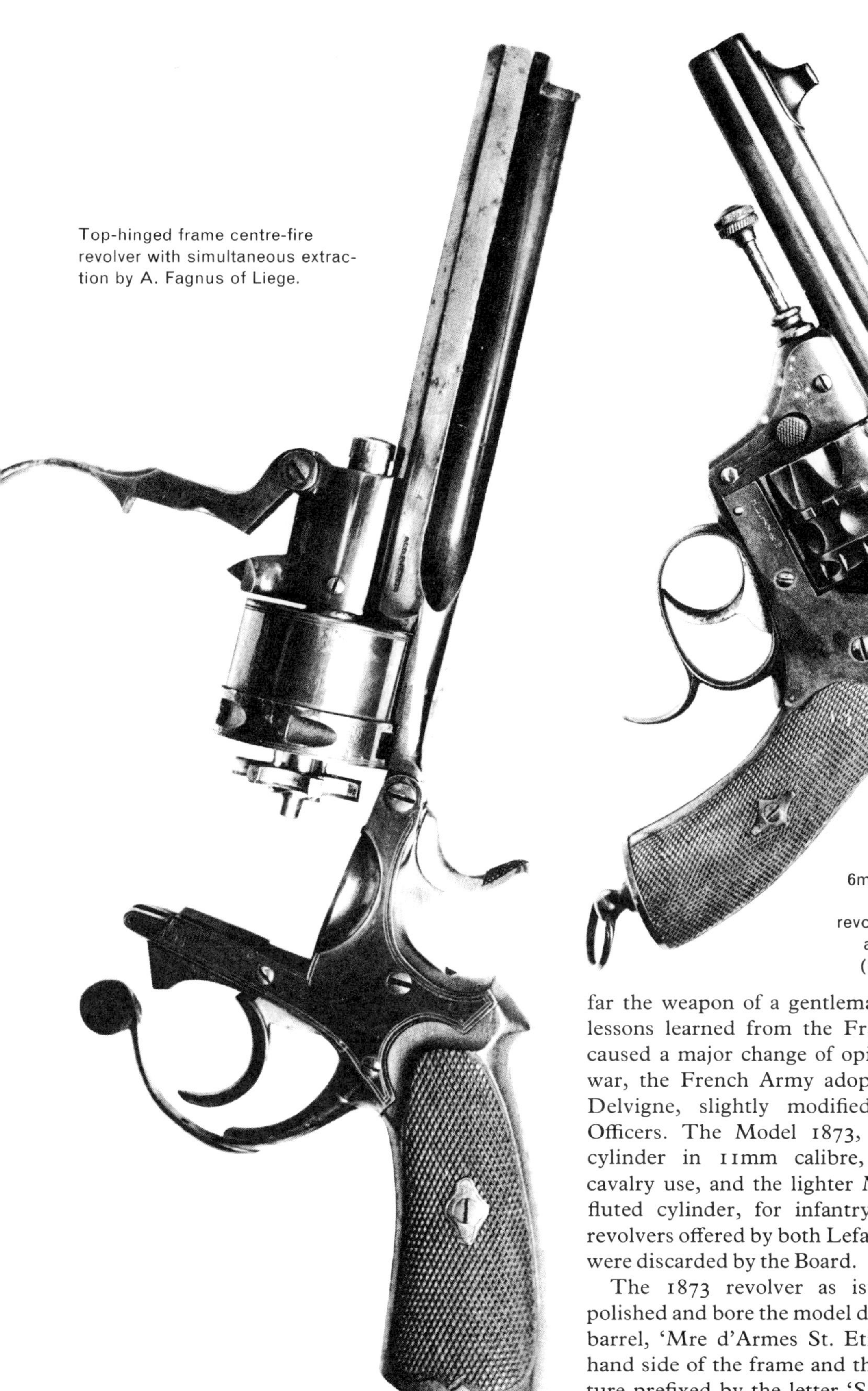

Top-hinged frame centre-fire revolver with simultaneous extraction by A. Fagnus of Liege.

6mm top-hinged twenty-four shot centre-fire revolver by Henrion, Dassy and Heuschen of Liege. (Musée d'Armes, Liege)

far the weapon of a gentleman, the sword. The lessons learned from the Franco-Prussian War caused a major change of opinion and, after the war, the French Army adopted the Chamelot-Delvigne, slightly modified by a Board of Officers. The Model 1873, with a non-fluted cylinder in 11mm calibre, was adopted for cavalry use, and the lighter Model 1874, with a fluted cylinder, for infantry use. Competitive revolvers offered by both Lefaucheux and Galand were discarded by the Board.

The 1873 revolver as issued was brightly polished and bore the model date on the top of the barrel, 'Mre d'Armes St. Etienne' on the right hand side of the frame and the date of manufacture prefixed by the letter 'S' on the right hand side of the barrel. The most important feature of the revolver was the lock. Mechanically it was

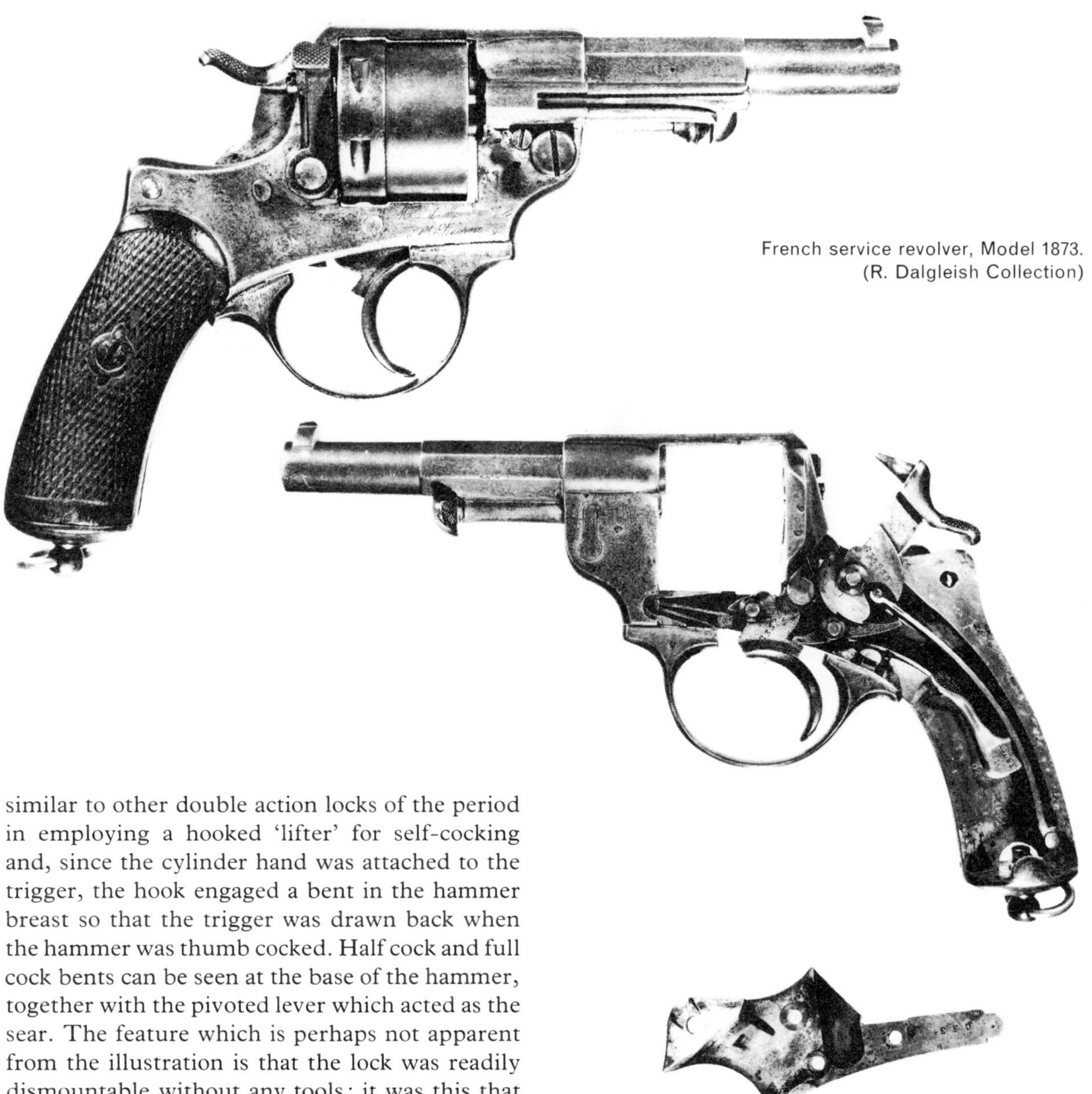

French service revolver, Model 1873.
(R. Dalgleish Collection)

similar to other double action locks of the period in employing a hooked 'lifter' for self-cocking and, since the cylinder hand was attached to the trigger, the hook engaged a bent in the hammer breast so that the trigger was drawn back when the hammer was thumb cocked. Half cock and full cock bents can be seen at the base of the hammer, together with the pivoted lever which acted as the sear. The feature which is perhaps not apparent from the illustration is that the lock was readily dismountable without any tools; it was this that appealed to the military mind of the time and probably accounted for the adoption of similar revolvers by Switzerland, Italy, Sweden and Holland. To dismantle the lock, a large screw at the top right rear of the frame was removed and the plate and left hand grip could then be detached. Tension on the mainspring was removed by rotating the lever attached to the grip frame, and all the limbs of the action could then be lifted out.

As is apparent from the illustrations, this revolver was of sturdy construction, the only point of weakness in service use being the trigger return spring (a similar weakness existed on British revolvers with a 'V' trigger return spring). The 11mm French Service black powder cartridge was also relatively weak, but present opinion regards the strength of the revolver itself as being more than adequate. The slightly different 1874 Model issued to infantry officers was finished in the traditional blue instead of being polished and left 'in the white'.

The French Chamelot-Delvigne was eventually replaced by the 'swing out' cylinder Model of

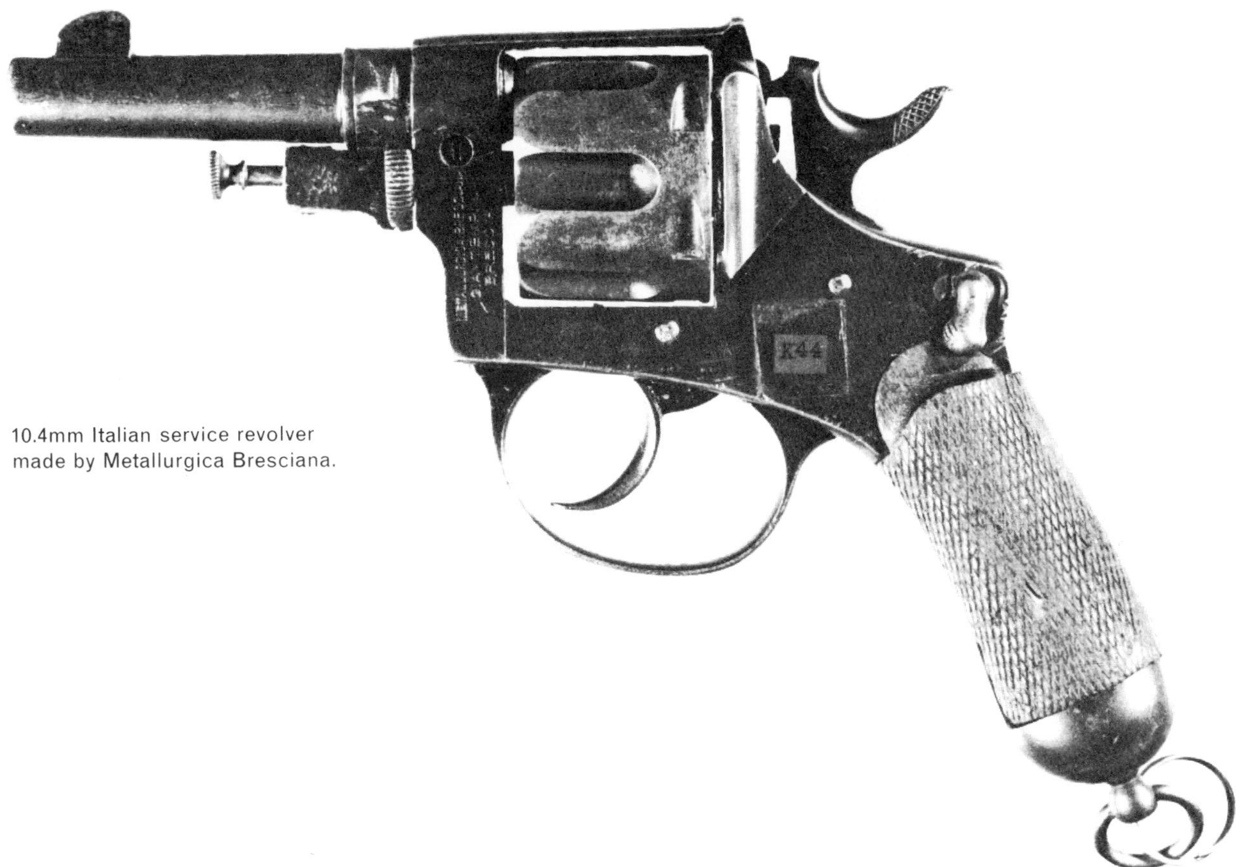

10.4mm Italian service revolver made by Metallurgica Bresciana.

1892, but it was still in use during the First World War and appears to command much the same affection amongst French enthusiasts as does the Colt Single Action Army among American and British students of firearms of this period.

The Système Chamelot-Delvigne was modified by Major Rudolf Schmidt and adopted by Switzerland as the Model 1873 in 10.4mm rim-fire. This was followed by the Model 1878 10.4mm centre-fire revolver, and the earlier rim-fire weapons were converted to centre-fire. The Model 1878 employed a lock mechanism similar to that in Galand's Patent No. 2308 of 1872 (page 266) and, because of this as yet unsubstantiated connection, some authorities refer to the Model 1878 Swiss revolver as the Schmidt/Delvigne. The Swiss retained rod ejection in the last of their military revolvers, the Model of 1882, in which the calibre was reduced to 7.5 mm. Black powder was used for early cartridges, but smokeless powder was later adopted and, from the first, metal-clad bullets were employed. Commercial ammunition was made with lead bullets and gallery round ball, and both shot and blank versions were produced. The cartridge is not normally encountered outside the country of origin, neither is the revolver.

The lock mechanism of the Model 1882 Schmidt was similar to the Nagant, but incorporated a very ingenious modification by Abadie, of whom unfortunately little is known. The Abadie modification would only operate when applied to lockwork which employed a hammer strut, but it was of particular value when applied to solid frame rod ejector type revolvers. The loading gate, which had to swing to the rear, was provided with an extended pivot which passed through the wall of the action body and terminated in a cam. When the gate was opened for loading or unloading, the cam rotated and pushed the hammer strut back against the breast of the hammer so that, in effect, the trigger was disconnected. This then permitted the trigger to be used to rotate the cylinder which would index appropriately for the extraction of cartridges by the rod ejector, and would also permit the introduction of new cartridges. Both loading and unloading were greatly simplified. The Abadie modification was applied to several revolvers and is most likely to be encountered on the French Modèle d'Ordonnance of 1892.

Yet another country to adopt the Chamelot-Delvigne system was Italy. The Italian Ordnance revolver (calibre 10.4mm, synonym 10.35mm

Dutch Model 1873 service revolver with the side plate removed.

Dutch Military revolvers.
Top: 9.4mm centre-fire Nagant, 1870 experimental issue only. Bottom: 12mm pin-fire Lefaucheux-Meyers, 1870 experimental issue only.

Chamelot Delvigne) was adopted in 1872 and some of these original revolvers were carried by Italians as late as the Second World War. Manufacture was carried out by a number of private firms, production continuing until 1926 and possibly later. The variations on the original are many and the quality is equally varied. Earlier versions used a side ejector rod similar to that found on the French Model 1873, others had a rod mounted on a barrel band which was rotated to the right so that the fired case could be pushed out of the cylinder. The loading gate, in common with most other revolvers made on this system, was hinged to be drawn back rather than outwards. The best specimens are those manufactured by Glisenti.

Known to the Dutch as the Chamelot-Delvigne but employing a modified lock, the Dutch Army revolver Model 1873 can be found in four variant types. The first, known as the Old Model, was six chambered and employed a 9.4mm centre-fire cartridge specially designed for it. A lighter version with a round barrel is known as the Model 1873 NM (New Model), and a five chambered version, the Model 1873 KlM (Klein Model—Small Model), was issued to auxiliary military personnel. A short barrel version intended for use with tear gas ammunition can also be encountered. These revolvers, made by Beaumont and P. Stevens of Maastricht and by J. F. T. Bar of Delft, replaced the Adams-Francotte and a percussion conversion known as the Adams-Wely. The 9.4mm cartridge was also used in the Luxemburger Gendarmerie revolver under the synonym 9.85×20.8. The Model 1873 was used until 1925 when it was replaced by the Browning Automatic Pistol Model 1925, followed by the Browning High Power 9mm automatic adopted in 1946.

The Dutch East Indies Police were issued with a 10mm revolver differing from the Model 1873. The cartridges for this were made at the Pyrotechnische Werkplants, Surabaja, Java.

Sweden also adopted the Chamelot-Delvigne in 11mm centre-fire as the 'Svensk marinrevolver m/1884' which was similar in all essentials to the original French version.

With so many rod ejector revolvers in use, it is not surprising that inventors and manufacturers of simultaneous extraction weapons sought to obtain military contracts and urged the adoption of more sophisticated systems.

In Germany the 10.6mm single action six shot Model 1879 was issued to the cavalry. The

Dutch Military revolvers.
Top: 11.2mm Adams-Wely percussion conversion, 1868 Netherlands Navy issue. Bottom: 11.2mm Adams-Francotte percussion revolver, 1865 Netherlands Navy issue. (Nederlands Leger en Wapenmuseum 'Generaal Hoefer')

Dutch Military revolvers.
Top to bottom: (left) 9.4mm short barrel 'tot traangaspatroon' Model 1873 revolver for use with teargas ammunition only, and (right) five chambered version of the 9.4mm Chamelot-Delvigne Model 1873 (Small Model) for issue to auxiliary personnel only; light round barrel version of the 9.4mm Chamelot-Delvigne Model 1873 (New Model); 9.4mm centre-fire Chamelot-Delvigne Model 1873 (Old Model). (Nederlands Leger en Wapenmuseum 'Generaal Hoefer')

10.6mm German service revolver with 7″ barrel. (R. Dalgleish Collection)

10.6mm black powder cartridge employed was similar to the .44 S & W Russian which would, in fact, chamber in the German 1879 pistol, although this was not advised. These were very simple single action revolvers—by no means as easy to use as the Colt SAA—but, in common with many European revolvers, they possessed the unusual feature of a lever safety catch on the left hand side of the frame. The later Model 1883 was identical except for the barrel length which was reduced from 7″ to $4\frac{5}{8}''$, the shorter model being issued to the infantry. A very similar double trigger revolver, both self-cocking and thumb cocking, was issued to officers. These weapons were manufactured by F. Dreyse of Sommerda and also by various Government Arsenals; the Model 1883, for example, was made at Erfurt.

10.6mm German service revolver with $4\frac{5}{8}''$ barrel, Model 1883.

Johnson's Patent No.922 (Mauser) of 1878.

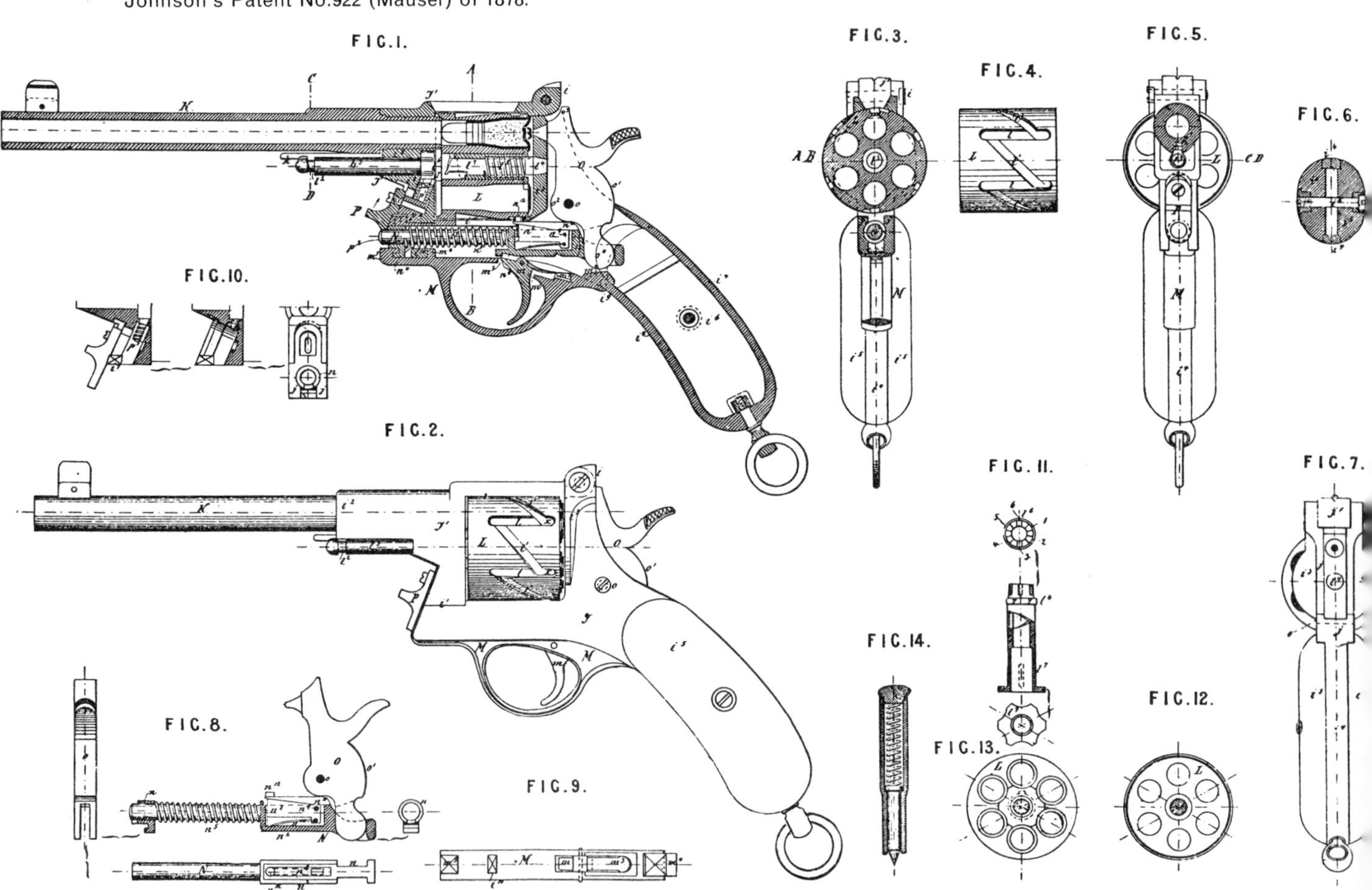

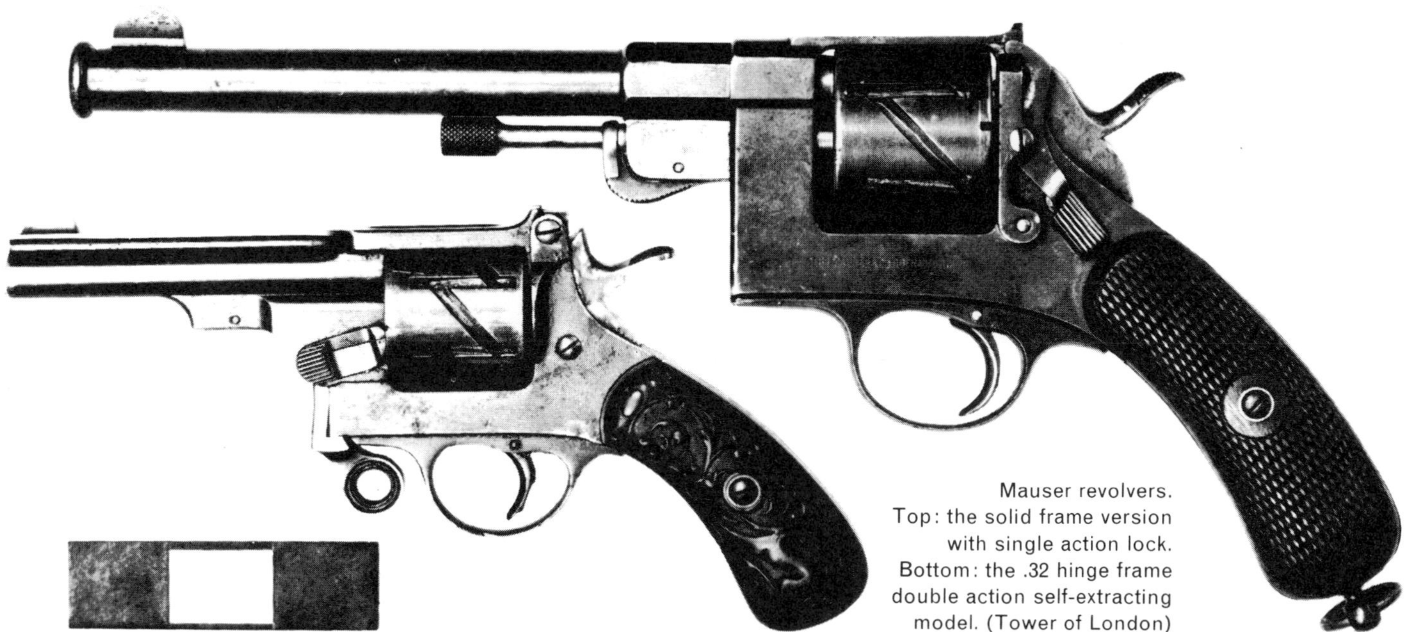

Mauser revolvers.
Top: the solid frame version with single action lock.
Bottom: the .32 hinge frame double action self-extracting model. (Tower of London)

The design of the German service revolver was the responsibility of a Commission and, as often happens when a committee designs anything, the results were unsatisfactory. Contemporary opinions regarding the German Service revolvers are lacking, but it is not surprising that one of the greatest armament firms in Germany mistakenly thought they could do better. Mauser revolvers, however, were never adopted officially and enjoyed little commercial success. Mauser had been one of the several firms responsible for the manufacture of the Model 1879/83 Commission revolvers and it must have been a source of some annoyance to them that their own simultaneous ejection revolver was rejected in favour of that proposed by the Spandau Military Commission.

Both solid frame and hinged frame revolvers were developed by Mauser, the hinged frame similar to the Spirlet. Single and double action models were produced, and the unusual feature of the mechanism was the use of a coil mainspring instead of the conventional flat spring. An additional feature was the unusual method of rotating the cylinder. Instead of using the conventional ratchet at the rear of the cylinder, a number of inclined and parallel grooves were machined on the outside. These grooves can be seen at Fig. 2 of the drawing accompanying Johnson's Patent No. 922 of 7 March 1878. This was later assigned to Paul Mauser of Oberndof and formed the basis for a number of revolvers made by Mauser which today are referred to as the Model of 1878.

The variant illustrated in the specification is the single action hinged frame model and, as the hammer was thumb cocked, the coil mainspring in the bar of the action was compressed and the mainspring carrier, on which was mounted the stud (n 12), moved forward in a diagonal groove to rotate the cylinder one sixth of a turn. When the hammer was fully cocked, the stud engaged a parallel groove and locked the cylinder in battery. This system was very positive in that the stud was always engaged with a groove unless the barrel was hinged upwards. The same system had been investigated by Samuel Colt (British Patent No. 535 of 1853—see page 132, and the Webley-Fosbery and Union Arms Company automatic revolvers also used a similar method of cylinder rotation.

The Mauser revolvers were reliable and, as one would expect, extremely well made. They were, however, very expensive to manufacture and the Mauser brothers' efforts to interest military authorities met with no success, although a few were sold commercially. The version normally encountered is chambered for the 9mm rimmed Mauser revolver cartridge, and is the hinged frame simultaneous extraction single action model distinguished by the ring locking lever in front of the trigger guard.

With the exception of the later Webley and Scott and the variants of the Smith and Wesson Model No. 3 adopted by Russia, Turkey and used to a limited extent by Austro-Hungary, the hinged frame simultaneous extraction system had little military success. In France the simultaneous ejector revolver was typified by Galand's design (British Patent No. 3039 of 1868). Although apparently not officially adopted by any major power, the Galand revolver was widely used in Europe as an officer's sidearm. Two types of Galand revolver can be easily identified. The first and earliest employed an

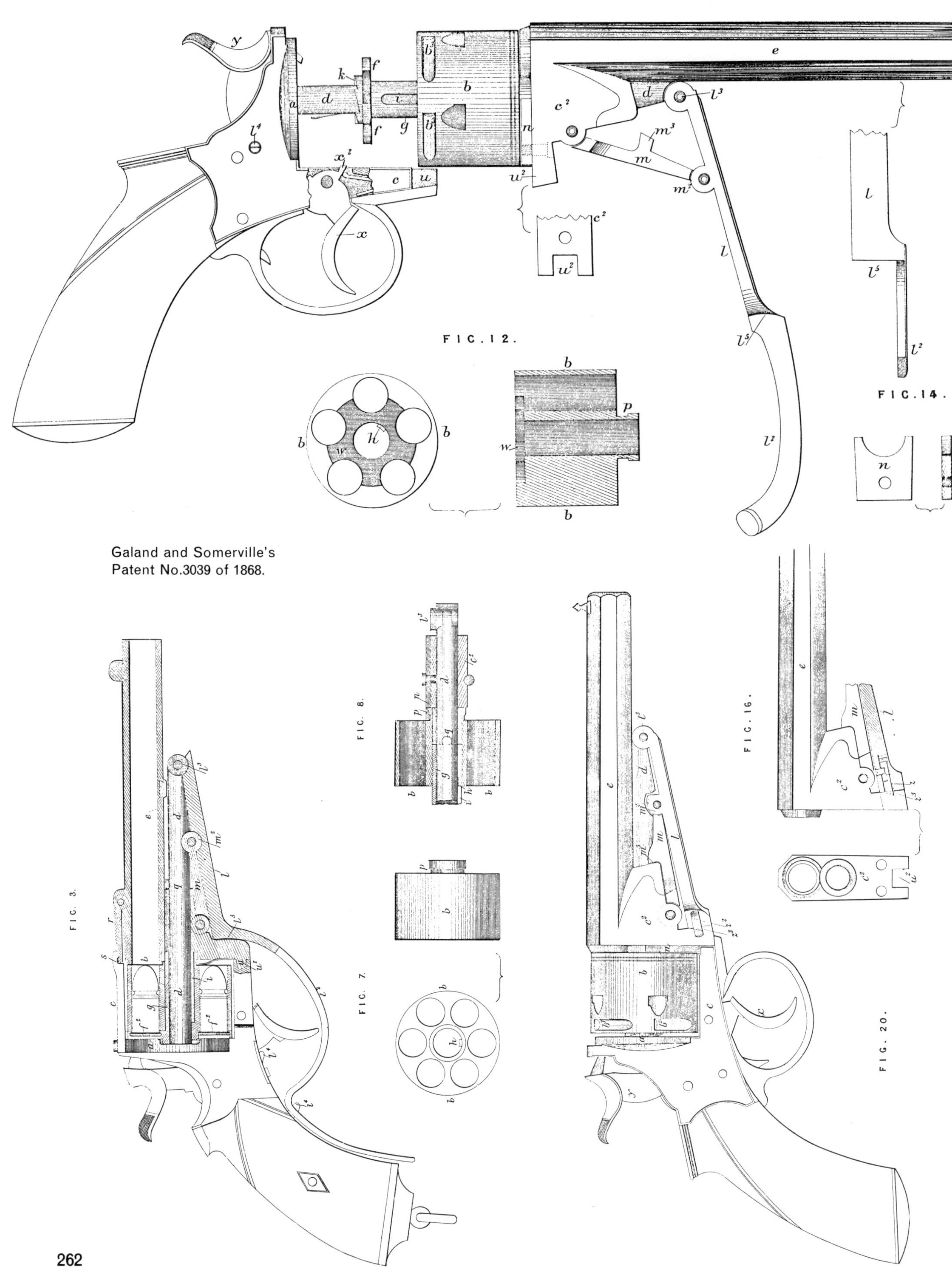

Galand and Somerville's
Patent No.3039 of 1868.

extractor plate instead of a 'star', while the operating lever formed the trigger guard and locked on a projection behind it (Fig. 3). These revolvers will be found in a variety of different models as to finish, method of locking the operating lever and also shape of stock. French sources indicate that the Paris gunmaker C. F. Galand invented his revolver in 1868 and, in an article published in 1868, M. Libioulle, the editor of *Franc tireur belge*, explained the method of operation and confirmed that the 'expulsion' of the fired cartridge cases was accomplished by a mechanism 'simple, solide, rationnel' and that the revolver operated with 'grande regularité', that it shot with precision and that reloading was speedy and simple.

I have not been able to discover much about the celebrated Monsieur Galand but, from contemporary literature, it appears that he was not only an inventor, but also something of a salesman in that his revolver received most favourable consideration from the press. At present there is no evidence to suggest that Galand revolvers were ever manufactured in France, since even those bearing the name 'Galand-Paris' or 'Galand, Fabricant d'armes—Paris' were undoubtedly made in Belgium. Galand's address in Paris was 13 Rue d'Hauteville, and premises were also acquired in Liege at 280 Rue Vivegnis—but whether as an office, saleroom or factory is not known.

Galand's first British Patent was taken out jointly with A. Somerville, a partner in a firm of Birmingham gun manufacturers trading as Braendlin, Somerville and Co., and was granted on 5 October 1868, some five months after his French patent appears to have been obtained. As well as protecting the self-extraction features of the Galand system, it also claimed an improvement, based on original ideas patented by Gevelot and Mathieu, for attaching a revolver to a single shot rifle.

The basic idea of moving the barrel and cylinder forward along the extended cylinder pin was not new; it had been thought of by the Belgian gunmakers Ghaye, and pin-fire revolvers using this system had been made by another Belgian gunmaker, Begueldre, the hinged locking lever lying alongside the barrel, the cartridges extracted by the pins. The origin of the system could well be taken back to the Colt method of attaching the barrel to the cylinder pin, and the Belgian percussion revolver by Ancion et Cie (see page 134) took the idea a little further by employing a locking lever under the barrel to drive a wedge into a dovetail cut into the cylinder pin. With the centrefire Belgian revolver illustrated, the principle was further developed. Here the locking of the barrel was done by a lever which operated a cam mating with a cut-out in the cylinder pin. The barrel was unlocked by pulling the lever downwards as shown, and the barrel was then manually pulled forward, the plate extractor withdrawing the cartridges from the cylinder.

Belgian centre-fire simultaneous extraction revolver.

By providing the lever with a small hook which engaged a depression in an extension to the frame, the forward movement of the barrel and cylinder could be made automatic, as with the .450 centre-fire double action revolver illustrated. Several of these revolvers have been encountered, all apparently identical except for the vendor's name engraved on the barrel. Birmingham proof marks are impressed on the barrel, cylinder and frame, but there are no other marks. The origin and indeed the identity of these revolvers is, as yet, unknown, but they are well made and well finished.

The Galand system introduced a link and lever to draw the barrel and cylinder forward, and a special version of the Galand was made with a folding shoulder stock, the 'Revolver Sportsman'. In addition to Galand revolvers of Belgian origin a similar revolver marked 'Galand and Somerville Patent' was sold in Britain. In this type, the lever extended only to the base of the frame (Fig. 20 on page 262) and did not form the trigger guard as on the Continental specimens. In addition a star extractor was employed and, although proof is lacking, there is reason to believe that these revolvers were made in Birmingham. On an even rarer variant, the locking lever was extended alongside the right hand side of the

.450 English centre-fire simultaneous extraction revolver.

A. Barrel.
B. Cylinder.
C. Locking lever.
D. Trigger spring.
E. Butt.
F. Hinge pin and bolt.
G. Trigger guard.

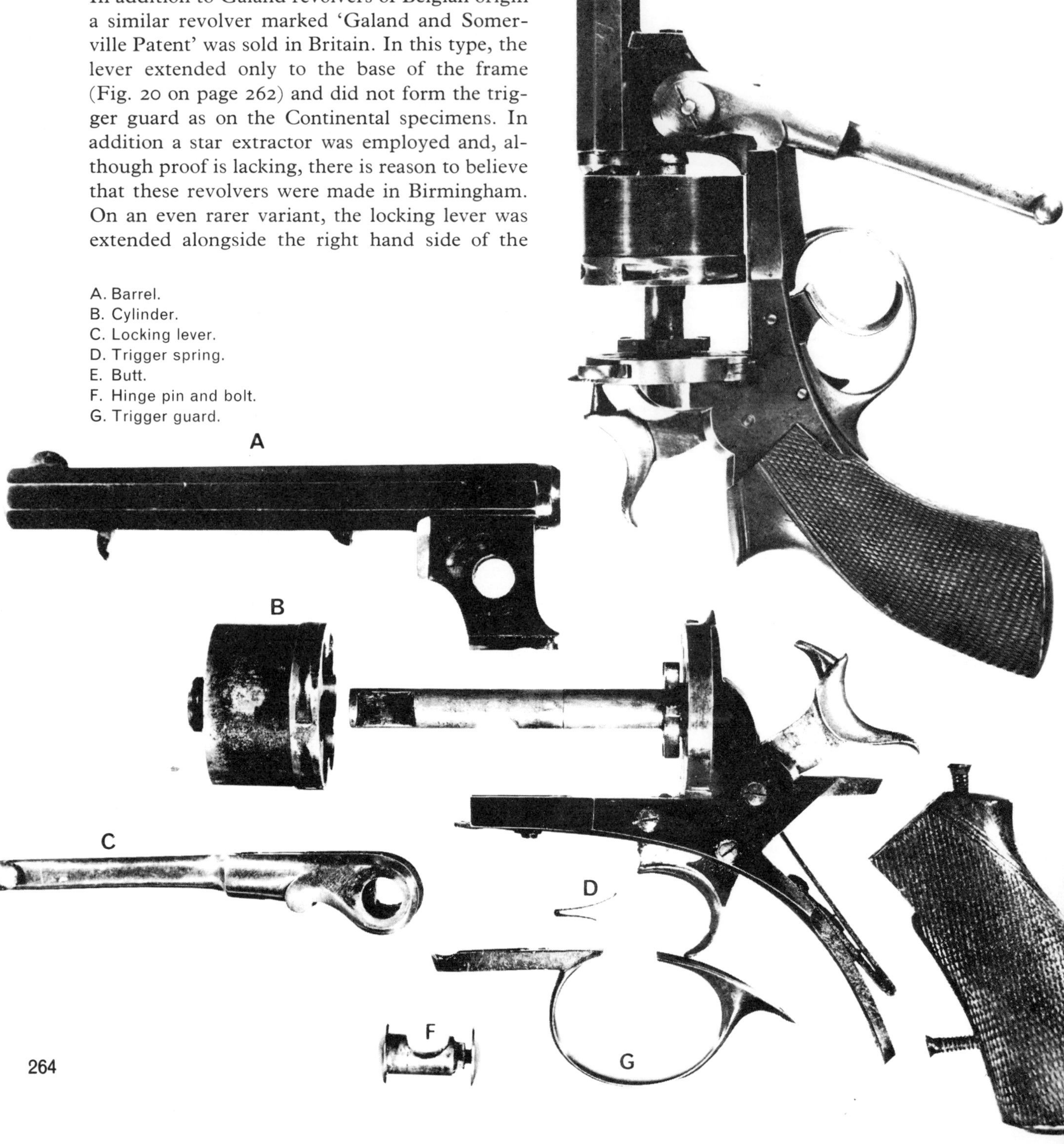

frame so that it could be operated by the thumb (Fig. 12). W. W. Greener illustrated the Galand and Somerville in *Modern Breechloaders* and commented that 'the revolver is made by machinery and the workmanship is very good. It has six chambers, and is double action; the large size is .450 and the small .380.' As was common practice in Britain, these revolvers were generally marked with the vendor's name along the top of the barrel.

Galand obtained a further British patent, No. 2308 of 1872, which was mainly concerned with improvements to revolver locks. A study of the lock, Fig. 1, illustrates the use of the 'lifter', but this can be more easily seen on the drawing of the hammer, Fig. 9. (The 'lifter', it will be recalled, was a feature of the Deane-Harding mechanism discussed in Chapter Seven.) Several other features of this lock are of interest. The 'V' trigger return spring, a troublesome feature on

Galand and Somerville revolver with the action open. (With acknowledgements to Peter Wright for the loan of his daughter as well as his revolver).

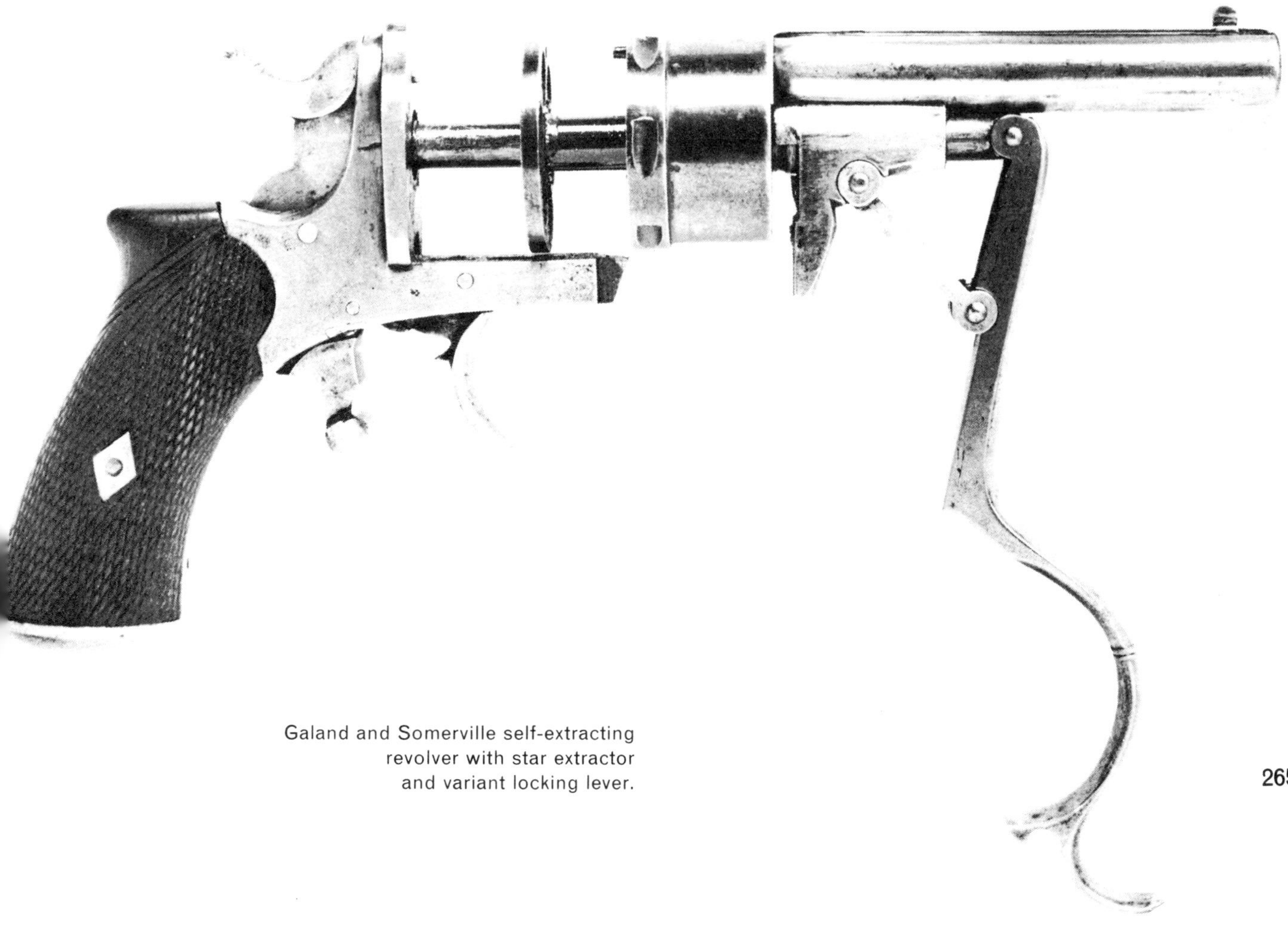

Galand and Somerville self-extracting revolver with star extractor and variant locking lever.

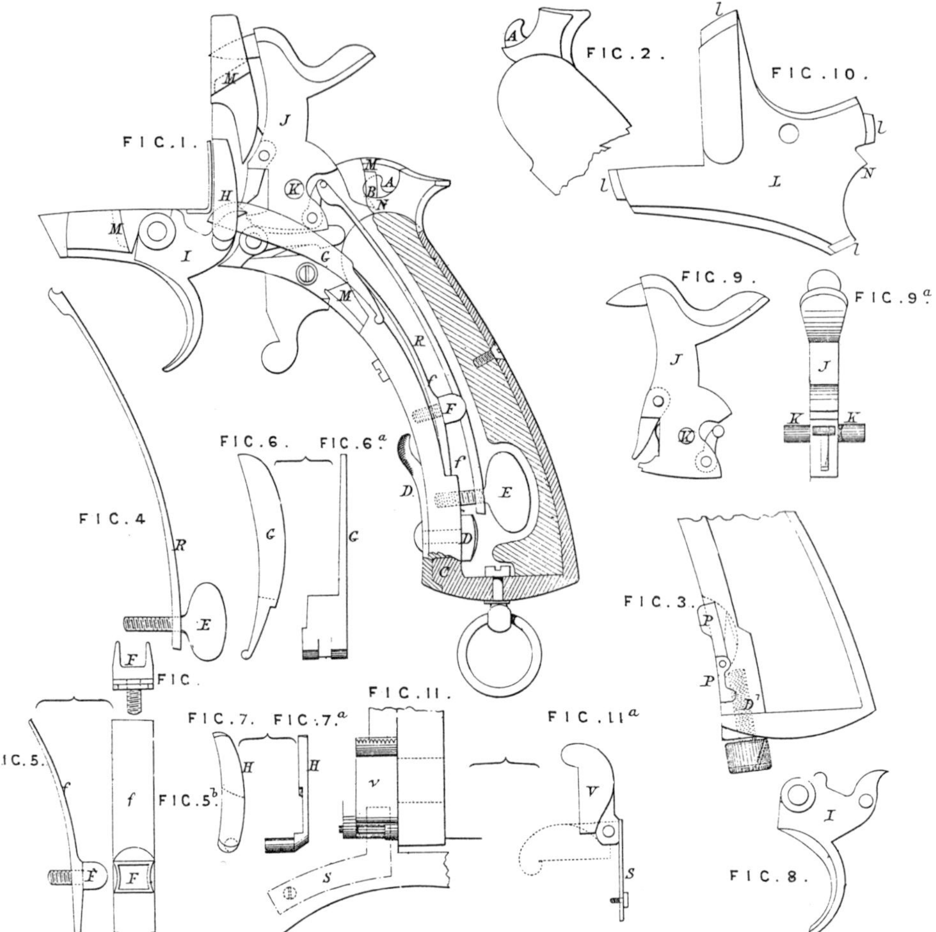

Galand's Patent No.2308 of 1872.

many revolvers, has at last been done away with and, although the lock appears complicated, the components were robust and not likely to break. The trigger return spring (R) was attached to the frame by a thumb screw (F) and operated by means of the lever (G), the shape of which is illustrated in Figs. 6 and 6a. The end of the lever bore against the cylinder hand (H) which was recessed, Fig. 7 (H), to accommodate it. In addition to action as a trigger return spring, it also performed the function of the hand spring and, in so doing, got rid of the oddly shaped little springs that did this job previously.

The 'secondary sear' which, on the French Model 1873 Chamelot-Delvigne lock, had provided the full cock position on single action was retained, but its function was now to provide the 'safe' or rebound position for the hammer, so that the cylinder could rotate and the firing pin be withdrawn from the indent in the cap of a fired cartridge.

A patent taken out by Bled, Richoux and Warnant (British Patent No. 5504 of 1881) illustrated the use of an extended mainspring which acted as a trigger return spring and also provided automatic hammer rebound when the trigger was released.

Because of their widespread distribution, the revolvers made under Emile and Leon Nagant's Patents—the first a simple solid frame rod ejection model, the second employing a reciprocating cylinder and special cartridges—are of considerable importance, as is the lock employed, even though there was nothing radically new about it.

The lock mechanisms of Continental origin already discussed illustrate the fact that the designers were to a great extent preoccupied with one feature, that of dismounting the lock without tools. On the Chamelot-Delvigne lock, a large side plate had been provided, and tension on the mainspring could be released by the lever cam so that the mainspring could be removed very easily without tools or risk of damage. Reference to the patent drawing for the Galand mechanism shows very clearly how the mainspring was retained by a large thumb screw and, in the case of the Nagant mechanism, similar provision was made to simplify the dismantling of the lock. Emile Nagant's British Patent No. 4310 of 1879 illustrated a simple solid frame rod ejector revolver, the mechanism of which was mounted on a plate which formed the grip. There was the usual full length removable side plate but, in addition, Fig. 1 of the patent drawing shows how

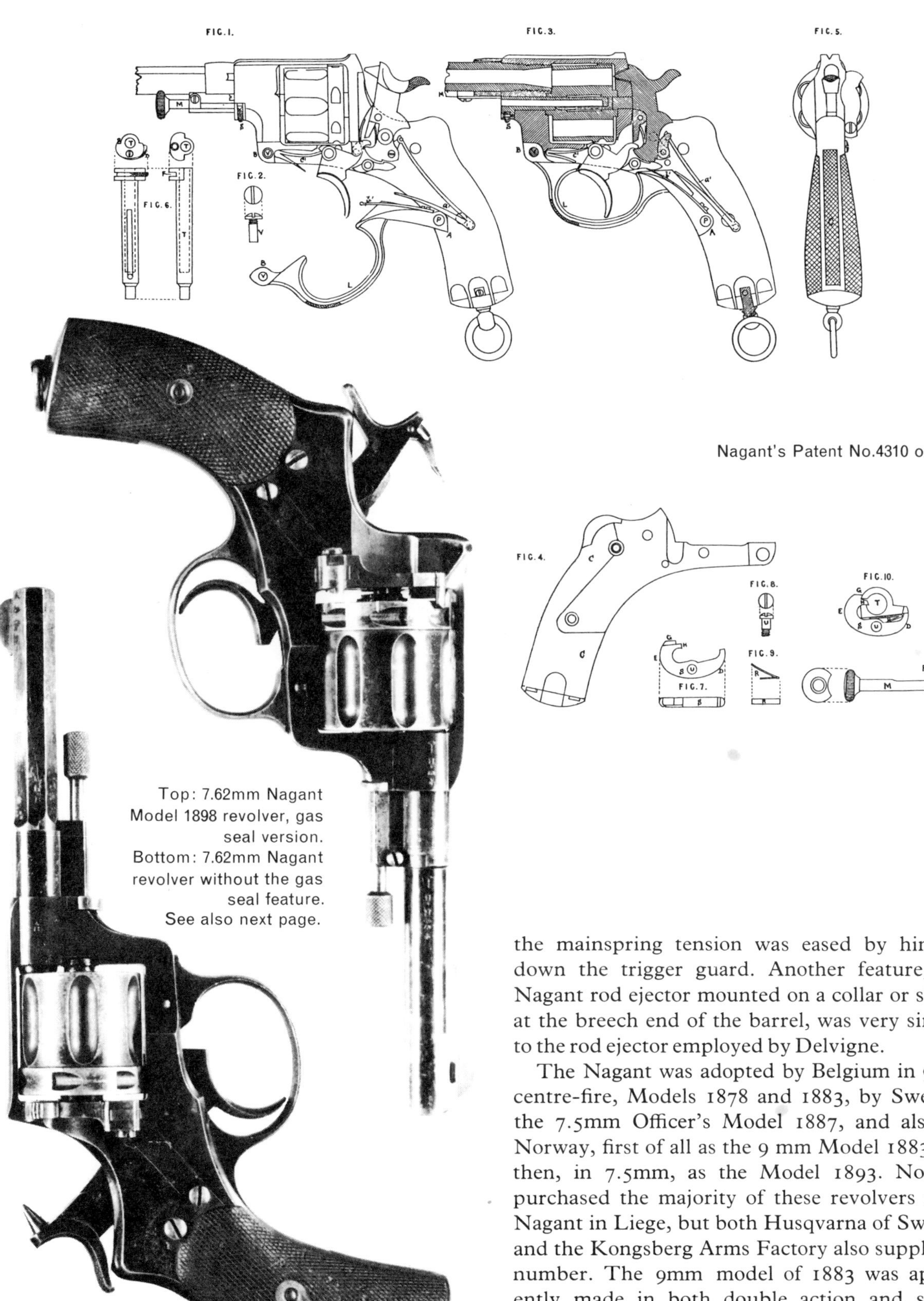

Nagant's Patent No.4310 of 1879.

Top: 7.62mm Nagant Model 1898 revolver, gas seal version. Bottom: 7.62mm Nagant revolver without the gas seal feature. See also next page.

the mainspring tension was eased by hinging down the trigger guard. Another feature, the Nagant rod ejector mounted on a collar or sleeve at the breech end of the barrel, was very similar to the rod ejector employed by Delvigne.

The Nagant was adopted by Belgium in 9mm centre-fire, Models 1878 and 1883, by Sweden, the 7.5mm Officer's Model 1887, and also by Norway, first of all as the 9 mm Model 1883 and then, in 7.5mm, as the Model 1893. Norway purchased the majority of these revolvers from Nagant in Liege, but both Husqvarna of Sweden and the Kongsberg Arms Factory also supplied a number. The 9mm model of 1883 was apparently made in both double action and single action variants. The double action model was for issue to officers and non-commissioned officers, the single action model for issue to privates. The

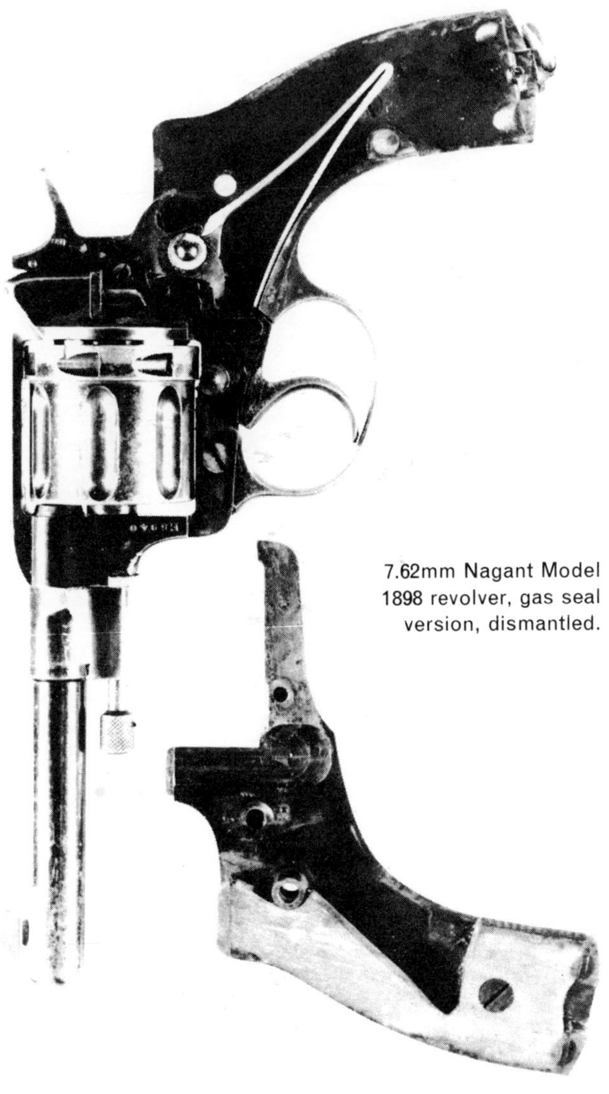

7.62mm Nagant Model 1898 revolver, gas seal version, dismantled.

7.5mm Nagant cartridge was similar to the .32 S & W long, except that the case length was slightly shorter, and it used a heel seated bullet of equal diameter to the outside of the case. Although .32 S & W cartridges can be chambered in the 7.5mm Nagant and can be fired, the practice is not advised as the smaller .32 cases have to expand in order to obturate, and the amount of swelling which occurs often causes the case to burst.

In 1894 Leon Nagant obtained British Patent No. 14,010 for a revolver externally similar to that shown in the drawings which accompanied his brother's previous patent of 1879, but exhibiting one important and unusual feature. This was the provision of a gas seal between the cylinder and barrel and, in addition to the modifications required to impart the necessary reciprocating motion to the cylinder (Figs. 4 and 5), there was a special cartridge in which the case extended beyond the nose of the bullet. The loaded 7.62mm Nagant cartridge appears at first sight to be a fired bottle-necked rifle cartridge. When this special cartridge was chambered, the case mouth protruded slightly from the front of the chamber, and the cylinder was recessed at the front so that, when it was moved forward by the mechanism, the tapered breech end of the barrel entered the cylinder recess and the mouth of the cartridge entered the barrel. The block (O) also moved forward to support the head of the cartridge. The forward movement of the cylinder took place after rotation, the cranked cylinder hand or pawl (L) exerting forward thrust against the rear. When the trigger was released, the lower arm of the mainspring returned it to the forward position and, since both the pawl and resistance plate were disengaged at the same time, the cylinder was free to move to the rear under the influence of the coil spring (R) and to withdraw the case mouth from the barrel so that the cylinder could again be rotated into battery.

The mechanism employed to achieve a satisfactory gas seal was ingenious and durable in actual use. Both single and double action versions of this lock were made and, to add to the confusion, there was a strong similarity between the normal and the gas seal models. Both loaded singly through a hinged gate and both employed the Nagant rod ejector mounted on a barrel sleeve.

The desire to eliminate the gas leak between the cylinder and barrel of revolving weapons had been pursued for a long time, and mention has already been made of the famous Puckle 'Defence', the Collier flintlock revolver and the later 'Lang' type revolvers. Throughout the percussion period, further efforts had been made by H. S. North and Savage, and by Moore and Harris in Britain, by Ghaye in Belgium and, in the cartridge era, by D. B. Wesson in America to solve the problem in a practical manner. Pieper manufactured double action 8mm seven shot revolvers with the gas seal feature, but the basic Nagant type, largely due to Russian interest, was the only gas seal revolver to be manufactured in large numbers.

The standard Nagant was marked 'Brevete Nagant' and bore the usual Liege proofmarks, as did the gas seal model which was marked 'L. Nagant Brevete, Liege'. The outstanding disadvantage of the Nagant was, of course, slowness of loading and, in an endeavour to overcome this

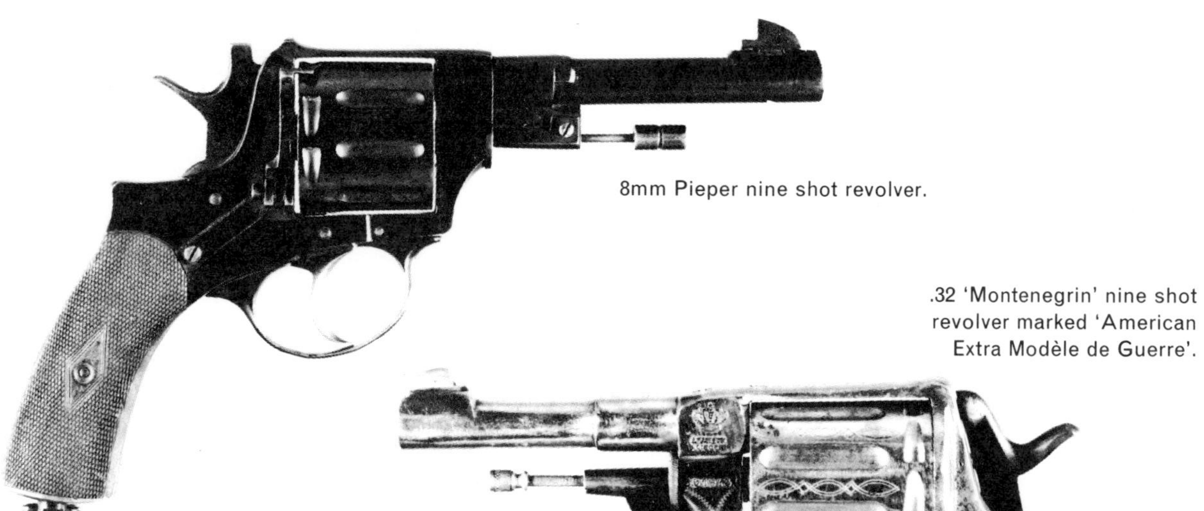

8mm Pieper nine shot revolver.

.32 'Montenegrin' nine shot revolver marked 'American Extra Modèle de Guerre'.

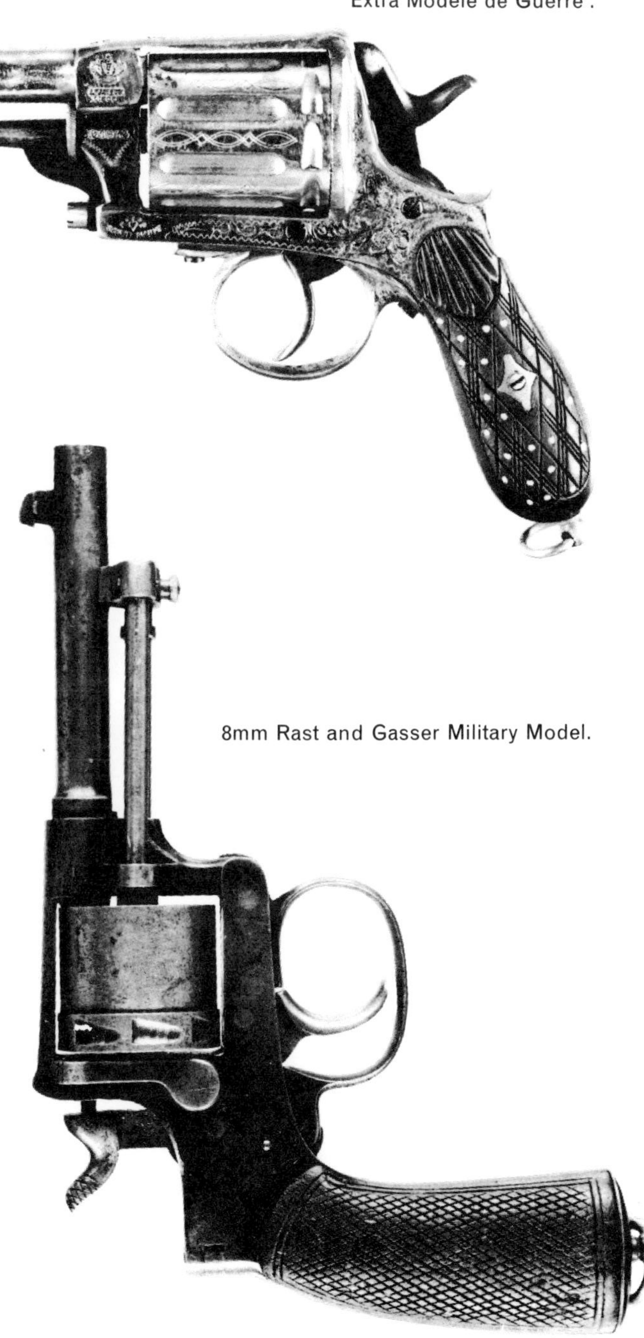

8mm Rast and Gasser Military Model.

Liege, perhaps the most distinctive were copies of the Austrian Gasser. The example illustrated is a nine chambered .32 calibre weapon marked 'American Extra, Modèle de Guerre'. For good measure it bears a copy of the original 'pierced apple' trade mark of Leopold Gasser of Vienna and is similar to the Montenegrin Infantry Model which appeared in the LePage catalogues. Undoubtedly the originator of this style of revolver, Gasser was born in 1836, served his apprenticeship as a gunmaker, and, by 1862, was manufacturing Adams type percussion revolvers. Later, he developed a revolver adopted by the Austro-Hungarian Army as the Model 1870. This was chambered for a cartridge similar in dimensions to the Model 1867 Werndl carbine cartridge. The Model 1870/74 was identical except for the use of crucible cast steel for the frame. In 1882 the Model 1870 was replaced by an improved version employing a cartridge with a shorter case length in an attempt to eliminate accidents caused by confusing the 11mm Gasser revolver cartridge with the 11mm Werndl carbine cartridge.

Surplus stocks of the Model 1870 type Gasser revolvers were sold to Montenegro, and the 11mm Gasser became known as the 11mm Montenegrin. The basic characteristics were derived from the Lefaucheux revolver. The overall length was 13″, the weight nearly 3 lbs, and the revolver was usually marked 'L. Gasser, Wien, Patent, Ottakring' (the location of one of the two Gasser factories). Gasser type revolvers in nominal .44 calibre were widely copied in Belgium and can be found with a variety of modifications, some with top straps, some without.

8mm Rast and Gasser eight shot Model 1898.

8mm Rast and Gasser Model 1898, showing (arrowed) the Abadie modification.

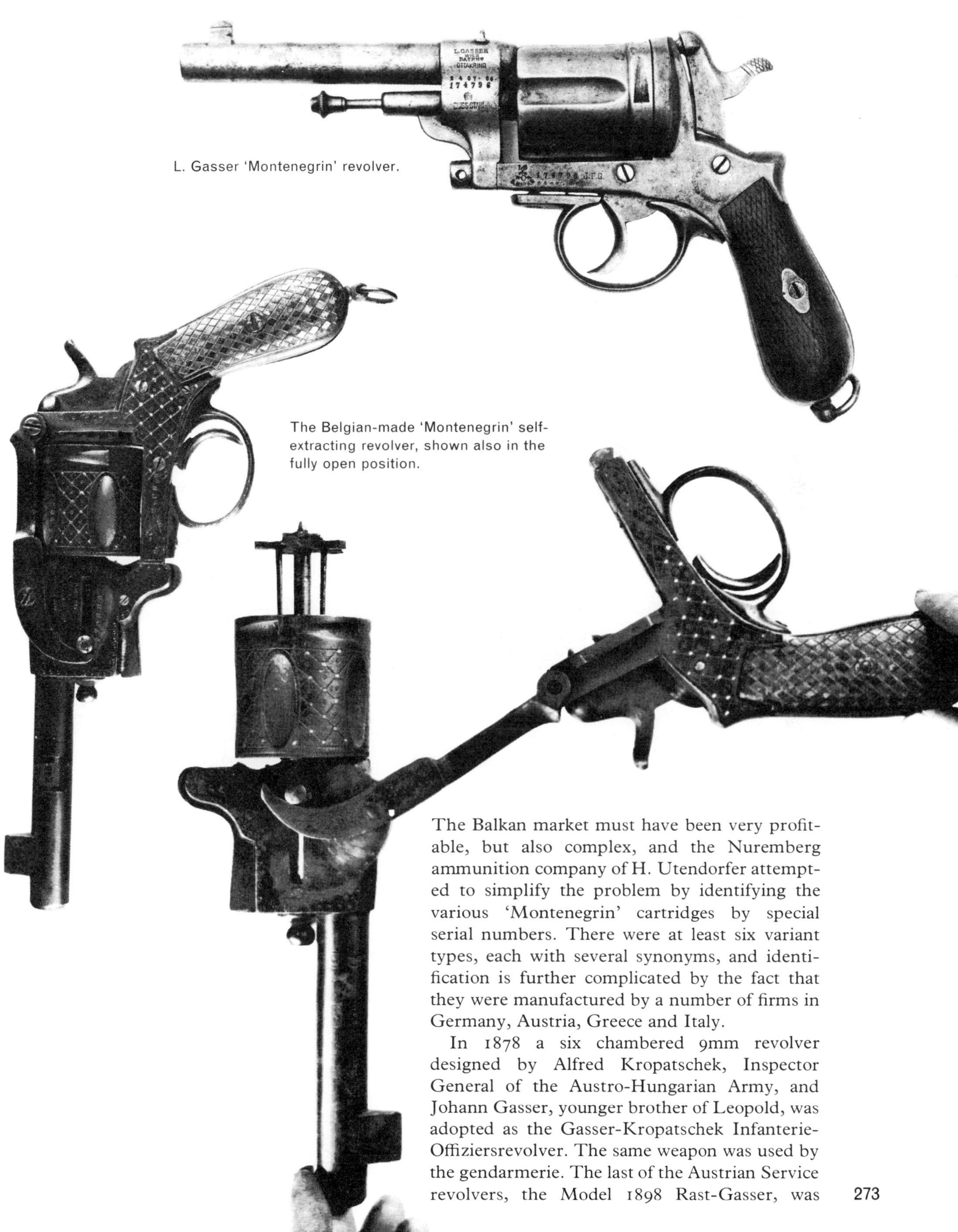

L. Gasser 'Montenegrin' revolver.

The Belgian-made 'Montenegrin' self-extracting revolver, shown also in the fully open position.

The Balkan market must have been very profitable, but also complex, and the Nuremberg ammunition company of H. Utendorfer attempted to simplify the problem by identifying the various 'Montenegrin' cartridges by special serial numbers. There were at least six variant types, each with several synonyms, and identification is further complicated by the fact that they were manufactured by a number of firms in Germany, Austria, Greece and Italy.

In 1878 a six chambered 9mm revolver designed by Alfred Kropatschek, Inspector General of the Austro-Hungarian Army, and Johann Gasser, younger brother of Leopold, was adopted as the Gasser-Kropatschek Infanterie-Offiziersrevolver. The same weapon was used by the gendarmerie. The last of the Austrian Service revolvers, the Model 1898 Rast-Gasser, was

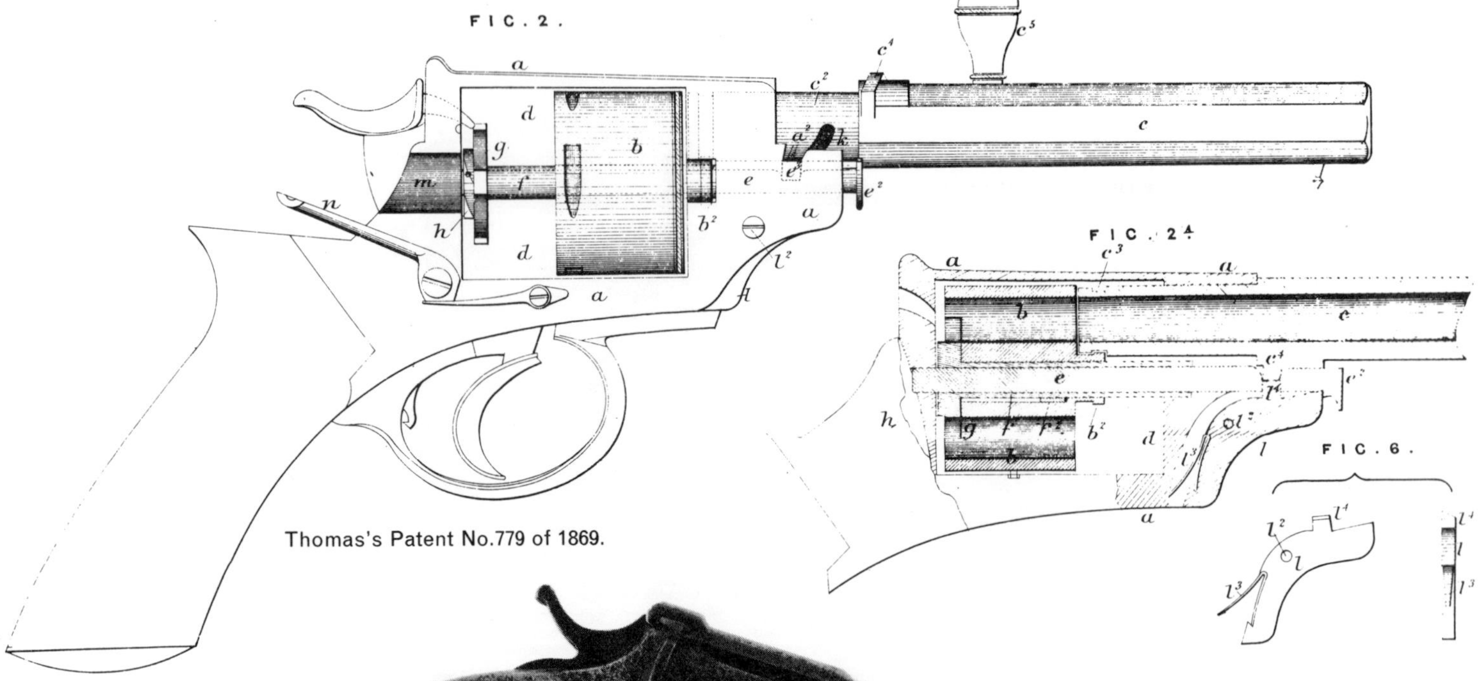

FIG. 2.
FIG. 2A
FIG. 6.

Thomas's Patent No.779 of 1869.

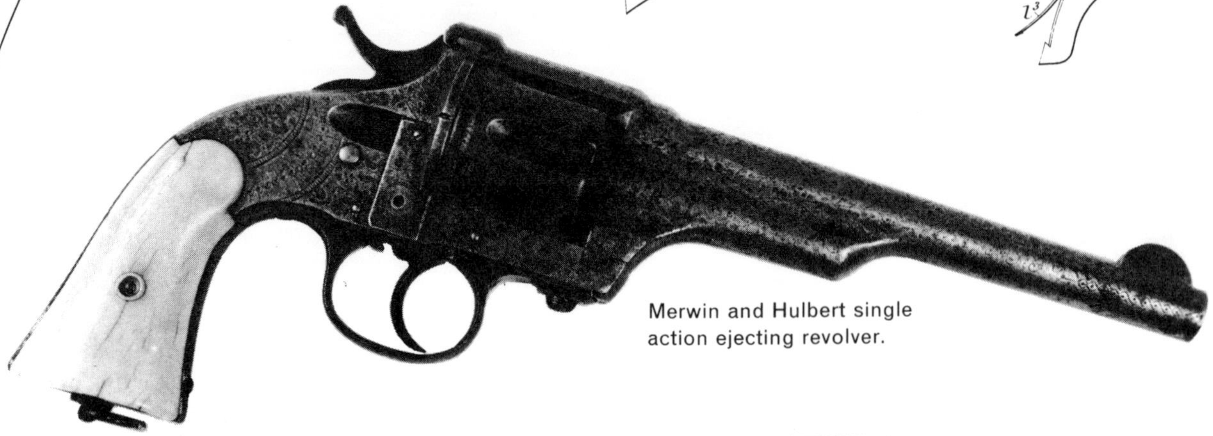

Merwin and Hulbert single action ejecting revolver.

SELF-EXTRACTING SOLID-BODY REVOLVER.

THOMAS'S PATENT.

'450
'380
'320
C
D
A
B

A DOUBLE-ACTION REVOLVER,

Simultaneously extracting the exploded cases—therefore can be loaded on horseback, in the dark, or while moving about in any way. The usual revolver, requiring a rod to eject each exploded case, is useless after being discharged until the operator can remain quite still to re-load it.

It revolves on an axis perfectly shielded from the effects of the powder, therefore is not liable to clog and have its action stopped, even though fired day after day without cleaning.

Is can be reloaded in less time than the exploded cases of others can be ejected.

It has a SOLID FRAME, forming an integral part of the body inclosing the chamber, without which no revolver can be depended upon for many successive discharges.

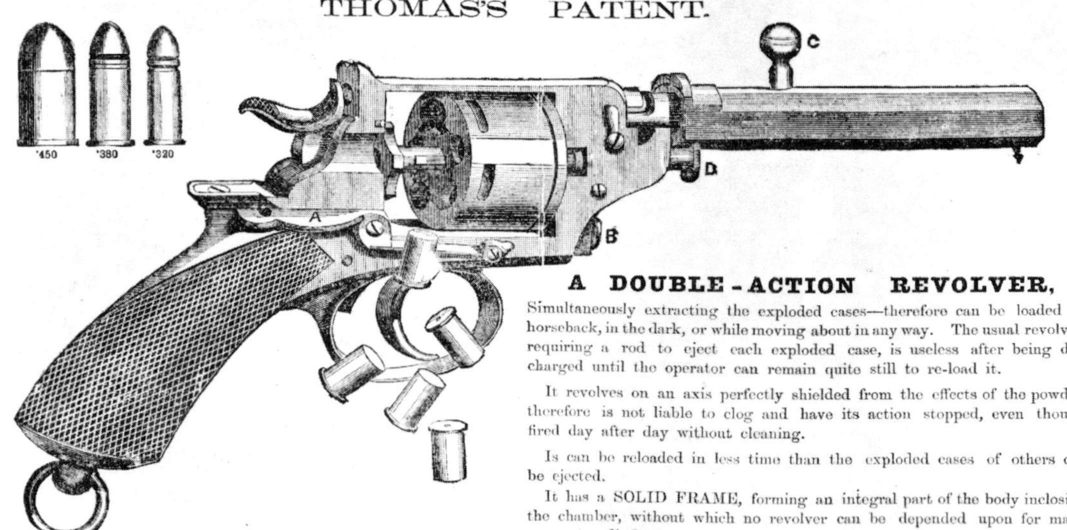

IT MAY BE PROCURED RETAIL FROM ALL RESPECTABLE GUNMAKERS.

WHOLESALE FROM THE MANUFACTURERS,

TIPPING & LAWDEN,

CONSTITUTION-HILL, BIRMINGHAM.

An advertisement for the Thomas self-extracting revolver as made by Tipping and Lawden.

designed by August Rast and made by Waffenfabrik Leopold Gasser (later known as Rast and Gasser) of Vienna. This was an eight chambered double action revolver with rod ejection, and was chambered for the 8mm Gasser cartridge. Capable of being rapidly dismounted without tools, the Rast-Gasser had the usual Abadie modification, and was ahead of its time in that the firing pin was in the frame and not attached to the hammer. This revolver was replaced by a self-loading pistol, but it continued to be used in Central Europe in considerable numbers as late as World War Two.

If we except the well-known hinged frame simultaneous ejection systems of Smith and Wesson, Webley and Tranter, we are still left with a number of designs the origins of which remain open to some debate; other are well documented but, after transitory success, they faded into relative obscurity.

One of the earliest of these designs was that patented by J. Thomas of Birmingham in 1869, British Patent No. 779. According to W. W. Greener, the Thomas revolver was made in three sizes, .450, .380 and .320. This information is confirmed by the advertisement published by the manufacturers, Tipping and Lawden of Constitution Hill, Birmingham, who manufactured the American Sharps four barrelled pistol (see page 350), and can really be regarded as 'makers to the Trade'. They were finally taken over by P. Webley and Son in 1877.

The revolver illustrated is the one normally encountered, but the patent does describe two other extraction systems neither of which appears to have been commercially exploited. The principle of operation with the production model was that, when rotated under the influence of a coarse barrel bolting thread, the barrel (and the cylinder) moved forward, the strong camming action 'unsticking' the fired cartridge cases so that they were retained by the star extractor.

The American Merwin and Hulbert was briefly mentioned in connection with the 1878 US Army tests and, although it was unsuccessful, it remains of interest because of the ejection system employed. The basic patent for the Merwin and Hulbert system was granted to Daniel Moore of Brooklyn, New York (US Patent No. 157,860 of 1874), and was assigned to Merwin, Hulbert and Co. of New York City who later obtained British Patent No. 277 of 1878 in the names of J. Merwin, M. Hulbert and W. A. Hulbert. As can be seen from illustrations, the

.44 Merwin and Hulbert double action simultaneous ejection pocket model revolver.

system relied upon the forward movement of the cylinder and barrel along a central pin projecting from the standing breech. The action was unlocked by releasing a spring bolt in front of the trigger guard, and the barrel was then rotated through 90 degrees, extraction being initiated by a camming action during barrel rotation. Both the barrel and cylinder were then moved forward until the fired cartridges were clear of the cylinder and could be removed.

The Merwin and Hulbert was made in three calibres, .32, .38 and .44, and in both single and double action variants. Some were fitted with a top strap and others without, and there were many combinations of barrel length and butt styles. Merwin and Hulbert were retailers, not manufacturers, and their revolver was made for them by the Hopkins and Allen Manufacturing Co. of Norwich, Connecticut, who also made revolvers to sell under their own name. The company was formed in 1868, and a percussion revolver was followed by a long line of pocket revolvers in various calibres bearing such names as Ranger, Dictator, Blue Jacket, XL, Expert etc. They also made single shot rifles and shotguns. One of the features of the Hopkins and Allen revolvers was the folding spur on the trigger, and the example shown, a .32 five shot double action XL 8 revolver, is fairly typical of their range. The company, controlled by the brothers Charles W., Henry H. and Samuel Hopkins, got into difficulties following the failure of the successors to Merwin, Hulbert and Co. (with whom they were financially involved), and the additional problems caused by a disastrous fire in 1900 proved too much for them. The Hopkins and Allen Arms Co. ceased to exist in 1915, and the assets were purchased by Marlin-Rockwell.

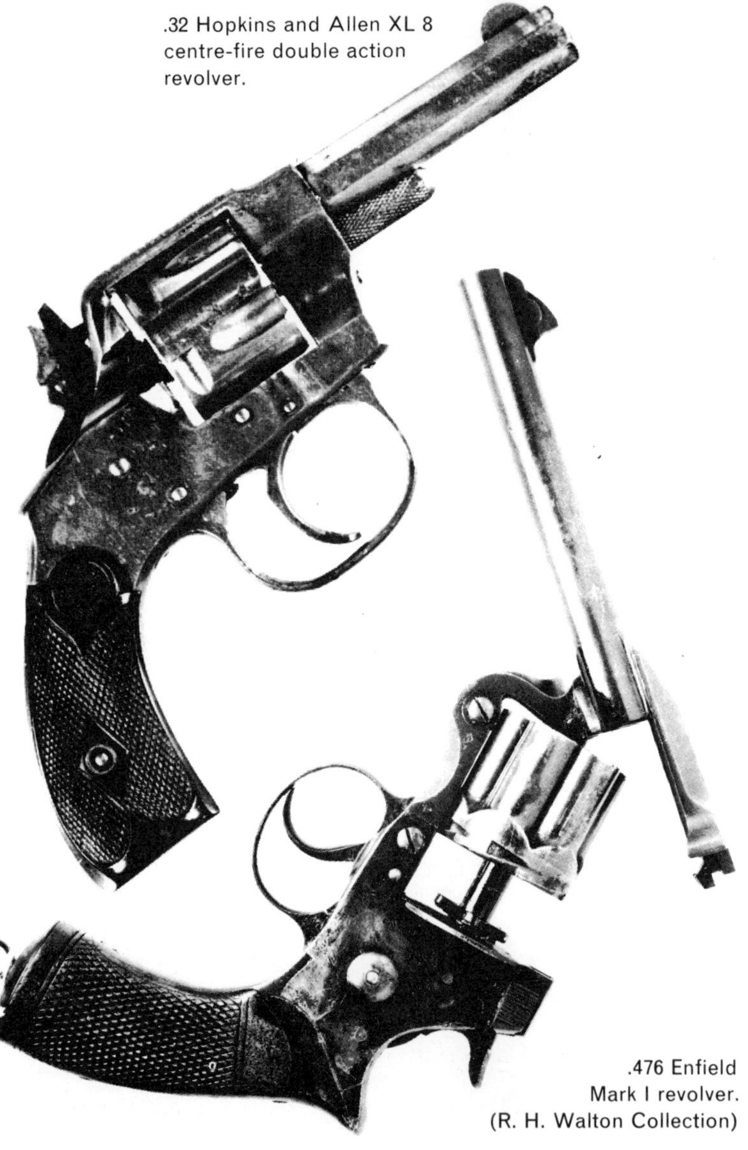

.32 Hopkins and Allen XL 8 centre-fire double action revolver.

.476 Enfield Mark I revolver. (R. H. Walton Collection)

The idea of a static extractor and forward moving cylinder was embodied in the British Enfield revolver, and the method of operation adopted can be seen from Owen Jones' British Patent No. 624 of 1878. An American citizen, Jones was a prolific inventor chock full of ingenious ideas, one of which is shown here—a 'tool tube' carried under the barrel (D) which contained among other things a double ended screwdriver.

The .476 Enfield Mark I was, as the name implies, manufactured at the Royal Small Arms Factory at Enfield (established 1804) and adopted as a replacement for the .450 Adams in 1880. To open the pistol, the thumb latch at the top of the frame was drawn back and the 6″ barrel hinged downwards. This drew the cylinder forward, but the extractor, attached to the breech, retained the fired cases until they cleared the cylinder and could be removed. A well made weapon, the Enfield was six chambered and double action. Although extraction was simultaneous, loading was not, and single cartridges were introduced through the loading gate which can be seen on the Mark II, a modified version adopted in 1882. The lock work was derived from Kaufmann and Warnant's British Patent No. 5031 of 1878 and, on the later Enfields, the loading gate also acted as a safety; with the gate hinged outwards for loading, the hammer could not be cocked—a refinement similar to that invented by Abadie. The external differences between the Mark I and the Mark II can be seen by comparing the illustrations. The shape of the top strap was

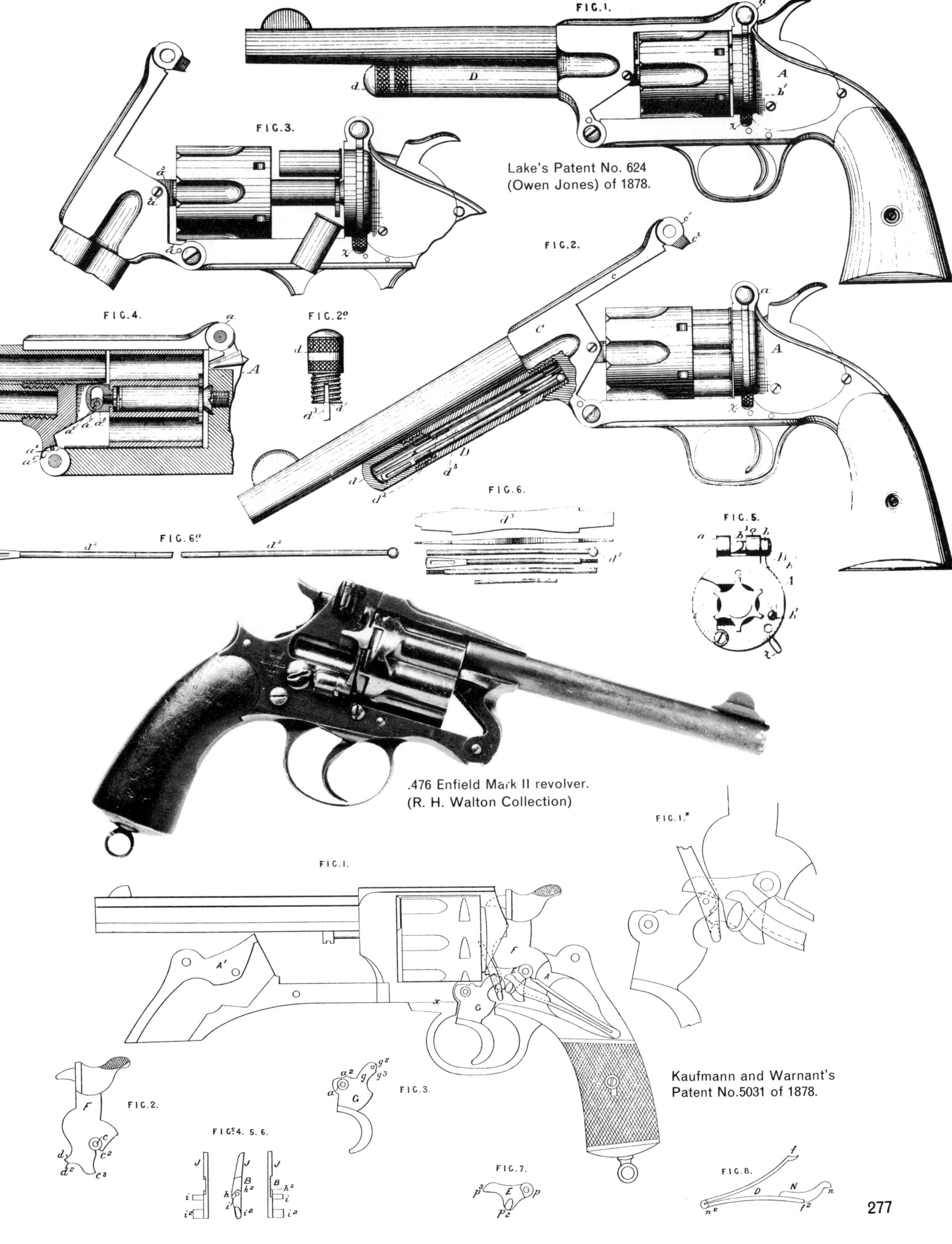

Lake's Patent No. 624 (Owen Jones) of 1878.

.476 Enfield Mark II revolver. (R. H. Walton Collection)

Kaufmann and Warnant's Patent No.5031 of 1878.

altered, as was the foresight, and a smooth grip replaced the checkered stock. According to Dowell, the Enfield was issued to the Navy, the Royal Irish Mounted Constabulary and the Canadian North West Mounted Police Force.

The Enfield has come in for perhaps more than its fair share of criticism, both then and now. It was certainly clumsy and lacked any pretence to beauty. My own feeling, having used it, is that the necessary complication did not result in any marked improvement in speed of loading. Although extraction was simultaneous, the cartridges were not expelled, and loading through the side gate was certainly no faster than with the solid frame rod ejector revolver which was both cheaper to manufacture and far less complicated. The Enfield remained in production until 1889 when it was replaced by the Webley.

Even granted that the Enfield was adopted by the Government, the system cannot be said to have been successful since it was never adopted for civilian revolvers. Several other unsuccessful revolvers also appeared about this time and should be considered before we come on to the designs of Webley and Scott.

One of several 'mystery' revolvers is marked Levaux, and is a hinged frame simultaneous extraction double action pistol, the principal features of which can be seen from the illustration. Several specimens have been encountered, some bearing Liege and some Birmingham proof marks. One is marked internally 'F. A. Braendlin' and also has Birmingham marks, while the one illustrated is marked 'D.D. Levaux Bte.' No patent has been found, however, which agrees with the design features, although Baron A. T. de Mouncie's British Patent No. 4163 of 1876 may have had some connection. Of the examples examined, over half had suffered damage to the barrel latch, but it can be assumed that this was one of the weaknesses of the design.

.380 Belgian Levaux centre-fire self-extracting revolver.

Mouncie also patented a rebounding lock mechanism (British Patent No. 3206 of 1876) which was later improved by Kaufmann and Warnant after Mouncie had assigned his patent to them (see page 290).

Far better documentation is available for those revolvers which bear the well known name of Tranter, whose pocket and solid frame Army revolvers have already been discussed. His hinged frame extracting revolvers were based on British Patent No. 3622 of 1868, and improvements were contained in his later patent No. 3577 of 1869. The basic idea was similar to that patented by Spirlet in 1870 and to the later patents of Mauser. No Tranter revolvers with rear top

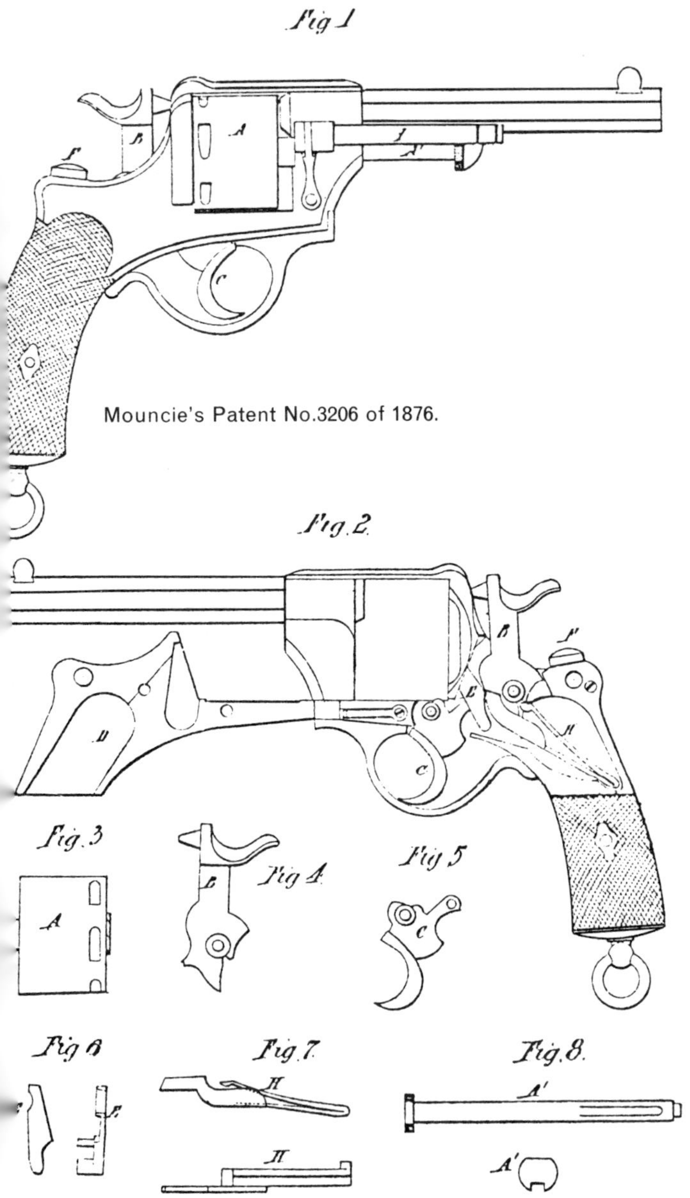

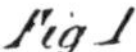

Mouncie's Patent No.3206 of 1876.

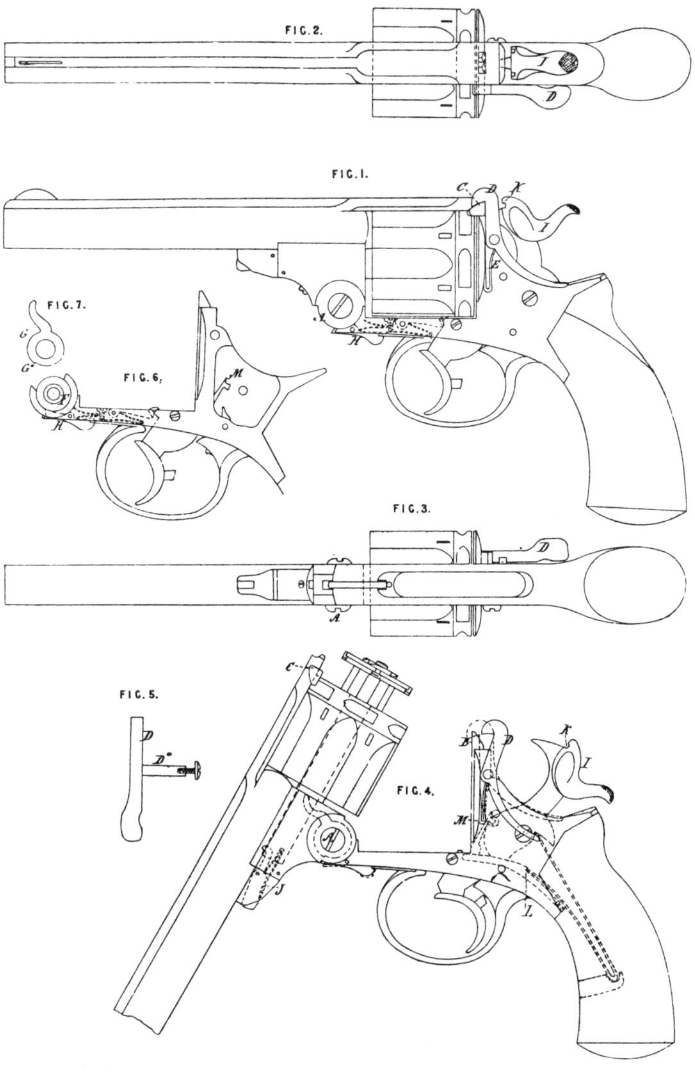

Tranter's Patent No.2855 of 1879.

hinged barrels have been encountered, and few, if any, can have been manufactured. A later patent taken out in 1879, No. 2855, did result in the volume production of a conventional hinged frame self-extracting revolver, the mechanism of which was undoubted Tranter, with locking accomplished by a thumb lever on the left hand side of the frame. A sturdy and well made revolver, its merits were not sufficient to save the fortunes of the company. William Tranter retired five years before his death in 1890 and, as we have already noted, the famous Tranter Gun and Pistol Factory passed into the hands of George Kynoch, the Birmingham ammunition maker. According to such records as are available, Kynoch purchased the business as a private venture, and a trade label of the period bears the famous Kynoch lion and the legend 'Kynoch Gun Factory, Aston, Warwickshire, Manufacturers of Military and Sporting Arms, &c — &c.' To my great annoyance the pistol case which bears this label was devoid of any contents when I acquired it, and we are left wondering exactly what the 'etc. etc.' might have been.

After the purchase of Tranter's factory in 1885, Kynoch appointed Henry A. Schlund as works manager, but then ran headlong into trouble with his board of directors, one of their complaints being 'that his attention is occupied with his private undertakings . . . and that there seems to be some confusion in the minds of outsiders between the limited company and private business which he carries on for his own benefit'. The Kynoch Gun Factory was undoubtedly one of these distractions, and further inroads into the time he should have been spending on the affairs

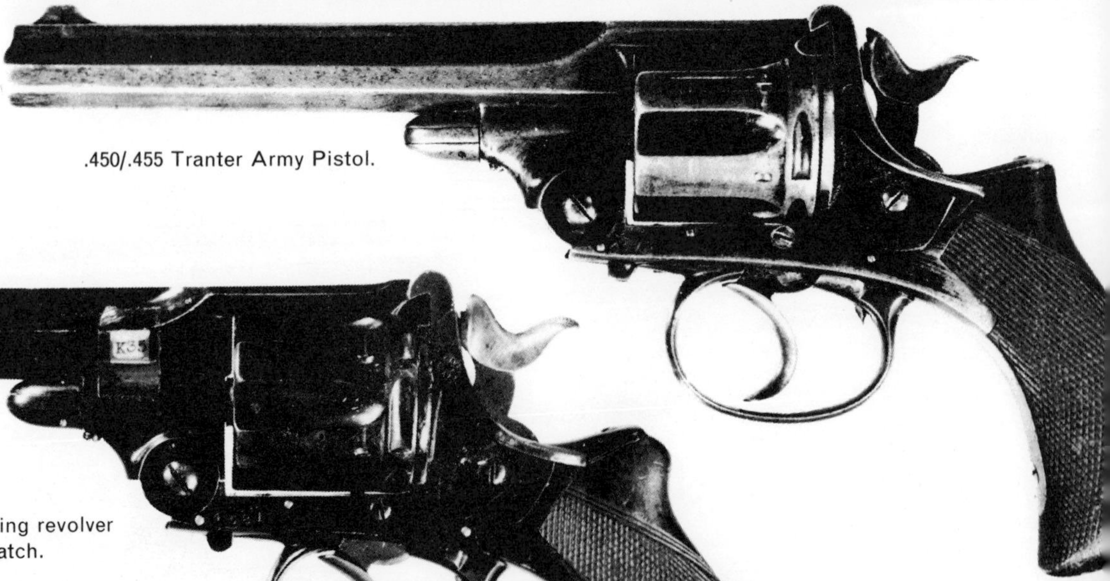

.450/.455 Tranter Army Pistol.

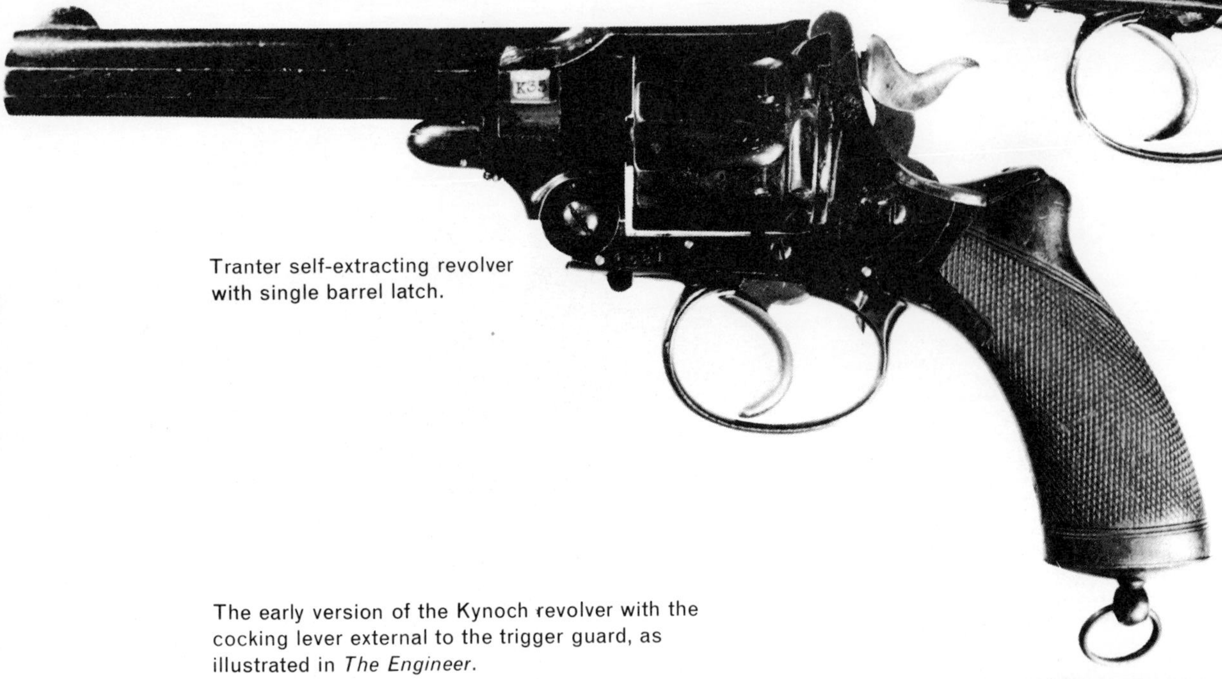

Tranter self-extracting revolver with single barrel latch.

The early version of the Kynoch revolver with the cocking lever external to the trigger guard, as illustrated in *The Engineer*.

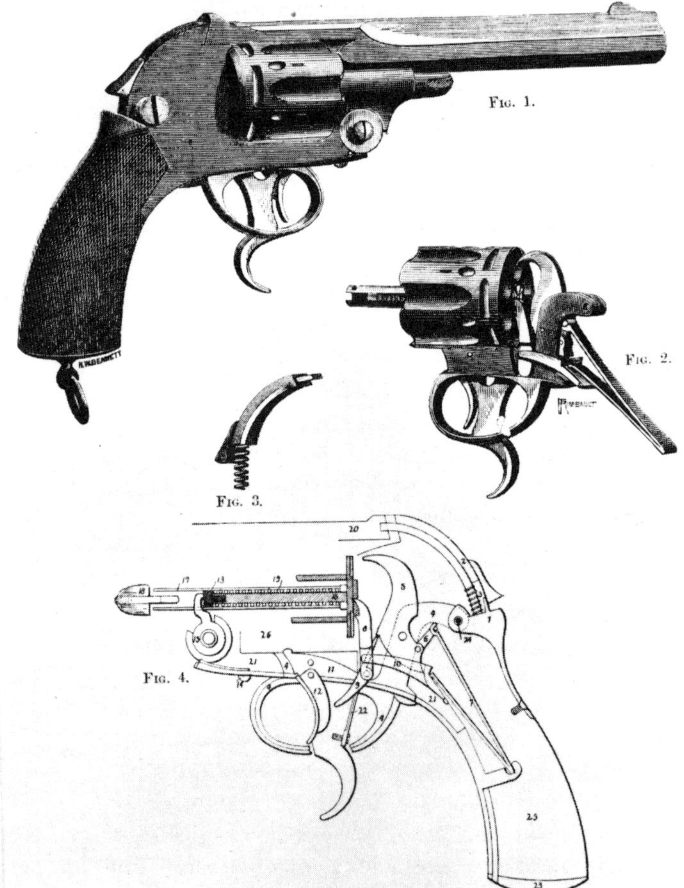

The trade label of the Kynoch Gun Factory

of G. Kynoch Ltd. were devoted to his political, and social activities—he was MP for Aston and also president of Aston Villa Football Club. In 1888, yielding to the pressure from his fellow directors, Kynoch resigned and, shortly before his death in South Africa in February 1891, Henry A. Schlund obtained control of the Kynoch Gun Factory, changing the name to the Aston Arms Factory. By 1900 the business had faded out and the premises were occupied by the Clipper Automatic Tyre Company; then, for a short time, it was occupied by Dunlop and used for making motor car tyres until, in 1926, it was finally sold to the Hercules Cycle Co. Tranter's factory was demolished in 1961 and yet another monument to the once powerful Birmingham gun trade vanished.

The period between 1885 and 1900 holds many

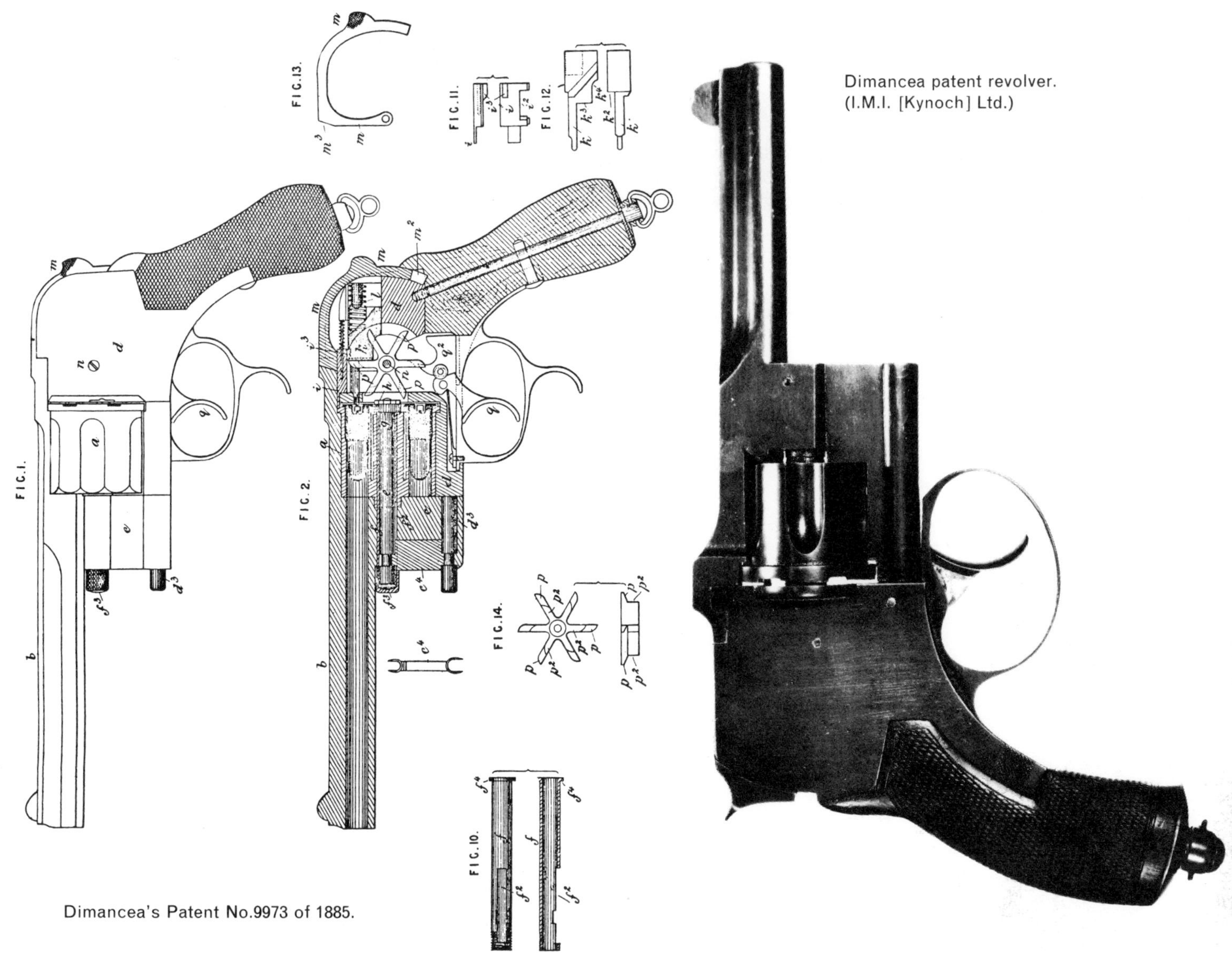

Dimancea's Patent No.9973 of 1885.

Dimancea patent revolver. (I.M.I. [Kynoch] Ltd.)

mysteries. The first of these is the unusual Dimancea revolver patented by Haralamb Dimancea in 1885, British Patent No. 9973. Despite considerable research, Dimancea remains somewhat of an enigma. From official Roumanian sources it is known that he was born on 1 October 1855, went to the Military Artillery School in 1874, was commissioned in 1876 and was decorated for bravery during the War of Independence. He was promoted Lieutenant in 1879 and Captain in 1883, and it must have been relatively soon afterwards that he came to England to patent and supervise the manufacture of his revolver. Why he came is open to conjecture, but it is possible that Kynoch, a much travelled man who had spent some time in Roumania and had been decorated by the King with the Star of Roumania, may well have invited him. While he was at Birmingham, Dimancea lived at 299 Aston Lane, Witton, near to both the Kynoch Gun Factory and George Kynoch's Lion Works.

Dimancea's revolver was undoubtedly made at the Kynoch Gun Factory and the example illustrated is marked 'Kynoch Gun Factory Aston, Revolverul Dimancea'. There are no proof marks, but there are three important and unusual features. The first is the extraction system. What at first appears to be the hammer shown (*m*) on the patent drawing, is actually the cylinder latch. When this was pressed downwards, the cylinder and barrel hinged to one side about the pin (*d3*), fully exposing the rear of the cylinder for unloading and loading. A star extractor was also provided. The second feature is the 'ratchet wheel' lock mechanism. This performed a dual function; it rotated the cylinder

Schlund's Patent No.11,900 of 1886.

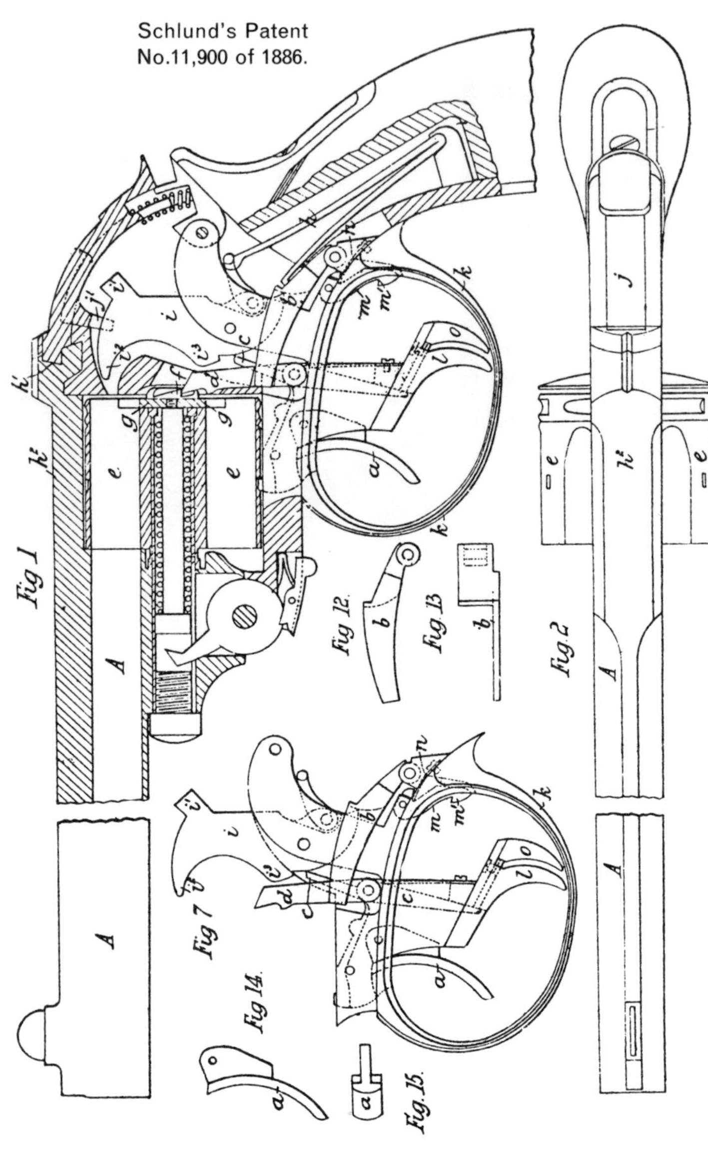

and also operated the firing pin. The third feature is the use of a long pin which passed through the butt into the action body. When this was removed, both the butt and trigger plate could be withdrawn, exposing the internal mechanism for examination.

According to Roumanian evidence, the Roumanian Government contracted with an English company to supply 1,000 revolvers to their specification. The English company then asked for the contract to be cancelled due to technical and manufacturing difficulties. If it is assumed that the 'English company' was the Kynoch Gun Factory and that the revolver specified was the 'Revolverul Dimancea', Dimancea himself may well have been sent over by his own Government in order to supervise operations.

Yet another equally interesting and unusual revolver was manufactured at the Kynoch Gun Factory. This was the Schlund revolver patented in 1885 by Henry Schlund, the Works Manager of the Kynoch Gun Factory. A later patent, No. 11,900 of 1886, incorporated improvements, and actual production appears to have been based on this. The presentation engraved example illustrated is marked 'Kynoch Gun Factory, Aston' and, on the shield on the right hand side of the frame, is engraved 'Presented to the National Rifle Association by the Kynoch Gun Factory for Revolver Competition'. Specimens examined of this revolver have been in .476, .450 and .380 calibres and of the 'improved' pattern based on Patent No. 11,900.

The mechanism of the Schlund undoubtedly owed something to Tranter. This is very apparent on the earlier model with the lower trigger

.320 Schlund revolver, presentation model. (I.M.I. [Kynoch] Ltd.)

external to the guard. On both models the lower trigger was pulled to cock the action and rotate the cylinder, while the top trigger fired the round in the chamber. A 'double action' effect was obtained if both triggers were pulled simultaneously. To uncock the later model (the top trigger would, of course, be in the rear position), the checkered surfaces on each side of the lower trigger were grasped, the trigger pulled slightly to the rear and then allowed to go forward under restraint. The barrel latch was at the top rear of the frame, and the small catch under the barrel hinge disconnected the extractor so that the pistol could be opened without ejecting the cartridges.

Exactly how many Kynoch-Schlund revolvers were manufactured it is impossible to say, but they do not appear to have been made by any other concern and, in the absence of significant contracts, it appears that the project was abandoned before the demise of the Kynoch Gun Factory. It is, however, possible that some may have been made by the Aston Arms Factory at a slightly later date.

The story does not end here, for Kynoch-Dimancea revolvers have turned up marked 'Gatling Arms and Ammunition Co, Ltd.—Dimancea Patent'. The Gatling Arms and Ammunition Company had premises at Holford about half a mile from the main gates of Kynoch's Lion Works at Witton. Originally the place name was Old Ford (where Ryknild Street, the old Roman road crossed the River Tame), but in course of time Old Ford became corrupted by the local inhabitants to Holford and a flour mill was established there, taking power from the river. Later, the flour mill became a gun barrel factory and, in 1872, the site was developed by the Westley Richards Arms and Ammunition Co., who erected several large buildings. This company was then taken over by the National Arms and Ammunition Co., manufacturers of paper musket and carbine cartridges and, at the end of the Franco-Prussian War, the company was fortunate enough to land huge orders from the German Government. By 1880 the company had become defunct and the premises were then taken over by the Gatling Company. A new company, the Gatling Arms and Ammunition Co., was subsequently formed in 1888, and it is at this time that the manufacture of the Dimancea revolver must have taken place. The Gatling-Dimancea at present in the Collection of the City of Birmingham Police was surrendered by relatives of a workman formerly employed by the company. This example, a demonstration cut-away model, had been made at the request of a Roumanian army officer prior to the placing of substantial orders which, in the event, never materialised.

Lack of orders no doubt contributed to the eventual failure of the Gatling Arms and Ammunition Co., and once again the premises changed hands, being acquired this time by Grenfell and Accles, manufacturers of patented weapons and fuses. A revolver bearing a strong resemblance to the Dimancea, except for the use of a conventional trigger mechanism, was patented by Grenfell in 1891, British Patent No. 17,993, but I have not been able to trace an actual example of it. In 1896 the manufacture of weapons appears to have been abandoned, and Accles Ltd. was formed to take advantage of the boom in cycles. This venture met with little success, Kynoch Ltd. bought the premises in 1901, and Holford Works is now part of I.M.I. (Kynoch) Ltd., Witton Works.

In the traditional centre of Birmingham gun-making—St. Mary's Row, Weaman Street, Whittal Street—there were no signs of despondency. The success of the Webley RIC and Bulldog series had finally been crowned with the adoption by the British Government, in 1887, of a hinged frame simultaneous ejection revolver, the Mark I Webley, the very success of which struck a final blow at the hopes and aspirations of the dwindling competition. Webley's interest in hinged frame revolvers can be said to have started with the introduction of the Webley-Woods revolver which employed a simple breech latch similar to the Levaux except that it was opened by a thumb lever on the left hand side of the frame.

During the evolution of the Webley hinged frame series, several distinct models appeared and Dowell's classification will be followed here. The first series can be easily identified by the barrel locking device consisting of two bolts which passed through the frame into the extension of the top strap; the bolts were withdrawn by two rocking levers, one on each side of the frame, the lower ends conveniently placed so that they could be grasped by forefinger and thumb. This series, known as the Webley-Pryse, still affords room for considerable conjecture since the identifying barrel locking device was not part of Charles Pryse the Younger's patent of 1876, No. 4421, where protection was claimed for part of the lock-work, in particular the cylinder bolt which

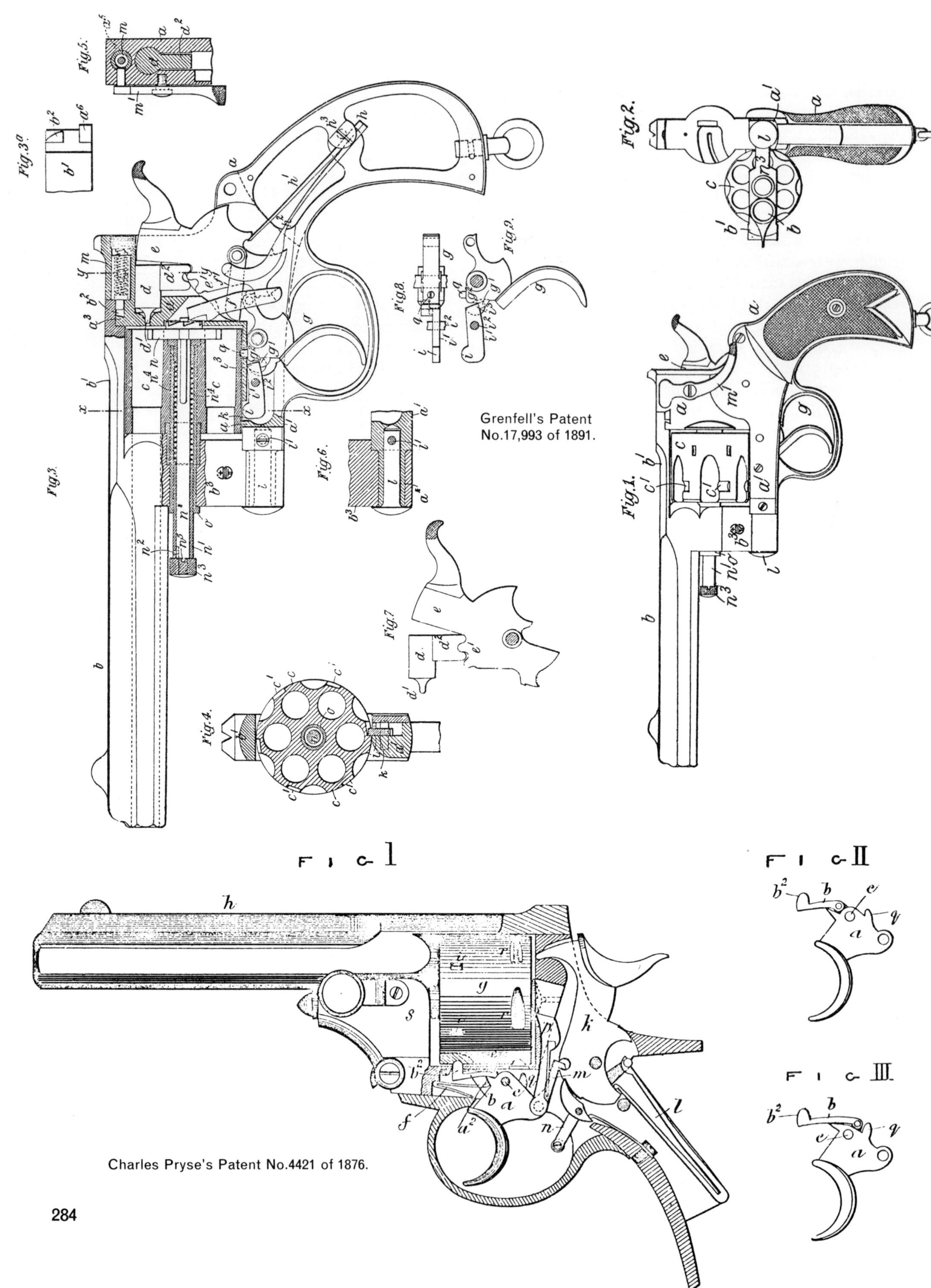

Grenfell's Patent No.17,993 of 1891.

Charles Pryse's Patent No.4421 of 1876.

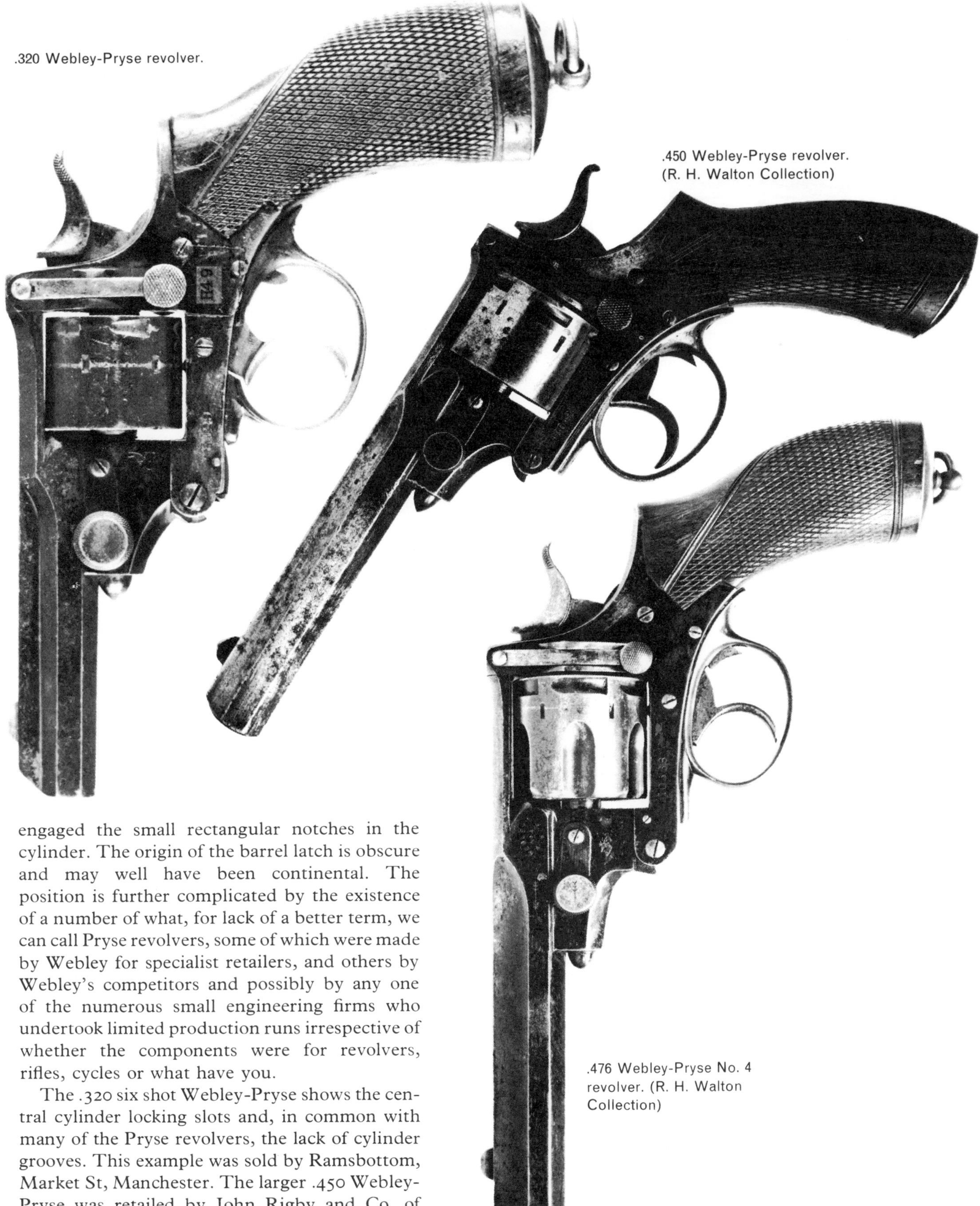

.320 Webley-Pryse revolver.

.450 Webley-Pryse revolver. (R. H. Walton Collection)

.476 Webley-Pryse No. 4 revolver. (R. H. Walton Collection)

engaged the small rectangular notches in the cylinder. The origin of the barrel latch is obscure and may well have been continental. The position is further complicated by the existence of a number of what, for lack of a better term, we can call Pryse revolvers, some of which were made by Webley for specialist retailers, and others by Webley's competitors and possibly by any one of the numerous small engineering firms who undertook limited production runs irrespective of whether the components were for revolvers, rifles, cycles or what have you.

The .320 six shot Webley-Pryse shows the central cylinder locking slots and, in common with many of the Pryse revolvers, the lack of cylinder grooves. This example was sold by Ramsbottom, Market St, Manchester. The larger .450 Webley-Pryse was retailed by John Rigby and Co. of Dublin (current opinion is that the Rigby-Pryse

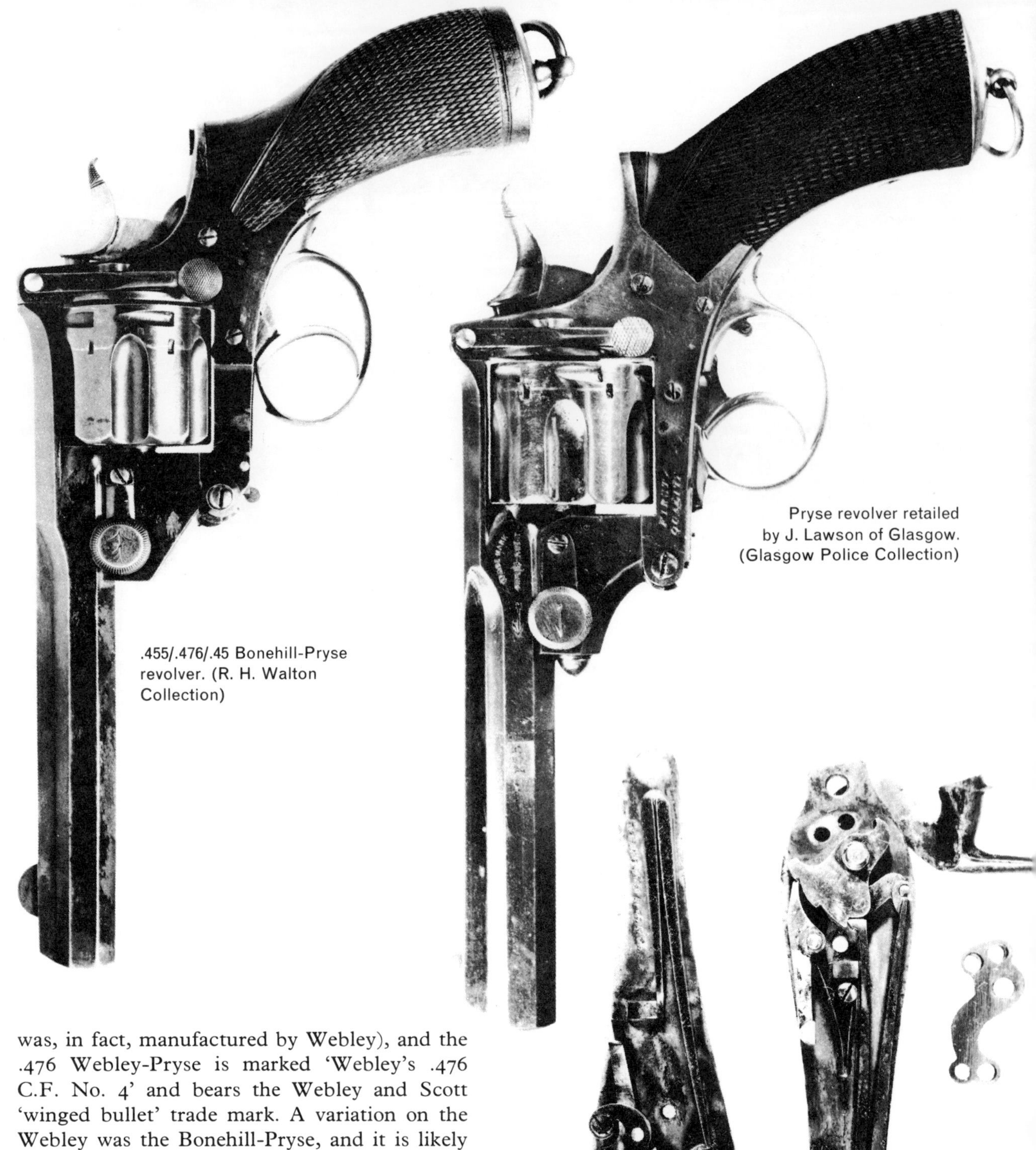

.455/.476/.45 Bonehill-Pryse revolver. (R. H. Walton Collection)

Pryse revolver retailed by J. Lawson of Glasgow. (Glasgow Police Collection)

was, in fact, manufactured by Webley), and the .476 Webley-Pryse is marked 'Webley's .476 C.F. No. 4' and bears the Webley and Scott 'winged bullet' trade mark. A variation on the Webley was the Bonehill-Pryse, and it is likely that this revolver was made under licence from Charles Pryse by Christopher George Bonehill, Belmont Fire Arm Works, Birmingham.

The revolver retailed by J. Lawson, 70 Argyle St, Glasgow, bears the 'arrow' trademark of Pryse together with the assertion 'First Quality'. The Pryse revolver may have been manufactured for Charles Pryse by Webley, but, irrespective of markings, the 'true' Pryse can be identified by the little roller bearing on the secondary sear which protrudes through the rear of the trigger guard. The locks on Pryse revolvers had rebounding hammers and were probably the first British

Back action sporting gun side locks by Stanton showing the rebound mechanism. The right hand lock (with the bridle removed) illustrates the principle of using both limbs of the mainspring, while the lock on the left employs an ingenious 'C' shaped tumbler.

revolvers with this feature. The patent shows this as claimed by Stanton, a man famous for his ingenious inventions, particularly with regard to side locks for sporting guns. Along with Brazier (also of Wolverhampton), he made more quality gun locks than anyone else in the country. The work of both has been sadly neglected; unless the locks are removed from that superb shotgun or rifle, it is assumed that the 'famous' maker whose name is prominently engraved on the barrel and on the outside of the lock plates, also made the gun locks. This was rarely the case. Take off the locks and inside will be found the name 'Joseph Brazier, Ashes' or perhaps 'I.B.' or 'Stanton'. A rebounding lock of the type used on sporting guns is illustrated, that on the left (with the hammer removed) showing an earlier method of rebounding the hammer by employing a hooked end to the tumbler. The right hand lock (the bridle of which has been removed), also by Stanton, shows how the lower limb of the mainspring bore against a projection on the tumbler, returning the lock to half cock automatically. Since the sear was engaged in the half cock bent, the hammer could not be pushed forward until the trigger was pulled. This was the system employed by Pryse, and revolvers like those illustrated often bore the legend 'Stanton and Co., Joint Patents'.

The Bonehill-Pryse was one of several variant revolvers which employed the Pryse type barrel latch but the one shown differs in that the mechanism is of the Schmidt type, immediately identifiable by the absence of a protruding secondary sear. Other 'Pryse' type revolvers were made by Webley for Henry Wilkinson and Son, 27 Pall Mall, and these revolvers are distinguished by the excellence of their finish. Webley's built the revolvers to Wilkinson's own pattern and they are unusual in that they bear London proof marks.

Thomas Horsley of York also sold Pryse type revolvers but I have not seen any evidence to indicate that Horsley actually manufactured these revolvers himself. It is possible that they were made for him by a Birmingham or even Belgian maker, or perhaps the components were supplied and finished by Horsley. Pryse type revolvers were certainly made in abundance in Belgium, the most notable makers being Auguste Francotte et Cie of Liege.

The chief defect of the Pryse locking system was the ease with which the barrel could be unlatched by accident. Since extremely large revolvers have been made employing this action, it was apparently sufficiently strong.

Solid frame double action revolver with rod ejector, marked 'Stanton & Co. Joint Patents'.

The Webley-Kaufmann represented an important landmark in the Webley revolver series. The previous hinged frame Webleys had employed a separate trigger guard attached to the frame by two screws; in the Kaufmann series the guard was forged as part of the frame and there was a great improvement in the comfort of the grip. According to Dowell, Michael Kaufmann was associated with Webley's during the 1880's, but little else is known and European works of reference do not mention him.

Kaufmann's British Patents were as follows: No. 5031 of 1878 (see page 277), taken out jointly with the Belgian maker Warnant, protected the lockwork used by the Enfield revolver but was admitted to be an improvement on the patent

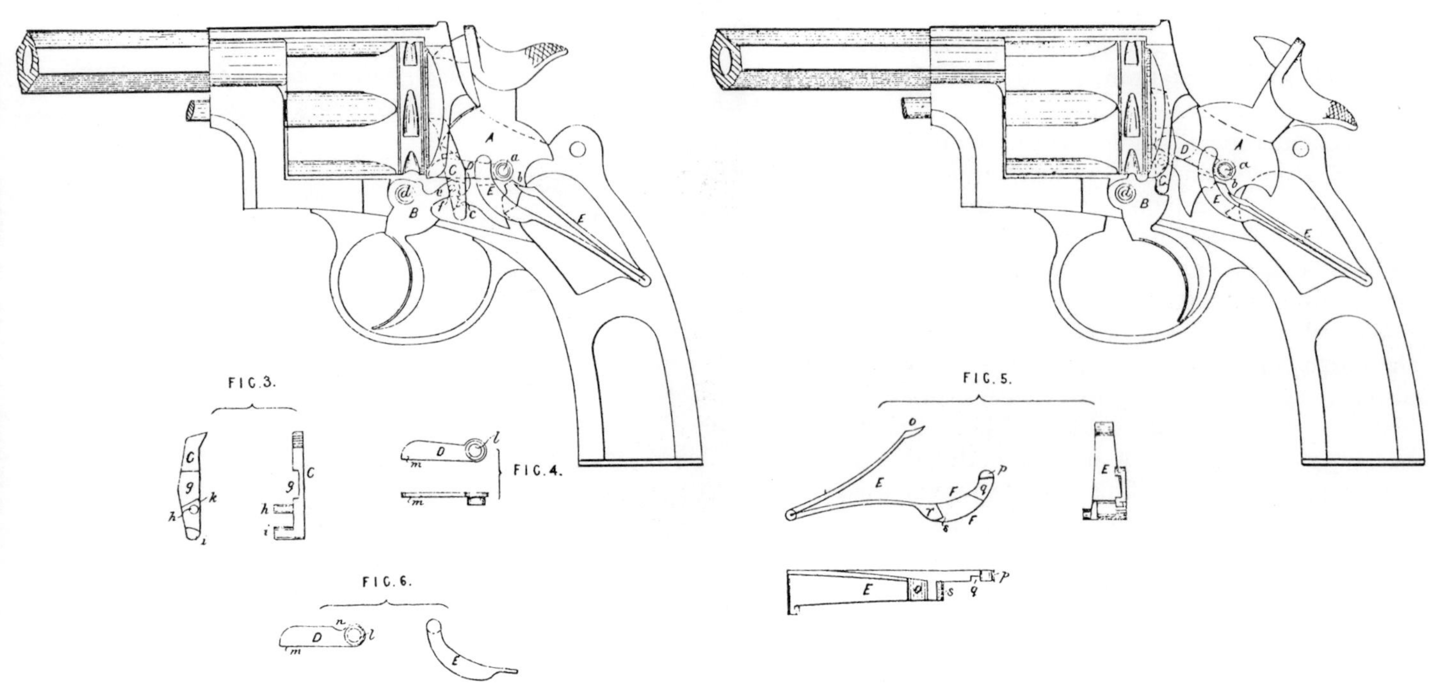

Kaufmann's Patent No.4302 of 1880.

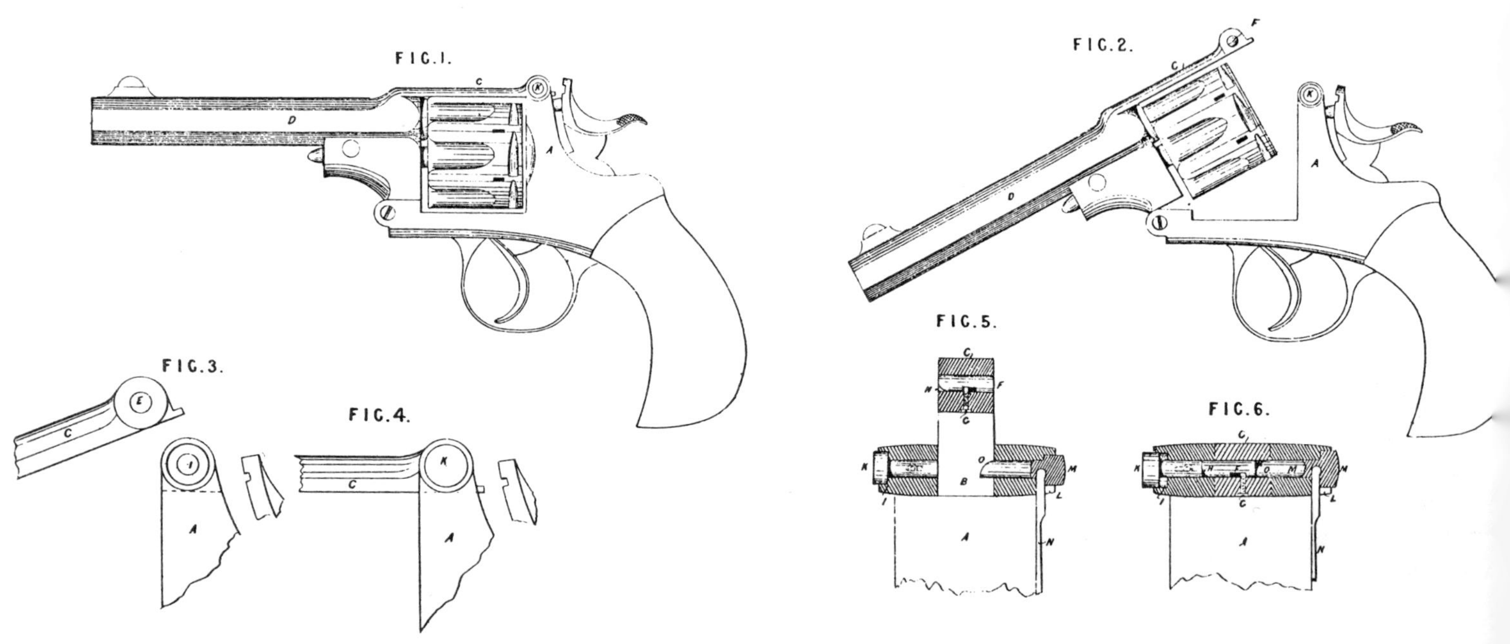

Gedge's Patent No.3313 (Kaufmann) of 1881.

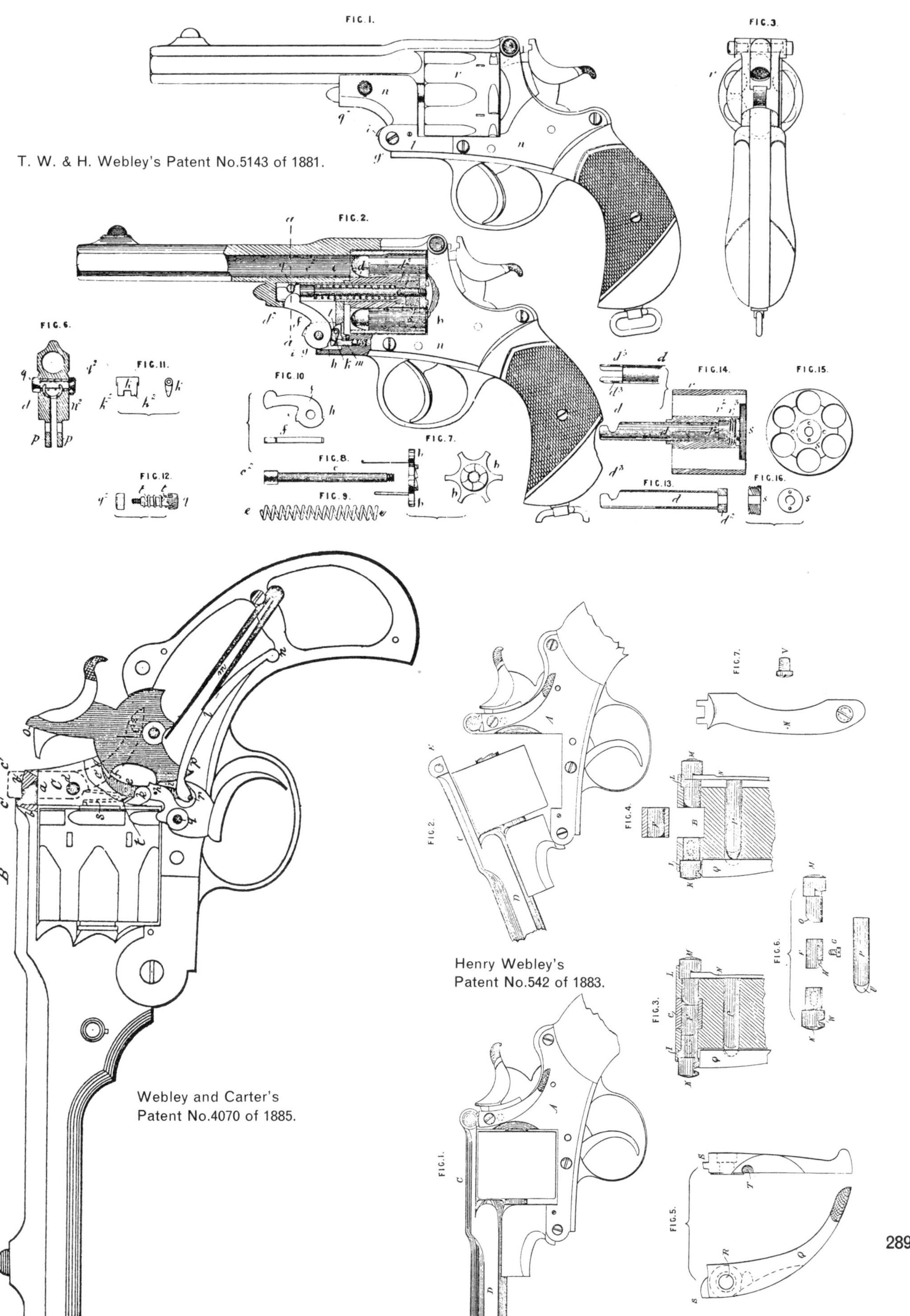
T. W. & H. Webley's Patent No.5143 of 1881.
Webley and Carter's
Patent No.4070 of 1885.
Henry Webley's
Patent No.542 of 1883.

assigned to Kaufmann by Baron A. T. de Mouncie; No. 4302 of 1880 covered the lock mechanism of the Webley-Kaufmann; No. 3313 of 1881 dealt with the original 'press button' barrel latch; No. 3913 of 1881 referred to a means of permitting the free rotation of the cylinder of solid frame revolvers during loading and unloading in a manner somewhat similar to the Abadie modification, and was used by Webley on the loading gate of the solid frame double action Army revolver. Two other minor patents were obtained by Kaufmann in 1884: No. 189 for a cylinder bolt, and No. 5308 for modifications to revolver stocks to permit removal of the side plates without tools.

The close connection between Kaufmann and Belgian interests can be inferred from the nature and scope of his patents. In the absence of positive information, however, the precise nature of his relationship with Belgian gunmaking interests remains a mystery and further conjecture, although perhaps of interest, would at present be unenlightening.

Kaufmann's barrel latch is shown on the illustration which accompanied Thomas William Webley and Henry Webley's Patent No. 5143 of 1881. T. W. Webley and H. Webley were the sons of Philip Webley, the founder of P. Webley and Sons, and the patent taken out jointly covered the cartridge extractor mechanism used on the Webley-Kaufmann, the operation of which can be seen from the drawing.

Henry Webley's patent of 1883, No. 542, referred to improvements in the barrel latch described by Kaufmann (Patent No. 3313 of 1881), and Dowell refers to revolvers with the Webley thumb latch as 'second' model Webley-Kaufmann.

In the writer's opinion, the finest Webley revolvers were the Webley WG series which introduced the famous Webley 'stirrup' or 'bridle' latch based on British Patent No. 4070 secured by H. Webley and John Carter (who described himself as an 'action filer') in 1885. According to Webley, the initials 'WG' stood for Webley-Green, and these revolvers appeared in an Army version with a 6″ barrel and in a Target Model with a $7\frac{1}{2}$″ barrel. Dowell refers to an 1882 WG revolver with a Pryse type cylinder release, and this was followed in 1885 by a modification to the cylinder release device, the large milled headed screw (as on the Bonehill-Pryse) being replaced by a much smaller screw with a wide slot which could be turned by a coin. In 1889 came the first WG Model which can be identified by the date stamp, 'W.G. Model 1889', on the left side of the top strap. The bird's head grip of the earlier model was replaced by a most comfortable flared grip, but the original cylinder fluting known in the Birmingham area as 'church steeple' was retained.

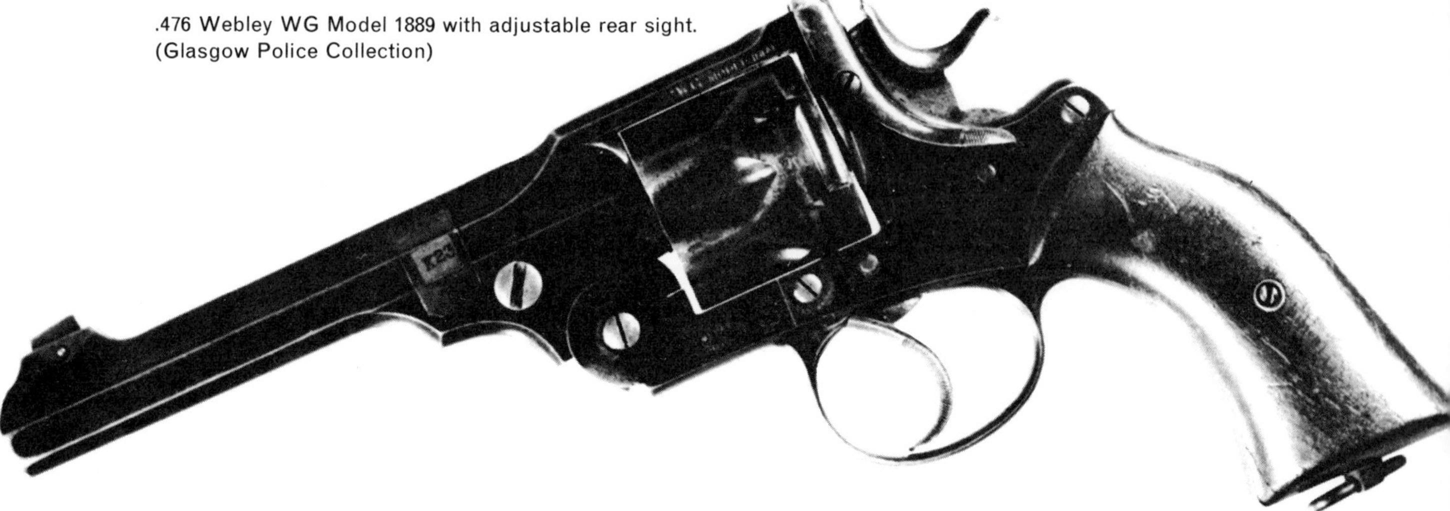

.476 Webley WG Model 1889 with adjustable rear sight. (Glasgow Police Collection)

The WG Model of 1892, incorporating W. J. Whiting's patent No. 3427 of 1891, employed a redesigned cylinder release which, with only minor modifications, has been used by Webley's to the present day. The Model of 1892 is illustrated (page 292), and a year later the Model 1893 introduced a spring-loaded striker instead of the conventional hammer with attached firing pin. After 1893 the practice of stamping the date on the revolver was discontinued, the separate striker was discarded and a grooved cylinder was used

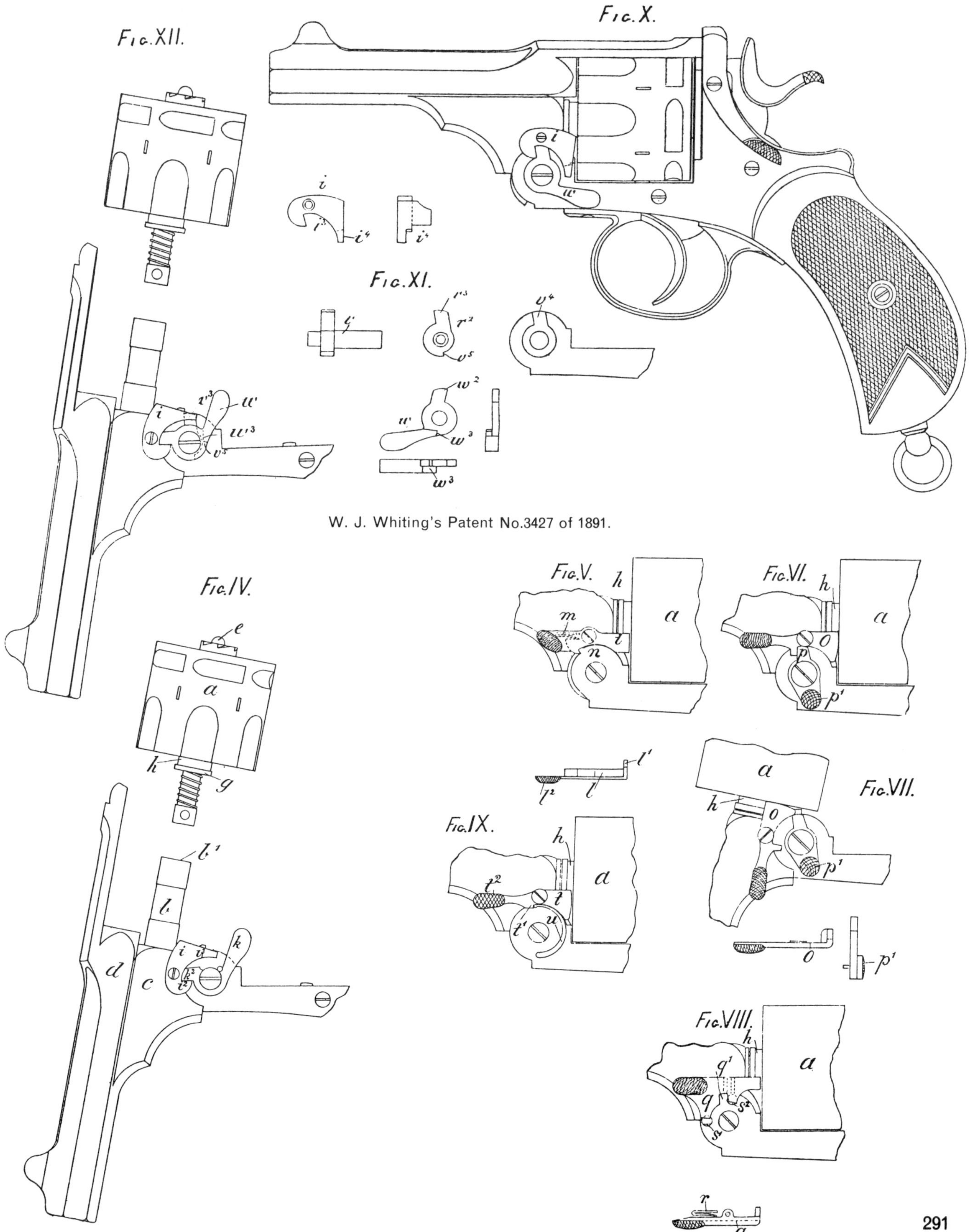

W. J. Whiting's Patent No.3427 of 1891.

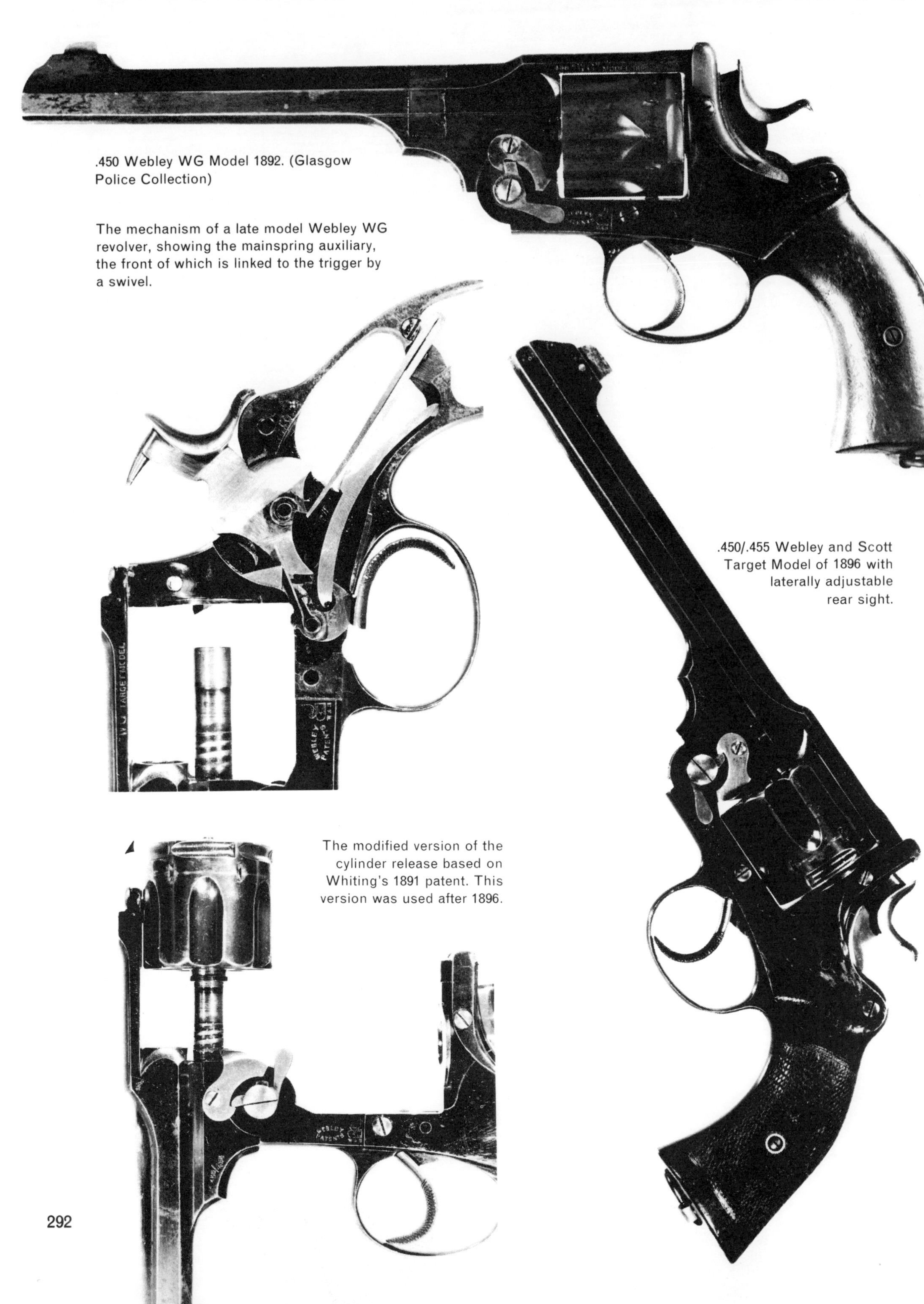

.450 Webley WG Model 1892. (Glasgow Police Collection)

The mechanism of a late model Webley WG revolver, showing the mainspring auxiliary, the front of which is linked to the trigger by a swivel.

.450/.455 Webley and Scott Target Model of 1896 with laterally adjustable rear sight.

The modified version of the cylinder release based on Whiting's 1891 patent. This version was used after 1896.

instead of the 'church steeple' fluting.

All of the excellent WG Models, with the exception of the first 1882 model, had the flared stock, and all models had the trigger guard machined as part of the frame. Both trigger action and thumb cocking action were particularly easy and pleasant in operation and, on the target models, a variety of sights could be had. This was also the case with the Webley's chief rivals on the target ranges, the Colt Target and Bisley Models and the Smith and Wesson No. 3 Target or 'Winans' Model'.

A type of sight which became very popular was the 'Patridge', originally used by E. E. Patridge, a well-known American pistol shot of the 1880's. This sight was first described by Patridge in a letter to *Shooting and Fishing*, 13 January 1898. In contrast to both the Paine and Winans sights, the Patridge consisted of a rectangular blade foresight and a rectangular rear sight notch. With the exception of a tendency for sights to be made broader, the target sight used today is of this pattern.

Rifling employed by both the WG Target and Army Models was of the Metford pattern with seven grooves 0.005″ deep, and calibres available were .450, .455 and .476. The last of the Target Models appeared in 1904 and was based on the Mark IV Government Model. Eventually, the 'WS' Bisley Model was built from the same components as the Mark VI Government or, as it was later known, the Mark VI Service Model of .455 calibre and with a 7½″ barrel and adjustable sights. This revolver was available in the 1939 catalogue, and then cost £7. In the late 1930's not only was the Bisley Target Revolver available together with the standard Mark VI, but Parker-Hale, for example, also offered re-finished Mark VI revolvers with adjustable Patridge sights and a 'converted' .455 Webley Target revolver, a Mark VI with a 7½″ target barrel.

When the name Webley is mentioned, the Webley British Government Models are those that spring to mind. The first of these was the Mark I which was adopted for both the Navy and Army in 1887. This was a .442 calibre six chambered top break revolver with a barrel length of 4″. Later versions of the Mark I were made in .476 and .455 calibres. Note the introduction of holster guides in front of the cylinder. On the original Mark I the recoil shield was formed as part of the frame; later a separate shield dovetailed into the frame was employed, and this modification resulted in the Mark I*. Further

.442 Webley Government Model Mark I with 4″ barrel. (Glasgow Police Collection)

Webley and Scott Mark II Government Model of 1894 (Glasgow Police Collection)

Webley and Scott Mark III Government Model of 1897. (Glasgow Police Collection)

.455 Webley and Scott Mark V Government Model of 1913. (Glasgow Police Collection)

.455 Webley and Scott Mark VI Government Model.

modifications produced the Mark II .455, which can be identified by the absence of the hump on the back strap and by the larger hammer spur introduced to permit easier cocking.

In 1897 the Mark III Government Model appeared, differing from the Mark II in the type of cylinder release and extractor mechanism employed. This model was the first of the Government series to employ the new extraction mechanism described in connection with the WG Target revolvers. The Mark III was chambered to take all the Service cartridges, whether they were .450, .455 or .476 calibre.

There is little difference between the Mark III and the 1889 Mark IV. The Mark IV was widely used during the Boer War and can be encountered in 3″, 4″, 5″ and 6″ barrel lengths. The Mark IV also saw service during the First World War, being superceded by the short-lived Mark V of 1913 where the standard barrel length was 4″, although, in the example illustrated, it is 6″. Apart from the markings, there is little difference from the Mark IV, but W. C. Dowell mentions that the cylinder diameter was slightly increased because of the use of nitro powder.

The last of the Webley and Scott Government Models was the Mark VI introduced in 1915. The standard model had a 6″ barrel, and the illustration shows that a change was made in the shape of the grip, which reverted very nearly to the design used on the original Mark I. The basic design followed that of the previous Mark IV and V revolvers, and the action was simple but reliable.

General instructions for cleaning and dismounting the Mark VI, together with an illustra-

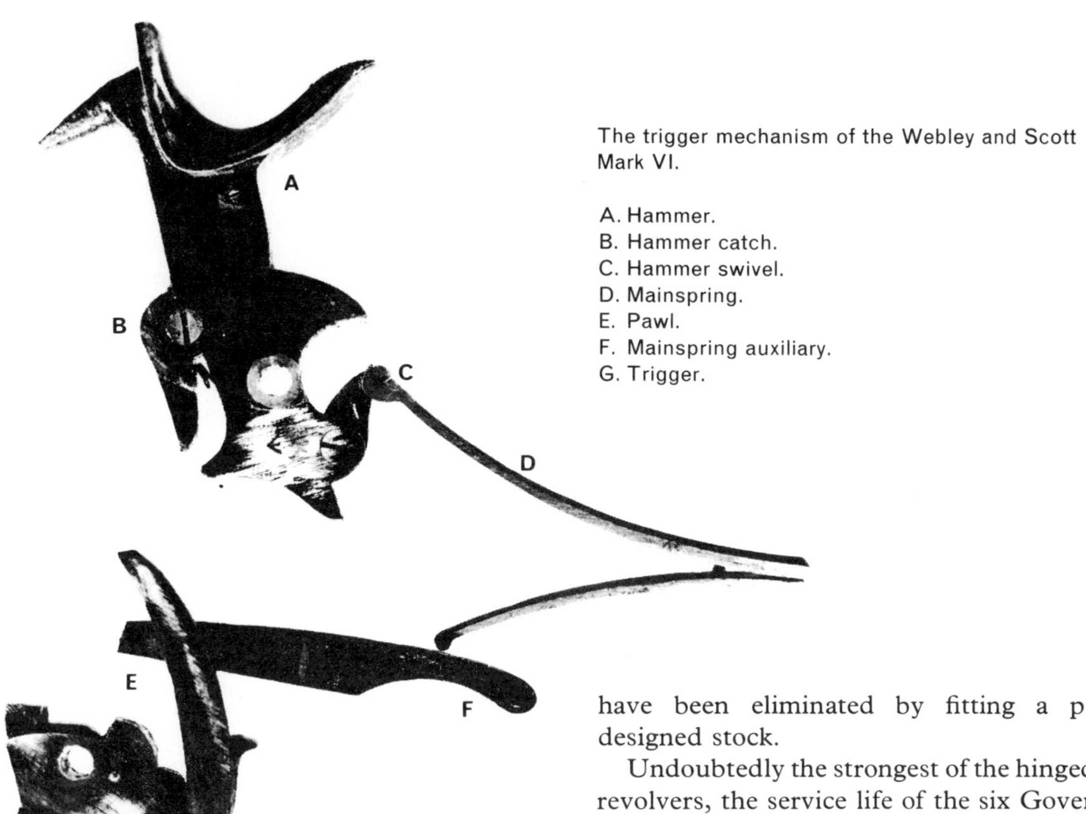

The trigger mechanism of the Webley and Scott Mark VI.

A. Hammer.
B. Hammer catch.
C. Hammer swivel.
D. Mainspring.
E. Pawl.
F. Mainspring auxiliary.
G. Trigger.

tion of the various components and their names, are shown on the Webley Instruction Sheet, and although, unlike the WG series, none of the Government Models had a side inspection plate, dismounting was far easier than might at first be expected. The mechanism consisted of five parts, the hammer (with the hammer catch or strut), the trigger, the pawl, the mainspring and the mainspring auxiliary. The only spring employed in the lock, apart from the hammer catch coil spring, was the mainspring, and this could be removed and replaced without tools. When properly adjusted, the lock functioned easily and, of importance in a military weapon, was very robust and not liable to go wrong. My only personal criticism is that the rear guard screw and the shape of the guard at this point could have been modified to increase the comfort of holding the pistol for prolonged periods, since irritation of the second finger is inevitable. This could have been eliminated by fitting a properly designed stock.

Undoubtedly the strongest of the hinged frame revolvers, the service life of the six Government Webleys was entirely honourable and there is no doubt that, if the same attention had been devoted to the stories and legends of the British Empire as has been devoted to the opening of the American West by the Movie Moguls, the Webley Government Models could truly be said to have been the 'Peacemakers' of the British Empire.

The revolver chosen to replace the Webley .455 Mark VI was the Enfield or, as described in the manual, the 'Pistol, Revolver .38 No. 2 Mark I'—a weapon for which I have no affection. Webley and Scott carried out the development work, and this revolver was Army issue from 1927 until 1957, when it was replaced by the Browning self-loading 9mm pistol. In 1938 the Pistol, Revolver .38 No. 2 Mark I* was approved, the star addition to the Mark resulting from a design modification which eliminated the spur and bent on the hammer so that trigger action only was possible. The pistol could not be cocked by the thumb. Two styles of grip were available: the first a conventional walnut stock as illustrated, and a later design, made in either walnut or bakelite, which had a thumb recess and was suitable for left or right handed shooting.

The general design of the action can be seen from the illustration of the Mark I pistol with the side plate removed. The provision of a side plate did not materially assist in dismantling since it was necessary to remove the barrel catch before the side plate could be removed.

"WEBLEY'S REVOLVER PISTOL" (MARK VI.)

FULL SIZE.

INSTRUCTIONS

FOR CLEANING AND DISMOUNTING

"WEBLEY'S REVOLVER PISTOL" (MARK VI)

GENERAL INSTRUCTIONS.

The parts of the revolver should be kept perfectly clean.

The nomenclature and parts of the revolver are shown in the annexed drawing.

DIRECTIONS FOR TAKING TO PIECES.

Unscrew the stock screw and remove stocks.

Unscrew guard screws and take off guard.

Full cock the hammer, press the slot of cramp over the mainspring, release the trigger, release stud of mainspring from stud hole. Take out the mainspring.

Take out mainspring auxiliary.

Unscrew trigger screw and take out trigger with pawl attached.

Unscrew hammer screw and take out hammer.

DIRECTIONS FOR REMOUNTING WEBLEY'S REVOLVER (MARK VI.)

Place in the hammer and screw in the hammer screw.

Replace trigger with pawl attached and screw in trigger screw.

Replace auxiliary.

Replace the mainspring, fix stud in stud hole, put the hammer to full cock and take off cramp.

Screw on guard.

Replace stock and stock screw.

To insure smoothness of action the cylinder must be kept free on its axis; should it work stiffly it should be dismounted, rust or fouling removed, and slightly oiled on bearing parts. (See directions below.)

In remounting cylinder see that the spindle screw is turned quite home, otherwise the extractor lever will not work properly.

DIRECTIONS FOR DISMOUNTING CYLINDER.

Open revolver to full extent, take out screw 9a, push round the cam lever (16), against the tooth of the cam (15), remove cylinder.

Remove the nut at end of spindle, take out spiral spring and extractor.

DIRECTIONS FOR REMOUNTING.

Care must be taken to thoroughly clean all the parts, and to insure that no dirt or grit be left inside cylinder or on the axis. The parts should be slightly oiled.

Drop in the spiral spring and replace extractor nut, turning the latter well home.

Replace cylinder on its axis, observing that the cam lever is pressed against the tooth of the cylinder, and replace screw 9a.

NOMENCLATURE

1	Body	10	Barrel Catch	20	Screw Shield	29	Pin Joint Axis
2	Barrel & Axis complete	11	Pawl	21	Spring Spiral	30	Nut Extractor Axis
3	Guard	12	Main Spring Auxiliary	22	Spring Spiral Extractor Lever	31	Screw Pin Joint Axis
4	Stock	13	Main Spring	23	Butt Swivel	32	" Cam
5	Cylinder & Extractor complete	14	Spring Barrel Catch	24	Screw Guard	33	" Cam Lever
6	Hammer complete	15	Cylinder Cam	25	" Stock	34	" Hammer Catch
7	Hammer Catch	16	Cam Lever	26	" Hammer & Trigger	35	" Hammer Swivel
8	Hammer Swivel	17	Extractor Lever	27	" Barrel Catch	36	" Trigger Stop Spring
9	Trigger complete	18	Extractor Lever Auxiliary	28	Blade Foresight	37	Trigger Stop
9A	Screw Cam Lever Fixing	19	Shield	28A	Screw, Blade Foresight	38	Trigger Stop Spring

Diagram and instructions for the Webley and Scott Mark VI.

Webley and Scott Mark VI with .22 Parker-Hale adaptor.

.38 Enfield No. 2 Mark I.

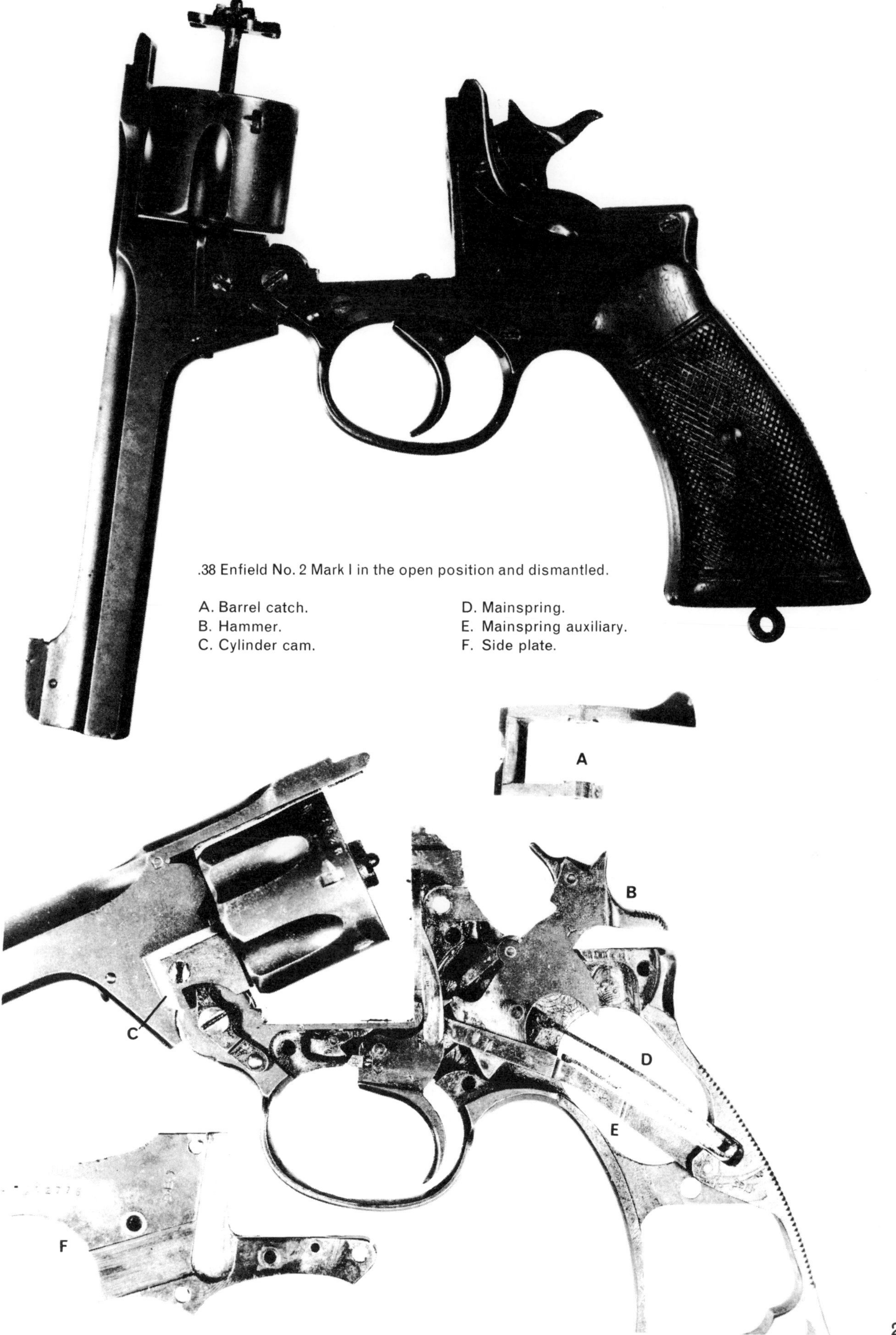

.38 Enfield No. 2 Mark I in the open position and dismantled.

A. Barrel catch.
B. Hammer.
C. Cylinder cam.
D. Mainspring.
E. Mainspring auxiliary.
F. Side plate.

During World War Two it became necessary to augment existing revolver production facilities, and firms with no previous experience of arms production were awarded contracts for the manufacture of the Enfield. The most important of these was the old-established Albion Motor Co. of Scotstoun, Glasgow. Additional premises were secured at Yoker and manufacture commenced in 1941. Considerable difficulties were experienced due to the use of untrained female labour and to an almost complete absence of dimensional standards. Although the Enfield factory employed mass-production, a great deal was left to the individual craftsman, particularly with regard to adjustment during assembly. Transmission of craft techniques is impossible without adequate training and, in the absence of a rigid processing schedule, errors were bound to occur which resulted in a high reject rate and overall poor quality. The pistols made by Albion are identifiable by the Albion trademark stamped on the right hand side of the frame above the rear of the trigger guard. There was certainly some excuse for the poor quality of the Albion Enfield manufactured under the stress of wartime conditions, but it is to be regretted that this, the last British Service revolver, was not a more worthy example of its type.

During the period when Webley's enjoyed the benefits of Government contracts, the civilian market was not neglected and, in the light of later events, this was perhaps just as well. Webley's had always been prepared to offer weapons suited to the requirements of particular customers, and this is best exemplified by the Wilkinson-Webley Models which succeeded the Wilkinson-Pryse. The first Wilkinson-Webley with the Webley stirrup barrel latch was the model 1892. The earlier version employed a single cam support on the left hand side of the frame and, when the release button just above the joint axis pin or hinge pin was pushed towards the muzzle, the cylinder could be withdrawn for cleaning—a very necessary job in the days of black powder cartridges. The distinctive feature of the revolver was, of course, the barrel with the well-defined top rib into which was dovetailed the foresight. On the later version of the same model two cam supports were fitted, one on each side of the frame. The example shown is nickel plated and has target sights. 'H.W.' in a six sided star, the Wilkinson Sword Co. trademark, can be seen on both, on the left hand side of the barrel towards the breech.

There were two further Wilkinson-Webley

Wilkinson-Webley Model 1892 with double cylinder cam. (Glasgow Police Collection)

Wilkinson-Webley Model 1892 with single cylinder cam and adjustable rear sight. (Glasgow Police Collection)

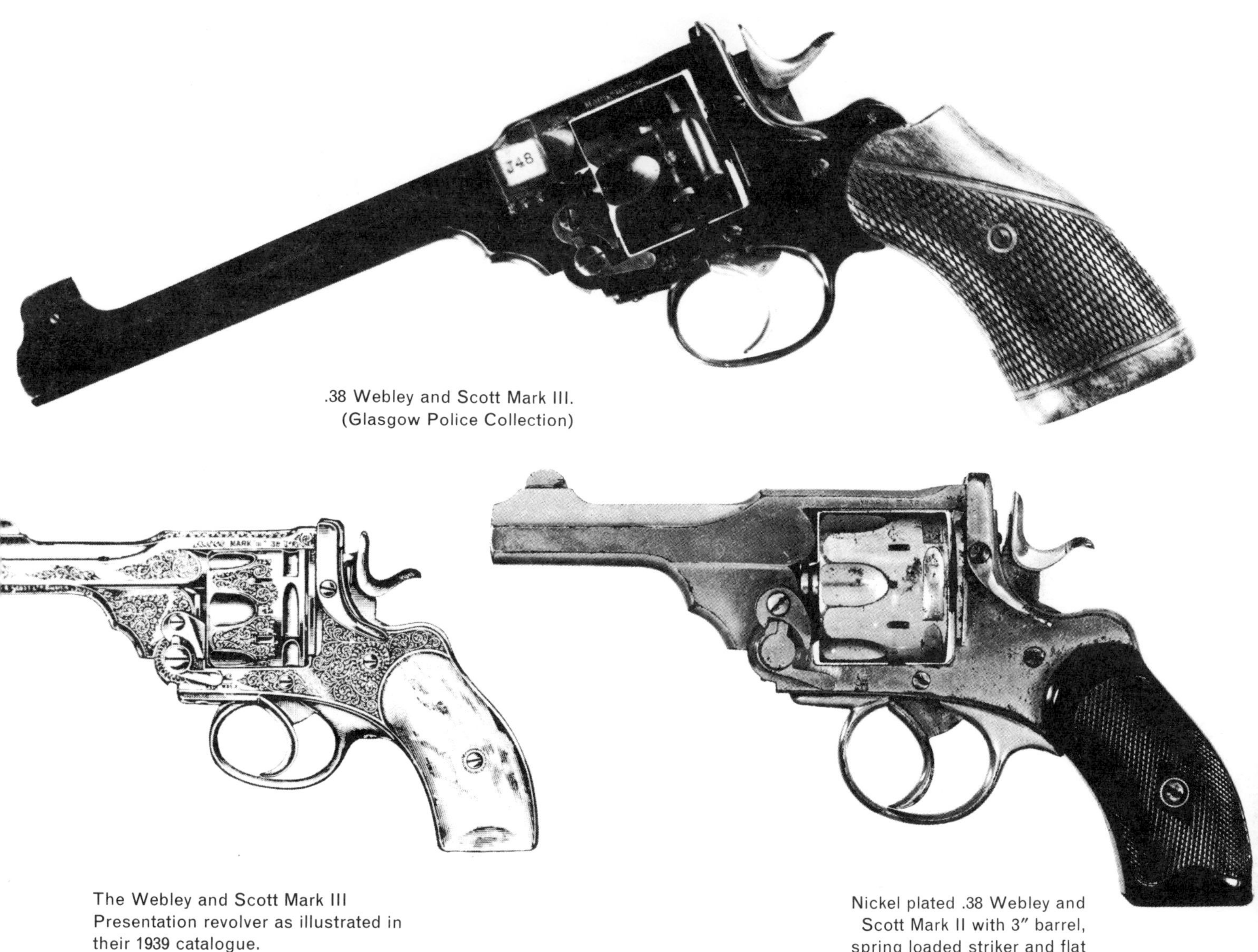

.38 Webley and Scott Mark III. (Glasgow Police Collection)

The Webley and Scott Mark III Presentation revolver as illustrated in their 1939 catalogue.

Nickel plated .38 Webley and Scott Mark II with 3″ barrel, spring loaded striker and flat hammer nose.

Models. The Model of 1905 was based on the Webley Mark VI, but had certain additional refinements such as a thumb cylinder release (a small fillet behind the trigger guard which eliminated the annoyance of the rear guard screw) and the provision of special sights. The Model 1911 was identical to the 1905 version except for the rifling, the later model having six grooves instead of the standard seven. The Wilkinson-Webleys lacked the holster guides of the production Webley and were better finished. Unfortunately the distinctive barrel contour with the top rib reverted to the standard Webley design in both the 1905 and 1911 models, and the Wilkinson-Webley eventually became indistinguishable from the common Webley and vanished from the scene.

From 1896 Webley's offered a range of Police and Military Models. The Mark II .38 will be found with a frame-mounted spring-loaded striker and flat hammer as well as with a fixed hammer nose. The Mark III continued in production as the Pocket Model with a 3″ barrel chambered for the .38 S & W cartridge, and was also available in .320 or .32, the calibre being marked on the left hand side top strap together with 'Mark III'. The Police and Military Mark III had either a 3″ or 4″ barrel, and there was also a 5″ target version with adjustable rear sight. Several stock shapes or 'butts' were available and, to special order, one could have the Presentation Mark III revolver with pearl or ivory stocks and either gold or silver plated and richly engraved. Complete with all tools, it was supplied in a fitted oak or leather case.

In 1927 the Mark IV was introduced, and it is

The WEBLEY "Mark IV" ·22 R.F. Target Revolver

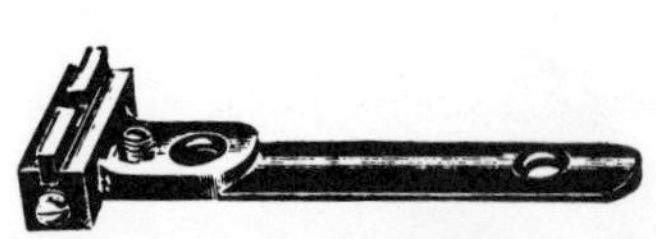

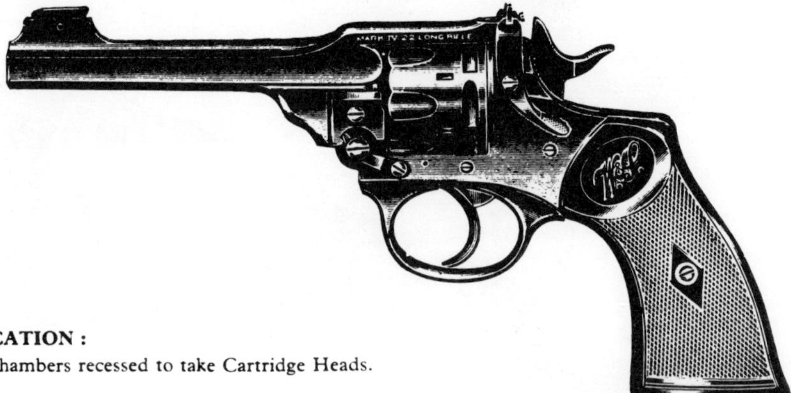

To meet the requirements of those desiring a sight capable of fine and accurate lateral and vertical adjustment a special sight, as per illustration above, has been designed and can be fitted at a small extra cost. The top strap of the Barrel is recessed to accommodate the sight.

SPECIFICATION :

CYLINDER – –	6 Shots — .22. Chambers recessed to take Cartridge Heads.
LENGTH OF BARREL	6 in.
LENGTH OVERALL	10¼ in.
WEIGHT – –	2 lbs.
PULL OFF – –	2 to 3 lbs.
TRIGGER – –	Serrated to prevent finger slip.
GRIP – – –	Steel portion of Grip is serrated. Stock Sides Vulcanite. Walnut sides fitted at extra cost.
TARGET SIGHTS –	Blade foresight, square notch rearsight laterally adjustable.
AMMUNITION –	Long Rifle and Short ; I.C.I. Non-Rusting .22 and the new American High Velocity .22 Cartridges.

The continued use of .22 Short Ammunition is likely to cause bad extraction with .22 Long. When Non-Rusting Ammunition is used the **Cylinder** should be cleaned. .22 I.C.I. Pistol Ammunition is now manufactured for target shooting and is specially recommended.

REGISTERED TRADE MARK.
W & S

The Webley and Scott Mark IV Target Model as illustrated in a pre-1939 catalogue.

.32 Webley and Scott Mark IV with safety catch.

.38 Webley and Scott Mark IV Police revolver with 5" barrel. (Webley and Scott)

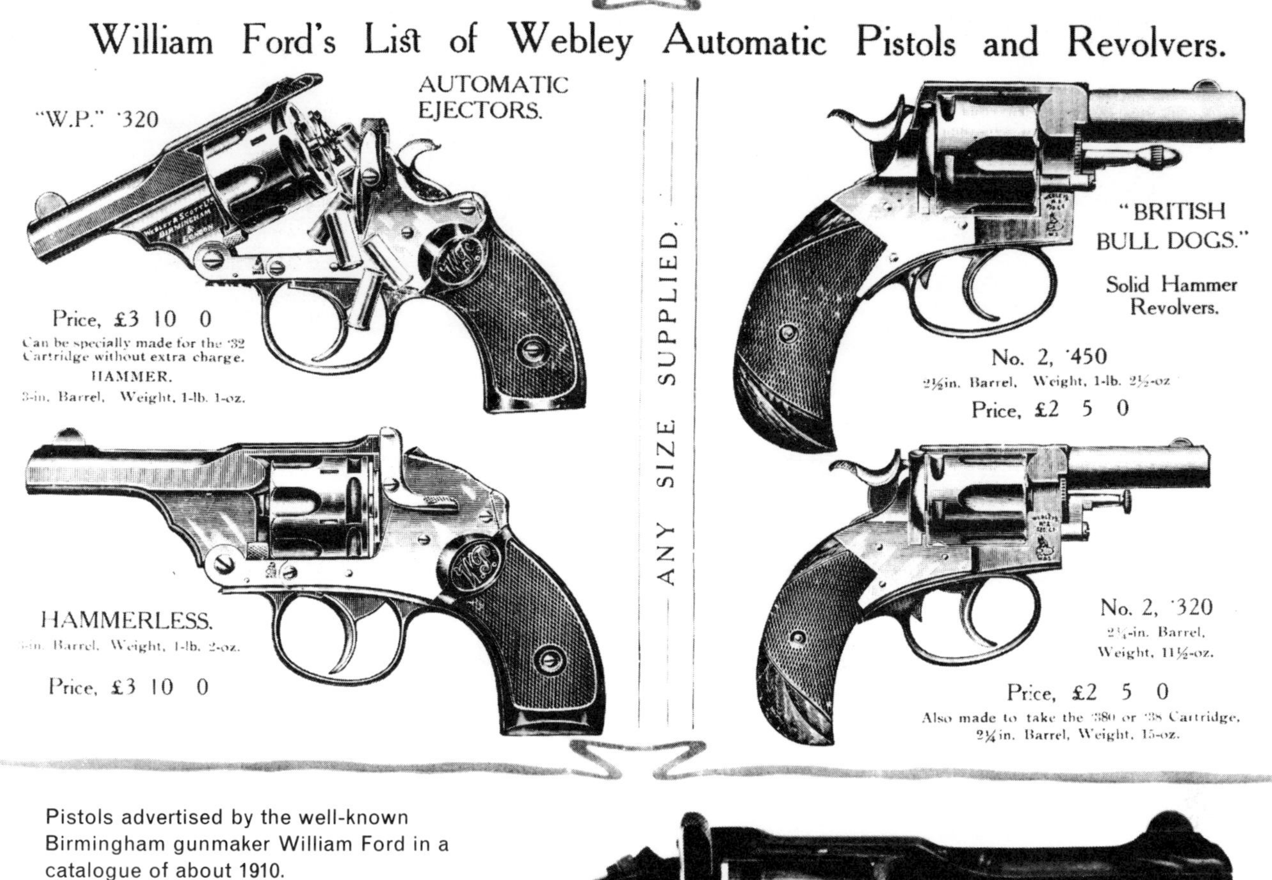

Pistols advertised by the well-known Birmingham gunmaker William Ford in a catalogue of about 1910.

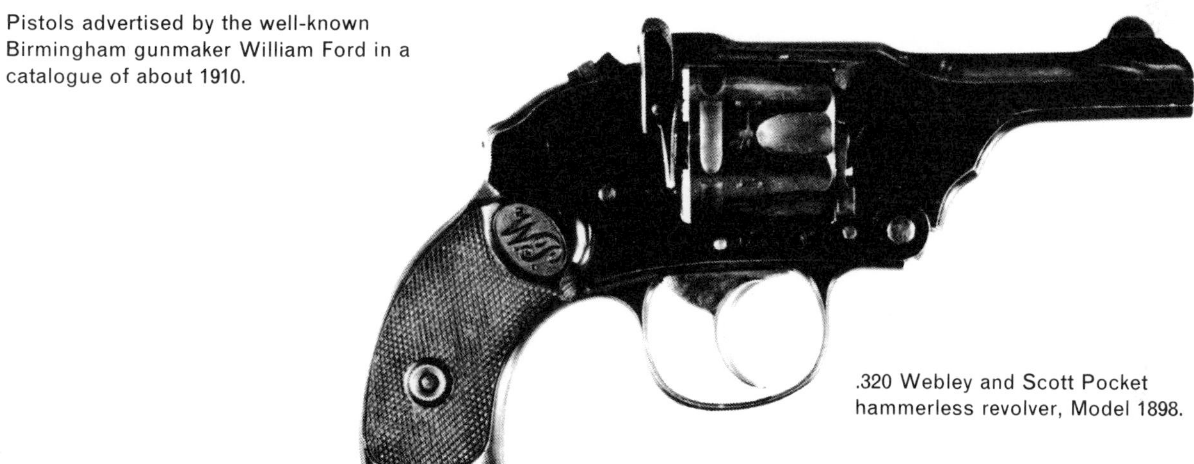

.320 Webley and Scott Pocket hammerless revolver, Model 1898.

pleasant to record that this revolver is still being manufactured by Webley and Scott at their new factory in Handsworth, Birmingham. The versions currently available are the Mark IV .22 rim-fire Target Revolver, the .38 Mark IV Police and Military Model chambered for the .38 S & W cartridge with either a 4″ or 5″ barrel, and the Pocket Model in .32 S & W, .32 S & W long or the .38 S & W. The barrel length of the Pocket Model is 3″ and alternative stocks are available. All the Mark IV revolvers can be fitted with a safety bolt device if required.

The last of the conventional Webley revolvers remaining to be described are the Webley Pocket Revolvers Model 1898. The first of these was the enclosed hammer or 'hammerless' type and, in 1901, an identical version with a conventional external hammer was put on the market. Available in the various .32 calibres, two types of barrel catch were offered, the normal type with thumb lever and a similar catch without the lever which was operated by pulling back the serrated top with the thumb. The hammerless model was fitted with a sliding safety catch.

Webley and Scott have remained staunch adherents of the hinged frame simultaneous ejection revolver. Today the manufacture of revolvers is carried out on a greatly reduced scale, and the decline of the domestic handgun trade is due to a number of factors—absence of Government orders, restrictions on the ownership of handguns and competition from overseas, particularly from America where a large domestic market permits economic production and consequently lowers export prices. Yet another factor has been the increased popularity of the

COMPLETE SPECIFICATION.

Mechanism for Automatically Withdrawing Empty Cartridge Cases from Revolvers and Pistols.

We HUGH ADAMS SILVER of Sun Court, Cornhill London, Merchant and Manufacturer and WALTER FLETCHER of the same place, Gunsmith, do hereby declare the nature of our said invention for "MECHANISM FOR AUTOMATICALLY WITHDRAWING EMPTY CARTRIDGE CASES FROM REVOLVERS AND PISTOLS" and in what manner the same is to be performed to be particularly described and ascertained in and by the following statement:—

The object of our invention is to withdraw and eject empty cartridge cases automatically from revolver pistols by the direct contact of the hammer upon a metal plate or bar pivotted or hinged to the body of the pistol in such a manner that as the fired cartridge is moved round to bring another or loaded cartridge into position the empty case is suddenly ejected by contact of the hammer on the metal plate or bar simultaneously as the loaded cartridge then in position is being struck by the hammer.

For the purpose of our invention we slot the back face or solid portion of the body and pass a pin through from the top of same. This pin forms a pivot on which a bar or plate which fits the recess can move in one direction when struck by the hammer in the act of firing a loaded cartridge and be returned to its normal position by a spring.

The bar has a blade projecting downwards and is so shaped that as the empty cartridge cases are brought round in succession by the ordinary rotatory movement of the charge chamber the edge of the blade engages within the rim of the empty cartridge case and when the hammer strikes the bar as the next charge is being fired, the empty cartridge case is suddenly ejected from its chamber and so on in succession after each successive firing.

The hammer may be of the usual construction with the striker as part thereof but the striker may be separate and enclosed within the hammer and be provided with a thumb piece capable of being set in a backward position or at "safety" by the thumb piece being set in a slot in the hammer.

Our invention will be understood by the annexed drawings in which at Figure 1 we show an ordinary five chambered revolver, the chamber block of which is shown at Figure 2. The back face of the body A is recessed and a bar B fits and is pivotted therein by the screw pin C upon which it has a movement when struck by the nose D of the hammer E when the striker F is in the act of firing a loaded cartridge which has been brought opposite it by the usual trigger claw.

G is the blade of the bar B whose edge is arranged to take into a cutaway portion I of the face of the chamber J and consequently under the rim H of the cartridge case to extract or eject it. The bar is held in position by a spring K which is fastened to the side of the body A and has a limb L which bears against the bar to hold the blade G in contact with the face of the chamber block except when the nose D of the hammer strikes the bar as before explained.

M is the usual gate which can be set open as at Figure 1 for charging the chambers in the usual manner and when the automatic ejection of the empty cases is not required the gate can be closed against the back face of the cartridge cases to retain them in position in the usual manner where it acts as a stop against the ejection.

Complete Specification. A.D. 1884.—Nº 16,078.

Silver & Fletcher's Mechanism for Withdrawing Cartridge Cases from Revolvers, &c.

We have referred to the bar B as fitting a recess but other means may be adopted for pivotting said bar B to the body A and the spring K may be arranged differently to that above described.

In the example Figure 3 we show the bar B pivotted to the body A and with a spring K fastened to the shield N with its free end behind the bar to press that end forward, the action corresponding to that described with reference to Figure 1.

If the extraction of the empty cartridge cases is not necessary the bar can be slid sideways on its pivot pin C as at Figure 4 so that the blade is free of the rim of the cartridge case.

Figures 5, 6, 7 and 8 represent other modified arrangements of the spring.

In Figure 5 the spring K is of helical form working against a shoulder of a stud P projecting from the bar. At Figure 6 the limb L of the spring is dispensed with. At Figure 7 another form of spring is shown and at Figure 8 the spring is fastened to the neck Q of the revolver frame, the object of the spring in all cases being to return the bar to its normal position so that the blade G may be made to engage with the rim of the next succeeding cartridge case in succession.

Figure 9 represents a hammer with the striker F fitted within the same and capable of being set at the position of safety by the thumb piece R being moved in the slot S Figure 10 to hold it back as at Figure 11, the thumb piece taking into a recess formed at the end of the slot.

By this invention empty cartridge cases can be extracted automatically at each successive firing of a full cartridge by opening the gate M or the empty cartridge cases may be retained within the chamber by closing the gate at the will of the person using the arm, this is with reference to the pistol shown in Figure 1 or if the gate be closed all the cartridges can be fired in succession and then the gate can be opened and all the empty cases extracted in succession.

The same remark applies to the pistol shown in Figure 9, but should by any error a loaded cartridge be left in, the placing of the striker F in the safety position prevents all possibility of accident happening at the time of extracting should a full charge be left in the chamber J.

Having now particularly described and ascertained the nature of our said invention and in what manner the same is to be performed We declare that what We claim is

1. Fitting an extractor bar B in or to the body A of a revolver pistol within the travel of the hammer for the automatic extraction of the empty cartridge case H simultaneously with the strike of loaded one by said hammer as set forth and substantially as shown in the annexed drawings Figure 1.

2. Fitting the striker F within a hammer of a revolver so that said striker may be set at a position of safety as and for the purpose described with reference to Figure 9.

The 5th day of September 1885.

H. GARDNER,
166, Fleet Street, London,
Agent for the said H. A. Silver & W. Fletcher.

LONDON: Printed by EYRE AND SPOTTISWOODE, Printers to the Queen's most Excellent Majesty. For Her Majesty's Stationery Office.

1885.

430 Silver and Fletcher's Patent No.16,078 of 1884.

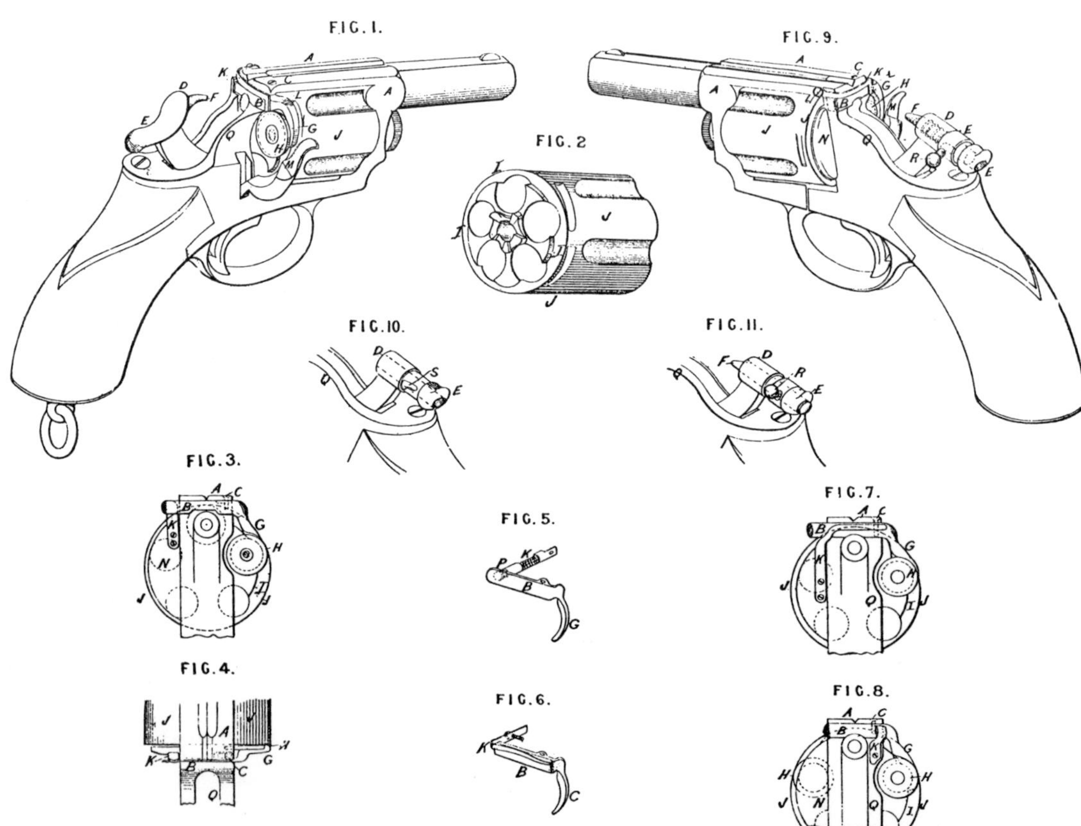

.450 Webley RIC Model of 1883 with S.W. Silver and Co's self-extracting system. (Tower of London)

self-loading or automatic pistol, although the revolver manufacturer did not let the threat from the auto-pistol go unchallenged.

One of the most bizarre schemes was that of 'automatic cartridge ejection', developed in the belief that self-ejecting revolvers would increase the speed of shooting. The earliest system was that of Drivon et Biron of St Etienne, and shortly afterwards, in 1865, Steiger of Thun in Switzerland obtained patent protection, while Bader of Mehlis developed a revolver invented by the Viennese, Sederl. In 1884, Hugh Adams Silver and Walter Fletcher obtained British Patent No. 16,078 for a similar system which covered automatic case extraction and a safety hammer. These devices were commonly applied in Britain to solid frame revolvers, the Webley RIC Model being the favourite.

Although, on the whole, little interest was shown in the idea in Britain, efforts to perfect automatic extraction continued on the continent. F. Praunegar of Graz in Austria developed a similar device, and the Swiss Model 1882 Schmidt revolver was modified to accept an automatic ejector 'Système E. Krauser'. Nicolas Pieper of Liege and an Argentine Army officer, A. Garcia Reynoso, also attempted improvements, as did A. Godin. The last attempt known to me was that of Manufrance of St Etienne who marketed a .25 ACP self-ejecting revolver which, according to the catalogue illustration, resembles the Webley Bulldog.

None of these valiant efforts proved successful. Like the gas seal revolver and the 'automatic' revolver, the self-extracting revolver added needless complexity and effectively cancelled the revolver's most important quality, that of simplicity.

Notes to Chapter Ten

Literature on European revolvers in English is regrettably scarce. In addition to the works mentioned in the notes to the previous chapter, information of interest is contained in *Small Arms of the World* by W. H. B. Smith (7th edition, Harrisburg, 1962) and in *The Book of Pistols and Revolvers* also by W. H. B. Smith (Harrisburg, 1962).

Reference should also be made to *Handfeuerwaffen* by Jaroslav Lugs (Berlin, 1962). Information on Norwegian military revolvers is contained in *Hoerens Handvapen* by Skaar and Nielsen (Oslo, 1954), on Danish military revolvers in *Gamle danske militaere vaben* by Th. Mollers (Copenhagen, 1963). Both of these publications have an English summary. Swedish military revolvers are covered in *Armens eldhandvapen forr och nu* by Joseph Alm (Stockholm, 1934), but unfortunately this has Swedish text only.

Austrian revolvers are mentioned in *Monographie der K.U.K. österr.-ung. blanken und Handfeuer-Waffen* by Anton Dolleczek (Vienna, 1896). This book should be read with caution since, in the light of later research, some of the statements made are erroneous. Detailed information on the bewildering variety of German service revolvers can be found in 'Reichsrevolver' by R. K. Edelmann, a series of articles in *Deutsches Waffen-Journal* 1968, issues 7/520, 8/593, 9/668, 10/747 and 11/854.

For their considerable assistance I must thank Prof. Dr. Heinz Zatschek of Vienna and Prof. Karel Konig of Bucharest. My thanks are also due to Noel Sherwood, Publicity Manager, Imperial Metal Industries (Kynoch) Ltd., for much of the information on the early history of the Tranter and Kynoch factories.

Chapter Eleven
The Revolver Today

The alternative to the sturdy hinged frame simultaneous ejector revolver as typified by the Webley and Scott was the solid frame swing-out cylinder revolver developed with conspicuous success by both Colt and Smith & Wesson in America. Colt had produced a double action revolver in 1877, first offered in .38 long and short Colt calibres. The .38 calibre DA models were known as 'Colt Lightnings' by the US distributors, and shortly afterwards a .41 model known as the 'Thunderer' appeared, once again in both .41 short and long Colt. A few .32 calibre DA Colts were manufactured but these do not appear to have been provided with 'trade' names. In 1878 the Colt DA Army and Frontier Model appeared, chambered for the .45 Colt, .44–40 WCF, .38–40 WCF, .32–20 WCF and for the British .450, .455 and .476 calibres. As can be seen from the illustration, the DA Models betrayed their Single Action Army ancestry, the noticeable differences being in the provision of the double action facility and the 'bird's head' grip. The DA models were made in the same profusion of barrel lengths as the Single Action Army, the short barrel versions dispensing with the rod ejector. The 1902 Army and Frontier Model can be identified by the over large trigger guard which was wider and deeper, the trigger being correspondingly lengthened from the 1″ of the 1878 model to $1\frac{3}{8}$″ on the 1902 model.

.38 Colt double action 'Lightning' revolver.

The man responsible for the development of the DA Colts was William Mason. Mason worked for Colt, Remington and Winchester, and was Factory Manager of Colt's Armoury at Hartford from 1866 until 1882, when he went to Winchester. Here Mason developed a revolver which could have had serious repercussions on Colt's dominance of the revolver market. Colt had already introduced a lever-action rifle, the Colt Burgess, and it appears obvious that Winchester employed a little intimidation when they made it known that they were interested in the revolver market for, shortly afterwards, Colt dropped the idea of making rifles and Winchester never marketed Mason's promising revolvers. The DA Series, however, never enjoyed the popularity of the Single Action Army and in 1910 manufacture ceased.

What was required was something entirely new, something which was the equal of, or preferably better than, the hinged frame Smith and Wesson.

The classic approach for a simple, robust alternative to the hinged frame self-extracting revolver was the solid frame, side opening revolver with a push-rod operated star extractor, and one early example of this was the design patented by Captain A. Albini in 1869 (British Patent No. 838).

With Colt, the first result was the Colt Double Action Navy Revolver, Model of 1889, which was largely the work of William Mason. Initially the design was for a fully automatic system, the cylinder being mounted on a crane which when opened also operated the extractor (US Patents Nos. 249,649 and 250,375 of 1881). This idea was abandoned in favour of a less complicated system in which the cylinder was mounted on a crane which pivoted outward to the left and downward, but the star ejector was manually operated. The design of the cylinder latch, an improvement on Mason's original idea, was due to Horace

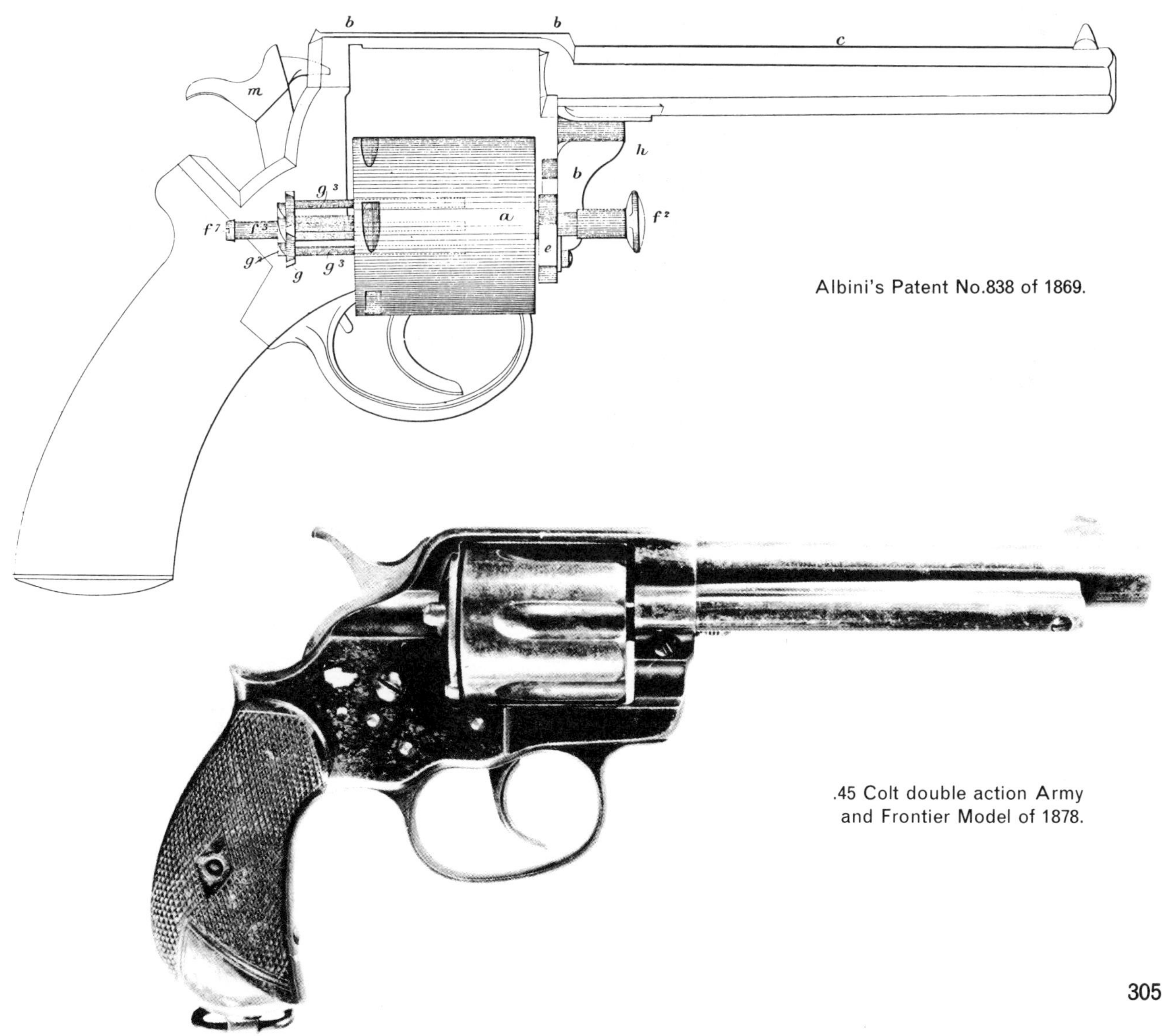

Albini's Patent No.838 of 1869.

.45 Colt double action Army and Frontier Model of 1878.

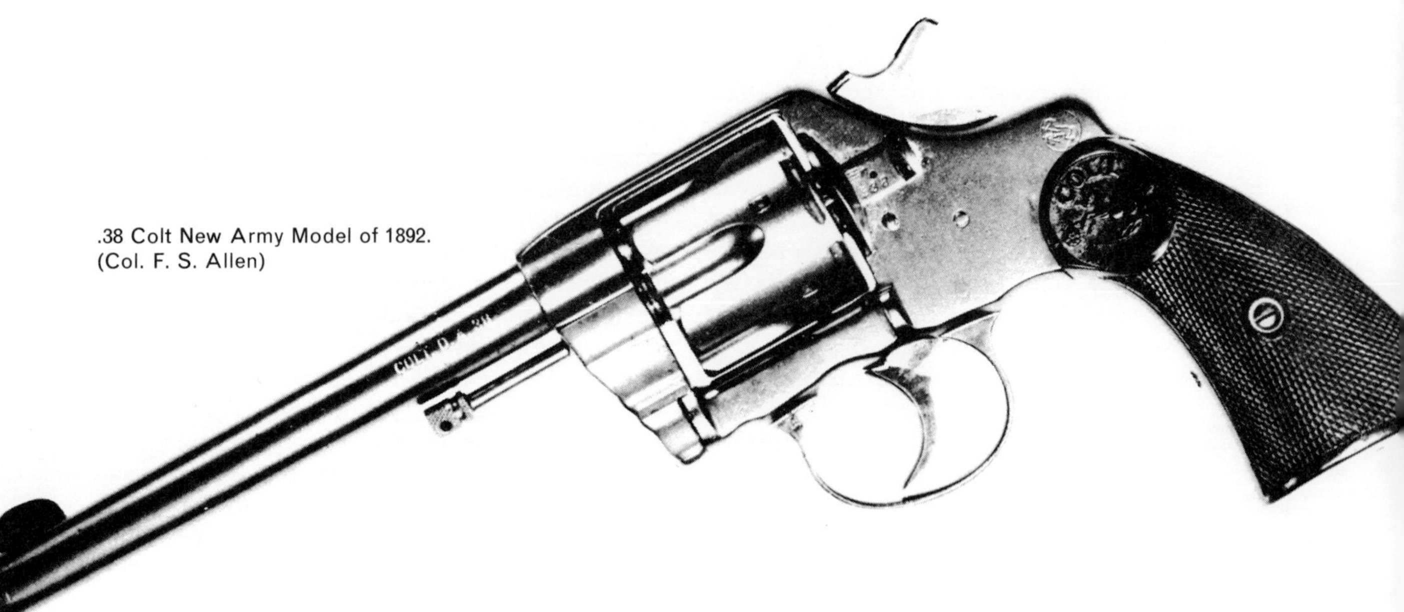
.38 Colt New Army Model of 1892.
(Col. F. S. Allen)

Lord, and C. J. Ehbets, Colt's patent attorney, was granted what could be called the master patent for the Model of 1889 on 6 November 1888.

The US Navy ordered 5,000 of this model which can be identified by the lack of locking slots on the outside of the cylinder. The Government issue had a 6″ barrel, but the Model 1889 was offered for sale with $3\frac{1}{2}$″, $4\frac{1}{2}$″ and 6″ barrels. Calibres were .38 short and long Colt and .41 short and long Colt.

In 1892, following minor mechanical improvements, the new DA Army and Navy Revolver appeared, and was similar in external appearance except for the locking slots in the outside of the cylinder. Two additional calibres were offered: .32–20 WCF and the .38 Special. The only difference between the Navy and Army versions was with regard to the stocks. The Navy was fitted with hard rubber stocks with the name Colt at the top. Army revolvers had the name Colt plus the trade mark, the rearing colt. The 1892 Model was progressively improved in 1894, 1895, 1896, 1901 and 1903. Manufacture ceased in 1908. The whole of this series were offered on the civilian market, the target version fitted with adjustable sights being known as the Officer's Model Colt DA. The .38 calibre designation was stamped on the left hand side of the barrel 'Colt D.A. 38' and Government Navy purchases were marked 'U.S.N. .38 D.A.' and included an anchor, the Army version being marked 'U.S. Army Model 1896'. The scarcest of the series was the DA Marine Corps Revolver, Model of 1905. The main difference was in the more rounded shape of the stock. All the DA swing-out cylinder Colts were unusual in that the cylinder rotated to the left, or anti-clockwise, unlike the previous models or the later New Service Revolver. Also the side plate was on the right hand side whereas all subsequent models had the plate on the left.

The service revolvers had plain walnut grips, and the Model 1894 incorporated a safety lock which prevented the hammer being cocked until the cylinder was positively closed and locked. All 1892 revolvers were eventually altered to the 1894 system. The models of 1894 and 1896 were apparently identical, the model 1901 had a butt lanyard swivel and the 1903 version had the bore diameter reduced to improve accuracy. The New Service Revolver introduced in 1897 was Colt's principal large calibre revolver until 1943. The side plate was on the left hand side of the frame and cylinder rotation was clockwise. Following their previous policy, Colt's introduced many alterations and modifications during the lengthy production run and, in order to differentiate between certain variants, modern collectors employ the terms 'old model' and 'improved model'.

The 'old model' New Service can be identified by a small dismounting hole through the ejector rod head, and was manufactured until 1905 up to serial number 21,000. In 1900 a target version appeared with a barrel length of $7\frac{1}{2}$″ and target sights. There was no provision for a lanyard swivel and, on those revolvers intended for the British market and chambered for the .455 cartridge, the sights lacked the adjusting screws fitted to the American calibre guns. This was due to the regulation in force which prohibited the use

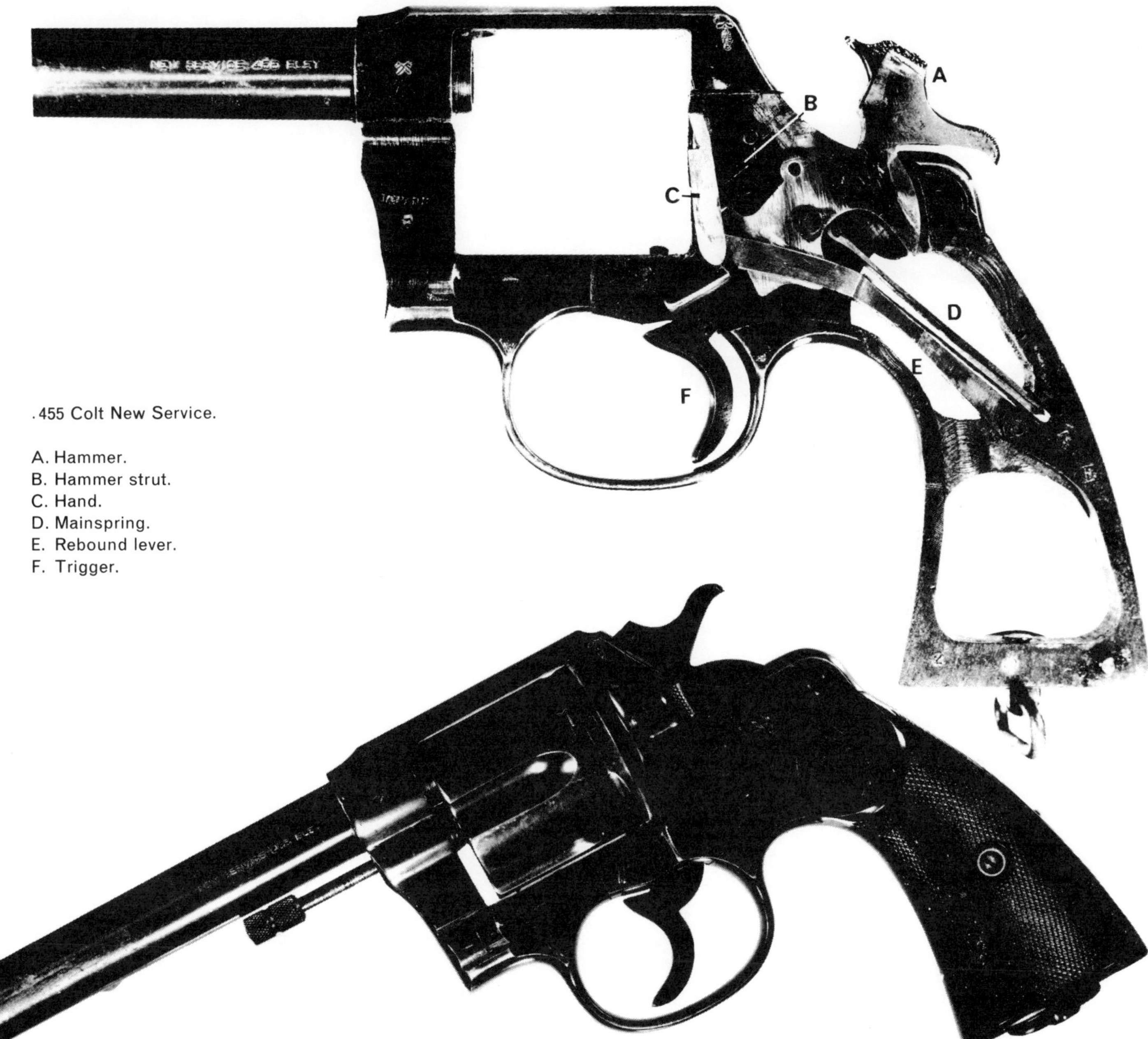

.455 Colt New Service.

A. Hammer.
B. Hammer strut.
C. Hand.
D. Mainspring.
E. Rebound lever.
F. Trigger.

of screw adjustable sights in British revolver competitions.

In 1905 the 'improved model' New Service was introduced and embodied several mechanical improvements: coil springs replaced flat springs for the cylinder bolt and hammer strut; a pivoted firing pin, first used on the old Target Model, was fitted; the ejector rod head was knurled and the dismounting hole eliminated. The obvious external difference was that the sides of the trigger guard joined the frame in a smooth contour. The basic lock mechanism incorporated an intercepting safety known as the 'Colt Positive Lock'. This was an additional feature to the rebounding lock, and the entire mechanism at this stage of development formed the basis for all subsequent New Service revolvers. Because of its ingenuity, it deserves further study.

In order to strip one these revolvers to the stage illustrated, the crane screw (on the right of the frame above the guard) is slackened until the crane can be pulled forward. The cylinder latch is then pulled back and the cylinder and crane can be removed. Stock screw and stocks are removed and the side plate screws taken out (two off). After tapping the frame to loosen it, the side plate can now be gently prised off. At this stage, the main lock components can be seen and identified. Both the trigger and hammer pins are screwed into the right hand side of the frame and, with care, the functioning of the lock can be verified. The cylinder hand is attached to the trigger and is tensioned by the 'rebound lever' (known by Webley as the mainspring auxiliary). This rebound lever performs two functions in addition to acting as the cylinder hand spring and

The Colt New Service with the hammer, mainspring etc. removed to show the positive safety lock.

A. Safety.
B. Safety lever.
C. Bolt.
D. Trigger.

Imray's Patent No.13,680 (Colt) of 1905.

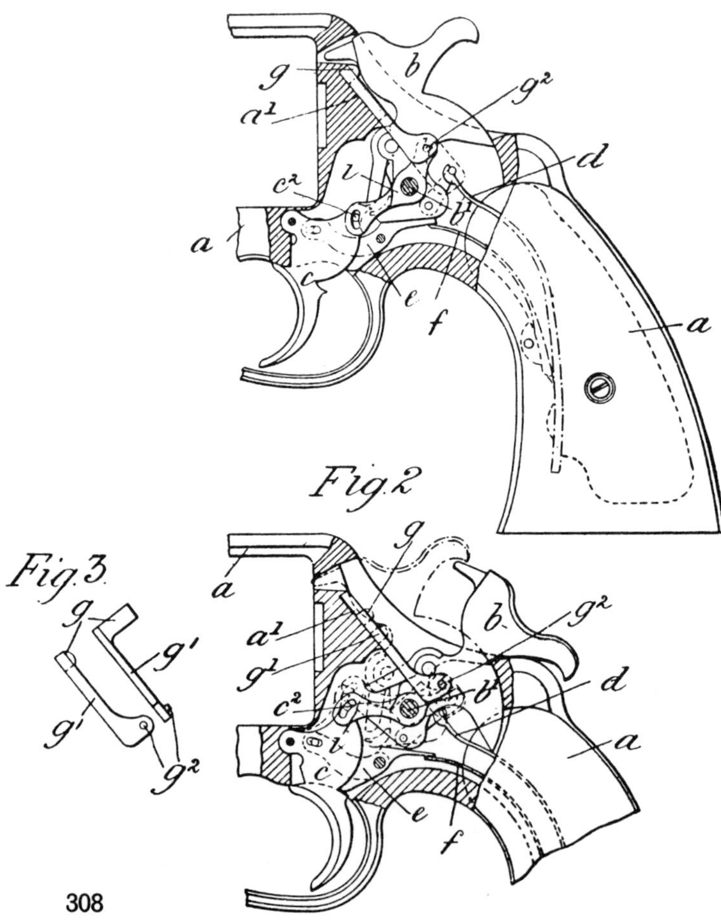

trigger return spring. The first of these is to return the hammer to the rebound position after firing. As the trigger is released, the rebound lever moves downward under the influence of the mainspring. As this happens, a portion of the lever where the section broadens pushes against the bottom rear of the hammer and causes it to rotate slightly into the rebound position.

The remainder of the safety lock work can only be examined after removing the hammer and trigger. The mainspring has to be taken out by drawing the hammer slightly back and disengaging the spring from the hammer stirrup, after which the spring can be removed. It is then necessary to remove the rebound lever by drifting out the lever pin securing it to the frame. The trigger, cylinder hand and hammer can then be taken out and the remainder of the lock work is revealed. At the bottom of the frame can be seen the cylinder bolt which is attached to the frame by the bolt screw and tensioned upwards by the coil bolt spring. This bolt is operated once again by the rebound lever, a slight projection on the right hand side contacting the rear tip of the bolt and raising it when the rebound lever moves upward as the hammer is drawn back. Since the lever is hinged at the bolt screw, the upward movement of the rear of the bolt drops the other end, so unlocking the cylinder.

The 'safety' or Colt positive lock can be seen above the cylinder bolt. It comprises two limbs, the safety lock itself and the flat safety lever which pivots about the hammer pin. The small pin at the top of the trigger enters the elongated slot on the left of the safety lever when the trigger is assembled. When the trigger is in the forward position, the safety bolt is at the top of its travel and lies between the hammer and the frame. In this position the hammer cannot come far enough forward for the firing pin to reach the cartridge in the chamber. A severe blow on the hammer (which might affect the rebound system) still cannot cause the revolver to fire since the safety would prevent any forward movement. When the lock is cocked, the bolt is drawn downwards and the hammer can move forward the full extent.

The safety lock performs yet another function. If the mechanism is cocked, the cylinder lock cannot be drawn backward since the position of the safety bolt prevents the latch pin moving to the rear. Alternatively, if the cylinder pin is not fully home and the cylinder securely locked, the revolver cannot be cocked. The operation of the safety bolt can perhaps be appreciated better from

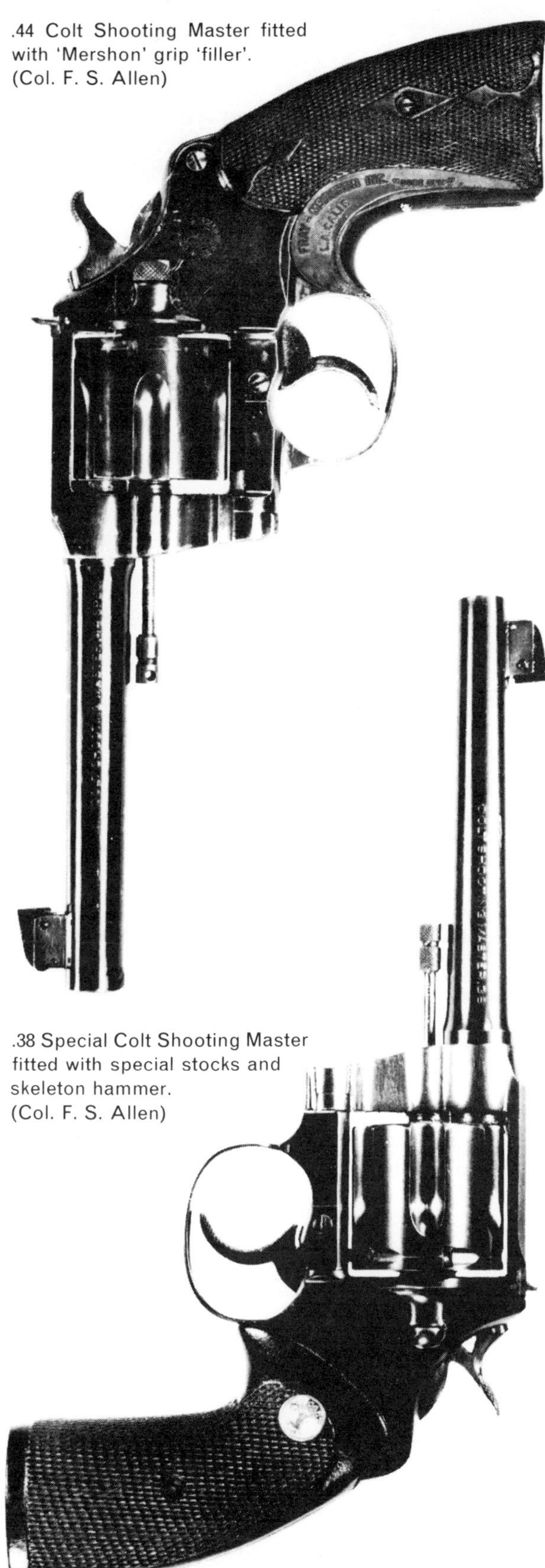

.44 Colt Shooting Master fitted with 'Mershon' grip 'filler'. (Col. F. S. Allen)

.38 Special Colt Shooting Master fitted with special stocks and skeleton hammer. (Col. F. S. Allen)

the patent drawing, British Patent No. 13,680 of 1905. Re-assembly is simple and can be done without special tools. Two points have to be watched. It is important that the tip of the rebound lever is in the recess on the inside of the cylinder hand and not merely resting on the hand pin. The trigger must also be correctly positioned so that the safety bolt lever is properly assembled; otherwise the side plate cannot be replaced.

When the side plate (which also carries the cylinder latch) is replaced, care must be taken to ensure that the latch pin enters the hole in the cylinder latch; otherwise, once again, the side plate will not seat properly in the frame.

Although I do not advise anyone deliberately to dismantle a new Colt revolver, the opportunity to strip an old model can give a most valuable insight into the operation and function of each part. The Colt action mechanism is a very fine one, simple, robust and trouble-free. The parts are large, not easily lost, and could be made with a hacksaw and file if the need were desperate enough. Perhaps the sole practical objection, and one which is still largely a matter of personal opinion, is the performance when used trigger action. More will be said about this later.

Four years after the introduction of the improved model in 1905, the Army and Navy New Service revolvers appeared. Chambered for the .45 Colt and also the .45 Colt Model 1909 cartridges, this version had a $5\frac{1}{2}''$ barrel and smooth wooden grips. The original .45 Colt cartridge was used in the .45 SAA with a rod ejector, but, as the star ejector of the New Service could ride over the rim of the standard .45 Colt, the later 1909 version had a slightly larger rim. Both the Army and Navy versions were marked on the strap adjacent to the lanyard swivel, and the similar Marine Corps Model bore the initials USMC in the same place.

There was also a target variant of the 'improved' or 1905 model, the American version having screw adjustable sights, the British version the usual Metford type rifling and sights adjustable by guess and by hammer.

The New Service Model 1917 manufactured during the First World War chambered the .45 ACP rimless cartridge. A $5\frac{1}{2}''$ barrel was standard and, in contrast to previous practice, was sharply tapered. Slight modification to the cylinder was needed to permit the use of the .45 ACP cartridge which was adapted for use in a revolver by three shot semi-circular steel clips. The automatic pistol cartridge can be fired in the late Model 1917 without the use of clips but, since the cartridge is rimless, it cannot be extracted and the fired cases have to be poked out singly. Clips had to be used with early models made with a straight chamber. During the latter end of the production run of the New Service, several minor modifications were made over a period of years. The tapered barrel of the Model 1917 was retained, the sight picture was improved by matting and altering the contour of the top of the frame, and the cylinder latch was altered from its rectangular shape to a rounded end less likely to cut the knuckle of the thumb in recoil.

An improved version of the New Service Target Model was introduced in 1932, the Colt Shooting Master, the normal calibres being .38 Special, .357 Magnum, .44 S & W Special, .45 ACP and .45 Colt. The Shooting Master had a slightly rounded butt and usually the cylinder latch was smooth instead of being checkered. Towards the end of production, Colt offered the New Service, New Service Target and Shooting Master with a choice of square or round butts and, throughout the period, there is always the possibility of some confusion due to revolvers being made to special order and components being replaced during service. The New Service revolvers were built on one of the largest Colt frames and are best suited to a big hand. The grip is very comfortable and is one of the few which can be used without alteration even when firing the heaviest loads. Blued or full nickel finishes were standard, but special engraved models were available on special order.

.32 Colt Pocket Positive. (Glasgow Police Collection)

Built on a smaller frame, the Colt Pocket revolvers were introduced in 1895. In 1905 the name was changed to Pocket Positive and modifications similar to those on the New Service were introduced. The Pocket Positive was six chambered and available in .32 Colt short and long, .32 S & W short and long and also the .32 New Police, a cartridge with the same case length as the .32 long Colt but with a heavier bullet and improved ballistics. Barrel lengths were $2\frac{1}{2}''$, $3\frac{1}{2}''$ and 6″, and manufacture was discontinued in 1943.

The Colt Police Revolvers have had a long and distinguished career. The New Police Model first appeared in 1896 chambered for the standard range of .32 calibre cartridges and designed to replace the sheath trigger single action New Line Police and House Pistol. Production life of both the standard and target versions was brief for, in line with the rest of the range, a new model appeared in 1905, known as the Police Positive revolver, which featured the Colt 'positive' safety lock.

The range of calibres was extended to include the .22 long rifle rim-fire, the .22 WRF and, at the other end of the scale, the .38 Colt New Police and the .38 S & W. The .22 WRF had been designed for the Winchester Model 1890 rifle and was unlike any other .22 rim-fire. Colt's discontinued this calibre in 1935.

Variants of basic models were introduced from time to time to meet the real or imagined need for slightly different versions to suit special demands. The 1886 catalogue featured the 'Ladies Target Model', offered with target sights and a 6″ barrel. Chambered for the standard range of .32 calibre cartridges, it was stated 'that this pistol has no perceptible recoil and shoots very accurately at 20 yards and above. Ladies have been very successful in making high scores with it.' This was, in effect, a special target version of the New Police Model. Similarly, the Colt Bankers' Special, introduced in 1928, was a 2″ barrel version of the Police Positive originally offered in .38 S & W and .38 Colt New Police calibres. In 1933 the Bankers' Special appeared in .22 rim-fire with a rounded grip. Rounded grips became standard for all calibres in 1934 and production ceased in 1945.

The practice of marking the model designation and calibre on the barrel aids identification, and there is no doubt that many of these short production run variants will become prized collectors' items of the future.

The need to increase the 'punch' of the Police Model resulted in the introduction of the Colt Police Positive Special in 1907. This model, like the Colt Police Positive, was a basic model and from it were eventually derived a number of variants. In order to accommodate the longer .38 S & W Special cartridge (which Colt's, with understandable reticence, called the .38 Special), the cylinder was made $\frac{1}{4}$″ longer, and this resulted in a correspondingly longer frame. Originally chambered for the .38 Special and the .32–20 WCF, the Police Positive Special was later available in .32 Colt and .32 S & W calibres. Barrel lengths were 4″, 5″ and 6″, but, in 1926, a 2″ barrel model was offered which, a year later, became known as the Colt Detective Special. It weighed 21 ozs. and had an overall length of $6\frac{3}{4}$″. After 1934 the grip was rounded at the toe and heel and, more recently, a detachable hammer shroud became available which could be installed on new guns or supplied as a kit. The shroud permits both trigger and thumb cocking and prevents the hammer from catching on clothing during a quick draw. Today this is also available on the Police Positive Special, Detective Special, Colt Cobra and Agent revolvers. The Detective Special can currently be obtained (Model D.1) in 2″ and 3″ barrel lengths chambered for the .32 New Police and the .38 Special cartridges.

The Police Positive Special is also retained in the current Colt selling range as the Model D.2 in .32 calibre with a 4″ barrel and in .38 Special with either a 4″ or 5″ barrel. The Police Positive Special was again modified in 1952 by fitting a heavy 4″ untapered barrel and a Baughman 'quick draw' ramp foresight. About four hundred of these

The current model of the Colt Detective Special. (Colt)

.38 Colt Detective Special with rounded butt and hammer shroud.

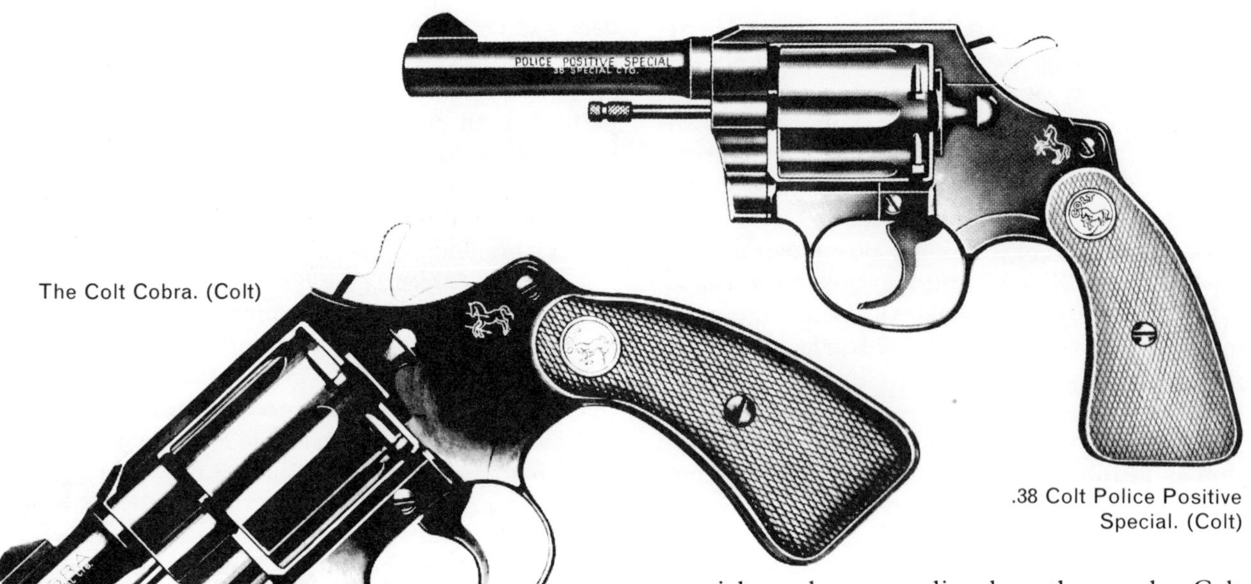

The Colt Cobra. (Colt)

.38 Colt Police Positive Special. (Colt)

.38 Colt Aircrewman. (Col. F. S. Allen)

special revolvers, not listed on the regular Colt range, were made for the Border Patrol, a branch of the US Treasury Dept. The sights were fixed and all were chambered for the .38 S & W Special cartridge. The barrel was marked in two lines on the left hand side 'Colt Border Patrol, .38 Spec.—Heavy Duty'.

If the 21 ozs of the Detective Special weigh too heavy, the answer may be the lightweight Colt Cobra Model D.3. Introduced in 1951 and currently available with 2″, 3″, 4″ and 5″ barrels, the 2″ barrel version, due to the use of a light alloy—known as 'Coltalloy'—for the frame and side plate, weighs only 15 ozs.

A slightly shorter stock makes the Colt .38 Special Agent Model D.4 the lightest in the range at 14 ozs. Introduced in 1955, the Colt Agent is similar to the Cobra and is currently on the selling range.

A very rare lightweight 'special' was the Colt Aircrewman developed by Colt at the request of the US Air Force during the Korean War. Both the frame and cylinder were made from aluminium alloy, and one thousand were ordered for test. Smith and Wesson then made up 500 Chief's Specials and 500 Military and Police Models, both with aluminium frames and cylinders. These revolvers were tested by the US Air Force as survival weapons for air crew who had complained about the weight and bulk of the .45 Colt Model 1911. In 1960 the special lightweight revolvers were recalled; it had been found possible to chamber the .357 Magnum in the Chief's Special and blown up guns had naturally resulted. Some of the guns had been sold as surplus and, in the hands of handloaders obsessed with velocity, had led to the usual disastrous results.

Currently available centre-fire lightweight revolvers have alloy frames and steel cylinders with an adequate margin of strength to accept all but the hottest of handloads.

In between the Police Positive Special and the New Service frame sizes comes the Colt Official Police Model. This medium size revolver started its life as the Colt Army Special in 1908 and was available in .32–20 WCF, .38 Special and .41 Colt. Similar to the New Service except for the frame size, this pistol was intended to interest the US Army. The military were, however, more interested in the New Service and later, of course, in the Colt 1911 automatic. But, if the Army were not interested, the American police certainly were and, in 1926, the New York Police Dept. adopted the .38 Special version of the Army Special in a 4″ barrel. Other Police Departments followed and, in 1928, the same revolver appeared as the Colt Official Police Revolver. At one time or another, the Official Police has been chambered for the .22 rim-fire, .32–20 WCF, .38 Special and .41 Colt. Various changes have been made during the long production run and today, as the Model E.3, the Official Police is made in .38 Special with a 4″, 5″ or 6″ barrel and in .22 rim-fire in either 4″ or 6″ barrel lengths. The 4″ .38 can be supplied with a round butt.

A short-lived variant of the Official Police Revolver was the Colt Commando, a wartime substitute which appeared in 1942 but was discontinued at the end of the war.

Built on the same frame as the Official Police, the Colt Officer's Model traces its ancestry back through the New Army Model of 1894 (the target version of which was designated the Officer's Model) to the Colt DA Model 1889. In 1908 production of the New Army, New Navy, Marine Corps Model and the 1904 Officers Model was discontinued and, as we have seen, the Colt Army Special was introduced. The target version of the Army Special introduced in 1908 again used the name Officer's Model, so that there are two distinct variants—that of 1904, where the cylinder revolved to the left, and the later 1908 model with clockwise cylinder rotation.

This revolver was and is Colt's pre-eminent target weapon. Over the years barrel lengths between 4″ and $7\frac{1}{2}$″ have been available, but today the standard length is 6″. In 1950 the Officer's Model Special appeared with a ramp foresight and, in 1953, minor improvements in sights, hammer etc. resulted in the Officer's Model

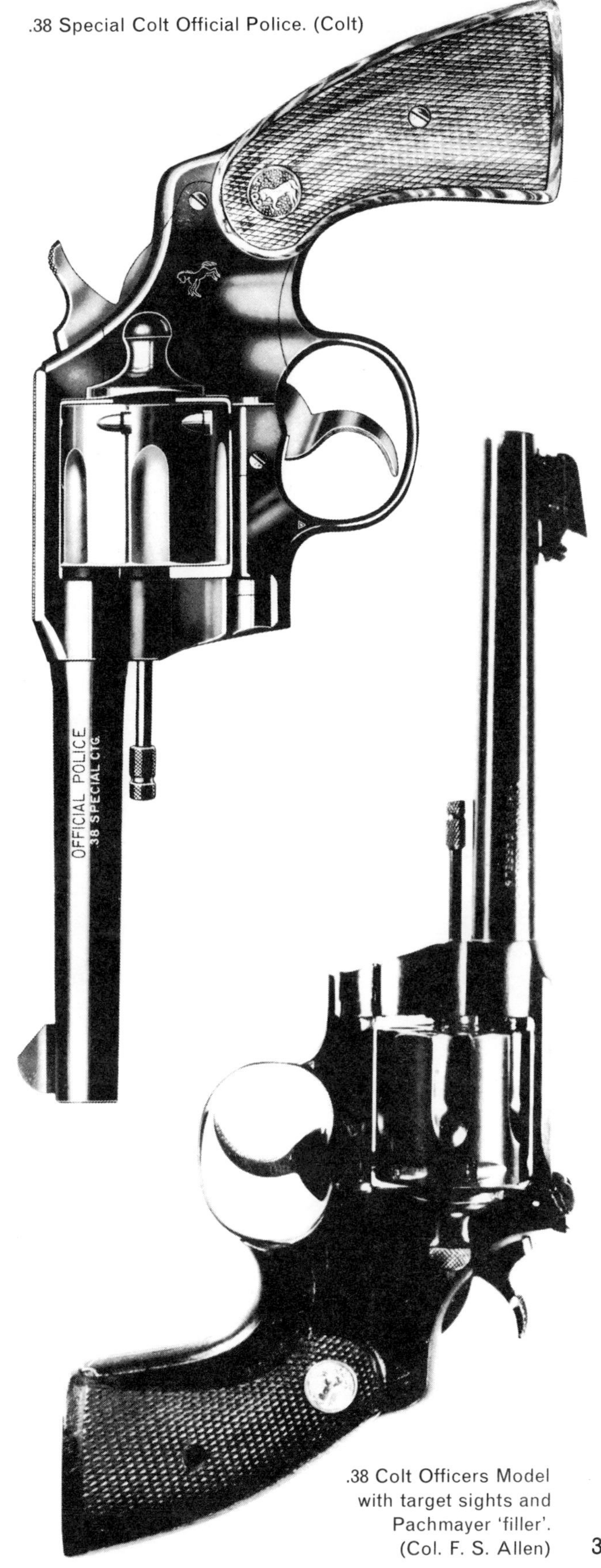

.38 Special Colt Official Police. (Colt)

.38 Colt Officers Model with target sights and Pachmayer 'filler'. (Col. F. S. Allen)

Match, currently in the Colt catalogue. A heavy barrel version was made available in 1935 and, although windage could be adjusted on the rear sight, the foresight was adjustable for elevation. On the Officer's Model Special both adjustments were incorporated in the rear sight. Throughout the years the calibres available have been restricted to .38 Special and .22 rim-fire long rifle and it is in these calibres that the Officer's Model Match is offered.

The demand for increased accuracy in what we might loosely term as 'work guns' has resulted in recent years in the appearance of revolvers designed for practical shooting but with the added refinement of target sights. It was to meet this demand that Colt, in 1954, introduced their Trooper revolver which is, in effect, the Officer's Model Match with adjustable rear sight and a ramp foresight. Two barrel lengths are at present offered, 4″ and 6″, and two calibres, the .38 Special and the .357 Magnum. The .22 calibre version originally available has been withdrawn since the Officer's Model Match in .22 meets the demand for this type of .22 revolver. Shortly after the introduction of the Colt Trooper, the Colt 357 was announced. This was a short-lived variant of the Trooper designed to take the place of the New Service .357 Magnum. With the availability of the Colt Trooper in .357 Magnum and the appearance in 1956 of the Colt Python in the same calibre, the Colt 357 was a needless extension to the range and was dropped in 1963.

Yet another of the short-lived .38 revolvers was the Colt Marshall which appeared in 1955 and appears to have been dropped in 1958. This was a standard fixed sight revolver chambered for the .38 Special and available in either 2″ or 4″ barrel lengths.

An attempt to meet the requirements of target-men resulted in the appearance of the Colt Officer's Model Match in single or thumb cocking action only. Due to the small demand and the high price in relation to the standard double action Officer's Model Match, it was taken off the selling range in 1965 after only a short life.

The Colt Python, the Rolls Royce of the Colt range, first appeared in 1955 and is a most imposing revolver with an integral ventilated barrel rib and an ejector shroud which extends from the crane to the muzzle. It is currently offered in $2\frac{1}{2}$″, 4″ or 6″ barrel lengths and is chambered for the .357 Magnum cartridge, but it can also be used with the .38 Special.

The current version of the .38 Special Colt Officers Model. (Colt)

This completes the current revolver range, and the models available are listed below.

Rim-fire
Colt Frontier Scout. SA .22 r.f. and .22 RFM
Colt Buntline Scout. SA .22 r.f. and .22 RFM
Colt Official Police. DA .22 r.f.
Colt Cobra. DA .22 r.f.
Colt Officer's Model Match. .22 r.f.
Centre-fire
Colt Detective Special. DA .38 Spl. .32 NP
Colt Cobra. DA .38 Spl. .32 NP

.357 Colt Python. (Colt)

Colt Agent. DA .38 Spl.
Colt Police Positive Special. DA and .38 Spl. and .32
Colt Official Police. DA .38 Spl.
Colt Trooper. DA .38 Spl. and .357 Mag.
Colt Officer Model Match. DA .38 Spl.
Colt Python. DA .357 Mag.
Colt SAA .357 Mag. and .45 Colt
Colt Buntline. SA .45 Colt
Colt New Frontier. SA .357 Mag., .44 Spl. and .45 Colt
Colt New Frontier Buntline Special. SA .45 Colt

This current list clearly shows not only the drastic reduction in the different calibres now available, the result of a long-needed standardisation, but also the virtual elimination of the .22 target revolver.

Before leaving the Colt revolver which, in either SA or DA form, has shown remarkable resilience in an ever changing world, one variant of the Officer's Model should be mentioned, the Colt Camp Perry Pistol, a single shot target pistol built on the Officer's Model frame. Introduced in 1926 and discontinued in 1941, this was an attempt to produce a target pistol with the minimum amount of disturbance to production and no need for expensive retooling. The idea was similar to that used on the Smith and Wesson Single Shot Model 1891, except that Colt based the Camp Perry on a solid frame revolver whereas Smith and Wesson were able to utilise their hinged frame revolver.

Sooner or later the question arises—which is best, the Colt or the Smith and Wesson? Both have quite distinct family characteristics. Since the double action series became established, very little change has taken place either in the Colt range, as has already been demonstrated, or, for that matter, in the Smith and Wesson range at which we must now look.

This is even larger than the Colt range. Taking into account all the variations of barrel length, calibre etc., the two major US revolver manufacturers between them offer nearly one hundred different models. Both ring the changes on a basic theme. The Colt Agent, the Police Positive and the heavier revolvers are based on the larger so-called .41 frame that started with the Colt Model 1889. Smith and Wesson use three basic frame sizes, and the light frame is based on the original .32 Model I Hand Ejector, although the large .38 calibres can still be accommodated in this frame by the simple expedient of reducing the number of cartridges in the cylinder from six to five. (Colt's lightweight revolvers have six chambers and Colt have made use of this in their advertising—'make that extra shot count'.) The next largest Smith and Wesson frame is the .38 which is used on the 'K' series, the Military and Police and the Combat Magnum. This frame size originated with the Model 1902 Hand Ejector. The larger revolvers use the .44 frame first introduced as the Smith and Wesson New Century in 1907.

The Smith and Wesson range is extremely

complicated, but a start can be made with Smith and Wesson's answer to the Colt solid frame revolver, the Smith and Wesson Model I Hand Ejector, introduced in 1896. Like the Colt Model 1889, the Smith and Wesson was six chambered, the cylinder swung out to the left on a crane, and the side plate was on the right (Colt changed over to the left). The Smith and Wesson was smaller than the .38 Colt and was chambered for the .32 S & W and the .32 S & W long, but could be used with the Colt .32. The method of latching the cylinder was also different.

The .32 calibre Hand Ejector went through a long series of production changes and development. Much of this work was in connection with the cylinder latch. Colt had patented their system and it was some time before Smith and Wesson were satisfied with their alternative. The basic idea was to use a rod which passed through the extractor stem, and to unlatch the split frame the rod was drawn forward against spring pressure. In 1899 two models appeared, the .32–20 Winchester Hand Ejector and the .38 Hand Ejector or 1st Model Military and Police. This .38 revolver was developed by Wesson in response to a request by the US Army and Navy Ordnance Boards and, for this reason, the Government purchase revolvers are also known as the Smith and Wesson Army and Navy Revolvers of 1889. The cylinder latch rod on these models, instead of being pulled forward from the front, was pushed forward from the rear (Wesson's British Patent No. 6184 of 1894, Fig. 8). This was the first stage in the development of the Smith and Wesson cylinder latch system where the centre pin is pushed forward, whereas on the Colt the cylinder latch is pulled to the rear.

In 1902 the next stage in the evolution of the cylinder latch system took place. This was the provision of a forward cylinder pin lock placed underneath the barrel through which operated a rear actuated pin. The system was covered by Wesson's British Patent No. 24,957 of 1901 and, except for the simplification of the thumb piece, this method of locking has been used by Smith and Wesson ever since. It will be remembered that, with the exception of one model, all the Colt DA revolver cylinders rotate to the right. On the Smith and Wesson, where the cylinder hand is on the right side of the frame, it tends, since it rotates it anti-clockwise, to push the cylinder to the left, in the opposite direction to the Colt. Different, yes, but as long as you remember which gun does which, of little importance. The additional barrel

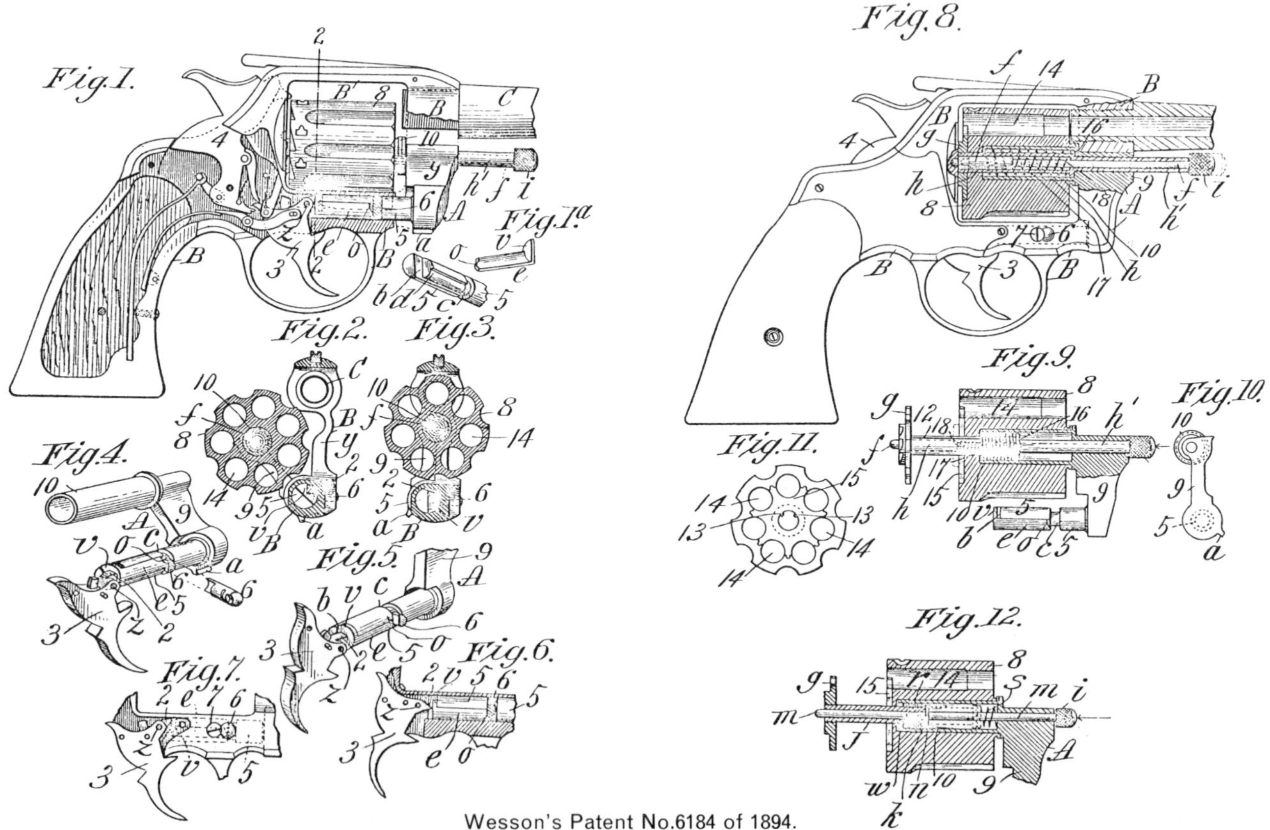

Wesson's Patent No.6184 of 1894.

mounted cylinder lock on the Smith and Wesson is important however; it results in a system which is marginally less liable to accidental damage and, since the centre-pin locks the rear and the barrel mounted lock fits into the front of the ejector rod to effect the front locking, it also helps to hold the crane in line. There are, of course, far more springs in the Smith and Wesson system, and one little one in the cylinder 'bolt' is quite weak (Smith and Wesson tend to cause confusion by calling the rear latch a bolt, and the cylinder bolt which locks the cylinder rotation a cylinder stop.) Its main job is to keep the cylinder latch or bolt in the forward position when the cylinder is unlatched; under its influence, a projection at the rear of the bolt (which can be seen in the illustration on page 318) moves forward under the rear of the hammer and prevents the hammer being cocked if the cylinder is not securely locked.

The centre-pin inside the extractor rod also has its spring which presses against a collar and causes the centre-pin to project to the rear. The centre-pin can be seen when the cylinder is open, and, if it is pushed forward by the finger, the spring pressure can be felt. As the cylinder is closed, the recoil shield pushes the centre-pin forward until it enters the centre hole in the standing breech. At this point, it overcomes the bolt spring and pushes the bolt and external thumb piece to the rear, while, at the same time, the front locking 'bolt', under the influence of its own little spring, enters the front of the extractor rod. The Colt system uses a stubby pin which is twice the diameter of the Smith and Wesson centre-pin and fits into a recess in the centre rear of the cylinder.

Irrespective of whether your revolver is a Colt or a Smith and Wesson, do not flick the cylinders in and out of the frame like the movie gangster. It might look very smart, but it does not do the latch or the crane any good. The Smith and Wesson is better able to take this punishment since the springs in the system do take some of the shock, but it is still bad practice. The best way to open either gun is to hold it in the right hand in the normal manner, press or pull the cylinder latch and, with the two fingers of the left hand on the right hand side of the cylinder and the thumb on the left, push the cylinder to the left. The fingers of the left hand will pass through the frame aperture and the left thumb is ready to operate the extractor rod. In this position, the pistol can be easily held by the left hand alone. When new cartridges have been inserted, the cylinder is relatched by pushing in with the left thumb.

In 1902 Smith and Wesson placed a very neat seven shot .22 solid frame revolver on the market. Known by the factory as the 1902 Model M Hand Ejector, it is perhaps better known as the Smith and Wesson Ladysmith. Three distinct models were produced in the comparatively short period of its manufacture. On the first model the cylinder was released by a round button-shaped thumb piece on the left hand side of the frame. Barrel lengths offered were $2\frac{1}{4}''$, $3''$ and $3\frac{1}{2}''$, and there was no front cylinder lock. The second model had a front cylinder lock with a knurled knob at the front which was pulled forward to latch the cylinder. There was no rear thumb piece, and it was offered in $3''$ and $3\frac{1}{2}''$

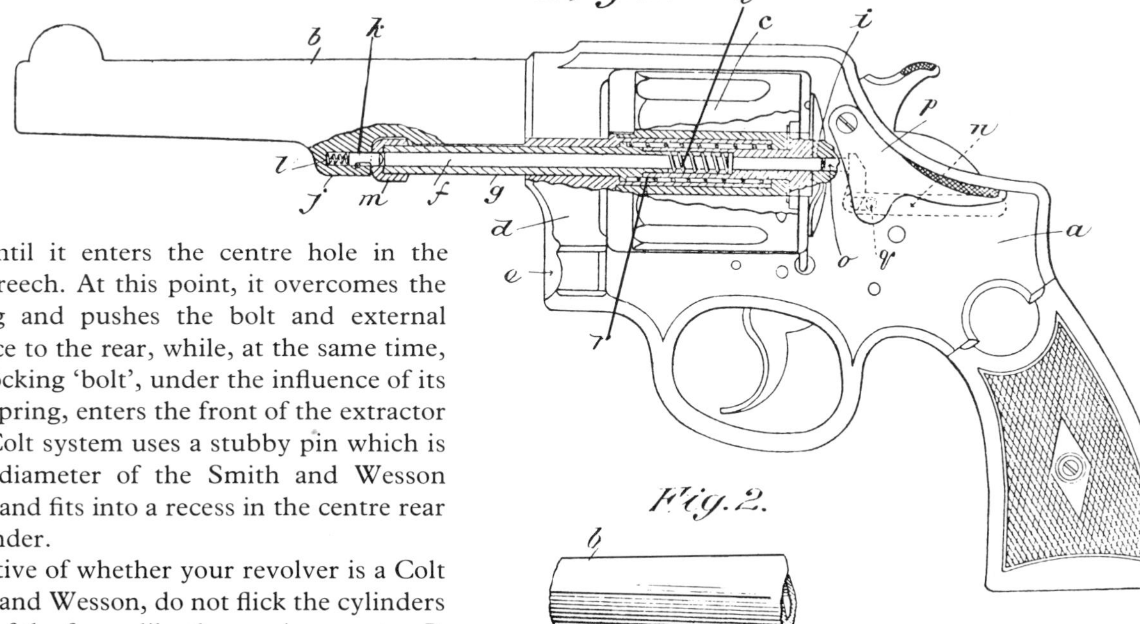

Wesson's Patent No.24,957 of 1901.

The trigger mechanism of the .455 Smith and Wesson New Century Model.

with an eye to a particular section of the market, the ladies, but its success was perhaps more than the sedate management had expected. Unfortunately, this was not entirely due to the interest of the fair sex in target shooting or, indeed, in protecting their virtue. It was, in fact, being used to ensure payment for loss of virtue by the ladies of the oldest profession who found that this little seven shot revolver fitted neatly into their handbags or could be tucked into a garter and, at close range, packed sufficient authority to produce the right amount of respect. Smith and Wesson promptly stopped manufacture, or so the story goes.

After Horace Smith retired in 1873, Daniel Baird Wesson guided the fortunes of the company until his death in 1906. His son Joseph Hawes Wesson then assumed control.

barrel lengths only. The third model, the production of which ceased in 1921, was similar to the previous model, except for a square instead of a round butt. A target version was offered of this model with a 6″ barrel and target sights. The diminutive Model M .22 Hand Ejector illustrated was originally used with the then standard .22 rim-fire long rifle cartridge. It was found in practice that, due to recoil, the bullets, which were not heavily crimped, jumped forward and tied up the cylinder. In order to overcome this problem, Smith and Wesson developed a special .22 rim-fire cartridge known as the .22 S & W long which was crimped to retain the bullet in place.

Some years ago the noted American writer Lucian Carey, writing the magazine *True*, told an interesting little story about the Ladysmith. Smith and Wesson had introduced this model

.22 Smith and Wesson Hand Ejector, Third Model.

An interesting variation of the .32 Hand Ejector was the target revolver known as the Beckeart Model after a San Francisco firearms dealer who had urged Smith and Wesson to produce a .22 target revolver. The Beckeart or .22/32 Hand Ejector was made originally in 1908 in a limited number but, from 1911, it was permanently introduced as a target model. Today the designation .22/32 is still used by Smith and Wesson for four versions which, like the original, are .22 calibre revolvers on the .32 frame.

Similarly, the .32 Hand Ejector has survived the years. In 1903 the Model I Hand Ejector was improved, in 1917 it was catalogued as the .32 Regulation Police Model, and it is still being currently manufactured.

In 1907 appeared one of the best looking revolvers made by anyone, the Smith and Wesson New Century or Triple Lock Model. This was based on the design of the .38 Model 1905 Hand Ejector, better known as the Military and Police Model, and was designed to take a new cartridge, the S & W .44 Special, based on the highly successful .44 S & W Russian cartridge. The powder charge was increased from 23 to 26 grains of black powder, the case was lengthened from 0.96″ to 1.15″ average, but the bullet weight was retained at 246 grains. This cartridge was highly successful in both black powder and smokeless loads, and work done on the cartridge in America later resulted in the appearance of a .44 Magnum.

The .44 Hand Ejector, the official factory designation, was made in .44 calibre and later in .455 and .450 British. A few were also made in .45 Colt calibre. The Smith and Wesson Triple

Smith and Wesson Hand Ejector chambered for the .455 British Service cartridge and fitted with special walnut stocks and an altered foresight.

.455 Smith and Wesson Hand Ejector Mark II.

.45 Smith and Wesson Hand Ejector, fitted with Mershon rubber stocks and an altered foresight.

Lock in .455 calibre was the first centre-fire large calibre revolver I owned. It had fixed sights and, shortly after it was obtained, I modified the foresight to the shape seen in the illustration. At a later date special stocks were made. The Smith and Wesson frame is much narrower than the Colt New Service and this, coupled with its greater length, caused the somewhat sharp corner to dig into the hand, into the soft flesh between the thumb and forefinger. Experience with the Colt dictated the need to modify something and the wider special stock was the result. These stocks also 'filled in' the space between the stock and guard and made the Triple Lock much nicer to shoot. Stocks of similar pattern are of course available from the factory today.

The triple lock feature of the .44 Hand Ejector was provided by an additional bolt housed in the modified ejector casing which bolted the cylinder yoke in addition to the normal front and rear lock.

In the .455 Mark II Hand Ejector the third lock and the casing round the ejector rod were discarded. Experience in the appalling conditions of the First World War had shown, on the Triple Lock models supplied to the British Government, that the ejector rod casing caused difficulty in closing the cylinder when it became choked with mud.

The .44 Hand Ejector formed the basis for the .45 calibre Hand Ejector which was manufactured from 1917. The casing and third lock were eliminated and the revolver was chambered for the Colt .45 ACP cartridge used in the US Government Model 1911 automatic. As with the Model 1917 Colt, the Smith and Wesson Army Model 1917 again employed the half moon clips and, in order to accommodate them, the cylinder was slightly shortened. These revolvers were marked 'D.A. 45' on the left hand side of the barrel and 'United States Property' under the barrel in front of the locking bolt housing. The recoil of the .45 ACP makes special stocks very necessary if prolonged firing is to be practised. The special stocks supplied by the factory first appeared in 1938 and were given the name Magna. These stocks were fitted to a commercial post-war Army Model and, to eliminate the use of clips, a special semi-rim .45 auto-rim cartridge was introduced. Known as the 1950 Army, this model is still in the current range.

The death of Joseph Wesson in 1920 introduced the third generation to managerial responsibility. Harold Wesson became President and Frank H. Wesson became Treasurer; both were nephews of Joseph Wesson.

In 1926 the basic .44 frame was used for a target model chambered for the .44 Smith and Wesson Special and, in 1930, the .38/44 Outdoorsman appeared, a .38 calibre revolver built on the heavier .44 frame. For this revolver, a high speed .38/44 S & W Special cartridge was developed by Remington. The .38/44 cartridge designation was later dropped and the two .38/44 revolvers currently sold by Smith and Wesson are both chambered for the .38 S & W Special. In 1933 the .38/44 Heavy Duty was introduced, the combination of cartridge and heavy frame revolver being thought especially valuable for Police Authorities faced with the criminal's increasing use of bullet proof vests and the appearance of auto body steels. This cartridge was the first of a long line of high-speed cartridges in nominal .38 calibre which culminated in the .357 Magnum. The .38/44 revolvers of this period were the first to be sold with the Magna grip.

Throughout the history of Smith and Wesson it will have been noticed that the Company either initiated or assisted in the development of a number of new cartridges, many of which were highly successful and established world wide standards. The .357 Magnum developed by Philip Sharpe and Merton Robinson of the Winchester Repeating Arms Co. in co-operation with Smith and Wesson was one of them. To handle this new and extremely powerful cartridge, the Smith and Wesson .357 Magnum revolver was developed, and the first Magnum produced was presented to J. Edgar Hoover of the FBI. Initial production was to special order only and barrel lengths from $3\frac{1}{2}''$ to $8\frac{3}{4}''$ were available, although they were later standardised at $3\frac{1}{2}''$, $5''$, $6''$, $6\frac{1}{2}''$ and $8\frac{3}{4}''$. American Police Authorities and Law Enforcement Agencies purchased the Magnum in volume and it became fashionable to use this revolver on big game up to and including moose and Alaskan bear.

Modifications and improvements continued to be made on established models. One of the most widely sold of these, the .38 Military and Police Model (in the improved Model 1905), traced its ancestry back to the .38 Hand Ejector of 1899, and was also the first of the series to incorporate the intercepting safety or 'hammer block' introduced in 1915. The original hammer block was far simpler than the Colt 'positive lock' and, when the hammer is drawn slightly back, the leaf interceptor can be seen inside the right hand side of the frame. As the hammer is drawn further back the safety retracts into the side plate and remains retracted until the hammer falls and the trigger returns to the forward position.

If you wish to see exactly how the Smith and Wesson mechanism works, first of all remove the stocks which are held together by a single screw on the left side, and are further positioned by the frame cut-out, with the stock pin in the base of the frame. It may be necessary to prise off the stocks and, if so, care should be taken not to damage them.

The side plate on the Smith and Wesson is on the right hand side and is retained by four screws instead of the two used by Colt. The front plate screw also serves to retain the yoke or crane in the frame, and, if this is removed first, the cylinder can be opened and the yoke drawn forward out of the frame. This screw and the one next to it are crowned, but the rear screw is currently flat headed. Earlier models employed a fourth screw at the top of the plate but, with present day models, a small lip on the side plate enters a rebate in the frame, so dispensing with the screw and, incidentally, resulting in a neater appearance. With the four screws removed (three on late models) the side plate can be carefully taken off. The fit of this side plate is a fetish with Smith and Wesson, and, as they go to a lot of trouble to get it exact, their workmanship should not be spoiled by efforts to prise the plate off. If it does stick, tap the frame with a wood or fibre hammer, or use a screwdriver handle (wood or plastic) to unseat the plate. Once this is removed, the works are exposed.

The hammer block (on later models) fits into a recess and has a rearward facing tongue which projects into the groove cut into the plate for the cylinder hand. The hand is, of course, on the right hand side of the hammer and is attached to the trigger. If the pistol is cocked, an inclined face at the rear of the hand will engage the tongue of the hammer block and push it rearward into the plate. In order to cock the pistol with the cylinder removed, it must be remembered that it is necessary to pull back on the cylinder frame latch in order to draw back the cylinder 'bolt'. A late model Smith and Wesson with the modified hammer block can be identified before dismantling by the fact that the hammer has a slot cut across the face below the firing pin. On this type, the hammer block is attached to the rebound slide underneath the hammer. It performs the same function as the old type but, as the trigger is pulled back, the rebound slide moves rearward and the hammer block, instead of moving inwards, now moves downwards.

If dismantling is to continue, the next step is to remove the mainspring. On the Smith and Wesson this is an easy operation since the mainspring has a strain screw which, when unscrewed, releases the mainspring tension and allows the spring to be taken out.

The most difficult job is the removal of the rebound slide with its internal coil spring. This can best be done by prising the end of the slide away from the frame with a small screwdriver, taking care not to let the spring clear the rebound stud. At this point, a screwdriver with a broader blade can be inserted to compress the spring so that, when it is clear, it will not escape. In replacing this spring the same technique must be used and the spring compressed before the slide can be got into position. The spring and rebound slide serve two purposes: the first is to return the trigger, the second to 'rebound' the hammer. The 'hump' at the foot of the hammer is lifted upwards by an inclined face on the top of the rebound slide as the slide itself moves forward. With the rebound slide removed, the trigger, hand and hammer can be taken out, together with the cylinder stop and cylinder stop spring.

It is seldom necessary to dismantle the revolver to this extent, but, if the pistol is old and likely to be returned to service, it is wise to examine the internal mechanism. It may be necessary to remove oxidised oil which can clog the mechanism and also, if the pistol has been accidentally soaked in water, it should be thoroughly cleaned.

The lean years between the two world wars substantially reduced the profitability of the Smith and Wesson enterprise, and a disastrous contract for a semi-automatic rifle which failed to pass British acceptance tests further strained the company's finances. Following the Dunkirk evacuation, however, Smith and Wesson received substantial orders for revolvers from the British Commonwealth and the debt incurred as a result of the ill-fated rifle contract was cleared.

The revolver supplied to the British Forces was the well-tried Military and Police Model under the guise of the Smith and Wesson K-200 or .38/200 British Service Revolver, and was chambered for the British 'Cartridge, SA, Ball, revolver, .380 inch, Mark I' to give it its full and somewhat unwieldy title. The cartridge was simply the .38 S & W which had first been introduced in 1876 for the hinged frame No. 2 revolver. As the .38 S & W it had become immensely popular and a wide variety of special purpose loads were developed. Amongst these was the .38 Super Police with a 200 grain jacketed bullet, and it was this version that was adopted by Britain. Unfortunately the terminology, although extensive, was not exact since the cartridge was not a .380; this designation had, by right of usage, been employed for the early externally lubricated cartridge. Much difficulty and trouble were caused during World War Two when, due to urgent need, .38 revolvers chambered for the smaller diameter S & W Special cartridges had to be purchased. The K-200 was designed to accept the British service .380 and was supplied with a 5″ barrel and a butt lanyard swivel. The commercial 'bright blue' employed by Smith and Wesson was used on some earlier deliveries, but pressure of production resulted first of all in the duller 'brush polish' blue, and finally in the substitution of sand-blasted and phosphated blue finishes. Issued with both checkered and smooth walnut stocks, the .38/200 Smith and Wesson became a great favourite and, by those who had to carry and use a revolver during the war, was certainly preferred to the .38 issue Enfield.

The .38/200 was marked 'Smith and Wesson' on the left side of the barrel and '.38 S & W Ctg.' on the right. British Government acceptance marks will also be found on the frame. Civilian models chambered for the .38 S & W Special and pressed into service were marked by a distinguishing red band round the rear of the barrel carrying the legend '.38 Specl.' This was a procedure similar to that adopted with the US Enfield rifles chambered for the .30/06 US service cartridge. On some .38 Special revolvers the chambers were bored out slightly to take the wider .38/200 cartridge and these 'conversions' were marked '.38/380' on the frame or barrel. Two of these wartime Smith and Wesson revolvers are illustrated, the first the standard K-200, the second a conversion from .38 S & W Special to .380 which was subsequently modified by the writer. These modifications consisted of shortening the barrel from the original 5″ to 2¾″ and fitting a ramp sight block and ramp foresight. The top strap was altered to accommodate an adjustable rear sight, the front of the trigger guard was cut off and the butt rounded. New stocks were made, the action was polished and hammer and trigger were 'engine turned'. This work was done at a time when new weapons could not be imported from America due to currency restrictions. I have had a lot of fun with this pistol and it can take its place in history since, at the request of the late Ian Fleming, it had its portrait painted and was used on the dust jacket of *From Russia With Love*, the fifth of the James Bond novels.

The .38 S & W Special 'Victory' Model was another wartime variant of the Military and Police Model which had both 4″ and 2″ barrels, a grey sand-blasted finish and serial numbers prefixed by the letter 'V'. Manufacture was discontinued with the resumption of commercial production at the end of the war, but it was with this model that the change in the design of the hammer block took place.

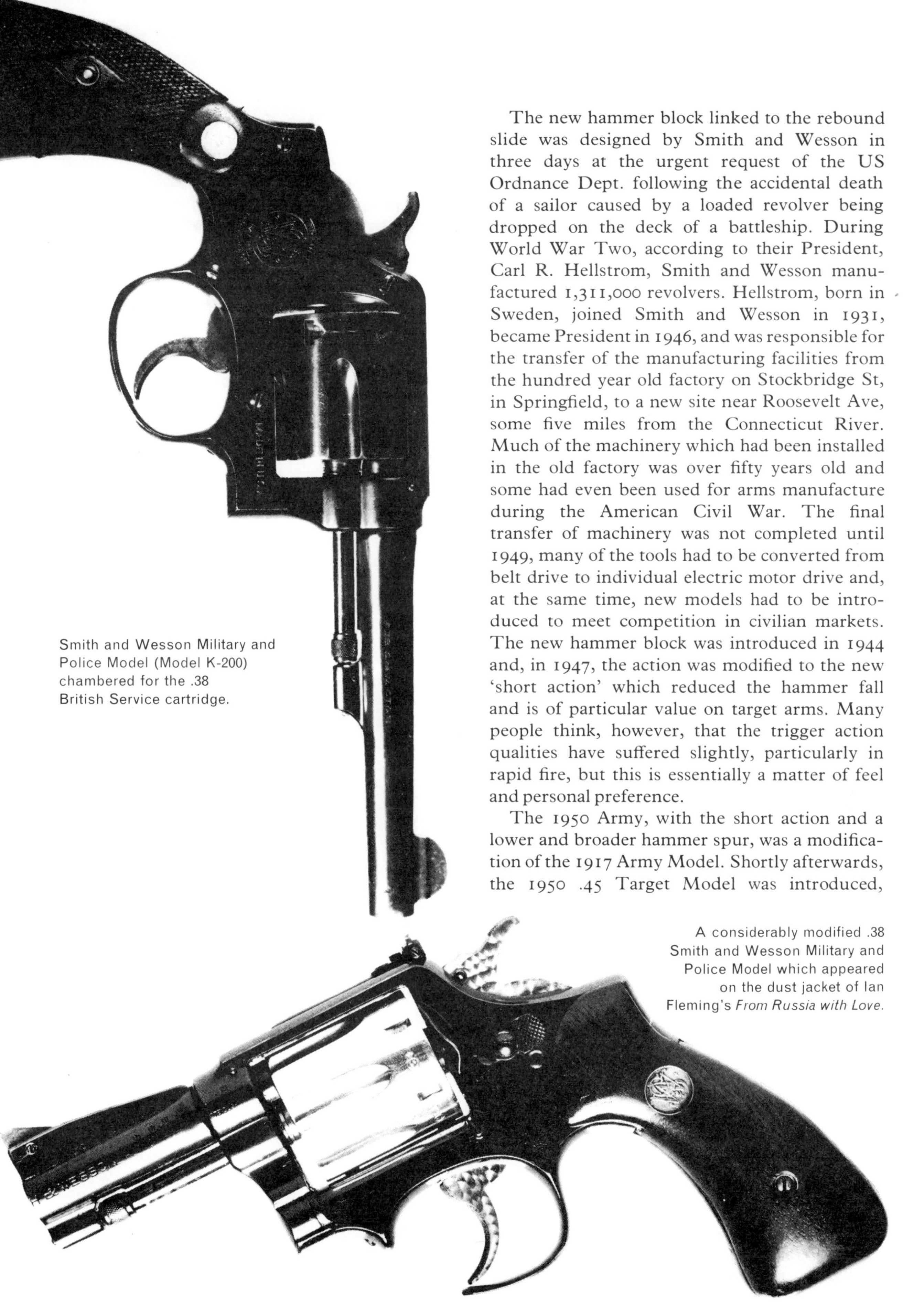

The new hammer block linked to the rebound slide was designed by Smith and Wesson in three days at the urgent request of the US Ordnance Dept. following the accidental death of a sailor caused by a loaded revolver being dropped on the deck of a battleship. During World War Two, according to their President, Carl R. Hellstrom, Smith and Wesson manufactured 1,311,000 revolvers. Hellstrom, born in Sweden, joined Smith and Wesson in 1931, became President in 1946, and was responsible for the transfer of the manufacturing facilities from the hundred year old factory on Stockbridge St, in Springfield, to a new site near Roosevelt Ave, some five miles from the Connecticut River. Much of the machinery which had been installed in the old factory was over fifty years old and some had even been used for arms manufacture during the American Civil War. The final transfer of machinery was not completed until 1949, many of the tools had to be converted from belt drive to individual electric motor drive and, at the same time, new models had to be introduced to meet competition in civilian markets. The new hammer block was introduced in 1944 and, in 1947, the action was modified to the new 'short action' which reduced the hammer fall and is of particular value on target arms. Many people think, however, that the trigger action qualities have suffered slightly, particularly in rapid fire, but this is essentially a matter of feel and personal preference.

The 1950 Army, with the short action and a lower and broader hammer spur, was a modification of the 1917 Army Model. Shortly afterwards, the 1950 .45 Target Model was introduced,

Smith and Wesson Military and Police Model (Model K-200) chambered for the .38 British Service cartridge.

A considerably modified .38 Smith and Wesson Military and Police Model which appeared on the dust jacket of Ian Fleming's *From Russia with Love.*

followed by the five shot .38 Chief's Special. The object was to produce the smallest and lightest all steel revolver which could handle what many regard to be the minimum cartridge for a combat handgun, the .38 S & W Special.

The 1888 Smith and Wesson Safety Hammerless or New Departure had been manufactured with several changes up until World War Two. In 1952 a new 'Safety Hammerless' based on the Model J or Chief's Special appeared, known as the Smith and Wesson Centennial. Designed for personal safety, the Centennial also incorporates a grip of squeeze safety in the rear butt strap. The cylinder holds five cartridges, as does the Chief's Special, but the Centennial can be fired trigger action only.

The Military and Police, Centennial and Chief's Special 'Airweight Models' were offered as supplementary special purpose revolvers in 1953. The reduction in weight made possible by the use of light alloys can be seen by comparing the 19 ozs. of the standard Chief's Special with the 10¾ ozs. of the Airweight version.

Mention has already been made of the contribution which Smith and Wesson have traditionally made in the field of handgun ammunition. In 1956 a bombshell burst, the Smith and Wesson .44 Magnum. Judged by contemporary energy figures, the new revolver was three times as powerful as the .45 Colt and nearly twice as powerful as the .357 Magnum. The .44 Magnum was built on the .44 Special frame but, if we take the 1950 .44 Special Target Model for comparison, the cylinder length of the Magnum was increased from 1.57″ to 1.75″ and a heavier barrel was fitted with muzzle diameter up by .15″. The Magnum also had different sights, a broader barrel rib, oversize stocks (designed to minimise the recoil) and a wider trigger and hammer spur. As originally offered with a 6½″ barrel, it weighed 3 lbs. as against the 2 lbs. 9 ozs. of the 1950 Model.

Finish and quality are beyond reproach, a remarkable achievement in this day and age of mass-produced mediocrity. Details of the .44 Magnum cartridge which was developed jointly by Remington and Smith and Wesson will be given later.

In 1964 the cartridge range was again increased by the appearance of the .41 Magnum. Introduced by the Remington Arms Co., it was designed to bridge the gap between the .357 Magnum and the .44 Magnum. As one would expect, the first revolver to be designed to handle this cartridge was a Smith and Wesson. Built on the same heavy frame as the .44 Magnum, details are given in the summary of present day Smith and Wesson revolvers below.

The production range in 1956, with the Model name and number, was as follows:

.44 Magnum. Model No. 29. Calibre .44 Magnum. Six shot, double action, available in 4″, 6½″ and 8¾″ barrel lengths. Click adjustable rear sight and red ramp foresight. Oversize Target stocks. S & W Bright Blue or Nickel finish.

.41 Magnum. Model No. 57. Calibre .41 Magnum. Six shot, double action, available in 4″, 6″ and 8⅜″ barrel lengths. Adjustable rear sight and red ramp foresight. Oversize Target stocks. S & W Bright Blue or Nickel finish.

Smith and Wesson Model No. 29. (Smith and Wesson)

Parts list for the Smith and Wesson Model No. 29.

5005 Bolt Plunger Spring
5014 Extractor Pin
5021 Extractor Rod Collar
5022 Extractor spring
5034 Hammer Nose Rivet
5036 Hammer Nose Bushing
5042 Hand Pin
5045 Locking Bolt Spring
5047 Mainspring
5049 Plate Screw, crowned
5053 Hand Spring Pin
5053 Hand Spring Torsion Pin
5053 Sear Pin
5053 Stirrup Pin
5053 Trigger Lever Pin
5054 Sear Spring
5055 Stirrup
5062 Stock Pin
5063 Stock Screw
5064 Strain Screw
5070 Thumbpiece
5071 Thumbpiece Nut
5073 Trigger Lever
5074 Rebound Slide Spring
5078 Trigger Stud
5079 Cylinder Stop Stud
5079 Rebound Slide Stud
5083 Rebound Slide Pin
5085 Rebound Slide
5091 Plate Screw, flat head
5102 Rear Sight Elevation Nut
5103 Rear Sight Plunger Spring
5104 Rear Sight Plunger
5105 Rear Sight Spring Clip
5106 Rear Sight Elevation Stud
5107 Rear Sight Windage Nut
5108 Rear Sight Windage Screw
5112 Hammer Stud
5113 Sear
5118 Hand Torsion Spring
5155 Rear Sight Leaf Screw
5191 Escutcheon
5192 Escutcheon Nut
5219 Rear Sight Leaf
5306 Trigger Stop
5357 Cylinder Stop
5389 Bolt Plunger
5390 Centre Pin
5418 Hammer Nose
5421 Hammer, wide Target type
5423 Hammer Block
5426 Hand
5429 Locking Bolt
5430 Side Plate
5431 Locking Bolt Pin
5448 Extractor
5456 Extractor Rod
5457 Centre Pin Spring
5461 Frame, with studs, bushing and lug
5500 Yoke
5608 Bolt
5750 Hammer Nose Spring
5810 Barrel Pin
5843 Trigger, wide Target type
5856 Cylinder, with extractor, pins and gas ring
5857 Barrel, 6½″
5859 Gas Ring
5900 Rear Sight Slide
5901 Barrel, 4″
5912 Stock, checked Goncala Alves Target, right
5913 Stock, checked Goncala Alves Target, left
5930 Frame Lug
5941 Barrel, 8⅜″
5953 Rear Sight Assembly
5959 Cylinder Stop Spring

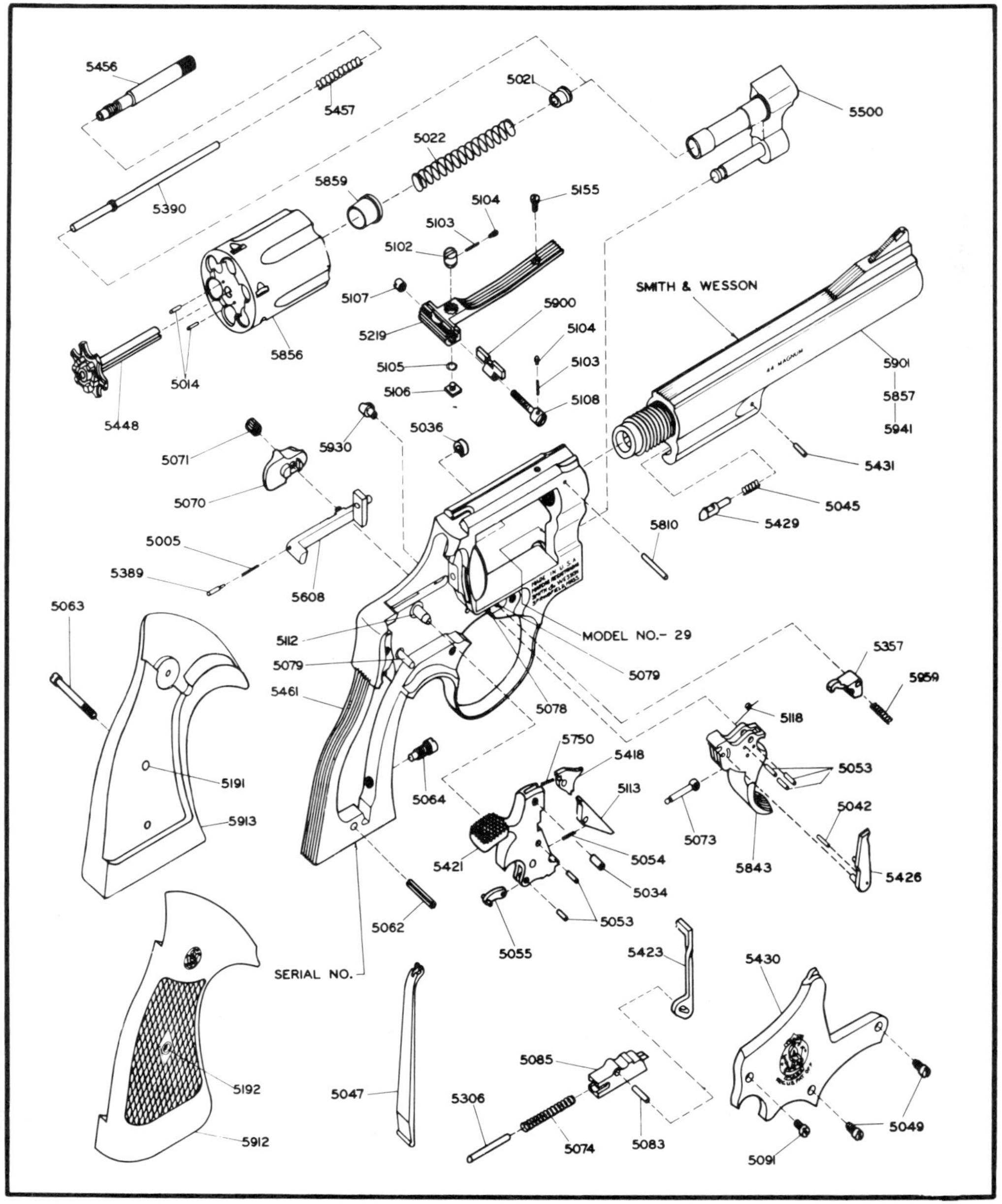

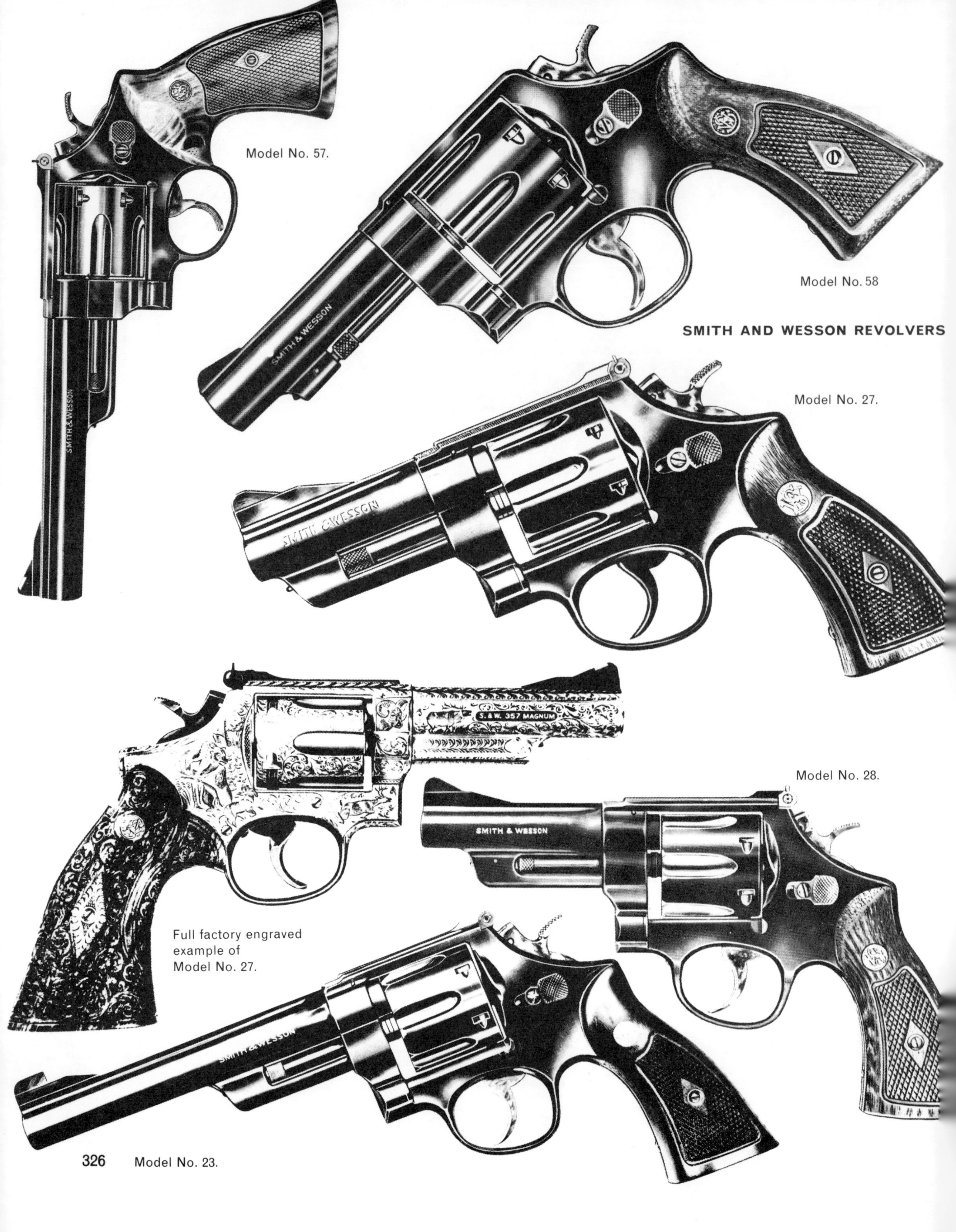

SMITH AND WESSON REVOLVERS

Model No. 57.

Model No. 58

Model No. 27.

Model No. 28.

Full factory engraved example of Model No. 27.

Model No. 23.

.41 Military and Police. Model No. 58. Calibre .41. Six shot with 4″ barrel. Fixed ramp serrated foresight and square notch rear sight. Magna stocks. S & W Blue or Nickel finish.

'.357' Magnum. Model No. 27. Calibre .357 Magnum (S & W Special can be used). Six shot, double action, available in 3½″, 5″, 6½″ and 8⅜″ barrel lengths. Any S & W target foresight, standard S & W click adjustable rear sight. Magna stocks. S & W Bright Blue or Nickel finish.

Highway Patrolman Model No. 28. Calibre .357 Magnum (S & W Special can be used). Six shot, double action, available in either 4″ or 6″ barrel lengths. Ramp foresight and S & W fully adjustable rear sight. Magna stocks (Target stocks can be supplied at additional cost). S & W Satin Blue finish only.

.38/44 Outdoorsman Model No. 23. Calibre .38 S & W Special. Six shot, double action, with 6½″ barrel. Patridge foresight, S & W adjustable rear sight. Magna stocks. S & W Blue finish only.

.38/44 Heavy Duty. Model No. 20. Calibre .38 S & W Special. Six shot, double action, available in 4″, 5″ and 6½″ barrel lengths. Fixed half moon service foresight, square notch rear sight. Magna stocks. S & W Blue or Nickel finish.

1955 .45 Target. Model No. 25. Calibre .45 ACP. Six shot, double action, with 6½″ heavy target barrel. Patridge foresight, S & W adjustable rear sight. Target stocks. S & W Blue finish only.

1950 Army Model No. 22. Calibre .45 ACP. Six shot, double action, with 5½″ barrel. Half moon service foresight, fixed notch rear sight. Magna stocks. S & W Blue finish only.

.357 Combat Magnum. Model No. 19. Calibre .357 Magnum (S & W Special can be used). Six shot, double action, available in either 4″ or 6″ barrel lengths. Ramp type (4″ barrel) or Patridge (6″ barrel) foresight, S & W adjustable rear sight. Target stocks. S & W Bright Blue or Nickel finish.

This completes the large frame models. With the exception of Models 22 and 58, all have ejector rod housings.

.38 Military and Police. Model No. 10. Calibre .38 S & W Special. Six shot, double action, available in 2″, 4″, 5″ and 6″ barrel lengths. Serrated ramp foresight, fixed square notch rear sight. Magna stocks. S & W Blue or Nickel finish. A round or square butt can be furnished, and a heavy barrel version of the Model No. 10 is offered with a 4″ barrel and similar specification.

.38 Military and Police Airweight. Model No. 12. Specification as for Model No. 10, but with only 2″ or 4″ barrel lengths. With the 2″ barrel the weight is 18 ozs.

.38 Combat Masterpiece. Model No. 15. Calibre .38 S & W Special. Six shot, double action, with 4″ barrel. Ramp foresight and adjustable S & W rear sight. Magna stocks. S & W Blue finish only. A special 2″ barrel version has been introduced with, otherwise, the same specification.

Tracing its ancestry back to the .22 Outdoorsman of 1931 built on the .38 Hand Ejector frame of 1905, the development of the K.22 series was carried out by Major Douglas Baird Wesson, a grandson of the founder of the firm. As with the .357 Magnum and the later .44 Magnum, this responsibility was shared between Remington, who provided the cartridge, and Smith and Wesson, who made the gun to fire it. Designed to handle the then new Remington Smokeless .22 long rifle rim-fire cartridge, the cylinder chambers of the K.22 had countersunk recesses for the cartridge rim, and the firing pin was in the frame. Countersunk chambers were necessary to provide support for the case head; otherwise lack of support caused the case to blow out around the rim.

The 1931 Outdoorsman in .22 rim-fire continued in production until 1940 when an improved model known as the K.22 Masterpiece was introduced. Similar to the earlier model the 1940 K.22 incorporated the short cocking action and was fitted with micrometer click adjustable sights. In 1947 a redesigned series of target revolvers was introduced, the K.22, K.32 and K.38. All the guns were the same size and shape, but they differed in weight and balance. In 1949, in response to the demand from target shooters who wanted the same feel and balance irrespective of calibre, the new heavy Masterpiece line appeared where the weights were the same and the targetman could change from .22 to .32 or .38 without having to adjust for balance variations.

The Masterpiece line has since been further

The Smith and Wesson revolvers on facing page and on pages 328, 331, 332, 333 and 334 (except Model No. 27 page 326, Model No. 53 page 331, Model No. 14 page 331, Model No. 36 with Herret stocks page 333) are reproduced from photographs supplied by Smith and Wesson.

SMITH AND WESSON REVOLVERS

Model No. 25.

Model No. 19.

Model No. 10.

Model No. 12.

Model No. 17

Model No. 53. See also page 331.

Parts list for the Smith and Wesson Model No.10

5002	Barrel Pin
5004	Bolt Plunger
5005	Bolt Plunger Spring
5006	Centre Pin for guns with barrels over 2″
5008	Centre Pin Spring
5009	Extractor
5014	Extractor Pin
5015	Cylinder Stop
5016	Cylinder Stop Plunger
5017	Cylinder Stop Plunger Spring
5018	Cylinder Stop Screw
5020	Extractor Rod for guns with barrels over 2″
5022	Extractor Spring
5023	Yoke complete
5027	Frame, square butt, for guns with barrels over 2″, stud bushing and lug
5030	Gas Ring
5034	Hammer Nose Rivet
5035	Strain Screw, round butt
5036	Hammer Nose Bushing
5038	Extractor Rod for guns with 2″ barrels
5042	Hand Pin
5043	Locking Bolt for guns with barrels over 2″
5044	Locking Bolt Pin for guns with barrels over 2″
5045	Locking Bolt Spring
5046	Frame Lug
5047	Mainspring
5049	Plate Screw, crowned
5051	Hammer
5053	Hand Spring Pin
5053	Hand Spring Torsion Pin
5053	Sear Pin
5053	Stirrup Pin
5053	Trigger Lever Pin
5054	Sear Spring
5055	Stirrup
5062	Stock Pin
5064	Strain Screw, square butt
5070	Thumbpiece
5071	Thumbpiece Nut
5072	Trigger
5073	Trigger Lever
5074	Rebound Slide Spring
5076	Hand complete with stud
5078	Trigger Stud
5079	Cylinder Stop Stud
5079	Rebound Slide Stud
5082	Centre Pin for guns with 2″ barrel
5083	Rebound Slide Pin
5084	Hammer Block
5085	Rebound Slide
5086	Cylinder with extractor, extractor pins and gas ring
5091	Plate Screw, flat
5094	Frame, round butt, for guns with barrels over 2″, studs, bushing and lug
5112	Hammer Stud
5113	Sear
5118	Hand Spring, Torsion
5129	Side Plate
5133	Hammer Nose
5135	Frame, square butt for 2″ barrels only, with studs, bushing and lug
5138	Frame, round butt for 2″ barrels only, with studs, bushing and lug
5147	Locking bolt for guns with 2″ barrel
5174	Barrel, 4″ (Heavy)
5178	Frame, square butt for 4″ Heavy Barrel only
5191	Escutcheon
5192	Escutcheon Nut
5200	Barrel, 4″
5205	Barrel, 6″
5206	Barrel, 5″
5307	Locking Bolt Pin for guns with 2″ barrels
5488	Stock Screw, round butt
5599	Stock Screw, square butt
5603	Barrel 2″
5606	Bolt
5629	Extractor Rod Collar
5822	Stocks, Magna, round butt left
5824	Stocks, Magna, round butt right
5830	Stocks, Magna, square butt left
5832	Stocks, Magna, square butt right

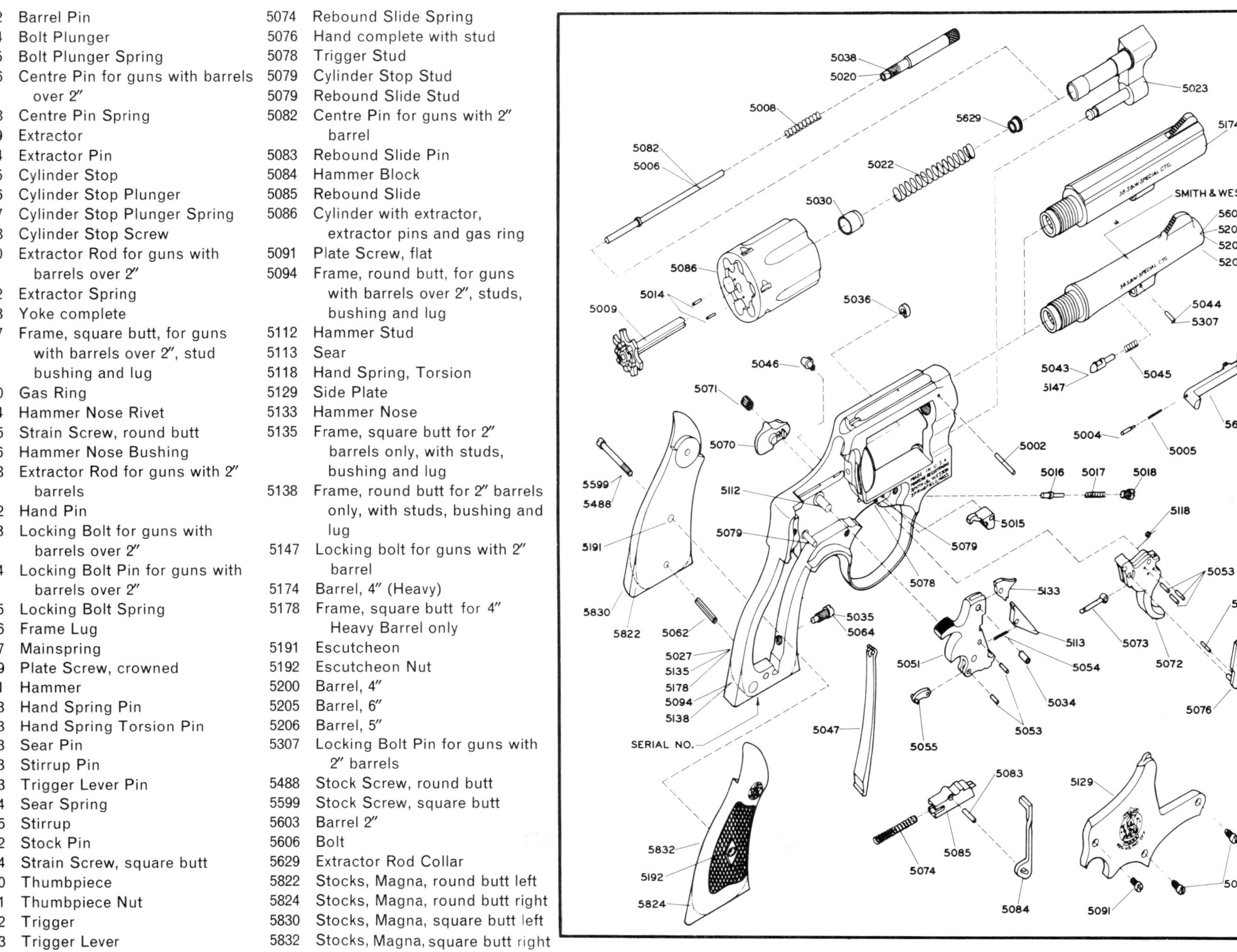

extended and now includes the following revolvers:

K.22 Masterpiece. Model No. 17. Calibre .22 long rifle. Six shot, double action. Available in 6″ or 8⅜″ barrel lengths, the weight with the former 38½ ozs. Adjustable S & W sights. Magna stocks. S & W Blue finish only. Two variants of this model are now available, the K.22 Masterpiece MRF, Model No. 48, and the '.22 Magnum' Model No. 53. The Model No. 48 is chambered for the .22 Magnum rim-fire, the Model No. 53 for the .22 Remington Jet centre-fire Magnum, or alternatively, when the special chamber inserts furnished with each gun are used, for the .22 rimfire short, long or long rifle. A third variant, the .22 Combat Masterpiece, Model No. 18, chambered for the .22 long rifle, is available with a 4″ barrel only.

K.32 Masterpiece. Model No. 16. Calibre .32 S & W long. Six shot, double action, with a 6″ barrel. Weight 38½ ozs. S & W adjustable sights. Magna stocks. S & W Blue finish only.

K.38 Masterpiece. Model No. 14. Calibre .38 S & W Special. Six shot, double action. Available in 6″ or 8⅜″ barrel lengths, the weight with the former again 38½ ozs. S & W adjustable sights. Magna stocks. S & W Blue finish only.

Smith and Wesson retain their single action variant of the K.38 in the range, unlike Colt who dropped the single action version of the Colt Officer's Match.

The next series in the range is the .22/32, .22 calibre pistols built on the .32 frame.

1953 .22/32 Target. Model No. 35. Calibre .22 long rifle. With 6″ barrel.

1953 .22/32 Kit Gun. Model No. 34. Calibre .22 long rifle. With 2″ or 4″ barrel.

1955 .22/32 Kit Gun Airweight. Model No. 43. Calibre .22 long rifle. With 3½″ barrel. Weight 14½ ozs.

All the .22/32 models are available in either S & W Blue or Nickel finish, as is the 1960 .22/32 Kit Gun MRF which, as the designation suggests, is chambered for the .22 Magnum rim-fire and has a 3½″ barrel.

The last series are revolvers based on the .32 Hand Ejector frame and designed for combat use where excessive weight might prove a disadvantage.

.32 Hand Ejector. Model No. 30. Calibre .32 S & W long. Six shot, available in 2″, 3″ and 4″ barrel lengths. Magna stocks. S & W Blue or Nickel finish.

.32 Regulation Police. Model No. 31. Calibre .32 S & W long. Six shot, available in 2″, 3″ and 4″ barrel lengths. Magna stocks. S & W Blue or Nickel finish.

.38 Terrier. Model No. 32. This is the first of the series of .38 calibre revolvers built on the .32 frame. All are five shot. The Terrier has a 2″ barrel and Magna stocks. S & W Blue or Nickel finish.

.38 Regulation Police. Model No. 33. Calibre .38 S & W Special. Five shot, with 4″ barrel. Magna stocks. S & W Blue or Nickel finish.

.38 Chief's Special. Model No. 36. Calibre .38 S & W Special. Five shot, with 2″ or 3″ barrel. Weight 19 ozs. The Airweight version, .38 Chief's Special Airweight, Model No. 37, has a similar specification except that the frame is light alloy.

Two remaining full-power lightweight revolvers have to be included to complete the remarkably extensive current Smith and Wesson range. The first is the Bodyguard Airweight, Model No. 38, and the illustration (page 334) shows how the sides of the frame have been extended upwards in order to shroud the hammer. The Bodyguard also differs from other Smith and Wesson revolvers in that coil springs are used instead of the traditional flat mainspring. Originally introduced in 1956 for a US Federal Law Enforcement agency, Smith and Wesson then stated that the reaction to the design was so favourable that it had been put on the selling range. As with the older revolvers in the Airweight range, the 19 ozs. weight was made possible by using light alloys for the frame and crane, while the barrel, cylinder and lockwork are of steel. The Model No. 38 is to all intents and purposes a Chief's Special with the frame extended. Chambered for the .38 S & W Special, it has the usual five chambers dictated by the use of the small frame, and is available in a 2″ barrel length only.

The second, and last of the current series, is the Centennial, Model No. 40, the development of which has already been covered. This pistol is now available as the Centennial Airweight, Model No. 42, and, at 13 ozs., is slightly lighter than the Airweight Bodyguard. Both models have 2″

SMITH AND WESSON REVOLVERS

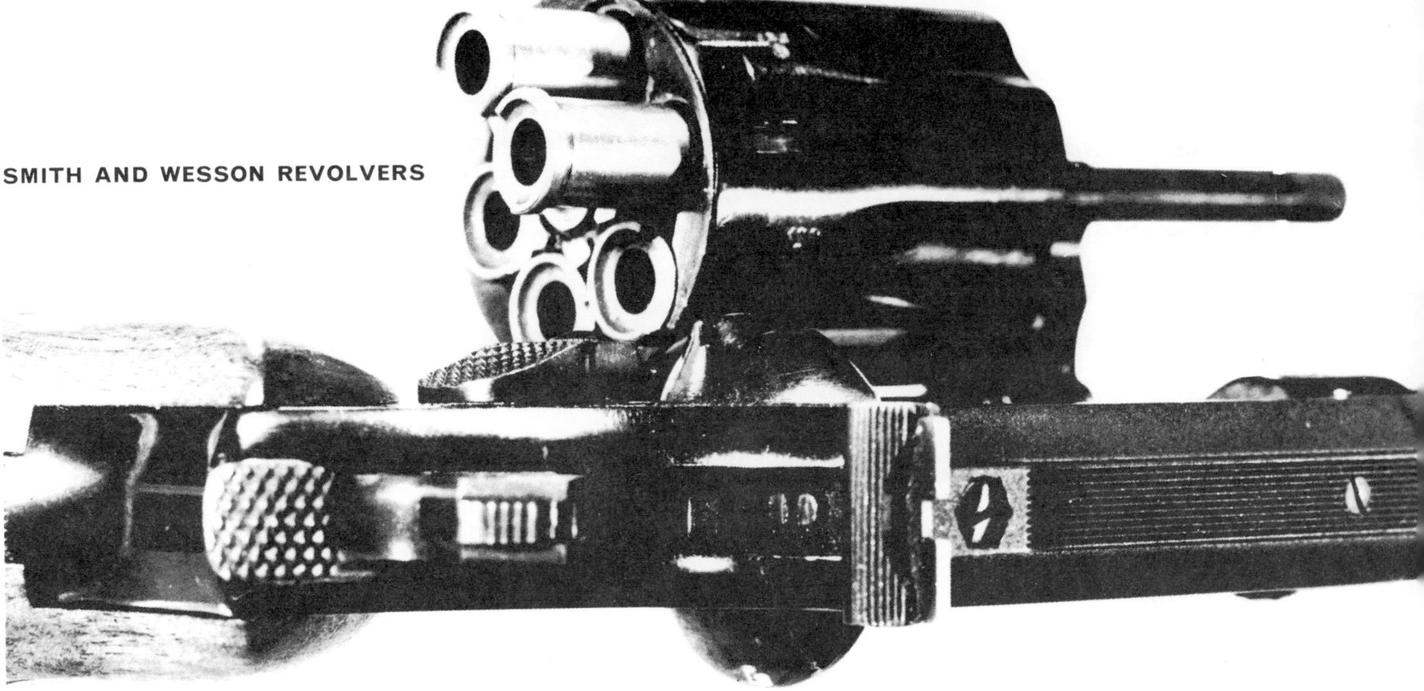

Model No. 53 showing the chamber inserts furnished for use with .22 rim-fire short, long or long rifle, and dual firing pins.

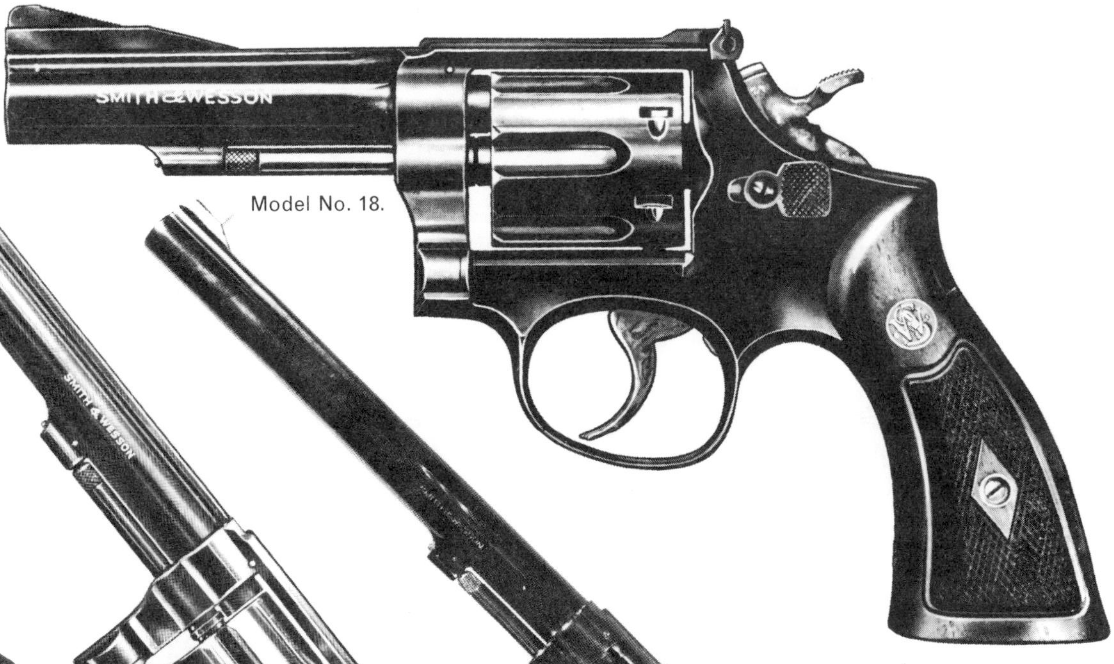

Model No. 18.

Model No. 14 with target trigger and hammer and custom built Herret stocks.

Model No. 16.

Model No. 14.

SMITH AND WESSON REVOLVERS

Model No. 34.

Model No. 35.

Model No. 43.

Model No. 30.

Model No. 3

Model No. 32.

Model No. 36 fitted with custom made Herret stocks. (K. McLeod)

Model No. 33.

Model No. 36.

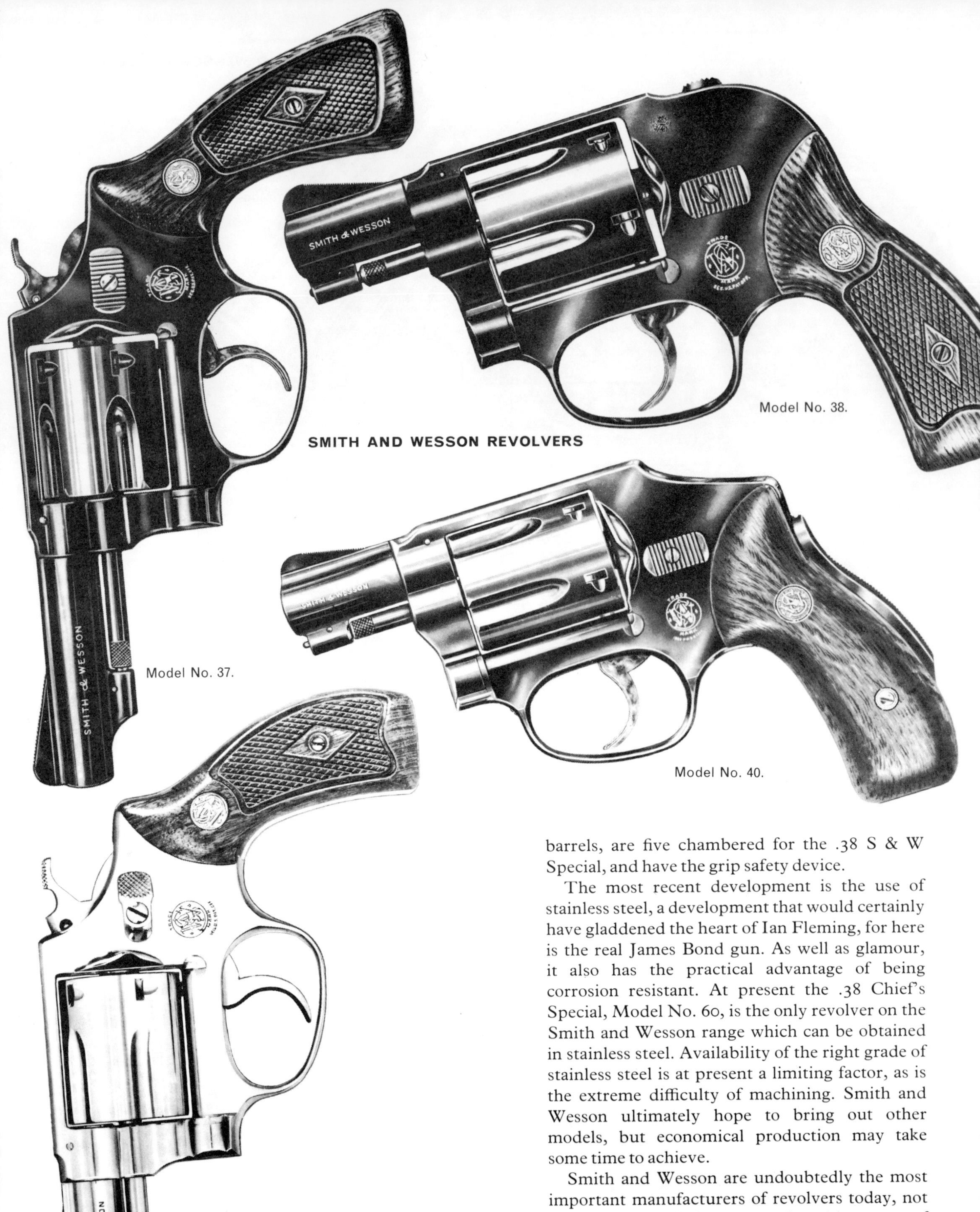

SMITH AND WESSON REVOLVERS

Model No. 38.

Model No. 37.

Model No. 40.

Model No. 60.

barrels, are five chambered for the .38 S & W Special, and have the grip safety device.

The most recent development is the use of stainless steel, a development that would certainly have gladdened the heart of Ian Fleming, for here is the real James Bond gun. As well as glamour, it also has the practical advantage of being corrosion resistant. At present the .38 Chief's Special, Model No. 60, is the only revolver on the Smith and Wesson range which can be obtained in stainless steel. Availability of the right grade of stainless steel is at present a limiting factor, as is the extreme difficulty of machining. Smith and Wesson ultimately hope to bring out other models, but economical production may take some time to achieve.

Smith and Wesson are undoubtedly the most important manufacturers of revolvers today, not only because of the extremely wide range of revolvers offered, but also because of their

Parts list for the Smith and Wesson Model No. 38

5014	Extractor Pin
5045	Locking Bolt Spring
5054	Bolt Plunger Spring
5054	Sear Spring
5074	Rebound Slide Spring
5091	Plate Screw, flat head
5147	Locking Bolt
5203	Barrel Pin
5216	Mainspring Rod Swivel
5220	Centre Pin
5227	Centre Pin Spring
5239	Extractor
5255	Extractor Rod
5260	Extractor Spring
5279	Hammer Nose Bushing
5291	Hammer Nose
5293	Hammer Nose Rivet
5294	Hammer Block
5301	Hand Pin
5302	Hand Torsion Spring
5303	Hand Spring Torsion Pin
5303	Sear Pin
5303	Trigger Lever Pin
5304	Hand Spring Pin
5307	Locking Bolt Pin
5309	Mainspring Rod
5311	Plate Screw, crowned
5315	Rebound Slide Pin
5317	Sear
5318	Yoke
5325	Escutcheon
5326	Escutcheon Nut
5330	Stock Screw
5336	Trigger
5337	Trigger Lever
5355	Bolt Plunger
5553	Cylinder Stop Stud
5553	Trigger Stud
5573	Cylinder, with Extractor and Pins
5577	Rebound Slide Stud
5580	Frame Lug
5581	Hammer Stud
5590	Barrel 2"
5594	Hand
5609	Bolt
5616	Rebound Slide
5659	Thumbpiece
5729	Stock Pin
5749	Mainspring
5839	Thumbpiece Screw
5875	Frame with stud, bushing and lug
5877	Side Plate
5880	Hammer
5907	Stock, magna, right
5908	Stock, magna, left
5924	Cylinder Stop
5959	Cylinder Stop Spring

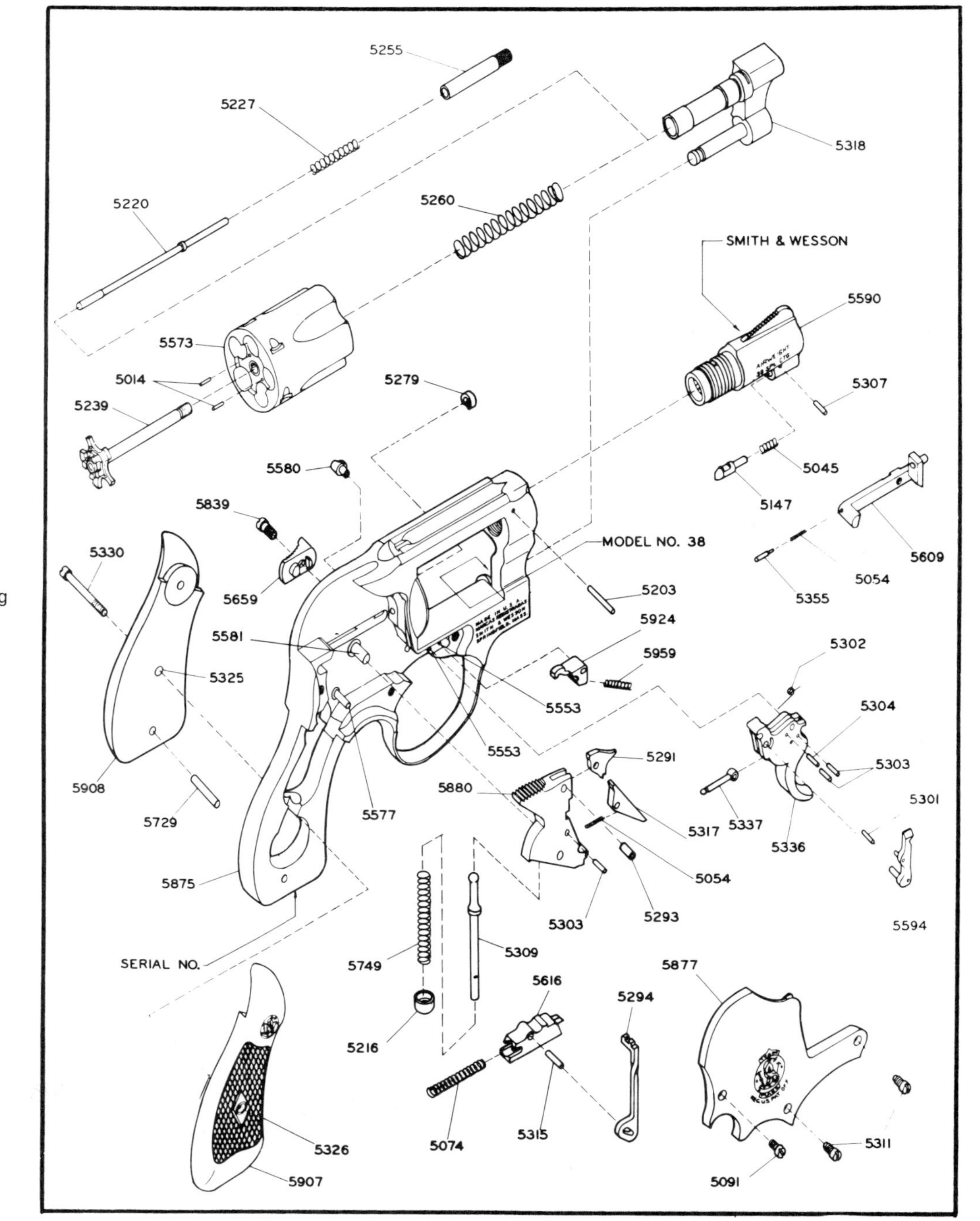

Parts list for the Smith and Wesson Model No. 40

5014 Extractor Pin
5045 Locking Bolt Spring
5054 Bolt Plunger Spring
5054 Sear Spring
5062 Stock Pin
5074 Rebound Slide Spring
5091 Plate Screw, Flat Head
5134 Barrel, 2″
5147 Locking Bolt
5203 Barrel Pin
5216 Mainspring Rod Swivel
5220 Centre Pin
5227 Centre Pin Spring
5231 Cylinder with Extractor and Pins
5239 Extractor
5255 Extractor Rod
5260 Extractor Spring
5277 Hammer Stud
5278 Cylinder Stop Stud
5278 Rebound Slide Stud
5278 Trigger Stud
5280 Hammer Nose Bushing
5281 Frame Lug
5289 Hammer
5292 Hammer Nose
5293 Hammer Nose Rivet
5296 Hand with Stud
5301 Hand Pin
5302 Hand Torsion Spring
5303 Hand Spring Torsion Pin
5303 Sear Pin
5303 Trigger Lever Pin
5304 Hand Spring Pin
5307 Locking Bolt Pin
5309 Mainspring Rod
5311 Plate Screw, Crowned
5313 Rebound Slide
5317 Sear
5318 Yoke
5320 Side Plate
5325 Escutcheon
5326 Escutcheon Nut
5336 Trigger
5337 Trigger Lever
5355 Bolt Plunger
5366 Safety Latch
5367 Safety Latch Pin
5368 Safety Lever
5369 Safety Lever Pin
5369 Safety Lever Disengaging Pin
5370 Safety Lever Spring
5493 Stock, Magna, Left
5494 Stock, Magna, Right
5610 Bolt
5659 Thumbpiece
5723 Stock Screw
5742 Frame, with Studs, Bushing and Lug
5749 Mainspring
5839 Thumbpiece Screw
5924 Cylinder Stop
5959 Cylinder Stop Spring

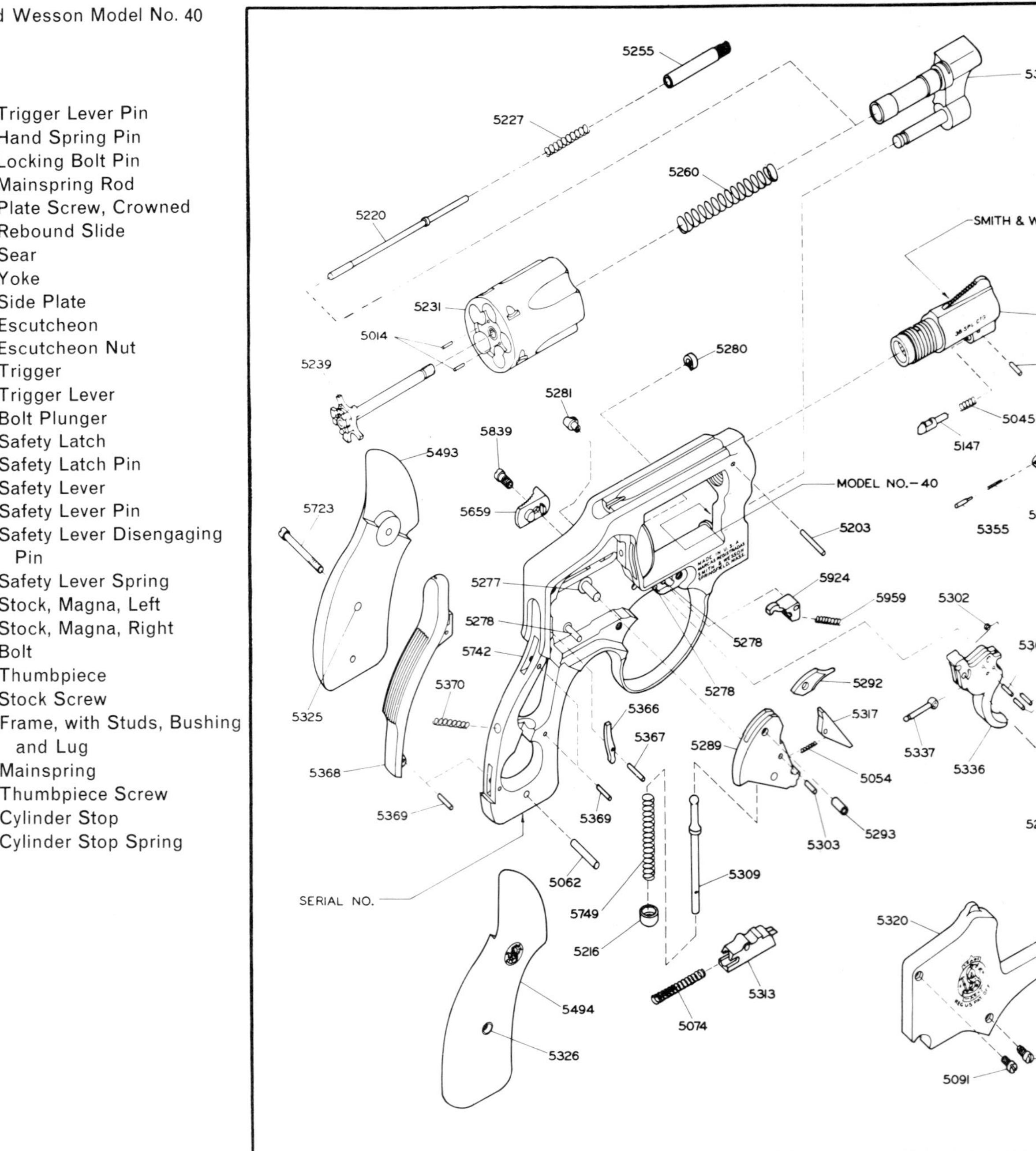

continuous efforts to promote new ideas and developments, both in materials and new calibres.

Such has been the success of Smith and Wesson that it is not surprising that their swing-out cylinder models have been widely copied. It would, however, be tedious to try and list all the variants, although those manufactured in Spain are without doubt the most numerous. The following short list of some of the trade names and makers indicates the extent of this business, most of which was conducted with South America.

Aranay Cia, Eibar, Trade Mark 'El Cano'. .22 copy of the Smith and Wesson.

M. Escódin, Eibar. Trade Mark 'Escodin'. .22 copy of the Smith and Wesson.

Fab. Material de Guerre del Ejercito. Trade Mark 'Famae'. This factory was in Chile, and the extent of Spanish influence is not known.

Trocaola, Aranzabal y Cia, Eibar. Trade Mark 'T.A.C.' Well-known maker of both Smith and Wesson and also Colt copies.

Armero Especialistas Reunidos, Eibar. Trade Mark 'Alfa'. Made copies of both the Colt and the Smith and Wesson.

Fab. de Armas Garantazadas, Trade Mark 'Apache'. Smith and Wesson copies made in Eibar.

Beistegui Hermanos, Eibar. Trade Mark 'B.H.'. Copy of Smith and Wesson.

Guisasola Hermanos, Eibar. Copies of the Smith and Wesson.

Suinaga y Aramperri, Eibar. Copies of the Smith and Wesson.

Antonio Errasti, Eibar. Trade Mark 'Oicet'. Copy of the Colt Police Positive.

Some of these copies will deceive unless closely inspected. The basis for most of them is the S & W Military and Police Model, but others share features of both Smith and Wesson and Colt. Quality varies considerably.

Since the last war the number of small makers has fallen and the Spanish firearms industry has realised that it is essential to improve the 'brand image'. In the absence of detailed knowledge of the individual makers, all the weapons, irrespective of quality, tend to be known collectively as 'Spanish', and often the index of quality is that

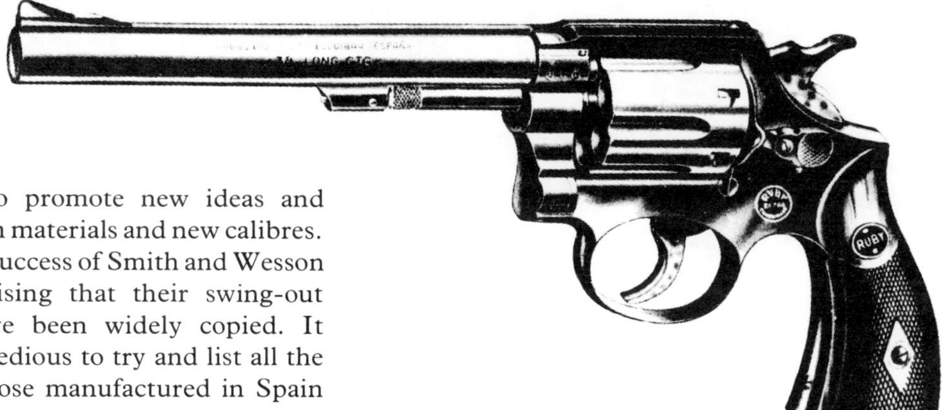

Ruby Extra revolvers by Gabilondo y Cia. (Gabilondo)

of the poorest specimen, to the detriment of reputable firms.

Two manufacturers are currently exporting quality revolvers. The first, Gabilondo y Cia, are makers of the 'Ruby' revolver, a copy of the Smith and Wesson made at their Eigoibar factory. In the US it is known as the 'Llama', the trade mark used for a range of automatic pistols manufactured by the same maker. Available in .22 rim-fire, .32 S & W long and .38 S & W Special, the normal finish is blue. Special finishes are, however, also available, including gold damascene.

The second manufacturer, Astra, Unceta y Cia SA of Vizcaya, Guernica, who are famous for their automatic pistols, make a .22 rim-fire nine chambered revolver, the Astra Model Cadix, offered in two barrel lengths.

Copies of the Smith and Wesson were also made in Belgium, particularly under the trade marks 'Bayard' and 'Hindu', in both .32 S & W and .38 S & W calibres.

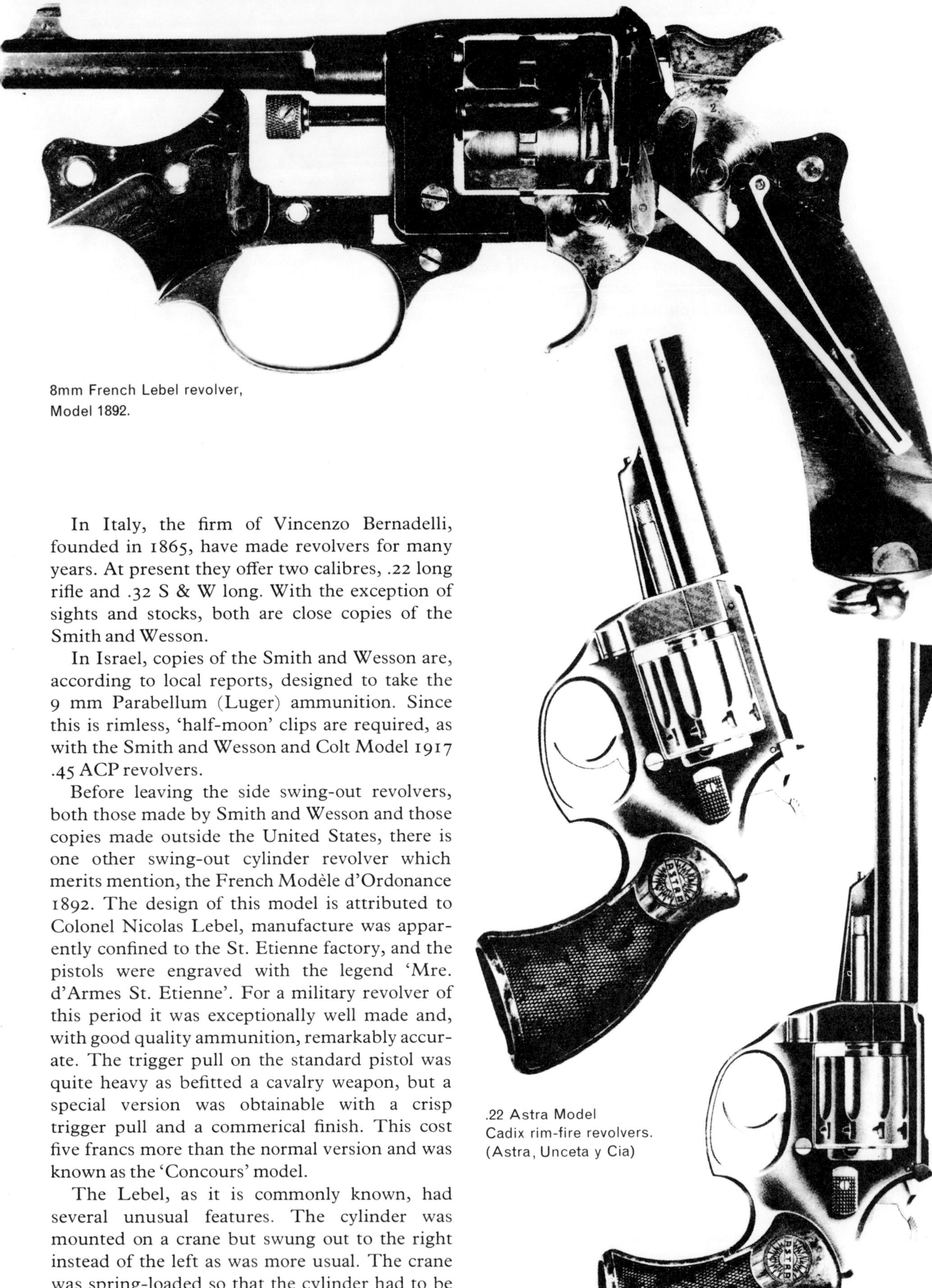

8mm French Lebel revolver, Model 1892.

.22 Astra Model Cadix rim-fire revolvers. (Astra, Unceta y Cia)

In Italy, the firm of Vincenzo Bernadelli, founded in 1865, have made revolvers for many years. At present they offer two calibres, .22 long rifle and .32 S & W long. With the exception of sights and stocks, both are close copies of the Smith and Wesson.

In Israel, copies of the Smith and Wesson are, according to local reports, designed to take the 9 mm Parabellum (Luger) ammunition. Since this is rimless, 'half-moon' clips are required, as with the Smith and Wesson and Colt Model 1917 .45 ACP revolvers.

Before leaving the side swing-out revolvers, both those made by Smith and Wesson and those copies made outside the United States, there is one other swing-out cylinder revolver which merits mention, the French Modèle d'Ordonance 1892. The design of this model is attributed to Colonel Nicolas Lebel, manufacture was apparently confined to the St. Etienne factory, and the pistols were engraved with the legend 'Mre. d'Armes St. Etienne'. For a military revolver of this period it was exceptionally well made and, with good quality ammunition, remarkably accurate. The trigger pull on the standard pistol was quite heavy as befitted a cavalry weapon, but a special version was obtainable with a crisp trigger pull and a commerical finish. This cost five francs more than the normal version and was known as the 'Concours' model.

The Lebel, as it is commonly known, had several unusual features. The cylinder was mounted on a crane but swung out to the right instead of the left as was more usual. The crane was spring-loaded so that the cylinder had to be pushed open. The cylinder lock was a hinged

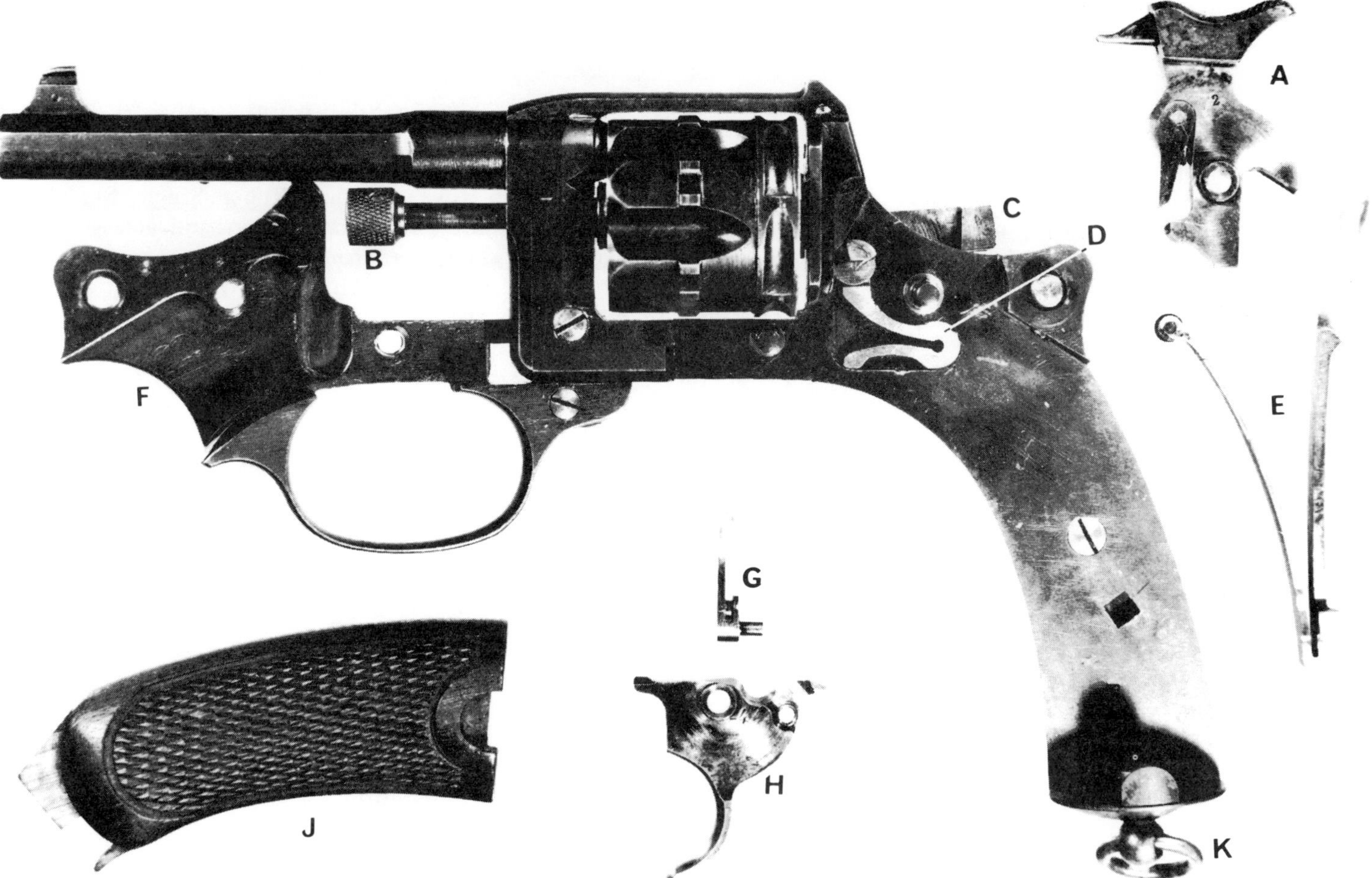

French Lebel Model 1892 dismantled.

A. Hammer.
B. Extractor.
C. Cylinder gate.
D. Cylinder gate spring.
E. Mainspring.
F. Side plate.
G. Pawl.
H. Trigger.
J. Left grip.
K. Lanyard ring.

lever/loading gate on the right hand side of the frame and had an internal cam to push back the hammer (the Abadie modification). This system was of value with solid frame rod ejector weapons since, by pulling the trigger repeatedly, the cylinder could be rotated and single cartridges extracted and retracted. Single cartridges could still be loaded into the Lebel, but the value of this feature was somewhat doubtful as a star simultaneous ejector was employed which did the job far more quickly. In this, the last of the French Service revolvers, the quick dismantling feature was retained. The large headed screw at the rear of the right hand side of the frame was unscrewed and the left hand side could then be hinged outward and forward, and the left grip removed at the same time. Further stripping of the pistol was easily accomplished and the illustration shows the principal features. The Lebel could be thumb cocked or fired by trigger action and perhaps the peculiarities of the design resulted from the fact that, as a cavalry weapon, it was intended to be used in the left hand, the right being occupied with the sword. The 8mm Lebel cartridge is rarely encountered outside France and the revolver is more common than the cartridge. Similar to the Winchester .32–20, Lebel cartridges can be made by sizing .32–20 brass. Loads must be kept moderate since the revolver was originally intended for black powder.

Since the last war, the tremendous effort made by Japan to enter world markets, particularly with regard to optical equipment, is well known. Less well known are the shotguns manufactured by the Japanese and, more recently, the revolvers. Such information as I have been able to obtain is meagre, and I cannot comment on either appearance or functioning from first hand. The revolver made by the Shin Chuo Kogyo KK of Tokyo bears a close resemblance externally to the Smith and Wesson. It is chambered for the .38 S & W Special cartridge and is five shot. Under the same brand name 'Nambu', the company also manufacture a copy of the FN Browning and the Colt auto-pistol. The Shin Chuo Company began manufacture as early as 1927 and made both Nambu revolvers and auto-pistols for the Imperial Government.

Copies of the Smith and Wesson have also been made in China. Their quality is uniformly poor and any maker's name impressed on the weapon, if indeed there is any, is undecipherable. The entire range comes under a special classification, 'Chinese Copies'.

Inevitably, throughout this history of the handgun, a great deal of time has been spent on weapons which are no longer in production. Companies have been formed to manufacture weapons, have risen to some eminence and then, for either political or economic reasons, have faded away into obscurity. Some, as we have seen, made major contributions and their products are either still in use or have been honourably retired.

It is particularly pleasant to be able to write about a newcomer, Sturm, Ruger and Co. Inc. of Southport, Connecticut, a company originally formed in 1949 to manufacture an interesting .22 automatic pistol. Bill Ruger designed the product and the late Alex Sturm looked after the financial side of the business.

The Ruger automatic pistol was very successful, and considerable interest was aroused when Sturm-Ruger indicated their intention of augmenting the range by the introduction of a revolver. In 1954 the first Ruger Single Six revolvers came off the production line and, at least externally, showed a strong resemblance to the Colt SAA. Designed to meet the demand for a high quality 'western style' single action revolver, the Single Six has been an unqualified success.

The basic design feature is the use of music-wire coil springs which, although they alter the 'feel' of the mechanism, are virtually unbreakable. As originally introduced, the Single Six was a six chambered, single action rod ejector revolver taking the .22 long rifle rim-fire cartridge. In the 5½″ barrel version the weight was 36 ozs. Patridge type sights were fitted, and the rear sight, dovetailed into the frame, could be adjusted by being driven sideways in the dovetail slot. The original version had a thin loading gate, but this was eventually modified to the design illustrated. In 1956 a lightweight version was brought out together with a special presentation model. Both have since been discontinued. In 1959 the Single Six was made available in .22 Winchester Magnum rim-fire and, in 1961, the Ruger Single Six Convertible appeared with two interchangeable cylinders, one for the standard .22 rim-fire and the other for the .22 WMR, which make it possible for .22 short, .22 long, .22 long rifle and .22 WMR to be used in the same gun. The range was further extended in 1965 by the introduction of the Ruger Super Single Six Convertible, available in either 5½″ or 6½″ barrel lengths, and with a fully adjustable rear sight and ramp type foresight. The Super Single Six Convertible completes the range of .22 single action revolvers.

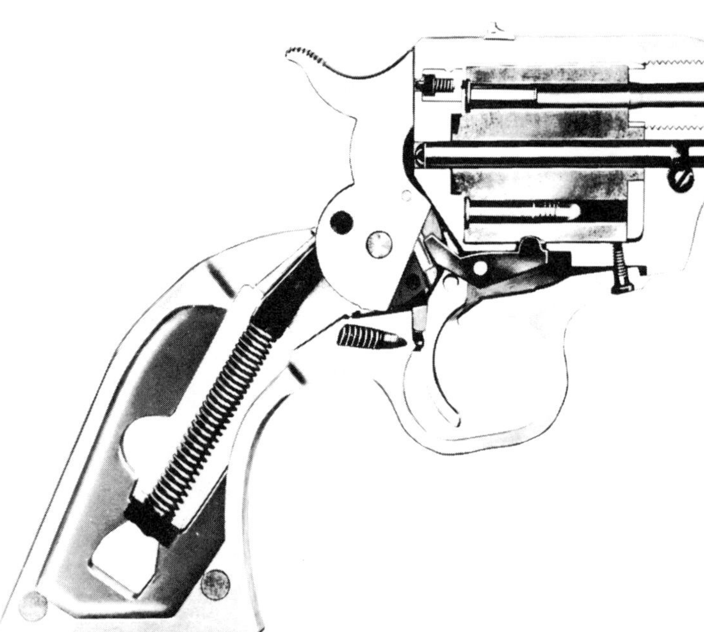

Sectional view of the Ruger Single Six. (Ruger)

To summarise, the Single Six range of .22 Ruger SA revolvers comprises:

No. RSS5W 5½″ barrel .22 long rifle.
No. RSSMW 6½″ barrel .22 WMR.
No. RSS5X 5½″ barrel Convertible.
No. RSSMX 6½″ barrel Convertible.
No. RSS9X 9½″ barrel Convertible.

No. SC5 $5\frac{1}{2}''$ barrel Super Convertible.
No. SC6 $6\frac{1}{2}''$ barrel Super Convertible.

In 1958 a companion to the Single Six appeared, the Ruger Bearcat, No. BC4. Differing from the Single Six in that the frame and grip straps are made in one piece from anodised cast aluminium alloy, the Bearcat is a miniature representation of the Remington percussion revolver. Like the Single Six series, it chambers six cartridges and has a firing pin assembly in the frame. An extremely neat and compact little gun with a 4″ barrel, the overall length is $8\frac{7}{8}''$, and the weight 17 ozs.

The Ruger series was further augmented in 1955 by the appearance of a very impressive .357 Magnum revolver, the Blackhawk, and the sectional illustration (page 342) shows the construction as originally manufactured. The same strong resemblance to the Colt SAA is again evident, and the provision of adjustable sights is in keeping with current trends. Basic design features follow the pattern established by the Single Six with regard to the simplification of the mechanism and frame construction, particularly in the use of a 'one piece' light alloy grip frame. In 1963 the early type frame (shown in the sectional illustrations) was replaced by the heavier 'Super' type frame with integral ribs to protect the rear sight. Slight dimensional alterations to the grip frame were also made to improve the comfort of the 'hold'. Two current versions of the .357 Magnum Blackhawk are available, No. BKH34 and No. BKH36, the first with a $4\frac{5}{8}''$ barrel, the second with a $6\frac{1}{2}''$ barrel. The original hard rubber grips fitted to the first model have been replaced by polished walnut. Finish is polished blue.

Ruger were quick to take advantage of the appearance of the .44 Remington Magnum cartridge and, in 1956, they placed on the market the Ruger .44 Magnum Blackhawk. This model was similar to the original .357 Magnum except that the frame and cylinder dimensions were altered to accommodate the larger .44 Magnum cartridge. In 1959 a modified version of the .44 Magnum Blackhawk appeared, the Super Blackhawk, and this was the model which introduced the 'Super' type frame with the integral protective rear sight ribs now employed on the .357 Magnum Blackhawk and the Super Single Six. The .44 Magnum Super Blackhawk also introduced the 'unfluted' cylinder which further adds to the truly majestic appearance of this revolver, and a square backed trigger guard which provides more room for the second finger and reduces the liability to bruised knuckles under the by no means insignificant recoil. The Super Blackhawk is very definitely the most comfortable factory .44 Magnum to shoot and, although the one in my possession has been re-stocked in polished Buffalo horn, the original stock dimensions have been retained. The Super Blackhawk has replaced the standard .44 Blackhawk and is available as No. S47 with a $7\frac{1}{2}''$ barrel only. Both the .357 and .44 Magnum will also use the .44 S & W Special without alteration.

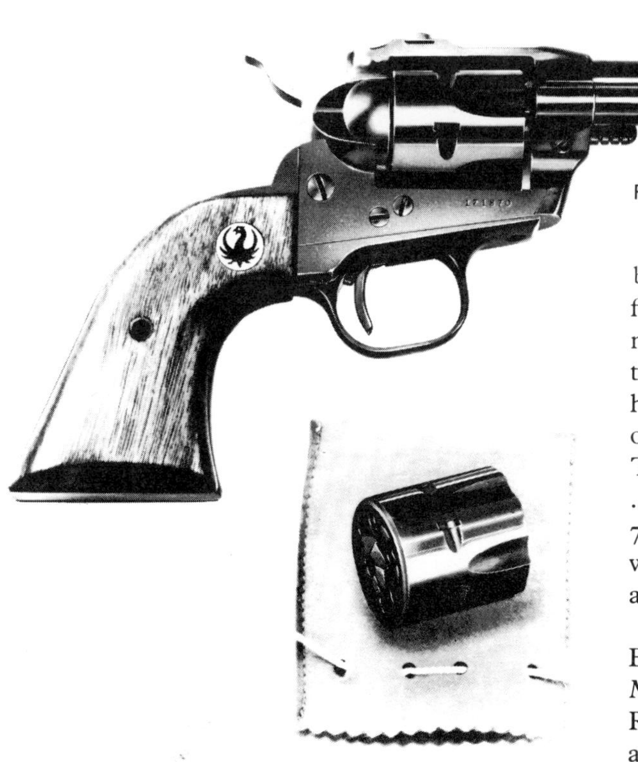

Ruger Single Six with $6\frac{1}{2}''$ barrel. (Ruger)

Lacking the square backed guard of the Super Blackhawk and with a fluted cylinder, the .41 Magnum Blackhawk, the latest addition to the Ruger stable, employs the .44 cylinder and frame and is available in $4\frac{5}{8}''$ and $6\frac{1}{2}''$ barrel lengths.

The Ruger Hawkeye should, strictly speaking, be discussed in a separate section devoted to

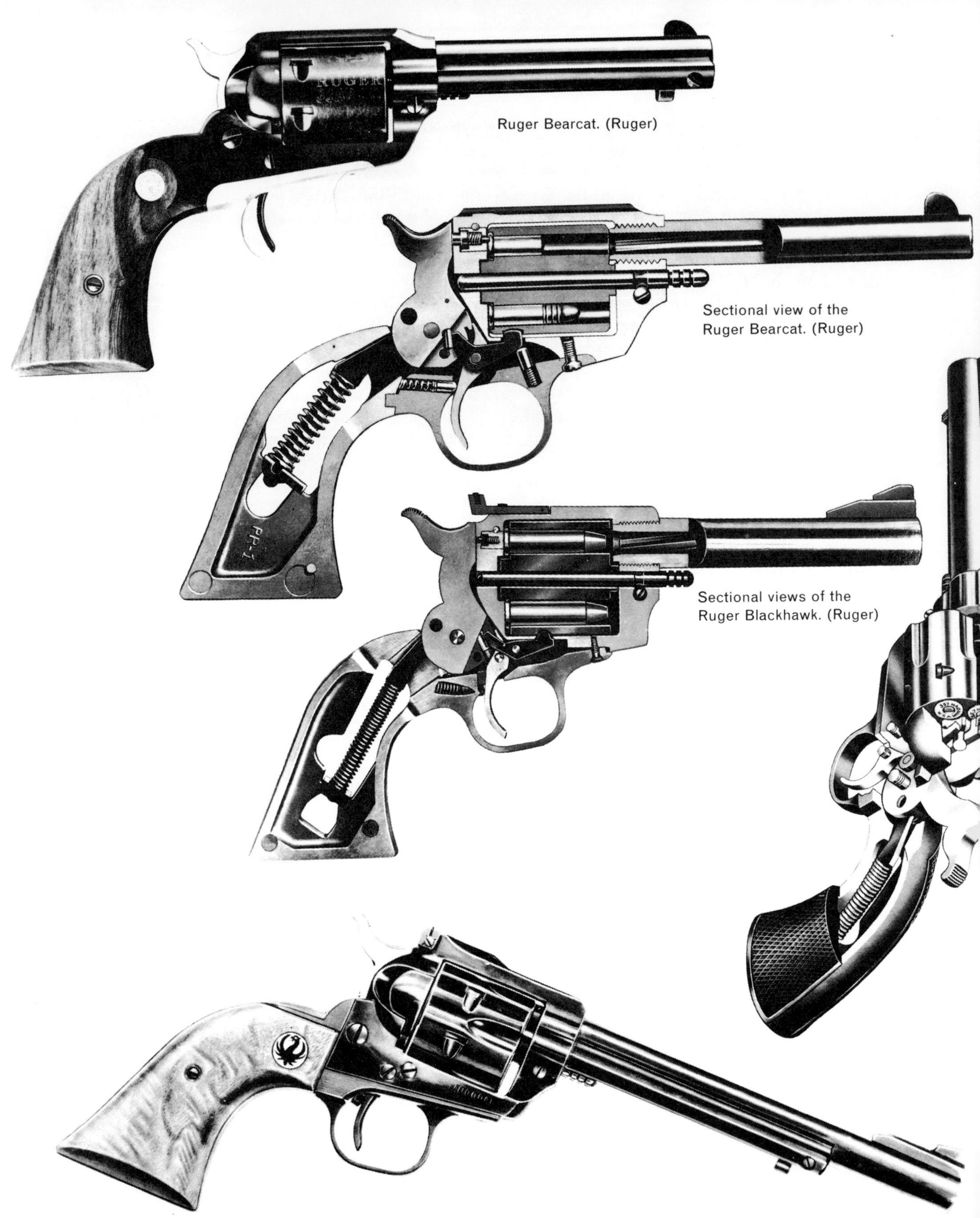
Ruger Bearcat. (Ruger)

Sectional view of the Ruger Bearcat. (Ruger)

Sectional views of the Ruger Blackhawk. (Ruger)

Ruger Super Single Six Convertible. (Ruger)

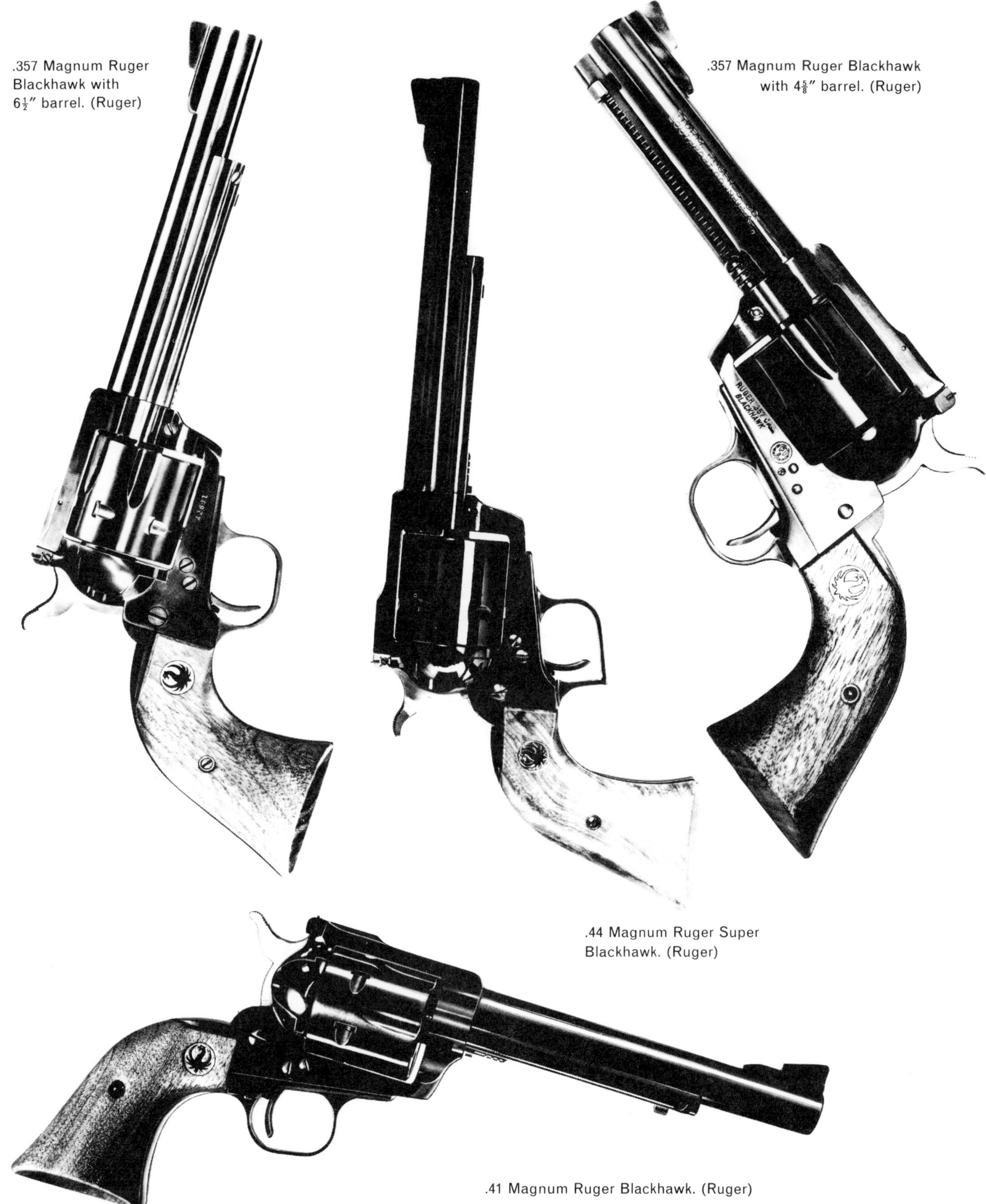

.357 Magnum Ruger Blackhawk with $6\frac{1}{2}''$ barrel. (Ruger)

.357 Magnum Ruger Blackhawk with $4\frac{5}{8}''$ barrel. (Ruger)

.44 Magnum Ruger Super Blackhawk. (Ruger)

.41 Magnum Ruger Blackhawk. (Ruger)

Single shot Ruger Hawkeye. (Ruger)

Single shot Ruger Hawkeye chambered for the .256 Winchester Magnum. (Ruger)

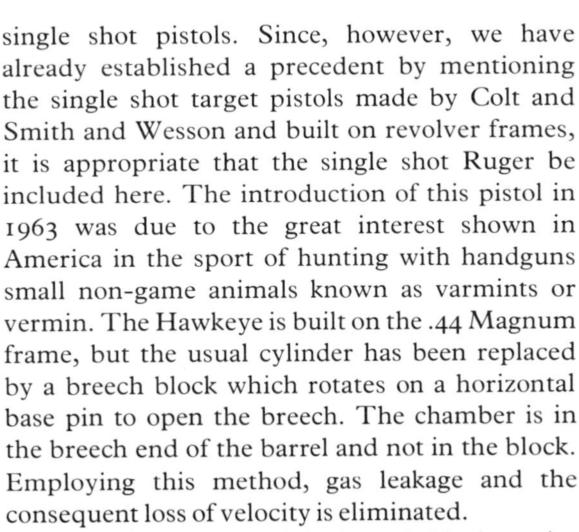

single shot pistols. Since, however, we have already established a precedent by mentioning the single shot target pistols made by Colt and Smith and Wesson and built on revolver frames, it is appropriate that the single shot Ruger be included here. The introduction of this pistol in 1963 was due to the great interest shown in America in the sport of hunting with handguns small non-game animals known as varmints or vermin. The Hawkeye is built on the .44 Magnum frame, but the usual cylinder has been replaced by a breech block which rotates on a horizontal base pin to open the breech. The chamber is in the breech end of the barrel and not in the block. Employing this method, gas leakage and the consequent loss of velocity is eliminated.

The left hand side of the breech block carries the locking plunger which has to be depressed to open the action for loading. On the right hand

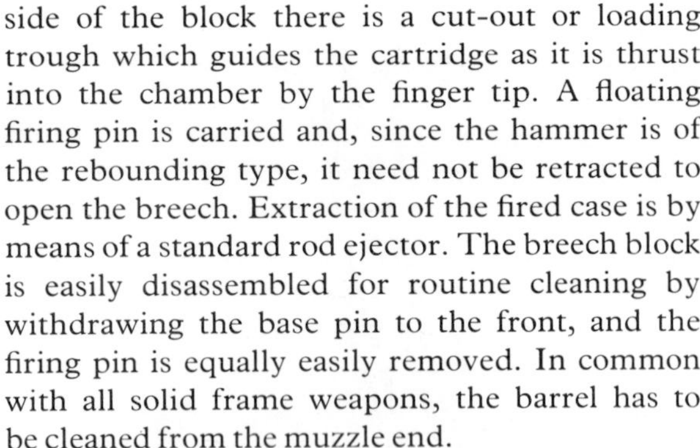

side of the block there is a cut-out or loading trough which guides the cartridge as it is thrust into the chamber by the finger tip. A floating firing pin is carried and, since the hammer is of the rebounding type, it need not be retracted to open the breech. Extraction of the fired case is by means of a standard rod ejector. The breech block is easily disassembled for routine cleaning by withdrawing the base pin to the front, and the firing pin is equally easily removed. In common with all solid frame weapons, the barrel has to be cleaned from the muzzle end.

The pistol is chambered for the .256 Winchester Magnum centre-fire bottle neck cartridge, and the case is derived from the .357 Magnum by necking down to calibre .25. With a 60 grain jacketed hollow-point bullet, the muzzle velocity of the .256 Winchester Magnum is 2,340 f.p.s.

The Ruger .256 Magnum Hawkeye is furnished with an $8\frac{1}{2}''$ barrel, walnut grips and adjustable target type sights. This pistol catered for a limited market and was discontinued in 1967.

The entire Ruger range adequately demonstrates how clever design allied with modern production techniques can result in the manufacture of revolvers at economic prices which possess those qualities that appeal to the civilian handgun user. It must be admitted that only in America would such a business flourish, but it reflects great credit on the Ruger Company that they do manufacture, and are not, like many other American firms, purely retailers of foreign-made firearms built to meet American requirements. Ruger have now entered the rifle field with a semi-automatic carbine, a range of bolt action centre-fire rifles and a single shot dropping block underlever rifle.

The relatively unhindered domestic market has been the dominant factor in the survival of several American firms who traditionally specialise in the manufacture of inexpensive handguns. Space does not permit a detailed examination of the fantastic number that have been made, but a brief history of three of the surviving firms will serve to indicate the type of revolver associated with the names of Iver Johnson, Harrington and Richardson and Hi-Standard.

Iver Johnson and Martin Bye went into partnership in 1871 and, in their original two room premises in Worcester, Massachusetts, they manufactured muzzle and breechloading pistols along with leg-irons and handcuffs. In 1883 the partnership was dissolved and Iver Johnson's Arms and Cycle Works took its place. Shortly afterwards, in 1891, the business moved to its present location in Fitchburg. The first revolver was the I-J Favourite, a single action pocket revolver made in .22, .32, .38 and .44 rim-fire. This was followed by revolvers bearing the names 'Tycoon', 'Encore', 'Smoker', 'Defender' and 'Eagle'.

An extremely interesting solid frame revolver appeared in 1879 in which the cylinder swung out to the right. It was unusual in that it was pivoted along the cylinder axis, the pivot being under the barrel so that the cylinder swung out in an arc. In 1879 the company began to manufacture shotguns, and shortly afterwards introduced the British Bull Dog revolver. In the 1890's the 'Swift' hinged frame five shot DA revolver appeared, to be followed in 1892 by the 'Safety Automatic Revolver'. This employed the famous 'Hammer the Hammer' safety feature which, along with the 'Owl's Head' trade mark, became famous the world over. In 1931 the 'Supershot Sealed Eight' was introduced which featured the counterboring of the chambers to recess the head of the .22 rim-fire cartridge. Variations on the 'Supershot' series of .22 revolvers continued to be manufactured, and Iver Johnson still make a hinged frame simultaneous extraction eight shot revolver today, the Model 67 Viking. A similar Viking revolver with a $2\frac{3}{4}''$ barrel, the Viking 67S, is currently available in .22 rim-fire, and also in .32 and .38 S & W calibres. A solid frame rod ejection eight shot revolver in the selling range is the Model 57A, first introduced in 1956 as the Model 57. This revolver incorporates the 'safety sealed' chamber, the counterboring to recess the cartridge head, and the 'sealed flash' control feature covering the raised rim which surrounds the front end of the cylinder to divert gas

.32 Iver Johnson 'Safety Automatic Revolver'.

.32 Iver Johnson double action hammerless revolver. (Kilmarnock Museum)

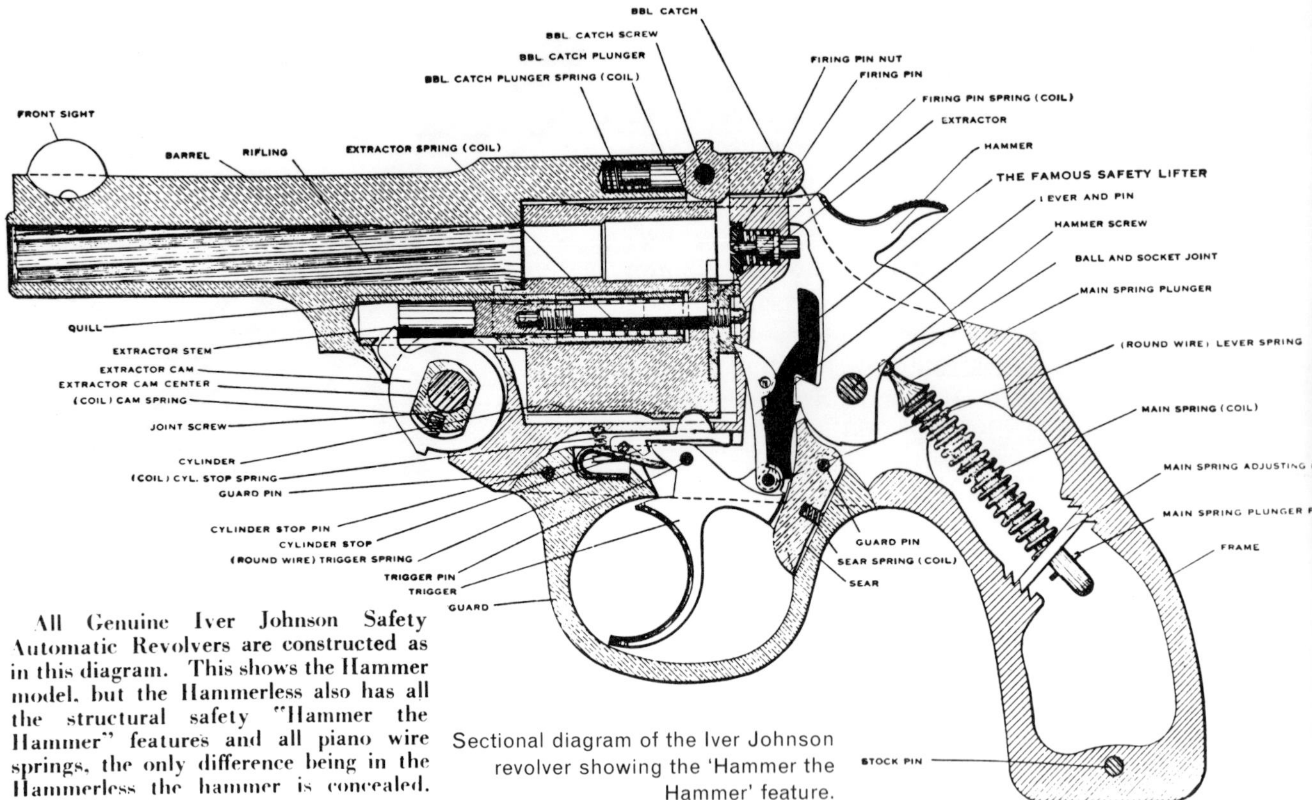

Sectional diagram of the Iver Johnson revolver showing the 'Hammer the Hammer' feature.

escape downwards and forward.

The firm of Harrington and Richardson have also been manufacturing firearms since 1871. Originally Franklin Wesson, a brother of Daniel B. Wesson, had formed a partnership with his nephew, Gilbert Henderson Harrington. But then William Augustus Richardson joined the company as factory manager and, in 1874, Harrington bought out Wesson and formed a new firm under the name Harrington and Richardson. The first revolver to be made was the Harrington ejector followed by a solid frame revolver in which the cylinder centre-pin could be quickly withdrawn, the cylinder slipped out of the frame, and the pin used to extract the fired cases. The first of the Harrington and Richardson double action revolvers was made in 1878 and this was followed by a whole range of five, six and seven chambered revolvers, most of which were made for .22 rim-fire, .32 centre-fire and .38 centre-fire cartridges.

Harrington and Richardson manufactured one of the most famous American target single shot pistols ever produced, the USRA Model. Made until 1941, this was designed by the late Walter Roper and incorporated a very light hammer having an extremely short throw. The Harrington and Richardson single shot pistol was, like its contemporaries, based on the frame of a hinged frame revolver and designed to compete with the Colt 'Camp Perry' target pistol. Special barrels were made for this pistol, the rifling tool not only cutting the grooves but also scraping the lands to eliminate any tool marks left from the previous boring operation. Considerable attention was paid to the provision of suitable target sights and, due to the design of the grip frame, it was possible to offer a wide range of factory stocks to suit individual requirements. At one time, eleven one piece stocks of various shapes and sizes were available. The USRA Model was capable of further development but, in 1939, J. W. Harrington, the younger son of the founder, died, and shortly afterwards the family control of the business ceased.

Solid frame and top break revolvers continued to be made and, from 1889, the Harrington and Richardson trade mark—a target with five shots scored on it—appeared on the stocks of most of their revolvers. Throughout the years a number of notable ones were manufactured. The Model 199 Sportsman, a nine shot single action version of the DA Sportsman was introduced in 1932, the single action version having appeared a year earlier. In 1938 a second model, the 777 Ultra Sportsman, appeared in which the cylinder was made only slightly longer than a .22 long rifle cartridge, so reducing the bullet jump from cylinder to barrel to a minimum. In 1940 this was superceded by the Model 196 Eureka, possibly the rarest of the Harrington and Richardson revolvers, since production was not recommenced after World War Two.

In 1956 Harrington and Richardson introduced the nine shot .22 calibre solid frame 'Side-Kick' which has a side-swinging cylinder with star extractor. This revolver is really a 'fungun' or 'Plinker' and cannot be considered for serious target work due to the absence of adjustable sights. The 'Ultra Side-Kick', introduced in 1959, retains the side-swinging cylinder from which the revolver derives its name and incorporates the Harrington and Richardson safety feature of a raised rim around the rear of the cylinder. A ventilated rib carries the front sight and the rear sight is adjustable for windage. A somewhat unusual safety feature is that the gun can be locked against use by means of a key inserted in a slot in the butt.

A solid frame rod ejector double action six shot revolver, known as the Model 660 'Gunfighter', appeared in 1959, which was obviously designed to take advantage of the vogue for 'Western' style revolvers, and Harrington and Richardson's current offering in this style is the nine shot Model 949 'Forty Niner'.

In addition to this range of .22 solid and hinged frame revolvers, Harrington and Richardson make the Model 925 'Defender' in a nine shot .22 long rifle version or a five shot .38 S & W. Their Model 732 'Guardsman' has a swing-out cylinder instead of the top break action of the Model 925, and is chambered for the .32 S & W or S & W long cartridge.

Hi-Standard commenced the manufacture of automatic pistols in 1932 and, after World War Two they diversified production to include revolvers, rifles and shotguns. The Hi-Standard 'Sentinel' range was introduced in 1955 to meet the demand for a moderately priced nine shot side-swing cylinder revolver. The frame is of aluminium alloy, the barrel and cylinder of steel. Designed for use with standard or high-speed .22 cartridge, the chambers are counterbored and coil springs are used throughout. Three double action 'Sentinel' revolvers are currently offered in either blue or nickel finish. All are nine shot and differ in barrel length: the Sentinel Snub has a $2\frac{3}{8}''$ barrel, and the Sentinel De Luxe is offered with either a 4″ or a 6″ barrel.

.22 Hi-Standard Sentinel de Luxe. (Hi-Standard)

.32 Harrington and Richardson auto-ejecting five shot hammerless revolver.

The Hi-Standard 'Double Nine' is based on the Sentinel but designed to give the currently popular 'Western' look. The standard model has a $5\frac{1}{2}''$ barrel, and the Double Nine 'Longhorn' a $9\frac{1}{2}''$ 'Buntline' barrel.

.22 Hi-Standard Double Nine. (Hi-Standard)

Hi-Standard also offer a most intriguing two shot derringer chambered for the .22 rim-fire (Model D 100) and for the .22 RFM (Model DM 101).

From time to time revolvers in this general class and price range appear on the American market which have been manufactured abroad, either in Germany or Italy. No mention has been made of these guns since they are usually transitory and manufactured merely to exploit a fringe demand.

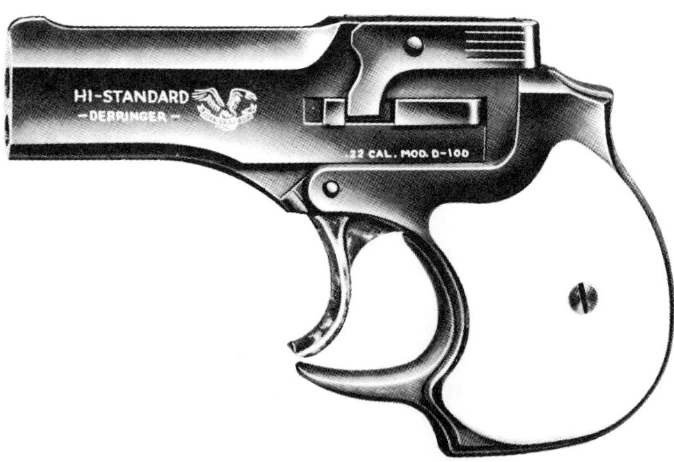

.22 Hi-Standard Derringer with over and under double barrel. (Hi-Standard)

Due to the intense demand for the high quality expensive products of the past, prices to the collector have risen tremendously, and certain models which the manufacturers sold off at reduced prices immediately before the war are now very desirable collectors' items. It is in the context of this new demand that some of these vintage revolvers should now be viewed. One of the results is that more interest is now being taken in the inexpensive revolvers produced by reputable manufacturers, and the extensive range of models which have been made by firms such as Harrington and Richardson and Iver Johnson certainly gives wide scope to the most penurious collector.

This type of revolver has, however, not been in great demand in Britain for many years now. The difficulties of obtaining permission to purchase are such that a casual desire to own a handgun cannot be justified, and, for serious target work, the advantages of specialised target weapons more than outweigh considerations of additional cost.

Only two other countries manufacture revolvers today. In Germany, the firm of Hermann Weihrauch of Mellrichstadt still produce their 'Arminius' revolver Models HW 5 and HW 9 in .22 rim-fire. Both are simultaneous extraction weapons with side-swinging cylinders and versions are made for use with special cartridges as 'Gas and Alarm' pistols. Cheaper .22 revolvers are also made by Rohm and under the trade name 'Em-Gee'.

In Czechoslovakia, a small arms industry was established at the time of the disruption of the Austro-Hungarian Empire following the end of the First World War. The development of this industry will, however, be dealt with in detail later, as it was mainly concerned with the manufacture of rifles and automatic pistols. Following the nationalisation of the Czech arms industry at the end of World War Two, revolvers were manufactured at the Zbrojovka Works in Brno. Two types are still made, the first being the

.38 Special Czech ZKR 551. (Omnipol)

'Grand', ZKR 590, which is manufactured in .22 long rifle, .32 S & W, .38 S & W Special and .357 Magnum. The design was by Necas and, externally, the ZKR 590 is similar to the Colt. The second is a special target revolver, the six shot ZKR 551 designed by the brothers Koucky, which is a solid frame side rod ejector with a short fall thumb cocking hammer. Chambered for the .38 S & W Special cartridge, it has gained important successes in the international shooting world.

Today, however, the undoubted home of the revolver is America but, even in the land of its first commercial exploitation, severe inroads are being made into many of the areas where formerly the revolver was pre-eminent. The automatic pistol is now the official service handgun of all the important military powers and, on the range, the .22 automatic has almost completely vanquished the revolver for competitive shooting and is seriously challenging the centre-fire target revolver.

The particular advantages of the revolver, as opposed to the automatic, can still, even now, be justified, although many of the arguments offered both for and against are based on personal experience and, at times, a deep-rooted but often illogical attachment for either one or the other.

It would be unfair to put forward my own feelings at this stage; fortunately, the revolver is still being manufactured in a wide range of types and styles, and a more final assessment will be left until we have examined that relative newcomer to the family of firearms, the automatic or self-loading pistol.

Notes to Chapter Eleven

In addition to the literature mentioned in the notes to the previous two chapters, reference can be made to *Pistols, a Modern Encyclopedia* by H. M. Stebbins (Harrisburg, 1961) and to *The Textbook of Pistols and Revolvers* by J. S. Hatcher (Small Arms Technical Publishing Co., 1935). On Colt revolvers, much of interest is contained in *The Modern Colt Guide* by Burr Leyson (New York, 1953) and on the Smith and Wesson, including historical data on the factory, in *Smith and Wesson, The Story of the Revolver* by Martin Rywell (Harriman, 1953). Articles of value on the 'swing-out' cylinder Colt revolvers appeared in the *American Rifleman* for August 1955 and September 1962. A definitive article on Harrington and Richardson revolvers appeared in the July 1962 issue, and on Iver-Johnson revolvers in that for May 1961.

Chapter Twelve
Multi-shot Pistols and the Birth of the Self-loader

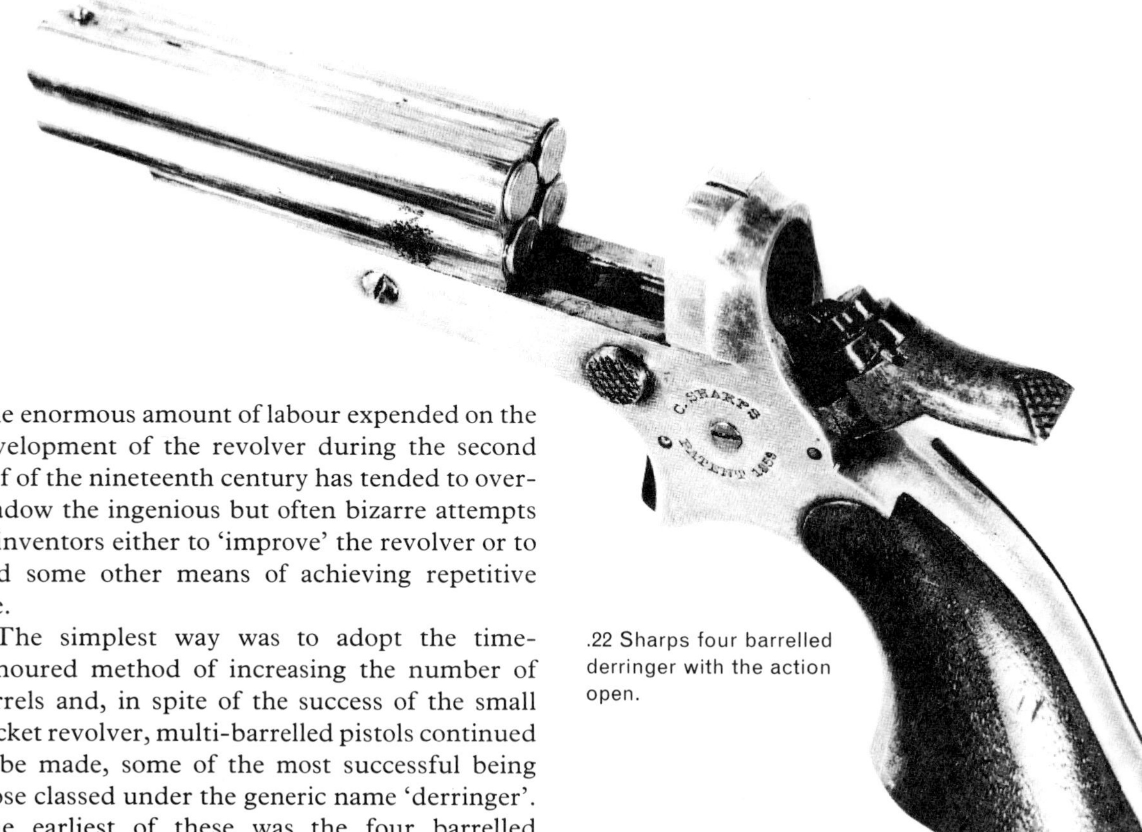

.22 Sharps four barrelled derringer with the action open.

The enormous amount of labour expended on the development of the revolver during the second half of the nineteenth century has tended to overshadow the ingenious but often bizarre attempts of inventors either to 'improve' the revolver or to find some other means of achieving repetitive fire.

The simplest way was to adopt the time-honoured method of increasing the number of barrels and, in spite of the success of the small pocket revolver, multi-barrelled pistols continued to be made, some of the most successful being those classed under the generic name 'derringer'. The earliest of these was the four barrelled Sharps, patented originally by Christian Sharps in 1849, US Patent No. 6960. This first patent referred to a percussion muzzle loading pistol in which a striker was simultaneously cocked and rotated so that it would strike each of the four nipples located at the rear of the group of stationary barrels. Sharps' patent of 1859, US Patent No. 22,753, described a method whereby a hammer with a revolving striker could be made to fire a succession of rim-fire cartridges, the chisel-shaped striker turning through 90 degrees each time the hammer was cocked. In order to load and unload the pistol, the hammer was brought to the half cock position and, on the earlier models, a small release button under the frame was pressed so that the barrel group could then be slid forward. On the later models there was a side

Replica of the .22 Sharps derringer made by Uberti.

button release which was pushed downwards. A rarer version had a lever release (similar to that on the American patent drawing) which also acted as a trigger guard. The guard was linked to a projection under the barrel and, when it was opened, the barrel slid forward. There were many minor variations in grip shape, frame contour etc. and, in America, the Sharps was made in .22, .30 and, later, in .32 rim-fire calibres. In Britain, it was manufactured under licence by Tipping and Lawden, a firm later acquired by P. Webley and Sons, who also made the Sharps for a short time. Here, the calibres were .22, 6mm, .30, 7mm and 9mm and the pistols were marked 'Tipping and Lawden, Sharps' Patent'. A large number of copies appeared on the Continent, the better quality examples bearing the name 'Grunbaum, Wien'. The popularity of the Sharps has not diminished; not only are the originals collectors' pieces, but excellent copies are being made in Northern Italy by Uberti.

On both of Christian Sharps' patents his pistol was termed a 'revolver'. The pedant would undoubtedly call it a 'pepperbox', but by common

.41 Remington Double Derringer.

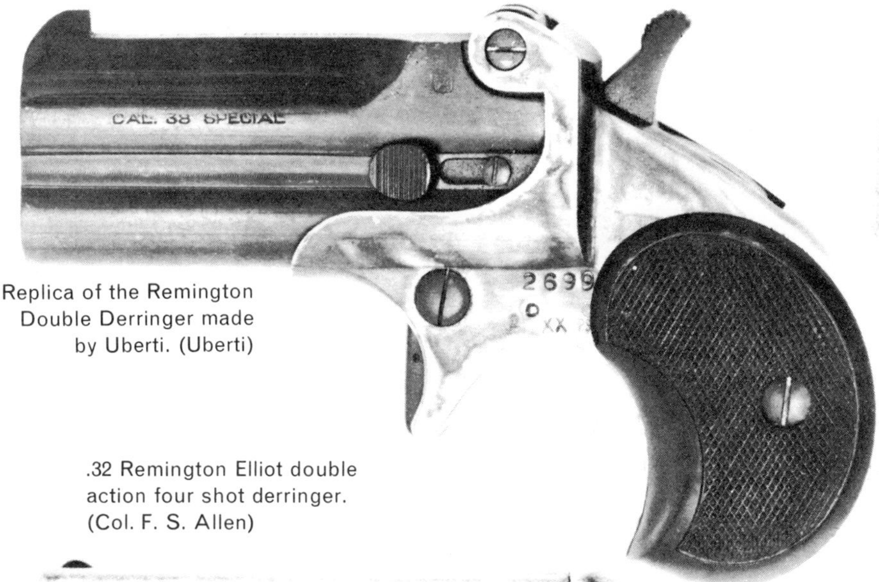

Replica of the Remington Double Derringer made by Uberti. (Uberti)

.32 Remington Elliot double action four shot derringer. (Col. F. S. Allen)

usage it is termed a derringer. A very similar pistol was made by Eben Starr and employed an external hammer and a button trigger.

It is probably true to say that few of the small calibre multi-shot derringers or pepperboxes would ever have been made but for the Smith and Wesson patent. Because this patent did not cover boring barrels through to the rear, the omission left the field open to Remington to place on the market the Remington Elliot or Remington Zig-Zag derringer. Made in .22 calibre and firing six shots, the Zig-Zag derringer got its name from the zig-zag grooves at the rear of the barrel group, while the group itself was rotated by a stud in the frame which moved back and forth in line with the barrel axis. When the ring trigger was moved forward, the stud slid along a straight groove and, when it was pulled to the rear, the stud slipped into a slanting groove and so rotated the barrel group. The Remington Elliot Zig-Zag pistol, made only in 1861 and 1862, was followed by the 'double action' Remington Elliot, a .32 rim-fire four shot pistol. A five shot .22 weapon on a similar plan was also manufactured, as were two vest pocket pistols, a small single shot .22 and a companion .41 rim-fire.

The most successful of the Remington derringers was the Remington Over and Under or Double Derringer based on William Elliot's US Patent No. 51,440 of 1865. The patent covered two points: firstly, a vertically oscillating firing pin, operated by a cam, for successive discharge; secondly, a cam and firing pin so constructed and operated that they served the purpose of ratchet and pawl.

A lever on the right hand side of the frame was swung downward and forward to unlatch the over and under barrels, which could then be swung upwards on the hinge at the top of the standing breech. Early models had no means of extraction and the fired cases had to be pushed out with a rod or pencil. Later versions had a simple extractor with two arms, and the most common, the last type, had a simple extractor dovetailed into the side of the barrels. This was operated by pushing a thumb catch to the rear.

The Remington Double Derringer enjoyed a remarkable production run. It first appeared in 1866 and, until 1888, bore the legend 'E. Remington & Sons'. Between 1888 and 1910 the wording was 'Remington Arms Co.' and, from then until production ceased in 1935, 'Remington Arms—U.M.C.CO.'

As made by Remington, the calibre was .41 rim-fire. Since the last war a number of copies have appeared, and one of the first was made in Germany specifically for the US market. Imported by the Derringer Corporation of Pasadena, the 'Double Derringer' was a reasonable copy of the original Remington but chambered for the .22 long rifle rim-fire cartridge. Since 1957 a number of similar copies have been chambered for cartridges from the .22 long rifle through the .38 S & W Special and .357 Magnum all the way up to a hand shattering version in .45 Colt.

The Remington Double Derringer was a highly effective 'hideaway' gun once the difficulty of cocking the rather strong mainspring had been overcome. The grip shape for so small a pistol was very comfortable, and modern, well-made copies in .38 S & W Special calibre have been used for serious work by responsible people who, for one

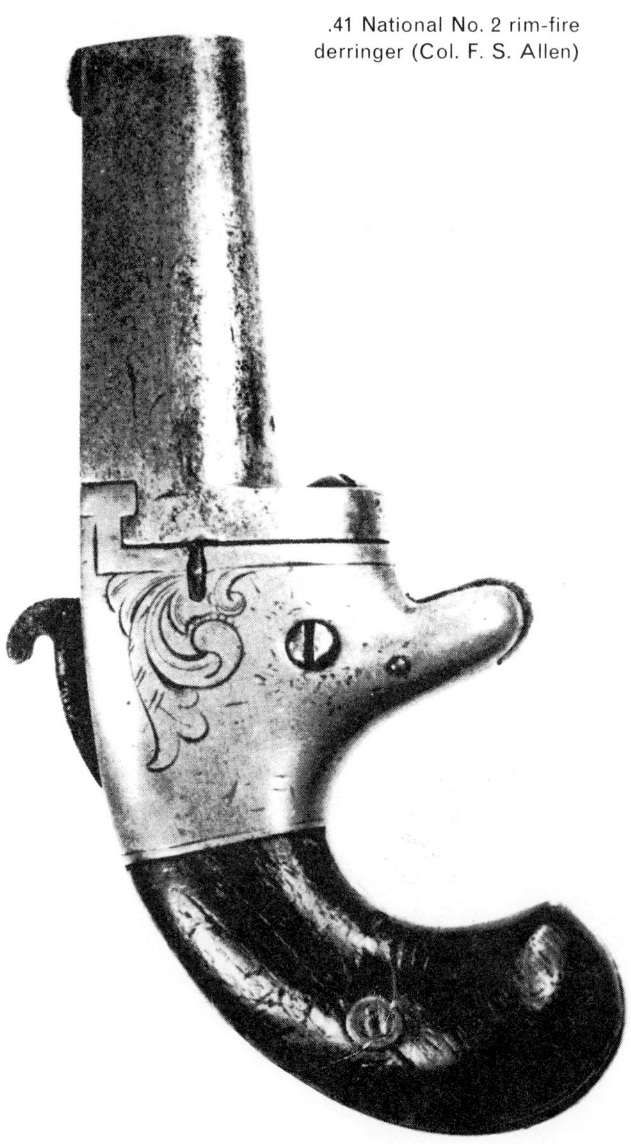

.41 National No. 2 rim-fire derringer (Col. F. S. Allen)

reason or another, could not carry anything larger.

The ancestor of the Colt Derringer, the first cartridge derringer of heavy calibre, was the Moore based on two patents that Daniel Moore obtained in 1861 and 1863. Production commenced just before the outbreak of the American Civil War and, in 1865, Moore's Patent Fire Arms Co. of Brooklyn became the National Arms Co. Two Moore-National models were made, the No. 1 with an all-metal handle, and the No. 2 with a wooden grip. In 1870 the Colt Company bought out the National Arms Co., retained the model designations, but also produced a Colt National No. 2. This can, however, be easily distinguished from the Moore-National in that the joint between the wood grip and the frame was rounded whereas, on the Moore-National, it was straight. Both the No. 1 and the No. 2 were .41 short rim-fire, the barrel length was standardised at $2\frac{1}{2}''$, and the barrel itself rotated downward to the left.

The Colt No. 3 or Thuer Derringer originated in the Colt factory and was designed and patented by F. Alexander Thuer in 1870. With a few exceptions, all were made in .41 short rim-fire and all employed a side-swinging barrel pivoted on the bar of the bronze frame. There were several minor production changes involving the shape of the hammer and grip frame, but all had the automatic cartridge ejection feature which expelled the fired case when the barrel was swung open to the right.

In 1960 Colt, alone amongst the original manufacturers, introduced a .22 calibre single shot pistol, the Colt Derringer No. 4, which bore

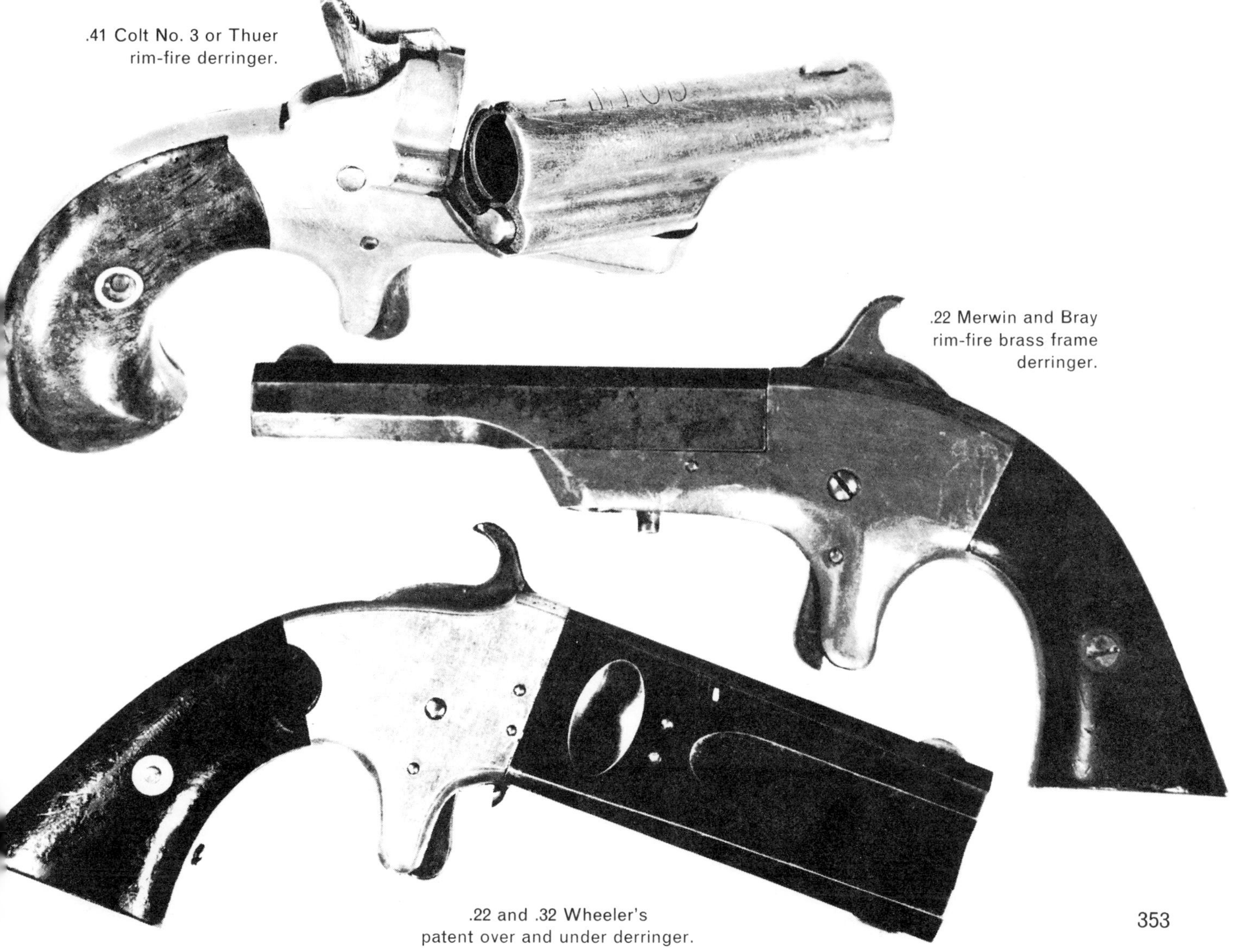

.41 Colt No. 3 or Thuer rim-fire derringer.

.22 Merwin and Bray rim-fire brass frame derringer.

.22 and .32 Wheeler's patent over and under derringer.

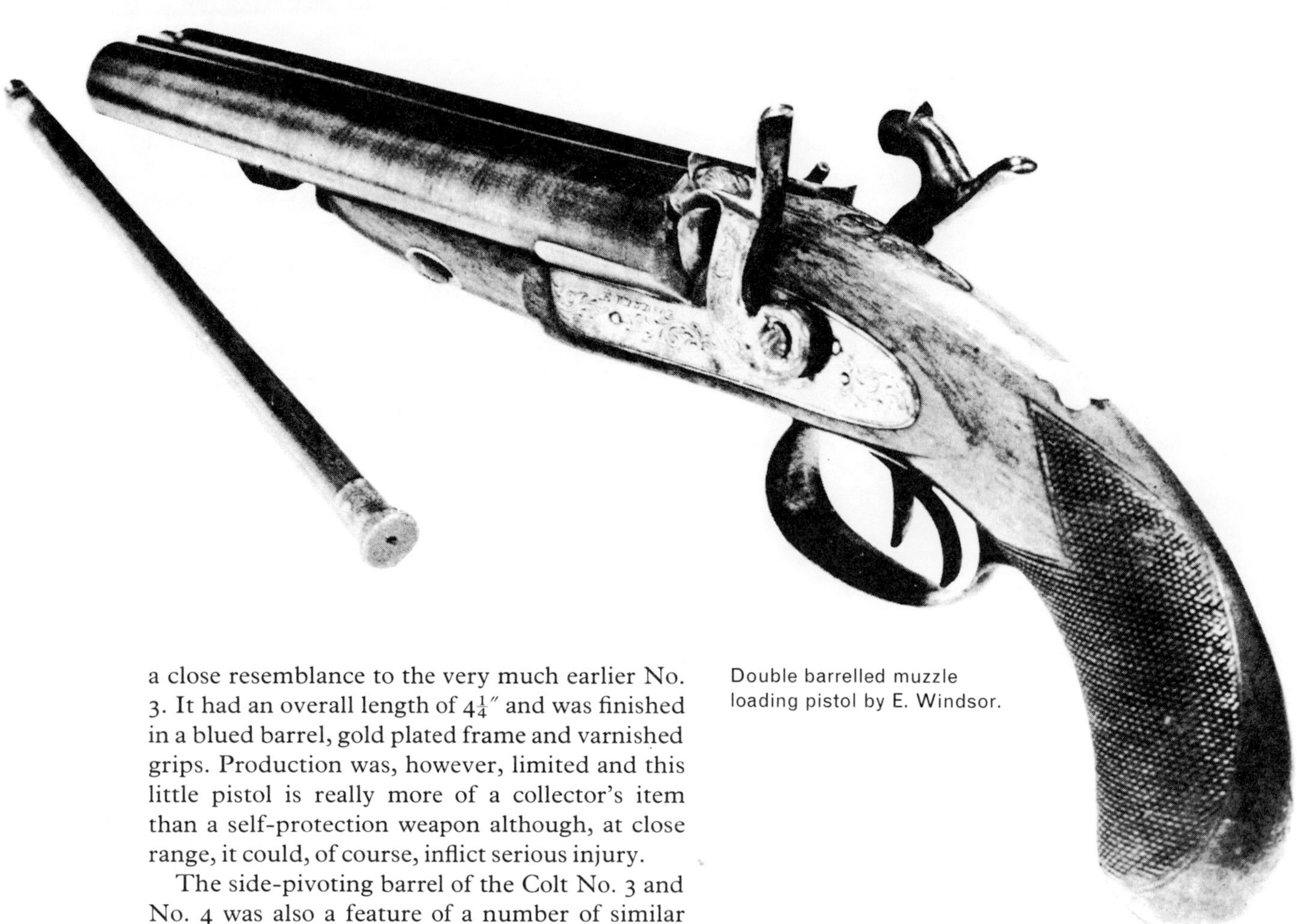

Double barrelled muzzle loading pistol by E. Windsor.

a close resemblance to the very much earlier No. 3. It had an overall length of $4\frac{1}{4}''$ and was finished in a blued barrel, gold plated frame and varnished grips. Production was, however, limited and this little pistol is really more of a collector's item than a self-protection weapon although, at close range, it could, of course, inflict serious injury.

The side-pivoting barrel of the Colt No. 3 and No. 4 was also a feature of a number of similar derringers manufactured by Ethan Allan, the Merrimac Arms and Manufacturing Co., Forehand and Wadsworth and others which bore names such as 'Victor', 'Southerner', 'XL' etc.

Among other derringers, the Starr employed a tip-down barrel, the Remington Double Derringer a tip-up barrel, and the ones produced by Frank Wesson and by the American Arms Co. an over and under revolving barrel. The American Nut and Arms Co. of Boston introduced their model in 1868, and this pistol, marked 'American Arms Co. Boston, Wheeler's Pat. Oct. 31 1865, June 19 1866', is of interest since it followed Wheeler's patent specification as regards the method of opening the breech. The barrels were first rotated and then pulled forward, and they were also of different calibre, one .22 rim-fire the other .32 rim-fire.

Of all the types of derringer made, the Perry and Goddard (manufactured under the name 'Double Header' by E. S. Renwick of New York) is undoubtedly the strangest. The barrel of this pistol was chambered at both ends and so arranged that it could be completely rotated about a central pivot. A cartridge could be introduced into the 'muzzle' and the barrel swung round through 180 degrees so that the muzzle became the breech. When the cartridge had been fired a new round was introduced at the muzzle and the barrel rotated again to permit the extraction of the fired case. If the user were sufficiently courageous, the spent case could be expelled from the muzzle by the discharge of the second cartridge.

Multi-barrelled pistols on a larger scale were popular in Britain—particularly the double barrelled side-by-side with either the common under lever locking or the later top lever snap action—and were to all intents cut down versions of sporting guns. They were chambered for a wide range of cartridges up to and including the standard 12 bore loaded either with round ball or buckshot. Such pistols were the descendants of the muzzle loading 'Howdah' pistols employed either for big game hunting or as a military weapon. Breechloading versions were either smooth-bored or rifled, and Lancaster's patent

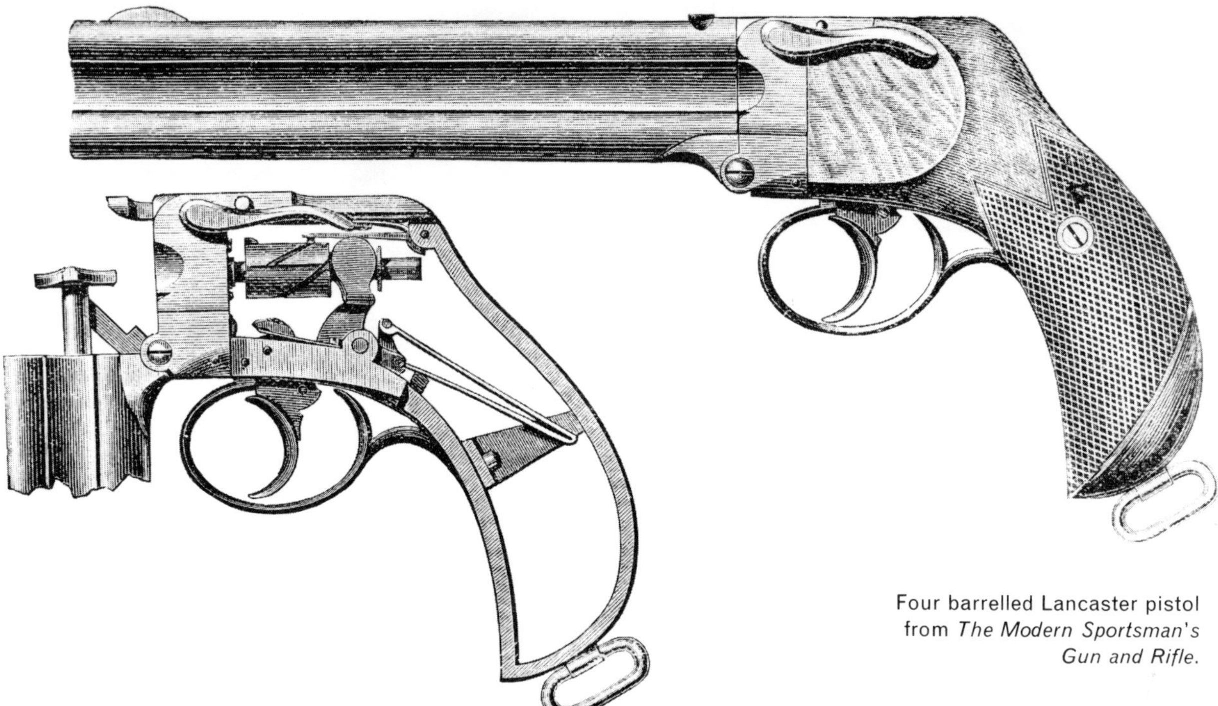

Four barrelled Lancaster pistol from *The Modern Sportsman's Gun and Rifle.*

'non-fouling smooth oval-bore' rifling can occasionally be encountered.

Charles William Lancaster was the eldest son of Charles Lancaster, a former barrel maker for Joseph Manton who started up on his own in New Bond St, London. When he died in 1847, he left the business to his two sons, but their partnership was dissolved in 1859 and Charles William carried on alone until his death in 1878. In 1850 he obtained British Patent No. 13,161 which described his oval or elliptical boring and the special rifling machinery which he also designed. Lancaster's rifling was used on pistols, rifles and field guns or cannon with some success although, of eight Lancaster rifled muzzle loading cannon sent to Sebastopol during the Crimean War, it is recorded that three burst during the siege. In mitigation it must be mentioned that these were old guns which had been re-bored on the Lancaster system.

On the death of C. W. Lancaster the business was bought by Henry A. A. Thorn who obtained patents in 1881 and 1882 covering multi-barrelled firearms with an ingenious rotating hammer lock mechanism. The illustration from J. H. Walsh's *The Modern Sportsman's Gun and Rifle* (1884) shows the early type of barrel latch, and the second illustration shows the later type which hooked over projecting lugs on the barrel. The early type was similar to the doll's head extension and was lifted out of a recess machined at the top of the breech by the thumb lever. Lancaster pistols can also be found fitted with both the doll's head and the hook lever system, as well as with both single and double trigger actions, the double trigger being similar in disposition to that employed by Tranter.

To load the Lancaster, the thumb lever was depressed and the barrel hinged downward exposing the four chambers. An automatic ejector ejected all four cartridges at once, the central rod fitting between the four barrels. The lockwork was rebounding and, as the action was cocked, the bolt was drawn back and a pawl engaged in a diagonal groove rotated the bolt one quarter turn. When the trigger was pulled further back, the 'hammer' went forward carrying with it the bolt which fired the cartridge. The Lancaster was also made in an over and under double barrel version and, since the Lancaster pistols were made by traditional methods which involved a great deal of hand work, variations as to the shape of the grip, trigger guard, barrel length and calibre were numerous.

A similar four barrelled pistol was invented by Abraham Martin, British Patent No. 1531 of 1880. The patent shows an eight barrelled pistol, but it is doubtful if any were made with more than four barrels. A feature of the design was the intended use of 'blocks' of cartridges which were to be made by riveting the heads to a perforated plate so that a complete 'charge' could be loaded in one operation. Martin was associated with Joseph Marres and J. A. Braendlin, and some of

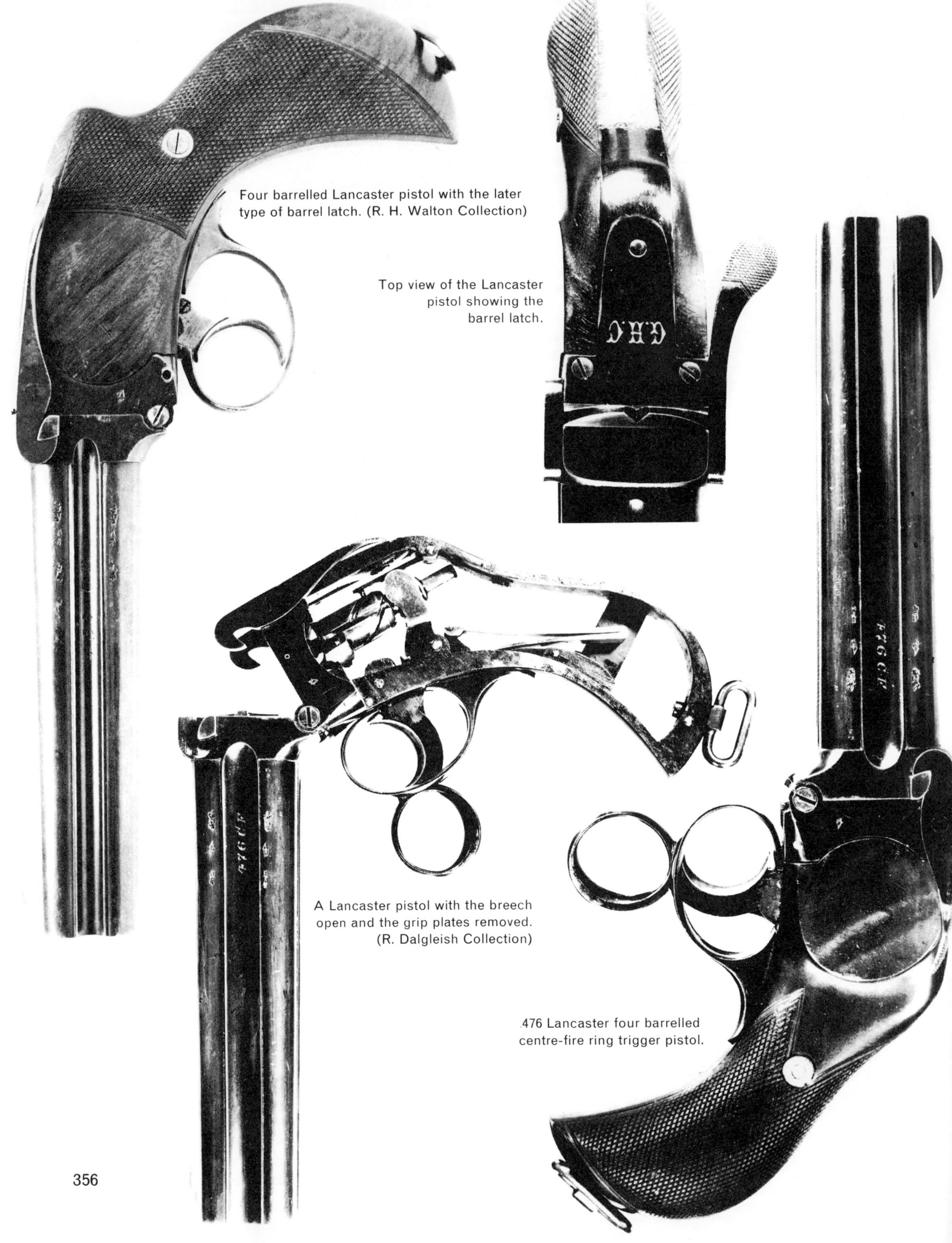

Four barrelled Lancaster pistol with the later type of barrel latch. (R. H. Walton Collection)

Top view of the Lancaster pistol showing the barrel latch.

A Lancaster pistol with the breech open and the grip plates removed. (R. Dalgleish Collection)

.476 Lancaster four barrelled centre-fire ring trigger pistol.

Four barrelled Martin centre-fire pistol. (J. Stewart)

the Martin 'Mitrailleuse' pistols which have survived were manufactured by the Braendlin Armoury Co. Ltd. Others were made by Thomas Bland and Sons who later manufactured their own multi-barrelled pistol. The Martin Mitrailleuse is dealt with at some length by W. W. Greener in *The Gun and its Development* where a note of caution states 'that it sometimes happens that the shock of the recoil prematurely discharges a second barrel'. This could not happen with the Lancaster but, since the Martin employed separate striker and springs for each barrel, Greener's warning may have been based on actual experience. The Martin pistol is by no means as common as the Lancaster, and even fewer examples of Thomas Bland's own pistol appear to have been made.

All these systems claimed the advantage of increased accuracy and fire power since the escape of gas between the cylinder and barrel which occurred with the conventional revolver was eliminated. That many of the claims made by the inventors were borne out in practice can be deduced by the number of these pistols, particularly the Lancaster, which saw actual service. The Lancaster was a favourite weapon in the 'little wars' of the late nineteenth century and it was chambered not only for the British service cartridges of the period but also for 20 bore and .500 calibre cartridges as well as the smaller .380 and .360.

Other methods of achieving repetitive fire were equally considered. The Iverson twelve shot percussion turret gun featured a radial cylinder which was revolved by manually cocking the hammer. The Josselyn, patented sixteen years later in 1866, utilised an endless belt of chambers to bring the cartridges under the firing pin, a system similar to that employed by Treeby who patented his idea in 1855. Turret and 'chain' guns were made in all possible manner of ways, the ultimate being patented by Joseph Enouy in 1855. Here, the inventor claimed a 'compound' magazine but the term 'ferriss wheel' used by Lewis Winant is far more descriptive. The pistol, which resembled an ordinary percussion pepperbox, had an additional revolving framework carried on an axle mounted between the barrel and butt. By means of this, forty-two shots were possible, and one at least of these contraptions was actually made.

As an alternative to turrets, chains and ferriss wheels, some people were of the opinion that it was better to have a series of barrels in a straight

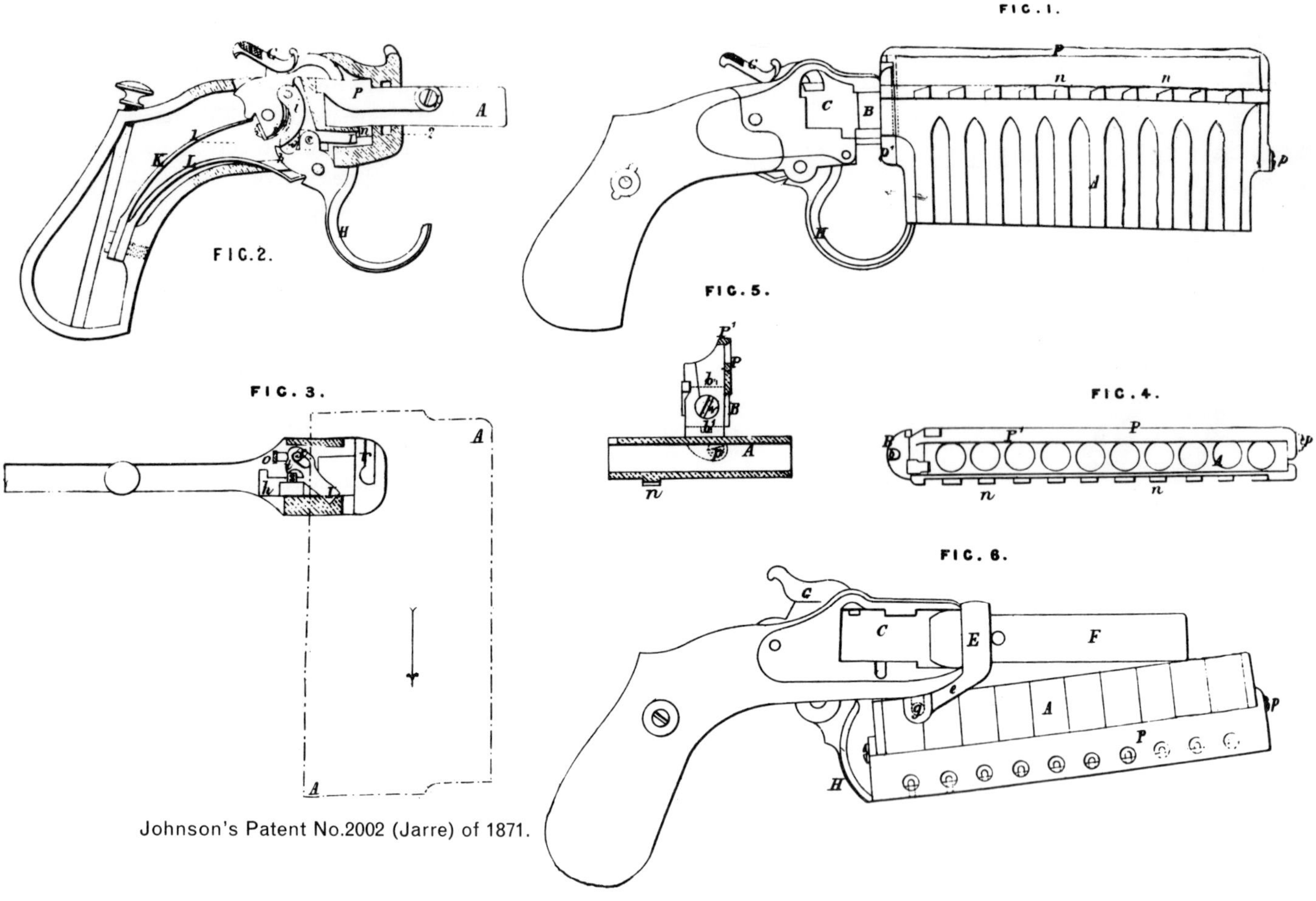

Johnson's Patent No.2002 (Jarre) of 1871.

line. The most widely known of these systems was that patented by Jarre in 1871, British Patent No. 2002. The Jarre system can be followed from the patent drawing, and the modern collector's name for this class of pistol, 'the Harmonica pistol', can be understood.

The German 'Reform' pistol is more modern, dating from 1911. Made under Richard Schuler's patents, the Reform, usually encountered in .25 ACP, fired one shot each time the trigger was pulled. After each shot, the mechanism elevated the vertical stack of four barrels until all four had been discharged. The barrels had to be removed for loading.

In this catalogue of the rare and curious we must not overlook the attempts which have been made from time to time to 'improve' or to increase the versatility of the revolver. John Walch of New York City was obviously not content with the normal six shot percussion revolver and he scorned the simple expedient of increasing the number of chambers and consequently the bulk of the cylinder. Instead, he turned back the clock and employed the old idea of superimposed loads. By this means he was able to increase the capacity of his revolver from six to twelve shots. To load, each chamber was charged with two bullets and two powder charges. Special cartridges were designed with a soap compound division between the sections which, when the cartridges were rammed home, would seal off the charges (Fig. 12).

Walch's British Patent No. 1764 of 1859 illustrates the common twelve shot Walch revolver in Fig. 7. This pistol employed two hammers, two triggers and twelve nipples (Fig. 10). Early Walch revolvers were similar to Fig. 2 and had had only one trigger. The nipples were set in two rows, one row in front of the other, and a special long nosed hammer was employed to fire the row fitted halfway along the cylinder. Unless, on the single trigger model, pressure on the trigger was released after the first shot had been fired, the second charge would follow immediately. To overcome this disadvantage, the later models were fitted with two triggers, and the production models followed the design of the patent arm illustrated in Fig. 7. The so-called Walch Navy

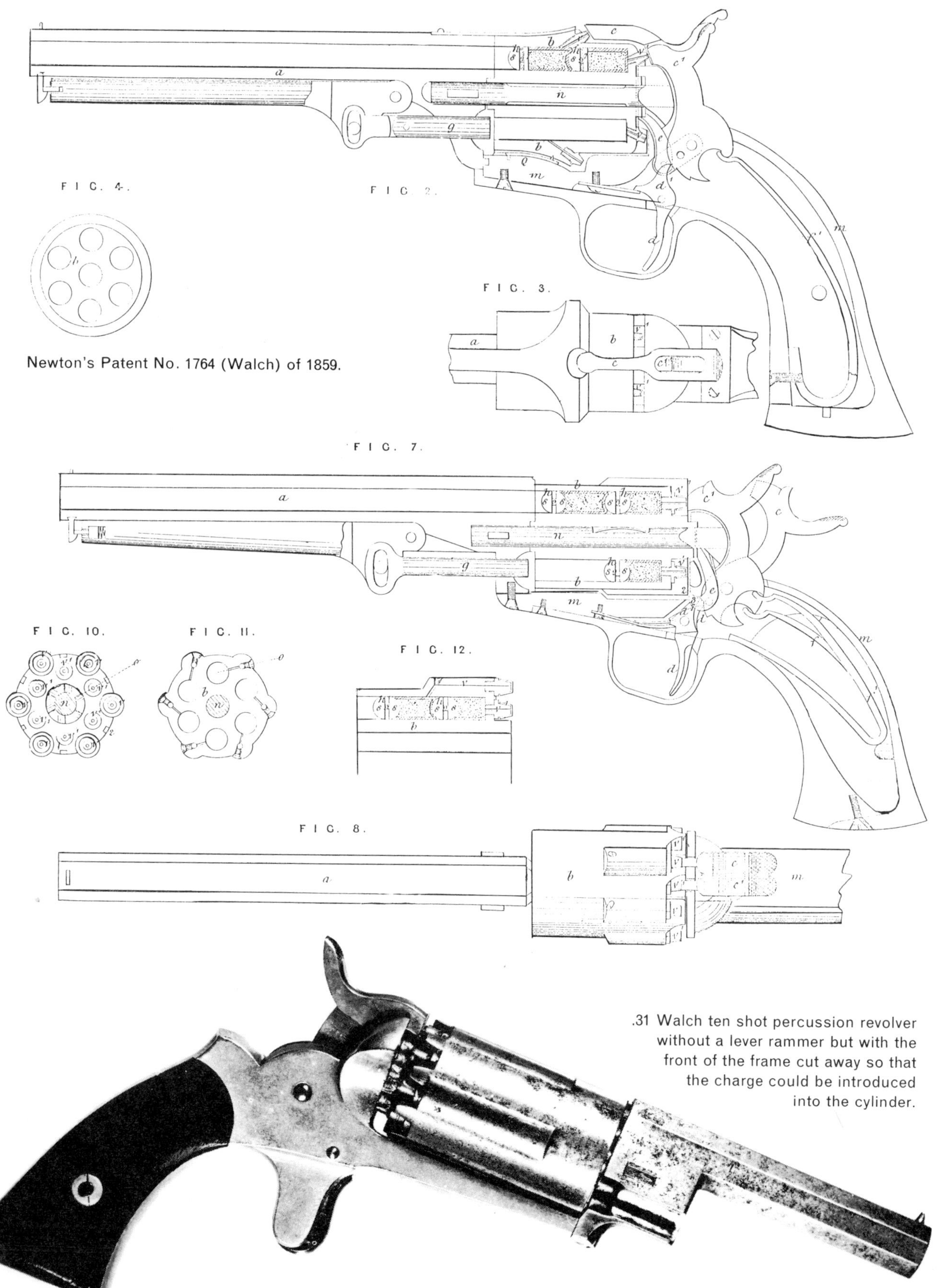

Newton's Patent No. 1764 (Walch) of 1859.

.31 Walch ten shot percussion revolver without a lever rammer but with the front of the frame cut away so that the charge could be introduced into the cylinder.

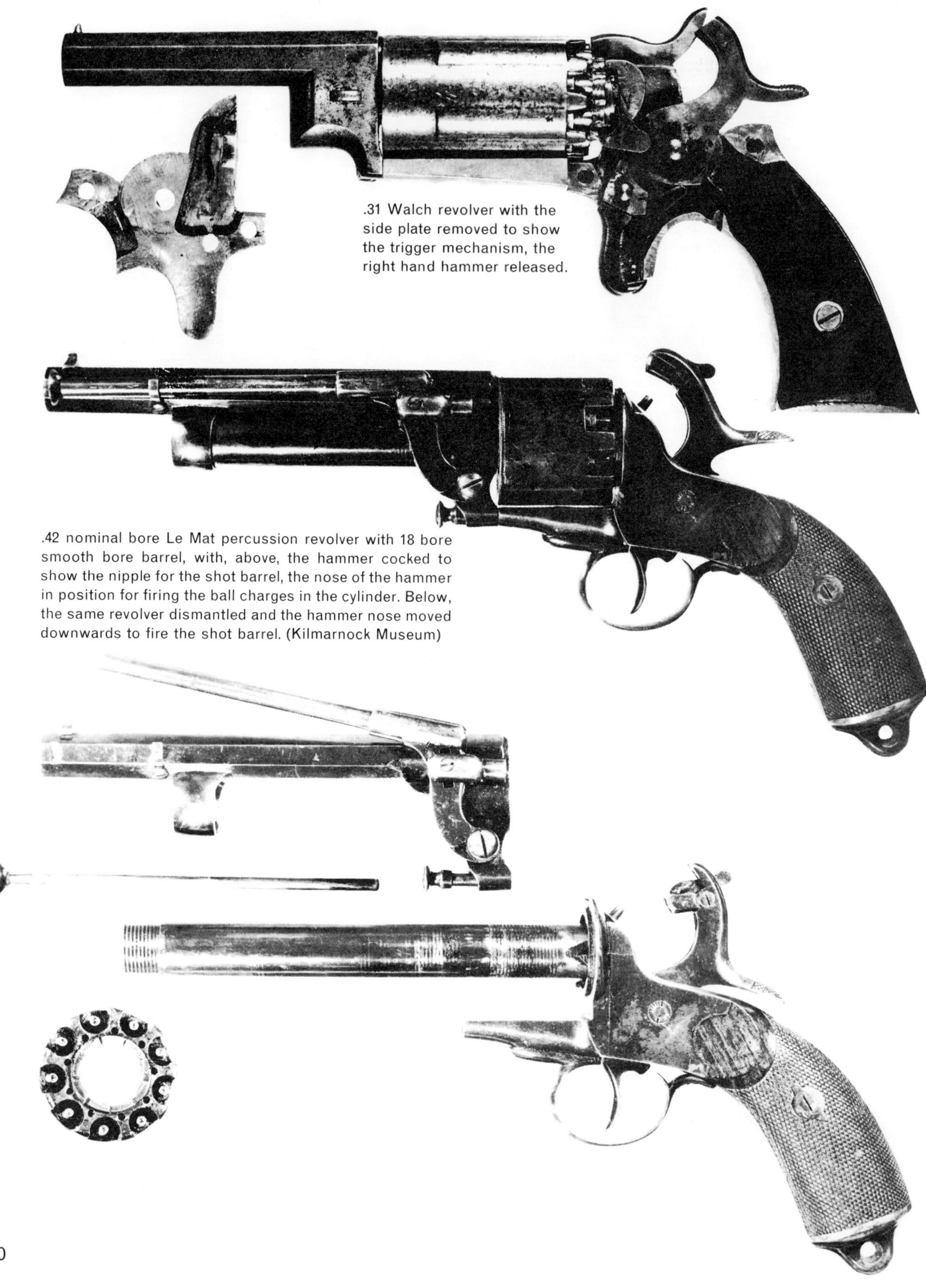

.31 Walch revolver with the side plate removed to show the trigger mechanism, the right hand hammer released.

.42 nominal bore Le Mat percussion revolver with 18 bore smooth bore barrel, with, above, the hammer cocked to show the nipple for the shot barrel, the nose of the hammer in position for firing the ball charges in the cylinder. Below, the same revolver dismantled and the hammer nose moved downwards to fire the shot barrel. (Kilmarnock Museum)

twelve shot pistol of .36 calibre was followed by the ten shot .31 calibre Pocket Model. Both reverted to the single trigger, but of an improved design attributed to Lindsay.

As with all superimposed load systems, the ever-present fear of the rear charge being fired first must have haunted all those intrepid souls who used these weapons. Walch, it must be admitted, took reasonable care to ensure against this, but Charles Edwin Wallis of London despised such mechanical involvement. In his system, provisionally patented in 1863, he relied on using two nipples to each multi-loaded chamber, both nipples being struck simultaneously by the same hammer. Wallis relied on special percussion caps with different ignition speeds to ensure that the foremost charge was ignited first. Undeterred by the apparent apathy which greeted this first invention, Wallis invented yet another system which allowed for three charges in each cylinder. A sliding firing stud was attached to the hammer and, provided the user remembered to locate the stud in the correct position, this system was possibly marginally safer than relying on special caps. It is doubtful if any Wallis pistols were ever made, and still more doubtful if any were actually fired.

But for the American Civil War, it is very doubtful if the Le Mat percussion revolver would have received the attention it later enjoyed. In 1856, Dr Jean Alexandre Francois Le Mat, a physician of French extraction living in New Orleans, obtained American Patent No. 15,925 which described a revolver with an upper and lower barrel, the lower barrel continuing to the recoil shield and serving as an axle upon which the cylinder revolved. The chambers of the cylinder fired through the top barrel. The same hammer, since the nose was manually adjustable, fired the charges both in the cylinder and in the lower barrel.

The normal Le Mat percussion revolver had a nine chambered cylinder, usually .42 or .36 calibre, which revolved around a .63 calibre smooth bore barrel loaded with 'buckshot'. As can be seen from the illustration, the revolver would function as a single shot pistol even if the cylinder and upper barrel were removed. The hammer nose in this illustration has been moved downwards to fire the shot barrel, the nipple for which can be seen behind the standing breech. The first Le Mat revolvers were manufactured in New Orleans by the inventor and Pierre G. T. Beauregard, who later gained fame as a Confederate General at Manassas and Shiloh. With the outbreak of the Civil War, Le Mat obtained Confederate orders for his revolvers, and these were manufactured in France and England. The revolver cylinder was loaded with the aid of the conventional side lever rammer into which was fitted a rammer for the shot barrel. Le Mat was also associated with C. F. Girard during the manufacture and promotion of his 'grapeshot' revolver and their joint British Patent No. 1081 was obtained in 1862. Later, in 1868, Colonel (or Dr) Le Mat obtained British Patent No. 3181 which covered a centre-fire version for 9mm ball and 14mm shot cartridges. Pin-fire Le Mat revolvers were also made although the shot barrel was still muzzle loading and discharged by the conventional cap and nipple. The pin- and centre-fire versions of the Le Mat enjoyed even less success than the original of which some 3,500 appear to have been manufactured.

Revolvers were also combined with knives, fitted with shoulder stocks and adapted for fitting to rifles (Mathieu, British Patent No. 3452 of 1862). Of the knife/pistol combination weapons the most successful were the Unwin and Rodgers percussion knife pistols made in Sheffield and the Elgin Cutlass pistol of 1837–38. James Rodgers and Philip Unwin had developed their percussion knife pistol by 1845, and their earlier models were discontinued. The percussion version was made until 1862 and was similar to the later breechloader in appearance. It is, however, of particular interest in that provision was made in the horn side plates for housing accessories, including a ramrod. In 1860 the firm patented their 'Saloon Barrel Knife Pistol' (Patent No. 2901) and here the emphasis was placed on the provision of a receptacle in the butt of the pistol to hold cartridges. This little compartment had a hinged snap action lid, and two knife blades were provided, one a 'self protecting dagger blade', the other a 'pen blade'. The barrel was of cupro-nickel and the side plates of polished horn. The cartridges were the No. 2 Bulletted Breech Caps and the manufacturers claimed an effective range of 100 to 130 yards. A simple breech mechanism was employed, the large hammer serving both to fire the cartridge and to close the breech. An equally simple hinged extractor was fitted to aid in the removal of the fired case, and the top of the extractor served as a rather crude rear sight. Using relatively modern cartridges, I found that this pistol shoots 10″ high at ten yards, in other words sufficiently accurately for close quarter self-defence; the knife blade, which lacked a self-locking device would have been of less value. The Unwin and Rodgers knife pistols were well made and are today an interesting and sought after curio.

George Elgin was granted protection for his ideas in 1837 and several firms undertook to manufacture his single shot percussion pistol. The US Navy purchased 150 of a .54 calibre version fitted with an 11½″ blade and a knuckle guard for the South Seas Exploring Expedition of 1838. The Elgin was the first percussion handgun and the first and only combination weapon of this type to be adopted by the US forces. The US Navy never purchased any more of these unusual weapons and the demand from the civilian market was so small that one of the firms, Morrill, Mosman and Blair of Amherst, Massachusetts, finally went bankrupt.

Before dealing with the magazine pistol, the last type of handgun before the true self-loading or automatic pistol, it would be appropriate to discuss the hybrid 'automatic' revolver. This type of weapon is greatly loved by newspaper reporters and thriller writers, but the only one ever to introduce it correctly was Dashiell Hammett in his excellent book *The Maltese Falcon*, first published in 1930. Thirty years earlier, the Webley-Fosbery Automatic Revolver had made its maiden appearance at the Bisley Meeting in July 1900, and had been placed on the market the following year.

Patents had previously been taken out for gas operated revolvers but these had never been commercially exploited. Colonel G. Vincent Fosbery, V.C., obtained his initial patents for a recoil operated revolver in 1895, British Patent No. 15,453. The pistol illustrated was based on the Colt SAA with the barrel and cylinder attached to a sub-frame which could slide freely in a grooved guide so that, when the pistol was fired, the barrel, cylinder and sub-frame recoiled independently, the butt remaining stationary. Fosbery's ideas were developed by the Webley and Scott Revolver and Arms Co. Ltd. and the production weapon was manufactured in two calibres, a .455 six chambered revolver designed for the service .455 cordite cartridge, and an eight chambered version which took the .38 Colt automatic pistol cartridge. It can be seen from the illustrations that the component parts of the Webley Government revolver were utilised as far as possible. The mechanism of the revolver was robust and the loading and unloading operation was carried out in exactly the same manner as for the conventional hinged frame Webley.

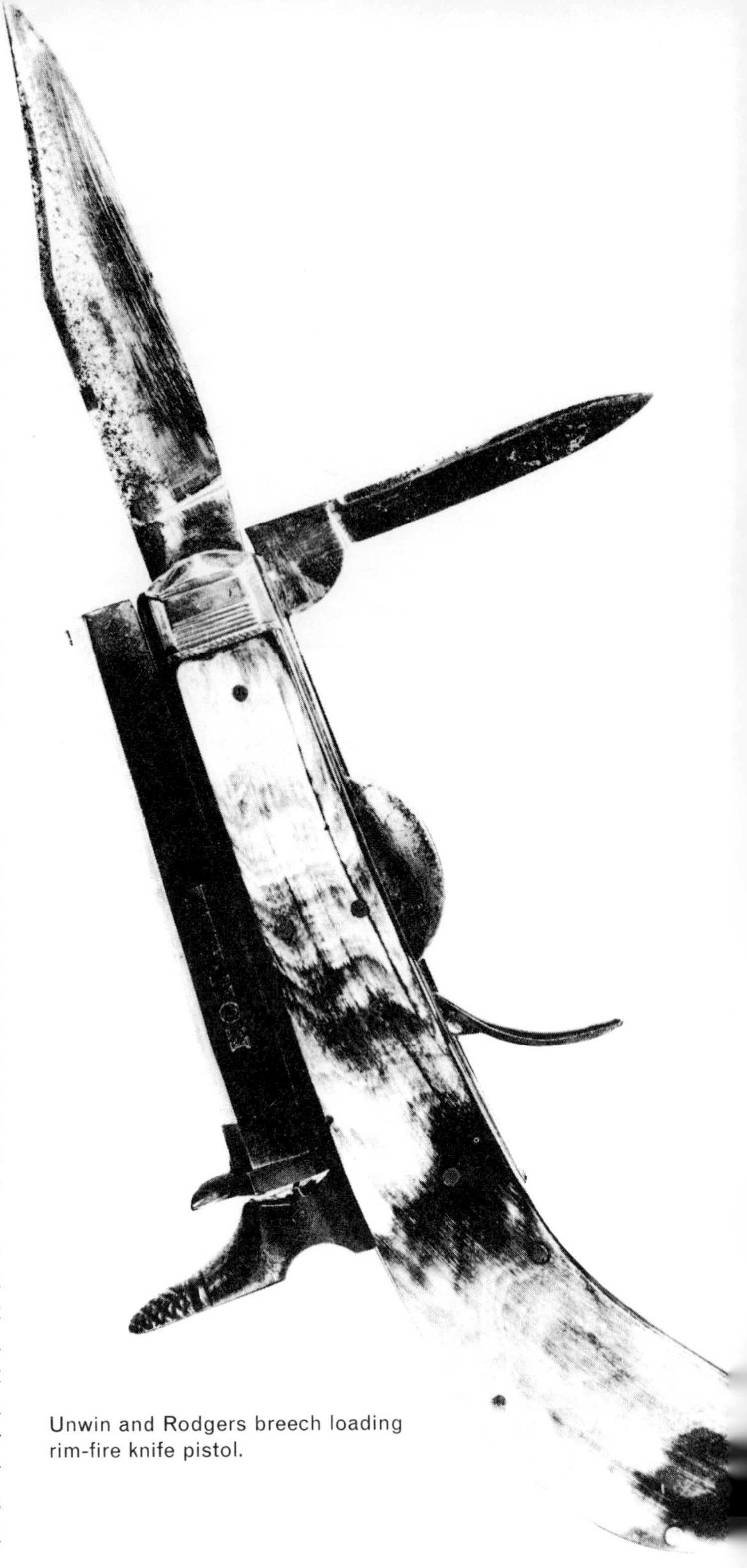

The process of development continued after production had commenced and, if we disregard both the special models manufactured to a customer's specific requirements and factory prototypes, two models can be identified. The first of these was the Model 1901 made in both .455 and .38 calibres. Early versions had a large

Unwin and Rodgers breech loading rim-fire knife pistol.

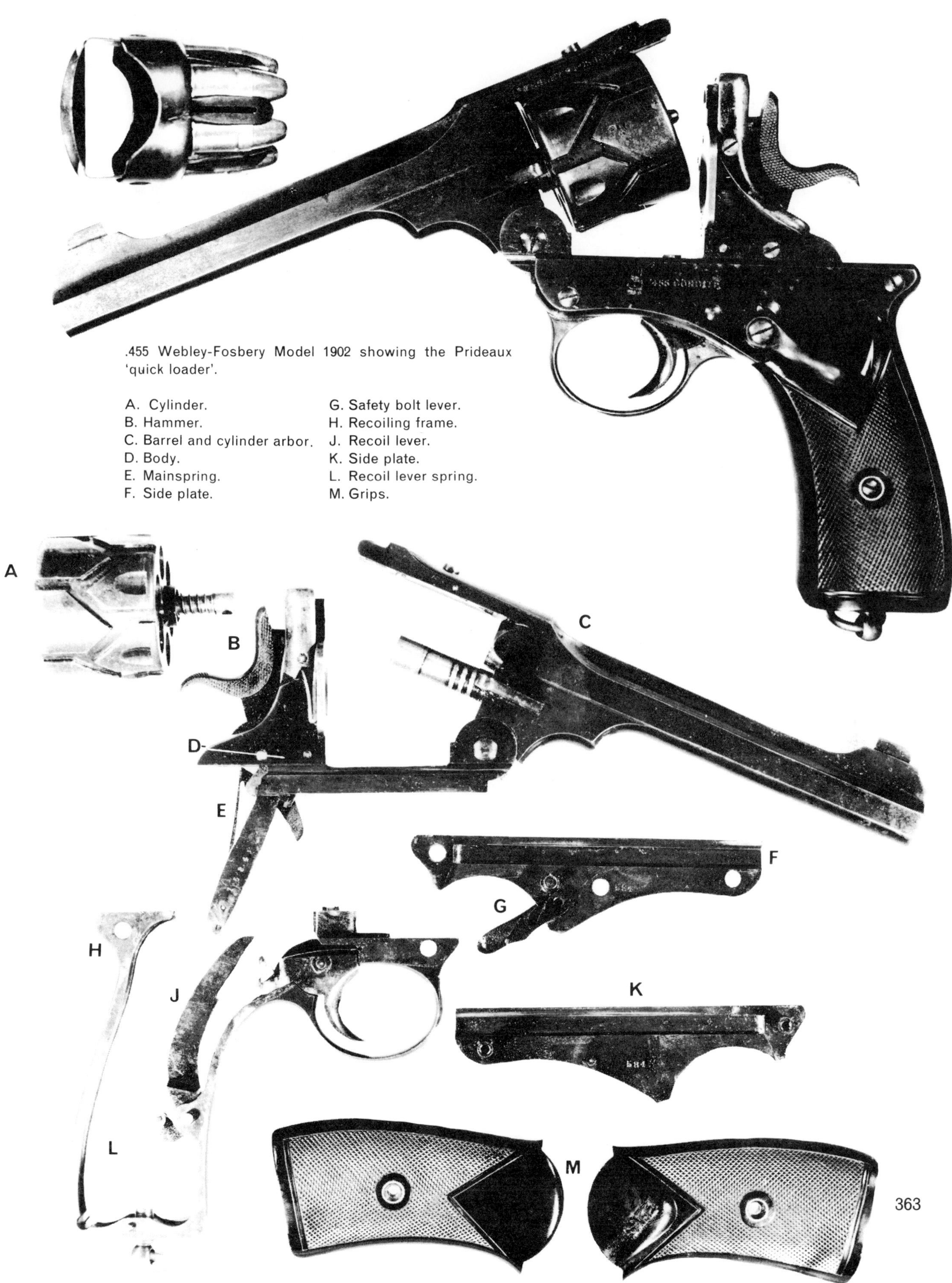

.455 Webley-Fosbery Model 1902 showing the Prideaux 'quick loader'.

A. Cylinder.
B. Hammer.
C. Barrel and cylinder arbor.
D. Body.
E. Mainspring.
F. Side plate.
G. Safety bolt lever.
H. Recoiling frame.
J. Recoil lever.
K. Side plate.
L. Recoil lever spring.
M. Grips.

hook shaped safety catch on the left hand side of the grip frame and the trigger guard assembly was separate from the grip frame. All the 1901 Models employed the standard Webley cylinder release and had wooden stocks.

The 1902 Models lacked the standard Webley cylinder retaining cam and, instead, the cylinder was retained by a spring catch, the button for which can be seen in the middle of the top strap. This device was part of the cylinder positioning catch. It will be appreciated that, since the cylinder rotating was affected by the actuating stud fitted into the middle of the grip frame (immediately above the trigger), it was important to position the cylinder correctly so that this stud entered a groove in it; otherwise the pistol could not be closed. The cylinder positioning catch performed this function and only when the pistol was closed would an indent in the standing breech lift the stud out of engagement and permit the cylinder to rotate clockwise. When the cylinder was correctly locked, the cylinder release catch entered a small depression in the front and, when the pistol was opened to eject the fired cases, it retained the cylinder in position. If it was necessary to remove the cylinder for cleaning, the button on the top of the barrel extension was depressed and the cylinder could then be drawn to the rear and removed. Replacement was simple; the cylinder had merely to be put on the cylinder arbor and pushed home. If the pistol was loaded and had to be opened without extracting the cartridges, the extractor lever at the knuckle was pushed upwards so that it was disengaged when the pistol was opened.

With the 1902 Model the recoiling frame carried the trigger mainspring on an extension, while an extension on the trigger engaged a stud on the left hand side plate so that the trigger was cocked when the recoil frame moved rearward. Immediately below the stud was the safety catch. The hook on the inside limb of the catch bolted the frames together by engaging a stud on the mainspring extension, against which the shorter limb of the mainspring rested. The rear of the internal limb of the safety catch locked into the recoil lever which, together with the trigger and actuating stud, was mounted on the grip frame. Stripping the pistol was simple. After the grip plates had been removed the side plates could be taken off, left hand side first, and the grip frame could be eased away from the recoil frame. Further stripping was not usually necessary. To reassemble, the grip frame was mated to the body or upper frame and the recoil lever pulled slightly to the rear so that the tip rested behind the end of the upper frame. If the back strap was sprung slightly so that the pins lined up, the right hand side plate could then be replaced, followed by the left, care being taken to locate the safety catch properly. The front and rear side plate screws were then tightened and the grip plates put back.

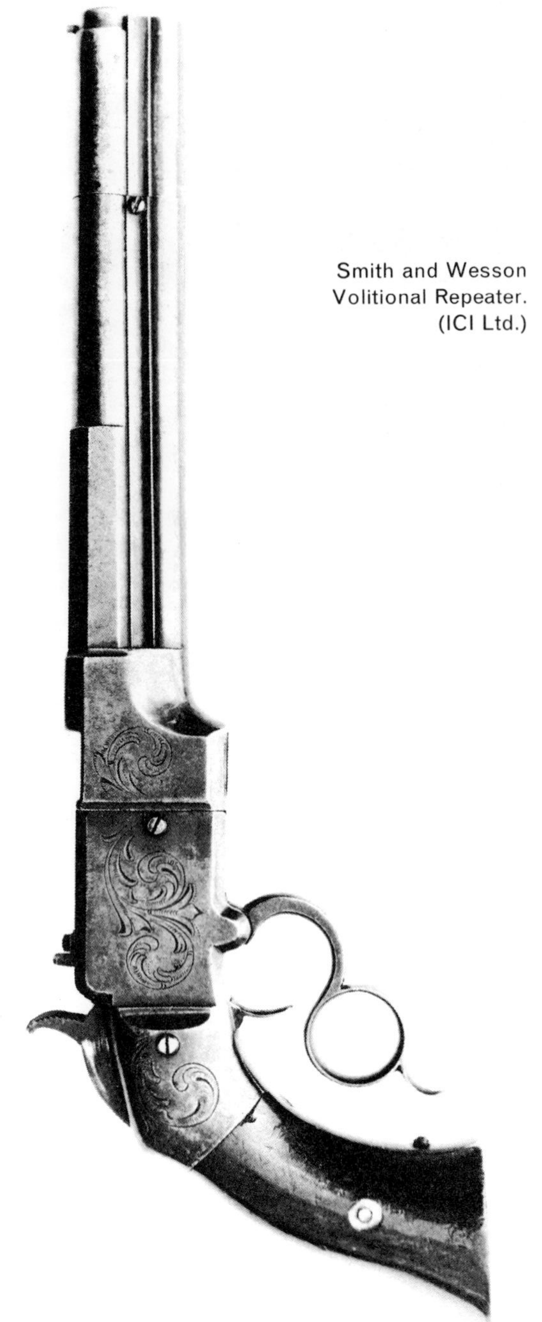

Smith and Wesson Volitional Repeater. (ICI Ltd.)

A special reloading device for the Webley-Fosbery was invented by W. J. Whiting, Webley's works manager, especially for the eight chambered .38 version. The most successful of the reloaders, however, was Prideaux's Patent Instan-

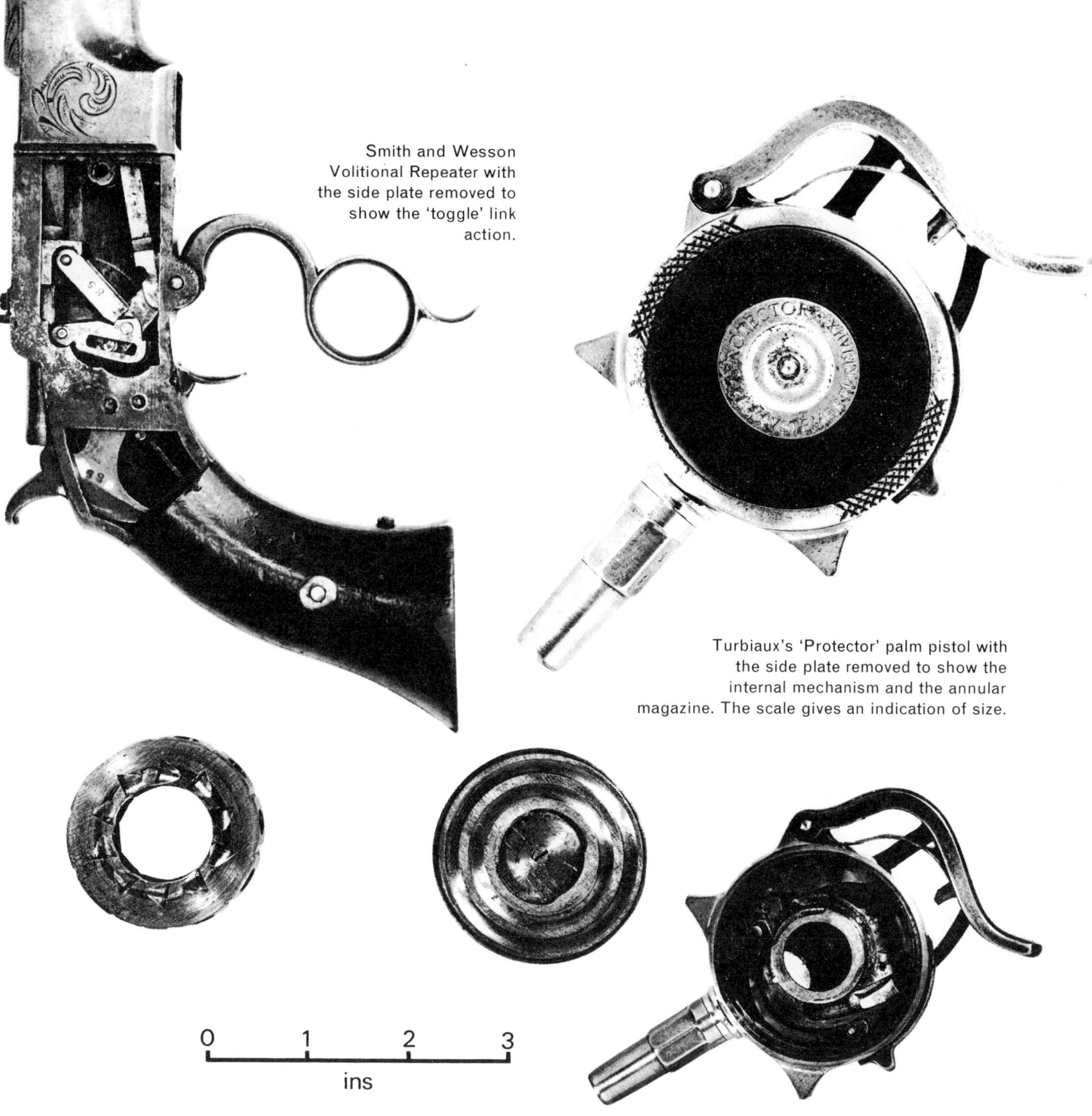

Smith and Wesson Volitional Repeater with the side plate removed to show the 'toggle' link action.

Turbiaux's 'Protector' palm pistol with the side plate removed to show the internal mechanism and the annular magazine. The scale gives an indication of size.

taneous Revolver Magazine patented in 1914. Provided a supply of loaded magazines was carried, reloading could be performed in one operation.

The Webley-Fosbery was entirely successful. In a target version it gained honours at Bisley and it was also highly regarded as an officer's side arm. The recoil of the top part of the pistol is scarcely noticeable and it is a pleasant pistol to shoot.

The only 'automatic' revolvers of a similar type were those made by the Union Arms Co., Toledo, Ohio, and also the .22 Zulaicai. Few, however, were manufactured and still fewer survive. The true forerunners of the present day self-loading or automatic pistol were the magazine pistols. If this term is used loosely, we could also include the flintlock Lorenzoni and Kalthoff systems, but percussion ignition and manufacture to close tolerances were, as we have seen, necessary before any magazine system could achieve commercial success.

One successful magazine pistol was the Hunt 'Volitional Repeater' as improved by Smith and Wesson, its only drawback being the limitations of its ammunition. This pistol later developed into the Winchester rifle, and it was not by chance that the first practical automatic weapon, the Maxim machine gun, was preceded by Maxim's patent modification of the Winchester which permitted recoil operation.

Many of the small magazine pistols, such as the 'Gaulois' and the watch-like 'Protector' palm pistols, were held in one hand and operated by the act of squeezing or compressing the pistol in the fist. Such personal defence weapons were popular during the 1880's, and the successful Protector series, invented by Jacques Edmond Turbiaux, was patented in Britain in 1882. European examples were marked 'Le Protector, Système E. Turbiaux' and also bore the legend 'Bte. S.S.D.G. en France et à l'Etranger, Paris'. The annular magazine, access to which was gained by removing the circular side plate, held ten centre-fire cartridges, and the construction of the pistol can be seen from the illustration which shows it partially dismantled. With the pistol held in the palm of the hand and the barrel protruding between the first and second fingers, squeezing the hand depressed the external lever, and this rotated the magazine, cocked the hammer, bolted the magazine, and then released the hammer to fire the cartridge. A safety catch or slide was provided which blocked the entry of the magazine bolt and so prevented the pistol from being fired.

In America the Protector was manufactured by the Ames Sword Co. of Chicopee, Massachusetts, and was sold by the Chicago Fire Arms Co. Several variants of the American made pistol can be encountered which are slightly larger than the European models. These are chambered for the .32 extra short rim-fire cartridge, and are seven shot instead of ten. The Protector was a well made and rather ingenious firearm.

Although the Protector was the best known of all the 'radial' revolver designs, a further example was that known on the Continent as the 'Rotovolver' which was patented by William Clark on behalf of Amédée Noël and François Guery of France in 1865 (British Patent No. 659). This was a self-cocking radial revolver with a folding trigger but, although it was compact and reliable in use, there is no evidence to show that it was manufactured outside France. Examples encountered were percussion weapons of approximately .30 calibre with a ten shot radial cylinder mounted on a horizontal axis, most of them bearing the legend 'A. Noël, Brevete'. Somewhat similar pistols having the radial cylinder mounted on a vertical axis were manufactured in America under patents obtained by John Webster Cochrane.

It was also during this period that further

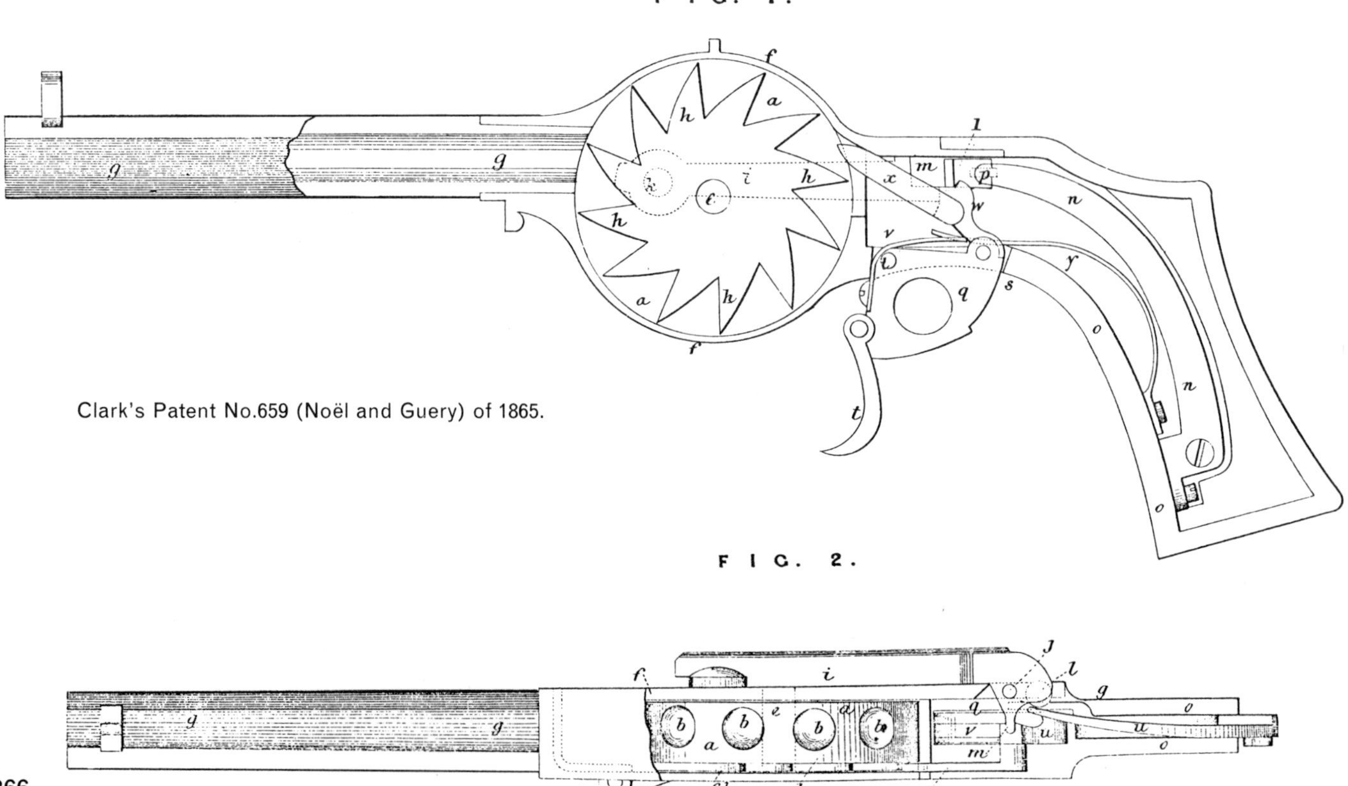

Clark's Patent No.659 (Noël and Guery) of 1865.

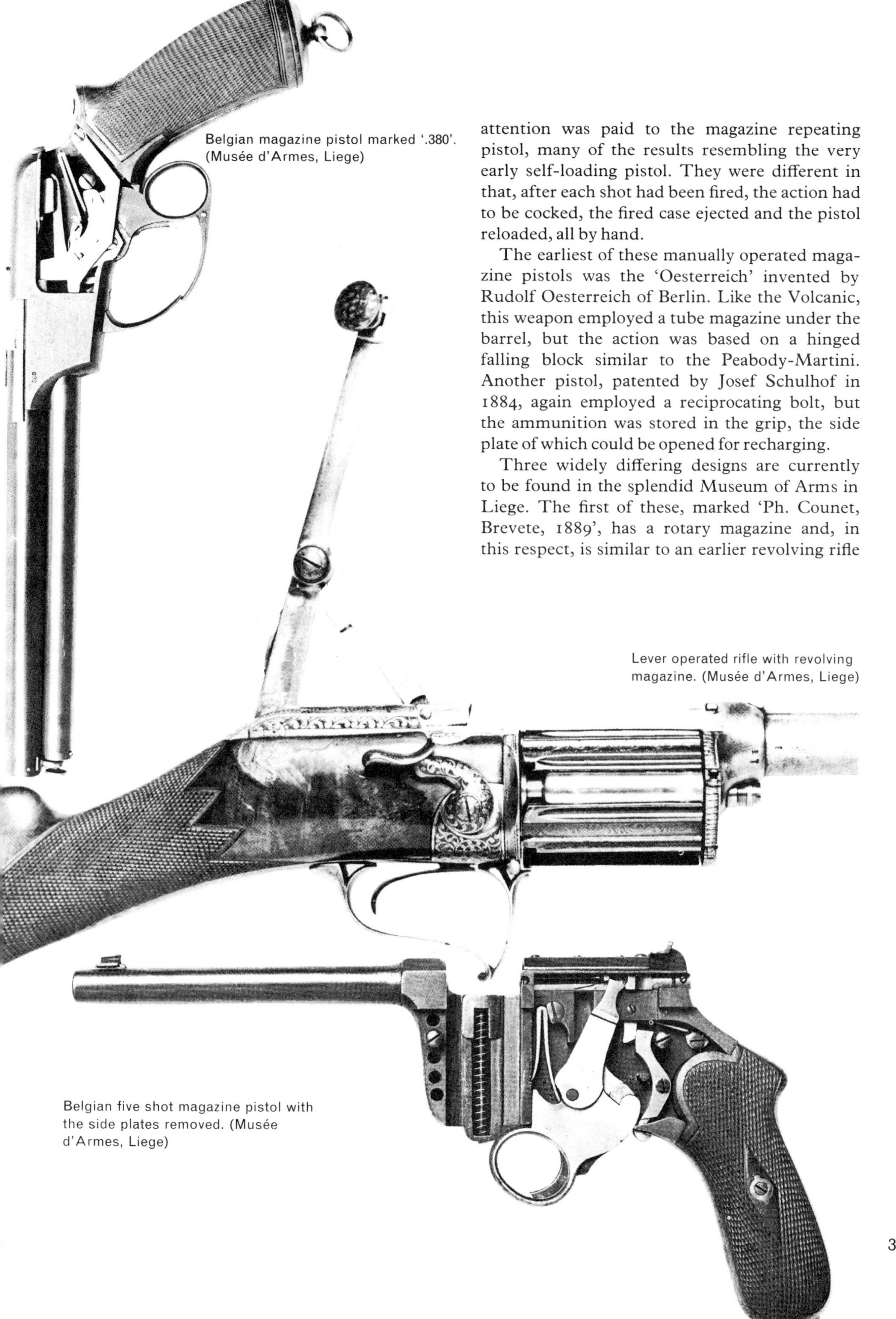

Belgian magazine pistol marked '.380'. (Musée d'Armes, Liege)

attention was paid to the magazine repeating pistol, many of the results resembling the very early self-loading pistol. They were different in that, after each shot had been fired, the action had to be cocked, the fired case ejected and the pistol reloaded, all by hand.

The earliest of these manually operated magazine pistols was the 'Oesterreich' invented by Rudolf Oesterreich of Berlin. Like the Volcanic, this weapon employed a tube magazine under the barrel, but the action was based on a hinged falling block similar to the Peabody-Martini. Another pistol, patented by Josef Schulhof in 1884, again employed a reciprocating bolt, but the ammunition was stored in the grip, the side plate of which could be opened for recharging.

Three widely differing designs are currently to be found in the splendid Museum of Arms in Liege. The first of these, marked 'Ph. Counet, Brevete, 1889', has a rotary magazine and, in this respect, is similar to an earlier revolving rifle

Lever operated rifle with revolving magazine. (Musée d'Armes, Liege)

Belgian five shot magazine pistol with the side plates removed. (Musée d'Armes, Liege)

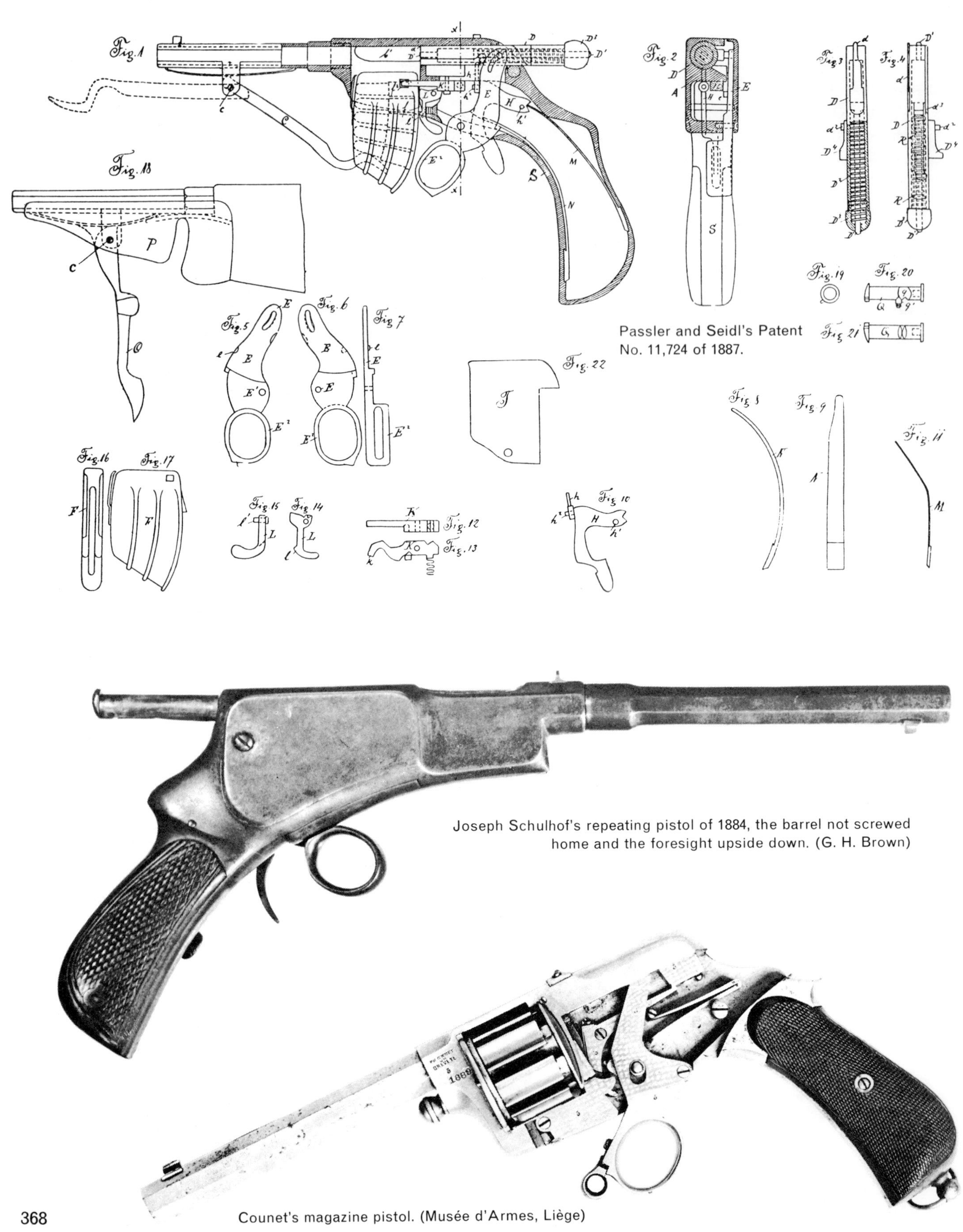

Passler and Seidl's Patent No. 11,724 of 1887.

Joseph Schulhof's repeating pistol of 1884, the barrel not screwed home and the foresight upside down. (G. H. Brown)

Counet's magazine pistol. (Musée d'Armes, Liège)

also in the Museum. The second magazine pistol, marked '.380', is operated by a ring finger lever, and the cartridges are stored in a tubular magazine under the barrel. This pistol is also attributed to Counet. The third pistol in this intriguing series, shown with the side plate removed, is operated by a combined trigger and finger lever and has a vertical magazine in the action body.

Fortunately, rather more is known about the activities of Karel (Carl) Krnka. The first of the many designs that originated in his fertile brain was also a lever operated magazine pistol patented in 1892. This was similar to the earlier Passler and Seidl magazine pistol except that the magazine was a rotary one. Karel Krnka, born in 1858, was the son of Sylvester Krnka, a gunmaker of Volyne in Bohemia, and served as an Infantry Officer with the Austrian Army. A military rifle he designed was rejected in favour of the Steyr-Mannlicher, and Krnka left the Army to stay in Britain where he worked for the Gatling Arms and Ammunition Co. in Birmingham. Following the failure of this company, he returned to Prague. In 1898 he joined George Roth, the famous Austrian ammunition manufacturers in Vienna, and his later patents were assigned to this company. During the formative years, Krnka was almost entirely preoccupied with automatic weapons, and several of his designs will be described where appropriate. He died in Prague in 1926.

It was in 1886 that the famous Paul Mauser took out his patents on repeating magazine pistols and carbines with tube magazines under the barrel, but relatively little is known about all these early magazine pistols and their study has been rather neglected. The Passler and Seidl, the Krnka and the later Bittner all exhibited a strong family resemblance, and their general design features can be seen from the patent drawing that accompanied British Patent No. 11,724 of 1887 granted to Franz Passler of Vienna and Ferdinand Seidl of Budweiss (Czech: Budejovice).

The most successful of these early transitional weapons was the Bittner. Manufactured by Gustav Bittner in 1893, it was again very similar to the Passler and Seidl and retained the vertical box type magazine in front of the trigger operating lever. Bittner's factory was in Vejprty in northern Bohemia, an area famous for metal working in the same way that Carlsbad (Karlovy Vary) had been renowned for fine gunmaking during the eighteenth century. A Proof House established at Vejprty in 1891, was one of five in the Austro-

7.7mm Bittner repeating pistol of 1893, the cartridges fed by the ring lever from a box magazine in the fore-end. (G. H. Brown)

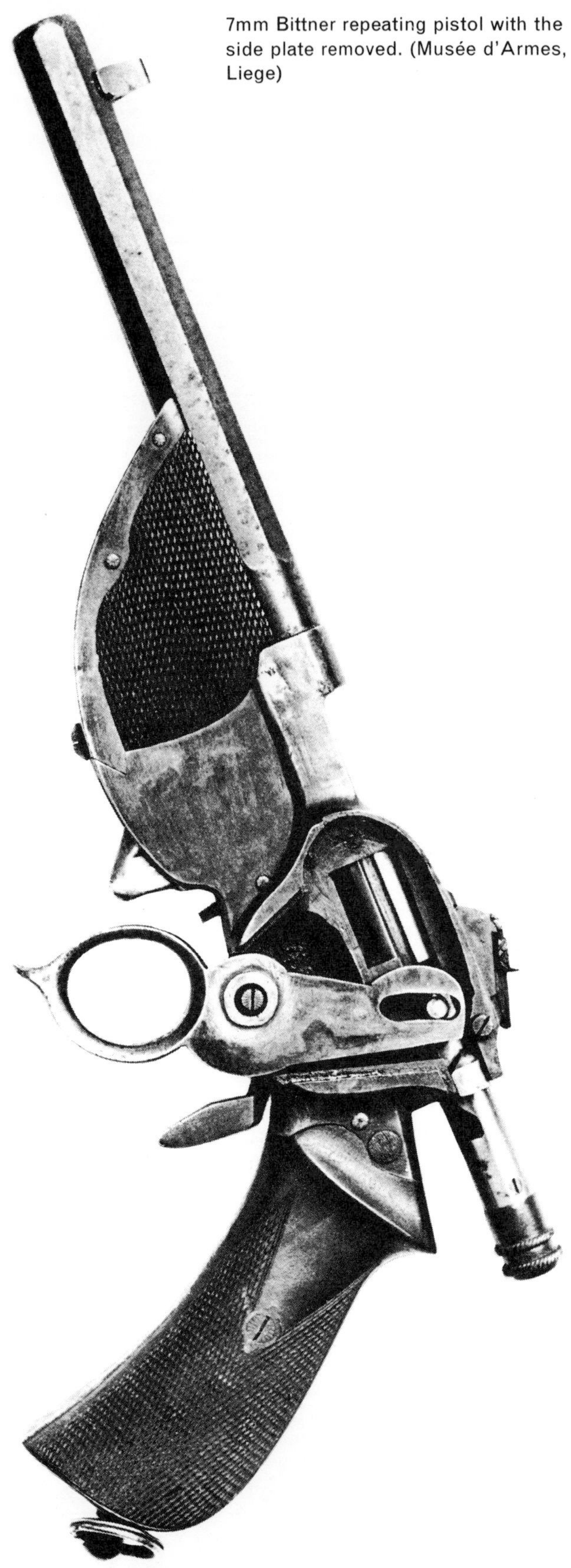

7mm Bittner repeating pistol with the side plate removed. (Musée d'Armes, Liege)

Hungarian Empire and continued in use until World War Two when facilities were transferred to Brno.

The industrialisation of the Habsburg Empire under the Emperor Franz Joseph was swift, painless and remarkably successful. In Vienna, the Kaiserstadt, the Imperial city, Joseph Laumann, gunmaker, was also working on a magazine repeating pistol which was later to become the Schonberger, the first practical self-loading pistol (see page 381) Although it was not a commercial success, this pistol did demonstrate the practicability of the recoil system and so influenced the design of the later European self-loading pistols.

Ideas alone, however, were not enough. To ensure both military and commercial success, manufacture by mass production techniques had to be possible, and the machine tools needed to create complicated shapes had to be available. As we shall see in the next chapter, many of the great European gun designers had to go to America for their machine tools; without them, the entire exercise would have been abortive.

Last, but by no means least, it was essential to have ammunition of consistently high quality manufactured to close dimensional tolerances and close metallurgical specification. If the self-loading pistol was not to be rapidly clogged and rendered inoperative by powder residue, an alternative to black powder had to be found. Fortunately, all these requirements were eventually met. Progress in one sphere influenced and promoted activity in another.

As far back as 1779, the great Swedish chemist Scheele had discovered glycerine or glycerol. By the beginning of the nineteenth century, organic chemistry was beginning to emerge as a definite branch of science, and a knowledge of such chemistry was essential before attempts could be made to prepare, manufacture and use an organic explosive. In 1846 the Italian chemist Sobrero prepared nitro-glycerine; in 1863 Alfred Nobel investigated the use of 'Nobel's blasting oil' as an industrial explosive. The manufacture, transport and use of nitro-glycerine were, however, attended by so many appalling accidents that many countries prohibited its use. Nobel set about trying to 'modify' his exuberant servant and found an excellent absorbent in a rather odd infusorial earth, known as kieselguhr or diatomite, which was able to absorb three or four times its weight of nitro-glycerine. Nobel named the mixture dynamite. Further work showed that, in addition to the original which employed an inert base, kieselguhr dynamites could be prepared with a combustible base such as charcoal or wood. This, in turn, led to the most important and varied group of dynamites, those with an explosive base.

At this point, however, we must retrace our steps somewhat and follow a parallel line of investigation which can be said to have started with the work of Pelouze who, in 1838, obtained a highly inflammable material by treating cotton with strong nitric acid. This gave rise to a whole new family of materials, the nitro-celluloses. Schönbein continued the work and, by nitrating cotton with a mixture of sulphuric and nitric acids, produced what was later to be known as guncotton. Based on nitro-cellulose, the first practical propellant was made by treating it with a mixture of alcohol and ether. This was the 'smokeless powder' known as 'Poudre B' (after the French General, Boulanger) and invented by Vielle. It was left to Alfred Nobel to show that both lines of research could be combined and that the properties of nitrated cotton could be modified by gelatinising the fibrous material with nitro-glycerine. Unlike black powder, nitro-glycerine and nitro-cellulose are chemical compounds, not simple mixtures.

The modern family of smokeless or nitro-powders fall into two groups, the first based on nitro-cellulose and mineral nitrates, the second containing both nitro-cellulose and nitro-glycerine in varying proportions.

Both black and smokeless gunpowders are known as 'progressive' explosives or propellants. Instead of exploding violently like high explosives, these propellants burn at a rate that can, within limits, be controlled by the manufacturer. They also burn only on their exposed surfaces, thus providing a means of controlling the speed of burning and, consequently, the pressure developed when used in a firearm. For this reason, modern propellants are made in a wide variety of grain sizes and shapes. The small pieces of explosive or powder grains can be cylindrical, with one or more holes or perforations running through the grain from end to end; they can be in cords or ribbons, or in thin, flat flakes; they can be diamond shaped or square, hexagonal or annular, or even—as in ball powder—roughly spherical.

Alterations can be made in the density by varying the proportion of nitro-glycerine used (or by eliminating it entirely), by incorporating chemical additives to modify the rate of burning, or by coating or 'glazing' the grains with ingredients which will again alter the rate of burning.

Powders based on nitro-cellulose alone are known as 'single base' powders, those based on both nitro-cellulose and nitro-glycerine as 'double base'. In the days of black powder, the charges were measured out by volume, and early smokeless powders were so made that an equal volume of smokeless powder would do the same amount of work as that of black powder. In other words, the space occupied in the cartridge case was the same for both. Smokeless powders, however, weighed less and, with the development of harder and denser grains, the principle of equal volume no longer applied.

Today, powders can be divided into three groups depending on their use: pistol, rifle and shotgun. Since a pistol barrel is short, and since, ideally, the powder should be entirely consumed at the precise instant the bullet leaves the muzzle of the pistol, smokeless pistol powders are relatively fast burning. This ensures that none of the energy generated by the burning powder is wasted and that unburned powder is not left in the barrel.

To recapitulate, gunpowder is a generic term for a propellant often abbreviated to 'powder'. Black powder is a mixture of charcoal, sulphur and potassium nitrate. The charcoal and sulphur burn with the aid of the oxygen in the potassium nitrate (KNO_3), and it is the solid residue of potassium salts that produces the smoke and fouls the gun. Smokeless powders consist of materials whose products are entirely gaseous—carbon dioxide, water vapour and nitrogen. They are divided into two groups, the single base nitro-cellulose powders and the double base, nitro-cellulose-nitro-glycerine powders. Their performance can be modified by changes in physical shape or chemical composition and by additives or coatings.

The number of smokeless powders available today is enormous; many are identified by an apparently meaningless number, and some can be recognised by their appearance. Many military and commercial powders are never seen in bulk by the ordinary individual unless he takes the trouble to remove the bullet from a loaded cartridge to see what is inside. Most of the firms who manufacture small arms propellants produce a special range of powders for handloaders. These are carefully regulated to agree with published data on their performances, so that we know that 2.7 grains of Hercules Bullseye (an American dense double based pistol powder) will give an accurate low velocity target load behind a 148 grain wadcutter bullet, and that 2.8 grains of Nobel Pistol Powder No. 3 (a British porous disc-shaped double based powder) will give about the same velocity behind a 158 grain bullet. For the factory this is a needless elaboration, since facilities exist to check each batch of powder and the charge (rather than the powder itself) is slightly altered to produce the standard ballistics for a particular cartridge.

A revolver will handle reasonable variations in powder charge and bullet weight without difficulty, but where, in addition to propelling the bullet, the propellant has also to operate the action, a greater degree of regularity is called for. Variation in performance may result in the cartridge not being properly ejected, in the pistol not being re-cocked or in failure to reload.

Auto-loading pistols introduced new shapes of cartridge case. The Bergmann, for example, lacked both a rim and a groove, and the seating or chambering was on the walls of the case. The .38 Colt auto cartridge is known as a semi-rim and, like the revolver, it seats on the rim in the same way as the .22 rim-fire. Cartridges like the 9mm Parabellum and the .45 ACP seat on the mouth of the case, while the 7.63mm Mauser, with a bottle-necked case, seats on the shoulder. As was explained in Chapter Eight, not only have all dimensions to be held within close tolerances, but the metallurgical properties of the brass have also to be closely controlled. If the brass is too soft the case tends to cling to the walls of the chamber, and extraction difficulties can also result in that the rim may be torn by the extractor. If, on the other hand, the brass is too hard, the case will split or crack and high pressure gas could leak into the action with unpleasant results.

These were only a few of the problems that had to be overcome before a satisfactory cartridge could be developed for the auto- or self-loading pistol. When some thought is given to the rather brutal treatment received by ammunition fed through the action of a self-loading pistol, it is apparent that a soft lead bullet would be totally unsuitable; most auto-pistol ammunition is therefore metal jacketed. For various reasons, expanding bullets are often called for, and here, although the cladding is retained, the lead core is exposed at the nose. An envelope covers the base to prevent the core being extruded (and the cladding left behind) with possibly disastrous results when the next shot is fired.

It is also imperative that the bullet is tightly seated to prevent it being driven back into the case when fed into the chamber, and also to prevent 'bullet creep'—the tendency for a bullet to move forward out of its case due to inertia effects resulting from recoil. Bullets can be secured against such movement by crimping the mouth of the case into a cannelure, but this method can only be used if the case is either bottle-necked or semi-rimmed. Another method is to 'stab' the case into a cannelure in the bullet, or simply into the bullet jacket. When the cartridge seats on the mouth of the case, as with the .45 ACP, the case can be crimped behind the bullet to prevent it being driven back into the case and, if sufficient bearing can be provided by the use of a long bullet, accurate manufacturing techniques and careful assembly result in entirely satisfactory ammunition without recourse to any additional crimping aids.

Cartridges used in revolvers, in spite of their different names, are often interchangeable. Some, such as the .44 S & W Russian and the .44 S & W Special can be used instead of the .44 Remington Magnum. This is, however, an example of limited interchangeability since the reverse is not possible. All the following are completely interchangeable: .32 Winchester, Marlin and Colt, .32 Winchester and Marlin, .32 WCF, .32 Winchester, .32–20 Winchester.

As will become apparent, a large number of nominal 9mm auto-pistol cartridges were developed, many of which are not interchangeable, such as the 9mm Parabellum, 9mm short, 9mm long, 9mm Roth-Steyr and 9mm Bergmann. Due, on the other hand, to widespread adoption, one particular cartridge may have several synonyms, and this only adds to the confusion since all are naturally interchangeable. An example is the 9mm Browning short which is also known as the 9mm M.34, 9mm Corto, Kurz or short, .380 Colt Auto Pistol, .380 ACP, .380 Auto Hammerless, .380 Automatic Webley Pistol, 9mm Browning Corto, 9mm Pistole Patrone 400 (h) and DWM 540. More common is the practice of employing both metric and inch calibre designations, as with the .25 ACP, (6.35mm Browning), .32 ACP (7.65mm Browning), .30 Luger (7.65mm Parabellum), .30 Mauser (7.63mm Mauser) and 9mm Luger (9mm Parabellum)—the last an example of where the metric calibre has survived but the name has changed.

The same cartridge under many different names may be used in a wide range of auto-pistols. The 9 mm Browning (.380 Auto) has been adapted to pistols made by Astra, Browning (FN), Beretta, Bayard, CZ, Frommer, Colt, Hi-Standard, Remington, Savage, Star, Llama, Walther and many others.

Of even greater importance, some pistols will accept ammunition for which they were not designed. But merely because the cartridge will work through the action and will chamber does not always mean that it is desirable or even safe to fire it. The temptation to fire a newly acquired 'collector's' gun is strong, particularly in the young. A cartridge, perhaps unidentified, may be selected from a box of 'oddments', in it goes, and then comes the temptation, will it go off? Such experiments can be dangerous and may result in a ruined pistol or worse. To quote the extreme, the 9mm Parabellum *will* chamber in the 7.63mm Mauser and, since the Mauser Model 96 has a very strong action, it can also be *fired*. But the 9mm bullet has to be swaged down to 7.63mm and the stress is high.

Ignorance and foolishness can result in a number of dangerous combinations of cartridge and pistol; unless both can be correctly identified, not always an easy task, the unknown and possibly unsafe should never be meddled with.

Fortunately, attempts are being made at rationalisation, some through purely altruistic motives, others because of hard economic fact. The high power .357 Magnum, for example, was made intentionally too long to chamber in the .38 S & W Special chamber. There are, no doubt, revolvers originally intended for a nominal .38 cartridge which will accept and fire the Magnum, and the manufacturer can only do his reasonable best. Other cartridges have disappeared since it is no longer economical to manufacture the limited number for which there is a demand. Satisfactory pistols have had to be retired because the ammunition lacked customer appeal, because of inadequate power or availability, or because of some other real or imagined defect. On the other hand, indifferent design, bad handling, high cost, undue complexity or just plain bad luck may have resulted in the manufacture of a particular pistol being stopped, although the ammunition intended for it was entirely satisfactory and was subsequently adopted for pistols made by other manufacturers. Most industrialised countries are able to support the commercial manufacture of metallic ammunition, others do so for military or prestige purposes. Some manufacturers are still able to offer a most impressive range of handgun cartridges, others only a few of the popular types or those for which there is a special national demand. The history of many of these firms is as fascinating as that of many of the great arms manufacturers, with whom, of course, several amalgamations and mergers have taken place.

As the quality of the ammunition improved, so the self-loading pistol became more reliable and further efforts were made to simplify and cheapen manufacture and, at the same time, to eradicate faults in both design and construction. At this stage, a word or two should be said about the nomenclature of this new form of handgun.

The term 'self-loading' should really be applied only to those pistols which rely on recoil operation to extract and eject the fired case and to re-chamber a new one. This would include the Schonberger, the Mannlicher Models 94 and 96, and the later Roth-Steyr and Roth-Sauer, even though some have to be cocked by hand and others, such as the two Roth pistols, employ trigger action.

Today, however, the terms self-loading, semi-automatic and automatic pistol are, to all but the purist, synonymous, since all modern pistols are both self-loading and self-cocking. The term semi-automatic was in vogue for a short time to differentiate between the pistol that required a separate trigger pressure for each shot, and the full-automatic one that would operate for as long as the trigger was pressed and there was ammunition in the magazine. The tendency nowadays is to use the term auto-pistol to describe the semi-automatic, and the term full-automatic to describe the 'machine pistol', even though the latter can also cover certain types of sub-machine gun or machine carbine. In the following chapters, 'self-loading' will be used for the early automatic pistols and 'auto-pistol' or 'automatic pistol' for the later models. Many other new terms will also have to be adopted to differentiate between the various systems.

Following the combustion of the propellant, the energy or power available to operate the mechanism is manifest in a number of ways:

1. Gas pressure within the barrel.

2. Reaction to the forward acceleration of the bullet and the powder gases. (Newton's third law

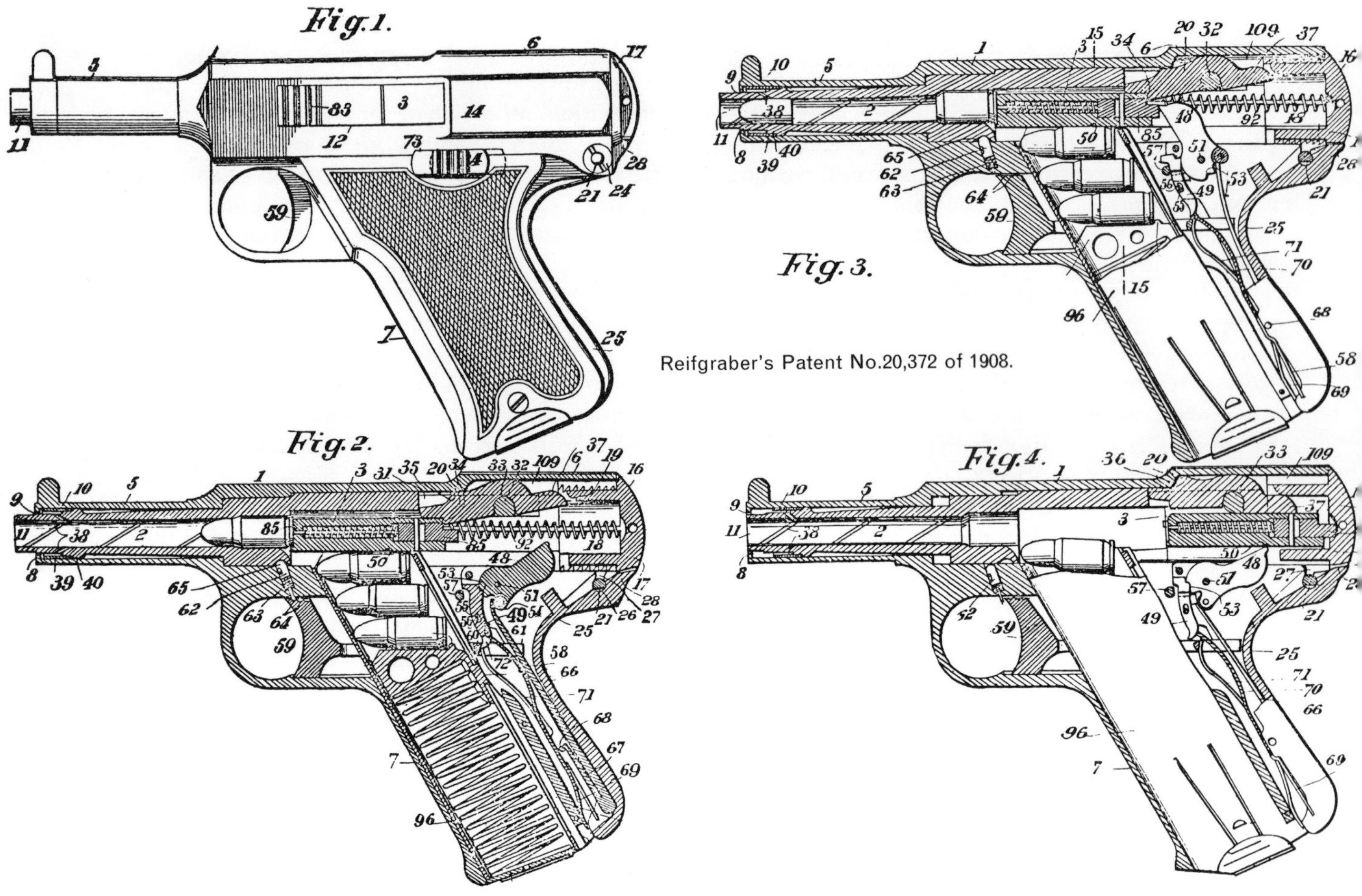

Reifgraber's Patent No.20,372 of 1908.

of motion: to every action there is always an equal and opposite reaction).

3. Heat resulting from the combustion of the propellant.

4. Noise caused by the expansion of the powder gases.

To the best of my knowledge, neither of the last two have ever been used to operate an automatic gun mechanism.

Gas pressure has been used very successfully for the operation of machine guns, rifles and, more recently, shotguns. Two pistols, the Clair, patented in 1892, and the McLean, patented in 1898, employed gas operation, but neither got beyond the experimental stage. One other pistol, the Reifgraber patented in 1908 (British Patent No. 20,372), employed a locked breech recoil action assisted by gas pressure, and the small ports in the barrel (marked 38) can be seen in the illustration. This technique was also used very successfully on machine guns, in particular the German MG 34 and MG 42.

All successful auto-pistols have employed recoil operation, and the various systems can be broadly classified as follows:

1. Locked breech actions in which the breech is mechanically locked to the barrel until the bullet has left it and the gas pressure has fallen low enough to permit the breech to be opened.

2. Semi-locked breech actions or delayed blow-back actions which employ a temporary delay lock.

3. Blow-back actions which rely on the projection of the spent case to the rear by the gas pressure in the barrel.

In its simplest form, the 'blow-back' system relies on a relatively heavy breech block and strong recoil spring to delay or retard the opening of the breech until the gas pressure has fallen to safe limits. A straight blow-back action could be built to handle the most powerful cartridges, but the weight of the recoiling parts would be excessive. Blow-back is particularly suitable for automatic pistols firing relatively low-powered cartridges, since the short barrel allows the gas pressure to fall quickly. Due to the type of

Remington Model 51 delayed blow-back automatic pistol.

cartridge commonly employed, the weight of the breech can be kept down, and the strength of the recoil spring need not be such as to result in difficulty in manually operating the action during loading or unloading.

There are exceptions to every attempt at classification and two pistols which could be described as 'blow-forward' types are the 1894 Mannlicher and the 1908 Schwarzlose. Here, instead of moving to the rear against the inertia of the breech and recoil spring, the case is retained against a fixed breech, and both bullet and barrel move forward.

Most pocket auto-pistols and .22 rim-fire pistols employ the straight blow-back system. It is also widely employed for machine carbines such as the Sten where the increased weight of the breech is acceptable.

Delayed blow-back systems have again been widely used for machine pistols, but the only major auto-pistols to use it were the Mannlicher Model 1900, which employed the frictional resistance of a cam against the breech slide, and the Remington Model 51 in which the breech bolt was separate and not part of the slide. When the cartridge was fired, the bolt recoiled at high speed and struck the slide which, under the impact, moved to the rear and lifted the breech bolt out of its locking recess in the frame. This type of delay blow-back is sometimes known as 'impinging action' or 'momentum block' action.

The locked breech system can be broken down into a number of different classifications, dependent on the type of lock employed and the method used for unlocking. All practical versions, with one exception, depend on a recoiling barrel. The exception, the primer 'set-back' system, relies on the rearward displacement of the primer forcing back the striker. This movement is utilised to unlock the mechanism. Special cartridges with deep primer pockets are used but, even so, there are practical difficulties. Manufacturing variations in the fit of the cap in the primer pocket are liable to cause erratic functioning, and caps can be ejected from the case entirely, so jamming the mechanism.

Classically, basic division is into long recoil and short recoil systems. The terms are often relative but the simple distinction is that, in long recoil systems, the barrel recoils locked to the breech for a greater distance than the length of the cartridge, while, in the short recoil systems, it recoils less than the length of the cartridge. In the long recoil system, extraction, ejection and cartridge feed must take place as the barrel moves forward from the full recoil position since, on the rearward movement, the barrel is locked to the breech. In short recoil systems, extraction and ejection can take place after the breech is unlocked but while the bolt or breech is still moving to the rear, the feed occurring as the breech moves forward and before it is locked to the barrel.

Ever since the practicability of recoil operation was demonstrated, the development of locking systems has exercised the ingenuity of a great many men. The following is a brief summary of the phases of this development; the individual systems will be covered in more detail later.

Predominantly of European origin, the rotary system of locking could, as in the case of the Steyr Model 1911, rely on rotation of the barrel. The locking effect was substantial, but there were other systems in which the locking was nominal and the result much the same as a delayed blowback. A rotating barrel was also the subject of one of Browning's designs in which the barrel rotated through less than five degrees before being unlocked (see page 434).

Instead of rotating the barrel, an alternative was to rotate the breech bolt, as with the short recoil Schwarzlose Model 1898 (see page 383). A different rotating breech bolt system was employed in the Mars (see page 411). In another variant, instead of the entire breech bolt, the head alone could be rotated in a manner similar to that employed by the 'straight-pull' bolt action rifles such as the Schmidt-Rubin and the various Ross designs. The Model 1901 Frommer was one example of this system (see page 405).

Wedges, blocks, lugs etc., for want of a better name or names, have all been employed for locking the breech instead of a rotary lock. The Mauser Model 1896 was a classic example of locking by means of a rocking lug and mating inclined surfaces (see page 392).

Yet another system was that developed initially by Maxim and employed to excellent effect on pistols by Borchardt and Luger (see page 485) and page 412). This system employed rollers or an inclined ramp to 'break' the toggle and unlock the breech but, although this type of lock was very strong, it required careful machining and first class materials. It was possibly for this reason that it was not extensively copied.

In the Bergmann Model 1897, the breech block was locked to the receiver body until it was laterally displaced, unlocked from the barrel and allowed to move rearward by itself.

Although, during the cycles discussed, the barrel moved, it was not displaced. In the Webley design, however, the barrel was displaced vertically by inclined grooves and, in the Browning, by parallel linkages. The Browning system as first employed used two linkages (British Patent No. 9871 of 1897, see page 434), the barrel moving both rearward and downward so that the locking grooves cut into the barrel and slide were disengaged (b5 and c8). This parallel linkage was later, in the Colt Model 1911, abandoned in favour of one rear link, and, in the Browning Model 1935 and the later Model 52 Smith and Wesson, the linkage system was finally discarded, inclined surfaces providing the necessary displacement.

In addition to locking systems, another field well tilled by the firearms inventor was that of trigger mechanisms. Automatic pistols may have an external hammer which can be cocked either by the recoil of the slide or breech or, if desired, manually. The hammer may be large and easily visible, as in the Mauser 1896 and Colt 1911, or vestigial, as in the Mauser Model HSc. Alternatively, the pistol may be of the enclosed hammer type, such as the Colt Pocket Model or Browning Model 1903 (see page 425).

The true 'hammerless' auto-pistol dispenses with the hammer, and the firing pin is released by a sear mechanism as in the FN Browning Model 1900 (see page 424) and many others.

The firing mechanism of any auto-pistol must incorporate a means whereby the trigger can be disconnected from the sear release of the firing pin, striker or hammer. Lack of such a device would result in repetitive firing or fully automatic operation. On pistols capable of full-automatic fire some means of neutralising the 'disconnector' is introduced, operated by the selective fire lever.

The majority of auto-pistols are, to use a revolver term, 'single action', whether they are striker fired or provided with an internal or an external hammer.

The firing mechanism is cocked whenever the slide is drawn to the rear. This can either be carried out manually when checking the pistol to see that the chamber is empty, or when the first cartridge is introduced into the magazine. The mechanism is also cocked when the pistol is fired, since the slide is driven to the rear to extract the fired case and to chamber a new cartridge.

Striker fired and internal hammer pistols may lack a cocking indicator and, consequently, there is no tactile or visible means of showing whether or not the mechanism is cocked. That one can see this at a glance is one advantage of the hammer auto-pistol.

Certain hammer auto-pistols have a further advantage: the pistol can be loaded, a cartridge introduced into the chamber and the cocked hammer let down on the firing pin. Admittedly this must be done with care and with the pistol pointing in a safe direction, and it is a procedure that can only be carried out on pistols which employ an inertia type firing pin—where the pin is shorter than the housing. To fire the pistol, all that is required is for the hammer to be drawn back by the thumb and the trigger pressed. Internal hammer and striker fired auto-pistols—if they are to be kept at instant readiness—have to be left cocked and with the safety applied.

More recently, 'double action' auto-pistols which provide for both thumb cocking and cocking by trigger action (Walther P-38, Mauser HSc) have become increasingly popular. Such pistols have the advantage of being as ready for use as a double action revolver.

The storage of ammunition in the auto-pistol is in a magazine, and immense ingenuity has been displayed in the design of magazine systems. Most of the ones that got beyond the experimental stage will be met as individual models and are discussed later.

In sharp distinction to the majority of revolvers, automatic pistols have been provided with a range of safety devices intended to eliminate human forgetfulness. In addition to the normal 'safety catch' which locks the firing mechanism and sometimes the slide or breech, auto-pistols have also been provided with butt safety devices intended to prevent the discharge of the pistol if it is not held correctly in the hand. One major source of accidental discharge and possible accident with the auto-pistol has always been the 'forgotten' cartridge in the breech. The uninitiated apply the safety catch, withdraw the magazine and pronounce the pistol 'safe'. Someone else picks it up, is assured that 'it is quite safe', releases the safety catch and pulls the trigger. The forgotten cartridge goes off and, at best, all concerned receive quite a fright. Safety devices were therefore introduced to prevent such occurrences. The first is an indicator to show that a cartridge is in the chamber. This, however, relies on the individual having some acquaintance with the weapon and recognising what the indicator is supposed to indicate. The second system is far superior. When the magazine is withdrawn, the pistol cannot be fired. The only disadvantage is that the pistol cannot, in an emergency, be used without the magazine as a single shot pistol.

The last of the common safety devices saves the user from presenting a pistol at his opponent in the mistaken belief that it is still loaded. Very useful for those who cannot count, a 'hold-open' device keeps the slide back when the last cartridge has been fired. In addition to preventing the 'I didn't know the pistol was empty' feeling, the 'hold-open' device also speeds up and simplifies changing magazines.

Unfortunately, there is no common requirement for safety devices. Some pistols are fitted with them all, others with only the simple and not always reliable safety catch. In spite of the impressive increase of interest in purely sporting and target shooting, most handguns are made with one purpose in mind: they are weapons of aggression. As such, certainty and reliability of operation are the prime desiderata. The addition of a number of mechanical devices designed to increase the safe handling of the automatic pistol can only be considered effective if the user is completely familiar with their function, a familiarity that must extend to an appreciation of their fallibility. Dependence on a defective safety device can all too easily create a greater hazard than the absence of that device.

Notes to Chapter Twelve

For further information on multi-barrelled cartridge loading pistols—for example the Sharps, Remington, Lancaster and Martin—reference should be made to Jack Dunlap's *American, British and Continental Pepperbox Firearms* (Los Altos, 1964). Some of the more bizarre inventions of this period are covered in *Firearms Curiosa* by Lewis Winant (London, 1956).

The Webley-Fosbery is dealt with in detail by W. C. Dowell in *The Webley Story* (Leeds, 1952) and information on the early magazine pistols will be found in the first volume of *Handfeuerwaffen* by J. Lugs (Berlin, 1962).

Early magazine and self-loading pistols are described in the *Textbook of Automatic Pistols* by R. K. Wilson (Plantersville, 1943).

Chapter Thirteen
The Automatic Pistol Perfected

The self-loading or automatic pistol as an abstract design is of European and predominantly Austrian origin. The practical application of the automatic principle, the utilisation of some of the energy of discharge to reload, recock and discharge the weapon is, however, undoubtedly due to an American, Maxim.

Apart from the noise, the main effect a person firing a gun is aware of is the recoil, and the first man to make use of the energy in this recoil was Hiram Stevens Maxim, the father of the first successful automatic system. Born in 1840 in Sangersville, Maine, of French Huguenot stock, Maxim's inventive mind turned first to the improvement of illuminating gas machines and, in New York City, he later formed the Maxim Gas Machine Company. When gas lighting was threatened by electricity, Maxim and his company turned to the manufacture of electric light bulbs and, shortly afterwards, Maxim himself joined the United States Lighting Company. Whilst in their employ he visited Europe and attended the Paris Exhibition of 1881, returned to America, and later visited London in order to re-organise a subsidiary, the Maxim-Weston Company.

During his visits to Europe, Maxim had been impressed by the interest shown in rapid fire weapons and, in 1883, he modified a Winchester Model 1866 rifle so that it would operate by recoil. A movable butt plate with a spring support was attached to the stock and connected by a series of levers to the finger lever of the rifle. When the rifle was fired, the recoil compressed the spring between the stock and butt plate and, at the same time, operated the levers which opened the action, ejected the fired case, and cocked the hammer. The compressed spring then took over the job of pushing the rifle forward against the butt plate, and the lever system closed the action on the chambered cartridge, leaving the rifle ready to fire again. As with many other inventors both before and since, Maxim adapted existing ideas and combined them in such a manner that the resulting mechanism was both practical and robust. The Winchester toggle link breech lock formed the basis of his later machine gun lock, and the general arrangement of the Maxim machine gun equally owed something to the earlier Gardner crank operated gun.

Maxim's first basic patent was obtained in 1884, and development work on his recoil operated machine gun was carried out in London at 57 Hatton Gardens. The first order for Maxim guns was received from the British Government in 1887, and these were made for him by Albert Vickers at Crayford, Kent.

Maxim subsequently obtained patent protection for very nearly every type of automatic operation and his machine gun, although 'improved' and altered to take various types of cartridge, remains, in its essentials, unaltered to the present day. Maxim also invented automatic rifles and automatic pistols; prototypes of several were made but none of them ever reached production. With the Maxim Model 1896 automatic pistol (of which there were several calibres), this is particularly a matter for regret since, in sharp distinction to its contemporaries, its design was of extreme simplicity. So few were, in fact, made that they are now exceedingly scarce.

Maxim's contribution was to demonstrate the feasibility of locked breech recoil operation as applied to machine guns and of recoil operation in its simplest form, straight blow-back, as applied to pistols. His reluctance to exploit his designs for self-loading pistols may perhaps be explained by his preoccupation with the task of promoting his machine gun. The appearance in Europe of the Model 1892 Schonberger was, however, the beginning of an intensive period of development and, although the automatic principle as applied to pistols was neglected in America, the American contribution to the actual manufacture of these European designs cannot be overestimated. As we saw in Chapter Four, America was the birthplace of the mass production technique, a technique peculiarly adapted to the needs of the gun manufacturer.

The Schonberger was made at Steyr, Upper Austria, where, in 1831, Joseph Werndl, the founder of the Austrian Arms Co., was born into a gunmaking family. Werndl, however, was ambitious and not content to stay in the family business. Instead, he worked both in Prague and in the State Armoury in Vienna, travelled to Germany and eventually went to America where he worked for both Colt and Remington. In 1853, having learned the techniques of mass production at the fountain-head, Werndl returned to Steyr, took over the family business, and bought additional premises on the banks of the three arms of the River Steyr where there was ample water power for the new machines.

The first contract was for the conversion of the Lorenz muzzle loading rifle to breechloading by the System Wanzel, and, in 1867, the Austrian Army ordered 100,000 Werndl breechloading rifles whose design was due partly to Werndl and partly to Karel Holub. Werndl's factory at Steyr grew rapidly, and breechloading conversions were carried out for many other European countries including Bavaria, France, Serbia and Greece.

At the request of the Hungarian Government, a branch factory was established at Pest to equip the Honvedtruppe (Hungarian Army). Even so, however, the main factories at Steyr continued to grow and, to finance further expansion and reorganisation, the business became a limited company, Osterreichische Waffenfabrik-Gesellschaft, with its head office in Vienna. Incorporated on 1 August 1869, the new company had a capital of six million gulden, and Werndl was appointed General Director. The next step was the buying up of the Vienna factory of F. Fruwirth together with that of Bentz in Freiland. Both factories were closed and plant and machinery were transferred to Steyr.

This new policy of concentration also led to the factory in Pest being shut down and to its equipment as well being moved to Steyr. It was a policy that paid off. Over and above the orders that continued to come in for the Werndl rifle (with improvements by Spitalski), the Prussian Minister of War ordered 500,000 Mauser Model 1871 rifles to the value of eight million gulden. At the time of this latter contract, Steyr employed over 5,500 people, had an output capacity of 8,000 rifles a week, and were exporting to Roumania, France, Persia, Montenegro, Chile and China. In 1878 the French placed an order for 10,000 magazine rifles and, following smaller initial orders, the Austrian Army placed one for 87,000. Every opportunity to extend machine manufacture and increase specialisation was eagerly seized and, by the 1880's, Steyr employed 10,000 workers on two twelve hour shifts and had an output capacity of 13,000 magazine rifles a week.

Werndl died in 1889, and it was shortly after his death that Steyr were licensed to manufacture the Schwarzlose machine gun which was to be adopted by the Austrian Army in 1908. Werndl left behind him a truly fantastic enterprise whose productive capacity was to be fully tested during the First World War when the payroll rose to 14,000 and output to over 4,000 guns a day. It was during the war that Steyr also made aero engines, an exercise that proved very valuable when, in the years immediately following, they started to manufacture motor cars. In 1934 came amalgamation with Austro-Daimler-Puch and the formation of Steyr-Daimler-Puch AG.

The German Anschluss of 1938 saw a further merger, this time with the Hermann Goering Group, but, at the end of World War Two, the factory was dismantled. Later, with American aid, it was restored, and Steyr-Daimler-Puch AG, after two world wars and the disastrous effects of occupation, are still in the business of making arms. Joseph Werndl would no doubt have been dismayed at the turn of events, but at the same time he would have been proud that the Steyr-Werke survived.

The name of this famous factory will frequently recur as we trace the development of the

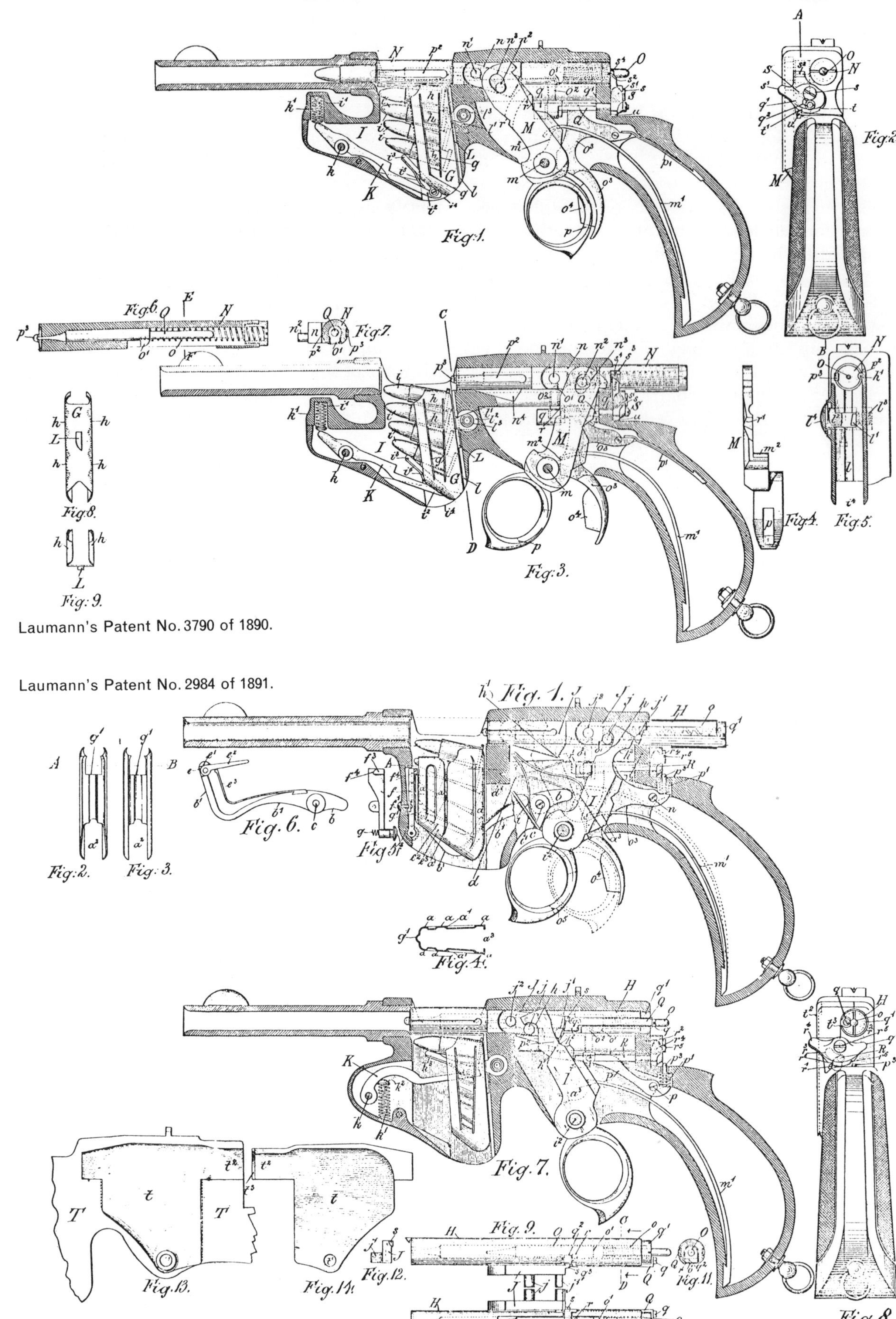

Laumann's Patent No. 3790 of 1890.

Laumann's Patent No. 2984 of 1891.

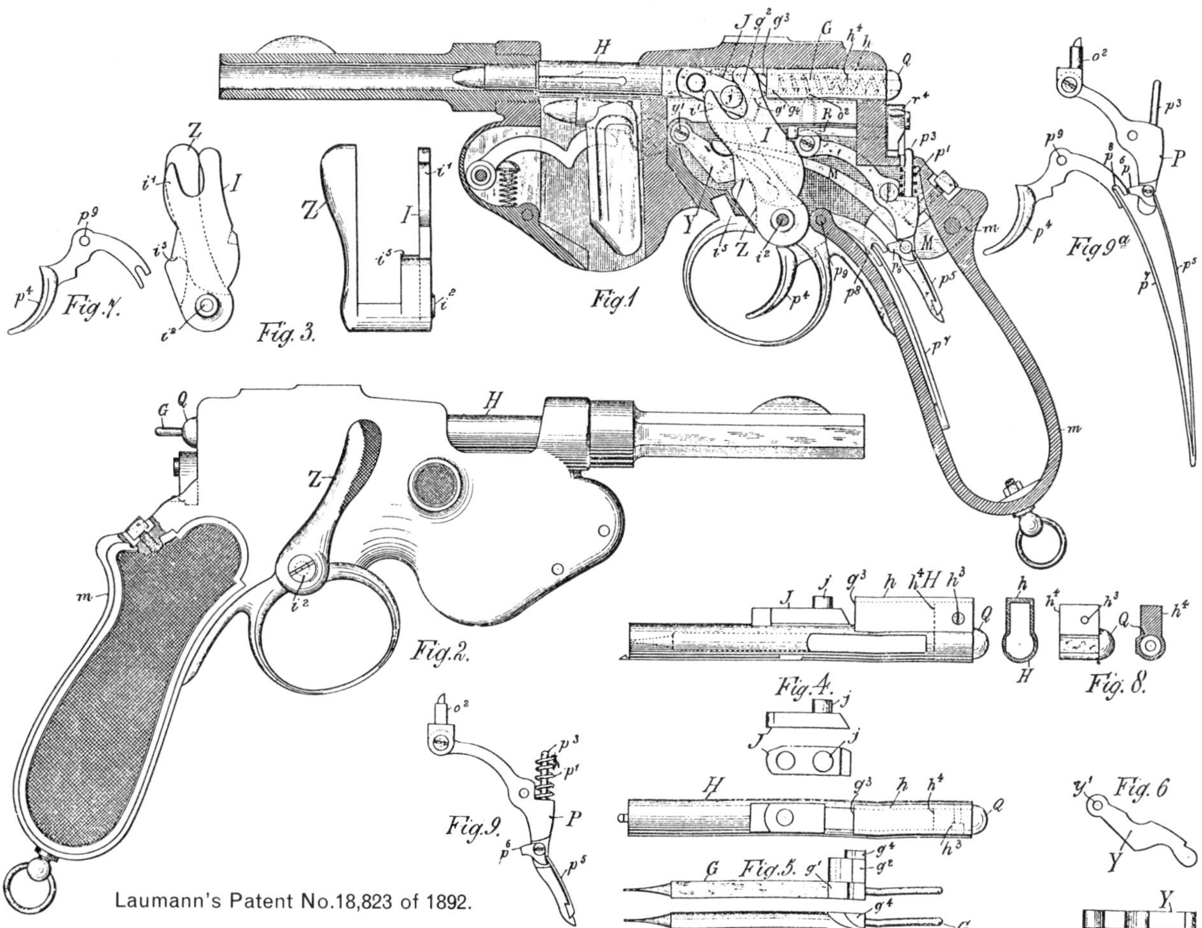

Laumann's Patent No.18,823 of 1892.

self-loading pistol. The Schonberger, for example, the first self-loading pistol to be manufactured as a commercial venture, was made there. Few examples have survived, but this pistol is of particular interest not only because it was a 'first', but also because of the unusual nature of its operation.

Although beautifully made, the Schonberger immediately betrays its ancestry by its appearance. The actual production pistol was not dissimilar to that illustrated in the patent drawing which accompanied Joseph Laumann's Specification No. 18,823 of 1892, and the transition from magazine pistol to self-loading pistol can be seen by comparing this with the drawings for Laumann's two earlier patents, No. 3790 of 1890 and No. 2984 of 1891. The Schonberger self-loading pistol based on Laumann's patents operated on the 'primer set-back' principle, a system subsequently used by Roth for both a pistol and a self-loading rifle. John C. Garand later designed a primer operated rifle which used a standard cartridge of conventional design. In the Schonberger the cartridge was provided with a special deep primer pocket to permit movement to the rear. When the cartridge was fired, the case itself, supported by the breech, could not move, but the primer was forced back by gas pressure and, in the Schonberger system, moved 0.18″ to the rear, sufficient to operate the mechanism which unlocked the bolt. Although heavy and ungainly, the Schonberger is pleasant to handle and is a pistol rather than a pistol masquerading as a carbine. The limitations of its ammunition were probably responsible for its early demise.

Andreas Wilhelm Schwarzlose is better known for his machine gun which, although originally made at Steyr, has seen widespread use throughout the world. Born in 1867 in Prussia, Schwarzlose experimented with a variety of designs for automatic weapons, the earliest of which was a pistol patented in Britain in 1892, Patent No. 23,881. As can be seen from the patent drawing (page 383), the rimmed cartridges were contained bullet downwards in a magazine under the barrel, and had to be swung round through 90 degrees to be chambered. This must have been a most interesting pistol to fire! Few of these exceedingly unusual weapons were made, but one has survived in the collection of the Musée D'Armes at Liege. Later, the surprisingly modern looking Model 1898 or Military Model appeared which was protected by British Patent No. 1934 of 1898. Recoil operated, it employed an unusual rotary locking bolt and was chambered for the 7.65mm Mauser cartridge. This model was produced in some quantity, but it is uncertain who was actually responsible for manufacture, and it was unsuccessful in that it was never officially adopted as a military pistol, the ultimate seal of approval. Today it is yet another rare but very desirable collector's item.

Regrettably there is no substitute for the actual handling of any pistol in order to learn as painlessly as possible how it works, but patent drawings do help considerably in understanding unusual and interesting mechanisms. The mechanism of the Schwarzlose Model 1898 comes into the short recoil, rotating bolt class and the various parts of the pistol can be recognised from the drawing. At Fig. 1, a live round has been chambered and the striker cocked. When the pistol was fired, both the barrel '*l*' and the bolt '*c*' recoiled together. As they moved to the rear, the bolt rotated, and the helical slot '*n*' which caused this rotation is shown in Fig. 2. The rotation unlocked the bolt lugs from the recesses machined into the barrel behind the chamber (Fig. 2 '*w*'). The separation of the bolt from the barrel allowed the barrel to move slightly forward under the influence of the return spring '*f l*' until forward movement was stopped by detent '*k*' (Fig. 6). Released from the barrel, the bolt continued to move rearward, opening the breech and extracting the fired case. After recoiling to the full extent of its travel, the bolt then moved forward under the influence of spring '*f*', picked up a fresh cartridge from the magazine and chambered it. At the same time, the bolt was locked to the barrel, the detent was released by the forward movement of the bolt, and bolt and barrel moved forward together ready for firing.

As with most of the self-loading 'dinosaurs', the Schwarzlose will work quite satisfactorily when kept clean and lubricated. A very well made pistol, it is a delight to handle, but the mechanism is too complex and there are far too many parts for it to function with any degree of reliability under anything but the most benign conditions.

The only other design to achieve series production was the equally interesting Schwarzlose Model 1908 Pocket Pistol (British Patent No. 10,222), one of the very few 'blow-forward' self-loading pistols. That Schwarzlose's main interest, however, was in machine guns is reflected in the machine gun trade mark impressed on the right hand side of the receiver. The Model 1908 was made in the Schwarzlose factory in Berlin and bears on the left hand side of the receiver the legend 'A. W. Schwarzlose G.m.b.H. Berlin'. It appears to have gained some measure of acceptance, but manufacture was discontinued in 1914, doubtless due to factory reorganisation caused by the outbreak of war.

The first self-loading pistol to gain any measure of commercial success was the Borchardt. Hugo Borchardt was born in Germany, but emigrated to America and took out American citizenship. Having worked for several firms on the Eastern seaboard, he joined the Winchester Company about 1870 and, by 1876, had developed several revolvers for them. One of these was a single action six chambered .44 calibre revolver with simultaneous ejection and a side-swinging cylinder which swung to the right instead of the left. Winchester submitted samples of the Borchardt revolvers to the US Navy and the Russian Ordnance Board, but no interest was shown and Borchardt's designs were never put into production. The possibility that Colt might go into the rifle market may also have influenced Winchester's decision to shelve the Borchardt revolver; it was certainly the reason why Winchester later shelved the equally promising revolver designed by William Mason in 1884. No doubt disheartened by this turn of events, Borchardt left Winchester and joined the Sharps Rifle Company who brought out the breechloading Sharps-Borchardt rifle in 1877. In the mid 1880's he returned to Germany and went to the firm of Ludwig Loewe and Co. of Berlin.

Ludwig Loewe, the founder of this firm, was born in 1837 and, like many of his contemporaries, went to America not to live but to learn. Returning to Berlin in 1870, he started the manufacture of sewing machines, but the new German Empire needed guns not sewing machines, and the manufacture of arms commenced in 1871 at the time of the Franco-Prussian War. Loewe died in Berlin in 1886, and his firm amalgamated with Pulverfabrik Rottweil-Hamburg and Vereinigte Rheinisch-Westfälische Pulverfabriken to form a new company, Deutsche Metallpatronenfabrik in Karlsruhe.

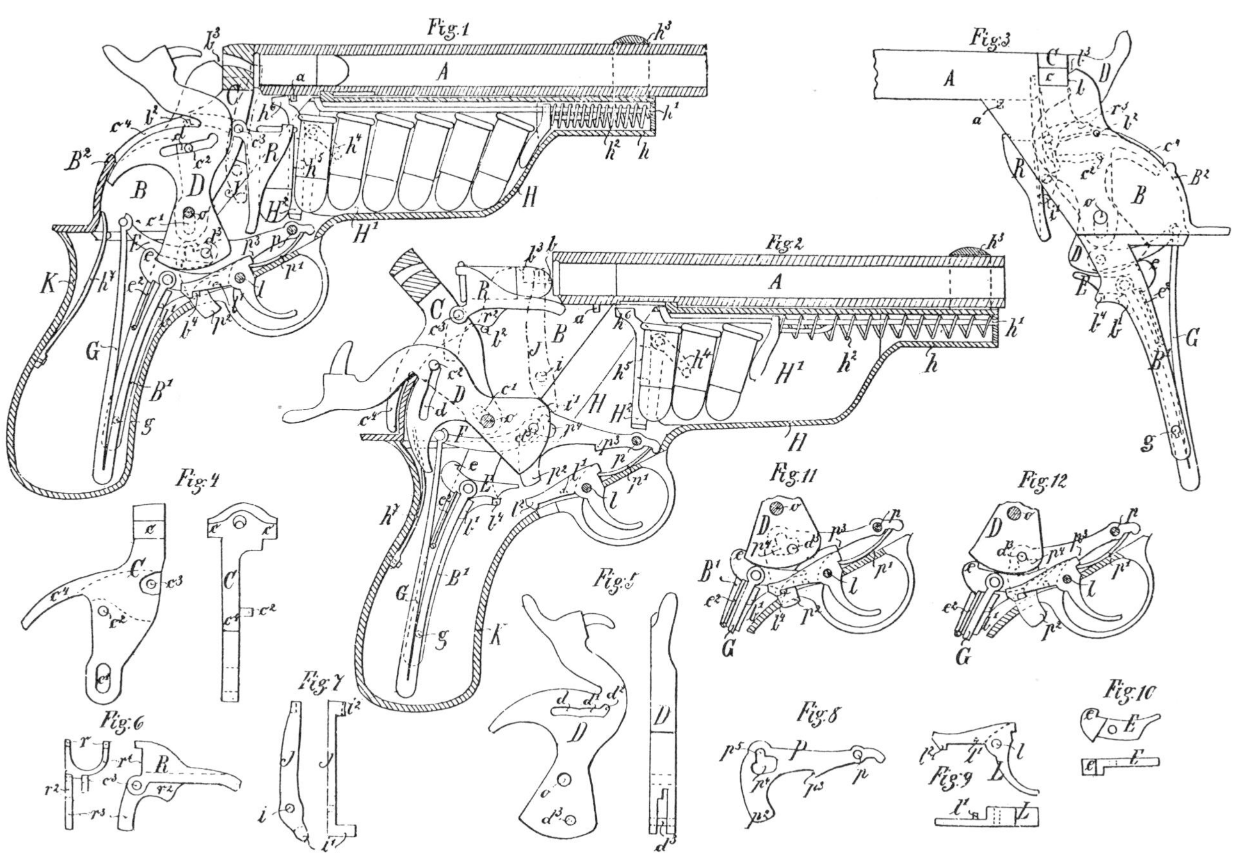

Schwarzlose's Patent No.23,881 of 1892.

Schwarzlose's Patent No.1934 of 1898.

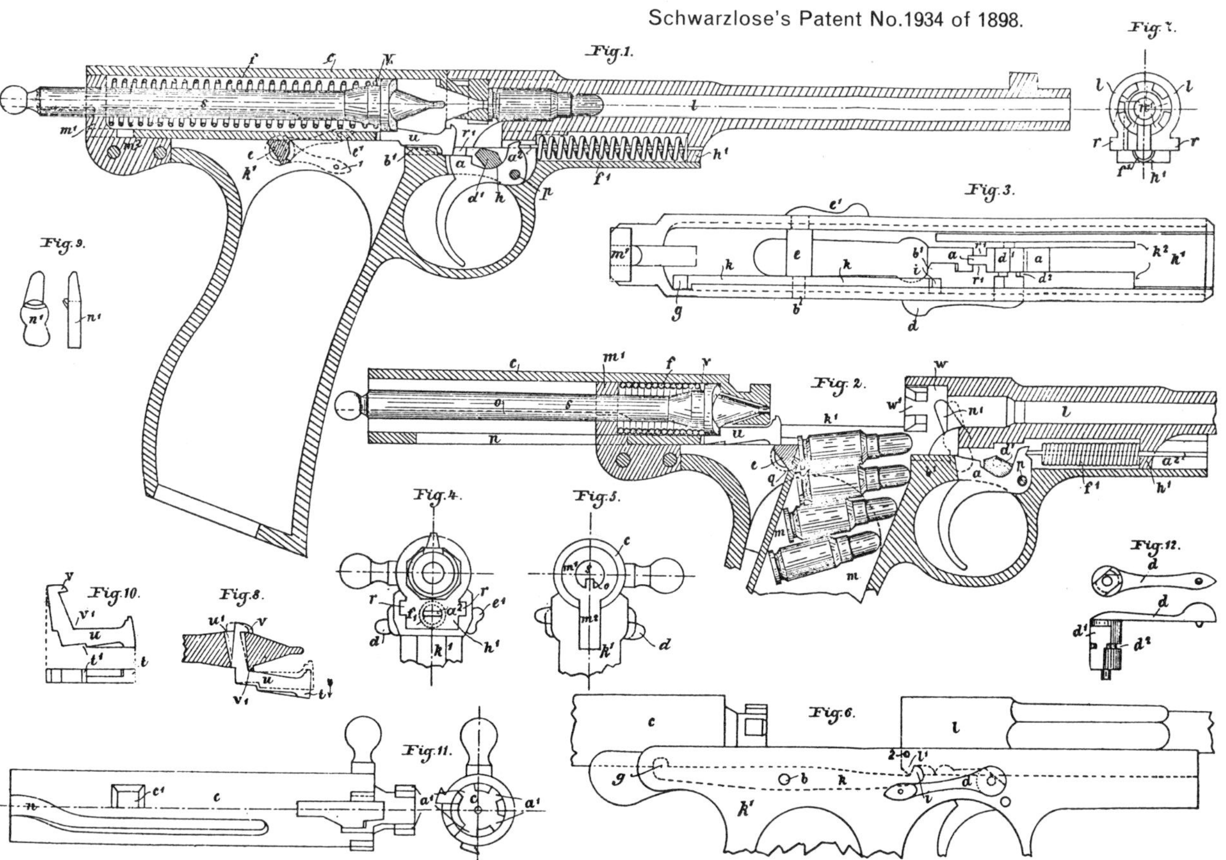

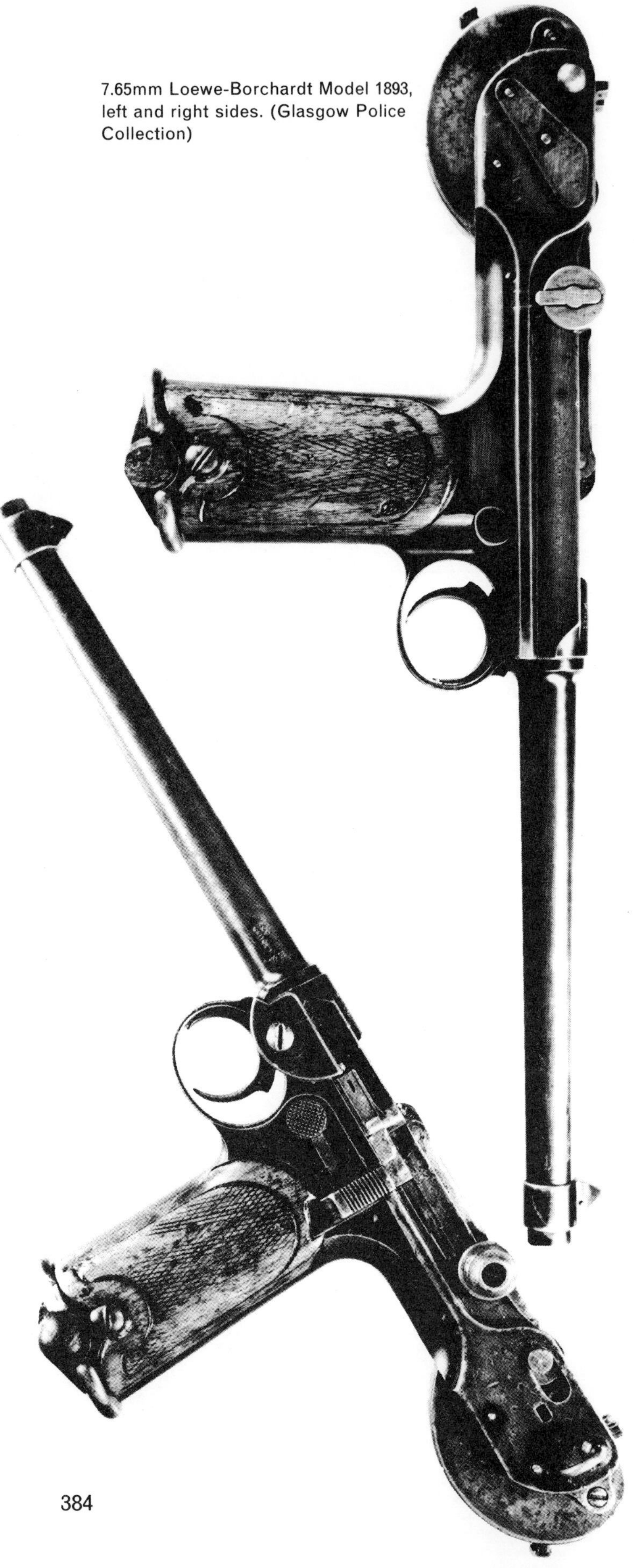

7.65mm Loewe-Borchardt Model 1893, left and right sides. (Glasgow Police Collection)

The merger took place on 14 Feburary 1889, and eight days earlier Ludwig Loewe and Co. had bought out the Deutsche Metallpatronenfabrik Lorenz with factories at Karlsruhe and Grötzingen. In 1896 the name of the company was changed to Deutsche Waffen-und Munitionsfabriken AG (DWM) and the centre of operations was transferred to Berlin, although the Karlsruhe factory was retained. An additional arms factory at Martinikenfelde, near Berlin, was also acquired, and two years later this factory commenced manufacture of Maxim machine guns. In 1899 DWM started to manufacture the Parabellum pistol adopted by the German Army as the Automatic Pistol m.08 in 1908. Wartime production of the combined DWM factories reached a total of 1,400 Mauser Model 98 rifles and 700 Model 08 pistols per day. In 1920 the manufacture of sporting ammunition was resumed and, in 1922, DWM changed their name to Berlin-Karlsruher Industrie-Werke AG, only to revert back again, in 1936, to DWM. After World War Two, the firm was administered by trusteeships, but these were cancelled in 1949 and the style again changed, this time to Industrie -Werke Karlsruhe AG (IWK) although the DWM trade mark was retained.

As made by Waffenfabrik Loewe, Berlin, and later by DWM, the Borchardt, following its introduction in 1893, was the first self-loading pistol to be widely advertised both in Britain and America. It was invariably supplied with shoulder stock and was double the price of a contemporary Colt .32 Police revolver. The 7.65mm Borchardt cartridge was the forerunner of, and interchangeable with, the famous 7.63mm Mauser cartridge and, in fact, the calibre of both the Borchardt and the Mauser pistols was the same at 0.3008. Much of the success of both can be attributed to the cartridge employed. Borchardt patented his pistol in many countries, his British Patent No. 18,774 being dated 6 October 1893.

As can be seen from the drawings which accompanied Borchardt's specifications, the box type magazine which held eight cartridges, was housed in the grip, and the Borchardt was the first self-loading pistol to employ such a magazine although this system has since become almost universal. Borchardt's magazine with the follower and magazine spring is shown at Fig. 11, and the magazine was retained in the pistol by a spring catch '*r*'. It was released by pressing the magazine button on the left hand side of the frame, and would then fall freely out of the grip frame.

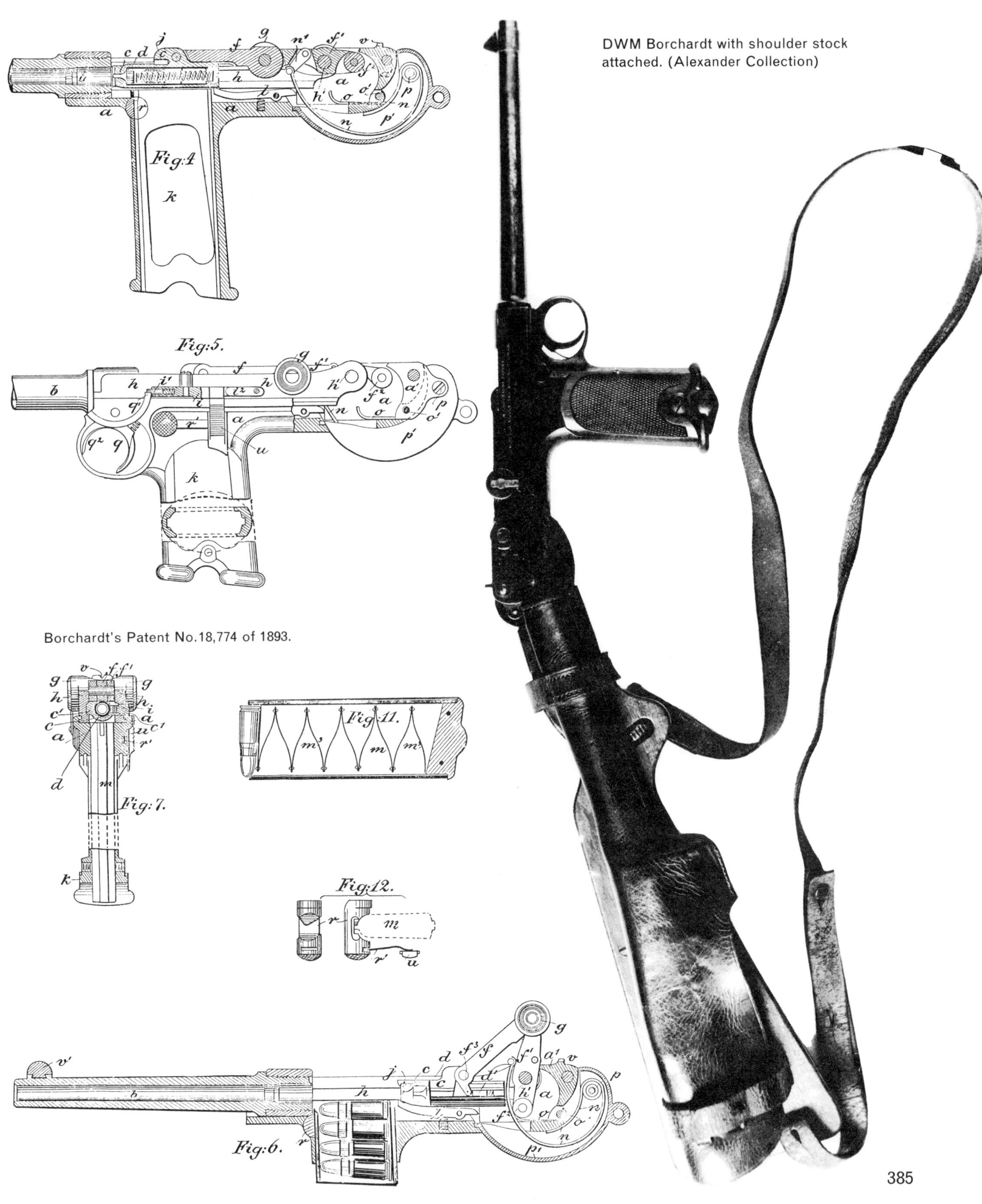

DWM Borchardt with shoulder stock attached. (Alexander Collection)

Borchardt's Patent No.18,774 of 1893.

Holes pierced in the sheet metal sides of the magazine allowed the number of cartridges to be verified. The Borchardt magazines I have examined have two parallel coil springs .38″ in diameter instead of the zig-zag rivetted flat spring shown on the patent drawing. Possibly the rivets gave trouble in service and coil springs were substituted. The magazine bore the number of the pistol impressed into the wooden base cap, and it was also the practice to include with the pistol a dummy wooden magazine which housed an oil bottle and a dismountable three piece ramrod. This dummy magazine was longer than the cartridge magazine and could be employed as a hold-open device; the only other way of keeping the action open was by hand.

The Borchardt was a locked breech recoil operated weapon employing the toggle joint used by Maxim, and was based on the system employed by Smith and Wesson in 1854. The principle of the Borchardt toggle link can also be seen in the patent drawing. When the pistol was fired, the barrel and breech block moved to the rear, the cartridge head being supported by the bolt or breech block '*c*'. By the time the bullet had left the barrel and the pressure was falling, the moving parts had recoiled to a point where the rollers '*f.2*' broke the 'knee' of the toggle by meeting the camming surface at '*a*'. This allowed the breech block to move rearward by itself to the position shown in Fig. 6 and, at this stage, the fired cartridge had been extracted and ejected from the action by the extractor '*j*' and ejector '*l*'. The breech block then moved forward under the influence of the flat spring '*n*' attached to the rear limb of the toggle by a link '*nl*'. As the breech block moved forward, it chambered the top cartridge from the stack in the magazine, the firing pin '*d*' having been cocked by an extension on the limb '*f*' of the toggle. The rollers were discarded in the later Parabellum design of Luger.

Another unusual feature of the Borchardt was that the sear mechanism was attached to the left hand side of the frame, and the sear '*i*' could be locked by a vertically sliding thumb safety piece '*u*' to prevent lateral movement of the nose and release of the firing pin.

The Borchardt was loaded by introducing one cartridge at a time into the magazine, and this was then pushed upward into the grip until retained by the magazine catch. With the pistol held in the right hand, the knob protruding from the left hand side of the toggle link was grasped

DWM Borchardt showing the cocking knob on the left hand side and also the three rollers that unlock the toggle.

What has been said about the "BORCHARDT" AUTOMATIC PISTOL.

NEW YORK TIMES, September 12, 1897.

From CREEDMOOR.—"A feature of yesterday's practice was the testing of a new magazine pistol, an invention of Borchardt. Col. Butt and Major N. B. Thurston, the latter supervising the day's practice, conducted the tests. Tests at 25, 100, and 200 yards were made, and proved highly satisfactory. At 100 yards Major Thurston fired eight shots in fifteen seconds, and the score showed seven bull's-eyes and one centre, a feat hitherto unaccomplished by a guardsman with an ordinary revolver. Col. Butt also made some high scores with the new weapon, and both pronounced it a marvelously accurate firing piece."

SHOOTING AND FISHING, September 30, 1897.

From WALNUT HILL, MASS.—"A very interesting exhibition was given during the afternoon of the capabilities of the new Borchardt automatic pistol, which has been adopted by the Swiss Government. It was shot by Herr Tauscher, and also by several members, one of whom, Mr. Francis, secured 39 out of a possible 40 at 50 yards, and made several bull's-eyes at 200 yards. In the rapidity test, the eight shots were delivered in less than half a second."

From the same paper.—"A Borchardt repeating pistol was taken to Walnut Hill, Mass., Saturday last, and shot at the various ranges. Ever since Mr. Rabbeth inspected one of these pistols at the office of *Shooting and Fishing*, he has had a longing to shoot one. On Saturday he had that privilege. In shooting at 50 yards, he scored 39 out of a possible 40. The arm was shot at 200 yards, and several bull's-eyes made. In shooting for rapidity, the eight shots were fired so quickly that the time could not be taken."

SHOOTING AND FISHING, October 21, 1897.

PITTSBURGH RIFLE CLUB.—"We were honored by a visit from Herr Tauscher, of Berlin, Germany, who exhibited to us the wonderful mechanism of the automatic pistol carbine that he is introducing. The rapidity of fire of this arm is simply wonderful, as it discharges eight bullets, one at a time, in such a short space of time as to appear incredulous; but seeing is believing, and the boys all agreed it beat everything they ever had the pleasure of witnessing. Messrs. Brehm and Hoffman did some very creditable work with it at 200 yards."

WESTERN SPORTS, San Francisco.

"The pistol, after being shown by Mr. Tauscher last Saturday, was shot by Thomas R. Barney, one of the well known sportsmen present. Mr Barney demonstrated that the pistol is wonderfully accurate, and all the gentlemen present were loud in praise of the perfect working of the mechanism."

COMMERCIAL ADVERTISER, January 20, 1898.

"The Borchardt magazine pistol, which is really nothing more nor less than a miniature Gatling gun, is one of the features of the Exhibit (Sportsmen's Show). The little implement of war operates with remarkable nicety. After the first cartridge in the magazine is thrown into the chamber and fired, the slight recoil automatically ejects the empty shell and reloads the weapon with the utmost rapidity, and this is repeated as fast as the trigger is pulled, so that eight shots can be fired in about half a second, or as much slower as the shooter likes. It is provided with a detachable rifle stock, which can be quickly adjusted and the weapon used as a rifle, with effective killing range of from 200 to 300 yards."

Other papers, such as the *Buffalo Express*, October 11, *Los Angeles Herald*, November 14, *Kansas City Star*, November 19, *Syracuse Evening Herald*, December 7, *Scientific American*, December 11, and many other papers that have had the privilege of seeing this pistol shot, praise it highly, and, in fact, consider it the coming weapon, not only for military purposes, but also as a sporting arm. We have given above only a few abstracts, and many more could be shown if necessary.

Write for copy of U. S. Government Test at Springfield.

AGENTS FOR THE UNITED STATES,

HERMANN BOKER & CO., 101 & 103 Duane Street,

NEW YORK CITY.

Some contemporary opinions of the Borchardt.

"Borchardt" Automatic Repeating Pistol and Carbine

The Ideal Weapon for the Woods—Light, Powerful and Effective.

ADAPTED TO WALSRODE SMOKELESS POWDER.

Nickel Full and Part Mantle Bullets, 7.65 mm. or .31 in. Calibre.

CUT SHOWING AS PISTOL.

CUT SHOWING AS CARBINE.

Price, complete, with three extra Magazines, Tools, Oilers, Holster, and Strap, ... $30.00

Leather Case extra, ... 5.00

Price for Cartridges, either full or part mantle, per 100, . $3.50

The "Borchardt" Automatic is a very simple weapon. The magazine holds eight cartridges. The only operation necessary is to draw back the bolt the first time, which cocks and loads the arm. After this the arm works automatically. The recoil of the first cartridge unloads, cocks, and loads the arm, and as fast or slow as the trigger is pulled the arm is discharged. Owing to its light weight and small size, it is a splendid sporting carbine.

Weight, complete, with stock, holster, and sling	3¾	lbs.
Total length of pistol	14	inches.
" " " carbine	27	"
" " between front and rear sight	12¼	"
" " of barrel to end of chamber	7½	"
Effective range	200–300	yards.

Agents for the United States,

HERMANN BOKER & CO.,

101 & 103 Duane Street,

NEW YORK.

An advertisement for the Borchardt of about 1900.

by the forefinger and thumb of the left hand and drawn upward and to the rear to the limit of its travel. The top cartridge then rose in front of the breech block, and, when the knob was released, the breech would close, carrying the cartridge out of the magazine into the chamber. The pistol was now loaded, cocked and ready to fire. To unload, the magazine release button was pressed and the magazine removed. A slow pull back on the toggle knob withdrew the cartridge from the chamber until it usually fell down through the grip. As with all self-loading pistols, it was not enough merely to operate the mechanism; a visual check had also to be made to ensure that the chamber was clear. Due to its shape, the Borchardt was clumsy and difficult to shoot, but one of its virtues was the rigidity of the shoulder stock attachment and, with this fitted, it performed very well as a carbine.

The Borchardt, particularly when complete with all accessories, is now a very desirable collector's piece. Its importance lies in the fact that it was the direct ancestor of one of the best known self-loading pistols ever made, the Pistole Parabellum or Luger.

Ferdinand Ritter von Mannlicher, undoubtedly one of the most prolific and most successful firearms designers, was born in 1848 in Most, Bohemia, a region renowned for metal working and with a tradition for skilled craftmanship. Bohemia was then part of the Empire of Austro-Hungary, and von Mannlicher was able to study in Vienna and then join the Austrian State Railways. In 1876 he visited the famous Philadelphia Exhibition, and this American visit appears to have had a decisive influence on his future career. Railways were abandoned and, in 1880, the first of many rifles bearing his name, a multi-tube magazine rifle with the magazine tubes in the butt stock, was produced in quantity by Steyr-Werke. This was followed by rifles with detachable magazines, with tube magazines in the fore-end and with gravity fed magazines, and then by the Model 1885 which introduced his famous clip or packet loading system. In 1894 came the first Mannlicher self-loading pistol to employ the 'blow-forward' system later adopted by Schwarzlose for his 1908 Pocket Pistol. The Mannlicher Model 94 was chambered for special 6.50mm and 7.60mm cartridges held in a five round charger. Unlike the Mannlicher rifle magazine system, the charger was not inserted into the magazine with the cartridges; the magazine was situated above the grip frame and the cartridges were stripped down into it. In the 1896 Mannlicher, the magazine was placed in front of the trigger and the cartridges were again inserted by means of a clip or charger which remained outside the pistol.

Both the Model 94 and the Model 96 represented an evolutionary step in the development of the automatic pistol since the utilisation of the energy of recoil, whether in the blow-forward Model 94 or blow-back system of the Model 96, did not extend to cocking the hammer, which had to be either thumb cocked or cocked by trigger action. This system was known as the Halbautomatische Repetier Pistole or semi-automatic, and the two Mannlicher designs can be truly said to have been *self-loading* pistols.

A Mannlicher automatic pistol which was both self-cocking and self-loading was first manufactured by the Steyr Armoury in 1896. This pistol is often called the Model of 1903 since that was the year in which it became generally available on the European market. The Model 96/03 was a short recoil locked breech chambered for the 7.65mm Mannlicher. In appearance it was similar to the Mauser Model 96 and will in fact chamber the 7.63mm Mauser cartridge, a practice which is not advised since the Mauser cartridge develops higher pressures than the correct Mannlicher cartridge. The design of the prop-up type locking system was unusual. The rear of the locking bolt or breech lock was pinned to the barrel extension which, unlike the Mauser, was made separate from the barrel. When the pistol was fired the recoil moved the bolt and barrel extension (locked together by the breech lock) to the rear. The bevelled mating surfaces of the rear of the bolt and the front of the breech or bolt lock tended to disengage, but were kept together by a recess in the lock frame. When the barrel extension had moved about $\frac{3}{16}$″ to the rear, the breech lock cleared the recess and dropped downwards unlocking the bolt so that it could move further to the rear and extract and eject the fired case. The 1896/03 Mannlicher was loaded in a similar manner to the 1896 Mauser, but its smaller magazine capacity allowed for six rounds only.

Made as a pistol, as a pistol carbine with detachable stock, and as a full stocked carbine, the Mannlicher was never as successful as the Mauser. If used with the 7.63mm Mauser cartridge, the Mannlicher was likely to suffer damage and, although it was a far better 'pistol' for shooting, the disadvantage of being able to handle the more powerful Mauser cartridge must have inhibited sales. Also the external cocking lever was perhaps not as popular as the more conventional Mauser external hammer. The correct cartridge was originally known as the Mannlicher Carbine M.96, as the 7.63mm Mannlicher M.1903 and, in Germany, as the 7.65mm Mannlicher. The DWM number for all synonyms was DWM 497. The most successful and most widely copied of the Mannlicher automatic pistol designs was the Model 1900. This was originally patented in 1898, British Patent No. 27,612, and, as with other Mannlicher pistols, the model designation was derived from the Steyr factory dating and not from the patent dates. The Model 1900 was made available in commercial quantities in 1901 and is sometimes referred to as the Mannlicher Model 1901, particularly by British and American authorities.

This pistol introduced further complexities on the ammunition side since it was chambered for yet another nominal 7.63mm Mannlicher cartridge which, fortunately, had straight tapered sides and was not bottle-necked like the Model 96/03 locked breech pistol cartridge (DWM 497). In Germany the straight sided M.1900 7.63mm Mannlicher cartridge was again known as the 7.65mm Mannlicher to avoid inevitable confusion with the more popular 7.63mm Mauser. The DWM number for the M.1900 Mannlicher cartridge was DWM 466.

As the illustrations show, the Model 1900 was graceful and pleasing in shape, and it is a most comfortable pistol to shoot. As one would expect from the Steyr factory, the general standard of finish, both external and internal, was of a very high order. The magazine in the butt was loaded from above by means of a charger holding eight cartridges. The charger guides were machined in the front of the breech block or slide, and the magazine contents could be removed, without having to work them through the action, by depressing the serrated slide on the right hand side of the frame with the slide held to the rear. The safety catch was simple and positive. A hinged bar at the rear of the slide was pulled down by means of the thumb catch and was interposed between the external hammer and the striker. When the safety catch was applied, the hammer could be released without fear of discharge since it would strike the bar and not the striker.

The lockwork was mounted on the left hand side of the frame and, once the cover plate was removed, was instantly available for inspection. The front of the cover plate also formed the cover for the recoil spring mounted under the barrel, and the whole was retained by a spring catch in front the trigger guard. The sear was in front of the hammer and, as the sear lever was moved to the rear by the trigger, it bore against a block machined in the action body and so provided the 'first' pressure. Increased pressure caused the sear lever to move slightly upward to rotate the sear and release the external hammer.

7.63mm Mannlicher Model 1905.
(Ian Frame Collection)

The lower arm of the mainspring bore against

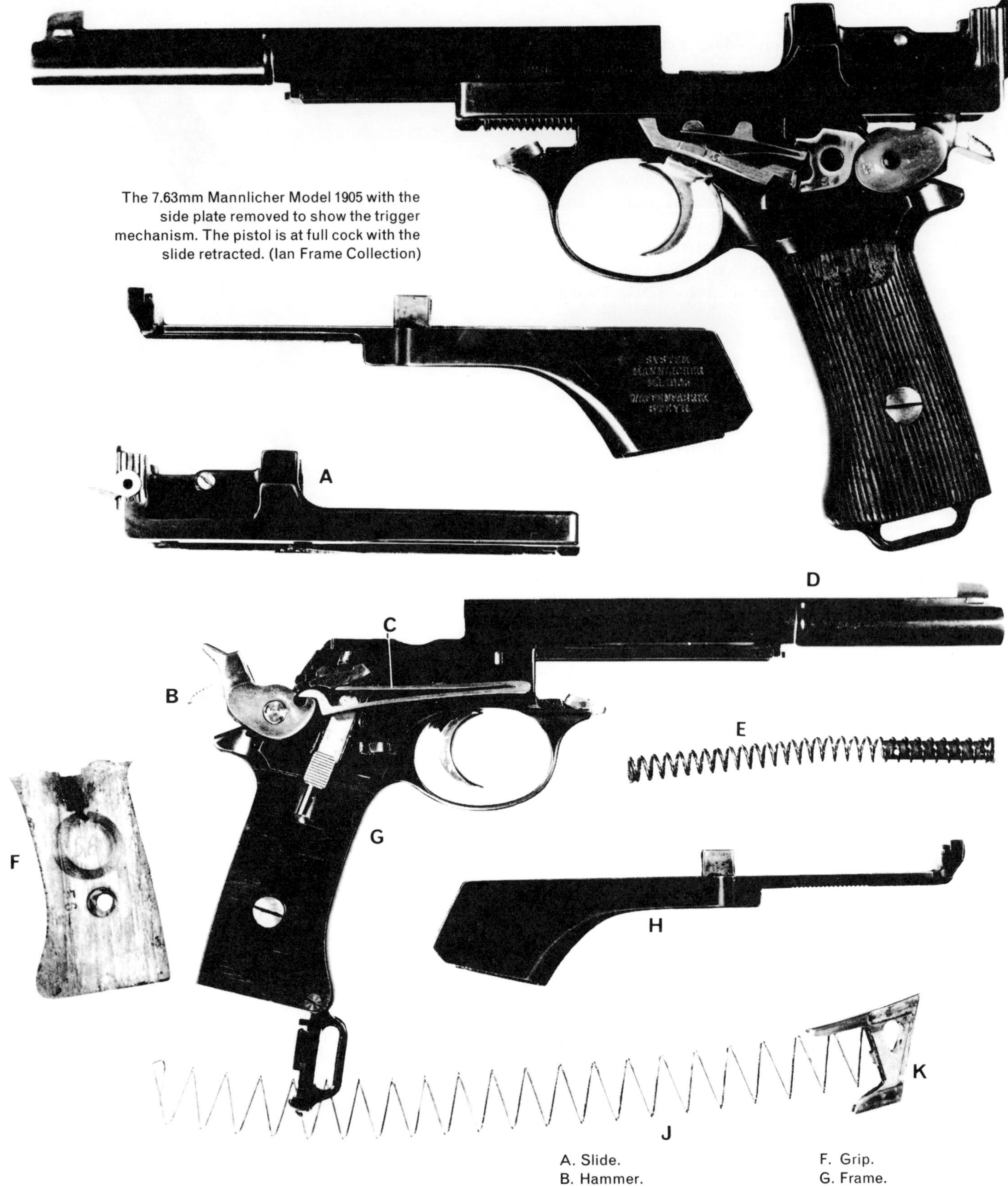

The 7.63mm Mannlicher Model 1905 with the side plate removed to show the trigger mechanism. The pistol is at full cock with the slide retracted. (Ian Frame Collection)

A. Slide.
B. Hammer.
C. Mainspring.
D. Barrel.
E. Recoil spring and spring guide.
F. Grip.
G. Frame.
H. Side plate.
J. Magazine spring.
K. Magazine follower.

the hammer, the upper against the delay cam. The cam itself bore against the slide which, as it moved to the rear under recoil, also compressed the mainspring at the same time as it cocked the hammer. By this arrangement, frictional resistance increased as the slide moved to the rear. When it had moved to its full extent, the cam engaged a notch cut into it, and this acted as a hold-open device so the breech could be left in the open position for loading or cleaning.

When the pistol was fired, the slide moved completely to the rear and the hammer pressed the hooked end of the mainspring against the tail of the cam so that the nose was depressed and disengaged from the notch. There was, of course, a hold-open device to keep the slide to the rear when the magazine was empty. To let the slide forward, the magazine follower was depressed and the hammer drawn slightly back so that the delay cam which acted as an additional hold-open device was released.

The pistol illustrated is marked 'System Mannlicher Md. 1905 Waffenfabrik Steyr', and is similar in all essentials to the Model 1900. The latter, although rejected for military use by the Austrian authorities in the 1904 tests, was extremely popular with officers of the Austro-Hungarian army and was sold in considerable numbers in South America. Variant forms can be encountered dated 1901, 1902 and 1905, but all are basically similar. Steyr appear to have discontinued manufacture in 1905, but ammunition was available up to the beginning of World War Two. As made by ICI in the years between the wars, the 7.63mm Mannlicher auto-pistol cartridge was loaded with four grains of revolver neonite and an 85 grain bullet. Muzzle velocity was given as 1,050 f.p.s. and it was not adapted for any other pistol. Copies of the Mannlicher Model 1900 were made in Spain, particularly for the South American market, and vary in quality from the acceptable to the impossible.

Having lived in Vienna for most of his life, Mannlicher was knighted by the Austrian State for his services and died in 1904. With the exception of the prototype of his first automatic pistol, made in Switzerland at Neuhausen, all his designs were manufactured at Steyr.

The blow-forward Model 1894 and the blow-back Model 1896 are excellent examples of the transitional 'self-loading' pistol; the design was improved in the locked breech Model 1896/03 and perfected in the final Model 1900 series which employed a delayed blow-back system where the inertia of the slide breech block and recoil spring was assisted by the additional friction resistance of the delay cam.

All these pistols are today desirable collector's items and deserve preservation if only as a tribute to their designer. Ingenious in design and carefully manufactured, none achieved the success of the Mannlicher rifles.

The credit for the design, manufacture and promotion of the first self-loading pistol to win lasting acceptance and world-wide popularity goes to yet another nineteenth century European firearms designer, Peter Paul Mauser.

Waffenfabrik Mauser, Oberndorf am Neckar in the former Kingdom of Wurtemburg, was founded by the brothers Paul and Wilhelm Mauser. Sons of Andreas Mauser, a Master Gunsmith at the Oberndorf Firearms Factory, both brothers learned their trade with their father. Peter Paul, the youngest of Andreas Manser's thirteen children, was born in 1838. The Government Firearm Factory at Oberndorf had originally been founded by King Frederick I in 1811, and was sited at Oberndorf primarily because of the availability of power from the River Neckar and also because of the presence of suitable buildings (formerly part of an Augustine Cloister dating back to 1775) which were easily converted to factory use.

Peter Paul Mauser displayed his talents as a gun designer shortly after he joined his father and brothers in the Oberndorf Factory, when his efforts, not surprisingly, were directed to improving the famous Dreyse Needle Gun. Wurtemburg joined the German Empire in 1871 and, in that same year, the Mauser rifle was adopted by the newly emergent German Empire as the first official metallic cartridge rifle. This resulted in a flood of orders, and the Mauser brothers were offered the Government Firearms Factory which, with the help of banking interests, they were able to acquire. Improvement followed improvement and, one by one, the armies of the world adopted the Mauser rifle in one model or another.

Wilhelm Mauser died in 1882 and the responsibility for the rapidly growing Mauser organisation fell entirely on the shoulders of Peter Paul. In 1884 Mauser Brothers and Co. became a stock company and the financial side of the business was taken over by Alfred Kaulla, a director of the Wurttembergische-Vereinsbank, leaving Peter Paul free to concentrate on the technical side. Undeterred by the lack of success of the Mauser

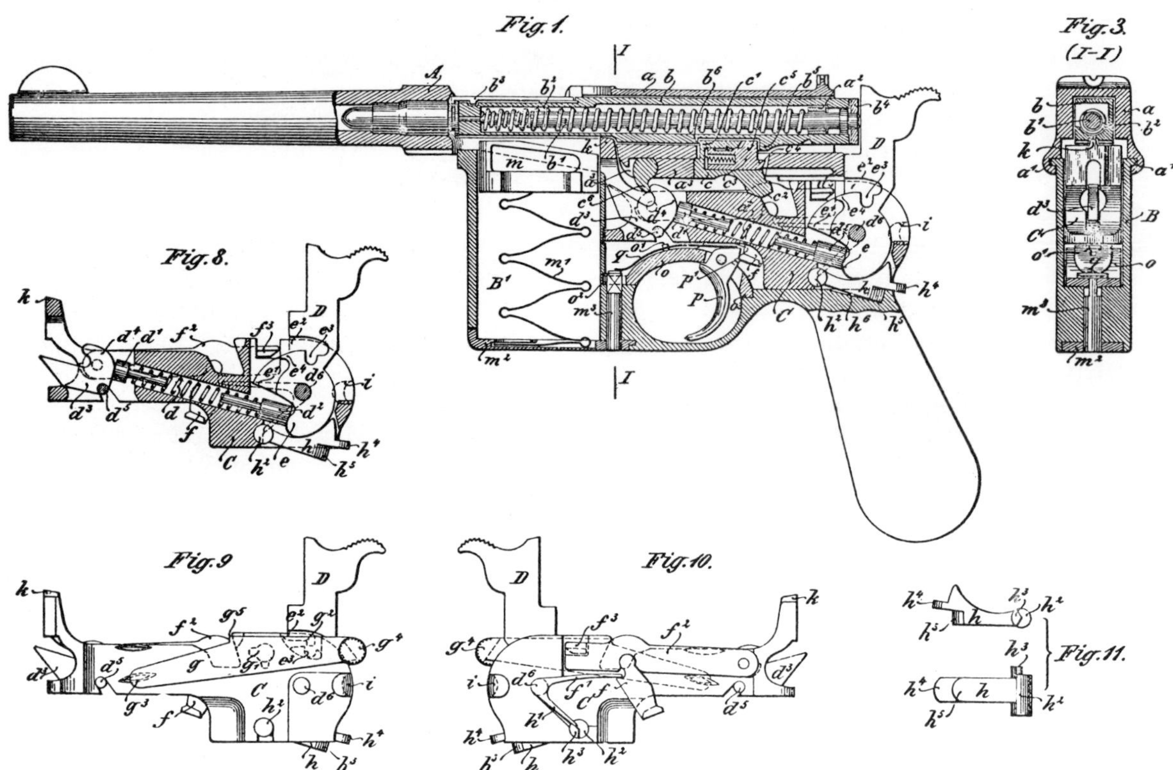

Mauser Patent No.959 of 1896.

Single Shot Pistol and the Model 1878 revolver, he developed, in 1886, a magazine pistol with a tubular magazine which operated in the then conventional manner by means of a finger lever, and then began work on a self-loading pistol.

The first true Mauser self-loading pistol was patented in 1896, and the general arrangement of the components can be seen from the drawing which accompanied Mauser's British Patent No. 959 of 1896. This pistol was quite remarkable in that it was the only 'first generation' self-loading pistol to stand the test of time. Production appears to have started in 1897 and was only halted in 1937 by the need for factory space due to re-armament requirements.

It is an adequate testimonial to the correctness of Mauser's original design that, throughout this entire period, only minor changes were made to adapt the pistol to new markets or to meet new needs. These changes included alterations to the barrel length, magazine capacity and general styling, and also slight modifications to the mechanism to improve safety and convenience, or to ease manufacturing problems.

Essentially the pistol consisted of four main assemblies. The barrel and barrel extension were forged in one piece '*A*' capable of sliding to and fro on the frame (Fig. 3, '*B*'). The bolt '*b*' was square in section and contained the striker 'b^1', striker spring and bolt spring. The striker spring, although shown on the drawing, is not identified, but can be seen at the front of the striker inside the larger diameter bolt return spring. The magazine was formed as part of the frame and models were made with six, ten and twenty round capacities. The standard model held ten cartridges staggered in two rows, and these were fed from the magazine by a follower with a bevelled top surface to ensure that the top cartridge was placed centrally so that it could be fed into the chamber.

To strip this pistol, having checked that it was unloaded, the first step was remove the magazine floor plate, spring and follower. This was done by inserting the nose of a bullet into the hole at the rear of the base plate to push up the locking stud. The floor plate could then be eased forward and removed, together with the spring and follower. The hammer was then cocked and the catch immediately under it pressed upwards so that the barrel, barrel extension and mechanism could be withdrawn from the receiver. The hammer mechanism was then detached from the bolt by gently pulling downward, and the bolt could be

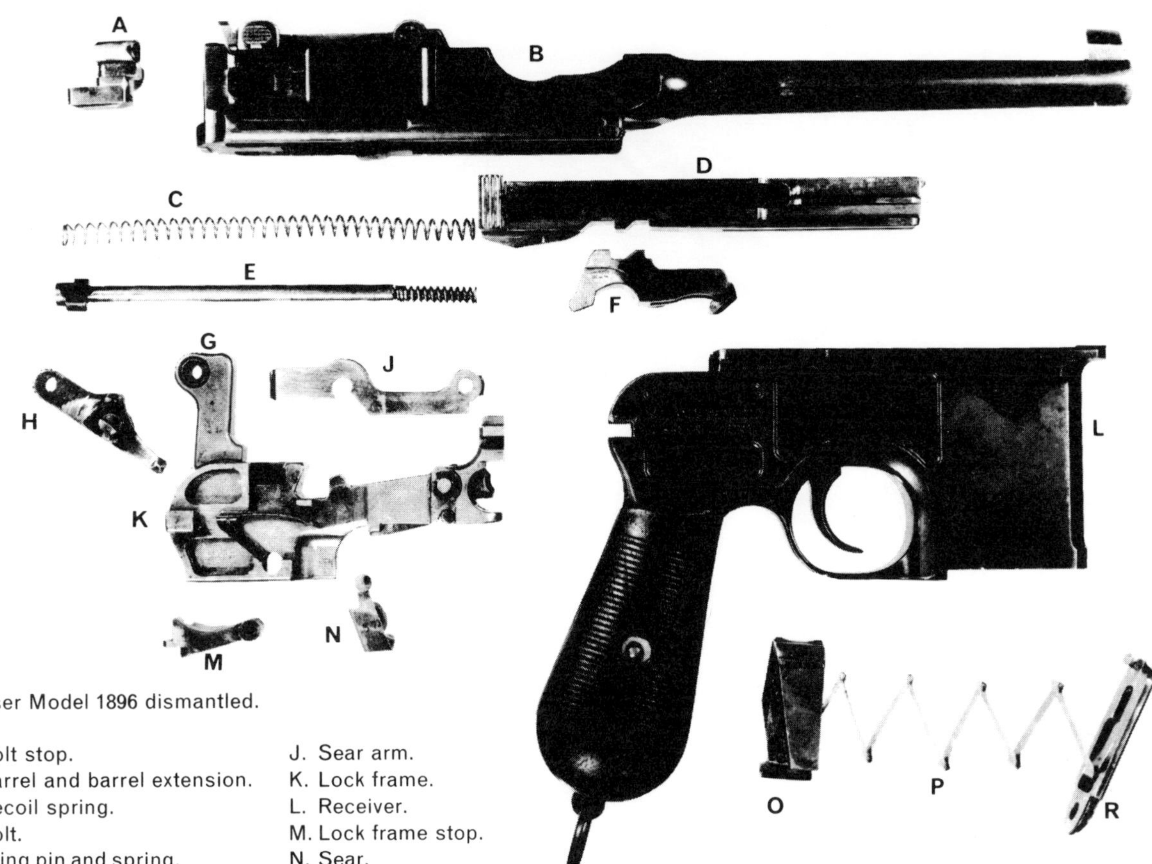

Mauser Model 1896 dismantled.

A. Bolt stop.
B. Barrel and barrel extension.
C. Recoil spring.
D. Bolt.
E. Firing pin and spring.
F. Bolt locking block
G. Hammer.
H. Safety.
J. Sear arm.
K. Lock frame.
L. Receiver.
M. Lock frame stop.
N. Sear.
O. Magazine follower.
P. Magazine spring.
R. Magazine floor plate.

removed from the barrel extension by using a screwdriver to push in the firing pin, at the same time rotating through 90 degrees clockwise. The striker or firing pin and spring were then withdrawn, and the bolt and mainspring removed by pushing forward the mainspring retaining block on the right hand side of the barrel extension and pulling out. The separate parts (note the smaller hammer) can all be seen in the illustration which gives some idea of the truly remarkable construction. Only one screw was used in the entire pistol, the one which holds the two sides of the stock together. The rest of the pistol fitted together like a three dimensional jigsaw puzzle. The sear mechanism, '*f*', 'f^2' and 'f^3', can be identified in Fig. 10, and the sear spring 'h^1', which also tensioned the dismounting catch, in Fig. 11.

The Mauser 1896 was a short recoil, locked breech action pistol, the locking system based on wedges or, more properly, rocking lugs. The method of operating was briefly as follows. When the cartridge was fired, the recoil drove back the bolt which was locked to the barrel extension by the bolt lock. As can be seen, the lugs on the bolt engaged the lugs on the bolt lock, but what is not easy to see is that the top rear bolt lock passed through a rectangular space machined in the base of the barrel extension. Hooked on to the barrel extension, the bolt lock could pivot downwards, so disengaging the lugs and allowing the bolt to recoil further to the rear. As this happened, the hammer was cocked and the bolt return spring compressed. The empty case, which had been withdrawn from the chamber by the extractor 'b^3', struck the ejector '*k*' machined into the lock frame and was ejected. When the bolt spring forced the bolt forward again, the tooth on the front of the bolt lock, under the influence of the mainspring '*c*', pushed the rear bolt lock upwards so that the lugs could engage the lugs in the bolt. The barrel extension could then move forward, the inclined surface at the rear of the bolt lock meeting the surface at the top of the lock frame 'c^2', so forcing the lugs to engage firmly. Fully repetitive fire was avoided since the sear lever '*f* in Fig. 10 was pivoted and could not move forward into the position shown in the drawing until the trigger was released.

To modern eyes, the Mauser pistol is rather clumsy, complicated, and by no means easy to shoot without the shoulder stock attachment. On the other hand, it is beautifully made to an extremely high standard, and a delightful pistol

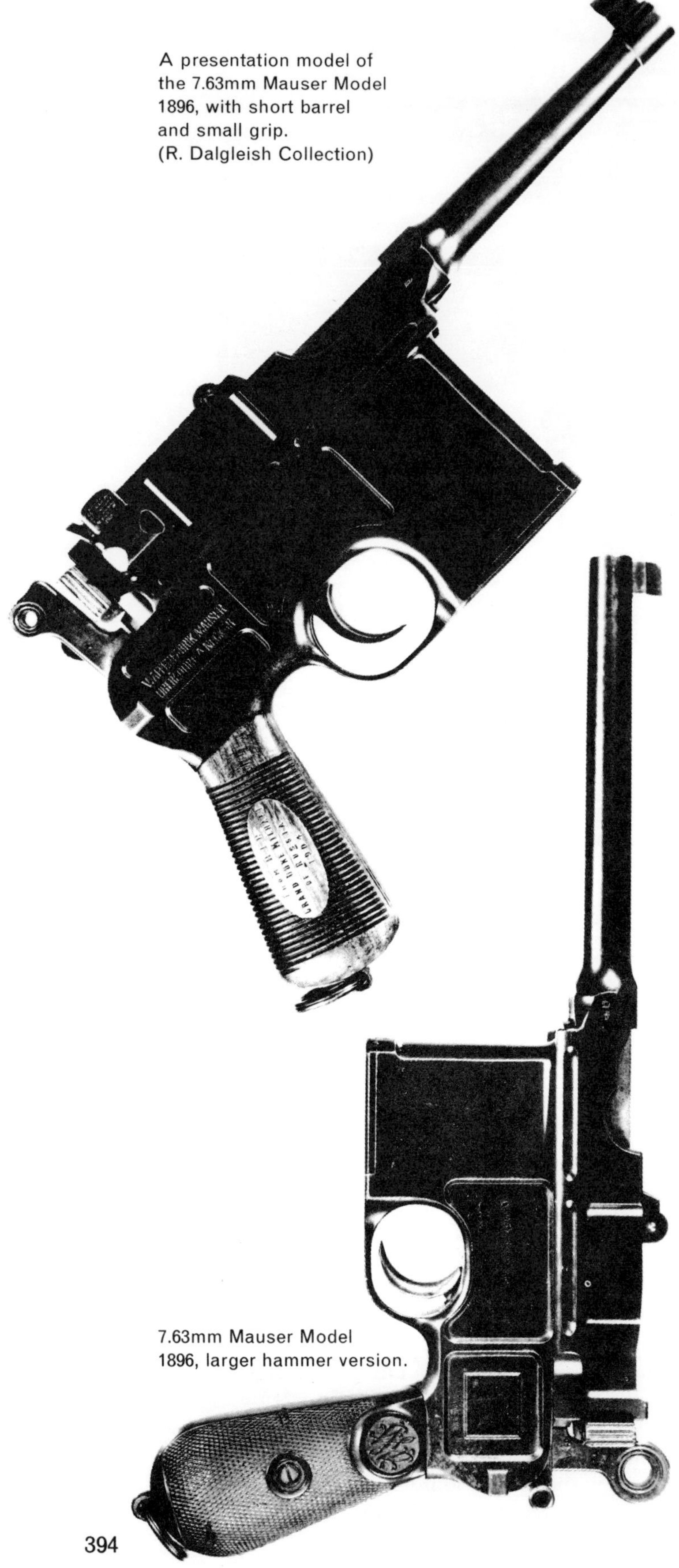

A presentation model of the 7.63mm Mauser Model 1896, with short barrel and small grip. (R. Dalgleish Collection)

7.63mm Mauser Model 1896, larger hammer version.

to own even if only for the pleasure of dismantling and the subsequent feeling of astonishment at the ingenuity with which it has been constructed. It was also the first pistol to incorporate a feature now considered essential, a hold-open device to ensure that the breech remains open after the last cartridge has been fired. This was achieved by a stop at the rear of the magazine platform which rose in front of the bolt when the magazine was empty. The other unusual feature was the design of the shoulder stock which also served as a holster. The front of this stock was provided with a metal tongue and catch which slid into a groove in the frame of the pistol. The other end of the stock was a hinged lid, and the whole interior was hollowed out to accommodate the complete pistol except for a part of the butt which protruded through a hole provided for it.

As a rough guide to identification, the earlier Model 1896 Mauser had a small hole through the hammer and large bosses with concentric rings on either side. (By the modern collector, this is sometimes called the cone hammer.) The safety lever head was solid, and the ridges which ran down each side of the barrel extension lacked any centre depression.

The 1896 type Mauser was made in six, ten and extended twenty round magazine versions, and also in a special carbine version with a long barrel. Few of these early 1896 pistols were manufactured and, in 1899, alterations were made which included the replacement of the original 'coned' hammer by a large-headed flat-sided hammer with a large central hole, and the provision of a hollow safety lever head. Two cut-outs were machined in the ridges at the side of the barrel extension.

The original grip plates were either checkered or smooth wood but, in 1898, serrated wood grips were introduced, to be followed by hard rubber grips with a floral pattern in 1899 and by hard rubber grips with the Mauserwerke monogram in about 1906. In 1902 the firing pin or striker retaining plate ('b^4' in Fig. 1) was dropped and wings were introduced on the rear of the pin.

The original Mauser and subsequent variants were only available in 7.63mm Mauser, although I believe that some were supplied in 7.65mm Parabellum. Some time after 1900 the 9mm Mauser calibre was introduced with the same case length as the 7.63mm Mauser, but the 9mm was straight sided instead of bottle-necked. This cartridge was adapted only to the 9mm Mauser and the Neuhausen machine gun and would not chamber in the 9mm Parabellum or Luger. The only specimens I have seen were made by DWM, carried the 487 identification code, and are described in English catalogues as being for the 'Export' Mauser.

About 1910 several improvements were made to the mechanism. The separate trigger plate retained in position by an extension to the magazine floor plate catch (Fig. 1 page 392) was discarded and a thinner trigger, with a flat instead of concave rear surface, was mounted directly on the frame. At about the same time, the safety device was altered, and, where the earlier safety lever had had to be pressed downward to engage, in the revised mechanism it had to be pushed upward. The earlier pattern had been liable to break internally, and it had also been necessary to push upward on the lever to release the safety and then downward on the hammer to cock the pistol. In the new design both the release of the safety and the cocking of the hammer were achieved by downward pressure. In addition to the variations in magazine capacity, barrel length etc., versions can be found without the inlet side panels, where the sides of the frame are quite smooth. In 7.63 mm, this is perhaps the most common of all the variants.

During the First World War a number of Mauser pistols were made for the 9 mm Parabellum cartridge, a rather belated attempt to secure a measure of uniformity. In order to avoid any confusion, these pistols had a large figure 9 deeply cut into the wooden grips. What would happen if the grips were changed is difficult to say, for, apart from the bore size, there are no other visible signs of difference between the 9mm and the 7.63mm versions. In this connection it is important to realise that the 7.63mm Mauser will actually chamber and fire the 9mm Parabellum cartridge. This, however, is a practice to be guarded against. Although the Mauser is immensely strong and will stand the pressures involved for at least one discharge, it will not survive repeated abuse.

Manufacture of the Mauser ceased at the end of the First World War, but was eventually resumed in 1922. In 1930 a selective-fire variant was introduced, known in Germany as the Schnell-feuer Pistole, the Model 1932 or the Model 712. When moved to the letter 'N', a selector lever mounted on the left hand side of the frame caused the pistol to operate as a normal semi-automatic, one pressure on the trigger firing one cartridge. When the lever was moved to the letter

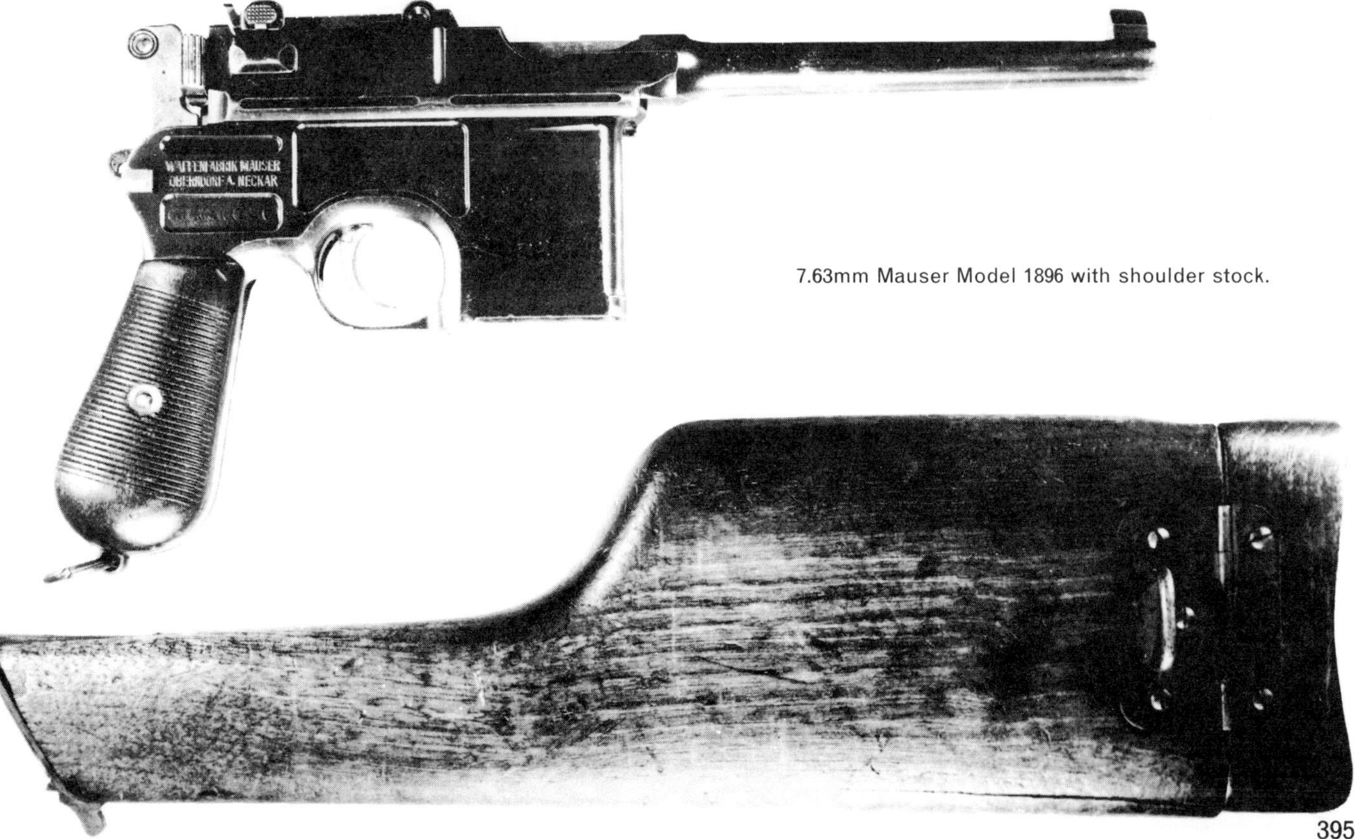

7.63mm Mauser Model 1896 with shoulder stock.

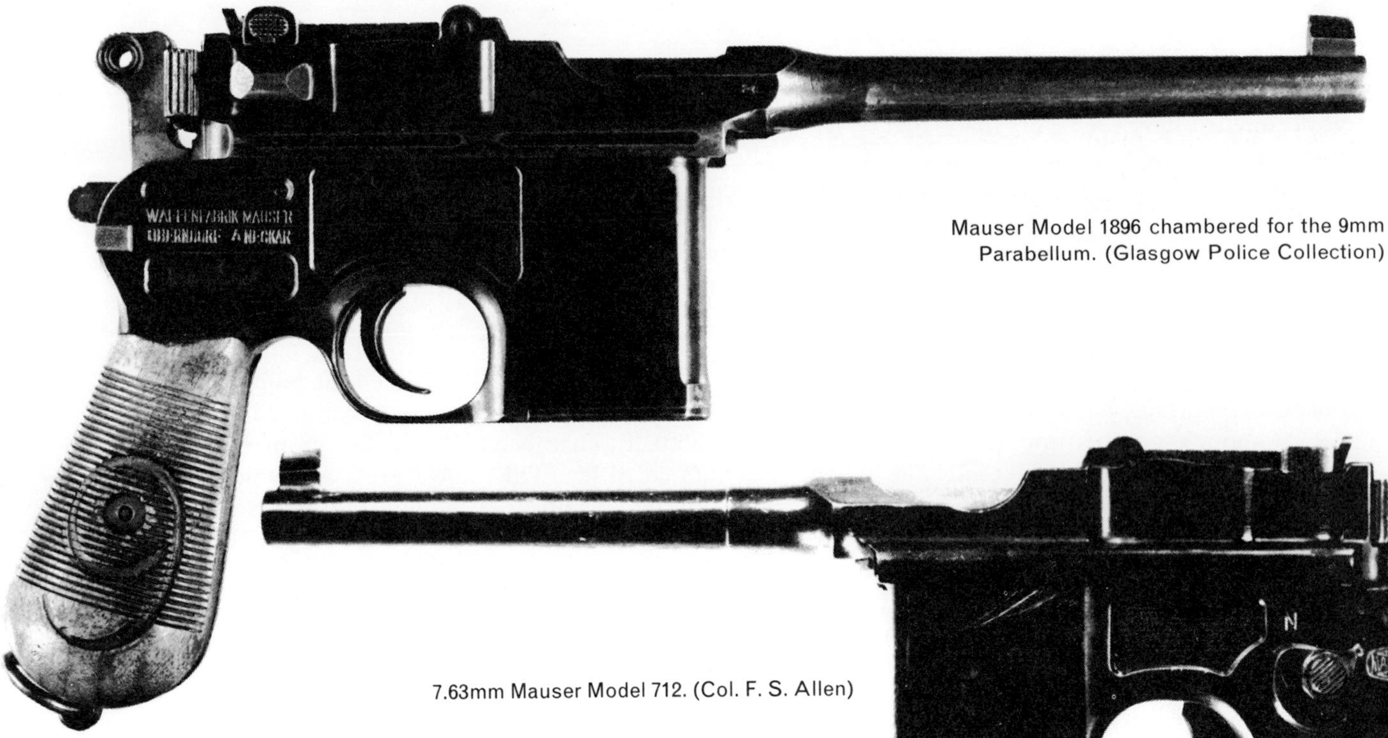

Mauser Model 1896 chambered for the 9mm Parabellum. (Glasgow Police Collection)

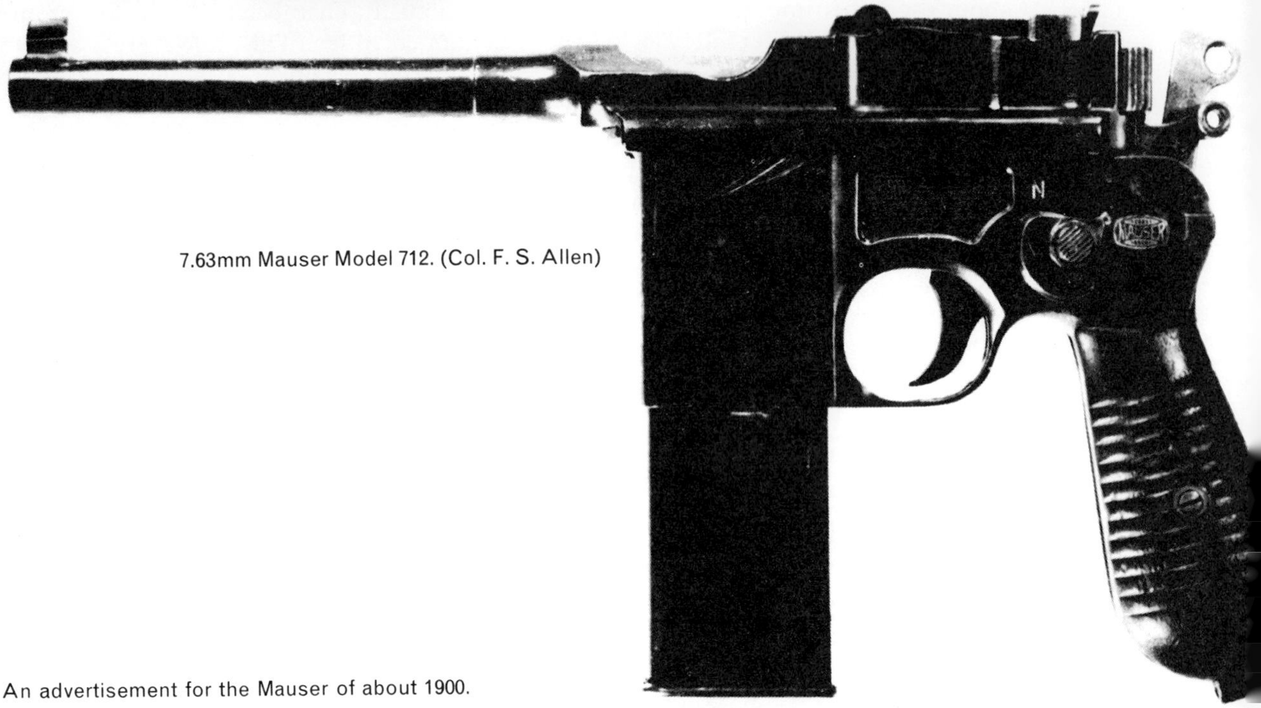

7.63mm Mauser Model 712. (Col. F. S. Allen)

An advertisement for the Mauser of about 1900.

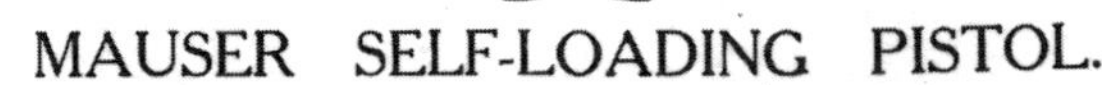

MAUSER SELF-LOADING PISTOL.

The Mauser Self-Loader as will be seen from the cut is of a compact form, and the magazine being flat, the Pistol can be carried on the person more conveniently than a revolver with its awkwardly projecting cylinder.

In this arm the force of the recoil opens the mechanism of the breech, ejects the empty cartridge case, cocks the hammer, introduces a new cartridge into the chamber and closes and locks the breech; the shooter having only to aim, press the trigger, and, after ten shots, re-charge the magazine.

The simplicity with which the functions are fulfilled and the substantial construction are the marked features of the system.

THE HOLSTER BUTT STOCK.

The Pistol is provided with a Walnut Butt Stock instantly attachable by a sliding tennon and spring catch to the back of the Grip. When not in use as a stock this Butt serves as a Holster its interior being hollowed out to the shape of the Pistol whose Grip projects about half its length outside to facilitate quick drawing.

Price £5 0 0

'R' (reihenfeuer-successive fire), the pistol operated as a machine pistol with fully automatic fire. The Schnellfeuer pistol is completely unmanageable on full automatic fire without its shoulder stock and, even then, is difficult to control. No doubt its chief purpose was for crowd control, the psychological effect of full automatic fire being considerable.

There are, unfortunately, few contemporary accounts of pistols in use under combat conditions, and rarely does the narrator actually describe the weapon used. It is fortunate therefore that one of the greatest Englishmen, Winston S. Churchill, in describing but one of the fascinating episodes in his extremely adventurous life, included the details of his personal armoury in such a manner that we know what type of pistol he used, and also under what circumstances. The following extract is from *My Early Life*, first published in 1930.

The time is September 1898; the place, the Plain of Omdurman in the Sudan. Churchill was with the 21st Lancers and he tells us exactly what happened. 'The troop I commanded was, when we wheeled into line, the second from the right of the regiment. I was riding a handy, surefooted grey Arab polo pony. Before we wheeled and began to gallop, the officers had been marching with drawn swords. On account of my shoulder (which had been dislocated in India) I had always decided that if I were involved in hand to hand fighting, I must use a pistol and not a sword. I had purchased in London, a Mauser automatic pistol, then the newest and latest design. I had practised carefully with this during our march and journey up the river. This then was the weapon with which I was determined to fight. I had first of all to return my sword into its scabbard, which is not the easiest thing to do at a gallop. I had then to draw my pistol from its wooden holster and bring it to full cock.' In the ensuing mêlée. Churchill, with dervishes all around, used his Mauser to good effect, the significant feature being the extremely close range. 'I raised my pistol and fired, so close were we that the pistol actually struck him.' With his last cartridge Churchill accounted for yet another dervish and then 'I found that I had fired the whole magazine of my Mauser pistol, so I put in a new clip of ten cartridges before thinking of anything else'. In the space of about two or three minutes the Lancers had lost, out of a total of 310 officers and men, five officers and sixty-five men killed and wounded, and 120 horses, nearly one quarter of its strength.

Several months later, in November 1899, Churchill, having resigned his commission, had become a War Correspondent in South Africa, but still carried his faithful Mauser. On this occasion, whilst assisting in clearing the line for an armoured train, he was surprised by a Boer horseman who had him covered with a rifle. 'I thought I could kill this man. I put my hand to my belt, the pistol was not there. When engaged on clearing the line, getting in and out of the engine, etc., I had taken it off. It came safely home on the engine, I have it now!' Unarmed, Churchill surrendered, and discovered that his captor was the famous Boer leader General Louis Botha, later to become the first Prime Minister of the Transvaal and a firm friend of his old enemy.

A Mauser pistol of the type that Churchill purchased in London (which could then be obtained for the princely sum of £5), is illustrated, and its success encouraged many imitations. In the period between the wars a genuine Mauser was selling for $37, the Schnellfeuer Pistole for $41. A Spanish Astra (made by Astra, Unceta y Cia of Guernica) sold for the same price, but a Royal (made by Zulaica y Cia) cost several dollars less. Although externally similar to the Mauser, none of the imitations and copies attempted to duplicate the intricate Mauser mechanism, and numerous short cuts were taken to avoid machining problems. The Astra Series 900 were usually marked 'Astra Automatic Pistol Cal. 7.63' and, in place of the beautiful interlocking parts of the Mauser, the design did away with expensive machining by having the various parts pinned to the frame. The Astra had a sliding plate on the left hand side of the action body and, instead of being made in one integral unit, the barrel and barrel extension were in two separate pieces. Shortly after the appearance of the Astra 900, the full-automatic 901 and 902 models were introduced with different barrel lengths. Both these actually preceded the Mauser Model 1932, although Mauser had produced an experimental full-automatic pistol during the First World War. The Astra 903 had a detachable twenty round magazine instead of the non-detachable type used on the 902 version, and the slightly later 903E had a modified magazine catch and was available in semi-automatic style only. A further version, the Astra Model F, was adopted by the Spanish Civil Guard in 9mm Bergmann, a straight sided cartridge slightly

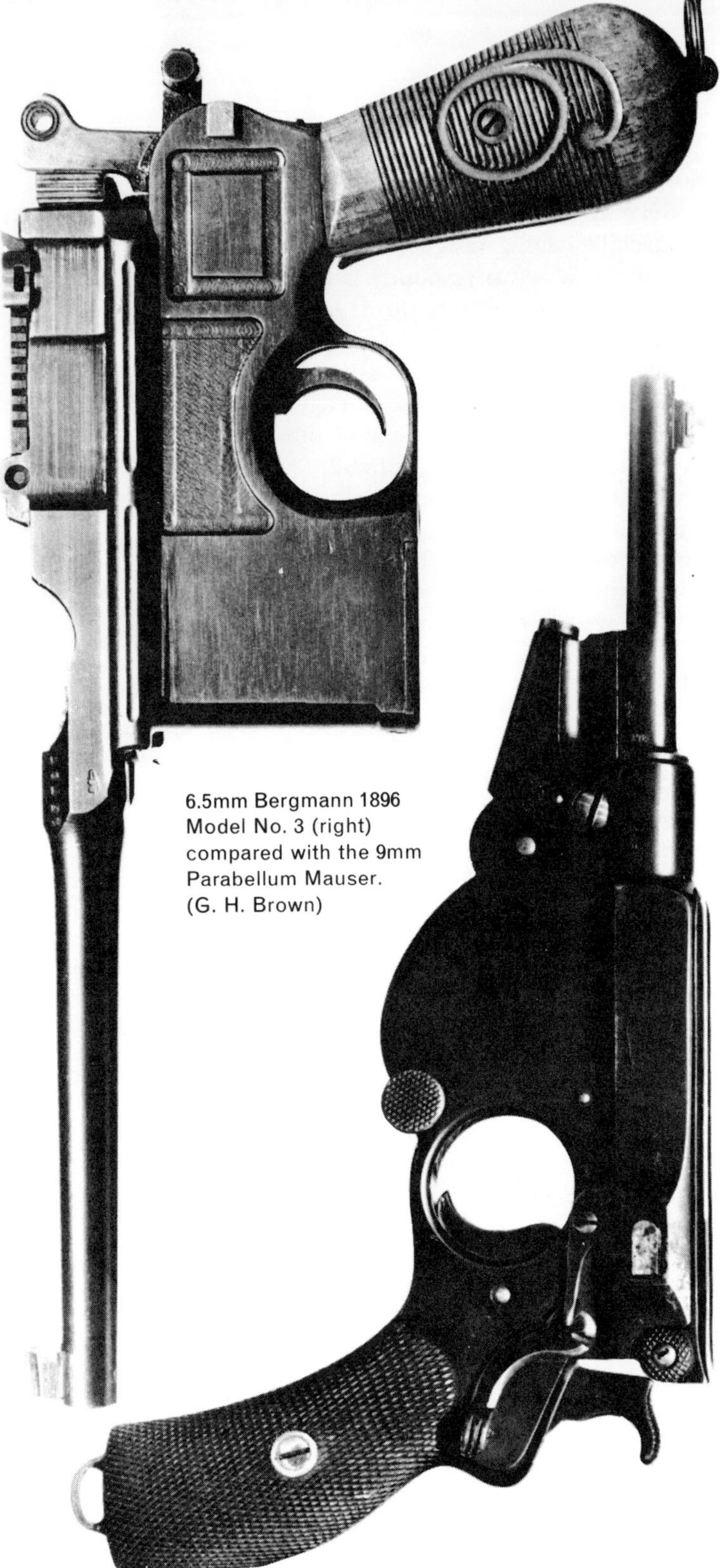
6.5mm Bergmann 1896 Model No. 3 (right) compared with the 9mm Parabellum Mauser. (G. H. Brown)

shorter than the 9mm Mauser. The Model F was selective-fire and, in common with the remainder of the Astra models, the selection lever was on the right hand side of the frame instead of the left as with the Mauser.

The Astra, Royal and the Azul (Eulogio Arostegui, Eibar) all took the standard Mauser type clip of ten cartridges. To load any of these pistols, the bolt was drawn to the rear until held by the hold-open device, the clip was placed in the guides at the top of the barrel extension and the cartridges were stripped down into the magazine. When the clip was withdrawn, the bolt travelled forward and chambered the top cartridge.

Copies of the Mauser were also made in India and China. Some of the Chinese copies made between 1925 and 1935 are of high quality, particularly those manufactured by the Hanyang Arsenal near Hankow and by the Government Arsenal in Shansei Province. In addition, the copies were themselves copied until only a nominal resemblance to the original remained.

Not unaware of the expense of machining the complicated Model 96, the Mauser factory introduced a new self-loading pistol, the action of which was based on one of their self-loading rifles. This, the Model 06–08, bore a superficial resemblance to the Model 96 series but it was not an inspired design, was never produced in quantity and was not further developed.

All the self-loading pistols so far discussed have been on the large side and, with the exception of the Mannlicher Model 1900, rather cumbersome. The kindest description would be 'Military Pistol'. Having also talked about the first successful automatic pistol and the first to be widely adopted, this is the moment to introduce the first pocket self-loading pistol, the Bergmann.

Theodore Bergmann was a successful industrialist whose factory manufactured a variety of articles which included air rifles and high quality sporting equipment. Many of the automatic pistols which will be encountered in the literature under the Bergmann name were not commercially exploited, and matters are further complicated by reference to purely experimental models and to those manufactured under licence by other firms. To simplify classification, the various models are designated by the calibre of cartridge used in ascending order of size, and also by the date of introduction (where known) and by number.

5mm Bergmann Model 94. Two models, the No. 1 and No. 2 Pocket Pistols, were designed to use this cartridge which was both rimless and lacked an extractor groove. DWM No. 416.

5mm Bergmann Model 96. Similar to the 5mm Model 94, this cartridge had an extractor groove and, until about 1930, was made by DWM under the code number 416A.

6.5mm Bergmann Model 94. Lacking both rim and

extractor groove, this was the original 6.5mm Bergmann cartridge for the No. 3 Model 94 pistol. DWM No. 413.

6.5mm Bergmann Model 96. The improved version of the Model 94 cartridge with extractor groove. This was designed for the improved Bergmann No. 3 or Model 96 automatic pistol which could be furnished with an extractor and was the most successful of the early models developed and produced at the Gaggenau factory. DWM No. 413A.

7.5mm Bergmann. Known as the Bergmann No. 4a, this cartridge was developed from the 8mm Bergmann No. 4 for an experimental pistol not manufactured commercially. DWM No. 451A.

7.5mm Bergmann. Known as the Bergmann No. 7a. Developed from the 8mm Bergmann No. 7, but neither the cartridge nor the weapon that fired it were made commercially. DWM No. 460A.

7.65mm Bergmann. Known also as the Bergmann No. 8 (DWM No. KK475), this cartridge was developed for the experimental Model 1901 pistol and was very similar to the 7.63mm Mannlicher. DWM No. 475.

7.8mm Bergmann. Known as the Bergmann No. 5, this cartridge was designed for the Model 97 automatic developed by Bergmann as a military pistol. Neither the cartridge (similar to the 7.65mm Borchardt) nor the pistol achieved a great deal of success, and distribution was limited to Germany. DWM No. 461.

8mm Bergmann. Known as the Bergmann No. 4 and designed for the largest in the Model 96 series of Bergmann pistols. DWM No. 451.

8mm Bergmann. Known as the Bergmann No. 7, this was an improved version of the 8 mm Bergmann No. 4. The experimental pistol for which it was intended was designed in 1898, but

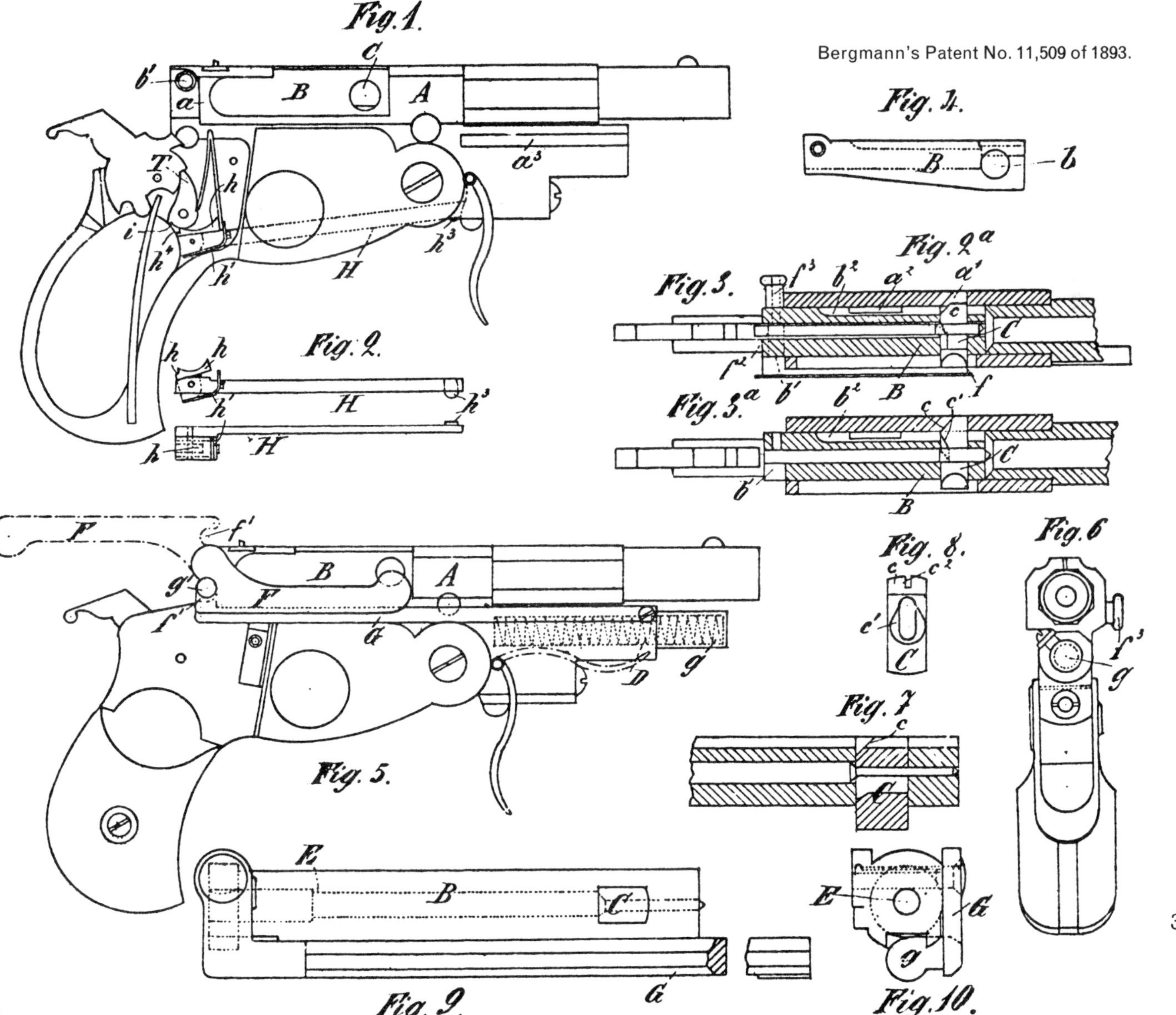

Bergmann's Patent No. 11,509 of 1893.

only limited numbers of both cartridge and pistol were ever made. DWM No. 460.

8mm Bergmann-Schmeisser. So designated to avoid confusion with the other 8mm cartridges in the Bergmann series, this was the largest of the original Schmeisser designs (5mm, 6.5mm and 8mm) and lacked both rim and extractor groove. It was replaced by the 8mm Bergmann No. 4 Model 96 cartridge.

8mm Bergmann-Simplex. This was developed in 1897 for the 'Simplex' pistol. DWM No. 488.

9mm Bergmann. Known as the Bergmann No. 6, this was a development of an 1898 military design. In 9mm, also known as the Model 1903 and as the Bergmann 'Mars' No. 6. DWM No. 456.

9mm Bergmann-Bayard. Developed from the 9mm Bergmann No. 6, this was perhaps the most widely distributed of all the Bergmann cartridge designs. It differed from its predecessor only in overall length, the bullet being seated to a greater depth. The 9mm Bergmann Model 1903 pistol was adopted by Spain in 1906 and was manufactured under licence by Pieper of Herstal as the Bergmann-Bayard. The pistol was later adopted by the Danish Army as the Model 1910. Due to its adoption by Spain, the cartridge can be found variously described as the 9mm largo, 9mm Astra and 9mm Star. It is very easily confused with the 9mm Steyr. DWM No. 456B.

10mm Bergmann. This cartridge was developed for an experimental version of the Bergmann No. 6 automatic pistol. Trials were carried out in Britain in 1902, but they were not successful and the cartridge was not manufactured commercially.

11mm Bergmann. Known also as the 11.35mm Bergmann, this was the largest of the experimental military series developed by Bergmann in his search for a satisfactory large calibre military automatic pistol. Further unsuccessful trials were carried out in Britain in 1903 and in America in 1907. The pistol was again the Bergmann No. 6 manufactured in this calibre for trial purposes. DWM No. 490.

To recapitulate, the earliest Bergmann pistol was the Model 94, known also as the Bergmann-Schmeisser. A simple revolver type lock mechanism was employed together with a side loaded magazine with pivoted cover located in front of the trigger guard. The pistol was loaded with a sheet metal clip which dropped out of the magazine when empty. The Model numbering system was not introduced until 1896, but it was then so organised that it incorporated the 1894 pistols—the Model No. 1 in 5mm (apparently never exploited commercially), the Model No. 2 in 5mm and the Model No. 3 in 6.5mm. Many of these pistols can be found with the marking 'V.C.S.' (V. C. Schilling, Suhl) and the Bergmann trade mark, a 'miner' (bergmann-miner: mountain dweller).

Early versions of the Bergmann No. 2 may be found with a folding trigger guard, and they may also lack an extractor. The factory of V. C. Schilling was taken over by Heinrich Krieghoff in 1904, and production of the Bergmann pistols was transferred to the new Bergmann factory in Suhl. The Bergmann No. 4 pistol was chambered for the 8mm Bergmann cartridge and was generally similar to the No. 3. At the turn of the century, the Bergmann-Simplex was introduced. Of straight blow-back design, this pistol was more compact and had a detachable vertical box magazine. Most of the examples I have seen have borne German proof marks, but some consider that this pistol was made in Belgium.

The No. 5 pistol was the first attempt made by Bergmann to produce a military pistol. Known also as the Model 97, it was similar to the Bergmann-Simplex, but employed a short recoil locked breech action. This particular model was also produced as a pistol carbine with a longer barrel and detachable shoulder stock. Ammunition for the pistol carbine was given the type number 5a and can be distinguished by a blackened case.

Undeterred by the lack of enthusiasm for his No. 5 pistol, Bergmann continued his efforts to develop a satisfactory military pistol and, in 1903, he introduced the Bergmann 'Mars' in a number of calibres, the most successful of which was the 9mm No. 6. A short recoil locked breech action was employed, and cartridges could either be loaded into the detachable box magazine from a clip or singly (if the magazine was removed from the pistol). Between 1907 and 1918 the Bergmann 'Mars' was also manufactured by Anciens Etablissements Pieper of Herstal, and the pistol was then known as the Bergmann-Bayard. After 1918, the Danes, who had adopted the Bergmann-Bayard as their Model 1910, decided to manufacture the pistol themselves at the Haerens Tojhus (Army Manufacturing Arsenal) in Copenhagen. These modified Danish-made Bergmann-Bayards were issued as the Pistol Pattern 1910/21 and were so marked, as they were with their place of origin, either 'Haerens Tojhus' or 'Haerens

Details of the construction of the Bergmann 1896 Model No. 3 as shown in a Gaupillat advertisement which also illustrates the Bergmann Model No. 2 with folding trigger. (G. H. Brown)

Rustkammer' (Army Storage Arsenal). The Bergmann-Bayard remained the standard service issue until the Browning Model 1935 was introduced in 1946.

In the years between the wars Bergmann continued to manufacture automatic pistols, and these will be dealt with later.

The first major power officially to adopt the self-loading pistol was, as one might reasonably expect, the Austro-Hungarian Empire. The pistol chosen in the year it appeared was the 8 mm Roth-Steyr Model 1907, the design of which is attributed to George Roth and Karel Krnka. There is, however, no evidence that the firm of Roth ever made this pistol, although they may have manufactured a very similar one, the Krnka Model 1895, on which much of the design appears to have been based. They did manufacture the Roth Model 1904, the immediate predecessor of the Roth-Steyr. The manufacturing facilities of George Roth were probably inadequate to handle sizeable Government orders, and the Model 1907 was produced at the Steyr factory of OWG and also at the arms factory in the Hungarian half of the Empire, Fegyvergyar (Arms Co.), Budapest. All official issue Roth-Steyr pistols bore the arms of the empire and the letters 'W-n' (Vienna) or 'B-p' (Budapest) and the year of issue.

The Roth-Steyr was loaded by means of a ten round charger inserted into the charger guides at the top of the receiver, the cartridges being stripped downward into the magazine with the bolt to the rear. The cartridges could also be loaded one at a time without using the charger. To unload, the bolt was drawn back to remove the cartridge from the chamber, and was then locked open by depressing the rectangular catch at the top left rear of the receiver. The cartridges in the magazine were then released by pressing the circular catch above the left grip. The 8mm Roth-Steyr cartridge was larger and more powerful than the .32 ACP and is now difficult to obtain.

7.65mm Roth-Sauer by J. P. Sauer and Son of Suhl. (Ian Frame)

Complicated and by no means cheap to manufacture, the Roth-Steyr is of interest because of its unusual locking system and 'trigger cocking' action. Locking was achieved by barrel rotation. Barrel and bolt recoiled about half an inch to the rear together while, at the same time, the barrel was rotated anti-clockwise through 90 degrees; at this point the bolt was unlocked and continued to recoil alone. Most self-loading pistols of this period were self-cocking, the exceptions being the Mannlicher blow-back Models 94 and 96. The Roth-Steyr retained this system, albeit slightly modified, and apparently this was done as a safety measure. Even after the pistol had been loaded and a cartridge chambered, the customary light pull on the trigger would not cause it to fire. During the long and rather hard pull, the firing pin was cocked, and only after a distinct 'pause' would increased pressure on the trigger result in the firing pin being released.

A pistol that can really be regarded as the pocket version of the Roth-Steyr was the Roth-Sauer manufactured prior to the First World War by the famous gunmaking firm of J. P. Sauer und Sohn in Suhl, Germany. With an overall length of $6\frac{3}{4}''$, as against the $9\frac{1}{8}''$ of the Roth-Steyr, the Roth-Sauer was chambered for a special 7.65mm cartridge also known as the 7.8mm Roth-Sauer bearing the code number GR 703. Today comparatively rare, the Roth-Sauer was beautifully made and had a most unusual action. With the pistol unloaded and uncocked, the large milled ring at the rear of the receiver was turned clockwise to unlock the bolt which could then be drawn fully to the rear to permit loading. This was done from a charger holding seven cartridges which were stripped into the magazine from the top of the receiver in the usual manner. When a button on the left hand side of the frame was depressed, the bolt was released to chamber the first cartridge and, as it moved forward, it was rotated anti-clockwise by the inclined slot at the rear of the actuator rod and locked. As with the Roth-Steyr, the striker was cocked by initial pressure on the trigger, and was only released by increased pressure following a pause. The barrel and bolt recoiled together and, in the full recoil position, the bolt was unlocked, allowing the barrel group to move forward again under the influence of the return spring. The cartridge was held against the bolt face by the extractor and, in effect, instead of the cartridge being withdrawn from the chamber, the chamber was withdrawn from the cartridge. As the barrel group moved forward, an internal ejector threw out the fired case and, as the bolt moved forward in its turn, a new cartridge was picked up from the magazine and chambered. A hold-open device was incorporated and was operated by a lever and an external stud on the magazine follower, the stud protruding through the side plate.

The pistol was dismantled by first of all pressing the serrated front of the side plate and withdrawing the pivoted catch. The side plate could then be removed, exposing the mechanism. After the actuator link and the bolt return spring had been taken out, the serrated barrel ring could be unscrewed and the barrel group and bolt withdrawn from the rear of the action. The left hand

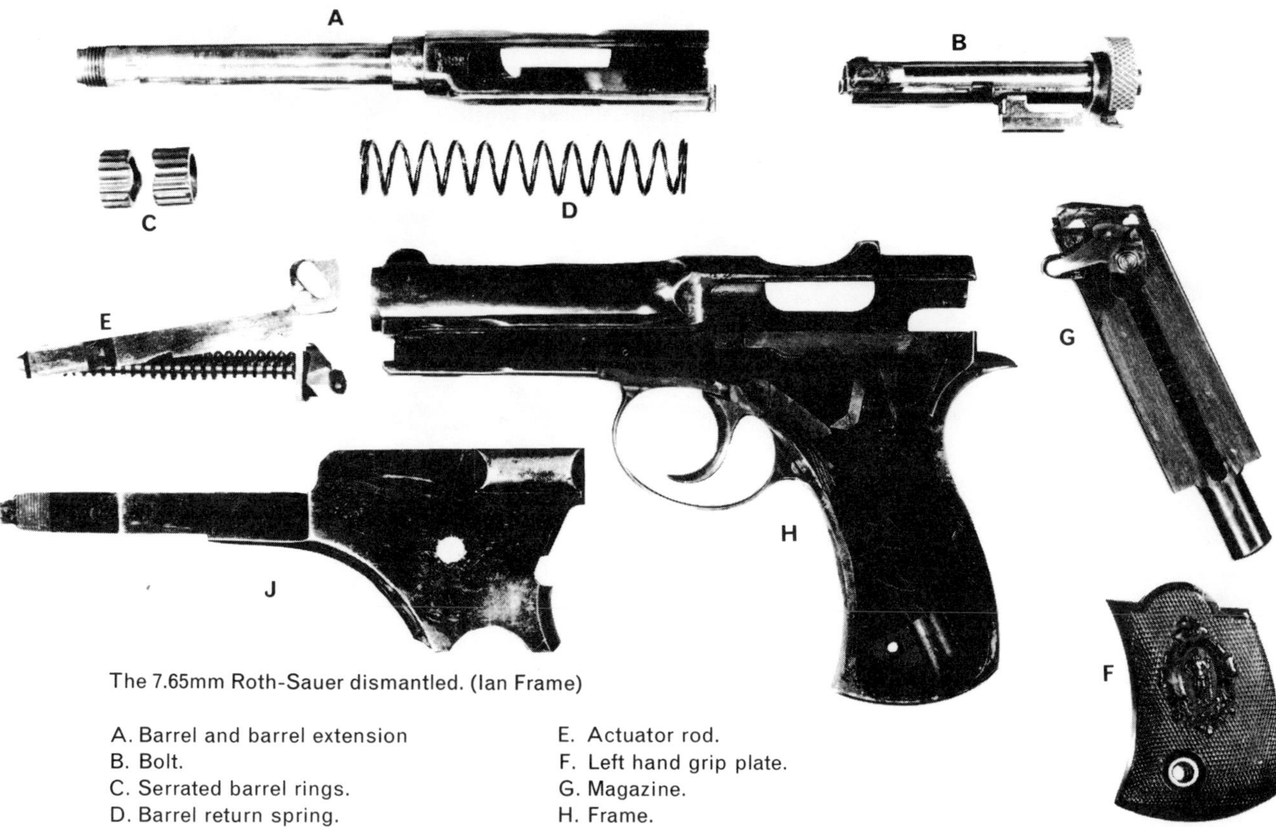

The 7.65mm Roth-Sauer dismantled. (Ian Frame)

A. Barrel and barrel extension
B. Bolt.
C. Serrated barrel rings.
D. Barrel return spring.
E. Actuator rod.
F. Left hand grip plate.
G. Magazine.
H. Frame.
J. Side plate.

grip plate could then be removed and the magazine lifted out of the grip frame. When rotated clockwise, the milled head of the bolt acted as the safety and, at the rear of the right hand side of the receiver, the magazine catch made it possible to remove cartridges from a loaded magazine without having to work them through the action. Somewhat complicated to operate and with a rather heavy trigger pull, the Roth-Sauer was nevertheless an adequate pocket pistol and has excellent 'feel' and grip. Examples I have seen were marked 'J. P. Sauer & Sohn, Suhl, Patent Roth'.

To sum up, the Roth-Steyr was a pistol with a short recoil action locked by barrel rotation, the Roth-Sauer one with a long recoil action locked by the rotation of the bolt.

In the third of these Central European pistols, the Frommer, yet another locking system was employed. Rudolf Frommer, who was born in Budapest in 1868 and made many important contributions to firearms design, became the Director of the Fegyver es Gepgyar Reszveny-tarsasag (The Small Arms and Machine Factory Ltd.), Budapest, and it was here that his pistols were made.

Externally the Frommer 1901 model (British Patent No. 20,363) looked very similar to the Krnka and the Roth-Steyr. The action, however, was completely different and, since only the bolt head rotated, was similar to the 'straight-pull' bolt action rifles such as the Mannlicher Model 1905, the Ross and the Schmidt-Rubin. The operational sequence was not unlike the Roth-Sauer—both were of the long recoil type—and barrel and bolt had to recoil fully to compress the recoil springs, that for the barrel being mounted around the barrel, and that for the bolt being coiled around the striker. At the full extent of recoil, the bolt was retained in the rear position (as with the Roth-Sauer) and, as the barrel moved forward, the bolt head rotated to unlock the action. The fired case was extracted and ejected and a new case chambered as the bolt, in turn, moved forward again. The 8mm Model 1901 Frommer was a complicated pistol and, probably for this reason, was rejected, following military trials, in America, Sweden, Britain, Austria and Spain.

Undaunted by these reverses, Frommer introduced a smaller and slightly simplified variant, the Model of 1906, chambered for a small 7.65mm cartridge developed by Roth, instead of the original 8mm Roth design. The 7.65mm Frommer is dimensionally similar to the Roth-Sauer cartridge, but differs in having a heavier charge. Further modifications were carried out in 1910 and the pistol was adapted for the 7.65mm

7.65mm Roth-Sauer in the full recoil position with breech and barrel locked together.

The bolt unlocked (but still to the rear) and the barrel forward.

7.65mm Roth-Sauer with the side plate removed to expose the action and with bolt and barrel fully forward. (All Ian Frame)

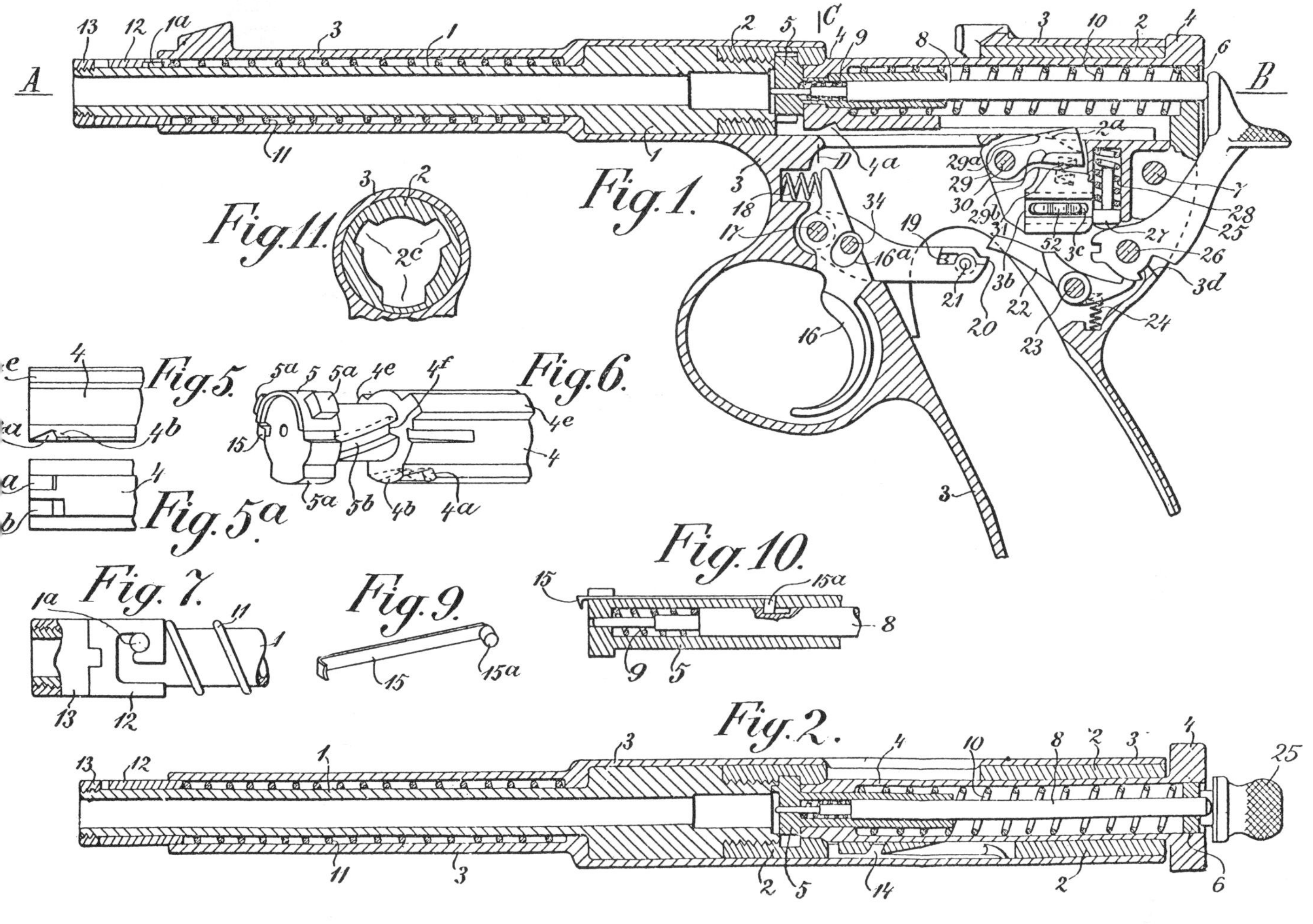

Frommer's Patent No.20,363 of 1901.

Browning cartridge. Very few 1901 series Frommer pistols were made and manufacture appears to have ceased prior to 1914. The 1912 Frommer Stop Model was of the 'straight-pull' long recoil type, but of a different, although still complicated, design to the earlier 1901 series. Two return springs were still required, but both were carried above the barrel, and the housing was the distinctive feature of the series. The sequence of operation was the same.

The Frommer Stop Model 1912 was made in tremendous numbers in 7.65mm and, in 9mm Browning short, was issued to the Hungarian Army of the Dual Empire, the Koeniglische Ungarnische Armee, and was made only by Fegyver es Gepgyar in Budapest and not by the Austrian factory at Steyr. In the years immediately prior to the First World War, the Hungarian half of the Habsburg Empire was becoming increasingly nationalistic and it seems likely that the Hungarian War Office adopted the Frommer Stop not because it was the most suitable pistol but because it was Hungarian.

A smaller version of the Model 1912 was also manufactured by the Small Arms and Machine Factory and, known as the Frommer Baby, was made in 7.65mm (.32) and 9mm Browning short. Some time after the First World War, the Frommer 6.35mm Lilliput Model appeared. This tiny pistol, with an overall length of just over 4″, was a forerunner of things to come in that the Stop Patent system was abandoned in favour of a simple blow-back design.

All the Frommer Stop series had detachable box magazines in the butt, external hammers and grip safety devices. Markings were usually

'Fegyvergyar-Budapest', but the model 1912 also carried 'Frommer Pat. Stop Cal. 7.65mm (.32)', the Hungarian War Office mark, 'B-p', the Austro-Hungarian Arms, and the acceptance date '17' for 1917. The hard rubber grips bore the letters 'F.S.' in an oval. The Frommer Baby was marked 'Fegyvergyar-Budapest Frommer Pat. Baby, Cal. 7.65mm (.32)', the grips bearing the letters 'FB'. The Lilliput was marked in the same way except for 'Lilliput' instead of 'Baby'; the grips bore the letters 'FL'.

A Browning type blow-back pistol was manufactured by the successors to the Small Arms and Machine Works Ltd., Femaru Fegyver es Gepgyar R. T. (Metalware, Small Arms and Machine Works Ltd.) and was adopted as the Pisztoly 29M (1929 Model). In 1937 a simplified variant appeared, the Pisztoly 37M, and both models were chambered for the Browning 9mm short cartridge. After signing of the 'Axis Pact' with Germany in 1940, the German Ordnance Department placed an order for the Pisztoly 37M in 7.65mm for the use of the Luftwaffe. Both the Hungarian 'Commercial' Model and the version

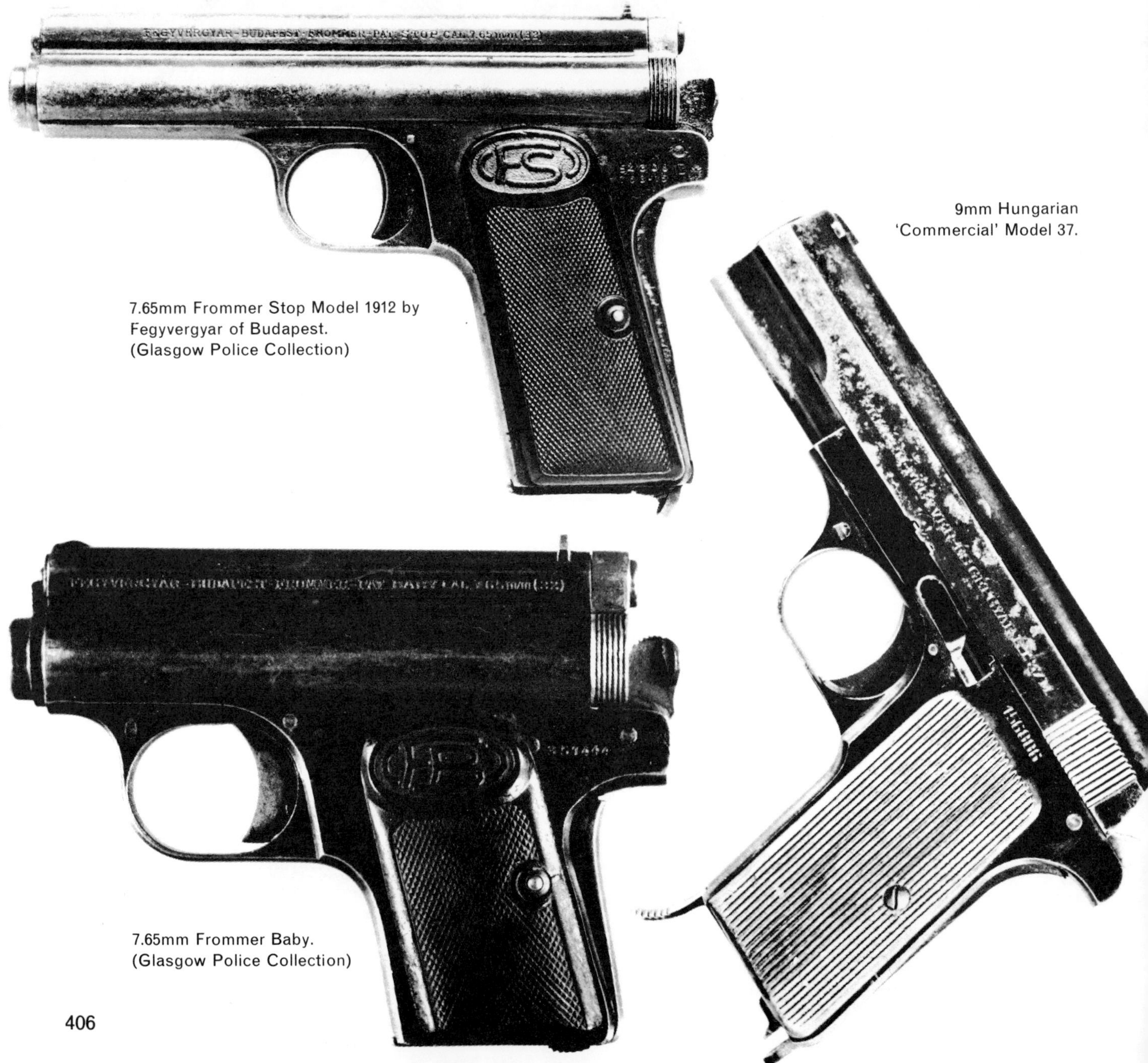

7.65mm Frommer Stop Model 1912 by Fegyvergyar of Budapest. (Glasgow Police Collection)

9mm Hungarian 'Commercial' Model 37.

7.65mm Frommer Baby. (Glasgow Police Collection)

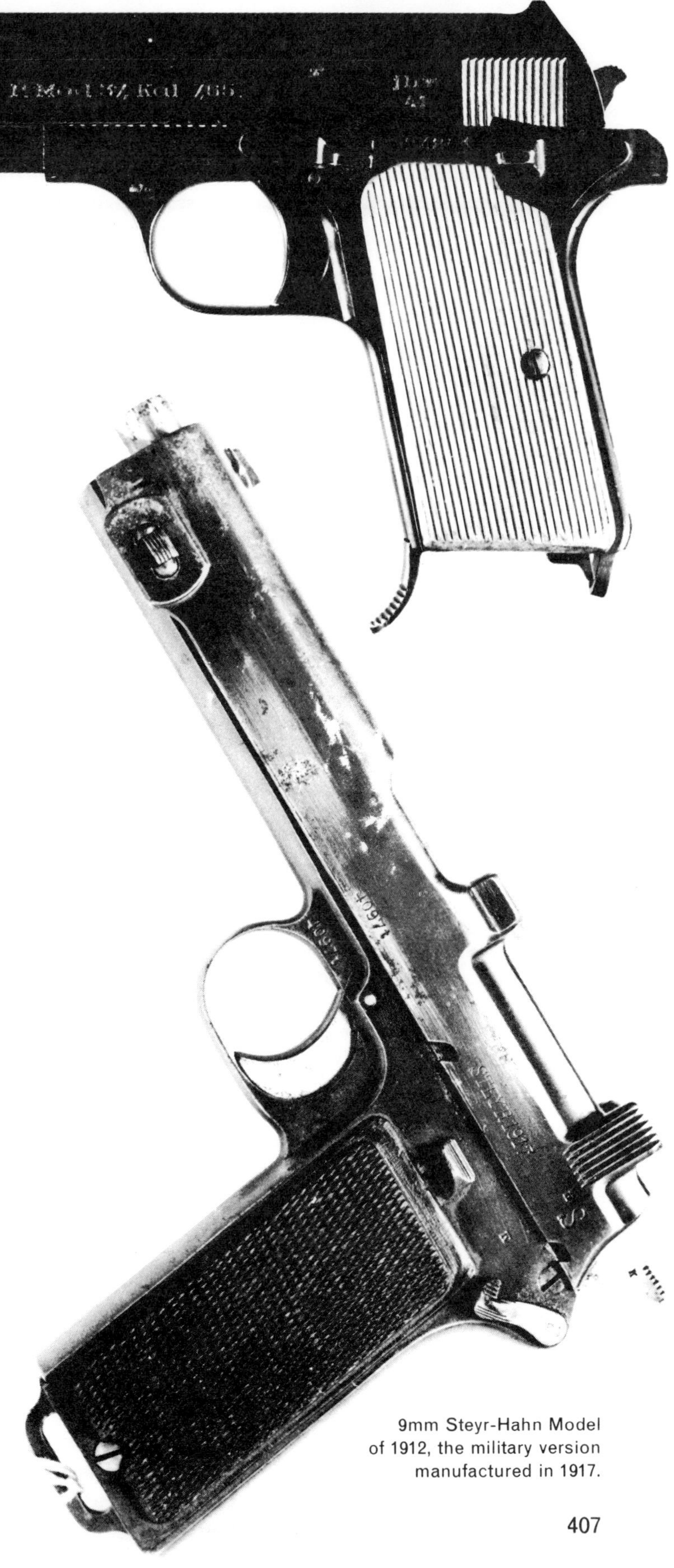

7.65mm Hungarian German Ordnance Model 37.

for the German Ordnance are illustrated, the latter having the German code 'jhv' (for the Metallwaren, Waffen und Maschinenfabrik) and the acceptance date '41' marked on the left hand rear of the slide and the pistol, as well as 'P. Model 37 Kal 7.65 mm'.

Subsequent production in Hungary is a matter for some conjecture. None of the pre-World War Two pistols are currently being manufactured and such information as is available indicates that unauthorised copies of the Walther, the Pistol W48, are at present being made for police use, military pistols being of Russian design.

The fourth in the Central European group of pistols is the Steyr Model 1911 known as the Steyr-Hahn (Steyr-Hammer) to distinguish it from the hammerless Roth-Steyr. The Steyr-Hahn was the third pistol (Roth-Steyr 1907, Frommer Stop 1912) to be adopted by the Austro-Hungarian Empire, and, being more robust and of simpler design, it was undoubtedly the best.

Nevertheless the Steyr-Hahn remains true to its ancestry, for it, too, had a rotating barrel locking system. When the pistol was fired, the barrel and slide (including the breech of the bolt) recoiled together, and lugs at the rear of the barrel engaged a helical groove cut into the receiver. The anti-clockwise rotation imparted to the barrel resulted in the release of the locking lugs engaged in recesses cut in the slide to lock slide and barrel together. Further rearward travel of the barrel was limited by a stop lug, while the slide was free to recoil to its full extent. Extraction and ejection took place on this recoil, the new cartridge being chambered on the forward return. As the slide moved forward, the breech face struck the rear of the barrel, forcing it forward, while the helical groove in the receiver rotated it clockwise so that the barrel locking lugs engaged the recesses in the slide.

The Steyr-Hahn was loaded by the usual Mannlicher type charger with a capacity of eight rounds. The slide remained to the rear when the last cartridge had been fired; it would also do so if the magazine was unloaded when the slide was pulled back. The slide release, on the left hand side of the pistol just above the grip, also

9mm Steyr-Hahn Model of 1912, the military version manufactured in 1917.

served to release the cartridges from a loaded magazine without their having to be worked through the action. The 9mm Steyr cartridge (DWM 577) was slightly longer than the 9mm Parabellum and almost identical with the Colt .38 ACP, except that the latter was semi-rimmed. The only other pistol which would accept the 9 mm Steyr was the Astra Series 400, and this had an omnivorous appetite for most nominal 9mm cartridges.

The Steyr-Hahn was adopted by the Austro-Hungarian Army as the Model 1912 self-loading pistol, Steyr, and the markings on the military models consisted of the word 'Steyr' followed by '17' for 1917, the date of manufacture. During the First World War, OWG at Steyr manufactured this pistol for the Roumanian Government, marking it 'Md. 1912', and, shortly before the war, the Steyr factory supplied a number to Chile with the legend 'Ejercito de Chile'. During World War Two many of the 9mm Steyr Model 1912 pistols were rechambered for the 9mm Parabellum cartridge and were issued to the Austrian Police during the German occupation. These altered pistols bore the additional marking '08' (for Patrone 08, the official service designation of the 9mm Parabellum-Luger cartridge).

The Steyr factory also manufactured pocket pistols under licence from Nicolas Pieper of Belgium, whose basic patents were taken out in 1906–1907. The Steyr-made pistols were of the 'basculant' type with the barrel hinged underneath, and two versions were made, one in 6.35mm and a larger version in 7.65mm. Those pistols made before the First World War bore the OWG monogram on the hard rubber grips; those made after the war bore the name Steyr.

Some authorities refer to the Steyr pocket pistols as the Model 1908, from the last patent date on the barrel; others use the term Model 1909, from the apparent date of commercial introduction. Manufacture started in 1909 and, with a break during the First World War, continued until 1939. During this period several minor design variations appeared, but the basic features remained unaltered. Unusual in that no extractor was employed, the Steyr consequently had fewer parts, but problems could arise with variable ammunition or in case of a misfire. With the latter, the barrel release on the left hand side of the pistol was depressed so that the barrel hinged downwards under spring pressure and the defective cartridge could then be pried out. The design of this pistol also allowed for it to be

7.65mm Steyr Model 1908 (Second Model). (Glasgow Police Collection)

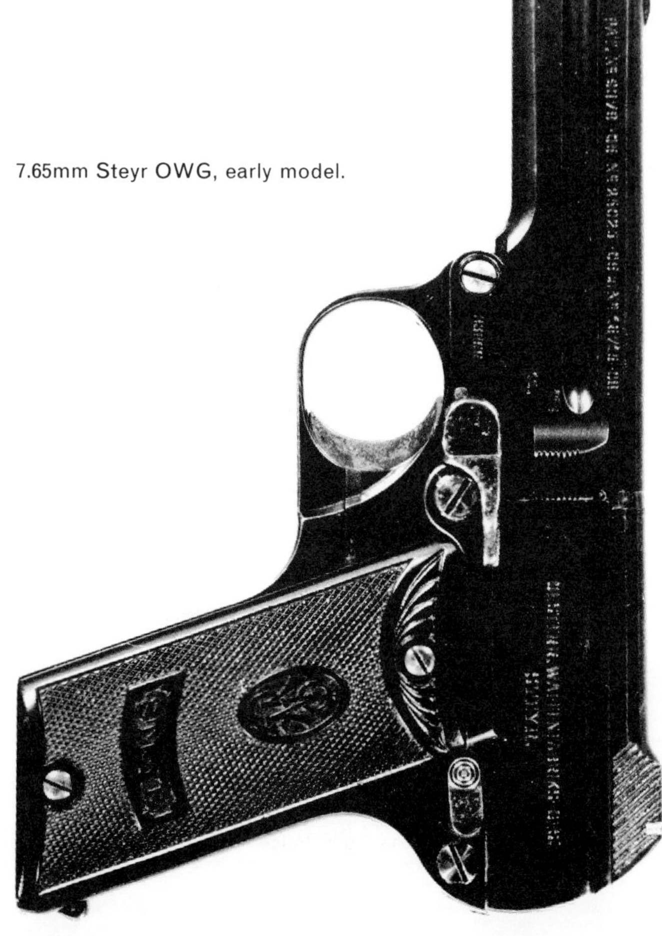

7.65mm Steyr OWG, early model.

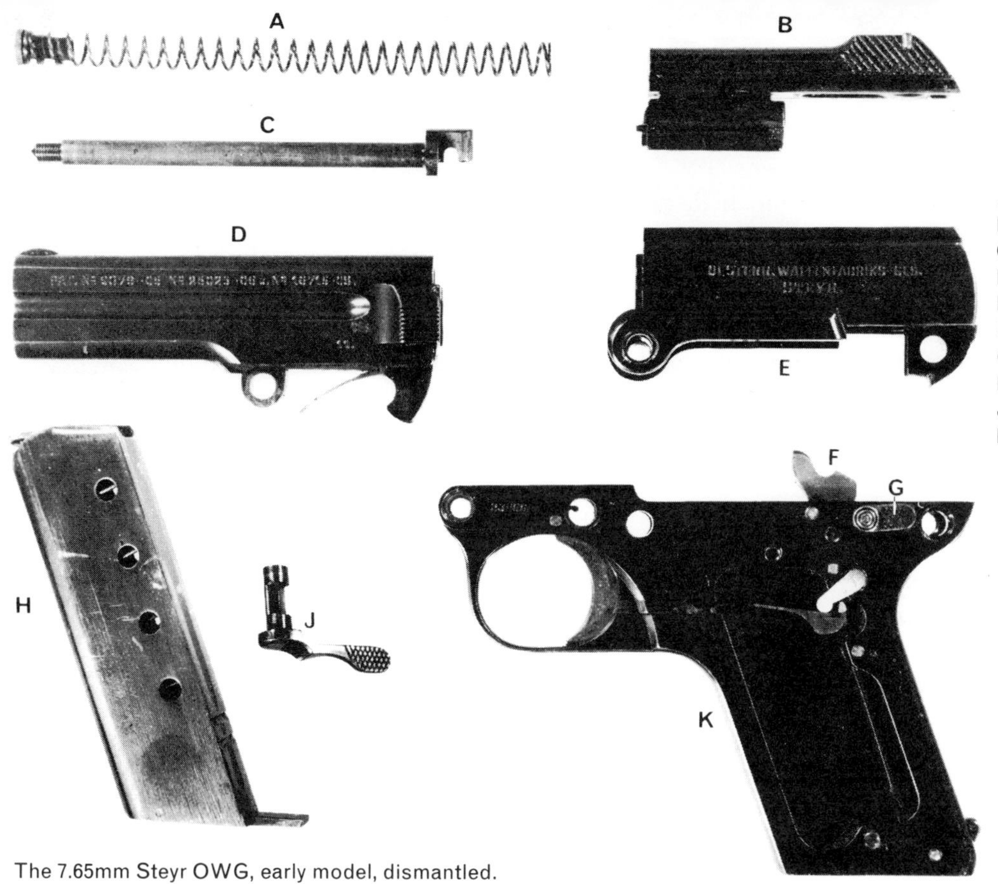

A. Recoil spring.
B. Slide.
C. Recoil spring guide.
D. Barrel.
E. Slide housing.
F. Hammer.
G. Safety.
H. Magazine.
J. Barrel latch.
K. Frame.

The 7.65mm Steyr OWG, early model, dismantled.

6.35mm Steyr OWG Model 1909, 'Basculant' type. (Glasgow Police Collection)

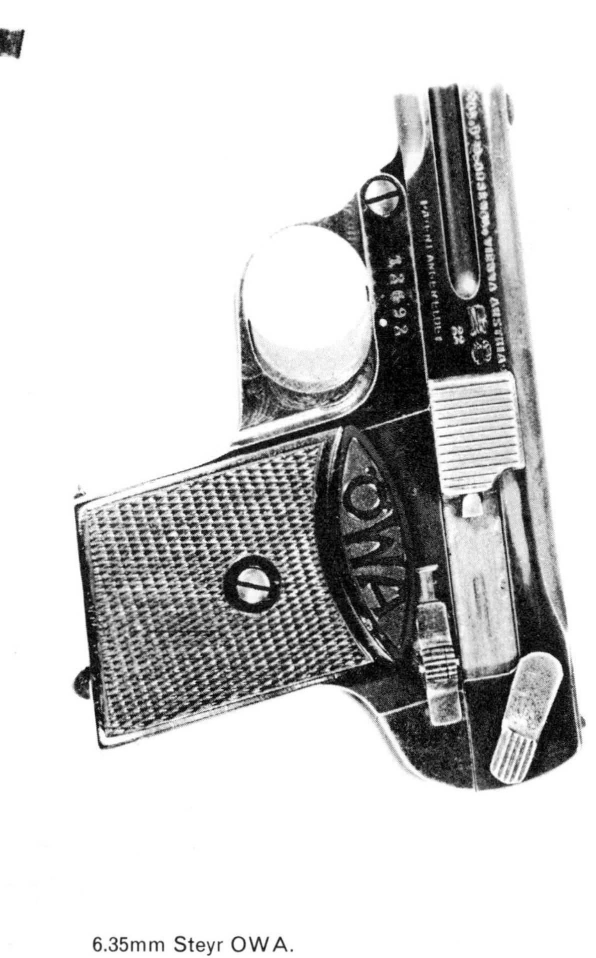

6.35mm Steyr OWA.

used single shot. If the barrel was opened, the recoil spring was disconnected from the slide and the internal hammer could be cocked by pulling back on the slide without having to compress the recoil spring. The 6.35mm model illustrated shows this operation in action.

An automatic pistol which bore a superficial resemblance to the Steyr was marketed in the years immediately after the First World War, and the grips bore the initials 'O.W.A.' standing for Oesterreichische Werke-gws-Antalt. Made only in 6.35mm calibre, examples seen were all dated 1922. Unlike the Steyr, both the barrel and the barrel extension hinged instead of merely the barrel. The locking lever was at the top rear of the barrel extension, and the recoil spring guide had a stud that engaged the front of the slide. This pistol owed something to the OWG Steyr, but it was unnecessarily complicated and lacked the Steyr's fine finish.

Two other pistols should be included here, the Gabbett-Fairfax-Mars because it was the ultimate in complexity and a failure, and the Parabellum or Luger because it was the last of its type and a resounding success.

During the evolutionary period of the self-loading pistol, inventors in both Britain and America appear to have largely ignored the developments which had taken place in Germany and Austria. Hugh W. Gabbett-Fairfax was obviously keen to change this state of affairs by designing a self-loading pistol with a locked breech of great strength for use with an extremely high velocity cartridge. A long series of patents obtained between 1895 and 1906 indicate how hard he and his collaborators strove to achieve this end. The many Mars variants are difficult to classify but, for the sake of brevity, they can be divided into three basic categories.

The first were those made for the inventor in 1898 by Webley and Scott, Gabbett-Fairfax having worked with J. W. Whiting who was later to design the Webley automatic pistols. The original design was modified, several prototype pistols were made, but, in 1901, Webley's lost interest in the project. The Mars Automatic Pistol Syndicate Ltd. of Birmingham was therefore formed to promote the sale of Gabbett-Fairfax pistols, and it was also intended to establish a factory for their manufacture. In fact,

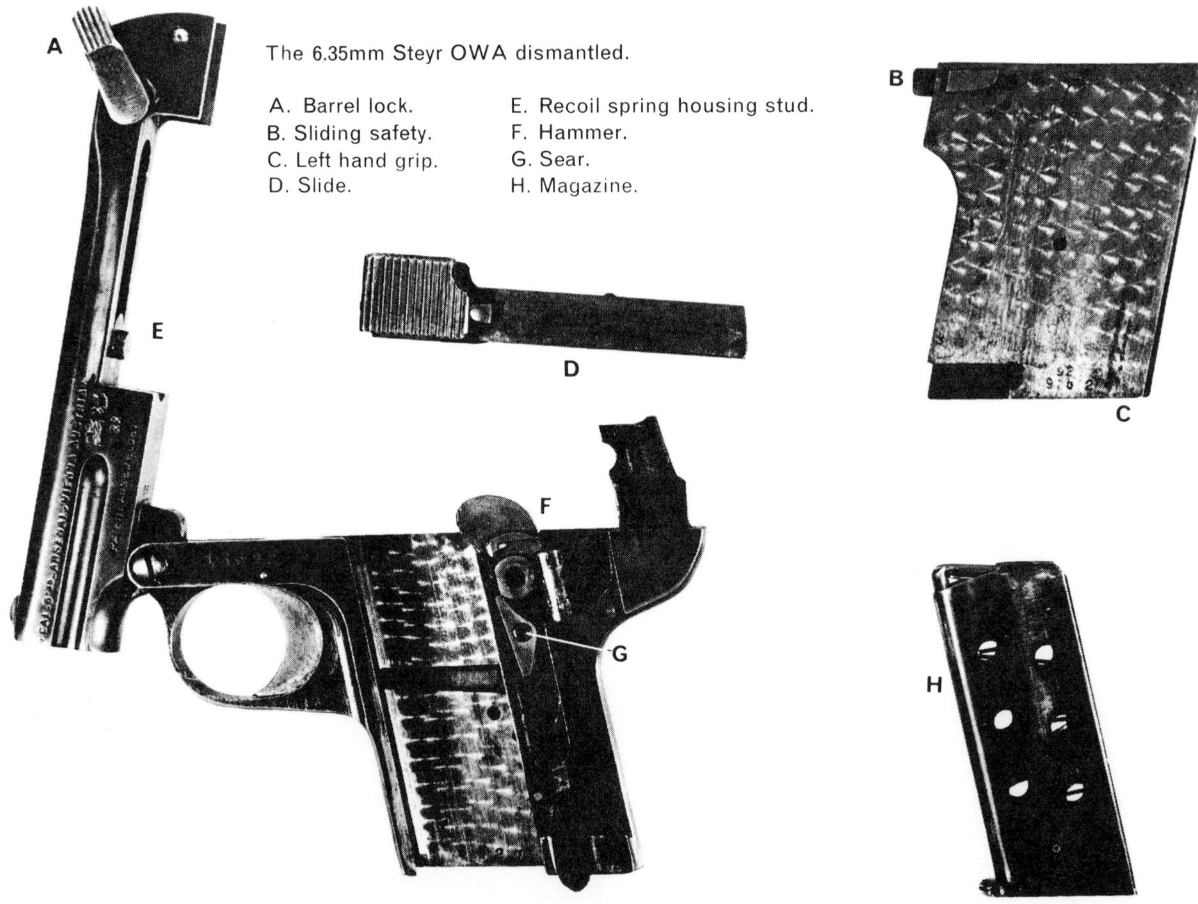

The 6.35mm Steyr OWA dismantled.

A. Barrel lock.
B. Sliding safety.
C. Left hand grip.
D. Slide.
E. Recoil spring housing stud.
F. Hammer.
G. Sear.
H. Magazine.

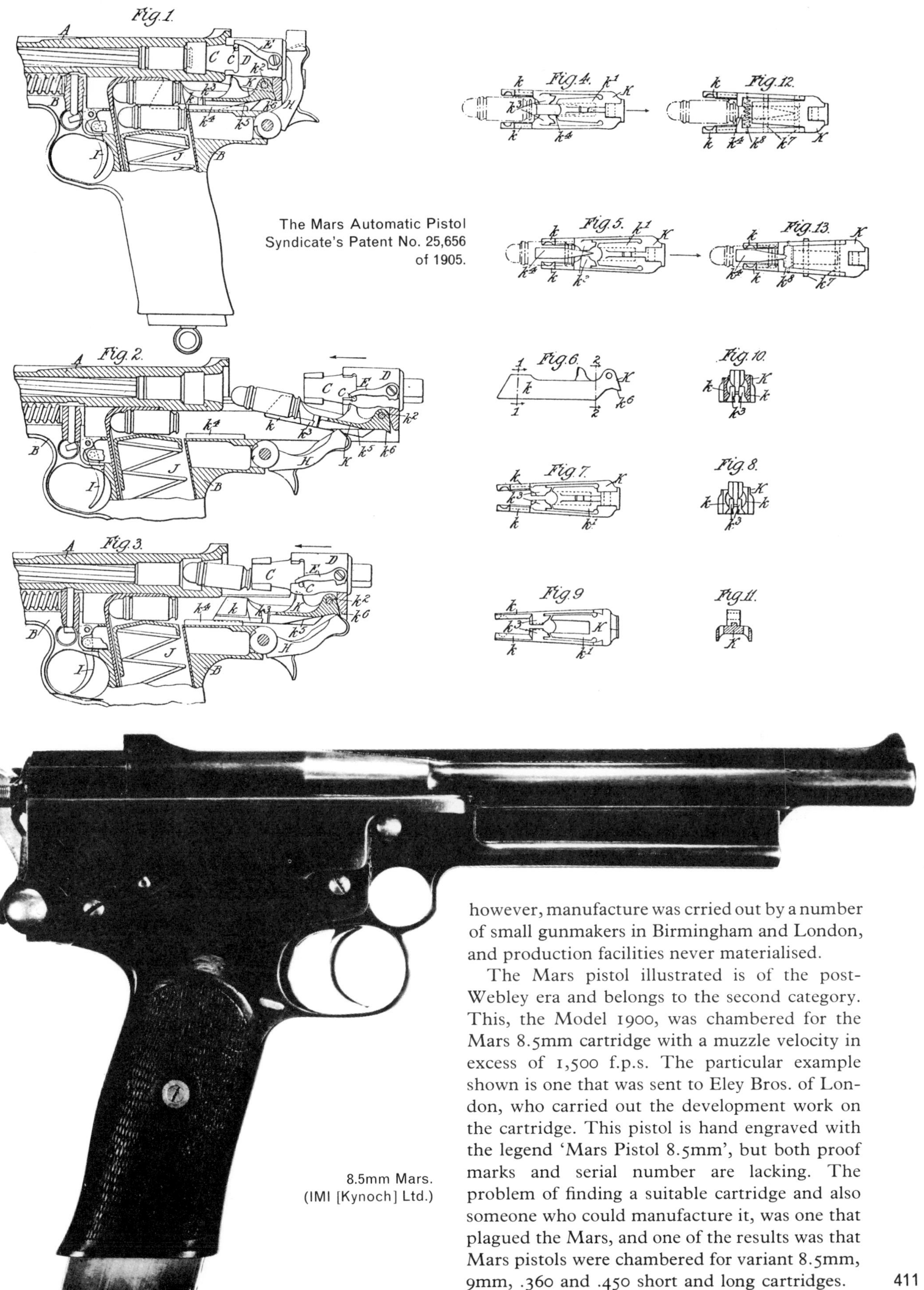

The Mars Automatic Pistol Syndicate's Patent No. 25,656 of 1905.

8.5mm Mars. (IMI [Kynoch] Ltd.)

however, manufacture was crried out by a number of small gunmakers in Birmingham and London, and production facilities never materialised.

The Mars pistol illustrated is of the post-Webley era and belongs to the second category. This, the Model 1900, was chambered for the Mars 8.5mm cartridge with a muzzle velocity in excess of 1,500 f.p.s. The particular example shown is one that was sent to Eley Bros. of London, who carried out the development work on the cartridge. This pistol is hand engraved with the legend 'Mars Pistol 8.5mm', but both proof marks and serial number are lacking. The problem of finding a suitable cartridge and also someone who could manufacture it, was one that plagued the Mars, and one of the results was that Mars pistols were chambered for variant 8.5mm, 9mm, .360 and .450 short and long cartridges.

The last of the Mars pistols was the so-called Mars Model 1906, based on improvements contained in the Mars Automatic Pistol Syndicate's British Patent No. 25,656 of 9 December 1905. As can be seen from the drawings, the Mars, at this stage in its development, had an external hammer, and the cartridges were contained in a vertical box magazine housed in the butt. Fig. 1 shows the mechanism immediately after the discharge of a cartridge. The barrel and breech block recoiled for 3″, compressing the recoil spring housed under the barrel and also two light springs which acted as breech block return springs. As the barrel and breech block started their return journey under the influence of the three springs, the bell crank '*E*' was depressed by an actuating rod operated by the returning barrel. The bell crank forced the stud '*c*' downward rotating the bolt head '*C*' anti-clockwise through 45 degrees so that the locking lugs on the bolt head were disengaged from their recesses inside the barrel. It can be seen from Fig. 2 that, as the barrel and breech block recoiled, the top cartridge in the magazine was drawn backwards by the carrier '*K*', the top of the magazine having a metal guide to prevent the cartridge being drawn forward. As the carrier rocked upwards, the fired case (which had been retained against the face of the breech) was ejected by the carrier, and the new cartridge remained in the position shown in Fig. 2 until the trigger '*I*' was released. The bolt, in turn, was then released to chamber the cartridge as in Fig. 3.

The Mars represents the ultimate in the pursuit of high velocity performance. The velocities obtained with many of the cartridges developed for it exceeded those of contemporary self-loading rifles, but a price had to be paid — in the cost of machining, in complexity and in poor handling. Gabbett-Fairfax made many efforts to arouse Government interest in his design but, although a number of trials were carried out, a report issued in 1902 by the Captain of H.M.S. *Excellent* (the Naval Gunnery School at Whale Island, near Portsmouth) listed the disadvantages and effectively damned the pistol. These disadvantages were its liability to jam, its weight, its unwieldy shape, the fact that it was difficult to hold steady, that the fired cartridges struck the firer in the face, and that the mechanism was complicated. The Captain also commented that 'no one who fired once with the pistol wished to shoot with it again; several of those who fired were good shots and in the *Excellent*'s pistol team'. In those days, the Naval personnel at Whale Island were not easily distressed by any sort of firearm, least of all a pistol, but their opinion is backed by R. K. Wilson who states that 'the 9mm Mars is a singularly unpleasant and alarming pistol to shoot with'. Today Mars ammunition is eagerly sought after by collectors, so much so in fact that, in the unlikely event of being offered a Mars and ammunition to shoot, the offer can be declined without loss of face, on these grounds alone. Actual manufacture of the Mars ceased after 1907, Gabbett-Fairfax having got into financial difficulties in 1903. When attempts to interest the Government failed and commercial interests were equally unresponsive, the first British self-loading pistol faded into obscurity. Despite its many failings it was, until the recent introduction of the .44 Magnum, the most powerful handgun ever made.

From failure, then, to success. George Luger's improvements on the Borchardt pistol were patented in Britain in 1900, Patent No. 4399. Only one of the ten pages of drawings can be shown, but this serves to indicate the general arrangement of the pistol and the fact that, although many of the features of the Borchardt were retained, Luger transformed an ungainly and rather impractical weapon into a pistol that has become one of the best known and widely used automatic pistols in military history.

As must already have become apparent, the identification of any pistol is not always entirely straightforward. Several pieces of information are often necessary before ambiguity can be dispelled, and the most important is the calibre of the cartridge which, as we have seen, may be a purely arbitrary figure bearing no relationship to actual bullet diameter or even to the bore dimensions of the barrel. The particular pistol we are at present considering was made in three calibres, 7.65mm, 9mm and 11.35mm or .45.

The 7.65mm cartridge was developed from the 7.65mm Borchardt and had an actual bullet diameter of .308″. For this reason it is often called a .30 calibre cartridge, particularly in Britain and America. The standard German loading by DWM bore the headstamp code 471 and the cartridge could variously be called a 7.65mm Parabellum, a 7.65mm Borchardt-Luger, a 7.65mm Parabellum-Borchardt and a 7.65mm Luger. The Swiss SIS auto-pistol and a number of machine carbines were also chambered for this cartridge.

The second cartridge, the 9mm Parabellum,

has been adapted to more military handguns and machine pistols than any other handgun cartridge. Introduced in 1902, it was loaded with a truncated conical bullet from 1908 until 1916, after which the round nose bullet was re-adopted. German commercial nomenclature was 9mm Parabellum, Military Pistolen Patronen 08, Pistolen Patronen 400 (b), and the DWM headstamp 480C. Also known as the 9mm long Beretta, 9mm long, 9mm M-38, 9mm Luger, 9mm Pour Mi. 34 e G.P. and 9mm M/34 (Sweden), it has been adapted to pistols manufactured by Walther, Browning (FN), Colt, Smith and Wesson, and Beretta, as well as to pistols made in Spain, Poland and Finland. As might be expected, variations are legion, especially if those developed for machine pistols and machine carbines are included.

The third cartridge, the 11.35mm or .45, is now apparently non-existent, less than 1,000 rounds having been originally manufactured in Germany for the US Army tests of 1907.

From the foregoing it will be appreciated that identification is only partially possible by calibre reference and that this often requires amplification. Something further has to be added, and this could well be a reference to the inventor or designer, or a note of the year in which the pistol was patented, first manufactured or marketed, or in which it was adopted as a military or official weapon. Where manufacture was subsequently licensed, or where it was pirated by another firm, the identity of the maker may also be necessary to prevent any possibility of confusion. Even granted all this, however, the correct identity of a weapon may still be difficult to record, and details of how and where it was used, coupled with the popular or even slang term for it, may have to be added to complete the picture.

All this might appear unnecessarily pedantic, but the difficulties we have already encountered with nomenclature pale into insignificance beside those of establishing the identity of the various Borchardt-Luger-Parabellum Models, even if the variant spellings of Luger are disregarded.

George Luger was born in 1849 in the village of Steinach in the Austrian Tyrol, not far from Innsbruck. He served as an officer in the Austrian Army, became acquainted with Von Mannlicher, and then, about 1891, joined the firm of Ludwig Loewe in Berlin for whom he went on several promotional trips to America—one visit, in 1894, being for the purpose of demonstrating the Borchardt. We have already seen how the firm of Ludwig Loewe, progressing from the manufacture of sewing machines to firearms, first acquired ammunition interests and then merged with other companies to form the firm of DWM. The Borchardt continued to be manufactured by DWM and, following the failure of the American Ordnance trials of 1897, they tried again in 1898 to obtain military approval, this time from Switzerland. The weapon put forward for consideration was the Borchardt-Luger, very possibly a transitional type. The Swiss held a further series of tests at Berne in 1899, when a 'much lighter pistol with a safety' was offered by DWM which weighed only 30 ozs. and had the overall length reduced from 14″ to 9″. A further result of these trials was the appearance of a modified cartridge, the 7.65mm Parabellum, the name apparently originating with the DWM factory since the pistol itself was known as the Pistole Parabellum

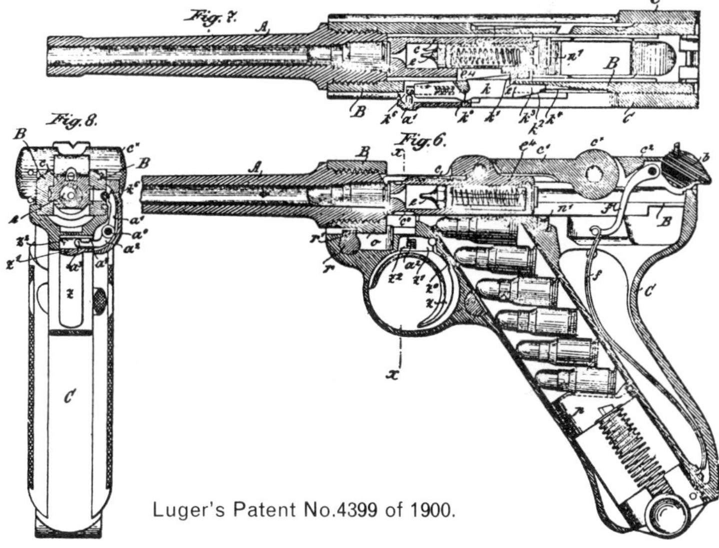

Luger's Patent No.4399 of 1900.

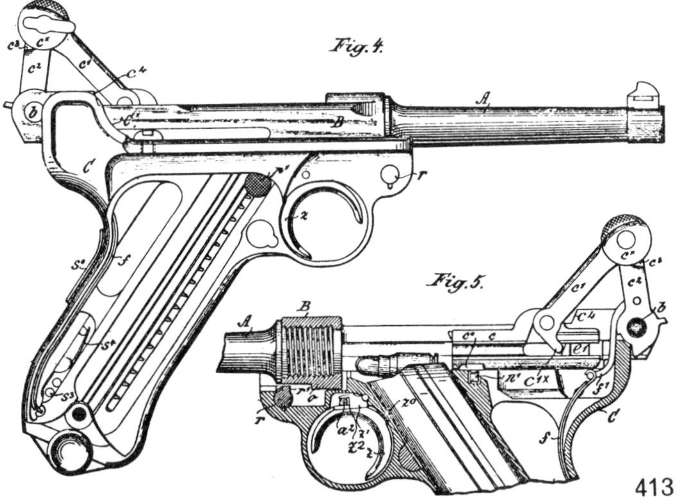

after a Latin phrase *Si Vis Pacem Para Bellum* ('If you want Peace, prepare for War') which, in German, becomes *Bereite Den Krieg vor Parabellum*. As far as the manufacturers were concerned the pistol had been christened 'Parabellum' and this was the name by which it was known throughout Europe.

The 7.65mm Parabellum (very similar to that in the patent drawing) was adopted in 1901, when an order for 3,000 pistols was placed with DWM, and the Swiss referred to their new military pistol as the Pistole 1900. At first glance it looks very much the same as any other Parabellum, but a closer inspection reveals the grip safety, the Geneva Cross (the Swiss National emblem) and, on the toggle link, the letters 'D.W.M.'. The success of the Swiss trials spurred DWM to further sales efforts. Trials were held in America and, as a result, a number of Parabellum Model 1900 pistols were purchased by the US Government and were later disposed of on the open market. These pistols differed from the Swiss Military Model in that they bore an American eagle stamped over the chamber in place of the Geneva Cross. In 1902 the pistol was chambered for the 9mm cartridge, and it was also slightly modified in that the slim 7.65mm barrel was replaced by a shorter (4″ instead of 4¾″) and fatter barrel. The Model 1900 was the first Parabellum to be adopted as a military weapon, the Model 1902 the first handgun to chamber the 9mm Parabellum cartridge.

Attempts to obtain official approval from the German authorities were crowned with success in 1904 with the adoption, by the German Navy, of the 'Marine Modell 1904'. Chambered for the 9mm cartridge, this was the first of the DWM pistols to be adopted by any of the German services. A six inch barrel, a grip safety, and a two position back sight (adjustable for 100 or 200 metres and mounted on the rear of the toggle linkage) were some of the main features, and the 1904 Model can be distinguished from later models by the fact that it still employed a flat mainspring and retained the toggle lock. Unlike the contoured grips of the previous models, the toggle grips were flat.

In 1904 DWM, in line with the policy of Mauser and Bergmann, also introduced a carbine model. This had an 11¾″ barrel, a wooden fore-end to house an additional recoil spring and, of course, a detachable shoulder stock. Standard-ised in 7.65mm calibre, the carbine variant is nowadays a most desirable weapon.

In 1906 several important alterations were made to the pistol. The flat mainspring was replaced by a coil spring which was less likely to break, and the original extractor was replaced by one which also, if the chamber contained a cartridge, acted as an indicator by exposing the word *Geladen* (loaded) or its equivalent. Not only was this indicator visual, it was also tactile, and the presence or absence of a cartridge in the chamber could be detected in pitch darkness without the breech being opened. The original toggle grips of the 1900 and 1902 Models were not easy to grasp and, on the 1904 Model, were replaced by the flat sided toggles that were to become standard. The toggle lock previously fitted to the right hand side and employed instead of the dummy wooden magazine provided with the original Borchardt, was also discarded.

When the Swiss placed a further order with DWM they were supplied with the 1906 variant, but in 7.65mm instead of 9mm. Portugal also ordered the same model, their pistols bearing a crowned 'M' with the figure '2' on the breech, standing for King Manoel II who reigned from 1908 to 1910. The extractor/indicator was marked '*Carregada*' instead of '*Geladen*'.

The 1906 Model was the first of many Parabellum pistols purchased by Holland, when it had a butt safety and the word '*Rust*' above the safety catch. A further batch of 1906 Models were purchased by the German Navy which differed from the 1904 Navy in that a coil mainspring was fitted.

Commercial sales of the 1906 model were satisfactory, notably those to America where the practice of stamping the breech with the American eagle continued. The American civilian market was apparently the only one honoured by having a special breech marking, such identification being normally restricted to military or police official purchases. In 1907 the DWM factory made a further attempt to interest the US military authorities who insisted that .45 was the minimum calibre to provide sufficient 'stopping power'. The DWM factory therefore made two prototype .45 calibre pistols to undergo trials in America, and one of these is still in existence in an American private collection. As a result of these trials, the American Ordnance Department ordered 200 Parabellum pistols from H. Tauscher, the DWM agent in New York, for extended field trials. Having accepted the order, Tauscher had to write again later regretfully declining it. Had he not done so, the standard military pistol

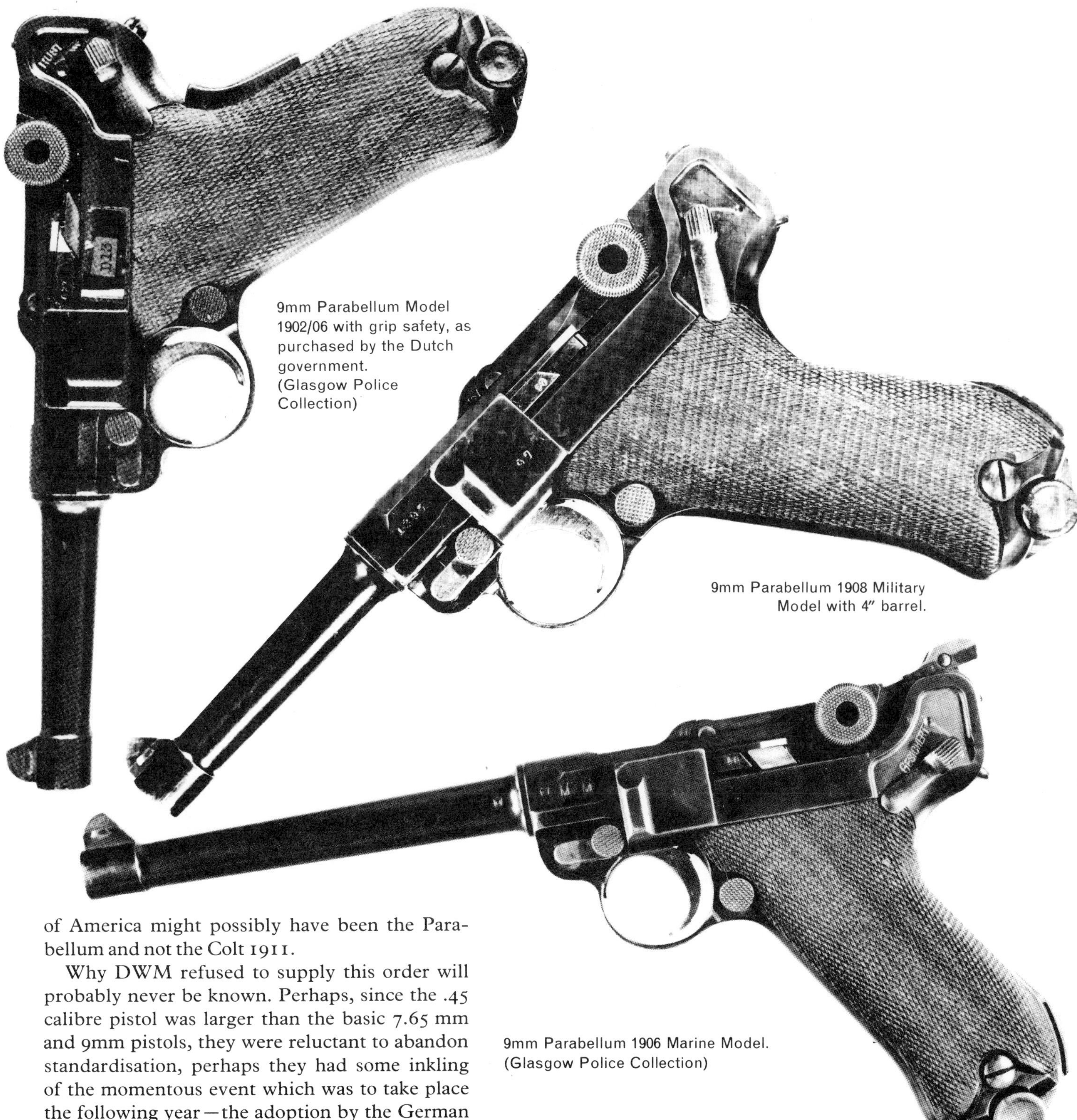

9mm Parabellum Model 1902/06 with grip safety, as purchased by the Dutch government. (Glasgow Police Collection)

9mm Parabellum 1908 Military Model with 4″ barrel.

9mm Parabellum 1906 Marine Model. (Glasgow Police Collection)

of America might possibly have been the Parabellum and not the Colt 1911.

Why DWM refused to supply this order will probably never be known. Perhaps, since the .45 calibre pistol was larger than the basic 7.65 mm and 9mm pistols, they were reluctant to abandon standardisation, perhaps they had some inkling of the momentous event which was to take place the following year—the adoption by the German Army of the 9mm Parabellum known in the future, at least in Germany, as the 'Pistole Model 1908' or 'P.08'.

Very little was changed from the previous 1902 and 1906 models, the most important alteration being that the grip safety was discarded. Consequently the P.08 safety catch had to be pulled downward to make the pistol safe, whereas, on models fitted with the grip safety, it had to be pushed upward.

For the first time too, a new name appeared on the Parabellum—'ERFURT' surmounted by a large crown—the insignia of the Royal Arsenal at Erfurt in Saxony. All the Model 1908 pistols were made with a 4″ barrel and were in 9 mm. There were, however, two variants. Since the old type

9mm Parabellum 1908/14 Model with shoulder stock and thirty-two round drum magazine attached.

of toggle link lock had been abandoned, the Model 08 had at first no device to keep the action open for cleaning or inspection, or when the magazine was empty. This was amended by fitting a spring-loaded lever which, when pushed upward by the magazine platform button, engaged a slot cut into the bottom of the bolt. Some of the original pistols supplied without this device were returned to the factory for modification, and these modified pistols bore an additional small proof mark on the frame.

The German Navy introduced a new model of the P.08, the Navy Parabellum, which lacked the grip safety of its predecessors but retained the 6″ barrel and the two position rear sight.

DWM supplied pistols to many countries in the period immediately before the First World War, and most of those reported bore the crest or insignia of the country which adopted them. The German Military models all bore the date of manufacture on top of the breech and were numbered in a special series, the numbers rising to 10,000 followed by a letter. Since more than 260,000 of the Model 08 were made, it is obvious that duplication must have occurred. For this reason it is important to note the number, the letter and also the date of manufacture. The complete number (i.e. including the letter) was marked on the underneath of the barrel and in front of the frame, the number alone on the side of the breech, and the last two digits on most of the components—the magazine base bearing a number which today is rarely the same as that of the pistol. Commercial pistols had the number underneath the barrel and on the front of the frame, and were, of course, numbered in a separate series.

The German Military 1908 model was supplied in a special holster with provision for a spare magazine and with a small pocket underneath the flap for the combination tool, a screwdriver (the only screws used being the two retaining the grip plates) and an aid for loading the magazine.

In 1914 an 8″ barrel version of the Navy Parabellum was produced which was known as the Model 08/14 or Model 1914. Identical to the Model 08 except for the longer barrel and the special elevating rear sight mounted on the rear of the barrel, this pistol was issued with a special long holster/shoulder stock and with a 32 round drum magazine. Although most impressive, this drum magazine was also cumbersome and prone to jamming, with the result that it was soon discarded.

During the First World War, development of the basic pistol continued. One interesting, rather rare variant was the Model 08 fitted with a magazine safety. Several pistols have been encountered either made or modified for this, but none had the device intact. The purpose of it was to render the pistol safe when the magazine was withdrawn, and so to avoid the accidents resultant on forgetting the cartridge left in the chamber. Pistols provided with the magazine safety were often fitted with an additional device to block the sear when the side plate was removed. This took the form of a flat spring with a stud which dropped down into a small hole in the sear. At this time, another modification also took place which was to cut back the tail of the sear so

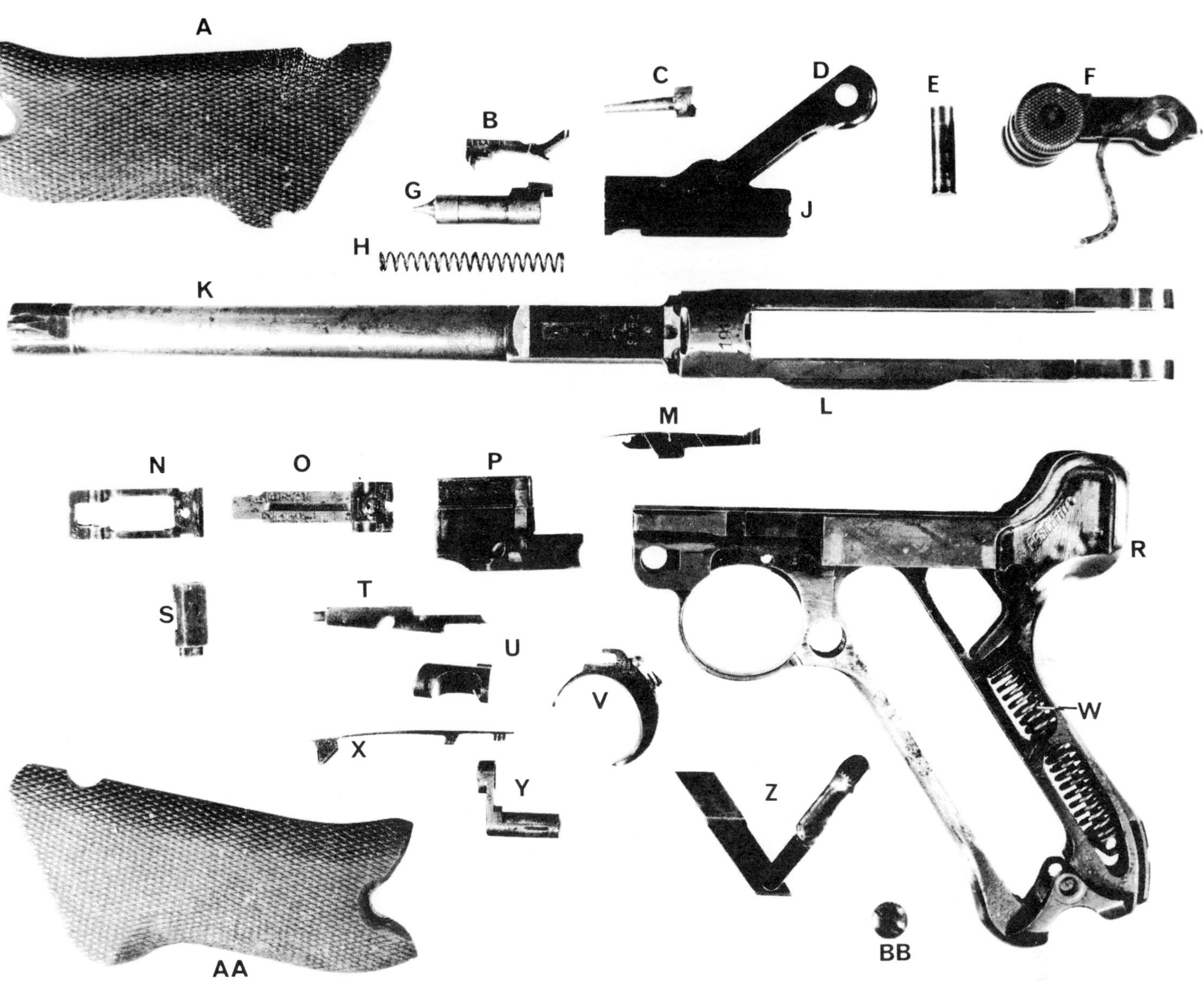

The 9mm Parabellum 1908/14 Model dismantled.

A.	Left hand gripl	O.	Rear sight leaf.
B.	Extractor.	P.	Trigger plate.
C.	Firing pin.	R.	Frame.
D.	Forward toggle link.	S.	Rear sight bar.
E.	Receiver pin.	T.	Trigger bar.
F.	Rear toggle link.	U.	Magazine catch.
G.	Firing pin.	V.	Trigger.
H.	Firing pin spring.	W.	Mainspring.
J.	Breech block.	X.	Ejector.
K.	Barrel.	Y.	Locking bolt.
L.	Receiver.	Z.	Safety bar and catch.
M.	Hold-open latch.	AA.	Right hand grip.
N.	Rear sight frame.	BB.	Grip screw.

that the pistol could be dismounted with the safety applied. This modification enabled the barrel to be pushed 9mm instead of 1mm to the rear, and soon became standard.

During the years which followed the First World War, the variant types of Parabellum pistol became increasingly diversified. Perhaps the most interesting are those which bore the legend 'Vickers Ltd.' in two lines on the top of the toggle link, and were made by Vickers for the Dutch Government at their Elswick Works. The components were, however, supplied by DWM, and, to German specifications, Vickers manufactured only the barrels. Initial deliveries appear to have been made during 1924. In contrast to the Parabellum pistols previously purchased by the Dutch from DWM, the Vickers models were 9mm instead of 7.65mm and had a grip safety; the stock lug was lacking.

The Parabellum pistol was considered to be of sufficient importance to receive mention in the Treaty of Versailles. Manufacture of pistols with

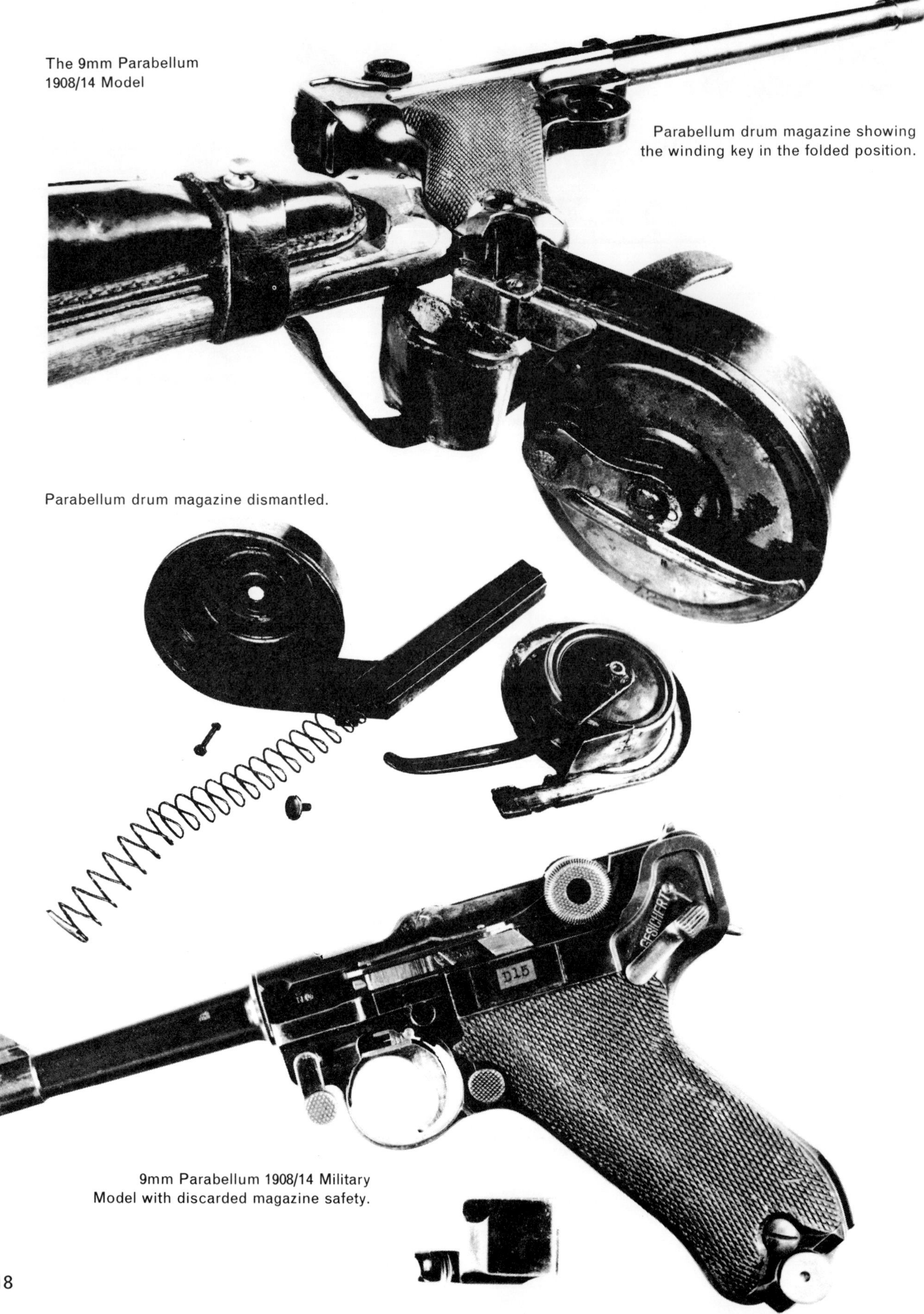

The 9mm Parabellum 1908/14 Model

Parabellum drum magazine showing the winding key in the folded position.

Parabellum drum magazine dismantled.

9mm Parabellum 1908/14 Military Model with discarded magazine safety.

a calibre greater than 8mm and with a barrel length in excess of 100mm was prohibited. It was for this reason that another variant Parabellum appeared with a barrel length of $3\frac{5}{8}''$ and in 7.65mm calibre. Under the treaty, Germany was allowed to retain an army of 100,000 men and, where necessary, these men were issued with pistols which bore both the original date of manufacture and the new date of re-issue. Many of these pistols were subsequently issued to the police and had further markings crudely stamped on the front or back strap of the frame.

Apart from the vast stocks of complete pistols, enormous quantities of parts were also available, and one famous firm who specialised in making up these parts was Simson and Co. of Suhl. Most of these pistols bore the legend 'Simson & Co. Suhl' on the toggle link in place of the DWM or Erfurt markings. Many post-war pistols can be found with the date markings ground off the receiver ring, and these were obviously made up from old models and components. In an attempt to meet a demand for 'carbine' style models, commercial long barrelled pistols were made up with barrels of up to 20″. All the post-war 'buntlines' lacked the wooden fore-end; if this was fitted subsequently, identification is still easy since none had the extra recoil spring and all had the coil recoil spring instead of the flat type fitted to the original carbines.

At the beginning of the story of the Parabellum, it will be remembered that the basic patents bore the name of George Luger. In the early 1920's, when A. F. Stoeger of New York became the distributer of DWM, he registered the name 'Luger', and DWM supplied pistols marked 'A.F. Stoeger Inc., New York, Luger Registered U.S. Patent Office', many of which also bore the American eagle crest on the receiver ring. The use of the name Luger to describe this pistol dates from this period and, although it was still known as the Luger-Borchardt in Britain, American influence has resulted in general acceptance of the simpler 'Luger'. It is short, convenient, and, when all is said and done, it is the inventor's name; as such, its use is entirely legitimate. In Germany, however, the terms 'Borchardt-Luger', 'Parabellum Pistole', 'Schweizer Parabellum', 'Luger P.08' and other variants remain in common usage.

In May 1930 the machine tools, jigs and fixtures employed in the manufacture of the Parabellum were transferred from the DWM factory in Berlin to Mauser Waffenfabrik at Oberndorf am Neckar. The pistols manufactured by Mauser bore the coding S/42 on the toggle instead of the Mauser name, and some also bore a 'K' (1934) or a 'G' (1935) date code. Subsequently, from 1936 to 1940, the date again appeared on the receiver ring. Commercial pistols bore the Mauser 'banner' trade mark and commercial proof marks, and the S/42 or 42 code was replaced by the 'byf' mark which also denoted manufacture by Mauser.

In the mid-1920's the Swiss decided to manufacture their own military pistols, and since they had been wedded to the Parabellum longer than anyone else it is not surprising that this was the pistol they chose to produce.

Known as the Model 1924, manufacture was undertaken by Waffenfabrik Bern, the Swiss Government Arsenal, and these pistols were marked 'Waffenfabrik Bern' on the toggle link. In 1929 the Swiss decided to make certain modifications to the design which resulted in a distinctive variant easily identifiable by the straight front grip strap, a round button type safety, and a stepped receiver ring. The toggle grips were not knurled and the grip safety was longer than conventional DWM practice. As far as is known, the Vickers and the two Swiss models were the only examples of foreign manufacture.

In the home of the Parabellum, renascent Germany, in the shape of the Third Reich, was crying out for more and more pistols. Production by Mauser was augmented by that of Heinrich Krieghoff Waffenfabrik of Suhl who assembled the Pistole P.08 from component parts until about 1939, and then started actual manufacture. In addition to supplying the German Government (mainly the Luftwaffe) Krieghoff also placed some of the production on the commercial market. All the pistols bore the Krieghoff trade mark, an anchor with the letters 'H.K.', and, beneath it, the words, 'Kreighoff, Suhl'.

Actual production of the Parabellum ceased in 1942 to make way for the Walther P.38 but, during the period of manufacture, it is estimated that over three million pistols were made in Germany, Switzerland and by Vickers. Even after the end of the World War Two, the assembly of components continued, and the Parabellum under one or another of its many synonyms is still advertised and still regarded as a desirable pistol to have either for use or in a collection. For the specialist collector it has many charms, and an initial collection can be built up for a relatively small outlay. Although, as we have seen, the major differences were confined to barrel lengths and calibre, the keen collector can pursue the variants (identifiable by markings only) for many years before a reasonably complete series is achieved. Added to the pleasures of collecting the pistols themselves, there are also the variant holsters and shoulder stocks. Equally, in both Germany and Switzerland, specialist suppliers produced a range of accessories, in particular sub-calibre conversion kits for both the 4mm centre-fire and .22 rim-fire cartridges.

A great deal has been written about the Parabellum, some people extolling its virtues, others decrying it. The Parabellum can and does jam, and parts do break, but it must be remembered that even the newest ones are now over twenty years old and many that are fifty years old are still in use. The major cause of malfunctioning is undoubtedly incorrect ammunition, and the 9mm Parabellum cartridge has been manufactured by many people, not always with the intention that it should function in a Parabellum. Most troubles are caused by the ammunition being low powered. DWM ammunition averages about 1,253 f.p.s. with 124 grain bullets, German military ammunition gives 1,250 f.p.s. and some European loadings push the bullets along at 1,335 f.p.s. British loads are slower at 1,100 f.p.s. and average American loadings are 1,130 f.p.s. Low powered ammunition will result in the breech block partially opening, with the result that the fired case is not ejected. On other occasions, the fired case can be ejected but the breech does not move sufficiently to the rear to pick up a new round from the magazine. Ejection but not loading results.

The use of low powered ammunition has been countered by cutting off one or two turns of the recoil spring, and this is satisfactory provided that high powered ammunition is not used subsequently. This could well result in damage to the pistol caused by the extra buffeting due to the reduced resistance to recoil. If correct ammunition cannot be acquired (it must be remembered that safety is the first consideration and that the ammunition companies have to manufacture 9mm ammunition for use in a very wide range of pistols, some of which are far less strong than the Parabellum), one solution is to load one's own. Here, the collection of fired cases for re-use is a major factor in dictating the economics. The normal load flings out the fired case with joyous abandon, and it is quite a task to collect the empties. More effort is spent in searching for

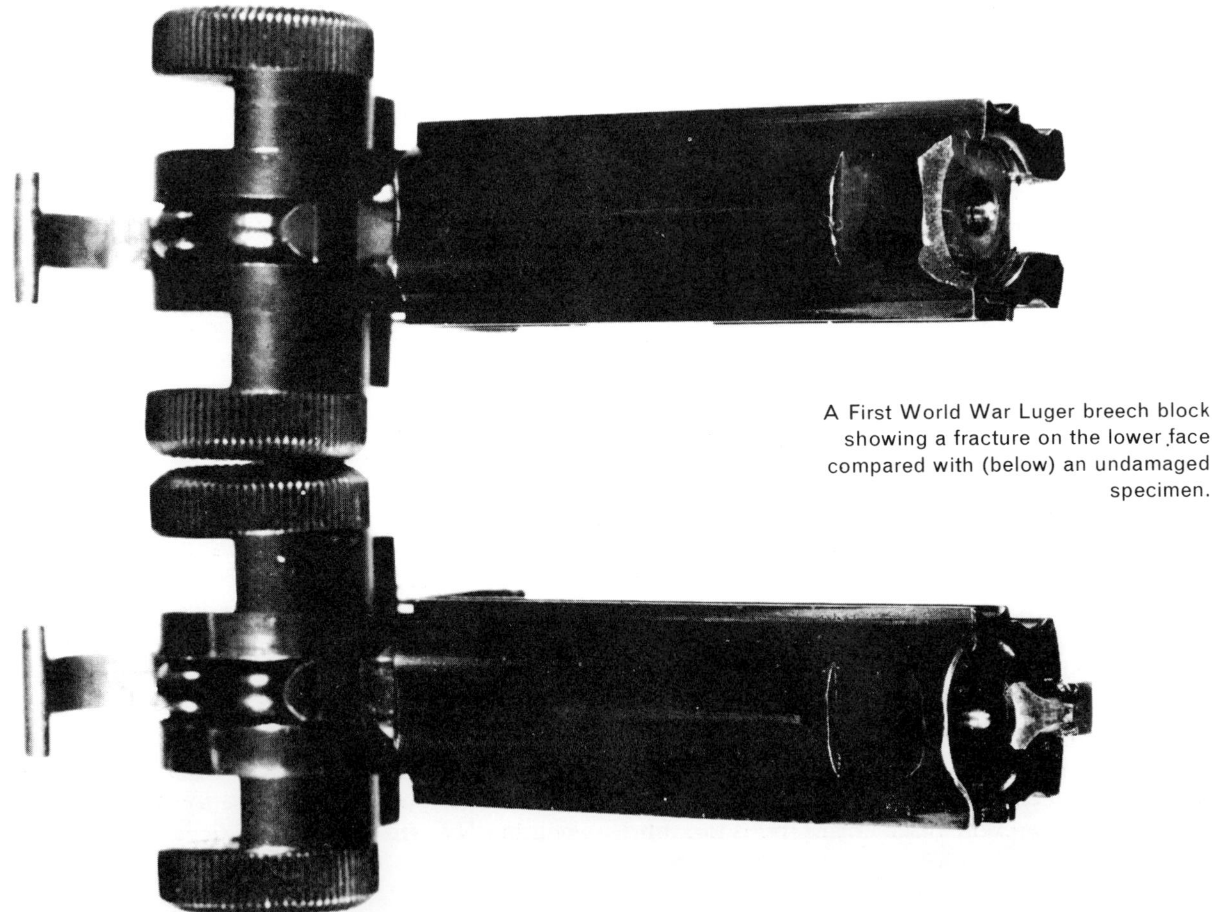

A First World War Luger breech block showing a fracture on the lower face compared with (below) an undamaged specimen.

them than in shooting, and ultimately the eye is on the ejected case rather than on the target—with disastrous results to the scoring. Yet another method adopted by aficionados is to load low power ammunition and use the pistol single shot. The official factory instructions for this technique are to remove the magazine, point the muzzle in a safe direction, pull back the toggle with thumb and forefinger, slip the forefinger on to the inclined toggle and slide the thumb to the rear of the action. The second finger is then crooked around the left hand toggle and the cartridge inserted into the breech with the right hand.

The pistol can be dismantled without the aid of any special tools apart from a screwdriver for the grip screws. To remove the barrel, first make certain that the pistol is unloaded by removing the magazine and operating the breech mechanism. The action is uncocked by withdrawing the breech about $\frac{1}{4}''$ (this is 'free' movement) holding the toggle grips, pulling the trigger and allowing the breech to move forward under restraint. (Excessive dry firing can damage the firing pin.) The barrel is pushed to the rear either by pressing the muzzle against a suitable flat surface or by gripping the pistol with the thumb underneath the rear of the frame and the fingers across the top of the toggle. 'Squeezing' the hand will cause the barrel to move to the rear until the toggle grips touch the cam surfaces of the frame. The small lever on the left side of the frame under the barrel is turned downward and the trigger plate removed. The barrel can then be taken off by pulling it forward.

To dismantle further, remove the link pin from the rear of the receiver. No pressure or tool is needed for this if it is remembered that it is withdrawn from the left hand side. Check again that the firing pin is not cocked by pushing the front of the trigger bar (the spring-loaded pin acts as the disconnector) before removing the link pin. The breech bolt and toggle can then be withdrawn from the rear of the receiver. To remove the firing pin, press in the breech block end piece either with the fingernail or with a small screwdriver and turn to the left. The breech end piece, firing pin and spring can then be withdrawn. On reassembly, it is important that the breech block end piece is replaced with the slot vertical. When replacing the breech block, press down the front of the trigger bar and re-insert the hinge pin from the left. When replacing the barrel, it is easiest to invert it to ensure that the coupling link is at the rear. The barrel is then slid on to the frame and, when turning the pistol over, care must be taken to ensure that the link falls into place in front of the hooks of the recoil spring bell crank. The barrel is then pushed to the rear against the recoil spring pressure, the trigger plate attached and the lock pushed upward. It is of the utmost importance to ensure that the recoil spring is operating properly by repeatedly working the mechanism.

A close-up of the case head failure which caused gas to leak into the action. The pistol was extensively damaged, but the firer was unharmed.

The Parabellum is a safe and entirely satisfactory handgun for most purposes. Demand, however, is still so high that many pistols which should be on the scrap heap—due to abuse, neglect or damage—are sold following only a cursory examination and re-blueing. Many have suffered from 'home gunsmithing' and so-called 'improvement', and accidents have been known to happen just because a slight distortion of the 'L' shaped trigger lever has caused

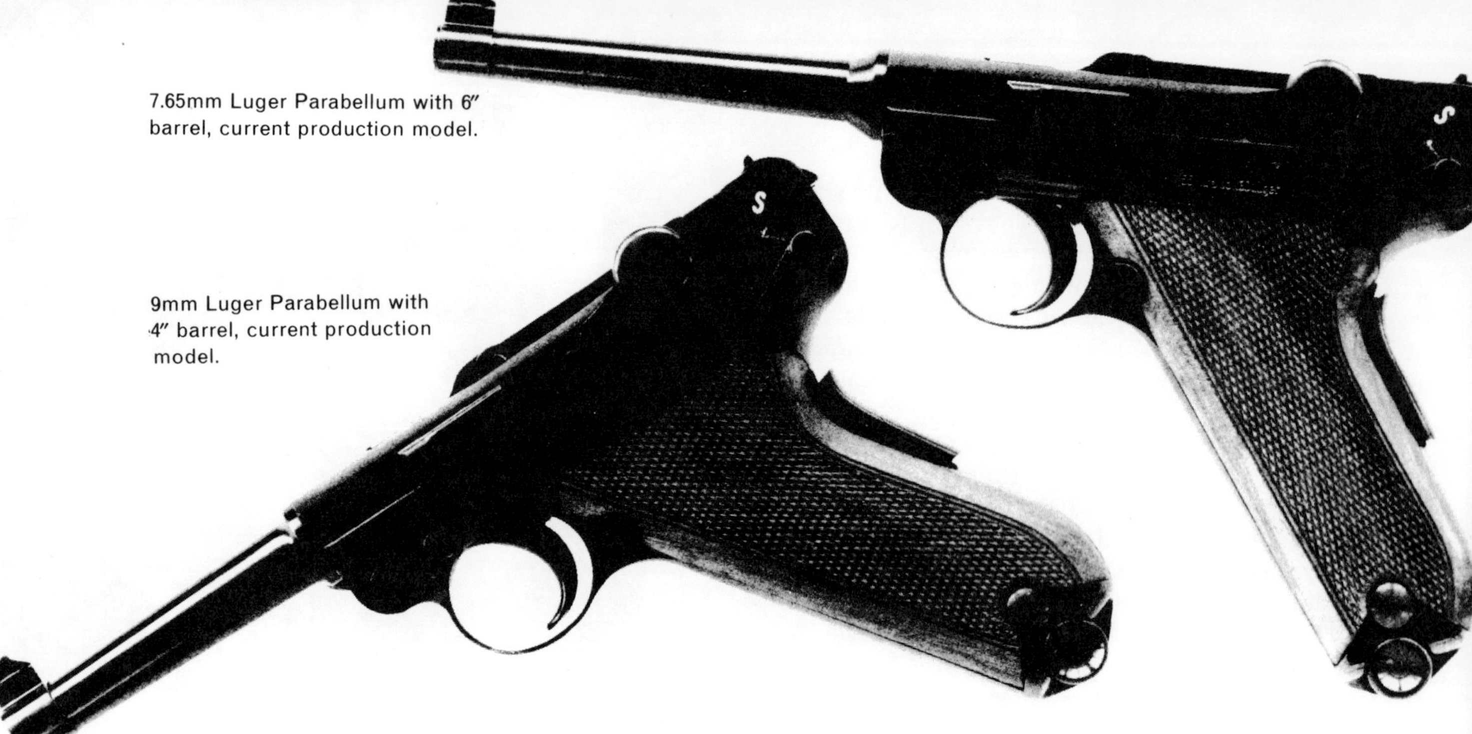

7.65mm Luger Parabellum with 6″ barrel, current production model.

9mm Luger Parabellum with 4″ barrel, current production model.

inadvertent discharge as the breech block moved forward.

The Parabellum was and is a fine pistol: the Governments of Brazil, Bulgaria, Chile, China, Holland, Iran, Luxemburg, Mexico, Norway, Portugal, Roumania, Russia, Switzerland and Turkey would not have adopted it for military use otherwise.

As the Colt SAA of the automatic pistol world it is not surprising that manufacture of so famous a weapon as the Luger-Parabellum has been recommenced by Mauser-Werke AG of Oberndorf-Neckar. This production must not be confused with the manufacture of replicas, imitations, or .22 calibre copies of the original.

It will be recalled that there were five basic variants of the Swiss Luger-Parabellum: first, the Model 1900 adopted by the Swiss in 1901; second, the Model 1906 which, like the Model 1900, was manufactured by DWM; third, the Model 1906/24 manufactured by Waffenfabrik Bern; fourth, the Model 1906/29 again of Swiss manufacture; and fifth, the Model 1906/34, the Mauser Commercial, made by Mauser-Werke AG, which, in common with the others in the series, was in 7.65mm Parabellum calibre.

According to current information, Mauser-Werke are to manufacture a new model essentially similar to the Model 1906/29 (the fourth of the above variants) in 7.65mm Parabellum and 9mm Parabellum, and in 4″ and 6″ barrel lengths. This pistol will be available towards the end of 1969 and, at a later date, other barrel lengths are likely to be offered. This will mean that old and abused Luger-Parabellums can be honourably retired along with equally dubious specimens of uncertain parentage. Interest in the Luger-Parabellum shows no sign of diminishing, but if you intend to use an old model for serious shooting, have it checked. Better still, buy a new one and accord the veteran its rightful place—in a collection.

Notes to Chapter Thirteen

Relevant works for further reading include *Textbook of Automatic Pistols* by R. K. Wilson (Plantersville, 1942), *Mannlicher Rifles and Pistols* by W. H. B. Smith (Harrisburg, 1947), *Mauser Rifles and Pistols* by W. H. B. Smith (Harrisburg, 1954), *The Luger Pistol* by F. A. Datig (Fadco, 1955), *Handfeuerwaffen* by J. Lugs (Berlin, 1962), *Luger Variations* by Harry E. Jones (Torrance, 1959) and *The Parabellum Automatic Pistol*, a reprint of the DWM instruction booklet (Follett, Chicago, 1964). Of particular value is the *Manual of Pistol and Revolver Cartridges* by Hans A. Erlmeier and Jakob H. Brandt (Erlmeier Verlag, Weisbaden, 1967), which deals with centre-fire metric calibres.

The *American Rifleman* contains the following articles on the Parabellum: 'Malfunctions' (June 1952), 'History' (July 1952), 'The Dutch Luger' (July 1953), 'The Erma Conversion Kit' (January 1957), 'The Model of 1900' (February 1958), The Portuguese Model of 1906' (October 1963), 'Accidents' (April 1964) and 'Bergmann Automatic Pistols' (October 1966).

Other articles of interest are 'The Luger Pistol' by F. A. Datig in the *Gun Digest* (1957), 'Parabellum Pistolen' by Otto Morawietz in the *Deutches Waffen Journal* (December 1965 and January 1966) and 'Mannlicher-Karabinerpistole M/1901' by Jurgen Pirkl also in the *Deutches Waffen Journal* (September 1966).

Chapter Fourteen
Browning's Pistols and their Competitors

It has been said that the simplest classification of automatic pistols is: those of Browning's design —and others. Although attributed to an American, there is some justification for this statement since Browning is regarded as one of the greatest gun designers not only of automatic pistols but also of rifles, shotguns and machine guns. The story of the Browning family starts with Jonathan, the son of Edmund and Sarah Browning, who was born in 1805 near Nashville, Tennessee. When in his late twenties, Jonathan moved to Illinois where he was engaged in farming, blacksmithing and gunsmithing. Later he moved to Kanesville in Iowa and, in 1851, was Captain of a wagon train which made the three month journey to Ogden, Utah, where he was to spend the rest of his life.

John M. Browning, who holds undisputed claim to the title of the greatest American firearm designer, was born in Ogden in 1855. He no doubt learned his trade at his father's workbench and, by 1879, at the age of twenty-four, had obtained his first patent for a single shot rifle later sold to Winchester.

By the time Browning decided to design an automatic pistol, considerable experience had already been gained with automatic weapons, and it is characteristic of the man that he patented several different types of action, only two of which were exploited commercially. These were a straight blow-back design for low powered cartridges and a locked breech action for medium and high power cartridges.

Browning was primarily associated with two companies, the Fabrique Nationale d'Armes de Guerre SA of Herstal, near Liege in Belgium, and Colt's Patent Firearm Mfg. Co. The history of Colt's has already been covered, but a word or two is necessary about FN. This independent limited company was formed in 1889 by a syndicate of manufacturers for the purpose of carrying out an order for 200,000 Mauser rifles for the Belgian Government. About 1898 an agreement was reached between FN and John Moses Browning which allowed FN to manufacture Browning shotguns, rifles and auto-pistols under licence. The first Browning auto-pistol was patented in 1897 and, as the FN Model 1900, was officially adopted by the Belgian Government. Two interesting features were, firstly, that one spring served as both mainspring and recoil or slide spring, and, secondly, that the breech block was separate and attached to the slide by two screws. The dual purpose spring was mounted above the barrel and its function can be seen from Fig. 4 and Fig. 5 in the patent drawings which accompanied British Patent No. 22,455 of 1898. (This patent, based on US Patent No. 580,926, was issued to S. Pitt acting on Colt's behalf.) The link arrangement which cocked the firing pin can also be seen. The cartridge was designed by Browning with the help of Winchester and became famous as the 7.65mm Browning or, in America, as the .32 Automatic Colt Pistol (ACP). It was subsequently manufactured throughout the world and thousands of pistols have been chambered for it. The FN Browning Type 1900 has been extensively copied, particularly by the Chinese. It was a unique pistol and the design was never developed further by either Browning, FN or Colt.

The next design was the famous Type 1903.

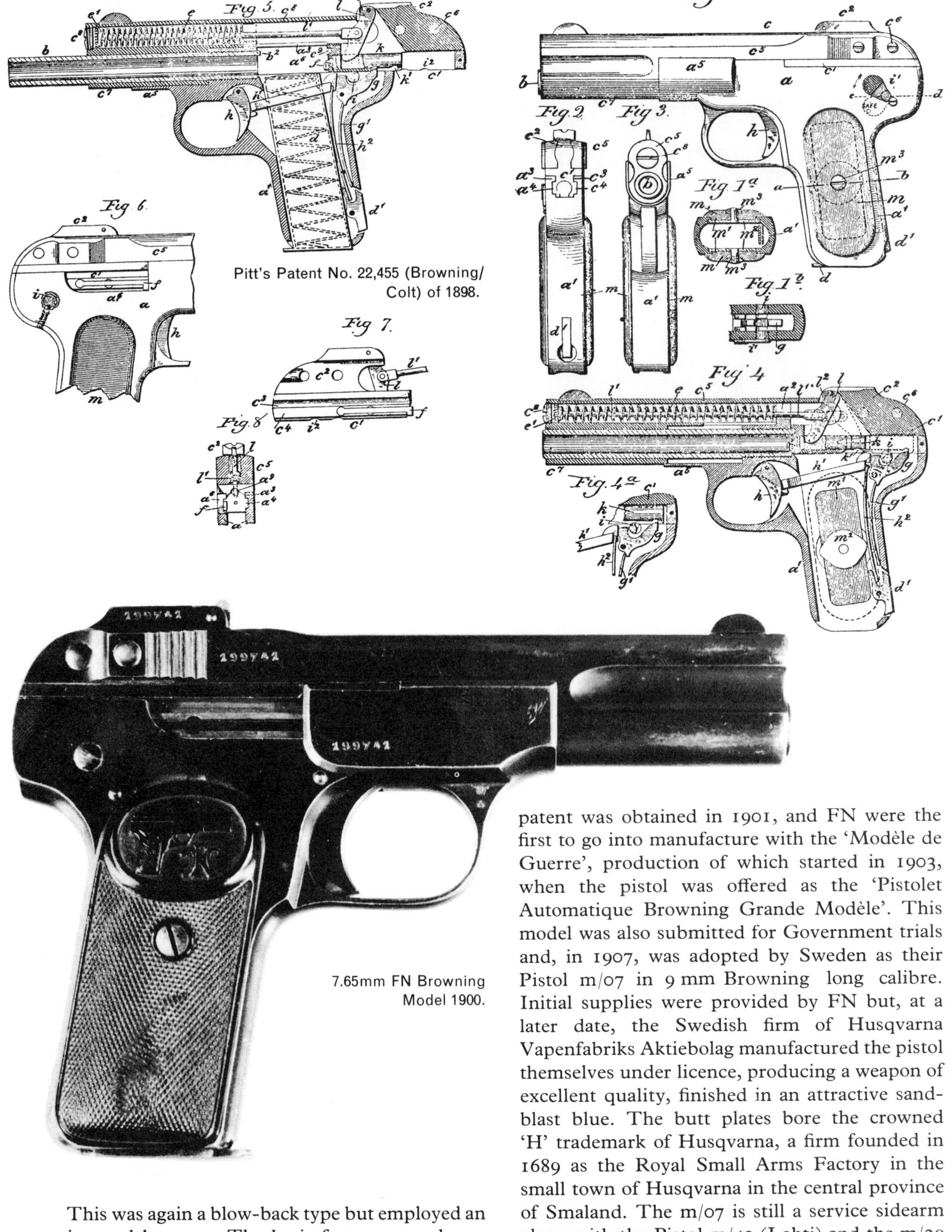

Pitt's Patent No. 22,455 (Browning/Colt) of 1898.

7.65mm FN Browning Model 1900.

This was again a blow-back type but employed an internal hammer. The basic features are shown in the drawings which accompanied British Patent No. 7188 of 1903. This was issued to O. Imray, Colt's British patent agent, and was based on US Patent No. 747,585 of 1893. The Belgian patent was obtained in 1901, and FN were the first to go into manufacture with the 'Modèle de Guerre', production of which started in 1903, when the pistol was offered as the 'Pistolet Automatique Browning Grande Modèle'. This model was also submitted for Government trials and, in 1907, was adopted by Sweden as their Pistol m/07 in 9 mm Browning long calibre. Initial supplies were provided by FN but, at a later date, the Swedish firm of Husqvarna Vapenfabriks Aktiebolag manufactured the pistol themselves under licence, producing a weapon of excellent quality, finished in an attractive sand-blast blue. The butt plates bore the crowned 'H' trademark of Husqvarna, a firm founded in 1689 as the Royal Small Arms Factory in the small town of Husqvarna in the central province of Smaland. The m/07 is still a service sidearm along with the Pistol m/40 (Lahti) and the m/39 (Walther) both of which are chambered for the 9 mm Parabellum cartridge. In order to ease the problem of having to deal with two types of non-interchangeable 9 mm ammunition, the m/07

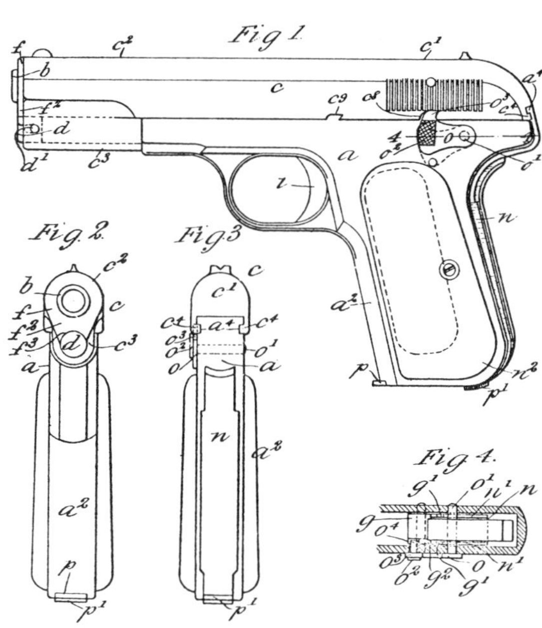

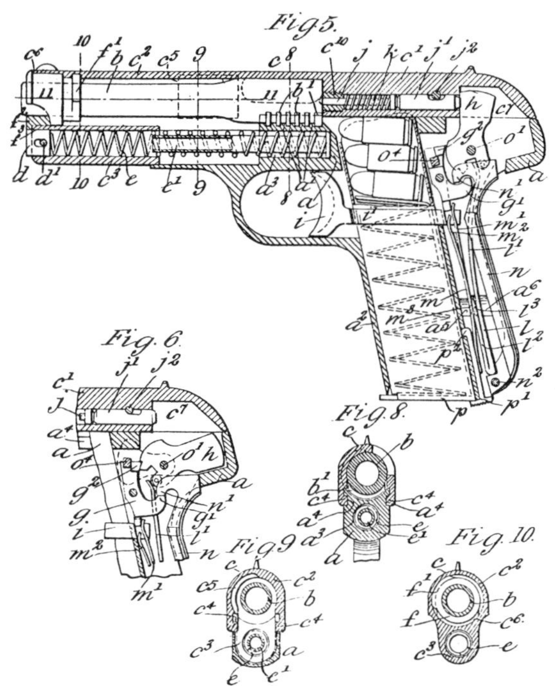

Imray's Patent No. 7188 (Browning/ Colt) of 1903.

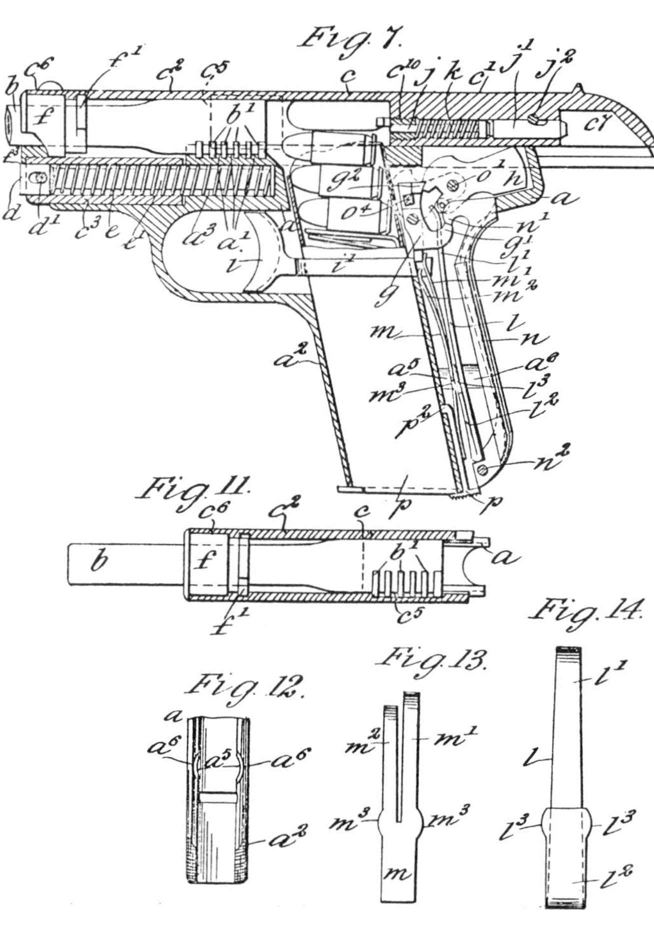

9mm Browning Model 1903 manufactured by Husqvarna as the Swedish Pistol m/07. (F. C. Curtiss)

9mm FN Browning Model 1903 as manufactured for the Turkish service.

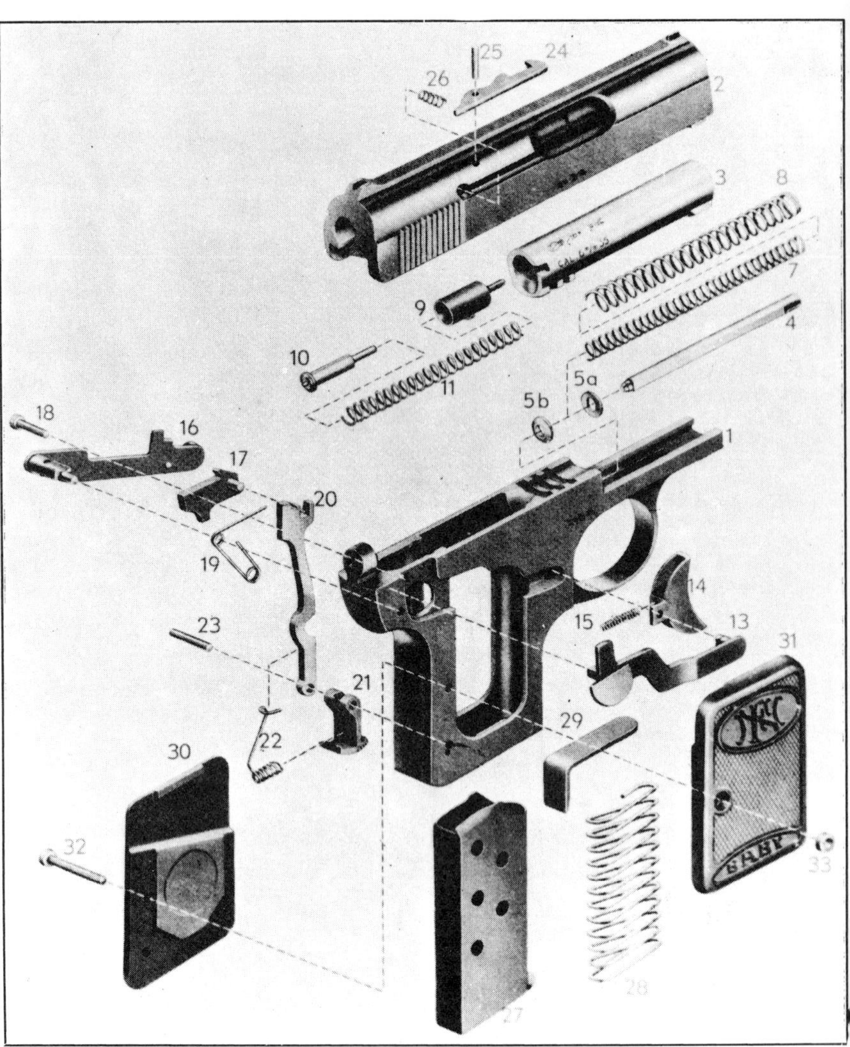

Component parts of the FN Browning Baby. (Fabrique Nationale)

1. Frame.
2. Slide.
3. Barrel.
4. Guide for recoil springs.

5a. Front washer for recoil springs.
5b. Rear washer for recoil springs.

7. Recoil inner spring.
8. Recoil outer spring.
9. Firing pin.
10. Cocking indicator.
11. Firing pin spring.
13. Loop.
14. Trigger.
15. Trigger spring.
16. Safety.
17. Sear.
18. Sear pin.
19. Spring for sear and loop.
20. Automatic safety.
21. Magazine catch.
22. Springs for magazine catch and automatic safety.
23. Magazine catch pin.
24. Extractor.
25. Extractor pin.
26. Extractor spring.
27. Magazine.
28. Magazine spring.
29. Magazine follower.
30. Left hand handle plate.
31. Right hand handle plate.
32. Handle plate screw.
33. Handle plate screw nut.

is issued to officers and the m/40 and m/39 to other ranks.

The manufacture of the basic FN Model 1903 was discontinued by FN around 1923 but, by then, a large number had been purchased by Denmark for police use, by Turkey for service use, and also by Czechoslovakia, Holland and possibly Russia.

The 9 mm Browning long cartridge, also known as the 9 mm Army Browning and the Swedish m/07, was not as popular as other Browning designs and very few other pistols were adapted to it, although these included the Spanish Astra, the French Le Français and a Webley autopistol. The Browning Model 1903 was also manufactured in variant types by Colt's and these will be discussed later.

In 1906 FN brought out a 'vest pocket' model

based on John Browning's Belgian patents. This diminutive little pistol was an immediate success and Colt's, after experimenting with their own design, eventually copied it. The Colt version appeared in 1908 as the Colt Automatic Calibre .25, and manufacture was discontinued in 1946. In Belgium the pistol was redesigned as the FN Browning Baby and is currently manufactured under the FN Baby name. In America, although still manufactured by FN, it is known as the Browning Calibre .25 and is sold by the Browning Arms Co. of St. Louis.

The present model weighs only 9½ ozs. and has an overall length of 4″. As well as being fitted with an ordinary and a magazine safety, it has an additional safety device to prevent discharge should the pistol be dropped. An external cocking indicator is also fitted to give both visual and tactile confirmation that the pistol is cocked.

To dismantle, the pistol is unloaded, the empty magazine replaced and the trigger pulled to release the firing pin. The magazine is then taken off again and the slide drawn to the rear until the nose of the safety catch can be pushed into the front notch. The now protruding barrel is given a quarter turn to the right and the slide is released by pushing down the safety catch. Slide and barrel are then withdrawn from the frame, and the barrel can be separated by giving it a quarter turn to the left and then pulling it forward through the front of the slide.

The 6.35mm Browning cartridge is also known as the .25 ACP and has the DWM number 508A. Widely used in both Europe and America for vest pocket and other small pistols, it has also, since it is ejected by the common type of rod

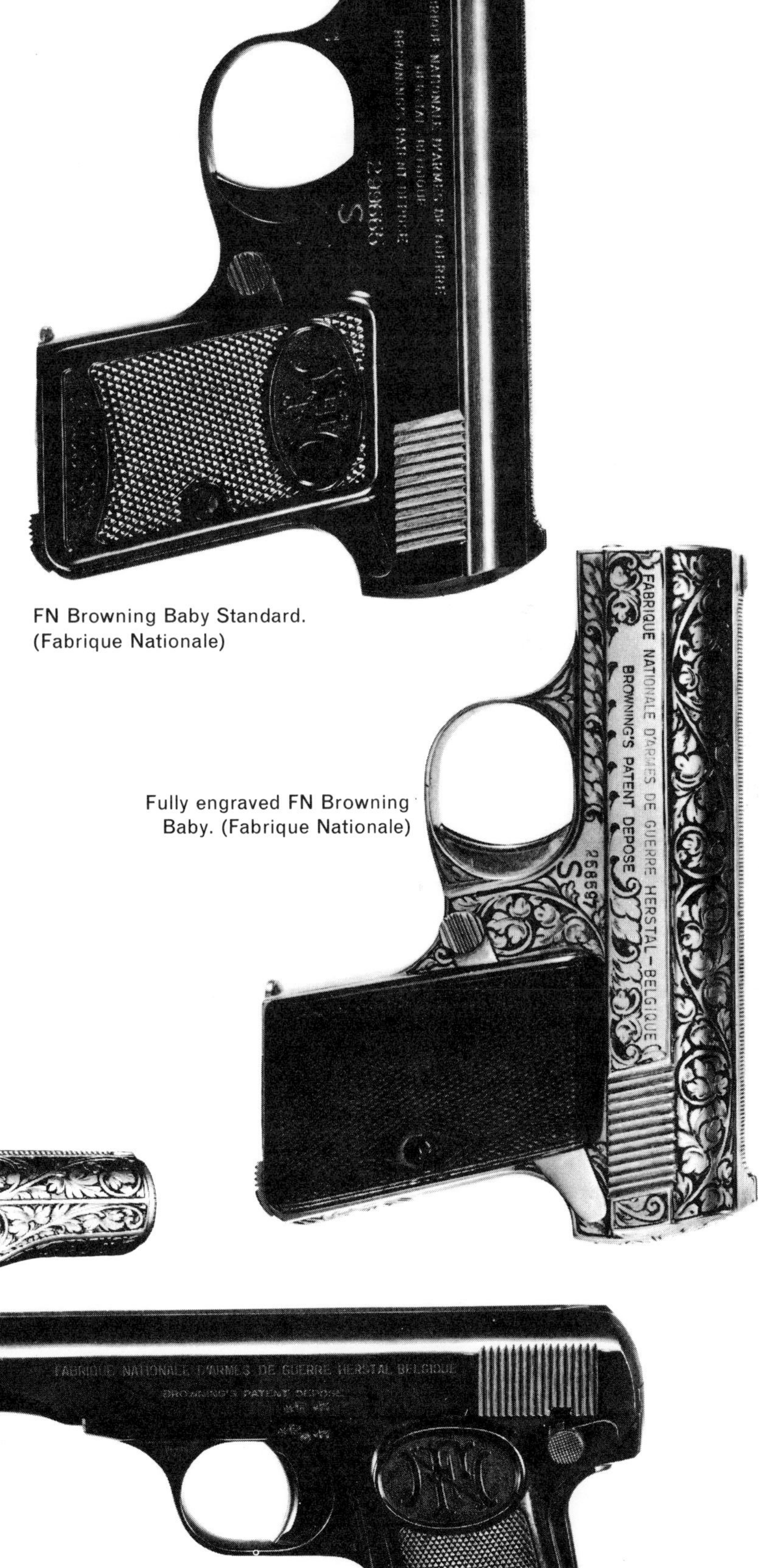

FN Browning Baby Standard. (Fabrique Nationale)

Fully engraved FN Browning Baby. (Fabrique Nationale)

Fully engraved FN Browning Model 1910. (Fabrique Nationale)

FN Browning Model 1910. (Fabrique Nationale)

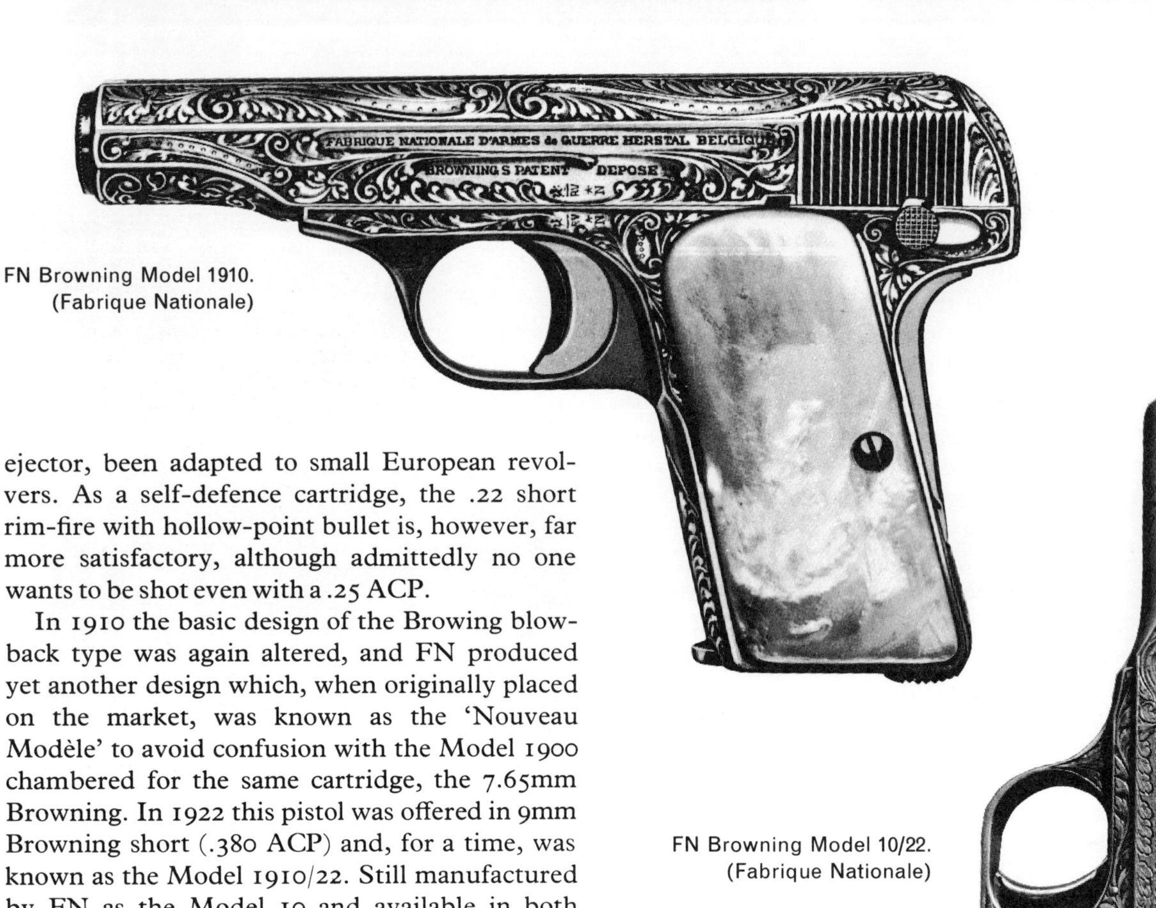

FN Browning Model 1910.
(Fabrique Nationale)

ejector, been adapted to small European revolvers. As a self-defence cartridge, the .22 short rim-fire with hollow-point bullet is, however, far more satisfactory, although admittedly no one wants to be shot even with a .25 ACP.

In 1910 the basic design of the Browing blowback type was again altered, and FN produced yet another design which, when originally placed on the market, was known as the 'Nouveau Modèle' to avoid confusion with the Model 1900 chambered for the same cartridge, the 7.65mm Browning. In 1922 this pistol was offered in 9mm Browning short (.380 ACP) and, for a time, was known as the Model 1910/22. Still manufactured by FN as the Model 10 and available in both 7.65mm (.32 ACP) and 9mm short (.380 ACP), it holds seven .32 and six .380 cartridges, has an overall length of 6″ and weighs approximately 20 ozs. It was never officially adopted as a service weapon by any major power, but it was widely used as a police weapon by many countries, and proved so successful that, by 1912, the older Model 1900 had been dropped from the range. Production of the Model 1910 ceased during World War Two, but was resumed by FN afterwards. Spanish copies can be encountered and several other pistols, such as the Czech Praga and the Hungarian M.29 and M.37, employ certain of its design features. Fitted with the normal safety, butt safety and magazine safety, initial stripping of the Model 1910 is done in the same way as with the Model 1906, but if it is necessary to remove the barrel from the slide, the recoil spring must first of all be removed by pressing in the slide ring and giving it a quarter turn. The recoil spring can then be taken out and the slide can be drawn rearward, the safety catch pushed upward into the slide notch and the barrel rotated one third of a turn in an anti-clockwise direction. The slide is allowed to move forward again, the barrel is turned back in a clockwise direction and then withdrawn forward.

In 1922 the Model 1910 was modified, the barrel length being increased from $3\frac{1}{2}''$ to $4\frac{1}{2}''$ and the overall length to 7″. As the Model 10/22 (not to be confused with the 9mm short version of the Model 1910), this pistol is still being currently manufactured by FN. The increased barrel length necessitates a barrel extension unit for the slide, but this, in fact, simplifies dismantling. For quick superficial cleaning, the pistol is unloaded and the firing pin released by inserting the magazine and pressing the trigger. The magazine is then removed again. The slide is withdrawn to the rear until the safety catch can be pushed upward into the front slide notch, and the barrel is then given a third of a turn anti-clockwise to release it from the grooves in the frame. Barrel and slide are removed from the frame by releasing the safety catch from the slide notch and pushing forward.

FN Browning Model 10/22.
(Fabrique Nationale)

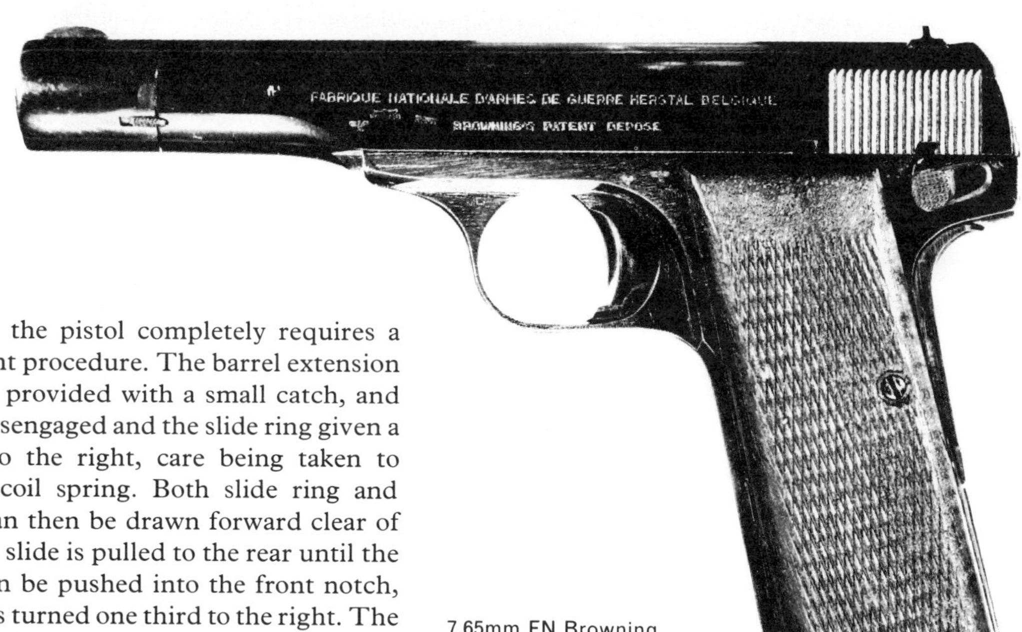

7.65mm FN Browning Model 1922, manufactured under German supervision.

Dismantling the pistol completely requires a slightly different procedure. The barrel extension or slide ring is provided with a small catch, and this has to be disengaged and the slide ring given a quarter turn to the right, care being taken to restrain the recoil spring. Both slide ring and recoil spring can then be drawn forward clear of the barrel. The slide is pulled to the rear until the safety catch can be pushed into the front notch, and the barrel is turned one third to the right. The slide is then released and the barrel is turned back and withdrawn. The slide itself can then be drawn forward off the frame.

The Model 10/22 is available in either 7.65mm Browning (.32 ACP), when the magazine capacity is nine cartridges, or in 9mm short (.380 ACP) when the capacity is eight cartridges.

The basic model of 1922 was adopted for Belgian military service as the Pistolet Automatique Browning Model 1922 calibre 7.65mm in place of the Browning Model 1903, production of which ceased in 1923. In 9mm short calibre, the Model 1922 was also used by the police forces of Belgium, France, Sweden and Czechoslovakia. During World War Two, it was made by FN under German supervision as the Pistol 626(b). This version lacked the excellent finish of the normal commercial FN production and was fitted with wooden grip plates.

Current commercial production offers both the Model 10 and Model 10/22 in various grades.

In 1925 and 1926, John Browning was working on a new recoil operated locked breech pistol which had been requested by FN, but, in the latter year, he died in Belgium. Between then and 1935, numerous prototype locked breech pistols were produced by FN which culminated in the appearance of the last of Browning's auto-pistol designs, the 1935 Browning High Power, or 'Pistolet Automatique Browning Modèle de Guerre Grande Puissance'. Two versions were offered by FN, one with conventional fixed sights, the other with a radial leaf sight and provision for a detachable shoulder

9mm Browning High Power with tangent rear sight and shoulder stock. (Fabrique Nationale)

stock/holster. Both were chambered for the 9 mm Parabellum cartridge. The Belgian Government adopted the fixed sight model as did the Latvian Army, whose pistol carried a crest on top of the slide.

The adjustable sight model was reported to have been purchased by the French Government, but was not apparently official issue. In 1936 FN produced a few experimental models, known today as the 'Browning Model 1936', for French Government trials. These pistols, chambered for the French 7.65mm long cartridge adapted for the French Model 1935A auto-pistol and also used by French sub-machine guns, were offered to the French through the FN subsidiary company in France, Manufacture d'Armes de Paris. In addition to its smaller calibre, the 1936 pistol was of different construction in that it had a single row magazine and a new sear and hammer mechanism in the form of a completely removable assembly similar to the Swiss Neuhausen SP 47/8. The FN Model 1936 was rejected by the French on the grounds of undue complexity and the pistol never got beyond the experimental stage.

Lithuania and Roumania adopted the standard 1935 pistol for military use, as did the Danish Army, although deliveries to Denmark were curtailed by the outbreak of war. The Danish order was reinstated in 1946 as the Pistol Model 1946. During World War Two the Model 1935 continued to be made by FN under German control, initial production being of the tangent sight model with shoulder stock groove, although the groove was later omitted. These pistols lacked Belgian commercial proof marks and bore instead the German Ordnance marks on the left side of the frame and slide, and on the barrel where it is visible through the ejection port. The finish of these pistols began to deteriorate and late production copies lacked the magazine safety device.

Production of the Model 1935 was undertaken in Canada by John Inglis Co. of Toronto, who manufactured the pistols for Canadian, British, Chinese, Greek and Australian use. These pistols were marked 'John Inglis' and originally carried a transfer on the front butt strap which incorporated the Canadian maple leaf insignia. With the radial or tangent rear sight, the Canadian manufactured FN is known as the Pistol No. 1 Mark I, and with the standard fixed rear sight, as the Pistol No. 2 Mark I. Modifications were carried out by Inglis and involved alterations to the

FN Browning Model 1935 with German Ordnance acceptance marks and fitted with an adjustable rear sight. (Glasgow Police Collection)

Browning High Power Model 1935, as manufactured by John Inglis of Toronto. This is the Pistol No. 2 Mark I. (Glasgow Police Collection)

FN Browning High Power Standard (Fabrique Nationale)

Fully engraved FN Browning High Power Standard. (Fabrique Nationale)

1. Frame.
1a. Locking shoulder.
2. Barrel.
3. Slide.
5. Slide bushing.
6. Foresight.
7. Rear sight.
13. Return spring guide.
14. Return spring guide cap.
15. Ball.
16. Spring of return spring guide.
17. Return spring.
18. Firing pin.
19. Firing pin spring.
20. Firing pin retaining plate.
21. Extractor.
22. Sear lever.
23. Sear lever axis pin.
24. Slide stop.
25. Trigger.
25. Trigger.
26. Trigger lever.
27. Trigger pin.
28. Trigger and magazine safety pin.
29. Trigger spring.
30. Magazine stop.
31. Magazine stop spring.
32. Magazine stop spring guide.
33. Sear.
34. Sear pin.
35. Sear spring.
36. Hammer.
37. Hammer pin.

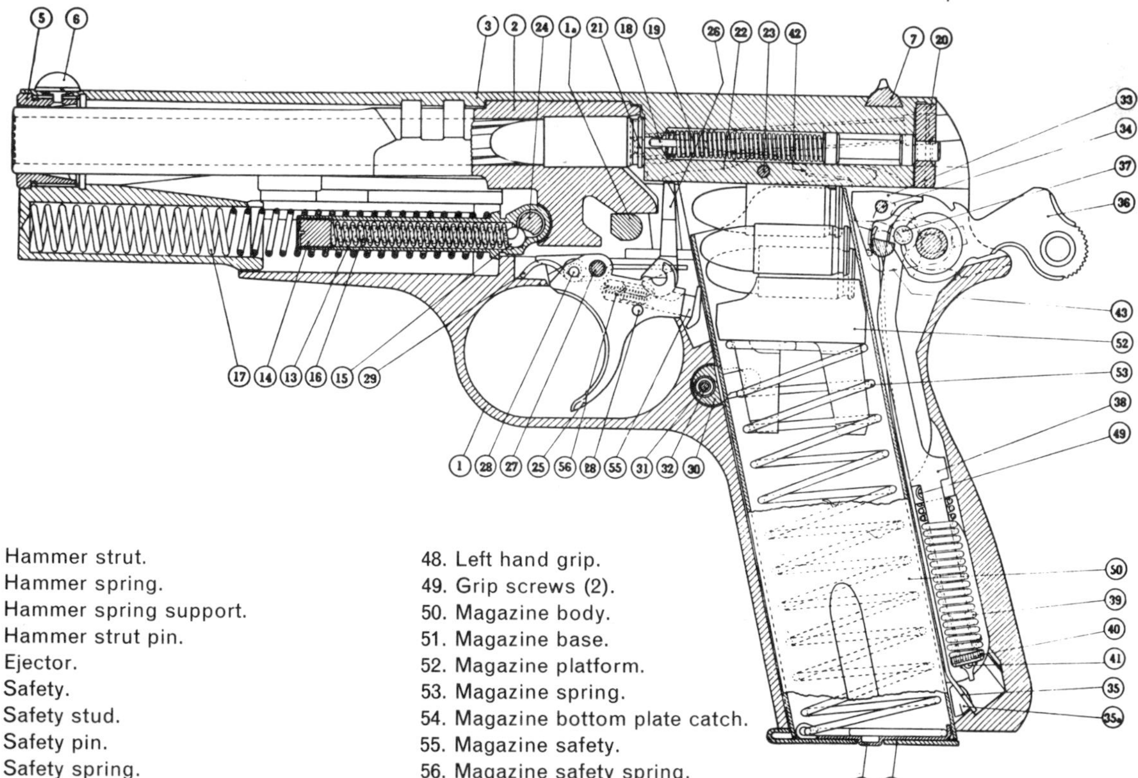

38. Hammer strut.
39. Hammer spring.
40. Hammer spring support.
41. Hammer strut pin.
42. Ejector.
43. Safety.
44. Safety stud.
45. Safety pin.
46. Safety spring.
47. Right hand grip.
48. Left hand grip.
49. Grip screws (2).
50. Magazine body.
51. Magazine base.
52. Magazine platform.
53. Magazine spring.
54. Magazine bottom plate catch.
55. Magazine safety.
56. Magazine safety spring.
(Fabrique Nationale)

hammer, ejector and extractor. These modified components are stamped '2' or 'II', and the pistols incorporating them carry an additional 'star' to the designation. The serial numbers bear an alphabetical code 'T' indicating Canadian forces issue.

In 1957 the Model 1935 was adopted by Great Britain to replace the .38 Enfield No. 2 revolver, Britain having been the last major power to use the revolver as a standard issue firearm.

The illustrated example of the Browning High Power or Grande Puissance Model Standard is of current Belgian commercial manufacture, and there is also the GP de Luxe with checkered wooden grips instead of the standard plastic.

The Model 1935 is a splendid pistol and its design features can be seen in the sectioned diagram. Locking is by the traditional Browning system except that the link employed on the earlier Colt 1911 has been replaced by a barrel extension provided with a camming surface. The recoil spring is mounted underneath the barrel and the trigger mechanism is also different to the Colt. The problem of transmitting the trigger pressure around the magazine has been solved by the use of a sear lever mounted in the slide instead of a trigger stirrup. Dismantling is easily accomplished without tools. The magazine is removed and the pistol checked to see that it is unloaded. The slide is drawn rearward until it can be held by the safety engaging the front notch. The slide stop is then pushed out from the right and, following disengagement of the safety, the slide is allowed to move forward under restraint. The recoil spring and its guide can then be removed and the barrel can be lifted out, breech first.

An ordinary and a magazine safety are fitted, and the external hammer provides an additional safety feature in that it is easy to verify if the pistol is cocked or not. Since an inertia type firing pin is used, the hammer can be carefully lowered on to the frame without discharging a live round in the chamber. (This operation must, however, be done with the pistol pointing in a safe direction and, preferably, only after practice with an unloaded pistol.)

Calibre is, of course, 9mm Parabellum, and the magazine holds thirteen cartridges. Overall length is 8″ and the weight unloaded 31 ozs. The barrel is rifled with six grooves, right hand twist.

As we have seen, Fabrique Nationale, with the exception of the Model 1935, did not manufacture any of John Browning's locked breech automatic pistols. These were manufactured in America by Colt's who also made several of the straight blow-back Browning designs as well.

Of the Colt blow-back models, the .25 Colt Automatic was, in most respects, identical to the FN Browning Baby. Manufacture of this ceased in 1942 and sales were discontinued after 1946. In 1959 the Model 0-6 appeared, the Junior Colt, available in either .22 rim-fire short or .25 ACP. This pistol, although sold under the Colt name, is actually manufactured in Spain and is currently in the selling range.

In the large calibre pistols, Colt's, as we shall shortly see, had concentrated on .38 calibre locked breech action weapons, which were all outsold by the FN Browning blow-back .32 and .380 pocket automatics. Colt must have taken their troubles to John Browning, for he produced for them a variant of his 1903 FN design in which the major change was the elimination of the slide hold-open feature of the Belgian version.

The Colt Model 1903 Pocket Automatic first appeared with a 4″ barrel and was chambered for the .32 ACP cartridge. In 1908 a new cartridge was developed, the .380 ACP (already known in Europe as the 9mm Browning short), and, in the following year, the Automatic Colt Pistol was adapted for it. While this pistol remained in production, there were various minor manu-

.25 Colt Automatic, the early commercial type fitted with grip safety. (Col. F. S. Allen)

facturing changes. To begin with, the section of the extractor was altered, and, for the .380 pistols, the end became broader; subsequently the broad type extractor was also used on the .32 calibre versions. Some time after 1910 the scallops on the grips were omitted and, after the First World War, the moulded rubber grips were changed for checkered wooden ones. In the mid-twenties a magazine safety was added. Manufacture continued until 1946 and large quantities were supplied to both the British and US Governments.

In Britain, Browning's designs were protected by Colt's in their Patent No. 9871 of 1897. This covered several types of action including one based on a rotating barrel (Fig. 21) and also Browning's famous parallel link action (Figs. 4 and 6). To these was added an unusual 'blow-forward' action designed by Carl H. Ehbets of Hartford (US Patent No. 580,935 of 1897) which had been assigned by Ehbets to Colt and was therefore included in their 'blanket' British Patent. The Ehbets action was gas operated and somewhat complicated, and Colt's, in fact, ceased development work on it in order to concentrate on the simpler Browning designs.

Colt Model 1903, late model. (Col. F. S. Allen)

.32 Colt Pocket Model 1903, First Model. (Glasgow Police Collection)

The Browning parallel link action embodying the basic principle of the locking arrangement between the barrel and slide was continually improved by Browning and Colt's who even purchased patents elsewhere if they appeared potentially helpful. The early Colt prototype locked breech automatic pistols and the commercial models of 1900, 1902 and 1903 were all based on this concept which reached its final form

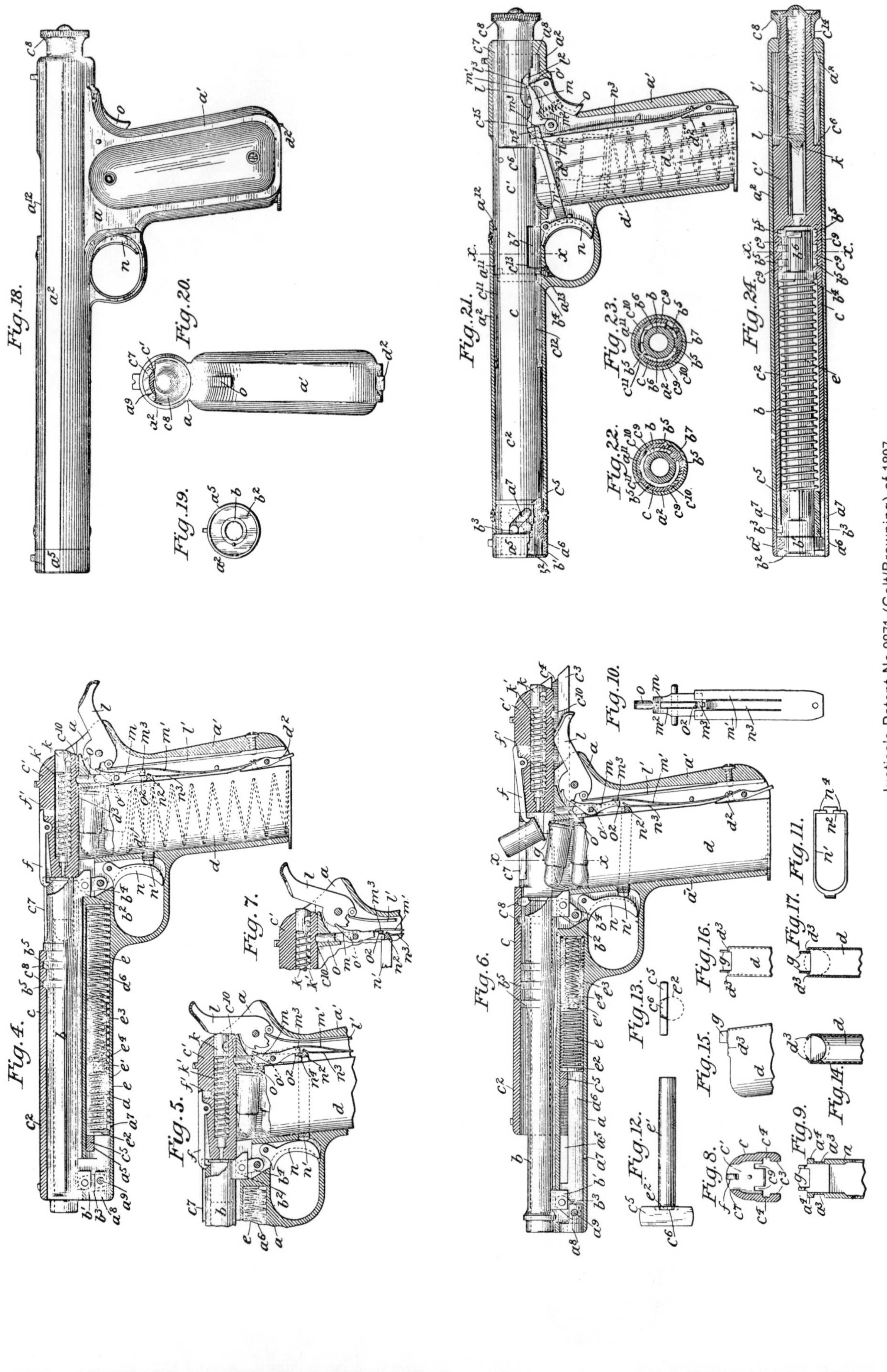

Fig. 4. Fig. 5. Fig. 7. Fig. 18. Fig. 19. Fig. 20. Fig. 6. Fig. 10. Fig. 12. Fig. 13. Fig. 8. Fig. 15. Fig. 16. Fig. 9. Fig. 14. Fig. 17. Fig. 11. Fig. 21. Fig. 22. Fig. 23. Fig. 24.

Justice's Patent No.9871 (Colt/Browning) of 1897.

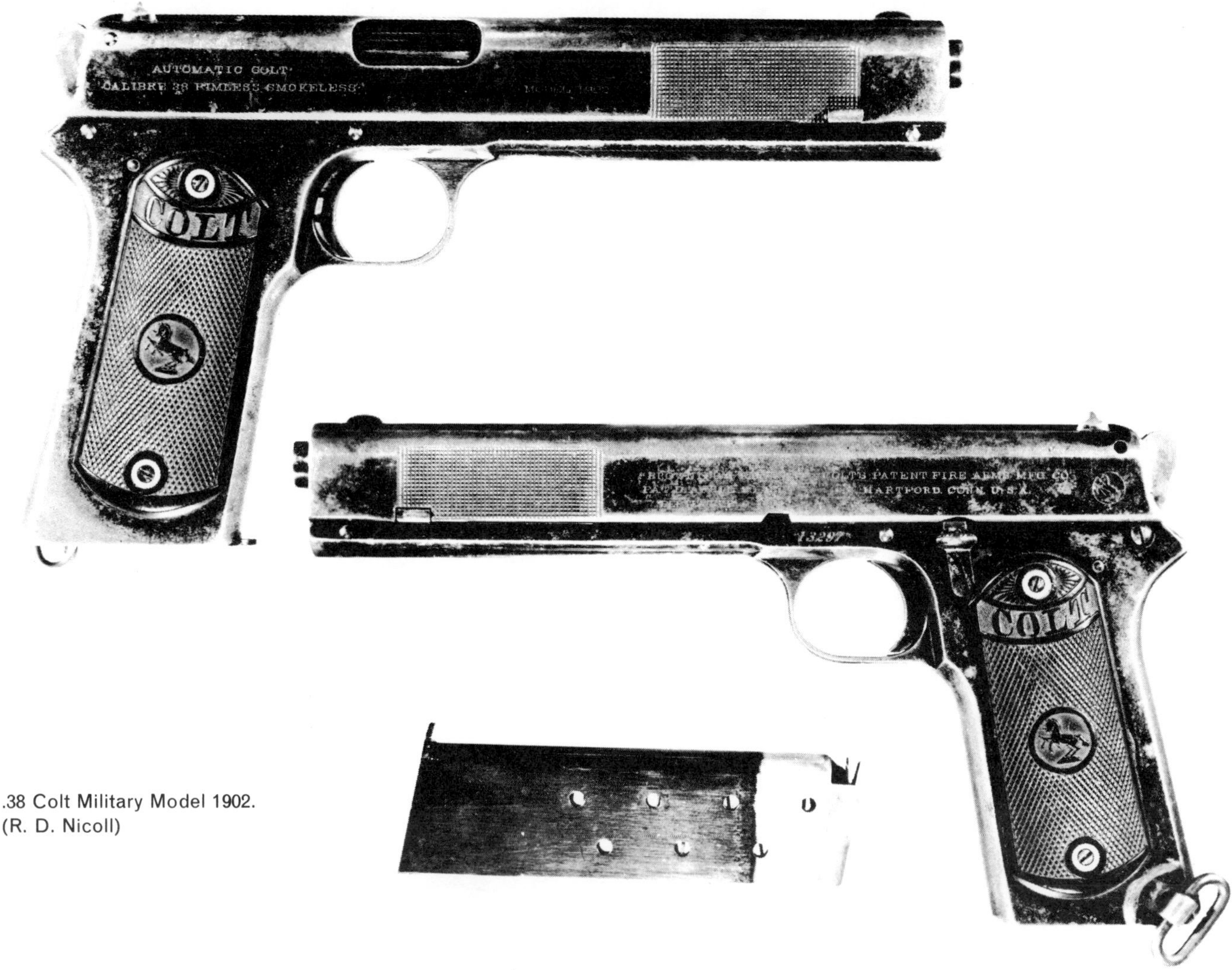

.38 Colt Military Model 1902.
(R. D. Nicoll)

in the FN Browning Model of 1935, a pistol that Colt's never manufactured.

The first commercial production, the so-called Model 1900, was chambered for the .38 ACP cartridge and was marked on the right hand side of the slide 'Automatic Colt Calibre .38 Rimless Smokeless'. Early production models can be recognised by the moveable rear sight safety device which, when pushed down, prevented the hammer from striking the firing pin. The hammer was of the straight spur type and the finger grooves were at the rear of the slide. In 1902 the Sporting Model was introduced which eliminated the rear sight safety and brought in a short 'inertia' type firing pin, a feature common to all the later Colt hammer weapons. Hard rubber grips replaced the smooth wooden grips of the 1900 model and a rounded hammer replaced the spur type.

The 1902 Military Model embodied further detail design changes. The grip was made longer and squarer and a slide stop was added to hold the slide open after the discharge of the last cartridge. Early production models of the 1902 Military had a checkered finger grip on the front portion of the slide and were fitted with a lanyard swivel. Later, the checkered grip was altered to a grooved pattern at the rear of the slide. The barrel locking grooves and the two link swivels can be seen in the partially dismantled specimen illustrated. In 1908 the round hammer was changed back to the more practical spur type.

In 1903 a Pocket Model was introduced similar to the Military Model except that the barrel was shortened from 6″ to $4\frac{1}{2}$″ and the back strap was again rounded. Both spur and round hammer variants can be encountered. The 1900 Model and Sporting Model of 1902 both had seven round

.38 Colt Military Model 1902 dismantled to show the barrel locking grooves and the two link swivels. (R. D. Nicoll)

magazines, as did the Pocket Model, but that for the 1902 Military Model carried eight rounds. The 1903 Pocket Model should not be confused with the straight blow-back Pocket Model: the former was locked breech with an external hammer, the latter was hammerless or, to be precise, had a concealed hammer. Although both were chambered for .38 nominal calibre cartridges, the 'hammerless' version was for the .380 ACP (9mm Browning short) and the hammer version was for the .38 ACP (later to become, in a more powerful loading, the .38 Colt Super Automatic). The .38 Military Model of 1902 was manufactured until 1928, the Pocket Model until 1927.

Following unsuccessful attempts to interest the US Government in the Model 1900, the Model 1902 did get as far as trials. The Ordnance,

The 1908 variant of the Colt Model 1902 with the spur hammer and altered location of the finger grooves.

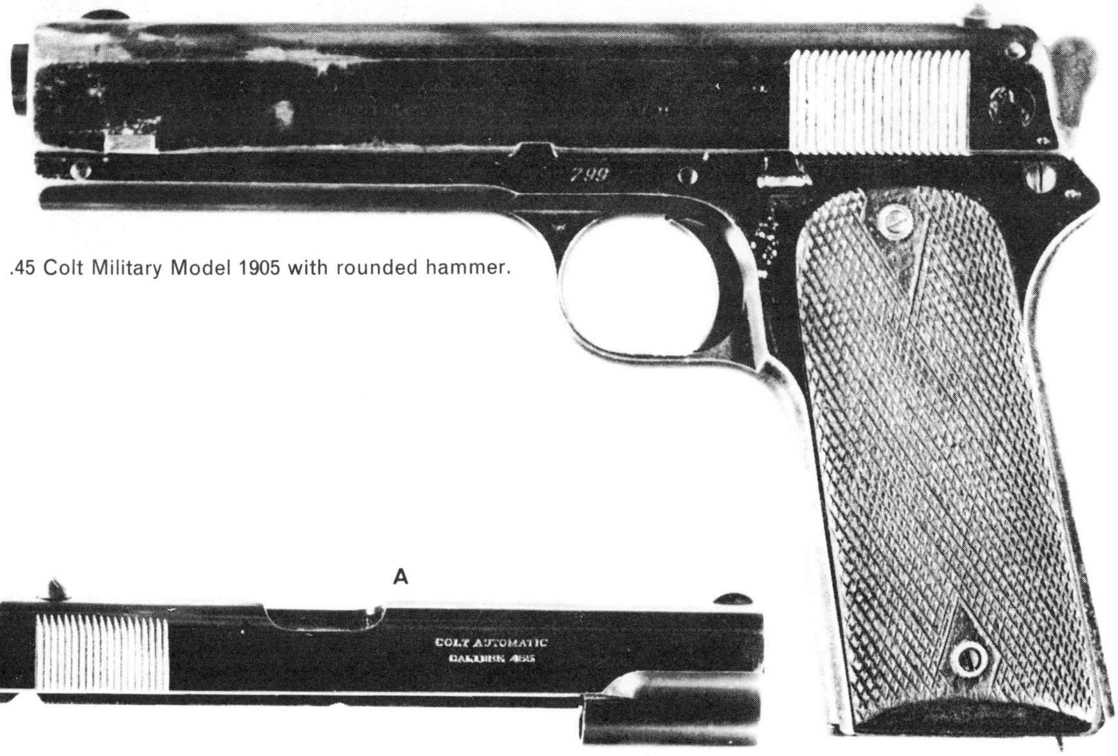

.45 Colt Military Model 1905 with rounded hammer.

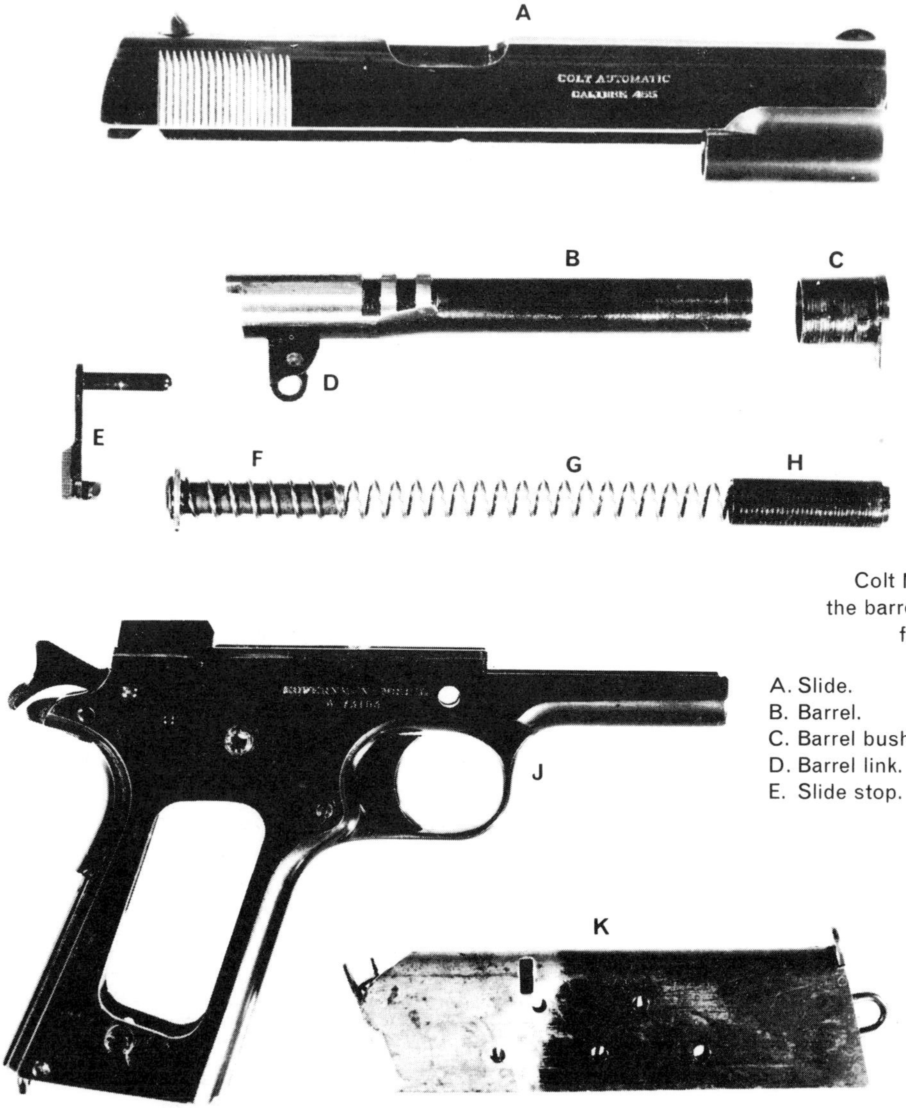

A

B

C

D

E

F

G

H

Colt Model 1911 dismantled showing the barrel locking grooves, a distinctive feature of the Browning system.

A. Slide.
B. Barrel.
C. Barrel bushing.
D. Barrel link.
E. Slide stop.
F. Recoil spring guide.
G. Recoil spring.
H. Plug.
J. Frame.
K. Magazine.

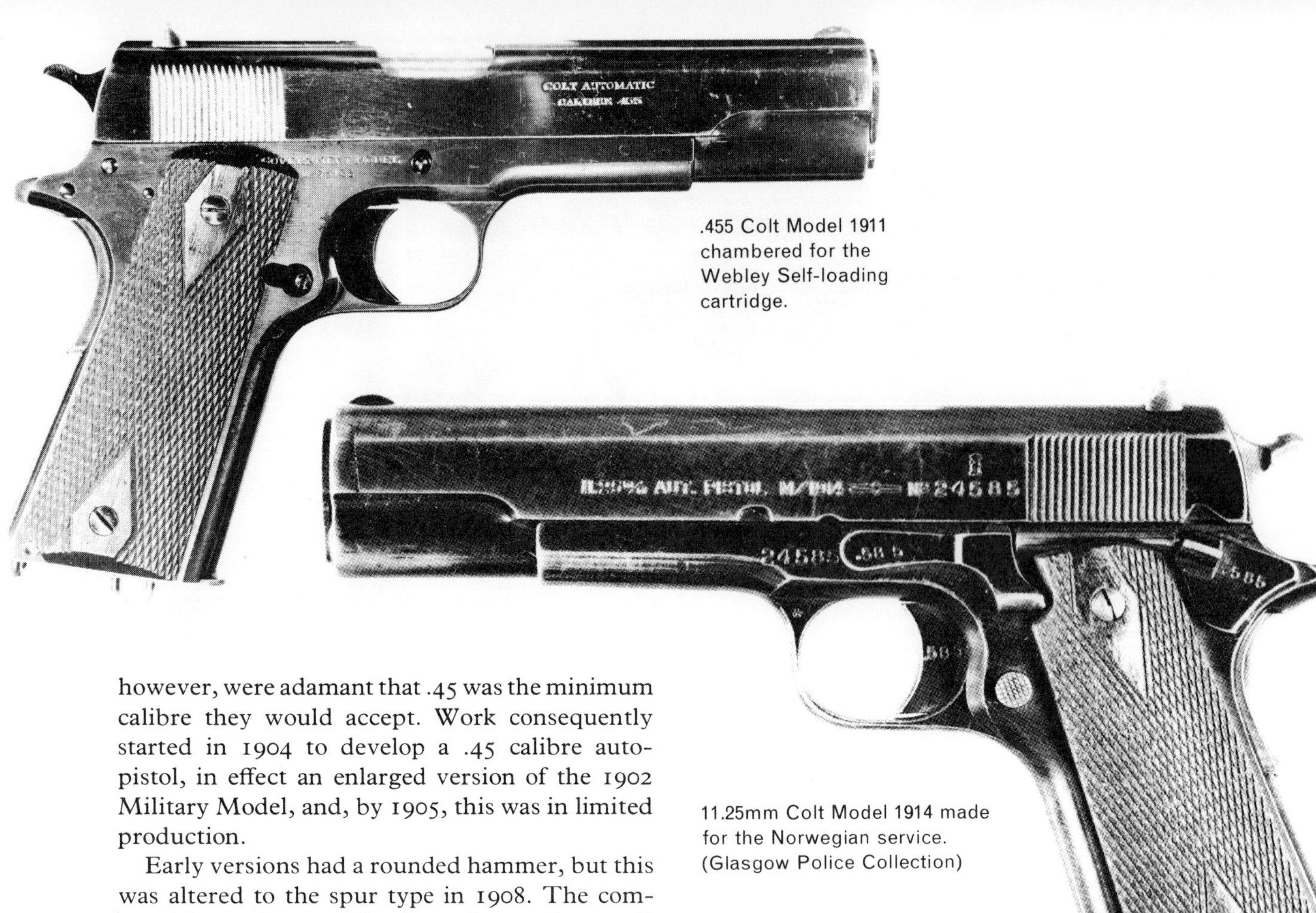

.455 Colt Model 1911 chambered for the Webley Self-loading cartridge.

11.25mm Colt Model 1914 made for the Norwegian service. (Glasgow Police Collection)

however, were adamant that .45 was the minimum calibre they would accept. Work consequently started in 1904 to develop a .45 calibre auto-pistol, in effect an enlarged version of the 1902 Military Model, and, by 1905, this was in limited production.

Early versions had a rounded hammer, but this was altered to the spur type in 1908. The commercial version remained on the market until 1911, while Colt's continued to try and produce a design that would really satisfy the US Ordnance Department.

In March 1911 their efforts were crowned with success, and the Colt Model 1911 was adopted for the US Army, Navy and Marine Corps. One of the inherent defects of the basic 1900 system, the use of two barrel links, was corrected in the experimental models manufactured in 1909, when the forward barrel link and take down key was eliminated, the muzzle end of the barrel being carried in a cylindrical bushing retained in place by a plug at the end of the recoil spring. Various other design changes were also made which both simplified manufacture and made dismantling in the field easier.

The basic 1911 type illustrated is a British contract model chambered for the .455 Webley self-loading cartridge. (The .45 ACP cartridge can be fired in the .455 version but the reverse is not true.) Supplies of these pistols were shipped to Britain during 1915 and 1916 and were marked on the left hand side of the slide with the patent dates, the Colt legend and trade mark, on the right hand side with 'Colt Automatic, Calibre .455' and on the frame with 'Government Model'. Serial numbers special to this contract were prefixed by the letter 'W'. In 1920 the .455 Colt 1911 pistols were withdrawn from the Navy and issued to the Royal Air Force marked 'R.A.F.'

A commercial version of the Model 1911 was placed on the market as the Colt Automatic Pistol Calibre .45 Military Model 1911 and was identical in design to the US Government contract. Commercial serial numbers were prefixed by the letter 'C' and the legend 'United States Property' was lacking.

In 1912, following competitive trials, the Norwegian Government adopted the Colt Model 1911, and three hundred pistols were ordered. The outbreak of the First World War and the subsequent involvment of America induced the Norwegians to manufacture the Colt 1911 themselves at the Kongsberg Arms Factory. Initial production was identical to the Colt but, by 1919, Kongsberg had tooled up for mass production and the final production version, marked '11.25mm Aut. Pistol M/1914', exhibited slight detail modifications including an alteration to the slide lock, the tail of which was extended downwards.

Colt also supplied the Model 1911 to the Republic of Argentina as the Model 1916 and, later, the Model 1911 A1 was supplied as the Model 1927. Both these pistols carried special slide markings, but were manufactured in America. Another version was made in Argentina under license and is interchangeable with the Model 1911 A1. In the 1930's the firm of Hafdasa, Buenos Aires, manufactured a simplified version of the Colt under Ballester Molina patents. This pistol lacked the grip safety of the Colt original and had a modified hammer strut, firing pin stop and safety lock. It is easily recognised by the absence of the grip safety and by the unusual slide serrations. The pistol illustrated bears the legend 'Pistola Automatica Cal. .22 Fabricada por "Hafdasa" Patentes Internacionales "Ballester Molina" Industria Argentina'. This version is a .22 adaptation using the Williams 'floating chamber' device.

.45 Colt Model 1911 A1, US Government issue.

During the First World War, Springfield Armoury tooled up to manufacture the Model 1911, and these pistols were clearly marked on the slide 'Springfield Armoury U.S.A.' The need to expand production to meet wartime demands

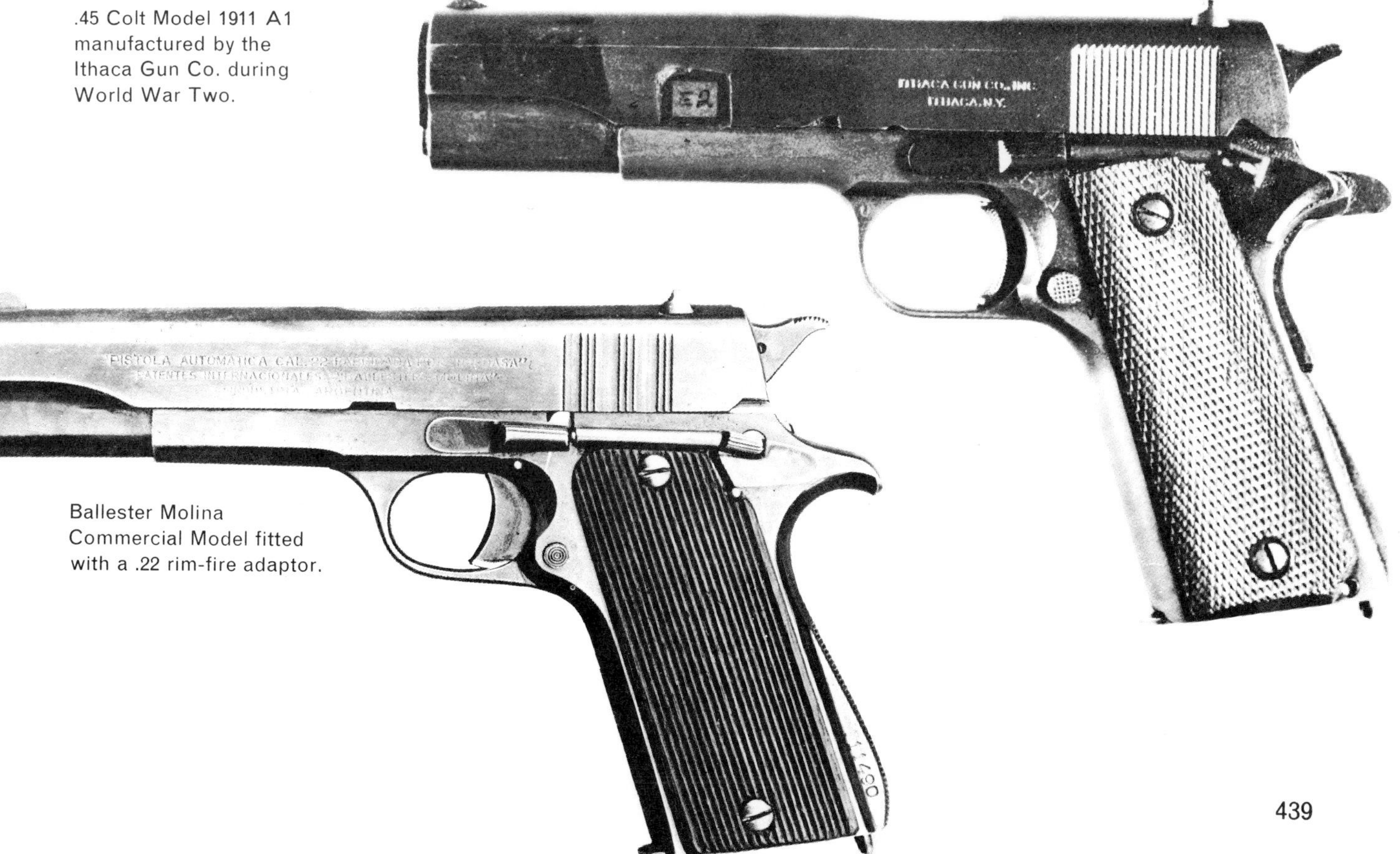

.45 Colt Model 1911 A1 manufactured by the Ithaca Gun Co. during World War Two.

Ballester Molina Commercial Model fitted with a .22 rim-fire adaptor.

Colt Model 1911 A1 fitted with special grips and trigger, and with sand blasted straps. (Col. F. S. Allen)

resulted in contracts being placed with several other American and Canadian companies, such as the Remington Arms UMC Co. of Bridgeport and the North American Arms Co. of Quebec. These two firms appear to be the only ones who actually got into production, although specimens bearing the name of the Caron Brothers Mfg. Co. of Montreal or the insignia of A. J. Savage Munitions Co. of San Diego have been reported.

During the First World War experiments were also carried out with long barrelled versions of the Model 1911 with increased magazine capacity. None were officially adopted, and it was left to the imitators of the Colt 1911 to introduce special versions of this type after the war.

In 1920 modifications were proposed and, by 1925, had been incorporated in the Model 1911 A1. Comparison of the Model 1911 with the Model 1911 A1 shows the 'clearance' cuts made in the frame behind the trigger, the reduced width of the trigger (the front surface of which was knurled), the extension to the tang of the grip safety, and the arching and knurling of the mainspring housing. In addition, the foresight was made slightly broader, alterations were made to the rifling, the land diameter was reduced and the height of the lands increased.

During World War Two production had again to be augmented and, to aid manufacturing, the traditional blueing gave way to a grey/green phosphate coating, and brown or black phenolic resin grips replaced the hard rubber ones.

The Ithaca Gun Co. were the first to produce the 1911 A1 in volume and marked their pistols 'Ithaca Gun Co. Inc., Ithaca, N.Y.' They were followed by Remington Rand who, well established in the production of business machines, were able to manufacture to the limits required with the marking 'Remington Rand Inc., Syracuse, N.Y., U.S.A.', and by the Union Switch and Signal Co., where the marking was 'U.S. & S. Co., Swissvale, Pa. U.S.A.' The last firm to manufacture under contract was the Singer Manufacturing Co. whose product was blued and marked 'S.M.Co.'

The establishment of manufacturing facilities for the 1911 A1 pistol on this scale was a considerable achievement, since over seven hundred machine operations and nearly two hundred visual and gauge inspections were needed to produce the finished pistol, as was a certain amount of 'know-how' which could only be gained from experience. The Government Model 1911 is still carried on the Colt commercial range and, as the Model 0-1, is available in Colt Blue with the standard 5″ barrel length.

In 1933 a special target version of the 1911 Model, known as the National Match Model, was put on the market to cater for those who shot in competition with the issue pistol. Patridge type sights were originally fitted, but were later replaced by a Stevens type adjustable rear sight and a ramp foresight. Discontinued during World

Colt Gold Cup National Match Model O-5 with target sights, special trigger, hand-fitted action etc. (Colt)

War Two, manufacture was resumed in 1957, since when the pistol has been known as the 'Colt Gold Cup National Match'.

In addition to those made by Colt's, the Springfield Armoury has also manufactured special target grade pistols, while a number of custom pistolsmiths in America have offered special quality weapons, the accuracy potential of which is higher than that of the standard military pistol. Each year Springfield Armoury produce several hundred .45 National Match pistols in support of the US Army Marksmanship programmes and the National Matches. Modifications continue to be made on an almost yearly basis and will undoubtedly provide the collector of the future with a king-sized headache. Much of the Ordnance work is connected with the need to check manufacturing divergencies from the Ordnance specifications. Both Colt's and the US Ordnance Department have designed a new type of slide in which manufacturing tolerances have been reduced and headspace control improved. These special slides have the slide grip serrations at an angle.

In addition to being offered in .45 ACP, the Gold Cup Model is also available in .38 Special. Colt-Elliason fully adjustable rear sights are now fitted, and the Colt Gold Cup in .38 Special (first introduced by Colt in 1960) allows the targetman who wishes to shoot with the light recoil .38 Special revolver cartridge in an automatic pistol to purchase a factory built model instead of having to use a conversion of the .45 ACP or the .38 Super.

The Colt Super .38 is almost identical to the 1911 Government Model. If first appeared in 1929 and is currently available with fixed sights as the Model o-2. In 1933 the Super Match appeared as the stablemate of the .45 National Match, but is no longer made, its place having been taken by the Gold Cup Model in .38 Special. The .38 Colt Super Automatic cartridge is a development of the .38 ACP and first appeared, along with the Super .38 auto-pistol, in 1929. The Thompson sub-machine gun was once chambered for this cartridge, but today, outside America, only a few Spanish auto-pistols are chambered for it.

A lightweight version of the Colt automatic, known as the Colt Commander and chambered for the .45 ACP, .38 Super and 9mm Parabellum cartridges, was put into production in 1949. The $4\frac{1}{4}''$ barrel length is shorter than the standard $5''$ of the Government Model and this reduction, coupled with the use of a special lightweight alloy—'Coltalloy'—reduced the weight from 39 ozs. to $26\frac{1}{2}$ ozs. Magazine capacity is nine rounds for the .38 and 9mm versions, and eight rounds for the .45 ACP model.

Conversion units or adaptors are by no means

new—witness the Parker-Hale conversion to .22 for the .455 Service Webley revolver and the Erma conversion unit for the Parabellum—and, before passing on to the .22 automatics, mention must be made of the .22 conversion unit for the Colt automatics. The Colt 'Ace' appeared originally in 1931 and, in 1937, the 'Service Ace' was marketed. This was an unusual pistol in that it employed a 'floating' chamber, the invention of David M. Williams, which increased the recoil of the .22 rim-fire long rifle cartridge four times and so simulated the recoil of the .45 calibre pistol. Manufacture was discontinued in 1941, but it was subsequently reintroduced as the Colt Conversion Unit which can be fitted to the receiver of and Colt Model 1911 or Colt .38 Super except the Colt Commander.

To fit the unit, the pistol must, of course, be dismantled, and the first thing to do is to remove the magazine by pressing the magazine catch on the left hand side of the pistol. Pull the slide to the rear and release, checking that the chamber is empty. Let the hammer down.Press the knurled end of the plug under the muzzle inward and rotate the barrel bushing a quarter turn clockwise. This frees the recoil plug and spring, and both can be withdrawn. Rotate the barrel bushing anti-clockwise until it is disengaged from the slide and then remove it. Pull the slide to the rear again until the slide stop is opposite the clearance notch (the first notch from the breech), push inward the rounded end protruding through the right hand side of the frame and remove the stop. Pull the slide off the front of the receiver and remove the recoil spring guide. Push the barrel link forward and the barrel can then be pulled out from the front of the slide. Further dismantling can be done by cocking the hammer and rotating the safety catch almost to the 'on' position; it can then be pulled to the left and away from the receiver. The hammer pin and the hammer assembly can be taken out, the mainspring housing pin can be pushed out by using the hammer strut, and the housing can then be slid downward off the receiver. The grip safety and the sear spring are removed, followed by the rear pin. Sear and disconnector can then be removed from the frame. Press in the magazine catch from the left hand side and, using the sear spring as a screwdriver, rotate the magazine catch lock one quarter turn so that the trigger can be withdrawn to the rear. Using the hammer strut, push in on the firing pin and then press down on the top edge of the firing pin stop and remove it from the recess in the frame. Using the hammer strut again, pry out the extractor from the rear of the slide and remove the firing pin and firing pin spring.

.45 Colt Commander. (Colt)

The remarkable feature of the Model 1911 is now apparent: full and complete dismantling can be accomplished without the aid of any tools. As an issue military handgun, the Colt 1911 has an enviable reputation. It is accurate within the needs of service use, extremely rugged and, should anything break, the part can be replaced without the need for skilled attention or the use of special tools or, indeed, the use of any tools at all.

At the other end of the scale is the Colt .22 automatic pistol, better known as the 'Woodsman'. The first .22 auto-pistol to be made by Colt's was based on patents taken out by two Colt employees, Francis C. Chadwick and George H. Tansley and owed much to the Browning blowback design. The first commercial model appeared in 1915 and, in March 1917, the legend 'The Woodman' was added to the left hand side of the frame. Originally offered with a $6\frac{1}{2}''$ barrel, a shorter $4\frac{1}{2}''$ barrel version became available in

1933. After 1935, the short barrel version was described as the Sport Model Woodsman. In 1936 further work was done on the design by William Swartz with the idea of introducing variable barrel weights, a feature of the Walther target pistols used at the 1936 Olympics. As it was decided that external weights would not be acceptable to the American shooting man, a heavy barrel was employed instead. This, coupled with larger grips and target sights, increased the weight by 7 ozs., but unfortunately the outbreak of war sharply curtailed both the use of this pistol and its further development. Although revised versions of the Sport Model and Target Model appeared in 1947, the Match Target Woodsman of 1938 was not manufactured after the war. In 1948 a new Match Target version of the Woodsman was introduced with a 6½″ barrel, but, by 1949, a 4½″ barrel length version was also available. Currently the Woodsman Match Target Model S-3 with a ten round magazine is offered with adjustable sights and either a 4½″ or 6″ barrel. A cheaper version, the Woodsman Target with 6″ barrel, the Model S-2 and the Model S-4 Targetsman complete the Colt series of .22 target pistols. The Woodsman Sports Model S-1 and the S-5 Huntsman, the latter with fixed sights, complete the range.

The earlier centre-fire Colt automatics acknowledged their ancestry on the slide by carrying the legend 'Browning's Patent'. Later models did not, and it is easy to forget the role of Browning in the development of the centre-fire Colt automatic pistols.

The Browning story is, however, not finished, for in 1962 the Browning Arms Co. announced a new line of .22 auto-pistols which were marketed in America under the name Browning Nomad, Challenger and Medallist. The cheapest in the range is the Nomad which features an adjustable rear sight mounted on a barrel extension so that

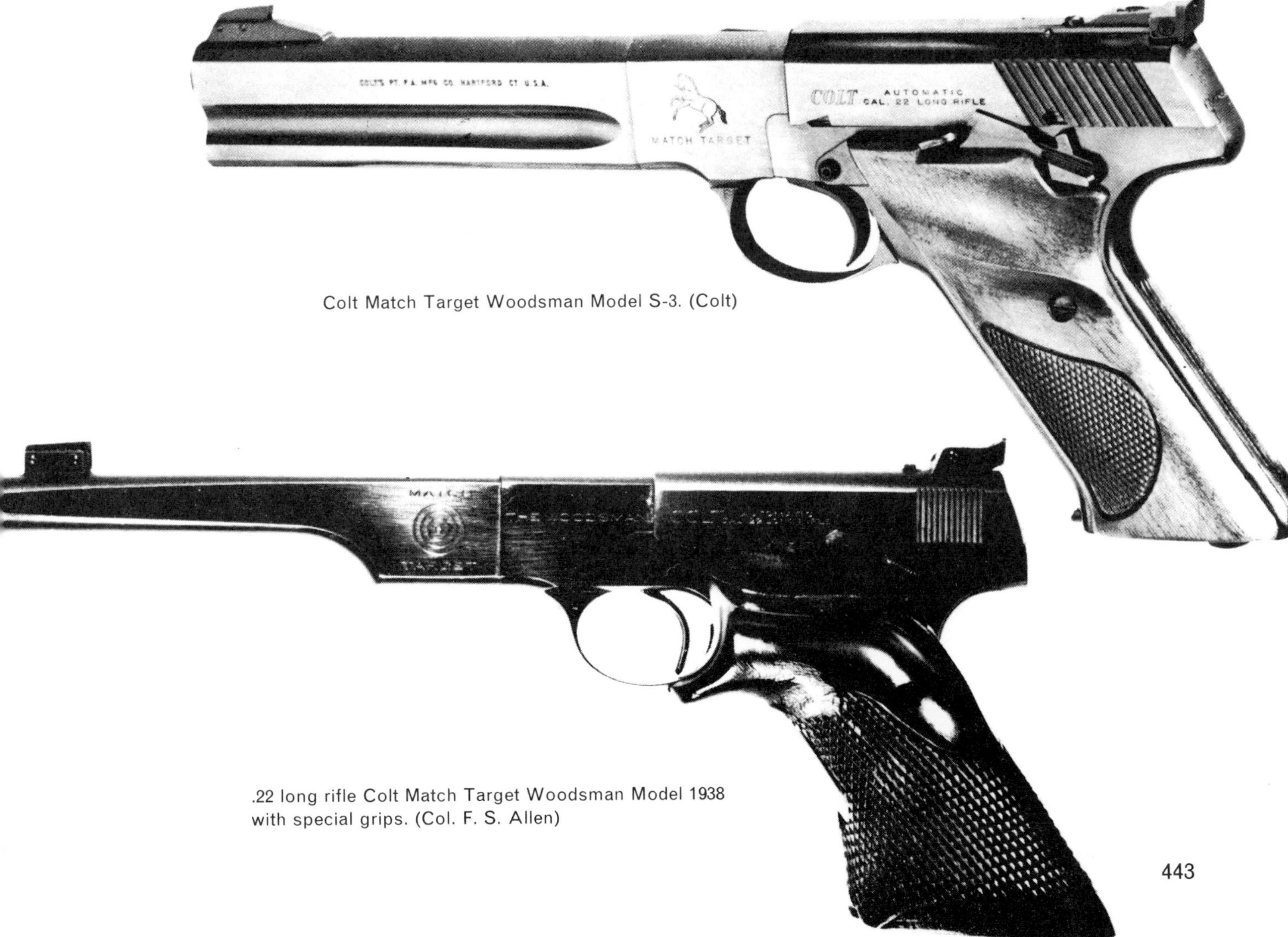

Colt Match Target Woodsman Model S-3. (Colt)

.22 long rifle Colt Match Target Woodsman Model 1938 with special grips. (Col. F. S. Allen)

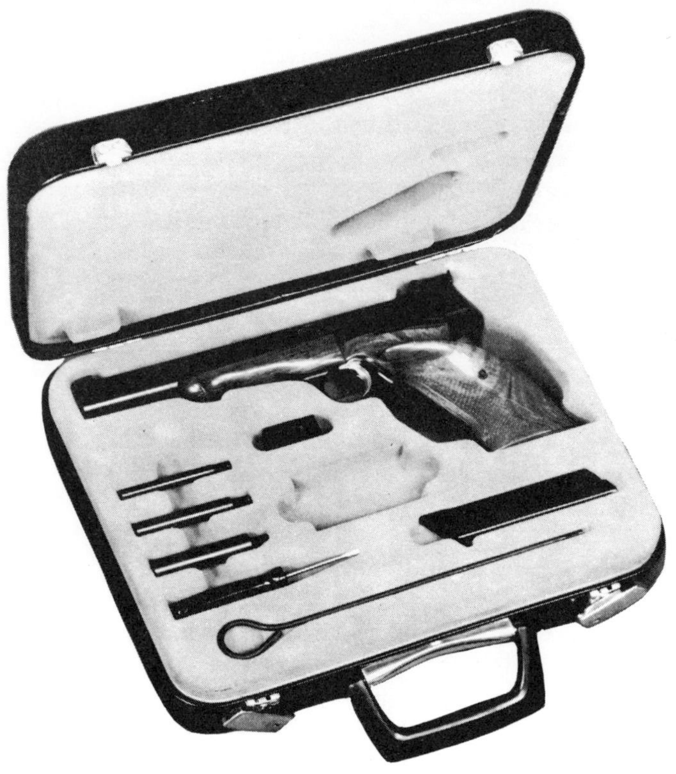

.22 long rifle FN Browning Concours or Match. (Fabrique Nationale)

it does not move with the slide, interchangeable $4\frac{1}{2}''$ or $6\frac{3}{4}''$ barrels and a lightweight alloy receiver. The Challenger specification includes a heavier steel frame and a manual or automatic slide stop with an adjustable trigger. The most expensive in the range is the Medallist with a heavier $6\frac{3}{4}''$ barrel with ventilated rib, micrometer click rear sight (sight base being $9\frac{1}{2}''$), fully adjustable trigger, target type walnut stocks and a walnut fore-end which holds additional barrel weights. A 'dry firing' mechanism—so that the trigger mechanism can be operated without releasing the hammer—is engaged by pulling out the safety catch after the pistol has been cocked and then pushing it forward and down.

The three variants are made by Fabrique Nationale at Herstal and, in Europe, are sold under the names 'Standard', 'Target' and 'Concours', except that, in Britain, the 'Concours' is known as the 'Match' model.

The name of Browning will always be associated with the Colt automatic pistol and the FN auto-pistols. Such was the strength of the Colt-Browning partnership in America that, until quite recently, Colt's undoubtedly dominated the auto-pistol field. Even so, in the period between the two wars, attempts were made by other gun manufacturers to get both a share of service pistol cake and also some of the commercial auto-pistol business.

In any review of this field three names emerge,

.22 long rifle FN Browning Target. (Fabrique Nationale)

Savage, Remington, and Smith and Wesson. The Savage Arms Co. of Utica manufactured a range of auto-pistols between 1907 and 1928 whose design was the work of William Condit and Major Elbert Hamilton Searle, a former ordnance officer attached to Springfield Armoury. Two basic types of pistol were developed, a fixed barrel retarded blow-back and a moving barrel locked breech. Production considerations were swept aside by participation in the 1907 US Ordnance Department trials. As mentioned previously, the minimum calibre for pistols was .45 and Savage were able to make up a special .45 calibre trial pistol in time. The Ordnance Board commented favourably on its performance and asked the company to furnish two hundred pistols for further trials incorporating certain additional features they thought desirable. Because of inadequate factory capacity, Savage were unable to do this. They were, however, geared to

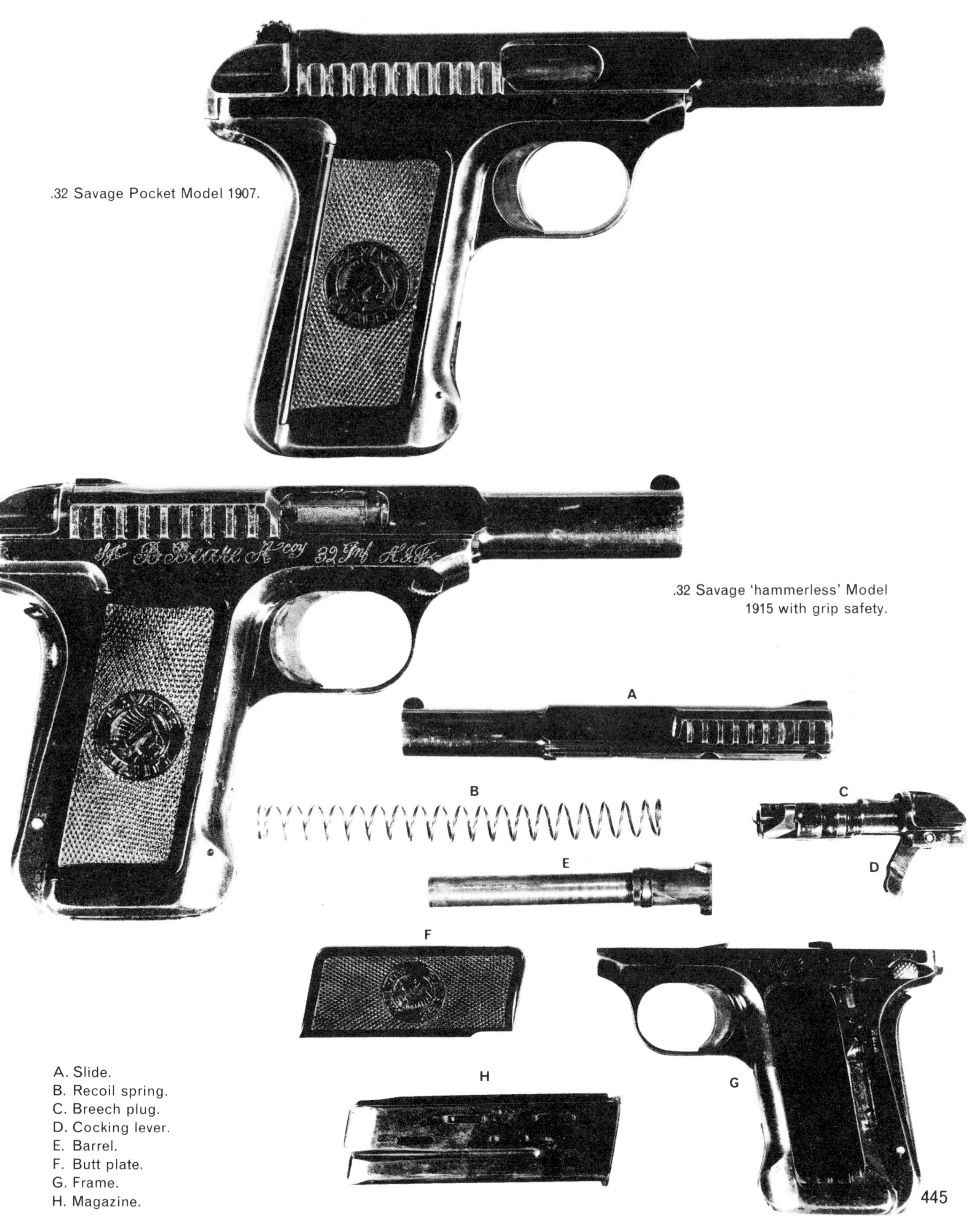

.32 Savage Pocket Model 1907.

.32 Savage 'hammerless' Model 1915 with grip safety.

A. Slide.
B. Recoil spring.
C. Breech plug.
D. Cocking lever.
E. Barrel.
F. Butt plate.
G. Frame.
H. Magazine.

manufacture pistols in .32 calibre and, in 1907, they introduced the .32 Savage Automatic Pistol, Pocket Model. In 1913 this was followed by a .380 calibre weapon but, in 1915, both designs were modified and an additional 'hammerless' model with a grip safety was introduced, although the term 'hammerless' is misleading since none of the Savage auto-pistols had a hammer. In the 1915 series, the rear of the striker was made smaller and covered with a shroud, and a slide hold-open device was fitted together with a slide release lever on the right hand side of the frame. Work was also carried out on a .25 calibre model, but it is very doubtful if this was ever offered commercially.

The Model 1907 continued in production, but the 1915 model was dropped in favour of yet another variant, the Model 1917. The late Model 1907 and the Model 1917 both had a spur cocking lever, but the former had different slide serrations. The Model 1917 had a larger, better shaped grip. The grip safety was eliminated and, although it still featured the Indian head motif, a new monogram was introduced on the butt plates. A .45 calibre model was produced in small quantities and in variant forms but was not adopted by the US Government. Savage were, however, able to interest the Portuguese Government in their .380 calibre Model 1917, and this was adopted as the official military pistol until manufacture was suspended in 1928.

The Savage was very well made and employed some unusual features, such as pressed steel grips on the early Model 1907. During its somewhat brief life, however, criticism was aroused by the lack of a magazine safety device, by the fact that it could not be carried uncocked with a cartridge in the breech, and because, on occasions, it could fire 'full-automatic' due either to dirt or to a weak sear spring.

A contemporary Savage catalogue gives factory data for the Model 1917, but an earlier catalogue extolled the virtues of the pistol in no uncertain manner. 'Inexperienced women have used it in defence of themselves, their homes and their children. Woodsmen, hunters, trappers, forest

9mm Savage Model 1917.

.32 Savage Model 1907 with 1917 type cocking lever.

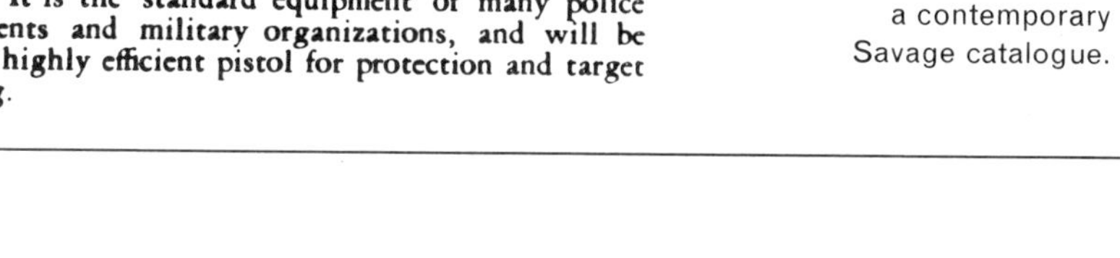

The Model 17 Savage Automatic Pistol

SPECIFICATIONS

Automatic action, hammer type, firing one shot at each pull of trigger. Finished by a special process in fine appearing carbonia blue, hard rubber grips.

MADE IN TWO CALIBERS AND SIZES AS FOLLOWS:

.32 AUTOMATIC, Rimless, smokeless; 3¾-inch barrel, total length, 6½ inches, **weight, 22 ounces. Magazine** holds 10 cartridges.

.380 AUTOMATIC, Rimless, smokeless; 4¼-inch barrel, total length, 7 inches, **weight, about 23 ounces. Magazine** holds 9 cartridges.

The Model 17, Savage Automatic Pistol, is a self-loading arm which combines **in the size and weight of a small pocket gun** the desirable features and qualities of **the best military pistols.**

The action of the pistol is semi-automatic, or self-loading. The recoil from **firing each cartridge automatically** extracts and ejects the empty shell, cocks the **firing pin, and puts a loaded cartridge** into the barrel, leaving the pistol ready to **be fired again. Only one shot** is fired at one pull of the trigger. The details of **design are most modern, and insure** the utmost reliability and durability. There **are no screws, and every spring** is spiral and unbreakable. The pistol may be completely **dismounted and assembled** without tools. The barrels are made of the same **grade of steel used for the barrels of Savage Hi-Power rifles**, and every part and point in the **mechanism subject to wear or strain** is properly tempered.

The stock is of unusual design and so shaped to fit the hand perfectly and **allows pointing with the wrist** in a natural position.

The pistol is of the hammer type, and can be carried with the hammer down **with cartridge in chamber.** Hammer can be cocked and safety manipulated by firing hand. The empty magazine may be expelled by one finger of the hand holding the pistol.

The Savage Automatic pistol is used and indorsed by some of the most respected authorities in the country and by many of the ablest firearm experts and critics. It is the standard equipment of many police departments and military organizations, and will be found a highly efficient pistol for protection and target shooting.

Data on the Savage Model 1917 from a contemporary Savage catalogue.

The Remington Model 51 from a contemporary Remington catalogue.

rangers etc. who require the most gun with the least bulk select it, and not only get small game regularly with it, but have on a number of occasions killed bear, mountain lion and elk.' As if this was not enough, the writer of this publicity puff went on to say that the Savage had 'proved its accuracy against the hottest competition from military and target revolvers'.

In contrast to the Savage, the Remington Model 51, throughout its production life, appeared in one basic type only. This incorporated three excellent safety features: firstly, an excellent manual thumb safety on the left hand rear of the frame; secondly, an excellent grip safety; thirdly,

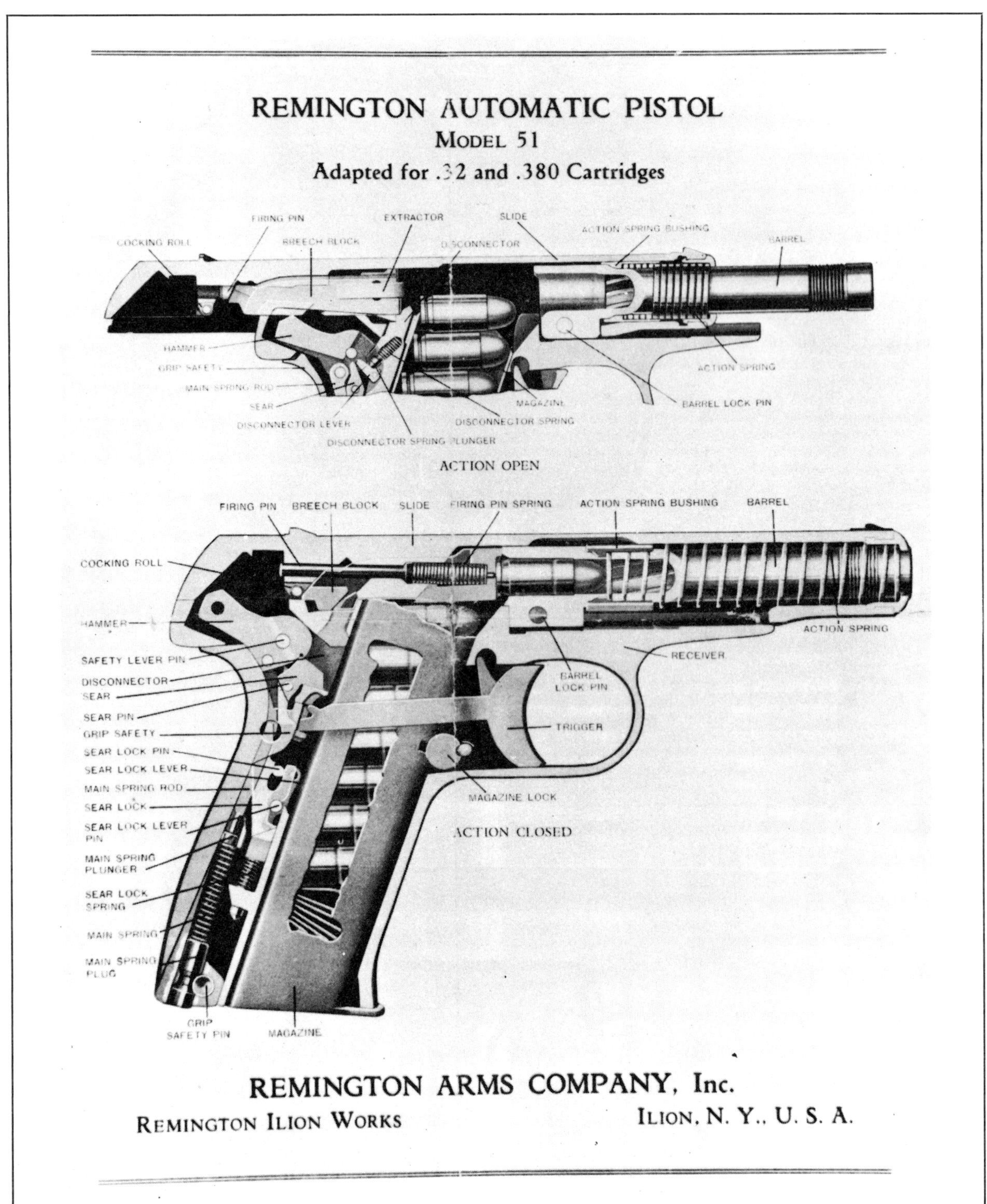

A sectional view of the Remington Model 51 from a contemporary Remington catalogue.

a magazine safety to prevent firing 'the forgotten cartridge' when the magazine was removed. Basic patents on this design were taken out by John D. Pedersen in 1915 and 1919, and the Model 51, first placed on the market in 1918, was offered in .32 ACP and .380 ACP, the smaller calibre having a magazine capacity of eight cartridges, the larger of seven. The action of the Remington was of the 'delayed' blow-back type or inertia lock, which, according to most authori-

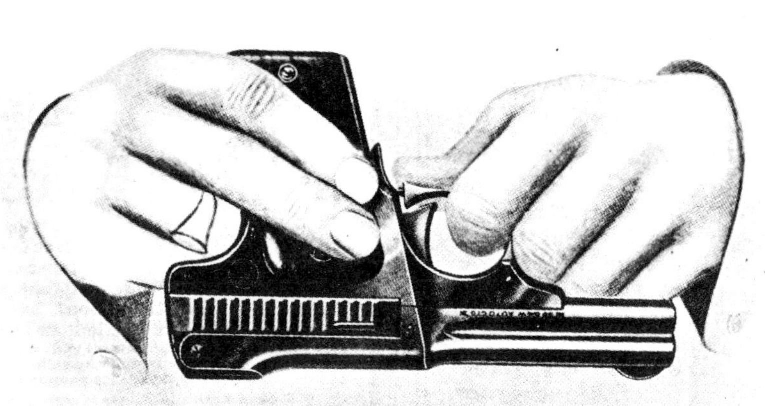

Ease of cleaning—

another exclusive S. & W. feature

You can open up the Smith & Wesson Automatic for *easy cleaning* in less than one second, and *without removing a single part*, not even a screw. Simply pull out the trigger guard as shown above, and barrel and bolt locking mechanism are readily accessible. The gun remains a unit—nothing to get lost.

Smith & Wesson Automatic

It's doubly safe

Fundamentally different

You can't discharge this gun *unintentionally*. The automatic safety under the trigger guard is operated by the *middle* finger, *not* by the trigger finger, *not* by the pressure of the hand in grasping the butt. And when the gun is not in use, you can lock the *entire* mechanism by means of the *non*-automatic safety on the rear of stock.

Other important features, found in *no other* automatic, are the *bolt release catch*, which makes cocking easy; *S. & W. mechanical perfection and accuracy;* and the *special calibre*, which protects from the trouble and possible danger of using cheap or unsuitable ammunition.

BY INVITATION MEMBER OF

You *need* an automatic pistol. You should investigate the *Smith & Wesson* before buying. Ask your dealer about it to-day.

Write for free booklet giving full details

SMITH & WESSON, 795 Stockbridge St., Springfield, Mass.

For over 50 years makers of Superior Revolvers

An advertisement for the Smith and Wesson automatic.

ties, lessened the force of the recoil and made the pistol more pleasant to shoot. Much attention was paid to the design of the grip and the pistol had excellent 'pointing' qualities. Fixed sights only were provided but the top of the slide was flattened and matted to avoid reflections.

Manufacture of the Remington ceased in 1927 and factory stocks were exhausted in 1934. Until

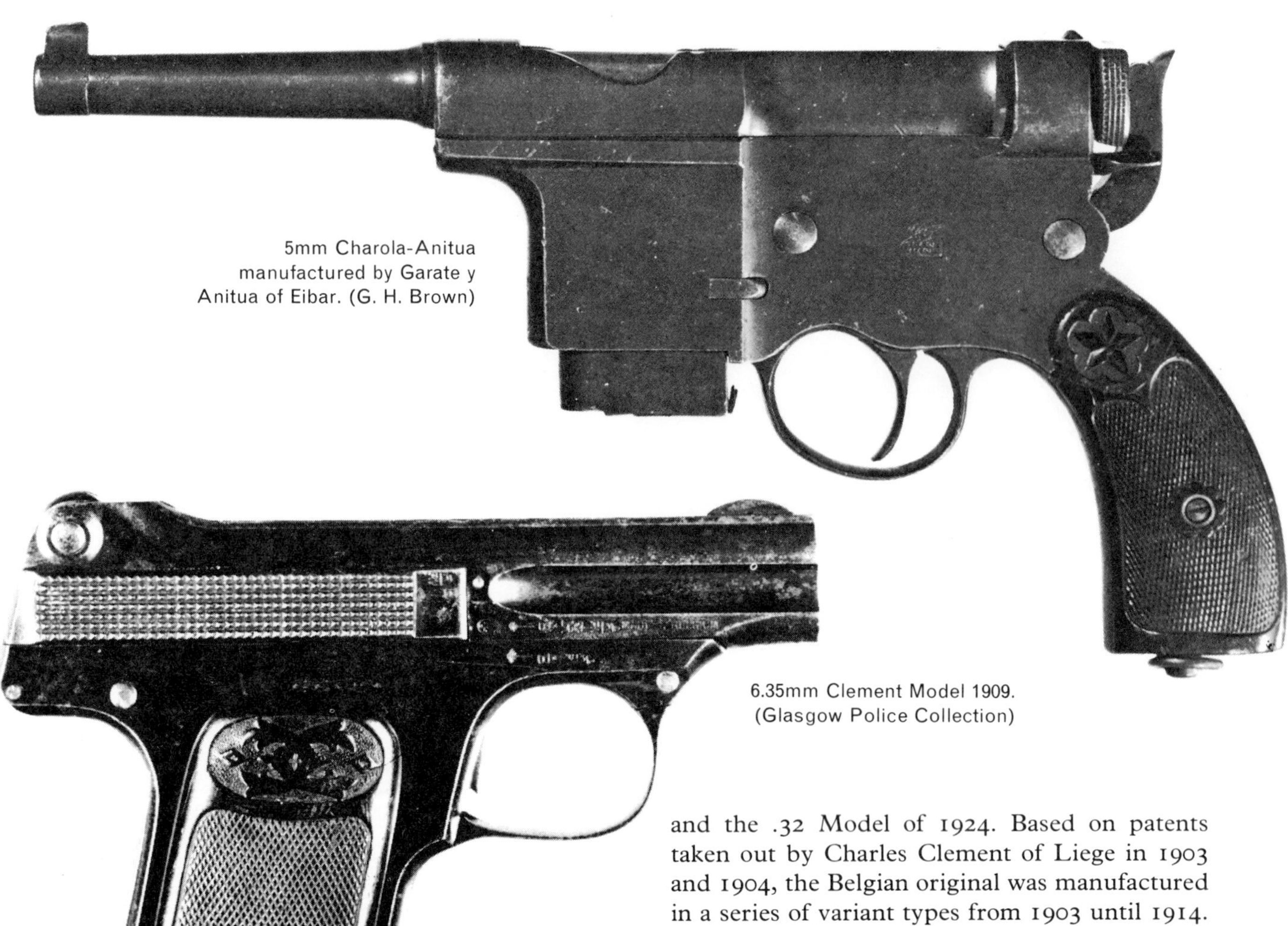

5mm Charola-Anitua manufactured by Garate y Anitua of Eibar. (G. H. Brown)

6.35mm Clement Model 1909. (Glasgow Police Collection)

1920 the pistol bore the Remington UMC style; after that date the style reverted back to Remington Arms Co. Inc. Calibre designation appeared on the barrel where it could be seen through the slide ejection port. Remington also manufactured an experimental .45 calibre pistol which appears to have been tentatively adopted by the US Navy.

Total production of the Remington Model 51 was under 65,000, and the decision to stop production was due more to the economic conditions of the times than to any defect in the design or manufacture of this slightly more complicated but nevertheless attractive weapon.

The rarest and most unusual of all the American production auto-pistols are undoubtedly the Smith and Wesson .35 Model of 1913 and the .32 Model of 1924. Based on patents taken out by Charles Clement of Liege in 1903 and 1904, the Belgian original was manufactured in a series of variant types from 1903 until 1914. All these were of the simple blow-back type with a fixed barrel and sliding breech block. The Clement, the smallest locked breech automatic ever made, was apparently manufactured in Belgium (although a small number were made in Spain), and was first adapted to the rather obscure 5mm bottle-necked rimless Charola-Anitua auto-pistol cartridge which originated in Spain in 1897. The pistol itself did not survive for very long, but the cartridge it employed did, and became more generally known throughout Europe as the 5mm Clement. It was still available as late as 1930, when the original Charola-Anitua had been forgotten and the Clement had been out of production for quarter of a century.

Why Smith and Wesson chose the Clement as the basis for their attempt to gain a foothold in the auto-pistol market will probably never be known. Perhaps its was due to existing patent protection, although the Smith and Wesson design was by no means a direct copy.

The grip safety was operated by a single finger on the front strap and was positioned directly below the trigger guard. A manual safety on the back strap, resembling a small wheel and operated by rotation, replaced the conventional slide safety used on the Clement. Smith and Wesson added $\frac{1}{2}''$ to the barrel length, and steel backed walnut grips replaced the Clement hard rubber ones. The .35 calibre cartridge was as unusual as the pistol. Not a true .35 calibre, the actual bullet diameter was .320″ compared with .312″ for the .32 ACP. The .35 S & W will not chamber in .32 calibre pistols but the .32 ACP will chamber in the .35 Smith and Wesson pistol. The bullet for the .35 cartridge had a cupro-nickel nose and an exposed lead bearing section with grease groove, the nose portion resembling that of any round nose jacketed auto-pistol bullet except for two slits in the jacket which helped to anchor the lead core to the half-mantle.

The Smith and Wesson Model 1913 was a most handsome pistol finished in the traditional deep lustrous blue, and the workmanship was, of course, beyond reproach. The advantages claimed for the pistol—sights attached to the barrel and non-moving slide, the safety system operated by the index finger, the bolt release catch which detached the light bolt from the recoil spring and permitted easy loading of the first cartridge—were to a great extent academic. Against the new pistol was its higher cost, about 10% more than the Colt or Savage .32 auto-pistols, and the fact that the ammunition was not readily available and was, in any case, ballistically inferior to the .32 ACP. The claimed reduction in barrel wear due to the use of half-mantle bullets did not turn out to be a useful selling point.

The last .35 Smith and Wesson auto-pistol left the factory in 1921, but the failure of this design did not prevent Smith and Wesson designing another auto-pistol which discarded many of the dubious features of the original. The Model 1924 was chambered for the .32 ACP cartridge, the manual wheel safety was discarded and the mechanism redesigned. Unfortunately, at $33.50, the cost of the new pistol was even higher, and Colt auto-pistols in the 1920's were selling for $20.50. The old pistol had about fifty components, the new model over sixty. Manufacture began early in 1924 and the last delivery was made in 1936.

Equally disappointing was the Smith and Wesson Straight Line single shot target pistol which appeared in 1923. American target pistols of this period were generally adaptations of a standard revolver frame with a single shot barrel and had been produced by both Smith and Wesson and Colt's. In the new Straight Line Model, however, Smith and Wesson produced what could, at first sight, be taken for an automatic pistol. The basic reason for its failure lay in the type of action employed. It is essential that any target pistol has a crisp and uniform trigger pull. The hammer of the Straight Line Model was a hollow plunger with a short coil spring inside and the sear notch on the bottom surface. Since the plunger had to be loose in order to slide freely, there was inevitably a certain amount of play resulting in a variable depth of engagement of the sear and varying trigger pressure. The Smith and Wesson Straight Line Model was rebuilt with a conventional swinging hammer and the performance was greatly improved. Even so, however, Smith and Wesson decided to cut their losses, and it was 1954 before they again entered the auto-pistol market.

Following the end of World War Two, there were persistent rumours that the US Army was contemplating a smaller calibre and, in 1954, Smith and Wesson unveiled the 9mm Parabellum auto-pistols. One was single action, the other double action, and both were very similar except for the position of the trigger. Eventually the double action version was placed on the market as the Model 39. The action is of the Browning recoil type; barrel and slide recoil locked together, the breech end of the barrel drops and the slide is free to move to the rear. Magazine capacity is eight rounds, and the overall length $7\frac{7}{16}''$. Weight without the magazine is $26\frac{1}{2}$ ozs. The slide mounted safety when put to 'safe' drops the hammer and, at the same time, introduces a steel block between the hammer and

Smith and Wesson Model No.39. (Smith and Wesson)

PARTS LIST

PRICES EFFECTIVE MARCH 15, 1967 – Subject to Change Without Notice – MINIMUM ORDER $1.00

No.	Name	Price
5107	Rear Sight Windage Nut	$ .10
5651	Rear Sight Windage Screw Plunger	.15
5652	Rear Sight Windage Sc. Plg. Sprg	.10
6001	Barrel	14.30
6005	Barrel Bushing	1.65
6011	Trigger Plunger Pin	.10
6013	Ejector-depressor Plunger	.55
6014	Ejector-depressor Plunger Spring	.10
6015	Ejector Magazine Depressor	.55
6017	Ejector Spring	.10
6018	Extractor	2.20
6019	Firing Pin	.65
6022	Firing Pin Spring	.10
6027	Frame Stud	.30
6031	Insert Pin	.10
6031	Trigger Pin	.10
6032	Magazine Tube	1.65
6034	Magazine Assembly	4.25
6036	Magazine Butt Plate Catch	.30
6037	Magazine Assembly—Military	4.25
6039	Magazine Catch	.85
6040	Magazine Catch Nut	.40
6041	Magazine Catch Plunger	.15
6042	Magazine Catch Plunger Spring	.20
6049	Manual Safety	3.85
6051	Manual Safety Plunger	.15
6052	Manual Safety Plunger Spring	.10
6056	Rear Sight Leaf	4.15
6057	Rear Sight Assembly	6.60
6059	Recoil Spring	.65
6061	Recoil Spring Guide Assembly	1.65
6066	Sear Pin	.15
6076	Rear Sight Slide	1.10
6077	Slide	24.20
6081	Slide Stop Button	.45
6083	Slide Stop Plunger	.20

No.	Name	Price
6084	Slide Stop Plunger Spring	$ .20
6095	Rear Sight Windage Screw	.55
6103	Sear Release Lever	.30
6106	Frame (factory exchange only)	35.20
6107	Disconnector	1.10
6108	Disconnector Pin	.10
6110	Drawbar Plunger	.55
6111	Drawbar Plunger Spring	.10
6113	Sear	1.95
6114	Sear Plunger	.15
6115	Sear Plunger Pin	.10
6115	Slide Stop Plunger Pin	.10
6116	Sear Plunger Spring	.10
6117	Sideplate	.60
6121	Trigger Plunger	.30
6122	Trigger Plunger Spring	.15
6125	Slide Stop	3.30
6126	Trigger Play Spring Rivet	.10
6127	Trigger Play Spring	.35
6132	Stock, Right	2.20
6133	Stock, Left	2.20
6141	Dust Shield—Military	1.10
6143	Drawbar	6.60
6144	Hammer	3.05
6145	Insert	4.95
6146	Magazine Tube—Military	1.65
6147	Magazine Follower	.65
6148	Magazine Spring	.90
6149	Mainspring	.35
6151	Stirrup	.45
6152	Stirrup Pin	.10
6153	Trigger	2.20
6185	Magazine Butt Plate	.45
6217	Mainspring Plunger	.30
6221	Stock Screw	.10

SPECIFICATIONS

Caliber 9mm Luger and Parabellum
Magazine Capacity 8
Barrel Length 4 inches
Length Over All 7⁷⁄₁₆ inches
Weight 26½ oz. without magazine
Sights Fixed, ⅛-inch serrated ramp front; Patridge type rear adjustable for windage
Stocks Checked walnut with S&W monograms
Finish S&W Blue or Nickel
Ammunition 9mm Luger and Parabellum

REFINISHING – SMITH & WESSON WILL REFINISH HANDGUNS OF ITS OWN MANUFACTURE AT THE FOLLOWING PRICES: Refinishing – either blue or nickel – $12.00 Change of finish – $15.50 No change of finish is offered on the Victory or Airweight models or on the Models 28, 39 or 60. The time requirement is usually less than 30 days, and if repairs are necessary the cost of parts would be in addition to the above figures.

SERVICING

Should your Smith & Wesson pistol require adjustment, repair or refinishing, we recommend most sincerely that the weapon be returned to the factory. There is no other way to insure that the work will be done in a properly equipped and staffed shop.

Charges are very reasonable, being based on the cost of parts replaced plus a labor charge for the time expended on the job. A labor charge for one hour is usually sufficient to cover all but very extensive overhaul jobs.

Pistols returned to the factory should be MARKED FOR THE ATTENTION OF THE SERVICE DEPARTMENT. A letter of instructions should be enclosed with the gun, and shipment by individuals must be made by Prepaid Railway Express. Adherence to these suggestions will prevent loss of time in handling at the factory.

When returning guns for service, please remove custom stocks and holsters. We cannot assume responsibility for these items.

When your pistol arrives in our Service Department, it will be very carefully inspected, together with your letter of instructions. Next, a quotation covering total cost of work to be performed will be sent to you. No actual work will be commenced before receiving your approval of our quotation unless you specifically authorize us to do so.

SMITH & WESSON

9MM AUTOMATIC PISTOL

DOUBLE ACTION MODEL No. 39

PARTS LIST • INSTRUCTIONS FOR USE • MAINTENANCE
SPECIFICATIONS • GUARANTEE

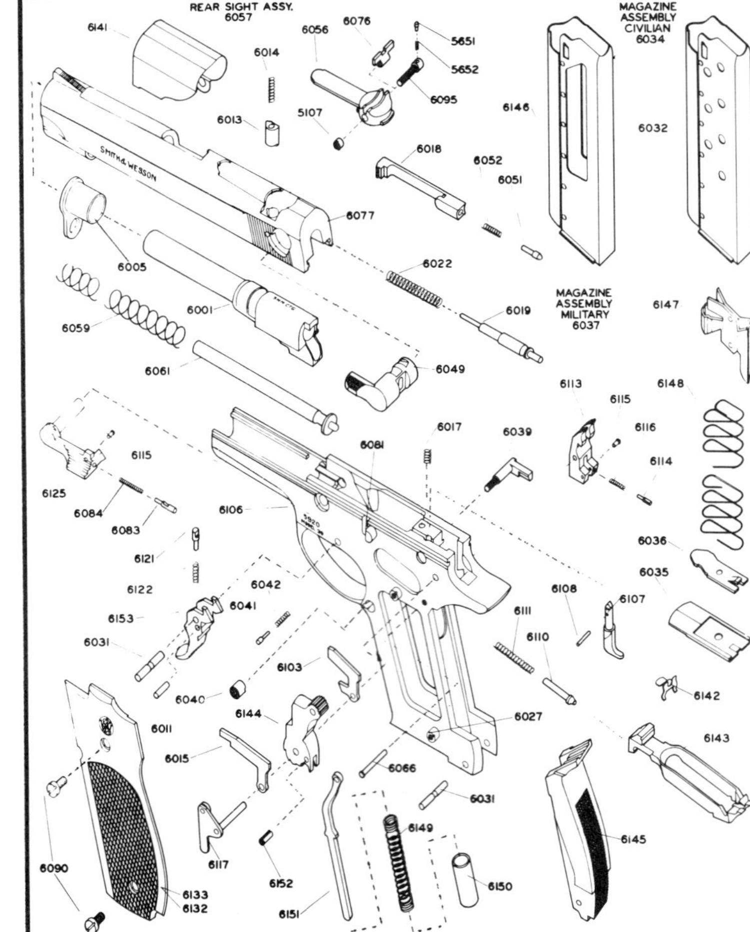

INSTRUCTIONS FOR USE

Before proceeding to use this weapon, a word of caution is in order. This pistol is as safe to handle and use as we can make it, but there is no fool-proof firearm. Be sure that the muzzle is pointing in a safe direction at all times, wbether the gun is loaded or not. Make safe gun handling a habit.

To Load

Magazine capacity is 8 rounds. If desired, an additional cartridge can be loaded in the chamber of the BARREL. Release magazine by pressing magazine catch nut on left side of frame back of trigger guard. Hold MAGAZINE in one hand with the rounded or forward edge away from the palm. Place a cartridge on the forward end of the FOLLOWER, press down and to the rear with the cartridge head or base toward the rear or flat edge of the MAGAZINE. Succeeding cartridges are loaded in the same manner, one on top of another.

If gun is to be fired immediately, place MANUAL SAFETY in upper or "fire" position. Insert MAGAZINE in butt until engaged with MAGAZINE CATCH. Simply press magazine into place – do not drive in forcibly, as this practice may in time cause distortion of magazine lips and resultant malfunctions. Draw SLIDE all of the way to the rear and release. The pistol may now be fired by pulling the TRIGGER.

If the pistol is to be carried ready for action, place MANUAL SAFETY in the lower or "safe" position before inserting MAGAZINE and drawing SLIDE to the rear. After releasing SLIDE put MANUAL SAFETY to upper or "fire" position, and the pistol may be carried ready for immediate action. Note that this obviates the dangerous practice of lowering the HAMMER manually with a loaded cartridge in the chamber. With HAMMER down and SAFETY in "fire" position, the first shot may be discharged by simply pulling the TRIGGER. The DOUBLE ACTION FEATURE cocks and releases the HAMMER in one operation as in firing a double action revolver. Subsequent shots may be fired as in traditional automatic pistols.

Upon firing the last round, the SLIDE STOP engages the SLIDE holding the action open. The MAGAZINE may now be withdrawn and reloaded. To release the SLIDE STOP press downward. When SLIDE STOP is disengaged, SLIDE will move forward to normal position. If it is desired to continue firing, the SLIDE may be left open and a loaded MAGAZINE inserted, in which case the slide can be released by drawing the slide rearward to its limit and letting it spring to battery position.

Note that a cartridge in the CHAMBER cannot be fired when the MAGAZINE is disengaged from the MAGAZINE CATCH. This is a valuable safety feature.

When unloading a loaded pistol, put MANUAL SAFETY in "safe" or low position. Press MAGAZINE RELEASE BUTTON and remove MAGAZINE. Next, draw SLIDE to rear, thus removing loaded cartridge from the CHAMBER.

The cartridges in the MAGAZINE may be removed by pushing forward on the head of each cartridge until it is released from the MAGAZINE LIPS.

To Disassemble (Field Strip)

1. Remove MAGAZINE by pressing MAGAZINE RELEASE BUTTON on left side of FRAME to the rear of TRIGGER GUARD, and drawing MAGAZINE out of BUTT.
2. Inspect CHAMBER to assure that pistol is not loaded.
3. Put SAFETY in "fire" or upper position.
4. While pressing to left on right end of SLIDE STOP (above TRIGGER on right side of FRAME) draw SLIDE to rear until RECESS in the lower left side of SLIDE is aligned with forward end of SLIDE STOP. Draw SLIDE STOP completely from FRAME.
5. Pull SLIDE forward off from FRAME.
6. With SLIDE upside down, compress RECOIL SPRING and lift out RECOIL SPRING GUIDE ASSEMBLY.
7. Remove BARREL BUSHING by rotating lower portion toward left side of SLIDE and drawing forward out of SLIDE.
8. Remove BARREL by lifting rear end back and out of SLIDE.

No further disassembly is recommended, as the pistol may be properly cleaned and lubricated when field-stripped as described above.

To Reassemble

1. Replace BARREL in SLIDE.
2. Replace BARREL BUSHING.
3. Replace RECOIL SPRING and RECOIL SPRING GUIDE ASSEMBLY, making sure that RECOIL SPRING GUIDE BUSHING is engaged in the small radius cut in barrel lug and properly centered. Failure to center properly will leave RECOIL SPRING GUIDE protruding from BARREL BUSHING after assembly.
4. Replace SLIDE on FRAME, depressing EJECTOR and SEAR RELEASE LEVER in turn, so that SLIDE will travel to the rear over them. When slide stop cut on SLIDE is aligned with slide stop hole in FRAME, insert SLIDE STOP and allow SLIDE to return to forward position.
5. Replace MAGAZINE.

Care and Cleaning

Pistols should be field stripped and cleaned at reasonably frequent intervals to insure proper functioning.

Use any good commercial solvent, and after cleaning, lubricate sparingly with a light weight gun oil. Outside surfaces may be protected from corrosion by coating lightly with a rust inhibiting oil or grease.

Be careful not to drop magazines, as they may be sufficiently deformed to cause failure to feed properly.

To Disassemble Slide Assembly

Press rear end of firing pin forward as far as possible with drift punch. Grasp forward end of firing pin with pliers and hold. Turn manual safety thumb-piece to point halfway between "fire" and "safe" positions and press right end of safety bar. Manuel safety may now be drawn out of slide. Hold thumb over rear end of firing pin and release grip on pliers. Firing pin and firing pin spring may now be removed. Manual safety plunger and plunger spring may also be removed from rear end of extractor.

Extractor may be removed by lifting forward end to clear hook, and pressing to rear.

To Reassemble

Place extractor in recess, with extractor hook forward. Press extractor down sufficiently to straighten slight bend and press forward to engage lug in slide cut.

Replace manual safety plunger and spring. Insert firing pin and spring. Push rear end of firing pin forward as far as possible and hold forward end with pliers. Insert manual safety until end of safety bar contacts manual safety plunger. Release grip on pliers and depress manual safety plunger, pressing manual safety bar into position.

To Disassemble Frame Assembly (After Removing Slide and Magazine)

Remove stocks by removing four stock screws. Drive out insert pin located just above lanyard ring. Remove insert. Mainspring and mainspring plunger may then be lifted out of insert. Pull out sideplate assembly on left side of frame. Lift out hammer and stirrup. Remove ejector, ejector spring and sear release lever. Push sear pin out from right side of frame, allowing sear to drop out. Drive trigger pin out from left side, allowing drawbar to slide back toward rear of frame. Let disconnector drop out, and pull drawbar and trigger play spring assembly out from rear of frame. Tip frame to vertical position, butt down, allowing drawbar plunger and spring to drop out. Push trigger upward and forward out of frame. Place frame on right side so magazine catch body is supported. Using drift, press down magazine catch plunger and hold. Turn magazine catch nut counter-clockwise to loosen.

To Reassemble Frame Assembly

Insert magazine catch body in frame. Support frame on solid surface and insert magazine catch spring and plunger. Depress plunger and assemble magazine catch nut. Turn until shank of magazine catch body is slightly below surface of nut. Release plunger and let it snap into notch.

Insert trigger downward through top of frame. Insert drawbar plunger and spring into hole forward of trigger. Insert drawbar through rear of frame, engaging drawbar plunger. Hold drawbar in position, and with frame bottom side up insert disconnector.

Grasp trigger and work drawbar and trigger play spring assembly all the way forward so that rear of drawbar is under the foot of the disconnector. Insert trigger pin. Be sure drawbar moves *under* foot of disconnector.

Insert sear and sear pin, headed end of pin on left side of frame.

Hold trigger back and insert stirrup and hammer. Release trigger. Insert ejector spring in hole and set ejector in place. Insert sideplate stud through left side of frame, ejector, and partially through hammer stud hole. Insert sear release lever. Press sideplate stud completely through hammer, sear release lever, and frame.

Place mainspring and mainspring plunger over stirrup. Bring insert into position by guiding mainspring plunger into recess in insert. Place top of insert in frame and swing base into place. Drive in insert pin.

Replace stocks and stock screws.

To Install Dust Shield—Military

1. Remove magazine and inspect chamber to assure that pistol is not loaded.
2. Put safety in "fire" or upper position.
3. Draw slide to rear until recess in lower left side of slide is aligned with forward end of slide stop. Press ball end of slide stop to left until flush with side of frame.
4. Slide dust shield down over muzzle and front sight until it seats firmly on slide with locking hole on right side and lugs engaged under bottom edges of slide. Slide dust shield rearward until locking hole is over ball end of slide stop on right side.
5. Again draw slide to rear until recess in lower left side of slide is aligned with forward end of slide stop. Press lever end of slide stop back through frame, thus restoring pistol to normal functioning position and securely locking dust shield in place.

Reverse above procedure to remove.

STATEMENT OF LIABILITY

This gun is classified as a FIREARM or DANGEROUS WEAPON and is surrendered by us with the express understanding that we assume no liability for its re-sale or safe handling under local laws and regulations. Smith & Wesson assumes no responsibility for physical injury or property damage resulting from either intentional or accidental discharge, or for the function of any gun subjected to influences beyond their control, and will honor no claims which may result from careless handling, unauthorized adjustments, defective or improper ammunition, corrosion or neglect.

For your protection, examine your gun carefully at the time of purchase, then fill out and mail to us promptly the registration card bearing your gun's serial number which accompanies all new guns.

WARRANTY

The company will replace or adjust to its commercial standard any gun or part thereof returned prepaid to the factory and found by us to be defective in either material or workmanship. Such service will be made free of charge for one year from date of registered purchase. This warranty and statement of liability supersedes all previous warranties and commitments.

April 15, 1955

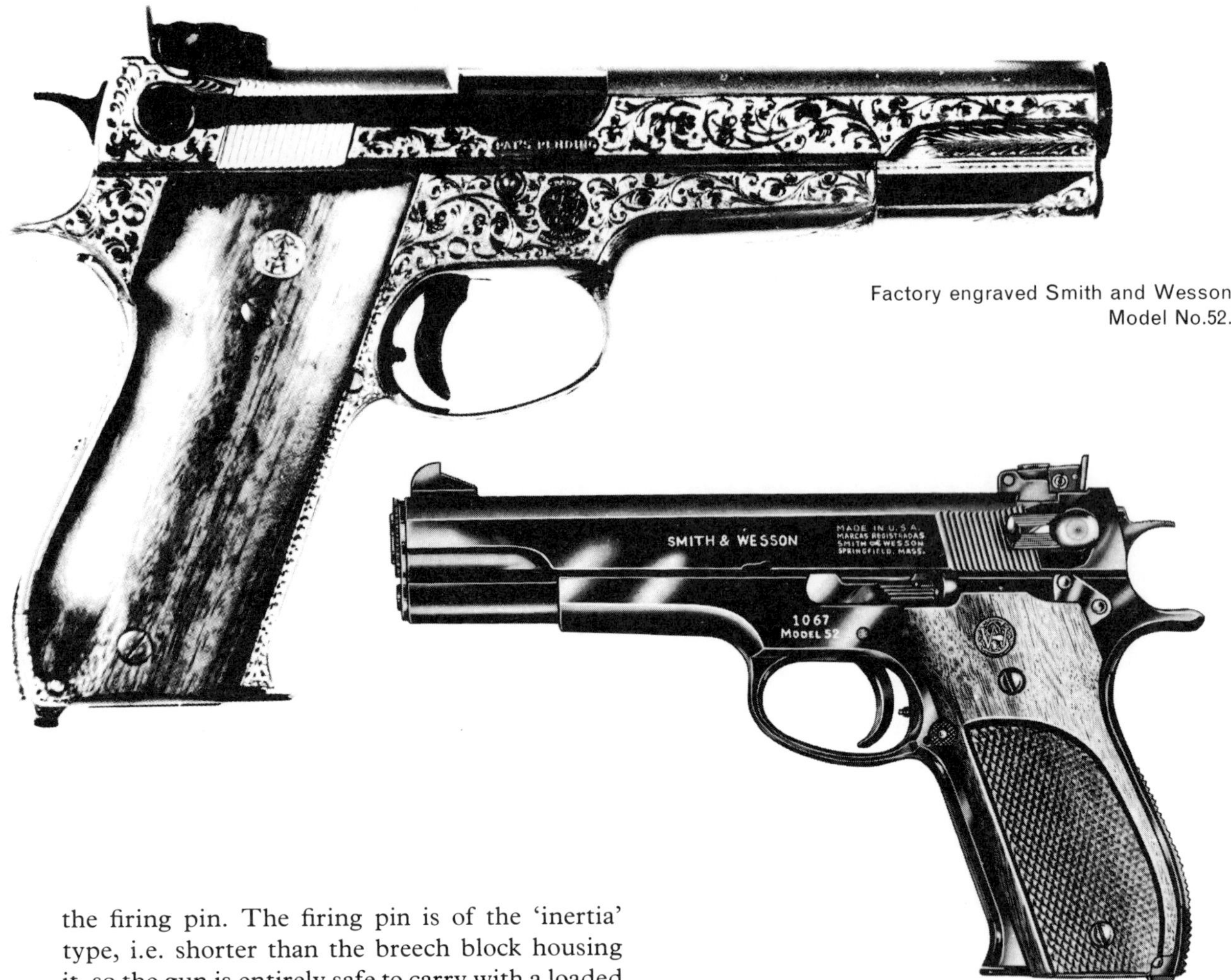

Factory engraved Smith and Wesson Model No.52.

Smith and Wesson Model No.52. (Smith and Wesson)

the firing pin. The firing pin is of the 'inertia' type, i.e. shorter than the breech block housing it, so the gun is entirely safe to carry with a loaded cartridge in the chamber and the hammer down. This arrangement makes loading equally safe, and permits that quick first shot, so long the prerogative of the revolver. Place the safety on 'safe', insert a loaded magazine, pull back the slide and let it go forward again. The gun is now loaded, hammer down and safety on. The safety can then be placed in the 'fire' position and the gun carried without danger. When needed, all that is necessary is for the trigger to be pulled, the double action lockwork cocking the hammer and firing the gun. The slide stop holds the slide open after the last shot has been fired and releases it when the thumb piece is depressed. Handling characteristics are good and practical sights are fitted, the foresight an $\frac{1}{8}''$ wide ramp, the rear sight adjustable for windage. Finish is excellent, the stocks being checkered walnut, and the pistol is offered in either S & W blue or nickel.

This is without doubt one of the best 'Combat' auto-pistols available today. The cartridge used is satisfactory and widely available and perhaps the only two points of adverse comment are cost and complexity.

Neither of these considerations are valid in our appreciation of the Smith and Wesson Model 52, the .38 Master. This special target version of the Model 39 is chambered for the .38 Special mid-range wadcutter cartridge, and the magazine will not function with cartridges longer than 1.19″, a limitation which must be borne in mind by those who handload their target ammunition. The lock mechanism of the original Model 52 could be adjusted for double action use by tightening the double action lockout screw, but the increase in initial trigger slack can be considered objectionable. As a result of recent internal changes, the current Model 52–1 is single action only. A new trigger linkage has been designed and the substitution of the sear spring permits adjustment of

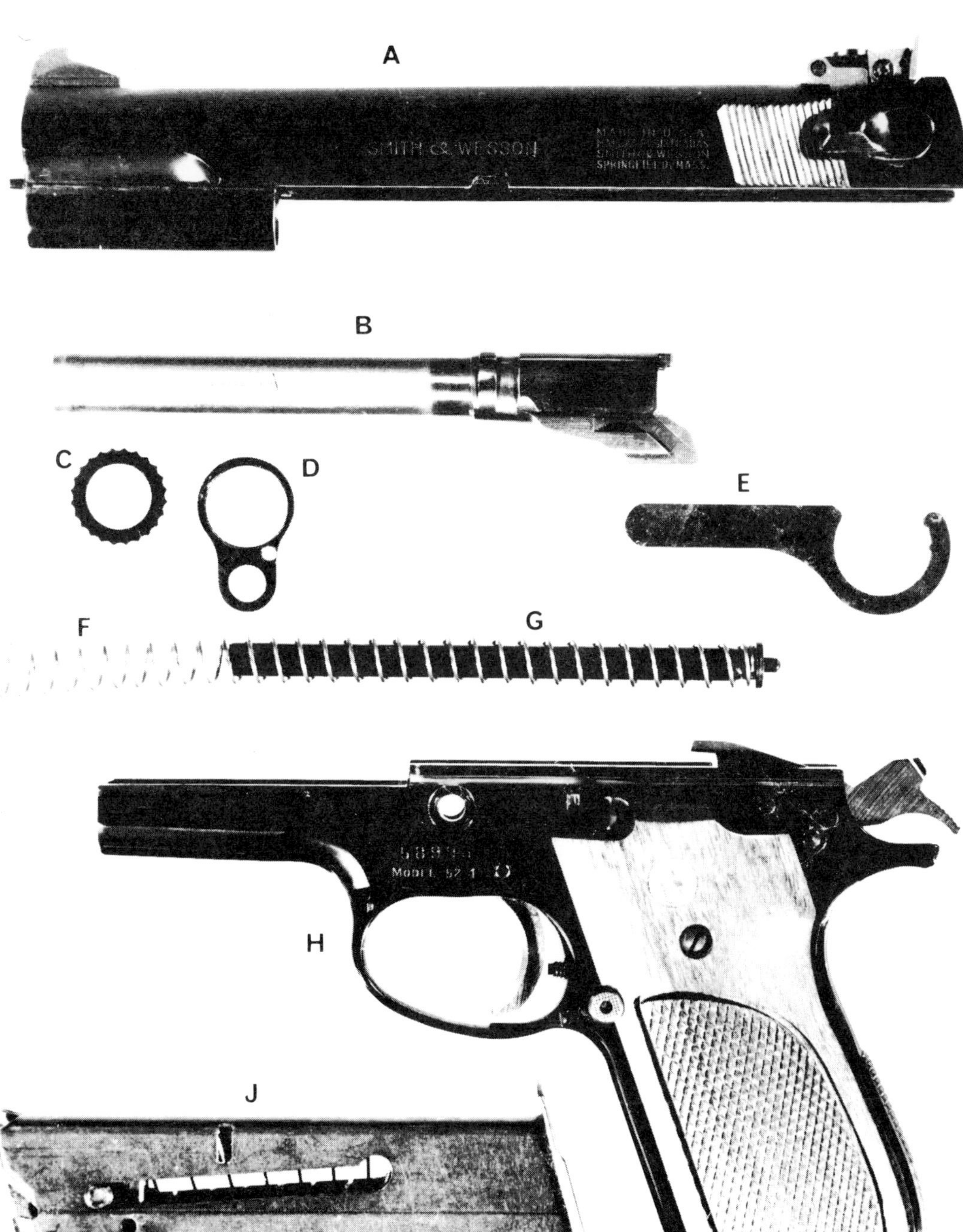

The Smith and Wesson Model No.52–1 dismantled.

A. Slide.
B. Barrel.
C. Barrel bushing.
D. Barrel bushing plate.
E. Barrel bushing wrench.
F. Recoil spring.
G. Recoil spring guide.
H. Frame.
J. Magazine.

the trigger pull. A visible alteration is the provision for the attachment of weights to the front of the frame. Magazine capacity is five rounds only and the pistol cannot be fired with the magazine removed. A feature of interest to the target shooter is that the pistol can be 'dry fired' with impunity since, as with the Model 39, engagement of the safety interposes a solid block between hammer and firing pin. A more sophisticated rear sight is fitted with provision for elevation and windage adjustment. Each click moves the point of impact approximately $\frac{3}{4}''$ in elevation and $\frac{1}{2}''$ in windage at fifty yards.

Partial dismantling is simple. First remove the magazine, checking the chamber to see that the pistol is unloaded. Place the manual safety in the fire or upper position and pull the slide to the rear, at the same time pressing the slide stop to the left. The recess on the lower left hand side of the slide is lined up with the forward end of the

Smith and Wesson Model No.41, the heavy barrel version. (Smith and Wesson)

Smith and Wesson Model No.41. (Smith and Wesson)

Smith and Wesson Model No.46. (Smith and Wesson)

slide stop which can then be pulled out of the frame to the left. The slide itself is withdrawn forward. Invert the slide and push forward the recoil spring guide to release it from the detent in the barrel lug. Withdraw the guide and recoil spring. Unscrew the barrel bushing from the slide with the wrench provided, remembering that the locking plunger must be depressed before the bushing can be turned. The barrel can then be removed from the slide. Reassembly is the reverse of this procedure.

Long before the centre-fire automatics were introduced, Smith and Wesson had been working on the design for a .22 calibre auto-pistol, the prototype for which was built in 1941. In 1957 they were able to introduce their Model 41 and the influence of the old Model 1913 can be seen in the general design features. The important feature of the Model 41 is that both front and rear sights are mounted on the same piece of metal, so eliminating the possibility of relative movement between them due to the action of the mechanism. Stripping of the pistol for normal cleaning purposes is again easy. Lock the slide back, remove the magazine and check that the pistol is empty. Pull down on the trigger guard and lift off the barrel assembly. Pull back the slide slightly, raise the rear and move the slide assembly forward for complete disengagement.

In 1959 a less expensive version of the Model 41 was introduced, the Model 46. The most noticeable change is the absence of the aluminium muzzle break and the use of nylon grip panels instead of walnut. The finish is S & W 'satin blue' instead of 'bright blue' and the barrel length is either 5″ or 7″ instead of the standard

SMITH & WESSON 22 AUTOMATIC PISTOL MODEL No. 41

PRICES EFFECTIVE JANUARY 1, 1960 SUBJECT TO CHANGE WITHOUT NOTICE.

PARTS LIST

Minimum Order 50c

No.	Name	Price
5102	Rear Sight Elevating Nut	$ .30
5103	Rear Sight Elevating Nut Plunger Spring	.10
5103	Rear Sight Windage Screw Plunger Spring	.10
5104	Rear Sight Elevating Nut Plunger	.10
5104	Rear Sight Windage Screw Plunger	.10
5105	Rear Sight Spring Clip	.10
5106	Rear Sight Elevating Stud	.30
5107	Rear Sight Windage Nut	.10
6041	Magazine Catch Plunger	.10
6045	Mainspring	.20
6069	Magazine Catch Spring	.10
6502	Barrel, 7⅜"	19.00
6504	Barrel Weight (Light) ⅜ oz.	.60
6505	Barrel Weight (Heavy) 1¾ oz.	.60
6508	Bolt	3.00
6509	Bolt Pin	.15
6510	Muzzle Brake	4.50
6511	Muzzle Brake Screw	.10
6512	Extractor	.50
6513	Extractor Plunger	.10
6514	Extractor Spring	.10
6515	Firing Pin	.65
6516	Firing Pin Spring	.10
6518	Frame	32.00
6520	Guard (accessory)	5.00
6521	Guard	4.50
6522	Guard Pin	.10
6522	Trigger Pin	.10
6523	Hammer	3.00
6526	Indicator Spring	.10
6527	Magazine Assembly	4.00
6528	Magazine Butt Plate	.30
6529	Magazine Catch	.35
6530	Magazine Catch Nut	.20
6531	False Muzzle	1.00
6535	Magazine Disconnector Spring	.10
6536	Magazine Follower	.50
6537	Mainspring Retainer Pin	.10
6538	Magazine Spring	.15
6539	Magazine Spring Plunger	.15
6540	Magazine Tube	3.00
6542	Mainspring Retainer	.60
6543	Sear Pin	.10
6545	Manual Safety	2.75
6547	Manual Safety Spring Plate	.15
6548	Pawl	.60
6549	Pawl Cam	$ .50
6550	Pawl Cam Plunger	.15
6551	Pawl Cam Spring	.10
6552	Pawl Pin	.10
6553	Rear Sight	4.50
6554	Rear Sight Assembly	7.00
6555	Rear Sight Elevating Spring	.10
6556	Rear Sight Pivot Clip	.10
6557	Rear Sight Pivot Pin	.10
6558	Rear Sight Slide	1.00
6561	Rear Sight Windage Screw	.50
6563	Recoil Spring	.15
6564	Recoil Spring Guide	.15
6565	Sear	1.50
6566	Sear Spring	.10
6568	Slide	12.00
6570	Slide Stop (& Ejector) Assembly	2.00
6572	Slide Stop Spring	.10
6574	Stirrup	.25
6575	Stirrup Pin	.10
6576	Stock—Left w/Escutcheon	5.50
6577	Stock—Right w/Escutcheon Nut	5.50
6579	Stock Screw	.30
6580	Trigger	3.00
6581	Trigger Stop Screw	.15
6586	Manual Safety Spring Plate Screw	.10
6589	Magazine Pin	.30
6591	Pawl & Trigger Spring	.10
6593	Trigger Bar Spring	.15
6595	Indicator	.30
6597	Trigger Bar	.50
6598	Magazine Disconnector	.75
6602	Trigger Pull Adjusting Lever	.20
6604	Counterweight Upper Section (Aluminum) 3 oz.	8.00
6605	Counterweight Upper Section (Steel) 7¼ oz.	8.00
6606	Counterweight Middle Section 4¼ oz.	4.00
6607	Counterweight Lower Section 4 oz.	3.00
6608	Counterweight Nut	.10
6609	Counterweight Screw	.10
6610	Counterweight Assembly With Steel Upper Section (6605)	15.00
6612	Counterweight Assembly With Aluminum Upper Section (6604)	15.00
6632	Barrel, 5"	19.00

SPECIFICATIONS

Caliber 22 Long Rifle.

Magazine Capacity 10 Rounds.

Barrel Length 7⅜", 5"

Length Overall 12" With muzzle brake attached.

Sight Radius 9$\frac{5}{16}$".

Weight 43½ oz. with muzzle brake attached, and an empty magazine. This includes also a ⅜ oz. aluminum weight in the weight recess under the barrel.

Sights Front sight—Patridge with an appropriate undercut. Rear sight—S&W Micrometer Click sight with sight slide tipped to the rear at approximately the same angle that the front sight is undercut.

Stocks Checkered walnut with modified thumb rest, equally adaptable to right- or left-handed shooters.

Finish S&W blue with sandblasting, matting and serrations around sighting areas to break up light reflection.

Trigger ⅜" width, with S&W grooving and an adjustable trigger stop.

Muzzle Brake Detachable.

NOTE: The 5-inch barrel provides exactly the same sighting radius as the Masterpiece Target Revolver. There are no provisions for muzzle brake, barrel weights or Olympic counterweights. This barrel is completely interchangeable with our 7⅜-inch barrel without fitting or adjustment.

SMITH & WESSON

22 AUTOMATIC Model No. 41

PARTS LIST • INSTRUCTIONS FOR USE • MAINTENANCE SPECIFICATIONS • GUARANTEE

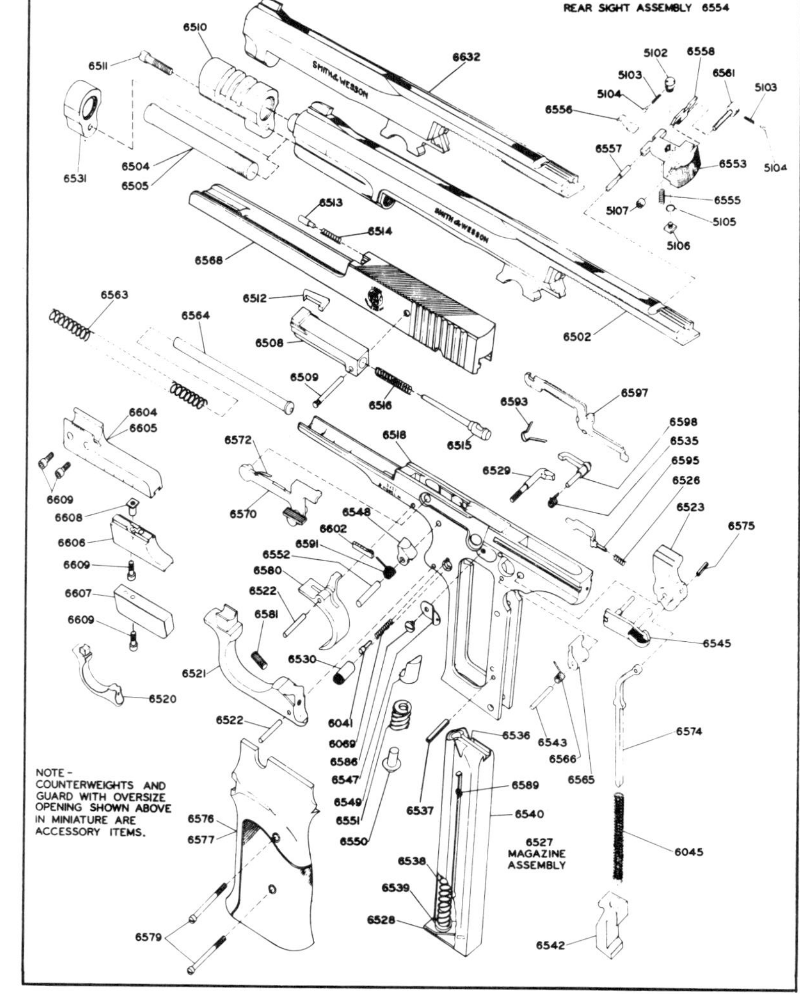

LOADING AND FIRING

1. Pull slide to rear until it locks open.

2. Press magazine catch nut on left side of frame back of trigger guard and drop magazine into the hand.

3. Holding the magazine in the hand, depress the follower with the buttons provided for the purpose and drop in or load the desired number of cartridges. These must be loaded with the primer to the rear, or flat edge of the magazine, and the bullet to the front or rounded edge of the magazine. It is important that all cartridges lie even and parallel when the follower is released. Competitive shooting indicates the loading of 5 cartridges. Full magazine capacity is 10 cartridges.

4. Replace the magazine in the butt of the gun, pressing upwards until it locks securely in place.

5. Holding the gun pointed in a safe direction, release the slide by pulling slightly to the rear and letting go. It will travel forward picking up the top cartridge in the magazine and loading it in the chamber. Keep finger off trigger during this operation.

6. The gun may now be fired by simply pressing the trigger for each shot desired. Its function is normal for a self loading semi-automatic pistol and the slide will lock and remain open after the last shot has been fired. The magazine may then be withdrawn and reloaded.

7. Should you desire to make the gun safe while loaded, press the manual safety on the left side of frame to its upper position with the hook engaging its notch in the serrations of the slide. This locks the slide, blocks the sear, and disconnects the trigger bar. This can only be done when the gun is cocked.

8. To unload a loaded pistol, first apply the manual safety as outlined in the preceding paragraph (#7). Remove magazine as outlined in #2. Then disengage the manual safety and pull the slide all of the way to the rear to eject the live round of ammunition from the chamber.

WARNING! Do not touch the trigger at any time while unloading the gun, and keep the muzzle pointed in a safe direction until the weapon is cleared.

FIELD STRIPPING

1. *Lock slide back.*

2. *Remove magazine.*

3. *Pull trigger guard down. Hold gun in position shown, so that barrel assembly will not fall off when released.*

4. *Lift off barrel assembly.*

5. *Pull slide back and raise slightly.*

6. *Move slide assembly forward to complete disengagement.*

This constitutes adequate field stripping for normal cleaning purposes. Reverse above procedure to reassemble.

NOTE: After reassembling slide assembly to frame, lock slide to its rearward or open position by holding back while you press upwards on the slide stop thumbpiece. This will facilitate the next step, which is the reinstallation of the barrel assembly.

SIGHT ADJUSTMENT

1. Front sight is fixed. All adjustments must be made at the rear sight.

2. Move the rear sight in the direction in which you wish the group on the target to move. (If group must be higher, elevate the rear sight. If group must go to the right, move the rear sight to the right, etc.)

3. To elevate rear sight turn top (elevating) screw to the left, or counter-clockwise. To depress rear sight turn top (elevating) screw to the right, or clockwise.

4. To move rear sight to right, turn side (windage) screw to the right, or clockwise. To move rear sight to left, turn side (windage) screw to the left, or counter-clockwise.

5. Each click of the rear sight moves the point of impact on the target approximately 3/8" elevation and 1/4" windage at 50 yards and half of that amount at 25 yards.

SERVICE

Should your Smith & Wesson pistol require adjustment, repair or refinishing, we strongly recommend that the weapon be returned to the factory. There is no other way to insure that the work will be done by a competent staff of trained technicians.

Charges are very reasonable, being based on the cost of parts replaced plus a labor charge for the time spent on the work. A labor charge for one hour is usually sufficient to cover all but very extensive overhaul jobs.

Pistols returned to the factory should be MARKED FOR THE ATTENTION OF THE SERVICE DEPARTMENT. A letter of instructions should be enclosed with the gun, and shipment by individuals must be made by Prepaid Railway Express. Adherence to these suggestions will prevent loss of time in handling at the factory.

When your pistol arrives in our Service Department, it will be very carefully inspected, together with your letter of instructions. Next, a quotation covering total cost of work to be performed will be sent to you. No actual work will be commenced before receiving your approval of our quotation unless you specifically authorize us to do so.

CLEANING AND OILING

Pistols should be field stripped, cleaned, and oiled at reasonably frequent intervals to insure proper functioning.

1. Field strip per instructions elsewhere in this booklet.

2. Clean all areas that have been in contact with the by-products of explosion, using for this purpose a good commercial solvent and appropriate brushes or swabs.

3. After cleaning and drying all exposed areas, oil lightly using an acid-free gun or watch oil designated for this purpose. At the same time oil lightly all pivot points and moving contact areas. The bore, chamber, and outside of the gun may be protected by coating lightly with a rust-inhibiting oil or grease.

4. If the gun is to be stored for a considerable length of time repeat this cleaning and oiling process several days later and before storage, as a certain amount of residue will work out of the metal, particularly the bore of the barrel, and this should all be removed and the gun re-oiled before it is finally put away.

5. Do not store guns for any length of time in a leather holster or case or in any type of container that will attract and hold moisture.

WARNING!

Before proceeding to use this weapon, a word of caution is in order. This pistol is as safe to handle and use as we can make it, but there is no foolproof firearm. Be sure that the muzzle is pointing in a safe direction at all times, whether the gun is loaded or not. Make safe gun handling a habit.

Beware of obstacles in the barrel. If, when firing, a weak or peculiar report is heard, cease firing and inspect the barrel for an obstruction. If the barrel contains a stuck bullet, cleaning patch, mud, snow, twig, or even heavy grease, a bulged barrel will probably result upon firing.

Be careful how you treat the magazine. In loading the magazine into the gun simply press it into place — do not drive in forcibly, as this practice may in time cause distortion of magazine lips and resultant malfunctions. And don't drop it, particularly on a hard surface like concrete or rock — the results will be the same.

Use extra caution in clearing jams in any automatic pistol. No fixed procedure can be quoted other than the fact that you should proceed in a commonsense and safe manner.

1. When the jam occurs, keep the gun pointed in a safe direction and wait for a few seconds to be sure you don't get a hang-fire with the breech open.

2. Pull slide back and lock it back by pressing the slide stop thumbpiece upwards.

3. Press magazine catch nut and release magazine, withdrawing it completely from the gun.

4. Remove jammed cartridge *with extreme care*, remembering that pinching the rim of the case could cause the priming compound to detonate and thus explode the powder charge in the cartridge being worked on.

MAKE SAFE GUN HANDLING A HABIT.

STATEMENT OF LIABILITY

This gun is classified as a FIREARM or DANGEROUS WEAPON and is surrendered by us with the express understanding that we assume no liability for its re-sale or safe handling under local laws and regulations. Smith & Wesson assumes no responsibility for physical injury or property damage resulting from either intentional or accidental discharge, or for the function of any gun subjected to influences beyond their control, and will honor no claims which may result from careless handling, unauthorized adjustments, defective or improper ammunition, corrosion or neglect.

For your protection, examine your gun carefully at the time of purchase, then fill out and mail to us promptly the registration card bearing your gun's serial number which accompanies all new guns.

WARRANTY

The company will replace or adjust to its commercial standard any gun or part thereof returned prepaid to the factory and found by us to be defective in either material or workmanship. Such service will be made free of charge for one year from date of registered purchase. This warranty and statement of liability supersedes all previous warranties and commitments.

April 15, 1955

SMITH & WESSON, INC.

SPRINGFIELD, MASS., U.S.A.

$7\frac{3}{8}''$ of the original Model 41. The Model 46 also lacks the grooving on top of the barrel and on the front strap. A detachable 2 oz. counterweight for fitting under the barrel is furnished as an extra.

In 1961 the Model 41 was offered in .22 short rim-fire for Olympic and International rapid-fire shooting, the differences being the reduction of magazine capacity from ten to five rounds and the use of a light alloy slide. The barrel is chambered for the .22 short and the recoil spring is matched to function with the short cartridge. Conversion kits are also available to change the Model 41 from .22 long to .22 short and vice versa. Each kit comprises five items: barrel, slide, magazine, recoil spring and slide stop-ejector assembly. Kits are available for both the Model 41 and the Model 46.

To complete the range, the Model 41 was offered, in 1963, in a heavy barrel version. Here, the barrel is $5\frac{1}{2}''$, and the pistol weighs $6\frac{1}{2}$ oz. more than the $5''$ barrel standard Model 41. The only external difference is in the contour of the slide at the muzzle, where the recess that all the other models have is missing.

Smith and Wesson can rightly trace their ancestry back to the beginnings of the metallic cartridge era. The High Standard Manufacturing Corporation of New Haven started out, in 1926, as tool makers making gun barrel drills. In 1932 they acquired the Hartford Arms and Equipment Co. of Hartford who had already produced a single shot pistol, a repeating pistol and an automatic pistol. The first High Standard automatic pistol naturally bore a close resemblance to the Hartford, but afterwards High Standard produced a bewildering range of simple blow-back .22 auto-pistols developed from the original Model A, Model B and the .22 short Model C. External hammer versions were also introduced, the model designation being prefixed by the letter 'H'. Variations in barrel length, barrel weight, stock shape and whether or not a safety catch was fitted, led to a number of variant pre-war model designations. During World War Two, High Standard manufactured a .22 auto-pistol for military training which was known as the H-D Military Model. Manufacture of this pistol ceased in 1951.

In 1947 a new series was introduced, the 'G' Series, the first of which was a straight blow-back pistol in .380 ACP calibre. Since it was too large for a pocket model, too expensive for casual use and lacked the accuracy necessary for a target

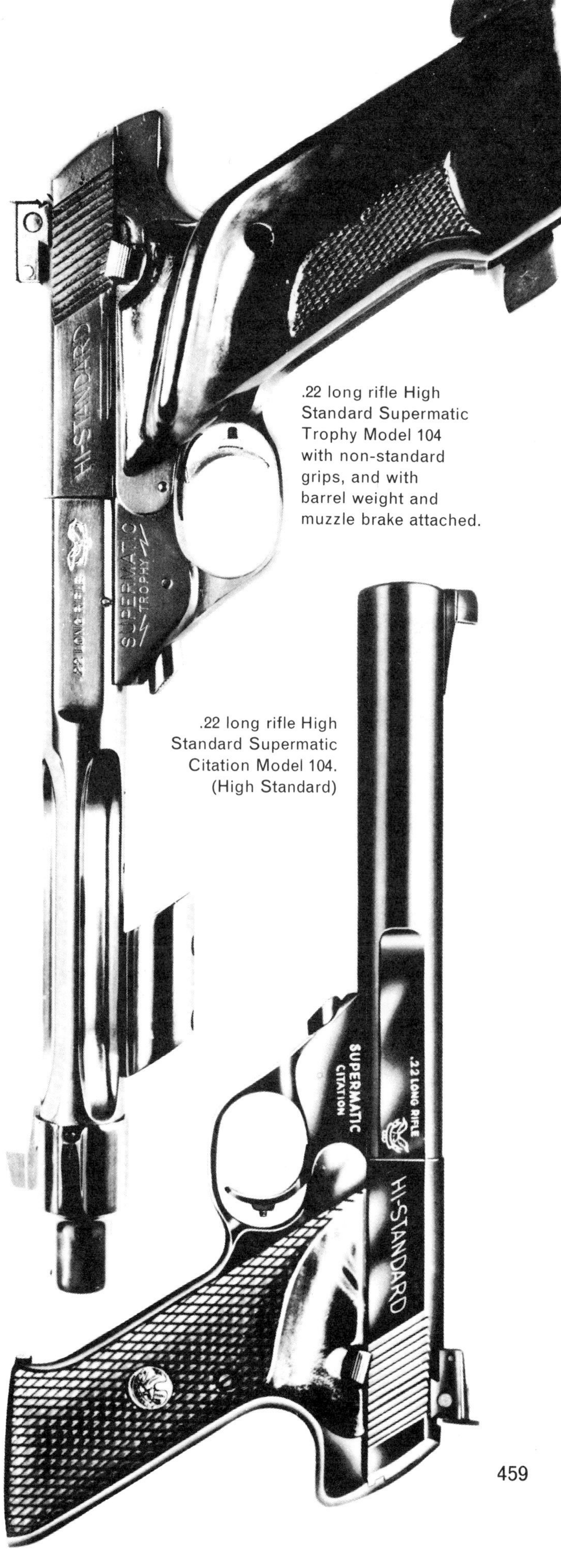

.22 long rifle High Standard Supermatic Trophy Model 104 with non-standard grips, and with barrel weight and muzzle brake attached.

.22 long rifle High Standard Supermatic Citation Model 104. (High Standard)

pistol, it never became popular. Manufacture was discontinued in 1950. In .22 calibre, however, with interchangeable barrels and target sights, the 'G' Series did attain some degree of popularity.

The next series, the Olympic Models, retained the interchangeable barrel feature, but progressive movements were introduced to meet specific requirements. The 1951 Olympic featured a light alloy slide and was chambered for the .22 short cartridge.

In 1958 the entire range was redesigned and the wide grooved trigger, new lockwork, automatic slide stop and improvements in the method of attaching the barrel all testified to the increasing demands made by target shooters on the manufacturers. Detachable barrel weights were offered, together with a barrel stabiliser, and the barrel lengths available ranged from 10″ to $4\frac{1}{2}$″.

This new range was known as the Supermatic series and three grades were available, the Tropy, Citation and Tournament. Finish on all models was first class, and the satisfaction that a great number of target men have found in these pistols has been to a large extent due to the excellent factory fitted sights.

The Supermatic 104 series is retained in the current range, but, in 1965, an additional series was added, the 106 or Military series. The controversial change in the bore to grip angle is noticeable immediately. Where the 102, 103 and 104 series had all retained the 123° angle, the Military 106 series has a grip angle of 107°, substantially the same as the .45 Colt Model 1911. The Military series is also graded into Trophy, Citation and Tournament models and, with the first two, but not the Tournament, the rear sight is permanently fitted to the frame. This sight has been slightly modified by increasing the depth of the sight notch, and the magazine catch has also been redesigned. The present range comprises:

Standard Models
Supermatic Trophy Model 104. With either $5\frac{1}{2}$″ bull barrel or $7\frac{1}{4}$″ fluted barrel.
Supermatic Citation Model 104. With either $5\frac{1}{2}$″ bull barrel or $6\frac{3}{4}$″ tapered barrel and stabiliser.
Olympic (ISU) Model 104. With either $6\frac{3}{4}$″ round tapered barrel or $5\frac{1}{2}$″ bull barrel. .22 short calibre.

Military Models
Supermatic Trophy Military Model 106. With $5\frac{1}{2}$″ heavy barrel or $7\frac{1}{4}$″ fluted barrel.
Supermatic Citation Military Model 106. Barrels as above.

.22 short High Standard Olympic (ISU) Model 104 with barrel weights and integral muzzle brake or stabiliser. (High Standard)

.22 long rifle High Standard Supermatic Trophy Military Model 106. (High Standard)

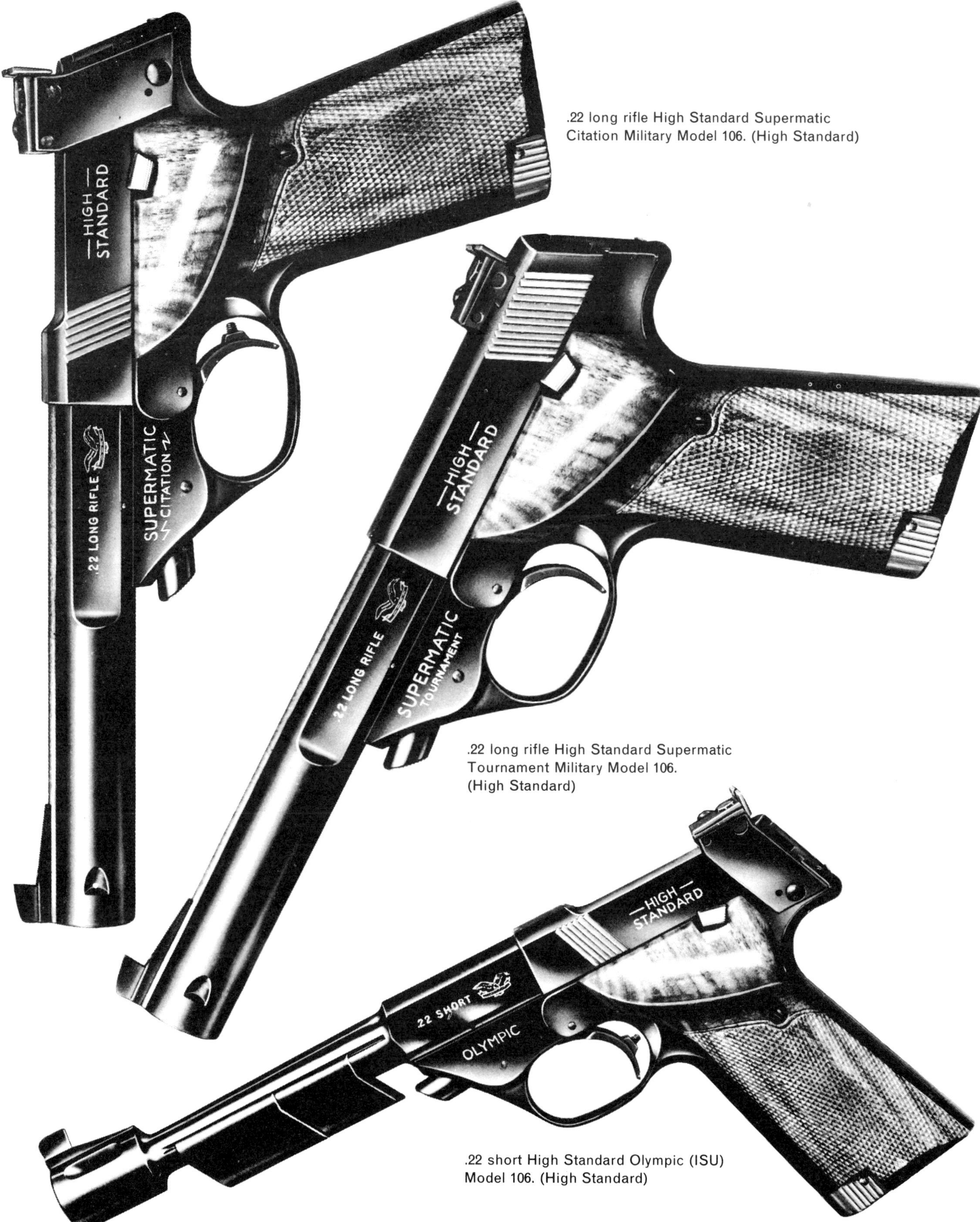

.22 long rifle High Standard Supermatic Citation Military Model 106. (High Standard)

.22 long rifle High Standard Supermatic Tournament Military Model 106. (High Standard)

.22 short High Standard Olympic (ISU) Model 106. (High Standard)

Supermatic Tournament Military Model 106. With $5\frac{1}{2}''$ bull barrel or $6\frac{3}{4}''$ tapered barrel.
Olympic (ISU) Military Model 106. With $5\frac{1}{2}''$ or $6\frac{3}{4}''$ barrel.

It is likely that the range of standard target models will decrease and that the Military Model will, in effect, be the 'standard' model of the future. High Standard's reasoning behind the change is entirely valid: the new 'square look' will be welcomed in America because it will make the transition from 'full bore' target pistol to .22 easier, although those who have become accustomed to the 'slant grip' of the present standard models may find the 'square look', particularly if they shoot .22 only, a real or imagined disadvantage.

At present, High Standard offer an extremely wide selection, with the added facility that the 'one pistol' man can purchase additional $5\frac{1}{2}''$, $6\frac{3}{4}''$ or $7\frac{3}{4}''$ barrels with integral stabilisers or with the built-in facility to fit one if desired, and variable barrel weights.

Two cheaper models, the Sport King and the Dura-matic complete the range. In 1960 High Standard announced their .22 single shot 'Free Pistol' with an electric trigger let-off. The trigger makes an electrical contact with the battery system, so energising an electro-magnet which pulls down the rear of the sear connector. This allows a rotary sear to revolve, releasing the striker. Whether or not this pistol will be produced commercially is still a matter for conjecture. High Standard pistols are deservedly popular; they offer extremely good value for money and a range of variant models wide enough to suit all pockets and personal requirements.

A rather rare American pistol of the 1920's was the Fiala made by the Blakslee Forging Co. of New Haven for the Fiala Arms and Equipment Co. Introduced in 1920, it went out of production in 1923. Well made and well finished, it was offered as a pocket pistol, as a target pistol, or, with a $20\frac{1}{2}''$ barrel and a shoulder stock fitted, as a carbine. Chambered for the .22 long rifle cartridge, an unusual feature was that, although it appeared to be an automatic pistol and had a magazine holding ten cartridges, it was, in fact, a single shot magazine pistol where the slide had to be pushed forward by hand to chamber a cartridge. After firing, the slide had again to be withdrawn to the rear by hand to extract the fired case. In spite of the claims made by the Fiala Company as to the advantages of this system as well

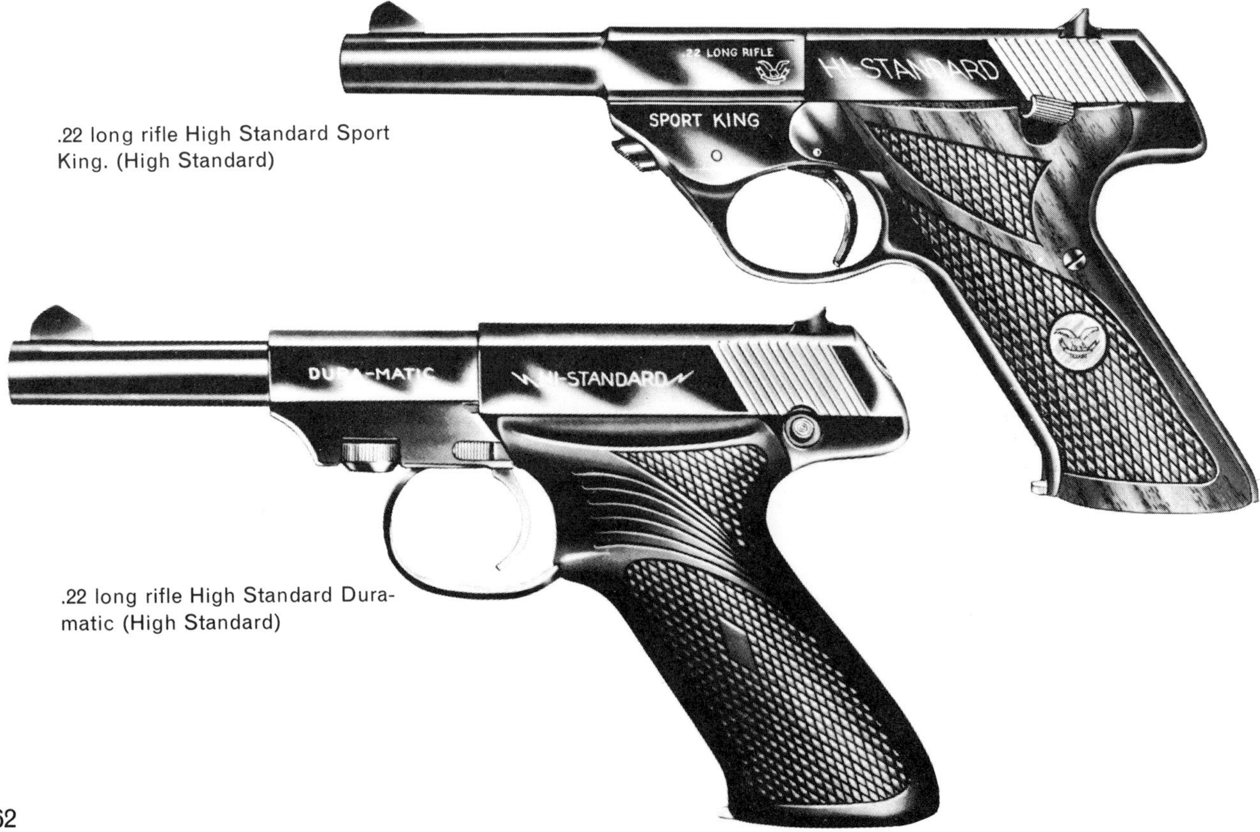

.22 long rifle High Standard Sport King. (High Standard)

.22 long rifle High Standard Duramatic (High Standard)

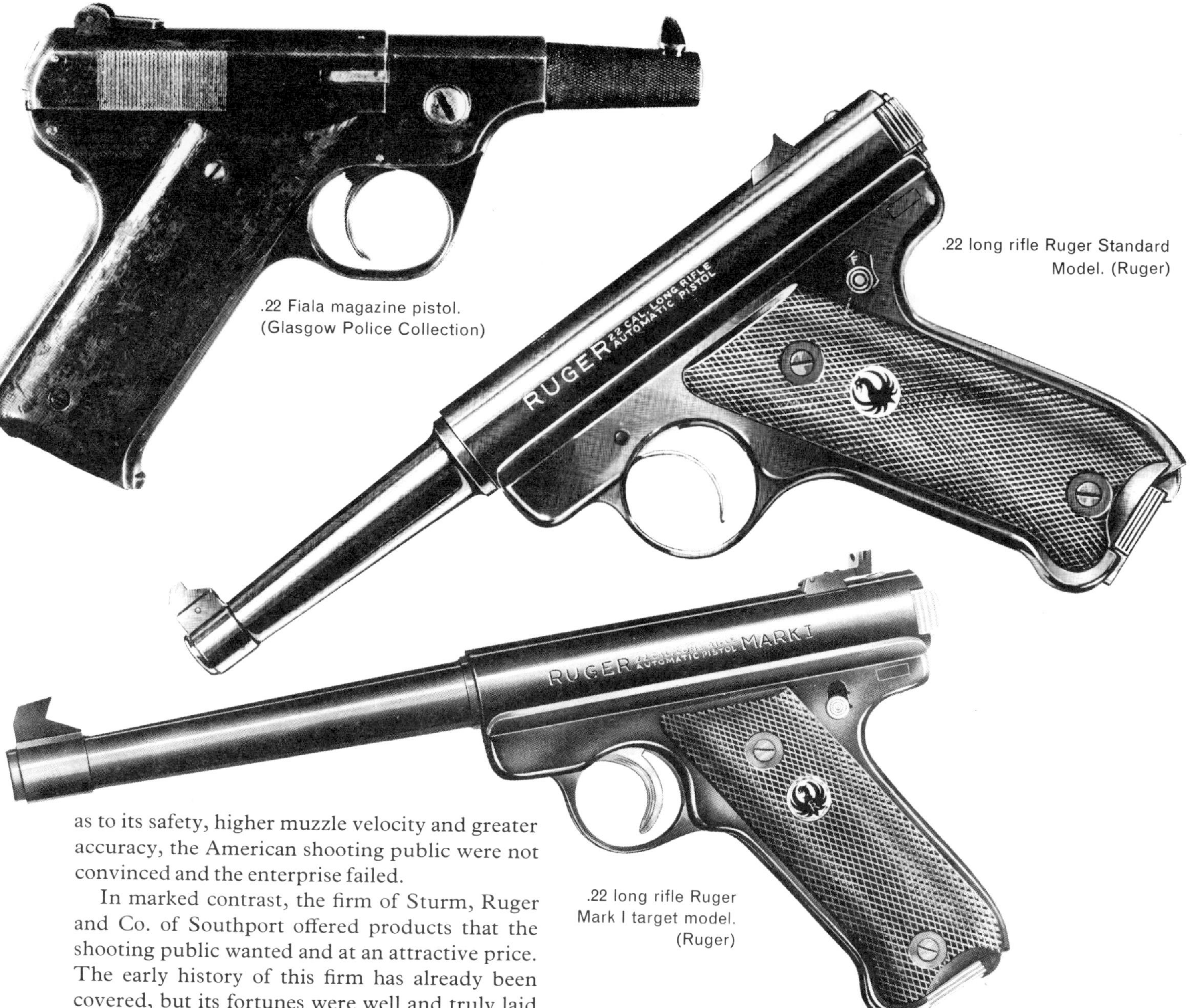

.22 Fiala magazine pistol. (Glasgow Police Collection)

.22 long rifle Ruger Standard Model. (Ruger)

.22 long rifle Ruger Mark I target model. (Ruger)

as to its safety, higher muzzle velocity and greater accuracy, the American shooting public were not convinced and the enterprise failed.

In marked contrast, the firm of Sturm, Ruger and Co. of Southport offered products that the shooting public wanted and at an attractive price. The early history of this firm has already been covered, but its fortunes were well and truly laid with the introduction, in 1949, of a .22 auto-pistol. In 1950 the success of the standard model prompted the introduction of the Mark I target pistol with adjustable sights and a heavier $6\frac{7}{8}''$ barrel.

The Ruger was designed with modern mass production techniques in mind. Stampings are employed for the frame, and the left and right hand frame shells are welded together. The barrel is screwed into the front of a simple tubular receiver forming a one piece base for the sights and assuring permanent alignment. The bolt is cylindrical in shape and has two milled projections at the rear for ease of cocking and loading.

Due to the use of modern techniques of fabrication, the cost of the Ruger is comparatively low. This factor, coupled with simple design and excellent performance, has ensured success. Soon after the introduction of the Mark I, the basic frame and receiver were used to build 'custom' target pistols with special target barrels and trigger assemblies; in 1954 a stabiliser or muzzle brake was made available, the fitting of which is easily carried out without tools. Ruger also introduced the Mark I woth a $5\frac{1}{2}''$ bull barrel.

Dismantling procedure for the Ruger auto-pistol is simple. After removing the magazine, the bolt is drawn fully to the rear to clear the chamber and is then allowed to return forward again. The trigger is pressed to uncock the hammer, and the housing latch on the back strap is prised open so that the main housing can be swung fully outward. The housing is pulled down to disengage the bolt stop pin, and the bolt can then be withdrawn to the rear. To remove the barrel assembly from the frame, grasp the barrel firmly and pull forward. On reassembly, be

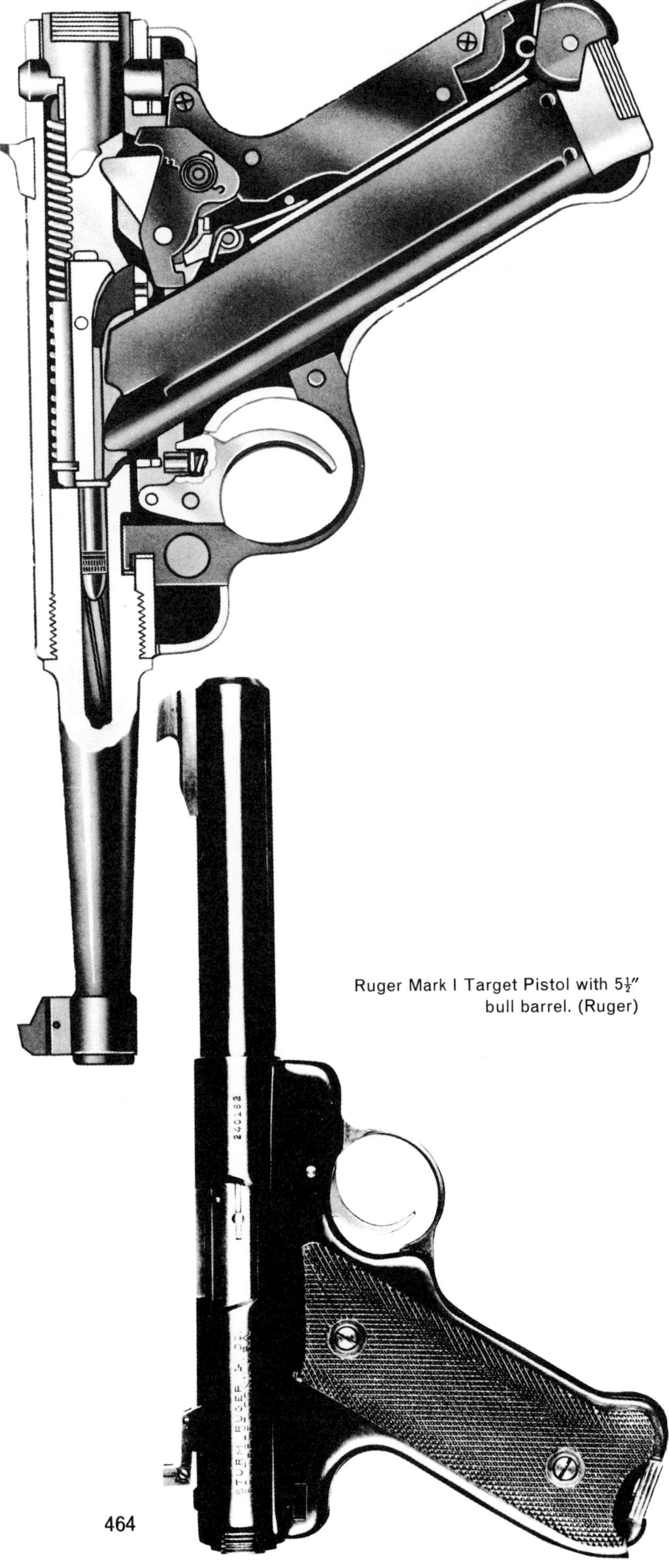

Sectional view of the Ruger Standard Model. (Ruger)

Ruger Mark I Target Pistol with $5\frac{1}{2}''$ bull barrel. (Ruger)

sure that the hammer is fully forward and that the hammer strut is aligned with the mainspring plunger.

The healthy position of handgun manufacturers in America is in sharp contrast to the gloomy picture in Britain.

Following the demise of the ill-fated Mars or Gabbett-Fairfax, it was left to Webley and Scott of Birmingham to introduce the only successful British made auto-pistols. The chronology of the various models is not exact and identification is not easy due to the absence of model designations on many of the pistols coupled with the absence of patent dates. To differentiate between types here, patent dates have been employed in general accordance with the system adopted by W. C. Dowell. There are, however, two main groups of Webley automatic pistols: firstly, the higher powered locked breech actions such as the .455 calibre series and the .38 (.38 Colt ACP) high velocity pistol, and secondly, the blow-back unlocked breech weapons in .25, .32, .380 and 9mm calibres.

The first of the locked breech models was the experimental Model of 1903 designed by J. W. Whiting, but only a few of these were made. The general design is apparent from the drawings that accompanied Webley's Patent No. 19,032 of 1903. Designed to fire the .455 rimmed service cartridge, the pistol employed a locked breech based on two external arms attached to the breech which engaged projections on the barrel.

In 1904 Whiting introduced a new design based on British Patents Nos. 3820, 17,856 and 25,028, all taken out in that year. The 1904 Model brought in the 'V' recoil spring (the forerunner of the standard Webley design) instead of the coil spring used on the 1903 Model, and was again of locked breech design. It was, however, very heavy, complicated in design and expensive to manufacture. Further attempts to simplify the design resulted in the 1906 Model, and this was the basis for the 'Pistol, self loading, .455 Mark I' approved in 1913 and adopted by the Royal Navy and Royal Marines.

A slightly different version, the Mark I, No. 2,

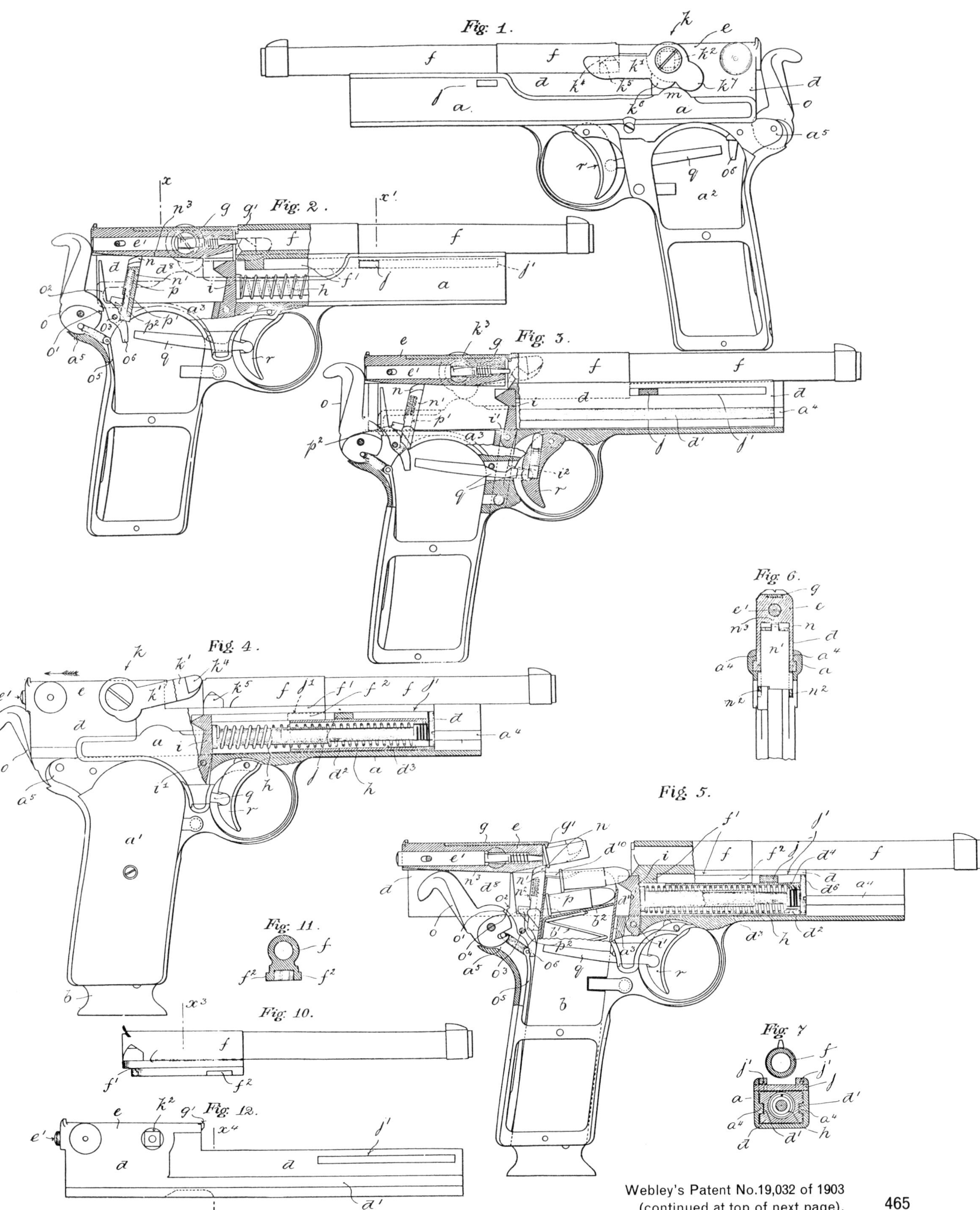

Webley's Patent No.19,032 of 1903
(continued at top of next page).

Webley's Patent No.19,032 of 1903 (continued).

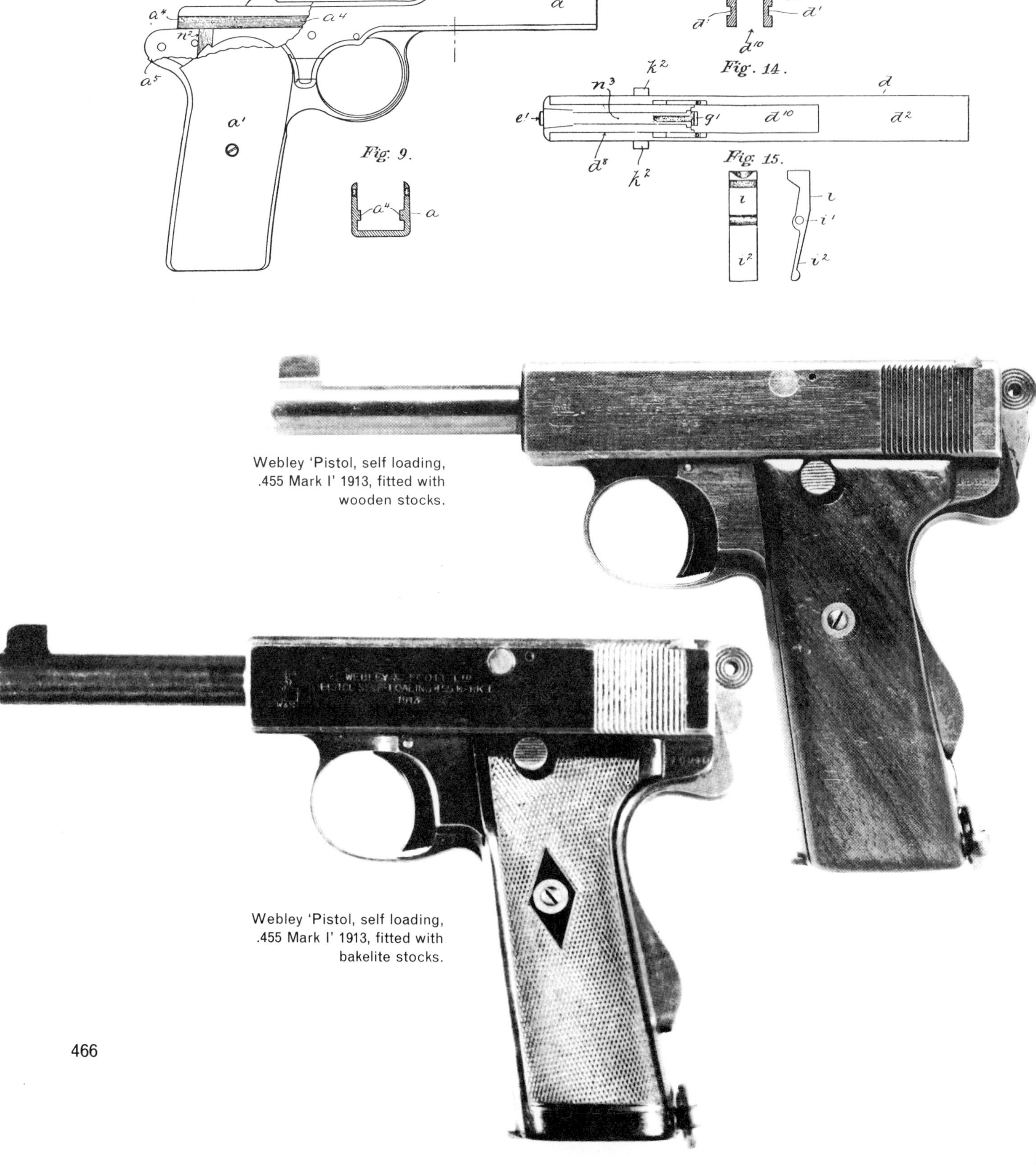

Webley 'Pistol, self loading, .455 Mark I' 1913, fitted with wooden stocks.

Webley 'Pistol, self loading, .455 Mark I' 1913, fitted with bakelite stocks.

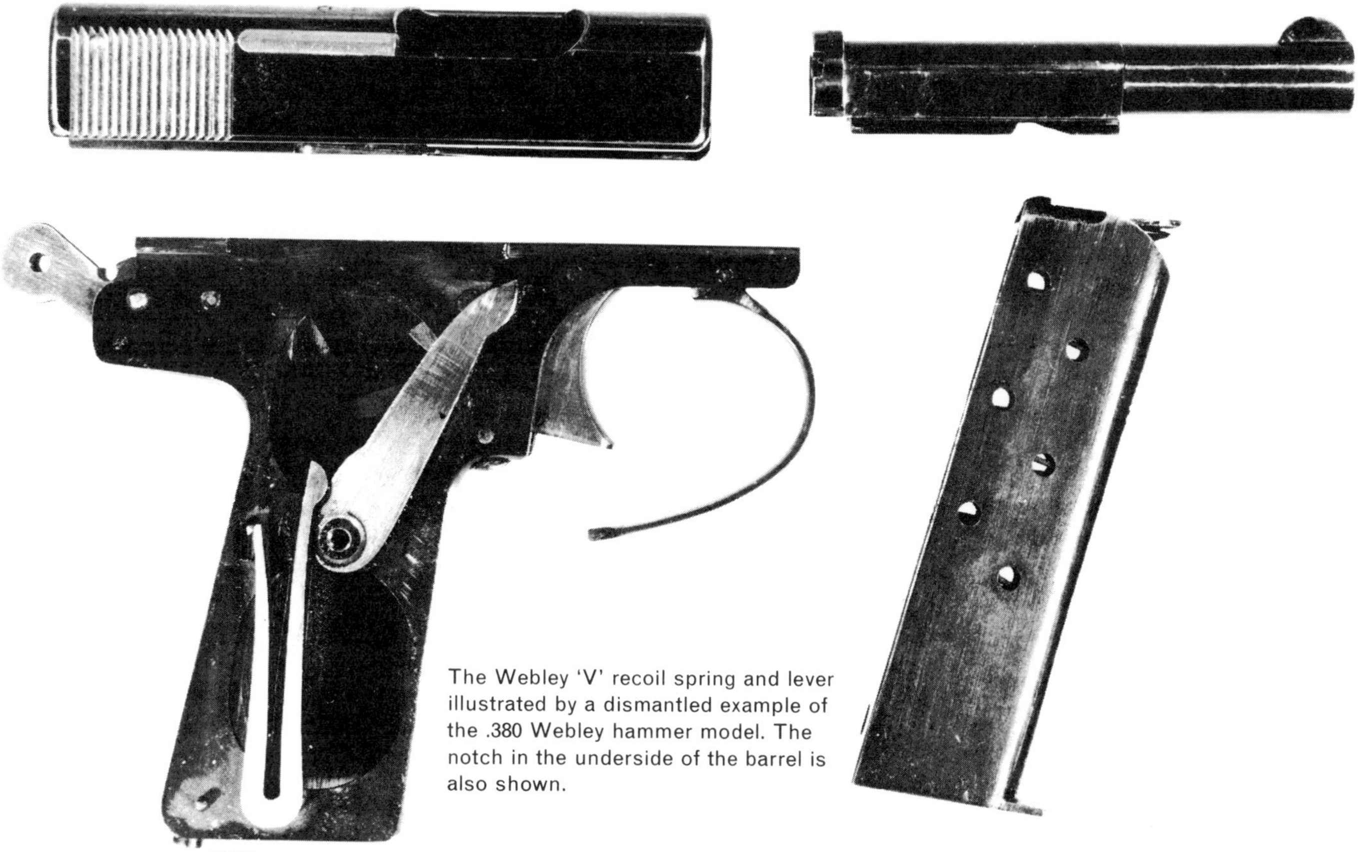

The Webley 'V' recoil spring and lever illustrated by a dismantled example of the .380 Webley hammer model. The notch in the underside of the barrel is also shown.

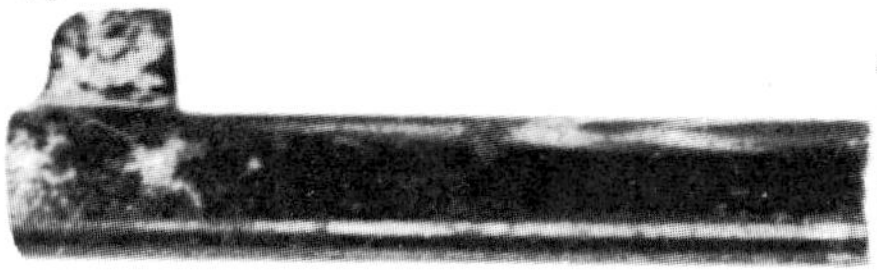

.38 Webley High Velocity 'hammerless' Model 1910. (Glasgow Police Collection)

was issued in 1915 to the Royal Flying Corps and was fitted with a shoulder stock and adjustable rear sight. The .455 military models had a grip safety device and a unique magazine feature which permitted single shot firing, the contents of the magazine being held in reserve. Of excellent workmanship, the .455 Webley and Scott auto-pistol cannot, however, be considered an entirely satisfactory military weapon since it was still too complicated and too expensive to produce.

A 'hammerless' automatic pistol chambered for the .38 ACP cartridge was introduced in 1910, the design similar to the locked breech Model 1913 or Mark I type. Magazine capacity was eight rounds and wooden or bakelite grips were furnished. A variant of the .38 high velocity hammerless model appeared in 1913 with a redesigned safety catch, but specimens of this are rather scarce.

The blow-back Webley automatic pistols can be sub-divided into the 'hammerless' and the 'external hammer' models.

.32/7.65mm Webley Police Model 1906.

.380 Webley external hammer model.

The external hammer models were based on Whiting's patent of 1905 and introduced the use of the trigger guard for locking the fixed barrel in position on the forward part of the frame. As can be seen from the illustration, the spring steel guard is hinged and can be pulled forward from its position where the lower part enters the frame. In the forward position, the specially shaped hinged end lies flush with the frame and disengages from the notch in the barrel, so permitting the barrel and slide to be taken off the frame by sliding both forward.

The 1905 Models were made in .32 (7.65mm) and .380 (9mm short automatic) calibres, the early versions having a safety catch on the left hand side of the hammer, the later (or so-called 1906 Models) having the safety on the left hand side of the frame above the grip. The .32 version was adopted in 1911 by the City of London and Metropolitan Police and, as the .32 Metropolitan Police Model, it remained in the catalogue until discontinued in 1940. The Police Model had a backsight at the rear of the slide, the civilian models having a groove and 'V' machined in the top of the slide instead.

The smaller calibre pistols were usually marked '7.65mm & .32 Automatic Pistol', the larger calibre bearing the legend '.380 Automatic Pistol'. The .32 calibre pistol had a magazine capacity of eight rounds, weighed 18 ozs. and had an overall length of 6¼″.

The 1909 external hammer blow-back 9mm pistol employed the same method of barrel attachment as the 1905 .32 and .380 calibre models, but was chambered for the slightly more powerful 9mm Browning long cartridge.

9mm Webley external hammer Model 1909.

Unlike the .380 Automatic or 9mm Browning short, the 9mm Browning long does not appear to have had an 'English' synonym; it was first introduced in 1903 and was adopted by Sweden in 1907. The 1909 9mm Webley was adopted by the South African Police in 1920, and production of a civilian version continued until about 1930. The civilian model was fitted with hard rubber grips, and later versions had the safety

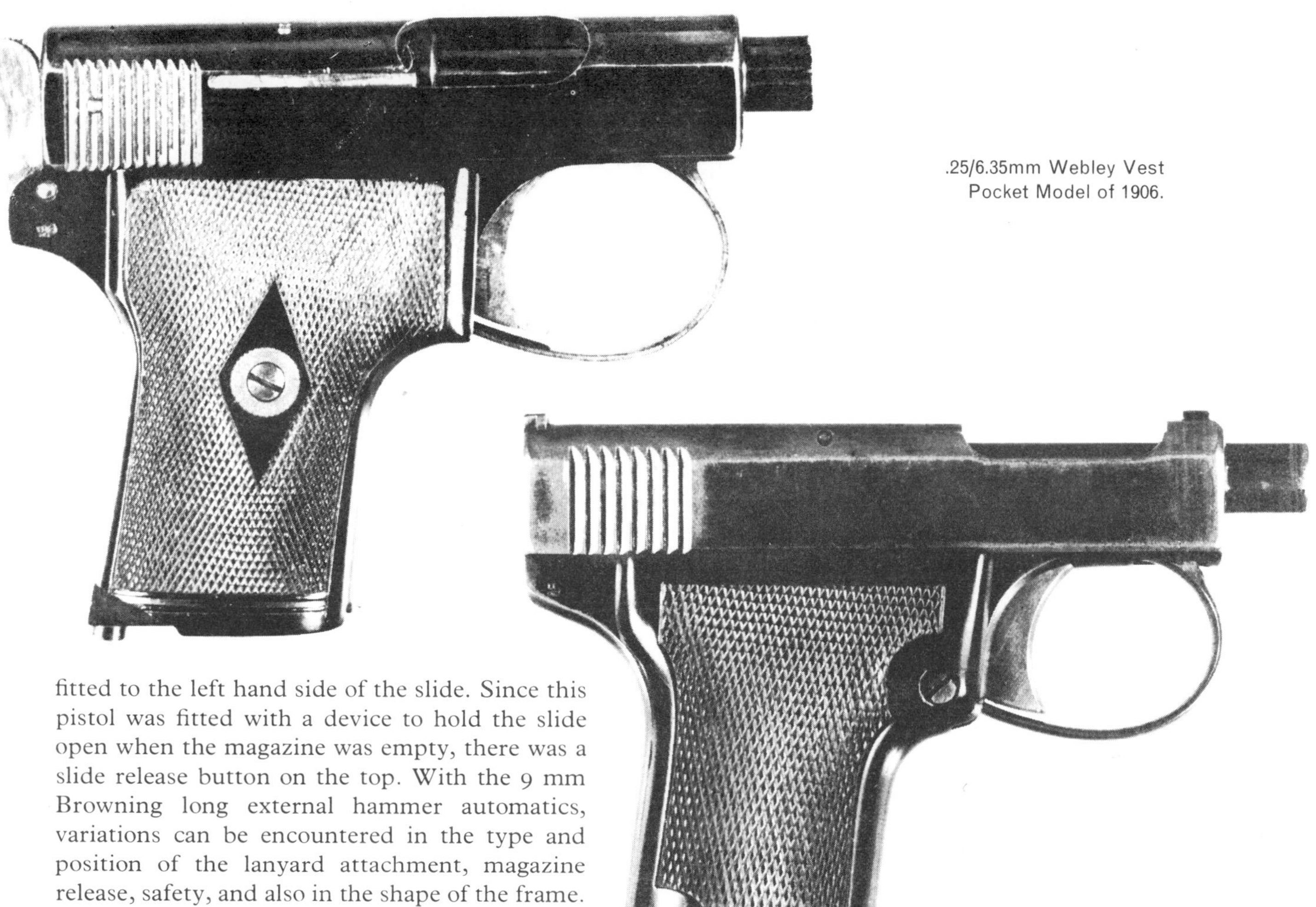

.25/6.35mm Webley Vest Pocket Model of 1906.

.25/6.35mm Webley 'hammerless' Model 1909.

fitted to the left hand side of the slide. Since this pistol was fitted with a device to hold the slide open when the magazine was empty, there was a slide release button on the top. With the 9 mm Browning long external hammer automatics, variations can be encountered in the type and position of the lanyard attachment, magazine release, safety, and also in the shape of the frame. The slide usually bore the legend '9 mm Automatic Pistol'.

The final series to be considered are the .25 calibre pistols, most of which, just to confuse the issue, bore the calibre designation '6.35 mm Automatic Pistol'. The .25/6.35 mm external hammer series were of blow-back design, the original 1906 Model departing from tradition in that the Webley 'V' recoil spring was not used; a conventional coil spring closed the breech slide after firing. The design was due to John Carter of Webley's revolver and pistol department, and the 1906 Model can be easily distinguished by the grip safety mounted on the front butt strap under the trigger guard. This pistol was, however, not developed, and a scaled down version of the .32/7.65 mm external hammer model was put into production instead.

The final range of external hammer blow-back pistols comprised the .25/6.35 mm 1906 Final Model, the .32/7.65 mm Model in the 1905, 1906, 1911 and 1913 variants, the .380/9 mm Browning short Model and the 9 mm Browning long Model 1909.

The smallest of the Webley automatics was the .25/6.35 mm Hammerless Model of 1909. The 'V' recoil spring in this series was discarded and two coil springs were used instead. These springs served a dual purpose, the first being to operate the recoil system, the second being to act as ejectors. As the slide moved to the rear in recoil, the recoil spring plungers protruded through holes in the breech and acted on the spent case which had been drawn back with the slide by the extractor. The case was then ejected from the top of the slide through the opening provided which, unlike that on the hammer versions (where it was on the right hand side of the slide), was symmetrical.

A rather more streamlined version of the Webley .25/6.35 mm Hammerless Automatic can be encountered from time to time. These pistols were marked 'H & R Self Loading, Calibre 25' and were made under Whiting's US Patents, the rights to which were assigned by Webley to the Harrington and Richardson Arms Co. The .25 calibre Harrington and Richardson automatic was introduced in 1912 and, like the Webley, should more correctly be known as a concealed hammer or internal hammer pistol, although the term 'hammerless' is now common usage. Internally, the Harrington and Richardson

.32 Harrington and Richardson 'hammerless' automatic with grip safety.

.25 was similar to the Webley; externally, the shape of the barrel and slide differed, and what appeared to be the top front of the slide was, in fact, part of the barrel. The Webley had sights; the Harrington and Richardson did not. Early Harrington and Richardson pistols had blued trigger guards, the later versions had polished steel ones. The .25 Harrington and Richardson was made for a period of three years and the total production was approximately 20,000.

In 1916, one year after the production of the .25 model ceased, Harrington and Richardson introduced a .32 calibre automatic or 'self loading' pistol, the latter term being that employed by the makers and marked on the slide together with the calibre. Unlike the 'hammerless' Webleys, the .32 Harrington and Richardson was a true hammerless automatic since it was striker fired. As with the .25 version, the recoil spring was a coil instead of the 'V' spring and lever that were the Webley trade mark. The Harrington and Richardson .32 was one of the first American made pocket pistols to have a magazine disconnector to ensure that the pistol could not be fired with the magazine removed. The .32 model was kept in production until 1939, the total quantity manufactured being about double that of the .25.

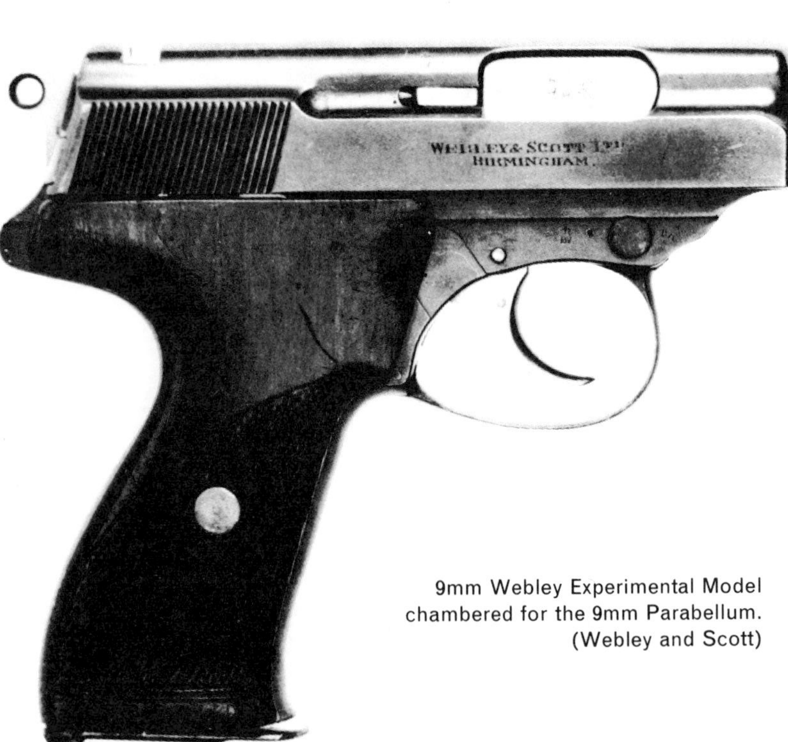

9mm Webley Experimental Model chambered for the 9mm Parabellum. (Webley and Scott)

The Webley .32 frame and slide were also used for a .22 single shot target pistol introduced by Webley's themselves in 1911. Built on a simplified retarded blow-back system, this pistol had to be operated manually for both extraction and breech closure. At least two versions were marketed, one with a $4\frac{1}{2}''$ barrel, the other with a $9''$ barrel. An unusual feature of this pistol was that the butt plate was machined to accommodate a shoulder stock. The $4\frac{1}{2}''$ barrel model was officially issued to police in the United Kingdom for practice and, both as regards 'feel' and weight, it approximates to the larger calibre .32 automatic.

The last Webley automatic pistol was the 9mm Experimental Model chambered for the 9mm Parabellum cartridge. With an overall length of $9\frac{1}{2}''$, this was a locked breech model and followed contemporary practice in that it was double action. Magazine capacity was eight rounds and the pistol was finished with the same high regard for standards that characterised all the Webley automatic pistols. Unfortunately, the 9mm Browning High Power auto-pistol was selected by the British Government to replace the .38 revolver and, although Webley's last auto-pistol was submitted to the Ministry of Supply, the decision in favour of the Browning meant that the Webley remained experimental and was never put into production.

The absence of government orders, coupled with a severely restricted home market, made it impossible to spend money on research and development and so to compete with foreign manufacturers. No auto-pistols have since been made in Britain, and it is unlikely that Webley and Scott—or, indeed, anyone else—will be able to re-establish themselves in this field.

Notes to Chapter Fourteen

For additional information on automatic pistols of Browning design, reference should be made to *Colt Automatic Pistols* 1896-1955 by Donald B. Bady (Beverly Hills, 1956) and to *Colt Firearms* 1836-1958 by James E. Serven (3rd edition, Santa Ana, 1959). Two articles in the *American Rifleman* are also relevant: 'John Browning's Pistols' by Jac Weller (November 1952) and 'An Early Colt Pocket Automatic' by D. M. Simmons Jnr. (April 1964), the latter covering the 1903 Pocket Model.

A definitive article on the Savage is 'Savage Automatic Pistols' by Daniel K. Stern which appeared in the *American Rifleman* for September 1962, with additional data in the August 1963 issue.

The Smith and Wesson Model 1924 is covered in 'Smith and Wesson Pocket Automatic Pistols' by Daniel K. Stern in the *American Rifleman* for October 1963, and the Remington Model 51 in 'Handguns by Remington' by Hershel C. Logan in the issue for May 1955.

The Gabbett-Fairfax Mars is treated exhaustively in 'Mars Automatic Pistols' by Larry S. Sterett in the 1961 *Gun Digest*. Additional information on Webley automatic pistols is given in *The Webley Story* by W. C. Dowell.

Full acknowledgement is paid to manufacturers' catalogues and to the makers who supplied additional data at my request.

Chapter Fifteen
The European Automatic Pistol

6.35mm Jieffeco by Robar. (See also facing page.)

In Europe, the birthplace of the auto-pistol, the pattern of production has changed over the years. Britain, as we have seen, still manufactures a revolver, but is armed with an automatic pistol of American design and, as far as new weapons are concerned, of Belgian manufacture.

In Liege, the centre of Belgian arms production, one manufacturer of auto-pistols remains, Robar, whose original 'Jieffeco' was, in 1921, replaced by a new series introduced under the name 'Melior'. These pistols were all simple blow-back types and sold for considerably less than the blow-back Brownings made by Fabrique Nationale. Currently, Robar are making a series of automatic pistols under the trade name 'Mercury'. Manufactured in .22 long rifle, 6.35mm, 7.65mm and 9mm short, these are again simple blow-back pistols of conventional design.

In Herstal near Liege, the long established firm of Anciens Etablissements Pieper (formerly Henry Pieper SA and generally known as AEP) had, in 1907, purchased the rights to manufacture the Bergmann Model 1903 Marspistole (see Chapter Thirteen). They later started production of the Bergmann Bayard Model 1908 for both civilian and military purposes and sold it to both the Spanish and the Greek armies who were, in fact, already using the Bergmann Marspistole as made by Bergmann Industriewerke.

In 1911 the Danish army adopted the Bergmann Bayard Model 1908 as the Pistol Pattern 1910 and were supplied by AEP until 1922. The Danish Government then decided to manufacture the pistol themselves as the Model 1910/21, and these pistols, marked 'Haerens Tojhus' (Royal Army) or Haerens Rustkammer' (Army Storage Arsenal), had minor modifications involving different grips etc. The Bergmann Bayard was replaced in 1940 by the FN Browning High Power as the Model 46, and then by the SIG 47/8 known to the Danes as the Model 1949.

In addition to the military pistols made under the name Bayard, AEP also introduced a series of pocket pistols which bore the name Bayard on

Advertising material enclosed with a box of 9mm short, advocating the Bayard. (AEP)

Pistola de repetición automática ,,BAYARD"

Una aventura de caza en el Africa Central.

La pistola BAYARD salva la vida a un cazador de búfalos.

De entre todas las pistolas automáticas hoy en dia existentes, la « BAYARD » posee las mejores cualidades de un arma de defensa y de plena confianza.

A un potente calibre en un tamaño reducido, reune la pistola « BAYARD » un funcionamiento exacto y un poder de contención máximo, siendo por tal el ideal de la pistola automática, fácilmente portátil.

Peso : 0.460 kg.

Dimensiones : 120 × 85 × 24 m/m.

Un solo tamaño en cal. 7.65 y 9 m/m.

En venta en las principales armerias.

7.65mm Bayard Model 1908.

.22 long rifle Mercury by Robar.

AUTOMATIC PISTOL ,,JIEFFECO"

6 Shots - Model 1909-1910 - 6,35 m/m Caliber

Advantages. — In the construction of the « **JIEFFECO** » pistol particular attention has been devoted to the size which has been reduced in such proportions as to make this pistol one of the lightest and the most handy «pocket pistol» ever made.

Notwithstanding its simplicity the « **JIEFFECO** » pistol is well known for its superiority and reliability. All wearing parts are made of the very best steel and tempered.

Accuracy. — The spiral spring being stronger than in any other similar arm, deadens entierely the effect of the recoil, which assures the accuracy of every consecutive shot.

Rapidity in shooting. — The trigger acting directly upon the hammer,

The original literature enclosed with the 6.35mm Jieffeco.

the grips. During the period 1910–11, three models based on patents by B. Clarus and identical in size were brought out and were known as the Models of 1908. The calibres were 6.35 mm, 7.65 mm and 9 mm short. The recoil spring was mounted above the barrel and the pistol was dismantled by pushing back the fore-sight block so that the recoil spring could then be removed. A variant design, similar to the Browning, appeared in 1930. AEP ceased to manufacture in 1957.

Not to be confused with AEP, the firm of Nicolas Pieper (also of Herstal) produced a wide range of pistols based on N. Pieper's patents of 1907 and 1908. Pieper licensed the manufacture of these pistols to OWG, which accounts for the similarity between them and the Steyr pistols. Unlike OWG, however, Pieper made pistols on both his 'basculant' (hinged barrel) and 'demontant' designs. These appeared in 6.35 mm and 7.65 mm and in several model variants as regards barrel length and magazine capacity. In addition, N. Pieper also produced a 6.35 mm Pocket Model (similar to the Browning Baby) which featured an extension grip magazine.

One of the oldest Liege makers was LePage, first established in 1848. This company began manufacture of automatic pistols in 1925 in the usual range of pocket calibres. These were simple blow-back weapons with a fixed barrel, the recoil spring located under the barrel. Sold under the name LePage, they did not have a wide distribution and the firm ceased operations in 1953.

Pieper Model 1919, 'demontant' type.

Yet another of the Liege makers, Fabrique d'Armes F. Delu, manufactured a small vest pocket 6.35 mm seven shot auto-pistol which, in the 1920's, was selling for $6.50 compared with $10.00 for the Browning Baby. F. Delu went out of business in 1945. Today, with the exception of Robar, Belgian automatic pistol production is concentrated at Herstal where, as we have already seen, Fabrique Nationale manufacture the Browning range.

The Liege arms industry manufactured a vast range of automatic pistols in a profusion of types, calibres and qualities. The companies engaged in this trade varied from large concerns like Fabrique Nationale to the smaller enterprises engaged in the manufacture of shotguns and revolvers by the older traditional techniques. Many were marketed by agents with no manufacturing capacity, some were copies of the more expensive automatic pistols backed by the integrity of a known name or trade mark, and there were also those attempts to introduce a new design the merits of which were insufficient to support series production. As we have seen, the smaller businesses have now disappeared, the names of many are all but forgotten, and any demand for the type of automatic pistol they produced is now met by the Spanish arms industry and by newly established indigenous industries in the countries that were formerly customers of the Belgians.

With the destruction of the old Austro-Hungarian Empire, the centres of small arms production have moved, and today the Steyr-Daimler-Puch AG at Steyr in Upper Austria manufacture only one automatic pistol, the Steyr Model SP. This was introduced in the late 1950's in 7.65mm (.32 ACP) calibre, is double action only, and the internal enclosed hammer must be cocked by trigger action after each shot. An unique feature of the Model SP is the cross bolt safety in the trigger which, when pushed to the left, engages the frame and so blocks the rearward movement of the trigger.

Whether or not this pistol marks the beginning of a renaissance of the Steyr factory in the field of automatic pistol production remains to be seen.

Czechoslovakia declared its independence as a separate republic in October 1918. In 1919 an arsenal for the manufacture of small arms was established at Brno in Moravia under the name

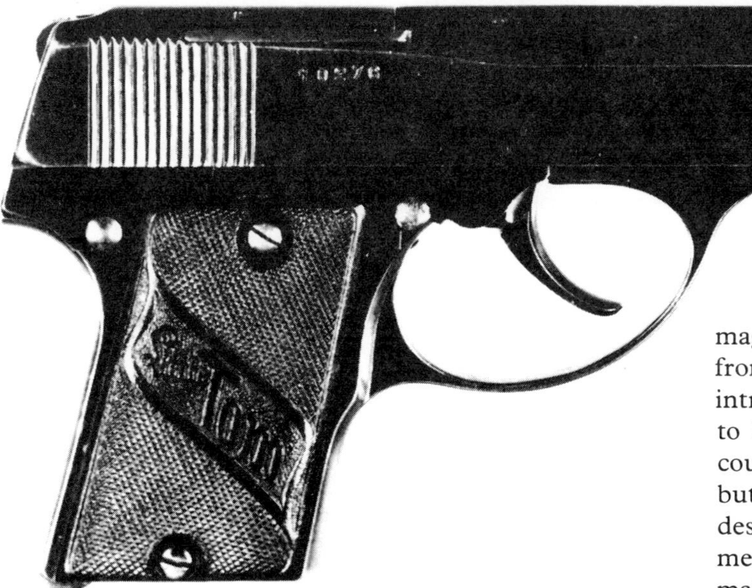

6.35mm 'Little Tom'
by Wiener Waffenfabrik.

Ceskoslovenska Zavody na Vyrobu Zbrani (Czechoslovakian Factory for Arms Manufacture) and, from that moment, the manufacture of small arms began to grow into a major industry. The Brno factory started with the manufacture of Mannlicher rifles, followed by the production of Mauser rifles under the direction of Josef Nickl, a former employee of the Mauser Werke at Oberndorf. The first military pistol, the CZ 24, employed a rotating barrel lock and was chambered for the 9mm short (.380) cartridge. It was based on a design produced by Nickl when he had been working for Mauser in 1916, and apparently Mauser had not been greatly impressed.

In 1923 the name of the Brno factory was changed to Ceskoslovenska Zbrojovka/Akciova Spolecnost (Czechoslovakian Arms Factory Ltd.) and, although the Government retained a controlling interest, it was reorganised as a limited company. Also it was decided to rationalise production, with the result that the manufacture of automatic pistols was transferred to Ceska Zbrojovka/Akc. Spol. (Czech Arms Factory Ltd.) at Strakonice in Bohemia. This latter firm had originally started out as Jihoceska Zbrojovka s.s.r.o. (South Bohemian Arms Factroy Ltd.) under the supervision of Alois Tomiska who had designed a pistol which sold under the trade mark 'Little Tom' and was manufactured by the Wiener Waffenfabrik in Vienna. This 6.35mm pistol incorporated a number of unusual features. It was one of the first double action automatic pistols manufactured and, although it employed a box magazine in the butt, the magazine was loaded from the top through the slide opening. To introduce or remove the magazine, the slide had to be locked in the rear position; the magazine could not be removed from the bottom of the butt. Tomiska was one of several Czech arms designers whose work contributed in no small measure to the emergence of Czechoslovakia as a major arms manufacturing country. He died in Prague in 1946.

In 1922 the South Bohemian Arms Factory Ltd. absorbed the Hubertus factory, and it was one year later that, as Ceska Zbrojovka SA, it became the largest pistol manufacturer in the country.

The third of the original Czech manufacturers was Zbrojovka Praga (Praga Arms Factory) in Prague, the capital city of the new republic. The first auto-pistol made by this firm, the Praga Model 21, is easily distinguishable because of its unusual shape and folding trigger guard. The next auto-pistol was a conventional .32 calibre weapon which bore a close resemblance to the Browning Model 1910 later adopted as the first official Czech Police Pistol, and was marked 'Zbrojovka Praga Praha' on the left hand side of the slide. The factory had been started by A. Nowotny who was soon joined by Karel Krnka (the designer of the Roth Model 1907 auto-pistol), by Vaclav (Wenceslas) Holek, later to become famous as the designer of the Bren machine gun, and by his younger brothers Frantisek (Frank) and Emanuel. The team was completed by Frantisek Myska. In spite of this galaxy of talent, economic conditions in the 1920's resulted in the Praga concern being taken over by the Prumyslova Banka (Industrial Bank). Even they were unable to save the company and, in 1926, it closed down. Myska immediately joined Ceska Zbrojovka SA and, in the same year, redesigned the Model 24 .380 pistol, eliminating the rotating barrel lock and converting the pistol to a straight blow-back 7.65mm automatic which went into production as the VZ 27

7.65mm Czech Model VZ 27.

9mm Czech Model CZ 38. (Glasgow Police Collection)

7.65mm Czech Model VZ 27 made under German supervision.

(Model-Vzor 27). As such, it was adopted as the standard Czech Police Pistol until 1951 and was manufactured in Prague. In 1939 the Model 27 was made under German occupation as the 'Pistole Modelle 27 Kal. 7.65'; early production copies were marked on the top of the slide 'Böhmische Waffenfabrik A.G. in Prag' and bore the German Ordnance code letters 'fnh' A special version of this pistol with a slightly larger barrel was made for the German Army for use with a silencer.

After the war manufacture of the Model 27 was resumed, the slide markings altered to 'Ceska Zbrojovka A. S. v Praze'. Following the Communist coup d'état, the name was again changed, this time to Ceska Zbrojovka Narodni Podnik (Czech Arms Factory, National Co-operative).

Frantisek Myska was also responsible for the design of a 6.35mm double action auto-pistol known originally as the Model 36. Later, this pistol was simplified by Jaroslav Kratochvil as the Model 45, and is currently being manufactured as the CZ 6.35mm Automatic Pistol.

The last auto-pistol designed by Myska was the Model 1938, which again employed the double action feature and was characterised by a hinged forward pivoting barrel assembly. Chambered for the 9mm short cartridge, the Model 1938 was adopted by the Czech Army and was being supplied in limited quantities when war broke out. All stocks were taken over by the German Army and the pistol was known as the Pistole 39(t); manufacture, however, was discontinued.

After the war and the subsequent nationalisation of the arms industry, a new double action 7.65mm blow-back pistol was introduced, the Model 1950. Designed by Jaroslav Kratochvil and bearing a superficial resemblance to the Walther PP pistol, the Model 50 is in current production for commercial sale and export with the CZ trade mark and 'Vzor 50' on the slide together with the legend 'Made in Czechoslovakia' in English.

The most recent pistol is the Model 52 chambered for the Czech 7.62mm bottleneck service cartridge which is interchangeable with the Russian 7.62mm and the German 7.63mm Mauser. The Czech cartridge is the most powerful of the three, and the Model 52 pistol is of short recoil locked breech design with dual locking rollers similar to the German MG 42 machine gun.

In the years between the wars a number of small blow-back pocket pistols were made in Czechoslovakia. Typical of these was the Mars (not to be confused with other pistols bearing this popular trade name) which can really be regarded as a copy of the 1906 Browning and, in 6.35mm, was made by Kohout at Kdyne in Bohemia. Initial production was sold under the name 'Niva'. The same company also made a 7.65mm copy of the Browning Model 1910 which lacked the grip safety of the original and the take down notches in the slide. Manufacture of both weapons appears to have ceased in 1945.

Also in Kdyne, the firm of Antonin Vilimec produced a small blow-back pocket pistol similar to the Browning Baby. This was sold under the name 'Slavia', but production ceased in 1938.

Another pistol similar to the Browning Baby

7.65mm Czech Model CZ 50. (Omnipol)

6.35mm Czech 'Duo' or Model 'Z'. (Omnipol)

6.35mm Czech Model CZ 45. (Omnipol)

(in fact, the magazines were interchangeable) was the 'Duo' which, manufactured by Frantisek Dusek of Opocno, Bohemia, was introduced in 1926 and was originally marked 'Aut. Pistole DUO Cal. 6.35 F. Dusek. Opocno'. Production of the 'Duo' continued during the German occupation when Dusek was allowed to go on marking his pistols with his own name, the only change being that the spelling of the town was altered to the German version, Opotschino. After the war and subsequent nationalisation, the manufacture was taken over by Ceska Zbrojovka, and pistols are currently exported with the markings 'Aut. Pistole "Z" R 6.35mm'. The letter R indicates calibre (Czech:raze). Due to the 'Z' marking on the slide and the use of the 'Z' monogram on the grip, it is often referred to as the 'Z' pistol, calibre 6.35mm, and is in fact known as the Z-6.35 by the Czech export organisation, Omnipol, Prague.

In addition to the two revolvers, the ZKR 590 and the target ZKR 551, the nationalised Czech arms industry manufacture a simple break open single shot target pistol chambered for the .22 short, long and long rifle or the 6mm Flobert. Originally made by Frantisek Pavlicek, this is currently known as the Model 'P'. A rather more sophisticated target arm, the 'Drulov' is marketed by Omnipol, but where it is manufactured is not at present known. Two target auto-pistols appeared after the war, the ZKP 501–11 and the ZKP 54, whose design, from the model designations, was the work of Joseph and Francis Koucky. There is some doubt as to whether these models ever went into full scale production.

In marked contrast to many of the older traditional centres of arms production, the Czech small arms industry appears to be in a very flourishing state, having survived both the German occupation and the radical reorganisation which followed nationalisation.

In Germany, in 1922, DWM, the manufacturers of the Luger-Parabellum, brought out a blow-back pistol based on the Browning Model 1910 and known as the DWM Model 22. The following year, when hard rubber grips replaced the wooden ones, the pistol was renamed the DWM Model 23, but manufacture ceased in the late 1920's.

Mauser Werke, following unsuccessful experimental work on blow-back models designed to use the powerful 9mm Parabellum cartridge, extended their range of automatic pistols by introducing a series of small blow-back models. The design features of the 9mm Model of 1909 were incorporated in a smaller 6.35mm version, now referred to as the Model 1910. In its original form, the Mauser Model 1910 was characterised by a small lever just above the trigger guard on the left hand side of the frame which combined the duty of trigger pin and side plate latch. Later versions of the pistol dispensed with the latch; the side plate was pushed up and out of grooves in the receiver. To strip this model, the magazine was removed and the slide pulled to the rear until it stayed open. The serrated portion of the takedown catch at the front of the frame was depressed and turned until freed from the lug on the frame. The rod could then be withdrawn and the barrel lifted upward and out of the frame. The magazine was then replaced and the slide eased

6.35mm Mauser Model 1910.
(See facing page.)

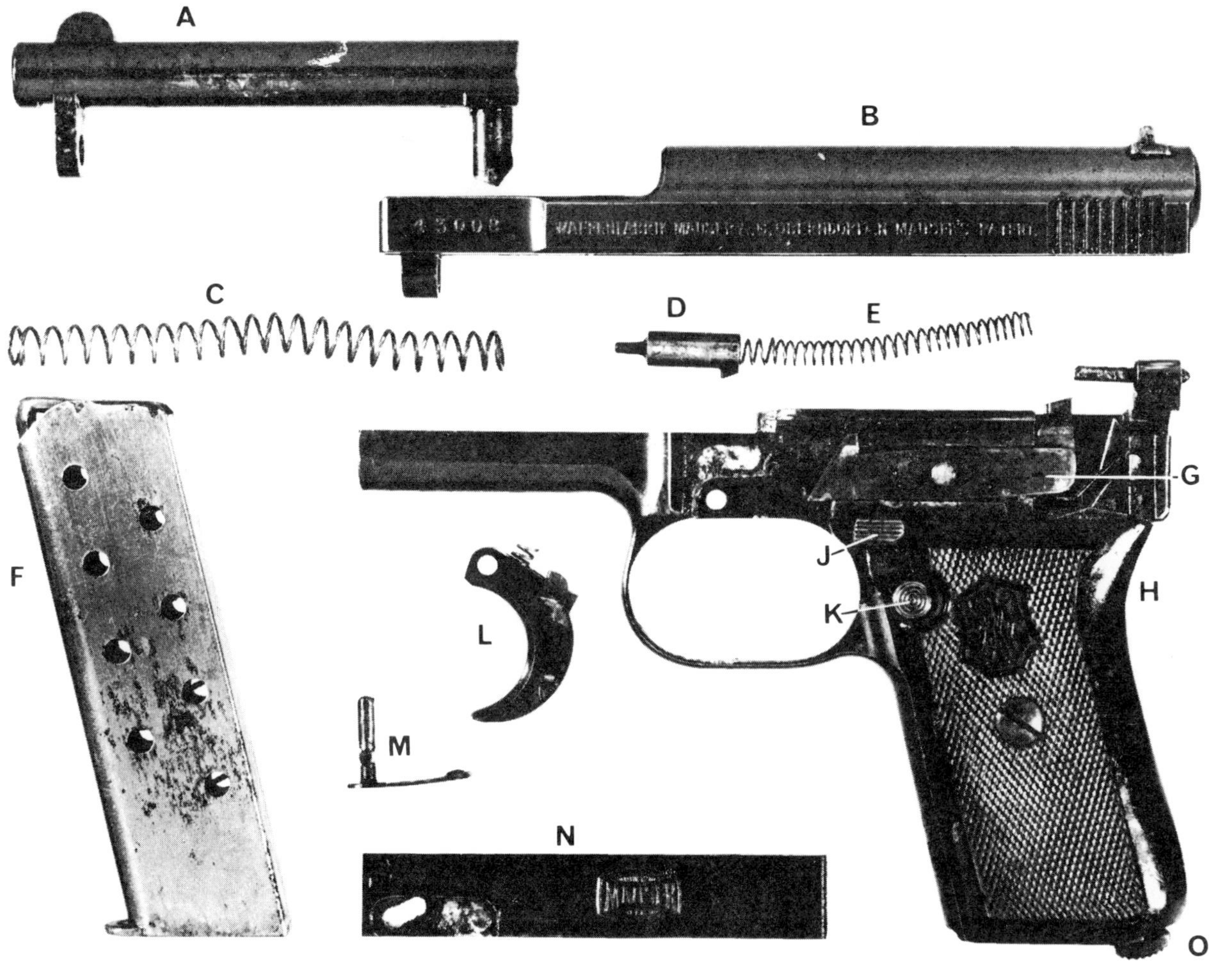

6.35mm Mauser Model 1910 dismantled.
A. Barrel.
B. Slide.
C. Recoil spring.
D. Firing pin.
E. Firing pin spring.
F. Magazine.
G. Trigger bar.
H. Frame.
J. Safety catch.
K. Safety catch release.
L. Trigger.
M. Side plate release latch and trigger pin.
N. Side plate.
O. Magazine catch.

forward off the front of the frame. During this operation the trigger was pulled to release the firing pin spring. In 1934 a new model was introduced which differed little from its predecessor. The obvious change was in the use of a wooden one piece grip which covered both sides of the frame and also the back strap. The first 7.65mm calibre pistol appeared about 1914 and, in 1934, was improved by the substitution of the larger one piece wooden stock. Both calibres were of the same basic design, straight blowback striker fired pistols. When the striker was cocked, the head protruded through the rear of the frame, giving visual and tactile indication that the pistol was, in fact, cocked. It did not show whether or not there was a cartridge in the chamber. A magazine safety was also fitted so that, when the magazine was withdrawn, the pistol could not be fired. The thumb safety on the left hand side of the frame, when pushed down to prevent firing, also locked the slide so that the breech could not be opened. A spring controlled button underneath the safety lever released the safety ready for firing. Of excellent workmanship, the Mauser pocket pistols were justifiably popular and competitively priced. De luxe engraved models were also available, but manufacture appears to have ceased in 1939.

Mauser also manufactured a smaller Westentaschen (Vest Pocket) pistol. The first of these, the WTP Model 1, was made until 1939. An improved version, the WTP Model 2, was introduced in 1939 and, as can be seen from the illustrations, is distinguished from the earlier model by the curved back strap and trigger guard. Both models embodied a magazine safety

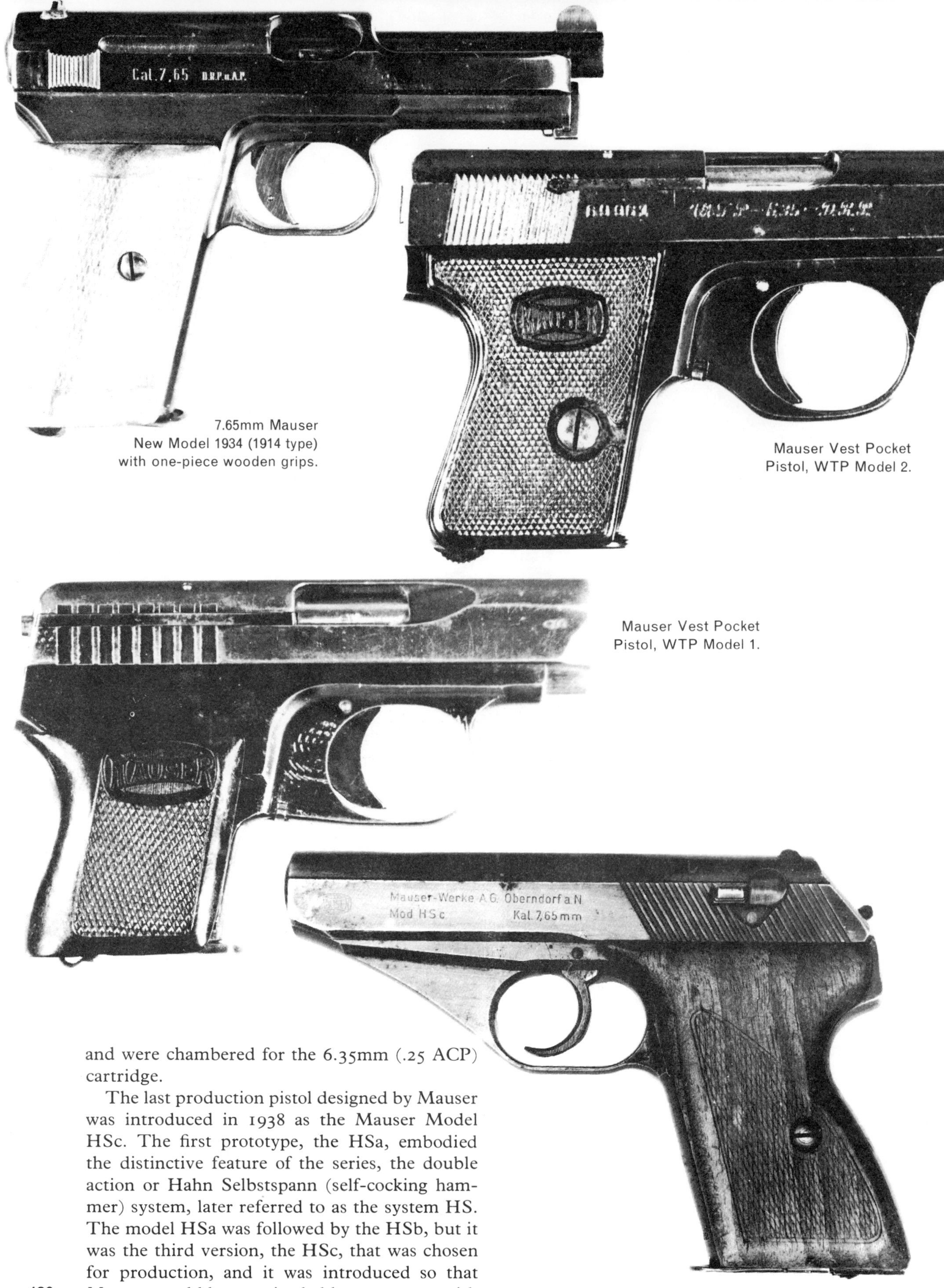

7.65mm Mauser
New Model 1934 (1914 type)
with one-piece wooden grips.

Mauser Vest Pocket
Pistol, WTP Model 2.

Mauser Vest Pocket
Pistol, WTP Model 1.

7.65mm Mauser Model HSc.

and were chambered for the 6.35mm (.25 ACP) cartridge.

The last production pistol designed by Mauser was introduced in 1938 as the Mauser Model HSc. The first prototype, the HSa, embodied the distinctive feature of the series, the double action or Hahn Selbstspann (self-cocking hammer) system, later referred to as the system HS. The model HSa was followed by the HSb, but it was the third version, the HSc, that was chosen for production, and it was introduced so that Mauser would have a pistol able to compete with

The top of the frame of the Mauser Model HSc.

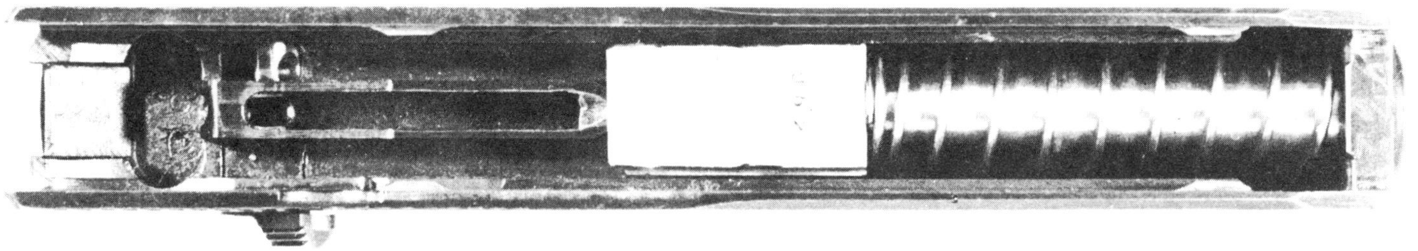

The underneath of the slide of the Mauser Model HSc, with barrel and recoil spring assembled.

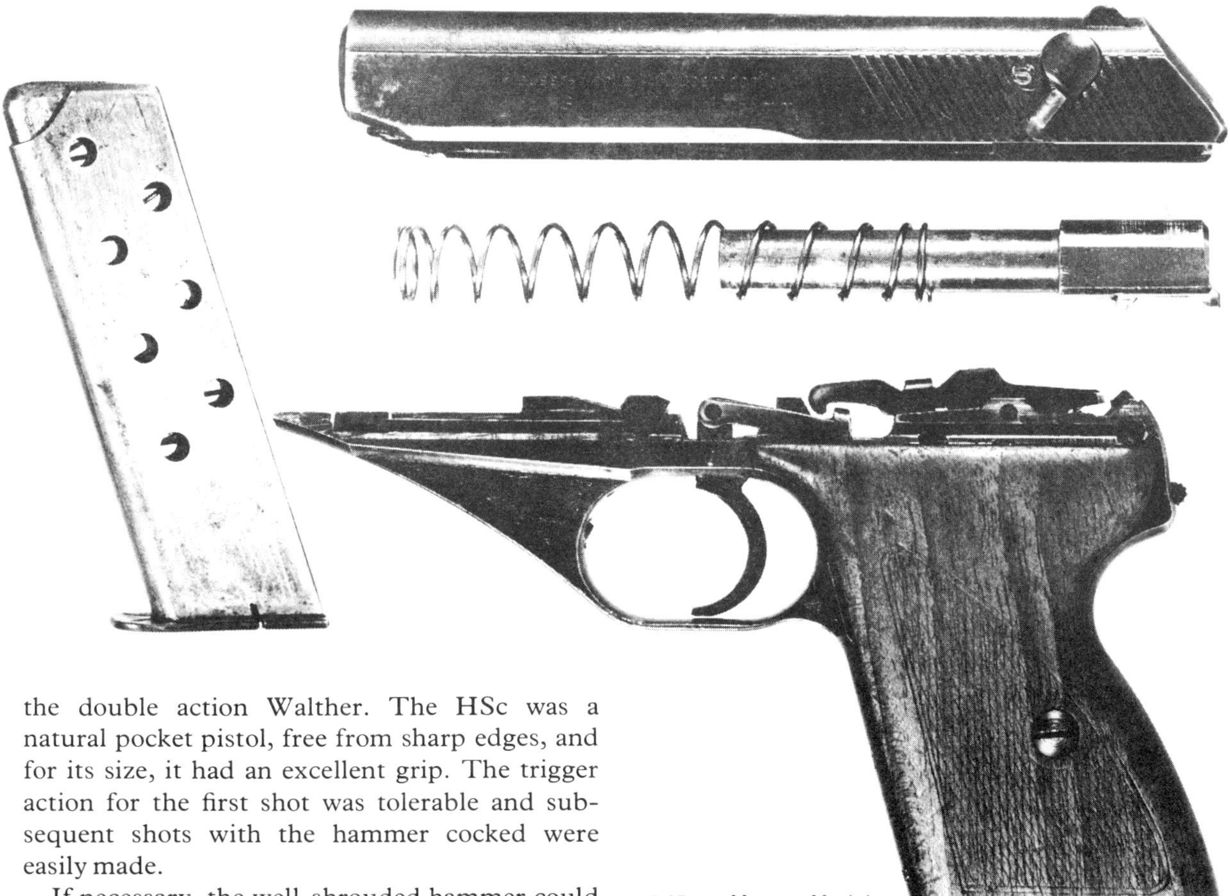

7.65mm Mauser Model HSc dismantled.

the double action Walther. The HSc was a natural pocket pistol, free from sharp edges, and for its size, it had an excellent grip. The trigger action for the first shot was tolerable and subsequent shots with the hammer cocked were easily made.

If necessary, the well-shrouded hammer could easily be manually cocked. The frame and slide were solid machined forgings, but much of the internal mechanism was stamped out, and simple music wire springs were used to reduce the cost of manufacture. Dismantling was simplicity itself. The magazine was removed and the chamber cleared. The hammer was put at full cock and the safety catch pushed down over the red dot marked on the slide. The slide was then pulled slightly forward and upward—the slide catch inside the trigger guard being depressed at the same time—until it was free of the frame. The barrel could be removed from the slide by pulling up the rear or breech end until it cleared the breech face.

Operation was straightforward. With the safety applied, a loaded magazine was inserted into the butt. The slide was drawn back and then released, chambering the top cartridge. The hammer did not remain cocked, and could not strike the firing pin since the cam surface of the safety pin shaft pulled the firing pin away. It could not be cocked with the safety applied.

When the pistol was to be fired, the safety was pushed upward disclosing the red dot, and the pull on the trigger both cocked and released the hammer. Subsequent shots were fired from a cocked hammer. This system provided a further advantage in that, with the safety applied, the hammer could be lowered on a loaded chamber without danger. Indication that the chamber was loaded could be obtained by visual or tactile means since, when a cartridge was in the breech, the extractor protruded from the side of the slide. Very few specimens of this model were available on the commercial market and, since almost the entire output was taken up by the German military forces, most bore military acceptance marks. Although the military production lacked the customary high quality Mauser finish, the 7.65mm HSc was an exceptionally fine pocket pistol.

In September 1968 the HSc was re-introduced into the selling range. It is now being offered in the original 7.65mm calibre and also in 9mm

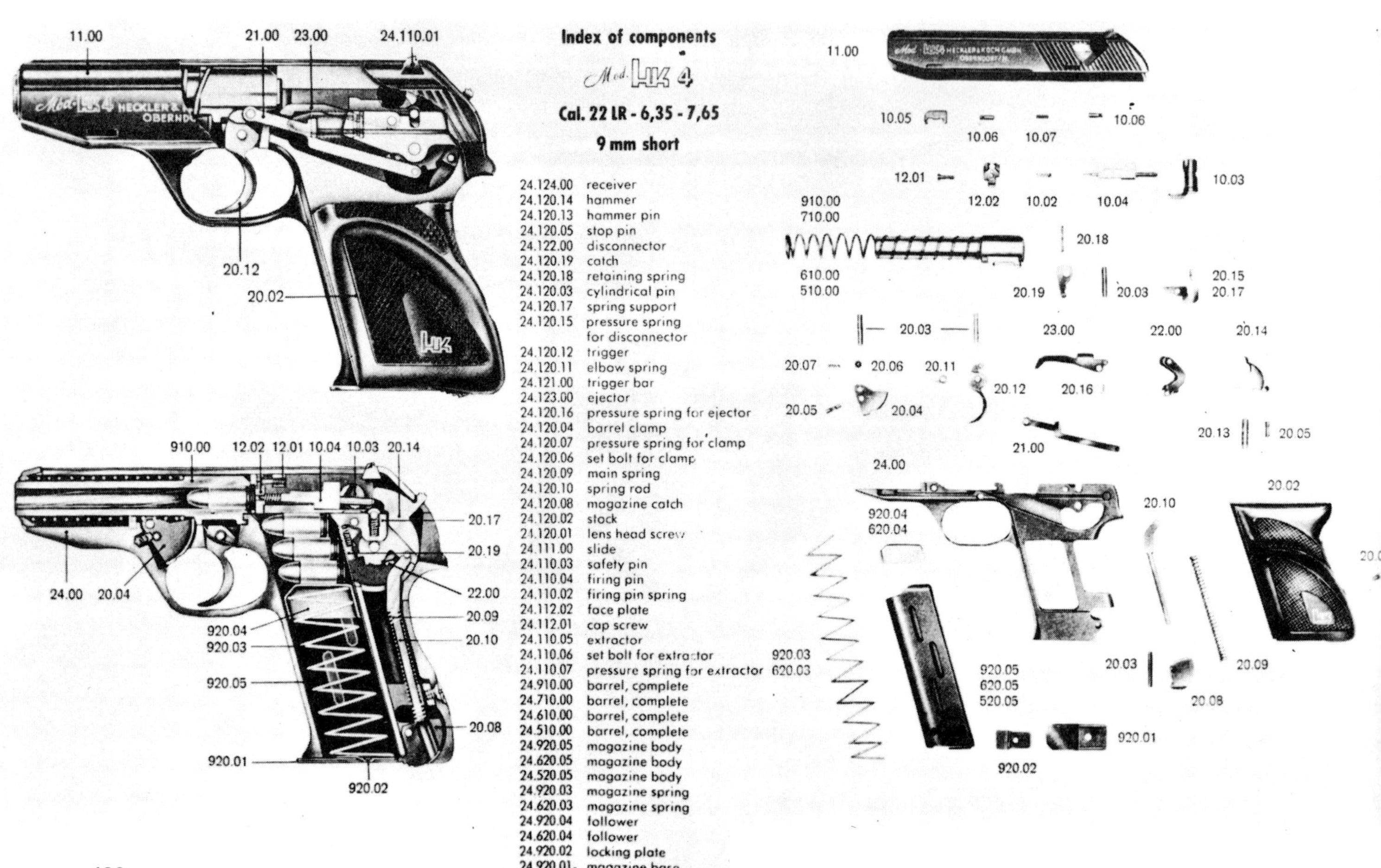

Heckler and Koch Model HK4 (Heckler and Koch)

short. Experimental models were made before the war in both 9mm short and .22 long rifle, and the latest information is that a .22 long rifle version will be introduced at the end of 1969.

In the 1960's the firm of Heckler and Koch, also in Oberndorf, introduced their blow-back double action automatic pistols which bear a strong resemblance to the Mauser HSc. The most interesting pistol in their range is the Model HK4 which is furnished in kit form with four interchangeable barrels and magazines so that the pistol can be used with 9mm short (.380 ACP), 7.65mm (.32 ACP), 6.25mm (.25 ACP) and .22 long rifle cartridges. The frame is an aluminium die casting, the slide is fabricated from a steel pressing with brazed internal components, and a replaceable plastic insert buffer is used to absorb the impact of the recoiling slide. A magazine disconnector device is incorporated to prevent the discharge of a cartridge in the chamber when the magazine has been removed, and the slide stays open when the last shot has been fired. When changing from centre-fire to rim-fire, the slide recoil plate has to be removed and reversed, an operation that also realigns the firing pin.

Similar conversion units are also available for the Swiss SIG SP47/8, and a popular conversion unit for the Luger was made before the war by the Erfurter Machine Works under the brand name 'Erma'. These were available for either .22 long rifle or for a special 4mm centre-fire adaptor cartridge. The .22 conversion unit for the Luger included a toggle breech mechanism, an insert barrel and a ten shot magazine. With the unit in

Details of the double action trigger mechanism and the safety system of the Heckler and Koch Model HK4. (Heckler and Koch)

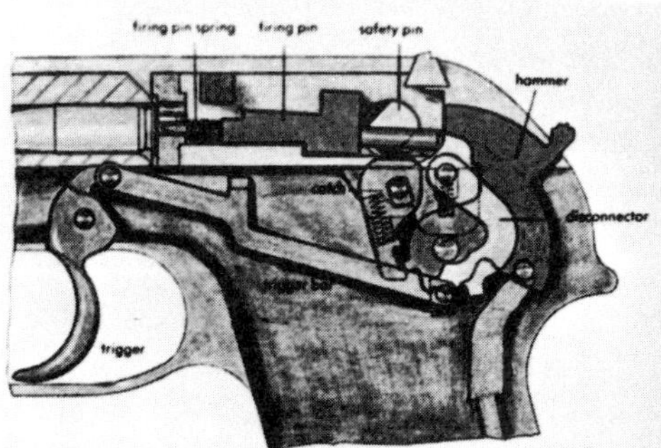

Illustration 1

Pistol loaded, locked and uncocked

Double safety: Through the shifting of the safety pin the firing pin is outside of the firing region of the hammer.
A longitudinal movement of the firing pin is impossible due to the solid blockage.

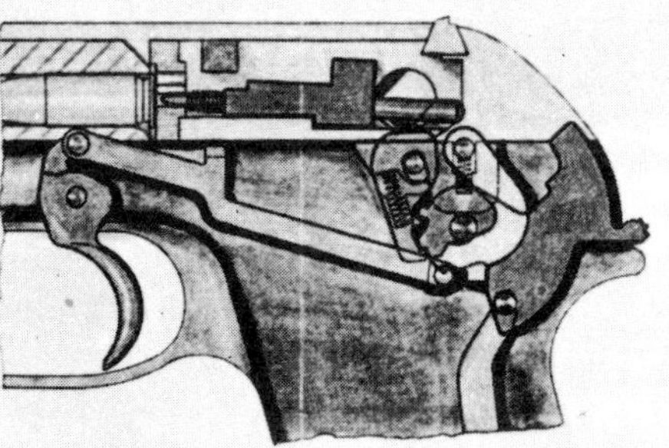

Illustration 2

Pistol loaded, locked and cocked

Since the firing pin is outside of the firing region of the hammer and solidly blocked, the pistol can be uncocked without danger by operating the trigger. There-by the disconnector presses against the catch and the hammer moves out of it's notch.

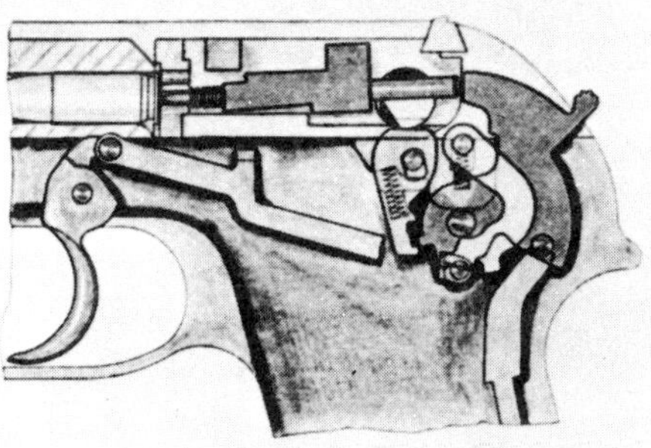

Illustration 3

Pistol loaded, unlocked and uncocked

The pistol is ready to fire through a cocking trigger. The firing pin is in the firing region of the hammer. By operating the trigger in connection with the trigger bar, the disconnector presses against the hammer and cocks it so far, till the disconnector moves through it's cam out of the hammer notch, the catch is held out of the turn region of the hammer and this way the hammer is able to precipitate.

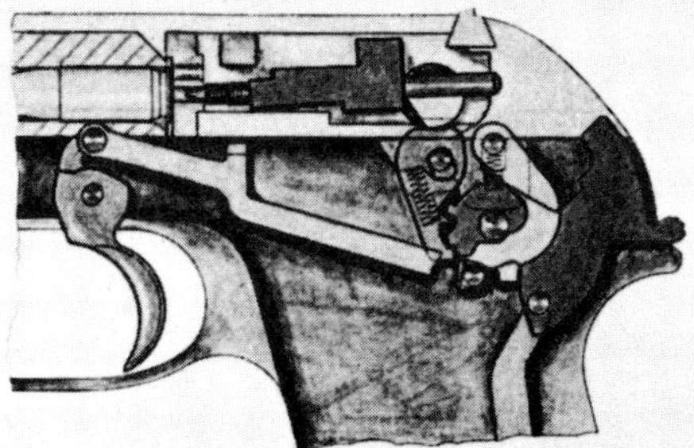

Illustration 4

Pistol loaded, unlocked and cocked

The pistol is ready to fire. The hammer is held in it's notch by the catch.
By operating the trigger, the blockage of the hammer is released by the catch over the trigger bar and the disconnector and the hammer hits the firing pin. The measurements of the firing pin and the firing pin spring are harmonized so, that the firing pin ignites the cartridge **laying bare.**

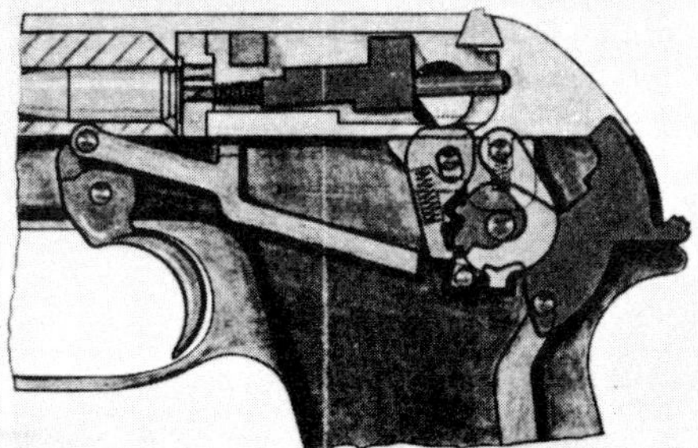

Illustration 5

Pistol loaded, unlocked, at the moment of the hammer release

By operating the trigger, the disconnector presses against the catch. The cocked hammer is released out of the hammer notch and hits the firing pin. The firing pin hits the cartridge and releases the shot.

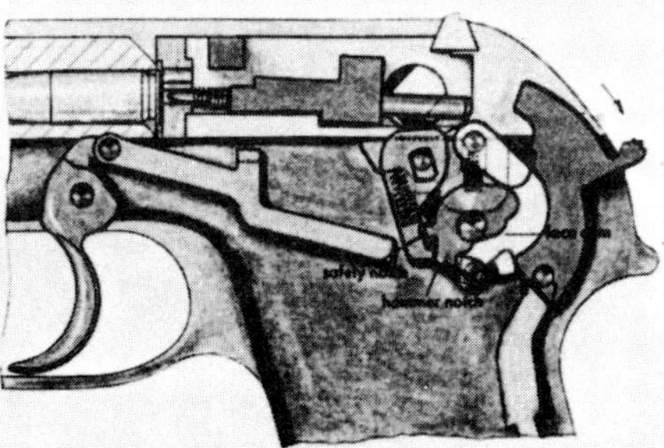

Illustration 6

Pistol loaded and locked

The pistol cannot be cocked neither with the cocking trigger nor by hand while secured, for the catch is solidely blocked by the safety pin. While cocking the hammer (in arrow direction) the hammer grasps into the notch at the catch and wants to push the catch up.

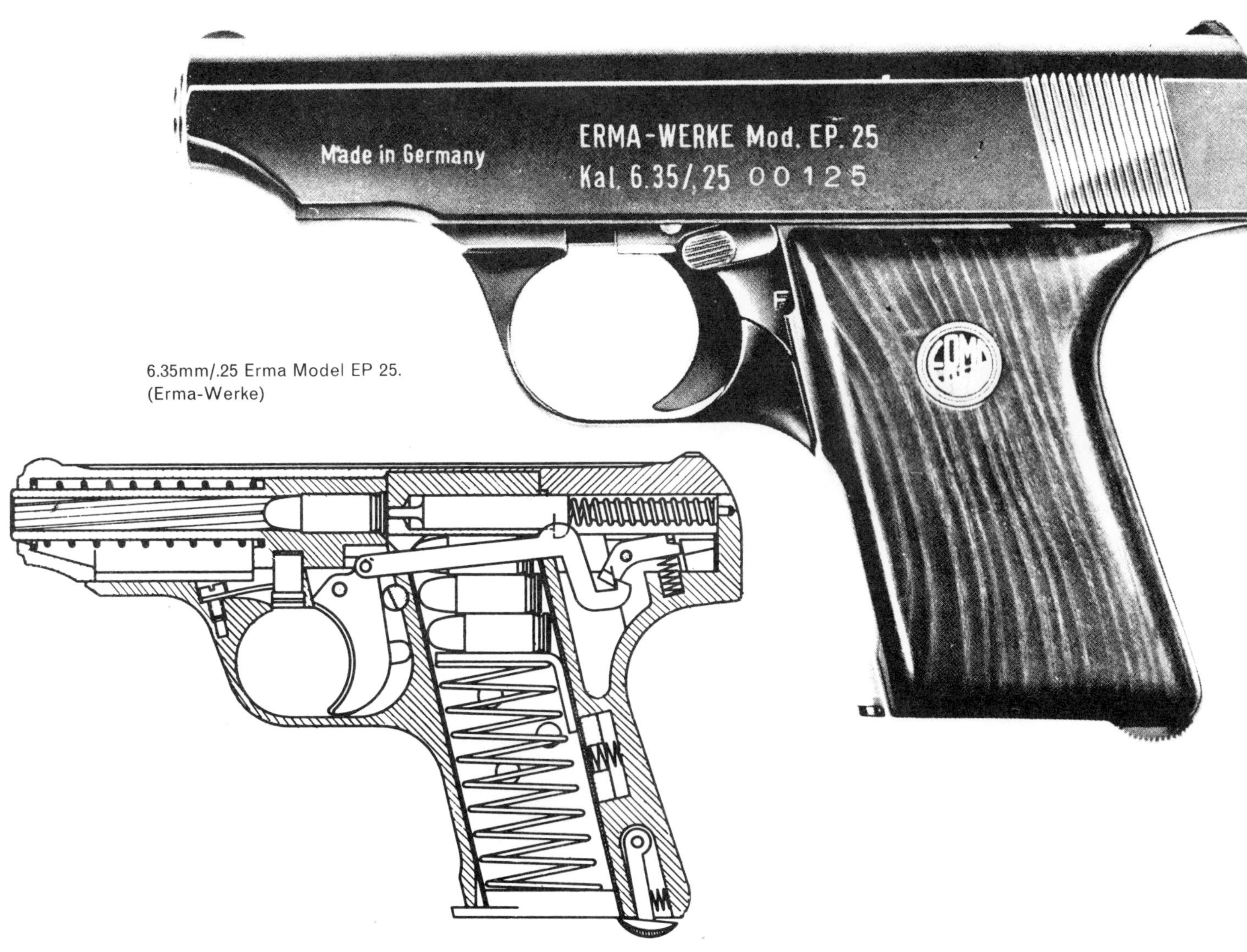

6.35mm/.25 Erma Model EP 25. (Erma-Werke)

place the pistol functioned just like any other automatic pistol.

Erma-Werke of Dachau currently manufacture a range of five pistols. The smallest of these is a straight 6.35mm blow-back pocket pistol, the Erma EP 25. Similar in appearance to the Ortgies (page 493), it has the familiar 'secret' grip plates but, after pulling down the slide bolt in the trigger guard, the slide is removed by pushing it forward instead of, as with the Ortgies, pulling it back.

In 1964 Erma-Werke introduced a .22 calibre pistol with a close external resemblance to the Luger Model 1908. But, although it employed a toggle-link mechanism to retard the opening of the breech, it did not provide the Luger's positive lock. The early Erma pistols were marked 'Erma Luger 22' but, in 1967, a redesigned version appeared, the .22 Erma 'Sportpistole' or Model EP 22, with checkered walnut grips and an improved trigger mechanism. Shortly afterwards, a longer barreled version, the Navy Model ET 22, appeared with a barrel length of 300mm as against the 80mm of the EP 22 and with an adjustable rear sight and wooden fore-end. Both pistols are chambered for the .22 long rifle and have a magazine capacity of eight cartridges. Equally, both models are largely constructed from non-ferrous die castings, with the exception of the barrel liner, breech block and minor steel pressings.

In 1968 a further model came out, the KGP 68, chambered either for the 7.65mm or for the 9mm short (.380). The KGP 68 and the basically similar KGP 69 (introduced in 1969 and chambered for the .22 long rifle) are different in design from the EP and ET models and both have 100mm barrels. Magazine capacity for the 7.65mm KGP 68 is six and, for the 9mm short, five cartridges. The KGP 69 magazine holds eight .22 long rifle cartridges.

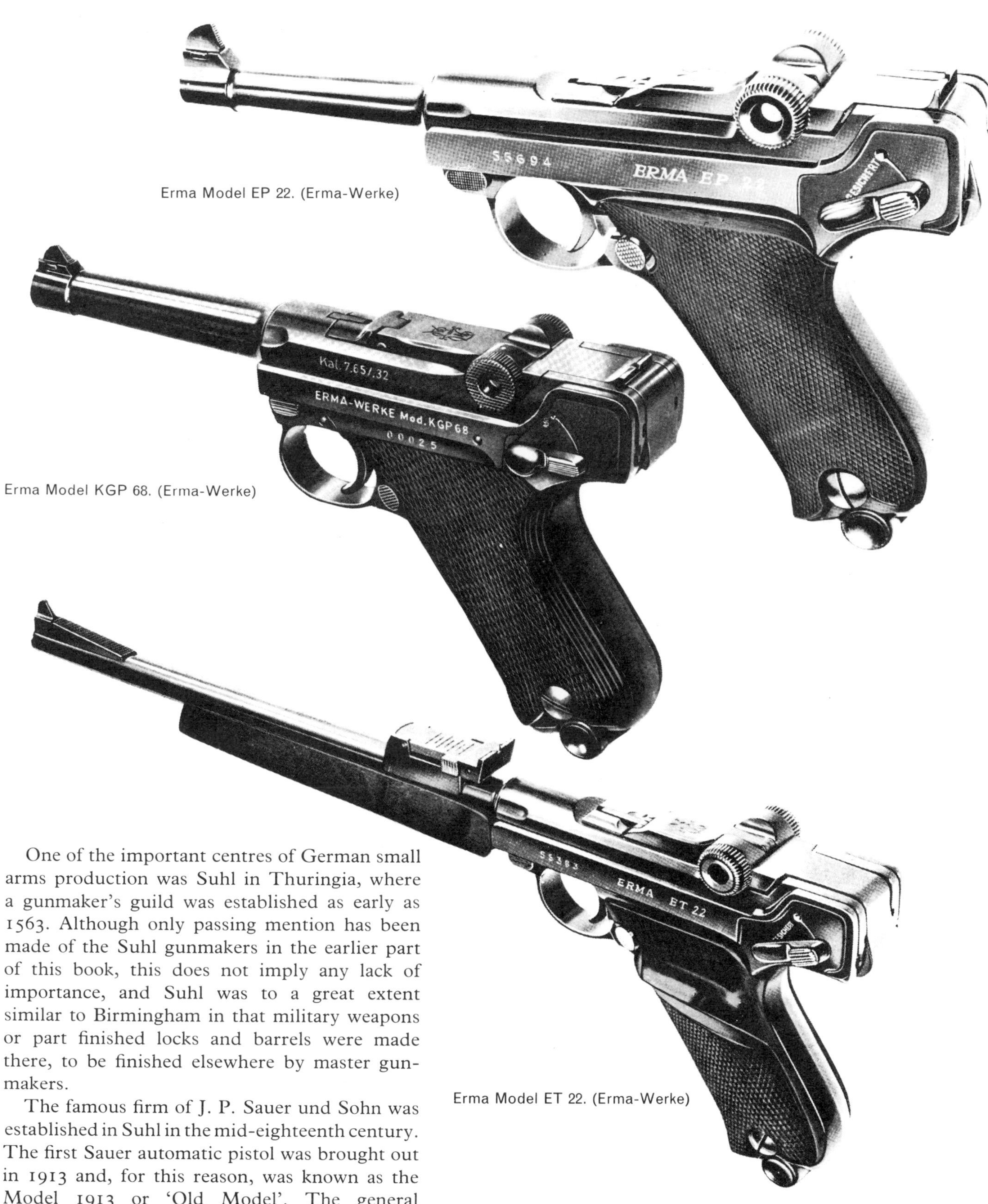

Erma Model EP 22. (Erma-Werke)

Erma Model KGP 68. (Erma-Werke)

Erma Model ET 22. (Erma-Werke)

One of the important centres of German small arms production was Suhl in Thuringia, where a gunmaker's guild was established as early as 1563. Although only passing mention has been made of the Suhl gunmakers in the earlier part of this book, this does not imply any lack of importance, and Suhl was to a great extent similar to Birmingham in that military weapons or part finished locks and barrels were made there, to be finished elsewhere by master gunmakers.

The famous firm of J. P. Sauer und Sohn was established in Suhl in the mid-eighteenth century. The first Sauer automatic pistol was brought out in 1913 and, for this reason, was known as the Model 1913 or 'Old Model'. The general arrangement can be seen from the illustration. To dismantle, the slide was drawn to the rear and locked by pushing the non-automatic slide lock

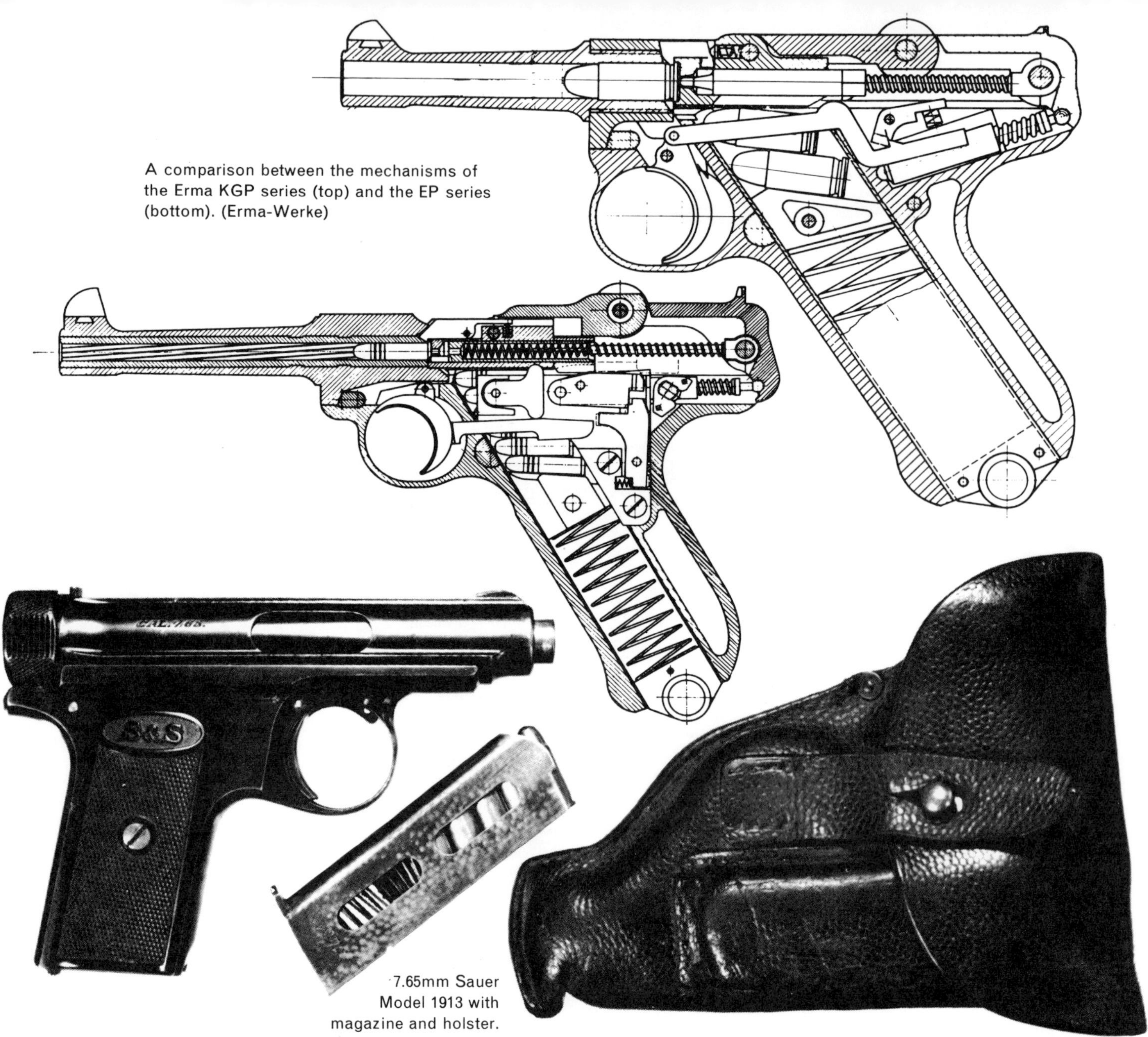

A comparison between the mechanisms of the Erma KGP series (top) and the EP series (bottom). (Erma-Werke)

7.65mm Sauer Model 1913 with magazine and holster.

inside the trigger guard upward. The magazine was removed and the rear sight depressed to release the milled take-down cap so that, held against spring pressure, it could be unscrewed. Breech block, striker and striker pin were then taken out. A pull on the trigger released the slide lock and the slide could be eased off the frame. On reassembly, the rear sight had to be kept raised to avoid engagement with the mainspring as the slide was replaced, and care had to be taken to ensure that the cap was screwed home and that the locking notch engaged with the rear sight. If a loaded magazine was inserted with the slide locked to the rear, the first pull on the trigger chambered the top cartridge, the second pull fired it. Neither magazine safety nor grip safety was fitted.

The original pistol was a seven shot 7.65mm (.32 ACP) calibre weapon, and, in 1920, a smaller 6.35mm version appeared. In 1930 it was redesigned as the 'Berhorden' or 'Authority' Model and was adopted for police use by the Dutch. The only difference between this and the earlier version was that the grip was improved to provide a better hold. One variant was manufactured with a light alloy slide. All the Sauer automatic pistols were very well made and satisfactory pocket weapons.

Somewhat in advance of the general trend, Sauer began experimenting with a double action auto-pistol as early as 1932. After prototype pistols had been made, the production version appeared in 1938 as the Sauer Model H, the designation later being altered to Model 38 (H).

Representing a further step in the evolution of this particular type of weapon, the Model H

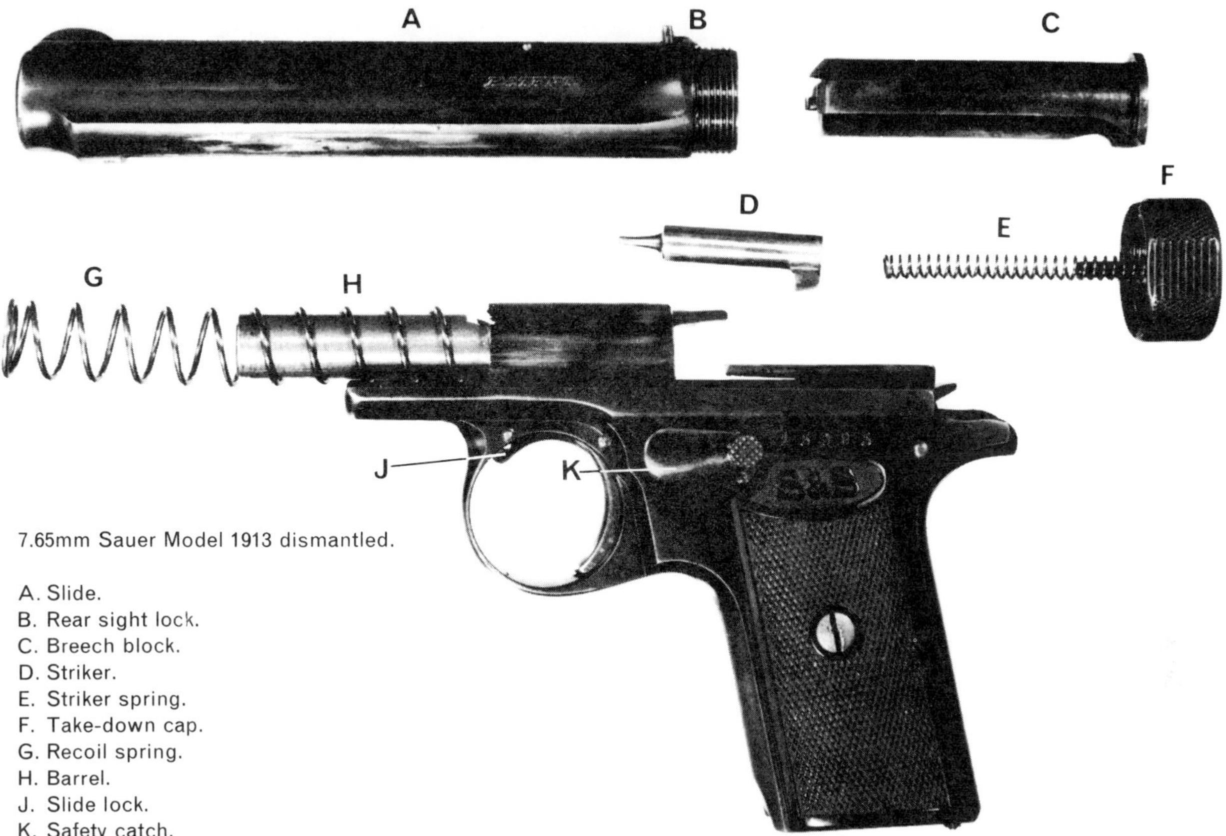

7.65mm Sauer Model 1913 dismantled.

A. Slide.
B. Rear sight lock.
C. Breech block.
D. Striker.
E. Striker spring.
F. Take-down cap.
G. Recoil spring.
H. Barrel.
J. Slide lock.
K. Safety catch.

embodied an interesting new feature whereby it could either be fired double action for the first shot by pressing the trigger, or else the internal hammer could be cocked by pressing the lever on the left hand side of the frame immediately above the magazine release button. Alternatively, the cocked hammer could be lowered by pressing the cocking lever until the sear was tripped, and then gradually releasing the pressure. To dismantle, the magazine was removed and the chamber checked to ensure that it was clear. The latch in the frame in front of the trigger was pulled down and the slide drawn to the rear and lifted until clear; it could then be allowed to slide forward off the barrel.

Made in 7.65mm calibre (6.35mm and 9mm short versions were projected but not put into production), this, the last of the J.P. Sauer pistols, was advanced in design and again well made. A magazine safety was fitted so that the pistol could not be discharged without the magazine, and the slide remained open after the last round had been fired. There was also a manual safety on the left hand rear of the slide. Towards the end of the production run the manual cocking lever was eliminated, most of the war production being for the Luftwaffe. After the war the original works in Suhl became the Fortuna Werke VEB (Suhl being in the Eastern Zone of Germany) and manufacture is confined to shotguns, accounting machines and pneumatic drills. The original company 'emigrated' to the Western Zone and, re-established at Eckernforde, are now making shotguns, combination guns and single shot rifles. The manufacture of automatic pistols has not been recommenced.

Another large and important pre-war manufacturer in Suhl was Waffenfabrik Simson, makers of shotguns, drillings, vierlings and several interesting vest pocket pistols. One of these is illustrated on page 488. It was of conventional design except that it was hammerless or striker operated and the barrel was removable. Simson are still in business in Suhl under the title of 'V.E.B. Fahrzeug-und Geratewerke Simson' and currently manufacture a range of shotguns, combination guns etc. on traditional lines. No automatic pistols are now made.

Typical of the smaller Suhl manufacturers was the firm of Becker and Hollander, makers of the Beholla 7.65mm blow-back pistol. Production started during the First World War and early examples had hard rubber grips with the 'BH'

7.65mm Sauer Model 38(H).

An automatic pistol by Simson of Suhl.

monogram. August Menz, also of Suhl, made a very similar pistol to the Beholla under the trade name 'Menta', and apparently a 6.35mm version as well.

August Menz was also the maker of the Lilliput automatic pistol which was manufactured in 4.25mm and 6.35mm calibres. A straight blowback striker fired weapon with a magazine capacity of six cartridges, both models were very much alike, the 4.25mm version being only $3\frac{1}{2}''$ long.

Although the 4.25mm Lilliput cartridge is not the smallest to have been used in an automatic pistol, it is today considered quite a scarce item and a collector's piece. It was originally developed for the Austrian Erika pistol made before the First World War by the firm of Pfanni, but the Erika itself was soon displaced by the Menz

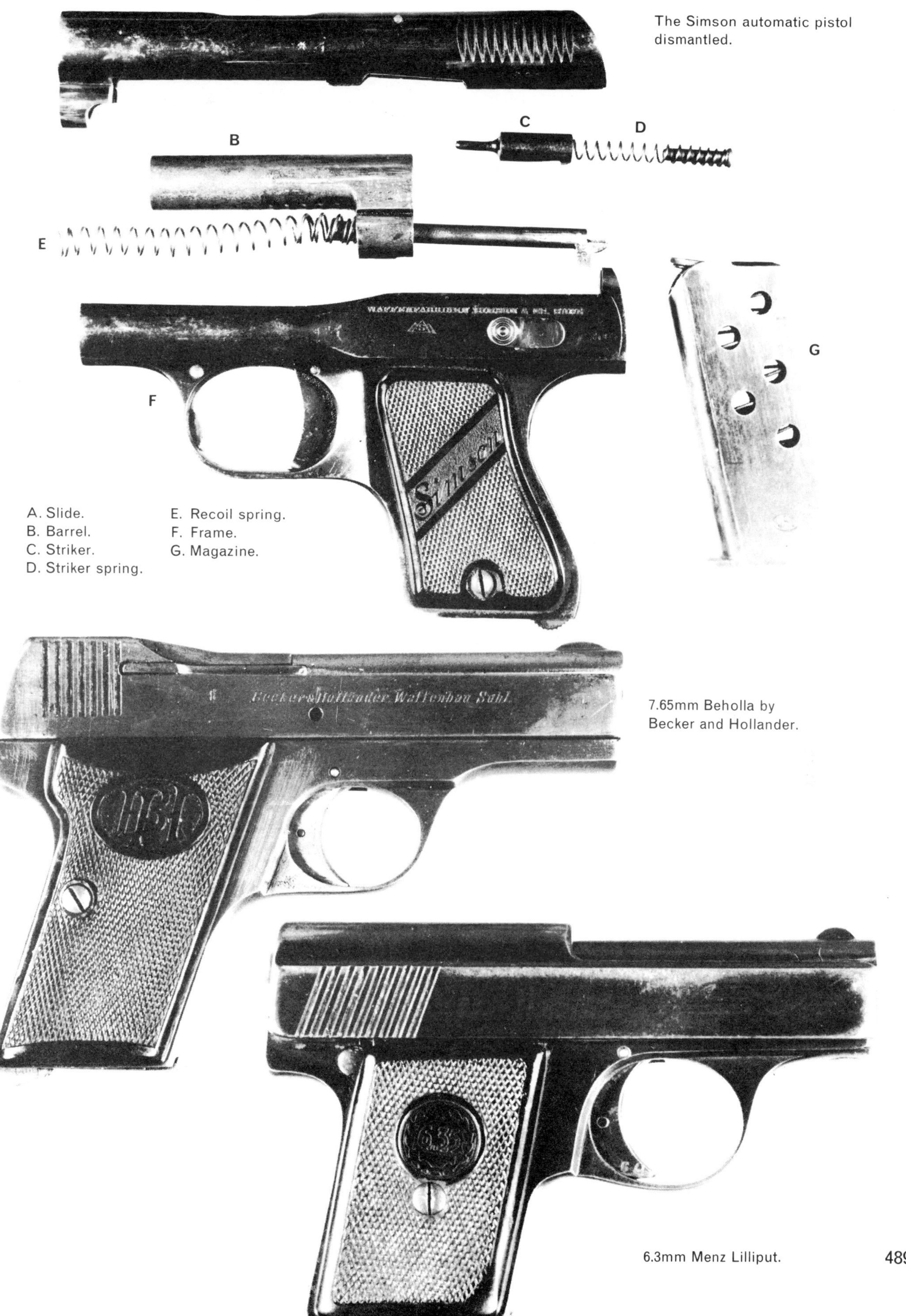

The Simson automatic pistol dismantled.

A. Slide.
B. Barrel.
C. Striker.
D. Striker spring.
E. Recoil spring.
F. Frame.
G. Magazine.

7.65mm Beholla by Becker and Hollander.

6.3mm Menz Lilliput.

7.65mm auto-pistol by Jager of Suhl.

6.35mm 'Einhand' Lignose by Bergmann.

7.65mm Dreyse Model 1907. (Glasgow Police Collection)

7.65mm automatic pistol by Franz Stock of Berlin. (See page 492.)

Lilliput. The smallest centre-fire cartridge manufactured commercially was the 2.7mm Kolibri made for the automatic pistol of the same name introduced about 1914. There was also a 3mm Kolibri, the manufacture of which was discontinued during the First World War.

The Suhl gunmakers were not, however, merely content to follow conventional patterns of design, and the Jager 7.65mm auto-pistol made prior to 1914 by Jager of Suhl was an example of advanced production techniques. The receiver of this pistol was fabricated from sheet metal and castings, with the result that costly forgings and machine operations were to a great extent eliminated. In spite of its unique design features, the Jager was both heavier and bulkier than contemporary 7.65mm pistols and, for this reason, was not a success. The magazine had a spur on the base which could be used as a tool to facilitate dismantling.

In the 1920's there was, as a result of the aftermath of war, considerable reorganisation of the many arms firms in Suhl, but the famous Theodor Bergmann continued to manufacture automatic pistols, some of which were sold by a sales organisation, Akt. Gesellschaft Lignose-Abt. Suhl, one division of a combine with headquarters in Berlin. Two new types of pistol appeared in 1920, the 'Taschen' or pocket pistol, and the 'Einhand' or one hand pistol. Both of these were made in Suhl, and the general principle of operation was based on the 1906 Browning. The 'Einhand' models are interesting in that they represented an attempt to overcome the basic problem with an automatic pistol, the need to pull back the slide to chamber the first cartridge. Several people, including Ole Krag, the Norwegian arms inventor, had experimented with 'one handed' operation, and the American White-Merrill, which competed in the US Army trials, had been another attempt to solve the problem. But neither of these designs got beyond the experimental stage. The principle adopted by Bergmann for the Lignose pistols was the invention of Witwold Chylewski, an Austrian.

Einhand pistols were characterised by the use of an extension to the slide which formed the front of the trigger guard. Pulling back on this with the trigger finger caused the slide itself to retract and cock the action. When it was released, a cartridge was chambered. The finger was then placed on the trigger and the pistol fired.

Pistols of this type enjoyed a brief popularity, but it was impractical to use the system for pistols of greater power than .25 ACP (6.35mm) since the effort needed to retract the slide was too great. Also the cartridge had to be relatively short so that slide retraction was not unduly cumbersome. For these reasons the 'one hand' system was restricted to small calibre weapons which, as later events have shown, turned out to be no more than a passing fad.

The name of Nikolaus von Dreyse, the famous inventor of the Prussian needle gun, was revered in the German Empire and, though he died in 1867, his name appeared on many weapons designed long after his death. The original Dreyse factory was known after 1901 as the Rheinische Metallwaren und Maschinenfabrik (often referred to as 'Rheinmetall') and, in 1907, a 7.65 mm auto-pistol was introduced bearing the name Dreyse. Designed by the famous Louis Schmeisser, then an engineer at the Sommerda Division of Rheinmetall, it was a rather awkward pistol and was soon made obsolete by the more advanced designs of Browning. Schmeisser also designed a smaller 6.35mm Dreyse pistol which bore a strong resemblance to the Browning 1906, and, in 1910, a straight blow-back pistol for the 9mm Parabellum. Due to the immensely strong recoil spring required, the slide could not be retracted with one hand, and the pistol was so designed that it could be disengaged for loading and only the mainspring had to be cocked. Once the pistol had been fired, slide operation was, of course, automatic. The last of the automatic pistols made by Rheinmetall was sold under the company name and marked 'Rheinmetall Abt. Sommerda'. Manufactured for only a brief period during the early 1930's, it was a copy of the 1910 Browning. In 1935 Rheinmetall combined with the firm of A. Borsig to form Rheinmetall-Borsig AG which became one of the largest arms and munitions industries of the Third Reich.

Hugo Schmeisser, Louis Schmeisser's son, became the Chief Engineer of the C.G. Haenel Waffen und Fahrradfabrik of Suhl, a firm known to most small boys of the pre-war period as makers of very desirable air pistols and air rifles. Haenel designed two small pocket pistols in 6.35mm calibre, Model I bearing the monogram 'HS' on the grip, Model II the name Schmeisser in full. The design originated about 1920, the Model II appearing in 1930. Both pistols were blow-back striker fired weapons, but they embodied one interesting feature that has not since been copied.

Many automatic pistols employed—and employ—a magazine safety device to prevent the discharge of the cartridge remaining in the breech after the magazine has been withdrawn. Hugo Schmeisser went one stage further. In his pistols the magazine could not be withdrawn unless the safety had been applied. The pistol could not be discharged with the safety applied and could not be fired after re-insertion of the magazine until the safety had been placed in the 'off' position.

In the early 1920's the firm of Franz Stock of Berlin introduced a range of simple blow-back pistols and, by March 1925, these were available in .22, 6.35mm and 7.65mm calibres. Only the 7.65mm has been examined but, from contemporary catalogue illustrations, all models followed the same general type of construction.

To dismantle the Stock, the magazine was removed and the slide pulled to the rear and locked by pushing the thumb safety upwards to engage a small notch on the left hand side. The large headed screw at the rear of the slide was unscrewed and the striker spring and striker removed. To disengage the catch locking the breech block to the slide, the front of the extractor had to be lifted; the breech block could then be pulled forward and raised, and the slide could be allowed to move forward along the barrel under restraint.

The Stock was a well made pistol of sound design, and the 7.65mm version is both pleasant and easy to shoot.

One pistol that was very popular during the inter-war years was the Ortgies, commercial manufacture of which was started by Heinrich Ortgies at Erfurt in 1920. The first pistol was a 7.65mm calibre, production of which was taken over by Deutsche Werke AG shortly after the business was established. A 6.35mm version was introduced later and, for a short time, a 9mm short model was also made. During the period of manufacture, which came to an end about 1926, the Ortgies became very popular in Central Europe and many were exported to America. The design was interesting since there was not a single screw anywhere; even the grips were retained by a spring-loaded catch. There was no fixed ejector and, after the fired case had been extracted from the chamber, it was ejected by the firing pin protruding through the bolt face. Once the procedure was known, dismantling was easy. The magazine was removed and the pistol checked to ensure it was unloaded. The slide was

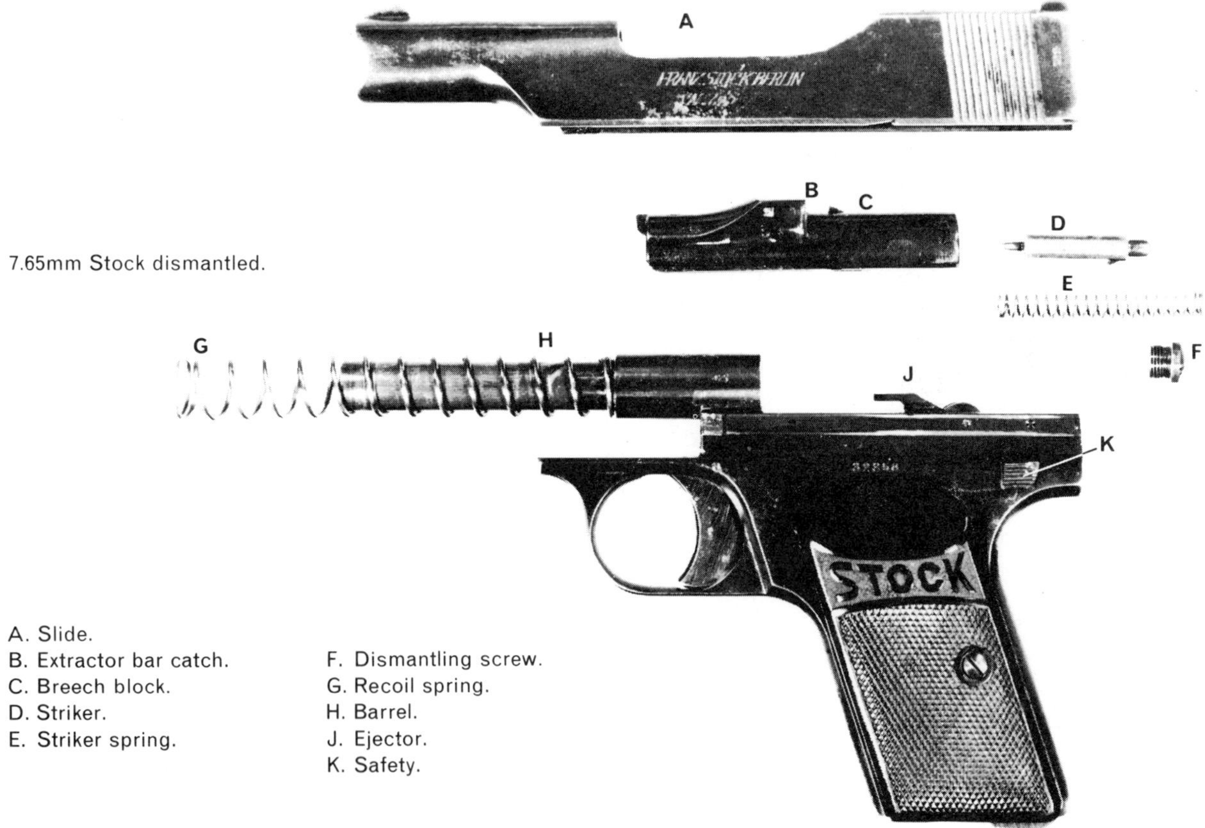

7.65mm Stock dismantled.

A. Slide.
B. Extractor bar catch.
C. Breech block.
D. Striker.
E. Striker spring.
F. Dismantling screw.
G. Recoil spring.
H. Barrel.
J. Ejector.
K. Safety.

then retracted until the slide serrations lined up with the rear of the frame, the take-down catch on the left side of the receiver was pressed in and the slide lifted free. The barrel was removed by turning it anti-clockwise until it was at right angles to the frame; it could then be lifted off. All Ortgies pistols, those made by the inventor and those made by Deutsche Werke, had wooden grips, some of which were plain, while others bore the monogram 'HO' or a 'lion couchant' in the shape of a letter 'D'.

Some five kilometres north of the great arms centre of Suhl are the twin towns of Zella-Mehlis. There, one of the earliest makers of automatic pistols was Langenham Gewehre und Fahrradfabrik, established in 1842. Early in the First World War, Langenham began manufacture of the FL automatic pistol, which was initially made for the German army. The FL was of the

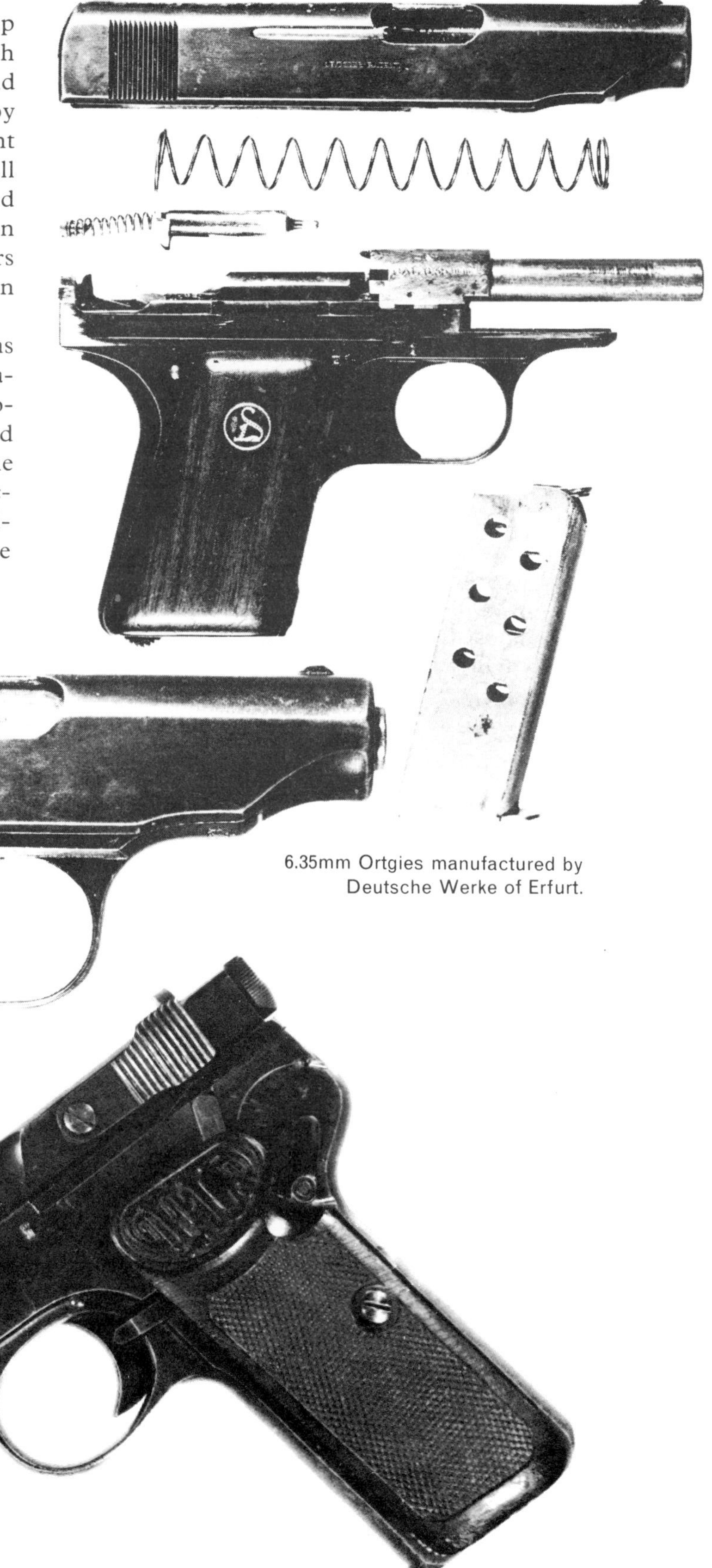

6.35mm Ortgies manufactured by Deutsche Werke of Erfurt.

7.65mm FL by Langenham.

blow-back type, with the slide and breech block made as separate units. A stirrup hinged to the slide locked both together, the stirrup itself being secured by a large milled headed screw. Slackening the screw allowed the stirrup to be hinged upward so that the slide and recoil spring could be removed, the breech block sliding off the frame to the rear. It was important to ensure that the take-down screw was properly tightened since, should it become loose, the stirrup could be released, with the result that the breech block would fly to the rear when the gun was fired. The FL was made in 6.35mm and 7.65mm versions, and several modifications to the design were introduced until the pistol went out of production around 1930.

If we compare a German catalogue of the 1930 period with one issued today, a quick glance through the section devoted to pistols and revolvers shows very clearly how many important manufacturers of automatic pistols are no longer in business. One name that will appear in both catalogues is that of Walther; from the current one, Lilliput, Menz, Schmeisser, FL, Kommer and Lignose have all vanished.

Carl Walther, the founder of the company which still bears his name, opened his own gunshop in Zella in 1886 to make precision target rifles. He was joined in the business by his three sons Fritz, Georg and Erich, and it was Fritz who, in 1907, designed the first Walther automatic pistol. This was their answer to the enormously successful FN Browning 'Vest-Pocket' Model of 1905, and it was placed on the market in 1908. The Walther was a simple blow-back striker fired pistol in 6.35mm (.25 ACP) calibre. Magazine capacity was six cartridges and there was a thumb safety on the left hand side of the frame behind the grip panel. To dismantle, the catch at the front of the trigger guard was pressed in and the slide was drawn to the rear and lifted off the frame; it was then eased forward over the top of the barrel.

The 6.35mm Walther Model 2 introduced in 1909 was slightly smaller than the Model 1. A knurled bushing retained the slide and, after it had been unscrewed, the slide could be withdrawn forward off the receiver. The Model 2 had the recoil spring arranged around the barrel instead of underneath it, as on the Model 1.

The first 'pocket model' was the Walther Model 3 (Models 1 and 2 were really vest pocket models). It was similar in appearance to the Model 2, but was of the larger 7.65mm (.32 ACP) calibre. An enclosed hammer was employed instead of the striker operation of the Model 2, but the magazine capacity remained at six rounds. The barrel bushing was not knurled as previously and had to be pushed in and turned for removal.

Also introduced in 1910, the Walther Model 4 was a larger version with an extended grip to allow for a longer magazine, the capacity of which was increased to eight rounds. The barrel was also extended and a special cylindrical slide extension was employed which was locked to the slide by a bayonet type catch. The first version had an external trigger bar on the left hand side of the trigger, but a later version had it enclosed. Dismantling was simple. The magazine was removed and the chamber checked. The slide extension was pushed inward against the recoil spring tension and turned to the left; it could then

6.35mm Walther Model 1 of 1908.

6.35mm Walther Model 2 of 1909.

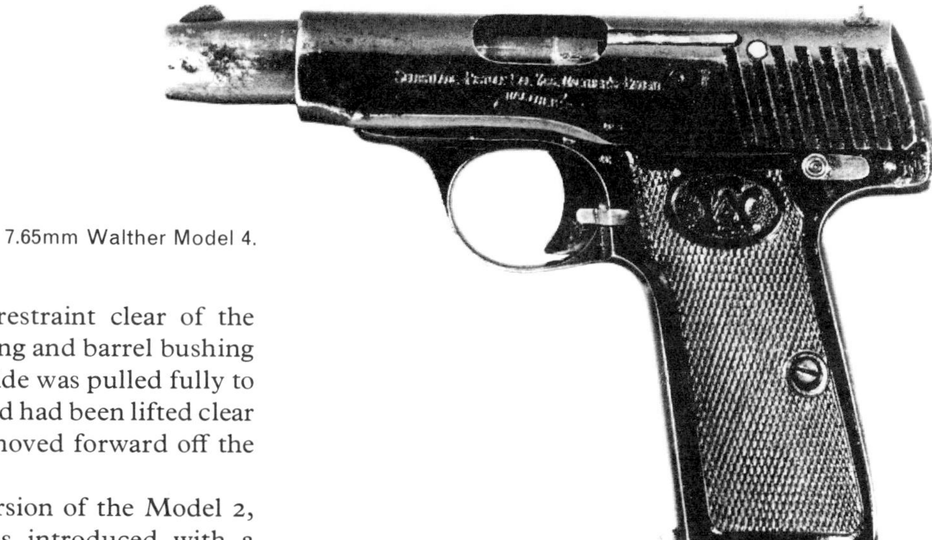

7.65mm Walther Model 4.

be drawn forward under restraint clear of the barrel. When the recoil spring and barrel bushing had been withdrawn, the slide was pulled fully to the rear and, once its rear end had been lifted clear of the guides, it could be moved forward off the barrel.

In 1913 an improved version of the Model 2, the Walther Model 5, was introduced with a similar general design but a much improved finish. The Model 6 can really be regarded as a war-time expedient. It was, in effect, a variant of the Model 4 designed to take the 9mm Parabellum cartridge. After only two years production, manufacture was discontinued in 1917 and examples are rather rare. If this pistol is fired today, it should not be used with 9mm Parabellum ammunition. There is now so great a variation in ballistics that damage to the pistol is

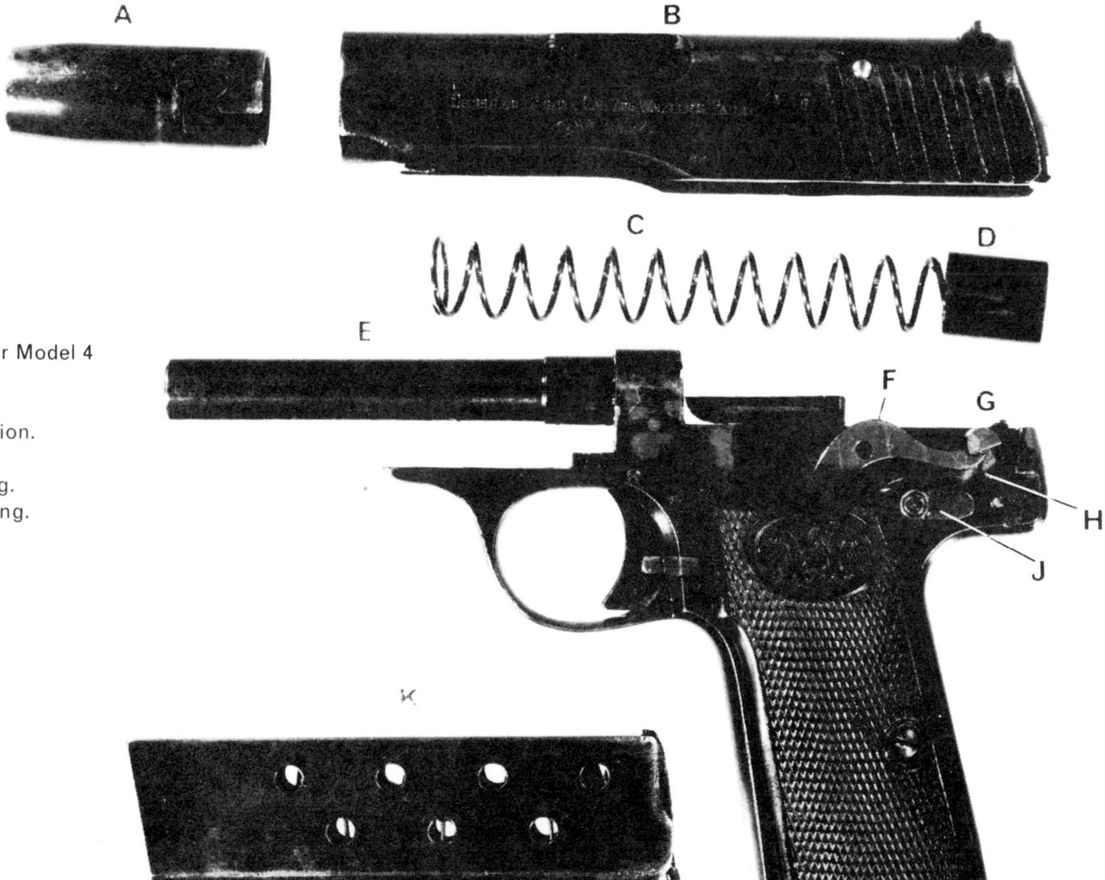

7.65mm Walther Model 4 dismantled.

A. Slide extension.
B. Slide.
C. Recoil spring.
D. Barrel bushing.
E. Barrel.
F. Trigger bar.
G. Hammer.
H. Sear.
J. Safety.
K. Magazine.

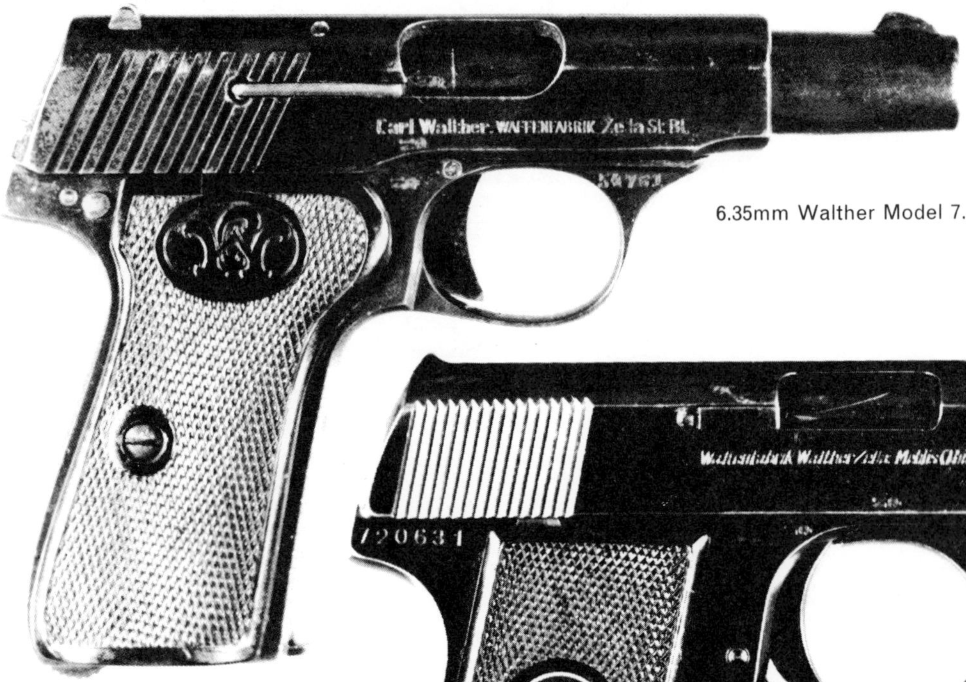

6.35mm Walther Model 7.

6.35mm Walther Model 8.

6.35mm Walther Model 9.

not unlikely and, with unsuitable ammunition, there is a possibility of actual hazard. An insufficient margin of safety, coupled with the margin of error created by wartime manufacture, typified the Model 6, and none were ever offered for commercial sale by reputable concerns.

The Model 7, smaller than but otherwise identical to the Model 4 except that the ejection port was in the right hand side, was introduced in 1917 and, as a small, easily concealable pocket pistol, was very popular with German officers. It went out of production, however, the following year.

One of the most popular of the Walther 6.35mm pistols, the Model 8, appeared in 1920 to mark the re-commencement of firearms production, and can be regarded as the direct ancestor of the PP series. It was this pistol that introduced unit slide construction and, although a takedown catch was employed on early models, later examples used the trigger guard itself as the slide lock. Manufacture continued until 1945.

The Model 9, a true 'vest pocket type' first marketed in 1921, had an overall length of just under 4″. In many respects it resembled the first Walther pistol and had the recoil spring under the barrel. There was no ejector, the firing pin serving this purpose, and the magazine capacity was six rounds. The 6.35 mm Models 8 and 9 were available in a variety of special styles with either pearl or ivory grips, and with engraved nickel or gold plated finishes.

In 1929 the Walther Model PP or Polizei Pistole was introduced, the first commercially successful double action automatic pistol. Initially made in 7.65 mm calibre (.32 ACP), it was

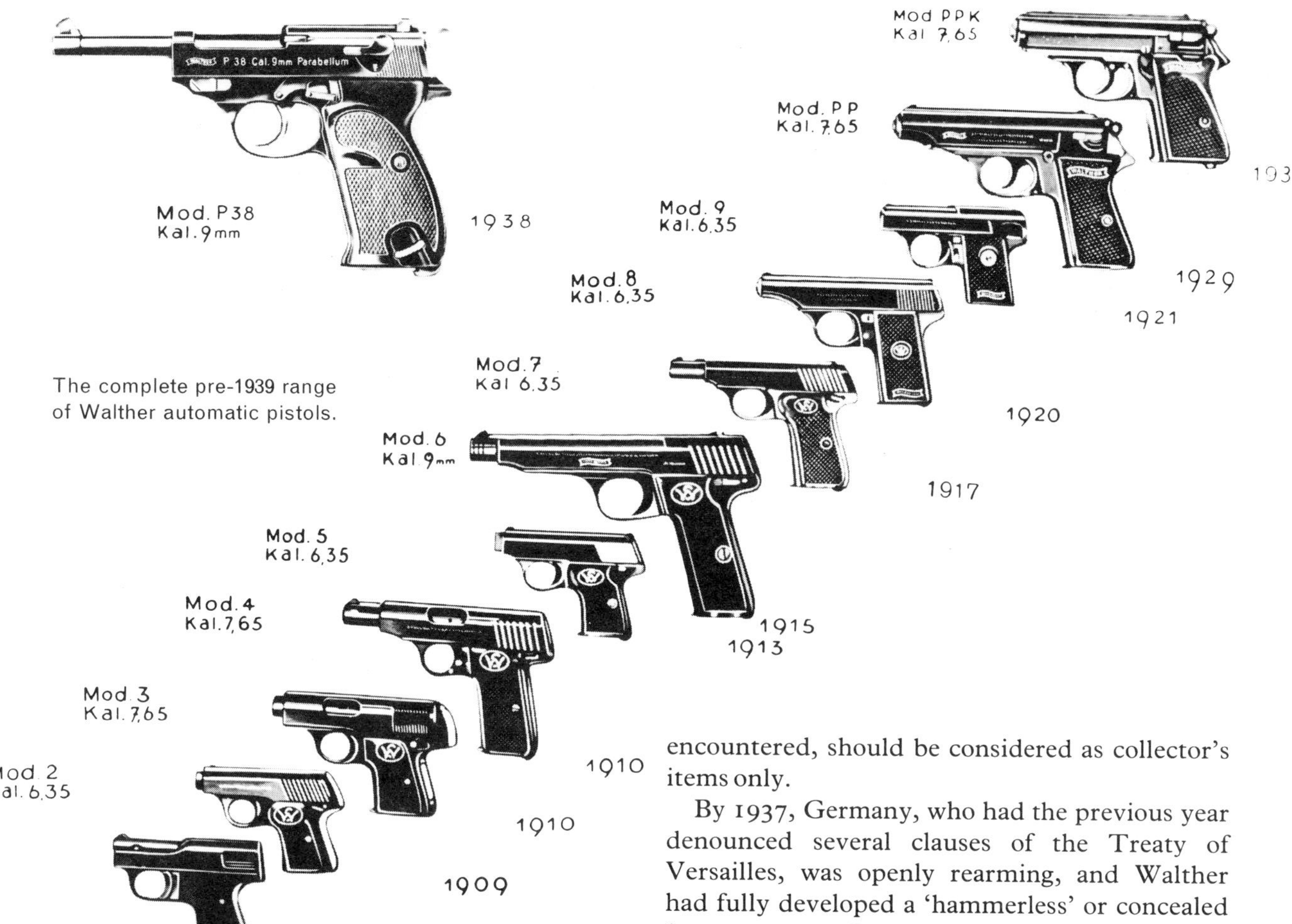

The complete pre-1939 range of Walther automatic pistols.

later offered in .22 long rifle and 9mm short (.380). A shorter and lighter version of the PP was introduced in 1931 as the PPK Model (Polizei Pistole, Kriminal) and was intended for concealed use. Calibres available were the same as for the Model PP and both versions were offered for a short time in 6.35mm.

In addition to the new double action feature, the PP and PPK models introduced the 'signal pin' which was mounted above the firing pin and protruded to the rear when a cartridge was in the chamber. The stress of wartime production led to the elimination of this device, but it was re-introduced again after the war.

In an attempt to evade the conditions of the Treaty of Versailles which prohibited 'the manufacture or sale of pistols or revolvers of 9mm Parabellum calibre by German or Austrian arms manufacturers', Walther produced a larger version of the PP model chambered for the 9mm Parabellum cartridge. Since the Model MP, as it was known, was a simple blow-back pistol, the strictures that applied to the Model 6 are equally valid here. The Model MP was never offered for sale commercially and specimens, although rarely encountered, should be considered as collector's items only.

By 1937, Germany, who had the previous year denounced several clauses of the Treaty of Versailles, was openly rearming, and Walther had fully developed a 'hammerless' or concealed hammer 9mm Parabellum pistol with a locked breech—the first they had designed. This was the rare Armee Pistole (Model AP) and it appeared in several variant forms and differing barrel lengths.

The Model HP or Heeres Pistole (Service Pistol) embodied the double action features of the PP and PPK Models and, with the exception of the external hammer, closely resembled the Model AP. The Heeres Pistole was the direct and immediate ancestor of the Walther P-38 and late production versions are indistinguishable except for the slide markings. The modified Heeres Pistole, which had plastic grips instead of checkered wood ones and also a repositioned magazine catch, was adopted by the German Army in 1938 as the Pistole 38 and manufacture was undertaken by Walther at Zella Mehlis, by Mauser at Oberndorf and by Spreewerke at Berlin-Spandau. The code number 480 or the code letters 'ac' were applied to those made by Walther, the letters 'byf' or 'svw' to those made by Mauser, and the letters 'cyq' to the smaller quantity made by Spreewerke. As the war continued the quality of the P-38 deteriorated. Most of them, except those marked 'cyq' (Spreewerke), bore the last two digits of the year of manufacture under the code letters.

9mm Walther Model HP or Heeres Pistole.

As with any pistol made under wartime stress, the military issue P-38 should be carefully checked before it is fired today. It is, for example, quite possible to reassemble the pistol without the locking block and, if the pistol is then fired, the slide will jam in the rear position; it is only prevented from being blown off the slide by the two recoil spring guide pins and the lugs inside the slide. On most of the wartime P-38 pistols a modified type of safety was employed, and these pistols can be identified by the round headed firing pin; earlier models with mechanical retraction of the firing pin had rectangular firing pin heads. When the safety lever is moved downward to 'safe', the 'relief piece' on the left of the frame is also pushed downward by the safety lever barrel; the internal cocking piece is lifted and the hammer released. But, since the barrel of the safety lever is arranged to lock against shoulders in the firing pin before the hammer is released (so preventing it from being impelled forward), the pistol, even with a loaded cartridge in the breech, will not fire. For this system to operate successfully, it is obvious that one must be able to rely on the fit and on the general tolerances of both the firing pin and the safety lever barrel. In addition, the metallurgical properties of both components must not be

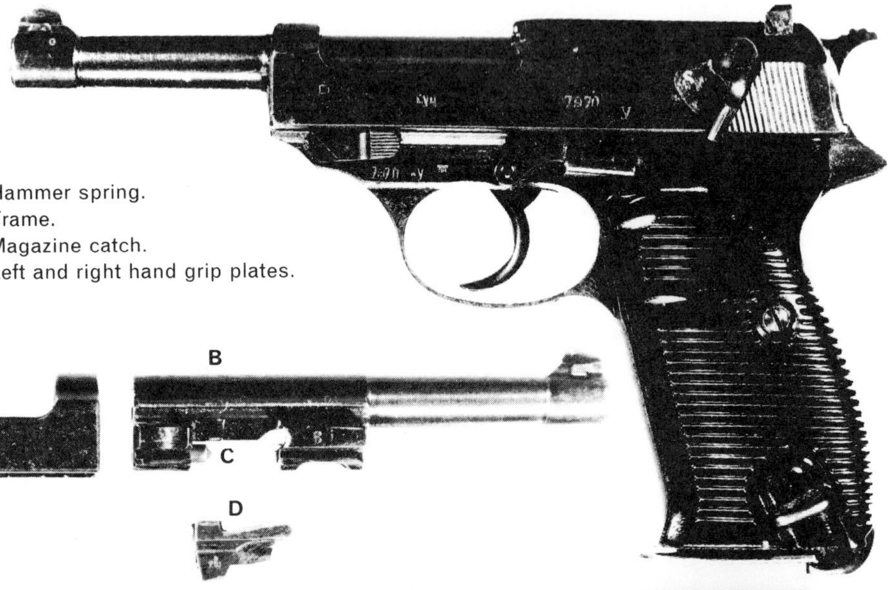

9mm Walther P-38

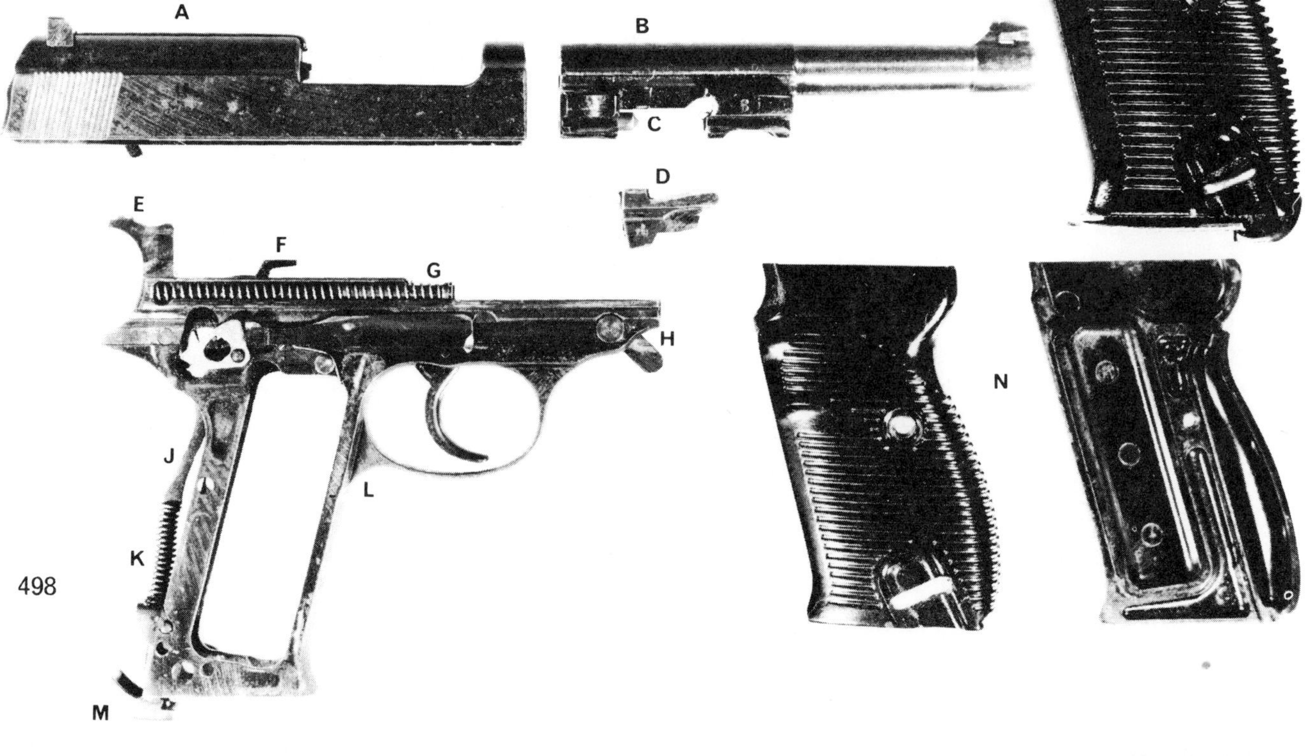

Walther P-38 dismantled.
A. Slide.
B. Barrel.
C. Locking block pin.
D. Locking block.
E. Hammer.
F. Ejector.
G. Recoil spring and guide.
H. Barrel retaining latch.
J. Hammer strut.
K. Hammer spring.
L. Frame.
M. Magazine catch.
N. Left and right hand grip plates.

suspect since a crack or softening of the material will adversely affect operation. In any event, the safety lever should only be used to lower the hammer on a live round when the muzzle of the pistol is pointed in a safe direction. Verification of the condition of the safety system can be obtained by lifting the slide cover plate and examining the signal pin, firing pin lock and the firing pin limit stop pin. It is emphasised that this safety system is one of the best devised, providing the pistol is of commercial manufacture.

At the end of the war the factory at Zella-Mehlis was destroyed. Fritz Walther fled the Russian occupation and, in a small village in Wurtemburg, he began to plan the manufacture of his calculating machines, production of which dated back to the 1920's. A factory was established at Niederstotzingen and additional premises secured in Gerstetten. In 1950 the first post-war Walther weapon, an air rifle, was designed and manufactured in a disused cavalry barracks at Ulm on the Danube.

Back in 1932 Walther had brought out the first of the Olympia models, a hammerless (or enclosed hammer) .22 blow-back target pistol with a ten round magazine which was first seen at the 1932 Olympics in Los Angeles. A .22 short version was also made with a light alloy slide, and it was an improved version of this model, the Fünfkampf, that appeared in the 1936 Olympics, the first to be held in Germany, and won the first five places in the competitions for which it was entered. The Standard version lacked the barrel weights of the Fünfkampf and, among other variants, a Rapid Fire version was chambered for the .22 short. Barrel length was 7.44″ (although a version was available with a 4″ barrel) and take-down was the same as for the PP and PPK models, the trigger guard acting as a slide lock. In 1945 Hammerli of Lenzburg in Switzerland were licensed to manufacture the Olympia—one of the truly outstanding target pistols of the world—and subsequent production by Hammerli will be dealt with later.

Walther also entered into an agreement with Manufacture de Machines du Haut-Rhin at Mulhouse in France who began to produce the Walther PP and PPK under the 'Manurhin' trade mark. The Model PP was made in .32, .380 and .22 long rifle, and the PPK appeared in a standard and also a lightweight version with a dural frame. The standard PPK was made in the same calibre range as the Model PP, but the lightweight model was not made in .380. In

The Walther PPK dismantled, the spare magazine lacking the extension grip.

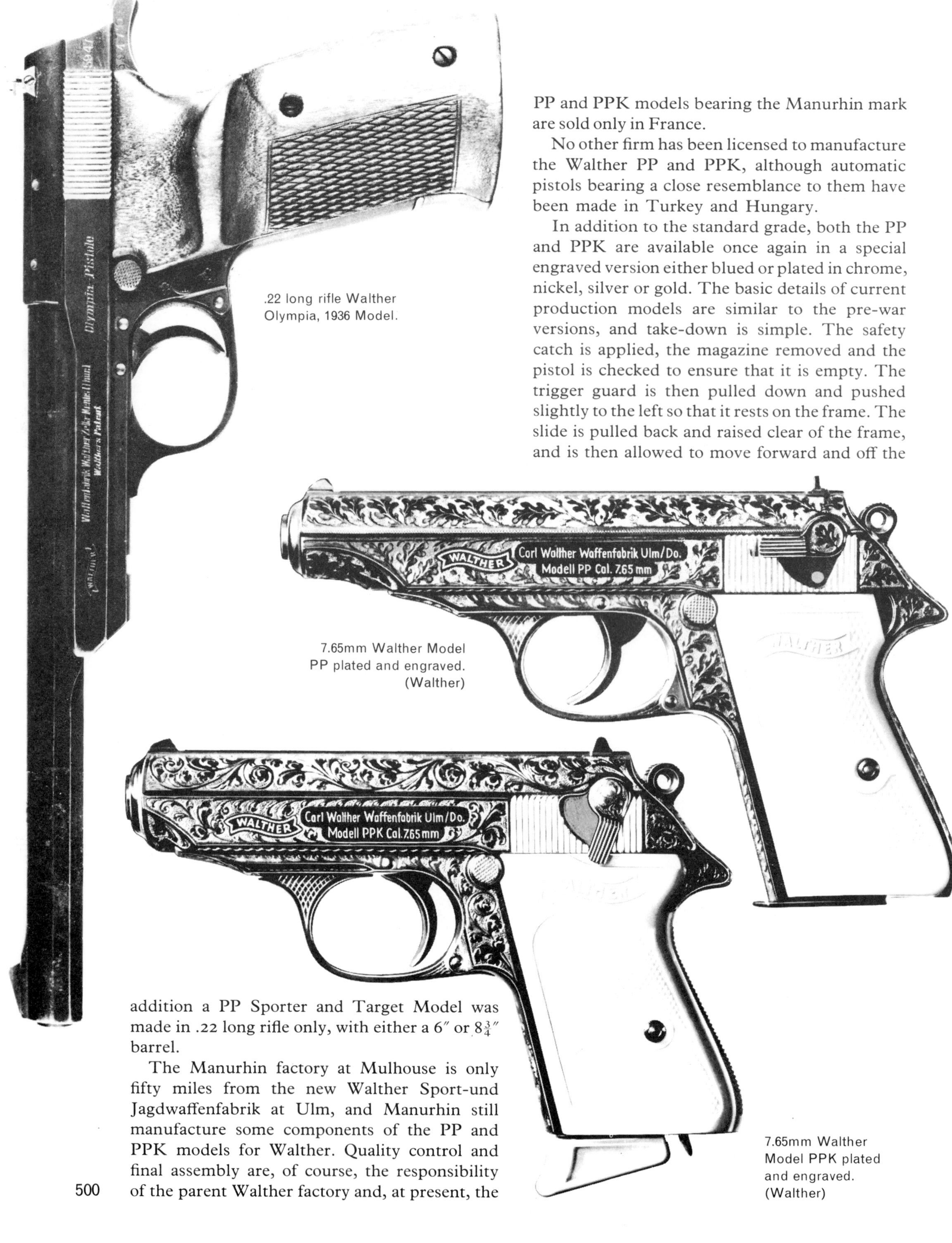

.22 long rifle Walther Olympia, 1936 Model.

7.65mm Walther Model PP plated and engraved. (Walther)

7.65mm Walther Model PPK plated and engraved. (Walther)

addition a PP Sporter and Target Model was made in .22 long rifle only, with either a 6″ or $8\frac{3}{4}$″ barrel.

The Manurhin factory at Mulhouse is only fifty miles from the new Walther Sport-und Jagdwaffenfabrik at Ulm, and Manurhin still manufacture some components of the PP and PPK models for Walther. Quality control and final assembly are, of course, the responsibility of the parent Walther factory and, at present, the PP and PPK models bearing the Manurhin mark are sold only in France.

No other firm has been licensed to manufacture the Walther PP and PPK, although automatic pistols bearing a close resemblance to them have been made in Turkey and Hungary.

In addition to the standard grade, both the PP and PPK are available once again in a special engraved version either blued or plated in chrome, nickel, silver or gold. The basic details of current production models are similar to the pre-war versions, and take-down is simple. The safety catch is applied, the magazine removed and the pistol is checked to ensure that it is empty. The trigger guard is then pulled down and pushed slightly to the left so that it rests on the frame. The slide is pulled back and raised clear of the frame, and is then allowed to move forward and off the

9mm Walther P-38, current production model (Walther)

1. Barrel. 2. Foresight. 3. Locking-piece. 4. Locking pin. 5. V-spring. Unit II: Slide. 6. Slide body. 7. Cover. 8. Signal-pin. 9. Rear sight. 10. Extractor. 11. Firing pin. 12. Firing pin lock. 13. Spring to No. 12. 14. Extractor pin. 15. Limit stop pin. 16. Firing pin spring. 17. Signal pin spring. 18. Extractor spring. 19. Safety lever unit. 20. Rest pin. 21. Rest pin spring. Unit III: Grip. 22. Frame. 23. Rest pin. 24. Rest pin spring. 25. Trigger connector. 26. Cocking-piece. 27. Barrel catch lever. 28. Striker rod. 29. Relief piece. 30. Release lever. 31. Ejector. 32. Recoil spring guide pins. 33. Hammer pin. 34. Cocking piece pin. 35. Recoil springs. 36. Striker rod spring. 37. Trigger rod spring. 38. Cocking piece spring. 39. Hammer. 40. Hammer trap. 41. Pins to Nos. 39 and 40. 42. Hammer trap spring. 43. Trigger. 44. Sleeve. 45. Trigger spring. 46. Magazine holder. 47. Catch lever. 48. Grip plate, right. 49. Grip plate, left. 50. Grip plate screw. Unit IV: Magazine. 51. Magazine casing. 52. Feeder platform. 53. Magazine bottom lock. 54. Magazine bottom. 55. Feeder spring.

.22 short Walther Model OSP. (Walther)

barrel. The PP and PPK can be fired 'single action' by thumb cocking the hammer or 'double action' merely by pulling the trigger. The safety lever permits the hammer to be let down on a loaded chamber; the safety lever barrel locks the firing pin, and the hammer is blocked by a locking piece to prevent contact. This most effective safety system, coupled with the double action feature, has made the PP and PPK models deservedly successful.

The income from the Hammerli and Manurhin licensing arrangements, together with the success of his post-war business machine venture, enabled Fritz Walther to start manufacture of the P-38 again in his own factory at Ulm. Initial manufacture was earmarked for the Army of the Federal Republic of Germany, but subsequent production was made available commercially. No basic changes were made in the design and the safety system is that of the wartime P-38 already referred to. When uncocking the pistol, current factory instructions advise that the following procedure should be carried out. Hold the pistol in the right hand with the index finger outside the trigger guard. Grip the hammer with the right thumb and push the safety lever downward with the left. Let the hammer down slowly under restraint, with the muzzle of the pistol pointing in a safe direction. Discretion is advised, but it is emphasised that the procedure is considerably safer than, for example, carrying out the same operation with the Browning Model 1935 or the Colt 1911 where there is no provision for locking the firing pin and where an accidental discharge could occur if, due to carelessness or fatigue, the hammer were to slip from under the thumb.

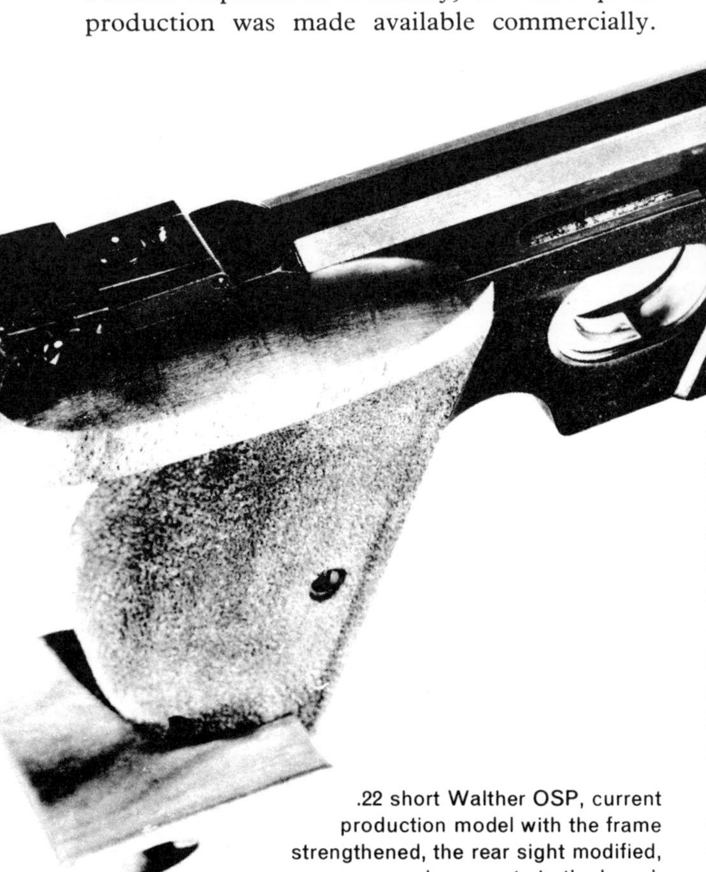

.22 short Walther OSP, current production model with the frame strengthened, the rear sight modified, and gas ports in the barrel.

When the last round has been fired, the slide stays open. If a loaded magazine is introduced, the slide can be returned either by easing it back slightly to release the slide lock or by pressing the lever on the left hand side of the frame. Dismantling is easy. Check that the pistol is unloaded. Insert an empty magazine, set the safety lever to 'safe' and pull the slide to the rear until it stays open. Then turn the barrel catch at the left front of the frame downward so that the slide can be moved forward clear of the frame. To remove the barrel from the slide, the latter is turned upside down and the locking belt is

.22 long rifle Walther Model GSP. (Walther)

6.35mm Walther Model TP. (Walther)

.22 long rifle Walther Model TPH. (Walther)

pressed forward with the index finger. This lifts the locking piece out of the recesses in the slide and permits the barrel to be removed.

The firm of Carl Walther are by no means resting on past successes. In 1962 the .22 short Olympia Schnellfeuer Pistole (Model OSP) was announced and, following slight modification, is currently in production. Its appearance is unorthodox, due mainly to the location of the magazine in front of the trigger guard. The bolt is cylindrical and operates inside the receiver; there is no recoiling slide. Because of the advanced stock design and the provision of a large adjustable hand-rest, it is an extremely pleasant pistol to shoot with. The action is hammerless and the bolt remains open after the last shot has been fired. One feature of this pistol is the fully adjustable trigger mechanism which can be easily removed from the sheet alloy frame following removal of the barrel and receiver. Take-down is simple. The pistol is checked to ensure that it is unloaded and uncocked, and the magazine is removed. The large barrel locking lever on the left hand side of the frame is rotated forward through 180 degrees, and the barrel is then pulled forward clear of the frame. The receiver is lifted slightly at the front end and pulled forward so that the trigger mechanism can be pushed upward out of the frame. The bolt is removed by pushing inward on the bolt stop retaining pin at the rear centre, under the receiver. The recoil spring and guide are removed and the transverse cocking piece is taken out through the receiver aperture. The bolt assembly can then be removed for cleaning etc.

Accuracy of the early production models was not outstanding, and modifications that have since been made to the barrel, rear sight and trigger assembly, have resulted in a marked improvement. As a specialised and expensive pistol made for a specialised type of shooting, the Model OSP, superbly designed and superbly manufactured, undoubtedly upholds the fine example first set by the Olympia Pistole Model of 1936.

In 1968 further modifications were made to the Model OSP resulting in the introduction of the Walther Model GSP (Gebrauchs und Standardpistole) chambered for the .22 long rifle cartridge and designed to conform with the International Shooting Union regulations for the 'Standard' pistol.

Also introduced in 1968, the new Walther-Taschenpistole (TPH) is a vest pocket model and, since the first Walther, the Model 1, was also a vest pocket pistol, the TPH can be said to complete the cycle. In styling the TPH is similar to the PP series, and it also has the double action feature and is available in .22 long rifle. Shortly before the TPH appeared, Walther brought out a more traditional vest pocket pistol, the Model TP, which is available in 6.35mm (.25) and .22 long rifle and has an overall length of 5.12″.

The latest Walther pistol is the Model PPK/S which has the slide and barrel of the PPK on the Model PP frame. This variant was introduced because of recent restrictions imposed by the US Treasury Dept. which prohibit the import of the original Model PPK.

Mention has already been made of the manufacture of Walther pistols under licence by Manurhin in France. They have also been made, not under licence, by the Hungarian firm Femaru es Szerszamgepgyar NV as the Pistol W48 (currently available in Germany in 9mm short), and by the Turkish firm Kirikkale Tufek Fabricular (the Government Rifle Factory of Kirikkale).

The outstanding manufacturer of Walther arms is without doubt the famous Swiss firm of Hammerli, founded by Johann Ulrich Hammerli (1824–1891) in 1863. Originally, the firm manufactured military rifle barrels for the Swiss Federal Military Administration, a job they have continued to do ever since. But, not content with merely making barrels, Johann Hammerli then began the manufacture of special rifles for target shooting, an art in which the Swiss excelled; they were truly a nation of marksmen, and rifles 'were as common as walking sticks'. It was, however, 1932 before the first Hammerli target pistol was made, the so-called Match or Free pistol. The term 'Free' had nothing to do with the price; it meant free (practically) from limitations regarding barrel length, sight radius, weight, trigger pull etc. Previous to the appearance of the Hammerli, the Swiss also made the Hauptli, Solothurn and Widmer pistols up until the outbreak of the First World War.

In 1947, with the death of Rudolf Hammerli, the last of the family, a limited company was formed. Rationalisation and reorganisation followed and Hammerli Ltd. made a concerted effort to increase sales, particularly in the export field. The design of the Match Pistol was improved in 1951 and, at the same time, Hammerli acquired the licence to manufacture the Walther Olympia Model. In 1958 the Match Pistol was again improved, resulting in the Models 101 and 102, both of which were equipped with round instead of the traditional octagonal barrels. The Model 103 appeared as the 'Grande Luxe' with special carved grips and engraved metalwork. The Match or Free pistol is traditionally based on the Martini 'falling block' action and the Hammerli range is no exception.

In 1963 the current Hammerli 104 and 105 models were introduced, the Model 104 with a round barrel and a non-reflective matt finish, and the Model 105 with the traditional octagonal barrel and a highly polished blue finish. Mechanically both pistols are identical. The Martini-type breech block is opened by means of a lever in the base of the grip, and when this lever is pushed forward to open the action the fired case is extracted. Closing the action cocks the firing mechanism. A five lever set trigger assembly of some complexity is fitted, which allows adjustment of the trigger weight to a fraction of an ounce. The Models 104 and 105 differ only from the preceding models in that they are fitted with improved grips, an adjustable rest for the trigger finger and a larger trigger guard.

Equally specialised are the Hammerli Walther International Rapid Fire pistols Models 206 and 207. Based on the original Walther Olympia Model 1936, this series started with the introduction of the Model 200 which had a $7\frac{1}{2}''$ barrel, muzzle brake and detachable barrel weights. The Model 201 was identical except for a $9\frac{1}{2}''$ barrel, and the Model 203 (again with a $9\frac{1}{2}''$ barrel) had an adjustable grip. Available in .22 long rifle only, the American Model (Model 204) had a 33 oz trigger pull and was therefore eligible for use in the normal American NRA competitions. In order to meet American range regulations, it was fitted with a slide stop to permit tabling the weapon with the slide open and the magazine withdrawn. The American Model 205 was similar except that adjustable grips were provided.

In 1965 the range was redesigned and the Models 206 (standard grips) and 207 (adjustable grips) were introduced. These pistols, like the Walther OSP, are specifically intended for a specialised type of target shooting, International Rapid Fire, and conform to UIT rules. Available in either .22 short or .22 long rifle, the only difference in design, apart from improvements in the grip shape and general styling, lies in the new fully adjustable rear sight which is rigidly attached to the frame and not to the moving slide. This eliminates any possibility of alteration in the relative positions of the sights due to movement of the slide.

Later developments of the series include the Model 208 which is described as a general purpose pistol, has a 150mm barrel and lacks a muzzle brake. It is chambered for the .22 long rifle cartridge and has a 3 lb trigger pull. Designed for Ladies Matches, it weighs only 35 ozs. Two

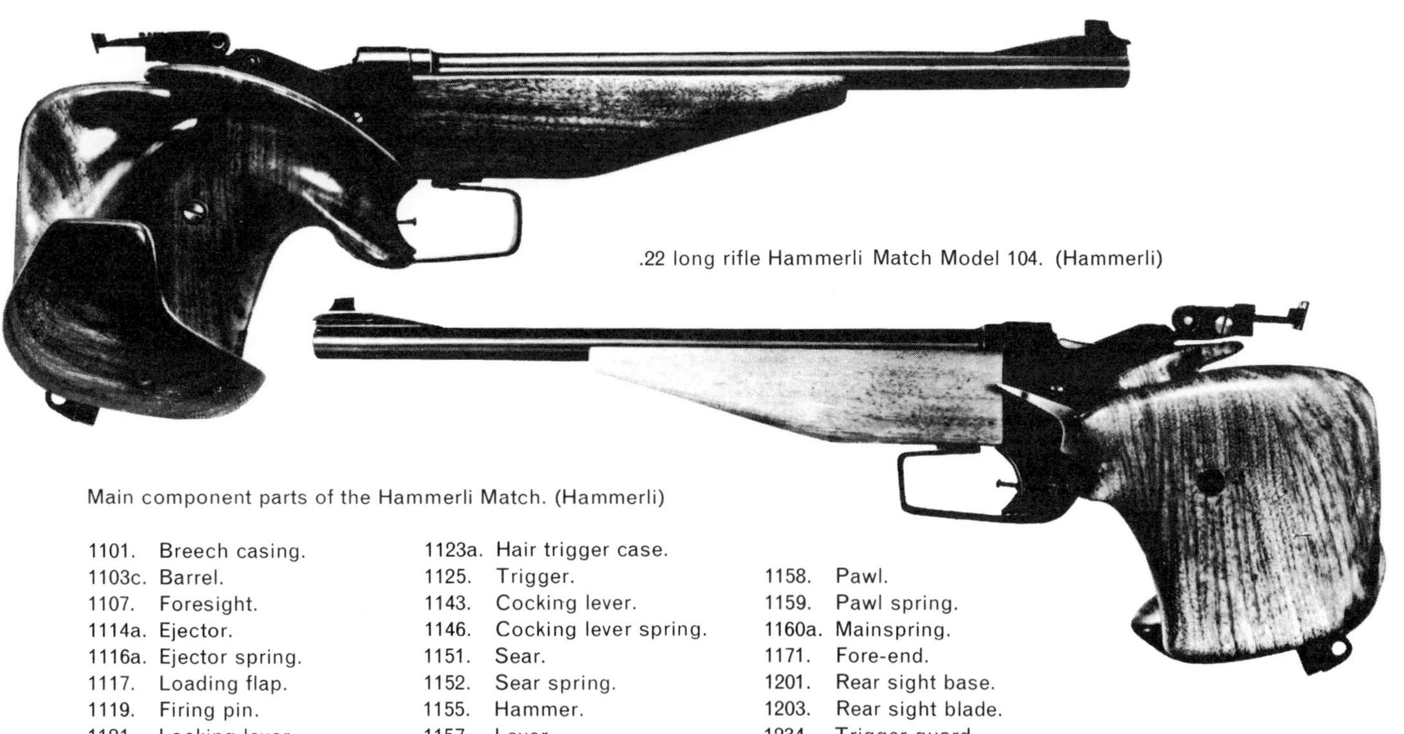

.22 long rifle Hammerli Match Model 104. (Hammerli)

Main component parts of the Hammerli Match. (Hammerli)

1101. Breech casing.
1103c. Barrel.
1107. Foresight.
1114a. Ejector.
1116a. Ejector spring.
1117. Loading flap.
1119. Firing pin.
1121. Locking lever.
1123a. Hair trigger case.
1125. Trigger.
1143. Cocking lever.
1146. Cocking lever spring.
1151. Sear.
1152. Sear spring.
1155. Hammer.
1157. Lever.
1158. Pawl.
1159. Pawl spring.
1160a. Mainspring.
1171. Fore-end.
1201. Rear sight base.
1203. Rear sight blade.
1234. Trigger guard.

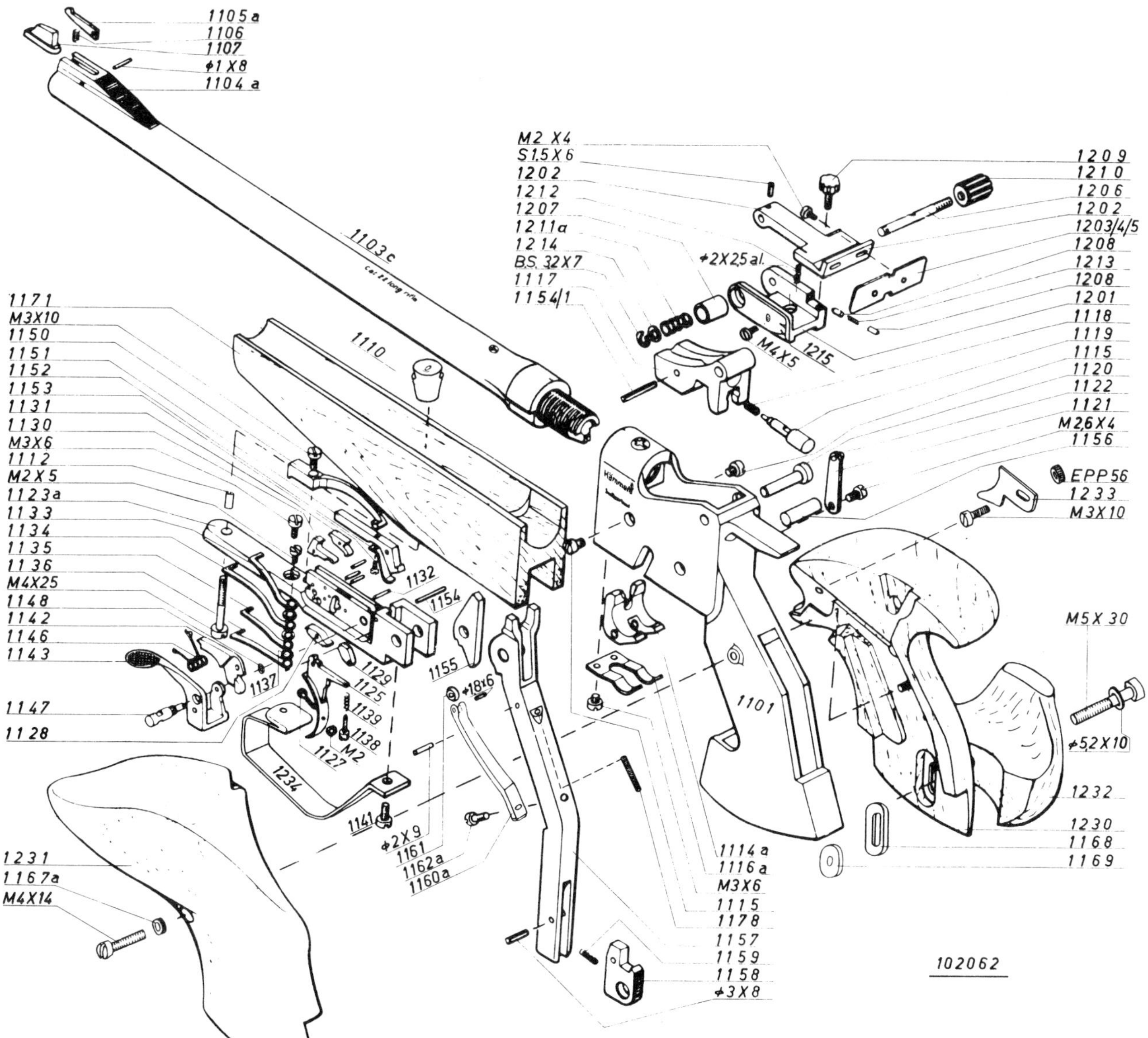

102062

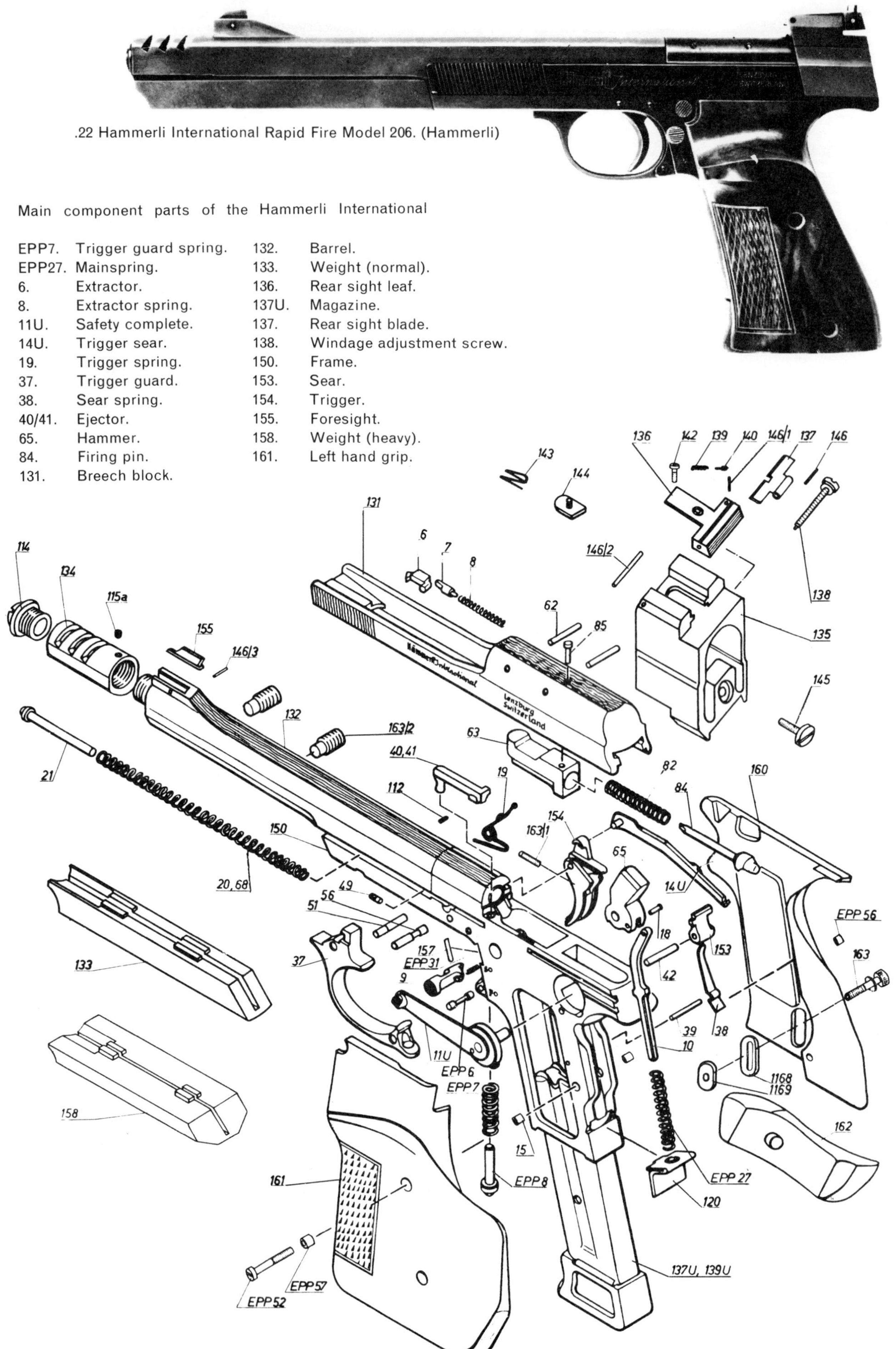

.22 Hammerli International Rapid Fire Model 206. (Hammerli)

Main component parts of the Hammerli International

EPP7.	Trigger guard spring.	132.	Barrel.
EPP27.	Mainspring.	133.	Weight (normal).
6.	Extractor.	136.	Rear sight leaf.
8.	Extractor spring.	137U.	Magazine.
11U.	Safety complete.	137.	Rear sight blade.
14U.	Trigger sear.	138.	Windage adjustment screw.
19.	Trigger spring.	150.	Frame.
37.	Trigger guard.	153.	Sear.
38.	Sear spring.	154.	Trigger.
40/41.	Ejector.	155.	Foresight.
65.	Hammer.	158.	Weight (heavy).
84.	Firing pin.	161.	Left hand grip.
131.	Breech block.		

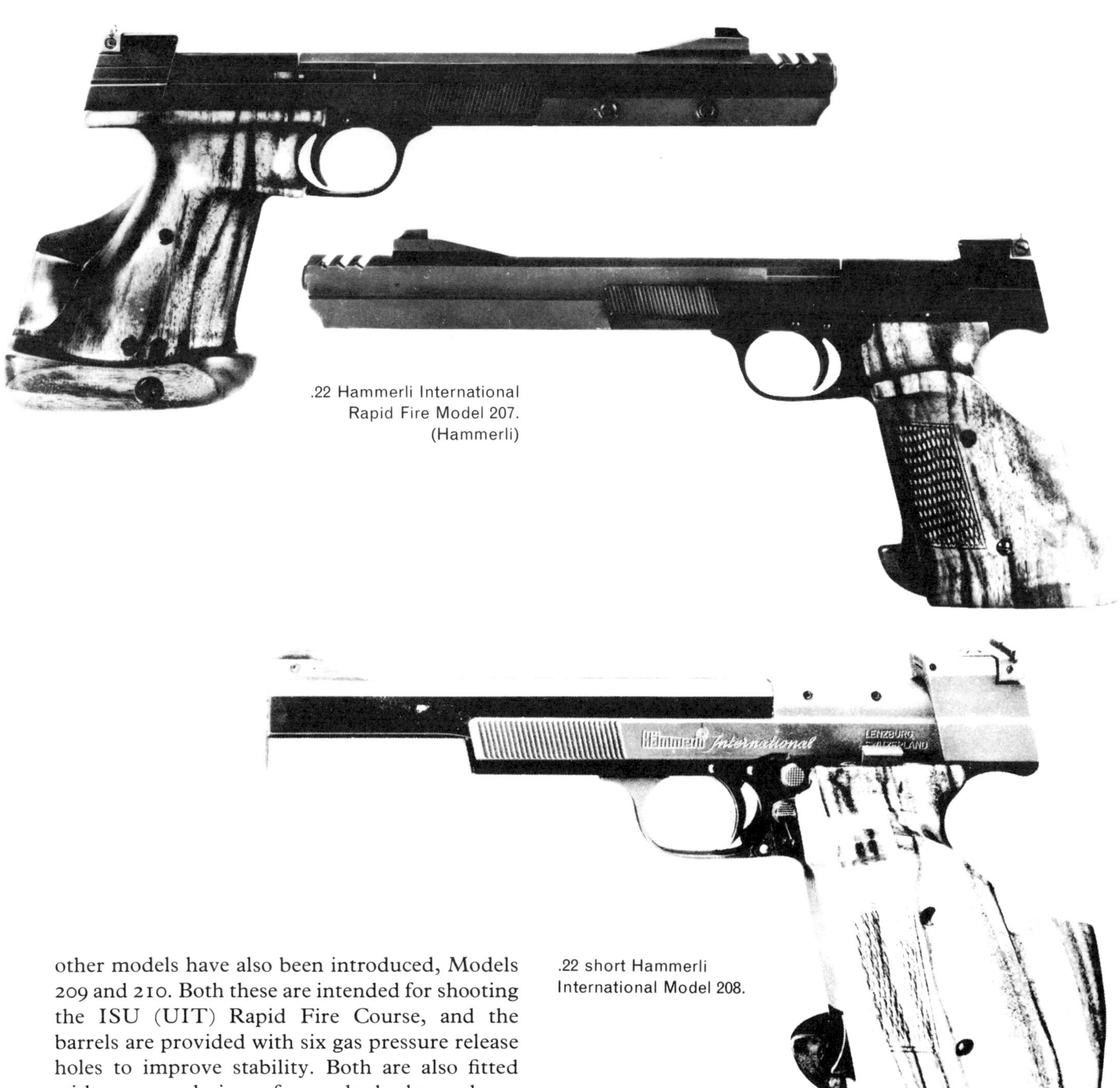

.22 Hammerli International Rapid Fire Model 207. (Hammerli)

.22 short Hammerli International Model 208.

other models have also been introduced, Models 209 and 210. Both these are intended for shooting the ISU (UIT) Rapid Fire Course, and the barrels are provided with six gas pressure release holes to improve stability. Both are also fitted with a new design of muzzle brake and are chambered for the .22 short. The Model 209 is supplied with standard grips, those on the Model 210 are adjustable.

Hammerli specialise in target pistols and have to deal with highly critical and selective customers. Their long record of success in International Competitions speaks for itself.

Situated to the north of Zurich, and about as far from it as Lenzburg, Neuhausen Rhine Falls is the home of the Swiss Industrial Company (Schweizerische Industrie Gesellschaft or SIG), the makers of the SIG P 210 series of automatic pistols. Before the war they manufactured the 6.35mm Chylewski 'one hand' pocket pistol which later appeared as the Lignose.

In 1937 SIG secured a licence from the French Société Alsacienne de Constructions Mécaniques (SACM) to manufacture and develop a pistol patented in France by Charles G. Petter, an engineer associated with SACM. The basic design became the French Service Model 1935 A in 7.65mm long calibre, and, at Neuhausen, SIG started to develop it. Since they supplied many of the parts of the Swiss 06/29 (Parabellum) Service Pistol, they had already gained experience in the manufacture of automatic pistols and, the Swiss Service cartridge being the 7.65mm Parabellum, they manufactured the 'Selbstladepistole Petter' (SP) in this calibre,

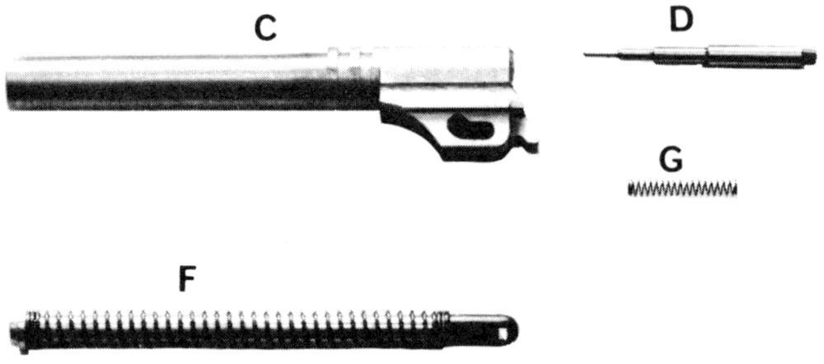

SIG Model P 210-1.

A. Slide.
B. Hammer, sear, hammer spring etc. in action casing.
C. Barrel.
D. Firing pin.
E. Firing pin stop.
F. Recoil spring and guide.
G. Firing pin spring.
H. Frame.
J. Magazine.
K. Slide stop.

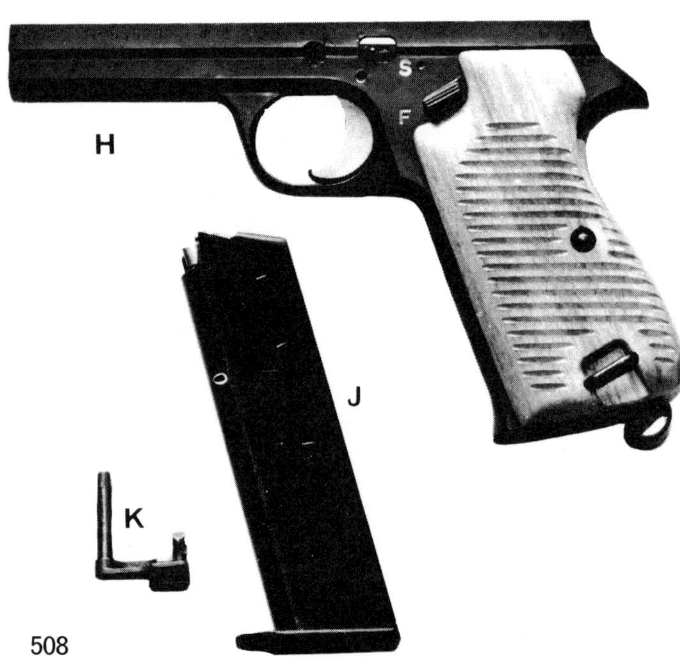

although a few specimens were also made in 7.65mm long and in 9mm Parabellum.

In 1942, following redesign, a series of pistols which, for lack of a better description, can be called 'Neuhausen' pistols, appeared. These were prototype designs and culminated in the appearance of the Neuhausen 44/16 in 1944. Never commercially exploited, this model was in 9mm Parabellum and had a sixteen round magazine. The SP 44/8 was of similar design with a reduced magazine capacity of eight rounds.

Further design changes occurred in 1947 after the SP 44 series had proved unsuccessful in Swiss Military trials. Commercial production of the Selbstladepistole 47/8 began in 1947 when it was offered, with interchangeable barrels, in both 7.65mm and 9mm Parabellum. The basic

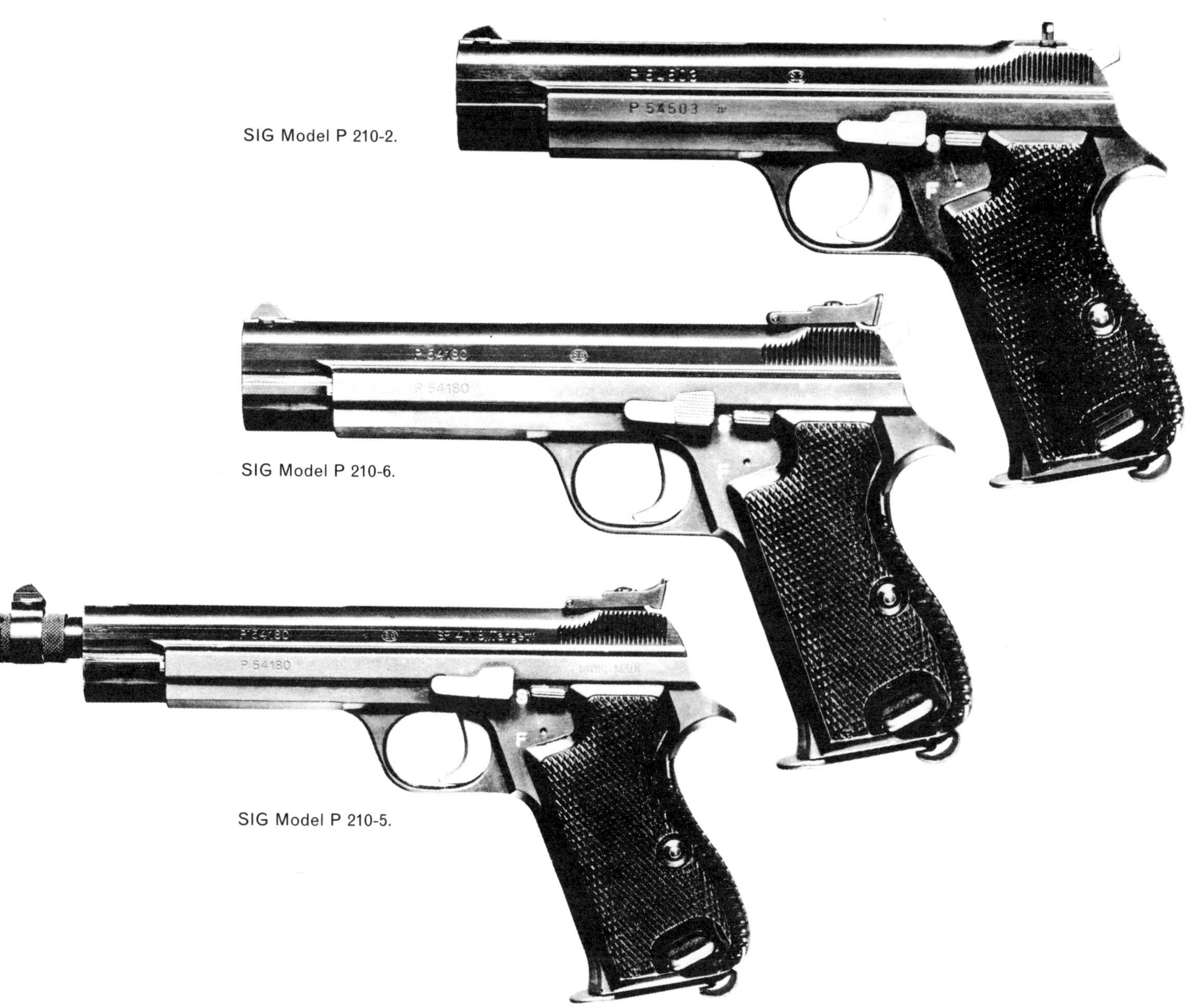
SIG Model P 210-2.

SIG Model P 210-6.

SIG Model P 210-5.

pistol was of 9mm calibre but, by changing the barrel and recoil spring, it could be converted to fire the 7.65mm cartridge. By changing the magazine, slide, barrel and recoil spring and guide, it could also be converted to handle .22 long rifle ammunition.

In October 1948 the 9mm version was adopted for Swiss Military service and was given the official designation Pistole Modell 1949. Issued to officers and NCOs, it was designed to replace the 7.65mm Parabellum and the old 1929 7.5mm revolver. Initial issue pistols had wooden grips, the later versions had plastic ones. A 9mm pistol of commercial pattern was adopted by the Danish authorities in August 1948 as the Pistol M/1949.

Current models are the SIG P 210–1 Standard Model with wooden grips and polished finish. The basic design features are illustrated, and are based on the Browning barrel locking system. The Model P 210–2 is similar but has a sand-blasted finish and plastic grips. Both models are available in 9mm Parabellum, 7.65mm Parabellum and .22 long rifle. Barrel length is $4\frac{3}{4}''$, and the 9mm and .22 long rifle have six groove rifling, the 7.65mm four groove. Magazine capacity for all calibres is eight rounds. Dismantling the pistol is simple. The magazine is withdrawn and the chamber checked. The slide is partially drawn to the rear and the slide stop pushed out, after which the slide can be pulled forward off the frame. The action casing is lifted out, the recoil spring is removed from the slide, and the barrel can then be taken off.

Target Models are also available. The Model 210–6 with the standard barrel length has an adjustable rear sight for both windage and elevation and is available in 7.65mm and 9mm Parabellum only. A 6″ barrel version, the Model 210–5 has the front sight mounted on the barrel instead of on the slide. All models have the conventional thumb safety, a magazine safety, and half cock safety on the external hammer. The slide remains open when the last shot has been fired. The SIG design is simple, the pistols are of the highest quality, and the fact that calibres can be changed quickly and simply is an important feature. The .22 conversion is of considerable interest and, although the action is unlocked, excellent accuracy is obtained, entirely adequate for small calibre training at reduced cost.

If we move south across Switzerland, we come to the Plain of Lombardy in Northern Italy and to the ancient town of Brescia. Arms have been made in this area since the days of the Romans who granted Roman citizenship to its inhabitants in 225 BC, together with the coveted title of 'colonia civica Augusta Brixia'. North of Brescia, in the quiet Val Trompia, is the town of Gardone, centre of the firearms industry of the valley, located on the banks of the fast flowing River Mella.

Here we find the oldest firearms manufacturing firm still in existence, Fabrica d'Armi Pietro Beretta SPA, founded in the year 1680, and the town of Gardone is dominated by their palatial office buildings and factory. Beretta are not just another gun manufacturing company, they represent a way of life, and how they have managed to survive wars, invasions, insurrection and the transition to modern industrial complexity is beyond comprehension. Traditionally, all the sons of the Beretta family are named Pietro but, to avoid confusion, are known by their middle names. Needless to say, even in the atomic age, a Pietro Beretta still guides the fortunes of the company.

The first Beretta automatic pistols, made in 1915, were of simple blow-back design with an internal hammer, wooden grips and a firing pin which acted as the ejector. This pistol, in 7.65mm Browning calibre, was made for the Italian Army and Police Force only. Marked 'PS' (Publica Sicurezza) for police use and 'RE' (Regio Esercito) for army use, manufacture was discontinued in 1919.

A larger version of the 7.65mm pistol, the 9mm Model 1915, was also manufactured for military and police use. This pistol was adapted for the 9mm Glisenti Model 1910 cartridge,

9mm Beretta Model 1915.

9mm corto Beretta Model 1934.

similar to the 9mm Parabellum but with a weaker charge. The muzzle velocity of this '1910' cartridge was 970 f.p.s. as against the Italian loading of 1,150 f.p.s. for the 9mm Parabellum.

The 7.65mm pistol was further modified and, in 1919, a grip safety device was added. In 1923 the first external hammer model appeared, and this was the first pistol to have an official Beretta designation, 'Modello 1923'. Of 9mm calibre (the reduced load 1910 cartridge), it was also available with a shoulder stock. The 7.65mm Model of 1931 was issued to the Italian Navy and bore the 'RM' crest. None of these models were sold commercially.

A more streamlined version of the 1931 Model appeared in 1934 in .380 ACP or 9mm corto (9mm Browning short). Adopted by the Italian

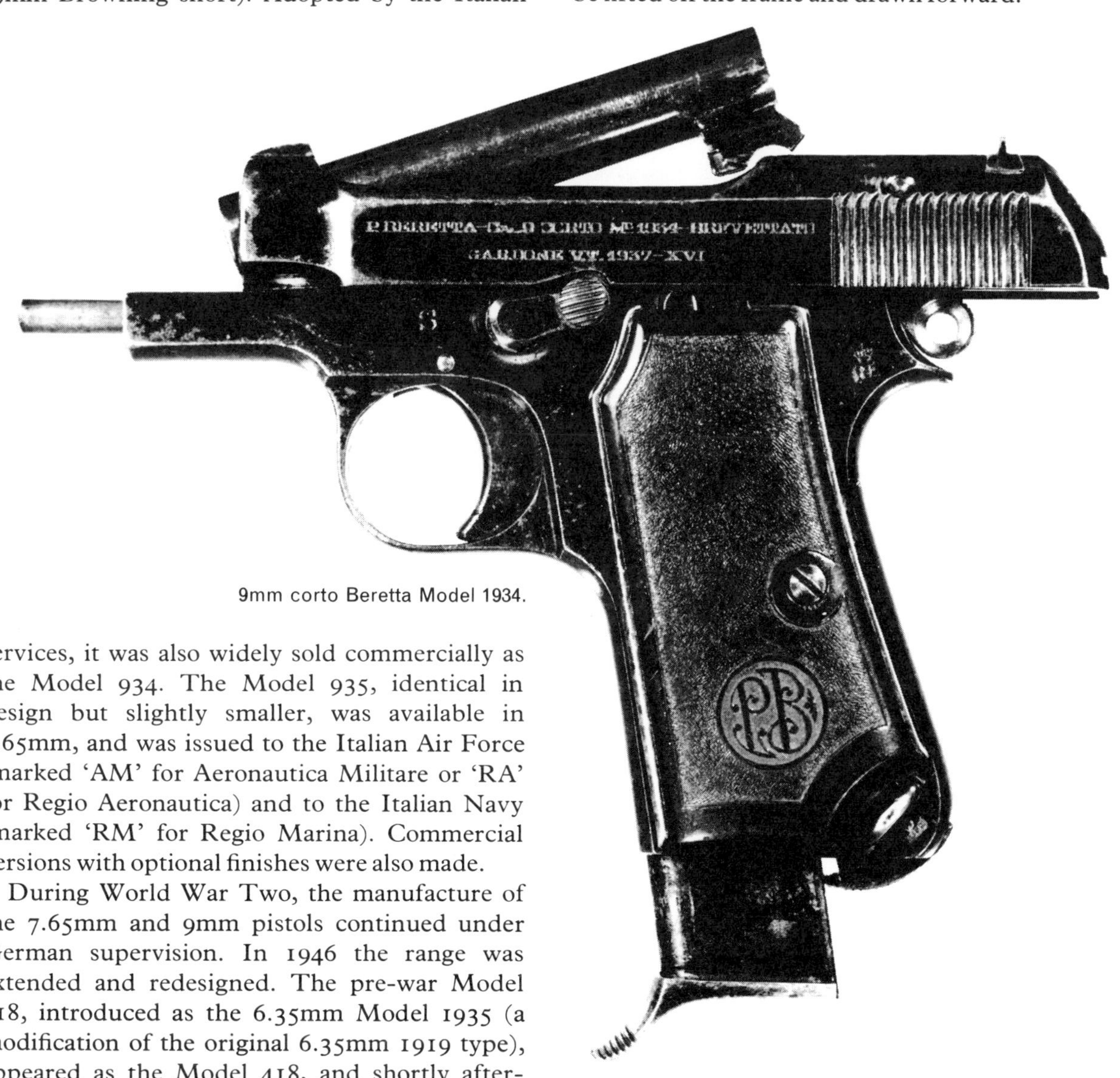

9mm corto Beretta Model 1934.

services, it was also widely sold commercially as the Model 934. The Model 935, identical in design but slightly smaller, was available in 7.65mm, and was issued to the Italian Air Force (marked 'AM' for Aeronautica Militare or 'RA' for Regio Aeronautica) and to the Italian Navy (marked 'RM' for Regio Marina). Commercial versions with optional finishes were also made.

During World War Two, the manufacture of the 7.65mm and 9mm pistols continued under German supervision. In 1946 the range was extended and redesigned. The pre-war Model 318, introduced as the 6.35mm Model 1935 (a modification of the original 6.35mm 1919 type), appeared as the Model 418, and shortly afterwards the .22 long rifle 'Pistola Modello 948' also became available.

Experimentation with the use of light alloys led to the development of the Model 1950 in 9mm short, and this was followed by the light alloy locked breech Model 951 designed for the Italian Navy and Air Force in 9mm Parabellum.

The current commercial range is based on the Series 950, an entirely new design quite different to those previously made by Beretta. The important feature of the Series 950 is the ease of dismounting. The barrel release lever (on the left hand side of the frame behind the trigger) is pushed forward so that the barrel is unlatched and springs upward from the hinge at the front of the frame. The slide is then drawn rearward for about a quarter of an inch until the front can be lifted off the frame and drawn forward.

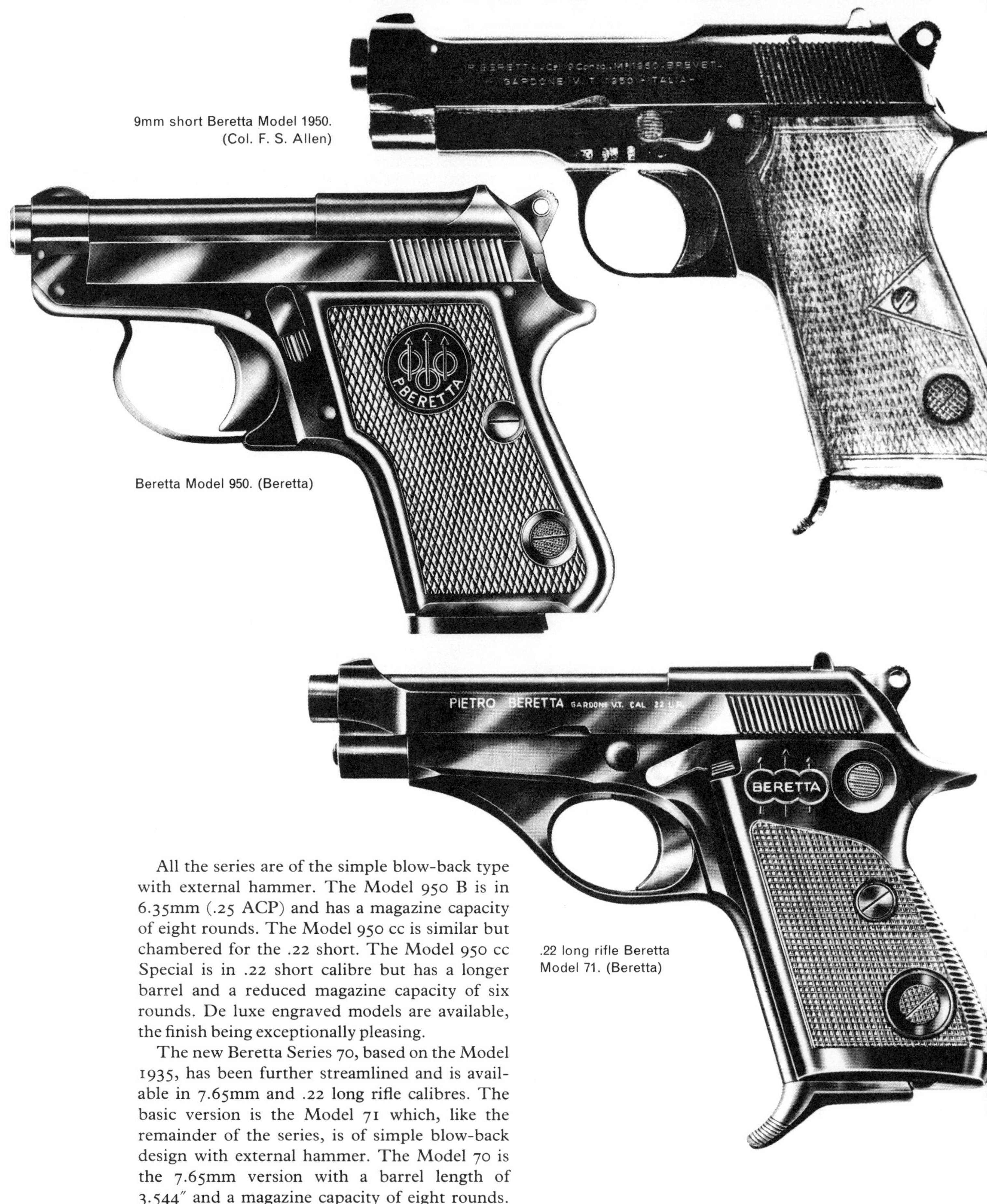

9mm short Beretta Model 1950. (Col. F. S. Allen)

Beretta Model 950. (Beretta)

.22 long rifle Beretta Model 71. (Beretta)

All the series are of the simple blow-back type with external hammer. The Model 950 B is in 6.35mm (.25 ACP) and has a magazine capacity of eight rounds. The Model 950 cc is similar but chambered for the .22 short. The Model 950 cc Special is in .22 short calibre but has a longer barrel and a reduced magazine capacity of six rounds. De luxe engraved models are available, the finish being exceptionally pleasing.

The new Beretta Series 70, based on the Model 1935, has been further streamlined and is available in 7.65mm and .22 long rifle calibres. The basic version is the Model 71 which, like the remainder of the series, is of simple blow-back design with external hammer. The Model 70 is the 7.65mm version with a barrel length of 3.544″ and a magazine capacity of eight rounds. The .22 long rifle version is the Model 71, also available with a spare 5.906″ barrel as the Model 72. The Model 73 is identical to the Model 72 except that the rear sight is attached to the barrel and not to the slide, and the magazine capacity is increased to ten rounds. The Model 74 has the added advantage of an adjustable rear sight on the barrel.

Beretta still manufacture the Model 949 in .22 long rifle and .22 short. This is a simple target pistol with special grips and barrel weights similar to the Walther Olympia. In 1964, during a visit to the Beretta factory, I was shown the new Beretta Olympic Pistol Model 80. This pistol is designed specifically for rapid fire silhouette shooting and is available only in .22 short. The action is straight blow-back with a cylindrical, almost totally enclosed bolt which is provided with wings at the rear to allow for loading. The barrel and receiver assembly permit the sights to be fitted so that they cannot move relative to one another once they are adjusted. The barrel also mounts a built-in muzzle brake. A muzzle weight can be introduced underneath and can be locked in any desired position by means of an Allen screw. A fully adjustable rear sight with clearly defined clicks is fitted, and the top of the barrel is ribbed to reduce glare.

The grip frame is of light alloy, and the wooden grips have a thumb rest and built-in palm rest. The safety is on the left hand side and has a 'red dot' indicator. The magazine catch is at the bottom of the grip. Dismounting is easily carried out by pressing out one spring located pin and pulling the barrel and action forward until they can be lifted off completely. Overall weight is 34 ozs., and the barrel length $6\frac{3}{4}$″ with a sight radius of $9\frac{7}{8}$″.

IN NOME
di S. M. l'Augustissimo Imperatore
Francesco I,
Re d'Ungheria, di Boemia, della Lombardia e di Venezia,
Arciduca d'Austria, ecc. ecc. ecc.
Partendo da ... il Sig.r ...
per recarsi a ...
S'invitano le Autorità Civili e Militari, e si pregano quelle delle Potenze amiche ed alleate a lasciarl... liberamente passare, o a darg... ajuto e protezione, offrendosi ad una perfetta reciprocanza.
Vale per ...
Dato in Milano il giorno ...
del mese di ... dell'anno mille ottocento ...

Il Ciambellano e Consigliere intimo attuale di S. M. I. R. A., Cavaliere di I.a Classe dell'I. Ordine Austriaco della Corona di Ferro, Commendatore del Real Ordine di S. Stefano d'Ungheria, Gran Croce dell'Ordine de' SS. Maurizio e Lazzaro di Sardegna e dell'Ordine Costantiniano di S. Giorgio di Parma, Presidente dell'I. R. Governo della Lombardia,

CONNOTATI.
Età
Statura
Capelli
Fronte
Sopraciglia
Occhi
Naso
Bocca
Barba
Mento
Viso
Colorito
Di condizione
Nativo di
Domiciliato in
MARCHE VISIBILI.
Firma del latore
Tassa lire due cent. trenta oltre il bollo

The original passport issued to Pietro Beretta in 1829. (Beretta)

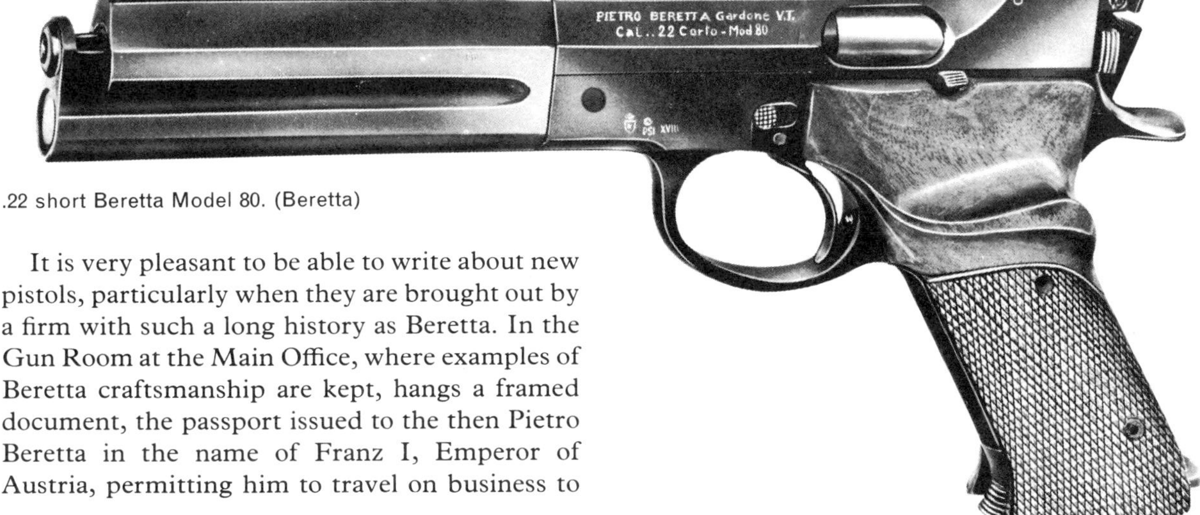

.22 short Beretta Model 80. (Beretta)

It is very pleasant to be able to write about new pistols, particularly when they are brought out by a firm with such a long history as Beretta. In the Gun Room at the Main Office, where examples of Beretta craftsmanship are kept, hangs a framed document, the passport issued to the then Pietro Beretta in the name of Franz I, Emperor of Austria, permitting him to travel on business to

Naples, Livorno and Genoa. The document is dated 1829 and illustrates just one of the many difficulties that this firm has successfully overcome in almost three centuries of gunmaking.

A comparative newcomer, at least as far as Gardone is concerned, is the firm of Vincenzo Bernadelli, founded in 1865 when Bernadelli, an employee of the Franzini Arms Factory, started making barrels on his own account in San Carlo. Vincenzo Bernadelli died in 1899 and the management was taken over by his sons, Pietro, Lodovico, Antonio and Giulio. The present premises on the banks of the River Mella, originally a textile mill, were acquired in 1908 and, following the First World War, the factory was again expanded and new machinery installed. In 1928 Bernadelli manufactured the 10.4mm Italian service revolver, the Model 89, and, after World War Two, two revolvers similar to the Smith and Wesson were put into production.

6.35mm Bernadelli Vest Pocket Model.

Bernadelli currently manufacture a vest pocket 6.35mm pistol originally introduced in 1945. Normal magazine capacity is five rounds, but a special extension magazine is available which increases the capacity to eight rounds and also extends the grip. A similar pistol, 'The Baby', was introduced in 1949 and is available in either .22 short or .22 long rifle.

The hammerless Standard Model was also introduced in 1949 and is now available in 7.65mm and 9mm short. In addition to the manual safety, it is fitted with a magazine safety and a cocking indicator. By changing the barrels the calibre can be altered, and special barrels 150mm, 200mm and 250mm in length can be had to order. Magazine capacity in 7.65mm is eight cartridges and, in 9mm short, seven. A special extended magazine with a capacity of seventeen cartridges is available in 7.65mm calibre only.

A new model with external hammer was placed on the market in 1959 and was called the Model 60. Basic design follows previous practice. The system is simple blow-back with a fixed barrel, and has the Bernadelli twin buffer springs in the frame to reduce the shock of the recoiling slide. The magazine has a finger extension and the general appearance has been modernised.

The Model 60 is made in .22 long rifle, 7.65mm and 9mm short. In .22 calibre a special long 200mm barrel is available, and this version has an adjustable rear sight. Dismounting is simple. Push the slide back slightly and then press the slide release button located on the frame behind the left hand grip. The slide is then raised and removed from the front of the pistol. On the special .22 long barrel model, the foresight has to be removed before the slide can be taken off the barrel.

The Province of Brescia, as might be expected, was also the home of the first automatic pistol adopted by the Italian Government for military use, the Glisenti. The Società Siderurgica Glisenti, founded by Francesco Glisenti in 1859 at Carcina, was initially concerned with the manufacture of iron and steel. By 1870, a section of the works devoted to the manufacture of small arms had successfully established itself and, in addition to the production of military and sporting weapons, a double action six chambered revolver, the 10.35mm Model 1874, was adopted for issue to Customs Guards, to the Artillery and to Government employees. This revolver employed

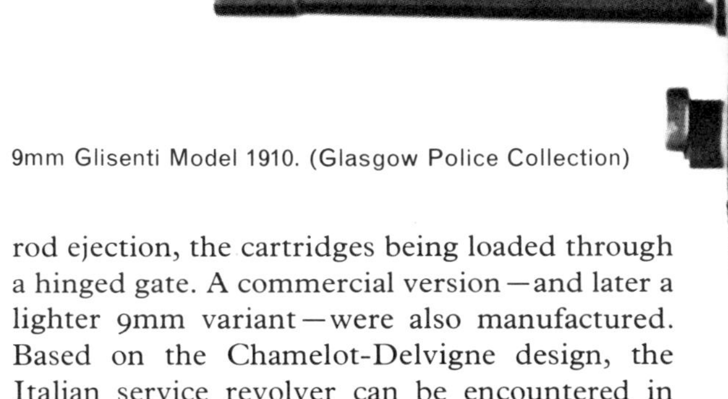

9mm Glisenti Model 1910. (Glasgow Police Collection)

rod ejection, the cartridges being loaded through a hinged gate. A commercial version—and later a lighter 9mm variant—were also manufactured. Based on the Chamelot-Delvigne design, the Italian service revolver can be encountered in numerous different models, the Model of 1917, for example, having a folding trigger. An interesting feature of the original design was the use of countersunk chambers. Other manufacturers produced similar weapons, but those bearing the Glisenti name were undoubtedly the better finished.

In 1905 Glisenti patented an automatic pistol designed by an ex-artillery officer, Revelli, who was also responsible for the Fiat Model 1914 machine gun. Originally manufactured in 7.65mm Parabellum, this pistol was adopted officially as the m.906. In 1909 it was decided to increase the calibre to 9mm and, as the m.910, it was adopted for service use by the Italian Government the following year. Earlier, both versions of the pistol had been submitted for trial to the United States Ordnance Board, but both had been rejected. The Glisenti m.910 was of locked breech construction and had features of both the Mauser and the Borchardt. The barrel and barrel extension were machined out of a single forging, the extension being of square internal section to receive the square section breech block. When the pistol was fired, the breech block and barrel extension recoiled to the rear along a groove machined in the left hand side of the frame. The opposite groove was machined in a thin plate or side cover attached to the frame by means of a hook and screw. This detachable side plate was a weak feature of the design. As the mechanism recoiled in the frame, the locking bolt rotated to the rear and, passing through a slot in the barrel extension, engaged the notch which can be seen in the breech block. When the locking bolt was disengaged from the breech block, the breech was free to travel to the rear, so extracting the fired cartridge. This rearward travel also compressed the recoil spring housed around the striker. The return motion of the breech block was accomplished by this spring—the lock, under the influence of a flat spring in front of the back strap of the frame, rotating anti-clockwise to engage the notch. The barrel was finally locked into battery by yet another spring, a short coil spring mounted under the barrel which abutted against a shoulder in the receiver.

To dismantle, the pistol was first checked to ensure that it was empty. An empty magazine was then inserted and the breech block drawn fully to the rear where, since the magazine platform operated a hold-open device, it would remain. The safety catch at the rear of the breech block was then unscrewed anti-clockwise and removed. The magazine was taken off again, and the breech block allowed to move forward. The trigger was then pressed, and the cross bolt at the rear of the barrel extension removed. In front of the frame there was a screw with a locking pin and, if the pin was depressed and the screw unscrewed, the side plate could be taken off. The left hand grip plate could then be removed, and the barrel group eased from the frame by disengaging it from the groove. The breech block was then withdrawn from the barrel extension and the striker unscrewed from the firing pin. If it was necessary to remove the firing pin, the dismounting tool (supplied with the

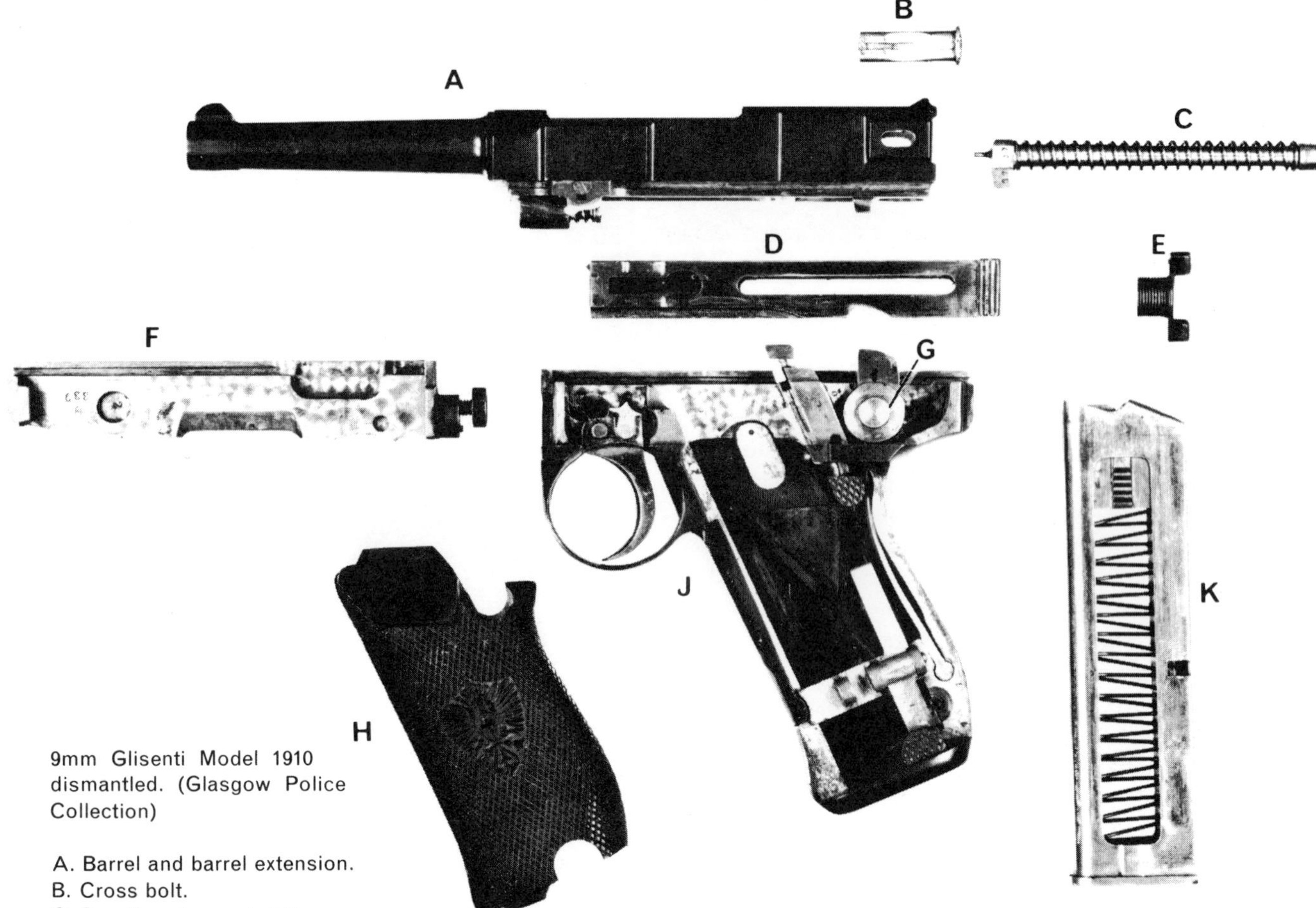

9mm Glisenti Model 1910 dismantled. (Glasgow Police Collection)

A. Barrel and barrel extension.
B. Cross bolt.
C. Recoil spring and striker.
D. Breech block.
E. Safety catch.
F. Side plate.
G. Locking bolt.
H. Left hand grip plate.
J. Frame.
K. Magazine.

pistol and carried under the left hand stock on the frame) was used. If this tool was missing, a small wrench could be used instead. The projection on the firing pin (which protruded through the breech block) had to be unscrewed in a *clockwise* direction, and the firing pin could then be taken out through the slot in the side of the breech block. On reassembly, it was important to ensure that the safety catch was screwed fully home; otherwise it would fail to function.

In addition to the normal safety catch which locked the firing pin, the Glisenti was also provided with a grip safety on the front strap, and this locked the trigger. The magazine had a capacity of seven cartridges and was provided with grips which allowed the platform to be moved downward to facilitate the introduction of cartridges. As can be seen from the illustration, it was open sided so that the contents could be checked; it was also plated. The magazine catch was on the left hand side of the pistol at the bottom of the frame; the upper catch operated the breech block hold-open device.

The Glisenti pistol has been treated in some detail since the Revelli rotary lock was yet another interesting variation of the locked breech system and should be compared, for example, with the Mauser locking system. The trigger mechanism represented an interesting variation of the Borchardt and later Parabellum systems. It was, of course, the first automatic pistol to be adopted by the Italian Government and, although the basic weaknesses of the Revelli lock coupled with the inherent weakness of the frame design (due to the detachable side plate) resulted in a pistol lacking certain desirable characteristics, the Glisenti should feature in any collection of early automatic pistols.

For anyone wishing to fire this pistol today, a word of caution is necessary. Since Italian loadings are considerably less powerful than the service or commercial loadings, 9mm Parabellum ammunition (which will chamber in the Glisenti) must not be used. The correct cartridge is variously described as the 9mm m.910 Glisenti, as the Beretta M.1915, or as the 9mm Brixia.

Although adopted for military use, the Glisenti was not a commercial success. The m.906 in 7.65mm was manufactured by Glisenti at their Carcina factory but, in 1907, the Glisenti Company sold its licence to manufacture to Metallurgica Bresciana ex Tempini (MBT) and gave them the right to impress the Glisenti mark on their weapons. Thus, from 1907 on, the name 'Glisenti' was purely a trade mark and did not refer to the actual maker.

The Glisenti Company is still in existence in Carcina and I am indebted to their Public Relations Officer, Dr Peroni, for much of this information. The Tempini Company discontinued the manufacture of firearms during the 1930's and was itself taken over by the Società Metallurgica Italiana in 1958.

This, however, is not the end of the story. In 1911 the MBT company patented several modifications simplifying the Glisenti, and marketed an automatic pistol known as the 'Brixia', this being the old name for Brescia. The front grip safety was abolished and a device was incorporated to prevent the pistol being fired without the magazine. The trigger mechanism was also redesigned to eliminate the flat springs—coil springs were substituted—and the design of the safety catch was altered. Whilst the Brixia was an improvement on the m.910 Glisenti, there were no substantial modifications to the design nor any attempt to eliminate the weakness which restricted the ballistics of the cartridge. Like the Glisenti, the Brixia should not be used with the 9 mm Parabellum. Despite the efforts of MBT, however, the Brixia was not a success and, with the appearance of the Beretta Model 1915, it was doomed to failure.

Not far from Brescia itself is the small town of Collebeato where the firm of Industria Armi Galesi was founded in 1910 by Nicola Galesi. The manufacture of a straight blow-back pistol on traditional lines was begun in 1914 and, in 1923, a second model appeared. Various minor design and styling changes were made over the years and, although the firm was relatively small, they offered a wide variety of finishes and styles in the three calibres, 6.35mm, 7.65mm and 9mm short. After the war Galesi offered a .22 rim-fire version as well as the 6.35mm (.25 ACP) and 7.65mm (.32 ACP) models, and all of them were well made and well finished vest pocket and pocket arms. Manufacture appears to have ceased in the early 1960's due to factory reorganisation and re-tooling. At the time of writing Galesi appear to have resumed production of automatic pistols in .22 and 6.35mm calibres. The pistols are available in either blue or chrome finish and have white plastic stocks with indented finger grooves.

Before we move on to France, some indication of the flexibility of the arms industry in Brescia

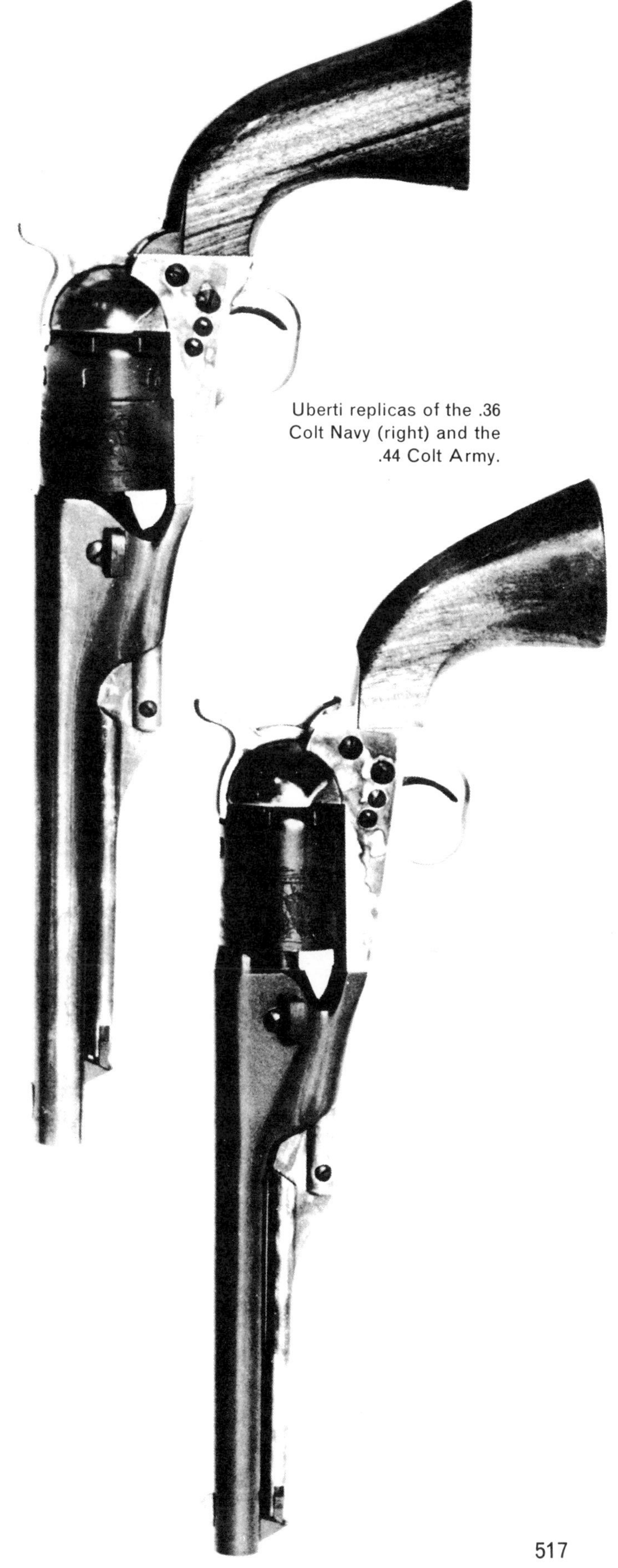

Uberti replicas of the .36 Colt Navy (right) and the .44 Colt Army.

can be gained from the fact that muzzle loading replica pistols, copies of the Remington and Colt, are currently being manufactured. A visit to the Aldo Uberti factory is bewildering; amongst the many modern machine tools lie parts of pistols similar to those which took part in the American Civil War.

Uberti, the founder of the firm, worked for Beretta until he went into partnership with Gregorelli shortly before the latter's death. The great interest in percussion arms generated in America during the centennial of the Civil War was seized upon by many small gunmakers in Gardone, most of whom were ruined by speculators. Uberti, however, has carefully maintained the quality of his replica arms which include copies of the Sharps four barrelled derringer in .22 rim-fire and the famous Remington over and under derringer in .38 S & W Special. Interest in shooting muzzle loading revolvers shows no sign of abating. For serious shooting the advantages of a replica are obvious, and the likelihood of damaging a rare and possibly valuable original by continued use cannot be entirely discounted. The Uberti replicas sold by the Navy Arms Co. of America are well made and, to avoid any possibility of misrepresentation, are marked with the names of both the vendor and manufacturer and bear the proof marks of the Banco di Prova at Gardone.

In France, the history of automatic pistol manufacture has to be considered from two standpoints: those weapons made by Government arsenals and those made for commercial sale. At the time of the First World War, the French Army was still dependent on the revolver. Due to the shortage of these, and in view of the success of German automatic pistols, the French pressed into service huge quantities of auto-pistols of Spanish manufacture. In addition, quantities of Spanish revolvers, copies of the Colt and the Smith and Wesson chambered for the 8mm French service cartridge, were also purchased. In the years between the wars, the French authorities began the development of an auto-pistol suitable for military use and, by 1925, St. Etienne had evolved a straight blow-back type pistol, the MAS 1925 Model No. I. This pistol was unusual in that a hinged grip frame was employed to facilitate cleaning and inspection, no doubt inspired by the traditional quick dismounting without tools long considered an important feature by the French military mind and exemplified by French Service revolvers.

Several versions of the Model 1925 appeared, but whether they were ever issued in quantity is unknown. By 1935 the Petter modification of the basic Browning system was put into production by the Société Alsacienne de Constructions Mécaniques (SACM) and, following Government trials, was adopted as the Model 1935 A and chambered for the 7.65mm French long service cartridge. This cartridge was apparently developed from the American Pedersen cartridge of 1918 used in the Pedersen device, an attempt to provide a pistol calibre conversion unit for the US service rifle which, although successful, was not adopted for military use. The French 7.65mm cartridge was also used in the Model 1938 sub-machine gun and has only recently been replaced by the 9mm Parabellum. The 7.65mm French service cartridge is slightly more powerful than the .32 ACP but no better than the .380 ACP, and one wonders why the change to the 9mm Parabellum was so long delayed.

In the Model 1935 S, a Government design, the usual Browning locking lugs were abandoned in favour of a simple step machined in the barrel which engaged a recess in the slide. The 7.65mm Model 1935 S was made by the Government Arsenal at St. Etienne (MAS), at the Tulle Arsenal (MAST), by SACM and by Manufacture d'Armes de Chatellerault (MAC). The Société d'Applications Générales Electriques et Mécaniques (SAGEM) made a variant model known as the Model 35 SM-1.

Current French automatic pistols include the several variants of the Model 1935 in 7.65mm calibre and the basically similar Model 1950 chambered for the 9mm Parabellum cartridge. The 9mm SE–MAS 1950 more closely follows the design of the Model 1935 A in that two locking ribs or lugs are used instead of the step of the 1935 S Model. No information is available from official sources on the Model 1950 but, in addition to being made by MAS, this pistol appears to have been manufactured by MAC and is advertised as second-hand surplus (armes d'occasion). The MAC version has plastic grips instead of wood. No new weapons are sold on the commercial market by Government factories.

The oldest manufacturer of automatic pistols is the firm of Manufrance, Manufacture Française d'Armes et Cycles de Saint-Etienne, not to be confused with the Government factory, Manufacture d'Armes St. Etienne (MAS). Manufrance currently manufacture three models, the

7.65mm SACM French Service Model 1935 A. (Glasgow Police Collection)

6.35mm Manufrance Modèle de Poche.

6.35mm Modèle de Poche, the 6.35mm Modèle 'Policeman' and the 7.65mm 'Le Français'. A 9mm Military model was introduced in 1928 but was rejected for military use and went out of production in 1938. There are minor differences in construction between the various models but all are based on designs by Président Directeur Général Mimard of Manufrance, dating back to 1913. All are of a simple blow-back type with a fixed barrel hinged to the frame. The design is unusual in that the recoil spring is housed in a tunnel in the grip frame in front of the magazine. Two levers, one on each side of the frame, connect the recoil spring to the slide. All models are striker fired, the striker being cocked by the trigger prior to release. Due to this 'double action' feature it is not necessary to pull back the slide to cock the action and, since the chamber can be reloaded directly by the hinged barrel, it is not necessary to operate the slide for this either. The 6.35mm models have no finger grips on the slide, and to load and fire the pistol the loaded magazine is inserted in the usual manner. The barrel opens when the magazine is withdrawn, and a cartridge can be directly inserted into the breech. The barrel is then hinged downward into battery and the trigger pulled to cock the striker and fire the pistol. The magazine of the current 6.35mm 'Policeman' Model is furnished with a clip at the base to hold an extra cartridge which can be placed in the chamber.

Manufrance also offer a single shot bolt action pistol, the Populaire, in 6mm Bosquette, a Flobert type rim-fire cartridge still used in France for twelve metre rifle and pistol competitive shooting. A rather more ornate version of

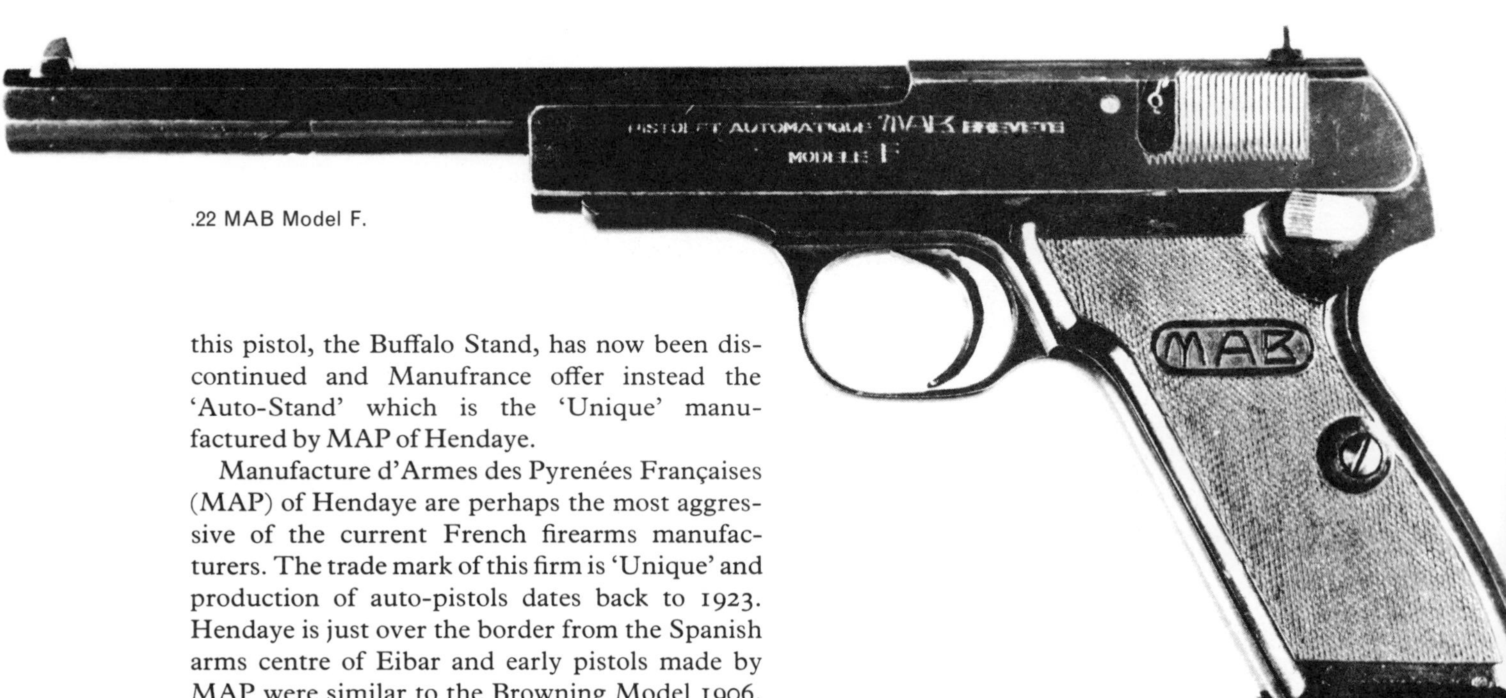

.22 MAB Model F.

this pistol, the Buffalo Stand, has now been discontinued and Manufrance offer instead the 'Auto-Stand' which is the 'Unique' manufactured by MAP of Hendaye.

Manufacture d'Armes des Pyrenées Françaises (MAP) of Hendaye are perhaps the most aggressive of the current French firearms manufacturers. The trade mark of this firm is 'Unique' and production of auto-pistols dates back to 1923. Hendaye is just over the border from the Spanish arms centre of Eibar and early pistols made by MAP were similar to the Browning Model 1906. During World War Two, production continued under German supervision and the present Chief Designer of MAP came from the Mauser factory. After the war, a range of .22 rim-fire automatics was introduced, the current E and D models appearing in 1954. These pistols are of the fixed barrel, simple blow-back type with external hammers, and are available in a range of barrel lengths from $4\frac{1}{4}''$ to $8\frac{1}{4}''$. The long barrel target versions can be supplied complete with barrel weights and a muzzle brake.

Prior to 1939, MAP manufactured the 'Mikros' auto-pistol and, in 1958, the name was revived for a vest pocket model which bears a resemblance to the Model 1934 Beretta. The 1958 Mikros is available in either .22 short or 6.35mm (.25 ACP) and, in the .22 version, a longer $4''$ barrel is available instead of the standard $2\frac{1}{4}''$ length.

The Model Rr-51 in 7.65mm (.32 ACP) and the Model Fr. .380 (9mm short) are conventional Browning type pistols with external hammers, and the somewhat similar Model L is also additionally available in .22 long rifle. Since the

7.65mm MAB Model D.

9mm MAB Model P.15. (MAB)

frame and slide of the pistol can be transferred to a light 18″ barrel rifle unit, the Model L forms the basis of the 'Combo' gun. The conversion from auto-pistol to auto-rifle takes about fifteen seconds, and the whole forms a simple and useful dual purpose weapon.

Not far from Hendaye, at Bayonne, the Société d'Exploitation de la Manufacture d'Armes Automatiques (MAB), founded in 1921 by the late M. Barthe, currently manufacture four models of auto-pistol. Early pistols resembled the Browning Model 1906, and the Model A, a six shot 6.35mm vest pocket pistol first introduced in 1925 and still manufactured, betrays its ancestry. So does the 6.35mm Model B, except that the front of the slide is cut away and ejection of the spent cartridge is upward instead of through the ejection port in the slide as with the Model A. Manufacture of the Model B began in 1932 and had only recently been discontinued.

The Model C resembles the Browning Model 1910 and the similar Model D, manufacture of which started in 1933, is still on the selling range in 7.65mm (.32 ACP) calibre. The Model E was introduced in 1949 in 6.35mm (.25 ACP) and manufacture appears to have been discontinued following the recent reorganisation of the company.

The 'R' series models have an external hammer and were originally made in 7.65mm, 7.65mm long French and 9mm Parabellum. The sole surviving example of the range is the Modèle R.22 which is offered in .22 long rifle with alternative barrel lengths of 4.4″ or 7.4″. The long barrel target version has adjustable sights. The Model F, introduced in 1950, has since been discontinued. This was a hammerless .22 pistol of simple design and available in several barrel lengths. Recently the range has been extended with the introduction of the Models P.8 and P.15. In contrast to previous production, the 'P' series are of locked breech design, but, instead of employing the Browning system, locking is accomplished by barrel rotation. The pistol bears an external resemblance to the Browning Model 1935, the P.8 having a magazine capacity of eight cartridges and the P. 15 of fifteen. Chambered for the 9mm Parabellum, the MAB pistols in the 'P' series are well made in a satisfactory military calibre, and their appearance, coupled with the recent acquisition of new and modern premises, augurs well for the future of this company. MAB pistols are currently listed in the Manufrance cataloque.

To what extent the rise of a firearms industry in the vicinity of Bayonne during the early part of the twentieth century can be attributed to the existing long-established Spanish gun industry across the border is not known, but certainly firearms were being made at Eibar near Bilbao as long ago as the fifteenth century. The town of Eibar, which lies in a valley of the Cantabrian mountains, possessed the necessary iron ore from Vizcaya, water power from the River Ego and, in the staunchly independent Basques, a source of high quality labour in which the skills associated with gunmaking became traditional. By the time of Charles V (1519–1556) Spain, enriched by the gold and silver of her American possessions, had become the most powerful nation in Europe. The gunmakers in and around the town of Eibar developed skills which were to arouse the envy of their competitors, particularly in the manufacture of gun barrels. The loss of the Spanish colonies engendered a feeling of inferiority which, coupled with the difficult transition into the machine age, resulted in a reduction in the standard and quality of work.

The first phase in the resurgence of the firearms industry, particularly with regard to the manufacture of pistols, took place immediately prior to the First World War. Probably the oldest of the three firms at present permitted to manufacture handguns is Gabilondo y Cia of Eigoibar, a small town not far from Eibar in the province of Guipuzcoa. Originally founded as Gabilondos y Urresti in 1904, the name was changed to Gabilondo y Urresti in 1909 and finally to its present form, Gabilondo y Cia, in 1919. Initial production was confined to shotguns and revolvers but, in 1914, Gabilondo started the manufacture of a simple blow-back internal hammer auto-pistol, a copy of the FN Browning Model of 1903. The company obtained from the Spanish Government the right to the exclusive use of the trade name 'Ruby' and the pistol was offered for sale in Europe and the Americas.

Shortly after the outbreak of war, the Ruby was offered to the French and, following trials, was adopted by the French Army as a subsidiary standard pistol. Orders were placed that called for delivery at the rate of 10,000—later increased to 30,000—per month and, since Gabilondo were unable to meet this, they subcontracted to a number of other firms in Eibar.

The quantity actually manufactured and supplied by Gabilondo themselves until the cancellation of the contract is reported as between 150,000 and 200,000. The number made by other manufacturers is not known but the demands made on the Basque firearms industry had a profound effect on the organisation and capabilities of the industry up until the outbreak of the Spanish Civil War in 1936.

After the war Gabilondo introduced a new type of pistol, patterned after the Browning Model 1910, which was sold widely under the names, Ruby, Danton and Buffalo. In the postwar period, the Browning 1903 type pistol was also made by a large number of firms in Eibar, so much so that these Spanish imitations are known as 'Eibar' pistols. Gabilondo themselves manufactured an Eibar type pistol under the name 'plus Ultra' until 1932, the outstanding feature being the extremely long grip frame which provided a magazine capacity (according to a contemporary catalogue) of twenty-three cartridges. The Danton, offered with magazine capacities of seven, nine and twelve cartridges, and in 6.35mm, 7.65mm and 9mm short, went out of production in 1933.

In 1931 Gabilondo decided to improve their range by introducing a recoil operated locked breech pistol with external hammer. Initially this was a copy of the Colt/Browning Model 1911 A1 and was offered in 9mm largo (9mm Bergmann) and .38 ACP calibres.

A series of straight blow-back auto-pistols was then introduced which retained the external appearance of the Colt/Browning, and the entire range was given the trade name of 'Llama', still currently employed by Gabilondo.

Details of current and obsolete Llama pistols are given below.

Model I. Introduced in 1934. A straight blow-back type in 7.65mm (.32 ACP) calibre with a fixed barrel.

Model II. A 9mm short version of the Model I.

Model III. A modification of the Model II in 9mm short. Went out of production in 1954.

Model IIIA. The current 9mm short (.380) locked breech auto-pistol. Magazine capacity is seven rounds and the pistol is fitted with a conventional pattern of grip safety in addition to the normal manual safety.

Model IV. The original Llama auto-pistol in 9mm largo.

Model V. Possibly the .38 ACP export version of the Model IV.

Model VI. Not known.

Model VII. As the Model IV in both 9mm largo and .38 ACP. Manufacture discontinued in 1954.

Model VIII. The current 9mm largo model with the addition of a grip safety. This model is not widely available in 9mm largo but is sold commercially in Super .38 Auto Pistol with nine round magazine capacity. Weight 2 lbs. 6½ ozs., barrel length 5″.

Model IX. Introduced about 1936. The locked breech model chambered for the .45 ACP cartridge.

Model IXA. An improved version of the Model IX and similar to the Model VIII with the additional grip safety. Currently offered in .45 ACP calibre with seven round magazine.

Model X. First introduced in 1935. The straight blow-back version in 7.65mm (.32 ACP) with a fixed barrel.

Model XA. The Model X with the addition of a

Gabilondo automatic pistols as advertised in a WUM catalogue of the early 1930's.
Top: 6.35mm Ruby.
Centre: 7.65mm Plus Ultra or Ruby Extra.
Bottom: Danton.

grip safety, and externally similar to the larger calibre Model IIIA in 9mm short, except that the XA is straight blow-back and the Model IIIA is locked breech. The .32 calibre Model XA has a $3\frac{11}{16}''$ barrel and an eight round magazine capacity.
Model XI. Still listed in the export catalogue in 9mm Parabellum. Differs from current production models in that a rounded hammer spur is fitted and there is no grip safety.
Model XII. .38 calibre Ruby Revolver. Also sold under the name Llama.
Model XIII. .32 calibre Ruby Revolver. Also sold under the name Llama.
Model XIV. .22 calibre Ruby Revolver. Also sold under the name Llama.
Model XV. Introduced in 1955. This is the current .22 long rifle model and is available in either standard or 'Airlite' versions. The steel version weighs 21 ozs., the Airlite Model 17 ozs. In effect a miniature version of the .45 Model 1911 A1 Colt, the Model XV has a barrel length of just under 4″ and a magazine capacity of nine rounds. A simple blow-back type pistol similar to the Model XA in .32 calibre.
Model XVI. The model designation for the Airlite version of the Model XV.
Model XVII. A recently introduced straight blow-back external hammer pocket pistol in .22 short calibre. Known also as the 'Executive' Model.
Model XVIII. The .25 version of the Model XVII.
Model XIX. Lightweight version of the Model IIIA.
Model XX. Lightweight version of the Model XA

Gabilondo y Cia, in addition to selling auto-pistols under the Llama mark, manufactured similar pistols sold by Jose Cruz Mugica (Manufacturas 'J.C.M.') of Eibar under the mark 'Mugica' and also the 'Tauler' pistols sold by Tauler of Madrid. Currently the .38 Super Model VIII and the .45 Model IXA are available with micrometer sights as the Super .38 Match and the .45 Auto Match, and, at extra cost, all models can be had silver or gold plated and in several styles of engraving.

The second important Spanish auto-pistol maker is Star, Bonifacio Echeverria SA of Eibar. The early history of this firm is in some dispute due to the destruction of the factory records, but they certainly manufactured automatic pistols of several types and in many variant forms. The early specimen illustrated (page 524) is the so-called 1919 type pistol in 6.35mm (.25 ACP) which was distinguished by the use of a safety at the top rear of the slide. Markings on these early models varied, but the most usual was 'automatic Pistol Star-Patent' followed by the calibre designation.

The Model CO can be regarded as an improved version of the 1919 type pistol. The slide safety was abandoned and the 6.35mm CO Pocket

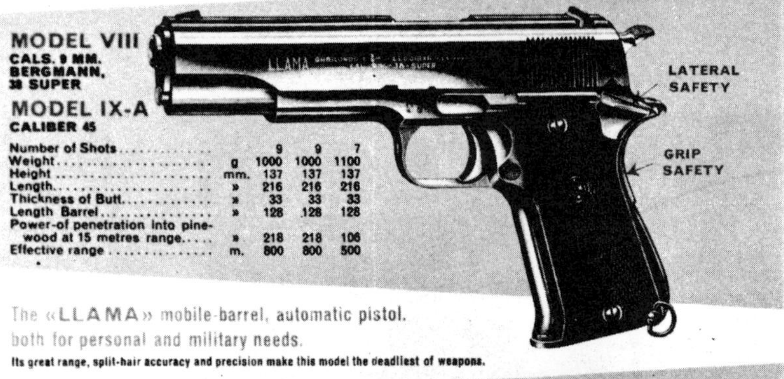

MODEL VIII
CALS. 9 MM. BERGMANN, 38 SUPER
MODEL IX-A
CALIBER 45

Number of Shots		9	9	7
Weight	g	1000	1000	1100
Height	mm.	137	137	137
Length	»	216	216	216
Thickness of Butt	»	33	33	33
Length Barrel	»	128	128	128
Power-of penetration into pinewood at 15 metres range	»	218	218	106
Effective range	m.	800	800	500

The «LLAMA» mobile-barrel, automatic pistol. both for personal and military needs.
Its great range, split-hair accuracy and precision make this model the deadliest of weapons.

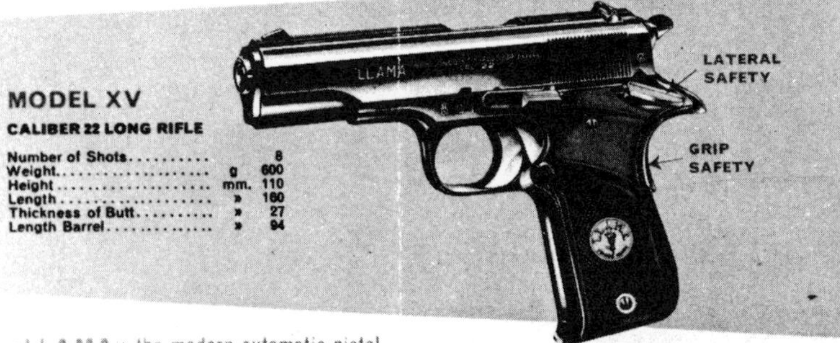

MODEL XV
CALIBER 22 LONG RIFLE

Number of Shots		8
Weight	g	600
Height	mm.	110
Length	»	160
Thickness of Butt	»	27
Length Barrel	»	94

«LLAMA» the modern automatic pistol, reduced size, high precision, fixed barrel.
The best for target shooting and general plinking.

LATERAL SAFETY

MODEL XVII
CALIBER 22 SHORT

Number of Shots		6
Weight	g	350
Height	mm.	85
Length	»	114
Thickness of Bull	»	25
Length Barrel	»	60

MODEL XIX
«AIRLITE»
Weight..... g 465

MODEL III-A
CALIBER 9 MM. SHORT (380)

Number of Shots		7
Weight	g	585
Height	mm.	110
Length	»	160
Thickness of Butt	»	27
Length Barrel	»	94
Power of penetration into pinewood at 25 metres range	»	70

The «LLAMA» officers' modern small-size, mobile-barrel, automatic pistol.
Specially designed for the Police-force, watchmen, etc. This model combines high penetrative power and perfect accuracy.

MODEL XI
CAL. 9 MM. PARABELLUM

Number of Shots		8
Weight	g	900
Height	mm.	127
Thickness of Butt	»	32
Length Barrel	»	122
Total length	»	193
Power of penetration into pinewood at 25 metres range	»	90

The «LLAMA» mobile-barrel automatic pistol, designed both for personal and military needs.
Its great range, perfect accuracy and deadly precision, make this model a most mortiferous weapon.

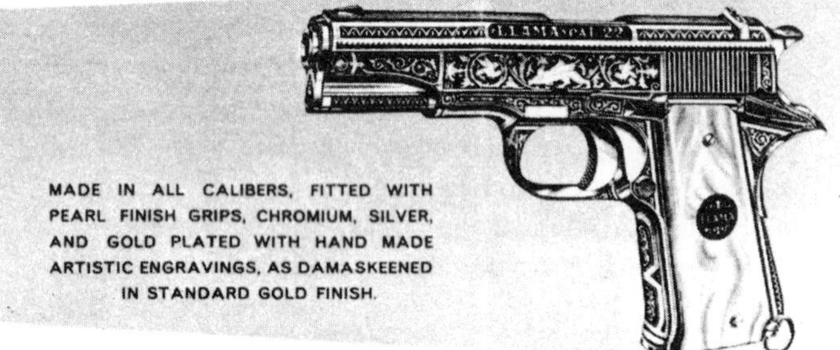

The «LLAMA» automatic pistol «Special de luxe».

Llama automatic pistols made by Gabilondo. (Gabilondo)

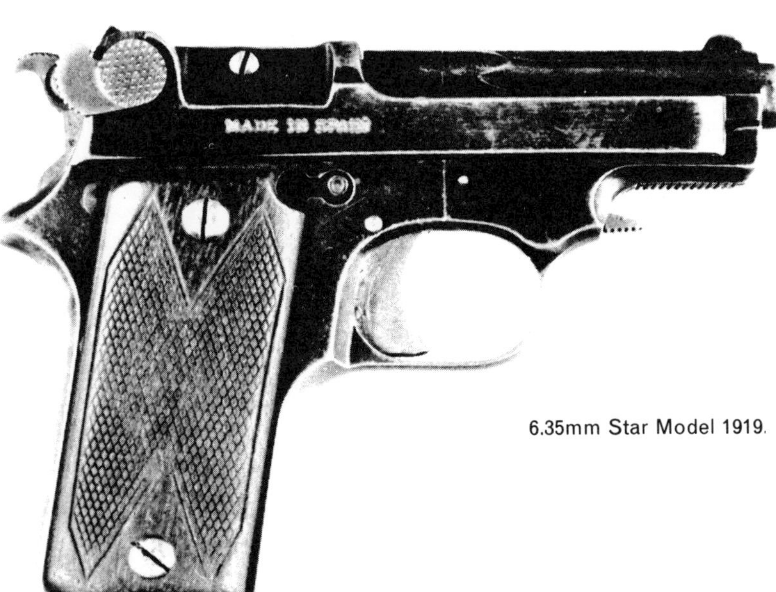

6.35mm Star Model 1919.

Model remained in production until 1957 when it was replaced by the Model CU. This is the current Star pocket hammer pistol, known also as the Starlet, and has a light alloy frame. The original type 1919 was the basis of the Star 1 Model which, in 7.65mm calibre, was known as the Modelo de Policia.

The Star 9mm Bergmann (largo) Military Model was externally similar to the Colt 1911 but retained the modified safety on the slide. The Star Models A, B and C were also similar to the Colt 1911 but lacked the grip safety device. Calibres available were 7.63mm Mauser, 9mm Parabellum, 9mm largo, 9mm (.38 ACP) and .45 ACP. Special magazines with increased capacity, either sixteen or thirty-two cartridges, were available for certain models and a 'case' type shoulder stock/holster could also be supplied.

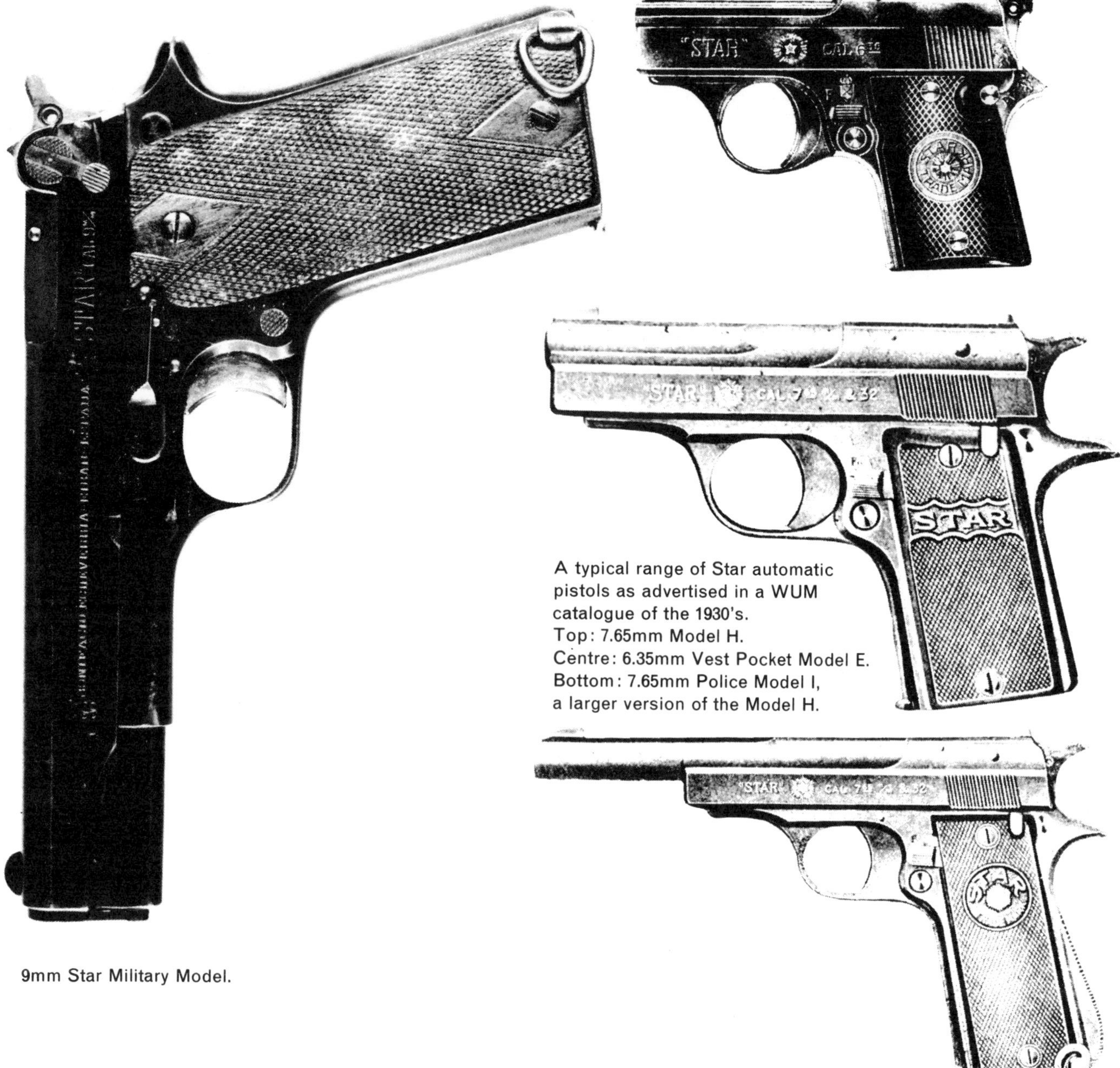
9mm Star Military Model.

A typical range of Star automatic pistols as advertised in a WUM catalogue of the 1930's.
Top: 7.65mm Model H.
Centre: 6.35mm Vest Pocket Model E.
Bottom: 7.65mm Police Model I, a larger version of the Model H.

The .22 'F' series Star blow-back pistols enjoyed considerable popularity and were made in 4¼″, 6″ and 7″ barrel lengths. There was also an Olympic version with barrel weights, adjustable sights and muzzle brake.

The Star commercial range at present includes the Model HF or 'Lancer', a short barrel lightweight version of the Model F with external hammer in .22 long rifle, the 'Starlet' or Model CU in .25 ACP, and the Model DK or 'Starfire', a 9 mm short (.380) auto-pistol with light alloy frame and external hammer.

The larger Star auto-pistols include the Pocket Model SI in 7.65 mm (.32 ACP), and the Model S Super in .380 (9 mm short) which incorporates a special quick take-down feature and a magazine safety. The Model A Super in .38 Super and the Model B Super in 9 mm Parabellum also have this quick take-down feature where the Browning link pin is replaced by a cam and ramp locking system. The locking lever on the right hand side of the frame is rotated to remove the slide.

The illustration (page 526) comparing the .38 Colt Super automatic and the Star Model B shows the different extractor. The Star also lacks the hold-open device of the Colt.

The Model P, an almost identical copy of the Colt 1911 in .45 ACP, is still on the selling range but the Model Super P appears to have been discontinued.

An interesting variant is the Model MD which was made in 9mm, 7.65mm and .45 ACP, had the conventional wooden shoulder stock/holster and could be converted from semi-auto to full-automatic fire.

The last of the important Spanish makers of

A comparison of the .38 Colt Super automatic (top) and the 9mm Star Model B. (Glasgow Police Collection)

automatic pistols is Astra, Unceta y Cia of Guernica. Both Eibar and Elgoibar lie on the main road between Bilbao and San Sebastian, but Guernica is nearer to the coast. Astra, Unceta y Cia started life in Eibar as Esperanza y Unceta in 1908. Don Pedro Unceta was in charge of administration and Don Juan Esperanza, a native of Aragon, was in charge of the manufacturing side of the business. About 1912 the firm, having made parts for other manufacturers and a simple blow-back Browning type pistol, the 'Victoria', began to suffer from growing pains, and these were aggravated by an order for the Spanish Military 'Campogiro' pistol. The need for additional premises dictated the move of the company from Eibar to Guernica where their new factory was established in 1913.

Don Venancio López de Ceballos y Aguirre, Count of Campo Giro, a Lieutenant Colonel in the Spanish Army, was a well-known firearms designer at the turn of the century. Experimental versions of his locked breech pistol were followed by the Model 1910 which, in 9mm Bergmann calibre, was adopted by the Spanish Army. One thousand pistols were purchased and, in 1913, a straight blow-back version of the pistol was adopted, again manufactured by Esperanza y Unceta. Further modifications and improvements took place until production was discontinued in 1921. In 1913, however, Don Pedro Unceta had begun to devote his time to other interests, and his son, Don Rufino, became the guiding hand of the growing enterprise.

The difficulties of establishing a factory in a predominantly agricultural community were many: machine tools had to be transferred, key personnel had to be housed, and an additional work force had to be trained. But there was also the compensating advantage of new and spacious factory premises instead of the motley collection of basements, courtyards, wine cellars, sheds and garrets that were characteristic of Eibar. There, due to the cramped conditions, every available square foot of space had had to be utilised.

At Guernica, the centre of a broad and fertile countryside, communications were also much easier for, 'since 1888 ran a train, wearily and at times at trotting pace, which with its mane of steam, tousled by the wind, shattered with its strident whistle the silence of valleys which it crossed'.

Esperanza y Unceta barely had time to reorganise their production before the First World War made its insatiable demands on the industrial capacity of the combatants. Situated close to the French border, Esperanza y Unceta were well placed to supply French orders for 7.65mm pistols of similar design to the 'Victoria' but marked 'Automatic Pistol—Astra Patent'. Several variants appeared with different barrel lengths, and the manufacturers state that Astra pistols were not only supplied to the French but also to the Italians. After the war, manufacture of the Victoria and related Astra Model 100 was discontinued and a new pistol was developed.

The new models, which date from 1921, were the Astra Models 300, 400 and 600, and the post-war series 3000 and 4000. Known also as the 'tubular' types, this series was a basic modification of the Browning, but was equally influenced by the 'Campogiro' pistol. The military Model 400, known also as the Model 1921, was normally manufactured in 9mm largo (Bergmann) calibre, but it was unusual in that other cartridges, such as the .38 ACP, 9mm Browning long, 9mm Parabellum, 9mm Steyr and 9mm Browning short (.380) could also be used. With the lower powered cartridge, however, it would not always operate semi-automatically. Although of straight blow-back construction, the Astra 400 and the basically similar Model 600 (chambered for the 9mm Parabellum) were able to handle powerful cartridges because they had both a heavy slide and a strong recoil spring. The Model 600, which was made for the German Army, was shorter than the Model 400 both in barrel length and in width of grip (due to the shorter 9mm Parabellum cartridge).

To field strip both models, the magazine was removed and the pistol checked to ensure that it was empty. The slide was then pulled to the rear and the safety catch rotated upward until it engaged in the slide. The barrel was rotated to disengage both barrel and slide lugs, the safety catch was released, and both barrel and slide could be pulled forward off the frame.

The Model 400 was adopted for Spanish Military service in 1921 and, during the 1930's, was supplied to the French Government. The Astra Model 600 had the marking 'Pist. Patr. 08' on the slide and bore German Ordnance acceptance marks.

The Model 300 which, oddly enough, post-dated the Model 400, was a shorter version of it, and, in 1922, was adopted by the Spanish Navy and Police in 9mm Browning short (.380) and was also sold to Germany during World War Two marked '9mm Kurz'. The similar Model 3000 was chambered for the 7.65mm cartridge.

During the 1930's a copy of the Mauser Model 1896 was marketed, the Astra 900. This had an integral box magazine holding ten rounds and, although externally similar to the Mauser, was different from it in that it had a sliding plate on the left hand side of the frame, and the barrel extension could be lifted off the frame instead of having to be slid off.

Early models had a one line inscription, 'Astra Automatic Pistol Cal. 7.63', on the side of the frame. Later models included 'Patented July 12, 1928' on a second line. The Model 901 was a full-automatic version of the Model 900. The Model 902, also a full-automatic, had the magazine capacity increased to twenty rounds and a longer barrel. The Model 903 was issued with interchangeable ten and twenty round magazines, and

9mm Astra Model 400 or Model 1921. (Glasgow Police Collection)

9mm Astra Model 300 with German Ordnance acceptance marks. (Glasgow Police Collection)

factory literature stated that, in addition to 7.63mm Mauser, it could be supplied in 9mm Parabellum, .38 ACP and 9mm Bergmann. The Model 1903 E was available in the semi-automatic version only. The only model of the 900 series which bore any model identification was the Modelo F in 9mm Bergmann, the standard sidearm of the Spanish Civil Guard. The change lever for the selective fire models 901, 902 and 903 was on the right hand side of the frame and was marked '1' and '20'. The markings for the Model F were 'A' for 'Ametrallador, (full-automatic) and 'T' for 'Tiro a tiro' (single shot or semi-automatic). Although the Astra was a copy of the Mauser it should not be forgotten that the ten round Model 901 and the twenty round Model 902 appeared on the market before the Mauser Model 1932 Schnellfeuer Pistol.

In spite of the general economic world crisis of the 1920's, the company developed the 900 series and made strenuous efforts to sell this pistol abroad, particularly in China where a branch office was opened in Shanghai under the name 'Astra China Company'. In 1926 the company title was changed to Unceta y Cia, and efforts were made to halt the decline in business which was aggravated by domestic political uncertainty. The precise role played by Unceta y Cia during the Spanish Civil War is still obscure. The Basque provinces, which include Vizcaya, were granted autonomy by the Republican Government in October 1936, but terrible retribution followed in April of the following year when Guernica, the ancient Basque capital, was completely destroyed by the Insurgents under General Franco.

When hostilities ceased, Franco's National Government issued extensive decrees for reconstruction, and the arms industry, hampered by restrictive legislation, attempted to regain their former export markets. Due to the efforts of Don Rufino Unceta, his company managed to survive and is today one of the three arms firms permitted to manufacture pistols by the Government. During World War Two, Unceta, as already mentioned, exported the Models 300 and 400 to Germany, and afterwards a successful attempt was made to diversify production with the manufacture of pneumatic tools and textile machinery.

In 1953 the world famous 'Astra' trade mark was incorporated in the company title, Astra, Unceta y Cia. The present range of pistols includes the Model 200, a 6.35mm concealed hammer vest pocket pistol with magazine and grip safety which is also sold under the name of Astra Firecat, and the Model 2000, similar except that it has an external hammer. The latter is also available in .22 short rim-fire as the Astra Cub, and an extended barrel version with a laterally adjustable rear sight, the Astra Camper, has recently been introduced.

Differing from the discontinued Models 300 and 3000 only in that an external hammer is now provided, the Astra Model 4000 (Falcon) is available in .22, .32 and .380 calibres and a conversion unit can be supplied to fit the .32 and .380 pistols with a complete slide unit and magazine suitable for the .22 rim-fire cartridge. Also now provided with an external hammer, the Model 800 (Condor), in 9mm Parabellum, is a revised version of the Model 1921 Military or 400 series. Astra, as we have seen, also manufacture a revolver and single and double barrelled shotguns.

The major firms of Star, Gabilondo and Astra, Unceta, now have a virtual monopoly in the manufacture of handguns in Spain. The very large number of much smaller companies who produced countless cheap automatic pistols and revolvers for the world markets have all disappeared. From small family industries, in Eibar, Guernica and Elgoibar, that flourished in cellars, courtyards, shops, attics and even in the narrow passageways between buildings, there used to flow a stream of pistols with such names as Atlas, Bronco, Buffalo, Bulwark, Cobra, Defender, Demon, Express, Frontier, Gloria, Imperial, Jupiter, Liberty and many, many others—names designed to appeal to the 'foreigner' and to disguise the Spanish origin. Many of these pistols are illustrated in the second volume of *Firearms Identification* by Howard Matthews, and one typical example is shown opposite, by Victor Bernedo y Cia of Eibar. But, as happened in both Liege and Brescia, the tendency has been to concentrate on better quality pistols produced by modern production techniques under controlled conditions.

The manufacture of firearms has been established in many parts of the world due to economic, nationalistic or military considerations. A classic example is the Polish 9mm VIS 35 auto-pistol (often incorrectly known as the Radom). Prior to 1935 the Polish Army had been supplied with a number of different types of handgun, many the legacy of the old Austro-

9mm Polish Radom VIS Model 35. (Glasgow Police Collection)

6.35mm Bernedo automatic pistol.

Hungarian Empire. For obvious reasons it was decided to standardise on one type of weapon and trials were therefore held in 1935. The pistol selected was an ingenious variation of the classic Browning short recoil action designed by two Polish engineers, Wilniewczyc and Skrzypinski. Manufacture was undertaken by the Government Small Arms Factory at Radom (Fabryka Broni w Radomiu) in 1936.

Pistols made until 1939 were marked 'F. B. Radom', followed by the year of manufacture, 'VIS-wz. 35' (wz=Model) and 'Pat. Nr. 15567'. The letters 'FB' (Fabryka Broni) were marked on the left hand grip and VIS, the Latin word for force or power, on the right hand one. This was also a play on the initials of the inventors, since 'W' and 'V' have the same sound in Polish. A large Polish eagle crest was stamped on the left hand side of the slide, and this particular model was made both with and without a shoulder stock groove in the back-strap. Manufacture of the VIS 35 continued under German occupation, but the Polish eagle was eliminated and the marks were altered to read 'F.B. Radom VIS Mod. 35'. Sometimes the stamp 'P-35(p)' was used, standing for 'Pistole 35 (polnisch)'. Later models showed a deterioration in the finish and slight modifications. These pistols usually had a phosphate finish instead of the traditional polished blue. Pistols made under German occupation bore German Ordnance markings.

Magazine capacity of the VIS 35 was eight rounds, and the calibre 9mm Parabellum. Bearing a close external resemblance to the Colt Model 1911 A1, the external hammer was rounded instead of having a spur, and the lever on the left hand side of the frame allowed the hammer to be safely lowered since it retracted the firing pin before releasing the hammer. All models had a grip safety, but the separate take-down latch at the rear of the frame was not fitted to examples of late German production. Since this latch was in the same position as the safety on the Colt Model 1911, it could sometimes be mistaken for a safety. On the VIS 35 it had no safety function whatsoever and was a disassembly aid only.

8mm Nambu Type 14, small trigger guard version.

The manufacture of yet another basic Browning design, the HAFDASA (Hispano Argentina Fab. de Automoviles) or Ballester-Molina has already been discussed, and this Argentine made pistol is illustrated on page 439.

In Mexico a variant of the basic Browning system, the Obregon, was made for the Government by Fabrica de Armas of Mexico City. The locking system of the Obregon was of the rotating barrel type, and the barrel did not hinge downward as on the Colt-Browning. Externally very similar to the Colt Model 1911 A1, the Obregon was very well made and had fewer parts than the Colt. The manual safety was in the same position as the Model 1911 and a grip safety was fitted.

The Colt Model 1911 A1 has also been copied more recently in Korea by the Pusan Jin Iron Works at Pusan, but traditional Oriental pistols (except those of Japanese origin) are copies of the Mauser 1896 type in both 7.63mm Mauser and .45 ACP calibres. The Chinese made excellent copies of the Mauser at Hanyang Arsenal and at the Shansei Province Arsenal, but the most widely used automatic pistol in the Far Eastern Communist block is the Russian Tokarev in 7.62mm calibre. Some have been imported from Russia, others made from Russian components; more recently, manufacture has been established in China using tools and machinery imported from Russia. During the Korean War, apart from the Tokarev, the Communist forces used the Mauser Model 1896 and Spanish and Chinese copies of it, Model 1911 and 1911 A1 Colts captured from the Chinese Nationalists, the Browning Model 35 of Belgian and Canadian manufacture (also captured from the Nationalists) and also the latest Russian Makarov and Stechkin auto-pistols. In addition, there were Chinese copies of various Browning models, in particular the Model 1900, and also copies of copies of the originals. Whether or not Communist China will standardise on Russian small arms or eventually develop her own designs remains to be seen.

The arrival of the American Commodore Perry in 1854 brought Japan from the matchlock to the cartridge breechloader in one vast technological leap. The first Japanese automatic pistol was designed by Colonel, later Lieut-General, Kijiro Nambu in 1904 and, in 1925, the Japanese Army issued a modified version of the original Nambu as the Pistol Type 14 (the 14th year of the Taisho reign or 1925). Manufacture was carried out by several Government arsenals and private firms with variations in the shape of the cocking piece and, about 1920, a version with a larger

8mm Nambu Type 14, large trigger guard version. (Col. F. S. Allen)

8mm Nambu Type 94. (Glasgow Police Collection)

8mm Nambu Type 14, large trigger guard version with a different cocking piece.

trigger guard was introduced. The Nambu Type 14 was in 8mm Japanese calibre, a cartridge which resembled the 7.65mm Parabellum, and employed a locked breech, using a system similar to the Italian Glisenti. Magazine capacity was eight rounds. This pistol had several bad features, the worst being that it could be reassembled without the locking block. If fired like this, damage to the gun and possible injury to the firer could result.

To strip the Type 14, the magazine was removed and, with the bolt held to the rear, the trigger guard was pulled down (it slid down the front strap). The muzzle was then pressed against a solid surface and the breech plug given a quarter turn and withdrawn. The bolt could then be pulled out of the sleeve and the firing pin could be removed from it. When the magazine was empty the bolt stayed to the rear, but when the magazine was removed, it flew forward. A magazine safety was fitted to prevent the pistol from firing when the magazine was withdrawn.

The Nambu Type 94 was designed by Nambu in 1934 and was intended for commercial export. After 1926 the method of dating was altered and models were given a date derived from the assumed date of the foundation of the Japanese Empire. On this basis, the Nambu Type 94 was adopted in the year 2594 of the Japanese Calendar, the last two digits being used for official nomenclature. With the entrance of Japan into World War Two, this pistol was adopted for military use and manufacture was carried out by Government Arsenals. It was, however, of inferior design and workmanship and, since the sear was exposed, a slight pressure could result in accidental discharge.

The same feature was present on the 7mm Nambu, a smaller version of the Type 14, but this weapon was not produced in great numbers. The three quarter size or 'Baby' Nambu retained the front grip safety originally a feature of the early Type 14. The cartridge was of special design manufactured only in Japan and is now a collector's item.

Following the end of World War Two, the Shin Chuo Kogyo KK of Tokyo manufactured, and still manufacture, a copy of the Colt 1911 A1 in both 9mm Parabellum and .45 ACP calibres. These pistols are marked 'New Nambu Model 57'. The New Nambu Model 57B is a close copy of the FN 7.65mm (.32 ACP) Browning and is of straight blow-back design. The Shin Chuo Kogyo KK have manufactured arms since 1927 and, in fact, made the Type 14 Nambu and the 'Baby' Nambu for the Japanese Government. Currently, production of both the auto-pistols and of a copy of the Smith and Wesson revolver is entirely taken up by Japanese Civil and Military Authorities, but no doubt these pistols will be exported in the future.

7mm Nambu Officers Model or 'Baby' Nambu.

Mention has already been made of the Finnish Lahti auto-pistol, but additional data is more than justified since the designer of this pistol, Aimo Johannes Lahti, one time Chief of the Government Arsenal of Finland, was an arms designer of some note. The pistol was designed in 1926 in 7.65mm calibre and was manufactured in 9mm calibre by the Valtion Kivaari Tehdas (State Rifle Factory) at Jyvaskyla. Adopted as the Finnish L-35, it was later also taken up by the Danish Army as the Model 40s and by the Swedes as the m/40 (to replace the German Walther P-38, supplies of which were discontinued on the outbreak of war). Both the Danish and the Swedish models were manufactured under licence by the Husqvarna factory in Sweden, but production was discontinued in 1944.

Chambered for the 9mm Parabellum cartridge, the Lahti is a heavy, rugged pistol admirably adapted to the conditions for which it

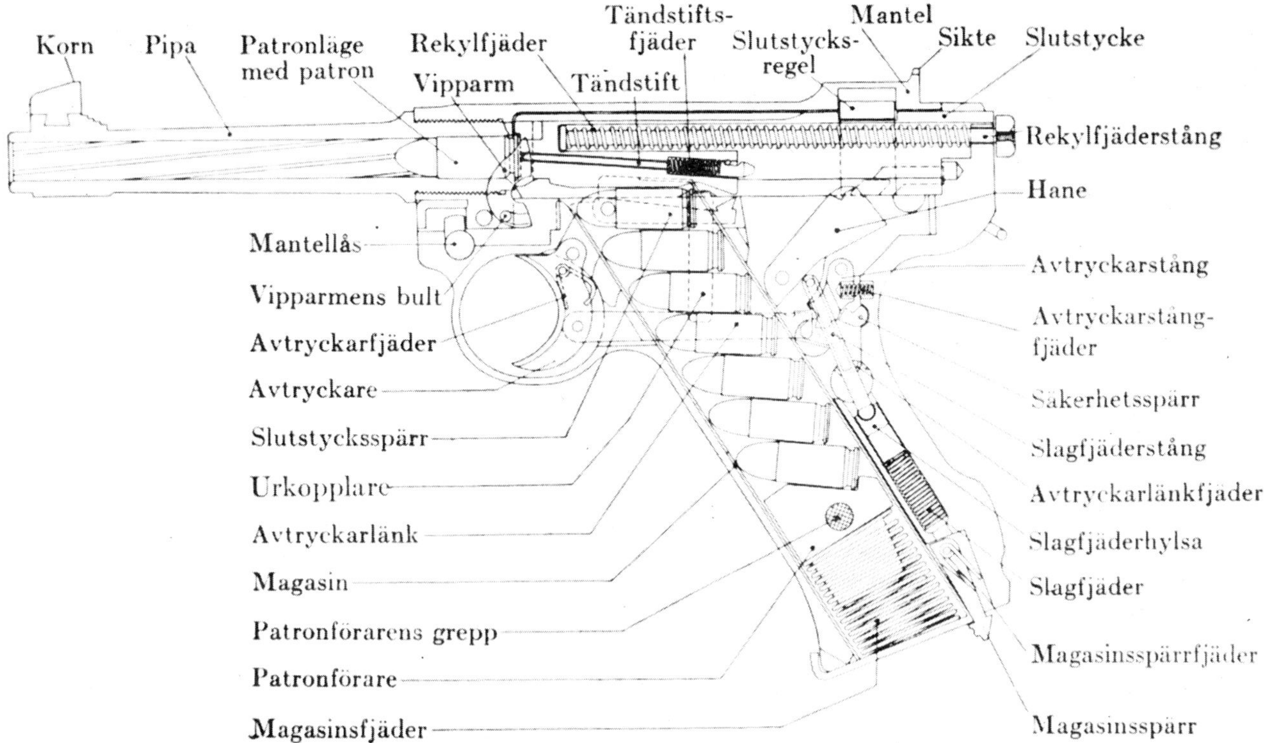

Sectional view of the 9mm Swedish Lahti m/40.

was designed. Take-down was simple. After the magazine had been removed, the barrel was pressed against a hard surface and the take-down catch at the left front of the frame rotated. The barrel assembly could then be slid forward off the frame. The locking block was removed from the barrel extension (when replacing the locking block, care had to be taken to ensure that the arrow underneath was pointing towards the muzzle) and the slide withdrawn. The pistol could, in fact, be reassembled without the locking block and would still fire. This was an undesirable feature of the pistol and, if a Lahti is fired today, a check should be made to see that the locking block is present.

Finnish pistols bear the marking 'VKT' on the grips and on the barrel extension. Some, marked 'Valmet', were made by the State Metal Works (Valtion Metallitehtaat), and others may bear the letters 'S.A.' (Suomen Armeija: Finnish Army). Those made in Sweden have a larger trigger guard and the grips carry the letter 'H' surmounted by a crown, the trademark of Husqvarna Vapenfabriks AB.

Information on weapons manufactured in the Soviet Union is restricted either on military grounds or because the selling organisation is State controlled and has little interest in the product.

The military use of automatic pistols dates from the introduction of the 7.62mm Tokarev developed by Fjodor Wassiljewitsch Tokarev, who served with the Czarist Armies in the First World War and was later employed at the famous Tula Arsenal. The TT-30 (Tula Tokarev) was quite a remarkable pistol. Much of the design was inspired by Browning, particularly with regard to the locking system. Manufacture, however, was made very much cheaper and simpler, and it was also cheaper to repair. The grip safety and mechanical safety of the Browning design were eliminated and the magazine was unusual in that it could be dismantled for cleaning and repair. In 1933 the original model was modified, and the Browning type locking lugs on the top of the barrel were discarded in favour of circumferential grooves which again simplified production.

To dismantle the TT-30, a cartridge nose was used to compress the recoil spring so that the barrel bushing could be rotated until the locking lugs disengaged. A cartridge or the base of the magazine could be used to release the spring locking clip on the right hand side of the frame. The locking pin was then withdrawn and the barrel and slide assembly were pushed forward free of the receiver. The receiver sub-assembly and hammer mechanism could then be lifted out of the receiver.

The Tokarev TT-30 was manufactured by several arsenals at Tula and production continued until the mid-1950's and possibly later. Most of the Tula-made pistols had serrated black plastic grips bearing a five pointed star with the letters 'CCCP' (USSR). Manufacture was also carried out in Poland at the Fabryka Broni w Radomi, and the grips on the Polish-made pistols had the letters 'FB' in a triangular panel on the left and the letters 'WP' on the right.

The TT-30 replaced the Nagant and Pieper revolvers and, in 1953, was itself replaced by the Makarov (PM). In 1958 the Stechkin Machine Pistol was introduced.

The 7.62mm Soviet pistol ammunition, which was similar to the 7.63mm Mauser (Mauser ammunition could be used in the TT-30), has now been replaced by the 9mm Soviet pistol cartridge similar in design to the experimental 9mm Ultra German cartridge in prototype stage at the end of World War Two. The 9mm Soviet has a bullet weight of 94 grains and is longer than the .380 ACP, but shorter than the 9mm Parabellum. It is not interchangeable with any other cartridge. Since the ammunition is not as powerful as the 7.62mm round formerly employed, both the new Soviet pistols are of straight blowback design.

The Makarov is an enlarged version of the Walther Model PP and operation and disassembly are similar. The Stechkin or APS is capable of semi- or full-automatic fire and is provided with a shoulder stock holster similar to the Mauser Model 96 type. The Makarov is issued to field officers and the Stechkin to officers in combat units and to NCOs and soldiers in special units.

Neither of these pistols is available for sale to civilians but, in recent years, the Soviet Union has made a considerable effort to introduce target pistols of Russian manufacture to world markets. Their efforts have been aided by the considerable success of Soviet marksmen in international competition.

Sales abroad are handled by V/O Raznoexport of Moscow, and both automatic pistols and single shot 'Free' pistols have been developed and marketed. As far as is at present known, the Soviet Union do not manufacture target pistols other than in .22 calibre, although the 7.62mm Nagant revolver is still used for domestic competition. Czech .38 calibre revolvers have been used by Soviet marksmen in international competitions, as have the Smith and Wesson K-38 revolvers.

The man responsible for the most widely used Soviet target pistols is Mikhail Margolin. Although blind, Margolin was invited to work at the great Russian arms centre of Tula (the first Superintendent of which was an Englishman, Trewhellar), noted throughout the years for the skill of its metal workers. (One of the Tula blacksmiths of old was so skilful that he is said to have shod a flea!) Margolin had the opportunity of meeting and working with the great Russian arms designers, Fjodor Tokarev, Georgi Schpagin and Serge Simonov. The early Margolin pistols were based on the Tokarev TT-30 and the first successful .22 automatic was developed shortly before Russian involvement in World War Two.

The first Margolin target .22 auto-pistol appeared on the range at the 1949 USSR Championships and, in 1954, at Caracas, Venezuela, the Russians achieved international success. This was repeated in the 1956 Olympics held in Melbourne when the Russians appeared with the now famous 'upside-down' pistol, yet another Margolin design. This pistol was specially designed for the .22 rapid-fire events. The five round magazine was loaded from the top, and the barrel was level with the middle finger of the hand holding the pistol. This type of pistol was, however, ruled out by the International Shooting Union in 1958, and consequently, unless the rules are amended, the 'upside-down' pistol will not be seen on international ranges again.

Current Margolin auto-pistols are a development of his earlier designs, the Margolin 'Vostok' MЦ. and MЦ.1. Since the Russian letter 'Ц' has no equivalent in English, two conventions have grown up. The first is to disregard the little 'tail' on the Russian letter and just call it 'U', the second, since the letter is pronounced 'tse', is to translate it as 'Tz' or 'Ts'. The problem is further complicated since the letter 'Ц' is sometimes translated as 'C'. The Margolin pistols have for this reason been described as the 'MЦ', 'MU', 'MTs', 'MTz', and the 'MC'. In Britain, pistol shooters refer to the 'MU' pistol, and small bore riflemen to the 'MTs' rifle. In the present text the

.22 long rifle Margolin Vostock MU target pistol with muzzle brake, barrel weight and palm shelf. (See next page).

7.62mm Tokarev Model of 1930. (Glasgow Police Collection)

term 'MU' will be used since it appears to have been sanctified by usage.

The MU pistol is chambered for the .22 long rifle and the MU-I for the .22 short cartridge. The MU also differs in that it is fitted with a trigger stop screw, a safety catch, steel slide and plastic grips. Both pistols are external hammer, simple blow-back types. The MU-I has a light alloy slide and wooden grips with a frame extension and adjustable hand rest. Magazine capacity for both pistols is six cartridges. Barrel length is the same at $6\frac{1}{4}''$ and the barrel is screwed into the frame. Both pistols are fitted with a muzzle brake and the rear sight is mounted on a 'bridge' attached to the frame. To dismount, the knurled take-down pin in front of the frame is pulled forward and turned, the 'slide cotter' can then be removed, the recoil spring and slide block pulled forward, and the slide itself pulled to the rear.

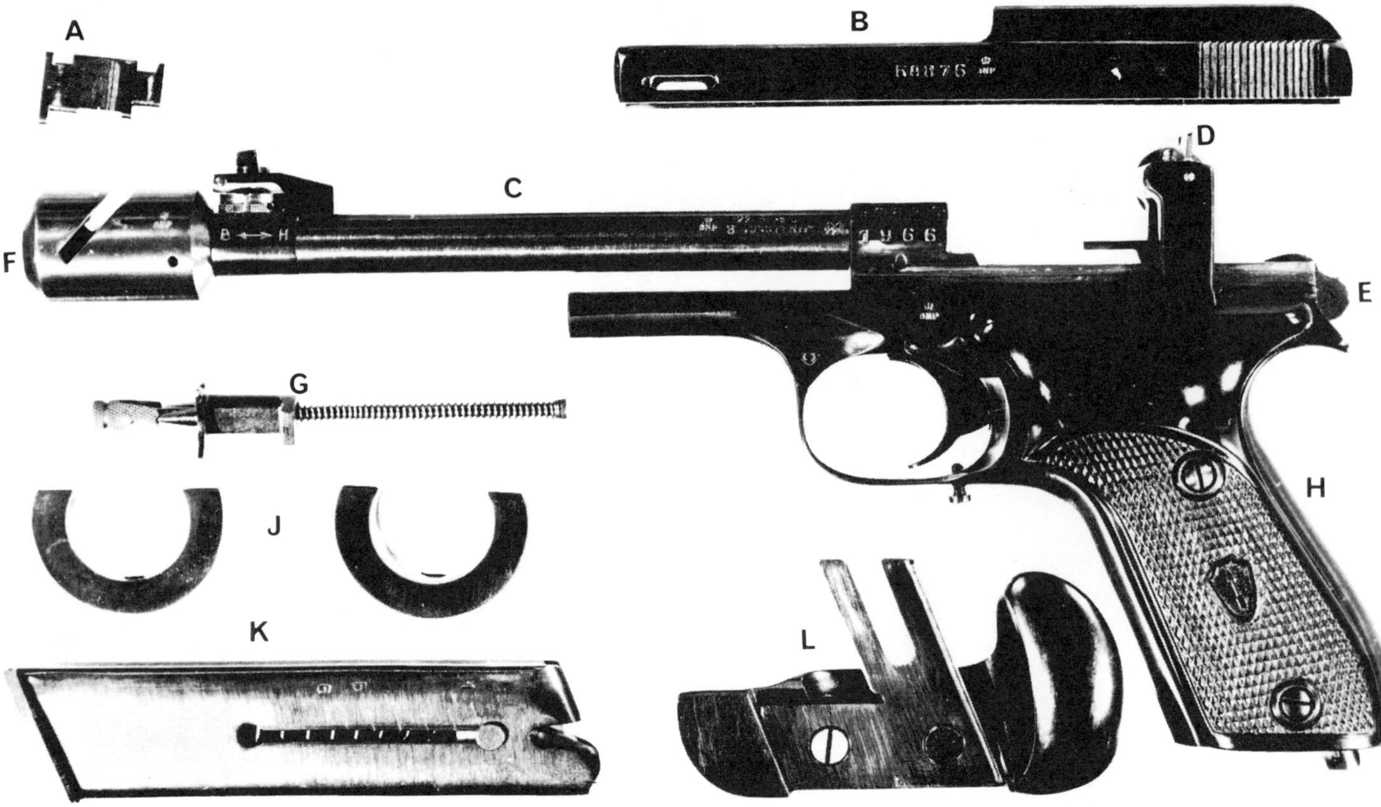

.22 long rifle Margolin Vostock MU dismantled.

A. Cross bolt.
B. Slide.
C. Barrel.
D. Rear sight.
E. Hammer.
F. Muzzle brake.
G. Recoil spring and guide.
H. Frame.
J. Barrel weights.
K. Magazine.
L. Adjustable rest.

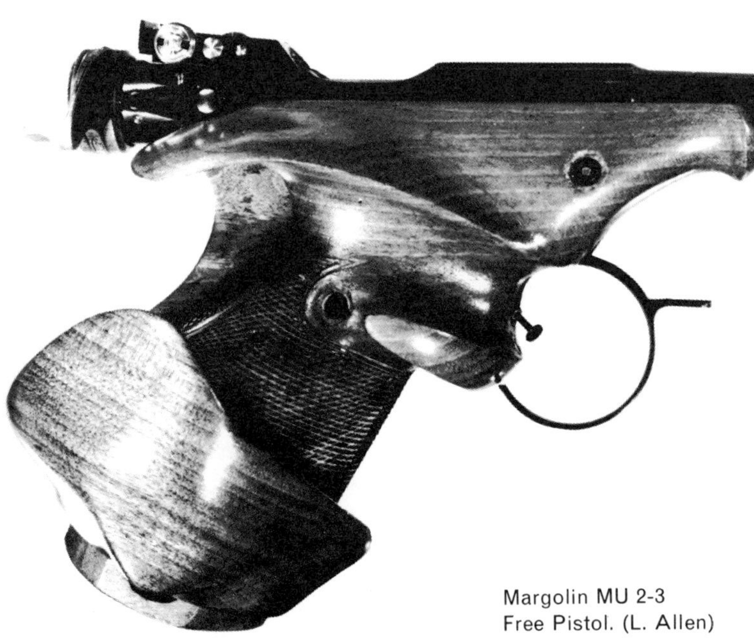

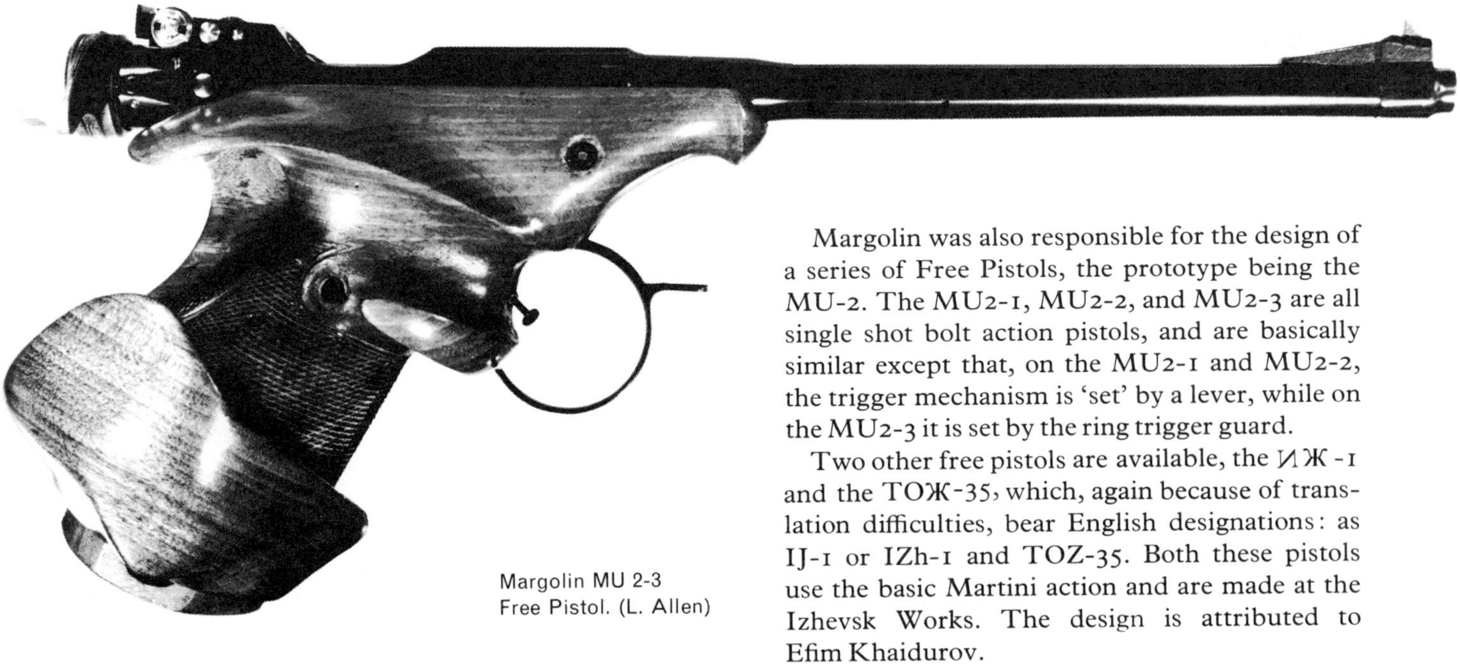

Margolin MU 2-3 Free Pistol. (L. Allen)

Margolin was also responsible for the design of a series of Free Pistols, the prototype being the MU-2. The MU2-1, MU2-2, and MU2-3 are all single shot bolt action pistols, and are basically similar except that, on the MU2-1 and MU2-2, the trigger mechanism is 'set' by a lever, while on the MU2-3 it is set by the ring trigger guard.

Two other free pistols are available, the ИЖ-1 and the ТОЖ-35, which, again because of translation difficulties, bear English designations: as IJ-1 or IZh-1 and TOZ-35. Both these pistols use the basic Martini action and are made at the Izhevsk Works. The design is attributed to Efim Khaidurov.

All Soviet pistols are sold in very stout wooden cases complete with accessories and spare parts. The finish is good and their considerable success in international competitions speaks for their functioning and accuracy.

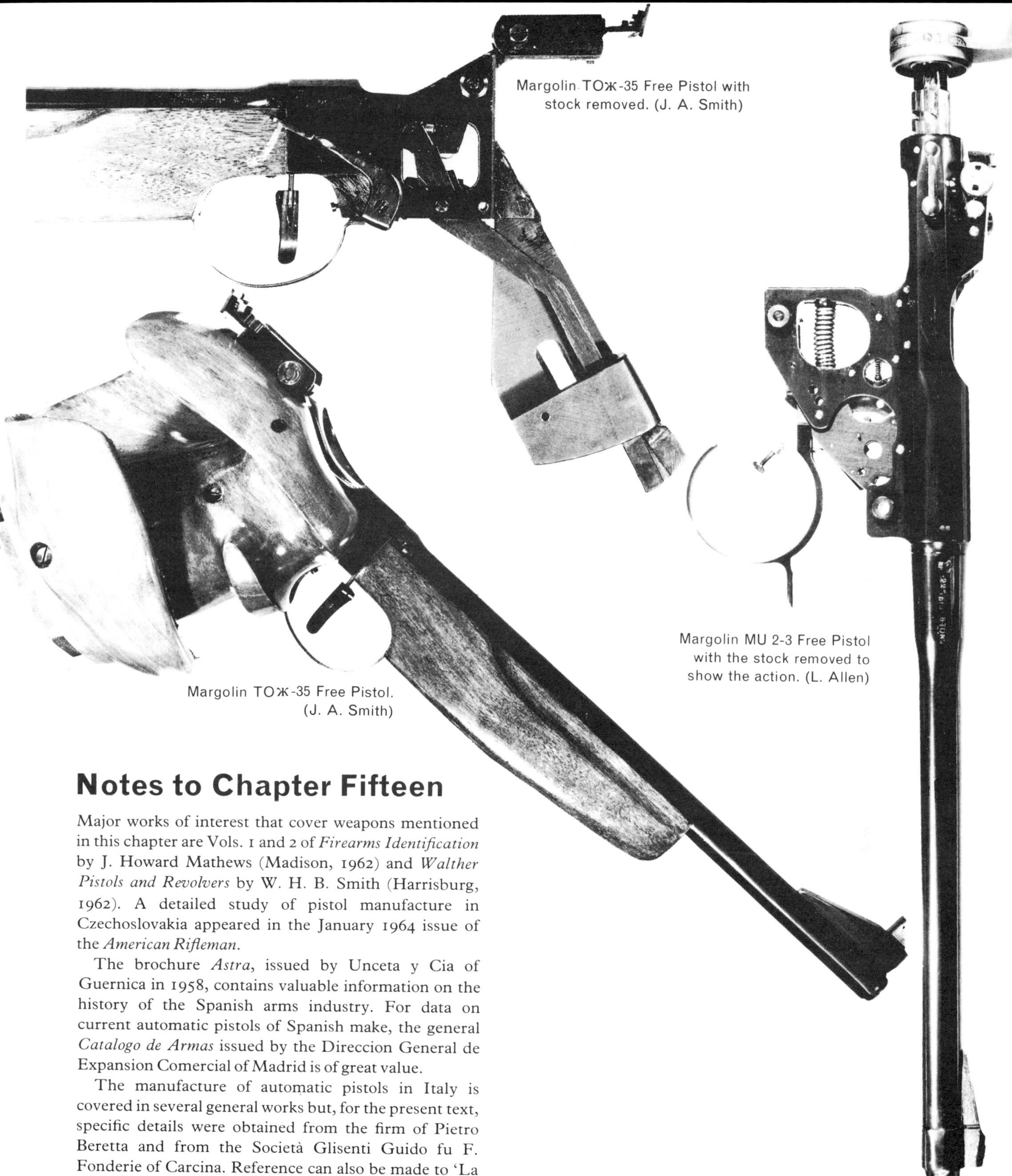

Margolin TOЖ-35 Free Pistol with stock removed. (J. A. Smith)

Margolin MU 2-3 Free Pistol with the stock removed to show the action. (L. Allen)

Margolin TOЖ-35 Free Pistol. (J. A. Smith)

Notes to Chapter Fifteen

Major works of interest that cover weapons mentioned in this chapter are Vols. 1 and 2 of *Firearms Identification* by J. Howard Mathews (Madison, 1962) and *Walther Pistols and Revolvers* by W. H. B. Smith (Harrisburg, 1962). A detailed study of pistol manufacture in Czechoslovakia appeared in the January 1964 issue of the *American Rifleman*.

The brochure *Astra*, issued by Unceta y Cia of Guernica in 1958, contains valuable information on the history of the Spanish arms industry. For data on current automatic pistols of Spanish make, the general *Catalogo de Armas* issued by the Direccion General de Expansion Comercial of Madrid is of great value.

The manufacture of automatic pistols in Italy is covered in several general works but, for the present text, specific details were obtained from the firm of Pietro Beretta and from the Società Glisenti Guido fu F. Fonderie of Carcina. Reference can also be made to 'La Pistola Automatica Glisenti' in *Tiro Armi Caccia* (Milan, 1966) and the history of the firm of Glisenti is dealt with in *L'arte del ferro in Valle Sabbia e la famiglia Glisenti* by Ugo Vaglia (Brescia, 1959). For information on current Soviet commercial pistols I am indebted to Mr. A. E. S. Matthews.

Apart from manufacturers' current catalogues, useful information on modern automatic pistols will be found in the *Gun Digest* published annually by The Gun Digest Company of Chicago. This lists all commerically available pistols, giving brief details and the prevailing US prices.

Chapter Sixteen
Recent Developments

We have traced the development of the handgun through four centuries, as a weapon for military use, for self protection and for sport. During this period patterns have emerged, some as a result of technical advances, others because of specific needs or requirements.

In this, the second half of the twentieth century, the self-loading or automatic pistol now dominates the military field and, even on the target ranges, the revolver has been almost vanquished by the rim- or centre-fire self-loading pistol. In general use the revolver is far from being relegated to the scrap heap, new models from both old and new manufacturers have continued to appear and to meet with success in the market place. After a period of near stagnation considerable changes have taken place over the last two decades, and in this chapter we can look at some of the changes and take a closer look at those people who manufacture handguns today.

On the broad canvas, two developments have occurred, both concerned with the materials of construction. The first is the adoption of stainless steel for handguns. The use of high chromium content steels for gun barrels was first proposed in 1912 and by the 1930s this material was used for sporting rifle barrels. The first handgun to be made from stainless steel in production quantities was the Smith and Wesson Model 60 revolver in 1965, and this material has now been used for the manufacture of automatic pistols. Its use for handguns has become well established, one of the leading advocates being Sturm, Ruger, who probably make more stainless steel models than any other manufacturer.

The term stainless steel can be misleading; it is not totally rust resistant but it is certainly more resistant to rust than ordinary alloy steels. The fact that your gun is made from stainless steel does not permit neglect and if the gun has been in a hostile environment the best way to clean it is still to use clean water or a water-based cleaner. In order to obtain a useful degree of rust resistance at least 12% chromium content is required. Other alloys are added to improve hardenability, machineability and to confer other desirable properties. Stainless steels are more difficult to drill and in milling operations, cutter angles have to be changed. The manufacture of handguns in stainless steel is not easy and this partially accounts for the higher costs which are reflected in the purchase price. The use of stainless steel does confer benefits, but it must be remembered that stainless steels can be attacked by salts, caustic chemicals and by neglect or abuse. Handguns made from this material can however withstand such attacks to a far greater degree than the traditional metals used in the manufacture of handguns.

More recently handguns have been made using plastics as engineering materials. Plastics have been used on guns for a number of years for rifle butt plates, handgun stock plates, rifle trigger guards and magazines. Possibly the most adventurous use of all was in the manufacture, some years ago, of the Remington Nylon 66 .22 rifle. The all-plastic pistol is not yet with us but the 9mm Austrian Glock 17 automatic pistol is durable, accurate and light and has a greater proportion of plastic components than ever before. This pistol has been adopted and issued by the Austrian Army and by 1990 the Norwegian Army will be totally armed with the Glock.

It is too early to say what the future holds for

the 'plastic pistol' but is seems likely that instead of substituting one material for another as happened with stainless steel, the use of engineering plastics will result in a complete rethink of the design and manufacture of automatic pistols. At this date military acceptance is apparent but whether the private citizen will follow suit remains to be seen.

The adoption by the military of the Glock caused a stir but an even larger one was created by the adoption of the Beretta Model 92 SB-F, in January 1985, as the 'official' personal defence weapon of the US Armed Forces. The trials were long and involved and aroused considerable adverse comment because of the manner in which they had been conducted. The 9mm Beretta, as the USM9, Service Pistol, is the first new military handgun since the introduction of the .45 calibre Colt Model 1911 in the year 1911. At the time of the announcement initial production was to be supplied from the Beretta factory in Italy followed by the assembly of Italian manufactured components in the Beretta factory in Maryland. It is planned that eventually the raw materials, manufacture and assembly will all originate in the American factory.

There were nine serious entries in the competition, three from Browning, one of which was the Model 1935 Hi-Power. Two pistols were entered by Heckler & Koch, the P9S and the VP-70, the latter pistol with selective full-automatic capability. From Spain came the Star Model 28 and Colt entered a stainless steel model, the SSP. The other American contender was Smith and Wesson, who entered a model similar to the Model 459. All the entries, with the exception of the Browning Hi-Power, had some form of double action and magazines capacities varied from 9 rounds in the P9S to eighteen in the VP-70. Both of these trends, to larger magazine capacities and DA capability, can be regarded as general during the period under review. According to an unofficial source, before final selection of the Beretta, the field had narrowed down to three, the Beretta, the Smith and Wesson and the DA version of the Browning.

In 1987 the US Congress directed that there be a follow-up competition to select a new M-10 Service pistol, applying the same specifications under which the Beretta was selected. Extracting some sense from the bureaucratic jargon it would appear that the Beretta will remain the selected Service pistol and will therefore not be required to be remeasured against other contenders. What is now regarded as the XM-10 trial for the M10 Service pistol could in theory again nominate the Beretta as the winner. Informed opinion does not consider this likely and the feeling is that there will be four or five contenders with the betting in favour of the Ruger P-85. This pistol was not submitted by Ruger in the XM-9 trials since, at that time, the company did not consider sufficient time had been allowed for development.

Another likely contender will be the Smith and Wesson M 459, the elimination of which from the XM-9 trials is one of the reasons why Congress ordered a new trial. This book will be in print before the results of the XM-10 trials are known; I shall certainly examine the results and conclusions with considerable interest since the series of trials will by then have cost the US taxpayer dearly!

Smith and Wesson were again in the news when this old-established American company was taken over by a British firm, F. H. Tompkins Ltd., of Walsall, a mini-conglomerate. The handgun scene was complicated by the number of small firms which appeared briefly on the scene, produced publicity handouts, prototype handguns and then vanished without a trace. Sadly, a number of old-established companies in America found the going rough and closed their doors. This happened to Hi Standard in February 1985 and as someone who has used Hi Standard .22 auto-pistols in competitive shooting for a number of years I felt this as a personal loss.

There is not the space available to cover all the developments of the past twenty years in detail, so I have chosen a number of makers of handguns whose operations during this period will be dealt with in detail and I hope that my choice, which is a very personal one, reflects the general scene as accurately as possible. The selected makers are dealt with in alphabetical sequence.

Armament Systems and Procedures Inc

This American company is located at Appleton, Wisconsin, and specialises in combat equipment. It was formed in 1976 to produce the 9mm ASP automatic pistol, which is intended to be carried concealed and is based on the Smith and Wesson Model 39. To produce the ASP the hammer has been bobbed, the barrel shortened to two and a half inches and the magazine capacity reduced to seven rounds, providing an overall capacity of eight. The pistol has been reworked to provide a smooth external surface further enhanced by the matt-black Teflon-S finish.

To further eliminate snagging the sights have been modified. The ASP sight is known as the 'Guttersnipe'; it is a simple groove running along the sight block which is 50mm by 20mm, the groove is tapered from 4mm to 1mm and is square in cross section. The walls of the groove are provided with a high visibility yellow finish with the outside of the sight finished a non reflecting matt black. Using this sight on the pistol and a special magnetic magazine holder 22 shots were fired in seven seconds (including reloading time), all hits grouping under the palm of the hand on a target at the regulation 6.4 metres distance. The weight of the pistol is a mere 24 ounces with a fully loaded magazine. Other useful features of this combat pistol are the tranparent polycarbonate grips which provide a constant indication of the number of rounds remaining in the magazine.

The ASP is not, at the time of writing, currently available, but it represents a significant trend in what one might call 'bespoke handguns'. Reworked pistols of this type, which will, for example, feed an empty 9mm cartridge case are very costly, since the work required is skilled handwork, and therefore expensive. The 'as issued' Model 39 has been extensively modified to produce a pistol which, above all, is reliable, has adequate stopping power, is user friendly and can be worn concealed. The work required to achieve these results is not cheap; in 1979 for example, you supplied a new M39 and six months later at an additional cost of $350 you acquired your ASP with three magazines and a magnetic magazine holder.

The ASP conversion of the Smith and Wesson. The long silhouette of the rear mounted 'Guttersnipe' sight can be seen and the transparent grips allow for verification of the cartridges in the magazine.

Astra-Unceta Y Cia, SA

From the beginnings, as outlined earlier in this book, Astra have maintained their position as one of the foremost manufacturers of handguns in Spain, a position amply substantiated by their current range of models. Such is the extent of the range that I have listed the more recent models below, together with the year of introduction. Those marked INOX are stainless steel.

1973 Model 7000 .22 RF, auto-pistol. Model 960 .38 Special revolver.

1976 Models Match, 250 & 250 INOX. The latter is a replacement for the 2″ barrel Cadix revolver.

1979 Model A-50, a single action .22 auto pistol. Double action .357 INOX revolver.

1980 Police Model .357 but with fixed sights.

1981 Models 680 and 680 INOX. Small frame DA revolvers in .38 Special. These replaced the 250 and 250 INOX and the A-80.

1982 Model NC-6 DA revolver in .38 special replaced the Cadix in 4″ and 6″ barrel lengths.

1983 NC-6 INOX and .44 INOX. Stainless steel versions of the NC-6 and Model 44 DA revolvers.

1985 Model 680 DA in .22, .22 Magnum, .32 S & W and .38 Special. The 680 AL (aluminium frame) is made in .38 Special only. Falcon INOX is a stainless steel version of the Falcon auto-pistol made in .380 and .32 ACP. The Cub INOX is a smaller version of the Model 7000 in .22 short and .25 ACP, and became available in stainless steel in 1985. Constable INOX is the stainless steel version of this double action auto-pistol and is available in .22 RF, .32 ACP and .380 ACP. The Model A-50 Sport is a long barrel target and sport version of the standard A-50 auto-pistol. Short barrel versions of the Model 44 DA revolver and the .44 INOX were introduced with 2¾″ barrel and rubber grips.

1986 The A-60 is a DA auto-pistol in .32 or .380 ACP and the A-80, A-90, A-90 INOX are state of the art DA auto-pistols with 15 round magazines (9mm) and 9 round magazines (.45 ACP). The A-80 and A-90 have the 'hook' trigger guard and the INOX versions are in stainless steel.

Today ASTRA operate from a modern factory with up to date machinery and test facilities. In addition to their wide range of pistols in both steel and stainless steel they also offer 'Deluxe Guns', silver or gold plated and engraved, and they also market a useful range of accessories.

Auto Mag Corporation

This stainless steel 44 Magnum auto-pistol appeared just too late to be included in the first edition. The

The DA Astra 'Police' Model with 3″ barrel. Calibres .38 Spl and .357 Magnum, an interchangeable cylinder can also be supplied in 9mm Parabellum.

The Astra 'Constable', available in .22, .32 and .380 calibres. Note the slide mounted safety which blocks the firing pin and hammer.

company appears to have been formed in 1968 by Harry Sanford. By 1972 production of the .44 Magnum had commenced and there were plans to extend the manufacturing base. However, the original cost studies were over optimistic and losses were made on each gun sold; in 1972 the factory closed down.

As originally manufactured, the pistol is based on a short recoil, rotary locked bolt system with an accelerator which throws the bolt back after it has been unlocked. The early standard models were fitted with a 6½″ barrel with 8 lands and 8 grooves rifled 1 turn in 18 inches. Adjustable rear sights were fitted and a non-glare ramp front sight integral with a full length ventilated rib. Magazine capacity is seven and overall weight 56 ounces, length 11½″. The pistol was sold in a black plastic carrying case with an extra magazine and a set of Allen keys at a price, in 1972, of $247.50. Initially, you had to make your own ammunition, using special dies from RCBS to rework rifle brass with a .30–'06 head. Special ammunition for the pistol was made by a Mexican company, Cartouches Deportivos de Mexico, SA or CDM, for short! This company was part owned by Remington.

Auto Mag announced a .357 Magnum version and also a conversion kit which allowed the .44 Magnum to be used with a special .357 Magnum cartridge, in effect a necked down version of the .44 Magnum. In addition, the company offered barrels in 6½″, 8½″ and 12″ versions in either calibre. All the barrels apparently weigh the same regardless of length or calibre since this equal weight is essential to the

The Astra A-90. A double action large capacity auto-pistol in 9mm or .45 ACP, slide mounted safety and 'Hook' trigger guard.

The .44 calibre Auto Mag pistol with the bolt fully unlocked. Note the target sights, non-glare front ramp and integrated ventilated rib which connects the two.

functioning of the Auto Mag pistol. Later, a further version in .45 ACP was heralded along with a number of wildcat calibres.

Throughout the brief history of the Auto Mag, promotion has been more effective than actual production. Estimates of the number of pistols made varies but it is certainly not large. The original Pasadena company went bankrupt as a result of the major financial backers pulling out; a large stock of finished parts and much of the tooling was then bought by Thomas Oil Co., who formed the TDE Corporation with the intention of assembling complete guns from the existing parts and having the missing parts made. Manufacture was recommenced in the North Hollywood factory before relocation to El Monte, California. In 1974 Hi Standard announced their interest and some pistols do bear the Hi Standard name; their involvement was short lived!

At the time of writing the .44 Auto Mag is not in production. Guns will be found with several addresses and the North Hollywood and El Monte Auto Mags will be found in both .44 and .357 Auto Mag calibres.

A new company, AMT, has now been formed and the Auto Mag Model II is in production in .22 Magnum. This is not the original Auto Mag but a more conventional 10 shot auto-pistol in stainless steel with a 6″ barrel. Whether or not the original .44 Auto Mag will ever be made is unknown. The cost would now be horrendous and, although the pistol starred with Clint Eastwood in the 'Dirty Harry' film *Sudden Impact*, even fame on this scale is unlikely to produce a demand which would ever make manufacture an economic proposition. Just in case you are wondering, the two .44 calibre Auto Mag pistols used in the film, were made up by Harry Sanford from available spare parts; one is a 'live action' pistol and the other has been altered to fire blanks. Both are, of course, instant 'Collector's Items' and they are valued at several thousand dollars each!

Beretta

Following the Series 70 pistols which were discussed in Chapter Fifteen, Armi Beretta introduced a range of double action auto-pistols in 1977, the Series 80. The Model 81 is in .32 ACP and the Model 84 is in .380 ACP. Both pistols are straightforward blowback designs but have large capacity magazines, 13 rounds of .32 and 12 rounds of .380. The design follows well-established Beretta practice except that the magazine release button on both pistols is on the front strap and the safety has extensions which permit operation by either hand.

In 1981, the Models 82B and 85B were introduced, characterised by the adoption of a single row magazine which, due to a reduction in the thickness of the butt, permitted easier carrying in a concealed holster. The single letter B was added to all models from 1981 to indicate a modification to the firing pin safety.

Frame modifications which took place in 1982 resulted in a second letter B being added and in the same year the Model 87 in .22 RF was added. That year also saw the introduction of the Model 92. Unmistakably of Beretta parentage, the Model 92 is double action with a 15 round magazine and is chambered for the 9mm cartridge. The Model 92 was a development of the single action Model 1951, sharing the same pivoting locking block which is not unlike that used on the Walther P38.

The Model 51 was the standard service pistol of the Italian armed forces and it was sold commercially as the Model 951 and also under the name

'Brigadier'. The Model 92 has an alloy frame which keeps the weight down but the use of the double column 15 round magazine puts up the loaded weight and increases the bulk. Both the double action and the large capacity magazine are features of interest for both military and police use.

No doubt with the intention of pursuing these outlets Beretta established manufacturing facilities in Maryland, USA, and these facilities will be employed in the manufacture of the later variant of the Model 92, the 92 SB-F. The ancestry of the Model 92 SB-F can be traced through the Model 92 S which got the 'S' designation because the safety was moved to the slide from the frame. This was followed by the Model 92 S1 with a reversible magazine catch and an ambidextrous safety; this model was tested by the US Air Force. In 1982 the designation was altered to Model 92 SB and a compact version appeared in the same year with the magazine capacity reduced to 13 rounds.

Just after the launch of the Model 92 series, Beretta introduced a version with a selector for fully automatic fire, the Model 93R. In order to improve control during fully automatic fire (1,100 rounds per minute) an additional hinged grip is fitted in front of the trigger guard and a folding metal stock can also be fitted. Another version of the Model 92 known as the 98F has been produced for the home market in 7.65mm Parabellum and this version is distinguished by the highly polished blue finish.

The Model 92 SB-F (one wonders if the 'F' indicates 'Final' version?) was known as the XM-9 in the selection trials, and in its final form, as the Model 92 F; it has a trigger guard which permits a two handed hold, a side-to-side pierced lanyard loop and a stronger aluminium floor plate.

Beretta have not neglected developments in other areas; they introduced a double action auto-pistol, the Model 90 in the late 1960s but this looked rather like one of the many copies of the Walther PPK and the Model 90 ceased to be manufactured in 1984 in favour of the Model 92 Series.

To end this brief discourse on just a few of the models made by this truly remarkable firm of gunmakers in recent years I have to mention the Beretta revolver. Largely inspired by the classic S & W the revolvers were manufactured in Brazil by an affiliated company under the Taurus trademark. They were imported into Italy under the Beretta name

The Beretta Model 92.

On the Beretta Model 92 S, the safety has been moved from the frame to the slide.

and then the factory in Gardone made a revolver to Beretta standards which was introduced in 1979. Never manufactured in any numbers, the revolver was discontinued since the directors of the company considered that the Beretta name was too closely associated with auto-pistols to permit the successful marketing of revolvers under the Beretta name, a name which has now been associated with gun-making for over three centuries!

Browning

The 1970s saw a revision of the famous Browning 9mm Hi-Power pistol. The Standard model continued on the range but with a new rounded hammer and the pistol is now available with adjustable click type target sights and a new ramp front sight, serrated to reduce glare. It will be possible to fit the new slides with ramp sights and adjustable rear sights to existing pistols. An engraved version of the Hi-Power was available, known as the 'Renaissance', fully engraved and chrome plated with polyester pearl grips and also available with either fixed or adjustable sights (see page 431 for an earlier example of engraving).

The Browning .22 auto pistols made by Fabrique Nationale of Belgium for Browning were the Medallist, Nomad and Challenger. In 1976 the company offered the Challenger II which, apparently, is made in America. The new model is lighter, the angle of the grip to the barrel is different and instead of a machined forging on the Belgian models the new version appears to be an investment casting.

In 1978 Browning introduced the Browning BDA in 9mm with ambidextrous safety and a magazine cavity of 12 rounds. This was followed by the BDA in .45 ACP (seven shot magazine) with a 'decocking lever' permitting the hammer to be lowered onto a locked firing pin. A year later the BDA was offered in .380 ACP and although one might have expected a similar pistol this was not the case: the BDA .380 turned out to be a small, compact double action pocket type pistol with an alloy frame and a slide mounted safety which drops the hammer and also blocks it. The original BDA in 9mm was the Swiss SIG P220 design but manufactured for Browning by Sauer & Sohn of West Germany. The BDA .380 is not made by Sauer but is a Beretta design; it is a modified version of the M 81/84 with a reworked slide (to remove the Beretta look) and has a slide safety, already mentioned.

Britarms

This small company, now one of the few remaining in Britain who actually make handguns, has had a fairly chequered history. Throughout its life it can be said that those connected with it have all been enthusiastic users of handguns and that the end product is based on the experience of many very knowledgeable shooting men!

The original Britarms target pistol was the brainchild of Tom Redhead and Chris Valentine and the company was formed in 1976. Early development of the pistol was beset by a number of problems not the least of which was the complex design of the Britarms Mark I. Some of the difficulties were solved with the appearance of the Mark II but the firm went bankrupt. The company was then bought by Jon Morgan, head of the Berdan Group. Further simplification of the design and production methods resulted in the Mark III version of the pistol and the vertical grooves on the bolt weights were replaced by a ball milled finger groove at the front of each weight.

Faults in the pistols magnified by a lack of factory back-up resulted in a loss of popularity, added to which were delays in the development of a .32 calibre model. Berdan pulled out and the factory was closed. In 1987 Alan Westlake bought the remaining stock, tooling etc., and he now has the .22 pistol in full production. This pistol has been renamed the Westlake-Britarms and in addition to significant improvements, which have restored reliability, there is now a very full and personal relationship between the factory and the owners of pistols.

Westlake Engineering modified the sear and trigger components and provided a means of adjusting the trigger weight without having to remove the trigger box from the frame. The pistol is provided with two top loading five shot magazines and can be furnished with a variety of finishes including gold plating! A lightweight barrel is offered as well as a vented barrel (to reduce muzzle flip) for rapid fire, and this type of barrel can be fitted to any of the earlier Britarms frames. The earlier models had adjustable Hoffman grips but on the Westlake Britarms pistols the grips are being made by Derrick Gent and will be standard on all Britarms pistols.

Berdan (Gun Makers) Ltd had offered a similar design, the Britarms 3000, in .32 S & W calibre, again with a five shot magazine. Alan Westlake has advised that, at the time of writing, he is not prepared to offer the .32 calibre model for sale until further development work has been carried out.

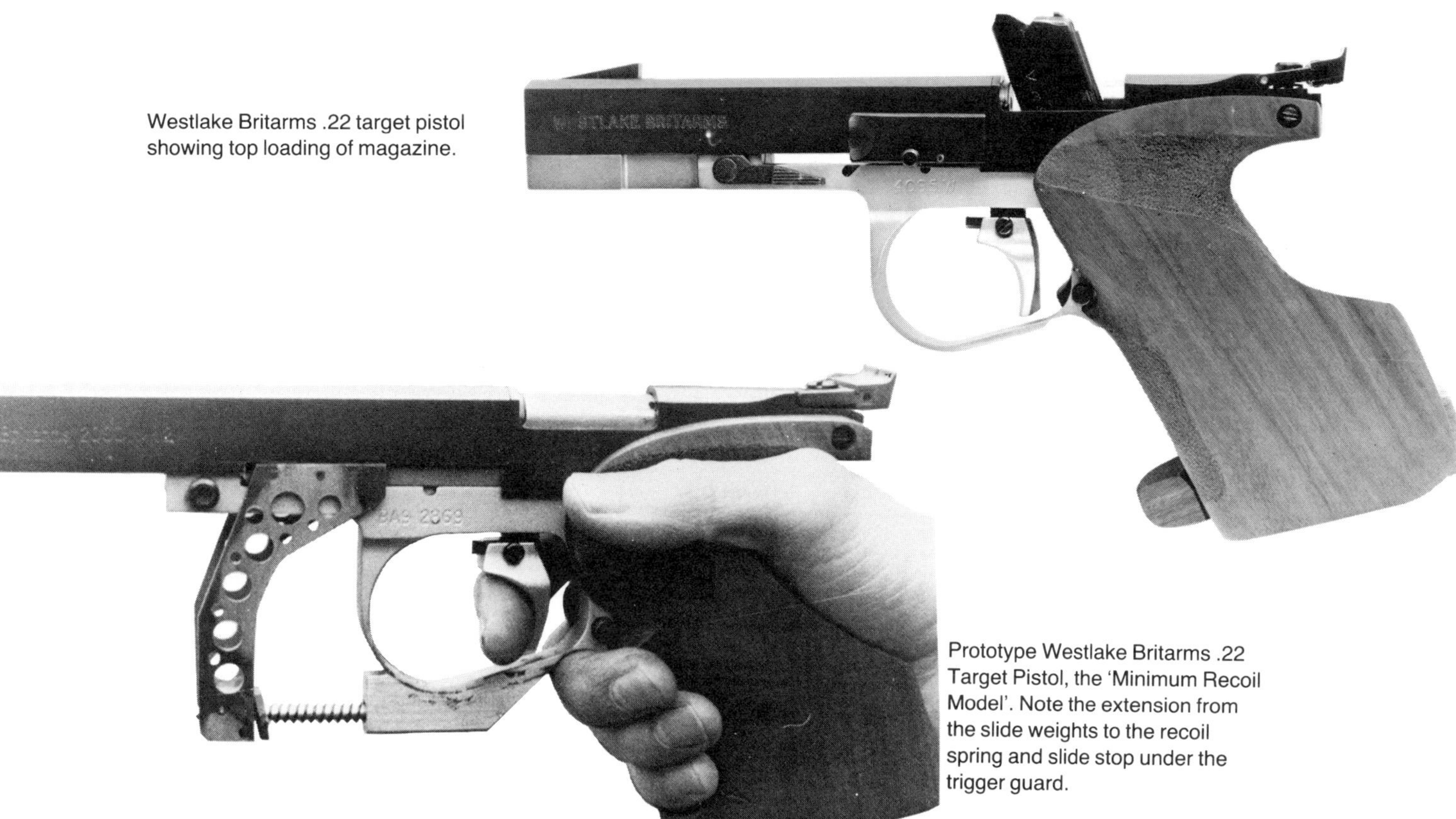

Westlake Britarms .22 target pistol showing top loading of magazine.

Prototype Westlake Britarms .22 Target Pistol, the 'Minimum Recoil Model'. Note the extension from the slide weights to the recoil spring and slide stop under the trigger guard.

This is not the only development work that is currently under way, as another pistol described as the 'Minimum Recoil' Model has now reached the prototype stage. The design concept is based on the fact that the recoil of an auto-pistol has two components. The first is the backthrust against the breechblock, which, although mitigated by various factors, causes recoil as a reaction to the forward travel of the bullet. The second component is due to the recoil energy contained in the slide; some of this is absorbed by the recoil spring but the remainder is felt when the slide impacts against the frame at the end of its travel. In the new design, this second component has been relocated well below the centre line of support, by means of two curved arms attached to the breechblock. These sweep down to the recoil spring housing and slide stop, located below the trigger guard. In use, the prototype has reduced muzzle flip, a softer recoil and, when the slide contacts the slide stop, the muzzle drops! This self correcting element is a valuable asset in rapid fire and once the design has been finalised it will be interesting to see what impact this design has in practical terms.

As we shall see during our review of pistol manufacture, if you build a better pistol, people will buy it. Westlake Engineering is not a large concern but they appear to have solved many of the problems which they inherited and have produced some interesting innovations. They have my best wishes for the future!

Charter Arms Corporation

This company was not included in the original edition. The first model which came to my attention was the .38 five shot, lightweight, 'Undercover .38 Spl'. The Undercover revolver weighs 16 ozs and its light weight is due partially to the short $1\frac{7}{8}''$ barrel (later versions could be had with a 3″ barrel) and the compact form is aided by the five chambered cylinder and rounded butt. This model was later made available as a 6 shot in .32 S & W Long and then as the Police Undercover as a six shot in .38 Special and .32 Magnum. All models are also available in stainless steel.

In 1976 the 'Police Bulldog' was introduced by Charter Arms to meet complaints by law enforcement officers that the traditional police issue revolver was far too heavy. The Bulldog, fully loaded, weighs less than 24 ozs while comparable police type revolvers weigh half as much again. This weight reduction is achieved by the use of a lightweight barrel shroud which incorporates the fore sight and the ejector rod housing. In addition, although the main frame is machined from a steel investment casting, the combined grip frame and trigger guard are made from an aluminium alloy die casting. The cylinder has positive locking both in front and behind the cylinder. The firing pin is independent and not in direct contact with the hammer. When the trigger is pulled back the hammer block rises in line with the firing pin and so transmits the hammer blow to the firing pin. When the trigger moves forward the block is lowered and even a hard blow on the spur of the hammer cannot fire the gun.

A 3″ barrel five shot .44 Special version of the Bulldog was also marketed, having a stronger chrome-molybdenum frame, solid steel barrel and a new cylinder. The five shot .44 Special Bulldog Pug followed with a shrouded ejector rod and all three Bulldog revolvers can be had in stainless steel. The .44 Special was followed by a .357 Magnum version, the 6″ barrel 'Tracker', since discontinued. Available in both .44 Special and .357 Magnum the Target Bulldog has the shrouded ejector but features fully adjustable sights and a four inch barrel. This model is not, at the time of writing, available in stainless steel. A .22 version of the Undercover was introduced, the 'Pathfinder', with 3″, 4″ or 6″ barrel options. This model was also offered in 1980, in stainless steel. This was then followed by .22 Magnum versions, since deleted from the catalogue.

Available with a number of options these revolvers represent new thinking in American handgun manufacturing techniques and the flow of new ideas shows no sign of abating. Charter revolvers have the Charter hammer block safety and the 'no side plate, solid frame' construction. In addition to walnut grips Charter offer a range of nine colour-enhanced laminated grips.

In 1981 Charter Arms produced the Explorer II, an eight shot automatic pistol similar in outline to the old 'Broomhandle' Mauser, with the magazine in front of the trigger guard. An 8″ barrel was standard with 6″ or 10″ barrels available as extras. Geared to meet the American market for varmint, plinking or informal target shooting the Explorer operated in a similar manner to the AR-7 survival rifle although unlike the AR-7, the Explorer didn't float! An interesting feature was the provision for a spare magazine to be carried in the grip. The company then introduced three additional auto-pistol designs to augment the Explorer: the Model 40 was a small .22 double action rim-fire auto loader; the Model 79K was a similar design but in .380 calibre and the third pistol was the 42 TGT, a .22 target pistol. At the time of writing these models are not

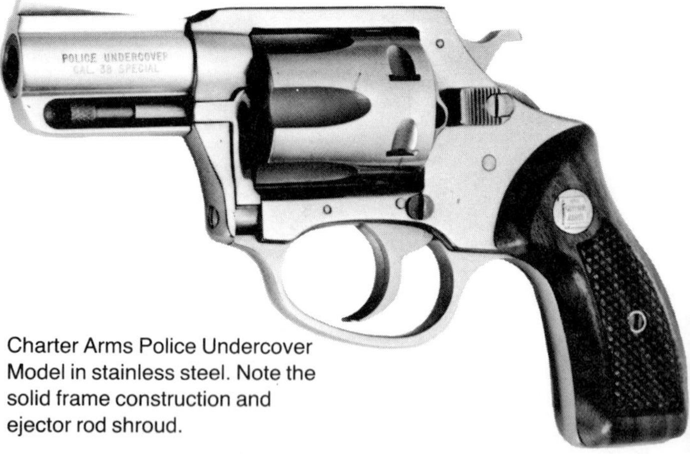

Charter Arms Police Undercover Model in stainless steel. Note the solid frame construction and ejector rod shroud.

included in the catalogue but whether this will be reconsidered is not known; the .22 AR-7 Survival rifle is however still available.

Colt

The casual observer of the handgun scene would probably comment that, over the past two decades, the most noticeable feature of Colt activities has been the flow of 'Commemorative' handguns from the Hartford factory. These have ranged from the 'Gold Spike', based on the .22 calibre rim-fire 6″ barrel Scout which commemorates the meeting of the Central Pacific and the Union Pacific railways at Promontory Point, Utah, in May 1869, to the four editions of the .45 Colt M 1911 commemorating US victories in WW1.

During the 1970s Colt re-started the manufacture of percussion revolvers at Hartford. The model, issued as a commemorative, is the Model 1851 Navy, and the guns are sold in special presentation cases, inscribed 'Robert E. Lee' and 'Ulysees S. Grant'.

The handguns produced by Colt during the '70s and '80s are best dealt with by looking at the revolvers first and the auto-pistols second. At the start of this review Colt marketed the following revolvers: the Detective Special, the Cobra, the Agent, the Police Positive, the Official Police and the Trooper. All were 6 chambered and available in a variety of calibres from .22 to .357 Magnum. The Single Action Army was available in .357 Magnum and in Colt .45. The smaller Frontier Scout was in .22 RF but could be had with dual cylinders, one in .22 RF, the other in .22 RF Magnum.

The important change in the revolvers was the introduction of the Mark III models, improved versions of the old established Official Police Models. The new models include the Trooper, the Metropolitan and the Lawman. All guns with the new action, which employs coil springs throughout (except for the hand spring) have a shortened hammer and trigger travel and a smoother double action pull. Along with the new double action revolvers Colt made available two .22 single action revolvers, $\frac{7}{8}$th scale versions of the .45 SA Army. Sold as the Peacemaker and the New Frontier these guns are of all steel construction; the New Frontier has adjustable Accro sights.

Colt maintained their involvement with target type revolvers, the Diamondback being offered in .22 and .38 Special with a ventilated rib and full extractor rod shroud. Available in the same choice of calibres, the Colt Officers Model Match revolver lacks these features, but the .357 Magnum New Police Python has them and offered an alternative longer barrel at 6″ than the Diamondback. The Colt Python, first introduced in 1955 remains the flagship of the Colt line and is arguably the most expensive mass produced revolver on the market.

In 1979 Colt announced that they intended to discontinue the entire range of D-Frame revolvers which included the Detective Special, the Police Positive, the Cobra, Agent, Viper and Diamondback. This was followed by an engineering update of the medium frame revolvers in 1983 with the appearance of the Mark V series, with the Trooper and Lawman being the first models to be upgraded. The Trooper retains the target sights and the Lawman the service sights. The modifications included new springs, a shorter hammer fall and physical changes to the grip frame.

The year 1986 saw the 150th Anniversary of the company, and, with their profitable line in commemorative models a well established feature of their sales philosophy, a number of Colt Python's and single action Army Models were suitably engraved and fitted out with ivory grips. The newest Colt revolver variant introduced in their anniversary year was the King Cobra which some US writers called 'the working man's Python'! It was available in .357 Magnum only.

Throughout the period models have been introduced, variants have appeared, models discontinued and then reintroduced. The Colt Agent was introduced, discontinued, the name reintroduced in 1982 and the model was again taken out of production. All that one can say is that the Colt revolver range in the second half of the nineteenth century will be a collector's dream, or perhaps future nightmare! When one considers the massive problems many of the old established handgun makers have had to overcome, not the least of which has been ferocious home and foreign competition, the fact that Colt have survived is a major feat in itself quite apart from the satisfaction its products have given to its customers during this period.

The complexity of the revolver and auto-pistol range is such that it would perhaps be a sound idea to stop before we look at the auto-pistols and pick out a Colt catalogue for, say, 1977 and take a look at what was on offer at that time. We are, in effect, taking a slice through historical time.

The Colt SAA with hard rubber grips and three different barrel lengths and in two calibres, .45 Colt and .357 Magnum, was the first gun in the catalogue. The New Frontier SAA in two barrel options and with wood stocks and adjustable sights and available in both calibres completed the Single Action Pistols on offer. In double action the top of the range was the Python in three barrel lengths and in one calibre, .357 Magnum (the .38 Special can also be used in this calibre). Available in blue or nickel, (no stainless steel as yet!), but with a fully shrouded ejector rod and ventilated rib. Then the Trooper Mk III with a 4″ or 6″ barrel, with adjustable sights, again in .357 Magnum and the companion pistol, the Mk III Lawman in 2″ or 4″ barrel lengths and with fixed sights. In medium

Colt Diamondback in .38 Special with 6″ ventilated barrel and target sights.

The Colt Government Model Mark IV Series 80 in bright nickel finish and .380 calibre.

Colt Delta Elite 10mm automatic pistol.

weight comes the Diamondback in .38 Special and .22 RF, again with target sights and the Police Positive in .38 Special only and a 4″ barrel with fixed sights.

Four snub-nosed self-protection pistols were next shown in the catalogue, the Detective Special, Cobra, Viper and Agent, all in .38 Special. The last three have aluminium alloy frames and all have fixed sights. Four auto-pistols are offered, the Gold Cup National Match for the target shooter, the standard Government Model and the Lightweight Commander, all in .45 ACP, the last with an aluminium alloy frame. Identical to the Lightweight Commander is the Combat Commander, available in .45 ACP, .38 and 9mm. This pistol has a steel frame. The .22 Woodsman pistols had been dropped from the line by this time but Colt still offered four grades of factory engraving and a range of alternative grips.

After that short detour we can now return to consider the range of auto-pistols Colt offered during the period under review. Colt introduced the Mk IV/Series 70 which incorporates improvements on the big .45 Government Models. The barrel bushing now has a spring loaded split collect which grips the barrel tightly at the muzzle and so improves accuracy. American competitive shooting in .45 ACP calibre was dominated by the Gold Cup National Match pistol. Upgraded as the Mark IV/ Series 80, it has remained in the catalogue up to the time of writing. Colt's other competition pistol, the .22 Woodsman, sadly did not survive and appears to have been last listed in 1977.

Legislation prevented the importation from Spain of the small .25 pocket automatic pistol which Colt sold under their name so this will now be manufactured, once again, in America. A .22 auto that was introduced in the late '70s was the Colt Ace. Based on the Colt Government Model (the 'O' Frame) the Ace is similar to the Ace conversion kit which Colt offered some years ago. The new Ace is based on the floating chamber principle just as the original conversion kit was, which provides near .45 ACP recoil from the .22 RF. Another .22 auto-pistol, which had a relatively short production life, was the .22 Huntsman, a low cost variant of the original Woodsman. Throughout the period under review, John Browning's basic 1905 automatic pistol design was continued by Colt under the name Colt Government Model, with an increase in the calibre variants to include 9mm, .380, .38 Super and, of course, the .45 ACP.

A new calibre was added in 1987, the 10mm. Made for the Bren Ten by Norma, Colt introduced their 10mm auto-pistol, the Delta Elite. This turned out to be a slightly modified Series 80 Government Model with a wrap around rubber grip bearing the delta logo.

The pocket model automatic pistols have always been an important line and they start back in 1908 when the existing .32 calibre pistols were modified to use the then new .380 cartridge developed by John Browning. Production of what was known as the Model M, or the Colt .380, continued in both .380 and .32 calibres until the series was discontined in 1945. In the 1960s Colt had considered the possiblilty of marketing a new .380 based on a Star design, but manufactured in the US (although not by Colt). In 1983 the problem was resolved by the introduction of the 'Colt Government Model Mark IV/Series 80–380 Auto'. The new pistol had a locked breech, but unlike the Model 1911 it does not employ a link and pin but an angle slot similar to the SIG SP47. The Government Model .380, to give the pistol its more usual name, was very favourably received and in 1986, a development of the pistol appeared, the .380 Mustang. Similar in design concept to the Spanish Star DK automatic, the Mustang is slightly smaller due to the shorter barrel and reduced five round magazine capacity.

What of Colt and the future? The Model 1911 A. 1, the Colt Government Model, will remain in use by the US Military for some time although, to the best of my knowledge, the last US Government purchases were made as long ago as 1945. Nostalgia, if nothing else, will ensure civilian purchases of the Model 1911 in the foreseeable future and such sales can be bolstered by Colt's skilled exploitation of the commemorative versions of this remarkable auto-pistol. The Colt entry in the competition won by Beretta was the Model SSP. I have not seen examples of this pistol and have no knowledge as to whether Colt intends to manufacture but failure in the competition is not a strong selling point to anyone other than a dedicated collector so its future, at the time of writing, seems somewhat obscure.

Detonics

A newcomer to the scene, the original product of this Seattle, Washington, USA, company was a compact .45 calibre auto-pistol aimed principally, it would appear, at the market offered by the off-duty law enforcement officer. The company feel that their compact auto-pistol firing a heavier bullet offers an attractive alternative to the standard 2″ barrel .38 Special revolver. The gun is, in essentials, similar to the .45 Colt/Browning Model 1911 but reduced in overall size and with a six round magazine giving a total weight of 29 ozs. The fixed sights have a sight base of four inches and the pistol has an envelope size of 6¾″ × 5″. The traditional Colt barrel bushing has been replaced by the muzzle end of the barrel seating directly on to the slide and the recoil spring is of different design, being two springs wound in opposite directions concentrically. The construction is based on an investment casting in 4140 chrome molybdenum steel. In 1980, a Mark VI series pistol was introduced, the Combat Master made entirely from stainless steel except for the grips and sights. This version is fitted with a three dot combat sight and the recoil spring has been modified. The Combat master was followed by the Scoremaster, a full sized stainless steel target/competition auto-pistol available in both .45 ACT and .451 Detonics Magnum. At the other end of the scale the company announced a 9mm Pocket double action auto pistol in stainless steel.

The .45 model was subsequently chambered for the .451 Detonics Magnum in a six shot clip as the original .45 ACP but in addition 9mm and .38 Super became available with a six shot magazine. The interesting six shot Pocket 9 double action pistol

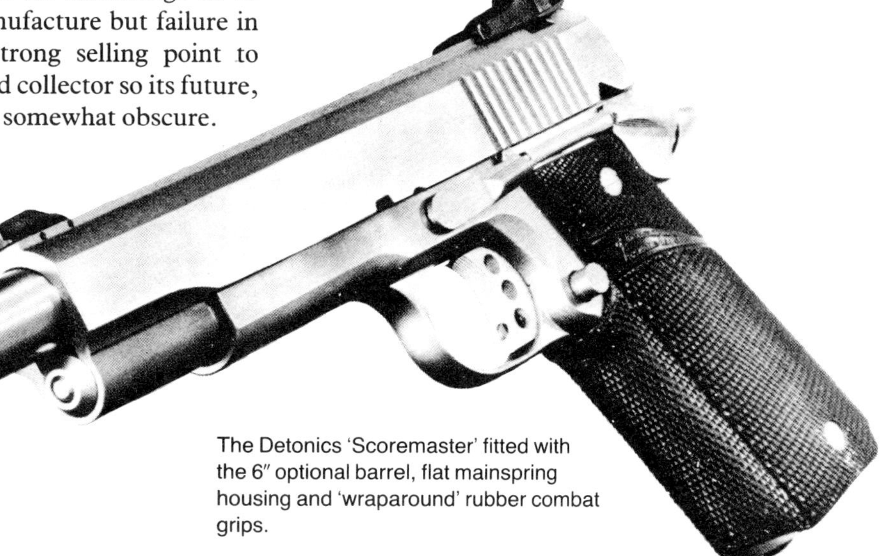

The Detonics 'Scoremaster' fitted with the 6″ optional barrel, flat mainspring housing and 'wraparound' rubber combat grips.

The 'Desert Eagle' .357 Magnum, gas operated pistol.

mentioned above remained in the selling line, a very business-like auto-pistol. In fact, for some customers this pistol in 9mm proved to be a little too fierce, so the company produced the Pocket 380 which is slimmer than the Pocket 9 and is easier on the shooting hand. It features what is now called a 'guard hook' where the front outside of the guard has a concave serrated curve to allow the index finger of the left hand to curl around the outside of the guard in a two-handed hold, a feature which is becoming increasingly popular. At the time of writing the last Detonics auto-pistol to appear was the stainless steel .45 Service Master.

In January 1988, the '1045 Investors Group Ltd' acquired the assets and marketing rights for all the Detonics firearms and advised that the range of stainless steel pistols, the Combatmaster, Servicemaster and Scoremaster would continue to be made. Following a review of current manufacturing techniques, I have been informed that some minor improvements, and a wider range of options for each model, will be introduced during 1988.

Desert Eagle

Rimless auto-pistol ammunition has been successfully used in revolvers, for example the 9mm Parabellum and the .45 ACP. The first widely used revolver cartridge in an auto-pistol was the .38 S & W Special and now we have the .357 and the .44 Remington Magnum, both rimmed revolver cartridges, in two new massive auto-pistols. Rejoicing in the name 'Desert Eagle' the .357 Magnum version was announced in 1982. This gas-operated auto-pistol is now chambered for both the .357 Magnum and the .44 Magnum. Made in Israel by Israel Military Industries this is a big pistol, over 10″ long and weighing in at just over 52 ozs (75 ozs for the .44 Mag.). Magazine capacity is nine, plus one in the chamber (eight in the case of the .44 Mag.) and usually this pistol has additional optional 8″, 10″ and 14″ barrels. An ambidextrous safety is fitted to the rear of the slide.

The operating principle of the pistol is of interest. Prior to firing, the bolt is locked by three lugs in the barrel assembly. When the pistol is fired some of the propellant gases pass through a port in the barrel, just ahead of the chamber, into a transfer port under the barrel. The gases push against a piston in the gas cylinder which, in turn, moves the slide rearwards and at the same time the bolt is unlocked. Case ejection, and the cocking of the hammer occur and the recoil springs are compressed. In the forward movement of the slide a new round is transferred from the magazine and chambered and the bolt is rotated to lock the action. The pistol has a number of safety features and owners are most earnestly requested to read the instruction manual in its entirety before handling the pistol! The standard finish is a dull black oxide on unpolished investment castings. A polished and blued version is available at extra cost. Standard fixed sights are fitted but both target and telescopic sights can be fitted as alternatives.

A gas-operated auto-pistol is an interesting venture for this Israeli company, when it might well be expected that the type of pistol most likely to be produced would be a version of some established design. The Desert Eagle joins a well respected family of firearms from IMI which include the UZI carbine and pistol and the GALIL rifles. I would not like to guess what the future holds for this unusual and quite expensive pistol apart from its potential use by handgun hunters.

Gabilondo y Cia, SA

The pistols manufactured in Spain by this long established company are probably better known under the names of 'Llama' and 'Ruby'. In the early 1970s the demand for .44 Magnum revolvers exceeded the supply and a number of new makers entered the field. Gabilondo y Cia had made pistols for many years, their range including a Colt Model 1911 'look alike' in various calibres under the

'Llama' name and a range of Smith and Wesson 'look alikes' under the 'Ruby' and 'Ruby Extra' names.

In 1980 the company introduced the large framed 'Super Comanche' for the .44 Magnum cartridge. The Ruby revolvers and the Llama (in the US the company appears to have dropped the Ruby name in favour of Llama for revolvers and auto-pistols) and the later Llama Comanche revolvers in .22, .38 Sp., and .357 Mag. all bear an external resemblance to the S & W range. The new Llama Super Comanche has the same external resemblance, in its case, to the S & W Model 29. Internally, the mechanism is different; coil spring lockwork is employed but the most important feature is the eccentric cam and lever assembly, employed as a safety measure instead of the conventional S & W type of hammer block. Only when the trigger is pushed to the rear does the hammer nose swing down so that it will contact the frame mounted firing pin. The other safety device blocks the hammer and trigger when the thumbpiece is pushed forward to unlock the cylinder. The Super Comanche shows considerable original thought, and is a well engineered and satisfactory revolver.

The latest auto-pistol of which I have details is the Llama XI-B, a 9mm steel framed derivative of the Colt Model 1911. Gabilondo have gone against the double action trend and this model is a fairly low cost auto-pistol which lacks the finish and refinement of the Comanche revolvers.

Glock

I have already referred to the Glock 17 auto-pistol and I would like to describe this interesting pistol in greater detail. When it first came to the attention of the non technical press the media in general referred to it as 'an all plastic gun' and that it would 'pass through metal detectors undetected'. In fact the Glock is, by weight, about 83% steel and the pistol with a full magazine would trip the normal metal detector.

The true facts about this pistol are nevertheless extremely interesting. The designer is Gaston Glock, chairman of the board of Glock GmbH, of Deutsch Wagram in Austria. The firm, founded by Glock in 1963, originally produced furniture and hardware. Eventually the company made combat knives, bayonets etc., for the Austrian Army, employing, where appropriate, synthetic materials, an area in which Gaston Glock specialises. Interest in manufacturing a military pistol was aroused in 1980 in spite of having no previous experience in

The Gabilondo 'Llama' revolver, The auto-pistols follow Colt in styling whereas the revolvers bear a strong likeness to Smith and Wesson.

The Gabilondo 'Llama' 9mm automatic pistol. The resemblance to the Colt Model 1911 is quite marked.

this field. In some ways this was perhaps an advantage since not only did the designer employ new ideas and materials, new machines were also required, of up-to-date design, to manufacture the pistol.

The firm make all the parts for the pistol except the springs, and of course, the basic raw material. The pistol is of hammerless, locked breech, recoil operated design with a magazine capacity of 17 rounds 9 × 19mm, which features a contents indicator and an optional 19 rounds capacity. It is not a true double action pistol in that the firing pin is held back when the slide is operated. This permits the firing pin to be blocked by the safety and also ensures that the pin does not come in contact with the primer. When the trigger is pulled the firing pin is fully retracted and released to fire the pistol. This design ensures that both the first shot with a manually operated slide and subsequent recoil operated shots operate in the same manner and that the trigger pull and pressure is also identical. The only manual safety is built into the trigger. Glock refer to the Model 17 as the 'Safe Action' pistol.

The Glock Model 17 'Safe Action' auto-pistol in 9mm Parabellum.

The plastic components of the pistol are the frame, which has integral steel stampings, for reinforcement where necessary. The barrel, as one might expect, is of steel but the rifling is unusual in that it is hexagonal, a series of six flats connected by small arcs, reminiscent of the rifling of the famous Whitworth rifle. Sir Joseph would be pleased! The large capacity magazine is of plastic construction as is the special holster provided for the pistol. There are two variants of the basic model, the 17L, a competition model with a 6″ barrel and the Model 19 'Compact' (overall length 7.30″) with a shorter 4″ barrel with a standard magazine capacity of 15 rounds.

Military use by both Austria and later by Norway will no doubt test the design concept of this pistol to the full and I, for one, will be interested to follow future developments.

Hammerli

The history of this Swiss company has been discussed in detail earlier in this book. They now produce an impressive range of target pistols in bewildering variety which have gained world wide acclaim and an enviable success rate in international competition.

In the 1970s Hammerli introduced their auto Model 230 Olympic Pistol chambered for the .22 short cartridge and designed for the Olympic rapid-fire contestant. The trigger pull is adjustable down to 5 oz (150 grams) and adjustment is provided for trigger slack, backlash, sear engagement and hammer engagement and, if this were not enough three trigger lengths are also provided! Wrap around walnut stocks have a fixed thumb rest and adjustable palm rest. The improved Model 232 has six gas ports in the barrel, the rear two of which are threaded and can be fitted with special choke plugs. This ensures clean recycling of the slide when light-load ammunition is being used. Full Wrap-around grips are available in small, medium and large sizes and they can also be provided for left handers! Owners of the earlier M 230s can have them factory modified to M 232 pattern.

The earlier single shot Hammerli Match pistols based on the Model 102 have now been phased out and are replaced by a new design, the Model 150 which first appeared in limited quantities in late 1973. This pistol features a low mounted barrel for near straight back recoil and it is fully floating to improve accuracy. A Martini type action is retained with a fully adjustable trigger and a loading/cocking lever is sited on the left hand side of the pistol. A version of the Model 150 is the later M 152 which features an electronic trigger mechanism which replaces the mechanical set trigger of the M 150. This new mechanism gives an extremely short lock time of 1.7 milliseconds coupled with an extremely light trigger pull, based on the use of an electro-magnet. Full wrap around grips are available for both models.

These are very expensive, highly specialised handguns, the high degree of specialisation render-

Hammerli Model 232.

Hammerli Model 215.

Hammerli Model 280.

ing them barely recognisable as pistols, but they are eminently suitable for the type of competitive shooting for which they have been developed over the years. Pistols of this type have to place all shots into the 25mm X-ring of the International slow fire target at a distance of 50 metres.

The current .22 target pistol is the Model 208 with adjustable grips and a variant, the M 211 is in all respects similar but has a conventional grip style. The range is further extended by the M 215 which is a lower priced version of the M 208, costs having been reduced by cutting down on finishing costs. Based on the M 208, the M 212 is a general purpose .22 but built to the same standards with a drop forged receiver and a cold swaged high precision barrel.

The latest in the line is the M 280, an entirely new concept for Hammerli with the magazine in front of the trigger guard. Hammerli have offered conversion units for their pistols in the past and, with the M 280 conversion units, the owner has the option of either .22 RF or .32 S & W Long Wadcutter. The use of carbon fibre components has reduced the weight of the pistol to 990 grams in .22 and the design has produced a pistol with a low bore axis relative to the hand, producing stable recoil and recovery characteristics.

Heckler & Koch GmbH

Located at Oberndorf, this company is at the centre of traditional firearms manufacture in West Germany. Mention has been made earlier in the book of their first handgun, the HK4. The interesting feature of this pistol was the fact that the pistol could be used with four interchangeable barrels, .22 RF, .25 ACP, .32 ACP and .380 ACP.

In the early 1970s H & K introduced the Model P9S, a locked breech, 'hammerless', double action 9mm auto-pistol with a single row magazine of 9 rounds capacity. Cocking is done by an external cocking lever on the left hand side of the the pistol in a manner similar to that of the Sauer Model H. The latest manufacturing techniques involving pressed steel parts, cast and sintered metal components are employed and the delayed blow back system is based on the double roller locking employed by the H & K G3 rifle and the first seen on the Spanish CETME some years ago. The long awaited .45 ACP version of the P9 finally appeared complete with the 'hook' shaped trigger guard in plastic for the increasingly popular 'double hold' and, as on the 9mm version, pressed steel components are widely used. Both pistols employ polygonal rifling.

Known for their innovation, H & K introduced the P7 (previously known as the PSP-Police Selfloading Pistol) around 1980. One of the smallest 98mm pistols currently in production, the P7 features a 'squeeze cocking' action. The lever forms the front strap of the grip frame and the pistol has to be squeeze cocked for each shot. This is a variation of the pre-war Einhand pistols made by Bergman under Witwold Chlewski's patents although the Einhand pistols were not only squeeze cocked but the slide was also drawn back to chamber the first round. A variation of the P7, the P7 M8 has been adopted by some US police forces as their standard sidearm. In the late '80s, H&K announced that they intend to discontinue the HK4 and that it will be replaced by the K3 in .380 ACP.

Heckler & Koch remain one of the most progressive manufacturers in Europe whose products have rightly received wide acceptance.

Heckler & Koch Model P9S double action 9mm lever cocking auto-pistol.

The Heckler & Koch Model p7 M8 'squeeze cocking' 9mm auto-pistol. The cocking lever forms part of the front of the grip frame.

Hi-Standard

Most of this chapter is taken up with recording new models and, of course, the demise of some of the older models. A feature of the last two decades has been the rise of small companies, the issue of exciting promotional literature, then the eagerly awaited appearance of the prototype gun to be followed by the collapse of the company!

It is rare to have to record the demise of a long-established and respected gun company. Sadly, this was to happen to one of the best known makers of handguns in America, Hi-Standard, after half a century of building .22 auto-pistols. To the informed, the writing was on the wall in the early 1980s, and by late '83, with sales and profits falling and interest charges climbing, it had become obvious that the company could not survive for much longer, the end was in sight and in November 1984 the assets of the company were sold at auction and the company ceased to trade in December of that year.

Most of the parts were purchased by PM Firearms, 514 East Burnside Ave., East Hartford, Conn. 06108, USA. The number of Hi-Standard pistols still in service is considerable and most of the parts for those made after 1960 are still available. Efforts have been made to manufacture some components, such as magazines, so that these pistols will continue to give good service for many years to come.

The Mauser 9mm Parabellum 'Luger' auto-pistol in its target guise with adjustable sights and a barrel weight.

Iver Johnson

This company, now a Division of the American Military Arms Corporation, is one of the few survivors of the old established American gunmakers with their roots in the nineteenth century. Now located far from the traditional centres of manufacture in Massachusetts, Iver Johnson is to be found in Jacksonville, Arkansas, just north of Little Rock. The early history of the company was detailed in Chapter Eleven. Iver Johnson at present manufacture a double action auto-pistol in 22 RF, the TP 22 and the TP 25, in .25 ACP, which they introduced in 1981. AMAC also sell a compact 'vest pocket' .25 calibre auto-pistol under their own name.

The Iver Johnson Model TP 22 double action, available in either .22 l.r. or .25 ACP.

Two simple centre fire auto-pistols, one in 9mm and the other in .380, the latter called the Pony, appeared in 1986. To the nostalgic delight of many, a .22 auto-pistol based on the now discontinued Colt Woodsman was introduced by them as the Trailsman in 1984. The Colt model upon which the Trailsman is based is the 1948–55 version with a round barrel. The new owners of Iver Johnson decided not to continue with the Trailsman and the 9mm and .380 models did not progress much beyond the prototype stage.

Mauser

The Pistole '08, Parabellum or Luger is not dead! Mauser-Werke of Oberndorf have reintroduced this famous auto-pistol in 9mm Parabellum. Available in the standard version with a 4″ barrel, Mauser also offer a 'customised' model which is engraved or inlaid and plated to the customer's requirements, with ivory grips and gold monogram plate.

In addition there is also the 'Erinnerungsmodell Lange Pistol '08' or 8″ barrel, 'Commemorative Model', with adjustable sights and a shoulder stock. And, most remarkable of all, Mauser offer a Target Model with a slab sided barrel, barrel weight and target sights.

Smith and Wesson

The history of this company has been dealt with at length in the earlier part of this book. As has been the case with much of American industry, Smith and Wesson encountered hard times and difficulties which they now seem to have overcome. The product range is wide and complicated and, as I did in the case of Colt, I will deal with the revolvers first of all, followed by the auto-pistols.

Early in the 1970s S & W introduced stainless steel versions of some of the revolvers on the range. These were the M 10 (Military & Police) which, in the stainless steel version became the M 64. The M 15 Combat Masterpiece became the M 67 and the M 19 Combat Magnum became the M 66. The five shot 'Bodyguard' hammerless models have been retained on the range. Using the 'J' frame, the Model 38 has an alloy frame with steel cylinder and barrel and the Model 49 is all steel. In line with other Models, the Bodyguard is also available, as the Model 649, in stainless steel.

What many consider to be the flagship of the S & W fleet, the Model 29 .44 Magnum, 'Dirty Harry's handgun', became available, as the Model 629, in stainless steel. The finish is a lustrous satin, which, in my opinion, is better-looking than some of the polished finishes found on the stainless handguns. Smith and Wesson also entered the commemorative handgun business so ably exploited by Colt. Commemorative revolvers bearing a Texas Rangers badge were issued to coincide with the 150th anniversary of the founding of the famous Texas Rangers.

Announced in 1982 was an interesting S & W revolver which, at first glance, looks very much like a Colt Python. This was the Model 586, Distinguished Combat Magnum, in .357 Magnum calibre, built on the new 'L' sized frame (which appropriately fits between the 'K' frame used for the .38s and the 'N' frame used for the .44 Magnum). The similarity is, of course, heightened by the use on the S & W of a full length ejector shroud as on the Python. As is common with S & W no sooner does a new model appear than it proliferates into a number of versions and the 586 is no exception. The stainless steel version is the Model 686, and with fixed sights the 586 becomes the 581 and the 686 becomes the 681. Where the S & W model wins is on price; it is nearly half the price of the Python!

An interesting revolver was introduced by the company in 1983, the 'K' Frame Model 547. This revolver started out as the M 13 and it was altered to take the 9mm Parabellum rimless cartridge in answer to a request from the French police. Instead of using the usual half moon clips S & W produced a modified extractor in beryllium copper built on similar lines to the extractors used on double rifles chambered for rimless cartridges.

The 1980s saw the re-introduction of models previously taken out of the catalogue. One of these was the Model 24 in .44 Special, returned 'due to popular demand'. Shortly afterwards, this model was upgraded in stainless steel as the Model 624. The Model 29 appeared with special four position sights designed to cater for the needs of the 'Silhouette Shooter' and in .22 Magnum, the Models 650 and 651 are Magnum stainless steel versions of the famous Kit Gun. The M 650 has fixed sights and the 651 adjustable sights.

Although, as we have seen, some models tend to appear, shine briefly in the catalogues and then vanish, some other models (or at least their names) appear immortal! One of these is the famous Military & Police Model which, with the .38 S & W Special cartridge, first appeared in 1899. It is still on the range as the Model 10, built on the 'K' Frame. By the mid '80s over six million of this model had been sold!

In the auto-pistol field one of the first new handguns introduced was the short-lived M 61 in .22 RF. Known as the Escort, this little pistol was similar to the M 1908 Bayard with the barrel below the recoil spring but S & W had brought it up to date with an alloy frame. At under 5″ in length this little gun apparently found few takers and was withdrawn from the line. In 1974 the Model 59 was

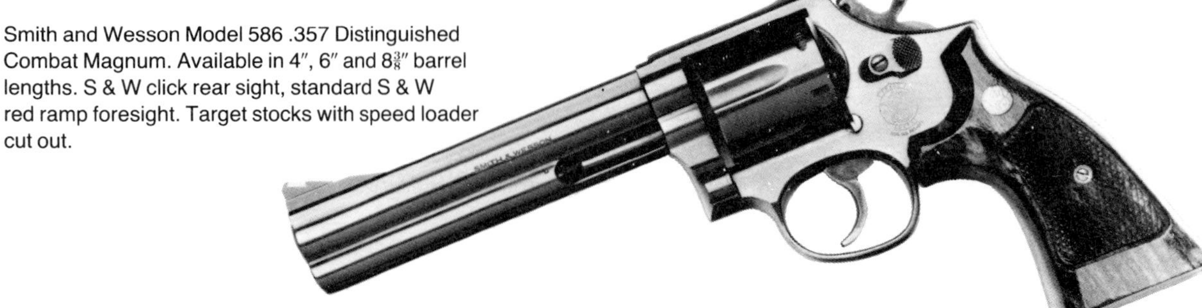

Smith and Wesson Model 586 .357 Distinguished Combat Magnum. Available in 4″, 6″ and 8⅜″ barrel lengths. S & W click rear sight, standard S & W red ramp foresight. Target stocks with speed loader cut out.

Smith and Wesson Model 469 9mm 12 shot semi-automatic pistol with alloy frame and 'bobbed' hammer. Fixed rear sight with white outline adjustable for windage only.

Smith and Wesson Model 645 in stainless steel with 9″ barrel and fixed rearsight. Double action semi-automatic pistol in .45 ACP with eight round magazine. Alternative version available with adjustable sights.

introduced, a double action 9mm auto loader with a magazine capacity of 14 plus one in the chamber. Similar to the M 39 the M 59 has been adapted to handle the double column magazine first made popular on the Browning Hi-Power. After a few years S & W announced both models were to be replaced by modified versions under the Model numbers 439 (8 shot) and 459 (14 shot). Modifications to the safety system and the provision of fully adjustable rear sights and a change in constructional materials are part of the re-design. The stainless steel versions are the Models 639 and 659.

Spurred by the activities of the custom pistolsmiths, S & W announced their 'Compact' 9mm Model 469, which became available in 1983/84. This is a 'reduced' version of the M 459 with an alloy frame and what S & W call a recurved trigger guard. Magazine capacity is reduced to 12 rounds. The stainless steel version is the Model 669 with an alloy frame and stainless steel slide. Both Models have a cropped hammer, hook guard and fixed combat type sights. In 1987 the company announced the latest example in the family of semi-automatic pistols, the Model 645 in .45 ACP. The new pistol weighs just 37½ ozs and is only slightly larger than the current 9mm auto-pistols. It is, of course, double action, but S & W also offer a single action version, the Model 745, for competitive shooting.

Of the .22 semi-automatic pistols mentioned in Chapter Fourteen, the Model 41 Target Pistol remains on the range but it has been joined by the Model 422 which is available in 'Field' or 'Target' versions and with either a 4½″ or 6″ barrel.

With eleven semi-automatic pistols and twenty-eight revolvers, each with several variants as to barrel length or sights, the present S & W range must be about the most extensive available to-day.

Star, Bonifacio Echeverria SA

Further research now permits some expansion on the history of this company. Jose-Cruz Echeverria made muzzle loaders in the Basque gun-making centre of Eibar. His two sons, Julian and Bonifacio, began the manufacture of automatic pistols based on Mannlicher and Browning designs in 1906. The first of these pistols was the Izarra (Basque for Star), which was designed around the then new Browning .25 ACP (6.35mm) cartridge.

A range of .22 pistols, the 'F' series, was produced as well as the .25 ACP models. In addition a range of auto-pistols in .32 ACP commenced with the Model No. 2 of 1908/9 and others were marketed in 7.62mm Mauser. The Model L was made in 7.65mm (.32 French long cartridge) in 1933 for the French Army and the U series in 7.65mm (.30 calibre Luger) during 1972. A further range of pistols in 9mm (.380 ACP) was introduced in 1914

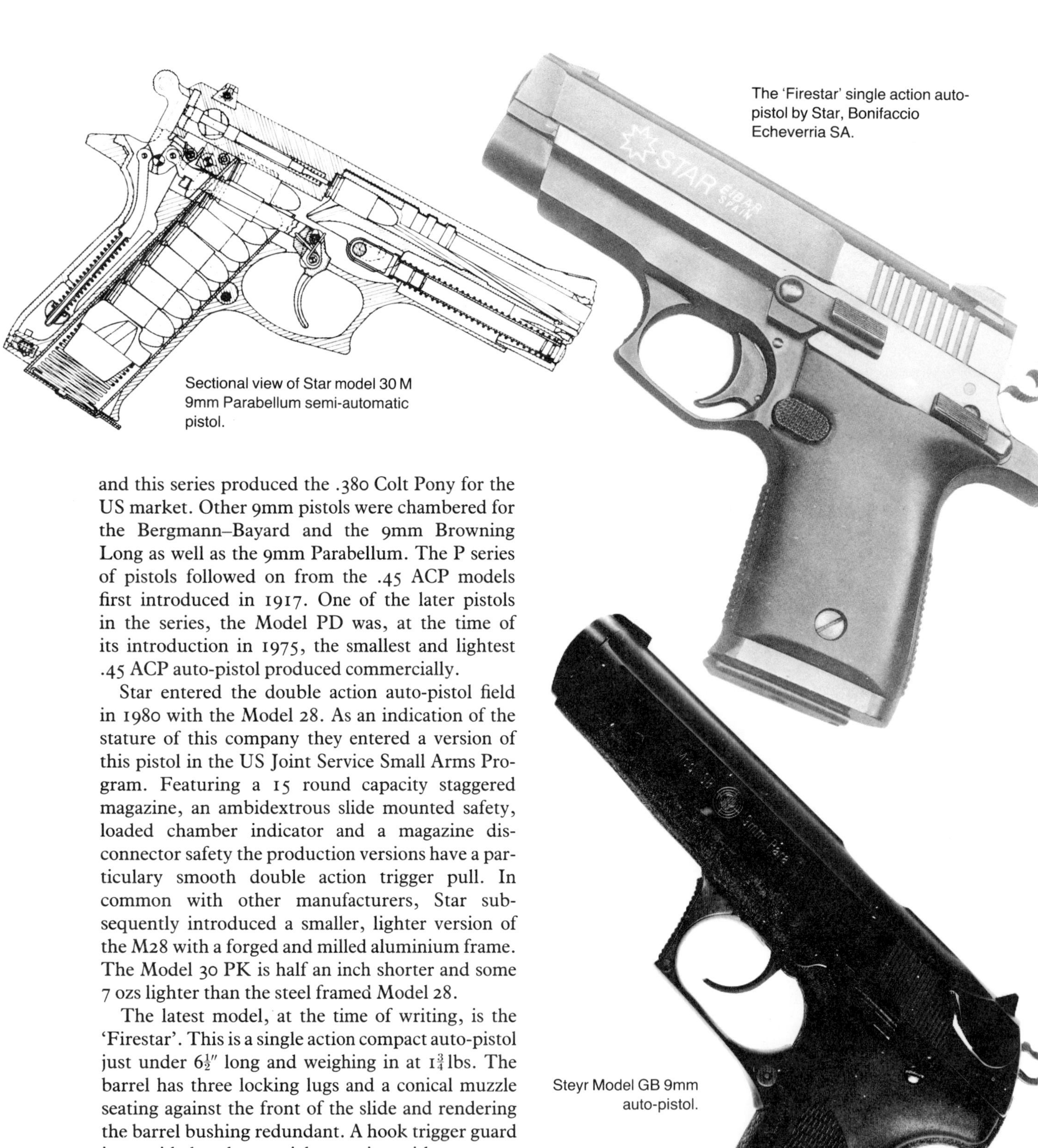

Sectional view of Star model 30 M 9mm Parabellum semi-automatic pistol.

The 'Firestar' single action auto-pistol by Star, Bonifaccio Echeverria SA.

Steyr Model GB 9mm auto-pistol.

and this series produced the .380 Colt Pony for the US market. Other 9mm pistols were chambered for the Bergmann–Bayard and the 9mm Browning Long as well as the 9mm Parabellum. The P series of pistols followed on from the .45 ACP models first introduced in 1917. One of the later pistols in the series, the Model PD was, at the time of its introduction in 1975, the smallest and lightest .45 ACP auto-pistol produced commercially.

Star entered the double action auto-pistol field in 1980 with the Model 28. As an indication of the stature of this company they entered a version of this pistol in the US Joint Service Small Arms Program. Featuring a 15 round capacity staggered magazine, an ambidextrous slide mounted safety, loaded chamber indicator and a magazine disconnector safety the production versions have a particulary smooth double action trigger pull. In common with other manufacturers, Star subsequently introduced a smaller, lighter version of the M28 with a forged and milled aluminium frame. The Model 30 PK is half an inch shorter and some 7 ozs lighter than the steel framed Model 28.

The latest model, at the time of writing, is the 'Firestar'. This is a single action compact auto-pistol just under $6\frac{1}{2}''$ long and weighing in at $1\frac{3}{4}$ lbs. The barrel has three locking lugs and a conical muzzle seating against the front of the slide and rendering the barrel bushing redundant. A hook trigger guard is provided and a special magazine with one extra round (8 round capacity) and extra length to provide a better grip for the bigger hand is available.

The traditional models based on the Model F are continued almost unchanged as the Models FR Sport and FR Target in .22 RF. The Model CK is a pocket .25 calibre auto-pistol with the D Series larger versions in .32 and .380 calibres. The B Series are in 9mm and the P Series in .45 ACP. All are compact traditional pistols, single action with external hammers.

Steyr

Founded in 1864 as Josef & Franz Werndl & Comp, Waffenfabrik, the name was changed to Oesterreichische Waffenfabriks Gesellschaft in 1869 (see page 379). The factory became known as Steyr-Werke AG in February 1926 and in May 1935 the name changed to Steyr Daimler Puch AG. In December 1986, it was decided to divide the company and Steyr Mannlicher GmbH was formed to concentrate the small arms interests in one company as part of the Steyr-Daimler-Puch AG group of companies.

Long associated with the design and manufacture of auto-pistols from the first commercially offered auto-pistol, the Schonberger, it is not surprising that the present auto-pistol produced by Steyr, the GB 80, is in many ways, just as remarkable! The GB is an advanced, gas retarded blowback operated, double action pistol, in 9mm Parabellum calibre. The prototype was, in fact, produced in America as the Rogak P18 and, in its perfected form, is now produced by the most modern manufacturing techniques at Steyr. The GB has an 18 round double row magazine and a 'hook' trigger guard. The frame is a two piece sheet steel stamping with a black crinkle finish. The thin frame walls coupled with the use of high impact plastic grip plates ensure that, despite the 18 round magazine, the overall width of the pistol is not excessive. The barrel has polygonal rifling and is screwed into a solid steel component in the frame. The design of the pistol requires gas seal swellings at the muzzle and mid point with gas ports forward of the mid point swelling.

The majority of the 9mm auto-pistols of recent years have short-recoil, locked breech mechanisms. The Steyr shares with the Heckler & Koch P7 the unusual, but by no means unique, gas retarded system.

SIG

Since we left this company in Chapter Fifteen a number of changes have taken place which deserve recording. The SIG 210 which we mentioned previously was considered by many to be a pistol manufactured to the very highest standards.

In the 1970s this Swiss company developed two new pistols, the P220 and the P230. As we saw in the case of the Model 210, the design was not original and the contribution made by SIG was to develop a design due to Petter. The two new pistols are a co-operative effort on the part of the Schweizerrische Industrie Gesellschaft of Newhausen and the old established firm of J. P. Sauer & Sohn of Eckernforde, West Germany, formerly of Suhl. This joint venture is, as we have seen already in the case of SIG Hammerli, a feature of European arms manufacture and one which, as development costs escalate, is likely to be even more common in the future.

The pistols are, in fact, manufactured in Germany and are sold under the SIG-Sauer name. The P 220 is a large double action 9mm Parabellum pistol, weighing in at just under 30 ozs. An unusual feature is the de-cocking lever, located at the top front edge of the left hand grip plate. To those who remember the Sauer Model 38H this will be nothing new! However, on the P 220, the lever lowers the external hammer from the full cock position only. On the original Sauer, it also cocked the hammer. The P 220 has an aluminium alloy frame and the slide is a stamped and welded assembly with a pinned in breechblock to reduce costs. Locking is by a modification of the Browning system and there are provisions for conversion units to other calibres as is established European practice.

The companion pistol, the P 230, has a more streamlined look. It is, like the P 220, double action, with a de-cocking lever. The pistol competes with the Walther PPK-S, the Beretta Model 90 and the Mauser HSc. Intended for personal protection, the P 230 can, of course, be considered for use by police forces in Europe and it will be available in a range of calibres from .22 RF to 9mm (.380 ACP).

These two pistols were the basis of a further design improvement intended for the US pistol competitions. Derived from the P 220 the SIG-Sauer P 226 has a double column magazine holding 15 rounds of 9mm ammunition and it retains the double action feature and the decocking lever of the P 220.

Sturm Ruger

This American company is without doubt one of the success stories of the industry. Details of the very successful .22 auto-pistol and of the range of single action revolvers have been given earlier in the book and perhaps the most important of the recent developments has been the introduction of double action revolvers and centre fire auto-pistols and, of course, the wide use of stainless steel in which field the company can be said to have been in the forefront.

The Ruger Double Action revolver first appeared in 1970 in .357 Magnum calibre. Later, a 9mm Parabellum version appeared with a modified extractor to engage the rimless cartridges (similar to the S & W M 547). Although the Ruger system worked well with US commercial 9mm ammunition in the Speed Six and Service Six DA revolvers some problems were encountered. Furthermore, the 'ring' extractor was not compatible with revolver speed loaders. The design of the pistols was altered to permit the use of half-moon clips similar to those used on Colt and S & W revolvers which were chambered for the .45 ACP cartridge.

The Ruger DA revolver has a solid frame and the six chambered cylinder swings out to the left on the conventional crane with simultaneous ejection of the fired cases by means of the ejector rod. The term 'solid frame' is perhaps a little more apt in the case of this pistol, since unlike current conventional US revolvers there is no sideplate; the lockwork is withdrawn from below the frame and the hammer is lifted out from above in much the same way as on the British Webley revolvers. Take down of the Ruger is simple and quick and can be accomplished without the need for tools other than a small coin to remove the grips.

Work on the new DA revolvers did not mean that the company abandoned work on the single action revolvers. In 1974, a new version of the Single Six appeared with a revised lock mechanism which included what Ruger call a 'transfer bar'. This device ensures that the pistol cannot be fired unless the trigger is deliberately held rearward. This permits the loading of all six chambers, which no prudent person did with previous single action revolvers. A further improvement is that with the

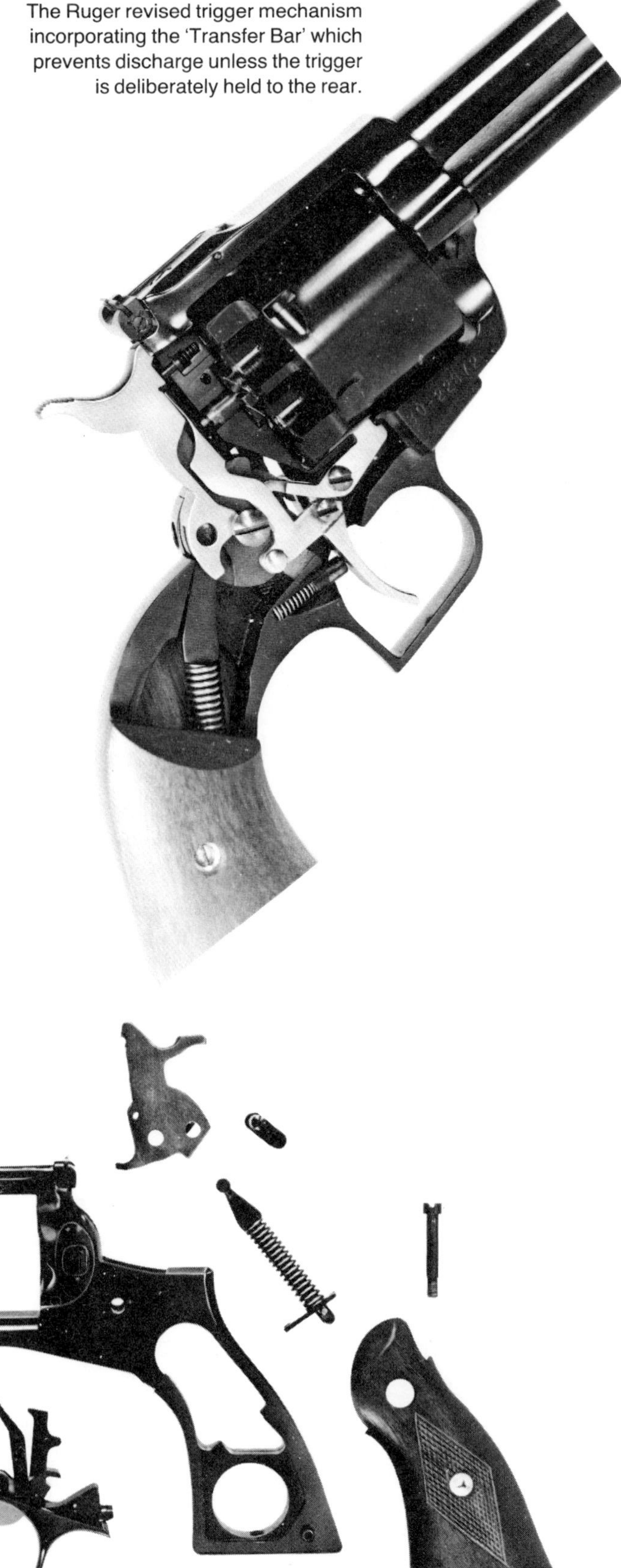

The Ruger revised trigger mechanism incorporating the 'Transfer Bar' which prevents discharge unless the trigger is deliberately held to the rear.

Ruger double action revolver.

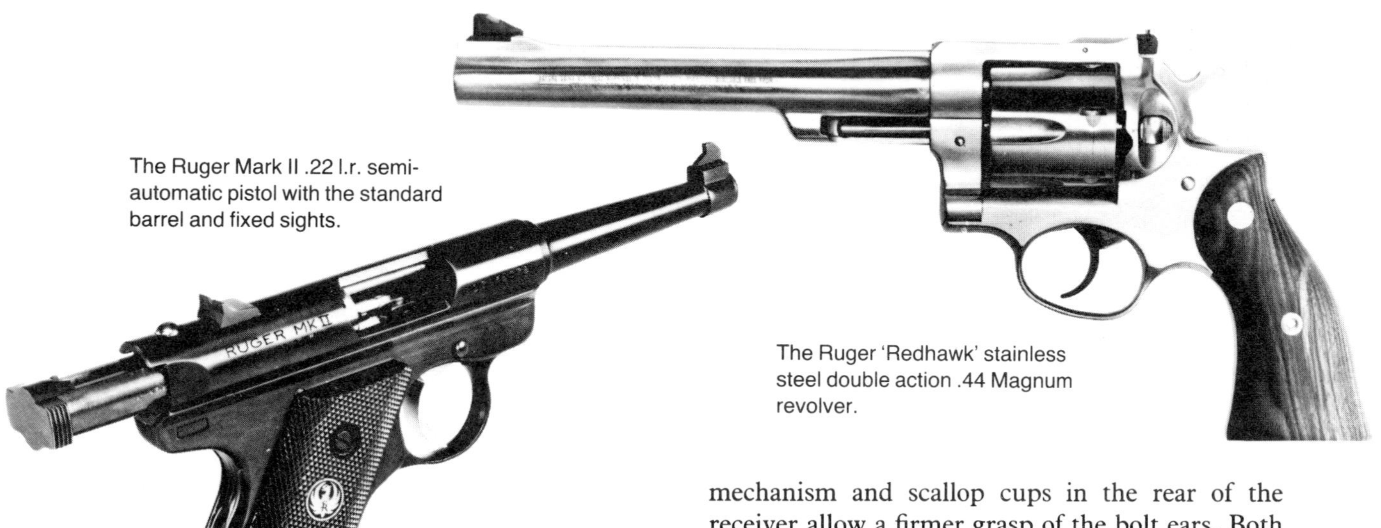

The Ruger Mark II .22 l.r. semi-automatic pistol with the standard barrel and fixed sights.

The Ruger 'Redhawk' stainless steel double action .44 Magnum revolver.

loading gate in the open position the cylinder is free to revolve for loading and unloading. Also, as another safety feature, the pistol cannot be fired with the loading gate open. Ruger was later to offer a conversion kit for the 'old model' single action revolvers, based on the 'transfer bar', for factory fitting, which brought the original single action revolvers in line with present day thinking on safety.

In 1980, advance information on a larger double action revolver was released, the .44 Magnum Ruger Redhawk. Made in stainless steel, with the top rib and ejector housing forged in one, the internal mechanism is based on the earlier DA revolvers and is unlike any previous revolver lockwork.

The Mark II version of the .22 Standard auto-pistol was introduced in 1983, the basic model on which it might be said that the Ruger fortunes were founded. Ruger produced 5,000 examples of the Standard pistol in stainless steel before production ceased in favour of the Mark II. This special series bears the legend '1 OF 5000' on the side housing. These pistols could, I suppose, be regarded as instant collector items!

The new Mark II version is offered in three versions, $4\frac{3}{4}''$ standard barrel, 6″ tapered barrel target model with adjustable sights and a 5″ bull barrel version. The Mark II has a bolt stop, a ten shot magazine instead of the original 9 shot, and changes in the manual safety now permit the bolt to be operated to check or unload the chamber with the safety applied. There are minor changes in the trigger mechanism and scallop cups in the rear of the receiver allow a firmer grasp of the bolt ears. Both the Ruger Mark I and II .22 auto-pistols have been used by the US military services as training pistols. A variant of the Mark II Bull Barrel Model was offered for sale in 1987 with a $6\frac{7}{8}''$ barrel instead of the $5\frac{1}{2}''$ barrel of the earlier version. This model bears the legend 'Government Target Model' at the rear of the ejection port.

The early nineteen eighties brought forth a new cartridge, the .357 Remington Maximum, some .315″ longer than the .357 Magnum. Developed by Elgin Gates of the Handgun Silhouette Association, the new cartridge required a revolver in which to shoot it and Ruger came up with the Blackhawk .357 Maximum single action, one variant of which boasts a $10\frac{1}{2}''$ bull barrel. Shortly after its introduction Ruger withdrew the .357 Maximum revolvers from the range due to erosion problems in the barrel and under the top strap of the frame.

In 1987, the new GP 100 double action revolver made its appearance in .357 Magnum calibre. Similar to the .38/.357 Security-Six and sharing some of the design features of the .44 Magnum Redhawk, the GP 100 has a new grip frame shape which allows for the use of a variety of 'custom' grips. A further, interesting departure from the conventional, is the use of rubber grips with Goncalo Alves wood panels. The GP 100 was heralded by Ruger as the first of an entirely new generation of DA revolvers. Also appearing in what might be regarded as a vintage year, the Super Redhawk DA revolver is provided with an extended frame to provide a base for a telescopic sight.

On the single action front, the Single Six and the Blackhawk have been provided with 'Bisley' variants; the smaller gun is offered in .22 RF or .32 Magnum and the Blackhawk can be had in .257, .41 and .44 Magnum. The Ruger Bisley follows the appearance of the original Colt Bisleys with a larger

The Ruger P 45 is a 9mm, double action, semi-automatic with a fifteen round magazine. The slide is head treated chrome-molybdenum steel and the frame is an aluminium alloy investment casting, subsequently hard coated. Featured are an ambidextrous safety and magazine latches, a grooved hammer spur and 'hook' trigger guard.

trigger guard, low set hammer spur and modified grip frame, although the Ruger is not quite as curvaceous as the original Colt Bisley. Just as Colt did in 1894, Ruger have managed to produce two usefully different guns by making a few simple alterations to existing models. Once again the benefits of the 'American' system are self-evident!

Sturm Ruger started to manufacture handguns in 1949 when they introduced their .22 auto-pistol, the design philosophy of which was a radical departure from the conventional. Now, nearly forty years later, Ruger have again entered the auto-pistol market but this time with an entirely new DA 9mm pistol, the P 85. Similar in many respects to the USM 9 (Beretta), the Ruger has an aluminium frame, a double row 15 round magazine, a slide mounted ambidextrous safety and at 7.85″ is slightly less in length and an ounce lighter in weight than the M 9. How the Ruger would have fared in the by now famous US Government tests I do not know. This pistol enters a market place with some stiff competition but with Ruger's track records on quality and value for money, I feel fairly confident that the P 85 or a variant will have a useful future.

Walther

The current trend towards double action automatic pistols has already been mentioned. Walther have been in the forefront of this development from the outset. The first Walther double action auto-pistol appeared in 1929, the Model PP. Details of this pistol, and the later PPK which dates from 1931, have already been given in Chapter Fifteen as have details of the P38 and Walther pistols made up to 1970.

An important market for Walther pistols is of course the United States. The PPK was a very popular model and US restrictive legislation on the importation of small pocket handguns from Spain closed the US market to this Walther model, but not the PP and P38. The regulations assigned a points value for importation qualificaitons designed in essentials to restrict the importation of 'Saturday Night Specials'. The US domestic industry has responded by turning out similar weapons, the S & W .22 M 61 and as we have seen, Colt started the domestic manufacture of the .25 ACP 'Junior' auto-pistol, formerly imported from Spain. Those foreign companies with US interests who wished to retain their market share have been stimulated to develop pistols which evade the regulations and which can therefore be imported.

The effectiveness of legislation on the control of handguns is a vast subject; suffice it to say that Walther overcame the problem it created for them by the introduction of a new pistol, the PPKS. The new model is heavier, longer and has a greater magazine capacity than the PPK and in essentials is the PPK slide fitted to a PP frame. It is offered in .221 RF, .32 ACP, and .380 ACP. The PPKS in .380 ACP is manufactured both in Germany and in the USA.

The company then went in the reverse direction for, after 'enlarging' the PPK, they then 'reduced' the P 38! The shortened P 38K has the front sight mounted on the slide bridge and the barrel shortened to very nearly the front of the slide, which has reduced the overall length of the P 38 from $8\frac{1}{2}''$ to $6\frac{3}{8}''$ for the K version. Manufacture of the P 38 K has now ceased. Another variant of the prewar P 38 is the P 1, a light frame version of the P 38 and the current German Service pistol. The latest contender for Service and Police use is the P 5, which can be regarded as a contemporary of the Heckler & Koch PSP and SIG P 225.

Walther have drawn on the P 38 design for much of the P 5; it has a light alloy frame and is a locked breech, recoil operated pistol. The magazine has a capacity of 8 rounds 9 × 19mm Parabellum ammunition and it is double action but with a new and unusual feature for Walther. The differences can best be explained by following the operating procedure. First, remove the magazine (the catch is under the butt), and then retract the slide and lock it in the open position by the use of the slide stop. This is on the left hand side of the pistol just behind the trigger and in front of the 'safety lever'. Load a full magazine and depress the safety lever which releases the slide and chambers a cartridge.

Press the lever again and the hammer, which was at full cock due to the retraction of the slide is lowered to the 'safe carry' position. The hammer cannot contact the firing pin until the trigger is pressed to raise and disengage the firing pin from its blocked safety position. The first shot is fired double action and subsequent shots are fired single action. The hammer can, of course, be manually cocked if required. There is no conventional manual safety device, since the design of the pistol permits it to be carried safely, with a loaded chamber and the hammer down.

Walther have had a long association with target pistols and the current models date back to a shooting system suited for each phase of the International Shooting Union (UIT) competition. The first of the series was the 'new' .22 short OSP, Olympia Schnellfeuer Pistol (see p. 502). This model was then later adapted for use with the .22 RF for the standard pistol course of fire and given the designation GSP. Then, in 1974, the same basic pistol was adapted to the .32 S & W long cartridge as the GSP-C centre-fire auto target pistol. This version has to be used with a flush seated wadcutter bullet and because of the larger diameter of the .32 cartridge, the five shot magazine, which retains its position in front of the trigger, has been extended downwards.

The latest auto-pistol for military and police use is the P 88. At present available in 9 × 19mm (9mm parabellum) the P 88 is a locked breech recoil semi-automatic pistol with double action lockwork and an external hammer. The pistol has multi-safety modes so that the hammer can only strike the firing pin when the breech is locked and the trigger is pulled fully to the rear. The locking system is modified Browning instead of the type familiar to users of the P 38. In addition the P 88 has an ambidextrous operation lever which closes an open slide and which will also uncock the hammer. This is the lever inlet into the top of the grips. The magazine release is also ambidextrous. The pistol can be fired both double and single action and the magazine has a capacity of 15 rounds.

The Model P 88 represents 'state of the art' in military and police pistols and one can only wonder where future stages of development will take this old-established firm.

Dan Wesson

Yes, they are 'related'! Daniel B. Wesson, the great grandson of the co-founder of Smith and Wesson worked for the company until it experienced a 'take

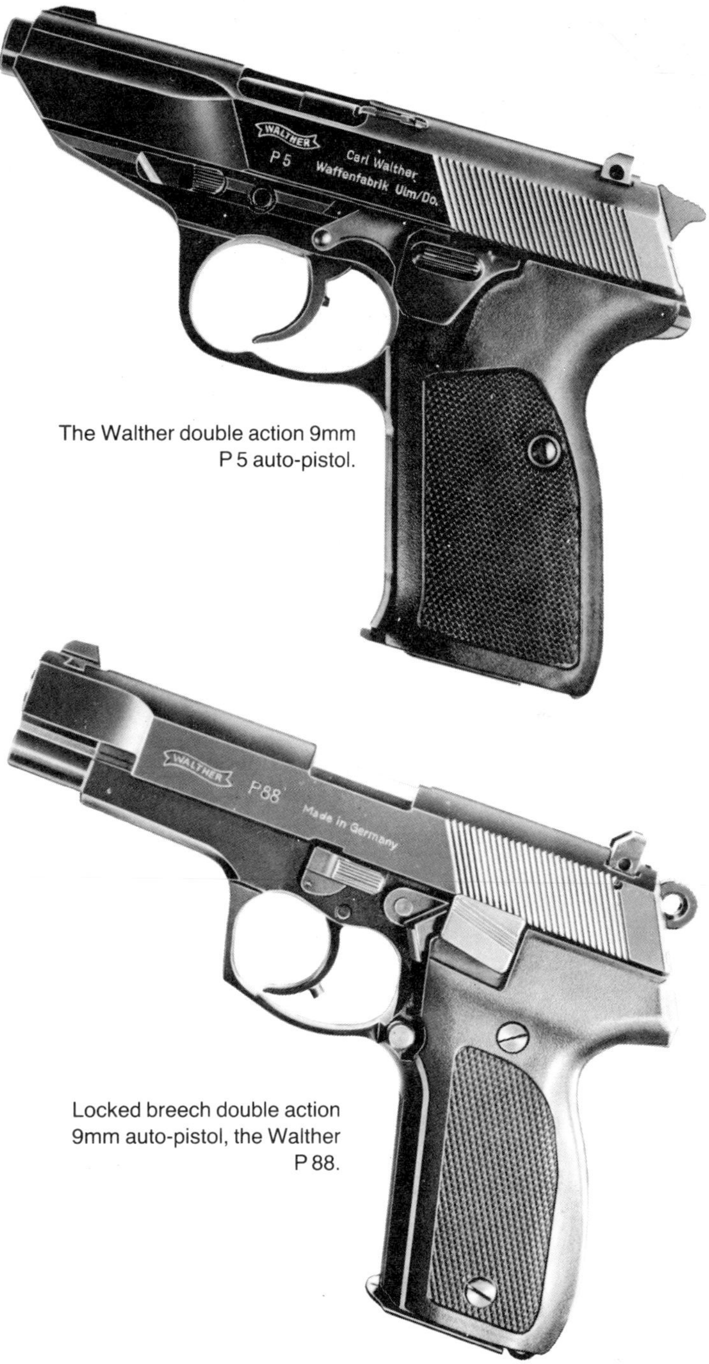

The Walther double action 9mm P 5 auto-pistol.

Locked breech double action 9mm auto-pistol, the Walther P 88.

over' and then he devoted his time to Daniel B. Wesson Co. Inc., who manufactured screw machines. Interest in handguns was maintained and a new company, Dan Wesson Arms Co., was formed as a subsidiary. The first Dan Wesson M 12 revolver has a number of interesting features, which combined, permit the owner to 'build' a revolver to suit his own needs.

The new revolver is built around a short double action mechanism with a low hammer spur to aid thumb cocking. The mechanism is contained in a solid frame with a right hand removable side plate,

held in position not by the conventional gun screws but by Allen screws, which permit the ordinary mortal who wields a screwdriver to tighten up the screws fully. The rear of the frame ends not in the usual grip shaped frame but in a square section hollow lug which contains the hammer coilspring. An Allen screw enters the base of the one piece grip and screws into the lug. Because of the design a variety of grip shapes are possible and since there is ample wood around the lug extensive alterations to the grips are both possible and practical. In front of the swing-out six chambered cylinder is a push down cylinder release latch. This location leaves the sides of the frame behind the cylinder free and allows even greater freedom in the design of the grips.

At the other end of the pistol there is freedom to choose a variety of barrel lengths. These will range from 2″ to 6″ at first and the barrels can be exchanged by first unscrewing the barrel nut by means of a special wrench which allows the barrel shroud to be removed followed by unscrewing the barrel. Each length of barrel requires the appropriate barrel shroud. A special gauge is provided to ensure that the correct clearance between the barrel and the cylinder can be maintained. The shroud carries the front sight, the base of which is integral with the barrel rib. The front sight is adjustable for elevation only, the rear sight for windage.

Later versions of the basic design included the Model 14 with a fixed barrel which can only be exchanged at the factory and the M 15, designed for target use, which has fully adjustable sights, with interchangeable barrels and stocks and a recessed barrel nut. In the mid 1970s the company produced a 'Pistol Pack' which consisted of a cased set including a revolver, three different lengths of barrel assemblies, two finished grips and one inletted grip blank. Subsequently, the company altered the design of the barrel shroud which permits the manufacture of an even greater variety of barrel lengths to now include 10″, 12″ and 15″ with the handgun hunter and the silhouette man in mind. In addition, a wider range of grips became available and the coloured fore sight elements could now be easily interchanged.

The Dan Wesson .44 Magnum revolver with the 4″, 6″, 8″ and 10″ interchangeable barrels.

The founder and driving spirit behind this company died on 24 November 1978 but the revolver which bears his name continues to evolve; the latest version being a .22. Built on the .357 Magnum frame the Model 22V with a six inch barrel weighs slightly more than the bigger calibre because of the smaller hole down the barrel. Nine grip styles are now available, plus of course, the extra blank just in case none of the factory ones are suitable!

In 1980 a new model appeared on the range, a large frame .44 Magnum with the interchangeable barrel system permitting 4″, 6″, 8″ and 10″ barrel lengths and solid or 'ported' barrels except for the 10″ length. The gas ports vent the gases through holes in the barrel shroud and have a beneficial effect on both muzzle jump and felt recoil.

Having gone up to .44 Magnum from the original

.357 Magnum Model 12, Dan Wesson Arms introduced a new revolver in 1986, the 32VH. Chambered for the .32 H & R Magnum, a cartridge introduced by the now defunct firm of Harrington & Richardson, this model has proved to be popular with the pistol silhouette competitors. The ability to change barrel lengths and grips has by now become well established and the popularity of the system is such as to ensure the continued success of the company.

Wildey

Developed by Wildey J. Moore, the Wildey gas operated, rotary bolt auto-pistol was first mentioned in 1975. Then came the announcement that Winchester were to develop two new cartridges, the 9mm Magnum and the .45 Magnum, based, of course, on the 9mm Parabellum and the .45 ACP cases and loaded to the ballistic equivalent of the .357 and .44 Magnums. Moving from the prototype to mass production revealed a number of time consuming problems not the least of which was the need for a degree of high precision engineering which was incompatible with volume production. The original company, Wildey Firearms Co. Inc., went out of business and the assets were acquired by an investment group. The new company, IFD, also foundered and the original principals were able to buy back the assets and are currently actively promoting the pistol in a range of calibres and barrel lengths.

To overcome the problems mentioned above, the pistol has been extensively redesigned. In essentials the pistol has a cylinder which surrounds the barrel in front of the receiver. An annular piston fits between the barrel and cylinder and to this is bled a small amount of gas when the pistol is fired. The gas pushed the piston forwards and this unlocks the breechbolt. The action opens under residual pressure and the fired case is ejected. A recoil spring returns the bolt into battery, chambering a fresh cartridge from the magazine. The trigger mechanism is double action with an external hammer which allows the pistol to be manually cocked.

The Wildey is a big gun: the weight is just over 64 ounces with the 5″ barrel and tests have shown that it is extremely accurate, one reason for this being the fixed barrel. It is intended to produce pistols with the following barrel lengths, 5″, 6″, 7″, 8″ and 10″. The range of available calibres has also been extended and now include 9mm Winchester Magnum, .45 Winchester Magnum, .457 Wildey Magnum and the .357 Peterbuilt Magnum. The latter is said to be the worlds highest velocity pistol Magnum cartridge.

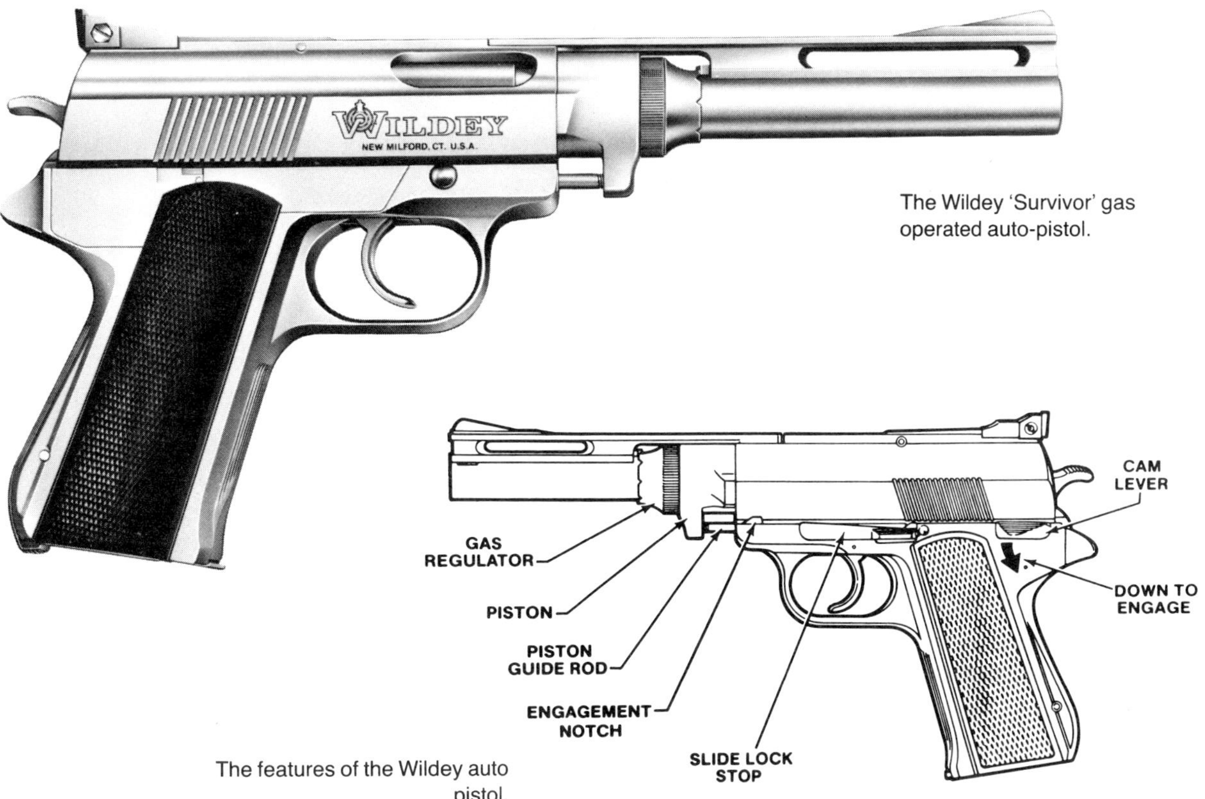

The Wildey 'Survivor' gas operated auto-pistol.

The features of the Wildey auto pistol.

The Wildey is an extremely interesting double action stainless steel pistol and is, I think, a fitting example of the art of pistol manufacture with which to end this update of the pistols of the 1980s.

Conclusion

This has been, due to the necessary constraints imposed, but a short discourse on later developments in the field of handgun design and manufacture. Hopefully, I have chosen, from the many available, those examples which illustrate the general trend in design and development over the last two decades and that the overall picture presented to you, the reader, is a representative one.

As I did in the original edition, I leave you with the following comments. Whether we collect old pistols or perhaps shoot them, whether our interest is confined to target shooting with a .22 or a centre-fire pistol or to a more serious involvement related to law enforcement or military use we are united by our common interest in that most fascinating of arms, the handgun.

The handgun is a dangerous weapon, it is meant to be! Let us ensure that our conduct when handling weapons is of a high standard so that we do not jeopardise the activities of those who share our interest.

Notes to Chapter Sixteen

Unlike the previous chapters, most of the material for Chapter Sixteen is based on illustrations and data received from the manufacturers. The majority of those to whom I wrote responded promptly and in a generous manner, and for this I am most grateful.

A number of individuals also provided valuable assistance and I have to thank Jurgen Lemm for his help in obtaining material from West Germany and also Peter Hambrusch of the firm of Josef Hambrusch, Ferlach, Austria and Alex Kerr of California. Jan and Judith Stevenson helped and advised at a critical time and some of the Britarms illustrations were supplied by Jim Harrison. I have to thank Phillip Pegram for bringing his Westlake Britarms for me to photograph and to John A. Feyk for an unending flow of material from America which kept my files updated. Lastly, I have to thank my old friend W. A. C. Paton whose generous help is greatly appreciated and happily acknowledged.

Index